PRAISE FOR

Against the Wind

"[Neal] Gabler's taste for the epic mode makes for some beautifully rendered chapters, such as his patient illustration, through the accretion of nifty anecdotes, of how Kennedy came to master the Senate's byways."
—*The Washington Post*

"Gabler's biography invites comparison to Robert Caro's volumes on Lyndon Johnson." —*The Economist*

"[A] smart, illuminating, and stirring portrait of a liberal champion."
—*Publishers Weekly*

PRAISE FOR NEAL GABLER AND

Catching the Wind

"As a character study it is rich and insightful, frank in its judgments but deeply sympathetic to the man. . . . *Catching the Wind* lends a cinematic sweep to Kennedy's legislative crusades. . . . Gabler makes these battles exciting." —*The New York Times*

"The rich narrative is studded with tasty factoids and lively quotes, anecdotes and vignettes." —*The Wall Street Journal*

"One of the truly great biographies of our time . . . Here is biography written at the highest level." —SEAN WILENTZ,
New York Times bestselling author of *Bob Dylan in America*
and *The Rise of American Democracy*

"A mammoth undertaking . . . Neal Gabler has brilliantly documented the rise of the most consequential legislator of our day, one who reached Shakespearean heights and tabloid depths. But the Ted Kennedy story is about much more. It is the tale of modern American liberalism and the shifting winds of political morality. . . . Deeply impressive."

—WALTER ISAACSON,
New York Times bestselling author of *Steve Jobs* and *Leonardo da Vinci*

"With his trademark elegance and insight, Gabler has crafted a moving portrait of the last Kennedy brother, which is also a portrait of the last great creative era of governance in the United States. Gabler has made a specialty of capturing the lives of architects of the culture, and now Ted Kennedy joins Walter Winchell and Walt Disney in a gallery of enduring biography."

—JON MEACHAM,
author of *The Soul of America*

"Gabler, a brilliant historian and prodigious researcher, grapples with all sides of Kennedy's complex personality. The result is a landmark study of Washington power politics in the twentieth century in the Robert Caro tradition. . . . Highly recommended!"

—DOUGLAS BRINKLEY,
New York Times bestselling author of *American Moonshot*

"Judicious and thoughtful, *Catching the Wind* will be essential reading for understanding the fate of political liberalism in American history."

—KAI BIRD,
Pulitzer Prize–winning author of *American Prometheus* and *The Good Spy*

"A triumphant achievement and essential reading for everyone fascinated by the Kennedys, politics, and governance."

—*Booklist* (starred review)

"A vigorous, highly readable . . . book full of triumph and tragedy and an exemplary study in electoral politics." —*Kirkus Reviews* (starred review)

AGAINST

THE WIND

Edward Kennedy and the Rise of Conservatism

NEAL GABLER

CROWN
NEW YORK

Published in the United States by Crown, an imprint of Random House,
a division of Penguin Random House LLC, New York.

CROWN and the Crown colophon are registered trademarks
of Penguin Random House LLC.

Originally published in hardcover in the United States by Crown, an
imprint of Random House, a division of Penguin Random House LLC,
in 2022.

LIBRARY OF CONGRESS CATALOGING-IN-PUBLICATION DATA
Names: Gabler, Neal, author.
Title: Against the wind / Neal Gabler.
New York: Crown, [2022] |
Includes bibliographical references and index.
Identifiers: LCCN 2022016140 (print) | LCCN 2022016141 (ebook) |
ISBN 9780593238646 (trade paper) | ISBN 9780593238639 (ebook)
Subjects: LCSH: Kennedy, Edward M. (Edward Moore), 1932–2009. |
United States. Congress. Senate—Biography. | Legislators—
United States—Biography. | United States— Politics and government—
1945–1989. United States—Politics and government—1989–
Classification: LCC E840.8.K35 G339 2022 (print) |
LCC E840.8.K35 (ebook) DDC 973.92092— dc23/eng/20220518
LC record available at https://lccn.loc.gov/2022016140
LC ebook record available at https://lccn.loc.gov/2022016141

Printed in Canada

crownpublishing.com

2 4 6 8 9 7 5 3 1

Once again, as always, to my beloved daughters,
Laurel and Tänne,
And to my equally beloved son-in-law, Braden,
And daughter-in-law, Shoshanna,
All of whom have devoted their lives to serving others.
And to my four grandchildren,
Sadie, Oren, Kaya, and Theo,
Who are the joys of my life.
No man is more fortunate than I.
May all of them live in a gentler, kinder, and more moral world,
And may they help make it so.

"If anyone has material possessions and sees a brother or sister in need but has no pity on them, how can the love of God be in that person? Dear children, let us not love with words or speech but with actions and in truth."

—I JOHN 3:17–18

CONTENTS

I BEGAN RESEARCHING this biography long ago, and by the time I finished writing, the political winds had shifted yet again, blowing the country into dark, dangerous, uncharted waters. We live now within an immense and profound cruelty, in a resurgence of white supremacy and the vile hatreds of racism and nativism and misogyny and homophobia and Islamophobia, in an anti-intellectual farrago in which large segments of the public display an aversion to indisputable facts and regard hard science as subversive, in a polarization so wide and hostile that Americans cannot even agree on protecting one another from a virus that, as I write, has taken the lives of one million citizens, in a bizarre, dizzying derangement that has a large number of self-described "patriotic" Americans extolling authoritarian dictators as heroes to be lionized and models to be emulated, and in a deep crisis for democracy itself, now surprisingly as fragile as an eggshell, and which virtually the entire rank and file of one of the nation's two major political parties now eschews.

None of these terrors came out of the blue, and the story I tell in these pages about the demise of liberalism and of the liberal consensus that had once been the prevailing American ideology, and the rise of conservatism, which, by the 1980s, had displaced liberalism as the dominant ideology, is certainly a predicate for the crisis in which the nation now finds itself— a crisis in which supporters of a former president march triumphantly with swastikas and wear T-shirts emblazoned with anti-Black and anti-Semitic slogans and insist an election—and, more, a nation—was stolen from them. Ronald Reagan oversaw a moral recalibration. This is something else: a moral extirpation. As Thomas Mann, a senior fellow at the Brookings Institution and a longtime political observer, recently put it, the Republican Party has undergone a transformation that precludes having a "moral sense: honesty, empathy, respect for one's colleagues, wisdom, institutional loyalty, a willingness to put country ahead of party on existential matters, an openness to changing conditions."

If this book tells how the foundation was laid for that extirpation, which threatens to move the tectonic plates of the nation's politics yet again, this time from conservatism to reactionary populism, so might it suggest a way back from the political and moral abyss that we face. Edward Kennedy was a deeply flawed man, for which he was reviled. But for all his faults, he was a good man, a caring man, an empathetic man, a man who sought to make this a better world. His were faults of the flesh, not the soul. He is arguably—an argument I have tried to make—the most consequential public servant of the last fifty years and the one who did more to help his fellow men and women than any other in that period. To the extent we reflect upon him and his times, I hope that perhaps, albeit in some small way, his political life might serve as a model for future public servants and for citizens generally; that it might remind us of our better selves; that it might show us how one individual can provide a ripple of hope in what seems an angry ocean of hopelessness; that it might challenge the ugliness that seems to have overtaken us; and, finally, that it might move us to rediscover our virtue and restore our nation's moral purpose when it is under assault.

A Countervailing Wind

IN THAT TENSE school year that ran from the fall of 1974 to the spring of 1975, Boston seethed as Federal Judge W. Arthur Garrity, Jr., tried to enforce a plan to desegregate the city's schools, and scores of white parents resisted the attempt—resisted it angrily, forcefully, resentfully, and even violently, until the seething erupted into explosion. Among the angriest, most forceful, resentful, and even violent of those parents was forty-three-year-old Elvira Palladino, or "Pixie," as she was known. But Palladino was no pixie. Though small of stature, she was loud, tough, coarse, vulgar, unfiltered, impolitic, and impolite—she once gave a monsignor who supported busing the Sicilian "kiss of death"—more a hellion than a sprite. Some called her "Garbage Mouth." The daughter of immigrants from the South of Italy, her father had worked in a shoe factory, and she sewed stitches in a clothing factory herself, which was where she met her future husband. Even after she became a civic leader, helping rouse those furious white parents against the establishment, she preferred to think of herself as a mother—she had two school-age children—and it was her children who had brought her to the forefront of the antibusing movement that year as the head of the East Boston chapter of Restore Our Alienated Rights, or ROAR, a perfect acronym for an organization that shouted down proponents of busing.

Palladino was blunt. She did not want her children bused out of East Boston, nor did she want Black children bused in. Races shouldn't mingle, she said. She had led a contingent at the antibusing rally on Boston's City Hall Plaza on September 9, 1974, three days before the opening of the schools and at the beginning of implementation of the desegregation plan—a rally at which Senator Edward Kennedy, who supported the court desegregation order, had foolishly waded into the restive crowd hoping to calm them and instead incited them, so that he was forced to retreat and race into the federal office building named for his brother John, under a torrent of vitriol and a hail of missiles, including a raw egg. And Palladino had led another contingent the following spring as tensions over busing were still thick, this one in front of South Atlantic High School in Quincy, where Ted had made a speech and where angry protesters, massing outside, deflated the tires of his car, rubbed dog feces onto the car's door handles, and chased him down the street when he exited the building, screaming at him, until he raced into a subway station, leaped through the doors of an incoming train, and survived. (A photo of another rally showed Palladino being forcibly carried away by two policemen.) All that year and into the next, at speeches and hearings and meetings, Palladino, sometimes wearing a tam-o'-shanter over her curly black hair, sometimes wearing a STOP FORCED BUSING T-shirt, showed up to harass Ted Kennedy, harass him for forsaking the white working class of Boston and favoring Black people, whom she called "pickaninnies" and "jungle bunnies." "First among his tormentors," the political scientist Ronald Formisano, who wrote a book about the Boston busing acrimony, would call Pixie Palladino due to her hostility to Ted Kennedy. Ted agreed, saying that she seemed to pop up wherever he was, shouting at him "at the top of her lungs." She came. She never stopped coming. She was even accused of punching him in the stomach during the fracas at the City Hall rally.

But Pixie Palladino and her army of angry Italian and Irish mothers who would drive their cars in motorcades through the Boston streets blasting their horns to protest busing were not anomalies that year. In fact, they had drawn encouragement from the new president, Gerald Ford, who had ascended to the office after Richard Nixon was driven from it by his Watergate depredations and who had argued forcefully against court-ordered busing for the purpose of desegregating schools. Far from anomalies, these women had become the face of America, ordinary folks, salt of the earth, a no-longer-silent majority, tired of being taken for granted, taking to the barricades, and their hostility toward Ted Kennedy, who had once been their champion and hero, was a sign of how dramatically the country had changed since he took office late in 1962. As a young senator, only thirty at his swearing-in, Ted Kennedy had caught the liberal wind and then, after his brothers' deaths, sought to be the voice of the dispossessed, which had, at the time, included these working-class ethnic Americans. Instead, the wind had died, and that voice belonged now to the Pixie Palladinos, who were carried by a countervailing wind.

Volume one of this biography, *Catching the Wind*, traced Edward Moore Kennedy's personal journey, which conflated with his political journey: how the youngest of the Kennedys, America's most famous family, was also regarded as the least of the Kennedys, a dull boy of little intelligence and even less character; how, after being expelled from Harvard when he asked a friend to take a Spanish exam for him, he enlisted in the army, returned to Harvard, was graduated, and then attended the University of Virginia Law School in hope of following his brothers into politics; how, by the dictates of the Kennedy family succession, he ran for the Senate when he was scarcely old enough to qualify for the office and had no legislative experience; how he entered the Senate with a cloud hanging over him and a preconception among his colleagues that he was a spoiled princeling; and how he used the deference he had learned in his own family as the youngest to ingratiate himself with the Senate leaders; and how he worked hard, very hard, to disabuse his colleagues of the impression they might have had of him; how, after the death of his brother John, the president, he took up John's causes, giving his maiden speech in support of the Civil Rights Act of 1964 that his brother had initiated; how he survived a terrible plane accident the very night the Civil Rights Act was passed and spent the next six months in the hospital with a broken back; how he used that time productively, inviting Harvard professors to his hospital room to tutor him, so that when he returned to the Senate, he was fortified with knowledge to go along with his charm and his drive; how his brother Bobby, who had entered the Senate in 1965, pushed him to be a better senator; and how, after Bobby's assassination, he assumed his brothers' mantle as a leading liberal, perhaps *the* leading liberal, even a prospective president, not only borne along by the liberal wind that his brothers had helped generate, but also now generating that wind himself, in no small measure because, as the least of the Kennedys and as someone who had suffered humiliations, he identified with the disempowered.

That was how Edward Kennedy entered 1974: no longer in his brothers' shadow but as a force in his own right.

That year, as the Boston busing protests would demonstrate, was a political inflection point. The coalition assembled by Franklin Roosevelt, a coalition forged largely between the white working class, people like Pixie, and Black Americans, had endured through the presidencies of Harry Truman and Dwight Eisenhower, a Republican, and of John Kennedy and Lyndon Johnson. It had not only endured in Johnson's but in many ways crested with it and with his Great Society—the most impressive legislative blitz since the New Deal. Some historians called the period of Johnson's early presidency the "liberal hour" and the political alignment at the time the "liberal consensus" because Republicans and Democrats were largely in accord about the fundamental purposes of government, if not on the means to achieve them. But now the coalition was beginning to splinter. Now Richard Nixon had managed to pry apart those white and minority cohorts, which had been bound by their economic affinities and by their reliance on government action on their behalf, and, projecting his own resentments onto those of the nation, Nixon had begun to replace the affinities with cultural divisions. The antibusing riots in Boston, where white citizens attacked Black citizens, even attacked those citizens' children with beer bottles and rocks and soda cans as those children sat terrified on their buses, were only one demonstration of Nixon's success in fracturing the country he had proclaimed he would bring together.

But Richard Nixon had only brought the fraction to fruition. The demise of the political coalition had been aborning for a long time, a story also told in *Catching the Wind*—the story of how, despite Ted Kennedy's best efforts, the end of the liberal hour was tolling. Whatever the politics behind it, the Great Society was primarily the product of something extrapolitical, of moral momentum propelled in no small part by the assassination of John Kennedy and the shock with which it had shaken the nation, and by Lyndon Johnson's desire to use that shock to create a legacy for himself that could stand beside Franklin Roosevelt's. Drawing on the national mourning for its lost leader and using his own considerable legislative skills, Johnson had created antipoverty programs, programs for neighborhood empowerment, a Medicare plan to provide health insurance for the elderly, and a Medicaid plan to provide it for the poor. Perhaps most important, he had engineered the passage of the Civil Rights Act of 1964 and then the Voting Rights Act of 1965, which bestowed the blessings of full citizenship on Black Americans. The political benefits of doing so were, for liberal Democrats like Ted Kennedy, scarce; the civil rights initiatives would cost the Democrats the South, which had been a fundamental part of the Roosevelt coalition. But the liberal hour wasn't just about politics. It was about doing the right thing. As the British journalist Godfrey Hodgson observed of that period, "From roughly 1963 to 1968, at any rate, the attention of the United States had been all but monopolized by two groups. One consisted of those—the poor, blacks, other underprivileged minorities—whose interests were served by posing the moral issue; the other—the young, intellectuals and the professional upper-middle class—was made up of people whose interests were in any case so securely protected by the status quo that they could afford the luxury of interpreting politics in moral terms. These two groups joined forces to put the issue of national morality at the center of American politics." And in those few years, with that moral focus, the nation had done the right thing.

It was powerful, even epochal, this moment of moral exhilaration, but it would be brief. Lyndon Johnson erected his Great Society and then, almost immediately, razed it with the Vietnam War, which came to be seen not just as a tragic military blunder but, by the very liberals who had supported Johnson's domestic efforts, as a moral catastrophe marked by the deaths of some two million Vietnamese civilians and the displacement of millions more; by the deaths of 58,000 American troops; by the use of flesh-burning napalm and by the decimation of the Vietnamese environment through chemicals like Agent Orange that also ruined the health of so many American soldiers there; by the slaughter of women and children by American soldiers at My Lai; and by a general sense of moral anomie, perhaps best captured by Eddie Adams's famous Pulitzer Prize–winning photograph of South Vietnamese national police chief Nguyen Loc Loan coolly executing a suspected North Vietnamese collaborator with a gunshot to the head in the middle of a Saigon street. Vietnam, it would be said, corrupted the American soul. Vietnam, it would be said, prompted doubts that Americans had seldom felt about themselves, even as Lyndon Johnson and then Richard Nixon encouraged their fellow citizens to see the war as a grand messianic mission to defeat Communism, promote liberty, and protect the world.

And so if the liberal hour was a product of moral fervor, it was a casualty, in no small measure, of moral abdication. Ted Kennedy, adhering to anti-Communist Cold War doctrine, had supported the war long after others, including his brother Robert, turned against it. Then he too flipped, though this was less a political decision (despite a growing chorus of

Democrats beginning to recognize the corrosive effects of the war), than a family decision (he didn't like being at odds with his brother), and finally a moral decision. Ted Kennedy was the chairman of the Senate Subcommittee on Refugees, which made him the trustee for the Vietnamese civilians whom the war had uprooted and who were caught between North Vietnamese forces on one side, and American and South Vietnamese ones on the other, and his opposition to the war was largely framed less as anger over the pointlessness of the war than as advocacy for those civilians harmed by it. When Bobby, in his own effort to end the war, announced his candidacy for the presidency in March 1968—after Senator Eugene McCarthy had, with more courage than Bobby, mounted an antiwar campaign against Lyndon Johnson and had embarrassed Johnson in the New Hampshire primary by coming close to defeating him—he called it a campaign for the soul of America, a campaign to restore the country's moral fiber. But the promise of moral restoration, which seemed to excite the country for the eighty days of Bobby's campaign, didn't succeed. The deaths of the Reverend Martin Luther King, Jr., and then of Bobby, just two months apart in the spring of 1968, removed two of the country's foremost leaders of conscience and sent America into a moral tailspin from which it never fully recovered, not even decades later.

That story was told in *Catching the Wind* as well—the story of how the liberal hour ticked down because it could not survive the waning of the morality that had seemed to drive it. Johnson, himself so undone by Vietnam that he chose not to stand for reelection, was followed into the White House by Richard Nixon, whom liberals had long viewed as deceitful and self-serving and who burned with personal vendettas against those who, he felt, seemed to think they were his social betters. Nixon had no interest in restoring America's soul, which, in any case, he felt had been lost not because of Vietnam but because of those who had protested the war and because of the civil rights movement and because liberal permissiveness—"permissive" became a conservative epithet—undermined traditional morality, and because cultural changes seemed to threaten white Protestant working-class and middle-class America with which he so closely identified, just as Ted Kennedy had identified with the underclass. In Nixon's view and that of his supporters, America had been a great country before the disruptions of the 1960s sent it off course, and it was still a great country, but the silent majority—those hard-working white Americans—had been shouted down, drowned out, marginalized by the left. And in this respect, Nixon was surely a man of his moment. He seemed to channel precisely how that so-called silent majority felt as their world seemed to be crumbling around them. After the death of Bobby Kennedy, a man who had seemed uniquely suited to maintaining the liberal coalition, many Americans concluded that Bobby had been wrong. America didn't need to restore its moral fiber. It needed to restore its past—the time before the 1960s.

Lyndon Johnson had helped kill the liberal hour through his hubris. His successor, Richard Nixon, made sure that it would not be resurrected. That too is a story told in *Catching the Wind*.

Ted Kennedy certainly understood what Nixon's project portended: To him, the end of the liberal hour meant the end of social and racial progress. And believing that, Ted Kennedy fought back. He had his brothers' legacies to maintain and his own legacy to begin. He spent the Nixon presidency carrying the "fallen standard" of his brothers, as he put it after he emerged from his seclusion the summer Bobby Kennedy was assassinated. *Catching the Wind* tells of that emergence—of how Ted, of whom so little was expected, turned himself into a sedulous legislator and became a kind of "shadow president," creating a liberal alternative to Richard Nixon's presidency; how he pushed liberal legislation and a liberal foreign policy; how he assailed Nixon for forsaking the country's moral traditions; and how he tried to champion the disempowered. And it tells how Richard Nixon, who both feared and despised Ted Kennedy, nevertheless tried to co-opt him so that Nixon's presidency, if not his rhetoric, turned out to be far more liberal than anyone might have suspected when he came into office.

But even as Richard Nixon was trying to blunt Ted Kennedy's assaults, Kennedy's own moral authority would collapse, and that is one of the stories of *Catching the Wind* as well. Ted was never the moral exemplar that his brothers purported to be. He was, in his own mind and in the minds of many, the most impaired and fallible of the Kennedys, which was why he worked so hard to convince them, and to convince himself, otherwise. And with that work, he seemed to expunge the doubts about him and inherit his brothers' moral authority. And then in July 1969, with Nixon only six months in office, Ted Kennedy squandered his authority on an automobile accident late at night on Chappaquiddick Island, off Martha's Vineyard, in which a young woman was killed—an accident he failed to report until the next morning. Kennedy had been one of the few bulwarks against the conservative enterprise to end liberalism, and the accident was a conservative godsend. (Nixon couldn't stop ruminating about it.) No one wanted to hear moral bromides from a man who seemed as morally compromised as Ted Kennedy now seemed. He had been the only national figure who might have revived the moral passion that Vietnam had destroyed—a Kennedy restoration was Nixon's deepest fear—and that Nixon had worked so hard to prevent. Now Ted couldn't.

After a triumphant reelection in 1972, in which he trounced Democratic nominee George McGovern and trounced liberalism, too, Richard Nixon seemed to construct a new political coalition for a new postliberal era. Pundits would later talk of "Reagan Democrats," white blue-collar workers who had abandoned the Democratic Party, but they were first "Nixon Democrats," and their defections were a harbinger of what was to come. And yet Richard Nixon, who seethed with resentments, was never a man to leave well enough alone. Determined not just to beat the Democrats but to eliminate them, he had encouraged his minions to sow discord among the opposition, to play "dirty tricks" on them, to sic the government on them, to investigate them—Ted Kennedy was a major target—to burglarize their headquarters. In the process he wound up undoing his own presidency when the burglary of the Democratic National Committee office at the Watergate office and hotel complex in Washington was interrupted by a security guard and when Nixon was revealed to have approved paying off the burglars with laundered money to buy their silence. Needless to say, in a period of uncertain morality, this also had moral implications, just not the ones most Americans might have thought. Testifying before the Senate select committee to investigate the administration's malefactions, Nixon's men, one after another, defended themselves on the basis that they had been conducting a moral mission themselves—a mission to save the nation from the permissive rot of the liberals. John Ehrlichman, the president's chief domestic adviser, called Nixon's henchmen "idealistic." Bob Haldeman, Nixon's chief of staff, admitted that he had penned "good" and "great" in the margins of a memo that predicted Nixon would be greeted by hostile demonstrators in North Carolina during a visit to the evangelist Reverend Billy Graham, not only hostile but "violent"—"good" and "great" notwithstanding that violence, because seemingly it would expose those demonstrators as dangerous. And G. Gordon Liddy, one of those Watergate burglars, would write: "To permit the thought, spirit, life-style of the '60s movement to achieve power . . . was a thought as offensive to me as was the thought of surrender to a career Japanese soldier in 1945." This was obviously politics wrapped to look like morality, but the sentiments were no less sincere for that. Conservatives genuinely feared the 1960s, feared the direction the country had taken then, feared the end of white Anglo-Saxon Protestant power (power that John Kennedy's election as a Catholic had seemed to imperil), feared the rise of Black Americans, feared the doubts that Vietnam had sown about the deployment of military force, feared feminism, feared what they saw as moral depravity that was the inevitable result of permissiveness—feared these things so much that they were willing to use covert, illegal means to arrest them. And added to the irony here of moralism defending itself against morality, there was another irony: Watergate, as the collection of Nixon's crimes would be called, would further undermine the sense of American morality, but rather than hurt the conservatives who had promulgated the crimes, it would undermine the very trust in government on which liberalism had been predicated. Richard Nixon went a long way toward destroying liberalism, just not the way he had wanted to. He did so by stripping Americans of their faith in their institutions and their leaders.

And that is a story told in *Catching the Wind*.

Richard Nixon's resentments, which had devoured him and led to Watergate, lived on long after he departed the White House. And when the liberal hour wound down, those resentments, now national resentments, would consume American politics and not just for a brief period, not just for a conservative hour, but for decades. Those resentments would trigger a backlash against liberalism—a backlash against the way it was transforming America and a backlash that John Kennedy's death had only delayed and muted.

And that backlash was what was transpiring in Boston in the mid-1970s, when Pixie Palladino led her demonstrations and hounded Ted Kennedy "like a banshee," as scholar Ronald Formisano would put it, and shouted him down, and chased him into the subway. Race was clearly a large part of that backlash, since liberalism was so closely associated with racial progress and since the white working class had come to see racial progress as a threat to its own neighborhoods, jobs, and schools. When the issue of integrating Boston's schools was first raised in the 1960s, the leader of those opposed to busing, Louise Day Hicks, disavowed racism—at least overt racism. She wanted only to maintain neighborhood schools, she claimed. But that was the 1960s, John Kennedy's decade, Lyndon Johnson's decade. (Later, in 1967, Hicks would run for mayor, lose narrowly, and lose again four years later, then win a seat in the House as the face of Boston's white ethnic citizens. "You Know Where I Stand" was her slogan in that first mayoral race, meaning where she stood on integration.) By the 1970s, when forced integration was on the table, Hicks, disappointed by the violent turn the movement had taken, both stepped aside and was pushed aside by protesters like Palladino who didn't hide their racial prejudice. "Sure we're racists," Formisano would quote protesters. "Isn't everybody?" And for those protesters, race was closely tied to crime—a conjunction that Richard Nixon had cleverly exploited, after dozens of American cities erupted in racial violence, using "law and order" euphemistically to refer to race, as if Black Americans posed a physical threat to white Americans. Black people had waited one hundred years after the end of the Civil War to gain their rights during the liberal hour. Over the following decade, working-class white Americans reacted with grievance, feeling they had been forgotten or been pushed aside, marginalized, stripped of *their* rights, as Black Americans were gaining theirs—losers of a giant zero-sum game. Decades later the political observer Thomas Edsall would describe what happened to America after the Great Society in terms that Pixie Palladino and her army would have understood and endorsed. "Beginning in the mid-60s," he wrote, "the priorities of the Democratic Party began to shift away from the white working- and middle-class voters—many of them socially conservative, Christian and religiously observant—to a set of emerging constituencies seeking rights and privileges previously reserved for white men: African-Americans; women's rights advocates; proponents of ethnic diversity, sexual freedom and self-expressive individualism." School busing seemed to both symbolize the transition and ignite it.

But Pixie Palladino, though a racist, had other resentments, even deeper than her racial ones, and in these too she reflected how America was changing. She not only detested Black Americans, who she feared were displacing white working-class Americans like her; she also detested those who had advanced their cause. In this, Palladino wasn't far from her predecessor, Louise Day Hicks. As J. Anthony Lukas wrote of Hicks, she had "tapped a much broader sense of grievance, rooted less in race than in class: the feeling of many working-class whites that they had been abandoned by the very institutions—City Hall, the Democratic Party, the Catholic Church, the popular press—that until recently had been their patrons and allies." *Abandoned.* And Richard Nixon, whose own resentments very much paralleled theirs, had known how to take advantage of their umbrage. And that sense of abandonment had only intensified when Hicks, who was still in many ways an establishment figure—her father had been a judge, and she was lace-curtain Irish who was a devout Catholic—gave way to the less rarified Pixie Palladinos, who roared against everything. Ronald Formisano would make the same observation as Lukas: "Pixie's pugnacious style was pure backlash," he wrote. But the greatest backlash was her "ferocious anger toward upper-class types such as [Ted] Kennedy and [Judge] Garrity," whom she scornfully called the "beautiful people." And Pixie and her troops would invade meetings of city committees—committees of "beautiful people" mainly from the Boston suburbs—and shout them down to shut them down. In a perfect blend of her racial and class antagonisms, Palladino would say: the "Kennedys look down on people of color like me."

So what happened in City Hall Plaza in September 1974 when Ted Kennedy was rattled by a crowd that pilloried him, and outside South Atlantic High School in April 1975 by a crowd that threatened him, and again and again over the following year pointed both to Ted's loss of moral authority among those ethnic white Bostonians and to the direction of the country now that the liberal wind was weakening. Bostonians like Pixie Palladino felt that they had been not only abandoned but also disrespected—that government, and the beautiful people who ran it, felt they knew better than the ordinary people, Nixon's once-silent majority. And that disrespect would ultimately release long-pent-up anger at having had to play by liberal rules. And now all the disaffected and aggrieved who had chafed at those rules, who had felt that their values were trashed by the permissiveness of the 1960s and by the rise of the young and the Black and the gay and the feminists, were getting their revenge—the revenge of the 1970s against the '60s.

And that revenge, intensifying, billowing, gusting, an angry political tornado roaring across the country and blowing down everything for which the Kennedys had stood and for which Ted Kennedy had fought—everything for which he would continue to fight—is the story of *Against the Wind.* If *Catching the Wind* was about the brief blast of moral wind that

filled the sails of the Great Society and that Ted Kennedy caught in helping advance that society as a tribute to his brothers and as an obligation
to those Americans whom, he believed, needed him, *Against the Wind* is
about how, despite Richard Nixon's disgrace after Watergate, the wind
shifted and reversed, and how Ted Kennedy attempted to defy it, then bent
into it, charged into it, even as he realized that the moral moment had
passed and the nation's values had changed, as Pixie Palladino so amply
demonstrated. Under Franklin Roosevelt and for thirty years thereafter,
America had been basically a liberal country, expounding a sense of charity and generosity and hope and community, even when it failed to live up
to those pronouncements, as it so often did. And while the turn against
that generosity began under Richard Nixon, the vestiges of liberalism
were still strong enough that he felt compelled to speak in code about his
racial animosities rather than openly about them, even as he sought to
divide the country along racial lines. But what Nixon had sown, his Republican successors would reap. Nixon dreamed of a permanent majority—
a majority that united traditional conservatives and Southerners with the
old working-class New Deal Democrats who now felt neglected. In his
wake, Republicans would very nearly achieve it. Beginning in 1980 under
Ronald Reagan, the deeply conservative but affable former governor of
California who largely eschewed racial appeals for more veiled and circumspect appeals to individual liberty, and whose deepest antagonisms
were expressed by inveighing against the alleged encroachments of government, encroachments that liberals had viewed as necessary to bring
the promise of the nation to all its citizens—under Reagan, and then for
more than thirty years thereafter, America would abandon the ideals that
had held the liberal consensus together. Reagan's America would embrace individual liberty over a sense of community, though it was lost on
no one that conservatives would be far less zealous in promoting the liberties of Black Americans than in defending the rights of white Americans
to deny those liberties. It would be a country in retreat from progressive
principles that had defined not only liberalism but also, for nearly four
decades, the nation itself. If, in *Catching the Wind*, Ted Kennedy, like his
country, had drafted behind a liberal wind, in *Against the Wind* he would
be sailing against a stiff conservative wind.

But this is not just the personal story of a man fighting for what he
believed in (conservatives, after all, had no less conviction in their cause
than Ted Kennedy had in his), or the political story of a country redefin-

ing itself, though it is certainly that, arguably the biggest political story of the last twenty-five years of the twentieth century and the first ten of the twenty-first, or the story of a society in upheaval as it faced those racial and class antagonisms that had animated Pixie Palladino, though it is that too. It is, perhaps most fundamentally, the story of how the basic moral precepts of the nation, those precepts that had driven liberalism, changed: a story in which Ted Kennedy was a central protagonist, both as the champion of liberalism, to his admirers, and as a symbol of the very disdain and hypocrisy against which the conservatives and their new populist allies were taking up arms. For as much as the national transformation that destroyed the old liberal consensus forged between moderate Democrats and Republicans in the 1950s had to do with race and with a sense of raw grievance against so-called liberal elitists, so too did it have to do with a rebellion against a certain kind of moral order they felt had been imposed upon them—an order that called for obligations to one another. The New Deal had begun with what Franklin Roosevelt, in his acceptance of the Democratic presidential nomination in 1932, called a "simple moral principle": namely that the state should serve the needs of the great mass of its citizens—*all* its citizens. And while in the post–New Deal period conservatives and liberals, Republicans and Democrats, would disagree on many things, on matters of political philosophy and policy and the means to achieve their ends, they generally agreed on the moral basis of national unity. The Republican Senate minority leader Everett Dirksen was a staunchly traditional conservative, but he nevertheless supported Johnson's Civil Rights Act, supported it powerfully and even movingly, and he brought twenty-six Republicans along with him to end a Southern filibuster on the grounds, as he declared on the Senate floor, that "we are confronted with a moral issue. Today let us not be found wanting in whatever it takes by way of moral and spiritual substance to face up to the issue." A *moral* issue. (Given the antipathy of Southern Democrats toward the bill, were it not for Dirksen and his Republicans, it would not have passed.) But when Richard Nixon in his quest for power and a permanent majority began dividing the nation along racial lines, he also divided it along moral lines. The consensus ended. Republicans increasingly saw and seized opportunities to nurse white backlash and to demonize liberals as Nixon's henchmen had, seeing them not as political opponents but as the gravest threat to the nation, akin, as Liddy had said, to the nation's enemies in World War II. The politics that would displace liberalism in the last quarter of the twentieth century, then, was not the old conservatism with which liberals had successfully crossed swords since the New Deal, the conservatism of small towns and big business, lower taxes, and less government; rather, it was something new that emerged in the late 1960s and '70s and that swelled in the 1980s when Ronald Reagan took power—the politics of anger and resentment that Ronald Formisano would call "reactionary populism." It was the politics of the Pixie Palladinos. And it would dominate not only America's political ecology but also its moral ecology for generations to come.

As I wrote in the introduction to *Catching the Wind*, Robert Caro's great multivolume biography of Lyndon Johnson uses Johnson's life to address the issue of power—how a political artist wielded it and toward what end. This biography uses the life of Edward Kennedy to address the issue of political morality—how a different kind of political artist attempted to wield it to ensure liberalism's survival and how liberalism ceded its power as its moral authority eroded under the assault of those white blue-collar populists who had once benefited from liberal programs but now felt targeted by them. In the second phase of his Senate career, Ted Kennedy dedicated himself to fighting this moral sea change, and he was as tenacious as any politician of his time in doing so. But he was a flawed proponent of the liberal standards he championed—flawed because his own personal morality—his seeming recklessness as evidenced in his college scandal, in his womanizing, in his drinking, and in his automobile accident on Chappaquiddick Island—gave his conservative opponents a bludgeon to attack his political morality and to discredit the Kennedy mystique that had done so much to advance liberalism.

Still, despite his own recognition of those flaws and of his own role in undermining the very values for which he advocated, as he became a Senate eminence in a chamber increasingly given to undoing the New Deal and the Great Society and undoing what he regarded as their moral underpinnings, he fought to preserve liberalism and what he saw as his nation's better angels. And like his brother Bobby, as he faced now a countervailing wind, that strong stiff wind of angry populism fanned by the conservatives who saw it as a way to seize power from the liberals, Ted Kennedy felt he was fighting for the soul of America. This book is about his fight and the country's, about the declining course of liberalism and the ascendant course of conservatism, and about the fate of the nation's soul.

AGAINST

THE WIND

ONE

A Man of the Senate

THE YOUNG MAN who entered the Senate in 1962 as one of its least impressive members, a thirty-year-old fledgling whose main recommendation for public office was that he was the president's brother, had, in the fourteen years since, risen to a level that none of his detractors or even most of his admirers could have foreseen. Ted Kennedy had become a member of the Club—that Senate inner sanctum of mostly senior senators, all of them committee chairmen, where true power was wielded. His brothers John and Bobby had hated the Senate. For them, it was a slow, grinding institution, an institution in which members had to wait their turn to achieve power or prominence—seniority was the congressional coin of the realm—an institution expressly designed by the nation's constitutional framers to slow or even halt progress rather than speed it. And if the Senate had been designed, in the likely apocryphal words of George Washington, to cool the more heated effusions of the House as a saucer cools hot tea, the Senate itself found ways to prolong that cooling, passing a rule that required a vote of two-thirds of its members to cut off debate, which effectively meant that it took only a third of the membership to stop a bill from coming to a vote. It was in the Senate, that reluctant institution, where Southern Democrats used the filibuster to defeat civil rights legislation again and again and to keep America's Black citizens in subservience until Lyndon Johnson and a liberal Democratic caucus abetted by moderate Republicans finally got cloture and pried a civil rights act loose. The two older Kennedy brothers preferred executive power—power that could get things done, even as John Kennedy as president quickly realized that the Senate could thwart executive power too. Ted Kennedy, however, had come to the Senate with a different agenda, a different attitude. He was no less desirous than his brothers of getting things done, no less desirous of making a difference. But when he got to the Senate, Ted Kennedy had patience. "It fills you with a heightened sense of purpose," he had said of the Senate, and as he got his bearings there, as he learned the legislative ropes—ropes that he became especially good at manipulating—he was determined to make the institution work for him.

But there was one other reason that Ted Kennedy became a Senate man: unlike his brothers, who made no bones about using the Senate as a stepping-stone to the presidency, he had no choice.

When Richard Nixon came to power in 1968, Ted Kennedy was in fighting trim—challenging him, parrying him, upholding liberal principles both for his own sake and for Bobby's, since but for an assassin's bullet, Bobby, not Nixon, might have been in that Oval Office making policy; creating a shadow presidency, like a parliamentary opposition, waiting to assume power when Nixon faltered; conducting, at times, his own foreign policy, even though that violated political norms; speaking out forcefully against the administration, so forcefully that Republicans took umbrage and felt he overstepped the bounds of civility, which might have been true; and biding, biding his time for his chance to enter the Oval Office himself, even if he was unsure whether he really wanted to occupy that office, though if he did, it would be not to restore Camelot, which he knew was a futile dream, a lost dream, but to rededicate the federal government to what he felt were principles of decency and compassion—the principles for which his brothers had stood.

But in 1976 Ted Kennedy surrendered his chance to become president. Though he had ruminated on the possibility after Senator George McGovern's historic landslide loss to Nixon in 1972, commissioning polls as early as 1973, and though he would boast to young staffer Richard Burke about the results of those polls and asked Burke what he was hearing on his campus (Burke was still a student), and though there were discussions of a possible candidacy, the deliberations had ended in September 1974, when Ted announced that he would not be running. At the time he cited family considerations. His son, Ted Jr., had recently had his leg amputated to prevent the spread of bone cancer, and the shadow of the deaths of John and Robert, both assassinated, always hung over the family and any possible candidacy. When Ted discussed a run with his sister Jean and her husband Steve Smith in the presence of Ted's mother, Rose, and of Kennedy family friend and historian Arthur Schlesinger, Jr., Schlesinger said that Rose immediately shrank, and Jean was "somber and silent." Schlesinger noted that the family seemed "deeply and genuinely opposed to Ted's running," but that Ted's brother-in-law "seems to think that Ted would be best for the country and that his candidacy may become inevitable and is fatalistic about the risks." As for Ted's own fatalism, Schlesinger thought that Ted "shifts according to the time of day from one of these positions to the other."

Ted had other concerns besides his son's health and his personal safety. His estranged wife, Joan, was an alcoholic who was often in recovery. It was questionable whether she could survive a campaign. And there was the ever-lingering issue of the automobile accident on Chappaquiddick Island, in which a young woman passenger had drowned when Ted drove off a narrow bridge and then failed to report the accident until the next morning, ten hours later. As the fifth anniversary of the accident approached in July 1974, *The New York Times, The Boston Globe,* the *Los Angeles Times,* and *The Philadelphia Inquirer* were all preparing new investigations of Chappaquiddick. "The hard truth is, as can be attested by almost any reporter who travels the country," wrote *New York Times* columnist Tom Wicker, "that there is a huge reservoir of doubt and resentment about what Mr. Kennedy called 'the tragedy' at Chappaquiddick, particularly among those who had given their allegiance to Spiro Agnew," Nixon's vice president who had been driven from office in disgrace for having accepted bribes, "and Richard Nixon," who had been driven from office for shenanigans in which he used the government to target opponents, "or both, and those who had seen both Mr. Agnew and Mr. Nixon brought low for 'cover-ups' rather like those of which they suspected Edward Kennedy." If Ted ran, Wicker suspected, the emphasis would be not on the misdeeds of Nixon and Agnew but on Ted's alleged misdeeds at Chappaquiddick. Ted, it was reported, didn't want to subject himself to that kind of scrutiny again. As Kennedy family adviser Milton Gwirtzman put it: "He is unwilling to take the personal risk that Chappaquiddick will defeat him."

But for a man as attuned to politics as Ted was, there was also a political element in his calculations: He understood how the temper of the country had changed since Lyndon Johnson's presidency and the heyday of the Great Society, and he recognized that America might no longer be receptive to his brand of politics. Years later he would write that while his supporters and Kennedy acolytes looked at the possibility of a Kennedy restoration romantically, he was too pragmatic to try to attempt one. "The eras that shaped them," he would write of his brothers, "had passed. The present era was quite different in mood, in collective experience and in the challenges the nation faced." Ted understood reactionary populism because he had confronted it during those antibusing demonstrations. He understood that the old New Deal coalition had fractured, that working-class white Americans and Black Americans were often at loggerheads, and that the liberal prescriptions of the past, however much he continued to believe in them and in the morality that he thought underlay them, had lost their appeal.

Those Democrats who did contend for the party's nomination after Ted's renunciation were a mixed but largely pallid group of retreads and opportunists hoping to catch lightning in a bottle. Among them were the liberal Arizona congressman Morris "Mo" Udall, neither a retread nor an opportunist but not a heavyweight either; the longtime Washington senator Henry "Scoop" Jackson; Indiana senator Birch Bayh, who had saved Ted's life in the 1964 plane crash by risking his own life to pull Ted from the burning wreckage; Pennsylvania governor Milton Shapp; former North Carolina governor and current Duke University president Terry Sanford; the segregationist Alabama governor George Wallace; and Ted's own brother-in-law, R. Sargent Shriver. None of them especially fired up the Democratic Party stalwarts who saw in Gerald Ford's reelection campaign an opportunity to seize the presidency after Nixon's Watergate scandal had soiled it, and many of them still pined for Ted, even after the race began and despite Ted's demurrals. "Teddy is the one who turns them on—the single incandescent presence, excepting only George Wallace, in the lackluster Democratic Presidential politics of 1976," *Newsweek* opined in June 1975.

Among the least known and least prepossessing of the contenders was a short, thin fifty-year-old former Georgia governor and one-time peanut farmer. Jimmy Carter admitted, when he announced he was running, that he was at the "bottom of the list" of aspirants, and he wasn't far off. He had grown up in the adjoining flyspeck hardscrabble farming communities of Plains and Archery, Georgia, at a time when segregation ruled; his own father, he said, was a racist. He got an appointment to the Naval Academy at Annapolis—his father, with political connections, helped arrange it—married a hometown girl, and then when his father died, left the service and returned to Plains to manage the family peanut farm and

associated businesses. Exactly why he decided to enter politics is unclear—he didn't seem animated by any particular social mission—but
one thing he did have was ambition. "Intense ambition," he was to call it
himself. He rose quickly—from chairing the county school board to state
senator, a contest he won after getting a court to invalidate fraudulent
ballots cast for his opponent, and, after losing a bid for a House seat, governor in 1970. Carter was no crusader for racial justice. As his biographer
Jonathan Alter would write, he "would do nothing to support what some
historians now call the Second Reconstruction"—the period from *Brown
v. Board of Education* in 1954 that desegregated schools through the Fair
Housing Act of 1968. He understood racial politics—his predecessor in
the governorship was the bumptious restaurateur Lester Maddox, a
"white trash dingbat," the writer Hunter Thompson called him, who had
won office after gaining notoriety handing out ax handles to his customers so they could resist anyone attempting to integrate his establishment—
and he understood reactionary populism, opposing school busing while
announcing that "conservatism is not racism," though in this case it
came perilously close. In his gubernatorial campaign, he decried "ultraliberals" in the Democratic Party, and his slogan was "Isn't It Time Someone Spoke Up for *You?*" with the implication that he would be speaking up
for them on race. But if Jimmy Carter was no stranger to the politics of racial backlash—in fairness, he couldn't have won in Georgia otherwise—
neither was he unacquainted with the politics of racial intolerance. In his
inaugural address, he stunned supporters in Georgia and won admirers
elsewhere by declaring, "The time for racial discrimination is over."

Though Carter was hardly a racist—he would later claim to have believed in integration but candidly admitted a certain cowardice in failing
to advance it—his new racial sensitivity might have been less a matter of
epiphany than a reflection of his intense ambition. Just as he had no
sooner become state senator than he plotted to become governor, so now
he plotted to become president, and he certainly realized that he would
have no hope of success if he didn't display his temporized racial views.
The Jimmy Carter who announced for the presidency on December 12,
1974, near the end of his gubernatorial term, was a member of what the
press had taken to calling the "New South"—enlightened governors like
Reuben Askew of Florida, John West of South Carolina, and Dale Bumpers of Arkansas, who contrasted with the racist demagogues among
whom George Wallace remained the most prominent example. Even so,

Carter's candidacy seemed preposterous. No one from the Deep South had been elected to the presidency in 130 years. But Carter might have understood more about the mood of the nation than many of the pols and pundits who dismissed him. In fact, he knew many of the same things Ted Kennedy had learned during those antibusing demonstrations. Democrats assumed that Watergate had so devastated the Republicans that it would hand the Democratic Party victory. Carter knew differently. He knew that the grievances of Americans, in particular white working-class Americans, ran deep, and that Watergate wouldn't necessarily obscure them.

Ted Kennedy was no particular fan of Jimmy Carter's. Nor was Carter a fan of Kennedy's. The two had met in May 1974 at the University of Georgia Law School, where Ted gave the keynote address at the Law Day observance and Carter delivered remarks of his own. In Ted's recollection, Carter invited him to stay at the governor's mansion—Ted also misremembered the date as May 1973, and the occasion as a speech on the Soviet Union—and offered Ted and his staff the use of his plane the next morning to fly from Atlanta to Athens, the site of the university, then suddenly rescinded the offer of the plane shortly before Ted was to board, forcing Ted to race seventy-five miles by car to his appearance, arriving just in time. "Puzzlingly changeable in his manner toward me" was how Ted recalled their meeting, "cordial one moment . . . and callous the next." (Ted surely didn't know that Carter had decided to run for president and saw Ted as his chief rival.) The writer Hunter Thompson, who was present that morning, said Ted was not so equable at the time. He was angry at Carter, and the "mood in the car was ugly," Thompson wrote. And later Thompson would note something else about the events that day that he said "stunned" him: He had seen Carter "push Kennedy around," just "pushed Kennedy aside, 'Get out of my way. I got work to do. Move aside.'"* Still, when Carter declared for the presidency, his chief of staff, Hamilton Jordan, suggested that Kennedy would probably welcome a

---

*Thompson was deeply impressed by Carter's speech that day—a seemingly extemporaneous speech, a scathing speech, about injustices in the Georgia legal system, that seemed to shock his audience—a heartfelt, no-holds-barred speech of a kind that Carter had never given. One of his advisers later said that he cut loose that day not because he had been repressing his true feelings but because he was angry and aggrieved at being relegated to a bystander by Kennedy's appearance. Peter Bourne int., July 28, 2015, quoted in Jon Ward, *Camelot's End: Kennedy vs. Carter and the Fight That Broke the Democratic Party* (New York: Twelve, 2019), 87.

candidate from the South who could take on Wallace and that Carter should talk to Kennedy on the day of the announcement, which Eleanor Clift of *Newsweek* said he did. (If so, neither man reported such a meeting.)

Now Carter was off and running. The "bottom of the list," he had said of his position upon entering the race, but the man at the bottom of the list rose rapidly, despite his liabilities, which were significant. Carter was no natural politician—no Ted Kennedy. He was stern, peevish, pious and even self-righteous, humorless, cold—"icy" was an adjective used to describe him—unforgiving, petty, and vengeful. Though he brandished a wide toothy smile that became the feature most identified with him and had a boyishly diffident manner that reminded some admirers of the Kennedys, Robert Shrum, a political adviser to Carter and later Ted Kennedy's press secretary, said, "Behind the reflex smile, there was steel," adding uncharitably, "but more about his ambition than his convictions."

This was Ted Kennedy's suspicion too: that Jimmy Carter was a man without convictions, though whatever convictions he might have had were certainly not the ones Ted had. Carter biographer Jonathan Alter, recounting how Carter's father had turned on Franklin Roosevelt when Roosevelt's Agricultural Adjustment Act had farmers plow under crops and slaughter livestock to reduce supply and thus raise prices, wrote of Jimmy that the New Deal "wasn't in his DNA." "Clearly the most conservative of the Democratic candidates in the '76 campaign," Carter's aide Stuart Eizenstat called him. (When Carter scaled back a statement on mine safety, to Shrum's consternation, Carter told Shrum sharply, "They chose to be miners.") But Carter didn't run as a conservative; he couldn't in a party as liberal as the Democratic Party was. He ran by espousing a moral agenda that would contrast with the amorality of the Nixon administration, though it was not the tenacious political morality of Ted Kennedy, the morality of compassion, but something more generalized and anodyne. He talked of honesty, integrity, fairness, liberty, justice, love—all of which no one could argue against. As late as May 1976, by which time Carter had dispatched his opponents in the primaries (his defeat of Wallace in Florida was especially significant, though Carter achieved it largely by convincing most of his rivals to step aside so he could take on the Alabama governor) and had all but clinched the nomination, Ted, when asked his assessment of Carter, told *The Washington Post*, "I still don't have any feel for the dimensions of the man, no sense of the human being. People ask me if I agree with his positions on the issues. I have to say 'what positions?' " Deliberately vague, "indefinite and imprecise" was how Ted described Carter's answers to the Democratic Platform Committee, so that, Ted believed, Carter didn't have to address the difficult, prickly issues of the day.

If Ted Kennedy was "restraining his enthusiasm" for Carter, as *Newsweek* put it with intended understatement, he wasn't alone. The entire liberal establishment harbored doubts about their enigmatic putative nominee and hoped he might be stopped. California governor Jerry Brown entered the race late to halt Carter's advance and won six primaries, but he was *too* late, and Idaho senator Frank Church made a brief run as well, with no success. Many of those liberals still yearned for Ted, and he might have yearned too. "Aching to be president," Speaker of the House Tip O'Neill had told a reporter of Ted's mindset a year earlier, ten months after Ted's announcement not to run but also eight months after Carter's decision *to* run. Now, with primary season over, the New York *Daily News* reported that Ted had told intimates he would accept a genuine draft at the convention. But this was wishful thinking among those who distrusted Carter. Ted's ambivalence toward Carter notwithstanding, there would be no late run and no draft. He had ceded the nomination to Carter. Carter, for his part, made no overtures to Ted, which, in a purely political sense, baffled Ted since Carter clearly needed liberal support if he were to win. ("I'm glad I don't have to kiss his [Ted's] ass," Carter had told the *Atlanta Journal*.) At a party at Steve Smith's New York apartment that July, just before the convention, Schlesinger found Ted "highly uncertain what to do about Carter." "I don't want to appear to be a bad sport," Ted told Schlesinger. "My brothers and I have always played by the rules. I can't change on that. But a lot of people have put a lot of work and belief in things. I can't go to them and say they must trust Carter or that he believes in the things they believe in. I don't know what he believes in myself." To unite the party, Steve Smith said that Ted would have even nominated Carter at the convention had he been asked, but he wasn't. He wasn't even asked to appear at the convention, saying years later of Carter's rebuff, "He wanted to be separated and clear from the Kennedys." "I want to make that clear," Ted told the *Los Angeles Times* in an article titled "Kennedy Almost an Afterthought at Convention," of his failure to appear. "I just wasn't asked." The next day Ted's aide Paul Kirk told *The Boston Globe* that the invitation had come too late and that Ted was already heading to the airport during the celebration on the podium, which might have been Ted's way of trying to ease the tensions between Carter and himself.

But Carter, clearly resentful of Ted, didn't seem eager to ease the tensions, possibly thinking he had already done enough to mend fences with the liberals by selecting liberal Minnesota senator Walter Mondale as his running mate. In truth, Carter didn't seem to care much for the party that had nominated him, nor it for him. "Their triumph was one of technique, not love," *Newsweek* reported of the Carter forces' victory at the convention, which was not something that would ever have been said of a convention that had anointed a Kennedy, "and was joylessly received by much of the party—at least till the hoarse victory bash on getaway night." The report went on, "Carter remains an outsider to many Democratic regulars—a strange man who owes them neither friendship nor favor." And Maryland governor Marvin Mandel might have been speaking for most of his fellow office holders when he told *Newsweek*, "You get the feeling he doesn't need you." That was precisely what Carter's own pollster, Patrick Caddell, had written Carter in a memo after the nomination: "To be frank, Jimmy Carter is not particularly popular with major elements of the Democratic Party, whether it be activists, the Congress, labor leaders or political bosses." Odd as it might have sounded coming out of a convention, that was more a boast than an alert. Carter ran as an outsider— someone who didn't abide by the traditional Washington folkways. He seemed to like to offend his fellow Democrats, whether as some form of personal retribution or as what he regarded as a sound political strategy to protect himself from liberal stigma. Ted said he reached out to Carter, offering to campaign with him anywhere, as long as Carter stood beside him, but Carter refused, Ted believed, because of Carter's own insecurities. (They did make an appearance together in Massachusetts.) Again, on his own initiative, Ted said he recruited his old campaign manager, Gerard Doherty, to head up Carter's general campaign in New York, and Ted appeared twice in the state at Doherty's behest. Still, Doherty said that Carter could have had Ted do more there, that Ted was a political savant who knew everything there was to know about New York politics, but again, Carter never asked.

It was an odd campaign, a campaign of two rather muted candidates both groping for the electorate and seeming wary of offending it rather than trying to excite it, because they both seemed to realize that the excitement in their parties lay elsewhere. Gerald Ford, though an incumbent, had limped into the general election, saddled with the unpopular pardon he had issued to his predecessor, Richard Nixon, for the crimes of Watergate and seriously wounded by a challenge mounted by former California governor Ronald Reagan, who viewed Ford as insufficiently conservative and also vulnerable. Ford had narrowly beat him at the Republican convention—by just 117 votes out of more than two thousand cast—but the damage had been done. He was now forced to win back conservatives in the general election, just as Carter was forced to win back liberals, and it left both of them foundering. As one journalist, looking back at Carter's campaign, put it, candidates typically veered right or left during primaries to shore up support among the party faithful, and then moved to the center during the general election. But Carter deviated from the plan by campaigning at the center during the primaries and then edging leftward during the general election. The journalist was only partly right. Carter did make small concessions to the left even during the primaries. He hesitated and then finally, late in primary season, endorsed national health insurance, one of Ted Kennedy's signature issues. But Ted was unimpressed, saying later that Carter "talked his way around it" and that he was "completely ambiguous about it and resentful of the pressure"—Ted's pressure—"that was being put on him for doing this." Rather, Carter, convinced that the country was moving rightward not leftward, remained vague, speaking in platitudes—"no ideology, no central informing political ideas," Robert Shrum, who left Carter's campaign staff, would say of him—avoiding discussing the recession and inflation that were plaguing the country and that had hurt President Ford and instead declaring that he wanted a government that was "as good and honest and decent and truthful and fair and competent and compassionate and as filled with love as are the American people," another implicit critique of Nixon and of Ford, who had pardoned Nixon, though with racial backlash rippling through the country, the terrible truth was that the American people might no longer have been as good as Carter portrayed them.

In effect, Jimmy Carter was running out the clock. He left the Democratic convention in July with a 62 to 29 percent lead over Ford and might have thought he could coast. That, however, was his high-water mark. Ford, an amiable if uninspiring candidate against whom attacks on Nixonian amorality were unlikely to land heavily, steadily gained on Carter, who had few of the party stalwarts, including Ted Kennedy, to fall back on. Were it not for a gaffe by Ford during the second of two debates—he declared that the Soviet Union had not dominated Eastern Europe and wouldn't in a future Ford administration, when it was clear that the Soviet Union had indeed dominated Eastern Europe—and were it not for a last-minute campaign swing for Carter by George Wallace, the threat of whose nomination had prompted many terrified Democrats to support Carter, Carter would almost certainly have lost. By election day, his thirty-point lead had shrunk to two points and to only 50.1 percent of the vote. "The Carter river is broad—and shallow," one Midwestern senator had said after the convention. He was right. The coalition that Carter assembled was not the durable one that he had hoped to construct of Black people and the increasingly conservative white working class. It was a narrower coalition. He won the South out of regional pride but received only 45 percent of white votes nationally, and while he improved upon McGovern's showing in 1972, which wasn't hard to do, picking up some poor voters and those without a college education, his biggest gains were among young college-educated voters, who were still a relatively small slice of the electorate. Among Democrats, Carter won only 80 percent of the vote, a poor showing, and he generally ran well behind local Democrats— in eighteen of twenty-three states where there was a senatorial or gubernatorial race, Carter received fewer votes than the Democratic candidates. (Among those candidates was Ted Kennedy, who stood for reelection that year against an antibusing Republican, Michael Swing Robertson, and won with 69 percent of the vote after easily fending off a primary challenge by another antibusing foe. "Well, this busing thing has hurt," Ted had confessed to biographer Theo Lippman as he braced for the campaign.) Carter had thought that distancing himself from his liberal party was good politics. He turned out to be wrong, not necessarily because he had misread the country—Ford's late surge probably meant he had read it correctly and that the national mood was conservative in spite of antagonism toward Nixon—but because he might not have been the best messenger for his message, which was mixed at best and fatuous at worst. Carter, whose disposition was too conservative to be liberal and too liberal to be conservative, had hoped to stand for everything by standing for nothing. His biographer, an admirer of Carter's, would nevertheless call his election a "historical anomaly."

But this was not the conclusion Jimmy Carter drew from his narrow election victory. The conclusion he drew was that liberalism was extinct. The pollster Patrick Caddell told him as much. Working-class white Democrats were disaffected because they were now focused on social issues rather than economic ones, meaning presumably issues like busing, and young voters were disenchanted with ideology, liberal or not, altogether. Old-line liberal Democrats like Ted Kennedy were "as antiquated and anachronistic a group as are conservative Republicans," Caddell prophesied, and he promoted a new Democracy, both postideological and postliberal—basically a future without Ted Kennedy. (Liberals repaid the contempt with contempt of their own. George McGovern was so distrustful of Carter that he voted for Gerald Ford.) Even after the long election season in which Carter was at the center of the nation's politics, even after spending some time campaigning with him in October in Massachusetts, Ted Kennedy told Arthur Schlesinger that he still had no sense of Carter. Ted said that when you meet most people, "you can make a connection. There's something they want to talk about, something they care about, something on their mind." But "I have never seen anyone like him. Once you get beyond the merely perfunctory and try to talk about something substantive, a glazed window seems to come down, and there it is." Ted, no doubt recalling Nixon's fierce Kennedy hatred, suspected that Carter, a small-town boy like Nixon and an avowed Washington outsider, resented the Kennedys too, and one of Carter's staff people, who was friendly with Ted, confirmed it: "He [Carter] is filled with disdain and contempt about the Kennedys." But Ted told Schlesinger that he didn't want to take it personally, so he asked McGovern, Humphrey, and Ed Muskie how Carter treated *them*—and "they all had the same treatment."

Carter, like Nixon, certainly disdained Ted Kennedy personally, but Carter also feared that Ted might derail the prospective postliberal world that Caddell was outlining for the new president and to which Carter subscribed, and sought to marginalize him. "Kennedy senses problems with Governor Carter and that Carter is unnecessarily antagonistic to him," Caddell warned, correctly, which was true both in that Ted sensed problems and in that Carter was unnecessarily antagonistic. But "he and others may develop a mind-set that enables them to build up seemingly rational arguments for opposing the president's policies and even instigating political opposition."

Ted Kennedy's arguments might have been only "seemingly" rational to Carter, but that assessment might have been another form of Carter's petulance, as well as projection since Carter himself typically viewed combat personally not politically. What neither Caddell nor Carter seemed to understand about Ted Kennedy was that he never took things personally, which was why he questioned McGovern, Humphrey, and Muskie about Carter's treatment of them. If he were to oppose Jimmy Carter, it would be on the basis of political disagreement; on the basis that Carter was passionless about the causes for which Ted was passionate; on the basis that if Carter had no real concern for the causes in which Ted believed, neither did he have real concern for the people for whom Ted advocated; on the basis that Carter seemed to believe in nothing but his own advancement (a charge, ironically, that had been made about John and Bobby and initially about Ted too); and on the basis that in the White House Carter would refuse to champion the issues that Democrats had traditionally championed. (During the campaign, Carter, like a Republican, talked ominously about the danger of deficits.) Ted Kennedy's opposition wouldn't be because he had personal distaste for Jimmy Carter, though he did. His opposition would be because the New Deal was not in Jimmy Carter's DNA.

II

"There was a certain sadness about Ted," Arthur Schlesinger observed in his journal as the campaign had headed to the home stretch. "One felt he could not escape the apprehension that history may have passed him by. The highest expectations have been instilled in Ted, and now it looks as if Jimmy Carter, whom no one ever heard of, will be President for the next eight years." And Schlesinger, like Carter, sensed that "Ted is quite clearly prepared to go into the opposition if he feels that Carter is moving too far to the right," which would make him, in Schlesinger's view, the "ideological conscience of the Carter administration." Ted had accepted that his own presidency, were it ever to come, was now deferred. "I can't sit around stewing about that," he had said when Carter's nomination was imminent. "I've accepted that." But accepting it and being comfortable with it were not the same thing. His old administrative assistant, David Burke, would tell biographer Theo Lippman that Ted was constantly measuring himself against his brothers—Jack had been forty-three when he became president; Bobby forty-six when he ran; and Ted was now forty-four. He constantly felt the pressure of people who would think—or at least Ted felt they were thinking—that Jack had been president and Bobby had led a "great crusade," in Burke's words, and "Look at you, futzing around in the Senate." Burke added, "I don't believe he will accept being just a senator."

But Ted Kennedy, having forsworn a presidential bid in 1976 and now with Carter in office, had no choice but to retreat to the Senate, despite the fact that it wouldn't be easy for him to do so, either emotionally or practically. Though Carter, like Nixon before him, would obsess over the threat Ted posed to his presidency, Ted understood just how limited his resources were in the Senate to move policy compared to the president's. The problem, besides the pace of the Senate, was the nature of senatorial power. It was partly extra-institutional—power that derived from popularity, media attention, charisma, and not least, the perception that one might someday very well be president. Ted had played upon that power, had often relied upon it. (The last of these was the reason he didn't want to bow out of the 1976 race until after the 1974 midterm elections.) Senators had deferred to Ted Kennedy because they knew he was a national power, a larger-than-life power, a power who drew upon his family history and the people's love of his family, but also because they believed he would likely be president someday, and they didn't want to cross him. (Those with presidential aspirations of their own, however, didn't necessarily want to assist him in getting legislation passed either.) A national senator, Ted Kennedy was. A "presidential senator," historian James MacGregor Burns called him. The senator to whom many people in need often turned, even though he didn't technically represent them. Most senators received a hundred letters a week; Ted Kennedy received a thousand by one estimate, five thousand by another, and five hundred to six hundred calls a day. One reporter watched him walk from the Senate Office Building to the Capitol and back rather than take the congressional subway, and noted that he was accosted continuously by Black supporters who stopped their cars and rolled down their windows and called out to him, and that a poor supplicant stood outside the Office Building waiting to hand him a letter.

But now, with Carter's election, that national power, that extra-institutional power, had diminished. Ted Kennedy wasn't going to be president anytime soon. And while he still had the aura of being a Kennedy, while he was still a celebrity as well as a senator, he would have to rely on the other kind of political power—institutional power, the slow accretion of power in that slow-moving chamber through seniority and ingratiation with his fellow senators and favors and hard work. Institutional power hadn't always mixed with the extra-institutional variety. Indeed, it was very difficult to combine the two. Institutional power seemed to require that one forgo extra-institutional power—that one not play to the galleries, that one not harbor ambitions outside the Senate, that one not self-promote, that one respect the Senate—though Richard Russell, the most inside of insiders, had harbored presidential ambitions, and so, blatantly, had Lyndon Johnson—so that the Senate wouldn't seem like a way station, a stepping-stone to higher office. Extra-institutional power, on the other hand, required that one not toil obscurely in the legislative trenches, that one be a showhorse rather than a plowhorse, that one attract attention, as Jack and Bobby had, not turn from it. Only the most dexterous of senators had been able to combine the two. Lyndon Johnson had managed to do so, to be both a national figure with presidential aspirations and the wiliest of Senate insiders. And now Ted Kennedy was another, though in an entirely different way. He couldn't help but be a national figure; he was born into it, and his aspiration was less something he sought than something thrust upon him. But unlike his two senatorial brothers, who ignored institutional power and even actively disdained it, Ted, the boy raised to defer to his elders and his betters, had cultivated it when he entered the Senate and continued to cultivate it, lest he be thought of as a kid, a spoiled princeling, an empty vessel, a prime example of political nepotism, which was exactly how his colleagues *did* view him, until they realized that he had no arrogance, little or no sense of privilege, and no desire to use the Senate for his own personal advancement, and that, unlike his brothers, he was an institutionalist, a man of the Senate, willing to work hard to earn their trust and to serve his constituents and his nation. He had been trained by his family to accept a low rung in the hierarchy, the lowest—to be the least of them. Now he did so in the U.S. Senate.

And yet as the years passed and as the possibility of the presidency continued to loom, Ted Kennedy's status rose on that ladder and his power expanded. Because of those extra-institutional expectations, he had to be taken seriously, and he was. And when he forswore running for the presidency in 1976, not only did his extra-institutional power diminish, but the entire shape of his career changed. Of Ted's presumptive presidential candidacy, Milton Gwirtzman, the longtime Kennedy political adviser, observed, "Everything he did was looked at with the idea that this person is going to run for president. And that was both a help and a hindrance, and it affected to some extent the things he chose to do, not always, but to

some extent." He was often more cautious with the presidency on the horizon, temporizing, often doing things he might not otherwise do were he
not looking to his presidential prospects, as he did when he courted the
racist Alabama governor George Wallace on a summer's afternoon in
1973 when Ted was contemplating a presidential run and hoped to lure
some of Wallace's admirers.

Now that the presumption was gone, Ted was what he himself called a
"free senator." "When everyone thinks you may be going after the White
House," he told the columnist Joseph Alsop the week he had renounced
running, "you can't take a single step; you can't make any move at all
that isn't interpreted in terms of presidential politics. Getting away from
that is what I mean by becoming a free senator." And he told Alsop he
wanted to go to work on a bill to provide national health insurance, a bill
he had first proposed in 1969, and that with "no one at either end of
Pennsylvania Avenue thinking that passing a Kennedy bill will help a
Kennedy nomination, I have a lot better chance of getting something
done that really needs to be done." And though he expressed interest in
wanting to be president someday, he reaffirmed that he still believed in the
Senate, believed fervently that it was not, as so many had come to think, a
place of inaction, a place where legislation went to be stalled, a place of
"verbose sterility," as Alsop called it, but rather he believed that, as his old
friend and Senate colleague John Tunney put it, "it's possible for individuals in the Senate to change things in a way that will help society in general." Tunney compared Ted's belief in the Senate to that of a priest in the
Church—a "higher calling," Tunney said of Ted's feeling about the Senate.

But if he was to realize that calling, and if he was to challenge Jimmy
Carter's rightward bent as he had challenged Richard Nixon's, Ted Kennedy, now that he was no longer an active presidential contender, had to
win the acceptance of his colleagues through institutional means—
acceptance that was a prerequisite to his real ambition, which was to accrue legislative power. He had worked at being a man of the Senate. Now
he desired to be an eminence in the Senate and to do what even the best
senators rarely did. He wanted to get things done.

III

Ted had entered the Senate in deference, realizing, as Lyndon Johnson had when *he* entered the Senate, where the power resided, which was in those old Southern bulls, like Richard Russell and James Eastland and John Stennis. Though Kennedy couldn't court them as Johnson had—couldn't because he was a liberal who disagreed with them on the fundamental policies of civil rights—he nevertheless paid attention to them, showed his respect for them, heeded the power structure as so many other liberals, who wanted to destroy that power structure, refused to do. Ted knew how the system functioned and knew that if he were to get anything done, he had to work within it. Robert Dove, the Senate parliamentarian, recalled a meeting at which a senator was beseeching Eastland, the head of the Judiciary Committee on which Ted sat, to confirm a nominee whom the senator supported to a federal court. Would the judge do what the senator asked him to do? Eastland wanted to know, point-blank. The senator said he had no control over that. And Eastland said, "Well, I do." Ted Kennedy was in the room that day. Ted Kennedy saw how power worked in the Senate. *Well, I do.* That was how power worked.

Dove said that Ted Kennedy "made his peace with the powers of the Senate" and became "comfortable" with those old Southern bulls, and the bulls appreciated it. Eastland might have been an "archconservative, arch white supremacist, and all the rest of it," Senator Charles Mathias was to say, but he was "actually an approachable fellow. You could sit down with him and discuss anything," presumably anything except race, and Mathias said that he and Ted did, that they got along well with Eastland despite the chasm that separated them on racial issues, and that there was never any animosity between them. "They all get along. They all try to do the right thing," Eastland would tell an interviewer tersely and blandly of his Senate colleagues. The only change in the Senate from the "old days," he said, was that it had become more liberal. And Ted, a liberal, knew how to work those bulls. When he needed authorization to send a staff member to Chile to investigate human rights violations there—an investigation that couldn't have interested Eastland—that staffer, Mark Schneider, remembered accompanying Ted to Eastland's office and then Ted instructing him to wait outside. It was the end of the day, and Schneider said he knew what was going on behind those closed doors—knew that Ted "went in to have a scotch or a bourbon with him," as Ted had done when Eastland had tested him by plying him with liquor to see whether Ted, a freshman senator at the time, should sit on Judiciary, Ted's tolerance for alcohol apparently being both a measure of his strength and a demonstration that he was a regular fellow. And Ted emerged that late afternoon with the signed letter to authorize Schneider's trip—the letter that Schneider himself had drafted. Ted had told Tunney that "you could really take the word of a Southern senator," which was not the case with all senators, some of whom, Ted admitted, "might give you their word, then renege on it when it was to their best advantage to do so." (He might have been thinking of those liberal senators who had promised they were with him when he ran for reelection as the Senate majority whip and then voted against him.) But not the Southerners. "Ted said once you got a commitment from a Southern senator, he would always be with you on that issue." And Ted Kennedy needed relationships with those bulls if he was to pass legislation, even as so many liberals disdained the bulls. Still, Ted wasn't above nudging Eastland, even sending him a clipping from the New Orleans *Times-Picayune* headed "Senator, Justice Head Private Schools Drive," which reported that Eastland and a judge named Thomas Brady had lent their names to a $1.25 million fundraising campaign to build three private white Christian schools to avoid integration. Clearly Ted sent the clipping to flag his disapproval of such activities. And sometimes Ted did more than nudge. Sometimes he fumed, as when the Senate voted to recommit a bill permitting voting registration by postcard back to the Judiciary Committee, and Ted pointed at Eastland's chair and "roared with anger," by one report, and bristled, "The Judiciary Committee has attempted to kill any progressive kind of legislation in this country for decades," clearly laying that on Eastland. (It was because of Eastland's intransigence that Senate majority leader Mike Mansfield had circumvented the Judiciary Committee and had the civil rights bill considered by the entire Senate.) But as the Senate tipped further to the left and Ted accrued more power, Eastland would use Ted just as Ted had used him, even inviting him in 1978 to give the commencement address at the University of Mississippi in order to help him win Black votes in a reelection bid that year, an invitation that Ted accepted, and then thanking Ted, with a note expressing that "I was deeply touched by the great friendship displayed for you particularly at the reception [—] a friendship which I share."

But it wasn't only Eastland with whom Ted ingratiated himself. Ted knew how to work those other bulls too, how to play upon their sense of sociability, which was very important to them. Ted's legislative aide Kilvert Dun Gifford recalled Ted pushing a draft reform bill and telling Gifford that they had to meet with John Stennis, the head of the Armed Services Committee, who was opposed to Ted's amendments, one of which would have integrated Southern draft boards. Gifford was terrified. "I thought they were going to chew us up, and we just had to take it, like when you get scolded in school." But it wasn't that way at all. Stennis was courteous, even friendly. "Teddy, my boy. Nice to see you," Stennis said with Southern bonhomie. And then while Stennis and a staff member sat behind his desk and Ted and Gifford sat in front of it, Stennis brought out a bottle of bourbon and tumblers and poured three or four fingers, even though it was only ten o'clock in the morning. And Gifford said they were "charming and funny." And that Ted was too. They drank bourbons for an hour, and Ted made much of the fact that Gifford had served three years in the navy, and when Ted and Gifford walked back to Ted's office, Ted said they had done well and that now they needed a "lot of strong Irish tea." And Gifford remembered another encounter on draft reform, this one after a long, hard day on the Senate floor, a depressing and exhausting day, when Ted had submitted amendment after amendment to the Selective Service Act, trying to liberalize it, trying to equalize it so that poor boys got the same advantages as rich boys, and Gifford watching nearly every single one of those amendments go down to defeat, and then seeing Ted approach Stennis as the session ended, at six or seven o'clock, and Stennis inviting Ted and Gifford and Stennis's own staff person into the cloakroom, where staff was by custom not allowed, and sitting down to drink a "couple of pops" of bourbon on the rocks. "Next year, we'll be right here again, won't we, Ted?" Stennis asked Ted. "You'll be back, won't you?," meaning that Ted would be introducing those amendments again in the next session. And Ted said he would, and Stennis said he would be "ready for you," but said it kindly. And then the four of them drank a toast to future combat and downed more bourbons and told stories. "They came out of a mold," Gifford would say of those bulls, racist though they were, a mold "now broken." "They were Southern gentlemen, comfortable with their power, and Ted was solicitous, but never craven."

And those bulls came to like Ted Kennedy, who was so different from them in nearly every way—liked him because he knew enough about human nature to give them the deference they felt they deserved. And

Ted, who liked people generally, liked them too, though the sociability was a means to an end, and the end was the power to get things done. This was how you won influence in the Senate when you didn't have time to wait for seniority.

But knowing how to curry favor with the Senate powers was not knowledge enough to become a Senate power oneself, which was Ted Kennedy's aspiration once he had, at least temporarily, suspended his presidential aspirations. One also had to prove oneself to them, and Ted Kennedy had had a lot to prove. He had come into the Senate as a hail-fellow-well-met—sweet, funny, happy, gregarious, very likable, but with little gravity. "He was a young, good-looking guy, a big guy, a huge personality, what somebody would call a 'room bender,' and everybody knew he was there," Senator Walter Mondale said of him. "Lots of energy, part of the Kennedy mystique, and was an all-out progressive, itchy and anxious to change and reform and get it done right away." (This last part was not quite true. Ted was a liberal, but when he entered the Senate, he was neither among the most liberal senators nor among the most aggressive. Not at the outset.) It was the persona he had developed to play his assigned role in his family and one he adapted to his assigned role in the Senate. But while his amiability was ingratiating, it also worked against him by creating another, less favorable impression: that he was an intellectual lightweight, a shallow man. And lightweights did not become Senate powers. "He is intelligent in the sense that he is shrewd, incisive, sensitive and retentive," a Republican senator said of him during Ted's first year in the Senate. "But not in the sense of depth." Arthur Schlesinger, Jr., who knew John, Bobby, and Ted well, said back in May 1965 that while he had come to admire Teddy—he hadn't always admired him—he realized that a "gap remains between Teddy and his older brothers." Ted told Schlesinger that he was trying to read the books that Jack had said were his favorites but was perplexed by those choices. "Could he really have enjoyed those books?" he asked incredulously. "I tried to read Bemis on John Quincy Adams and Allan Nevins on the coming of the civil war, and I just couldn't get through them." His was not a searching mind, a cultivated mind. An adviser to the Kennedys told biographer Burton Hersh that Ted "takes in everything you tell him and gives it back to you exactly as you told it to him. Bobby takes it in and you get that and something more. With John Kennedy, of course, you had a discussion." "The dumbest of the three brothers," independent journalist I. F. Stone called him. Another journalist, Richard Reeves, put it bluntly in *New York* magazine as late as 1974, when Ted had already been in the Senate eleven years: "The impression is abroad that Kennedy is some kind of dope."

And unlike many of his Senate colleagues, Ted Kennedy had no illusions about his intellectual capabilities. If anything, he was so lashed to the idea of his own inferiority that he might have agreed with those who denigrated him. He admired intelligence, deferred to men of intelligence as he had deferred to those Senate bulls, sought out men of intelligence to advise him, and never put them down, as Lyndon Johnson had done to the "Harvards," or resented them, as Richard Nixon had. There was no anti-intellectualism in him. One of those intellectuals he sought out to brief him, or, more accurately, educate him, on constitutional issues, was Harvard Law professor Laurence Tribe, and Tribe would talk him through those issues—Tribe remembered schooling him on how Congress could enforce constitutional rights through the enforcement clauses of the Civil War amendments, which amounted to federal preemption of state sovereignty—and Tribe concluded this about Ted Kennedy from those sessions: that Ted was "bright, but he's not 'brilliant.'" And yet there was something else Tribe observed of him, something that, in the Senate, might have been more important than brilliance: He was "serious and dedicated," Tribe said of him, so much so that he described it as "really impressive." He wasn't quick, but he would think things through— "worked at issues with a dedication that I've just not seen other people do." And Tribe said that Ted was one of those people who has "certain core insights and deep values" and also "the commitment and energy to take those insights and values and figure out what kind of staff and help do I need; what do I need to learn; how could I move this issue." "There is some force in himself that filters the world," another Harvard Law professor, Charles Haar, who had also tutored Ted, said of him, concurring with Tribe while also disputing the idea that Ted simply parrots back what he hears. He "comes out with his own conclusions." His wasn't conventional intelligence, Haar concluded. "He's also bringing something that nobody else brings, bringing his personality, his experience, his life, his contemplation of it, and the end result is fascinating." He called Ted "brilliant" in terms of his "decision-making power and excellent judgment." Tribe said he observed the same attributes when Ted was questioning witnesses at Senate hearings. He was not "among those who used the interrogation process as a way of actually thinking through something. It was a rehearsed exercise in which he wanted to get certain things on the record, wanted to make sure he covered certain bases." And Tribe said he did that well—that, in effect, his real intelligence was *political*, which was what that Republican senator meant when he said Ted was "shrewd" and "incisive," if not deep, and what Haar meant when he praised his "decision-making." Shrewd, Ted Kennedy was, which was also one of the reasons he was never intimidated by his staff, most of whom he knew were smarter than he—because while they might have been smarter in raw intelligence, they were not smarter in political intelligence, which was what really counted in the Senate, and which was why he would bridle at the aides who often accompanied him to those hearings—many observers assumed that he was just a mouthpiece for those staffers—and would scribble "TMBS"—"too many blue suits," his favorite acronym for the off-putting self-possession of his own staff—or just say it to them, "Too many blue suits," and then tell them, "I don't need this." And Ted wasn't just trying to protect himself from the impression that he needed a praetorian guard of staffers because he wasn't smart enough. He didn't need those staffers passing him questions because his political intelligence was so acute. He knew what he needed to ask, knew what he needed to ascertain, knew not only how to make himself look good, though he knew how to do that too, as all Kennedys did, but also how to leverage himself to get things done. He might not have been the smartest senator in the room, but he might have been the most astute. He knew systems, and he knew people.

And through the strength of that political intelligence, Ted Kennedy had impressed his fellow senators and won those Senate powers over. "Very intelligent," James Eastland would say of him.

And if Ted Kennedy's outsize personality led his colleagues to underestimate his intelligence at first, so did the way he spoke to those colleagues. Jack Kennedy had spoken eloquently, beautifully, soaringly, and though the rhetoric was often that of his chief aide, Ted Sorensen, not his own, he had a gift for language and the rhythms of language. Bobby was less eloquent, more halting in delivery, shy at times, but what he lacked in fluency and lapidarian construction, he compensated for in passion. Few delivered speeches that seemed more passionate, more heartfelt, than Robert Kennedy. Ted could deliver a speech well, too, as he demonstrated in his heartbreaking eulogy to Bobby at St. Patrick's Cathedral. Some compared the timbre of his voice and his style to Jack's and said that the two were indistinguishable, but it was not an apt comparison. The pitch of Ted's voice was higher than Jack's, his dramatic flair less than Jack's, his patterns less varied than Jack's, with his sentences typically rising then falling at the end, almost singsong, and there was more Irish in Ted's delivery than in Jack's, more of the street and saloon. And when he got going, which is to say when he was feeling it, when he really got on a roll, when he was jabbing an opponent in faux indignation, and his voice rose even higher, sometimes trilling in exaggerated astonishment at the opponent's transgressions, his voice quavering with incredulity at those transgressions, and the declamations grew louder, he could bring a crowd to its feet, cheering and laughing simultaneously with Ted laughing right along with them, which was a gift that neither Jack nor Bobby had. They had the gift of dignity. Ted had the gift of an old-fashioned Irishman, the gift of a Honey Fitz, his grandfather and onetime Boston mayor, the gift of a politician who was one of the boyos.

A very good speaker, a dynamic speaker, an entertaining speaker, a speaker who knew how to press the right buttons in a crowd and get a reaction from it—Ted Kennedy was all those things when he spoke from a prepared text in front of a large group or when he was telling one of his stories. But when Ted Kennedy spoke extemporaneously, when he spoke one on one or to a small coterie, it was different, very different. He stammered, the slightest remnants of eloquence disappeared, the syntax was mangled, the words garbled, sentences ended before the period—he seldom spoke in whole sentences—and some sentences lacked a noun or a verb. One of his press secretaries joked to reporters about his stocking a "closet of unused verbs" from which they could choose after an interview with Ted—and all this made him seem not only inarticulate; it sometimes rendered him unintelligible. "Better in amphitheaters than in living rooms" was how one reporter put it. "When the groups are not large, when the adrenaline is not flowing, his mind seems adrift." His staff called it "Kennedyspeak" or the "Kennedy/Eisenhower," referring to President Dwight Eisenhower, who had many of the same verbal tics as Ted, many of same syntactical meanderings. "A personal dialect," one reporter called it, "his mind skipping like a flat rock across a lake while his language lumbers behind." The "code," aide Gregory Craig called it, and warned a new staffer, that the "biggest thing you have to understand is the code"—a "choppy code" that's "hard to figure out." And Craig told the new staffer how many times he would get a call from the senator at eight in the morning, and Ted would say, "Greg, I need you, da da da," and "he'll go on for a paragraph, and I have no idea what he's talking about. And you just want to shout into the phone, 'Topic sentence, Senator. Give me a topic sentence. Just let me know what the subject is.'" And Craig advised this to the new staffer: "Just work hard at figuring out the context, and then you can figure out what he's talking about."

But to those who hadn't cracked the code, Ted Kennedy was inarticulate. "Inarticulate"—that is what the junior senator from Massachusetts, Edward Brooke, called him when he first met him: "inarticulate and lacking in confidence." "One of the loudest and least articulate debaters," Senator Robert Dole's chief of staff, Sheila Burke, said of Ted, again citing the fact that he seldom spoke in full sentences. It was worst when he was "launched," in the word of Senator Alan Simpson, meaning all wound up, as he often was during those floor debates. When Ted was launched, he would career out of control on the floor, shouting—Ted said Republican senator John Chafee had told him he was "wrong at the top of my lungs"—waving his hands, pacing, his face reddening, the words tumbling forth, sometimes connected, sometimes not—the inarticulate Ted. (Of course, when Ted was prepared, rehearsed, when he knew exactly what he was going to say, he could be one of the most effective debaters.) Simpson remembered late one evening on the floor when Simpson was on the dais presiding over the Senate, counting seconds because he had an engagement to attend, and Ted had launched, even though the chamber was nearly empty. Simpson finally asked a page to take a note to Ted and to tell him that it was imperative he read the note immediately. It said: "Dear Ted, I'm sitting here on my ass, listening to you babble. You're standing there, but when you're walking, you don't realize your fly is open. I think you need to get back to the podium and end all this!" And Ted did.

And it was the inarticulateness that had led to that inevitable conclusion. Not terribly bright was the verdict at first, especially compared to his brothers, else why did Ted Kennedy have so much difficulty with simple English? Ted himself was so concerned about his garbled speech that he had gone to a speech therapist for help early in his Senate career, thinking his difficulty might be the result of a learning disability, but he decided he didn't want to subject himself to the regimen the therapist recommended. Instead, he studied oratory, became a student of oratory, reading his way through *Elliot's Debates,* which Jack had given him, and through David Brewer's *The World's Best Orations,* Jack's own set, which Jackie had given Ted as a gift—not just reading through them but, as he often did, reading them closely, studying them, telling one biographer how, looking at a Charles Francis Adams speech, he could see the "music of that speech, the rhythm," and discovered something in it that he recognized in his brother's inaugural address. But it wasn't oratory that was his problem. It was ordinary speech. One friend said his drinking made him get a "little bit inarticulate from time to time," when he could be so articulate at other times, though Ted seldom drank when he was conducting Senate business. One reporter said that he seemed to be "more than one person" when it came to his speech, alternately articulate and not. Others who knew him said it was a matter of Ted's brain outpacing his tongue. He has a "tendency at times, particularly in private, to talk as he is thinking, and he is thinking through his thoughts," his friend John Tunney observed, "and therefore he gives people the impression of being inarticulate." But Tunney also observed, as many others had, that "when he knows what he wants to say and is focusing through, he speaks extremely clearly and with excellent diction," and he cited his experience with Ted in a moot court competition during law school—a competition he and Ted won. Ted Sorensen agreed, comparing Ted to a favorite law client of Sorensen's, a "very, very smart businessman," who is "always three sentences ahead of where his mind and my mind are. And so I have great difficulty understanding him." Ted's mind, Sorensen felt, was similarly "full of so much information" that his mouth couldn't process it quickly enough. One Senate colleague, John Danforth, always had a "sense that he knows exactly what he's thinking and talking about on the points that he's making, but he can't verbalize them as well as he's thinking them." Still others thought Ted's obfuscation was at least semi-intentional—a "fog machine," reporter Tom Oliphant called it, that allowed Ted to blur subjects he didn't want to talk about. His nephew, Christopher Lawford, said the same thing: "Whenever we came close to exploring the realm of things better left unsaid, the discussion veered into ambiguous 'Teddy Speak' or another funny story." And so Ted Kennedy, not a man to introspect publicly, a man who abhorred intimacy, might have learned to use language not only to express but also to conceal. And to all these theories, Ted had one of his own: At the Kennedy family dinner table when he was a boy, his siblings would all be talking, all of them articulate, and he, the youngest,

the least, had to develop a verbal shorthand in order to get a word in edge-
wise. His was a childhood of half-sentences that became an adulthood of
half-sentences.

And yet as his colleagues got to know him and as they came to realize
that he was a close study who, despite his syntax, knew what he was talking about and that he was anything but dumb, Ted Kennedy won those
Senate colleagues over.

And if Ted Kennedy's colleagues had initially thought him unintelli-
gent and inarticulate, there was a presumption as well when he entered
the Senate that, as the youngest Kennedy and one scarcely qualified for
his office, he would follow in his brother Jack's footsteps, that he would be
a shirker as Jack was, that he would do as little as possible as Jack had, that
he would spend his time advancing his career and appealing to the extra-
institutional power. "Always having to live down his reputation as a pam-
pered kid brother," journalist William Honan would say of him. But Ted
Kennedy had not been a shirker. Ted Kennedy felt he could not afford to be
a shirker like Jack because he lacked the self-confidence of Jack, the
aplomb of Jack, the style of Jack, the ability to coast that Jack had had.
Jack, as their mother Rose had said, was the boy who could fall into the
mud puddle in a white suit and not get dirty. But not Ted. Even in his
school days, Ted had been something of a plugger when he finally buckled
down to work. It was, said his nephew, Robert Shriver III, the theme of his
life: He was shaped by his sense of inferiority. "He was never a wunderkind," Shriver said. "He never was the smartest kid in the class; he wasn't
the fastest kid in the class; he had siblings who were smarter, faster, and
taller than he was, yet he was able to continue to plug along, plug along,
plug along, even when he got smacked down." And Ted plugged along
when he got to the Senate—"worked very hard, very insatiably," one of
his aides, Robert Hunter, said. "This amazing capacity for work," said another, Dun Gifford. He lived and worked like a fatalist. "He always operated as if tomorrow was going to be his last day," Hunter said, which
might have been another Kennedy inheritance, since tomorrow *had* been
the last day for his three older brothers. And he worked hard to prove himself not just to himself and his colleagues but to his voters. His legislative
assistant Carey Parker said that Ted learned early on that in order to
"please" his Massachusetts constituents, to "make them love him," he
"would have to show that he was working for them in the Senate," and
Parker said that in order to do that, Ted told himself, "I need to understand

how these legislators work and what they think and what the issues are that they are concerned about," which was more political intelligence, but also a function of hard work since the "more he knew about an issue, the better he could do, because most of his colleagues don't understand the issues as well as he does." "Some people who didn't care for the Kennedys used to say, 'Teddy's a good senator, but Bobby's all over the lot.' It was only a question of time before I got put in the same position," Ted would say, which was the position of a legislative dilettante, spread too thin. So, when he did expand his legislative portfolio, as he did after Bobby's death, he had to work even harder to master a number of issues. Parker said that in the office, the aides would remark of him, "He can keep one hundred balls in the air." And Parker said Ted had a "knack for seeing which one is about to hit the ground and burst, and he can reach out and flick that one back up into the air to give it a little more time." And *that* took work—hard work. But Ted was a plugger. His son, Ted Jr., once asked him why the two of them were always the only boat on the water late at night as they were preparing for the weekend's sail races. And Ted told him they were the last because the other sailors were "smarter" and "more talented" than they were, but that intelligence and talent didn't matter. He and Ted Jr. would win because "we will work harder than them and be better prepared."

And Ted Kennedy, who entered the Senate with his colleagues having all those preconceptions about his lax work ethic, had worked so hard—"very insatiably," as his aide had said—that he impressed those colleagues. "One of the hardest-working men," James Eastland would say of him. "Very effective," Eastland would say. "He's grown very fast."

In those fourteen years in the Senate, Ted Kennedy, the plugger, won them over.

IV

But having won his colleagues over, he couldn't relent, especially now that he had, for the time being, forsaken his presidential prospects and devoted himself to making his mark in the Senate. Even if he had wanted to relent, by this point in his career—by the mid-1970s—many people looked to him, needed him, thought of him as their leader, which placed an obligation upon him, especially when the administration itself, now a Democratic administration, had its doubts about liberalism. That obliga-

tion was to keep liberalism alive. And as a Kennedy, he took that obligation seriously. His days began early. Sometimes a staffer would arrive at
the McLean house at 636 Chain Bridge Road at six o'clock in the morning
to brief him before a hearing or a markup session on a bill. And usually
that staffer would ride with him from his house to his office or to the Capitol. "We would be talking all the way in," David Boies, the chief counsel of
the Judiciary Committee, the chairmanship of which Ted would later assume, would say. "Sometimes he was driving and paying more attention
to talking than he should have been, when he was driving. Sometimes
somebody else was driving him, and he was giving the person constant
directions as to where to go to get around traffic, and at the same time, he
was carrying on very complicated discussions about antitrust policy or
the *Illinois Brick* case or airline or trucking deregulation." Other times it
was reversed. Ted would arrive early at a staffer's house. "I am just getting
used to the idea that I can now be certain that I will come down my staircase to prepare breakfast and not find Edward Kennedy sitting in a living
room chair waiting for my husband to appear," the wife of a former staffer
told biographer Burton Hersh. "This guy worked our tails off," Stan Jones,
a health policy adviser, recalled. When there was a hearing at nine, Jones
said he and the other staffers would be at Ted's house by seven or seven-
thirty, briefing him over breakfast. "And I mean he would go through it
and through it. Here are the questions. Here are the people. Now where
are they coming from, why are they saying this." And again, on the drive
in to Washington, "briefing him all the way in, take him to the hearing
room, sit down, and of course there would be two staff people waiting to
remind him of what he was going to do after the hearing, give him a piece
of paper to read when things were slow during the hearings so he could
get ready for the next thing. And the whole day was like that. By the time
we let it go, I mean, you were exhausted."

A *hundred balls in the air.* That was what had been said about him and
what impressed Thomas Rollins, the chief counsel of the Labor Committee, after Ted assumed its chairmanship. "He would grind through some
committee thing until noon," Rollins said, "and then I would walk him
back to the main office. Man, he'd be off doing a press conference on Nicaragua. He would go from that to an arms control briefing. He would go
from that to a Judiciary Committee [hearing]. I mean, the guy could move
among and between subjects and care about all of them all day long." It
was a "presidential schedule," Melody Miller said, who served various

functions from receptionist to deputy press secretary over a long career in Ted's office. "He was scheduled every fifteen minutes, every ten minutes almost, with so many demands on his time." The "Senator from the United States," she called him. "The Senator from the entire world . . . because from all corners came demands for him to take leadership on various issues." "There was never a moment from the day he became a senator," said his friend Lee Fentress, "that he didn't have a daily, typed-out schedule, by the hour"—though it was really by much smaller intervals—"of what he was going to do that day." The daily agenda would be written on three-by-five-inch cards that he would carry with him, and on some days, it might take five of those cards to list his appointments.

A demanding schedule it was, an unrelenting schedule, but Ted Kennedy could not relent, not if he wanted to prove himself, which he did, not if he wanted to be a great senator, a senator who mattered, which he did, and not if he wanted to pressure Jimmy Carter, which he did. And Ted Kennedy did not relent. "Energy pours out of him," a staffer said. He would break from the grind only at four or five o'clock each day to repair to the baths in the Russell Senate Office Building to soak his aching back that had been broken in the 1964 plane crash. Then he was back at it. "He'd want to go home at six o'clock," his onetime press secretary James Manley said, "and then somebody would come in and say, 'Hey, the pension conference is about to start. We need you to go over there.' He'd maybe whip off a few swear words, then he'd say, 'OK. Let's go.'" But there was no surcease, no moments of just sitting quietly in a hearing or a conference or a markup session because, as Manley observed, "everybody was watching him." And that meant "he had to know his issues, he had to talk to the Republicans because they wanted to talk to him." He couldn't afford to be distracted, couldn't afford to be at less than his best. So he would work all day and into the evening, tirelessly, uncomplainingly, save for those curses. The only time he would get upset was when he felt he was wasting time—"if somebody didn't show up for an appointment, for whatever reason; somebody on the staff didn't get something to him when he needed it; the airplane didn't take off, and he was stuck in it on the tarmac," said Melody Miller. And though Ted was usually even-tempered, slow to ignite—except for those impromptu floor debates, which were part performance—he could get "loud and angry" in those idle moments, according to Miller. Still, he made a point of yelling only at people he knew could take it and who would not take it personally, and he made a point to apologize to them later. Some believed, understandably, that he tired by the end of those long days and lost his edge. Thomas Rollins said, "His battery never seemed to run out before about nine o'clock at night, and then he would start getting really irritable, which I learned the hard way. Just don't ask him for lots of stuff after nine o'clock at night. It's not going to happen."

But that wasn't entirely true. He didn't tire, at least not visibly. And the work didn't end when he left the office. It often continued at the McLean house at night—late-night meetings with his staff, long discussions of policy, more briefings. And there were dinners, issue dinners, that he would begin to arrange soon after he entered the Senate, several of them each week, starting promptly at seven and ending promptly at ten, to which he would invite experts who would debate one another and with whom he could brainstorm on bills and positions. "The liberal intelligentsia [regarded him] as the person who could get their ideas accomplished," Carey Parker, Ted's chief legislative assistant, said of these dinners, "and they were eager to lay out their ideas in front of him. They'd drop everything and take a plane in or a train down from Boston or whatever." These would be small dinners, intimate dinners—four or five experts, many of them from Harvard, and a few staff members and Ted. But on some occasions, he would also invite members of the advocacy community, people with a stake in the outcome of these bills, so they would hear what was practical and what wasn't. And Ted, who had been carefully briefed before the dinner, would sit, mainly listening, sometimes asking questions, breaking in only occasionally when policy touched on politics, to say what he thought could be accomplished—*his* expertise. "That approach won't work, so you have to go back to the drawing board," he might say. Other evenings he would invite Senate colleagues to his home for dinner, including Republicans, but this time without staff. "Kennedy was very sensitive to the importance of member-to-member communications," said Carolyn Osolinik, another staffer, "that things would be said in those member-to-member conversations that wouldn't be said with staff, and that it was also a matter of respect for a colleague that it be principal to principal." And in those meetings, he won over his colleagues, too, by showing them that respect, even as he was trying to win their respect himself by doing so.

But Ted Kennedy knew that respect wasn't a function just of collegiality. Once one of the least respected senators himself, he realized that he now had to be the best-prepared senator in the room, the one who knew the issue inside and out, the one who could impress his fellow senators with that knowledge—had to be because that was expected of him. Before a hearing or a markup session or a meeting or a press conference, his staff would prepare briefing books for him—fat books with numerous tabs. If he was scheduled for a markup session, the book would contain the bill and the amendments to that bill and the arguments for and against that bill and a background memo explaining what the staff thought his position should be on that bill. If he was scheduled for a hearing, the book would contain the witness statements and the questions Ted might ask and briefings on what the intention of the hearing was and "plenty of back-up reading" as well, according to another staffer, Stephen Breyer. An "enormous amount of material going back from the committee to him"—from the Dirksen building, where the committee staff was headquartered, to the Russell building, where his office was, said one staffer. His "homework," Ted called it. And Ted wouldn't just skim those books; he would pore over them, usually late at night, mark them up, underline passages, write questions in the margins, or scribble in blue felt-tip pen, so thick as to be often illegible, "Want more on that" or "Didn't quite understand this" or "See me" on the bottom of the page—the "ubiquitous 'See me,'" one staffer called it—which meant that Ted wanted further discussion of the issue, and then the staffer would have to hunt for some time in Ted's schedule to have that discussion, usually fast-walking with him between the elevator and the Senate floor when Ted was racing to a vote. And Breyer said that Ted not only read through these briefing books, not only pored over them, he ruminated on them, thought them through, because doing so gave him confidence—the confidence Brooke said he had lacked—and "then he can make a decision fairly quickly." And for all the gibes over the years that Ted wasn't very smart but his staff was, for all the gibes that Ted didn't know very much but his staff did, Ted Kennedy not only read through those fat books, not only pored over them, not only ruminated on them, he also absorbed them until he understood everything in them. "Not a details man," it was said of him. But Ted Kennedy *was* a details man. "If you watch Kennedy at a committee hearing," Republican senator and later majority leader Robert Dole, said, "he's not reading the questions. He may look down or maybe have notes. Some senators, if they had lost their paper on the way to the hearing, might as well go home." But not Ted Kennedy. He didn't need those notes because he had held those issue dinners, had talked with those experts, had scrutinized those briefing books, had had lengthy discussions with his staff on the issues, so he knew what he was talking about.

And now his fellow senators knew it.

And Ted Kennedy lugged those fat briefing books every night from his office, lugged them in what became the repository of his knowledge and the nerve center of his operation: The Bag. That is what everyone in the office called the worn leather briefcase: "The Bag." The Bag was totemic. The Bag was iconic. The Bag was the primary form of communication between the staff and the senator, and the surest way into the senator's mind. The Bag was the receptacle of every input—the memos, the briefing books, the correspondence. Whatever came to Ted got stuffed into The Bag. "If you talk to him and say, 'So-and-so really wish [sic] you would do such-and-such,' he says, 'Give me a note.' That goes in the briefcase. Everything went in the briefcase, and he had it with him, and he studied it," said his friend Doris Reggie. And those communications would then be organized into compartments in The Bag—first a general cover letter from his administrative assistant, then compartments for memos from each issue group on his committees, and one for news clippings, and another for correspondence, and one titled "Must do," which was self-explanatory. And yet for something that was invested with as much importance as The Bag, there was nothing elegant about it. At the beginning it was actually an old green leather briefcase embossed with Ted's initials—or two briefcases, depending on the period. (In a later iteration, it was a black leather bag.) Heavy was The Bag—twenty pounds when full, and it was nearly always full. Bulging was The Bag. At the end of Ted's office day, remembered Dun Gifford, The Bag was so overstuffed that you would see him "sitting on that briefcase to close it, trying to snap it closed before he left," the way a person might sit on an overstuffed suitcase. Omnipresent was The Bag. "Whenever he had a spare moment, on the floor of the Senate, in the backseat of his car, on an airplane, or even as he ate his lunch," said one of his administrative assistants, "the Senator maximized his time by digging through the paperwork, reading, amending, approving, and signing." His longtime Hyannis neighbor Melissa Ludtke said, "You'd walk in through the kitchen, and there'd be like a little pantry, and then The Bag, you know, would kind of be there." A friend, Tim Hannan, recalled that whenever the two of them traveled together, "you sit down on the airplane, and he pulls out The Bag. He's not reading *The New York Times*. He's got a briefing book there that he's digesting." He frequently carried it with him even on social occasions, lest he waste a moment.

The Bag had an aura of its own. Every staff member genuflected before The Bag as if it were a shrine, and every staff member understood the rigid protocol—or had to come to understand the protocol—that surrounded The Bag if he or she was to have any influence with the senator. The Bag "drives the day," health staffer Michael Myers would say, and once computers came into use, "one of the first messages we get on our computers"—from Ted's secretary Angelique Voutselas—"when we come in in the morning is what time The Bag is expected to be [leaving]. You've got to have your stuff into the briefcase before he heads out the door. So Bag Time—you plan your day so that you don't miss Bag Time. Make sure you get your memos in by Bag Time." "You'd always say, *The Bag* would be leaving," Scott Ferson, onetime press secretary, recalled, "not that the *Senator* would be leaving, but *The Bag* will be leaving at seven o'clock, if that was the case." Every night Ted took The Bag home. Every night after dinner, he would read everything that had been stuffed into it—often as many as one hundred memos, as well as those briefing books. Every night he would scribble his comments on those memos and briefing books and pieces of correspondence and newspaper or magazine articles with his blue felt-tip pen. *Every night*. And every morning Ted would carry The Bag back to the office, and Voutselas would distribute the memos—all of them now annotated by the senator in that blue felt-tip pen with his "See me's" and "Let's talk's" or, if he was especially displeased, "Ugh!"

And the staff fretted over The Bag, fretted over the protocol of The Bag. Was it better to submit a memo early, when it might be pushed to the bottom of The Bag, or later, and as one staffer told a reporter, risk having it miss The Bag altogether? One of Ted's legislative assistants noticed that other staffers were doing "all kinds of stunts" to make sure their memos attracted Ted's attention: "big check marks, or times circled with brightly colored marking pens, especially red and yellow, or writing 'Must do' or 'Must read' on their memos." And then there was the "mad dash" for The Bag, as one staffer called it, every Friday because the staff knew that Ted would be spending his weekend digging through The Bag, boning up for the week to come, giving every item greater consideration in the leisure of that weekend than he did on weeknights, and no one wanted to be left out.

And then there was the deciphering of the comments on those memos and briefing books. Sometimes this was just a matter of getting to know Ted's shorthand. If he left a checkmark, it meant he had read it and either was not interested in it or had put it on hold. If he wrote "See me," in very large letters in the upper-right-hand corner of the memo, according to one staffer, it meant "See me." But if he wrote "See me" in "letters so small that you can barely make it out," it meant "I'm angry" and you'd better see me. Other times, most of the time, it wasn't a matter of understanding his shorthand but of deciphering the comments, because Ted's felt-tip pen was as illegible as his verbal maunderings were often unintelligible. And this could prompt great consternation among those who had no idea what he had written. "You'd get a memo back and say, 'Well, what does this say?'" recalled staffer Mark Schneider. "In that room, we'd all go around, take each other's memos [and ask], 'Can you read this?'" "Grand debates," another staffer called the disputations over what Ted had written. And in the end, if they failed to decipher the scrawls, they would take the memos to Angelique Voutselas, who was the "ultimate translator," as Schneider put it, which was also a source of her power in the office. But Schneider also realized this: that "I was there too long when I could interpret" the scrawls.

A great deal was riding on The Bag, not just for the staff but for Ted Kennedy. The Bag was a monument to his work ethic, to the fact that he had to keep pushing himself, had to keep proving himself, both to himself and to his colleagues, that to rest might be to fail. And that near-desperation made The Bag a monument to something else—to the fear that continued to grip Ted Kennedy: the fear that, even after all those years in the Senate, he would never measure up.

But he *was* measuring up, even after having to start from scratch after the car accident on Chappaquiddick Island in which Mary Jo Kopechne had died and that had all but dashed his presidential hopes and his senatorial ambitions. He impressed his own staff with his indefatigability. "You worked for Kennedy knowing that he was working just as hard as you were," recalled onetime press secretary James Manley, though Ted was almost certainly working harder than his staff, putting in longer hours, and Manley said that "it made you feel even better when you walked into a room knowing that you were better and smarter than anybody else in that room, and that you were going to win." "He took his standard twelve-hour day and turned it into a fourteen-hour day," another staffer, Paul Donovan, said of Ted. And Donovan said "countless times" he would be sitting at home late at night, at ten-thirty or eleven o'clock, and the phone would ring, and Ted would be on the line with a question. Ted impressed the press too—those Beltway cynics who had seen so many politicians come and go and who had been as skeptical of Ted as those old senators had been of him when he entered the Senate. "On any given day, he can absorb two twenty-pound briefcases of memos and background papers," wrote Richard Reeves, "take a couple of dozen verbal briefings, ranging from thirty seconds to an hour, handle a dozen confrontational situations with other senators, reporters or bureaucrats trying to make their bones by trapping him, juggle the egos of fifty talented staffers and ex-officio advisers, interrogate the presidents of four drug companies and their counsel about their business, debate Senator John McClellan about the death penalty and Senator Jesse Helms about handgun production in the South, read a half-dozen newspapers, remember five hundred faces and names, and be canny and witty at dinner. You try it." Thomas Oliphant of *The Boston Globe*, who observed Ted's career for decades, said, "My real bias is that I never stopped being stunned by his work ethic, his relentlessness and diligence, not to mention his kindness."

But most of all, he impressed his colleagues. "I was astonished when I came to the Senate, quite frankly, and came to know him intimately," recalled Senator James Sasser of Tennessee, "about how hard he worked there at the job of being an effective United States Senator—the hours he would spend in preparation, the passion he felt about the issues." And Sasser said he was impressed too that Ted "never seemed to grow tired or cynical or apathetic," which were occupational hazards of the Senate. "Nobody works harder than that man and his staff. Nobody," Senator Lowell Weicker of Connecticut said. "One of the hardest working men," Eastland had said. And Eastland said more: "He's a leader." And even more: "Very effective. . . . To be effective, you've got to get legislation passed." But the highest professional accolade, the sign of greatest respect, might have been this. By the mid-1970s, his Senate colleagues had stopped calling him "Teddy." Now he was simply "Ted."

V

A man of the Senate. That was what he had aspired to be before his presidential aspirations took hold—a man who, in the words of journalist Clayton Fritchey, "never permits ideology, party loyalty, or even personal conviction to supersede his dedication to promoting the Senate's primacy in the American constitutional system, whether the Constitution calls for it or not." That dedication was what would separate him from his brothers. And a man of the Senate was what he *needed* to be now that Jimmy Carter was in office with the intention, Ted feared, of derailing Ted's liberal agenda. And in those fourteen years he had been in office, Ted Kennedy had become a Senate man, though his dedication to the Senate was different from that of so many other men of the Senate—as much a function of his desire to *use* the Senate to advance his political goals as it was the kind of civic religiosity that Fritchey described and that characterized the old Senate bulls who ran the place. Ted Kennedy might have loved the Senate. Ted Kennedy might have respected the traditions of the Senate. But Ted Kennedy's love and respect were in the interest of giving him the perquisites to get things done. Showing those bulls that he respected the institution and perforce them, that he was one of them and not an opportunist, was a way of getting them to help him move legislation through an intransigent institution. And help him they had.

But the power of those bulls had been ebbing. Because the source of Senate power was its committees—"The true and ultimate power in the Senate resides in its standing committees," William S. White had written in his 1957 classic on the institution, *The Citadel*—and the committee chairmanships were distributed on the basis of seniority; young senators used to have to wait for the bulls to retire or die before they could ascend to power. And though many of the bulls *had* retired or died by the mid-1970s, the new generation of Democratic senators was not as patient as its predecessors. As *New York Times* Senate reporter Martin Tolchin put it, they weren't going "to sit around forever and wait their turn." Instead, they did something that would have been unthinkable just a few years earlier—unthinkable and impossible: They decided to challenge the Senate rules that had bestowed and then protected the bulls' power. In an institution in which custom had always prevailed, they launched what amounted to an insurrection to shift the balance of power from the senior aging members, nearly all of them conservatives, to the younger members, nearly all of them liberals.

The bulls, however old, however ailing, would not relinquish their power readily. Lyndon Johnson, as majority leader, had been impatient too and might have begun the transformation by centralizing power in his office, which meant taking it from the bulls. But they hadn't begrudged giving it to young Lyndon because they trusted him, and they trusted him because he was their protégé and because he was a conservative who would not push too aggressively on civil rights. When Johnson became vice president in 1961, he anointed as his successor his whip, Mike Mansfield, who was more liberal than Johnson, which meant he was less enamored of the bulls' foot-dragging to slow progressive legislation, and also more democratic than Johnson, which meant he was more interested in redistributing power to the entire caucus. (Johnson had been chiefly interested in aggregating power to himself.) But Mansfield, liberal and democratic as he was, was also politic, and he understood the danger of riling those old bulls. The reforms he implemented he implemented slowly, incrementally, like nearly everything else in the Senate. And Mansfield's pace ran up against the liberals' increasing impatience too. Now they took dead aim at seniority. There had been attempts at reform—attempts at blunting the bulls' horns. Robert Byrd, who as majority whip and later majority leader was not only a Senate officer but also an historian of the Senate, credited Pennsylvania Democrat Joseph Clark, the "poet laureate of the Senate establishment," as Byrd called him, with laying the groundwork for a revolution when, in February 1963, just after Ted's entrance into the chamber, Clark proposed that a majority of members be allowed to call meetings, and that chairmen be selected by secret ballot rather than by seniority, and that committee chairmanships terminate at age seventy, which would have displaced most of the bulls. Clark's proposals didn't pass—the bulls were still too powerful and Senate tradition still too strong—but those proposals led to the Joint Committee on the Organization of Congress, which in turn led to the Legislative Reorganization Act of 1967, adopting many of the committee's recommendations: letting members call committee meetings if the chairman had ignored calls for ten days; opening all sessions, save executive sessions, to the public; putting all committee votes on record; limiting new senators to membership on two major committees and one minor one. And now for the first time, the bulls were on the defensive. Another Legislative Reorganization Act, this one in 1970, further dispersed power, limiting senators to chairing only one committee and one subcommittee and further democratizing a previously highly oligarchic, undemocratic institution, where seniority and cabals had prevailed.

For decades the bulls with their seniority had run the Senate, and the liberals had agonized over their own powerlessness. "More liberal," James Eastland had complained of the new Senate, and now those liberals were in full revolt. And Mike Mansfield, who had deferred to the bulls but who now saw the tide turning against them, was willing to bless the challenge without taking active control of it. Committee assignments had been the responsibility of the chairmen, which was why John Kennedy had sent Ted to Judiciary chairman James Eastland to beseech for a seat on that committee. But just because Ted Kennedy was an institutionalist didn't mean he was a traditionalist, and now Ted and his cohort of young liberal senators proposed that assignments be vested in the Steering Committee—a committee of committees appointed by the majority leader. Not at all incidentally, Ted sat on that committee—he had been appointed in 1971 as a consolation prize after he ran for reelection to the Senate whip and lost to Byrd—though it was still, he said of the committee's power, a "very insider process," basically, as he described it, "three or four chairmen and the majority leader." And Ted said that he worked to democratize the Steering Committee, to make it representative of the entire caucus geographically, which meant, in practical terms, to make it representative ideologically as well, and a rule was adopted to make the committees themselves also representative of the caucus, which was now, especially after the post-Watergate class of freshmen, appreciably more liberal than it had been, as Eastland had griped.

Ted Kennedy was to call himself one of the "real reformers," along with Iowa senators Dick Clark and Ted's old Harvard classmate and close friend John Culver, the latter of whom had moved from the House to the Senate in the 1974 midterm elections. But if Ted was an architect of the reforms, he would also be a major beneficiary of them. Those reforms would enable him. With Mansfield now appointing younger members to the Steering Committee, even a freshman senator like Dick Clark, Ted and his fellow liberals pressured the Democratic leadership to let the committee seize from the conservatives the right to make committee assignments.

Clark went further. He had organized a group of liberal senators to challenge the seniority system itself. "The only reason in the world that made anyone a chairman was that they had served in the committee longer than anyone else," Clark would later complain, and he complained as well that younger senators had been loath to change the system for fear of reprisals by those committee chairmen if they tried. Having worked secretly with Ted and other liberals, lest the bulls discover their plan, Clark, at a momentous Democratic caucus on January 17, 1975, sprang his proposal: a rule that would, beginning with the next Senate, vest the selection of committee chairmen in the Steering Committee but subject to approval by a secret ballot if one-fifth of the caucus anonymously petitioned Majority Leader Mansfield for that vote. The bulls, realizing that their positions and power were in jeopardy, were outraged by the plan, with Majority Whip Robert Byrd leading the opposition. It was a sign of just how the balance of power had shifted in the Senate that the reformers, by voice vote, carried the day. And at the organizational meeting of the now-seventeen-member Steering Committee later that month, Ted struck too. He got it to place liberals on the most important committees, even clashing fiercely with Byrd himself, who, as a way of currying favor with his Southern base, wanted Alabama senator James Allen named to Judiciary, where he would undoubtedly attempt to halt civil rights legislation. (A "one-man wrecking crew," Allen, perhaps the single most important obstructionist in the Senate, had been called.)* Instead, Ted and his allies got liberal James Abourezk of South Dakota appointed, and when Byrd proposed adding another seat at a session the next day, so that Allen could join as well, Ted managed to beat it back, which was a blow to the conservatives—a blow they had not previously suffered. (Meanwhile Ted got himself appointed to the Joint Economic Committee, further increasing

---

* Allen exacted revenge shortly after the caucus meeting. A brilliant parliamentary tactician who was determined to stop the Senate from enacting progressive legislation, he beat back an effort led by Senator Walter Mondale to end the filibuster by filibustering the bill itself and holding the entire Senate hostage for nearly two months as he did so. In the end, Mansfield and Senate Republican leader Hugh Scott negotiated a compromise that reduced the number of senators required for cloture from two-thirds to three-fifths. The filibuster, the primary obstacle to progressive legislation, remained. James Wallner, "Senators Nuked the Filibuster in 1975. Then They Changed Their Minds," *Legislative Procedure,* March 2019, https://www.legislativeprocedure.com/blog/2019/3/8/fb2te1chy6lsoiyqw5 tehw82es9pnw.

his power.) Similarly, the caucus named liberals to the Armed Services and the Finance and Foreign Affairs committees, important committees, even pressing successfully to add a seat to Armed Services and Finance to do so.

Since it was a fight for power, Ted admitted that these were not easy battles to win. There was blood on the floor—Southern blood. "We had the most extraordinary kind of tension in that caucus," he was to say, understandably since the entire locus of power in the Senate was shifting, and the bulls knew it. "It was enormously divisive and very heated and very acrimonious." (A photo in *The New York Times* the next day showed reformer Frank Church, in seeming fighting mode, leaning into bull John Stennis—Stennis's arms akimbo, his head tilted back, and his jaw jutting—the very image of arrogance.) In the end, Ted and his fellow reformers, who had tired of waiting their turn, won. In the end, seniority took a beating. A "quiet revolution," *Washington Post* reporter Spencer Rich called it, though it hadn't been so quiet. A big revolution, really an epochal revolution, one in which the democratizers had prevailed. (A similar revolution was taking place in the House, where three longtime committee chairmen were ousted; "The End of an Oligarchy," *The New York Times* editorialized.) And while Ted had the assistance of those young liberals like Clark and even of Mansfield, he was as responsible as anyone for the revolution because he had a stature that none of those other young liberals had. (Clark would say that the would-be reformers had actually not thought of putting Ted on the firing line because he had much more to lose than they did, but Ted put himself on the firing line anyway.) Rich quoted a detractor of Ted's who groused that "Kennedy utterly dominated the sessions. . . . He had learned every nook and cranny of the rules we use for appointments." And Rich himself called it a "milestone in his [Ted's] recovery from the Chappaquiddick incident and embarrassment of his ouster by Byrd from the whip job in 1971." And Rich closed his report this way: "It is clear to most observers that, at forty-two, he is rising in the estimation of many senators." But the reforms of that January in 1975 proved he had already risen.

Although Ted Kennedy prioritized gaining respect and banishing the impression that he was a lightweight, he wanted power no less than Lyndon Johnson had, though it was not power to advance his presidential prospects, as it was for Johnson. Ted wanted power to enact his liberal agenda whether Jimmy Carter endorsed it or not and, in a more personal sense, to close the gap between himself and his brothers' legacies. And while power in the Senate was in some measure a function of respect, institutional power was also largely a function of one's control over the committees, through which legislation either flowed or was bottled up, which was why the bulls' seniority, the seniority that had given them that control, had been so important. And part of that power, a not inconsiderable part, was the power of staffing, since committee and subcommittee chairmen were the ones who appointed staff. Ted was especially adept at using this perquisite; the two subcommittees that he chaired, the all-purpose Administrative Practices Subcommittee and the Refugee Subcommittee, by one account, spent more on staff than Appropriations, Agriculture, or Armed Services, three of the Senate's major committees, whereas AdPrac and the Refugee subcommittees were decidedly minor ones. This too became a generational issue. The power that derived from committee staffs meant that junior senators, who didn't have their own committees to staff and who weren't as adept as Ted at leveraging their minor subcommittees, were largely powerless. And chafing at their powerlessness, those junior senators staged a revolt of their own while Ted was leading his organizational reform. This one was largely instigated by Senator Mike Gravel of Alaska, who proposed a resolution to give junior members their own committee staffs, which was yet another way of reducing the chairmen's power. Gravel's revolt acknowledged that staff had become kind of a coin of the legislative realm. Good staff, active staff, staff that could gain the institution's respect redounded to the credit of the senator who hired them. In many respects, it could be said of a senator that by his staff would one know him.

Nowhere might this have been truer than with Ted Kennedy. He had come early to appreciate the importance of staff; it was one of the lessons Bobby had taught him when Bobby came to the Senate and scolded Ted for not having what Bobby regarded as a first-rate staff. "Always looking for the best," Ted said of him. But Ted said it was also a lesson that his father had taught him. Joe Kennedy always surrounded himself with a superb staff, and Ted said he had been exposed to those luminaries at a very young age. William Douglas, later Supreme Court justice William Douglas, was on Joe Kennedy's staff at the Securities and Exchange Commission. So was John Burns, the youngest professor at Harvard Law School and a man Ted called the "ablest, most gifted" lawyer in New England.

But that was the executive branch, where power was necessarily delegated. In the Senate, when the bulls ran things, staff had been less meaningful. For one thing, staffs had been small. Before the Legislative Reorganization Act of 1946, which authorized four aides for each senator, there were fewer than two hundred staffers in the entire Senate. Even when Ted entered the Senate in 1962, he had only roughly a dozen aides, and those included his secretaries. But that number had more than quadrupled since, as the Senate decentralized and each senator sought his or her own center of power, power that could be measured by the size of one's staff and the number of areas into which a senator could extend his or her influence through that staff, as Ted himself had done; the number of staffers in the Senate had soared to a total of nearly 2,500 personal aides and 900 committee staffers by 1972, and from those numbers to 3,251 and 1,534 respectively just four years later. Huge staffs, ballooning staffs—and this even as yet another Senate reorganization committee, this one headed by Senator Adlai Stevenson III in 1976, made recommendations endorsed by Majority Leader Byrd and Minority Leader Howard Baker, that reduced the number of standing committees from thirty-one to twenty-four and the number of subcommittees from 174 to 117, in an effort to streamline the system.

But while the system might have been streamlined, the staffs were not. When Ted first entered the Senate, he recalled that a committee chairman would call him in with only one staff member present, and "if you weren't up to speed," meaning if you hadn't anything to contribute, "the bill would go forward." A "barebones system," Ted had called it, a system with little staff, a system in which the senators themselves did most of the work and prevailed. And with fewer staff members, the relationship between a senator and his staff was different then, less formal, less hierarchical than it was to become—closer. (Ted's Harvard friend John Culver was one of his first staffers.) In Ted's case, he and the staff were, at the beginning, literally close. Ted's own office in room 431 of the Senate Office Building was large, with a large desk, but the rest of the office space was cramped. A connecting door from Ted's office led to the tiny staff office, into which the staff were "packed," as Kilvert Dun Gifford told it—"packed like sardines." And the room was smoky because nearly everyone on the staff smoked then. "You couldn't even see." "Too crowded," Robert Bates, who joined the staff in 1969, recalled. "We were all stacked on top of each other." Bates's own desk was squeezed outside the restroom that Ted used, and when people asked Bates if he saw much of the senator, he would quip, "I was privy to everything that went on." And close the staff and Ted were figuratively as well—bound in spirit. Melody Miller, who joined the staff at roughly the same time as Bates, when she was twenty-four, remembered that one could look out through the back windows of the office in the winter, when the trees were bare of leaves, and see President Kennedy's eternal flame marking his gravesite on the hillside at Arlington Cemetery, and she said that view had its effect on them all, forging a sense of common purpose. It was a young staff for a young senator. And in those early years of his Senate career, Ted, still in his mid-thirties, was the eldest of the group. "Everybody was growing up together," said Miller, "so we were very close and very tight." They would socialize. Ted would invite them to shows, or out to his house during the summer when he would throw open the pool. The staff played softball, and Ted would come to the games. And when it rained, they would repair to a nearby restaurant, often the Dubliner, and Ted would come there too and tell stories of his early days as a Suffolk County assistant district attorney, and he would have "all of us in stitches." "Great fellowship and bonding among those of us who were with him from the earliest days," she said.

But just a few years later, the barebones system was barebones no longer, and Ted was one of the contributors to that change, enlarging his staff to enlarge his power and influence. By the mid-1970s, his office staff and his subcommittee staff had swelled to just under sixty—the typical senator had around twenty—at a cost of $500,000. And as Ted himself described it, the new system operated very differently from the old system, the barebones system. It was much more complex, with the staff taking a much larger role in Senate operations and the senators themselves taking a smaller one. "So much staff," Ted was to say, "that they have to justify their presence; they have to come up with five amendments on these issues." But that was Ted's system, Ted's staff, Ted's ambitions, Ted's way of gaining power and influence and respect—always respect. The old staff hadn't needed an organization chart; each of them met with Ted directly and hashed out the agenda. A larger staff with a larger agenda—and Ted's agenda was constantly growing—had more layers, but in Ted's office at least, he retained the initial informality because Ted thrived on it. Ted's chief legislative aide at the time, Paul Kirk, described the organization as a circle with Ted at the center, which meant that most staffers had access to the Senator, as he was always called. *The Senator.* Even as the Senate

became far more bureaucratic than in Lyndon Johnson's day, when senators themselves struck bargains over bourbon and branch water—as Ted
had himself in getting his committee assignments from Eastland—and
when comity meant clout, and even as, with the decline of the bulls, staff
often filled the vacuum, Ted's office was loose and unbureaucratic, with
only two chains of command. One was the administrative chain headed
by the administrative assistant, or AA, essentially the chief of staff, who
was responsible for running the office, and the other was the legislative
chain headed by the legislative assistant, who was responsible for all the
legislative matters. The AA, as Paul Kirk, who had gone from the whip
staff to the AdPrac staff to Ted's personal staff, described his duties when
he held that post, took care of the political details: "the schedule, what
appearances, what invitations to accept, what invitations to generate or
to seek out because it would be the right kind of forum for a particular
speech." The AA was Ted's surrogate when visitors came to the office and
Ted couldn't see them, and the AA then maintained contact with them
and drafted correspondence that was political in nature. The AA provided
input on speeches and on policy and served as a sounding board. The AA
served as liaison to the other side of Capitol Hill and to advocacy groups
with whom Ted worked, often attending their events when Ted couldn't.
"I sort of kept the network together" was how Kirk put it. And the AA ran
staff meetings and organized the practical staff—the secretaries and receptionists and schedulers. And more. One AA, Ed Martin, said he would
have supper at eight and then type all the answers and "everything else,"
presumably anything that Ted needed, until eleven at night, and not just
the Senate work but personal work. "See, when you work for a Kennedy,"
Martin would later say with a large dose of exaggeration, "you not only
do all his work, but you're working also for the Kennedy family."

Two chains, both reporting to Ted. The AA handled the political work
(and personal work); the legislative assistant handled the substantive
work of the committees and the bills. The staffs of the subcommittees that
Ted chaired technically belonged to their respective committees—they
were paid out of the committee budgets—but they were hired by Ted, followed Ted's instructions, and reported to Ted. (In time, as the staff grew in
number, the staff director for the committee would recruit his or her aides
before presenting them to Ted for his approval.) They researched issues,
tracked bills that other senators had introduced and those emanating
from the White House as well, traced legislative history, including Ted's

own positions on issues in the past, followed hearings, served as liaisons with other staffs, and raced to the Senate floor when the bell rang for a vote so that they could inform Ted on the issue. As Dun Gifford described it, as the aides were running for the Senate subway, their senators were alongside them asking, "What the hell is this bill all about? What are the issues?" They supplied material for speeches. "Gee, I'm going to Holyoke," Ted might tell his legislative assistant "Is there anything in the pipeline about Holyoke?" And the legislative assistant, or one of the subcommittee staff, would have to provide it. "So you race around and get memos pulled together for him," Gifford said, though his job description was even less specific: "You do everything. You really do everything."

And that was the additional burden on the staff. There was a lot of everything because Ted Kennedy was no ordinary senator—no ordinary politician even. He was the nation's leading liberal, with all the attendant obligations; he was a president-in-waiting; he was a Kennedy, with all that entailed; and he was a celebrity over and above his political status. The staff had to serve that figure too—to serve what was now the *industry* of Ted Kennedy.

And if by his staff he would be known, Ted Kennedy had to woo that staff, find the best, as his father and brothers had. When he began his Senate career, it had been difficult to woo them. When he began, when he had been the least of the Kennedys, working for him was considered a comedown. But that had changed early on, when Bobby pushed him to raise the quality of his staff, and it changed even more dramatically upon Bobby's death, when Ted assumed the Kennedy mantle, the Kennedy legacy, and then became the shadow president with Nixon's election. At that point, Ted Kennedy's office became the center of the opposition. And at that point, Ted Kennedy no longer had to fight for staff. That was how it was to remain through the course of his Senate career. One aspired to work for Ted Kennedy. His power exalted his staff. His staff exalted his power.

A "Harvard" himself, though an admitted cheat there, he admired other Harvards, the loftier ones, and sought them. Paul Kirk, one of them, was both Harvard and Harvard Law. A young attorney, he arrived on Ted's staff via Bobby's presidential campaign, which, after Bobby's death, left him "too wrung out for more politics." But Dave Burke, Ted's AA, kept badgering him to join Ted's staff, and Kirk finally decided that if Ted could

keep going after that tragedy, he could too. But there was more to his ac-
quiescence: "You just had the dynamic of another Kennedy in the Senate
and the wonderment about what his political plans might be." (Of course,
most expected those plans were presidential.) Kirk's was a common refrain. Ted was a big senator now. Ted had big plans now. Another staffer,
Sharon Waxman, who would become Ted's senior national security adviser, had served Senator Frank Lautenberg, who sat on the important
Appropriations Committee but lacked foreign policy credentials. Mostly,
though, she left Lautenberg's staff because Lautenberg wasn't Ted Kennedy. "He's a leader in the Democratic Party," Waxman said of Ted. "He's
a national leader, and it's just a different environment and a different ball
game," meaning different from Lautenberg's staff. Jan Kalicki, who had
served on the Policy Planning Staff under Henry Kissinger in the State
Department and then under Secretary of State Cyrus Vance in the first
months of the Carter administration, was also persuaded to join Ted's
staff. He met with Ted at the McLean house, where they discussed very
little about the prospective job but a great deal about history—Kalicki
said others had a similar experience with Ted—and felt "instantly close
and connected." Kalicki assumed his bosses at State would do everything
to dissuade him from leaving. Instead, they told him, "Look, we'd really
love you to stay, but if you are going to go anywhere, to work with Ted
Kennedy is really, really something."

Among these stars of the staff, however, the brightest was the quiet
man, the diffident man, the inscrutable man, another "Harvard" and a
Rhodes scholar as well, a young sage named Carey Parker, whom Jim
Flug, Ted's staff person on the Judiciary Committee, had recruited from
the Justice Department after Nixon's election, and who had also said after
he took the job, "I probably wouldn't have come to work for any other
senator." Parker wanted "to be under the radar," as one staff person put it.
He stayed there. Other staffers trailed Ted to hearings or markups or even
occasionally followed him onto the Senate floor for important debates—
those blue suits buzzing around him. Parker almost never left the office,
never even left his desk, would never go on the floor or attend a hearing or
a markup unless, as one staffer put it "there was a crisis brewing." Other
staffers, at least those at the top of the organization chart, would meet
with senators. Parker never met with senators. Carey Parker sat at that
desk, day in and day out, sat there unobtrusively, sat there quietly, sat
there and wrote most of Ted's speeches and provided many of Ted's

ideas—a silent power. A "great writer and a great thinker," said Ed Martin, Ted's onetime AA. But Parker had something more important than brilliance, something that made him the first among equals. It wasn't any particular personal connection like the friendships Ted would form over the years with a few esteemed staff persons; Ted's relationship with Parker was primarily professional. It wasn't because they were kindred spirits. Two men could have hardly been more dissimilar. Parker was an introvert where Ted was an extrovert; Parker a man of no seeming great ambition while Ted's ambitions were large; Parker a man of moderate temperament where Ted's temperament was outsize. And yet whatever the reason, Carey Parker had this ability: He always managed to have his finger on Ted's pulse. The man who was so dissimilar from Ted Kennedy in so many ways would become Ted Kennedy's alter ego.

VI

An elite staff it was. A well-trained staff. A staff of professionals. A staff of the best and the brightest. "The highest caliber staff I have ever seen work for any senator," John McCain called it. But despite the impression one might have had, it wasn't all Harvards or Brahmins. Ted had an affinity for the streetwise too. Ed Martin had been a political reporter at the *Boston Herald* when Ted asked him to become his press secretary and then, later, his AA, replacing Dave Burke when Burke left in 1971. Dick Drayne, who served as Ted's press secretary for ten years, from 1965 to 1975, went to Georgetown for a year before leaving for Penn State and then working as a journalist. Richard Burke was a freshman at Georgetown when he volunteered at Ted's office, began running errands for him, and eventually, after seven years as an apprentice, and without any formal government training, became his AA in 1978. "It wasn't the blue-blood type of thing," another staffer was to say, "so much as just exceptionally smart, high energy, creative people."

If there was no secret as to how Ted Kennedy attracted these staffers—as Paul Kirk had said, it was the power he wielded and the promise of a future presidency—there was a secret nevertheless as to how he kept them. Ted paid them well—or at least better than most senators paid their staffs. There was a Senate allowance for personal staff, based partly on the size of the state one represented. And there were other allowances for committee staff, which Ted used creatively, moving staffers around from his personal staff to committee staffs or from one committee staff to another as need be to fit the budget. "Judiciary had very large budgets for its subcommittees," said staffer Thomas Susman, and "there wasn't much attention paid to whose payroll you were on." "There was a lot of back and forth," Susman said. None of the staffers were particularly well paid in the beginning. Top staffers made less than $25,000, which, even in the late 1960s, was not an exorbitant sum. But to attract and hold better staff, Ted began doing something that most senators did not do, could not do, because they didn't have the resources to do so. Ted had that great staff—staffers who could have worked elsewhere in other departments of the government or in the private sector, could and later would—because he supplemented their incomes occasionally out of his own pocket. "A very limited way," he would say, "on some special, special occasions," he would say, but then would admit, "in an important way." Ted financed his shadow government out of his own pocket. And he did that, too, for power and for respect.

And having paid for that staff, Ted Kennedy worked that staff. But even as he worked them, and worked them hard, he was never a martinet. It wasn't in his personality. "Teddy doesn't demand," his old campaign manager Gerard Doherty said. " 'This is what I want you to do,' or 'I'm ordering you.' He's never done that." Instead, Ted would set his staffers out on their own with little instruction. "Just put you in the pot and then set the water on high heat to see how you do" was how Dun Gifford put it. When Gifford joined the staff, Ted told him his first project would be draft reform, and Gifford responded enthusiastically, saying he had been in the service. To which Ted snapped, "The rest of these people up here are all on deferments. You and me, we served, and we're going to figure this out." So Gifford stayed up that night and wrote a speech for Ted to deliver on the floor about the military draft and handed it to him the next morning at the office. An hour later, Gifford said, Ted opened the door and invited Gifford into his office and told him how bad the speech was and how he couldn't deliver it and how he should go downtown and talk to Milton Gwirtzman, Ted's quondam adviser and frequent speechwriter. So Gifford, who was utterly exhausted and now dispirited, headed off to Gwirtzman's office, where Gwirtzman said the same thing as Ted: the speech was awful, undeliverable. What was missing, he said, was a five-point program. And the two of them sat there and worked one out. Then Gifford returned to Capitol Hill and began sounding out people, experts, and talked to Bobby's staffers, who had worked on draft reform, and learned that one of the most salient issues was the fact that Southern draft boards were all white, which explained in part why white college students received deferments and young Black people didn't. But he had had to figure this all out on his own. Ted had never told him.

And Ted had never told him because by that point—the early 1970s—Ted Kennedy didn't want his staff to regurgitate his ideas. "He wanted new ideas with continuing problems," Carey Parker said. "That's what the staff was supposed to do: to scout, to go around and talk to the experts, find the experts *he* should talk to, and then pare it down, and put together a realistic strategy." "We would go to him at the beginning of a year with an agenda," said health staffer Stan Jones. " 'Here's the issues we think you should be getting into.' And, of course, we're reading and hearing about stuff and looking for both opportunities, for visibility, for making a difference." (And then, said Parker, Ted would take the plan to a Republican senator who he thought might be receptive and say the two them should work together.) But that was just the beginning of the process. After the strategy had been presented, Ted wanted to argue that strategy, test it out in internal debate to make sure that it was sound, that the staff hadn't missed anything. That was part of his earning respect too—showing that you were prepared to parry disagreement, should it arise. "When Kennedy got up to speak—I don't know whether that was the first time he'd read the speech, maybe the second or third," Senator Bob Dole later said, "he could rely on it being accurate. . . . It was just a given that when you were going up against Kennedy, you'd better have some good staff work, because he's got it." "You don't just serve something up to the Senator," an aide told one reporter. "Half the job is arguing things out with him, discussing every issue. He has more deeply-held views than the staff does, to a large extent." And these would be vigorous sessions, tough sessions, sessions with whoever on the staff knew the most about the issue. And those staffers would jam into his office—fifteen or so of them—and the discussion would bounce around the room, everyone having a word or two, so that Ted could, as Carey Parker put it, "digest that, condense it, and say, 'Here's where we go.' " "One of those uncommon politicians who genuinely want some people around who say what they think instead of what will please the principal," said Robert Shrum, who served in several staff positions. And Ted had asked Shrum, "What good does it do to have a bunch of advisers who just agree with you? I can agree with myself if that's what I want." And it wasn't just the chief counsels of his subcommittees who attended these debates. Among those attendees were junior staffers, and Parker said that was "extremely helpful" to attract staff because "word gets out that if you go to Kennedy's office, there isn't a hierarchy that you're at the bottom of and that you have to painfully work your way up. You can start right out talking to Senator Kennedy." And Parker added this: that Ted Kennedy *loved* those sessions with his staff, *loved* to consider new ideas, *loved* the give-and-take of the debates.

But if Ted Kennedy wasn't a martinet, if he was collaborative, the Ted of the mid-1970s had also grown impatient. "Like a shark," one longtime staffer said of him. "He's got to keep moving all the time. That's part of Ted Kennedy metabolism." Even the debate sessions in his office seldom lasted longer than fifteen or twenty minutes. And the staffer noted that his spare time, Ted's relaxation time, of which there was little, was spent sailing. "That's relaxing? You're constantly in motion, moving around, raising this and lowering that. It's fairly tense, an on-the-edge kind of sport." But Ted needed action, and he hated wasting time. He appreciated the preciousness of time. "We have a limited amount of time to do things," Stephen Breyer, his onetime staffer, said of Ted's mindset. "Let's organize and get something done." And if whatever he was working on fell apart, Breyer observed, "he'll go on to something else." And Breyer said that meant that the way to "win some of his time is to get something done." Another aide, Paul Donovan, noted how rapidly Ted would resolve decisions. "Oftentimes people would just come in for short fifteen- to thirty-minute updates, and Kennedy would say, 'Okay. Of the three things you're asking to do . . . two of them I'll give you permission to do and you can act on this, and the third one, I agree I should do it, and I will call Senator so-and-so, I'll call the White House.'" One reporter cited him snapping to his staff, "Get me an energy program by next week. I'm sick of Scoop Jackson being called 'Mr. Energy.'" But it wasn't just impatience that drove Ted Kennedy, not just the consciousness of the awful scarcity of time that he had learned from his brothers' deaths. Ted Kennedy had always thrived on speed and on tension. He was always in a hurry, until his early days in the Senate when the institution had forced him to slow down; his hell-bent driving attested to that. His onetime AA Richard Burke recalled speeding from a party with Ted behind the wheel of his car to make a Senate vote. "He just laughed as he hustled in for the vote," Burke said, "and I realized then that much of his personality was driven by an enjoyment of life on the edge." Now he ran his office that way too.

And if Ted Kennedy was impatient with the legislative process, he could also be impatient with his staff, now that he was a Senate man— a man to whom one deferred, a man who had a reputation to uphold. In the early days, when less was riding on Ted, his health aide Stan Jones said that Jones had arranged to take his family to the Canadian wilderness for their annual canoeing trip, but he had been forced to postpone it several times due to the press of Senate business. Finally, he importuned Ted to let him go—his last chance, he said—even though a bill was coming up for a hearing. Ted sent him back a brief poem: "It's okay. Paddle away. We'll pass the bill another day." And when Jones returned, he said that Ted wanted to know all about the trip. But that was the young Ted. The older Ted was less forgiving. Thomas Rollins, the former staff director of the Labor Committee, compared how Ted used his staff the way the Pony Express used its horses: "Ride 'em hard and then leap to another horse." Ted had always been kind with people, ordinary people, people at risk, people who needed something from him. He was less kind and pricklier with people from whom he needed something. "Brusque and imperious" was how a reporter described him with those staffers, snapping his fingers at an aide during hearings or dressing down an aide who whispered information to him in front of reporters, thereby reinforcing the idea that Ted was the puppet of his staff. One Foreign Service officer complained to a reporter that Ted had treated him like "shit" when he was assigned to accompany Ted through a country and how Ted was "bellowing at him profanely" when the country's phone system broke down, even sticking the officer with a lunch bill. But then, that was a Foreign Service employee, not one of his own. (John Culver said that Ted would never permit anyone other than Ted himself to criticize a staff member, and he would explode at anyone who did.) "Snitty," one acquaintance called him, after Ted complained sarcastically about a dinner guest who dominated the conversation. "Very nervous and upset," said health aide Dr. Philip Caper, if Ted felt he had been insufficiently prepared for a hearing or markup or House-Senate conference. "He'll turn to you and expect you to have the answer, and if you don't have the answer, you're in trouble." On one occasion, when a staffer didn't know a prospective vote count, Ted shouted on the Senate floor, "What do you mean you don't know? Why can't I get a staff that knows what it's doing?" A reporter watching him at a hearing said he kept asking for "obscure facts," almost as if he were probing to make certain that the aides knew what they were talking about. One of those aides said, "Heaven help you if you are unprepared. He has a very sharp temper, and he uses it very effectively." This was the new Ted Kennedy, the ascendant Ted Kennedy, the Ted Kennedy who feared any slippage. And this Ted Kennedy was much more demanding than the younger one. This Ted Kennedy felt he had much more at stake. And this was the Ted Kennedy who would square off against Jimmy Carter.

But by the same token, Ted knew what it was like to be dressed down, remembered those dressings-down, and despite his occasional snittiness, almost no one on his staff accused him of being cruel or callous or caustic, and almost all of them said that he was deeply regretful and apologetic after he did dress them down, so that no one on the staff trembled in fear, as staffers of, for instance, Lyndon Johnson had, sometimes being brought to tears. "Forgiving," Phil Caper said of him if you botched something. "You blow up, you realize instantly that you've done the wrong thing, that you were a jerk, and you need to go apologize right away" was how Thomas Rollins described Ted's sense of remorse after upbraiding a staff member. "Within a half-hour, you would hear from him." "Fall all over himself apologizing," Bob Shrum said of him. "He does not have any meanness." "He never lost his temper without apologizing for it," said another staffer. "If you screwed up, it wasn't a matter of being punished," Bob Bates said. "It was a matter of 'Okay. What do we do to make it right?'" Bates recalled one episode where he had done something wrong and felt it necessary to explain himself to the senator. Ted's response: "Peace," scribbled on the memo. Reporter Tom Oliphant noticed that often when Ted did scold a staff member, he would shift into a "semi-whiney" voice and crank up his "fog machine" in which the criticism was nearly unintelligible, "which took a little of the edge off," almost as if he couldn't really get himself too worked up, even if a staff member deserved it. Other times, he undercut his tongue-lashings with humor. "He could really laugh about these things [mistakes] that would happen," recalled another staffer. "I'm sure he was upset about it, but he got over it in a big hurry, and then, of course, enjoyed telling the story hundreds and hundreds more times." When Shrum fed him some erroneous information just before an interview with the *New York Times* editorial board, Ted told him in the car afterward, "I'll thank you to let me make my own mistakes. As you may have noticed, I'm quite good at it."

And if he chewed out his staff for errors, he was not one to compensate by lavishing praise on them for their successes, a habit he no doubt inherited from his father and his mother, both of whom were stern taskmasters. "Rarely, as I discovered, he would write, 'Good note!' on a memo," said one staffer, but this was so infrequent an occurrence that the staffer also said that "someone in the personnel office would affix a red star on it" when it did happen. And yet, when staffers drafted a piece of legislation and Ted managed to get that legislation passed, particularly if there had been a floor fight to achieve it, Ted would get copies of the bill and write across them, "To Jim"—if, for example, it had been Jim Flug—"I couldn't have done this without you," and he would have these framed for those staffers. And Ted would write thank-you notes for those who helped engineer successes—this too an inheritance from his mother, who was diligent about thank-yous and impressed that diligence upon him. And he would have photographs taken with his staff when they had been at an event together. But these appreciations were not given out liberally, only after those successes. With others, Ted could be sweet, grateful. With his staff, he was grateful largely for results—because he needed results in order to measure up, needed results to avoid that slippage, and needed results to accomplish his political mission.

And measuring up affected his relationship to his staff. He had been forced to adjust his behavior toward them from the informality and socializing of the early years, when he was the least of the senators, to greater formality fourteen years later, when he was a Senate man, a Senate leader. Ted had two states of mind, said one staffer during the senator's ascendant years: "jovial and light-hearted, or focused and pissed." "He either wanted to talk about me or his staff and laugh and joke, or he wanted to talk about work, in which case he was all business." It was a difficult balance to strike for a man who was naturally outgoing and gregarious and who loved to joke and tell stories, but his Senate reputation, which was increasingly important to him, depended on his drive and his success, which in turn he felt depended on his getting the most from his staff. With some of them, like David Burke or Paul Kirk, he had developed a chemistry, even a friendship, and they would get invitations to the McLean house. Others wouldn't. But even with these chosen few, Ted was always wary that friendship would undermine discipline. The man who once loved to pal with his staff became increasingly aloof from them outside the office. A "brisk approach to subordinates," *Time* called it, and reported that he often told his staff how his father would have dealt with a situation, almost as a warning to keep them at arm's length. Bobby, said Nance Lyons, who had worked for him and for Ted, was deeply involved with his staff. He would sit on the receptionist's desk and inquire what she had done over the weekend, or tease Lyons when she asked to use his long-distance line to phone her mother, interrupting her jokingly to ask if he might use his own phone—Bobby, who was usually characterized as hard and abrupt and humorless. But Ted, who was usually characterized as warm and approachable and funny, Lyons said, was the one who could now be cold. In crowds, she said, he was boisterous and comfortable. Around staff, now that he bore the pressure of being a Senate leader, he was no longer his old self. Lyons said she couldn't remember Ted ever asking anyone in the office, "How are you?" And she said he seemed nervous around his staffers.

And he *was* nervous—nervous because he had so much for which to atone, so much he had to prove if he were to become an important senator.

There were certainly easier senators for whom to work, but the staff tolerated the long days into night, the relentless pressure to be better than anyone else's staff so that he could be better than any other senator, the criticisms and the dearth of praise, the aloofness, because they received something in return—besides the combat pay—that no other senator could possibly provide. They got the power that derived from working for Ted Kennedy. "What I loved about doing the big legislation was you could call anybody in the world," said Nance Lyons. "You could call up and say, 'I'm from Senator Kennedy's office,' and they would share all their knowledge with you. 'How can I help?' They couldn't do enough to educate me"—all of which spoke to how Ted Kennedy had ascended outside the Senate too. Bob Bates even complained that between Ted's constant pressure for more and the willingness of experts to provide more—"everybody wants to be feeding stuff to Kennedy"—you could actually get "too much information." "Your problem was, after the day was over, and you'd spent all of your time on the phone talking to people, you had to spend a good part of the evening learning what it is you had dug up and then be prepared to present it to him in a way that he could use it and be forceful and direct." They had the same kind of access to most other senators' offices as they had to experts. And because of the relationships Ted had forged with his Senate colleagues and because of Ted's growing importance, those senators' staffers were usually eager to help. "We're trying to do something for North Adams. Can you give us a hand?" was how Dun Gifford relayed a typical call. "And you'd go to lunch with the staff guy." And then they would try to work out a deal because senators wanted to work out a deal with Ted Kennedy and gain his favor. And there was another benefit, other than access, from working on Ted's staff: Ted Kennedy really did speed up the slow institution. He got results. Other senators could work on bills, but Ted was already becoming known for bringing his bills to passage. "It's a bill; it's a hearing; it's on the agenda; it's out of committee; it's now on the floor; it's up on the floor; it's bipartisan. Fabulous!" said Kenneth Feinberg, once an AA of Ted's, of the process. "You saw every day that you worked for him, the progress, instead of just spinning along, and got great personal satisfaction out of that, and he did too."

There was little doubt of that. The consensus was that Ted Kennedy, the senator with a hundred balls in the air, the senator who got results while so many of his colleagues were, as Feinberg put it, "spinning," had the best staff in the Senate, which was a far cry from the opinion of his staff during his early days there. But there was a complaint as well among many of his colleagues and especially among their staffs: that Ted Kennedy's staff *knew* they were the best and flaunted it. "Very smart, very ideological, very hard-driving, very sure of themselves, and difficult," Senator John Danforth said of the staff. Always difficult. Unpleasant, many senators felt. Being on the staff, one reporter said, so inflated those staffers' egos that it engendered arrogance, even rudeness. "Kennedy staff people get a reputation for being very pushy and obnoxious," one of them admitted. "You hear things coming out of your mouth at times that you can't believe you're saying." Still, the staffer defended the arrogance the way Ted might have: "No matter whose feathers you have to ruffle, just get it done." Senate staffers could generally be pompous, certainly compared to House staffers; the pecking order was much stricter. But Ted's staffers were the most pompous of all. And more. They were cutthroat. His staff was the "most aggressive," said one longtime lobbyist, and he added that other staffs and even advocacy groups had a "fear of being outmaneuvered" by them. *Boston Globe* columnist Tom Oliphant recalled an episode where Secretary of State Henry Kissinger had proposed extending the territorial water limits to two hundred miles to thwart Russian and Japanese fishermen, and Massachusetts congressman Gerry Studds opposed the recommendation—the "first of the block to see and then push" his opposition, Oliphant said. And as soon as Ted heard about Studds's public denunciation, Ted had his own aide, Mary Murtagh, whose responsibilities this legislative area was, seize the initiative from Studds, just as he had asked his aide to seize the energy initiative from Henry Jackson. "Believe me," Oliphant said, "Mary caught up in a matter of hours." Ted was generous in handing out credit. He was not generous in seeing someone else co-opt him.

But the staff not only competed with other staffs. It was so competitive that members even competed among themselves. The personal staff might want Ted to attend a press conference in Massachusetts. His committee staff might want him to chair a hearing. Both are on the same day. "His press person and I end up in a knock-down, drag-out fight because of these kinds of conflicts," said Leroy Goldman. "Tremendous staff competition," one staffer called it, and laid it on Ted. "He promotes internal intrigue. He relished playing one of us off against another to get the most good work out of us. If something goes wrong, he'll say, 'Jesus, what's wrong? Why haven't you straightened that goddamned thing out?'" It was the way Franklin Roosevelt had run his White House staff—goading members, pitting them against one another. But that staffer told Burton Hersh, "We do it because the rewards, the recognition, are tremendous." The "closest thing to being a clerk on the Supreme Court," one lobbyist said of being a Kennedy staffer. And John McCain said something else about Ted and those staffers. He said Ted "inspired in them a degree of devotion and affection that I have not seen for any other senator." In the end, they were loyal to him. Once a Kennedy staffer, always a Kennedy staffer, it was said. And in the end, for all his vicissitudes, they loved him.

Amid the intrigue and the competition and the arrogance and the aggressiveness—all in the interest of making Ted Kennedy matter—there was one other feature of Ted Kennedy's staff, and it did not redound to his credit. The champion of the marginalized, the voice of the powerless, had a staff that was nearly all white and all male. Bob Bates, the first Black staffer, who came aboard in 1969, said that while Ted had the "public image of his being empathetic and concerned and all," neither he nor his staff had had much contact with Black people, and Bates felt that he was "treated somewhat with kid gloves" as a result. And if Black Americans were underrepresented, so were women, and those who were on the staff—and there weren't many in the 1970s—felt the sting of sexism. "It

was very sexist at that time, both in his office and throughout the Senate,"
Bob Bates said. Women were secretaries and receptionists, and advancement for them was restricted. Anne Strauss said she had worked in the
office for nearly ten years—this was a bit of exaggeration—before Dave
Burke, then the AA, offered her the "legislative correspondent's" job,
which was essentially handling mail, and she said she got it only because
Burke had made a deal with her that she would get it if she agreed to stay
for a year as a secretary after Burke left. Many of the women in the office,
who were called secretaries or caseworkers—which meant handling constituent requests and complaints—were already doing much more without getting the title or the pay. Nance Lyons, who went to work for Ted in
1967 after graduating from college, was ambitious and energetic and not
easily intimidated and would not accept secretarial or receptionist work.
Instead, she worked on Massachusetts projects. But when Ted asked her to
set up dinners to retire Bobby's debt from his presidential campaign, she
insisted that she be appointed a legislative assistant—the first woman legislative assistant in Ted's office. Still, she didn't feel the men considered
her the equal of the male legislative assistants because they all had secretaries and she didn't. She had to write, type, and mimeograph everything
herself. "It was horrific," she recalled, because no woman in the office was
doing professional work, and, she believed, none would have been allowed
to do so, if she hadn't demanded it. A woman aide was such a novelty that
when Lyons attended one of Ted's issue dinners at McLean, Joan assumed
she was there to serve cocktails. And women were paid less than the male
staffers too. Anne Strauss remembered that when a friend of hers in the
office asked for a raise, the woman was told that she didn't have a mortgage and didn't need the money as much as one of the male staffers. Even
into the 1970s, Strauss said, there was no job review and no schedule for
raises. She said she was notified of a raise on a Post-it note. Later, when
Congress awarded cost-of-living increases to staff and Ted announced
that he was going to use those increases to hire more staff, Strauss and
Barbara Souliotis, another staffer, decided to confront him, especially
since they had to work on Saturdays and the men didn't. Ted, according
to Souliotis, was practically "shaking in his boots." "It had never been that
two women had come in to confront him on some serious matters having
to do with salary and payroll and office stuff." Souliotis said that Ted was
so stunned he simply muttered, "Okay. Yes. That's fine. Yes, everybody
should do Saturday work. Yes, of course, you should get a cost-of-living

increase. Yes, all that should be fine." Years later, when there was an opening to head Ted's Boston office, and it was just assumed that a man would
be appointed, Ted scotched the idea. "No way," he said. "It's Barbara's."
And Souliotis became the head of that office.

It wasn't just that Ted Kennedy was a chauvinist, though he was, and
though most of the men he hired were. "Very male chauvinistic," Souliotis said of the AAs. It was also that Ted Kennedy had always been uncomfortable around women, his growing up with four sisters and his
serial romances notwithstanding. Even before she attended the Chappaquiddick party, Nance Lyons said that Ted was "not willing, pretty much,
to communicate directly with me for a long time." And she felt it had
nothing to do with her personally. "I felt it was because I was a girl." Part
of the discomfort he seemed to feel around professional women, no doubt,
was an effect of his own mother's attitude that women controlled the
house but had no function in the office; that was how she operated with
her husband. And part of it, almost certainly, was his own reputation as a
womanizer. Had he appointed more women, he might have felt he would
likely have invited gossip. But it went deeper than Rose's sexism or practical political considerations. Ted had little sensitivity to women. He didn't
spend a great deal of time with them, and while he had many female supporters, he had few female friends, save for the wives of friends. Ted could
understand grievances of Black Americans and the grievances of the
poor because he had felt marginalized himself. He had a harder time with
women's grievances. Women's issues hadn't initially interested him, as
his resistance to the Equal Rights Amendment and his early waffling over
abortion rights attested. The Senate was a male domain, and Ted Kennedy, a Senate man, was not about to change that.

It had been a process—a long process—this ascension of Ted Kennedy
from a callow young senator of little promise into a man of the Senate.
Good at ingratiation, he had ingratiated himself with the Senate powers
and won their affection and then their respect. He had worked tirelessly to
change the preconceptions about him by showing his colleagues his
mettle—worked harder, it was said, than any other senator. He had expanded his portfolio rather than specialize, as most senators did, so that
his purview ranged as widely as that of anyone in the chamber. He had
studied to master issues, priding himself on knowing more about most of
those issues and bills than his fellow senators, to the point where many of

them dared not debate him without boning up themselves. He had surrounded himself with what was generally acknowledged as the best staff in the Senate, a brilliant staff, and he worked that staff nearly as hard as he worked himself, which was very hard. And he had, in an audacious move, led the young liberals of the Democratic caucus into battle against the bulls to whom he had always shown deference and, in winning that battle, helped change the power structure that had stood unchanged for decades. And by doing all this, he had by the mid-1970s made himself not only into a man of the Senate; he had arguably made himself into *the* man of the Senate—the most influential.

But no matter how much admiration he won from his colleagues, no matter how assiduously he worked the Senate, most of Ted Kennedy's power was still extra-institutional. It derived from his being a Kennedy and from his being a prospective president, which was largely a function of his being a Kennedy. Now those presidential prospects had dimmed and, with that, his ability to promote his causes. In any case, the real power, as Ted Kennedy fully understood, resided in the White House, Jimmy Carter's White House, and because he doubted Carter's commitment to those causes, Ted Kennedy wanted power to advance liberalism and, if need be, check Carter. And he knew that if he was to gain that power, the power to bend the Senate to his will, he needed to do one more thing. He needed to be not just a man of the Senate. He needed to be what Lyndon Johnson had been when Johnson was Senate majority leader. He needed to be a master of the Senate—a virtuoso of legislative politics.

And Ted Kennedy, who had the instincts to be a master, now set his sights on that lofty objective.

The Chemistry of the Senate

A FTER NEARLY FOURTEEN years in the Senate, Ted Kennedy was determined to acquire the kind of power that would allow him to *use* the Senate, not necessarily for his own personal ends, though there was no discounting his ambition, but to implement the liberal agenda he believed was imperiled. To do so, he would rely on the lessons he had learned about the operations of the Senate and had bent to his own personality. Lyndon Johnson, wrote his biographer Robert Caro, could read men— read them as if they were a text. And it was Johnson's reading of those texts, his assiduous and astute reading of them, that was the primary source of his power. Lyndon Johnson knew what men wanted and then played upon that knowledge. Ted Kennedy was not an especially avid reader of men. He read quickly, the way he did nearly everything else except prepare for hearings and markups and conferences. He made snap judgments about people. One of his administrative assistants said that Ted relied on first impressions, and that if a relationship between a new staff member and Ted was going to work, it had to work immediately, though Ted's judgment was hardly infallible and those relationships not infrequently sputtered. Ted Kennedy's primary source of power, then, was not reading men but reading the institution in which those men operated and appreciating the interpersonal relationships among those men—appreciating how much those men *wanted* interpersonal relationships. Ted frequently referred to the complex interactions among those men—and they were complex—as the "chemistry of the Senate." Lyndon Johnson was a student of men—of what men wanted. Ted Kennedy was a student of the chemistry of the Senate—of what men valued in one another. And Ted Kennedy might have understood that chemistry better than any of his colleagues—understood it and used it.

Ted Kennedy had to understand the chemistry of the Senate because the Senate had changed significantly since the days when Lyndon Johnson and those Senate bulls could control the chamber. Johnson's mastery of the Senate was a function of his keen political skills but also of his role in the Democratic Senate leadership, first as whip and then as the Democratic leader, and he deployed that role to consolidate his command of the chamber. The new and more liberal Senate class of 1974 and the reforms it instituted in the mid-1970s had made the Senate less hierarchical and less reliant on seniority and deference and party discipline; they had made the Senate more individualistic, more collegial, more democratic. And though Lyndon Johnson was a master manipulator, a master at reading men's minds and knowing what they wanted and knowing what he could give them and then take from them, he would have had a difficult time operating in this environment where Senate men, men who had deferred to the institution of the Senate, were few and far between, and most senators were out for themselves. This new Senate was no longer an institution in which a leader could stare men down or threaten or cajole or even wheedle—no longer an institution in which hard power prevailed, which was the sort of power Lyndon Johnson best wielded. (Of course, Lyndon Johnson, the most adept master of the Senate, also knew how to use honeyed words when it suited him.) The new Senate was an institution in which a leader had to coax and tempt and stroke—an institution in which soft power prevailed, which was the sort of power Ted Kennedy best wielded. And this was what Ted meant by chemistry. He meant finding ways of getting colleagues to work with him, bringing people along, not because they felt they had to, or even because they felt they would gain something from doing so, the old-fashioned horse-trading, though that was certainly part of it, but because they wanted to, and often they wanted to not because they thought he would be president, though many did, but because they had succumbed to the charm of Ted Kennedy.

And Ted Kennedy, having sought and won acceptance from most of his Senate colleagues through his hard work and diligence and deference, now would use that chemistry to get something more than acceptance. He would use it to get power—power that would lead to legislative results.

• • •

The chemistry Ted Kennedy practiced arose from the new comity of the Senate. Despite the premium placed on Senate decorum—the presiding officer was always called "Mr. President," and senators were prohibited from launching personal attacks on the floor—members in the past could and did erupt at one another, betraying that decorum, violating those prohibitions. During a heated exchange, Senator John McClellan once pointed a finger at Jacob Javits of New York, a Jew, and declaimed, "We don't need your kind in the United States Senate." But those were breaches. Normally, senators behaved cordially to one another, even if they had by custom kept their office doors closed to one another. (It was Senator Margaret Chase Smith who introduced an open-door policy when she hung a WELCOME sign on the entrance to her office decorated with a hand-painted scene of the coast of Maine, the state she represented.) And that comity grew from the late 1950s onward. When Joe Biden entered the Senate in 1973, he asked James Eastland what was the most important change he had seen during his years in the Senate, and Eastland answered, "Ahr-conditionin'," and explained that before air conditioning, the Senate chamber would begin heating up around April, heating up to 140 degrees, he said, and the heat was so unbearable that the senators would have to "just up and go home." But when the chamber was air-conditioned, the senators could stay in Washington year round and "really mess up the country," Eastland said, though what he didn't say was that the longer sessions also contributed to a greater sense of community among the senators. South Carolina senator Ernest Hollings, who entered the Senate in 1967, also recognized a blossoming comity at that time: "Senators would have get-togethers for a drink or a barbecue or other social settings." And because there were no television cameras in the chamber reporting the proceedings then, senators had to keep tabs on what was happening on the floor, which, he said, meant that they would congregate in the cloakroom at the rear of the chamber and "swap stories" while they followed the debate. "The Senate was a club," he said, meaning not the exclusive club the Senate had been in the 1940s and 1950s, that club of bulls and insiders, but a club of the whole—clubby. "We looked out for each other." Hollings also felt that when incumbents were more secure from electoral challenges, as they were back then, they could spend less time on fundraising and more time "to talk and listen to each other." (Of course Ted Kennedy never had to worry about fundraising.) Ted adduced another reason for the sociability of the Senate. He felt that Vietnam and civil rights, the most salient issues of the mid-1960s, extended the length of the Senate year, because there was so much that needed to be done about them, and that extension, Ted believed, contributed to camaraderie, saying, as Hollings did, that it "helped senators listen to one another, and sometimes even to take action on matters they might otherwise have avoided." Senators interacted now, even with those across the aisle. (Ted had those McLean dinners.) And these were times when the Senate could be so friendly and the socializing so normal, Ted said, that senators allowed their children to caper through their offices.

But within that comity, Ted Kennedy was the *most* social of senators, the friendliest, the most charming, the best-liked. The "thousand little personal touches that are old-time politics" was how *Boston Globe* reporter John A. Farrell described that charm. Little personal touches like having a spouse's name on his call sheet next to that of the person he was phoning, so that he could ask after him or her when he placed those calls; or having his aides accompany him to gatherings and whisper the names of people he was meeting and some personal details so that he could address them as if he knew them; or sending a fellow senator a painting that Ted had done, after Ted took up painting, as a token of appreciation; or even going over to the House side of the Capitol, as he had done when he was working on healthcare with House Ways and Means chairman Wilbur Mills, when virtually no senator would make that trek because it was considered beneath him to go to the lower chamber. And though he and Robert Byrd had had their tiff when Byrd beat Ted in the Democratic caucus in 1971 for the position of whip, which Ted held at the time, they had long since made peace, and Ted would frequently visit Byrd's office, especially after Byrd succeeded Mike Mansfield as majority leader in 1977. (Ted didn't contest for majority leader; unlike Johnson and Byrd, he abhorred the dull housekeeping chores of being the leader, and he realized the real power of the Senate was no longer located there.) When he did visit, one of those little personal touches was that he always brought Byrd a gift— a "very soulful" gift, Ted's chief counsel of the Labor Committee, Nick Littlefield said—or he would recite a poem he had learned specifically for Byrd. But he was just as thoughtful to the Senate aide who had helped Senator William Proxmire reform the tax code, sending that aide a gift, another of those little personal touches: a framed copy of the old tax code, a book three inches thick, in which Ted had had holes punched, so that the code looked like a block of Swiss cheese. And on the bottom, Ted wrote a tribute to the aide for helping close tax loopholes.

And Ted Kennedy, the student of the chemistry of the Senate who understood the soft power of courtesy, responded with little personal touches whenever someone did a favor for him. In 1956 House member Tip O'Neill, at Jack Kennedy's request, had sacrificed his delegate's seat at the Democratic National Convention so that Bobby could be seated in the delegation instead—and O'Neill had already promised seats to others so that, in giving up his seat, he didn't have one for himself. But Jack never thanked him. "Never expect any appreciation from my boys," Joe Kennedy later told O'Neill. "These kids have had so much done for them by other people that they just assume it's coming to them." But that was not true of Ted Kennedy, who made a point of giving thanks for almost everything, save to members of his staff for their labor. "If you don't get a thank you note within twenty-four hours, it's because the mail system is broken," said one bureaucrat, who had worked with Ted and received a "stack of these notes" over the years. "He is just completely courteous with everyone." And Ted told Tom Oliphant of the *Globe* that "as far as he was concerned, the key to politics and governing—*the key to it*—was saying, 'Please and thank you.'"

And those courtesies were elements of the chemistry of the Senate.

And Ted Kennedy with his little personal touches made a point of ingratiating himself not just with the leaders of the Senate, as young Lyndon Johnson had, but with all the senators, even the ones with no power whatsoever. "Very willing to embrace a new young Republican who shows up in the Senate and is sort of doe-eyed," John Farrell of the *Globe* would say. "Kennedy comes over like this big shark and puts his arm around him and says nice things to him, and the guy goes home at night and says, 'You know who said nice things to me today on the floor? Ted Kennedy said I did a nice job with that amendment.' Then the guy's mother gets a signed book of Rose Kennedy's memoir." Precisely because they felt lost, Ted, who had known what it was like to be lost, would always approach those freshmen senators—the senators whom most of the Senate elders neglected. One of Ted's staffers remembers freshman senator John Chafee, a Republican from Rhode Island, a former Rhode Island governor, sitting forlornly in his Senate chair while other senators were in the well "yucking it up." And Ted walked over to Chafee, sat down with him, chatted with him for maybe twenty minutes, and in those twenty minutes, they cemented a relationship that would last for years. At a reception for the new freshman class in 1979, Alan Simpson, a Republican member of that class, remembered that Ted was the first person in the Mansfield Room to greet them. And Simpson said that he had been in the Senate scarcely a month when Ted introduced him to his staff and told him, "These people of mine are here. They're professionals. They can help you." And Simpson said that from that point on, he would phone Ted's staffers with questions and requests, and "they would get back to me and they would get back to my staff." And Ted loved to give those freshmen tours of his office, adorned with memorabilia from John and Bobby Kennedy. "If he had done it a thousand times, he still made it seem as if it were the first," said one reporter "—the framed letter from President Hoover when he was born," which always was accompanied by the story of how the letter arrived with postage due, and the framed note from fourteen-year-old John Kennedy asking if he could be his baby brother's godfather.

And with his office, so with his "hideaway." Hideaways were small offices in the Capitol itself intended to let the lawmakers stay in the building rather than return to their formal offices during Senate business. (They were also called "escape rooms" because they allowed senators to escape Senate business.) Hideaways conferred prestige—"extensions of the old ego," Bobby Baker, the secretary to the majority leader when Lyndon Johnson held that post, would say. They were parceled out on the basis of seniority, and until the East Front of the Capitol was extended in 1982 and storage space was converted to office space, freshmen seldom got them, and lower-ranking members were likely to be stuck in the basement. ("My older brother said that by the time you get one of these offices, you're too old to enjoy it," Ted had joked to columnist Jimmy Breslin when Breslin visited him there.) Johnson, it was said, had seven hideaways on two floors of the Senate—"LBJ Ranch East," they were called—which testified to the ego that Baker had cited. Ted Kennedy's ego was smaller. His hideaway was located on the third floor of the Capitol, up a massive marble staircase from the Senate floor that took him past a large oil painting of Abraham Lincoln signing the Emancipation Proclamation, then through the radio-television room, then through a narrow tunnel of windows, and then down a short tiled hallway. Inside, its windows gave out, said a visitor, to a view to the west of the Mall, the Washington Monument and the Lincoln Memorial, and to the right, of Pennsylvania Avenue, past the National Archives and the FBI Building and the Treasury Building all the way to the White House. It was spacious as far as hideaways went and comfortable. "Elegant," another visitor called it.

But it wasn't really just a hideaway. John McCain would later call it a "tactic." It was a tactic because Ted Kennedy used his hideaway not to hide away from the Senate but to embrace it. As he would invite colleagues to his office, he would invite them to his hideaway, which, like his office, was decorated with Kennedy memorabilia—a "museum," McCain would say, with "pictures of his brother, the table is the rudder of a boat, pictures of his dad, his family, all kinds of stuff." And McCain said that "he started out doing it with me and then I watched him do it with others." Ted would show them around the hideaway and say, "Now here's a picture of Bobby when we were doing such-and-such, and here's a picture of Jack. He was in his naval uniform—and then here's—." (In the mid-1970s, however, there was only one photograph on his desk: of Joan.) He would walk his visitors, often Republicans, through his family history, and in this way, he would soften them but also remind them of his own history—of the giants with whom he had lived.

And that ingratiation, combined with the aura of the Kennedys, which he was not averse to using when it suited him, was an element of the chemistry of the Senate.

But it wasn't just the little personal touches, the pro forma gestures of hospitality, which weren't pro forma for anyone else in the Senate, in which Ted Kennedy specialized. It was the larger gestures too. Joe Biden said that when he entered the Senate, just weeks after his young wife and infant daughter had been killed in a car accident, and his two sons seriously injured, Ted phoned him every day, even though the two hadn't really known each other, and when Biden's sons were recuperating in the hospital, Ted would send specialists down to Delaware from Boston. And throughout his first year of anguish, Biden said that Ted made "regular trips" to his office in a faraway corner of the Dirksen Office Building. "He'd squeeze through the too-small anteroom and poke his head into my office" and ask Biden to join him in the Senate gym, and when Biden told him that he didn't feel like working out, Ted, giving him a lesson on the chemistry of the Senate, explained that this wasn't a weight room, that it was a "good place to get to know some of my colleagues." So Ted took him there. "Joe, I want you to meet some of the guys," Ted said, introducing him to Jacob Javits and Stuart Symington, "legendary senators," as Biden described them. And Barbara Mikulski, a new senator from Maryland, said that when she was about to go before the Steering Committee for her committee assignments, Ted told her he was going to be her "precinct organizer." And when Mikulski asked whether they were playing by "Baltimore rules" or "Boston rules," Ted told her they were playing by "Ted rules." And Ted got her the committees she desired, even the coveted Appropriations Committee. "I've got [Tom] Harkin on the committee," he said. "I'm going to get you on the committee." And he did.

And that solicitousness was an element of the chemistry of the Senate.

And it wasn't just the things Ted Kennedy *did* that made him a master of the chemistry of the Senate, one of the most well-liked of the senators, but who he *was*. No senator was more gregarious. One of Jack Kennedy's favorite maxims was "In politics, you don't have friends; you have allies." But Ted Kennedy, far less cynical than his brother, did have friends, and many of them were his allies. One of *his* favorite proverbs was an Irish one: There are no such things as strangers. Strangers are just friends you haven't met. "If you're Teddy, you win by talking to a whole lot of people, because it helps you," said Dun Gifford, an early member of his staff. "When you're up there at that level, if you just read the newspapers and talk to your close staff, you're dead meat. You get narrower, narrower, narrower, and Ted was never that way. He talked to everybody." And not just talked or talked Senate business; because he understood the chemistry of the Senate, he joked with everyone, enlivened the somber institution. "We always knew when Ted was in the cloakroom," recalled Senator Patrick Leahy, "because every so often you'd hear these bellows of laughter." Leahy said that once Ted was in the cloakroom with Senator Dale Bumpers of Arkansas and a few others, all telling stories, and the laughter growing louder and louder—so loud that the presiding officer in the Senate chamber called for order and banged the gavel hard—twice—and called for order in the *cloakroom*. "Somebody had to come in and say [to Ted], 'I think that means you.'" He was often jocular with colleagues, often chiding them gently. "Leavin' early today, Senator," he quipped to a colleague leaving his office. "M'gosh, the farmers back home are still workin'."

The trick—a trick Ted Kennedy had mastered—was not seeming manipulative or insincere, even on those rare occasions when, like Lyndon Johnson, he had ulterior motives. He respected New York Republican senator Jacob Javits, an intelligent man, a moderate, a doer, but, said Ted's friend William vanden Heuvel, Ted also "played him like a Stradivarius." Javits had an outsize ego, so large that "by asking his advice and counsel and working with him—a thing Bobby never would have done—Teddy then earned his friendship and respect." And Vanden Heuvel said that "Javits was quite prepared to do a lot of things to help Ted." But if Ted did not show his hand, in large part it was because there was seldom a hand to show, no guile, and his Senate colleagues knew and appreciated that too. He genuinely liked people, genuinely cared about them, which was one reason he could work the chemistry so well. "It was always with a personal twist," his son Patrick would later observe. "It was always asking them about their families. It was always about intervening in some way that would be helpful to them and their respective politics. It was always sharing something of a personal connection somewhere along the line such that they could begin from that to build a personal relationship that could become the basis for a political relationship."

And that personal warmth was an element of the chemistry of the Senate.

And added to that warmth was another characteristic: Ted Kennedy was never malicious, never retributive. "He doesn't have any enemies in the Senate," Carey Parker would say of him, which Parker attributed to Ted's having to get along in a family of eleven and having to make accommodations. "Most politicians, I'm sorry to say, spend a large share of their time bad-mouthing other politicians, including their own party," Ted Sorensen said. "But the Kennedys did much less of that, and I'd say Ted does it less than anyone else," possibly because Ted Kennedy knew what it was like to be the target of spite. Reporter Tom Oliphant, who covered Ted for years, said he couldn't come up with a single example of Ted disparaging people either, "whereas in this racket, you hear this stuff all the time." Senator McCain, a frequent adversary of Ted's, said, "Ted doesn't have a mean bone in his body." "He'd get really mad and be incensed at somebody in public or in private, in closed session, open session, or on the floor," recalled John Podesta, a longtime Democratic operative and later chief of staff to President Bill Clinton and counselor to President Barack Obama. "He'd get really furious." But for all that fury, Podesta said he couldn't think of anybody that Ted Kennedy hated. "I think he kind of liked everybody. He found something to like about everybody, and that gave him a connection to virtually everybody." And Podesta averred that it wasn't "fake charm." It was his deep feeling for others, his deep interest for and enjoyment of others. "Very, very few people, not just in politics but in life, have that capacity to seize on and find that bond and find something to like about somebody who basically would have very little to like about him." Ted Kennedy did. He was not, as Podesta put it, a "good hater." "It didn't wear well for him to hate people."

And that equanimity was an element of the chemistry of the Senate.

Nor did Ted Kennedy, a master of soft power, try to throw his weight around, as Lyndon Johnson, the master of hard power, had. "He's not a bully," Senator Jay Rockefeller of West Virginia said of him. "He was Lyndon Johnson without the muscle" was the way Tom Oliphant put it, "because you could say 'no' to him if you were a colleague, and it's not like a mark went down next to your name forever, because there was always tomorrow." John Tunney, perhaps Ted's closest friend and later a Senate colleague, had told a reporter that he didn't think Ted's health insurance plan, the most fervent cause of Ted's political life, was affordable. Tunney said that Ted called him up and asked incredulously, "Did I read that right?" And Tunney said he had. But Tunney said that Ted "never tried to argue with me . . . never said anything more about it." He simply said, "Okay. If that's the way you feel about it, all right." Another Senate friend, James Sasser, said, "He is not a mean-spirited person," and "he doesn't carry grudges over, and that's known by people in the Senate." (No one would have ever said that of Lyndon Johnson.) Joe, Jack, and Bobby were thought of as vengeful. But Ted would never take revenge if someone didn't go along with him. And it was known.

And that lack of vengefulness was an element of the chemistry of the Senate.

And if his fellow senators knew that Ted Kennedy was not vengeful, they also knew he could be gracious, even magnanimous. Ted Kennedy had an ego. Ted Kennedy wanted credit for what he had done, and even sometimes for what he had not done. Senator Walter Mondale complained that Ted had a habit of "hogging good issues," and he cited a Teachers' Corps program initiated by Senator Gaylord Nelson, who had worked on it for years. One day Nelson arrived on the Senate floor to hear Ted introduce his own Teachers' Corps bill, co-opting Nelson's. Mondale said that "Ted did a lot of that" and that his fellow senators "got used to it, but it didn't mean that people were very happy about it." Ted's staffer Bob Bates recalled a similar situation where he was talking with one of Senator

Charles Mathias's staffers about an amendment to an education bill, and Bates mentioned it to Ted, only to find Ted offering the amendment himself. Bates said Ted was "impetuous" that way. "He would just do something on the spur of the moment." Another staffer complained to Kennedy biographer Theo Lippman that while a chairman might add an amendment to a committee member's bill, Ted would have his staff redraft the entire bill and then call it his own. "He's the biggest thief on the Hill," the individual said. Some of this thievery might have had less to do with stealing a fellow member's bill than with sponsoring a bill in which he believed because he felt he would have greater clout in gaining its passage—greater clout in part because of his greater appreciation for the chemistry of the Senate. But that thievery changed over time. The longer he was in the Senate, the less personal need he had for putting his name on bills, and as he had handed the National Cancer Act over to Peter Dominick, who had had practically nothing to do with it—handed it over because he knew it would be easier to bring the Republicans on board by doing so—he was increasingly willing to sacrifice his own sponsorship if that meant gaining passage for a bill. "If you would like it to happen," he told Stephen Breyer, when Breyer was a member of his staff, "then don't worry about their getting credit for it. That's fine. If in fact they know they'll get credit, they will work harder. Even if it's a different senator, a different party— that's all right if you accomplish something." "He is willing to do all the work and share the credit," another staffer agreed, "to the point of maybe even not getting very much credit." And he would tell her: "You can get a lot done if you're willing to not take credit for it."

And for the Ted Kennedy of the 1970s, that magnanimity had become one of the elements of the chemistry of the Senate.

And there was another, less notable element to the chemistry of the Senate, one for which Ted had great respect, one he said he had learned from a colleague. That was the soft power of moral authority. Unlike his brothers, who wanted to get out of the Senate as quickly as they could and had little use for mentors, Ted had a model senator—one whom he tried to emulate, one who moved the institution, not through bullying or manipulation or horse-trading or raw demonstrations of power or even through Ted's great social magic, but who moved it through the force of his moral standing. Phil Hart of Michigan was a quiet man, a diffident man, quite the opposite of most of the Senate power brokers, including Ted Kennedy. He was so diffident that the secretary of the Senate during much of Hart's tenure, Francis Valeo, called him "one of the least success-ful of senators," and Valeo said that Hart "knew it," and that "towards the end of his life, it really embittered him." But Ted disagreed with that assessment. "I think he reflected sort of a Jesuit training where he believed in hope and was basically an upbeat person, although he was very quiet and soft-spoken," Ted was to say. And Ted said that Hart had a way of ask-ing simple questions at hearings that captured what everyone wished they could capture, citing the time that Hart asked Alabama governor George Wallace if he thought heaven was segregated. Not effective, Valeo had said of Hart. But Ted Kennedy felt that Hart was the "only man who can, with quiet argument and comments, actually change votes. That's not usually done in debate, where minds are already made up and there is only the formality of the vote. But Phil can do it, with intelligence, reason-ing and compassion." And Ted Kennedy felt that Hart seemed ineffective only because he was so modest and didn't need to take credit for his ac-complishments. The Senate liberals loved Hart, said Chuck Ludlam, who was counsel to the AdPrac Subcommittee that Ted chaired—loved him, as Ted did, for his dignity and sense of principle. And when Hart was dying of cancer and trying to get the Senate to pass an Antitrust Improve-ments Act, which he had steered through his Antitrust Subcommittee and to which he was deeply committed, and Alabama senator James Allen was filing one amendment after another, even once cloture had been in-voked, to stop its passage,* Senator Byrd, who might have been the only senator who knew more about procedure than Allen, circumvented Allen—circumvented him as a way to prove himself to the liberals in his caucus—and then, rather than prolong the ordeal with more procedural maneuvers, made a bargain with Allen that he would make a concession to Allen in return for Allen's letting the measure pass. During the debate, Hart, debilitated from the cancer and the chemotherapy, had, against doctors' orders, been sitting on a couch at the rear of the chamber with his staff, and Byrd and Senator Gaylord Nelson and Ted would join him there, discussing whether they should approve of the compromise with Allen. Hart finally asked them, "I want you to tell me whether you would do this deal if I wasn't dying," because Hart, even near death, didn't want

---

* Allen, a parliamentary genius, had perfected use of a loophole in the Senate rules that allowed debate to continue even after cloture if an amendment had been introduced before the cloture vote. It was called a "post-cloture" filibuster.

that compromise otherwise. And they said they would. That was the sort
of thing that Ted admired: Hart's fear that pity for him would lead to his
principles being compromised. And when Hart was wasting away in the
hospital in those last days, and his wife asked him whom he wanted to see,
he would request to see Ted, and Ted would come to his room and reassure
him that he was taking care of Hart's legislation. And at those times, Ted
would weep for him—weep for one of the Senate's last great men.

And that moral authority that Phil Hart exemplified would be an element in Ted Kennedy's understanding of the chemistry of the Senate—
a major element, as it had been a major element in liberalism itself.

II

But the chemistry of the Senate wouldn't have mattered to Ted Kennedy
had his understanding of it not contributed to his real aim and the only
reason for his working it so aggressively: the passage of legislation. He
was a people person, a glad-hander, a socializer, a storyteller, a joker, the
dispenser of a thousand little personal touches, and those things endeared
him to his colleagues. But above all, Ted Kennedy wanted to be a legislator, and he used the chemistry of the Senate to pass his bills as Johnson
had used terror and threat and bribery to pass his. For this, his charm and
conviviality were not incidental. Most senators liked doing business with
Ted, and as John Danforth put it, he was "easy" to deal with. Those sentiments notwithstanding, some Republicans complained that he was ideological to a fault. Orrin Hatch of Utah even called him the thing that most
insisted he wasn't: a bully. "If he has the votes, and he knows he's going to
win, he'll tramp all over you." This, however, was Republican pique when
Ted did have the votes and didn't have to make compromises. Ted Kennedy was no bully. He was, however, relentless when it came to the things
in which he believed, and by the mid-1970s he was a devout believer in the
liberal catechism. "He comes at you like a wind of a hurricane," Dun Gifford said, "not just every once in a while; it's always there. He just has this
energy and strength and conviction." What Orrin Hatch couldn't counte-
nance was that, as Gifford said, Ted had a "point of view." And he was
"convinced of it, he fights for it." But Gifford also said this: "He doesn't do
it in a nasty way." In fact, Ted had that gift for separating the political from
the personal—a profound gift. "He never made it personal," CBS correspondent Bob Schieffer said of him. He could give a rousing liberal speech,

one of those speeches where his face reddened and his voice rose to a shout, and then leave the Senate floor and joke with the opposition. He did that repeatedly. Some Republicans, those who couldn't separate the personal from the partisan, couldn't fathom how he could. And some Republicans couldn't fathom either that Ted could go on the offensive without being a rabid ideologue. He never seemed happier in the Senate than when he was either attacking, as his health staffer Stan Jones, put it, "some rich, powerful, entrenched interest," or when he was fighting for the interests of the dispossessed. He liked big battles, even those that on the surface seemed unwinnable. "It's what gets him up in the morning," his longtime staffer Melody Miller said of him. "When I saw him really, really, really angry, it was because something was just not fair." And she said that Ted would say, "We can't let that stand. We have to do something about it."

And yet for all that, Ted Kennedy, though a proud liberal, though a believer in the moral authority of liberalism, was not a rigid ideologue, even if Republicans found it politically advantageous to portray him as such. And that was another critical quality of his in working the chemistry of the Senate, where ideology could doom accomplishment by dividing prospective partners. He was a pragmatist, and this was as important to his eventual mastery of the Senate as his likability. Ted seldom wanted just to score points. "I can stand up and speak out and get credit for that, but is there something else I can do that will really *help*," he asked one interviewer, "that will get something done about it?" Getting things done— now that he was firmly a Senate man, that was his mission—the impulse that drove him to master the Senate. And the mission made him not only a pragmatist but also a compromiser, which infuriated some of the more vehement liberals in the chamber. "I don't think you can be a very strong ideologue and be a good leader," William Hildenbrand, the secretary of the Senate, said. Despite what some conservatives might have thought, Ted, strong of liberal conviction, would likely have agreed with Hildenbrand. Ted liked to tell a parable of his legislative approach. It was about three geography teachers interviewing for a job before a school board whose members were divided between whether the earth was flat or round. The first teacher was rejected because he said the world was flat. The second because he said it was round. The third said, "I can teach it flat or I can teach it round." And Ted said so could he. Flat or round was how one became a master of a body full of believers in each.

It wasn't that Ted Kennedy didn't care. No one would have accused him of that. He cared and cared deeply. It was that, understanding the chemistry of the Senate, he knew he would never get everything he wanted—a lesson he had learned painfully with the demise of his national health insurance plan in 1974, when he had failed to reach agreement with Nixon. By the same token, John Podesta said that Ted didn't compromise in advance. "He'd start [legislative] fights by staking out a liberal position but being open to working with conservatives to try to get there," which also gave him the opportunity to tell his liberal allies that he had tried to get whatever he could. "I can't imagine how many thousands of compromises, or how many times his heart has been broken [as] he tried to put together not all that he wanted, but what he could get," said Senator Richard Durbin. *What he could get.* That was his position. He would tell his staff repeatedly, "Let's get half a loaf or three-quarters of a loaf. They'll be back." And he would say repeatedly, "The perfect is the enemy of the good." Another staff member, reacting to criticisms of Ted from the left, said, "Yes, we settle for what we can get, but we get something." The "art of the do-able," Senator Tom Daschle called it, "and there's no one who does it better." Senator Mike Enzi, a Wyoming conservative who often worked with Ted, said that the two of them never really compromised. "We leave out what we can't agree on, so we can get things done." And yet Paul Kirk would say this: that for all his bargaining to get what he could get, "I don't think there's anybody that you'll talk to who would say that in order to accomplish something, he gave up a fundamental value or principle that he believed in."

And so if his pragmatism and willingness to compromise were two of the elements he used to work the chemistry of the Senate, so were his principles. Everyone in the Senate knew Ted Kennedy was sincere in his devotion to the battles he waged—that he never initiated a campaign for political gain because he didn't need political gain. He needed results.

And there was the *form* his pragmatism took, which became a central factor in Ted Kennedy's working the chemistry of the Senate too, especially as the country moved rightward. The days of liberal hegemony were gone—gone with the election of Nixon and the conservative drift of the Republican Party. He needed Republicans in order to get legislation passed. And this was where his affability and his pragmatism converged, and where Ted had to deploy every personal resource, so that he didn't seem doctrinaire, so he didn't seem as if he were repackaging old liberal solutions, so that he really seemed as if he were reaching out to his adversaries. A longtime aide, Larry Horowitz, said that at every staff meeting on any major issue, Ted would always ask, "How can we go against the grain?" by which he meant, Horowitz said, the conventional liberal grain with the conventional liberal approaches that he knew Republicans would reject. And: "Who could he recruit to advance his agenda? It was how he got Republicans to sign on." And Horowitz added, "If it's a conservative Republican, even better." Stan Jones said it more directly: Ted would tell the staff, "You've got to get me a Republican on this." This was not exactly a secret. It was, everyone knew, Ted's way of doing business. Years later Republican House majority leader Dick Armey would fulminate over Ted Kennedy's "script," which "never varies": "He has this idea to make government bigger or [raise] taxes, and, lo and behold, out of the woodwork, there's this Republican co-sponsor, and then exactly what Kennedy wants passes the House and then he does the best he can [to get Senate passage]." Even among Ted's staff, it was an office joke how he got those Republicans to work with him. "When the wooing was going on," *Boston Globe* columnist Tom Oliphant said, "and when things got almost to the point of closing," Ted's aides would say, "It was time to bring out Mother's china" at the McLean house and invite that Republican for dinner and show off pictures of the family. Dale Bumpers of Arkansas, a Democrat, pointed to these interparty collaborations as the "thing that makes him . . . the master legislator. He invariably finds a Republican that has a lot of influence on that side, a lot of credibility. . . . He learned a long time ago that most of the time out here, unless you've got a Republican co-sponsor with him, someone who's willing to stand up with him, you're not going to succeed." Mike Mansfield's old aide Charles Ferris put it differently. He said that "some senators have bigger umbrellas than others, and Teddy has a big umbrella." In fact, Ted, the strident liberal, might have had the biggest umbrella in the Senate—one that could fit both Democrats and Republicans, both liberals and conservatives, underneath. The "consensus go-to guy when it comes to sitting down and actually hammering out legislation," said one Republican Senate aide.

But there was one last quality of Ted's without which the compromises and the recruitment of Republican co-sponsors would have failed. And it was this: Ted Kennedy could be trusted. They could make deals with him—Howard Baker on passing legislation to enforce one-man, one-vote;

or Orrin Hatch, a conservative, on health legislation when Hatch headed the Senate committee overseeing such legislation; or John McCain on immigration reform—and Ted Kennedy would never renege. Senators, *Republican* senators, spoke of this even years later when Ted was the face and voice of American liberalism, the very personification of liberalism, and when the Republican Party had been commandeered by conservatives who made a point of demonizing Ted to satisfy their partisans. "A handshake with Ted, and you take the risk," Republican Alan Simpson said, meaning that you were *willing* to take the risk with him. "That is what goes wrong with legislation when it fails: It's because you failed to trust. That sounds naïve. It sounds phony, but it's true. There are some guys out there you just don't trust. Not Ted." "I never had him back out of what he told me he was going to do," another Republican senator, Lindsey Graham, was to say years later. "Ted always keeps his word," said a third Republican, John McCain. "There is no bullshit with Ted. You know exactly where he is coming from. He does what he says he will do. He is a great listener in a body of poor listeners. This makes it easy to deal with him." Citing the "manipulation and conniving" in the Senate, Stephen Breyer said that the policy in the Kennedy office was always "Open Conniving Openly Arrived At." And he explained, "There are no secrets. That is, if the Republicans want to know, or the unions want to know what you're doing, tell them. . . . No dishonesty. No deception. Explain to anyone willing to listen. We'll bore them to death. But there are no secrets."

No secrets.

You could always trust Ted Kennedy.

III

That was inside the Senate—what Ted himself called the "inside game." But when it came to pushing legislation, to becoming a master of the Senate, there was another locus—what Ted called the "outside game." The players in the outside game, as Nick Littlefield, who would later be the chief of staff of the Labor Committee, explained it, are "all the interest groups and advocates and public interest community and people in Washington and across the country who can help provide the grassroots support for legislative initiatives." (There were also the campaign contributors and the corporate lobbyists whom most senators had to court, but Ted, who had the luxury of being independently wealthy, didn't need the former, and he had the temerity as the Senate's foremost liberal to resist the latter.) And Littlefield said, "Whatever it is, you need that whole political world"—the insiders and the outsiders—to pass a piece of major legislation. Ted, then, not only had to work the chemistry of the Senate, orchestrating how to bring legislators together, even across the aisle, he also had to work the chemistry of those groups and individuals outside the Senate who could bring pressure to bear on legislators now that the party discipline on which Lyndon Johnson had relied had frayed. And Ted Kennedy had a chemistry with those outsiders too. "He and his staff were among the people who worked the kind of infrastructure of Washington advocacy groups and national advocacy better and in a more witting way than most," John Podesta said. Ted would invite representatives from those groups to his office to discuss strategy, incorporating them as part of the legislative process. Podesta, who was close to many of these groups, said that Ted's staff would call him weekly. Tom Rollins, who would become the chief counsel of the Labor Committee, said that "no one [in Ted's office] would make a move without checking with the groups." And even though Rollins said that the groups "tend to represent the most extreme views," if the groups didn't agree with a strategy or position, "then often nothing could move forward," which meant that Ted had to convince them—convince them that he was serving their best interests, even when he was compromising with Republican colleagues, convince them that the compromise was the best deal he could make. "A huge magnetic grid" was how Fred Dutton, an old Kennedy adviser, described the Kennedy network to Ted Kennedy biographer Burton Hersh. "Everybody in touch with everybody." And comparing that network to Lyndon Johnson's, Dutton said that with Johnson, "everything came down from the mountain," while with the Kennedys, they didn't necessarily send orders; they received intelligence.

No one in the Senate might have been better at receiving that intelligence than Ted Kennedy.

And it wasn't only the advocacy groups to whom Ted listened. Sometimes his chemistry was with a single individual who had a grievance. Senator Bob Kerrey said that for him the moment that best captured the way Ted Kennedy operated occurred in the course of one hour when Kerrey said he received back-to-back phone calls from Edgar Bronfman, the CEO of the Warner Music Group; Jack Valenti, the president of the Motion Picture Association of America; and Lew Wasserman, the chairman of the Music Corporation of America and Universal Pictures. And each one made basically the same plea: "All we want is for Ted to return our phone calls." So Kerrey approached Ted on the Senate floor and told Ted that he really didn't care if Ted called these men back, but that if he did, would he be so kind as to tell them it was due to Kerrey's intervention, so Kerrey could get some credit. And then Kerrey, curious, asked Ted why these powerful men were imploring him. Ted explained that he was in the process of writing enabling legislation in the Judiciary Committee for an international treaty on intellectual property—a treaty that clearly impacted Bronfman, Valenti, and Wasserman. And Ted said that the other evening just before the legislation was about to be sent to conference with the House, he happened to run into a man at an event who said he had written *Casablanca*, presumably Julius Epstein, and the man complained that the treaty as written was "screwing" him. So Ted made a note of the issue and took it to his staff and asked them to explore it and then prepare an amendment to the bill and then took the amendment to Strom Thurmond, the committee's ranking Republican, and asked if he would approve the amendment, which Thurmond did. "Kennedy went to bat for some guy who was getting the shaft," Kerrey said. "One guy getting the shaft, and he would go to the wall for you." And Kerrey said, "Everybody knew it, by the way"—knew that Ted would stand up for the little guys no matter how formidable the opposition was, and in this case, it was very formidable.

And that was chemistry too, just chemistry of a different kind.

But the chemistry didn't end with the Senate or with the outside groups or even with an aggrieved petitioner. There was also the press with which to contend, and which could determine the course of the progress of legislation—once again now that party discipline had largely broken down and senators were looking out for their own interests. And Ted worked the press too. He had been press-shy when he first entered the Senate, wary that courting the press might seem to be grandstanding for so young a senator and might offend the senior senators. As time passed, he became more confident and loosened up with them. But after Chappaquiddick and the treatment he received in the media, where he was assumed to have lied, Ted had become suspicious of the press. One of his press secretaries called him "cautious" with reporters, less apt to accept interview requests than most senators, who eagerly sought those requests, and when he did accept, he was studied, on script. And the press secretary said that Ted might stop to chat with reporters, "if he was in the mood," but that, if not, he would rush right past them. And while most staff might have encouraged their senator to court the press, Ted's staff, also wary, also concerned that Ted's halting and stammering and mangled syntax might make him look less than intelligent, didn't push him. "Innate caution," the press secretary called it. Instead, Ted made sure that his staff kept on the press, so he wouldn't have to, not only to buff his image, though that was certainly part of it, but also and primarily to press his agenda. "They had very, very explicit marching orders to vigorously pursue their point of view with reporters," Tom Oliphant of *The Boston Globe* said. "I never operated under the illusion that any of this had anything to do with me. It had to do with them." And Oliphant said that when he did get a call from Ted, it was always with a specific legislative purpose and with Ted making no bones about using the press to advance his cause, so there were no secrets there either.

But for all that caution, Ted Kennedy was still a people person, even with a group he distrusted. And he was still a chemist. Ted would invite twenty-five or thirty reporters to his annual Christmas party, and according to James Manley, one of his press secretaries, "He'd just charm the hell out of them." Manley said Ted would "stick around afterwards to talk to everybody . . . and just work the room." That softened those hard-nosed reporters because it was very difficult to resist Ted Kennedy's bonhomie. And if he could work a room, he could also work his charm one on one. Martin Tolchin of *The New York Times* scheduled an interview with Ted at the McLean home, and Ted told him to bring his children. "They adored him," Tolchin said. And then, while the children went off and played, Ted and Tolchin sat on the deck, and Ted did an impression of a patient sitting in a dentist's chair, which was how he said he felt about being interviewed. He "went from laughing and enjoying himself to wondering how painful the interview was going to be," Tolchin said. But Ted wound up winning over Tolchin too, as he so often won over his fellow senators.

And that was his chemistry with the press.

IV

Despite his years of studying the Senate, of learning both its folkways and its folks, Ted Kennedy, like Lyndon Johnson, had something else that enabled him to become a master, something that couldn't be learned: an instinct for wrangling people. Ted Kennedy was a natural politician. A natural charmer. A man who genuinely enjoyed mixing with people. A man who had an inborn talent for wooing and winning people. A social virtuoso. When he first entered the Senate, some of his staffers had worried that he might be too much the good-time Charlie, too social to be taken seriously or to be effective. But by 1976, after fourteen years in the upper chamber, Ted Kennedy had come to understand the chemistry of the Senate, had come to understand how often things got done because of personal interactions—how the Senate was an institution of personal interactions and how successful a legislator he could be there if he was good with people.

But to realize his legislative aims, he had to master not only the chemistry of the Senate but also its physics—its mechanics. He needed to create not only the social conditions for passing legislation through the charm offensives at which he was so skilled, but also the parliamentary ones—the drafting of bills, the negotiating and horse-trading, the debating, the questioning during hearings, the conferencing. One observer said of John Kennedy that he always thought in terms of grand design, what the observer called the "imperial pretensions of the administration." But Ted Kennedy couldn't have been more different. He didn't look to grand designs. He was granular. He looked to nuts and bolts, to the machinery of getting things done, to winning. A far better athlete than either Jack or Bobby, he was a closer—the one who knew how to bring home victory. Ted said that the *New York Times* political sage James Reston would talk to him about who the "serious" men in the Senate were, and Ted said that he would counter that seriousness wasn't the issue. "There are a lot of serious people"—he told Reston he could name two or the three of the "brightest"—"but they are not the ones who are moving this place." And Ted Kennedy had come to understand that, too, in his years of observing his institution: The Senate wasn't about seriousness or intelligence or high-mindedness or reputation. It was about "moving this place," which meant gaining legislative victories.

And so the master of the chemistry of the Senate became a master of its physics too in order to *move this place.*

Mastering physics was different from mastering chemistry—one was born with the conviviality that inspired chemistry, while one had to learn how to work the mechanisms of the Senate—but Ted Kennedy, a quick study, proved as adept at physics as he was at chemistry. In committee, those who did not succumb to him—primarily conservative Republicans—would criticize him. One colleague told a reporter that Ted was a "weak senator," one "who has not thought seriously about the serious issues," who was "doctrinaire," who has "this vague, high-powered staff that leads him around by the nose," who is "not well-prepared" and is "spread too thin" and "embarrasses himself frequently." But this was a decidedly minority opinion—a partisan opinion, finally an erroneous opinion. Another Republican senator, Charles Mathias, said, "I thought at the time that [impression] was so wrong, because sitting with him on the bench at committee hearings, I was aware of the questions that he asked during hearings, and I could see which questions were those that had been concocted by his staff. When he got to the list of the staff-concocted questions, he was on his own, and he was just as good or better in probing for information when he was on his own." It was Robert Dole, no ally, who marveled that Ted knew the issues so well that during a hearing, he seldom glanced at his notes, much less read questions verbatim, preferring instead to look at the witness. House Democrat George Miller, who sat on many conference committees with Ted, called him the "best-prepared person in the room." And Miller qualified that opinion, "without exception," even though the author of the bill or the chair of the House committee often sat in those conferences. And as time passed, even the criticism that he had his aides behind him passing him notes became inaccurate. The man who had complained about TMBS—"too many blue suits"—kept his aides to the side, as a way of proving his mettle to those doubting colleagues.

Nor was he only adept during the hearings. He was adept in executive session—the behind-the-door meetings where a Senate committee would mark up a piece of legislation before it headed to the floor or where a piece of legislation would finally be hashed out by representatives of the House and Senate when the chambers had passed two bills with different provisions and the bills had to be reconciled. George Miller said that on the first day of a conference, Ted "had a wonderful way" of raising an issue and having other conferees argue that the issue was not germane. "And he'd just say, 'I just want to raise it. I just want to make sure that we have the right to bring it up, because it's very important to me, and I've got to do this.' And he'd start moving his hands around, and they would say, 'Oh, OK, OK, that's fine.' And then, just as sure as hell, just as you were getting ready to close the conference, everything's done, he'd say, 'Excuse me.

Just a minute. I told you that I had to do this, and I want to bring it up now.' And they'd go, 'Oh, my god!'" But Ted would say that they had agreed. And now they were heading for the airplane, headed home, and they would relent: "Oh, Ted. Just put it in. Go ahead." And Miller recalled another occasion, at the conference on education for disabled children. Ted kept hammering about the things to which these children should be entitled and what would happen to them should they be denied these services—hammering away until he changed the minds of the conferees in that room or wore them down. In either case, he won his points. And sometimes Miller said he would attend conferences to which he had not been appointed, attend them just to watch Ted in action—watch how he "was able to weave people in those meetings," meetings which could last from four in the afternoon to two-thirty in the morning, as Ted would leave and then return, but always able to keep after people, to raise his points. John Kerry, the junior senator from Massachusetts, said the same thing: that he loved to watch Ted in operation. He would go to an executive session of a committee where the discussions could drag on for two hours and were "not making a lot of headway." But then Ted would arrive, after having sat in two other "execs" earlier that morning. And Kerry said Ted would sit down and listen for a few minutes about what had already transpired and then say, "OK. I'll tell you what I'll do. I'll do such-and-such, if you do thus-and-so. I'll have my staff have a memo on your desks tomorrow to do this. If we can agree here, I can bring so-and-so on, and I think we can make it happen this way." As Kerry put it, "He would do in ten minutes what the rest of us couldn't pull together in an hour-and-a-half of bickering. Then he'd get up and leave and would go to the next one and do the same thing, and those memos would be on our desks the next day, as he said they would be." Ted called this bargaining and bartering "heavy lifting," though it was not so heavy for him.

On some occasions, the physics of the Senate didn't have anything to do with heavy lifting; it had to do with environment. Al Simpson remembered Ted holding a hearing in the Capitol basement, where the "vaulted ceilings looked like the sewers of Paris." When Simpson asked why the hearing was being held there, Ted told him it was because the space was too confined for disgruntled citizens to come and "bitch and protest," which might have derailed the legislation. When those citizens asked the sergeant at arms why the hearing was in the basement, he told them that it was the only available room. Tom Oliphant, observing Ted when Oliphant first arrived in Washington, said that it "dawned on me that this guy really knows what he's doing. And to me that's what initially made him so interesting in the sense that you would always rather go to a major league baseball game than a minor league game because you just loved to watch the major leaguers play." By the mid-1970s, Ted Kennedy was one of the best of the major leaguers in the Senate.

And he was adept on the floor of the Senate. That floor had not been of much importance prior to the mid-1950s; it was essentially a stage on which senators could perform. But along with the other changes in the Senate in the mid-1970s came a change in the function of the floor. A "much more active decision-making arena," a Senate scholar called it, saying that the "highly-restrained activism that characterized Senate floor behavior in the 1950s was replaced by the 1970s by a widespread unrestrained activism." The sheer number of bills considered by the Senate increased appreciably, from 55 in the eighty-fourth Senate to 176 in the ninety-sixth, the session beginning in 1979, and the number of roll calls from 217 to 1,027 in that same period. And along with that, more senators were likely to offer more amendments on the Senate floor—many more—prompting the Senate scholar to call them, Ted included, "hyperactives." That sheer number of amendments was one of the things that changed the floor from a stage—though Ted still loved to perform there—to an arena of real combat, where there was often as much legislative decision making as in the committee room—the place where, in the heyday of the bulls, most of the decisions were made, only to be ratified on the floor. And Ted knew how to win that combat with his skillful combination of chemistry and physics. As their seniority increased, senators typically moved from the back of the chamber toward the front and center; doing so was one of the prerogatives of seniority. But Ted Kennedy, who occupied what was assumed to have been his brother Jack's seat in the back row, did not advance. He chose to remain in that back row, just off the cloakroom, among the freshmen, where he could see whoever entered the chamber, in case he needed to buttonhole one of them, and where he could retire to the cloakroom to conduct business if need be. The natural on the floor loved to conduct business on the floor or just off it—loved to conduct it face-to-face. "This is a goal line we want to cross," he would tell his staff, according to Carey Parker. "Now you tell me the plays we need to run in order to get to the goal line as fast as possible." And Parker said that he was likely to "throw a touchdown pass in about a week."

Throwing a touchdown pass meant getting a bill on which they had been deliberating through the Senate, which in turn meant getting his colleagues to operate as a team. Ted would tell his staff that there would be a vote on various bills that day and that he wanted to see Senators A, B, C, and D to discuss points on each of the bills they were sponsoring. And he would have the staff prepare cards with those points, three-by-five cards, on which the staffers wrote the points that Ted had told them he wanted to discuss. And then Ted would head to the floor with his cards, usually eight or ten of them, reviewing the points quickly with the staffers on the floor who were engaged in those particular issues. But Ted had memorized those points by then, knew them by heart. "He knew it perfectly," one of his aides was to say—the man allegedly not interested in details having mastered the details. "A master of detail" was how John Podesta put it. But Ted not only knew the issues; he also knew the senators. "He knew where everybody stood on the substance," recalled Podesta. "So he was always: 'What do you [think] about making this switch, because I think we could get, you know, [Senator Mike] Enzi, if we move, if we give a little on this. What do you think of that switch?'" Always "thinking tactically," Podesta said. Always thinking about how to turn the chemistry into physics. "How to bring them along," said a staffer of Ted's knowledge. "Nobody second guessed that." The staff was capable, Podesta said, but Ted always "cut the deal." And Carey Parker said that Ted was "at his best" when he was handling "six or seven different" issues and would find those senators on the floor or in the cloakroom and discuss his points with them and hand them his cards with the reasons he thought something should be done. And the senator would frequently agree with Ted, would ask him with a degree of wonder how he found the time to devote to that arcane issue—Carey Parker felt that Ted's ability to converse knowledgably about esoteric provisions in a piece of legislation gave him a "leg up" on those senators—or the senator would say, "I think you have a good point there. We'll take care of that," or he would take the cards back to his office to discuss the points with his staff and then phone Ted and tell him, "It looks like a go." "Thousands of examples of that," Carey Parker would say. "It's a way he has an impact that is not seen by the public," Parker said, "but it's a way that some of the lesser, though still important provisions of legislation get written." And sometimes it wasn't even legislative points but political ones. Ted might wander the cloakroom before a vote and tell a colleague, "If we could change the language just a little bit, I'll go to that fundraiser for you down in Pennsylvania." John Tunney said that for Ted, these floor sessions were substitutes for Ted's old football days—a way of channeling his energy. Working the Senate now, sometimes physically working it, was like scoring a touchdown, as Carey Parker had put it. An "extraordinarily good legislator," Senator Patrick Leahy was to say of him. "He knew what would work and what wouldn't. He knew how to put people and things together": the chemistry and physics. And Leahy said that Ted had developed a "shorthand" with other senators. Leahy could ask whether Ted thought they could get a certain amendment passed. Ted would immediately tell him what he thought could pass. Ted knew. Ted had learned.

And Ted Kennedy was a natural at the "vote-a-rama"—those sessions where bills that have been debated for a week or so but haven't yet been voted on, all get thrown into a long session as the Senate nears its recess, a two- or three-hour or longer session, with all the senators on the floor, mixing, talking, convincing, while one senator offers his amendment and gets a minute to explain it, and another senator gets a minute to explain his opposition. Sometimes votaramas could tackle twenty-five amendments in a single sitting. And Ted Kennedy loved the votaramas because he knew the issues and he enjoyed the combat mixed with camaraderie. Ted Kennedy was in his element during the votaramas, buttonholing senators, clapping them on the back, handing out his cards and giving them his points. A Senate man, but now more than a Senate man: a Senate mover, even a Senate master.

And Ted Kennedy was adept when the bills were debated. His old administrative assistant David Burke said that Ted was always courteous on the floor—"so hesitant to be discourteous that as a staffer, I'd be furious with him. 'Why don't you rap that guy upside the head? He's so wrong on this.'" But Ted Kennedy, who knew the chemistry of the Senate, seldom lit out against another senator, and on the rare occasions when he did, it was likely to be one of his fellow Democrats, who he felt should know better, rather than a Republican. (He once castigated John Kerry at a Democratic caucus when Kerry called the minimum wage an "old" idea, shouting at Kerry that anyone who felt that wasn't much of a Democrat.) On the floor, Ted could boom. "What I remember most vividly is Ted's voice," said Senator John Warner. Most senators used microphones on the floor. Ted didn't. "His voice just rattled the chandeliers. There was no snoozing when Ted was speaking." The volume was largely for effect, as were the theatrics that accompanied it: the quavering voice, the head-shaking, the arm-waving, the face-reddening. The floor might no longer have been the stage it once was, but Ted still knew how to give a melodramatic performance there. And at times the performance and the emotion converged—times when Ted Kennedy was angry, not at a person, never at a person, but over an issue, times when he felt he had to declaim to show that he meant business. *Time* reported Ted marching with a full head of steam to the Senate floor, puffing on a small cigar, to debate a regional health planning bill that he had proposed and the American Medical Association opposed. Ted "cut loose," as *Time* described it, "his voice booming, his arms reaching into the air." He yelled, "No, I will not yield," when Orrin Hatch of Utah, an opponent of the bill, asked him to do so. And then, when the vote began, *Time* said, Ted "planted himself in the well of the Senate, head constantly moving, always checking the remaining time, persuading certain Senators, among them Ohio's John Glenn, to change their negative votes." And Ted won. That was Ted Kennedy in action. That was Ted Kennedy throwing a touchdown.

And for all his congeniality, he had this capability too: He was willing to fight on the floor, willing to sacrifice chemistry for physics, politics for principle, if he couldn't combine the two. His opponents decried this as partisanship. Orrin Hatch said there were two sides to Ted Kennedy: a "caring, compassionate, considerate, kind, thoughtful, personal" side, and a "partisan, sometimes mean, tough, sometimes vicious" side, which, Hatch felt, became over time the "dominant Kennedy." Hatch liked the chemistry of Ted Kennedy but not the physics—the backslapper but not the legislator, not comprehending that Ted saw the two as inextricable. Jan Kalicki, a foreign policy adviser, recalled accompanying Ted to the floor for the first time for a debate on an amendment that would end military assistance to the Argentinian junta—a debate for which Kalicki had drafted a memo. Ted fought heatedly with Senator Jesse Helms, one of the most conservative members of the Senate. Kalicki said he was surprised by the vehemence of the debate, even though "everybody knew the Senator had strong views." But he was even more surprised by how expeditiously Ted managed to attach his rider to the bill and get it passed. A lobbyist who worked with Ted on the campaign finance bill said the same thing of him. "He's a fighter. He understands what Jim Allen"—the Alabama conservative who used every possible procedural resource to defeat liberal legislation—"understands, and what too many liberals don't: that you have to do battle to win." And Ted Kennedy was adept when it came to those floor fights because he believed so sincerely and so passionately in his causes. When he arrived in the Senate, South Dakota senator James Abourezk said that he had a decision to make: "You must decide whether your Senate office will be conducted within a moral framework, or whether it will be used merely to advance your own ambitions." Abourezk felt that most senators chose the latter. Ted Kennedy always chose the former. He always worked within a moral framework. "There isn't anybody that's as passionately devoted to what he believes in as Ted Kennedy," Senator Dale Bumpers said of him. "Sometimes you have politicians come along, and they sort of talk about it, but they don't feel it," Representative John Lewis, a hero of the civil rights movement, said. "This man feels it."

Ted Kennedy's outsize personality was often cited as the source of his power—bigger than life he was, like Lyndon Johnson—and on many issues, issues of no great consequence, issues on which a senator might be willing to horse-trade, issues where Ted could charm a colleague to his side, this might have been true. He had entered the Senate as the least. He had become one of its most formidable forces. As one of his administrative assistants was to say of him, "The power of his personality was like a black hole—once you were sucked in, there was little chance of a way out, so strong was its gravity." It was this very power, the social power of Ted Kennedy, that made freshmen senators, especially Republicans, wary of him. John McCain said that when he first arrived in the Senate, he kept his distance from Ted, fearful of him because "he's just one of those larger-than-life figures that you tread carefully around." But there was also this other power—the power that emanated from his devout belief in the ability of government to better the country, that emanated from what he saw as the moral basis of the legislation he proposed to help the poor and marginalized, and that emanated from the idea, as Dale Bumpers put it, that we "would all be infinitely better off if we would commit ourselves to the kind of values that he believes in," and that emanated from his faith in the Senate itself, his "physical love of the place," as he described it, but also his spiritual love of it. ("It's like a fix every day to go to the United States Senate," Robert Dole said of Ted.) It had taken Ted Kennedy well over a decade to acquire this power—that decade of study and growth and redemption; that decade of a change in the Senate that now rewarded those who got the institution moving, as Ted did, rather than those who attained power through seniority; that decade of Ted rising from a man of the Senate to a budding eminence in the Senate. There were still those who doubted him. There were still those who thought him a lightweight or a rabid partisan. But Joe Biden would say that the real source of Ted Kennedy's legislative power was something larger than either chemistry or physics: "People didn't want to feel small in front of him."

And that was because in those fourteen years in the Senate, despite all his lapses and all his failings and all his misdeeds, Ted Kennedy had been transformed. He had managed to grow larger—large enough to make people feel small by comparison.

THREE

"A Special Place in His Animus"

A ND NOW TED Kennedy watched the new president, Jimmy Carter, and watched him warily. Though Carter was a fellow Democrat, the two men couldn't have been more different. Ted Kennedy was a student of human chemistry—of interactions among individuals. Jimmy Carter, a strident moralist, had very little feel for that chemistry. He entered the White House riding the backlash against Watergate, and in promising to undo the damage that Richard Nixon had done, he presented himself as a figure of rectitude, incorruptibility, transparency, and candor—as much a minister as a political leader. He had pondered using his inaugural address to ask Americans to repent and had even considered citing II Chronicles 7:14: "If my people, which are called by my name, shall humble themselves and pray, and seek my face, and turn from their wicked ways, then will I hear from heaven, and will forgive their sin, and will heal their land." He wisely reconsidered, but the notion that Carter would chastise the country for the sins of Richard Nixon seemed to set the tone for his presidency. It was not the tone of a man who appreciated human fallibility. It was the tone of one who scorned it.

A political skeptic, Carter also distrusted ideology and sought to replace it with moralism and competence. A "natural extension of the change in American politics," Carter's pollster, Patrick Caddell, said of him, by which Caddell meant a less ideological, more technocratic approach to government. "He lacked a unifying political philosophy that had been affirmed through the election," his campaign manager and top adviser, Hamilton Jordan, a fellow Georgian, would say, though he meant it as a compliment. "Non-ideological," Jordan called him. And: "Moderate." He made decisions, Jordan said approvingly, ad hoc, and he made

them "at the expense of the consensus in his own party"—a consensus
that Carter disdained. "No ideology, no central informing political ideas,"
political consultant Robert Shrum, who had briefly been an adviser to
Carter's campaign, said of Carter, though Shrum believed, as Jordan did,
that this was an "asset, not a liability in 1976, because it let him transcend
the polarities of the Democratic Party—and the country." Senator James
Abourezk, an ardent liberal and no fan of Carter's, was less charitable.
"His entire national career," Abourezk would write, "was based on sniffing the wind to see what was momentarily popular, a technique that he
tempered with a pious attitude that he thought would carry him past the
political rough spots. To him that was the way smart politics was done."
The "last progressive," the historian Leo Ribuffo labeled him, because Carter had the characteristics of an early twentieth-century progressive
rather than of a late-twentieth-century liberal: moralistic, concerned
with efficiency over equality, a scourge of special interests. When Carter
listed his own priorities, they were not especially liberal-sounding:
"achieving maximum bureaucratic efficiency, reorganizing the government, creating jobs, deregulating major industries, addressing the energy
problem, canceling wasteful water projects, welfare and tax reform, environmental quality, restoring moral fiber for the government, and openness and honesty in dealing with the press and public." Carter had none
of the liberal messianism of a Franklin Roosevelt, a John Kennedy, or a
Bobby Kennedy, a Lyndon Johnson or a Ted Kennedy. His call, instead,
was a refutation of that messianism. (There was, significantly, no mention of healthcare, Ted's signal cause, among his priorities, though he
had, in a concession to Ted, discussed it during the campaign.) Where
John Kennedy had said that Americans could accomplish anything, Carter said, "We have learned that more is not necessarily better" and that
"we must simply do our best." He had been trained as an engineer at the
U.S. Naval Academy, and his list was an engineer's list—making government work, not expanding government's role. A "Republican in Democrat clothing," consumer advocate Ralph Nader called Carter. Reading
the national mood as one less generous than the liberals thought, he envisioned his presidency in terms of limits, a theme he sounded in his inaugural address, of which he was to write, "In some ways, dealing with
limits would become the subliminal theme of the next four years." But it
wasn't so subliminal. Arthur Schlesinger, Jr., had terrible premonitions
about the impending Carter presidency. "His mind seems managerial, not

innovative," Schlesinger wrote in his journal, echoing the idea that Carter was a small-bore president rather than a large-bore one, "and his passion will be government reorganization, not social invention." And Schlesinger concluded the entry with this damning indictment: "He reminds me too much of Nixon."

None of these things endeared Carter to his fellow Democratic officeholders, nor they to him. He blamed the Democratic reforms following the disastrous 1968 convention for turning the party into a welter of special interests, decrying the very diversity that the liberals had strived so hard to achieve and telling his aide, Hamilton Jordan, that the party couldn't survive "if we don't figure out some way to nominate [he meant elect delegates for] a convention that also represents the mainstream of American life in this country," meaning, apparently, white male moderates, who had been plenty represented in party conclaves. (Of course, politically speaking, Carter may very well have been right; white backlash against liberals was unmistakable.) And pollster Patrick Caddell in a preinaugural memo had already warned Carter to stay away from old-line liberals like Morris Udall, who had contested the nomination, and Ted, calling them "as antiquated and anachronistic a group as are conservative Republicans." But Carter didn't need to be nudged. By temperament, he was not just nonideological but also actively illiberal, no more a believer in liberal moral authority than the Republican conservatives were, and he listed "fights with the Democratic party's liberal wing" as one of his "problems," identifying himself with his hero, President Harry Truman, who, Carter said, had had to battle those same stubborn liberals. (Among Carter's inner circle, only Andrew Young, his United Nations ambassador and a former associate of Martin Luther King, Jr., had been an early opponent of the Vietnam War.) Carter kept his distance from liberals. Ted said that Carter "baffled" him when the nominee rejected Ted's offers to campaign for him, and he had baffled others too—Humphrey, Muskie, and McGovern—who had made similar pledges and met similar rejections. "Carter had a way of making me feel like he couldn't trust me," Joe Biden was to say of him, "despite the fact that I'd gone way out on a limb to endorse him in the primaries against a number of my senate colleagues." And Biden said that Carter, once in office, met with him only grudgingly, and then, during the meeting, kept checking his watch, which he wore on the underside of his wrist, so that he had to twist his arm to see it. When the Senate Democratic caucus invited the new president to speak to them, Biden said he was struck by how edgy Carter was before his own party faithful. "He was bent uneasily forward at the waist, and his hands seemed to be shaking."

Shaking because Carter had run not only as a nonideologue and a moderate but also as an outsider—a man against Washington, the Washington that he felt had given rise to Watergate, and he seemed determined to show his superiority to those sullied pols. "They were parochial," Speaker of the House Tip O'Neill said of Carter and his Georgia minions who followed him to Washington. "They were incompetent. They came with a chip on their shoulder against the entrenched politicians. Washington to them was evil. They were going to change everything and didn't understand the rudiments of it." When O'Neill arrived at the White House for a get-acquainted breakfast, the parsimonious Carter served him a continental one, after which the rotund O'Neill told Walter Mondale, "I did not get as big as I am on croissants and orange juice." Ted came to feel that Carter invited legislators to the White House not to listen to them but to vaunt and show them how much of the minutiae he grasped, as if they would be impressed. "In contrast, when you read about Franklin Roosevelt," Ted would later write, "you realize that he was the master of the situation he needed to know about. He didn't know every name and every place, but he knew what was worth knowing: the key people, and what motivated them, and why they were doing what they were doing"—in short, the chemistry of people. But, then, Roosevelt had no need to show off. Jimmy Carter, the outsider, did.

What Carter seemed to miss was that while one could get elected by posing as an outsider, it was extremely difficult to govern as one, since a president needed insiders to advance legislation. And though he arrived in office with overwhelming Democratic majorities in the House (292 to 143) and the Senate (61 to 38, with one independent), Carter soon squandered that advantage with his contempt for the chemistry of the House and Senate and the chemistry among those men and women. When new Senate majority leader Robert Byrd and House speaker Tip O'Neill publicly complained that Carter was not consulting them on policy, Carter felt aggrieved, as if they had no right to be consulted. Senator Fritz Hollings complained that Carter tried to run the government the way he had captained a nuclear submarine. "Once policy was set, like a command onboard ship, there was not much follow-through with personal calls or conferences to cajole lawmakers to vote with the President. Carter just didn't hobnob with Senators or Congressmen. He didn't cultivate confidants on Capitol Hill." He wanted to do it alone. "I think he had simply convinced himself that he was going to do it his way," Ted would write. "He was an outsider, and he was going to run things from an outsider's point of view," which was why, Ted believed, he could never win the cooperation of his own party's legislators. Instead, Carter not only ignored those legislators; he was openly antagonistic to them, trying to show them who was boss. "Actually working against us" was how Tip O'Neill felt about the attitude of the Carter White House toward congressional Democrats. And O'Neill said that when he asked the White House for assistance on a grant to build new roads in Boston to help his constituents, "they did everything possible to block my way."

Certainly, if Jimmy Carter had any feeling for the chemistry of the Congress, he would have had a far better chance of advancing his agenda rather than having it be stymied, as it was, at almost every juncture. O'Neill said Carter had "moral zeal" and "intelligence" but lacked another, essential ingredient: "political style," which was O'Neill's way of saying chemistry. At one point, one of Carter's advisers convinced him to invite Senators Fritz Hollings and Lloyd Bentsen to the White House for a game of tennis and an opportunity for Carter to ingratiate himself with them. Instead, Carter played a game and abruptly left the court. "You told me to play tennis with them," he said to the adviser peremptorily. "I played tennis with them."

But even if he had had style, Carter labored under one more deficit, an enormous deficit: He was out of phase with his own party. The Democrats after Richard Nixon and Gerald Ford were in no mood for retrenchment. They had welcomed Carter to Washington with the hope that they could restore liberal government—the government of Roosevelt and Kennedy and Johnson. But Jimmy Carter, not altogether unreasonably in a political sense, had no interest in restoring liberal government or pushing liberal initiatives. He believed primarily in fiscal prudence, and he said that when he met with O'Neill, who was "much more liberal than I," the speaker "flinched visibly whenever we talked about balancing the federal budget or constraining any of the Great Society programs." And Carter, the outsider and the moderate, was especially loath to make promises and commit money to programs for fear of seeming fiscally imprudent—again believing, not unreasonably, that he had been elected not to recharge the Great Society, but to bring temperance to government. Robert Shrum, who quickly soured on Carter, believed that on "almost every policy [Carter] wanted to make sure 'it doesn't commit me too much.'" Committed he wasn't.

And if none of this endeared him to his fellow Democrats, it especially did not endear him to one of those Democrats: Ted Kennedy, among the most liberal of them. Even so, Ted made common cause with Carter that first year. They agreed on challenging a bill that had been reported out of the Senate Finance Committee to cut taxes on the oil industry, and the two, at the president's suggestion, met at the White House, where Carter assured Ted that he had not struck a deal with Finance chairman Russell Long, a strong proponent of lower taxes on the oil industry. And Ted was supportive of Carter's campaign for human rights, introducing amendments that terminated arms agreements with Chile and Argentina for violating those rights, and asking Carter both to press Latin American leaders to promote democracy and to welcome opposition leaders to the White House. And Ted commended Carter for his Panama Canal treaty, the treaty that would pass the following year and surrender the canal to Panama. The two even met late in 1977 to discuss a healthcare bill. Overall, Ted backed Carter legislatively. But even as he attempted to work with Carter, Ted Kennedy was still suspicious of Jimmy Carter—had been suspicious of him since the presidential campaign. And he had come to feel that Carter, while scornful of liberals generally, "reserved a special place in his animus toward me." William vanden Heuvel, a close Kennedy associate who had also served in the Carter administration, noted of the president's attitude toward the Kennedys that "there was something he didn't like and appreciate" about them, and wondered whether it was because the Kennedys might have been too cosmopolitan for Carter, or had come out of a "too-sophisticated set" for him, or had too flamboyant a lifestyle for him, given Carter's self-righteousness. But Vanden Heuvel felt that whatever the reasons, Carter did "not go out of his way to accommodate the Kennedys," which meant accommodating Ted Kennedy. And Vanden Heuvel said that during the 1976 election, Carter had *wanted* Ted to run against him so that he could beat him and establish himself as the national candidate. The animus, however, could have been sparked by something simpler, even by something as simple as envy. "When the Senator walks into a room, it changes," Harvard Law professor Charles Haar observed of Ted, noting a "charismatic charge of energy." But "when Jimmy Carter walked into a room, it did not change. I remember several occasions with a group in the

White House, whenever President Carter came in, and the people keep on talking, keep on doing what they're engaged in doing." Carter was not too myopic to have noticed that too. Or it might have been a clash of temperaments: Ted's disdain for political trimmers like Carter, and Carter's disdain for expansive, free-spending liberals like Ted. Ted Kennedy might have disagreed, and disagreed strenuously, with Richard Nixon, but Kennedy, who had suffered so many of his own humiliations, could at least understand Nixon and Nixon's resentments at *his* humiliations. He could not understand Jimmy Carter's cribbed political outlook, any more than Carter could understand Ted's generous one. Both men were arrogant. Both believed in the rightness of their cause. Both felt they represented the best interests of their party and their nation.

All of which was why the two Democrats were headed for a reckoning.

II

It came as early as May 1977. In his presidential bid, Carter had courted Walter Reuther's successor as United Auto Workers (UAW) president, Leonard Woodcock, and by Good Friday 1976, Woodcock had pledged his support to Carter. According to Woodcock, one of the primary lures for that support was a national health insurance program, which Carter had endorsed in a speech before a Black medical student association earlier that spring during his campaign and then again on the CBS Sunday-morning interview program *Face the Nation*. Carter, usually fixated on cost, said that how such a program got financed was "not very important to the voters." Rather, they wanted to know if "we are going to have a national, comprehensive, mandatory health insurance program," and Carter said, "I'm committed to that, and will work hard as president to get it implemented." Woodcock didn't necessarily think that Carter was a true believer in national health insurance, as Ted Kennedy was. What he knew was that the UAW had 160,000 retirees in Florida where Carter was facing George Wallace in an upcoming primary. So Woodcock agreed to work "day after day" for Carter, on the condition that Carter become a "leader" in national health insurance. Woodcock upheld his end of the bargain. But once elected, Carter's professed enthusiasm for health insurance seemed to wane, and no one was more cognizant of it than Ted Kennedy, who had begun the new congressional session, as he had begun every session since 1971, by reintroducing S.3, his national health insurance bill, which he considered the single most important potential government initiative and for which he had continued to fight tenaciously. Ted felt that during the campaign, Carter had "talked his way around" healthcare; that he had used "artful" words to avoid a full-throated endorsement of national health insurance; that he "didn't really want to stand up on it"; and that he was "completely ambiguous about it and resentful of the pressure that was being put on him." "Bet on what you think a man will do rather than what he says he'll do, and you'll be right more often than not," Joe Kennedy had told his son. Ted Kennedy thought Jimmy Carter, despite his pronouncements, didn't care much about health insurance. Carter had said it was going to be his first priority but then focused on energy policy instead, which, Ted averred dismissively, was "basically deregulation" and was "not very well done" and which simply added to Ted's doubts about Carter and increased the tension between the two men. When Carter did turn to healthcare, he prioritized small changes: an extension of the Hill-Burton Act, a 1946 law that dedicated federal funds to hospital construction; and the Hospital Cost Containment Act that capped the costs hospitals could receive from payees but that, under pressure from hospitals and Republicans, was compromised from compulsory to voluntary compliance, limiting increases to the rate of inflation.

Carter's secretary of Health, Education and Welfare, the former Lyndon Johnson aide Joseph Califano, was more sympathetic to Ted's cause, and Ted viewed him as a "pipeline," in Carey Parker's word, to Carter. But Califano had few illusions about Carter's commitment to the issue either. He believed that Carter had endorsed, however wanly, a health insurance program only because he needed votes in industrial states, and that for Carter, "as for most elected Democrats, national health insurance was more political than potential reality, a part of the national Democratic catechism more to be recited than honored." Califano moved on it, but given Carter's reluctance, he moved slowly, practically grinding the process to a halt, setting up an advisory committee that would collect more data, though his real motive, he admitted, was partly to demonstrate to Ted that he was doing *something* as a way of keeping Ted from asking him to do more. Meanwhile Califano approached one of Ted's health aides, Stan Jones, to head up the administration's national health insurance initiative, but when Jones asked how much money was being earmarked for the effort, and Califano said $12 billion, Jones declined, saying that there was no way that a system could be constructed for so little money. It further demonstrated how little enthusiasm Carter had for a real health insurance plan.

Part of the national catechism, Califano had called national healthcare. Political rhetoric, he had called it. *But not for Ted Kennedy.* As early as February 16, less than a month after taking office, Carter told his HEW staff that he would be working on a national health insurance program, but one that would "phase in" national healthcare, beginning, it would develop, with care for low-income children and catastrophic care for the elderly on costs that were not covered under Medicare. Ted was not pleased, thinking that this was a delaying tactic. He didn't want a phase-in. He wanted a full bill. On May 2 he invited Califano; Congressman James Corman, who had introduced a single-payer plan in the House back when Ted introduced S. 3; Hale Champion, the head of Califano's advisory committee; and several of Ted's staffers, including a young doctor named Larry Horowitz, to his house to discuss healthcare. It was, even so early in the new administration, a testy meeting. When Califano insisted that the issue needed further study and that the administration was working up a new plan, Ted told him that they didn't need a new plan. "We already have a program we've been working on for years," meaning his S. 3, which was full-scale health insurance underwritten by payroll taxes, as Medicare was. And he said that the supporters of his plan were willing to negotiate with the administration, but their question was, "Is the administration willing to negotiate with us?" Califano explained that the Senate Finance Committee and the House Ways and Means Committee were tied up with the administration's other priorities, energy and welfare reform. Ted snapped that he would hold hearings himself and get things moving. Califano said Ted was "amicable" during the discussion. Horowitz, however, said he was anything but. Rather, he had thrown down the gauntlet. "If we're not going to move on health care," Ted warned Califano—and Ted told Califano he knew that Carter had no real interest in it—"I'm going to fight you publicly every step of the way."

But still Carter, despite having been forewarned, took no action. And now Ted, not an especially patient man when it came to his legislative priorities, had run out of patience. Two weeks later, on May 16, at the UAW convention in Los Angeles, Ted delivered what even Califano called a "rousing" speech, in which he called out Carter for not submitting a healthcare plan and said that "health care has been left behind." A "missing promise," he called it, though what he really meant was a "broken promise." "The American people should not tolerate delay on national health by Congress," he railed to his appreciative audience of six thousand delegates, "simply because other reforms are already lined up bumper-to-bumper." And he asked Carter—he had warned Carter he would do so—to make a "firm commitment now" to comprehensive health reform. Carter, who had been under liberal siege for several weeks, spoke the next day at the convention, with uncharacteristic spiritedness, telling those delegates that he was "committed to the phasing-in of a workable national health care system" (Ted found risible the two conditions "phasing-in" and "workable") and that he would send a bill to Congress in 1978 (the dilatory schedule Ted had protested), and Carter then tempered expectations further by invoking limits again and saying that he would have to "make some hard choices about how we spend taxpayers' money." "We can't afford to do everything," he told them, sounding his now-constant refrain. Still, the crowd, desperate for some Democratic revival, responded with a fifty-second standing ovation.

But the realization of Carter's vow was, by Carter's own intention, far off. In the meantime, on June 16, exactly a month after Ted's UAW speech, Ted and Woodcock's successor as UAW president, Douglas Fraser—Woodcock had been named Carter's ambassador to China—met with Carter at the White House to discuss healthcare. That led to meetings between Ted's staff and Carter's staff to hash out a plan, though Carter was clearly stalling again, as his pronouncement at the UAW convention about submitting a proposal in 1978 had signaled. Max Fine, the coordinator of the still-extant Committee of 100, which the late UAW president Walter Reuther had originated in 1969 to push for national healthcare, said he would sit in Ted's office trying to craft a bill on which both the administration and the congressional liberals could agree. Fine said Ted was accommodating. He understood that the final bill would be regarded as Carter's bill, and Ted didn't mind that. Having failed to strike a deal with Nixon, he seemed especially eager to strike a deal now with a president of his own party and with an overwhelmingly Democratic Congress. And he enlisted labor, even Carter's own ambassador, Woodcock, to press the issue with the administration. Meanwhile Carter's people kept working on a bill of their own—a bill that eschewed a comprehensive insurance plan for the incremental plan that Carter kept touting—and as they did so, Carter rejected any input either from Kennedy's staff or from the Committee of 100, even though such input would be a practical necessity if any heathcare plan was to advance in Congress. "Creeping incremental-ism," Ted called Carter's approach with unconcealed contempt, because Ted, who knew the chemistry of the Senate, realized that no incremental plan could possibly pass. Incrementalism, he believed, was just a way to provide opportunities for healthcare's Republican and industry oppo-nents to thwart it. "Carter was scared" was how Max Fine characterized the effort—scared that he would be attached to and attacked for a new government program; scared that there wasn't sufficient money for such a program; scared that a program would wind up wrecking his mission for fiscal prudence and political moderation; in short, scared that a plan would undermine him politically. Even as he was laying the groundwork for preventing national health insurance, Carter made a pretense of seri-ousness about it because it was the only way to pacify his own party. He met several times with Woodcock to find some common ground on healthcare before Woodcock left for his China station. But Woodcock was unconvinced. He would tell Ted, "He's equivocating." As Ted put it, citing evidence of that equivocation, Carter would announce, "I'm going to put out principles" on which a healthcare plan could be constructed, but then failed to put out those promised principles. Ted had even agreed to a major concession—to forgo his single-payer system—and had wrung the same concession from Doug Fraser and Lane Kirkland, the president of the AFL-CIO, admitting that it would be "politically impossible to pass." But none of this seemed to sway Carter. As the year wore on, Ted said that organized labor, which had given Carter that ovation at the UAW conven-tion, was losing faith that he would enact a health insurance plan, and the UAW leadership had even met with Carter to tell him so. "Voices were raised," Max Fine said of that meeting. But Carter, as Fine had said, was scared and willing to sacrifice labor if the alternative was sacrificing white conservatives. According to Califano, Treasury secretary Michael Blu-menthal and Council of Economic Advisers chairman Charles Shultze both advised Carter to drop health reform, and some conservative Demo-crats in Congress were less than enthusiastic as well. "Where are you going to get the dollars?" Representative Dan Rostenkowski, the chair-man of the Ways and Means Subcommittee on Health, asked. And with Carter scared and backing off, labor realized that national health insur-ance had collapsed yet again.

But this time it wasn't Richard Nixon who was thwarting Ted; Nixon had in fact been amenable to some compromise for a national health insurance plan. It was a fellow Democrat. And as Max Fine put it, Ted was angry—very angry. Califano had a prophecy: "It was only a matter of time before Carter and Edward Kennedy became a redux of Johnson and Robert Kennedy."

Passionless. Too tepid. Not sufficiently bold. Not sufficiently liberal. Those had been Ted Kennedy's primary criticisms of Jimmy Carter. He had supported him legislatively. He was, by voting if not by voice, one of the president's staunchest allies in the Senate. But he felt that Carter was never fully engaged and never willing to push the boundaries, that he was saving political capital not to do things but to get reelected. On domestic policy, Carter always seemed to Ted to stop short. It was no different on foreign policy. There were many areas in which the two men agreed—particularly on the importance of human rights in American foreign policy, which had not been an interest of Johnson or Nixon. It was the foot-dragging of the administration that frustrated Ted. Nixon the red-baiter had opened China in a bold stroke—a stroke that Ted had partly precipitated by planning to go to China himself—but relations between the United States and China had yet to be normalized, in part because of a dispute between Secretary of State Cyrus Vance, who was eager for rapprochement with the Soviets and felt that any overtures to Red China could derail that, and special assistant to the National Security Council, Zbigniew Brzezinski, a fierce cold warrior who wanted to use those overtures as a pressure point against the Soviets, and in part because of the thorny issue of Taiwan. Red China had made full diplomatic relations contingent on the United States withdrawing its recognition of Taiwan, with which the United States had a mutual defense treaty. Such a withdrawal would have had severe political consequences for Carter. So Ted did what he had done so often during the Nixon administration. He began conducting his own foreign policy in an attempt to move Carter's, only this time he did so with the assistance of allies within the administration. That summer, while he and Carter were squabbling over healthcare, Ted delivered a major address to the World Affairs Council in Boston, in which he laid out guidelines for normalization with China, timed just days before Vance was leaving for Beijing for negotiations. The speech, according to Ted's new foreign policy adviser, Jan Kalicki, had been developed "with great care" and "with a lot of external and internal input." Richard Holbrooke, the assistant secretary of state for East Asian and Pacific affairs, and Michael Oksenberg, the senior director of the National Security Council, had both seen the speech prior to Ted's giving it, as had a number of China experts from academe. Ted's prescription was that America could no longer behave as if Mainland China were a phantom state and Taiwan were the real China, and he called for the withdrawal of recognition of Taiwan on the basis that China and Taiwan would eventually resolve their differences and that the United States would retain the option of aiding Taiwan should Red China attack it. More specifically, Ted called for a 1978 deadline for the exchange of embassies and announced that he would submit a resolution of his proposals the following month. *The New York Times* called the speech the "most forthright and detailed proposal made by a politician who is influential with the Carter administration," though Jerome Cohen, a China expert from Harvard and adviser to Ted, had another take. He called it a "blatant challenge to Carter and Vance— as well as to China—to show more flexibility in their bargaining." And Cohen said that Ted had now exerted pressure on the administration, just as he had exerted pressure on Nixon when he had kept demanding recognition of Mainland China during the early years of Nixon's presidency.

Whether or not Washington was listening, China was. That public pressure convinced China to issue an invitation to Ted for a visit—an invitation that it had previously withheld for fear of compromising relations with the sitting president. On Christmas Eve 1977, Ted, Joan, Kara, Ted Jr., and Patrick; Caroline; Bobby's son Michael; Ted's sisters Pat, Eunice, and Jean; the China expert Jerome Cohen, two Boston reporters, and several of Ted's aides left for China. Ted went believing that the invitation was not merely a courtesy to a prominent senator but, as Kalicki put it, "part of a larger view of the relationship with the U.S.," and Ted treated it as such. He was heavily briefed—at least eight or nine briefings at Ted's home, Kalicki said—by experts on a variety of fields, including a number from the administration, and even from ideologically different points of view. The mission was not entirely diplomatic. Ted was given permission to visit prisons and a school, where he polled the students on which of China's "four modernizations" they felt was the most important. (They voted that military modernization was the least important.) And he met with low-level political functionaries in an effort to get to know the country from its roots. But the centerpiece of the trip was a meeting with Chinese leader Deng Xiaoping—a "hard-won" meeting, Jerome Cohen called it. (Carey

Parker had said that Ted had been led to believe that if he showed an interest in getting to know the Chinese people, Deng would meet with him, and Ted was always willing to get to know people.) In his ninety-minute meeting with Deng—during which the Chinese leader, as was a custom among men of his generation, kept expectorating into a large spittoon, while the Kennedy children, amazed, laughed—Ted did not make concessions to China but rather explained to China the deep American commitment to Taiwan, even as he and others were desirous of an accommodation with the Communists, and asked China for its assurance that if the United States were to offer recognition, China would renounce any intention to invade Taiwan—a renunciation that Chinese leaders would not offer, though they signaled that they had no intention of attacking Taiwan. And Ted clearly made himself available as what Carey Parker called a "peacemaker" who could advance American-Chinese relations. This did not necessarily please Jimmy Carter, since it demonstrated that Ted Kennedy seemed able to do things that Carter could not. Still, Carter picked up the effort, and a year later, on December 15, 1978, China and the United States jointly announced normalization.

But Ted had made a pledge to Taiwan too. Even as he was seeking diplomatic relations with Mainland China, he was working with Senator Alan Cranston, another liberal, to strengthen America's commitment to Taiwan. This was not a traditional liberal position. "People would have expected that from a [Barry] Goldwater," Jan Kalicki would say, "but not from a couple of liberals." (Indeed, Goldwater was among a group of legislators who brought suit against Carter for unilaterally abrogating the Sino-American Mutual Defense Treaty with Taiwan.) Still, Ted and Cranston worked, and worked hard, and Ted invited to one of his McLean dinners, on January 25, 1979, the head of the Chinese Liaison Office, Chai Tse-Min, who was the equivalent of an ambassador, and representatives from the administration, including assistant secretary of state Holbrooke and Ambassador Woodcock, to discuss how America could honor its commitment to Taiwan without jeopardizing its hope for an accord with Red China. The Taiwan Relations Act (TRA), the product of Kennedy's and Cranston's joint efforts, effectively permitted the United States to have diplomatic and commercial relations with Taiwan without calling Taiwan the Republic of China, which had been its official designation, or without having formal relations with it, though in every other respect the relations between the two countries remained unchanged, including the provision of "defense articles and defense services." And it declared that any attempts to undermine Taiwan save through peaceful means would be viewed by the United States as a "grave concern." The liaison officer, according to Kalicki, criticized the language of the act at that dinner but "not too strongly," which the participants took to mean that the act "would fly." Carter was enraged by what he saw as Ted's preemption of presidential prerogatives, especially a provision of the TRA that required the president to inform Congress of any Chinese aggression against Taiwan. Carter's attorney general Griffin Bell said that Carter had asked him if he thought Ted might accept an appointment to the Supreme Court, apparently as a way to get rid of him, and Bell said he replied, "I did not believe he would want to give up being co-president." Given the momentum behind it, Carter had little choice but to support the TRA. It sailed through both houses of Congress that March and was signed into law by President Carter on April 10, 1979. But it was Ted Kennedy, not Carter, who had been the primary instigator in reconciling China and the United States and Ted Kennedy who had reassured Taiwan of its continued independence.

The Soviet Union was different—different because Carter's policies toward it were variable, at turns conciliatory and bellicose, and because Ted Kennedy also had his own dual objectives, one of which was finding areas, particularly on arms control, where there was mutual interest with the Soviets, and the other of which was forcing the Soviets to allow Russian dissidents to leave the country. Historian Sean Wilentz speculated that Carter's vacillation was an attempt to pacify both the left and the right with his policies, as he so often did on domestic issues. He signed a Strategic Arms Limitation Agreement with the Soviets, then supported the MX mobile missile system. He demanded that the Soviets remove their missiles from eastern Europe or risk the United States positioning Pershing missiles and cruise missiles in western Europe. But the vacillation was also the result of very real divisions within the administration, as there had been on Chinese relations, between those who wanted to engage the Soviets, like Vance, and those who wanted to punish them, like Brzezinski. Carter could never quite make up his mind which to do. Kalicki said that the one advantage to the discord among Carter's advisers was that Ted could always find allies within the administration, as he had done on China. Ted had already been deeply involved in helping Russian dissidents as part of his concern with refugees. Early in 1974, while he was still pondering whether to run in 1976, he had made his European tour, which included a trip to Moscow to discuss the emigration of Jewish dissidents with Soviet premier Leonid Brezhnev. The trip had been preceded by petitions from a score of Americans, some of them prominent, like Random House chief Robert Bernstein, former Supreme Court justice Arthur Goldberg, and New York Philharmonic conductor Leonard Bernstein, and other friends and relatives of refuseniks, asking for Ted's intercession with Brezhnev to allow dissidents to emigrate. Ted met with Brezhnev over lunch for two and a half hours—Ted said immodestly he was accorded this courtesy because Brezhnev expected him to be president— and the two chatted about the siege of Stalingrad during World War II, Joe Jr.'s death, and nuclear weapons. (When Ted proffered a draft treaty banning nuclear weapons and had it translated for the Soviet leader, Brezhnev told him that if Ted were president, they would sit in front of the fire, drink vodka, and sign the treaty.) Brezhnev became "defensive," however, when Ted raised the issue of Jewish emigration. And when, at Leonard Bernstein's request, Ted asked about letting the famed classical cellist Mstislav Rostropovich, a Jew, leave the country, Brezhnev said that the Soviets had trained Rostropovich, and that after he was finished playing for the Russians, he could play for the Americans, but that he would let Ted know about the disposition of the matter before Ted left for America. But Ted hadn't come to Russia only to meet with government officials. Even though his Soviet handler had warned him that doing so would jeopardize his relationship with Brezhnev, late one night, and much to the consternation of the secret police, Ted visited a group of refuseniks at the apartment of a mathematician named Alexander Lerner and spent three hours with them, sipping tea, discussing their situation, and leaving them with a promise that he would continue to press their cause and publicize it. It was on his way back to America, when his plane touched down for a layover in Copenhagen, that the Russian ambassador boarded and informed Ted that Rostropovich would be released. He was.

Now, a little over four years later, Ted returned to Russia, returned to Brezhnev, with the same causes: nuclear arms limitation and Jewish emigration. In the intervening years, Ted had become even more aggressive for the refuseniks. He compiled lists of émigrés from the Jewish Community Council and the American Jewish Congress and the Alliance for Soviet Jewry, then had Kalicki negotiate with the Soviets over the list, and the Soviets would argue with Kalicki, trying, as Kalicki put it, to "bully" the senator, telling him that there were things in the backgrounds of some of these refuseniks that disqualified them from emigrating. But Kalicki said he insisted that these were members of divided families—families with relatives in the United States or in Israel—and that the issue was a humanitarian one, not a political one. And he said that the Soviets would grudgingly concede, saying that they knew Ted would, for his own political advancement, have to show some results if he were to go to Russia. (The Chinese, Kalicki said, were much more informal; Ted would hand over a list of possible émigrés when he met with them, and there was no prior vetting.) And Ted also exchanged letters with Brezhnev, long letters, passing on Brezhnev's to President Carter. Once again, this time on a Saturday morning after what Ted called a "series of rather blunt private messages stating my wish for further easing of restraints against dissidents," Ted had a long meeting with Brezhnev, but there was little of the chattiness of the first visit. Brezhnev was clearly ill—in "extremely bad health," Kalicki said—and rather than speak freely, the Soviet leader read his remarks, read them slowly and deliberately, and his words were slurred. Ted said Brezhnev complained about Carter's human rights campaign, with which Ted told him, he was in agreement. And then Brezhnev fell asleep. The next morning, as he had on his first visit, Ted made a point of visiting with the dissidents, an "intense" visit, Kalicki called it, and informed several of them, including Boris Katz, who had petitioned for exit visas every six months, that he had secured those visas now, which was especially important since Katz's daughter was ill and in need of medical care. Katz was speechless. "The impression was inescapable," wrote the *Los Angeles Times*, "that Kennedy had achieved in his brief visit a result in the field of human rights—an area of special interest to the Administration—what had escaped Carter during 20 months in office." Ted's interest, however, was not in showing up Jimmy Carter, however great his distaste for him. Ted's interest was in those refuseniks. "He said to me once that he almost had never got more satisfaction [than] in seeing those people leave and come here and be reunited with family," said George Abrams, his old refugee aide, years later. Ted Kennedy had become their personal savior.

III

"Government cannot eliminate poverty or provide a bountiful economy or reduce inflation or save our cities or cure illiteracy or provide energy," Jimmy Carter declared in his State of the Union address at the beginning of his second year in the presidency, thus sounding a retreat from forty years of Democratic liberalism. It had been a quiet year compared to the turbulent times of the Vietnam War and then Watergate, but it had not been an easy one. The economy, while picking up from the recession of 1974–75, was still faltering. "The character of this recovery is perplexing," observed the senior economist at the Minneapolis Federal Reserve Bank, "for while production and civilian employment have been high, so, too, have inflation and unemployment. For this, there are no postwar precedents." Part of the inflationary pressure, a large part, was a rise in oil prices, since America was largely dependent on foreign oil and those foreigners were gouging the country. Carter, however, a fierce deficit hawk, also blamed government spending—typically a Republican answer—and he proposed austerity. In a time of growth, he believed, the Keynesian economics in which the government pumped money into the economy—the economics that had been a basis of liberalism since Roosevelt's New Deal—was not needed. Carter's new budget, he said, would be "lean and tight." He would, adjusting for inflation, be submitting the smallest increase in four years: just 2 percent.

But as far as Ted Kennedy was concerned, this was less a matter of financial prudence than a way to pacify conservatives, whom Carter seemed to fear much more than he feared liberals. And there was a cost for doing so—a huge cost. In arguing for austerity and tax cuts, Jimmy Carter, whom the UAW had cheered a year earlier, was also striking a blow at Ted Kennedy's single most cherished legislative initiative: his national healthcare plan. The two had already spent much of Carter's first year squabbling over national health insurance, with Carter continuing to promise to submit a plan in 1978. He had made the same promise personally to Ted at a meeting on December 20, 1977. But Carter was clearly just placating Ted and Ted's labor allies, especially Doug Fraser of the UAW, who had been lobbying Carter's vice president, Walter Mondale, for action. As his State of the Union three weeks later plainly stated, Carter had no real enthusiasm for healthcare or any other government program and no real plan to pass any. His enthusiasm was for budget cutting and for curbing inflation, the latter of which he viewed as the major problem besetting the country and the major problem he had to solve to be reelected. That put him and Ted on the collision course Joseph Califano had predicted.

But Ted Kennedy, however much he might have distrusted Carter, did not seek that collision because Ted, as much as he relished legislative combat, did not relish personal combat. He had charged his staff with drafting a bill that would meet Carter's main criteria—mainly keeping costs down, incorporating a private insurance component, and rolling out a plan slowly, in stages, rather than all at once, so long as there was a predetermined schedule set in the legislation and it couldn't be halted suddenly once it had been set in motion. That was an essential condition. And his old health adviser, Rashi Fein, and his new health aide, Dr. Larry Horowitz, worked hard to achieve those ends. "The part that I knew," Fein recalled, "was that Kennedy was willing to say, 'We don't have to do it all at once. But we do have to do it with a timetable. We don't want to have the same debate every two years or every four years. I can live with: Let's begin with children, let's then go to age twenty-five, age thirty-five. But I want it in the law.'" And that was the biggest difference between Ted's approach and Carter's—the sticking point. For Ted, *it had to be in the law.*

Ted wasn't necessarily happy about having to compromise, not just because he didn't believe in Carter's rationale for the phase-in but because doing so was complex and most likely self-defeating, which might have been Carter's aim. Rashi Fein, who claimed to be largely responsible for Ted's new jerry-built plan and who said he knew it "forward and backward," nevertheless also said later that "on pain of death, I could not tell you now what it was" because "it was so complicated that I suspect I forgot it within six months." And when Fein explained the bill to Ted and a group of thirty or so labor union presidents after a dinner at Ted's house, Ted's immediate comment was, "That's very good. But, Rashi, will it work?"

In any case, Carter and his people didn't seem particularly interested in devising a plan that worked—or any plan at all. Their main goal now was to keep Ted and labor at bay. And while Ted's staff tweaked their own plan and Carter's staff purportedly were working on their plan, nothing moved forward, which was Carter's way of avoiding a collision—by moving so slowly that there could be no crash. And despite Carter's commitment to Doug Fraser and to Ted to have a plan in 1978, Califano told a press conference on December 6 that he did not know whether a bill would be introduced in late 1978 or, now, early 1979. Ted, very much displeased, asked Carter's chief domestic adviser, Stu Eizenstat, for a clarification, which was: Califano doesn't speak for the administration. But that seemed to be a dodge—Califano seemed very much to be speaking for the administration. That January, the January of Carter's 1978 austerity State of the Union, Carter met with Doug Fraser, who pressed Carter to submit a bill so that Ted could hold hearings on it that summer, and apparently Carter gave Fraser his word that he would. But before that meeting, Eizenstat wrote a memo to Carter telling him there was not enough time to build support for a bill and counseling Carter to push back on Fraser's likely requests, especially his desire to pay for a plan out of payroll taxes and general revenues. Meanwhile Califano, whom Ted had seen as a partner among the Carter procrastinators, turned out not to be a partner after all. Califano met with Carter on March 2 and urged him to delay any bill until after the midterm elections that fall. By Califano's own account, he told Carter, "There is little stomach on the Hill for any national health insurance legislation this year," adding, "except for Kennedy." Congress, he said, wouldn't pass such a bill anyway, if doing so meant new taxes. (Califano might very well have been right, which was a sign of how spooked Democrats now were, even so-called liberal Democrats, by Republican calls for smaller government and steeper tax cuts.) Carter, who had no stomach for healthcare himself, agreed with Califano but countered that he had given his word to Fraser that he would introduce a bill, and that Fraser had vowed to support any Democratic congressman who pledged to vote for it. And then he wiggled out of his commitment to Fraser by saying that he thought it would be satisfied if he set up *principles* for a healthcare plan instead of a full plan—principles he had long promised to deliver but never did. And according to Califano, when Califano warned that principles wouldn't satisfy Ted, Carter snipped, "Kennedy is wrong." Carter now deputized Eizenstat to break the news to Ted that Carter would be announcing principles and phasing in a plan, but instead, Ted announced his own plan to Eizenstat and asked for a meeting with Carter, while having Larry Horowitz tell *The Washington Post* that Ted, in the spirit of compromise, had backed away from his comprehensive plan of the past and was negotiating with the White House, thus putting the onus on Carter.

And the onus *was* on Jimmy Carter—a heavy onus, since he was doing everything he could to avoid a national healthcare plan while seeming to support one. Nixon, a Republican, had tried to preempt Ted on healthcare to protect his presidency. Carter, a Democrat, was cagily trying to block him to protect his presidency. And unlike foreign policy, where Ted had conspirators within the administration, he had none when it came to this. Inside the administration, almost everyone had signed on to Carter's budget cutting, which precluded healthcare. Office of Management and Budget director James McIntyre, a stern foe of national healthcare, wrote Carter on April 5 that there was a consensus: "no plan will significantly improve the nation's health status," which seemed on the face of it absurd. How could providing health insurance to those who could not afford it *not* improve healthcare? And McIntyre, not coincidentally, had delivered his verdict the day before Ted, and labor leaders George Meany, Lane Kirkland, and Doug Fraser, were to meet with Carter at the White House to advocate for a plan. That day, April 5, Carter received four plans from his health advisers: a federal mandate with employers paying 75 percent of the premiums; a plan targeted at the poor; a plan combining tax credits and vouchers for the poor to purchase private insurance; and a public corporation to administer benefits while those benefits would be provided by private insurance. At the same time, Ted's plan was dismissed out of hand as too costly, which amply demonstrated how little Carter cared about Kennedy's objections.

But this time Ted Kennedy had not come to the meeting in a spirit of compromise. He had come to the meeting in a spirit of challenge. He explained to Carter that he had already compromised, and so had labor. He described the work as "agonizing"—agonizing because both he and labor had had to sacrifice some of their most cherished principles—but he said he had devised a plan that included a central role for private insurance, as Carter desired. But then, as Califano reported it, Ted, "fixing his eyes firmly on the President," told him that there were three things on which he could not compromise: universality, comprehensiveness, and tough controls. Califano would later recall that when Ted said that, he was not talking with Carter; he was making a speech to him—a speech, Califano said, for the benefit of labor. But Califano certainly misread Ted's intentions. Ted didn't need to win the labor leaders' confidence. They had full confidence in Ted Kennedy. He was speaking to demonstrate to Carter the urgency of Carter's staying the course and the consequences if he didn't. And then Ted began making demands on Carter, wanting to know when Carter would finally set a timetable for his bill, and insisting on a working group consisting of Ted's staff, labor, and the administration to negotiate the bill. He addressed the president in a "tone so insistent," Califano would write, "it was almost disdainful to the President." And Califano, who had worked for Lyndon Johnson, said, "Certainly no one had ever talked to Lyndon Johnson that way." And Califano came to a conclusion: He thought that Ted "wants to take over the presidential decision-making process," which was exactly what he wanted to do. Ted was tired of Carter putting budgetary restraints above providing healthcare.

"Soft," Califano called Carter in his response to Ted. But Jimmy Carter was not soft. He was canny. He promised Ted action, knowing full well there would be none. Rather, Eizenstat warned, as Califano had done, in a memo after the meeting, that a bill not be submitted before the midterm elections in 1978. "It is one thing to honor a commitment," he wrote Carter. "It is quite another to have the UAW and Kennedy dictate the date on which you send the proposal up," and he cited the "conservative climate" of the country, which Ted continued to ignore. Califano said that after the April 6 meeting, he went to Capitol Hill and found unanimous opposition to a healthcare plan—opposition that he said now included James Corman, the sponsor of Ted's own bill in the House. (Califano might have misread Corman, too. Corman, who, if anything, was more vehement than Ted when it came to healthcare, opposed Ted's compromises to Carter.) All the congressmen and senators to whom he spoke, he said, "made the point that the only person the President seemed to be talking to was Kennedy, and Kennedy was out of touch with Congress." It was a remarkable statement—that Ted Kennedy was out of touch with his fellow senators—remarkable because Ted Kennedy understood the chemistry of the Senate as well as anyone, understood what should and should not be proposed, what could and could not pass, which was not to say that he necessarily thought national healthcare would pass, but that it was important for a bill to be introduced and debated and supported by the administration. And even if Ted Kennedy was out of touch, as Califano believed, Carter himself was not quite ready to break with Ted, realizing that despite Califano's assessment, Kennedy did have supporters in the Senate, and he would continue to fight for healthcare no matter what. So Carter instructed Joe Onek of his domestic policy staff to continue meeting with Ted's staff, with labor, and with the Committee on National Health Insurance—the Committee of 100—not so much to find a modus vivendi with them as yet again to placate them, and Carter agreed to a "series of meetings" with Ted and labor to discuss their proposal—again, less to advance it than to *pretend* to be working on it as a way of slowing its advance. But Carter's goal wasn't only to placate Ted Kennedy and labor and to waylay healthcare. For all Carter's talk about his understanding the conservative temperament of the country, his own approval rating had dropped precipitously that April as he was vying with Ted over healthcare—down in a single month from 48 to 40 percent. Though a good deal of that drop could be attributed to rising inflation—a rate of 7.4 percent that month—largely as a result of that rise in oil prices, which was why Carter was so fixated on budget cutting, he was clearly not winning any adherents for his fiscal belt-tightening, which also clearly was not having its intended economic effect.

The summer of 1978 was to be the summer of healthcare for Ted Kennedy. Ted, who seldom relented, would not relent, quite possibly because he felt that with a large Democratic majority in Congress and a Democratic president and with so few accomplishments already, the time would never be more auspicious for some kind of healthcare bill—*if* Jimmy Carter would only support one. (There was also almost the certainty of losing seats in Congress because sitting presidents, with few exceptions, typically did so and because Carter's economic distress put him in extreme peril.) Moreover, labor, having worked for Carter's election, also needed something to show for its efforts beyond budget cutting. And despite Carter's intransigence and his belief that an increasingly conservative country would balk at healthcare, Ted was winning the battle of narratives. A *Newsweek* piece that May praised Ted for not trying to "upstage" the president, even though that was exactly what he was trying to do, and said that when Carter and his fellow Georgians came to Washington, they had thought of Ted as a "playboy and putative rival" and that Hamilton Jordan had largely "cold-shouldered" him the first year, but that Ted had won them over for his "team play," and that Attorney General Griffin Bell, one of those Georgians, called Ted the "most effective man in the Senate." Ted, *Newsweek* said, had come to Carter's aid on tax reform and the Panama Canal treaty, convincing fellow liberal James Abourezk to vote for the latter.* But Ted has "impressed the White House most of all" by compromis-

---

* Abourezk did say that Ted, at Carter's behest, called him to lobby for his vote on the treaty, but that he hadn't needed convincing. He had been withholding support because Carter had reversed himself on an issue that was as near and dear to Abourezk as health insurance was to Ted Kennedy: the deregulation of energy. In effect, Abourezk was using his treaty vote to bargain with Carter. James Abourezk, *Advise and Dissent: Memoirs of an Ex-Senator* (Lincoln: Univ. of Nebraska Press, 2013), 144.

ing on healthcare and said that Carter was so grateful that during a recent
meeting—presumably the tense April 6 meeting—he stopped calling Ted
"Senator" and began calling him "Ted." A piece in *The Washington Post* the
following week reported that momentum was finally gathering for health
insurance, and that Ted's staff had met with the White House staffers
eighteen times since December to hammer out a joint bill. But the piece
also quoted Max Fine, the head of the Committee of 100, that he still
didn't know if the administration was "for real or not on this," despite the
administration's professed commitment, and he added that "if there is no
national health insurance legislation in the next two years, the issue will
be dead for a decade."

It was to be a long summer of jousting between two intractable politicians, but it wasn't just their sense of the country's priorities that was
different. They had two very different sets of moral priorities. Carter believed in a personal morality, a traditional Protestant morality, in which a
virtue like frugality was deeply valued. (This was the progressive moralism of Carter's that historian Leo Ribuffo had seen in him.) Ted Kennedy,
whose personal morality was often reviled, nevertheless believed in a
communal morality, a political morality, in which compassion was deeply
valued. Still, the two kept trying to co-opt each other. While Carter
shrewdly kept declaring his commitments to healthcare as a way of fore-
stalling Ted's more aggressive approach, Ted shrewdly kept praising Carter and declaring that with Carter's leadership there would be an
"important educational experience over the next eighteen months" that
would end in passage of a health insurance law, as a way of forcing Carter's hand. Early that June Dr. Peter Bourne, Carter's health adviser, announced that the administration was "pretty close" to agreeing on a
"modified form" of the Kennedy health plan—one that relied heavily on
private insurance—but this too was a kind of bluff. Whatever the public
stance, the private discussion, as Eizenstat and Onek wrote Carter early
that June, was about economic conditions, especially concerns about rising inflation, and whether any health plan in these circumstances would
work, and they advised that when Carter and Ted next met—a meeting
had been scheduled for June 28—the main objective should be not achieving some rapprochement on healthcare but avoiding a "rupture" with
Ted and urging him to exercise "patience," not on economic grounds, but
on the practical grounds that some Democrats might repudiate a health
plan and that that would set back the cause for a long time, as Fine pre-

dicted. In short, Eizenstat and Onek were trying to convince Ted that they and the administration shared his goals, just not his process—no doubt because there were now rumors, just whispers at the time, among pols and in the press about Ted challenging Carter for the nomination. (This also spoke to something else: to Ted Kennedy's legislative power now that he was increasingly a master of the Senate, someone who knew far better than Carter did how to work the institution.) In a phone conversation with Carter two days before their scheduled meeting, Ted took the opposite tack. He laid out to the president "how politically untenable his position was," meaning Carter's continuing insistence that healthcare be phased in depending on economic circumstances and cost control benchmarks. In Ted's view, you couldn't begin a massive program only to pull the rug out from under it in midcourse. Effectively, it would mean passing the legislation again and again and again. Ted, who understood the chemistry and physics of the Senate, knew that that wouldn't work. "Opponents would pick it off bit by bit," he told Carter.

But there was no rupture—yet. Despite his growing frustration with Carter, Ted didn't want to break with the administration because he knew that without its support, a bill was unlikely to pass, and the administration didn't want to break with Ted because of its fear that Ted might mount a campaign against it, and even if he didn't, that labor would be unhappy. At the June 28 meeting, as Califano reported it, Ted brought his health aide Larry Horowitz, a tough, feisty infighter, though Carter asked if he and Ted might be alone, and for the next hour, the two of them wandered the White House grounds. Whatever they had resolved—neither ever said—the next morning Carter told Califano that he and Califano would examine Ted's health plan before Ted made it public and that Califano would be working with Ted the last two weeks of July to arrive at a set of principles—yet again principles. And however tentatively, healthcare now seemed back on track.

At least that was the way it seemed when Carter and Ted next met, at nine-thirty a.m. on July 28 in the Oval Office in the Cabinet Room to hash out, once again, their last differences on healthcare—differences that Califano, after weeks of conferring with Ted, told Carter still amounted to whether there would be a single bill, as Ted wanted, or a phase-in of several successive bills, as Carter had wanted. Ted brought Horowitz again. Throughout the year, Horowitz had been meeting with two administration groups—a sign of the disarray around Carter's healthcare initiative—one headed by Eizenstat and another appointed by Califano and headed by Ben Heineman, an assistant secretary for policy at HEW. Horowitz thought he and Eizenstat might still reach some consensus, and the two had worked until midnight supposedly to hash out the last details. Carter had Califano, Mondale, Onek, who had once been on Ted's staff, an aide named David Rubinstein, and Eizenstat at the table. It was meant to be a peace session—a session at which each side could consider the other's proposals and find some common ground. In the event, it was anything but, in large measure because by this time Ted and Carter had been arguing over the same issue again and again without resolution, and Carter had come to feel that Ted was determined to run no matter what the administration did on healthcare. "From the minute we walked in the door," Horowitz recalled, "it was clear he," meaning Carter, "did not want to solve the problem" of the phase-in triggers. As Ted recalled it, Carter told him, "I want to work with you. I know that we are not going to have a chance to get any bill passed unless we have your help and our support." (Eizenstat's version of Carter's appeal was more conciliatory. "It will doom health care if we split. I have no other place to turn if I can't turn to you.") But then Carter said, "I'm facing serious problems with this," and he asked Ted to explain to Eizenstat "why it is in the interest that we do this before the election." But Carter, who insisted that "I must emphasize fiscal responsibility if we are to have a chance," had stopped listening to explanations. He said he would announce principles for a bill within the next twenty-four hours—not a bill but, again, *principles* for one, which was what he had been saying for months. Then Carter grew resolute—"fingers tightly clasped, cold blue eyes fixed directly on Kennedy," as Califano described it. "I don't fear criticism," he said. "I take crap every day, criticism every day." Ted didn't respond in kind, at least not at first. (Horowitz actually chewed Ted out later for not being more forceful with Carter.) He said he still wanted to work with Carter and that he read Congress similarly: "Unless we develop the right kind of constituency, I don't think we'll get legislation passed probably even during our lifetimes." But then Ted did grow resolute and did challenge Carter. "If it is not one bill," he said, "then your words have very little meaning—especially when phasing is based on forces we have very little control over"—those economic forces. Horowitz argued that labor wanted certainty. Carter refused to promise it. As Ted later put it, "He had made the judgment and the decision that health care was going to be put aside," even after all the work and all the commitments. "He was just backing out of that."* As Ted quoted Carter, "We'll get one bill, and if we meet the economic points test further on down, then we'll submit it so that it can have a second phase and a third phase and a fourth phase." And Ted was to say, "That was the break." The big break between the two of them. Ted told Carter that it would never get through Congress. Years later Ted told biographer Burton Hersh, "My own sense was—after sixteen years in the Senate—that the House and Senate would pass the easiest part of this bill and leave it."

But Ted Kennedy would not walk away empty-handed. He phoned Califano after the meeting and asked him if Califano might announce Carter's principles on healthcare that very afternoon instead of waiting until tomorrow as planned, since Ted was being besieged by the press for comments. Califano countered that the charts weren't ready yet. So Ted said he was going to face the press himself, along with George Meany and Lane Kirkland, and announce his own plan, which had been drafted by his old healthcare aide Stan Jones and former House Ways and Means Committee chairman Wilbur Mills's former aide Bill Fullerton. When Califano told Eizenstat about Ted's threat, the latter snapped, "That bastard." (In the event, Ted forced Califano to call his own hastily arranged press conference that same afternoon to counter him.) Carter recalled it differently. He said that during the meeting Ted had asked for a stay of Califano's presentation the next day so he could study the proposal, and Carter had agreed. "We shook hands and parted in fairly good spirits." And then, Carter said, Ted, who would never have betrayed any of his Senate colleagues, betrayed him. Carter wasn't wrong, though it would be one of the rare times that Ted reneged on a promise. Now that Ted and Carter had broken—the rupture Eizenstat and Onek had warned against—Ted wanted to get out front and shape the story so that it didn't look as if he was the one who had sunk healthcare. The president had "misread the mood of the people," he told the press. Carter had shown a "failure of leadership." He, Ted, had agreed to nearly every provision of Carter's, even those he disliked, save one, that there be no "self-destruct buttons" that could kill a phase of the plan depending on the state of the economy,

*Though it is not entirely certain to which meeting Horowitz was referring, he would later say of Carter, "It was clear he didn't give a shit. That he almost wanted Kennedy as a foil." And he said that Carter's error—a "classic error"—"was doing it in front of organized labor, right there, who had come in shoulder to shoulder." Horowitz int., May 29, 1992, H Folder, Box 3, Series 2, Clymer Papers, JFK Lib.

and that "special interest groups with overflowing war chests" could oppose serially, he told the press. He had his own health plan, he told the
press. But when asked, he said that in spite of his anger, he still expected
to support Carter's renomination in 1980.

As he had had a different version of the break, Carter read the causes
of the break much differently. "It was a tragedy that his unwillingness to
cooperate helped spell the doom of any far-reaching reforms of the healthcare system," he was to write of Ted in his memoir. This was not true. Ted
had compromised—had compromised a great deal, had compromised on
almost every issue, including the role of private insurers, had even agreed
to stages of healthcare over time so long as those stages were not subject
to any revocation. In fact, labor had bristled at the compromises, had leveled criticisms at Ted, but had finally agreed to go along with him, and
Horowitz flew out in February to get Lane Kirkland to sign off on them.
And Carter wrote too that he had "struggled for months" to provide a
comprehensive healthcare bill, but that Ted's opposition to his plan was
"one of the major obstacles," which was half true—Ted did throw up
speed bumps for the plan—and half untrue—Carter had not struggled for
months to enact healthcare, but largely to see that it was postponed. Carter was on firmer ground when he claimed that Ted's bill was expensive
and would be unlikely to pass. But Ted himself had admitted he wasn't
sure he could pass his bill. He simply wanted an opportunity to do so at a
time when he felt that the wind might possibly be at his back, even if it
wasn't gusting. At worst, Ted thought he could turn it into a political
issue for the next election, but only if it was a single, comprehensive bill.
A phase-in, he felt, would never stir the grass roots.

In the end, the rupture was the result less of politics, though some politics was involved—Carter didn't want to give Ted an advantage that Ted
could use to challenge him—than of vastly different and equally sincere
and valid visions of government and of the country. Party Democrats had
misread Carter in 1976 as a Southern liberal because he was enlightened
on race. But Carter was no liberal when it came to government activism,
and once he was elected, he had made no effort to conceal his priorities.
After the July 28 meeting, and even as Califano was finally announcing
the principles on which a healthcare plan would be based, Carter said that
reducing inflation was more important than passing healthcare. (One of
those principles was not to involve additional government spending in
any plan until after 1983.) To Ted Kennedy, that was perfidy. To Carter, it

was both common sense and good political sense. "We looked prudent and careful," he told Califano after the press conference, as opposed to how he felt Ted had looked. And Ted and Carter had different visions of the national mood—Carter believing that the country was increasingly conservative and that it had no real appetite for healthcare; Kennedy believing that the country might have listed right but that it nevertheless desired a healthcare plan, even if only as a way of curbing inflation, since healthcare costs had contributed significantly to rising costs. As columnist David Broder assessed it, their real division was over what each thought the middle class was in favor of: economic stringency or government healthcare, which in many ways mirrored the nation's shifting tectonic plates over whether government activism was still popular or whether the Republicans had convinced the public that the government needed to retrench. There was no simple answer. Broder concluded, "A great political story—with a class act on both sides—is in the making." Finally, the great political story was a difference in temperaments. Ted was impatient now, aggressive, bold, but also willing to make almost any concession, regardless of what Carter said, so long as he didn't concede away the basic purpose of his mission. Carter, as historian Leo Ribuffo analyzed him, was more implacable—divided between his will and his intelligence, and when the two clashed, Ribuffo wrote, the will almost always won, as it had with healthcare. But it was a pyrrhic victory. As one Carter aide told *Los Angeles Times* reporter Jack Nelson after Ted's and Califano's warring press conferences, "It certainly didn't help us politically to fall out with Kennedy and labor over this issue. God knows we need Kennedy and labor."

And now Jimmy Carter, already besieged, didn't have them.

During the congressional recess that summer of 1978, Califano would say, the drive for healthcare reform faded into the vituperation between Ted and Carter, though this might have overstated the case since the issue hardly boiled down to just two men. Carter met with Meany, Fraser, and Ted on August 6—a "heated" meeting, Carter called it—at which, in another wan effort at appeasement, he pledged to work out the principles before the following May, even though, in what was more political déjà vu, Califano had already announced vague principles. But it was hard for the proponents of healthcare to take Carter seriously now, and Carter, for his part, like Califano, thought Ted was "posturing" in front of the labor leaders, though once again, what he would be posturing for—unless, Carter felt, it was for a presidential challenge—was difficult to say. But Ted was not posturing. Ted Kennedy believed more fervently in the need for national health insurance than in any other issue—believed in it not only morally, but now that inflation was soaring, economically too. He spent most of the late summer and fall stumping for his healthcare plan and attacking Carter's amorphous plan, telling the National Medical Association, "The President and his economic advisers and the Secretary of HEW want to launch a ship of national health insurance with a hole beneath the waterline," meaning those trigger provisions. The last week of September, representatives from more than one hundred liberal organizations and from labor unions gathered at Cobo Hall in Detroit, where they were whipped up by Douglas Fraser to promote a healthcare plan and to hold Carter accountable for not presenting a satisfactory one. "We had a big victory in '76," said one UAW official, "and wound up with a pile of shit." A few weeks later Ted kicked off three days of hearings, at which Meany was one of the witnesses, who again struck at Carter. In late November, after the midterm elections—in which Democrats lost only three Senate seats and fifteen House seats, a small victory of sorts for President Carter—Ted took to the road again for hearings in Chicago and Denver (a California swing was postponed due to the murders of San Francisco mayor George Moscone and Board of Supervisors member Harvey Milk) and again flogged his own bill. Through all this, Carter had continued to sell austerity. *Time* ran two pieces that October that cited a public desire for tax cuts. "Taxes, taxes, taxes! Ever since the resounding triumph of California's Proposition 13 last June"—a proposition passed by two-thirds of California voters to reduce their property taxes by 57 percent—"the nation has been shuddering with a kind of tax-cutting fever," the magazine said. And it reported that "poll after poll shows Americans in a mood of irritation and resentment about the money they have to spend on the public needs." (In short, the public was irritated and resentful about having to support the liberal agenda.) This had been Carter's argument too. But Ted was unmoved. He thought Proposition 13 was a "cry against bigness in all forms" and not against big government in particular, and he asserted that if there had been a proposition to cut big business, it too would have passed. Other polls showed that while taxpayers wanted budget cuts in government waste, they actually desired increases in healthcare and education. During his hearings tour, Ted called the national parsimoniousness "transitional" and said the country would return to a more "humane" course. And he declared something that Jimmy Carter certainly would have contested: "I think I am in the mainstream."

IV

And though Jimmy Carter had insisted that his fellow congressional Democrats were just as opposed to a national health plan as he was—Eizenstat had written a memo to him to that effect, citing the "anti-inflation, anti-regulation mood of the country"—Ted Kennedy was right about being in the mainstream, at least the Democratic mainstream, and about being much closer to the old generous New Deal spirit of the party than Carter. Indeed, Carter, who had largely eschewed Congress, left the party rudderless. During the Roosevelt administration, the number of votes in which a majority of Democrats opposed a majority of Republicans was just under 60 percent. During Carter's administration, it was under 40 percent. All along, Ted felt that Carter had kept backsliding from the promises he had made, first as a candidate and then as a president. All along, Ted had clashed with Carter without looking for a breach until the clash over a healthcare plan created one. And yet Ted insisted that he had no desire to challenge Carter for the nomination, even as Carter seemed increasingly willing to goad Ted into doing so. Carter suspected that every time his own popularity declined, Ted's presidential ambitions rose.

Despite the break over healthcare in July 1978, Ted said that it wasn't until the fall, when someone in the administration leaked him the upcoming budget and Ted saw that Carter intended to "starve" some of Ted's pet programs, that those ambitions were relit. As one of the reforms passed by liberals at the 1976 Democratic convention to allow Democrats a forum at which to challenge a Democratic president if need be—they were clearly thinking of Carter—the party had scheduled a midterm "mini-convention" in Memphis, where 1,633 delegates were to meet to discuss the direction of the party. Ted hadn't thought of that convention as a launching pad for any presidential bid—or so he said—and Ted's brother-in-law, Steve Smith, told Arthur Schlesinger, Jr., that there was no premeditation whatsoever to rally support there. But then, Smith said, John Culver, Ted's old Harvard friend and now Iowa senator, visited Ted one night, and the two began railing against Carter's slashing of social programs while beefing up the military budget, "thereby placing," as Smith said Ted put it, "the burden of a fiscal attack against inflation on those least able to bear it." It was then that both Ted and Culver decided to use Memphis as a platform to protest Carter's priorities. "You will hear a lot from Kennedy every time he thinks Carter has gone too far," an aide told *Newsweek.* Now Ted Kennedy thought Carter had gone too far.

Ted headed to Memphis that first week of December bristling with indignation. His speech, to be delivered at a session on healthcare, had been written by Max Fine, the healthcare specialist, at Larry Horowitz's request, and then was edited by Horowitz. Neither man was disinclined to use fire and brimstone. And neither was Ted. "He wanted to stir the pot" was how Horowitz put it. It was, Horowitz said, to be a "big speech," but not a "watershed speech"—a speech in which Ted could prod Carter, but not one in which he would give credence to the idea that he would consider running against Carter. Carter, who had spoken the night before, had drawn what *Newsweek* called a "lukewarm" response. "He creates no great enthusiasm and he creates no great hostility," Senator Paul Simon observed. "This is the orneriest audience," Robert Strauss, Carter's U.S. trade representative and a longtime Democratic operative, said of those passive delegates. After two years of inflation and austerity, Carter was no longer the party's hero, and at two workshops he attended in Memphis, workshops that captured the growing mood of liberal discontent, he was bombarded by questions about cuts to social programs—the cuts about which Ted had both fretted and boiled—and increases in the military budget. Said one Northern state chairman: If Carter had been born anywhere but in Georgia, he would have been a Republican. The next morning, when Ted took to the dais after a droning recitation by Califano on the administration's plans to deliver a healthcare bill next year, and another by Eizenstat, who reiterated that the administration could not move too quickly or too improvidently on healthcare, Ted was in fighting form. And though he didn't mention Carter by name, there was no doubt whom he was fighting. After citing how Vietnam had torn apart the party, he said, "There could be few more divisive issues for America and for our party than a Democratic policy of drastic slashes in the Federal budget at the expense of the elderly, the poor, the black, the sick, the cities and the unemployed." And he said, "We cannot accept a policy that cuts spending to the bone in areas like jobs and health but allows billions of dollars in wasteful spending for tax subsidies . . . and defense." And he declared that it was time to enact a healthcare plan that "would make health care a right for all our people now." *A right.* But it wasn't all stirring the pot. At one point Ted softened, lowered his voice, and with his half-rim glasses at the edge of his nose, began extemporizing about his family's own health crises, telling the crowd, "There probably has not been a family in this country that has been touched by sickness, illness and disease like my own family," and mentioned his sister Rosemary's mental disability, and his father's stroke, and Ted Jr.'s cancer treatment, and his own months in the hospital with his broken back—health issues, he said, that "would have bankrupted any average family in this nation." And he asked: "What about others who cannot afford such care?"

He reserved his severest criticism for the idea—Carter's idea—that the Democratic Party had to retrench, that it could no longer be the party of the dispossessed, the party of moral authority. And even if the country was drifting rightward, as Carter and others believed, he called for resistance. "Sometimes a party must sail against the wind," he said, a line that he had added to the speech shortly before delivering it. "We cannot afford to drift or lie at anchor. We cannot heed the call of those who say it is time to furl the sail." And he said this: that he would continue to speak out "as long as I have a voice in the U.S. Senate." Then he concluded by shouting: "The Democratic Party must choose!" And as he did, the crowd rose as one in a thunderous endorsement, so energized that Horowitz said even Ted was "startled" by the reception.

It was a loud speech, delivered at the top of his lungs, save for that family passage, and without a microphone, a "stem-winding speech," *The New York Times* called it, a speech in which he flailed his arms and pounded the lectern, a speech as unruly as his long hair, hair he had let grow because he was no longer a presidential hopeful, at times an almost stream-of-consciousness speech in which he "winged it quite a bit," as Horowitz put it—at one point he flipped a chart in the air that purported to show that healthcare was too expensive, then smiled broadly, and the crowd roared—and a speech in which he followed his heart. It was a speech that galvanized the previously somnambulant crowd of 2,500 that had packed the session and cheered Ted, even rewarding him with two ovations, in contrast with Carter's polite reception, many in the crowd wearing blue and white Kennedy buttons that had, reported *The Washington Post*, "mysteriously appeared." "Where the President had won respectful applause," Hedrick Smith wrote in *The New York Times*, "the Senator enjoyed rousing cheers." Max Fine said he could feel the "surge" as Ted gave the speech. "He had that audience in the palm of his hands." An "electric effect" was how Smith described Ted's appearance. "The stage literally trembled," said Califano, who watched abjectly and in awe. Perhaps the country had taken a right turn. Perhaps inflation had become the nation's preoccupation, as Carter believed, and fiscal responsibility was the answer, as Carter believed. But Ted Kennedy had touched the moral nerves of the Democratic faithful in that auditorium in Memphis, while Jimmy Carter had aimed for their fiscal ones. "God, in His infinite wisdom, did not design the Democratic party as His instrument for budget-cutting and inflation-fighting," David Broder wrote in his postmortem, pointing to the Democratic tradition of social activism and saying that it is a "tradition that Kennedy—and only Kennedy—now invokes." And he wrote that when Ted finished with his declaration that the "Democratic party must choose," the hall was filled with "more passion and personal commitment" than "Carter or Mondale can generate in a month with their historically correct analysis of what the times require." Historically correct, thought Broder. But it did not touch the hearts of those Democrats.

None of this was lost on Carter's men. Ted had scarcely finished speaking when Hamilton Jordan, who was in the hall, turned to Carter's pollster, Pat Caddell, and said, "The son of a bitch is going to run against us." Caddell didn't disagree, but thought they should try to make peace with Ted, and he was not alone. Before Ted's speech, Carter's representatives had insisted that they would make no concessions to the liberals on resolutions that called for no budget cuts in social programs and a firm timetable for when a healthcare plan might be implemented, and they said they expected a floor fight. An hour after the speech, they reversed themselves and agreed to a resolution that called for a healthcare plan within two years. Carter eventually beat back the other resolution—the resolution about the budget. But 40 percent of the delegates voted against their president on that plank, and Carter's aides left Memphis "relieved to have contrived some compromises on social issues and to have salvaged a respectable though hardly ringing victory for his tight-budget strategy," as the Times's Smith put it. There was no doubt, however, that Ted Kennedy had been the star of the convention—the heart of the convention, the one who stirred the passions of the convention. "If Kennedy would run, I'd vote for him tomorrow," a Carter supporter gushed.

Carter tried to put the best face on what, despite the vote on the budget, was a repudiation. He insisted at a press conference later that week that his differences with Ted were "very minor." Ted disagreed. He told The New

York Times's Adam Clymer that the economic difficulties the country was enduring were "basic and fundamental in determining the political structure of our society." Carter insisted at the same press conference that he was dedicated to reducing the budget deficit to less than $30 billion in 1980, and an aide said that the "public mood is behind the President's budget-cutting, not the liberals' spending proposals." Ted felt the cuts Carter would have to enact to achieve that goal would harm Ted's people. Still, Carter dispatched Eizenstat to meet with Ted at McLean to smooth over disagreements, and then he had the OMB director, James McIntyre, Jr., meet with Ted toward the same end, while Caddell, on his own initiative, met with Kennedy advisers Paul Kirk and David Burke, who told Caddell, "This is not a war. Why are you guys saying it's war?" But for Jimmy Carter, it was war. At a Cabinet meeting on December 11, after the Democratic National Committee chairman, John White, pronounced himself happy with the Memphis convention, Vice President Mondale countered that he was unhappy and that the administration would have to reach some accommodation to win over the liberals. Carter dismissed the warning, and the meeting ended with Carter telling Califano that this was only the beginning. He would later say of Ted's address in Memphis that it was "throwing down the gauntlet." And this time Jimmy Carter was right.

FOUR

Sniffing the Wind

LESS THAN TWO years into Jimmy Carter's term, Ted Kennedy, the man who had so often vacillated about running for the presidency and who had squandered several chances to do so, now had another decision to make: Should he run in 1980? The national goodwill toward Jimmy Carter had evaporated rapidly as the economy stubbornly refused to recover completely from the recent recession, and inflation continued to rise steadily. Polls earlier that spring of 1978 had shown Democrats preferring Ted to Carter overwhelmingly. Another Gallup poll in May, while showing Carter defeating likely Republican opponents Gerald Ford and Ronald Reagan—only a four-point lead over the latter—showed Ted with huge leads—ten points over Ford and twenty over Reagan. Another poll, in California that September, showed Carter running twenty-three points behind Ted in that state, and even after Carter had held a summit at the presidential retreat, Camp David, between Egyptian president Anwar Sadat and Israeli premier Menachem Begin, a summit that ultimately resulted in a peace treaty between the countries—Carter's signal foreign policy triumph—Ted still led him by double digits. Moreover, while Democrats were spared the large losses one might have imagined in a midterm election with an increasingly unpopular president, the ranks of Senate liberals were depleted, making Ted Kennedy's task of sustaining liberalism in the face of conservative headwinds all the more difficult. Dick Clark in Iowa, Thomas McIntyre in New Hampshire, and William Hathaway in Maine all lost their seats that fall, while James Abourezk decided not to seek reelection in South Dakota. But the biggest blows had already occurred with the deaths of Senate giants Philip Hart, Ted's model senator, in December 1976, and Hubert Humphrey in January 1978, both of cancer. If one needed a sign of liberalism's decline, it could be found in the fact that both Humphrey's and Vice President Mondale's vacated seats— seats in the liberal state of Minnesota—were won by Republicans. "Being a liberal today is like having a disease," one Democratic official told *Time*. The political arm of the AFL-CIO, the Committee on Political Education (COPE), opined in a memo that a "lot of Democrats seem to have gone squeamish," though it went on to say that the "attitude is not so much reflected in the real and justified concern about getting your money's worth out of government," which had become an increasingly loud and politically effective grievance among Republicans. "It's more a bending to the demagogues of the right and the pressures of the business community." And COPE predicted a "long and tough two years coming up in the ninety-sixth Congress"—the two years before Jimmy Carter's reelection campaign.

But Ted Kennedy, despite the blows, was not squeamish, as his speech at Memphis demonstrated. Instead, he redoubled his efforts. He had spent the first two years of Jimmy Carter's presidency acquiring power, becoming a master of the Senate, for the very purpose of stemming the conservative tide to which so many of his fellow Democrats, including his Democratic president, had been succumbing, and if anything, he had been further empowered as his fellow liberals departed the chamber— further empowered and emboldened by the vacuum that had been created by their departures. Once the Senate's preeminent liberal, he had become one of liberalism's only full-throated voices. After Hart's death, Ted assumed the chairmanship of his Antitrust and Monopoly Subcommittee when Ted's friend Birch Bayh, who had wanted the post, accepted the Constitution Subcommittee instead. Now Ted finally left AdPrac, his small all-purpose subcommittee that had provided him with the purview to investigate everything from the draft to the marketing practices of pharmaceutical companies to natural gas deregulation to the Watergate break-in. Though AdPrac's hearings had attracted attention in the media and given Ted a legislative stage, Antitrust, the largest of the Judiciary subcommittees, was a much higher-profile committee than AdPrac, a much more significant committee when it came to legislation, notwithstanding that Hart, for much of his tenure as chairman, had been circumscribed by its powerful conservative members: Everett Dirksen, John McClellan, and Sam Ervin. Ted would not be similarly circumscribed. Upon taking the chairmanship, he almost immediately announced that he would be looking into antitrust laws that permitted large corporations to take over companies whose business had nothing whatsoever to do with the business of those corporations but whose acquisition would constitute control over a large segment of the economy generally. And then, putting action behind his words, he introduced a bill that prohibited large oil companies from merging with any business—not just energy companies—whose assets exceeded $100 million.

Power to move the Senate—that had been Ted Kennedy's ambition when he surrendered his presidential ambitions. In all his years in the Senate—and he had been there fourteen years at the outset of Carter's presidency—Ted, like most junior senators, had been biding his time, hunting for ways to augment his power, keeping one hundred balls in the air, as Carey Parker had said of Ted, to maintain a broad portfolio that would allow him to investigate nearly everything. He did have advantages. As a Kennedy, he had gained influence because of his presidential prospects and the attention he attracted—extrainstitutional power, soft power. But even after the democratizing Senate reforms of the early and mid-1970s—reforms that Ted had been instrumental in pushing and that he had used to weaken the muscle of seniority—it was still the chairmen of the major committees who continued to exercise the real power—the power to spend money and hire staff; the power to hold hearings and sparkle in the media; the power to challenge the president; above all, the power to draft and then move legislation or stop it. Lyndon Johnson seized power by joining the Democratic Senate leadership and transforming that leadership from one that served the caucus to one that often controlled the caucus. Ted Kennedy had already been in the Democratic leadership, as whip, and had lost the position—lost it largely because he was indifferent to it, and because Robert Byrd, who beat him, enjoyed it, even seemed to enjoy the tedium of it. Even without a leadership position, though, Ted had gained status in the Senate, had used his personal charm and his experience to become a master of the Senate, but he had one deficit: He had no vehicle with which to work the levers of legislative power as Johnson had. That vehicle would have been the Judiciary Committee, on which Ted had sat since he entered the Senate, but he was blocked from taking the chairmanship by a formidable, insurmountable obstacle: James Eastland, one of the last of the Senate bulls, who had held that chairmanship for nearly twenty-three years. As the 1978 midterms approached, however, Eastland had seen the handwriting on the wall. He knew that Southern Democrats were threatened by Southern Republicans, whose national party was dedicated to slowing racial progress rather than advancing it, and though Eastland attempted to enlist Ted in helping him make inroads with Black voters to compensate for the white drift to the Republicans—hence Ted's commencement speech at the University of Mississippi—Eastland, at seventy-three, had finally decided not to stand for reelection. Thad Cochran, a Republican, won Eastland's seat in the 1978 midterms, and Eastland resigned in December before his term ended, as Ben Smith had done for Ted when Ted was first elected, to give his successor seniority over other incoming freshmen. And with that resignation, and with Ted's lobbying with the ranking Republican on Judiciary, Strom Thurmond, Ted Kennedy had won his chairmanship—the chairmanship of one of the Senate's most important committees.

Now he had his lever—institutional clout, hard power, to go along with his social clout, his soft power. And Ted Kennedy was prepared to use that power.

That clout, considerable clout, changed a great deal about how Ted Kennedy would function within the Senate, even as Ted changed a great deal about how the Judiciary Committee would function in the Senate. Judiciary was the largest of the Senate committees, the committee with the most extensive jurisdiction, the committee to which one-fifth of all measures were referred, and the committee that dealt with some of the most critical issues, from constitutional matters to civil rights to passing on candidates to the federal judiciary. That alone would have empowered Ted. But Ted was not relying on that alone. Eastland, an unregenerate racist, had maintained his control as the Democratic Party and the Senate shifted leftward by delegating power and money to the subcommittee chairmen. This was how he had pacified Ted and the other liberals on the committee—by trading perks for less vocal opposition. Ted intended to operate the committee differently—Johnson-like. "It's ironic," one of Ted's aides told a reporter when Ted took over the reins at Judiciary. "Eastland, the great conservative from Mississippi, was a real democrat in running the committee. Kennedy, the great liberal from Massachusetts, is going to be a real tyrant." Ted readily admitted that he was going to be a "taskmaster." Now that he had at last gotten his chance, he wanted full control of the committee. Part of that control would come from the members of the committee. Ted didn't want conservatives on it. By one account, he tried to persuade Republican moderates to petition their caucus to be placed on Judiciary but had little success. He was more successful with his own caucus. He interviewed fellow Democrats, "carefully sounding them out," according to one account, until he settled on his close friend John Culver, Patrick Leahy of Vermont, Max Baucus of Montana, and Howell Heflin, a moderate from Alabama. (The last three replaced three departing Southern conservatives.) And having selected the new members, part of that control would come from reconfiguring the committee, even braving the wrath of freshmen senators who sought subcommittee chairmanships, by, in another Johnson-like move, trimming the number of subcommittees from ten to seven—he had originally tried to trim it to four—as yet another way of shifting power from the subcommittee chairmen to the committee chairman—*him*—and a way of making certain that his favorite bills, as one reporter put it, "were not left to atrophy." And then he named two allies, Culver and Howard Metzenbaum of Ohio, to chair AdPrac and Antitrust respectively, two of Ted's old subcommittees. (Ted's own Immigration and Refugee Subcommittee was one of those subsumed by the whole committee.) And part of that control was Ted changing the rules of the committee—rules that Eastland had enforced as a way of reducing liberal power but that Ted would now rescind to increase that power. Ted would let senators vote by proxy and let a majority of the committee cut off debate—Eastland had used prolonged debates to stall civil rights legislation—and he would change the longtime tradition of permitting a senator from a state to blackball the appointment of a federal judge from that state by submitting what was known as a "blue card," and he would hire investigators to examine prospective judicial nominees rather than rely on the FBI and the American Bar Association for vetting. (He and ranking minority member Thurmond formed a two-man committee to work out these issues.) And part of that control—a large part—was reapportioning the committee's budget. Eastland had discretionary power over $1 million of the committee's $5 million budget, and he had used it to buy off other members by financing their pet projects, as he had often done with Ted in the Refugee Subcommittee and AdPrac. In Ted's reapportionment, he was personally to control $3 million. Together with the $400,000 he was appropriated as head of the Health and Scientific Subcommittee of the Human Resources Committee, and the influence he had as chairman of the Office of Technology Assessment over the $11 million staff budget, and his own staff budget of $650,000, Ted now had a financial war chest larger than Eastland's, in all likelihood larger than any other senator's, and he could use it to promote his agenda.

And Ted Kennedy was not shy about seizing his moment, however uncharacteristic it might have seemed coming from Ted, who had so patiently waited his turn, despite his inherent impatience when it came to legislation. Colleagues knew that Ted Kennedy had an ego and ambition, but his sudden aggressiveness—this from a senator who had been unusually deferential, collegial, and cordial—surprised many of them and made some of them furious with him; few senators heretofore had ever been furious with Ted Kennedy. When he unilaterally transferred jurisdiction on antitrust and criminal law from those subcommittees to the full committee, the subcommittee chairmen boiled, and Birch Bayh, a good friend of Ted's, was so livid when Ted proposed moving his Constitution Subcommittee to a smaller office that, by one report, Bayh had a staffer measure the square footage of the new office and then argued that Ted had more square footage per staff member than Bayh had. Ted forced him to move anyway. When Ted's Judiciary staff refused to cooperate with Joe Biden, a committee member, on an amendment to the Law Enforcement Assistance Administration, which provided funds to local police departments, Biden, in an attempt to circumvent his own chairman, went to the Budget Committee and asked for a $100 million limit just to get Ted to listen. And when Ted announced that Judiciary would be tackling trucking deregulation, he enraged Howard Cannon, the chairman of the Commerce Committee, who felt his committee should have jurisdiction. "Eyebrows raise, pulses quicken, adrenaline and a suppressed anger surge," wrote syndicated columnist, Nick Thimmesch, of Ted's new aggression. "Is it a bird? Is it a plane? No, it's EMK, the senator with that name. Since when did anyone in this clan ever shrink from political power?" But Ted had always shrunk from *flaunting* political power in a way his brothers hadn't, and one might have presumed that he had actually been seething all that time while his path to power was blocked. But Carey Parker, his alter ego, saw it through another lens. He thought Ted had not seized the moment, as Lyndon Johnson had, to feed his ego or his political prospects. Ted Kennedy didn't need to do that. He had seized the moment to *move the Senate* at a time when it needed moving. And he said of Ted, "He didn't want to be just a go-along senator."

• • •

In inheriting the Judiciary Committee from Eastland, Ted also inherited staff, though he was quick to say that he expected most of Eastland's staff "to be looking for employment." At AdPrac, Ted had had a staff of only three—albeit three who produced results out of all proportion to their numbers. At Judiciary, he had a staff of sixty, with another sixty working with the minority, and another sixty with the subcommittee chairmen and other majority members. (Under Eastland, the committee used to be called the Plantation, it had so many staffers.) As he had with his own personal staff, Ted wanted a great staff, an aggressive staff, a staff, he said, that would feel comfortable airing its opinions. In 1974 he had recruited Harvard Law professor Stephen Breyer to be his chief counsel on the Ad-Prac subcommittee. In the summer of 1978 Breyer had returned to Harvard and was teaching in Salzburg, Austria, when Ted called to tell him that he would be taking the Judiciary chair and he wanted Breyer to return to Washington to be that committee's chief counsel. Breyer hesitated. He had other obligations, but it was too tempting an offer to refuse. So Breyer came aboard after the Harvard term ended, and he came with an agenda. Both Ted and he wanted the committee to be proactive—so proactive that, as Breyer put it, "when people ask, 'What is it that Senator Kennedy is doing with the Judiciary Committee?' we answer, 'In the Constitution Subcommittee, we have a fair housing proposal. In the Antitrust Subcommittee, we have a trucking deregulation proposal. In the Criminal Law Subcommittee, we have FBI reform, and we have the criminal code. In the Judicial Practices Subcommittee, we have several projects including reform of the judicial ethics law, so there's a system that citizens can complain about judges; the creation of the Federal Circuit; the Court of Appeals for the Federal Circuit will be the place where the patent law is decided.'" And then, Breyer said, the mission wouldn't be just to propose issues but to guide the committee to send bills to the floor and bring them to a vote—"something that is significant." *To move the Senate.* And to that end, at Ted's behest, Breyer would meet over breakfast each morning at eight o'clock with the minority counsel, Retired General Emory Sneeden, Thurmond's man, and the two would collaborate on the daily committee's agenda. "No secrets," Breyer said. And they would try to focus on issues on which the Democrats and Republicans could agree, issues on which disputes could be minimized. "That's what the chairman wanted," Breyer said. "He liked it when people would agree about things."

It was an "awfully full legislative platter," as one reporter put it: trucking deregulation, the revision of the federal criminal code, a revision of the Law Enforcement Assistance Administration, the expanded jurisdiction of federal courts, the new and more expansive antitrust laws, a new FBI charter, and a bill about illegal aliens, as well what one reporter called a "flood" of judicial nominations—45 percent of the federal bench was being appointed. The last of these had always posed a threat to Senate comity—the comity about which Ted cared so deeply and upon which he had so often relied to gain allies. But maintaining that comity had sometimes come at the expense of judicial excellence. Eastland had avoided controversy and contention by honoring the "blue cards" that denied any judicial nominee a hearing unless that nominee had the support of both senators from his state, even if one were a Republican and the other a Democrat. So cozy was the system that for forty-two years, no nominee to the federal district court had been rejected by the Senate. But Ted Kennedy was especially sensitive to the quality of the judiciary since his embarrassment over the nomination of Francis X. Morrissey, for whom he had advocated at the behest of his father, a Morrissey friend, but who was clearly not qualified for the federal bench and who was forced to withdraw from consideration. And Ted Kennedy was not necessarily pleased either by the politicization of the process or by the lack of scrutiny of the nominees. And now that he was the Judiciary chair, the person responsible for overseeing the vetting of those nominations, he acted upon that displeasure. He not only removed the veto power from each state's senator, which he had done when he eliminated the "blue card" blackball, he also insisted on holding a hearing for each nominee, whether that nominee was ultimately reported out to the floor or not. And to ensure fairness and to professionalize the approval of judges, Ted also insisted that each nominee be investigated by both a Democrat and a Republican on the staff.

Almost immediately, however, the new process provoked an eruption over the record of one nominee, Charles Winberry, Jr., who had the support both of President Carter and of Winberry's senator, Tom Morgan of North Carolina, for whom Winberry had been campaign manager in Morgan's last Senate run. Ted's staff had found what they called "stains" on Winberry's record—ethical stains. Morgan, following the old rules—Eastland's rules—demanded that the committee override the objections and approve Winberry anyway. To mollify Morgan, Ted countered that the ABA, which had initially endorsed Winberry, would be given the staff's report and be allowed to render a revised judgment. But Morgan was not mollified. So Ted asked Republican Orrin Hatch and Democrat Patrick Leahy to conduct a new investigation and write a new committee report. (Later, Ted had Breyer circle Winberry's "stains" in the report to show Morgan why Winberry was unfit.) Comity yielded, and in the end, Winberry became the first nominee to be rejected in those forty-two years. The *Christian Science Monitor* dubbed it the "day they threw the rubber stamp away," though it might also have been named the day Ted Kennedy took command of the nominating process, now that he was a master of the Senate.

And now that he finally had some hard power, a committee chairman's power, Ted Kennedy did not tread lightly. His Judiciary Committee was a rejuvenated committee, a reimagined committee, a committee with a newly expanded agenda, a committee dedicated to the professionalism on which Ted had always insisted—a committee designed to move the Senate. It was a very different committee from the one he had inherited. For the twenty-two years of Eastland's reign, it had been, despite its jurisdiction, a relatively quiescent committee, erupting only when its liberals and conservatives butted heads on civil rights. Otherwise, Eastland had mostly gotten his way by placating his left-wing opponents with those subcommittee assignments and budgets. But Ted Kennedy, who was centralizing authority and consolidating power, didn't want to buy peace or need to. He took a different approach—an approach based on his understanding of the chemistry of the Senate yoked to the underlying hard power of the chairmanship. Breyer recalled a time, as the 1980 presidential election grew nearer, that Strom Thurmond had ordered Emory Sneeden, the aide with whom Breyer had been meeting every morning for nearly two years, not to cooperate with Breyer any longer, apparently so that the Democrats couldn't gain any electoral advantage and so that a possible new Republican president could make the judicial appointments rather than Jimmy Carter. Sneeden apologized to Breyer but told him that he, Sneeden, was powerless to countermand the order. This was politics. But it was not Ted Kennedy's politics, and he was not about to sacrifice those judgeships. Sneeden had broken this news to Breyer just before Ted was to arrive for an executive session of the committee at which four judicial nominations were to be discussed. Once the cooperation was shattered, Breyer anticipated the worst, and he was right. "It was total chaos," with committee members vehemently arguing over the nominations. John Culver even shook his fist at Thurmond. Breyer said that Ted looked at him and quipped, "What did they teach you about how to deal with this at Harvard?" Breyer admitted that they hadn't taught him very much. So Ted, working off the chemistry of the Senate and armed with his new hard power, said he would show Breyer what to do. And then Ted, taking command, said, "Birch," speaking to Birch Bayh, "you're going to head the first subcommittee, and that'll consider these two judges. And Strom, you're on the subcommittee with Birch." And he continued, "Orrin," speaking to Republican Orrin Hatch of Utah, "you're on this subcommittee over here with the other two, and we'll appoint somebody else to be on that subcommittee," presumably a Democrat. What Ted had done, Breyer recalled, was suddenly decentralize the decision making on these nominations, knowing full well that the subcommittees he had appointed would most likely never meet because Thurmond would realize that it would be much easier ultimately to just get all the staffs together and work it out the way Breyer and Sneeden had previously done rather than to argue over the appointments. In effect, Ted had demonstrated that he wasn't going to let overt politics derail nominations.*

And he had shown the committee something else: that the days of James Eastland were over and that days of consensus had arrived. But it was a strange consensus—a consensus arrived at under the hard power and the iron command of the committee's new chairman: Ted Kennedy.

II

Now as the chair of the Judiciary Committee, Ted Kennedy had ascended into the uppermost ranks of the Senate, ranks from which he once again saw himself as the opposition, as he had been during the presidency of Richard Nixon, when the primary source of his power was his prospective presidential run. This time, however, there was a difference to the opposition—a big difference. This time he was opposing the president of his own party and that president's budgetary tightfistedness. The "unquestioned leader of the liberal bloc," *Time* called Ted, and said, "He has

---

* A time was to come, however, when, during a Supreme Court nomination battle, Ted would be accused of politicizing judicial appointments in a way that would change them for decades.

not appeared to give an inch to the conservative tide. With evocative, emotional, near-demagogic oratory"—*Time* was no doubt thinking of Memphis—"that lifts supporters to their feet cheering lustily, he has positioned himself to the left of Carter in case he chooses to run for the presidency." But as much as the Democrats were inclined toward Ted's liberalism, there were doubts in the ranks—serious doubts—that Ted Kennedy's ardent liberalism would help the Democratic cause. In the same article, *Time* quoted one senator, a "prominent Democrat," who claimed that Ted's advocacy for the dispossessed and his legislative efforts to help them were at cross purposes, and that the former could undermine the latter; he seemed to be speaking about the general notion that Americans seemed more interested in lower taxes than in lower poverty rates and that Ted's liberal measures would only incite voters to turn even more vigorously against liberalism and the disempowered it served. That prominent Democratic senator said that Ted was unlikely to get more than twenty-five votes on any of his legislative initiatives, and that while, on his charisma alone, he was able to attract public attention for his bills, he could not get them passed—a criticism that took dead aim at Ted's new hard power and at a source of Ted's pride: that he was an effective legislator. Another senator told *The New Yorker*'s Elizabeth Drew that many of his fellow senators were "not sure they want a guy who comes on as strong as Ted does. They worry about what happened with the rising of the decibels. Politicians used to like excitement; now most of them are gray, want to play it safe." And he said they were afraid of the "mouthy people," the gun lobby and the anti-abortionists and other special interest groups, who would be united against Ted—that countervailing wind growing ever stronger. "There is a feeling Ted would arouse the dogs in the campaign."

In short, they saw Ted Kennedy, the man who had not so long ago excited the party faithful, the man who not so long ago was the very face of the party, as an anachronism—a moral voice at a time of increasing moral deafness.

But this was only partly true—another sign of Democratic fear of reactionary populism. While some Democrats were certainly wary of him, it was hardly true that Ted would get only twenty-five votes for his legislation—the Senate's liberal bloc was considerably larger than that, even after the 1978 midterms—but even if it had been true, Ted was staking a marker by promoting his liberal agenda. And that marker might have had less to do with legislation, though Ted was always more interested in gaining passage of his bills, in moving the Senate—than with setting the nation's agenda—or in resetting Carter's. With the wind blowing against him, Ted felt he had to stoke liberalism lest it die. And some Democrats were wary about that—wary that the country had turned so far right that Ted Kennedy, for all his charisma, might even be as much a liability as Carter. On the other hand, other Democrats, seemingly more Democrats, were even more concerned about the electoral prospects of Jimmy Carter, whose difficulties with the economy—both high inflation and halting economic growth, a toxic combination that had been labeled "stagflation"—beclouded his presidency. And with those difficulties of Carter's, a seeming conservative who would never be as conservative as the Republicans, the prospect of Ted Kennedy as a candidate was beginning to percolate again. With Carter, the party seemed rudderless. With Ted at the helm, it had a direction, even if, as those nervous Democrats fretted, it might be the wrong one for the times.

Ted had publicly forsworn running against Carter. He had said repeatedly that, for all their differences, he fully expected to support Carter's renomination. Yet again gun-shy about a presidential run, he made no comments whatsoever privately about challenging Carter either. But whether he was girding for a run or not, Ted had no compunction about attacking what he saw as the administration's illiberalism, especially after the midterm elections and especially after becoming the Judiciary chair. In January 1979 Ted had gone to the Ebenezer Baptist Church in Atlanta, Martin Luther King, Jr.'s, old church, on the fiftieth anniversary of Dr. King's birth, and delivered a stirring call to arms, *Newsweek* wrote, in "cadences that summoned up the hopes of the '60s and the dreams of the Reverend Martin Luther King": "Now is the time to redeem the promise of the Humphrey-Hawkins Act," which called for full employment. And the congregation shouted, "Amen." "Now is the time to move forward with comprehensive national health insurance," Ted said. And, according to *Newsweek*, the congregation cheered. "Now is the time to move forward toward . . . all the other unfinished business of our society." And to that, Daddy King, Martin's father, yelled, "Preach." And when reporters afterward asked if this meant Ted was going to challenge Carter, he smiled and said, "No," which prompted *Newsweek* to ask, "Just what is Teddy up to?"

It was a good question, but not one for which he had an answer. He baited Carter. He felt that Carter, as one Kennedy aide put it, would "throw out an idea and then back away from it." And he had always thought that

Carter never was tenacious enough in fighting for Democratic principles. When Carter submitted a new windfall profits tax to recoup the money oil companies were likely to reap after Carter lifted price controls (he had done so unilaterally, over the objections of Congress and of Ted Kennedy), Ted said that Carter had knuckled under to Big Oil and then tried to hide his surrender under the "transparent fig leaf" of the tax. Carter's press secretary Jody Powell rushed into Carter's study to relay Ted's remarks while Carter was preparing for a press conference. Carter snapped, "That is a lot of baloney," a riposte he then repeated to reporters. That outburst heartened his inner circle. "Jimmy's had a bellyful of Ted Kennedy," one of them said. But after attending a Law Day ceremony at the White House, Ted got the last laugh, repeating his attack on the windfall profits tax and telling reporters on the lawn that the president must have been "confused" when he called it "baloney." "I wasn't talking about food prices. I was talking about oil prices."

And while Ted Kennedy in his frustration with Carter baited and goaded him, Carter responded with pettiness, trying to "sequester" Ted, as political columnist Joseph Kraft put it, with silly indignities like refusing to invite Ted to a state dinner honoring Chinese leader Deng Xiaoping, whom Ted had met in China—refusing until Secretary of State Cyrus Vance got the president to relent at the last minute. Normally "gracious," Kraft wrote, Carter turned "rivalrous and vulgar" when it came to Ted. Carter scotched a research center for child health and development that Califano had promoted—scotched it even though Congress had appropriated the money—because, Califano said, it was a pet project of Sargent Shriver and Eunice Kennedy Shriver. And in May, Ted and Carter skirmished bitterly over the possible appointment of Archibald Cox, the longtime Kennedy friend and Watergate prosecutor, to the First Circuit Court of Appeals. Cox had been ranked first among five candidates for the vacancy by a commission that was appointed by the president and designed to depoliticize the nomination process in conjunction with Ted's efforts as Judiciary chair to do so. But Cox was sixty-six, older than the recommended sixty-four-year age limit, and would need a special presidential dispensation. Attorney General Griffin Bell told Ted that Carter would not give that dispensation. Ted was furious and importuned Griffin, but Griffin told him, "The President isn't going to do it." So Ted went to the White House for what he thought would be a fifteen-minute conversation in which to plead Cox's case. Instead, Carter expatiated widely on his presidency for over an hour before finally coming to Cox. Though Carter would later claim that Cox was disqualified solely by age, Carter, Ted said, gave him a different reason: Cox, he said, had supported Ed Muskie in the New Hampshire primary instead of Carter. (Actually, Cox had supported Morris Udall.) And Carter, as Ted recalled it years later, concluded, "I'm just not going to do it. And I'm not going to support national health insurance. I know that's the thing you care most about. I'm just not going to do it." (Though this was Ted's recollection, for Carter to be this frank doesn't seem entirely credible.)

And now, two years into Carter's presidency, Ted Kennedy, incensed over the direction of the administration and over the pettiness of Jimmy Carter, did finally begin to consider the possibility of running against him, though he was still only considering it and was not sure, as when he had considered the presidency so often in the past, that he really wanted it.

And as he did so, others, especially the party's liberals, finally exasperated with Carter's liberal rebuffs and his fiscal conservatism and, more, much more, by the worsening economy and, perhaps most of all, by Carter's ever-falling approval rating—28 percent in June 1979—were making noises about Ted Kennedy as a possible rival to the president. As early as 1978, when the healthcare negotiations collapsed, Doug Fraser on at least two occasions, according to Larry Horowitz, who was present, urged Ted to challenge Carter, to unseat him, saying that Carter couldn't win, that he was a "disaster." And Fraser, disgusted by Carter, launched the Progressive Alliance, an umbrella group that he hoped would convince other advocacy groups and labor unions to join forces to fight the New Right by way of usurping Carter. By the spring of 1979, when Ted and Carter were having their tiffs over the windfall profits tax and the Cox nomination, the *Los Angeles Times* was reporting on a "Kennedy fever," albeit still low-grade, in the Democratic Party: draft movements from Florida to Iowa, a pro-Kennedy resolution from the Cuyahoga County Democrats in Ohio, local union agitation, and perhaps most telling of all, five Democratic congressmen publicly calling for a nominee other than Carter (and presumably meaning Kennedy) and announcing the formation of a Coalition of Democratic Alternatives. Democratic National Committee chairman John White excoriated the congressmen for driving a "wedge into party ranks," but one of them, Richard Ottinger of New York, was unbowed. "To those who say Senator Kennedy will not run, we say let us develop a national mandate for his candidacy that is irresistible." But by that same report, Ted, yet again a vacillator when it came to the presidency, continued to insist that he intended to support Carter, and he had his administrative assistant Rick Burke phone activists in an effort to dissuade them from promoting his candidacy. Burke's efforts were ineffective. In June, Americans for Democratic Action, the erstwhile liberal group, officially issued a call for an "irresistible national mandate" for Ted to run. Joseph Rauh, the civil rights attorney with whom Ted had often worked in the past, said, "If we liberals don't want to take a stand, then something is wrong with us. The point is we want Teddy Kennedy to be president." After Carter received a lukewarm reception at the NAACP convention in Louisville that same month, one member complained that Carter was "just not putting out the effort that Hubert Humphrey and John Kennedy put out for Black people. Now, if you ask me about Senator Kennedy—" and the man beamed without having to finish the sentence.

And pressure was building from Ted's fellow senators too. Ted said George McGovern told him to "go," and that New York senator Daniel Patrick Moynihan "made a big point" of pulling Ted aside at the Special Olympics, an athletic competition that Ted's sister Eunice Shriver had organized for the disabled, and telling him that he had to run, that "he'd do anything for me." (According to Califano, Moynihan, who might have been hedging his presidential bets, told Carter that May that unless the president took charge, he would find "he's governing by the sufferance" of Senator Kennedy.) Henry Jackson also encouraged Ted to run. So did Ohio senator John Glenn and New Jersey senator Harrison Williams. One senator told Elizabeth Drew that Ted's turnout in big states would help downticket Democrats even if he didn't win the presidency. Tom Wicker, writing in *The New York Times* that June, called Ted the "popular favorite of the Democratic Party" and said that those disappointed in Carter—which was a sizable and ever-growing group—"seem to be looking to Ted Kennedy for salvation." And Wicker cited a remark—one he said that Carter had clearly leaked to the press: that he would whip Ted Kennedy's ass if Ted ran against him. "This is the kind of thing that took Muhammad Ali," the former world heavyweight boxing champion, "a long way," Wicker wrote, "but it may not work as well for what some ringsiders think is no more than a light-heavyweight from Georgia fighting over his weight."

III

For all the brewing frustration with him, Jimmy Carter hadn't done anything egregiously wrong. The country wasn't at war. There was little corruption in his administration, no serious scandal. He didn't work the
divisions in the nation, as Nixon had, to help his political prospects. He
hadn't taken on too many big issues, so he didn't exactly fumble them,
and in any case, his presidency never seemed large-scale to begin with. It
was, by his own admission, a presidency of limits. He had had two major
foreign policy successes, the Middle East accord between Egypt and Israel
and the Panama Canal treaty. The economy was a shambles, and Carter
hadn't been able to tame it, but much of that was due to circumstances
beyond his control—namely, rising oil prices, dictated by oil-producing
nations, that resulted in long gas lines that, fairly or not, became an annoying daily symbol of Carter's seeming inadequacies. Still, the problem
wasn't Jimmy Carter's inability to meet the massive problems of the day,
in part since the problems, like energy dependence, were difficult to frame
as massive. The problem was that nothing seemed to be going right, and
the country was losing its self-confidence. What Carter lacked, what Carter had always lacked, was the quality that might have bailed him out:
that personal chemistry, not only with his fellow Democrats in Congress,
but also, and more important, with the American people. Jimmy Carter
wasn't weak, though he was sometimes portrayed as such. He was in fact
tough-minded, as he demonstrated by taking on Ted Kennedy. But he
didn't appear tough-minded. "To the public he appeared weak," former
senator James Abourezk, no fan of Carter's, would later recollect, "an
image that presidents cannot convey and remain popular." And Jimmy
Carter had not remained popular.

But as Democrats agonized throughout 1979 over Carter's presidency
and what they perceived as his diminishing chances for reelection, and as
many of them seemed to pine yet again for a Kennedy, they also continued
to wonder, as they had wondered repeatedly, whether Ted Kennedy was
the answer or was too liberal to be in step with the American people. Ted,
who seldom overestimated himself, harbored the same doubts. Analysis
of his voting record showed Ted to be the *most* liberal senator in the chamber. Even before the calls for a Kennedy candidacy, long before, years before, Ted had begun reexamining his political situation, and while he
didn't want to tailor his own beliefs to fit the national mood—by this point

in his career, he couldn't have if he *had* wanted to—he did do something that was unusual for him, unusually timorous: He began to think of ways of tempering his liberalism to better fit that mood, clearly for fear that were he not to do so, he faced the extinction of which Patrick Caddell had warned. "Didn't give an inch to the conservative tide," *Time* magazine had marveled of Ted when it came to the nation's growing disaffection for the compassion that had been a liberal hallmark. But Ted Kennedy *was* giving an inch. For years, he had been sniffing the wind, which was what James Abourezk had accused Jimmy Carter of doing—testing it to see which way it was blowing or rather, since it was clearly a conservative wind now, how strongly it was blowing and what accommodations he might have to make to it. (This from the man who had exhorted his fellow Democrats to sail against the wind.) He had made few enough of those accommodations, but now, realizing that he would strengthen his Senate hand and his larger electoral prospects, he was more amenable. "Asserting his independence from liberal orthodoxy" was how Milton Gwirtzman, Ted's longtime adviser, characterized Ted's reevaluation, putting a more positive spin on it, which was in line with Ted's directives to his staff to repackage liberalism in ways that might attract Republican senators to his legislative campaigns. Gwirtzman dated Ted's independence from traditional liberalism to the early 1980s, after Massachusetts's junior senator, Paul Tsongas, delivered a critique of traditional liberalism and argued for a more growth-oriented, deficit-cutting approach, not unlike that of Carter. (He had actually begun that reevaluation as early as 1974.) He certainly hadn't abandoned liberalism. But he was shifting his emphasis, even pandering. At the University of Mississippi commencement in May 1978, the commencement he attended at James Eastland's behest, he echoed his host, saying that the "challenge now is to find paths toward solutions which do not begin and end in Washington, which rely on units of action in government small enough to permit the influence and participation of the individual citizen." At a conference convened by *Time* magazine later that year, he backed a cut in the corporate tax rate to a maximum of 44 percent. (The House had called for a 46 percent maximum.) And as he called for greater federalization and lower taxes, he also promoted free-market solutions to problems—this from the man who felt the market often generated problems that government alone could correct. "There are two sides to Kennedy," one Democrat told *Time*. "People tend to focus on his liberal votes. But there is another side that pushes hard for an open, competitive market." By 1979, he was going further, declaring what he called a "clean break with the New Deal and even the 1960s," his brothers' time, and saying that he shared a "growing consensus" that "government intervention in the economy should come only as a last resort"—yet again, a seeming embrace of the very things for which he had criticized Carter and the Republicans.

Ted justified these positions not as a repudiation of liberalism or a fundamental change in his political vision, but as evidence of his pragmatism, to which he had always been committed, in the service of furthering that vision. He may very well have believed that, but it was hard to look at his new views without seeing hypocrisy there too. Ted Kennedy had devoted his entire political career to pushing liberal solutions—to making sure that the lessons of the New Deal were not forgotten. Now that those solutions had become increasingly untenable politically, he was resorting to the trimming politics of the day, even as he was assailing Jimmy Carter for submitting to them. Republican congressman Barber Conable of New York called Ted a "centrist," a label that had not often been attached to him, and a "pragmatist, not an ideologue," which was a label Ted would have attached to himself. Ted Kennedy loved to be thought of as a pragmatist—a man who didn't care what route he took so long as he got to his desired destination. But for the first time in his career, pragmatism looked very much like political expedience or something worse. It looked like opportunism.

And this was more than Ted Kennedy giving lip service to accommodate the adverse national mood. In sniffing the wind, Ted Kennedy had begun *legislating* for the first time with a conservative tilt. Two of his primary legislative campaigns during the Carter administration, alongside health insurance, might have seemed to qualify as pragmatic rather than liberal—might have to those who admired Ted Kennedy—but they would have qualified as conservative too in their results, pragmatic or not. One, a big one, a daunting one, was a reform of the massive federal criminal code. Beginning in the 1960s with a national commission appointed by Lyndon Johnson, whose liberal supporters thought the code too harsh on criminal defendants, and headed by former California governor Edmund Brown, there had been a strenuous effort to reform the federal criminal code—the code that governed federal criminal law: defining crimes, laying out procedures, determining penal provisions, and providing sentencing guidelines. The effort had been strenuous because the code had been largely untouched for two hundred years, with laws simply accumulating over that time, and because even proposed minor changes triggered major debates. The efforts were strenuous but not successful. Judges had had wide discretion in meting out sentences, but that also meant there were wide disparities in sentences, which the reforms were meant to repair. Brown's commission led to bills that included standardized sentencing, allegedly an improvement in the catch-as-catch-can process, but civil liberties groups attacked its reforms, fearing that judges' hands would be tied and the convicted would suffer, especially minorities who always suffered, and the bills failed to pass. (Those fears would turn out to be largely justified.) Richard Nixon had tackled the problem in 1973, but his reforms met the same fate—in part because, as *The New York Times* editorialized, he had turned the reform effort into "a prosecutor's laundry list designed to enhance official secrecy, stifle the press and generally ride roughshod over individual rights." Ted Kennedy had had no particular interest in criminal code reform. But in the fall of 1975, with Gerald Ford still president, Ted's chief Judiciary aide, Jim Flug, who was primarily interested in civil rights issues, was leaving the staff, and a Massachusetts-born, New York federal prosecutor named Kenneth Feinberg had applied for the opening. Feinberg was interviewed first by Carey Parker and then by Ted. Feinberg was candid. He told Ted that while he was a liberal himself, he wasn't sure his own views on criminal justice, which he said were more conservative, comported with the senator's. Ted fired back that Feinberg shouldn't assume he knew what Ted's attitude might be. (This was when Ted was looking to repackage his liberalism.) "You may find, Ken, that all is not what you perceive." A week later Feinberg was offered the job.

Feinberg arrived with an agenda of his own, and it concerned those views on criminal justice about which he had warned Ted. He told Ted that there was one issue that needed immediate attention: that old issue of reform of the criminal code. To press the point, Feinberg arranged to have Judge Marvin Frankel, from the Southern District of New York and an expert in sentencing, come to McLean for one of Ted's issue dinners. Ted would later say that Frankel made a "very powerful impression on me [about] what was possible and the iniquities of sentencing." "A roll of the dice for the defendant" was how Carey Parker described federal sentencing. And Ted admitted that he now saw an "important kind of opportunity to try and make some difference" in the criminal justice system.

But that explanation wasn't the whole of it. No doubt Ted was sincere in the concern he expressed about the iniquities of the system for defendants. Yet already there was also considerable political calculation, which indicated Ted's sensitivities to the conservative wind he had been sniffing. Feinberg admitted that Ted was troubled by the fact that he was pigeonholed as a liberal and as a left-wing ideologue when Ted insisted, even as he was espousing liberal positions, that he was a pragmatist and a legislator first—a politician who knew how to get things done. And Ted, who had shown no interest in the issue, now appreciated that taking on criminal code reform, a legislative task that had not engaged most other liberals either, was a way for him to change that ideological reputation of his, and to co-opt the conservatives as Nixon had tried to co-opt him—basically stealing their issue.

And there was no doubt one more reason for Ted's new interest, this one a matter of ego: The bill was huge, the effort a herculean one at which no previous senator had succeeded and no other current senator likely would. Which meant that its passage, were Ted to manage it, would be an extraordinary testament to his skill to move the Senate.

So now, in 1976, Ted Kennedy joined forces with Senator John McClellan, a law-and-order conservative, with James Eastland, and with the Ford administration to draft a reform bill.* Some of his fellow liberals regarded this as heresy. But in a speech that October before the Chicago Crime Commission, Ted defended himself: "Let us not confuse social progress with progress in the war on crime," he declared. "We fool ourselves if we say 'no crime reform until society is reformed.'" Sounding like anything but a die-hard liberal, he insisted that a recent rise in crime had to be addressed, though again, how much of this was political posturing, either to enhance his future presidential prospects or to strengthen his hand as a master of the Senate in a liberal eclipse, and how much a sincere turn is impossible to determine now that Ted Kennedy was beginning to sniff the wind.

Whichever it was, and it was likely both, for the next three years, beginning with the Ford administration and then into the Carter administration, Ken Feinberg worked almost exclusively on two initiatives: the

---

*McClellan had already drafted and submitted a bill with the conservative Republican senator Roman Hruska, and that became a basis of compromise with liberals, but no final compromise could be reached. See EMK, "Reforming the Federal Criminal Code: A Congressional Response," *North Carolina Central Law Review* 8, no. 1 (1976): 1–16.

criminal code reform and the Foreign Intelligence Surveillance Act
(FISA), which arose out of congressional investigations of Nixon-era
abuses of intelligence and law enforcement agencies against Nixon's perceived enemies, and which established procedures for judicial oversight of
government surveillance of foreign governments and possible foreign
agents. And to those liberals who objected to Ted working with the Ford
administration and with McClellan, Ted answered that he was there to
"bridge differences and get something done"—always to get something
done, always to move the Senate, even if he was now moving it in a different direction. The Criminal Code Reform Act, S.1, which had been blocked
repeatedly in the past, that heavy legislative lift, introduced additional di-
vides to the traditional ones between liberals and conservatives and provided a plethora of issues, the result of three thousand different laws that
constituted the code, over which to quarrel—from the death penalty to
penalties for marijuana possession to provisions against pornography
(Ted wanted to eliminate all three) to punishments for national security
violations to limitations on wiretapping, just to name a very few. (These
were in fact among the very disagreements that had stalled the McClellan-
Hruska bill in the Senate late in 1975 and early in 1976 until Majority
Leader Mike Mansfield pleaded for concessions. His pleas, however, went
unheeded.) But it was this divide, the fact that code reform disassembled
the traditional conservative-liberal coalitions, that was a reason Ted had
wanted to wade into the field. This was pragmatism, not ideology, and because it was pragmatism, it was, Ted felt, good politics too—again, his way
of disassociating himself from the liberal stereotype.

The heavy lift would not pass in 1976. But Ted, again realizing the
enormity of the bill and the fact that credit would redound to anyone who
could gain its passage, was not discouraged. He reintroduced it during
Carter's first year, when Attorney General Griffin Bell strongly supported
it. And seeing a prospect for passage at long last, this time McClellan, the
no-holds-barred crime-stopper who had worked with Bobby in the 1950s
to root out union corruption, and Ted reached agreement on a patchwork
bill, a bill of trade-offs, many trade-offs, that Ted hoped might do enough
to appease the civil libertarians, who had continued to attack any reform
because those reforms were so riddled with compromise, while also doing
enough to appease conservatives, who wanted to make sure the code still
had teeth—sharp teeth—which Ted and McClellan had sharpened with
new provisions to fight white-collar crime and even a section called the

"Ehrlichman Defense," after Richard Nixon's former adviser, John Ehrlichman, that would have disallowed government officials accused of felo-
nies to claim that they were only following orders. The compromise
reinstated the insanity defense, which conservatives had attempted to remove, put new curbs on police entrapment, extended the death penalty
rather than eliminate it (a concession to the right), subjected labor unions
to extortion laws (a McClellan addition), and perhaps most important,
instituted a sentencing commission of experts to standardize those sentences and remove judicial discretion—this last being one of the reasons
Ted Kennedy had taken on the reform in the first place, since, again, sentencing often worked to the disadvantage of Black defendants. But neither the civil libertarians nor the conservatives were appeased, no matter
how much Ted tried to meet their objections—he worked closely with
Norman Dorsen, the head of the American Civil Liberties Union, especially on bail reform—and no matter how vehemently he argued that his
bill would actually expand civil liberties. Ted's bill, as he outlined it, rescinded the notorious Smith Act, an anti-Communist relic that criminalized advocacy to overthrow the government, decriminalized marijuana
possession, modernized civil rights laws by making them more easily en-
forceable (under previous federal law there had to be a conspiracy to deny
civil rights; the reform included individuals violating those rights), en-
larged privacy rights, removed stigmas that had sapped rape laws, provided for victims' compensation, and outlawed the electoral dirty tricks
that had led to Watergate. And he argued that nearly every provision the
liberals opposed—placing curbs on the press if they refused to disclose
confidential sources; broadening solicitation laws; imposing new laws on
individuals who disobeyed orders during natural disasters; criminalizing
making a false statement to the FBI—were either mischaracterized or
would be revised before the bill was voted upon. Still, liberals found the bill
too conservative, while conservatives found it too liberal.

But just as he enjoyed tackling issues that were not strictly liberal or
conservative, this was exactly the kind of situation that Ted, a natural
mediator, loved to navigate—the kind in which he was forced to search for
a way to split the difference between opponents, especially on something
as large as this bill and as epochal as this bill. Though Ted had yet to rise to
the Judiciary chair—that wouldn't happen until after the 1978 midterm
elections—he sat on the Subcommittee on Criminal Laws and Procedures, which held sixty hours of hearings that year of 1977. And Judiciary

held sixty-seven hours of markups on the bill—elsewhere Ted said eighty-six, which he admitted was unprecedented—markups on which the attorney general occasionally sat in, and Ted, as the bill's sponsor, assured every member of the committee that if it were to go to conference, and any member expressed an objection to the conference report, Ted would personally pull the bill. "It was the only way that you could try to begin to build enough confidence so that they would permit the process to go forward," Ted was to say. And Ted, whose mastery of the Senate was now being tested, eliminated the most controversial provisions, including the death penalty. And he told his Judiciary colleagues that he would take those "hot button" issues, as he called them, and put them on a different track, separate from the bill. (Feinberg said that Ted voiced his legislative mantra again, "The perfect is the enemy of the good," and kept horse-trading provisions on the basis that "we can improve it later.") And then, with liberals offering amendment after amendment to gut the bill, and with Ted blocking them, it finally passed the Judiciary Committee, 12 to 2, on November 2, 1977—the two dissenters being liberal James Abourezk and conservative James Allen, which perfectly characterized Ted Kennedy's achievement of uniting the middle against the extremes.

And now, after years of wrangling and years of defeat—eleven years since the Brown Commission—it finally came to the Senate floor following the Christmas holiday recess—a 382-page bill, the bill worked out by Ted and McClellan and the Justice Department. The debate took eight days, but it didn't exactly rage, largely because Ted had cobbled together the liberal-conservative coalition. "One of the best examples in the history of the United States of the legislative process functioning at its best," said Strom Thurmond, the Judiciary's ranking minority member and deeply conservative, adding that he and Ted would brook no controversial amendments. In the end, few were offered. But James Allen, one of those two Judiciary dissenters and arguably the most conservative member of the Senate, was not about to partake in the display of unity. As Ken Feinberg described it, Allen vowed to stay on the Senate floor "every day, for ten hours a day, to make sure the bill didn't blow through in his absence." And Feinberg said that Ted, who understood the physics of the Senate and understood that Allen was prepared to take the Senate floor and filibuster as he had in the past, presumably no matter how long he had to do so, looked at Feinberg and told him, "We'll outwait him. We're going to sit here as long as he sits here. We will make him blink. He thinks we'll quit.

We're not quitting. Be prepared, Ken, to tell your wife you're here for dinner." And Ted was right. After two days of stalemate, as a sop to Allen, the Senate restored the Logan Act of 1799, which made it an offense for private citizens to engage with foreign governments. And with Allen pacified by this small sacrifice—he must have realized that Ted would not be outlasted—the Criminal Code Reform Act passed the Senate on January 22, 1978, by a vote of 78 to 12.

This bill that had failed repeatedly in previous sessions of the Senate even after Mike Mansfield had asked for concessions, this bill that had divided liberals and conservatives on some of the most basic issues of criminal rights, this bill that had few adherents and many opponents, this bill that had taken longer to mark up than just about any bill in the Senate's history, this bill that had been blocked by one of the Senate's most astute and tenacious parliamentary tactitions, James Allen—this bill, the Criminal Code Reform Act of 1977, had been shepherded through the Senate by Ted Kennedy. "It would have never passed [without Ted]," Eastland said. He was right, especially since its co-sponsor, John McClellan, had died two months earlier and was not there to lend conservative support, though Strom Thurmond took his place as co-sponsor. One aide to a Democratic senator said of Ted, "He cut some deals there that were almost uncuttable." "There were a number of conservative-type amendments that simply had to be passed or it wasn't going to get through committee," Nevada Republican Paul Laxalt, a conservative himself, said. "And he compromised." *The Washington Post* called it "one of the greatest legislative feats of modern times." He had done what no one else had ever done in the Senate, though many had been working for more than a decade to do so. He had done what no one else in the Senate at the time could have done because no one else understood the chemistry of the Senate well enough to do so.

An impossible piece of legislation. A divisive piece of legislation that nevertheless passed overwhelmingly. A piece of legislation that couldn't be labeled conservative or liberal. It was a testament to how skillfully Ted had led his Senate colleagues that the bill died later that fall in the House, where there was no one as skillful; there the bill's civil libertarian antagonists were much more effective in pressuring liberals to oppose it, despite entreaties by both Ted and Thurmond for the House to pass it. (Ted, who certainly wouldn't have worked on the bill as doggedly as he did if he thought the House would sink it, said he was "extremely disappointed," but introduced it again in the next session of Congress.) Meanwhile Feinberg had worked out FISA, which had been another hotly debated bill for years. (He said that Ford's attorney general, Edward Levi, with whom he had begun work on FISA and who had approached Ted for his help, had "great confidence in Kennedy's abilities and in his word.") It passed the Senate, 95 to 1, three months after the passage of the Criminal Code Reform Act, giving Ted a second major legislative triumph and certifying a transformation in its sponsor.

Unquestionably, Ted Kennedy had become one of the great masters of the Senate.*

IV

Not just a doctrinaire liberal. That had been one of Ted Kennedy's objectives in spearheading criminal code reform. But Feinberg believed that Ted had another objective in wanting to change his image as an ideologue— a more practical objective. He believed that Ted· already had "his eye on 1980" and "thought he'd better develop a position on one of the leading issues at the time: crime, violence in the streets." (If so, Feinberg was crediting Ted with remarkable foresight, since that election was five years away when Ted took on the issue, though the Kennedys often did demonstrate remarkable foresight when it came to the presidency.) But it hadn't been just a matter of developing a position on crime. It had been a matter of developing a position that demonstrated he wasn't another hopeless bleeding-heart liberal who sympathized with criminals. And Ted had done so, convincing even Strom Thurmond. But if Ted Kennedy was to change his image in an attempt to appeal to an increasingly conservative electorate, he was faced with another equally large test: He needed to show that he was no longer the big government liberal he had long been accused of being (and was)—someone who had been portrayed by opponents as gouging big business while spending taxpayers' money profligately. When Ted had first recruited Stephen Breyer as AdPrac counsel in 1974, Ted and Breyer had a get-acquainted dinner at McLean, where the

---

*But not a master of Congress. Ted Kennedy's Criminal Code Reform Act would never gain passage in the House. Instead, in 1984 Congress passed the Comprehensive Crime Control Act, sponsored by Strom Thurmond, which was a much scaled-down version of the Criminal Code Reform Act. It did, however, include a bipartisan, independent U.S. Sentencing Commission to do away with the sentencing disparities that had so rankled Ted.

two discussed possible areas that AdPrac could investigate. Breyer suggested procedural changes necessitated by Watergate and airline deregulation. Ted was unenthusiastic about both, and Breyer readily conceded that airline deregulation was a "nonglamorous" subject—certainly less glamorous than Watergate—but he insisted that it was nevertheless important, primarily because it affected the prices that ordinary people paid for their flights. Liberals had generally regarded deregulation contemptuously, viewing it as a way for Republicans to protect business from government oversight rather than a way to protect consumers from business greed, which was how Breyer was posing it. Moreover, Breyer said, the time for hearings on airline deregulation was auspicious—obviously meaning in terms of getting results but also in terms of getting media attention, which was always an appeal for Ted. Nixon had appointed a conservative named Robert Timm to head the Civil Aeronautics Board (CAB) that had regulated the airline industry since the board's creation in 1938, and Timm was especially close to the airline industry—*The New York Times* wrote that airline executives considered his appointment "one of the best things that had happened to the industry since the invention of the jet engine." Timm had argued against deregulation—argued against it since the airlines had benefited from regulation that minimized competition and gave them control over routes and fares—fares that were generally higher than those a competitive market would have set. (This was not entirely new territory for Ted. One of his earliest legislative efforts was in restoring airline service from Miami to Boston that had been cut by the self-dealing relationship between the airlines and their regulators.) AdPrac's counsel at the time, Thomas Susman, warmed to Breyer's idea; with conservatives gaining ground, he thought that liberals needed to address government regulation, which conservatives had long attacked as interfering with market forces and thus hurting business, though the conservatives' opposition, liberals pointed out, was selective; they were less avid foes of regulation in those cases, like that of the airlines, where circumventing competitive market forces actually helped businesses profit at the expense of consumers. And Ted, sniffing the conservative wind, began to warm to the idea, too, because supporting deregulation challenged the liberal shibboleth that regulation was invariably for the public good. Rather, Ted had come to see that some regulation—the regulation that let businesses manipulate the market by lessening competition—hurt consumers. The bottom line was that airline deregulation "would help average people," as Breyer put it in assessing Ted's reasoning to move in a direction that might have seemed conservative but really wasn't. "Sometimes this deregulation will work," Breyer would later say of those situations where regulation had actually allowed businesses to cheat the market. "Sometimes less government will mean more help" for the consumer. But even after Ted waded into deregulation, Breyer said he was struck by something else Ted mentioned—something important. He told Breyer that "this governor," referring to Jimmy Carter when Carter was first gaining attention as a potential presidential candidate, was "going around talking about too much government, and he's getting a very good response." And Breyer said that he remembered thinking to himself that this was all good: "It's less government, consumer benefit, and people are interested in airlines, so maybe there will be a little publicity." And last, he thought, "You can make a name for the subcommittee. The subcommittee will mean something because it will have accomplished something significant," which had always been Ted's reasoning too. And the significance wasn't just lowering airline fares. Breyer thought that Ted's establishing AdPrac's jurisdiction in deregulation would lead to AdPrac deregulation hearings in other industries where it might also be beneficial—beneficial not only to the effort but, though Breyer didn't mean this, beneficial to Ted Kennedy.

And this was another step away from liberal orthodoxy.

Taking on the airlines was not an easy task. Criminal code reform had been hard because it had so many moving parts and so many people had something at stake. Airline deregulation was hard because the airlines vigorously opposed even holding hearings, claiming that the industry was accustomed to being regulated and that any transition to deregulation would be disruptive. And it was hard for another reason: The airlines had clout of their own—big financial clout with senators. But that was the sort of challenge Ted welcomed, the sort of challenge he enjoyed, just as he had enjoyed mediating among the different factions on criminal code reform, only this was the challenge of taking on a behemoth. Though there was no money for airline deregulation hearings and Eastland didn't seem to have any interest in them, Ted corralled Strom Thurmond to support his hearings, and Thurmond helped Ted get the funding from the minority on the Judiciary Committee. As Ted told biographer Theo Lippman, both he and Thurmond wanted deregulation—Ted to lower fares and

Thurmond, who *was* being a doctrinaire conservative, to get government off the airlines' backs, even though the airlines *wanted* the government on their backs to secure those higher profits. The Ford administration, at the airlines' bidding, was initially opposed to hearings. Ted ignored them. Breyer said he received a call from the assistant secretary of commerce, who asked him to call off the hearings because they could bankrupt Pan American Airlines, and when Ted asked Breyer if it was true, Breyer admitted that without regulation Pan Am might very well go bankrupt. But when Ted asked if the hearings would be the cause, Breyer said they wouldn't, so Ted plowed ahead. And to the airlines' resistance, there was also the matter of jurisdiction. By now Ted Kennedy was gaining the reputation of someone who would bull his way into any issue that interested him legislatively. (Senators didn't yet seem to think that he was bulling his way into any issue that might help him politically, though he was doing that too.) Howard Cannon, who headed the Aviation Subcommittee of the Commerce Committee, was indignant that Ted was poaching on his territory, and he had his staff director draft a huffy letter, which both he and the Commerce Committee chairman at the time, Warren Magnuson, signed, asking Ted to postpone his hearings while international airfares were being negotiated between the airlines and the CAB. (Not surprisingly, after the negotiations, the fares were increased.) Ted, a Senate man, did so begrudgingly, then rescheduled the hearings a month later, for November 1974, while telling the press Cannon was fearful that the AdPrac hearings would expose the sweetheart relationship between the CAB and the airlines. As an associate of Ted's put it, "I think he got a big kick out of the fact that two senior senators"—Magnuson and Cannon—"didn't want him sticking his nose into what they regarded as their business, but they couldn't stop him." Then, almost as if to provoke them, he scheduled another round of hearings for February. As Cannon's staff director, Robert Ginther, put it, "They play a tough game over there," meaning, of course, Ted played a tough game when he realized that his usual ingratiation wouldn't get results.

A tough game it was. Just days before the second round of hearings, and two days before he was to testify, William Gingery, the head of the CAB's bureau of enforcement, committed suicide, leaving behind a ten-page note that accused Timm, whom President Ford had refused to reappoint as CAB chairman, and the former head of enforcement and current acting chairman, Richard O'Melia, of ordering Gingery to shutter an investigation into illegal campaign contributions by the airlines during the Nixon administration. (This was an example of the clout the airlines had.) Timm and O'Melia then both testified in direct contradiction to each other—Timm saying that he had never ordered any investigation to be stopped, O'Melia saying that he had received a letter initialed by Timm telling him to block the investigation. Now the CAB's corruption was a public matter. Meanwhile Ted had done his customary homework, parrying airline executives who decried the potential effects of deregulation— thus putting the shoe on the other foot. Breyer said that when Ted asked acting CAB chairman O'Melia why deregulated fares in California were so much lower than regulated fares, O'Melia had no answer, no doubt because he was afraid to answer: The answer was competition.

The hearings, which addressed the very basis of airline fares, lasted only seven days. But they were consequential days. The "nonglamorous" subject, as Breyer had called it, the subject that seemed so dull and insignificant that Ted had to be convinced to take it up, attracted major press attention—in no small part because Breyer courted *New York Times* reporter David Burnham, who provided coverage, even front-page coverage, of the hearings, saying he realized they were "really aimed at substance"—and they sent a shock wave through the airline industry. Breyer called Ted's decision to hold the hearings the "crucial factor in the emergence of airline deregulation as a politically viable and important issue" and said that "politicians felt they had to take a position upon or deal with the issue." The hearings had demonstrated unequivocally how the regulators had been corrupted and how airline deregulation was a boon to consumers because regulation had actually kept fares artificially high. Helping the average American, Breyer had said of deregulation in selling the idea of hearings to Ted. And the hearings had. Meanwhile Ted had forced the hand of the Ford administration, and on April 18 the president announced that he would introduce a bill to facilitate deregulation. When that failed to materialize, Ted wrote Ford in frustration, saying that the "delay . . . suggests to some a lessening of the Administration's commitment to genuine reform" and that it was making it difficult "for me to maintain the same momentum on the congressional front." This was Ted Kennedy's way of warning the Ford administration to act or he would blame it for those higher fares. But already he had put the Republicans on the defensive. As Breyer later assessed it, "Deregulation played a big role in changing the terms of the political debate" on how to manage the economy. And Ted Kennedy, arguably the nation's foremost liberal, had played a big role, perhaps the leading legislative role, in deregulation.

But if Ted Kennedy had an outsize effect on deregulation, deregulation would also have an outsize effect on him. "I am convinced," he would write of his newfound belief in selective deregulation, "that the key lies in agency-by-agency examinations of specific regulatory programs." And he said that "government bodies should be governed by 'regulation as a last resort philosophy,'" which hardly comported with old-fashioned New Deal liberalism. One of his aides said of him, "You could really call him Mr. Free Enterprise," though what the aide might have said more accurately was that Ted Kennedy, the quintessential liberal, was sniffing the wind, and the wind was blowing from the right.

But now there arose another matter: the matter of legislation. Ted had shined a light on airline deregulation through hearings. He had pressured the Ford administration to come up with a bill. He hadn't, however, *achieved* deregulation, which meant that ordinary Americans were still overpaying for their flights—the very reason he claimed to have taken on the fight. The following year, in April 1976, he testified as the leadoff witness before Cannon's Aviation Subcommittee, which was holding hearings on a bill that Ford had finally and reluctantly proffered, and on another introduced by Ted that called for a more intensive deregulation than Ford's—out-deregulating the deregulators. In testifying and essentially acknowledging the Aviation Subcommittee's primacy on the issue, Ted was once again demonstrating his understanding of the chemistry of the Senate. He had taken on deregulation because he had been convinced that it needed to be done and that no one else in the Senate was doing it (his own political considerations aside), and he did it, even though it required him to ruffle Cannon's feathers. Now he needed to smooth those feathers to get Cannon's cooperation. And he needed that cooperation. AdPrac, despite its hearings, had no jurisdiction over airline deregulation. All it could do was publicize it. The jurisdiction, as Cannon had protested, belonged to Cannon's Aviation Subcommittee. So Ted now waged a charm offensive on Cannon to get him to take up the legislation. According to one account, Ted's new AdPrac counsel, Phil Bakes, and Cannon's Aviation counsel, Bob Ginther, did not feel especially warmly toward each other, given their territorial disputes. But Ted had instructed Bakes to work with Ginther on legislation. And when the two had drafted a bill, Ted then began stroking Cannon, phoning him, commending his leadership. "A year-long process of stroking," Ginther called it, one that he said was so successful—Ted Kennedy was hard to resist when he turned on the charm—that a "remarkable" camaraderie developed between the two. Ted and Cannon co-sponsored the bill in February 1977. Ted, as was now customary as his Senate muscle had grown, put Cannon's name first and let Cannon introduce it on the floor, where he called it "one of the most important pieces of legislation in the past several decades." Ted lauded Cannon publicly, saying the bill was the "result of the effort and skill of the chairman of the Commerce Committee"—that chairman who had been so reluctant to take on deregulation. But it wasn't Howard Cannon's legislative acumen that advanced airline deregulation. It was primarily Ted's understanding of how the Senate functioned. The bill passed the Senate, 83 to 9, then, like criminal code reform, got hung up in the House.

Undeterred by the House defeat, Ted had already been working the incoming Carter administration—pressuring them to endorse airline deregulation, lobbying new Transportation secretary Brock Adams to appoint Breyer as deputy secretary to oversee airline deregulation (he failed), and pushing hard for Alfred Kahn, an economist and leading proponent of deregulation, to be appointed the new chairman of the CAB. (He was.) And Carter, who distrusted regulation, was amenable. With Carter's backing, Cannon reintroduced the deregulation bill the following year, in February 1978. The airlines, however, did not intend to go gently. As recalled by Charles Ludlam, the chief counsel of what was now, with Ted's move to the Antitrust Subcommittee, John Culver's AdPrac Subcommittee, the airlines insisted that they would continue their opposition, which had proved so effective in thwarting the bill in the House, unless a portion of a federal tax on tickets—a hefty $4 billion portion—was earmarked for them to buy new, quieter planes. A "massive bribe," Ludlam called it. The bill had passed the Senate without the "bribe" on April 19 over the opposition of a few liberals, among them George McGovern. Then it passed the House easily on September 14 with the new provision. (Effectively, it seemed, the airlines had bought off the House.) When the bill returned to the Senate, Ted reluctantly agreed to the bailout in order to gain the bill's passage, even though his staff encouraged Ludlam to take every procedural measure he could to remove it. (It was a very tangled legislative web since the bailout involved a tax, and Finance had jurisdiction over tax measures in the Senate, though the bill was sent to the Commerce Com-

mittee, where it had originated.) In the end, the House bill arrived on the
Senate floor just prior to the end of the session, and James Abourezk, a
liberal who had been recruited by Ludlam for this very task, was able to
separate the "noise" provision, as the bailout for quieter airplanes was
dubbed, from the deregulation provision by threatening to sink the entire
bill if it wasn't. (Ludlam literally used a scissors to cut the funds out of the
bill.) It passed the Senate on October 14 and was signed by President Carter on October 24, eventually resulting in the disbandment of the CAB—
all because Ted Kennedy had prodded Howard Cannon into action.

And now Ted Kennedy, who had been sniffing the wind, had gotten the full
whiff of deregulation and liked it. When he moved to the Antitrust Subcommittee, he began investigating the deregulation of the trucking industry. This time he faced formidable opposition both from the Teamsters
union and from the trucking industry, each of which had benefited from
regulation and the price fixing that went with it—price fixing that allowed
truckers, like the airlines, to set higher rates than those a competitive
market would have set. "This is not something that's going to be easy,"
warned Cannon, now the chairman of the Commerce Committee, which
had jurisdiction over trucking deregulation as it had over airline deregulation, though in predicting difficulties, Cannon was also giving voice to
his own wishful thinking. *The New York Times* described Cannon, an ally
of the trucking industry, as "skeptical" of trucking deregulation, and he
insisted it would take years to pass. Nor was Cannon about to make it any
easier, once again clashing with Ted over jurisdiction and, ending their
legislative honeymoon after airline deregulation, sniping over Ted's trespassing, "What will be next? Will Senator Kennedy want to take the bank
merger act away from the Banking Committee, or political action away
from the Rules Committee?" But Cannon, in a rare bit of congressional
candor, admitted that Ted had shouldered his way in because there was
concern Cannon did not want to move on trucking deregulation, any
more than he had wanted to move on airline deregulation. (This was also
an admission of the kind of power Ted Kennedy now wielded.) Ted had
already held hearings in Antitrust to dispute the contention by the trucking industry that there was no appetite outside Washington for deregulation. To show there was, he went on the road, visiting trucking depots and
food markets, and returning with the message that there was indeed an
appetite. And having once again forced Cannon's hand on an issue about

which Cannon had been less than enthusiastic—the trucking industry had contributed heavily to Commerce Committee members' campaign funds—Ted eventually ceded jurisdiction to Cannon, who was now, Cannon said, prepared to investigate the matter, claiming he had an "open mind," clearly meaning an open mind to continue regulation, while insinuating Ted did not have an open mind to do so.* This time, however, Ted had an ally in President Carter. In June, with Ted at his side, Carter submitted a bill deregulating the industry—it was the Interstate Commerce Commission that was the regulator—and when the truckers, fearful of losing their monopoly, railed against it, Ted threatened to use his subcommittee to remove their antitrust immunity, which was the mechanism that had allowed them to legally price-fix. With some liberals seeing the consumer benefits of deregulation, which is to say the political benefits, and now joining conservatives, it was hard to defeat deregulation. Carter's bill was passed the following year and was signed into law in the Rose Garden on July 1, 1980. At the ceremony, Carter singled out Ted, who stood behind him, saying, "There's one person who has worked on this legislation for at least two years, sometimes alone, sometimes facing discouragement, but never giving up on the concept."

By this time, however, Jimmy Carter seldom had kind words for Ted Kennedy. By this time, they were locked in mortal political combat.

V

For the last two years, even as he concentrated on deregulation as "Mr. Free Enterprise," it was a sign of how ambivalent Ted really was about running against Jimmy Carter—he was hardly champing at the bit—that he had not given up hope of gaining passage for health insurance as "Mr. Health Care." By 1979, 23 percent of Americans, fifty-one million, had inadequate health insurance, and thirty-one million had no access to healthcare, while twenty-three million had no health insurance whatsoever. Ted was dedicated to rectifying that. Still hoping to head off Ted from any challenge, even after all the sparring and heated exchanges throughout 1978, Carter had instructed Califano to devise a health insurance plan

---

*Ted was right to be concerned about Cannon's zeal for trucking deregulation. Cannon would later be implicated in a scandal in which the Teamster union president, Roy Lee Williams, had allegedly offered Cannon a bribe to derail legislation.

by January 1979 that, as Calfiano described it, called for an employer mandate, an expanded and federalized Medicaid program, and basic care for every American, which was no different from the earlier principles he had announced when he and Ted conducted their dueling press conferences the previous July, and still with a gradual phase-in, which had always been the deal-breaker with Ted. When, again at Carter's instruction, Califano floated the plan with Congress, he met with resistance, some of it over fears of inflaming inflation, some of it over the unlikelihood that it would pass, some of it over the desire to pass a less comprehensive plan. None of it, however, was because the Carter plan was too timid, as Ted was arguing. Russell Long, the chairman of the Finance Committee, which had Senate jurisdiction over a health plan, was still touting his catastrophic insurance with a $15,000 deductible, the plan he had first introduced in the early 1970s, and Califano said Long had even agreed to compromise and accept the employer mandates and expanded Medicaid. But Carter didn't trust Long, and instead of taking the risk of being double-crossed by him, the president pursued his own plan. At the same time, Ted was still pushing his comprehensive plan, and to keep pressure on the administration, he met with Carter at the White House on March 21. As Carter described it, he began by telling Ted that he would be opening campaign headquarters soon for his reelection, and he said that Ted promised support. (At least that was Carter's version.) Then they talked healthcare. "It's almost impossible for me to understand what he talks about because he's been using this special jargon for the last fifteen years," Carter was to tell Kennedy biographer Adam Clymer, seemingly indifferent to the fact that Ted had a special jargon because he was so deeply entrenched in healthcare. But Carter came away from the meeting realizing there is a "basic difference between his approach and mine." (Of course, Carter could have come to the same realization a year earlier.) Ted, he said, wanted a mandatory payroll tax to finance his plan "which is different from what we have in mind." Ted came away realizing that over the last year, the two of them had made no headway. Carter continued to insist, as he always had, that in order to get anything passed, healthcare had to be phased in and that each phase had to be reauthorized in Congress separately as the time arose, which Ted believed as firmly as ever was a prescription for no progress. ("To hold out for comprehensive insurance is simply to deny millions of Americans any improvement in health care coverage for perhaps a decade," Stu Eizenstat had written Carter the day before the meeting.) Carter's proposal also seemed to confirm to Ted his conclusion that the president was not serious about healthcare and was just stringing him along. Moreover, Ted thought Carter was squandering an opportunity. And he felt that "under different leadership we would be able to get this passed." Carter obviously felt that Ted Kennedy was the one squandering an opportunity.

"Different leadership" seemed like a euphemism for Ted Kennedy's leadership, but Ted still, after all the standoffs, hadn't lost hope that he could rally Congress around some consensus plan without having to run for the presidency. Carter felt otherwise. As Caddell characterized the president's attitude, "I wasn't going to kiss his [Kennedy's] ass to keep him from running." Despairing of reaching any compromise with Carter, Ted and his labor allies drafted their own plan—the UAW's Doug Fraser said that he and UAW general counsel Steven Schlossberg would discuss healthcare at McLean all night—this one drawn up largely by I. S. Falk, now a professor emeritus at Yale, who had drawn up Ted's original single-payer healthcare plan in 1969. Falk's new plan relied largely on payroll taxes, and it incorporated private consortiums both to compete with one another and to bargain with states and hospitals on costs, and individual insurers to sell group policies in which the premiums would be scaled to one's ability to pay. (This was Ted's retreat from a single-payer, Medicare-like government system and his compromise with the private health insurers.) Welfare recipients would be covered by state subsidies, thus obviating the need for Medicaid. There were to be no deductibles, and annual premiums were not to exceed $1,950 for a family of four. Ted pegged its cost, from both government and private contributions, at $39 billion but claimed it would eventually save that much in negotiated fees with hospitals and doctors. Carter thought Ted had vastly underestimated the cost.

Now, with intimations of his presidential intentions swirling around him, Ted challenged Carter directly and publicly. He introduced his bill, the Health Care for All Americans Act, on May 14, 1979, surrounded by sixty-five representatives of various interest groups and labor. It was lost on no one that Ted made the introduction in the cavernous Senate Caucus Room where both his brothers had announced their presidential candidacies—a venue he had chosen, said *Time*, "with an eye for drama and history." The proposal grabbed front-page attention in *The New York Times*, but behind the scenes, Ted's staffers still insisted the rollout was not a presidential preview. "The exercise is moving the President, not kicking him in the behind," said one of them. A month later, on June 12, the president had been moved. As one of Carter's aides put it, "Kennedy leveraged Carter into expanding health care. I concede that. And I just hope it will be enough to help us with the liberals." Surrounded by his own group of representatives from interest groups, including the NAACP, the National Council of Senior Citizens, and the National Association for Retired Persons, Carter, assisted by Eizenstat and Califano, introduced at long last his health plan. Since Ted's proposal, Carter had been pondering two options: a catastrophic plan, similar to Russell Long's, and a comprehensive plan with employer mandates. As Califano told it, Carter agonized over the issue at a two-hour meeting on June 1 and finally wound up asking Califano to draft a phased-in program that began with catastrophic insurance and added broader health insurance as inflation abated. Califano admitted that he felt as if comprehensive insurance were no longer on the table. "In a time of budgetary restraint amid concern about inflation, it is not possible to enact a full, universal, comprehensive plan," the administration announced. (Long, who had had his own deep antipathy to Ted since 1969, when Ted beat him as the Democratic whip, was one of Carter's guests at the introduction.) Ted objected not only to the scale of the program as too small, but also to the fact that it set fee limits for the elderly, disabled, and poor, who would be serviced through a new organization called HealthCare, which merged Medicare and Medicaid, thus setting up what Ted called superior healthcare for those with private insurance, inferior care for those without it. Carter responded to the criticism by saying, "The idea of all or nothing has been pursued now for nearly three decades. No one has benefited from that."

Some in the press saw Carter's frugal plan as a way of taunting Ted, almost begging him to run by rejecting any compromise with him. "If Carter had said, 'Let's do it,'" meaning healthcare, "there would have been no race," said Carl Wagner, a political consultant whom Ted had brought aboard after the Memphis convention, and whose hiring had given impetus to the idea that Ted would run. As always, Carter felt Ted had been the stubborn one—the one who had taunted *him* while looking for a pretext to run. The day of his healthcare rollout, Carter wrote in his diary that Ted, "continuing his irresponsible and abusive attitude, immediately condemned our health plan." And he crowed that Ted couldn't get five votes for his own plan and that he told "Stu [Eizenstat] and Joe Califano to fight it out with him through the public news media." Califano, taking the cue, said Ted's Healthcare for All Americans had as much chance of gaining passage as "an elephant had of fitting through a keyhole," which prompted Ted to send Califano a large posterboard with a keyhole cut into it and a tiny toy pink elephant attached dangling from a string. On the side, he had written: "Joe—It looks to me like it fits." When Califano phoned Ted to thank him for the joke, Ted said, "If you don't have a sense of humor in this business, you'll go crazy."

But when it came to Jimmy Carter, Ted Kennedy's sense of humor had disappeared along with any hope that the two of them might come to an agreement, and when the Healthcare for All Americans Act failed to get any traction, Ted decided to go back to his original single-payer bill, telling his old health staffer Stan Jones that "there's no point in laying a compromise on the table when nobody's compromising." Years later Carter was still complaining about Ted's obstructionism. He told Lesley Stahl of *60 Minutes* that "we would have had comprehensive healthcare now, had it not been for Ted Kennedy's deliberate blocking of the legislation that I proposed. It was his fault. Ted Kennedy killed the bill."* Carter seemed to think of Ted's opposition as petulance or politics—his alleged obsession with running for president. (So, for that matter, did Ted regard Carter's opposition that way.) But the disagreements between them had always gone much deeper, to the very heart of policy. "Kennedy saw national health insurance as an opportunity to reconstitute the health system on a new framework of incentive and bargaining relationships," the social historian Paul Starr would write. Carter "regarded national health insurance as an onus the system could bear only if cost controls preceded it and the economy prospered," which was why he only reluctantly proposed a plan. And the disagreements went deeper than that—again, right to the moral obligations of government and the meaning of leadership and the sense of national crisis, which Ted saw as the danger to social services and Carter saw as the danger to the economy. And they went

---

*Carter biographer Kai Bird agreed with Carter's assessment: "In retrospect, Kennedy's refusal to support Carter's incremental, catastrophic national health insurance bill in 1978–79 condemned the country to wait three decades for meaningful healthcare reform." And Bird cited how closely Barack Obama's healthcare plan, which did pass, tracked Carter's, though, in fact, Kennedy's compromise bill was nearly identical to Obama's and Carter's phase-in, had Obama adopted it, would have surely destroyed so-called Obamacare. Kai Bird, *The Outlier: The Unfinished Presidency of Jimmy Carter* (New York: Crown, 2021), 310.

deeper even than that—very deep—to the kind of men they were and how they approached problems: one bold and expansive, the other proudly prudent and austere. In the final analysis, they didn't understand each other, and they didn't like each other; Ted had his "special place" in Carter's animus, and Carter had his place in Ted's. Carter might have been right that Ted's healthcare bill didn't have a chance of passing and that Ted, the pragmatist, was being impractical in proposing a comprehensive bill. Ted might have been right that Carter's bill would ultimately have thwarted national health insurance rather than promoted it. Carter felt Ted didn't have the common sense to see that his plan could never pass. Ted felt Carter didn't have the political will to get a bill passed, only, as Leo Ribuffo had said, his personal stubbornness. So nothing passed.

And now the tension between Ted Kennedy and Jimmy Carter, which had been building since Carter first declared his candidacy in 1975 and continued to build throughout his presidency, was coming to a head. When Jimmy Carter entered office in January 1977, Ted Kennedy had accepted that his job now was to work the Senate, to become a master of the Senate, to encourage Democrats to fight for their liberal principles while trying to prevent Jimmy Carter from abandoning them. Throughout Carter's presidency, he had done that, but not only that. He had edged rightward as the country had, shaking off some of the old liberal verities, covering his political bases, maintaining his liberal identity while working on establishing some conservative credentials by toughening law and order with criminal code reform and by lifting the alleged onus—alleged by conservatives—of government oversight on businesses with his push for deregulation. (Ted, of course, saw the onus being lifted on consumers.) Part of this, no doubt, was a legislative tactic—a way of strengthening his bargaining position with Republicans to enhance his mastery of the Senate and increase his ability to move that recalcitrant institution. And he had, in those few years, used his newfound might to pass legislation— difficult legislation, important legislation, legislation that Jimmy Carter could not have passed were it not for Ted Kennedy. But if Ted Kennedy was building his Senate muscle, he had, through those same efforts, also never been far from positioning himself as a presidential alternative should Carter fail.

And the general perception was that Jimmy Carter was failing. Carter had tried to stem the backlash against liberalism—a backlash that was largely the result of white Americans' anger over perceptions that racial progress was endangering them—by replacing liberalism with moderation. He invoked traditional values and reduced the growth of government programs. But Carter was no racist, and he could never trump conservative Republicans who were stoking that anger. In any case, those racial tensions had been simmering in America for decades. But there were now economic tensions—tensions that Carter had largely inherited but that he seemed impotent to defuse. When he entered the White House, the annual inflation rate was already running at 5.76 percent. By 1980, when he was running for reelection, the rate had risen to 13.50 percent. Since he had little power over the rising oil prices that had contributed to the inflationary spiral, Carter determined that the most effective means of beating back inflation over which he did have control was cutting the federal budget, hoping to slash that budget from 4 percent of the gross national product in 1976, before his election, to 0.5 percent by 1981. "My new goal," he was to write in his memoir, "was to reduce the deficit to zero." It was this budget cutting, which hacked at many programs cherished by Democrats, that had initially put him at odds with Ted Kennedy, and not only with Ted but with a large segment of the Democratic rank and file, who understood the nation's conservative drift but nonetheless clung to the remnants of liberalism that Carter seemed to be undermining. In the event, Carter's plan hadn't worked, though it is unlikely that any plan would have worked, at least any politically feasible plan—Ted Kennedy offered no serious remedy—and with the election approaching, Democrats were despondent at the state of the economy with its high inflation, the sputtering growth of the gross national product, and an unemployment rate stuck above 6 percent. And they were despondent at Carter's futile attempts to cure these ills, which was why they had cheered Ted at the Memphis midterm convention—cheered him for providing some flicker of hope.

As 1978 turned to 1979, Carter continued to founder, relying on a Council of Wage and Price Stability to tamp down inflation, which proved no more effective than Gerald Ford's feckless Whip Inflation Now campaign, and appointing Paul Volcker to be chairman of the Federal Reserve Board, which, under Volcker, threw the economy into recession as a means of reining in inflation. (In truth, it might have been the only option, though it would be too long a process to help Carter in his reelection effort.) "From the right, with Governor Reagan as its chief spokesman, came demands for unprecedented tax cuts and defense expenditures," Carter would later complain, like a man besieged, which he was. "From the left, Senator Kennedy orchestrated the cry for an expensive new round of government programs for jobs, housing, health, welfare and the like." Carter positioned himself as the responsible one, the one with common sense, the one who resisted the Republicans' draconian cuts and yet the one who sought austerity when others in his party were calling for profligacy, but there was no wide support for such a centrist approach in either party. (His biographer, Kai Bird, would title his book *The Outlier*.) "Carter's economic policies are not shaping events," *BusinessWeek* would later comment, in what could have been a description of Carter's entire presidency. "They are being shaped by them." And *BusinessWeek* prophesied this: "A Democratic President who is locked into a fiscally conservative stance will be highly vulnerable in the political battles that will come in the winter and spring."

Carter was in an untenable position. "We are in an essentially conservative period," *The New York Times*'s Anthony Lewis had written as early as 1977, less than a year into Carter's term, "continuing the swing to the right noted at the end of the turbulent 1960's. The country is hardly eager for social experiment. There is a backlash against sexual permissiveness. Further steps to help Blacks and other minorities are difficult. Economic fears have aroused protectionist feelings and resistance to environmental safeguards." And with Americans in a testy mood and largely hostile to liberal palliatives, Lewis believed that "one of Jimmy Carter's principal functions in history may be to keep the reaction from going too far." By his own lights and those of his supporters, Carter had tried through his moderation to save as much of the liberal program as he could, though that moderation was not enough for Ted Kennedy and his fellow liberals. And even Anthony Lewis concluded that "there is a basis for the feeling of disappointment in the President." The times called for vision, Lewis said. Carter, a trained engineer, offered technical solutions instead, partly out of temperament, partly out of trying to avoid being labeled a liberal. Carter did not disagree. On May 20, 1979, at a meeting on the Truman balcony at the White House with his advisers—a meeting that had been prompted by a memo from Carter's pollster Patrick Caddell so pessimistic that it was known as "Apocalypse Now"—he fulminated, according to Theodore White, that the "country is going to hell. The government has fucked up from end to end." And Jimmy Carter would have to take the blame because Jimmy Carter was the government.

. . .

Now, with nowhere to turn and his popularity in free fall, Carter asked for network time to deliver a national address about energy—yet another address about energy—on July 5, 1979. But on the eve of the speech, Caddell brought the president a new poll and a "voluminous memorandum," as Carter described it, very much like the earlier memo, that nudged him in a different direction. What Caddell had found in his surveying was that whatever ailed the country was much larger than the issue of inflated oil prices that had led to those shortages and long lines at the gas station— a gas "panic," it was called that summer—and that had pushed inflation ever higher. Caddell had discovered a crisis of confidence, a loss of faith among the people "in themselves and in their country." So Carter canceled the energy address, realizing he had said it all before anyway, and instead retreated to Camp David where he spent the next eleven days, "some of the most thought-provoking and satisfying of my presidency," he said, meeting with what he called "small groups of people"—people from government, from business, from labor, from academe, from religion—and pondering his next move. It was an unusual move—in some ways a Hail Mary—a move that left Vice President Mondale "distraught." Carter emerged from his sequestration to ask for television time once again—for July 15—but this time he wouldn't be talking chiefly about energy or policies, though he *would* lay out another energy plan. Despairing of any political solution to the national gloom that had settled over the country, Carter, after his days of reflection, had arrived at a spiritual one. He had run for the presidency calling for a government that was as good as the American people. Now at ten p.m. on that July 15, three years to the day after he accepted the Democratic presidential nomination, sitting sternly before a television camera at his desk in the Oval Office, he reprimanded those people for the faithlessness Caddell had found in them. Carter told the nation that he had tried hard to implement legislation to fix the nation's problems. But "all the legislation in the world can't fix what's wrong with America." That problem, he said, wasn't a broken economy. It was a broken spirit and an erosion of confidence. And now Carter delivered a sermon: "In a nation that was proud of hard work, strong families, close-knit communities, and our faith in God, too many of us now tend to worship self-indulgence and consumption. Human identity is no longer defined by what one does, but by what one owns." In a not-so-veiled criticism of liberalism, he said that the people had turned to government, and government had failed them. "You see every extreme position defended to the last vote, almost to the last breath by one unyielding group or another. You often see a balanced and a fair approach that demands sacrifice, a little sacrifice from everyone, abandoned like an orphan without support and without friends." His solution began with something one of those visitors to Camp David had told him: "We've got to stop crying and start sweating, stop talking and start walking, stop cursing and start praying. The strength we need will not come from the White House, but from every house in America," thus taking the burden off himself and placing it on the American people. We can be selfish and self-interested, he said, which leads to fragmentation. Or we can look for common purpose and the restoration of our values. Then, almost as an afterthought, he enumerated the points of a new energy program. And he closed by saying: "I will do my best, but I will not do it alone. Let your voice be heard. Whenever you have a chance, say something good about our country. With God's help and for the sake of our nation, it is time for us to join hands in America. Let us commit ourselves together to a rebirth of the American spirit. Working together with our common faith we cannot fail."

Carter had spoken the way politicians seldom do—in fact, it was the way Bobby Kennedy had spoken during his presidential campaign in 1968 at a time of crisis—talking about the national soul, and not making promises but trying to exact them. There was, no doubt, a good deal of truth in Carter's diagnosis, however impolitic it might have been for him to say it. The country had lost its way, had become selfish, obsessed with material success, disunited. In fact, reactionary populism was a symptom of all these afflictions. Carter thought he had struck a nerve. "The response was very good," he wrote in his diary. "Instantaneous poll results on the West Coast were the best they've ever had for a half-hour program, and I think the people were getting the message." But one of those who was watching and was not impressed was Ted Kennedy, despite the fact that he himself had often called for moral rededication. This, however, wasn't a call, he felt. It was a reprimand. He had watched the speech alone—watched it, he said, "with mounting incredulousness and outrage"—then phoned friends for several hours afterward to canvass their reactions. He found Carter's message to be "contrary to—it was in direct conflict with—all the ideals of the Democratic Party that I cherished," and though he didn't say it, of liberalism itself. It was a conservative speech, a speech without uplift even as it called for uplift, a speech that demanded soul-searching, which, Ted felt, was the province of religion, but not bold action, which was the province of government. And he felt that it was in "conflict with what the country was about," or at least what Ted felt the country was about. Nothing so delineated the difference between Ted Kennedy's idea of governance and Jimmy Carter's as this: Ted felt that the "essence of political leadership . . . is basically challenge and response. Constantly. . . . You are trying to challenge and move the process, and then you are getting response to the challenging." This was what his brothers had done. Meeting that challenge, he believed, was what made the country great. Carter hadn't issued that kind of challenge. He talked instead about how Americans had fallen short and asked them to look into their hearts to do better. *Americans had fallen short.* In Ted's view, it was *government* that had fallen short. And he said, "Any thoughts I still held about supporting Jimmy Carter in a reelection bid I firmly put to rest on July 15, 1979."

Even so, Carter had been correct in thinking the speech was a success. His approval rating rose eleven points overnight. For three days, it recalibrated the political calculus and seemed to resurrect Carter. But just for three days. Because Jimmy Carter then did something that rapidly undid any boost the speech might have provided. He had asked for resignation letters from his entire Cabinet—a move that replicated what Richard Nixon had once done—a comparison that did Carter no favors. And then having gotten those letters, he effected, in *Newsweek*'s words, a "purge as complete and bloody as any in recent Presidential history—an upheaval that swept away nearly half his Cabinet"—five members—"in twenty-four hours and put practically everyone else who counts on notice, except his closest Georgia comrades." And then he named Hamilton Jordan his new chief of staff, a move that one House Democrat compared to the "dummy taking control of the ventriloquist." It was a debacle.

Among the Cabinet casualties was Joseph Califano, the Health, Education, and Welfare secretary with whom Ted had tried to find an accommodation on national health insurance, and among the legislative casualties was that health insurance. Ted felt that this too was a personal affront to him and another way of sabotaging his passion project. He thought Califano was forced out because he and Ted would attend Mass at Holy Trinity Church every Sunday and then drop their children off at Sunday school and attend a kaffeeklatsch at the church at which someone would be invited to speak. "Califano was always there," Ted recalled, and the two would discuss healthcare, which Carter, Ted suspected, might have seen as Califano consorting with the enemy. In truth, Carter disliked Califano, and so did Rosalynn, both of whom thought him disloyal but not particularly because of his relationship with Ted. In any case, once Califano was gone, any small lingering hope of collaboration between Ted and the president on healthcare was also gone.

But hopes for Carter's presidency were plunging too. Carter had managed to snatch defeat from the jaws of victory. The Cabinet shake-up created an image of "instability," Senator Henry Jackson said, and he added that he thought it would be "very, very difficult" for Carter to win renomination, and Jackson was a moderate, not a rabid liberal. George McGovern agreed. Ted was the "most logical" candidate for the presidency, he said. Republican John Connolly predicted that Ted would now win the nomination, saying blandly, "President Carter has difficulties and will continue to have difficulties." As Carter conducted his purge, his favorability rating, which just days earlier had soared, fell back to a dismal 32 percent in the Gallup poll. By September, it had fallen to 19 percent in an NBC/AP poll—the lowest ever recorded in presidential surveys.

Carter had issued no call for greatness. Now Democrats wondered whether Ted Kennedy could and, more, whether the call would be answered. The future of liberalism seemed to depend upon it.

"In the Lap of the Gods"

JOE KENNEDY HAD had a succession plan in place for his sons and for the presidency they sought. But fate had broken the succession, with the deaths of Joe Jr. and Bobby. And the accident at Chappaquiddick had seemed to blight any chance that Ted would enter the White House. It had *seemed* to—but it hadn't. After refusing anointment in 1968 when the nomination might have been his for the asking, he decided not to run in 1972, when Chappaquiddick still hung over him. For 1976, Ted Jr.'s cancer and Ted's obligations as the Kennedy paterfamilias had prompted him to renounce a run as early as 1974. Now, however, the blight had lifted. Now Chappaquiddick seemed like ancient history—or so Ted thought. Now Ted Jr. had recovered. Now there was pressure, intensifying pressure from his own party, for him to challenge Jimmy Carter, whose presidency was deemed a failure, whose leadership had, by consensus, proved inept, whose calls for national soul-searching had seemed self-serving. "Different leadership," Ted had declared after Carter's July 15 speech, in a not-too-subtle hint of his own predilections and intentions. And now Ted Kennedy had to make a decision—once again, yet again, in the quadrennial ritual with which he, his party, and his nation had become so familiar: Should he run? Should he finally run?

The polls were favorable—exceptionally so. (The fact that as early as 1978, there was polling of Ted against Carter was itself an indication of Carter's weakness.) In January 1979 a *Los Angeles Times* poll had Ted leading the field among Democrats in New Hampshire, the first primary state, with 57 percent, to 21 percent for Carter and 12 percent for California governor Jerry Brown, and nationally he led Carter by 42 to 34 percent. By May, Ted led Carter by twenty-three points in the Gallup poll. By July, just before Carter's speech on the crisis of confidence, Ted had the highest favorability rating he had had since Chappaquiddick—75 percent overall—and he had increased his lead among Democrats, 53 to 16 percent over Carter. Another poll at roughly the same time found that 64 percent of Americans wondered if Carter had the "basic competency to do the job." By August, Ted's lead over Carter was larger than any Gallup had ever polled of a potential nominee over an incumbent. By September, with Ted continuing to hold a 53 to 16 percent lead over Carter, CBS correspondent Bruce Morton remarked, "The consensus among political professionals here is that Edward Kennedy can have the Democratic nomination any time he wants it." According to Ted's administrative assistant, Richard Burke, pollster Lou Harris told Ted that Carter's numbers were plummeting and that he was "presiding over the destruction of the Democratic Party." And Harris added that voters didn't seem to care any longer about the accident at Chappaquiddick, which had cast so long a shadow over Ted's presidential prospects. Indeed, the press, which had questioned Ted's veracity after Chappaquiddick and buried him, now seemed eager to have him run, so much so that *Newsweek* ran an article that October titled "Teddy and the Press" that examined whether the press itself was conducting its own Draft Kennedy movement, and answered that it was. "Throughout much of September, Kennedy appeared to use the media like a yo-yo, spinning out the ultimate answer"—the answer to the question of whether he would run—"to within a tantalizing inch of the end of the string, drawing it teasingly back, and getting heavy coverage all the way." It got to the point where *The New York Times*'s Tom Wicker was asking whether Carter might actually decide not to run—a question to this effect was actually asked of Carter at a press conference—and announce that he was dedicating himself to governing the country rather than politicking.

Ted's move. Ted's decision. That was the way the press was characterizing it. In June, Martin Schram of *The Washington Post* wrote, "Democratic politics has come down largely to a matter of watching for signs—signs that Kennedy really will not challenge Carter." But Ted had never jumped at the presidency the way Jack had. A friend of Ted's told writer Elizabeth Drew of Ted's Hamlet-like consideration of whether to run that "he's kind of walked around the question of his candidacy for a long time; a good power operator is always walking around that kind of question, sensing the possibilities." He had been walking around it for so long that it had even become a joke among his staff. One afternoon he was enjoying a quiet lunch in his office when several of his former aides, including his former press secretary Richard Drayne, barged in with a cake. Drayne explained they had come "to recognize the tenth anniversary of the first time you denied you were running for president." Written across the cake was, "If nominated I will not . . . Wm. T. Sherman 1884; Ted Kennedy 1968." Ted exploded in laughter.

Ted was a man torn. He professed to love the Senate, especially now that he was not just a man of the Senate but a leader of the Senate, a master of the Senate. "I enjoy the work and am looking forward to it," he told *The Washington Post* in August 1978 when he was beginning to be pressed on a presidential run against Carter. That same month, on the ABC public affairs program *Issues and Answers*, he said, "I will let the future take care of itself. But certainly, for any foreseeable future, my work will be in the Senate." When the syndicated columnist Nick Thimmesch asked him if the presidency didn't mean as much to him as it meant to his brothers, he answered evenly, "That's about right." And when Thimmesch asked him if he wanted to become the Irish Daniel Webster, the great nineteenth-century Massachusetts senator and orator, Ted laughed and said, "Read those speeches, and you'll see no one can ever be that again." He was more expansive with Robert Ajemian of *Time*, that same month, August 1978, when, talking and broiling steaks in his kitchen, he waved his big fork and said, "Why should I be talking about running for President? There's a Democrat in the White House, there's no moral crisis in the country. What's the reason for running? For power? For what?" And he said that if Carter hadn't been sinking in the polls, no one would be asking him these questions. "The press made Jimmy Carter, and now they're trying to destroy him. I'm going to set my own course."

Ted wasn't being coy when he disavowed any consideration of running. But things had changed since the summer of 1978. There *was* a moral crisis now. The country was desperate. And Carter was not only foundering, he was also regarded as a sure loser in a general election. And there were all those people—labor leaders, congressmen and senators, ordinary rank-and-file Democrats—talking up a Kennedy run, pressing Kennedy to run, telling him he had an obligation to run. Elizabeth Drew said that she had spoken to a number of people who reported conversations with Ted "in which he gave implicit or explicit indications that he was seriously thinking of running this time," indications that included his hiring Carl Wagner, the brilliant young political operative, after the Memphis convention. While on his trips he was sending postcards to friends who said that they hadn't heard from him in years, and when the newly elected Democratic chairman of Ohio's Cuyahoga County, a party stronghold, asked Ted if he might consider delivering the keynote address to a large gathering in October, never expecting Ted to say yes, he was "startled" at how quickly Ted agreed. California controller Kenneth Cory said he visited Ted in Washington that September to discuss energy policy, but the conversation soon pivoted to presidential politics. Kennedy even joked about his intentions with Carter when he phoned the president that month to congratulate him—one of the first to call, Carter said—on the success of the treaty Carter had brokered between Egypt and Israel, joking to Carter that he'd "had to cancel his speech to the Democratic convention in New Hampshire." Later that month one of Carter's associates wrote the president to report on a meeting in Boston among Gerard Doherty, Ted's first campaign manager; Paul Kirk, his former aide and friend; and Dave Burke, Ted's former administrative assistant. "They are clearly planning," the associate said.

But these were steps, not a commitment. His close friend John Tunney, who knew Ted as well as anyone did, believed Ted when he said he had no presidential aspirations, that he didn't have that "fire in the belly that just demanded, or required that he be president," the fire that Jack and Bobby had had, and that he saw his future in the Senate. But Tunney also believed something else: that it was "expected" of Ted that he run for president, had always been expected of him, and that those expectations had only intensified with the deaths of his brothers. Dave Burke agreed that a presidential run was "an event that had to occur," basically was fated to occur, though it wasn't necessarily an event that Ted wanted to occur. Burke said, as Tunney did, that "it was expected of him to run. People were saying, 'When are you going to do it? When are you going to do it? Why not now?' He could never escape, 'When are you going to do it?' He may have succumbed or reached the point when he decided to get it done," which, of course, made a decision for a possible run sound like a surrender rather than a choice. Harris Wofford, who had served Jack Kennedy as special assistant for civil rights, thought Ted had been "programmed by history (and family)" to run, to be the "receptacle for years of accumulated resentment and skepticism about the Kennedys," and had been told a run would clear the "political air," "although he seemed also to fear it and draw back from it." The conservative columnist George Will, observing Ted at this time, saw a man with a "large laugh," and "large cigars," and a man "heart happy in Senate toil." "Time is a great healer of life's bruises," Will wrote as the speculation was heightening, "and today he walks jauntily, with the slightly rolling gait of certain large-framed men, half sailor, half cop. He is the personification of vigor and animal spirits. When he meets constituents, his buoyancy becomes like that of the Graham Greene character who resembled 'a warship going into action, a warship on the right side to end all wars.' " In such a man, Will felt, "whatever fires once burned hotly within him have been banked for the foreseeable future."

But Ted Kennedy had never been a man who controlled his own destiny. The editor Lewis Lapham, in an otherwise damning analysis of Ted in *Harper's,* allowed himself this bit of sympathy: "He always gave the impression of a man who had lived his life for everybody but himself." And now, as the election approached and the day of decision with it, Ted Kennedy was being borne once again by the current. "I think competition, whether it's in the private sector or the public sector, is a healthy ingredient," he told one reporter in September 1979, speaking not of deregulation but of his deliberations, almost as if he were trying to convince himself. "I think the key to the question of success for the President will be in how he handles the economy." Ted said he believed that if Carter was "perceived as someone able to deal with this," no Republican would be able to beat him. But after all the months of telling the press that he would be supporting Carter—this was after Carter's July 15 speech, when Ted had told himself he couldn't support Carter's candidacy—Ted said he had reconsidered and was now telling politicians, "I don't foreclose the possibility of a candidacy." He was still being cautious. He wondered whether he was up to the presidency—a question that had never gnawed at his brothers but always gnawed at him. And he wondered just how quixotic a run against an incumbent might be, though Bobby had taken on an incumbent, and their beloved grandfather, Honey Fitz, had taken on the anointed Democratic machine candidates, both in his congressional and in his mayoral races—taken them on not because Bobby or Honey Fitz needed higher office to satisfy some personal ambition, but because they felt it was the right thing to do—in Bobby's case, the necessary thing, to rescue the country from Lyndon Johnson and save it from the prospect of Richard Nixon. Quixotic quests were not bred into the Kennedys. Winning was bred into them. As one former aide to Ted told biographer Burton Hersh, "The Kennedys never shit themselves. There are no daydreams." Was taking on Jimmy Carter a daydream? Or was it a mission?

II

For all his waffling and for all the questions among intimates over whether Ted really wanted the presidency or was being forced into running against his wishes, there was one person who was to say, years later, after Ted's death, that Ted Kennedy did want to be president: his second wife, Victoria Reggie Kennedy. "I asked him if he really wanted to be president," she told an interviewer, "because everybody assumes he really didn't want to be president. He said, 'Oh, no. I wanted to be president.' He really wanted to be president, and I believe that. I believe that." The fire did burn. His hesitations weren't over desire. They were over practicalities. As he pondered whether to run, the first question—it had always been the first question—was whether he should risk his life. (California State Assembly leader Jesse Unruh, who had been in the Ambassador Hotel when Bobby was shot, raised that very issue with Ted when the two of them spoke about a possible run in September 1978.) David Ormsby-Gore, a close friend of Jack Kennedy's, thought Jack had a kind of preternatural calm because he had escaped death so many times—in World War II, in his illnesses, in his back problems that put him on his deathbed. "I have always noticed," Ormsby-Gore said, "that people who have that kind of experience have a sort of calm; not quite a detachment from life, but a calm attitude to anything that life can throw at them." William vanden Heuvel, another Kennedy confidant, described it as a "legendary quality of the Irish, where death is not an intimidating force and fear is not part of your personality. You just move forward in a strong and continuing way." And Ted, the fatalist, the man who was sure he would be next, the man who had survived a near-fatal plane accident and then an automobile accident, did move forward fearlessly, although not obliviously. John Tunney and Ted took a trip after Bobby's death, and Tunney said that Ted suffered under a grief that "he hid pretty well from the public" but that was "emotionally self-destructive." "I think he really thought that he was going to get it too, and this was—it wasn't fear. It was a sense of the futility of what was going on in his life"—a sensitivity to the senselessness of the deaths of Jack and Bobby and possibly of his own. He knew a campaign for the presidency would be an invitation for assassination. It would permit, as Lewis Lapham wrote, "his fellow citizens to enjoy the guilty pleasure of guessing at his chance of being murdered" and "impart to the election the excitement of a gladiatorial show in the Roman arena." He stands "within the penumbra of death, a smiling and Dionysian figure playing out the last act of a fearful tragedy."

His family suffered from the same fatalistic chill—expecting his death. He once asked a reporter, "Do you know what it's like to have your wife frightened all the time?" Joan's father, Harry Bennett, told Joan's biographer, Lester David, "Over and over, Joan keeps saying she hopes he does not run." He said they all "pray he doesn't." Patrick said as a boy he had no idea of the magnitude of his father's fame until the Secret Service arrived to guard him—in short, when he saw how his father needed to be protected. And Patrick said he had once seen someone stab his father's hand when Ted was walking a rope line. When Ted was campaigning for the Senate, he would pull over every night to a pay phone and call the children and tell them stories and do imitations, just to let them know that he was all right, to assuage their fears, to show them that he hadn't suffered the fate of their uncles.

Ted himself was skittish. By one account, when a toy cannon was fired at the observance of the one-hundredth anniversary of Haverhill, Massachusetts, he doubled over. Others said that when a car backfired, he would dive down and put his briefcase, The Bag, over his head. Even the Senate's quorum buzzer call would cause him to jump. He lived with danger even as he tried to suppress his fear of it. "If you took it"—the possibility of assassination—"lightly and said there was nothing to it, you'd be a fool," Ted told journalist William Honan. "On the other hand, if you worried about it all the time, you'd be valueless, so you have to bring these two things into balance and make an evaluation. And you have to think of what that means to the other people in your life." But he once told a friend this too: "All I want—if someone's going to blow my head off—I just want one swing at him first. I don't want to get it from behind."

There had been hundreds of threats over the years, more death threats against him than against any public figure outside the president. The first recorded by the FBI—in March 1964, after Jack's assassination—was from a Montana group that had lost money to the Castro regime and, it was feared, for some reason might take vengeance against Ted. Some FBI reports listed people who heard voices ordering them to kill him. Another report discussed a minister of the Universal Metaphysical Church who had visions of Ted's death. Many people told the FBI of overhearing conversations between individuals plotting his death. Still others discussed meetings at which his death was bruited about. One reported threat was allegedly made by Sonny Capone, possibly the son of Al Capone, at a telephone booth outside a restaurant in Coral Gables, Florida. Among the would-be assassins were seers, inebriates, white supremacists, mental patients, and some people who just hated Ted's liberal politics. Some sent threatening letters to him. Others phoned his office with threats. His security was so tight that when two men stole a pistol from a local sporting goods store in Lowell, Massachusetts, where Ted was scheduled to deliver a college commencement address, police provided a heavy guard, lest that gun be used against him. Whenever he traveled, his advance men would make arrangements with local law enforcement. Even when he attended Martin Luther King, Jr.'s, funeral in Atlanta, he publicly announced he would not be attending, then flew to Florida and back up to Atlanta to foil any potential assassin. Many of these threats were frivolous, but not all. One woman arrived at his office and "blasted" through his private office door, as his aide Melody Miller described it, even tearing away from the police who had been summoned. Ted was at his desk when the woman burst in, yelling that she would "get" Miller and "get" the senator, and he began speaking very softly, making everyone strain to hear him, and that quieted the room and subdued the woman. And that very November 1979, a mentally disturbed woman carrying a five-inch hunting knife barged into his office and had to be subdued by the Secret Service agents who had been assigned to him in prospect of his presidential run. Ted's staff, with gallows humor, would joke that they were going to get a sign with an arrow pointing to him.

And there was another issue that gave Ted pause, which had to do not just with the logistics of a campaign, including his safety, but with the logistics of life: Joan Kennedy. It had long been a troubled marriage, an increasingly distant and loveless marriage, to which both Joan's alcoholism and Ted's womanizing contributed. As Ted described it in his memoir, "My parents and siblings were all well disposed toward Joan," which wasn't exactly true since the sisters particularly felt that she wasn't "Kennedy" enough for the Kennedys. "Yet as time went on, the awareness deepened among all of us that something fundamental was not working right," Ted wrote. "Our relationship atrophied," and the two of them "remained together for many years longer than we were happy." But they did not consider divorce. "The reasons were many: our children, our faith, my career, and perhaps fear of change." Still, the marriage was untenable, and in July 1978, when Ted was being pressured to contemplate a presidential run, Joan publicly confessed in an article in *McCall's* magazine that she was an alcoholic—though she said at the time that she had been sober for a year—and that some eight months earlier she had moved to a Back Bay apartment in Boston, where she began taking classes at the Lesley College. She never discussed this as a separation—"The truth is, I just needed some space to work on my sobriety"—though a separation was what it was. She made it sound like a breather. She talked about her distaste for the Washington political scene—"I like going to a party and not talking just politics"; and about having to escape the gravitational pull of the Kennedys and declare her independence—"She realized that the only way she could save herself from total destruction was to leave behind her husband and everything Kennedy for a new life," a friend said; about the slower pace of life in Boston, which enabled her "to find out who I am and what it is I want to do for the next forty years of my life"; and about the anonymity she could find in Boston that she couldn't find in Washington, now that she was regularly attending Alcoholics Anonymous meetings, though, in truth, the anonymity was Ted's decision as much as Joan's. As she told the writer Laurence Leamer, Ted did not want her to attend AA because he feared she would talk about the family. ("They don't want any part of AA," "they" being the Kennedy brain trust, presumably that group of advisers including brother-in-law Stephen Smith, Paul Kirk, Dave Burke, and Milton Gwirtzman, who, she said, made decisions for her as if she were a "nonentity," because AA "means public to them.") Instead, she said Ted wanted her to see a priest/psychiatrist who they knew would be discreet. But Joan wasn't as compliant this time as she had been in the past. She sought out Del Sharbutt, a Washington broadcaster who was also active in AA, and he guided her. Ted was not happy about Joan's confession either, about which she hadn't consulted him before making it. Secrecy, after all, was the Kennedy curse, and Kennedys didn't reveal their weaknesses. "Our family has always kept things private," he told *Time*, "but once Joan decided it was best for her to talk openly about the problem, I thought it was very brave," though this remark too was for public consumption. He did not praise her bravery privately. He scorned it.

And Joan was candid. She told *McCall's* that she had just drunk so-cially at first, but it became a pattern that "starts to creep up on you." "Little by little," she said. There were times when she would be out with friends and drank too much and embarrassed herself and embarrassed Ted. But there were times, too, when she felt she had risen to the occasion, as she had when Ted Jr.'s leg was amputated and she didn't take a drink beforehand. "But as soon as he was well and back in school," she told *McCall's*, "I just collapsed. I needed some relief from having to be so damn brave all the time." And if she was candid about her drinking, she was candid too about rumors of her husband's womanizing—she said she never believed those rumors, though that was Joan protecting Ted—and the devastating effect they had on her. Ted, who didn't exercise much dis-cretion when it came to his affairs, had seemed to stop caring about that effect as he had seemed to stop caring about Joan generally. (Years later she would say that his infidelity had driven her to flirt and that when she returned from a trip once, she had smelled a woman in her bed.) And now, as he contemplated the presidency, those rumors of infidelity resurfaced, though in Washington, they were no longer regarded as rumors. He was linked to the blond Olympic skier Suzy Chaffee, with whom he had been seen on the slopes of Aspen the previous February. Chaffee denied any relationship other than a professional one, saying that she had met with Ted to work on women's issues in her capacity as head of the World Fed-eration of Sports. "Kennedy is essential for getting anything done in Washington," she told the *Los Angeles Times* in a tone that seemed less than professional. "He gets the job done like he skis—fast, smooth, strong, and with a great sense of humor." "People think I'm living apart because I'm furious with him," Joan told *Newsweek*, shortly before her *McCall's* confession, "but they don't know what's going on. Sure, I asked him about Chaffee. We discussed it, resolved it, and are happy about it. It's a lot of nonsense."

Joan would tell Ted's biographer, Adam Clymer, that when she moved to Boston in 1977, "I hadn't left him." She said she intended to return to Washington after her treatment, but her doctor advised against it. So she developed a new life in Boston—attending the AA meetings "often," driv-ing to McLean Hospital in Belmont once a week for group therapy, seeing a psychiatrist, Dr. William Hawthorne, three times a week, picking up her interest in piano and attending her music classes and working toward a master's degree. Ted would fly up as often as once a week to attend family counseling sessions—"It's brought us so much closer," Joan would say. "We all talk about it."—and he would sometimes ask her out to dinner. "In Washington, when we were out for dinner, it was always with our children or my in-laws or his friends or invariably a large group. Now we go out alone together. It's almost like having a date." That was Joan Kennedy's gloss on her dissolving marriage.

Independent. Making decisions for herself. Sober for a year. Finding her way. These were the achievements of Joan Kennedy when she spoke to *McCall's* in 1978. "At 41, Joan Kennedy has the recharged vitality and easy smile of a convert," *People* gushed the same month as the *McCall's* piece, in an article titled, "A Second Chance." (No doubt Joan was launching a media campaign of her own to demonstrate her rehabilitation, possibly as part of her therapy, possibly even as a way to prove her resilience to her husband.) But by the time the articles appeared, she had suffered a relapse—"badly," according to *Time*. Joan had not recovered. Joan had not found her way. And Joan could never win back her philandering husband. She needed to be attended to. According to Marcia Chellis, who was Joan's personal assistant at the time, Joan had a junior high school counselor coming to the apartment to help her out and take her to the movies and later even move in with her, and a cook named Kitty Gillooly, who also watched over her. She made frequent trips to McLean Hospital, and she lost her privileges to drive. A year after that, just when Ted was coming to a decision on the race, she had another relapse and went to another treatment center, Appleton House, where, she told Chellis, a room was reserved for her at all times. And Ted, who seemed to feel that Joan was a lost cause and who had moved on, showed little concern, which was a very Kennedy-like attitude—a Joe Kennedy–like attitude. Joan was a nuisance. As Chellis told it, all communications between Ted and Joan were now handled through Ted's administrative assistant, Rick Burke. Ted hadn't even provided her with a telephone number when he was out of town. Asked how he thought she was doing after her latest relapse, Ted would only say, "I think she's making great progress," which was also a Kennedy response—a rote response, not a sincere one.

Now life had changed. For the last year and a half, from late 1977 through the summer of 1979 when his presidential considerations were ramping up, Ted Kennedy had lived at McLean with his children but without his wife. In his new daily routine, he would get up and have breakfast with

Patrick. Then Patrick would take the bus to school, and Ted would do twenty-five push-ups and swim or run a mile or play a game of tennis with friends, whom he invited to his court. "You'd drive in the driveway, and the Senator would always be waiting in the driveway, and it would often be in the teens—the temperature," said his friend Lee Fentress, who was one of the regular tennis partners for these early morning doubles games, along with occasional players like Senators Claiborne Pell and Fritz Hollings. "We always used to kid if he ever put on long pants, because he used to wear shorts and it would literally be thirty degrees outside. I remember sliding over that tennis court with ice, all of us saying, 'My god! We're going to break a neck here.'" Then the group would shower and eat a light breakfast and Ted would head to work. He made an effort to be home in the evenings for dinner with the children—Kara and Ted Jr. were eighteen and seventeen respectively at the time, the first headed off to Trinity College that fall of 1978, the second getting ready to go to Wesleyan University the following year—where they would discuss current events as Ted had done as a boy at his father's table, and then Patrick, only eleven, would do his homework, and Ted would help Ted Jr., who was at the private St. Alban's School, with his homework, and Ted would say his prayers with Patrick and then make himself a scotch and soda or two, retire to the library, sit in his high-backed wing chair, and dig into The Bag or make phone calls before heading to bed, watching television, and going to sleep.

The absence of Joan was hardest on Patrick, the youngest, though he said his mother had never really been a presence in his life. "Honestly, I don't remember my mom being around a lot when I was growing up, so it's not as if I saw them as a couple," he was to say. "That's because she was constantly off trying to get treatment." Joan understood and Joan regretted. "I knew the older children would be fine, but Patrick was my little boy," she would say of her decision to leave Washington. There was no maternal presence in his life, only a series of governesses, young women, just out of college or graduate school, who would come for a year or a year and a half and then move on. But Ted tried hard to compensate by doubling his affection. "Both Mom and Dad to Patrick," even Joan would admit of Ted during this period. There was a special bond between him and Patrick, special because, like him, he was the youngest, special because, like him, he was seemingly the weakest, the one who had the most to overcome, the one of whom the expectations were the lowest, and because, unlike him, he was small and unathletic, skinny, red-haired, and freckled rather than robust and movie-star handsome like the other Kennedys, the most "sensitive" of his three children, Ted said, "more so than the others." Patrick said he felt "awkward, anxious, separate, like a loser." And Patrick said this of their relationship, which was incongruous in the Kennedy family, where strength was valorized: "He felt that I was his guy."

And Patrick had one more deficit. He was sickly. Ted said that when Patrick was administered an allergy test with twenty-four pinpricks along his arm, the arm "looked like a nuclear meltdown; it just absolutely reddened, all of it. He was allergic to everything." Above all, Patrick suffered from a virulent form of asthma—so debilitating that he had to take steroids daily to treat it, so debilitating that Ted had to lug a twenty-five-pound Maxi-Mist nebulizer everywhere he went with Patrick, and that Patrick was constantly being hospitalized, and that he had to sleep occasionally under an oxygen tent, and that he had to be held back in school. And Patrick said he fretted as a boy that when he was traveling with his family, he would have an attack and that it would "ruin everything," so he would wait and wait and wait until the asthma got so bad that he could no longer deal with it. (Every year, sometimes twice a year, until Patrick graduated from the Phillips Andover Academy, Ted convened a group of asthma experts to examine Patrick and determine if they could improve his treatment.) The asthma adumbrated the Kennedy family. Joan would say that when she was still living in Washington, Ted demanded that she not "baby" Patrick, and that when he and Ted would return from a function and Patrick would be breathing heavily and she would run to fetch medication and turn on his nebulizer, Ted would bark, "You're just giving in to him," which would have been a typical Kennedy response. But Patrick didn't recall it that way, certainly not after his mother left. He said that his father was often overtaken by "emotional turmoil" and was sometimes unavailable to him. But he also recalled that the asthma was "lucky" for him because "it gave a focal point to his [Ted's] being attentive to me" and because Ted showered him with that attention. The two of them would share separate accommodations from the rest of the family when they traveled. And often, after dinner, Ted would pull Patrick onto his lap, and Patrick would "lay my head on his chest while he held me tight"—Patrick said, "I seemed to fit perfectly"—and Ted would finish his dessert and his Sanka decaffeinated coffee with Patrick nuzzling against him. And sometimes, after taking his medication in the evening, Patrick would be stricken with terrible headaches, often in the middle of the night, and Ted would sit beside him and gently apply cold compresses to his forehead until he fell asleep. Other times he slept beside him because the wheezing was so bad that Ted simply wanted to be near him. Every summer, from the time Patrick was eight to the time he was fifteen, Ted would take him on a four-day camping trip—just the two of them. (Kara and Ted Jr. complained that Ted never took them.) They would sail on the *Victura*, Jack's old boat, to Menemsha or Tuckerknuck or Meskeget or Naushon Island or one of the Elizabeth Islands or Cuttyhunk, and set up a tent on the beach and fish and at night watch the stars. And even when the Senate was in session, Patrick said that no matter how busy his father was, he would drop everything if Patrick had an asthma attack. But it wasn't just the asthma that had Ted put everything on hold, even though Patrick often talked as if it was. Ted's administrative assistant Rick Burke said that Ted "would stop whatever he was doing and take time to call them [his children] every afternoon," but he remembered best Ted talking to Patrick, making animal noises—"I'm here with a little doggy, woof-woof"—and entertaining him. He called him "Dippity Dawg" because Patrick's favorite cartoon character was "Deputy Dawg." And in a family where Rose Kennedy had been cold, distant, and unloving, Ted, Patrick said, "just hugged me all the time." (He would continue to do so years later when the two would meet in the halls of Congress.) It was the "kind of intimacy that was an antidote for me" amid the family turmoil, Patrick would say. And he would say that without it, he would have been "lost."

Should he run? All through the year, 1979, Ted had been meeting with family and friends, to discuss that very question. There had been a parade of them: Steve Smith and his former aide Paul Kirk and his legislative assistant Carey Parker, of course; former administrative assistants Eddie Martin and Dave Burke; Bobby's old colleague at Justice, John Douglas; another of Bobby's close friends, Fred Dutton; Bobby's old press secretary during his presidential campaign, Frank Mankiewicz; and John Culver. "A number of sessions," Culver would say, at the McLean house. Now, as summer arrived, Ted was moving toward a decision about challenging Jimmy Carter, but he wasn't moving quickly. Patrick's needs had been one reason Ted adduced for why he had decided not to run in 1972, and Ted Jr.'s cancer one reason he adduced for not running in 1976. This time Ted discussed the prospect with Kara, Ted Jr., and Patrick in the Squaw Island house in Hyannis. But it was different this time. A "much higher tempo at the house," Patrick recalled. And Ted seemed more decisive, as if he relished the idea of running. When Ted broached the idea with the children, Larry Horowitz said Ted thought they might "blow up" at him. Instead, Patrick said he thought the idea was "just exciting," and while Kara and Ted Jr. were "not wildly enthusiastic" and expressed their fears about their father's safety, they didn't try to nix it. But there was that other consideration, a major consideration, and they discussed that too. "It wasn't about personal safety or whether we could hack it as kids," Patrick said of their conversation with their father. "It was more about, 'Can your mother handle it?'" Joan was the issue now.

As a practical matter, especially with the media floating rumors about his womanizing and the disrespect his behavior demonstrated toward the woman to whom he was still married, he could not run without Joan. As Joan herself described it to Adam Clymer, she and Ted took a walk on the beach at Hyannis in either July or August 1979, after Jimmy Carter's speech that had so infuriated Ted, when Ted was seriously pondering a run. By her recollection, Ted told her that he was proud of her for staying sober for two years—even though she had had several relapses over that period of time—and asked her if she would be up for a campaign. Joan said she was "delighted" by the question because she felt she had been a problem to him—he had certainly made her feel that way—and "I wanted to give something back to him." (Five years earlier, when he was thinking of a 1976 run, she had said, "I am not ambitious for my husband. I'm not that kind of woman. But I don't want to be a drag.") That, however, was hardly the end of it. Ted's advisers and the elder Kennedys, especially Ted's sister Eunice Shriver and his brother-in-law Steve Smith, had their doubts. Smith told Arthur Schlesinger, Jr., that Joan's "loose lips" were the "gnawing and perhaps inhibiting uncertainty in Ted's situation," and Smith was worried that she might say something damaging, not because she wanted to but because she was not in full control of herself. The exact timetable for resolving those doubts is unclear. Ted said of Joan, "I had to get the green-light, which we got that summer, in the early summer, that this was going to be all right, because the last thing I wanted to do was to tip things over."

By "green-light," however, Ted did not just mean Joan's consent. He approached this decision the way he approached his legislative decisions: with great deliberation. With her permission, he collected all Joan's medical records and asked a panel of three psychiatric experts, and Joan's own psychiatrist, Dr. William Hawthorne, to review them. "We spent a lot of time on this," Ted was to say, in order to make sure that "there was a much better chance than not that she would make it through and be satisfactory," though, according to Larry Horowitz, not just that she would make it through but that "whether, in some strange way, it [her participation] would be helpful," though Horowitz did not say helpful to whom, Ted or Joan. If the panel thought a campaign would be deleterious to her health, Ted agreed not to proceed with one. In all likelihood, his children wouldn't have let him proceed with one anyway. By Horowitz's account, the conclave, an all-day session, took place in mid-September at a hotel in Crystal City, Virginia, with Joan, Kara, Ted Jr., Patrick, the Kennedy sisters, and Ethel all in attendance. Late that night the panel delivered their verdict: A campaign would not adversely affect Joan. (Yet again Joan seemed to be left out of the decision making, which was clearly tilted to Ted's benefit.) At least that was Horowitz's version. In Rick Burke's version, Joan expressed some hesitation, saying that while she didn't want to do anything to impede Ted's chances, and while she wanted him to be president, she wasn't sure she was up to the rigors of a campaign. In her defense, Dr. Hawthorne said a decision could wait, even though, politically speaking, it really couldn't. And then, as Burke told it, the family met for a weekend at McLean, after which Ted told Burke to call Paul Kirk, his longtime aide, and instruct him to begin staffing a campaign. And that ended the deliberations about Joan. She was onboard, by her own volition or not.

But there had been other deliberations that spring and summer and other efforts on his behalf, even as Ted had remained tentative about a run. Paul Kirk said that a Washington attorney named Mark Siegel, who was well connected to the Democratic National Committee, had "ginned" up a draft movement, and Ted had asked Kirk to keep tabs on it, without encouraging it. When supporters called Kirk to gauge Ted's feelings, Kirk would tell them, "If you want to mark time, mark time." Ted, however, was the one who was marking time. In April he had met with New York attorney general Robert Abrams and Abrams's executive assistant, Ethan Geto, at the Carlyle Hotel in Manhattan and told them that he did not expect to run. But Geto said that he used words like "drift" and "malaise" to describe the national condition, and told them that he was deeply worried that a conservative Republican might capture the White House. And he said more. He said the Democratic Party of Jimmy Carter did not reflect the values of his brothers. Geto used that statement as a prompt to join the draft movement that had been developing and that was being encouraged by William Winpisinger, the president of the International Association of Machinists. "Pressure is building on Teddy," Arthur Schlesinger, Jr., reported in his journal after visiting with Steve Smith in May, and Smith told him that Ted's posture—saying that he expected Carter to be renominated while not ruling out a challenge to him—was increasingly untenable and might wind up preventing another liberal—Mo Udall had said he was willing to take on Carter—from joining the race. Smith said that the problem wasn't political but rather personal: the fear of assassination and the issues of Joan and the children. And yet the rest of the family had already come to terms with his run, even Rose, who had been set against it.

Still Ted drifted, dropping hints of a run, giving speeches in which he jabbed at Carter, even, in one of the old tell-tale signs of a run, going on a diet with only soup and a salad with lo-cal dressing for lunch and dropping twenty pounds in six months—this for a man, once nicknamed "Biscuits and Muffins," who scoured the office for peanuts and crackers and of whom Ethel had said that he could describe a meal with so much gusto that "you feel you've eaten it yourself." But for all that, there was no commitment to a run. The "biggest tease in politics," *Time* called him that June. He admitted he had ramped up his rhetoric against the president, but said he had not done so out of political opportunism but because the circumstances of the nation had changed and because he and Carter were no longer "moving along the same track." "If I were silent," he told *The Washington Post*, "I'd be violating my responsibilities as a senator to speak out on what I am for and what I am against."

And that remark only further heightened speculation about his intentions. The big tease delivered the commencement address at Boston University that June, saying he would forgo any criticism of the presidents, either of BU president John Silber, who had been under fire, or of Carter. "It is hard being president these days. At least that is what I'm told," Ted joked in his loud, hyperbolized register that he reserved for sarcasm. "I, of course, don't have any firsthand experience at it." Then he paused with a deafening silence, the audience poised for the punchline. "Yet!" And the crowd roared.

And as Ted teased, Carter himself vacillated over what he thought Ted might do—one day certain that Ted had been planning to challenge him since 1978, another day convinced that Ted would not take him on. "This Kennedy game of pretending to run doesn't scare Jimmy," said one aide. "He doesn't believe it." But then Carter later that month told a group of congressmen who had come to the White House for a dinner at which he briefed them on the Panama Canal treaty that if Kennedy ran, "I'll whip his ass." (This is the remark Tom Wicker had cited in his column.) And though he professed in his memoir that he was "surprised" to see the quote appear in the news afterward, he had actually made certain that the remark was widely circulated. To which Ted quipped, "I think what he meant to say was that he was going to whip inflation." A few days later, speaking before the Iowa State Bar Association, Ted chuckled, struggling to get out the line through his own laughter, "I always felt the White House would stand behind me, but I didn't realize how close they would be."

That was how the nascent, possible campaign proceeded into the summer—jauntily, desultorily, uncertainly. Carey Parker said that Ted was seriously thinking about it but didn't seem headed toward a definite deadline, unlike Jack's presidential bid, which had been years in the planning. (Of course, Ted's slight shift rightward as early as 1975 on the criminal code and deregulation prefigured a possible presidential run.) The process just kept going as if the decision would arrive by itself, and the party's liberals waited. "I can't think of a particular time when the decision was made," Parker said. Paul Kirk said something of the same. "If you had to do it over again, and you knew you were really going to plan a campaign, this would not be the way to go." Ted spent the summer speaking—at the National Urban League convention in Chicago that July, he joked about accusations that Carter was playing politics with his policies: "Now, I ask you, 'Who at a time like this would be thinking about presidential politics?'"—and discussing the presidency with friends and advisers who came up to Hyannis. He had set Labor Day as a target because he didn't want to come back to the Senate after the summer recess and "still be sort of back and forth," but he still didn't exude any sense of urgency about it. Arthur Schlesinger, Jr., visiting him that July, found him "cheerful and unconcerned." Unlike the long detailed planning sessions that had preceded Jack's run and even Bobby's, Ted held a cookout on Squaw Island where the presidential run was the main topic of conversation. The process seemed so lackadaisical that even after all the months of discussion and debate, Horowitz still thought it was only fifty-fifty whether Ted would run.

But that changed after Carter's speech on July 15—the speech Ted had so detested, the speech he felt that had betrayed everything in which his brothers had believed and everything he had believed about America. "It just seemed to me that we were moving in a direction where incompetency was just taking hold," he would later say of that period. And there was by that time an inexorable, nearly irresistible force building that militated for a run: the polls that August showing Carter losing to Reagan while Ted beat Reagan; the overwhelming preference by Democrats for Ted over Carter; the mounting pressure by Democrats who told him "You've got to run"; the sense that it would be easy to beat Carter and that, as one aide predicted, "The Carter campaign will be like the French army in World War II, an obstacle but not a deterrent"; and perhaps above all, the peril he thought the economy was facing—a peril underscored by a meeting at his home of leading liberal economists, including John Kenneth Galbraith, who warned him that the country was heading toward recession. (It turned out it was.) Most important was not how his advisers felt or how the Democratic partisans felt or how the economists felt or even how Ted Kennedy himself felt. It was how the American people felt, and they did not feel, as Carter himself had observed, especially confident. The country seemed dispirited, and Carter couldn't rally it. And rallying the nation was precisely the sort of thing that Kennedys had always done.

Ted knew that. He batted away the obstacles that had prevented him from running previously: his vow to his mother not to run ("I've always been mindful of the strain Mother's under, but she would support any decision I made"), or the concerns over his safety (he said he had to keep a balance between being paralyzed by threats and being insensitive to them and concluded, "It's not hard"). Paul Kirk, who argued against his running, felt Ted was almost too casual. (During a cookout at Hyannis, Ted had taken Kirk aside, told him he had decided to run, and said, "If the thing doesn't work out, I think I'll just be able to live with myself better for having taken up the cause that's drifting away.") "Overconfident," Carey Parker said. Almost as if to shock him out of his complacency, Ted Sorensen, who wrote a paper analyzing a run, warned Ted that he should expect his poll numbers to fall, and Milton Gwirtzman later said that Ted "wouldn't have run if it had been more even." ("The Kennedys never shit themselves.") But Ted seemed unconcerned that there was any possibility of Carter overtaking him now—now that Carter seemed to be flailing and Ted was clearly ascendant. Pat Moynihan said, "It's beginning to be an open scandal in Washington that the administration makes its decisions on how Kennedy will react. The President is governing at the sufferance of Senator Kennedy"—the very thing Moynihan had said to Carter privately and now felt emboldened to express publicly. (This was how Nixon had reacted to Ted as well.) And one close Carter associate even accused Ted of intentionally "poisoning the political atmosphere" against Carter to force him to step aside. Meeting with Ted and a small group of advisers at McLean after Labor Day for what he thought was yet another discussion of the potential race, Sorensen arrived to find that Ted had already come to his conclusion and that there were "pieces of paper" being handed out—"strategies and so on"—for Ted to sign off on. Sorensen, like Kirk, thought it unwise to run—thought that the combination of Chappaquiddick and, recalling Bobby's fight against the Democratic establishment in 1968, Carter's incumbency made it a difficult proposition. (He said that Steve Smith agreed with him.) Despite all the deliberations, albeit desultory, the decision also seemed impulsive. At an earlier meeting, Sorensen had originated a term, "lap of the gods" strategy, by which he meant that Ted's decision on whether to run would seem to be left to fate: "No, we weren't going to organize a campaign. We don't think it's likely [that Ted will run]—the problems, the obstacles, and so on, but it's in the lap of the gods. If events propel him in that direction, we'll be ready." Now events had propelled Ted in that direction. And now the campaign was in the lap of the gods. Carter was a weakened president; his approval rating that September stood at 19 percent, the lowest rating in the AP/NBC poll in three decades. Ronald Reagan seemed the likeliest Republican nominee, but there were serious doubts about Reagan and whether he was *too* conservative, even for a country headed rightward. The presidency seemed to beckon to Ted. Joe Kennedy had taught his children: "If you see a piece of cake on the table, you take it."

Given Jimmy Carter's missteps and Ted Kennedy's belief that the country was headed in the wrong direction, the presidency was now Ted's piece of cake. He had to take it.

III

Having finally made his decision, Ted now had to announce it. The first person he had to inform was Jimmy Carter. Ted asked to meet with Carter shortly after Labor Day, on September 7, at which time he intended to break the news.* But before he went to the White House, he told Larry Horowitz that he still hadn't fully committed, and he said that "if Carter was willing to be conciliatory in some way"—he was thinking obviously of national health insurance—that he would be receptive. The two met along with Carter's wife, Rosalynn, for a lunch of broiled fish on the White House terrace. (Carter had suggested lunch *and* dinner to give them more time to talk. Ted declined.) Ted said that he and Mrs. Carter discussed mental health care, which was a priority of hers, and when she left, he and the president "got down to business," in the words of Steve Smith, to whom Ted had apparently reported the luncheon. Carter asked Ted to issue a "Sherman-like" statement that he would not accept the Democratic nomination. Ted refused, which, Ted said, seemed to take Carter aback. Ted said he had come to the White House to inform Carter of his intentions. But judging from Carter's reaction to the meeting, from Steve Smith's conversation afterward with Schlesinger that he was 85 percent certain Ted was going to run—not 100 percent—and from the reaction of Ted's own staff when, after the lunch, he told them he was going to run, this doesn't seem either to have been planned or to have occurred. In all likelihood, Ted had told Carter that he wouldn't refuse the nomination if proffered, that he wasn't going to endorse Carter, and that he was considering running, just considering it. And then the two went to the Map Room—Ted now accompanied by Richard Burke, and the president by Hamilton Jordan. Carter had made no attempt at reconciliation and hadn't even mentioned healthcare, which had clearly pushed Ted over the line. The next day Carter told his staff to assume that Ted and California governor Jerry Brown would be running against him—to assume it, not that Ted had told him he was going to run. Even after all the endless speculation about his running, when Ted announced to his staff, after the Carter lunch, that he was going to be a candidate, they were surprised

---

* Steve Smith told Arthur Schlesinger, Jr., that Carter was the one who extended the invitation. Arthur Schlesinger, Jr., *Journals: 1952–2000*, eds. Andrew Schlesinger and Stephen Schlesinger (New York: Penguin Press, 2007), 470.

because, as Larry Horowitz put it, "there had been no work on defining the issues for a campaign, the message for a campaign, the logistics of a campaign, the personnel for a campaign. There had been none of that. None of that went on during the summer in any meaningful way, except spinning around in the back of your mind." It was a "lap of the gods" decision and now a "lap of the gods" campaign. Ted suddenly became a candidate almost without having chosen to be one.

Officially, however, he wasn't a candidate yet. He had made no public announcement. He was still teasing, saying that while he was not a candidate, both his mother and his wife had given their blessing to a run, which led the press to treat it as if his candidacy were a foregone conclusion. And he acted like a candidate, giving what amounted to campaign speeches before the American Newspaper Publishers Association, in which he laid out a comprehensive economic plan, highlighted by strict wage and price guidelines and a big windfall profits tax on oil companies; before the Investment Association Dinner (the speech in which he declared that the New Deal was over); and the very next day, before the Massachusetts AFL-CIO, where he railed against "unconscionable" profits to an enthusiastic crowd that had already passed a resolution urging the national union to endorse him. To which Ted said, "You'll be hearing my response to that resolution in the not-too-many days and weeks to come. I don't think you'll be disappointed." The cheer nearly drowned him out before he finished. Meanwhile Larry Horowitz, a doctor himself, arranged through Carter's physician to provide Secret Service protection for Ted.

Jimmy Carter remained obstinate and unimpressed. Discussing the expected run with Vice President Mondale a week after the lunch, he ticked off Ted's deficits: "As a student he was kicked out of college; he's my age but unsuccessful; as majority whip in the Senate, he was defeated after his first term; his preoccupation with national health insurance while never able to get a bill out of his own subcommittee in twelve years, et cetera." (Ted's subcommittee, AdPrac had no jurisdiction over healthcare.) And then, almost as if to convince himself, he told Mondale, "When the issues are debated we will be okay," but he derided the weekend newspapers for "practically anointing Kennedy as president and claiming the 1980 election is already over."

In truth, it hadn't begun, not because Ted wasn't finally ready to make a public announcement, but because he had prevented himself from doing so as a courtesy to Jimmy Carter. Ever since Jack's death, Ted had worked on raising money for his brother's presidential library, which had finally been erected on the Columbia Point peninsula off the water in Dorchester, beside the University of Massachusetts Boston campus. Dorchester had not been the family's first choice. They had wanted the library built on the Harvard campus, but Cambridge residents had revolted, fearing the influx of tourists; Ted's former administrative assistant Dun Gifford was among the most vocal opponents, and it caused a breach between him and Ted that never fully healed. When Ted finally capitulated to the outcry and visited other sites, he came to Columbia Point, with John Culver, one wintry morning, looked out at the sea and the Boston skyline in the distance across the bay, and said, "I think Jack would like it here." The library's dedication was scheduled for October. The previous May, before his presidential plans had gained full steam, Ted had invited Carter to speak at the ceremony, and despite the tension already mounting between the two men, Hamilton Jordan encouraged Carter to accept because he realized that if Ted was planning on running, he would have to postpone his announcement until after the dedication. Jordan was right. Though his advisers were pressuring him to announce as soon as possible, Ted felt that by inviting Carter to the dedication, he had invited Carter to his home, and as he told it to Larry Horowitz, "you don't trash people in your own home." So he delayed his announcement. Still, presidential politics hung over the event, and Carter cited an old interview with Jack in which he was asked if he had to do it over again whether he would seek the presidency, and whether he would recommend the job to others. Carter said the president had responded, "Well, the answer to the first question is yes, and the answer to the second question is no. I do not recommend it to others"—and here Carter paused—"at least for a while"—which drew laughter from the crowd. "As you can see," Carter continued, "President Kennedy's wit and also his wisdom is certainly as relevant today as it was then."

"Sort of a paralyzed period," Ted called the time between his decision to run and his announcement of it. He began phoning Democratic officials— between 150 and 200 of them—to notify them of his decision. He continued to speak out, now even more forcefully, more unmistakably a candidate, even if an undeclared one. At a fundraiser for Philadelphia mayoral candidate William Green, he assailed Carter for his July 15 speech, saying, "We want action, not excuses. We want leadership that inspires people, not leadership that . . . blames people for malaise," and without naming him, he labeled the president a counsel of "defeat and despair." At a rally afterward in South Philadelphia, he bounded onto a table and spoke extemporaneously while the crowd chanted, "We want Teddy!"

At long last, with the announcement imminent, he finally began forming a campaign organization, though still haphazardly and with none of the vaunted efficiency of Jack Kennedy's presidential run. He recruited former aides of his and former aides of Bobby's, but it was a combination that didn't quite blend. Dave Burke, one of the first to join the campaign, said Bobby's office had been "disjointed and acrimonious," rife with aggressiveness, as Bobby was—an "uncomfortable atmosphere"—while Ted's was more harmonious, and that led to sniping between the two camps. (Actually, Bobby's staff had been aggressive, as was Ted's, but there had not been acrimony.) And during this period of paralysis, Carter and the still-noncandidate Ted Kennedy had their first face-off. That October, Florida held a straw poll and caucus, basically popularity contests since delegates wouldn't be chosen until March. As early as August, the Carter forces had met at the Maryland home of a supporter and, among other things, decided to target Florida with resources, among them his vice president, Mondale, and his press secretary, Jody Powell, while Ted didn't even have a campaign organization yet. The "battle of the buses," *Time* called the straw vote, because people were shuttled to the state convention by bus. But it was a battle less of buses than of largesse. Carter spent heavily, not only campaign funds—one woman disembarked from a bus and asked for the free lunch she had been promised by the Carter campaign—but also federal money that suddenly rained down on the state. Carter won handily. "Carter did what he had to do in Florida: avoid disaster," wrote *New York Times* columnist Anthony Lewis. "He had a great deal at stake, for a bad loss to Kennedy in delegates chosen at the caucuses"—actually, no delegates were chosen—"would have been widely seen as humiliation. That did not happen." So overhyped was the race already, even before Ted's official entrance, that *Newsweek*'s chief political writer, James Doyle, pronounced that a Kennedy loss would have a "very large, major impact," and when he did lose, a Carter campaign leader crowed, "Camelot is over!," though that was wishful thinking.

Having stalled so long, first out of indecisiveness and then out of courtesy, even as the campaign was under way, Ted was finally ready to declare. But there was nothing joyful about the anticipation, none of the exhilaration that had accompanied Jack's announcement or even Bob-by's. Melody Miller recalled talking to him shortly before his declaration. He was looking out his office window, lost in thought. "Where are you? What are you thinking?" she asked him. And he said, "I'm somewhere between happiness and sadness, and life and death." Miller said she would never forget those words—"between happiness and sadness, and life and death." And she thought, "He knew what was expected of him. He knew, reluctantly, that he probably had to go forward and do this, but he knew, too, that it was dangerous. He loved the Senate and would have much preferred to be able to stay in the Senate."

But it wasn't really his choice to make. It had been in the lap of the gods.

All along, for nearly three years, the question had been: Should he run? The question had not been: *Why* should he run? Hamilton Jordan had felt for over a year that Ted was going to run, and he advised Carter to do what Gerald Ford had failed to do when Ronald Reagan mounted a similar challenge in 1976: build a big enough war chest to dissuade Ted from running. Jordan's rationale was that "Kennedy's decision would be based simply and only on whether or not he thought he could win." That was how the Kennedys were perceived: as opportunists. Tom Oliphant of *The Boston Globe,* who knew Ted well, believed that Ted was torn about running and really didn't have a well-defined reason, other than that Carter had been "duplicitous" in reneging on health insurance and that, in any case, Carter was now vulnerable to a challenge. Flying back with Oliphant from an AMA meeting in Chicago after Carter's July speech, Ted was despondent over Carter's national diagnosis but also impelled by it. "There's just nothing I can say or do that changes this reality or alters it in any way," he told Oliphant about the state of the country. "It's just happening." The only thing he could do is run. Ted Kennedy certainly wanted to win, and as Gwirtzman had said, he might not have countenanced a run if he didn't think he could win. But both Jordan and Gwirtzman had overestimated Ted Kennedy's political drive and underestimated his moral passion. He ran not because he wanted to—despite what he would later tell his wife. He ran because, like Bobby when he declared against Lyndon Johnson, Ted felt he needed to. With hubris of his own, he needed to as a way of saving the country from its worst impulses.

In some ways, that constituted a political problem—a problem that would surface when he was later questioned about his reasons for running. Over the three years of Carter's presidency, a presidency he had found so disappointing, he had no single grievance with Carter, but rather many, many disagreements. Some were on policy: Carter's oil deregulation and his insufficient, by Ted's standard, windfall profits tax; his alternative energy policy, which Ted thought too large; his substantial tax cuts and simultaneous budget cuts on social services; his opposition to Ted's antimerger legislation; and the symbol of all Carter's priorities and all his policy failings, his intransigence on national health insurance, which Ted, rightly or wrongly, thought was motivated as much by personal animus against Ted as by budgetary stringency. If a president wasn't willing to exercise his power for the powerless, then why was he president? Ted had asked after the 1979 State of the Union address. (The line about the limits of government to which Ted had reacted had been written by Pat Caddell, and Caddell said that the Kennedys took it as a personal affront. Steve Smith, he said, was "literally foaming at the mouth about it.") And Ted took exception to Carter's foreign policy, which seemed to him unfocused, willy-nilly.

Still, some Carter supporters felt that Ted protested too much and that he and Carter were actually in agreement on most issues. While still HEW secretary, Joe Califano said that the Office of Management and Budget had restored most of the cuts to HEW about which Ted had complained, and that Carter had actually increased HEW's budget more substantially as a percentage of the entire budget than had Lyndon Johnson. "Kennedy seemed to be bickering about nickels and dimes," Califano groused, in support of the idea that Ted was being unfair to Carter. New York lieutenant governor Mario Cuomo, a strong Carter supporter, called Carter and Kennedy "doctrinally identical." "Who do [the people] want as a new leader," he asked, "Kennedy, [John] Connally, or Benito Mussolini?" (Carter himself was to say that he only had two really substantive disagreements with Ted: on the pace of national health insurance and on Archibald Cox's judicial nomination.) One study showed that on seven key votes in 1977, applying the criteria Americans for Democratic Action used to determine whether a bill was liberal or conservative—among the bills were the B-1 bomber, food stamps, and gas deregulation—Carter and Ted had taken the same position on all seven, which seemed to support Cuomo's contention. But the following year, 1978, on nine key votes, Carter and Ted did diverge: Ted voted 100 percent with the liberals, Carter only two-thirds of the time with them. Carter had shifted right, but then so had the congressional Democratic Party and so, on some issues at least, if not on these specific ones, had Ted himself. Another study showed Ted had voted with Carter 156 times and against him only twenty-nine times.

But Ted had never made policy the central reason for his challenge. He himself admitted that he didn't differ substantially from Carter when it came to economics. Instead, he usually cited Carter's lack of leadership—by which he meant his lack of a leadership style that deployed the exhortations Jack and Bobby had used to call the country to greatness, a style that inspired the American people rather than scolded them. "The American people will respond to leadership, direction," he told *Newsweek* in discussing his reasons for running. "They understand there are no magic wands, no simple, easy solutions. But they do expect leadership." And when asked directly if Carter failed to inspire confidence in the American people, he answered without hesitation: "That's right." In another interview, sounding like one of the Republican presidential contenders, Ronald Reagan, he said Americans wanted a "feeling of progress in which they are involved—that you don't overpromise, that you don't try to solve the problems with massive government programs, but that you involve them, and there is a sense that we're moving along on these issues." The Kennedys had always fired up the American people. Carter hadn't. A "passionless presidency," columnist William Raspberry had called Carter's, and Raspberry quoted a public relations expert that "if the nation will want passion in its next leader, and if Kennedy won't be the one to supply it, it will not be unlikely, in my opinion, for the voters of this nation to seek to find its passion with an extreme reactionary-type leader." Theodore White, seeing little ideological difference between Kennedy and Carter, concluded that what separated them was, "very simply, the growing contempt Kennedy developed for Carter as a national leader, the contempt of a master machinist for a plumber's helper," and White said that Ted, after giving a detailed and "stunning" explication of how laws are passed and how Carter and his lobbyists kept botching their own legislative program, fumed to him about Carter's political ineptitude: "We wanted the same things," he said, but "this . . . this *outsider* can't solve our problems. . . . Even on issues we agree on, he doesn't know how to do it."

But it was more than leadership—much deeper than leadership. It was something as nebulous as but as powerful as moral authority. Carter had come to the presidency after the amorality of Richard Nixon as the one who would restore morality to politics and subsequently to government. But he couldn't succeed because he had felt that morality didn't inform politics; it was in opposition to politics. Hence his disdain for the pols. Ted thought otherwise. For Ted, the two were inextricably bound up. The purpose of politics *was* morality, not as Carter understood it, with his seemingly stifling sanctimoniousness, as a form of pride in one's personal uprightness and devout religiosity—which might have been why his July 15 speech so rankled Ted—but as a means to help those who most needed help. And this was where, as Ted had been saying for three years, Carter had suffered his greatest failure. He had always been more interested in the machinery of government than in its soul. "I did not become Speaker of the House," Tip O'Neill declared, "to dismantle the programs that I've fought for all my life, or the philosophy I believe in. I'm not going to allow people to go to bed hungry for an austerity program." And neither did Ted Kennedy become senator to do so. He could understand austerity on the part of Republicans, most of whom, he knew, had little interest in the poor and who had preached fiscal responsibility for years—meaning not spending money on the poor. But he could not understand it, could not tolerate it, coming from a Democrat. For him, there was no other reason to *be* a Democrat, and he attributed Carter's poor polls to the fact that he hadn't "come to grips with the concerns of Americans," meaning their social concerns. (Of course, from Carter's perspective, trying to curb the deficit and halt inflation were ways of dealing with social concerns.) And he said that if Carter's polling numbers had been low because he was fighting for a vision—obviously a vision to help the poor—"I would not have run. I would have stood on the barricades with him." Hamilton Jordan might have thought otherwise. Hamilton Jordan might have thought that Ted Kennedy was running only because he believed Carter was vulnerable and Ted could win—actually felt entitled to win. But Jordan was wrong. Ted Kennedy had no great lust for the presidency. If Carter had advocated for the vulnerable, Ted would have been on those barricades alongside Carter. He had in fact been manning them without Carter.

So Ted Kennedy, whatever personal ambitions might have lurked within him, was running less to win an office than to redeem a promise—a promise his brothers had made and that he felt duty bound to keep, as he had since their deaths. It was a promise to vouchsafe the Democratic Party's moral commitment. He had been deeply concerned that Carter's disregard for that commitment, Carter's obsession with budget cutting and his seeming lack of compassion for the dispossessed, had led to weakness and that the "weakness will deliver the country next year to a far-right Republican, a Ronald Reagan or a John Connally," as Anthony Lewis described the fear. "That could undo basic policies, foreign and domestic, that John and Robert Kennedy fought for and that Edward Kennedy has cared about in his seventeen years as a Senator." And Lewis said the key question for Ted was "whether President Carter will be a viable Democratic candidate in 1980." But Lewis wasn't entirely right. The question wasn't so much viability as decency: not whether Carter would be a viable candidate but whether he deserved to be the Democratic candidate in 1980. And that was a very difficult thing to articulate simply or clearly, certainly not without sounding like a liberal zealot.

Ted had long postponed the decision and then, having made it, postponed his announcement—postponed it for weeks, even after the JFK Library dedication—because he had hoped fate would make the decision for him. He had worried that running might divide the party so badly that a Democrat might not be able to win, but he had concluded that the "things that are troubling people are troubling them irrespective of whether I run or not," and that the divisions were already deep. He knew Carter had all the advantages of incumbency, even if he had frittered away many of them, but as Dun Gifford had described Ted, he was a "heavy weather" sailor, one who liked to take chances. Now the time had come. As he prepared to announce, he was sailing in heavy weather and against the wind.

IV

After months of foot-dragging, they were suddenly in a hurry. One campaign aide joked to *The New York Times* that Ted had to get into the race because the "Carter people had a massage parlor in one room and a rack in the other room to work on people they wanted to hold with the President. The Senator felt he just couldn't leave people out there alone to take that, not knowing if he was running. He felt he had to go and go quickly." The remark fit the tone of the campaign: jolly and a bit fly-by-night. On October 27, Ted's top aides met at McLean over chicken soup and cheese sandwiches to lay out strategy and arrived at the unsurprising conclusion that they had to pick up the pace. An announcement, for which everyone had been waiting for months, was soon to come. "I want to get it done," Ted told the press. "I'm tired of screwing around." Four days later, on Halloween, Steve Smith announced the formation of a Kennedy for President Committee, and Ted's Senate office at 2241 Dirksen was, as Elizabeth Drew reported, a "beehive of activity," packed with former aides, while Carey Parker sat in a staff room solemnly putting together briefing books. Ted had already collected $150,000 of pledges at a party at his sister Pat's New York apartment (Carter intended to file a complaint with the Federal Election Commission to have the money count toward Ted's allowed spending), and he had the direct mail specialist Morris Dees preparing a mailing.

But it was a game of catch-up. Carter had been working on his reelection almost since his election, and he had been working to counter Ted at least since the fall of 1978, when he began to think that Ted might be gearing up for a run. "He had always felt that, somehow, he was entitled to be president," Carter wrote then, "because of the tragic legacy of his brothers, and to be presented with an almost certain victory in the Democratic race was a temptation too attractive to resist." By January 1979, Carter and his aides were strategizing against Ted, and Jordan wrote Carter a memo asserting, "The best way to discourage a serious challenge from within your own party is to expect one and prepare for one." And Jordan's main advice was for Carter not to act as if he feared Ted, which he thought is what Ford had done in trying to fend off Reagan in 1976. Many in Carter's camp, including Carter, still weren't certain as the year went on whether Ted would really mount a challenge; Caddell, media adviser Gerald Rafshoon, and longtime Democratic operative Robert Strauss all thought he wouldn't, that he would finally chicken out. But Jordan was certain. He wrote Carter in another memo that Kennedy had a "gleam in his eye and a tone in his voice that added up to the conclusion that this guy is running."

By September, after Ted and Carter had met and Carter had concluded that Ted would run, gloom settled over the White House. "Like a morgue," Jordan said. Carter himself seemed jittery, testy, even more ungracious toward Ted than Ted had been toward him. Speaking at Queens College in New York late that month, he alluded obliquely to Chappaquiddick, saying he had a "steady hand" and "I don't think I panicked in a crisis." And when Ted told reporters that he had gotten the go-ahead for a run from his mother and his wife, understandably concerned about his safety, Carter mocked him at a fundraising dinner, saying, "I asked my mama. She said it was OK. My wife, Rosalynn, said she'd be willing to live in the White

House for four more years." Meanwhile by one account, Carter was battening down the hatches and preparing to purge from the administration anyone he suspected might be backing Ted. "If they are not loyal to the President," an aide told the *Los Angeles Times*, "they can go to work for Kennedy, but we don't want them on the federal payroll."

It was going to be rough. The day before he was to announce, Ted phoned Vice President Mondale to notify him. "I'm very sorry to hear that," Mondale said he told Ted. "I'm sorry for us, and I'm sorry for the Democratic Party." Even though opposing candidates might say that this was "going to be civil and pleasant on the issues," Mondale continued, "it never gets that way. I've been through it. It's going to get mean as hell, and we're all going to be hurt in the process."

And then the campaign almost went off the rails before it had even begun. As Ted recalled it, he had attended a reception earlier that year for the Mexican president, José López Portillo y Pacheco, at the Waldorf Astoria in New York and was leaving when he ran into CBS News correspondent Roger Mudd. According to Ted, Mudd said that he was locked in a battle with fellow correspondent Dan Rather over who would succeed the legendary anchorman Walter Cronkite, and it would help his chances if he could land an interview with Rose Kennedy, especially if he could interview her up at the Kennedy compound on Cape Cod. Ted protested that Rose was aged and didn't grant interviews now, but he promised to think about it, a courtesy he extended because he and Mudd had had a personal relationship, and Mudd had often been to Bobby's house for fundraisers, and Mudd's son, Dan, had even interned in Ted's office, and, lastly, probably because he wanted to help Mudd land the anchor job. (When another of Mudd's sons was hit by a car, Ted arranged to have him treated by the best specialists.) A short time later, after Ted discussed the proposition with his sisters, they decided that Mudd could have his interview, but it would not be a formal sit-down interview—she would be walking—and it would not be with Rose alone—Ted and his family would be accompanying her. Mudd acceded, and that was the way it was to be, at least in Ted's version of events. But then in late September, Rose fell ill, and Kara headed off to a Hopi reservation, and Ted Jr. had an engagement of his own, so it was only Ted and Patrick. Still, Mudd said, he would like to conduct an interview with Ted alone, against the backdrop of the ocean in Hyannis—an interview on Ted and the sea. A "friendly interview," Mudd supposedly had told Ted. "Casual." Larry Horowitz had already discussed the matter with the segment's producer, Andrew Lack, who assured Horowitz that "it was not going to be [a] hard-hitting, hard-pressing interview." And even though Ted was complaining then about needing some downtime and even though he expressed reluctance, his press secretary, Tom Southwick, and others encouraged him to do it, as did Lack, who visited with Ted during a trip to New York to give him the same assurances he had given Horowitz. When asked by his aides which staffers he might want present, Ted said he didn't need anyone to run interference for him for this kind of interview—for an interview about Ted and the sea. "It's just Roger," he allegedly told his administrative assistant Rick Burke. He didn't prep. He didn't have time. He had just returned from a family rafting trip the day before.

Mudd would later call Ted's recollection "complete fiction" and assert, "There are no pieces of truth in it. It's almost beyond preposterous." Mudd's own account was entirely different and seemed more plausible. In Mudd's version, CBS News president Bill Leonard had commissioned a one-hour documentary under the *CBS Reports* banner on Ted Kennedy, whether he decided to run or not. Leonard tapped Mudd to report it, and Mudd put another assignment aside. Instead of a softball interview with Rose, as Mudd told it, Lack and Howard Stringer, the executive producer of *CBS Reports*, met with Ted to explain the project and told him that "this was to be a serious undertaking by serious TV journalists," and they intended to make the program whether he cooperated or not. And Mudd said that before the interview, Lack was already shooting footage of Ted in the halls of the Capitol, and that Mudd himself had coordinated with Steve Smith when Ted might announce his candidacy, since the documentary had to air before that announcement, or under the equal time provision, CBS would have to give an hour to Jimmy Carter. But Mudd said Smith scuttled that schedule by telling him that Ted planned to announce on November 7, the very day that the documentary was to air. (Mudd obviously suspected that this was by intention, to draw attention away from the documentary.) Mudd rushed to tell Bill Leonard about the announcement, and the network moved the airtime to Sunday, November 4. There was, in this account, no mention of the Cronkite position, no mention of Rose, no mention of Ted and the sea.

Smith had good reason to want to scuttle the schedule, and the reason was what transpired on September 29, when Mudd arrived at Ted's Squaw

Island home and conducted his interview. They spoke for a half-hour, and Mudd, Lack, and Stringer all agreed during a break that it was a "disaster." Ted, who was usually so boisterous, so charming, so funny once he agreed to talk with the press, had said nothing of value, and he was uncharacteristically grim. As Mudd told it, they hoped he would be more forthcoming when they resumed and discussed Chappaquiddick—though why Mudd might have thought that about a very sensitive subject is inexplicable. According to Melody Miller, who had obviously gotten the information from Ted himself, the reason Ted was so flat was that he was seething. Mudd had asked him not about the sea but about rumors of an alleged drug problem that Kara was suffering. As Ted relayed it to Miller, he told himself, "I'm just going to clam up and not give him a very good interview at all. I'm just going to be monosyllabic. . . . I'm going to show him, because this is outrageous, that he would do something like this." And that was precisely what Ted did. Ted would say that after the first thirty minutes, he thought the interview was over and sent Patrick down to the boat for a sail, but Mudd pressed him to shoot another reel, and Ted reluctantly accommodated him. And now, when Mudd continued by asking him about Chappaquiddick—he gave the same answers he had always given, though clearly irritated now as he gave them—and then about why he was running for president (a question that Mudd thought was the "slowest pitch I've ever thrown at a presidential candidate" but that Ted thought broke the rules of their agreement) and then asked him about his marriage (which Ted felt was off limits), he wound up wounding himself and wounding himself badly on a program on which he was to make his introduction as Carter's challenger. He knew the reel spelled "trouble." He said he had "compartmentalized" his thoughts about running, and he wasn't prepared to go public with them. So he rambled and fumbled and stammered and double-talked and sounded like the Ted Kennedy who spoke in a code that no one could decipher. Ted realized his error immediately. He was both mortified with himself and livid with Mudd. Immediately afterward, he phoned Southwick and said that he had blown the interview, that he had gotten so mad, he'd just clammed up. When Mudd arrived, Ted had been on the phone with Richard Goodwin and had to get off. When the interview was over, he called Goodwin back and remarked mordantly, "I should have stayed on the phone with you." Seeking peace, he took Patrick out on the water—the place where Ted had always sought relief. "But he just kept shaking his head," Patrick recalled, "looking out to sea and muttering to himself. He was replaying the interview over and over in his head." Patrick called it "painful to watch," and said, "I had never seen him so upset with himself." And then Ted did something he never did. He phoned Joan, complaining that no one but Patrick was there to help him and confessing that he had never felt so down in his life.

There was a redo. Mudd said it had always been part of the plan to continue the interview in Ted's office, which they did on October 12. Horowitz would say that wasn't the plan and that Lack and Mudd accorded Ted the opportunity to reshoot parts of the interview then so that Ted could repair the damage. But Horowitz said Ted's redo was "just as bad if not worse than the original." Asked why he wanted to be president, he was incoherent. "Well, I'm—were I to make the announcement and to run, the reasons I would run is because I have a great belief in this country. That it is—there's more natural resources than any nation in the world; there's the greatest education population in the world; the greatest technology of any country in the world; the greatest capacity for innovation in the world; and the greatest political system in the world." But other countries were exceeding us. "We're facing complex issues and problems in this nation at this time and that we have faced similar challenges at other times. And the energies and resourcefulness of this nation, I think, should be focused on these problems in a way that brings a sense of restoration in this country by its people to—in dealing with the problems that we face." He said that leadership could galvanize "an effort with a team to try and deal with these problems that we're facing in our nation, and can be effective in trying to cope with the problems that we'd face." He called it a "watershed period," primarily "from an energy point of view and from an economic point of view." But this was nonsense. At one of the biggest moments in his political life, he had spoken gibberish, leading Mudd to conclude that "he doesn't know. He doesn't know why he's running." And Mudd would later tell *The Boston Globe*, "It was like I want to be president because the sea is so deep and the sky is so blue."

Mudd wasn't the only one who drew that conclusion. When *Teddy* aired—it was up against a broadcast of the blockbuster movie *Jaws*—the reviews were uniformly devastating, even among Kennedy admirers. Columnist Jimmy Breslin, a Kennedy pal, said he watched with uneasiness: "I suddenly found him to be annoying, wanting, and disturbing." He thought he dodged the Chappaquiddick question. "To me, he seemed insecure,

which was fine, and insincere, which is maddening and unacceptable."
Washington Post columnist Richard Cohen called him "cold and lifeless"—
this of Ted Kennedy!—and said he talked "like a zombie." At the *Times*,
Anthony Lewis found him "stumbling, inarticulate, unconvincing." And
not just on Chappaquiddick: "His responses in general seemed to be those
of a man unsure of the why's and where's in his life—unsure who he
was." And Lewis added, "The curious thing is that after all his years in
public life Edward Kennedy performs these days as if he were under some
troubling inhibition." The Carter people rejoiced. Carter wrote in his
diary, "It showed him not able to answer a simple question about what he
would do if elected"—which was not true—"or why he should be
president"—which was true. Hamilton Jordan had worried that *Jaws*
would swamp the interview—worried because "I wanted everybody to
see what I saw: the Kennedy legend reduced to a bumbling, inarticulate
man." And he hoped that Ted might now "get the message at last" and
drop out, though he hadn't yet opted in. *Teddy* rapidly became the primary
meme of the Kennedy campaign, even though there was no campaign as
of yet. He was now viewed as a candidate without a cause.

Even members of Ted's own staff subscribed to the now widely circulating idea that he hadn't thought through his reasons for running. "An
instant embarrassment," the normally imperturbable Carey Parker called
the interview, and said that "there was a sense that once he decided to
run, we could pull it together. But once he decided, there was a lot to do
that wasn't getting done." "He had never really seriously thought about
being president and why he should be president," Milton Gwirtzman
would say. "It was just something that was thrust upon him." Dave Burke
thought that if running for the presidency was like a legislative hearing,
Ted would have prepared assiduously "because he would have to prove
something—that substantively he's on par with so and so." But Burke
also thought that Ted took a different attitude when it came to politics:
"Oh, that's not a tough question." "I can do this." "I can do that." Burke's
conclusion: "The preparation wasn't there." John Tunney agreed that
Ted was "always getting himself prepared, prepared, prepared, and then
he starts off the biggest campaign of his life, and he doesn't prepare himself." And Tunney reasoned that he didn't prepare because "he initially
had only half his heart and half his mind into the campaign." In another
interview Tunney said, "It's almost as though he felt that he had to run,
but really didn't want to." *The lap of the gods.* Even Ted later admitted that

during his long deliberations about running, he had been "slow to accelerate," and that he had always taken a long time to get into campaign mode. He hadn't gotten up to speed by the time of the Mudd interview.

All those reasons for his bungling debut: He was ambushed; he had never given the question any thought and was unprepared for it; he had compartmentalized; he was overconfident; he was half-hearted; he was not in campaign mode. There was probably some truth in all of them, as well as the possibility that he thought the interview, like nearly everything else in the campaign, was in the lap of the gods. Whatever would happen would happen. But there was likely also truth in the idea that Ted Kennedy knew precisely why he was running and had expressed it repeatedly, though it was that amorphous idea, very difficult to articulate and not the stuff of normal politics and not something that might necessarily have resonated with voters at a time when liberalism was often treated like a plague—the idea that America needed a leader with a bigger heart than Jimmy Carter was willing to show, a leader who was willing to summon the American people to some moral conscience, as Bobby had attempted to do, and whether he was right or not, Ted Kennedy felt he was that leader. That had been the reason he was running: to stir the moral conscience of the country. "EMK's vision of the nation transcends a single administration; define country's purpose, articulate it, provide assurance to people and nudge them beyond their personal concerns," Ted Sorensen had advised Ted in his preparatory memo. And Bob Shrum, his former staffer and now one of his campaign chiefs, thought it wasn't that Ted didn't realize all this—he obviously did—but that his strategy was "based on the premise that since he was far ahead, he should measure his words carefully to avoid sounding too 'liberal' or taking sharp issue positions." But Shrum said it was unnatural for Ted to operate this way—calculating every move and trying to conceal what he really felt. When he wasn't operating from the heart, he was vague and lost. When he was obfuscating, he couldn't hide it. "Edward Kennedy is the worst politician I've ever seen at saying nothing," Shrum understood, but too few of Ted's other campaign advisers did.

But if Ted was the victim of his own deficiencies, he was also a victim of the press, which had heretofore been abetting him in his battle against a president for whom the media had no particular affection, but which was always alert for weaknesses and looking to pounce on them. The press had been easy on Ted as he weighed his run. They were going to be harder on him as he made his run. As Garry Wills was to write, "The very charm of John Kennedy, the intensity of Robert, worked against Edward. Their success at contriving appearances now put journalists on guard, made them adopt a compensatory harshness." (Mudd had tried a similar trick on Bobby Kennedy to the one he had used on Ted, asking him in a 1967 interview whether it was true he was ruthless. "No," Bobby answered then. "What did you think I was going to say?") The Mudd interview was referenced repeatedly throughout the campaign as proof of Ted's inadequacy, making it quite possibly the campaign's defining moment. Ted had given an interview on *Meet the Press* that very morning, before the Mudd interview was broadcast, in which he delivered a defense of his behavior in crisis—obviously in reaction to Chappaquiddick—that *Washington Post* television critic Tom Shales, who felt that Mudd had been unfair to Teddy, called "moving and electrifying," and Ted gave a one-hour interview on ABC's *20/20* the same week as the Mudd interview, but neither of these appearances engendered any press coverage. Rather, the Mudd interview became a kind of journalistic Chappaquiddick—a stain from which Ted could not escape, a misstep that kept surfacing again and again and again.

The long-awaited announcement came, finally, on November 7, a drizzly gray morning, at historic Fanueil Hall in Boston—a site Ted had chosen rather than the Senate Caucus Room, where both Jack and Bobby had announced their presidential bids, because, he said, he wanted to demonstrate that he was his own man. ("I don't want nostalgia to be part of this thing," he told *Time*. "I'm the person who will be judged, not them," meaning his brothers.) "Enveloped in the moment" was how he would recall that morning, with a festive crowd of 350 inside the hall and several thousand outside, and with his family sitting behind him, including Rose and Jackie Kennedy. The 350 estimate was Ted's; others reported four hundred journalists and four hundred supporters inside, and *The New York Times* reported a total crowd of five thousand packed into the adjacent Quincy Market. By one account, construction workers paused and sat on the scaffolding to hear him, and children climbed on top of cars and fences to get a glimpse of him when he entered and left. But if the crowd was festive, Ted was not. He spoke with an oil painting of George Washington and a bust of Daniel Webster looking down upon him, and he wore his customary dark blue suit and dark-rimmed glasses as he read his statement. Somber was the tone, at the advice of his campaign, which, by one account, thought that a cool demeanor would play better on television than Ted's usual heated one, though the sobriety had the effect of deflating the room. It was a short statement, only seventeen minutes, drafted largely by Richard Goodwin, Lyndon Johnson's old speechwriter and a close Kennedy friend, a statement that stressed, as Ted had in the run-up to it, Carter's deficiency of leadership and Ted's own strength. "For many months, we have been sinking into crisis," he told the crowd. "Yet we hear no clear summons from the center of power. Aims are not set; the means of realizing them are neglected. Conflicts in direction confuse our purpose. Government falters. Fears spread that our leaders have resigned themselves to retreat." "I question no man's intentions," he said, "but I have a different view of the highest office in the land—a view of a forceful, effective Presidency, in the thick of the action, at the center of all the great concerns our people share." He chided Carter for letting subordinates carry the fight against inflation, and for laying the country's problems on the people's crisis of confidence rather than on his own insufficiency, when just three years earlier Carter had lauded those people and called for a government as good as they were. And he invoked Franklin Roosevelt's famous dictum from Roosevelt's first inaugural, that Americans had nothing to fear but fear itself, by saying, "The only thing that paralyzes us today is the myth we cannot move." He closed by reassuring the crowd that he would not moderate, even though he had been moving to the center, and implicitly drawing a contrast between himself and the president, he said that his were "convictions rooted in the life of my family and in my own career."

He loosened when he fielded questions, loosened when he could just be himself, even mocking himself with a purposely convoluted answer to an inquiry about the Mudd interview that had the crowd laughing. But then came a moment—a moment the advisers had anticipated and a moment that sent a shudder through the crowd. A reporter asked about Joan's role in the campaign. A week earlier Milton Gwirtzman, staffers Sarah Millan and Sally Fitzgerald, and Ted's old administrative assistant Ed Martin had met at Joan's apartment to discuss her presence at the announcement and determine whether she should make a statement or answer questions or do anything. Marcia Chellis, Joan's assistant, said they talked about Joan as if she weren't present, but she was, and she spoke up, saying that she thought making a statement at the announcement might take the pressure off Ted. To which Gwirtzman, as Chellis told it, snapped that it wasn't Joan's day, it was Ted's, and that people cared more about the possibility of his being assassinated than about the state of his marriage. Fitzgerald then wrote a brief statement for Joan, but Joan, who was enjoying her longest sustained period of sobriety in some years, objected that it didn't reflect her feelings, and the meeting broke with the solution that they would plant a question, asking if Joan intended to campaign. Ted and Joan spent the night before the announcement in the apartment—Joan on the bed, Ted on the couch. And when they headed toward Fanueil Hall under those gray skies the next morning in a sixteen-car motorcade, Patrick recalled that the tension between his parents was so thick, "you could have cut the air with a knife." When the question about Joan was asked after Ted's statement, the audience groaned and some even booed. But Ted shushed them, and Joan rose from her seat, squeezed his arm as she approached the lectern, and said, her voice quavering, "I look forward to campaigning for him. Not only that. I look forward very, very enthusiastically to my husband being a candidate and then to his being the next President of the United States." Joan performed admirably. And then Ted headed off to a rally at Manchester, New Hampshire, and a four-day campaign swing—"the beginning of the last act in the longest, most painful political drama in American history," as *Washington Post* reporter Haynes Johnson called it.

But the gods in whose laps Ted Kennedy had laid his campaign were not kind. On November 4, CBS aired *Teddy*. That same day a group of irate Iranian students seized the U.S. embassy in Tehran and took fifty-two Americans hostage. The crisis had actually been simmering since Carter returned to the presidential retreat at Camp David from the JFK Library dedication and received a "super sensitive" memo from Warren Christopher, the acting secretary of state while Cyrus Vance was on a trip to Bolivia. The memo informed Carter that the shah of Iran, who had recently been overthrown in a religiously inspired revolution, was suffering from lymphoma and jaundice, and a Dr. Kean of the Cornell Medical School had examined the shah, then in exile in Mexico, and advised that he undergo further tests in the United States. The State Department was willing to agree. And Carter said that he was confronted by a "whole phalanx of my people," including Vance and presumably others in the administration, but also others like former secretary of state Henry Kissinger and David Rockefeller, who were pushing Carter to approve. "It was a momentous decision to make," he would later say of the decision he made reluctantly. But he would also say, "I didn't know it at the time." By deciding to admit the shah, whom the Iranian people detested and whose admission to the United States the radical elements in Iran regarded as a hostile act, Carter invited retribution. And he got it.*

How serious that retribution would be, Carter clearly hadn't calculated. One of the first thoughts after the hostage taking, Hamilton Jordan said, was, "It'll be over in a few hours, but it could provide a nice contrast between Carter and our friend from Massachusetts in how to handle a crisis." Jordan was wrong—very wrong—about how long the hostage crisis would last. He was right, however, about its effect on the Carter-Kennedy contest. Carter's approval rating stood at 32 percent at the beginning of November, and in the last Gallup poll before Ted's announcement, Ted led Carter 54 to 31 percent among Democrats. After the hostages were taken, Carter's approval rating climbed to 51 percent, and by the end of November, it reached 60 percent, the highest leap in a single month since Gallup had begun polling, while 80 percent of Americans expressed confidence in Carter's ability to handle the crisis. The country had been divided and dejected. Now the Iranian students had brought America together and ignited its spirit. "The days of infamy in Tehran have infused the country with an unmistakable sense of provocation and common cause," wrote Thomas Matthews in *Newsweek*. "From New England to the Pacific last week, church bells tolled out for the 50 Americans held hostage more than 6,000 miles from home. In New York City and Washington, D.C., cabdrivers kept their lights on round the clock, signaling the country's aggravated distress over the fanatic works of Ayatollah Ruhollah Khomeini [Iran's new leader]. Down South, red-necked country boys and city folks alike said that it was time for closing ranks. Out

---

*It was later revealed that the shah's condition was nowhere near as serious as his advocates had told Carter and that he could have received treatment elsewhere. Carter had resisted before finally giving in to the pressure, so, despite his disavowals, he actually did have some sense of how momentous the decision was and of how it could go wrong. "What are you guys going to advise me to do if they overrun our embassy and take our people hostage?" he had asked while deliberating. Kai Bird, *The Outlier: The Unfinished Presidency of Jimmy Carter* (New York: Crown, 2021), 488–90.

West, people seemed to agree that the situation called less for John Wayne than Gary Cooper, a calm man at high noon. And Jimmy Carter apparently fit the bill."

For Ted, the Iran crisis, like the *Teddy* documentary, was a sudden political blow delivered even before the campaign had begun, even before he had caught his breath. As Elizabeth Drew was to put it, "The Kennedy campaign was premised on the idea that Carter was not a leader; then, of all things, just as the campaign began, he was being hailed as one." Everyone rallied around the president. His congressional liaison told Drew, "You go up to the Hill now, it's like you're a rock star. People are coming up to you—they all have a message for you to give the President." Days earlier Carter had been a pariah. Now he was Gary Cooper. And Ted had to hold his tongue. With the nation on what amounted to a war footing, he couldn't criticize the president's approach, even though one could certainly have wondered why Carter hadn't anticipated the Iranian reaction to his letting the shah into the country. (He had and did it anyway.) But if Carter had underestimated the reaction to his invitation to the shah, Ted said that he himself underestimated the impact of the hostage crisis on the election. "We didn't see it, but that really ended the campaign," one of Ted's staffers, Mark Schneider, said of the hostage taking, "because you couldn't go out and run against the president of your country when you were 'at war.' . . . We should have recognized that and rolled it up right then." But they didn't. Instead, Ted, as Schneider put it, "held himself back," speaking in platitudes, careful in those first few weeks not to undermine Carter, which blunted the attack at the very time when he should have been on the offensive. "The worst politician I've ever seen at saying nothing," Robert Shrum had called him. And now Ted Kennedy had launched his presidential campaign by effectively being forced to say nothing.

"Just Another Clark Kent"

AFTER NEARLY TWO years of Ted Kennedy's contemplating a presidential run, the Kennedy forces weren't ready when it began. "Everybody wanted him to run," said William Carrick, a political professional who had signed on to Ted's campaign as a strategist. "It was crazy. But there was no centralized campaign authority capturing names of donors, workers—nothing to fall back on." "Kennedy had been drafted by the power structure of the Democratic Party," Carey Parker recalled, which wasn't entirely true. "At that point we were doing the homework we should have done in April, May, June. These people were appalled that we couldn't run a good campaign." Even before Ted announced his candidacy, little things kept going wrong—harbingers of what was to come. The Secret Service lost his luggage on a flight to New York to address a formal dinner for a business group, and he appeared wearing a suit and not a tuxedo; elsewhere, his motorcade was blocked by a fire truck; and the sound system wouldn't function at a Boston Bar Association meeting. And after he announced, a charter pilot couldn't find an airport, and Larry Horowitz, Robert Shrum, and another campaign aide, Denny Shaw, pored over a road map near the front of the plane to see if they could spot it.

And if the campaign wasn't ready, neither was the candidate. At a birthday party for the Democratic patriarch Averell Harriman, Harriman's wife Pamela told Arthur Schlesinger, Jr., that she had concerns about the race, believing that Ted had jumped in too soon. Schlesinger said he agreed, saying that Ted had not fully formulated the themes of his campaign—the criticism that had dogged him after the Mudd interview. And Schlesinger, who had generally admired Ted, now compared him unfavorably to his brothers. "Ted himself lacks the grasp of things his brothers had," he wrote in his journal that November. "His staff is far more conservative than their staffs were. All this prevents him from developing themes distinguishing himself from Carter." He thought Steve Smith was the "great hope for remedy," but Smith was absorbed with the logistics of the campaign, not its message. Meanwhile, on his four-state campaign swing after his announcement, Ted kept on assailing Carter's leadership—"I say it isn't the American people that are in a malaise; it's the political leadership that's in a malaise"—and smoking a long cigar on a flight to Chicago, he told the press that the theme of the campaign would be the "failure of leadership," rather than the failure of Carter's dedication to policies and programs that would put the government at the service of its people, especially the most powerless of them. But even Ted conceded that he didn't know how to get the leadership message across—the safer, more conservative message his staff had advised he stress in this more conservative environment, so that at the very outset, he was basically running against his own instincts and his own record.

Like the campaign's message, everything had been hastily assembled once it was launched. Ted's campaign headquarters was a defunct Cadillac dealership on 22nd Street NW and N Street, with linoleum floors and cream-colored walls, the paint slapped on them so carelessly that green splotches from the previous paint job showed, and the windows plastered with posters that the supporters and volunteers painted. The whole thing had been retrofitted into offices with plywood cubicles that barely allowed breathing space. Steve Smith, who was the nominal head of the campaign, said that when he got there, he didn't have a phone line, and his office didn't have a window, so he couldn't tell if it was day or night. He decided to have one cut right into the wall. The shock of it all was that the Kennedys were noted for their proficiency when it came to campaigns. Jack had been elected by a smoothly efficient machine, or so the Kennedy myth went. Nothing was left to chance. That myth meant that Ted was running not only against Jimmy Carter and, inevitably, against the image of his brothers, which had been burnished brightly by the years, often by Ted himself, but against the campaigns that they had purportedly run. He was not only expected to win; he was expected to coast to victory, the beneficiary of that purring, potent political machine, while Carter slogged along.

But the myth of Kennedy efficiency was just that—a myth. "When their things worked out," said Harris Wofford, who had been a staffer on both Jack and Bobby's presidential campaigns, "it was not because of a great machine, but because they released energy in a lot of directions and sort of trusted that . . . the general goal was right." In any case, while Jack's campaign was years in the planning and state-of-the-art for its time, its time, when Ted ran, was twenty years ago, and a lot had changed since. And Bobby's campaign was anything but efficient. Like Ted's, it was assembled at the last minute, jerry-built, and unlike Jack's, it didn't have to bear the weight of victory since Bobby, tragically, never got that far. Ted's campaign resembled Bobby's much more than it resembled Jack's, but Bobby's had a clear objective—end the Vietnam War and renew America's moral sensibility—and that papered over a lot of mistakes and a lot of disorganization. There was no papering over disorganization in Ted's campaign. He had asked Steve Smith to run it since Smith was the closest Ted had to a brother. But Smith, as close as he was to his brother-in-law, was not a Kennedy; rather, he served the Kennedys. "He was like the Robert Duvall character in *The Godfather*," Ted's nephew, Christopher Lawford, said of Smith. "He was the consigliere to the Kennedy family. He brokered the power of the family, and was in the family. He ran the family business, which basically amounted to trying not to screw up what my grandfather had created and keeping the beneficiaries happy. He asked people for favors, not just money and votes." And Lawford said, "It made him a pretty angry guy." Smith could scarcely say no to Ted, any more than Bobby would have said no to Jack—or would have wanted to—or Ted would have said no to Bobby. But Smith knew his limitations. Milton Gwirtzman said that Smith hadn't run a campaign since Bobby's, twelve years earlier, and that even then he hadn't wanted to, though it went by so quickly that he had hardly had time to get it organized, and in any case, Bobby had recruited many of Jack's old hands, including Larry O'Brien, who was a campaign mastermind.

But Ted's campaign was different. Many of those old hands were gone. The new aides were people like thirty-three-year-old Carl Wagner, the young staffer Rick Stearns, Bill Carrick, and Robert Shrum—people, as Gwirtzman described them, "who had been very successful and knew the whole new group that was becoming important in politics: younger people, younger organizations, different organizations, ethnic organizations, black organizations, gay organizations." Steve Smith didn't know any of that, though he did know that politics had changed dramatically since

Jack's election and that he hadn't kept pace. And just as the combination of Bobby's old staffers with Ted's new ones was uneasy, so was the combination of the 1960s operatives with the 1980s operatives. The older hands derisively called the younger ones "McGovernites," referring to defeated 1972 Democratic presidential candidate George McGovern, meaning too ideological and not sufficiently loyal to the Kennedy brand, while the younger hands thought the older ones were, as one reporter put it, "living in a fantasy world, 1960 all over again." "You could win West Virginia back in the '60s by going in there and getting the bosses to turn out the people," said Tim Hanan, a close friend of Ted's who worked on his campaign. "That didn't work in 1980. They no longer had the power they used to. The whole system had changed. . . . The old political party structure was beginning to disintegrate." And Hanan said, "Teddy's people just never got up to speed, and it got ahead of them."

"Decentralized," pollster Peter Hart called the campaign from the outset. "Here it was like dealing with modern Russia. There were all of these various little satellite states out there and there was nothing that was centralized." A better word might have been *disorganized*. Smith could never quite wrangle all the parts of the campaign into a single unit—the Bobby people and the Ted people, the old people and the new people, the Senate staff and the draft-Kennedy organizers, and even the field operation, headed by Paul Kirk, and the campaign office, headed by Smith. There were a half-dozen or more bailiwicks. As Kirk described it, "Everything was sort of necessarily grab-ass, if you will, because we didn't have a media guy, we didn't have a media plan, we were raising money, it was coming in one door, going out the other." It was Smith's job to get the money, but he was an anachronism there too, as he was with the campaign organization. "In the old days, you could go into Chicago and get together a bunch of Jewish leaders and raise half a million dollars and go line up Mayor Daley and that was Chicago and Illinois" said one longtime Kennedy associate. Money didn't come that easily now. Still, Smith handed out large salaries to the top staffers, $45,000 to $50,000 by one account, which rapidly depleted the funds. Even the media operation was balkanized: The nominal authority was Phil Bakes, a former Civilian Aeronautics Board counsel and onetime AdPrac staffer who had no media experience. The result, said a veteran political media adviser, Joe Napolitan, were ads that were an "embarrassment, probably the worst television ever produced for a Presidential candidate in American history." It was weeks before the operation was consolidated under another veteran producer, David Sawyer, but by then the campaign had lost valuable time when there was no time to lose. Less than two weeks after his announcement, Ted's lead in the polls was already slipping, though he still led Carter by twenty-two points (down from thirty-four) and would have beaten Ronald Reagan easily in a match-up. Carter had said earlier, during the summer when Ted's lead seemed insurmountable, that he was "running against a myth of perfection now, but I'll do better when I am compared to another human being." Carter was right. Kennedy's disorganization made him seem entirely fallible in the eyes of the Democratic pols and even, since his halting start was being reported in the media almost to the exclusion of anything else in his campaign, in the eyes of the public as well.

The campaign was already a disaster, and it had hardly begun.

But there was a worse disaster than the campaign chaos—a disaster that largely undid Ted Kennedy altogether. Ted had been campaigning across the country that first month, campaigning tirelessly, but he had been cautious not to undermine Carter on the Iran hostage crisis, which was dominating the news—cautious even though he was privately boiling about what he regarded as Carter's misstep in admitting the shah of Iran for medical treatment in the United States, and compared his own self-imposed silence to the silence that had led to the escalation in Vietnam. "The more time one spends with Kennedy," David Broder wrote, "the more one senses the extent to which he has been left dangling by the Iranian crisis." Reporters kept trying to draw him out. Ted kept shutting them down. This was partly politics; he knew there could be no possible upside in criticizing the president at a time of crisis. And it was partly Ted Kennedy's natural civility that you didn't jump on someone publicly at a time of crisis. That was the Kennedy way. But on the night of December 3, at the end of a long day, a fourteen-hour day in which Ted had granted five interviews on the Iran hostage crisis, each time saying that it was not "useful or wise" to discuss the hostages while they were still being held, he granted one last interview to a local newsman named Rollin Post of television station KRON in San Francisco. Post was no more successful than the others in getting Ted to say anything meaningful, until his last question, when he asked Ted his reaction to a comment by Republican presidential contender and former California governor Ronald Reagan that the shah was a loyal friend of the United States and should be allowed to stay in the country. Others would later claim in Ted's defense that he was tired, which he undoubtedly was, but Post had clearly struck a nerve—the shah was precisely the kind of despot for whom Ted Kennedy had little sympathy—and Ted, tired or not, let open the floodgates. The shah, Ted vented, "ran one of the most violent regimes in the history of mankind." He asked how we could possibly consider allowing him to stay in the country "with his umpteen million dollars that he'd stolen from Iran, and at the same time say to Hispanics who are here legally that they have to wait nine years to bring their wife and children to this country?" And then as soon as he had unloaded, he got up and left the studio, "as if he had a cab outside with the meter running," as *Time* described it.

It wasn't necessarily that Ted knew he had made a gaffe and was trying to escape. Post didn't even realize the importance of the story he had; one report said he was "surprised" by the outburst, but if he thought it was a scoop, he didn't act like it. It didn't even make the KRON news broadcast that evening. But Post had invited *San Francisco Chronicle* reporter Larry Liebert to sit in on the interview, and as Liebert listened to Ted's blast, he did realize what he had. He wrote the story that evening for the paper's morning edition. The United Press International news service picked it up at eleven that night, by one account when its reporter, Clay Richards, ran into Ted's press secretary Tom Southwick, who alerted him about it. (It was yet another sign of the amateurishness of the campaign that Southwick would call attention to the outburst.) CBS ran the KRON news feed after learning about the tirade from the UPI story. By morning, it was the headline nationally. Ted's foreign policy adviser, Jan Kalicki, realized instantly how damaging Ted's remarks were. He and Ted had never had any discussion about the hostage situation before Ted leveled his attack on the shah. When Kalicki was called by a campaign aide almost immediately afterward and asked what he thought—apparently the aide was hoping for some assurance to quell the coming storm—Kalicki said that it was a mistake both on policy grounds and on political grounds. "You do not say something like that," even if it were true that "our history with Iran is a deplorable one in many ways."

But it wasn't only that Ted had fulminated against the shah. What was worse, the statement was picked up in Tehran, where one of the leading newspapers, *Ettela'at*, saw it as signaling a shift in the American position toward Iran and the hostages. Now Ted was accused of giving aid and comfort to the enemy. "Worse than Chappaquiddick," one Democratic senator called it. As his trouble deepened the morning after his remarks, Ted tried to clarify at an appearance before five hundred supporters in Reno, saying that Ayatollah Khomeini, the new Iranian leader, was himself a terrorist and distinguishing between the necessity for getting our hostages out of Iran and understanding the legitimate grievance of the Iranian people against the shah. But again, the damage had been done. The State Department said that he had possibly endangered "delicate" negotiations. *The Washington Post* editorialized: "It wasn't right, it wasn't responsible, and it wasn't smart"—the last of these certainly true. The *Atlanta Constitution* called it a "cynical campaign ploy" and accused Ted of having "publicly sided with the Khomeini anarchy in Iran," neither of which was true, but both of which might have seemed true. The *Houston Post* opined that the remarks would "remain on his record." The conservative *New York Post* tabloid headlined: "Teddy Is the Toast of Tehran!" A week later a bogus letter, allegedly written by Ted and pledging his support to the revolutionary government—"I pledge my blood to you"—was released by another newspaper in Iran and "authenticated" by the Ayatollah. Even though Ted had clearly not written it, it underscored his blunder.

But the remarks had an even greater effect on the infant campaign than the charges of intemperance and possible encouragement to America's Iranian enemies. The statement reinforced the meme first introduced by the Mudd interview, the meme that was already dogging Ted's efforts to get his campaign in gear: that he was error-prone, unready, unsteady, a walking catastrophe. "Kennedy's performance last week stirred old questions about his steadiness under pressure, raised new ones about his talent for statecraft—and lengthened the winter-book odds a bit on his prospects for unmaking a President in 1980," *Newsweek* said in its Iran gaffe postmortem titled "Kennedy's Blooper." When questioned about the balky start, he told *Time* that "there is a problem moving from the day-to-day life of a Senator, where you are involved in the details of legislation, to a campaign, where the expression of issues is quite different," which was an admission that in becoming a Senate man, an insider with Senate instincts, coupled with the fact that he hadn't had a competitive Senate race since 1962, he had let some of his electoral instincts atrophy. "The best politician in the family," his brother Jack had called him. That was true no longer. By this time, less than three weeks into the campaign, his seemingly insurmountable lead over Carter had evaporated. In an ABC/Harris poll, the day after Ted's gaffe, Carter led him by two points among Democrats. Ted had complained privately that the Iran hostage situation kept him off the news pages—and, not incidentally, kept the poor economic news off the front pages too. Now Iran had gotten him on those pages with withering effect.

But Ted was not entirely hamstrung as he waited for the hostage situation to play out. On December 6, three days after the Iran gaffe, he was contacted by someone claiming to be an intermediary to the Iranians who said that Ted Kennedy was the one person to whom the Iranians might release the hostages. Ted himself was skeptical and had the intermediary see Ted Sorensen at Sorensen's office. As Sorensen recalled, "He came to me in the dark of one night, and I have no idea if his credentials were genuine." But Sorensen thought it was worth a chance that Ted might secure the release of the hostages and, thinking politically, that it "might be a tremendous breakthrough for his presidential campaign." But the "mysterious" intermediary—as Sorensen called him—didn't promise the release of all the hostages, only some of them—only one of them, Sorensen was to say in his book *Counselor*—and Sorensen thought that would be a "highly dubious road for Ted to go down." He reported on the meeting to Ted and never heard anything more from the intermediary or from Ted. Still, Ted continued to look for a way to gain the hostages' release, and he sent the former senator and his onetime Judiciary Committee colleague James Abourezk, who had left the Senate and become head of the Arab Anti-Discrimination League, to Iran. (Abourezk would later say that Ted made no direct contact; he had John Culver, Ted Sorensen, and Jan Kalicki make the request.) In Iran, Abourezk met with the foreign minister, Sadegh Ghotbzadeh, who told him that "Kennedy is a good man," and that Ghotbzadeh would try to gain the hostages' release. But the foreign minister was overruled by Khomeini, and that was the end of that effort. Ted made one more attempt, contacting European liaisons to Iran, but that failed too. The hostages remained in captivity. The campaign stalled.

And then came another blow. A Communist-led insurrection in Afghanistan the previous year had led to a coup and to the installation of a Soviet-backed government there, headed by the former journalist Nur Mohammed Taraki. Taraki's regime, however, was highly factionalized, and he was killed in October by his second-in-command, Hafizullah Amin. On Christmas Eve, the Soviets airlifted troops into the Afghan capital

Kabul, killed Amin, and installed a puppet who was charged with putting down a rebellion of aggrieved citizens. Carter immediately responded by imposing a grain embargo on the Soviet Union—"All it means," Ted said in opposition, "is that the Soviets are going to eat a little more chicken and a little less meat"—after asking Congress to approve an increase in the defense budget of 4.5 percent for each of the next five years, and declaring, "We must understand that not every instance of the firm application of power of the United States is a potential Vietnam." (The following month, January, Carter would call for a boycott of the Summer Olympic Games scheduled for Moscow if the Soviets did not withdraw their troops from Afghanistan.) After the Iranian hostage taking, the country rallied around Carter, even though polls showed that Americans thought he had precipitated the event by admitting the shah into the country. After the Soviet invasion and Carter's resolute response, he was being lionized. A forklift operator in Auburn, New York, named David Hopkins captured the mood when he told *Time,* "Carter seems to be getting a little more tough with the Soviets, more forceful and dynamic. I don't turn off the TV now when Carter is talking." Ted could make little headway, especially since he had staked his campaign on leadership rather than on Carter's unwillingness to help Americans who were underwater economically— leadership that most Americans felt Carter was now demonstrating against Iran and the Soviets. Moreover, Carter used his new obligations to forswear actively campaigning against Ted. He was saying, in effect, that he was too busy saving the country to argue with his opponent and that instead he would campaign from the White House Rose Garden. Through back channels, Ted tried persuading the Soviets to leave Afghanistan as he had tried to persuade the Iranians to release the hostages. "We worked very hard on that," Kalicki said, and when those efforts failed, Ted made public statements, encouraging the Soviets to leave, and Kalicki said he hoped they might view those speeches as "not simply a political campaign speech, but as a real policy effort that would lead them to make some comment of a more positive nature." But they didn't. Instead, Carter used the Soviets' intransigence to build more momentum. He was a president in crisis and now he was a president in ascendance. And Ted Kennedy, who had predicated his campaign on the perceived weakness of his opponent, was now running against his opponent's perceived strength.

II

While Jimmy Carter's campaign soared, Ted Kennedy's campaign was in steep descent from the heights it had held as a noncampaign before he declared. "The striking development in the first month of Kennedy's race for the White House has been the rapid demise—both inside and outside the campaign staff—of the once widely-held notion that Kennedy, heir to the nation's richest political legend, is unbeatable," wrote T. R. Reid, who was covering the Kennedy campaign for *The Washington Post*. "Almost overnight, the perceived Superman of American politics has turned into just another Clark Kent." That sense of invincibility had been an important element of Ted's campaign, perhaps the central element, among both the pols and the public, just as seeming invincibility had been an important element of the Kennedys' aura generally: Kennedys didn't lose. "The initial strategy was to demonstrate an early strength," Steve Smith would later say. "If you could start strong and demonstrate that strength, you'd have an opportunity to keep it going, to show the ineptness on the part of the Administration." Iran changed all that, as Smith acknowledged, and the timing couldn't have been worse. (What Smith didn't say was that it was *Ted*'s ineptness that kept being revealed.) Peter Hart, Ted's pollster, believed that voters made their decisions within a "small window," and that window for Ted was between his campaign launch in early November, when he was knocked off stride by the Mudd interview, and the Iran situation a month later. But instead of righting himself, Ted kept stumbling. He was "just awful at the beginning," Larry Horowitz said, calling a speech Ted delivered at a South Carolina movie theater the "worst speech I ever heard him give anywhere, ever. I don't understand a word he said." Time and again on the stump, he misspoke and garbled his language, which had long been among his deficiencies—"Kennedy-speak," his aides had termed it—but which he and his advisers had kept largely hidden from public view in the past by not having him speak extemporaneously. But that was hard to do on the campaign trail. Time and again Ted couldn't find a comfortable style, B. Drummond Ayres, who covered the campaign for *The New York Times*, observed, and he "seems undecided whether to read his speeches or deliver them off the cuff, whether to pound the podium or play things low key." And Ayres observed too that the expectations for his speaking were so high, the demands for soaring rhetoric so great, that he not only couldn't meet them but couldn't have won the presidency with that kind of Sorensenian prose if he had. Time and again he rushed through speeches, David Broder said, so that when he implicated Carter in helping the Middle Eastern powers raise oil prices, the press didn't catch it. Carter's press secretary Jody Powell countered the charge and got coverage for doing so, but by the time Ted marshaled evidence to refute him, the issue had already died. Time and again he was off his game. *Boston Globe* columnist Ellen Goodman cringed that "I feel embarrassed, as if I were watching a great athlete striving for a comeback with bad knees. I want to change the channel." Time and again he seemed unready for the national stage—a stage he had occupied for well over a decade. Political veterans from Jack's and Bobby's campaigns came aboard to fix Ted's, and Ted, on vacation at Palm Beach late that December, held a summit with fourteen of his advisers to discuss remedies, but as Peter Hart said, the window was closing. "The first reviews are, at the very best, mixed," wrote syndicated columnist Mark Shields. "The crowds have been good, but not great, more curious than committed. One month into his long-postponed pursuit of the presidency, Edward Kennedy has confronted an immutable political commandment: there are no 'New Havens' "—the city where shows headed to Broadway often tried out—"in a genuine national campaign, no chances to rewrite the second act." There were reports that he had already conceded Florida and that instead of delivering the knockout punch he had been hoping for, he would now be fighting a campaign of attrition.

No New Havens in which to sharpen his message, which was muddled and which, in any case, at his advisers' suggestion, muted the real reason for his run—the need for a more vigorous, reenergized liberalism—that reason his advisers continued to distrust in a more conservative environment. Peter Hart said that Ted lost his grip on his message, and his grip on his only possible advantage in a race against Carter. "He saw everything falling apart in terms of the gas lines and the inflation and the hostages," Hart said. "And then he started to look at the race in a tactical manner. And as he looked at it in a tactical manner, he lost the strategic advantage that he really had. Which was his strength, his voice. And his voice was his vision." And Hart would say that early in his campaign, having abandoned his liberal cause, "Edward Kennedy lost his way," even though Hart was one of the advisers who had encouraged that abandonment. And having lost his way, Ted Kennedy seemed to have lost his passion, which was the Kennedy hallmark and a critical distinction between him and the bloodless Carter.

A tactical campaign was not a Kennedy campaign. A tactical campaign was one in which he began thinking of maneuvers to win, not reasons to win, sniffing the wind and moving to the center again, at times attacking big government, saying on *Meet the Press* that November, "More doesn't necessarily mean better. Less doesn't necessarily mean better. Better means better," because that was what the political wisdom dictated, even though Ted had chosen to run precisely because Carter was too squarely in the center for his liking. ("It's time to have a real Democrat in the White House again," he had said at the outset of the campaign, lumping Carter with William McKinley, Herbert Hoover, and Richard Nixon, but then he retreated from that message.) Now not even his supporters could tell why he was running. "The Kennedys feel they can charge the political system with enough voltage so that they can get things done," said historian James MacGregor Burns, who had traveled with Ted during an early campaign swing. "This is not adequate." The left-wing sociologist Norman Birnbaum, who was working on Ted's campaign, questioned in *The Nation* whether Ted had yet shown the "capacity to promulgate an alternative vision of our society in concrete terms," but also excused him on the basis that the "progressive social movement" was itself "notably inchoate" and that asking Ted to lead the movement was "decidedly asking too much too soon." One of Ted's own campaign aides was more direct: "He just hasn't given the voters a reason for moving away from an incumbent president." Ted himself seemed confused, caught between advice that he temporize his liberalism and his own instinct that he promote his liberalism, which was the reason he ran.

And there yet was another problem beyond the muddled messaging, perhaps the central problem, an inescapable problem, a problem that hung over him constantly: Ted Kennedy was not John Kennedy or Robert Kennedy. Those were the standards to which he was held, to which he had always been held, the standards to which he himself readily admitted he didn't measure up, at least not in his public image. He had always been the least. And when he launched his campaign at Faneuil Hall rather than in the Senate Caucus Room, where they had launched theirs, explicitly to escape comparisons, when he said that he would not invoke his brothers during the campaign, though he had always invoked them throughout his political life, he was doing everything in his power to avoid those comparisons—with no success. "I think he psychologically had staked out his own role, his own identity, his own stature, his own status in the United States Senate and was comfortable with that," Bobby's old Justice aide and close family friend John Siegenthaler said. And Siegenthaler was right. Ted had done all that. He had sought separation by being a better senator than his brothers, an institutionalist, a Senate master, which his brothers had not been. And he had asked to be judged by his achievements there, which were considerable. But now he was being judged not as a senator but as a potential president. And not just as a president but by a sterner standard: as a Kennedy. "Each day Kennedy was faced with what was probably the most painful criticism of all," wrote Elizabeth Drew of *The New Yorker*, "that he was not as good as his brothers," and she felt that it made him tense, less relaxed and affable than he had been in his Senate campaigns. Because the worst of it was that he believed it, had always believed it.

Not as good as his brothers. It became a press mantra. "Kennedy was being forced every day to demonstrate that he was as good as his brothers," Garry Wills would later write of the campaign. "His every effort at recommending himself worked to condemn him," and Wills compared Ted to the last mountain climber in a chain with four men above him, but the four men fall and the "very strength that had been drawing him upward now hung a dead weight below him." For Ted, as Wills put it, the " 'Kennedy legacy' had become a very literal burden."

Not as good as his brothers. He didn't speak as well as they had spoken. He wasn't as witty as they had been—the "witty aside that reinforced the air of dignity," in Wills's words. He didn't have the intellectual command they had, despite his very real intellect. (An aide to Republican presidential aspirant George H. W. Bush said that Ted could be "rattled" if "you force him out of his set piece.") But Ted wasn't being compared only to his brothers; he was being compared to people's memories of his brothers, which was not just a difficult standard to meet but an impossible one. Just as his campaign was astonishingly sloppy in comparison to the memories of John's and Bobby's campaigns, even though Bobby's was every bit as sloppy, his entire demeanor was compared to what people remembered of John's and Bobby's demeanors, which in reality were far less perfect than the memories of them. "He can't be as good as people's fantasies," one of his former aides said. "Look at old tapes of Bobby Kennedy—he had a herky-jerky delivery with lots of ums and ahs." Ted was up against what the former aide called "distorted memories." Jack had been nervous, fidgety, when he spoke on the stump. Bobby had stammered, and his speeches could trail off into hectoring. People saw Ted, also nervous, also stammering, also trailing off, and they couldn't imagine he was cut from the same Kennedy cloth. But he was.

And there was another issue—not an aesthetic problem, like the ghosts of his brothers, but a physical one. Campaigning was agony for him, literal agony. His back—the back that had been broken in the 1964 airplane crash—caused him unceasing pain, especially when he was forced to stand for long periods, as he was during the campaign. He asked not to be scheduled in factories with hard floors because standing on those hard floors hurt his back. He ached bending to get in and out of cars. A Secret Service agent was assigned to hold the back of a chair against Ted's back when he stood for a period, and he had to soak the back in a hot bath each day before dinner to loosen the muscles. "He would be limping more, or you could see it in his face," his Boston office manager, Barbara Souliotis, would say, speaking not specifically of the campaign but of Ted's daily situation. Heading into a reception, Ted would tell Souliotis, "I can't stand that long. Make sure I get seated," but then he stood because he didn't want to be seated when everyone else was standing. When he gave a long speech, he would have to adjust himself so that he was leaning against something, however inconspicuously. And the back worsened during those long campaign days, worsened more because he was forced to wear a stiff bulletproof vest and the Secret Service ran a line through it so that if he were attacked, they could pull him back from danger.

And that threat, a constant threat, affected him too. He traveled with a doctor and nurse, not just for his back but in case an attempt was made on his life—the threat of which also seemed to tighten him and make him less agreeable. His first week, marching through Chicago, a woman hurled an egg at him and hit him on the shoulder. He didn't look well either—not the handsome, robust Ted Kennedy that most people thought of when they thought of him. A prodigious drinker, he had sworn off alcohol during the campaign, but he compensated by eating again, after losing so much weight in preparation for the run. Biographer Burton Hersh said that Ted and Bob Shrum worked their way through a two-pound cheese in short order. Ted had never been as fastidious as Jack about his appearance, and he no doubt missed a female presence with Joan gone, but Elizabeth Drew, on the trail with him, found him surprisingly wobbly, unkempt, and disheveled. "Kennedy's face is pale and blotchy; his body seems chunkier than usual; his suit is rumpled, and the breast pocket is coming loose, and another jacket pocket has been unartfully mended; the leather of his shoes is cracked and worn," she wrote. She could have added that his hair was long and usually over his collar, but not fashionably so as it had been. Even with his blotchy complexion, he didn't want to wear makeup for television appearances and agreed to do so only if his administrative assistant Rick Burke applied it—a "masculinity thing," Burke surmised.

Nor was he as mentally sharp on the trail as he normally was—he was clearly distracted. That first swing in November Ted flew into Nashville, and his good friend Senator Jim Sasser was invited to greet him at the airport, where the dignitaries lined up on the tarmac. Sasser had somehow been pushed to the end of the line, behind former senator Ross Bass and, in Sasser's words, "a few other political has-beens." "When he got off the airplane," Sasser recalled of Ted, "he was really, I thought, extremely uptight, and when he was coming down the line, when he got to me, he couldn't even remember my name." This of the man who called everybody, even Boston precinct captains, by name during his Senate campaigns.

Many of Ted's own campaign staff felt it wasn't the campaign that was awry; it was the candidate. And many of them had come to feel, as some had expressed even before the campaign, about Ted's long deliberation and his postponement of a decision and then of an announcement, that there was something amiss about Ted, that he wasn't his typical buoyant self, that he hadn't charged into the campaign with his normal gusto. *It was almost as if he didn't want to run for the presidency.* An "inhibition," Anthony Lewis of *The New York Times* had sensed in him. "An enormous inhibition," a friend said, but then predicted that once he got to the primaries and was actually campaigning for votes, "he'll be in familiar territory, doing what he likes to do and does by instinct." But the instinct hadn't been functioning. "It was clear to me as soon as I got there and saw him," said Robert Bates, his civil rights aide, that "his heart was not in it at all. It was all of us who wanted to be connected to this person who could be president that was pushing him. And it just didn't work. It was not him. He was more like a shell." Bates called him "robotic," "doing what people were telling him to do." "He was not doing what he did in the Senate,"

Bates said. "See, he wasn't making jokes about it, or making fun about it. His gut wasn't in it." Bates said he hesitated to use the word *manipulated,* but he nevertheless felt that Ted was being manipulated by those around him, just as he had been manipulated by his father to enter politics in the first place, which might have explained his reticence to be a full-throated liberal and to emphasize instead leadership, a soft, anodyne campaign theme, and which might have explained his uncertainty over whether to be the old, hot, bellowing Kennedy, who had dominated Memphis, or a new, cooler Kennedy. He was circumscribed and confused by constant suggestions of what others thought he should be. Another former aide said, "At some level, I think he doesn't want to win." William vanden Heuvel said that several close Kennedy observers felt that way, that "he didn't want to be successful, that this was something he got into, but this wasn't the determination that one would have expressed if the presidency was your consuming objective." And Vanden Heuvel felt that "you had a feeling that he was truly not unhappy" about losing. Ted's close friend and former Senate colleague John Tunney had said the same thing—that his heart wasn't in it, that he was doing it because he felt he had to since it was expected of him. "He did not so much declare his candidacy," columnist Joseph Kraft wrote, "as assent to his fate."

Ted himself said very little about his situation and expressed few misgivings, but even that was unusual for him; though he had always been reticent about his personal matters, he had also been open and expressive about his political ones. He was less so now, as if he were marching not toward victory but toward a kind of grim political catharsis, and he might have sensed the country was watching that march. Lewis Lapham had talked about how the campaign would enable the voters to enact a kind of ritual sacrifice of the Kennedys and purge them from the national consciousness. Sally Quinn of *The Washington Post* thought that *Ted* might have been the one wanting to enact that sacrifice: "It's as if he's doing some awful penance for his sins, forcing himself to go through the motions. As if the campaign is an anguished barefoot walk to Rome, the speeches a string of tormented Hail Marys." This would have been consistent with Ted's life. He was the man, filled with Catholic guilt, who sinned to be redeemed, the man who constantly subjected himself to punishment as penance.

Now the punishment was the campaign he had waited so very long to wage.

• • •

Ted Kennedy, who had made so many miscalculations when he got into the race, had made one more miscalculation—a major one, it turned out. He had entered the race thinking he might issue a clarion call for liberalism versus Carter's pinched centrism and deficit hawkishness, until the brain trust dissuaded him from doing so and convinced him to focus on the leadership issue instead because they felt liberalism had been discredited. (Carter had based his entire presidency on the same conclusion.) Ted bowed to their expertise, but the brain trust had been wrong, especially after the Iranian hostage taking and the Soviet invasion of Afghanistan enhanced Carter's leadership credentials. Even so, the capacity to be president had never really been the factor the brain trust thought it was. At the outset of the campaign, Pat Caddell had conducted interviews in Iowa that indicated Ted would overwhelm Carter if people imagined Ted as president. A "fantastic" president, they effused to Caddell. When Caddell informed Carter, the president told him simply to burn those interviews: "No one is ever to see them."* (Instead, Caddell put them under lock and key.) But if the brain trust was wrong in focusing on leadership, Ted was wrong in thinking liberalism was the issue. Trying to stir a liberal conscience in the electorate, as Bobby had tried to do in 1968, was not a road to success in 1980 either. In a survey conducted after the campaign, three political scientists found that the "Senator's compassion for the less fortunate, long considered to be an attribute, generated more criticism than praise." The moral moment had long since passed.

Most of the liberal establishment knew this, even as it tried to push Jimmy Carter further leftward. And it was why Ronald Reagan was gaining momentum in the Republican nominating contest. *The moral moment had passed.* It had passed in no small measure because the nation was reeling economically—the high double-digit inflation rate (over 12 percent in 1980), the slowing growth rate (a negative growth rate in 1980), an unemployment rate of 7.2 percent that year—and there was little appetite now for the kind of grand programs to help the poor and the marginalized that were the trademarks of liberalism and among the signs of government morality. Americans were now worried about their own economic

---

*In his presidential memoir, Carter directly contradicts this, writing of Ted that "much of his voter approval melted away even among his own supporters when they faced the prospect of his actually serving in the White House." *Keeping the Faith*, 530.

survival. And the moral moment had passed not just for economic reasons but for cultural ones too—because many Americans, white Americans, increasingly viewed liberals' entreaties for morality as a call to disenthrone white Americans from a position of primacy, while others saw it as a call to disenthrone their traditional morality and replace it with a kind of moral license for people to do whatever they pleased. Nixon's Watergate misdeeds might have derailed his larger objective, to create a permanent majority of disaffected white Americans, as Jimmy Carter's election seemed to attest, but that derailment had been only temporary. Though Jimmy Carter had inherited a weak economy from the Republicans, the forces of conservatism—and especially the forces of reactionary populism—had gotten back on the tracks and had been picking up steam since Nixon's resignation, and while those reactionary populists were largely impelled by racial animus, which also had a good deal to do with their growing animus toward the government for having promoted civil rights, they were now joined by other clusters of crusaders who were fighting their own battles against a changing, diversifying, democratizing, liberalizing America—a new and seemingly terrifying America—the America whelped in the 1960s, in part, politically speaking, by the Kennedys and Lyndon Johnson. Pollster Peter Hart, in a survey taken for Carter in Wisconsin before the primary race began, found citizens there worried about "moral threats which cut right through the social fabric"— not the threats about which Ted Kennedy worried, the threats of poverty and racism and lack of healthcare and economic inequality and injustice, but a "lack of morality and religion and the breakdown of family structures." These were the very things on which conservatives had been attacking liberals: a kind of moral lethargy. And so came a new force— a force of coalescing moralists. In addition to the racial antagonists, the soldiers of these massing armies were anti-abortion activists, antifeminists, evangelical Christians, antitaxers, homophobes ("God made Adam and Eve, not Adam and Steve"), pro-militarists, and those adherents of what had been the fundament of modern conservatism, anti-Communism, the last of whom were certain that in any pact with the Soviet Union, the United States would be hornswoggled. Individually and divided, these groups had been marginal; except for the last group, they hadn't even been able to commandeer the Republican Party. But a Venn diagram of American conservatism in 1980 would have shown that almost all of them now overlapped—after all, despite their separate battles, they were generally fighting the same war against liberalism—which intensified their power exponentially. Republicans, awakened to the possibilities of cultural warfare, encouraged that massing and benefited from it, turning conservatism from a gaggle into a movement. As historian Rick Perlstein would put it, "Movements become powerful enough to change history when they merge diverse tributaries." Perhaps Democrats could have survived if there hadn't been the double blow of a faltering economy and brewing cultural warfare. But there was.

And there might have been no single political figure who so symbolized the forces this movement despised as Ted Kennedy.

Ted Kennedy, who had always had such sound political instincts, had miscalculated that either of the things on which he hoped to campaign, leadership or moral mission, really mattered to the public; if they had, Ted might have beaten Carter. Caddell found that the deciding factor was not leadership or liberalism or any policy considerations at all, since exit polling during the primaries showed that voters preferred Ted's policy prescriptions to Carter's, at least his economic prescriptions, and since, if policy mattered, Carter would not still have been accruing delegates as the economy continued its tailspin throughout the election. People vote on character, Caddell told Elizabeth Drew, not issues. And the American people had found Ted Kennedy's character wanting. "Character is the only explanation for Kennedy's enormous negative ratings," an aide told *Newsweek,* affirming what Caddell had discovered. "The issues are coming around to us, but it's not helping." One Kennedy supporter, who had counseled Ted not to run, given the state of his marriage and his womanizing and the haze of Chappaquiddick that still, even eleven years later, hung over him, said that the "American people will see him as someone who does not have his life together." B. Drummond Ayres of the *Times* said the same thing: The character issue was paramount, and it didn't work in Ted's favor. Those three political scientists who conducted an election postmortem found that the "more people thought (and perhaps the more people knew about Kennedy) the less they liked him," though a lot of that might have had to do with knowing more about his campaign and their disenchantment with its failings, which they conflated with his sullied character: A failed campaign spelled a failed person. As pundit William Schneider stated it, "Kennedy's main problem is that people don't trust him."

Obviously, despite pollster Lou Harris's assurance that interest in the issue had declined by 1980, Chappaquiddick, not unreasonably, played a significant role in damaging the perception of Ted's character. Ted had thought he had put the incident to rest, or at least the passage of time had. A *Time* poll in August 1978, found that 79 percent of Americans did not feel Chappaquiddick should disqualify him from the presidency. On the tenth anniversary of Chappaquiddick, in July 1979, he had granted several interviews, including one with *The New York Times*, in which he continued to express his regrets and accept responsibility but provided no new information, save for the fact that he had instructed his cousin Joey Gargan and his friend Paul Markham not to report the accident that night because, he said, he felt it was his responsibility to report it. A CBS/*Times* survey published at the same time found that only 23 percent of the 80 percent of voters who remembered Chappaquiddick said they would be less likely to vote for Kennedy because of the accident, and a higher percentage, 53 percent, thought that he would show "good judgment under pressure" than said the same of the president, 40 percent. That same anniversary week the Kopechnes granted an interview to *The New York Times*, their final interview on the subject, they said, in which they claimed they "more or less" believed Ted's version of events, even though they felt they still didn't know the "whole story," and that they wouldn't commit to supporting him for president, despite the fact that he had "grown up" in the last few years. None of this seemed to stir very much public interest, in part, because the anniversary fell on the same week as Carter's speech on America's crisis of confidence and his purge of his Cabinet, which overshadowed the Chappaquiddick anniversary—possibly overshadowed it not least because the press was not particularly sympathetic to Carter's bungling and didn't seem keen on undermining Ted's possible candidacy at the time. As speculation on Ted's decision intensified that summer, the Kopechnes did grant another interview, in which they told *Newsweek* that Ted would be a "leader" and that "everyone makes mistakes," while Ted told *Time* shortly after announcing that the "essence of the event for me is that the girl is dead."

But Ted Kennedy was not going to be let off so lightly by the media. The media saw the chance to revive the Chappaquiddick story partly as a way to intensify the campaign narrative itself, that story it wanted to tell, and partly as a way to develop the narrative of Ted's ineptitude and incompetency that the Mudd interview had established and that the press had continued to promulgate. The *New York Post* had attempted to centralize Chappaquiddick as early as November 8, the day after Kennedy's announcement, by featuring yet another interview with Mary Jo Kopechne's parents headlined, "Tell the Truth, Teddy" and under that, running another article, "The Story That No One Really Believes." (The Kopechnes were little quoted in the piece; it was the words of Representative Robert Dornan, a virulently anti-Kennedy Republican who had camped out on the Kopechnes' doorstep, that were chiefly reported.) The *Chicago Tribune*, another conservative paper, also ran a series of negative columns and editorials, several of which mentioned Chappaquiddick. Referencing Chappaquiddick, *Tribune* columnist Bob Weidrich wrote, "Ted Kennedy should adopt the white feather of cowardice as the logo for his presidential campaign."

But as much as Chappaquiddick was bruited about, it didn't seem to be a *public* obsession; it was a national *media* obsession. (Carter's people seemed to know as much. One Carter adviser told Theodore White, "We don't have to attack [Kennedy] on his character; the press will do that for us.") T. R. Reid, who was on the hustings with Ted for *The Washington Post* on those first campaign trips, said that Ted was seldom asked about Chappaquiddick by voters—never, not even once, in his question-and-answer sessions with those voters—and that even the local press scarcely mentioned it—only once in his fourteen-state swing that first month that included dozens of interviews. But, Reid observed, the national press, of which he was a member, was obsessed with Chappaquiddick—especially now that Carter had rebounded—and he cited an ABC interview on *Issues and Answers* with Ted in which eight of the thirteen questions were about Chappaquiddick. (Ted bristled at the hypocrisy of reporters asking about his personal life when he knew many of those reporters had personal problems of their own. "Hey, how's *your* first wife," he said he wanted to ask one television moderator.) Shortly after his announcement, a *Time* poll showed that 76 percent of respondents felt, "It is time to forget Chappaquiddick and judge Kennedy by what he has done since then," and a *NYT/CBS* poll found that 69 percent of Democrats thought favorably about him. A survey conducted by *Newsweek* before the Iowa caucuses, just two months later, found that 98 percent of respondents were aware of the accident and that 50 percent had followed the case closely. Of those, 65 percent thought he had acted improperly at the time—a significant rise in the past six months, which spoke to how steeply his star had fallen. Sixty-eight percent of those who believed he had acted improperly said they would not be likely to vote for him in November. And of those who had seen his explanation, only 19 percent felt more sympathetic to him. "The Drag on Teddy" was what *Newsweek* labeled the report. A drag it was. But barring some subterranean animus toward Ted because of Chappaquiddick, subterranean because it hadn't previously surfaced, Ted's numbers didn't drop because the public's interest in Chappaquiddick had spontaneously flared and their opinions spontaneously changed; they had had ten years to ponder it. The only plausible explanation was that the interest flared and the opinions changed because the national press was now focused so heavily on Chappaquiddick. The national media had insisted that Chappaquiddick would hurt Ted Kennedy. "Chappaquiddick is politically, a ticking time-bomb," Martin Schram had written in Reid's own *Washington Post*, after the *Post* ran a six-thousand-word reexamination of Chappaquiddick in two front-page stories on November 11 and 12. Whether it had been ticking before Ted's candidacy, it certainly was after he declared.

But however heavily Chappaquiddick weighed on Ted Kennedy's campaign, Arthur Schlesinger, Jr., had another observation: that it was only one element of many that had tarnished the Kennedy brand, and that if Ted, in the eyes of most people, wasn't perceived as being as good as his brothers, his brothers were no longer perceived as being as good as they were once thought to have been either, since by that time revelations about John Kennedy's philandering and Bobby Kennedy's wiretapping of Martin Luther King, Jr., among other transgressions, had been made public. "I think there is a deep resentment of the Kennedys in the land," Schlesinger wrote in his journal. "I guess we like dynasties up to a point, but then begin to hate what are taken as dynastic pretensions and expectations. Ted Kennedy is the victim of the same backlash that destroyed TR Jr. in the 1920s and FDR Jr. in the 1950s," though Schlesinger didn't consider whether it wasn't so much dynastic pretensions that had done the Kennedys in or a dented mythos, as it was their relationship to liberalism, which had once elevated the Kennedys, and now seemed to reduce them, as liberalism itself had been reduced. Of this diminished Ted Kennedy, Caddell told columnist E. J. Dionne, Jr.: "If it's Carter versus Kennedy, we win. If it's Carter versus Carter, we lose." In short, the effort for the Carter campaign was to keep the focus on Ted and off the president.

·   ·   ·

The nature of the Chappaquiddick coverage revealed something else that added yet another log to the inferno that was engulfing Ted Kennedy's campaign: The press had turned on him. "They expected Camelot," one campaign staffer said of the press the Kennedy forces thought Ted would receive. "They expected reporters to fall all over themselves for Kennedy." The press had liked Ted, and Ted had always enjoyed a cordial if sometimes guarded relationship with them, except for the period after Chappaquiddick when there was little cordiality. But that was a decade ago. With the press, he had been one of the boys—again, at least when he was in the mood. "He loved the back and forth," said Tom Oliphant of *The Boston Globe*. "He found it invigorating." By the same token, Oliphant said that Ted "did his outreach diligently, just like he did in the Senate," learning whom he could trust and whom he could use. "He respected journalists who worked hard," and he "preferred the company of reporters to [that of] columnists," who were basically opinionators, in his view, rather than working journalists. But the press, however friendly, had nevertheless been wary with him, worried about "getting swept up in the magical moving parade," as one reporter put it, and worried that in so doing they would lose their objectivity. They called him "Senator" or "Sir," never "Ted" or "Teddy," and none of them were particularly close to Ted, as, for example, Charles Bartlett and Ben Bradlee had been close to Jack, or as Jack Newfield had been to Bobby. And though Ted had received that generally favorable press during his long ruminations over whether to run, once he made the decision, the press changed its attitude toward him and changed it decidedly. Now he was a subject to expose, not a fellow to pal around with. (Ted changed too with the weight of a presidential candidacy bearing down on him. During an early campaign flight, Drummond Ayres recalled Ted and the reporters on the plane tossing a football late at night, and Ted "got into it." But then, Ayres recalled, "all of a sudden, it was like a curtain was drawn down—almost in mid-throw, he stopped, handed the ball to somebody, went up to the front of the plane. It was like, 'Can't engage in this.' ") The reporters seemed to fear that they might be accused of "flacking" for Ted if they gave him positive press, as reporters had once been accused of "flacking" for his brothers. Columnist Haynes Johnson questioned whether, having covered the Kennedys for so many years, he and his fellow journalists would even be "capable of fairly covering this intensely personal contest." Instead, they were not only capable; there was a backlash. *Washington Post* television critic Tom Shales called it the "Petty for Teddy" bias and said it was "another case of the press sensing its role in having created a legend, trying to break it down again," while the *Post*'s ombudsman, Charles Seib, asked if the "press [is] leaning over backward to the point where it is now unfair to the man it was accused of favoring." And when Ted was looking as if he might blow Carter away, they became, by one account, suddenly sympathetic to the president whom they had been bashing for months. There was a consensus that with a Kennedy in the race again, the public interest in the campaign would be much greater than if he had not entered. But as Shales noted, it also meant that there would be an additional race to watch besides the one between Kennedy and Carter: "Kennedy versus the boys on the bus, a square-off held to determine who will be able to make the more advantageous use of whom." Throughout, however, it was almost always the press taking advantage of Kennedy, using him, as Roger Mudd had, to score points and gain attention since the best story, the new story, was Ted Kennedy's ongoing slips rather than his challenge to a sitting president. Put simply, the demise of Ted Kennedy was a compelling story.

And while some reporters wanted to ensure their objectivity by coming down harder on Ted than they might otherwise have, another cohort in the press, weaned on Vietnam and Watergate and skepticism toward public officials, young reporters, didn't remember Jack or Bobby and had none of the reverence for the Kennedys nor swooned under their spell as older reporters might have. "The people who chewed him up," columnist Richard Reeves said, "were kids in grammar school when John Kennedy ran."* And there was another factor, an ideological factor, that might have affected the coverage Ted received. As a liberal in a nation where antigovernment sentiments were rising, he was an anachronism. As one reporter put it, speaking of the "illiberal times" in which Ted was running, the times of those massing armies of conservative interest groups and racial backlash, "It is not fashionable for either a reporter or a candidate to have liberal thoughts." Even the so-called progressive press now

---

*By one study, in addition to becoming younger, the number of journalists increased dramatically in the 1970s, by 69 percent; their geographical distribution had come to resemble the national population distribution, which lowered the number of reporters in the Northeast where they might have been more favorable toward Kennedy, and their political orientation had changed from 38 percent who regarded themselves as "pretty far to the left" or a "little to the left" in 1971, to 22 percent by 1982. David Weaver and G. Cleveland Wilhoit, *The American Journalist in the 1990s: U.S. News People at the End of an Era* (Mahwah, N.J.: Lawrence Erlbaum Associates, 1996), 2–25.

seemed hostile to Ted, some because of what they regarded as his sniffing the wind and being insufficiently liberal, like Nat Hentoff reprimanding Ted for his attempt at criminal code reform, others because they regarded his campaign as an embarrassment, like Robert Sherrill and Alexander Cockburn. Moreover, Ted was running into the chainsaw of the newly emerging right-wing media. The *New York Post,* under the ownership of the conservative Australian-born newspaper magnate Rupert Murdoch, was especially unrestrained and antagonistic toward him. One headline story, coming just before the Iowa caucuses, featured a phony countess who claimed to have been Ted's mistress and had gone with him to Chappaquiddick before Mary Jo Kopechne's accident. (This was pure make-believe.) "Such a story represents more than the outpourings of the current scandal sheet," Haynes Johnson commented. "It reflects a blood-in-the-water syndrome that has the sharks circling the Kennedy presidential campaign."

But it reflected something else that undermined the Kennedy campaign—namely, that Ted Kennedy wasn't just another presidential candidate espousing positions and trying to provide a vision for the country. He was different from Jimmy Carter. He was a celebrity, a star of the ongoing soap opera of "The Kennedys," a man whose personal life overshadowed his policies. The media had long created narratives to turn an electoral campaign into a television series in order to hold the public interest. Harvard political scientist Thomas Patterson said that the press had four stories to tell during a campaign: "a candidate is leading, or trailing, or gaining ground, or losing ground." And he said that the press had a "distinctive narrative for each situation," most notably, that "the press joined the bandwagon and chipped away at the candidate who was losing ground." Ted had certainly been victimized by the narrative of his losing ground to Carter just as Ted's campaign was beginning. And Patterson noted too the increasing prevalence of the story function in political coverage, quoting NBC News president Reuven Frank that "every news story should, without any sacrifice of probity or responsibility, display the attributes of fiction, of drama. It should have a structure and conflict, problem and denouement, rising action and falling action, a beginning, middle and an end." None of this worked to Ted Kennedy's advantage, not only because he was losing ground, which meant the press was likely to jump on him since the media, by one study, tend to "slide away from surprise losers," and not only because the story function came at the expense of the issue function, when on the issues the electorate seemed more favorably disposed toward Ted than toward Carter—"If I give a funny remark, or put my arm around my family you know, that's what's going to be on the morning news"—but also and perhaps primarily because Ted's "story," the soap opera of his life, was filled with melodrama that raised doubts about the things that voters seemed to like least about him—most important, questions about his character, fed by accounts of his cheating scandal in his freshman year at Harvard, by his womanizing as reported in the tabloids, by his peculiar relationship to Joan, and by Chappaquiddick. The Kennedys had been beneficiaries of their celebrity. It endowed them with movie star glamour. (John Kennedy's Camelot was a by-product.) Now Ted Kennedy was a victim of his celebrity. It endowed him with movie star tabloid turpitude.

Finally, the press seemed to turn on Ted because he had disappointed them. "Journalists see themselves in the business of evaluating campaigns, not candidates," two media scholars, Michael Robinson and Margaret Sheehan, observed, and Ted Kennedy's campaign had definitely fallen short by the media's evaluations. Reporters had expected a Superman. When, as T. R. Reid had written, Clark Kent arrived instead with his bungling campaign, they were more than disappointed; they felt betrayed. And in that betrayal, they seemed to feel that they had to disenchant the country as they believed Ted Kennedy had disenchanted them—to awaken everyone from the spell of the Kennedy myth. Story after story after story featured Ted's missteps: "Kennedy Myth Gives Way to Hard Realities" (*Washington Post*); "Troubled Kennedy TV Effort Changes Direction" (*New York Times*); "Teddy's Ragged Start" (*Newsweek*); "Kennedy Makes a Goof" (*Time*); "Kennedy's TV Style, or Lack of It Is a Surprise" (*Los Angeles Times*). Moreover, Ted was struggling against another media bias—this one not personal but systemic. As Harvard's Thomas Patterson found, "Journalists reason from effect to cause," so that Ted's sudden drop in the polls had to be attributed to some failing of Ted's, despite the Iran hostage situation and the Soviet invasion of Afghanistan, which had clearly boosted Carter at Ted's expense. "A man who had become accustomed during his entire career to receiving praise for his political acumen and ability, suddenly, according to press reports, could do nothing right," Elizabeth Drew observed that December. "A man who used to be able to bring crowds to their feet, suddenly, it was said, could hardly deliver a speech." And Ted reacted to the endless criticisms, as he so often reacted to criticism, not by recognizing the press dynamics at work that generated the negativity but by internalizing the barbs. Drew said that Ted became so self-conscious about making any slips of the tongue that he made more slips, which moved his staff to tell him to read his speeches, "which led to wooden delivery and loss of contact with his audience." Hunting for his mistakes—that was what the press did after the Mudd interview erased fifteen years of eloquence, at least when Ted gave formal addresses, and created a narrative of Ted's inadequacy. No nit seemed too small to pick. Phil Jones of CBS, as evidence of Ted's lack of spontaneity, made a point of showing a teleprompter for one of Ted's speeches, as if using a prompter, which every candidate did for major addresses, were a sign of deception or weakness. Every slip of the tongue became news, and Drew noted that even when Ted vastly improved as a speaker, the press was still portraying him as inarticulate because once having created the narrative, they were reluctant to change it. And more personally, the press would take those bloopers and play them over the plane's public address system on the next flight—Ted's flight—play them over and over. By one account, Ted "laughed as loud as anyone," but in all likelihood he was hurting underneath like the boy he had been who was the butt of jokes and had to laugh along, rather than the proud senator, the master of the Senate, who was sensitive to slights. One reporter told Tom Shales of the "phenomenal" anti-Kennedy bias, "We turn on the nightly news to find out how badly Teddy is doing today." "Pack pressure," *Post* reporter Myra MacPherson called it, and claimed not a single reporter that December, when Ted was being ridiculed, dissented. Not one. Even the conservative *New York Times* columnist William Safire, who had been a speechwriter for Richard Nixon, couldn't help but sympathize with Ted now that the press was tearing into him. "The trend in wolf-pack journalism is to savage Mr. Kennedy," he wrote, "while treating Mr. Carter's Rose Garden campaign with awe and reverence."

As Ted Kennedy headed into Iowa for the caucuses that would be the first test of his and Carter's strength, he faced overwhelming discouragement—the discouragement that the press read into his tension. By mid-December, his favorability rating had dropped thirty-four points to 50 percent in a *Los Angeles Times* poll, and only 33 percent of Democrats favored him as their nominee, while 54 percent now favored Carter. (The media focus on Chappaquiddick apparently had an effect; Chappaquiddick was cited as a central factor.) Gallup called the drop "one of the most dramatic turn-abouts in its four years of polling" the 1980 race. It now had Carter ahead of Ted by eight points among Democrats and ahead of Ronald Reagan, the leading Republican presidential contender, by twenty-four points, while Ted had fallen from a twenty-eight-point lead over Reagan to a slim five-point lead. But it wasn't just the voters who were losing enthusiasm for him. His fellow Democratic officeholders, those very people who had encouraged him to run for well over a year, who had told him he must run to save the party, were losing enthusiasm. As one Democratic senator put it, "Carter's low point was just after Labor Day, and Ted's high point was right up until he made his move." Senator Daniel Patrick Moynihan, who had pulled Ted aside a year earlier at a Special Olympics event and pressed him to run, now was noncommittal and refused to meet with Ted on his first New York campaign trip, in mid-December. New York governor Hugh Carey, who had also been an early Ted booster, also refused to meet with him. According to Ted, the Democratic chairman of the House Ways and Means Committee, Daniel Rostenkowski, had come over to Ted shortly after Ted's announcement to run and told him, "We're going to do the same for you in Chicago that we did for John Kennedy. You can relax. You can depend on me to do it." About ten days later Ted said he saw him at the White House at a meeting of congressional leaders, but Ted noticed that Rostenkowski kept his distance. Four days later he endorsed Carter. The civil rights leader Jesse Jackson had also pledged his support to Ted, then Mondale visited Chicago, where Jackson lived, and pledged federal funds to his organization. One of the most galling of the deserters was House speaker Tip O'Neill. O'Neill had said in May that if Kennedy were to run, he would beat Carter, but he had had a "fatherly" talk with Ted trying nevertheless to discourage him and wait for another time because Carter had too much largesse to dispense and because Chappaquiddick was still a live issue. O'Neill had had a contentious relationship with Carter, a relationship not unlike that between Ted and Carter—contentious because O'Neill found Carter insufficiently liberal too. But when it came time for Ted's run, O'Neill didn't back him. (*New York Times* Senate correspondent Martin Tolchin said it was because O'Neill considered the Kennedys privi-leged Brahmins rather than working-class Irish like him. Ted said it was because, as Judiciary chair, he had chosen another nominee for an open-ing on the bench, one who had been endorsed by a special selection panel that Ted had organized, over the one for whom O'Neill had lobbied, Congressman Ed Boland's brother.) When Bobby was considering taking on Lyndon Johnson for the nomination in 1968, the Democratic committeeman of New York, Jack English, warned him, "With an incumbent president, these old-line leaders would go with the Presidency because somebody wrote in a book or their mother told them, 'You know the rule says you don't dump an incumbent president.'" Now Ted was learning that lesson. He was going it alone. Carter would have the pols who wouldn't dump an incumbent president.

III

Jimmy Carter's plan was no different than Ted Kennedy's: win early and win big. Establish momentum. Puncture the Kennedy myth of invincibility. Hamilton Jordan wrote in his January 17 memo to Carter that "if we win the early contests, it is difficult to see how anyone could defeat us for the nomination." But Jordan was leaving little to chance either. He had already devised a primary schedule that set the Southern state primaries early in the year, so that Carter could accumulate those delegates. That meant Ted's best chance of generating his own momentum was winning the Iowa caucuses, scheduled for January 21. "Step one was, let's really make Iowa the big deal," campaign adviser Bill Carrick was to say. "We'll throw everything in there. That became the number one imperative of the campaign." But if Ted thought he would be able to test his ideas against Carter's and even meet Carter face-to-face, he was mistaken. The day before Ted's announcement, Carter's press secretary Jody Powell accepted on the president's behalf an invitation from *The Des Moines Register* to debate Ted and California governor Jerry Brown, who had also declared his candidacy. But that was when Ted still had a lead over Carter. With the hostage taking and the Soviet invasion of Afghanistan, Carter and his staff were mulling over the wisdom of facing Ted. On January 4, Carter decided to cancel the appearance, telling Hamilton Jordan, "I go out there as a President and return as just another political candidate." (Powell then wrote and leaked a memo with Carter's handwritten notations saying that he couldn't debate because of Iran and Afghanistan, and "we will just have to take the adverse political consequences," as if not going to Iowa were a sacrifice rather than a boon.) Ted responded to Carter's decision not only not to debate but also not to engage in any political activities while the hostages were being held, with a sarcastic note, inviting him to a joint discussion before the Consumer Federation of America meeting but limiting the subjects to "non-political, non-campaign matters, i.e., that is [sic] exclusively to the substance of subjects which you and I deal with and take positions on in the course of our official legislative and executive capacities," and he cited a pamphlet, "The Record of President Jimmy Carter," that the White House had mailed "at taxpayer expense"— "presumably non-political, non-campaign."

But if Jimmy Carter wasn't physically present in Iowa that December and January, he was present nonetheless. That September, when Ted's entrance into the race seemed all but assured, Caddell had sold Carter on the fruits of negative campaigning, citing campaigns by New York governor Hugh Carey, New Jersey governor Brendan Byrne, and Connecticut governor Ella Grasso, all of whom had been down in the polls and then rebounded by attacking their opponents. "This campaign could get very bloody," he told Carter. (Carter, by his own admission, was a ruthless campaigner, his smile, as Robert Shrum had said, notwithstanding.) And the Carter campaign compiled a list to contrast the president to Ted, with such items as "Big Spender," "Very Liberal," "Changes positions," "Ineffective Senator," "Grandstander," "Won't take on tough fights," "Never worked a day," and "Panics in a crisis"—the last in obvious reference to Chappaquiddick. Meanwhile Carter had begun running television ads in which he said, with a not-too-subtle poke at his opponent, "I don't think there's any way you can separate the responsibility of being a good husband or a father or a basic human being from that of being a good president." Other ads exploited the foreign crises and a new hawkish mood in the country by saying, in effect, that a vote for Carter was a vote for America. It was a powerful two-pronged attack on two of Ted's vulnerabilities: his character and his patriotism, which was questioned because he was challenging a sitting president while the president was fending off foreign adversaries.

It was an attack that was difficult to parry, and Ted Kennedy did not parry it, especially since he was now committed to silence about Iran after his San Francisco blunder. Though Iowa was the "big deal," his chance to turn things around, and though he usually arrived with a large press contingent in a long caravan and before packed houses—one thousand at the high school auditorium in Ottumwa, five hundred at the community center in Oscaloosa, a jammed bingo parlor in Knoxville and an equally crowded coffee shop in Indianola—that turned his appearances into media events, he was every bit as ragged in Iowa as he had been during his whirlwind stumping throughout November, and he roused none of the excitement that Jack and Bobby had generated. He appeared at the University of Iowa and read a speech so mechanically—this was when his handlers had pushed him to read rather than speak extemporaneously—that one reporter said it sounded as "if he had never seen it before, seldom looking up to make eye contact with the audience." The applause at the end was as "perfunctory" as the speech, and when Ted began a question-and-answer session, the reporter noted that students began to exit or sat reading their textbooks. Paul Kirk said that the modulation was by design. A "tender time," Kirk called it, saying, "It's hard to launch a blitz attack against an incumbent president when things are like this," meaning the hostage crisis. But the modulation made Ted look weak and uneasy, and according to an account in the *Los Angeles Times*, when he did shake off the restraint, at the Knoxville bingo parlor, and raised his voice—"I'm getting all excited here"—he seemed "taken aback" by the applause he received. "Programmed and reprogrammed," Elizabeth Drew would write of him in those early days in Iowa, "battened down and unnatural," "his hands tied behind him," "defensive, tentative, explaining himself." "Cold and lifeless," columnist Richard Cohen wrote of Ted's demeanor at rallies. "He refers to himself mostly as 'we' and talks of 'our' administration—the one he will have when he wins. He speaks in clichés. He says Iowa is in the 'heartland of the country' and the 'crossroads of the nation.' It is not stirring stuff." "Lifeless, humorless, totally without passion," Cohen reported, which had been the very charges against Jimmy Carter. And when Cohen asked him on the plane afterward what had happened to him—an indelicate question—Ted said that campaigning had once been fun but was fun no longer. "The basic joy of it went out with my brothers," he told him, as he had told others before him. In effect, he was going through the motions.

And going through the motions, he couldn't catch fire. He said that the "more I went to these towns"—he specifically cited Ottumwa—"the more I fell behind," and he asked Iowa's popular former governor and senator, Harold Hughes, a supporter who, as the head of a national drug rehabilitation program, was prevented from getting involved in the campaign, why. And Hughes said that when he was campaigning and he would drive up to, say, Ames, he would arrive in a car or a truck, and he would be by himself, and he would go into the venue himself, and he would introduce himself and shake hands with everybody there himself. Then he would write down everyone's name when he got back into his car, and late that night back in the motel, he would go over them with an aide and later write each one a handwritten note. "Folksy," he said. But Ted couldn't be folksy. He would have that press caravan and the Secret Service agents and all the cameras around him—"in case something would happen to me," meaning an attempt on his life—and they would all be pushing these folks around, and, Hughes said, the folks became resentful. Resentful, but also disappointed, as the press had been, that Clark Kent had arrived and not Superman. A young high school teacher told *Time* that he had hoped the "Kennedy excitement would come forth again. It didn't." (It couldn't. Ted didn't feel it.) An industrial cleanser salesman said, "He seems more mortal now." Running in to Ted on a visit to Washington during one of Ted's breaks from Iowa, and joining him in Ted's office for a chat, former UAW head and now U.S. ambassador to China Leonard Woodcock found him dismayed, and Woodcock too got the impression that Ted had been "shoved" into the race "to defend his honor or whatever." Ted had just returned from a UAW rally in Waterloo, Iowa, the largest local in the state—twenty thousand strong—that had endorsed him. But he complained to Woodcock that "with friends like that, I don't need enemies." He said, "All I got was [questions about] abortion, gun control." Even when Carter announced, in a televised address, that he would be embargoing grain to the Soviet Union as punishment for its Afghanistan behavior—an embargo that would hurt Iowa farmers and one, Ted said, that he never would have imposed—Ted couldn't agitate them. One operative, echoing Caddell, said the farmers cared more about "Ted's makeup" than about economics. And there was one last indignity. Ted left the campaign trail in Iowa and flew through an ice storm to make an appearance at a tribute for Birch Bayh, the Indiana senator who had rescued him from the plane wreckage in 1964 and who was now in a tight reelection race to hold his Senate seat. At the event, Bayh gave what Robert Shrum called a "windy" speech that ended with an endorsement of Carter. Shrum said he was upset at the ingratitude. Ted, who by this time seemed inured to ingratitude, said that Bayh would always have a pass for having saved his life, though he must have been hurt.

Ted did not fool himself either about his performance or his prospects. He realized early on that he was almost certain to lose Iowa. His own internal poll in December showed him losing three to one. Still, he did his best to salvage the election. He brought his mother, now eighty-nine, into the state where she thanked a crowd in Davenport for helping Jack and Bobby and said she was "delighted you are going to help my youngest son—my last child." He tried changing his style, being less robotic, more himself, looser, relaxed, more of the old Ted Kennedy. He tried changing his tone, invoking the new national concord over Iran to tackle other problems, as a way of addressing Iran without criticizing Carter directly. A "spirit of unity," he called it, and "who is to say that we cannot do it in trying to come to grips with our economy or trying to fashion an energy policy that's going to be fair?" He tried changing his message, exasperated with the one he felt he had been persuaded to adopt, leadership, and he asked Bob Shrum, who was traveling with him and writing his speeches along with Carey Parker, to give his stump speech more edge, to go on the attack, to make it more of a liberal case for his candidacy: "It is time to put a real Democrat back in the White House."

Hopeless. That was the feeling in the Kennedy camp. And that was the feeling in Ted Kennedy. *"The basic joy went out of it with my brothers."* Interviewing Ted during a campaign break in Washington two weeks before the caucuses, *New York Times* columnist James Reston found that the "inner leisure is gone, and he talks like a man who fears he cannot afford another indiscretion," which, of course, he couldn't. And Reston found Ted's fatalism rising, with Ted telling him that "so many things were beyond his control or anybody else's" and "he would just have to work away and see what happened," so that the entire campaign now was in the lap of the gods. He said something similar the following week to T. R. Reid of *The Washington Post*—that he had a "reasonable expectation" he would lose the caucuses and that "one of the things you learn in politics is that there are a lot of things you can't control" and that you must "do the best you can and wait for things to change." Ted Kennedy had long been fatalistic about himself; he had never been fatalistic about politics. Now he was. And Reid noticed something else in Ted now that hadn't been there before—the same thing Vanden Heuvel had noticed: "Kennedy did not look very devastated." Reid said Ted joked with reporters before going before the cameras to assert that if Carter won any less than 50 percent of the vote, it would have to be considered a loss for the president. His mood lightened, as if not carrying the burden of having to win were the elixir to make him a better candidate.

And he *was* a better candidate now—now that the burden was lifted and even he conceded he had little chance of victory in Iowa. Hugh Sidey, the veteran *Time* political correspondent, watching Ted that January, wrote that he is "not so bad a performer as his Eastern drama critics make out," and he even said that "one can pick up echoes of some of the old magic from John and Bob," which, given his early reviews, was a major reevaluation. He said, "Ted is a presence," when it was precisely his lack of presence that had sent the press into a frenzy. And Sidey reported that when Ted arrived outside the Perry City Hall one morning, there was a "small shock wave of anticipation," the sort of anticipation, though Sidey didn't say it, that had preceded Bobby's campaign stops in 1968. "Young women shifted, craned, raised themselves to tiptoe. Wisecracking high school students shut up. Then a little of the Kennedy legend walked through the door. There was impact." And now when he spoke, he was bellowing again, "pumping the air with that familiar Kennedy gesture, fingers folded, thumb on top"—Jack's gesture. "The Kennedy on the stump tonight is markedly different from the Kennedy of two months ago," Haynes Johnson concurred. "Today he delivers a superb political speech, crisply and confidently, handles question adroitly, draws enthusiastic responses from audiences, and campaigns with what appears to be obvious enjoyment," though he had shown little enjoyment earlier in the campaign. "There is no faltering, no fumbling, no vague wandering from issue to issue," Johnson continued, and Ted's new "coherent message" hammers at the president from Ted's liberal perch and reaches an "emotional peak" when Ted, the old Ted, pounds his fist on the lectern and says, "Enough is enough." When Ted finally got the chance at the Black Hawk County Democratic dinner to go toe to toe with Jerry Brown and, in Carter's stead, Vice President Mondale, Tom Oliphant called him "brilliant—clear and focused," and Elizabeth Drew said of his speech that night, "He delivers it as if it were coming from somewhere deep within him. 'I am a candidate for President of the United States because I have a sense of hope for the future of our nation. I reject the counsel of voices, no matter how high in government, that talk about a malaise of the spirit,'" referring to Carter's speech of July 1979. And he said, "I haven't seen it in Iowa. And I haven't seen it in the ten weeks of traveling the length and breadth of the nation." And he closed by asking Iowans on caucus day, eight days hence, to "walk across that room and join with us, join with us, and try to ensure that this great nation of ours can come to grips with the problems that we're facing today" and show the world that "America is on the move again." This was the Kennedy that voters had expected—a fiery, inspiring, passionate Kennedy. This was the Kennedy that Ted had become now that he had nothing to lose because he was destined to lose, the Kennedy who didn't have to bear the weight of victory, the Kennedy who had been freed from expectation.

But as good as he was, as energized as he was, there was little hope of escaping the miasma that had settled over his campaign, and even if there had been, the press, with its growing antipathy to Ted, would not allow him to escape. As the Iowa caucuses approached, the *Washington Star*, *Reader's Digest*, and the *New York Post*, all of them conservative publications, ran stories challenging Ted's account of Chappaquiddick—in the case of *Reader's Digest*, conducting forensic studies of the water conditions at the time of the accident and the speed his car must have been traveling; in the case of the *Star*, taking aerial photographs of the sandbar opening through which the tides ran to prove that the current could not have been as strong as Ted had contended in preventing him from rescuing Ms. Kopechne; in the case of the *Post*, refuting the story that Ted had not previously visited Chappaquiddick by reporting on the "mistress" with whom he had once visited the island. Larry Horowitz said that Ted was surprised by the renewed preoccupation with Chappaquiddick, thrown by it, at the very time he needed to concentrate on the campaign. "I can't tell you the number of hours of key staff time that went into that," Horowitz said, meaning the refutation of the *Digest* and *Star* stories. "Worry time, in his mind." Determined to challenge these accounts and save his candidacy, Ted hired his own engineers, including MIT oceanographer Jerome Milgram, and obtained his own aerial photographs from the very time of the accident to disprove the *Star*'s contention. (The *Star* had conveniently neglected to print another photo that would have supported Ted's account.) And a week before the caucuses, Ted was forced to hold two press conferences, both staged in a room of the Judiciary Committee, where he sat nervously biting his nails and chewing on a pen or waving a cigar and, with Milgram and two admiralty lawyers beside him, presenting evidence to rebut the charges against him, large blowups of the photographs of the channel—the first day *Reader's Digest*, the second, the *Star*. The press conferences served only to focus even more attention on Chappaquiddick. "If there were new facts that would conflict with that testimony," the testimony he had given at the inquest, he told *The New York Times*, "I never could have been a candidate for the presidency." But the damage had been done. The "Campaign Issue That Will Not Go Away," *Time* called it that week, while an aide to Ted said, "It may already be fatal."

His impending defeat might have liberated Ted Kennedy, but it didn't make campaigning any easier. He still hoped against hope that he might turn the tide. But that tide was running strongly against him. A *NYT/CBS* poll in mid-January, five days before the caucuses, showed that for the first time in twenty years, Americans wanted to spend more money on defense, while two-thirds wanted cuts in domestic spending—the very cuts that Ted was fighting, showing how much the national mood had seemed to shift away from liberalism. Carter's approval rating stood at 52 percent, his highest since the Egyptian-Israeli Camp David accords. Still, Ted wouldn't surrender. Shortly after he declared, he had pressed his close friend John Culver, who was in a tight race for reelection in Iowa, to endorse him, but they had "mutually decided," as Culver later put it, that he would remain neutral. But now, days before the caucuses, late Friday night, Ted met Culver at Culver's Washington office and asked him if he might reconsider and endorse him. This wasn't Moynihan or Carey or even Tip O'Neill. Culver was one of Ted Kennedy's closest friends, practically family. Culver told Ted he would think about it, then discussed it with advisers and phoned people in Iowa, all of whom told him it would be a "disaster" for his reelection chances and wouldn't help Ted anyway. So Culver had to tell his old college friend the next morning that the endorsement would not be forthcoming. Ted left Washington and returned to Iowa. "There was some sensitivity there, at the time," Culver said, with what was surely some understatement. Not even Ted's "brother" dared support him.

But there wasn't much Ted could do in Iowa now. He had visited every hamlet, dragged Joan and Kara and Ted Jr. and even Rose around the state, had spent ten weeks there. When he had started and a colleague asked him how the campaign was going, Ted lifted his hand like an airplane taking off and said, "Whooosh!" Now, as the Iowa campaign neared its end, his strategists met at his home in McLean, and Carl Wagner said that Ted had thirty thousand voters identified as backing him, which would have been enough to win previous Iowa caucuses. Ted in his memoir said he was sure he was going to win, contrary to those accounts at the time that he knew he had no chance to win. He said he sensed it. But Bob

Shrum had a different recollection. During the McLean meeting, he said, Ted called Shrum into the foyer and "put out his hand, wobbled it toward the floor like a plane falling from the sky, and offered this prediction: 'This baby's going down.'"

Down it did go. Ted got his thirty thousand votes. Carter got sixty thousand in an unprecedented turnout. And there was more bad news. That night, the night of the caucuses, Steve Smith told Ted there was no money left: "We're in debt." And he advised that if Ted pulled out now, there would be no real consequences. "Your career is still intact. You go back to the Senate, and it's not a real knock." But Smith said—a "very tough conversation," Ted would later call it—that if he continued in the race, Smith's new polling showed him losing the Massachusetts primary—his Massachusetts—to Carter by twenty-five points. "And if he beats you in Massachusetts, your career is gone. Finished. That's what you're looking at." And Ted, surprised and chastened, told Smith that he needed to think about it—needed a couple of days to think about it. And Ted said he walked around the field at his house and ruminated on what his brother-in-law had told him.

For months, the question had been: Should he run? Now suddenly, the question was: Should he withdraw? The night of his loss, he gave a concession speech that was called both gracious and humorous but got little television coverage because the networks cut away to an interview of George Bush, who had stunned Republican frontrunner Ronald Reagan by upsetting him in the caucuses. (When Ted conveyed news of his defeat to his mother, he said she told him, "Oh, that's all right, Teddy dear. I'm sure you'll work hard and it'll get better," and then she asked him that if he hadn't worn the blue sweater she got him for Christmas, would he kindly return it to her because she had found a cheaper one, which Ted called a "reality check.")* And when Ted arrived back in Washington at two a.m., and roughly one hundred campaign workers were at Dulles airport to greet him, he said, with his gallows humor, that he thought they were anti-abortion protesters. Meanwhile Carter gloated that Ted had squandered his lead by being "incompetent and confused" in the Mudd interview and ill-advised in his comments on the shah and the Soviet in-

---

* In his memoir, Ted says he called his mother with the news that he was the first Kennedy to lose an election, which suggests how much, even decades later, he felt the albatross of his failure. In fact, Bobby had lost the Oregon primary to Eugene McCarthy in 1968. EMK, *True Compass* (New York: Twelve, 2009), 375.

vasion, in which he pushed back against Carter's sanctions, and Carter's staff thought that, having lost, having been humiliated, Ted would now exit the race. And Carter privately contacted supporters in labor and the civil rights movement and in Jewish groups—supporters who might have had ties to Kennedy—and urged them to push him to withdraw "quickly and gracefully" so as not to polarize the party and hurt Carter's general election chances. "There's a death rattle now to Kennedy's campaign," a Carter aide told the *Los Angeles Times,* no doubt wishfully.

But Ted was not yet ready to concede. The next day, after the defeat, the Kennedy brain trust—Smith, Kirk, Horowitz, Parker, Shrum, Rick Burke, Kalicki, and former Bobby aide and Ted campaign adviser Peter Edelman— met in Ted's Senate office to determine what to do now that they had no money and few prospects of victory. Smith argued again that Ted needed to quit to preserve his senatorial power. Shrum argued for him to stay in the race despite the likelihood of his continuing to get "clobbered." Ted was uncertain, and the first session ended inconclusively, but Ted ordered his speechwriters to prepare a draft of a statement withdrawing from the race. The next morning the brain trust reconvened at his home for more deliberations, while other advisers met at the campaign headquarters in the old Cadillac dealership on 22nd Street NW. After a full day that began with breakfast and continued that evening over a roast beef dinner at McLean, the group—which now also included John Tunney; Bobby's Justice colleagues, John Siegenthaler and John Douglas; Ted's former administrative assistant Ed Martin; and a contributor named William Dunfey—was still debating whether Ted should stay or leave. When, by one report, an adviser encouraged him to stay because, "You represent the hopes and aspirations of huge numbers of people," Ted smiled and said with more gallows humor, "Yes, I noticed that in Iowa." Later that night, however, Carter delivered his State of the Union address, in which the president called for a boycott of the Olympics to be held in Moscow and threatened, as Ted saw it, to reignite the Cold War by providing American assistance to Afghan resistance fighters—two more ways of punishing the Soviets for the Afghan invasion. And, as Shrum described it, Ted, watching the address, was furious. The next morning, Ted was in his office yet again with the eight brain trusters, still without having come to a decision. Shrum now argued that Ted had run because he represented the liberal traditions of the Democratic Party and that if he abandoned the race, he would be branded a "quitter"—the sort of gutless individual his critics, including Carter, had accused him of being. Ted smiled at Shrum, then took a vote. The advisers were evenly divided: four to four. Ted broke the tie. "Let's get ready and go," he said.

He was going to remain in the race—remain even though he told reporters that he knew his chances of winning were gone, remain even though some of his closest friends—Vanden Heuvel and Tunney had had a conversation to this effect—felt that he would destroy the Democratic Party as well as any future he might have as a presidential candidate. He was going to remain even though he might have preferred sparing himself the further humiliation of defeat. He was going to remain, almost surely because he was a Kennedy and Kennedys never quit (Shrum's prod), but also because, as he was to say, it wasn't about victory, which was an odd thing not only for a Kennedy but for any politician to admit. It was about delivering a message, a "strong message," he called it, no longer the feeble one about leadership but a message about something much more important to him. He wanted to campaign for "social progress," even as his fellow Americans were turning their backs on that progress. He wanted to campaign to revive the promise of American liberalism.

SEVEN

"Keep the Rudder True"

TED KENNEDY, HAVING determined that he would continue to run, now had to determine *how* he was going to run. He had suffered "one of the most dramatic turnarounds in American political history," *The New York Times* declared after Iowa. If he were to turn it around again, he would need to start fresh, reboot the entire campaign—a "new type of campaign," in Carey Parker's words. "The Senator often does something when things are going the wrong way on issues," Parker said. "For example, he'll suddenly decide, 'We have to give a major speech on issue X,' and he'll choose an eminent forum—say, New York or the National Press Club in Washington. . . . He'll give a major speech, and we'll sell it to the press beforehand as 'Kennedy's going to give a major speech on this issue.' Usually, it gets a lot of attention, and it shows that Kennedy will at least continue to fight on the issue. Even though the odds are against him, he will not give up." But Parker conceded that this time it was different—not a single issue, not a single fight. This time it was a "test of a lifetime of politics." This time he had to show that "he wouldn't throw in the towel," even though that was exactly what some were expecting. Now Ted announced that he would give a major speech at Georgetown University on January 28, a week to the day after the Iowa caucus drubbing. He didn't say what kind of speech it would be, and when two reporters asked him at his headquarters that week whether it would be a withdrawal announcement, he snapped in irritation, "No!" It would be a different kind of speech than the ones he had been giving so far in the campaign. It would not be a cautious speech—a speech designed to "modulate," as Paul Kirk had said of Ted's approach through most of the Iowa campaign when he was circumspect lest he make another blunder. It would not be an anodyne speech, touting the virtues of the leadership he could provide that Jimmy Carter had not provided, which was what he had been touting through most of the Iowa campaign. It would not be a speech that veered away from liberalism or from criticizing Carter, not just for Carter's leadership deficiencies, but for his deficiencies of policy, which, to Ted, meant Carter's deficient sense of commitment to the poor and marginalized who were Ted's real constituents. It would be the kind of speech Bobby might have delivered in 1968 when he was summoning the country to rediscover its moral sense. It would be a speech appealing to the better angels of America at a time when those angels seemed to be dormant—a Hail Mary—because, as one of Ted's aides later told biographer Burton Hersh, "Once it became apparent in the polling data that all these nice calculations about whether you should or shouldn't come out for price controls and the rest weren't going to affect the outcome one way or the other, you might as well just throw everything at it because you weren't at a point where it was even worth calculating risks anymore." He had campaigned, at his advisers' suggestion and against his own instincts, to hide his passions, until midway through the Iowa campaign, sensing any chance of victory slipping away, he had asked Bob Shrum and Carey Parker, his speechwriters, to toughen up the message, sharpen the tone, to give some sense of his passions. But for all that, he was still relatively restrained. "It's been like punching a pillow," he told reporters of waging his fight against Carter. "I have to get a spark going." The Georgetown speech was designed to unleash those passions and ignite that spark.

A classic liberal speech in illiberal times—that was what both Shrum and Parker had been pushing while Ted was talking numbly about leadership. And now Ted—livid over Carter's State of the Union address that had convinced him to continue his fight, a speech in which the president saber-rattled against the Soviet Union, in which he called for a reduction in the deficit and balancing the budget, in which he asked for labor to "restrain pay increases," in which he spoke, as he had spoken so many times, of American limitations but introduced not a single effort to help the American people in their economic distress, save for a vague mention of a job program for minorities—agreed with his speechwriters, freeing himself from the caution that had constricted his campaign. As Shrum would later write, "Kennedy was determined to run, to win or lose, on the basis of what he really believed, in a campaign that would demonstrate his resolve in adversity and the strength of his commitment to progressive values." If he was going to lose, Ted said, he would "go down honorably." Another aide put it that Ted was going to "let it all hang out."

The speech, a "last-ditch effort to set the themes and issues for the campaign," as Adam Clymer called it in *The New York Times*, required a mobilization. He phoned Arthur Schlesinger, Jr., the day after the State of the Union, complained that "foreign policy is swallowing everything else up," and asked Schlesinger to help draft a speech—a "foreign policy speech," he called it, in which he ostensibly hoped to put those issues to rest. Schlesinger arrived to find Ted in "very good form." He was energized. Though the speech was to center on foreign policy, it would not stop with foreign policy. Stephen Breyer sent a memo on wage and price controls, which Ted had been considering as a way to stanch inflation, and Paul Kirk sent a memo with other ideas. Peter Edelman, Bobby's old aide who now headed the campaign's domestic issues staff, contributed, as did New York congressman Allard Lowenstein, who, Shrum said, showed up at Ted's house uninvited and began working on the speech. It was a sign of just how important the speech was to Ted that he canceled a four-day campaign swing through New England and spent the time instead taking briefings with deputy secretary of state Warren Christopher, Defense secretary Harold Brown, head of the Joint Chiefs of Staff General David Jones, and CIA head Stansfield Turner, and he later met with UN secretary general Kurt Waldheim in New York. (When Ted phoned Carter to request the briefings, Carter thought he was phoning to tell Carter he was leaving the race.) It was also a sign of the speech's importance that there were three days of strategy sessions in preparation, and for the speech itself, there were at least four drafts. Shrum and Parker were still working on it through the night the day before its delivery, though by one account, Ted himself "topped" it off with a "cri de coeur" over what he saw as the "strain of indifference" in Carter's State of the Union.

Speaking the morning of January 28 at Georgetown's Gaston Hall, Ted Kennedy began what he hoped would be a "re-do" of his campaign launch—the first of which had failed so spectacularly. He spoke for forty-five minutes. He spoke of Carter's new "doctrine" that the president had declared in his State of the Union, in which the Persian Gulf was now of vital strategic interest for the United States, and Ted said that many Americans thought we should "stand silent" in the face of that doctrine, though Ted, who had largely stood silent during Carter's foreign crises, said that "if we could discuss foreign policy frankly when Hitler's panzers were poised at the English Channel, surely we can discuss foreign policy when the Soviet Union has crossed the border of Afghanistan." And now Ted did. He questioned whether this was, as Carter had asserted, the "gravest threat to peace since World War II," and he blamed Carter for letting the Soviets mass their troops on the Afghan border before invading without Carter's taking any action. He called for multilateral action against Russia and for strength, not symbolism, in dealing with them. And Ted worried that Carter, in his pique, would fail to pursue nuclear arms limitations with the Soviets now. His voice "dripping with scorn and sarcasm," as the *Times* reported, Ted said that less than a year earlier, at Vienna, Carter had kissed Soviet premier Brezhnev on his cheek: "We cannot afford a foreign policy based on the pangs of unrequited love." And when he turned to the crisis in Iran, Ted returned to his criticism—the criticism that had been so costly to him—of Carter's admitting the shah into the United States when the administration had been "warned that the admission of the Shah would provoke retaliation in Tehran." And he now called for a UN commission to investigate Iranian grievances. And then, pivoting from foreign policy, he said that the silence that had descended on critics of that foreign policy had also descended on critics of Carter's domestic policy. "Last week we heard a State of the Union message that left behind the problems this President was elected to resolve." And he said this: "Someone has to speak for all the Americans who were ignored in the State of the Union address." Ted promised to speak for them, and then rattled off a few of the things that Carter had ignored: inflation, rising unemployment, high energy prices for consumers while oil companies made huge profits. He called for gas rationing and a six-month freeze on prices and wages, but also on profits, dividends, interest rates, and rents. But it was in his peroration that Ted Kennedy sounded his theme—his new theme for his relaunched campaign. "I believe we must not permit the dream of social progress to be shattered by those whose promises have failed. We cannot permit the Democratic Party to remain captive to those who have been so confused about its ideals.

"I am committed to this campaign because I am committed to those ideals."

He closed with a long and stirring list of commitments, virtually a liberal litany—to justice and equality and full civil rights and tax fairness and healthcare for all and the strengthening of America's farms and cities and a safe environment and peace. And "for all these commitments," he said, flashing a huge smile, one of the few in the campaign so far, "I have just begun to fight." He said he was convinced, rejecting Carter's crisis of confidence speech, that the American people were not "selfish" or "hopeless," and that government was not "helpless to serve the public interest." He returned to the sea for his closing metaphor, citing a New England poet: "Should the storm come, we shall keep the rudder true." And he said: "Whatever comes in the voting of this year, or in the voyage of America in all the years ahead, let us resolve to keep the rudder true."

And now he was free.

Unabashedly liberal was the speech, even though his ardent liberalism earlier in the campaign had been one of his miscalculations. It made no concessions to the idea that America had forsworn liberalism, even if it were true that America had. It had its policy prescriptions—two economists he consulted, Walter Heller, Jack's chief economic adviser, and Arthur Okun, who advised Lyndon Johnson, warned Ted that wage and price controls would not work, but Ted was not about to trim his sails—though it was not primarily a speech about policy. It was a speech about Carter's errors, which was an old song, and then about the role that a vigorous government should be playing, and a speech about the candidates' different visions of the country. Carter thought he had to work within reality. Ted thought his job was to change reality. The reception among the five hundred who heard it that morning—a "roiling sea," Shrum called them—was enthusiastic, and Ted got cheers throughout. Students even packed the stairwells, though Georgetown's president, the Reverend Tim Healy, said that Kennedy staffers had already sent two hundred supporters into the auditorium before students were admitted.

After two months of receiving relentlessly derogatory reviews, Ted got positive ones for the Georgetown speech from outside the hall too. An "elegantly drawn and uncommonly well-delivered return to the liberalism Kennedy had muted in the days when he thought he was winning," wrote Peter Goldman of *Newsweek*. Columnist William Raspberry, sounding like Shrum, said it was the "real" Kennedy who spoke at Georgetown, and Ted's deputy campaign manager, Ron Brown, used the same word, "real," to describe him—the "old Kennedy people have been looking for." "Not only has he dared to say that the emperor has no clothes," Joseph Kraft opined, "but he has said it in a way that is comprehensive and weighty." And Kraft seemed to speak to a liberal renewal: "His words will come home when the storm breaks and the country stands helpless amidst the desolation of shattered dreams." Mary McGrory opined that the "man who could not shake Chappaquiddick is being reborn as the conscience of his party." Conservative columnist William Safire's verdict was also a positive one: It "revived the art of political speech, which has been dormant for a decade. The Kennedy oration was written by people with a feel for vivid prose; it was delivered with force and style; and it has meat for everyone to chew on." Safire concluded that "Kennedy, sitting Job-like atop a political dunghill, has evidently decided to run as a Kennedy." Arthur Schlesinger, Jr., thought it gave the whole campaign a "genuine lift," most of all Ted himself. Ted had phoned him afterward, and Schlesinger asked how he was feeling. Ted said he felt much better. "Free at last?" Schlesinger said. "Yes, that's exactly right," Ted answered. Drummond Ayres of *The New York Times,* watching him on the stump the week after Georgetown, found him a different man. "There's a sharp edge, a fresh enthusiasm in his stumping. His tone is alternately dead-serious and mock-hearty"— the tone Ted had always balanced in the past—"as he detailed his controversial gas-rationing plan, then taunts President Carter to 'come out of that Rose Garden.'" "Reborn," Ayres said, from the candidate who had been "mouthing noncontroversial, middle-of-the-road ideology" to a "classic, free-swinging Boston Irish politician," which was what Ted Kennedy had always been. And Ayres said the man who had dropped the football in midthrow on a plane, because he felt he shouldn't be doing that sort of thing, now began riding the press bus when his limousine failed to appear one day. The empty limousine, Ayres noted, trailed behind the bus. "Voices should not be muffled, as they had been muffled in the past," Ted told students at Northeastern University shortly after the speech, referring to his own self-imposed muffling to which he no longer submitted.

And it wasn't only Ted who felt revived. Bill Carrick was to say that it "really rallied people to his side, particularly blue-collar Catholic voters." Shortly after the speech, the Reverend Ralph Abernathy of the Southern Christian Leadership Conference endorsed Ted, as did Rabbi Andrew Schindler of the Union of American Hebrew Congregations. The Carter forces were nonplussed. They had fully expected the speech to be a withdrawal, despite Ted's disclaimers. "We kept knocking him down, and he kept getting up," Jordan would later complain, "obviously not knowing he was beaten."

But for all the tonic effect of the speech, for all the positive reviews and the new endorsements and the revivification of his campaign staff and of the candidate himself—a Ted Kennedy who was finally enjoying his stumping—the unavoidable reality, one he couldn't change, was that his campaign was still in deep trouble. (The Carter people thought even the timing of the speech, early in the morning, was yet another Ted blunder, since it gave them time to respond. The response was that "it represented the latest attempt to develop a rationale for his candidacy.") Ted had raised $4 million before Iowa, but the money, as Steve Smith had told Ted, had run out, so that staff checks had been canceled on January 15 and only half-pay was given on February 1, three days after Georgetown. It had been a "deluxe campaign," with a large staff—sixty-five in Washington, forty advance workers, one hundred in the field—and a well-paid staff. The chartered jet had phones and electric typewriters and a videotape machine. But even during Iowa, money was an issue. The press was charged exorbitantly for places on the plane—225 percent of the cost of the seat, as opposed to 150 percent in most campaigns—and some news outlets had to cut back. After the Iowa loss, there was no more charter jet; Ted flew commercial. In a story titled "Sinking Feeling in Camelot," *Newsweek* reported that the staff now ate stale Dunkin' Donuts and used recycled coffee grounds for a "muddy" brew. Campaign literature piled up in stacks, unmailed because there was no money for postage and little enough for gas. By the same account, when Ted drew a huge crowd in Concord, New Hampshire, the staffers passed around cardboard fried-chicken buckets for a collection. New campaign reform finance laws hurt too, since they limited the amount of money Ted could funnel into his own campaign and the amount he could spend on each state, while Carter lavished tax dollars for projects in primary states. (When Carter gave a grant to Lynn, Massachusetts, to revive its downtown, Tom McGee, the speaker of the Massachusetts House and the man who represented Lynn, endorsed the president.) And with the staff thinned, and the Maine caucuses and the New Hampshire primary hard upon him, Ted was forced to concede the South and move his Washington operatives to those states where he felt he still had a chance, emptying his headquarters. And while the Georgetown speech had generated a small infusion of money, it had not generated enough to fire up the campaign again. "We can keep going as long as the liberal left can keep their wallets open" was how one aide put it. Instead, Ted relied on artists—James Rosenquist, Andrew Wyeth, Andy Warhol, the last of whom, as Ted put it, "sprinkled some dust" on a portrait of Ted, and "we'd sell it for a big chunk of change—$1000, I think." He said he raised a "couple of million dollars" by selling art, or rather using the art as collateral, which was "enough to keep the pace going along," but still not enough to pick up that pace and be competitive with Carter.

Nor had the personal resurgence led to a political resurgence. As he headed to New Hampshire after Georgetown, polls showed him even farther behind Carter, unable to make a dent in Carter's foreign crisis shield. "The swing is all to the right," one of Ted's aides told *The New York Times*. "There isn't much left or middle in the polls," and he added that "most people feel Carter hasn't been tough enough," rather than too tough, on defense spending. And Chappaquiddick still dogged him, with a *NYT/CBS* poll in February finding that only 16 percent of voters believed his Chappaquiddick story and 24 percent said they could not vote for him because of Chappaquiddick. Ted purposely did not mention Chappaquiddick in his Georgetown speech, realizing that it would only detract from his message, but he did mention it in a half-hour video version of the speech that he taped to be televised in the northeastern states. "I know there are people who will never believe me, no matter what I say," he said in his commercial. "I do ask you to judge me by the basic American standards of fairness, not the basis of gossip and speculation." But it was a little late for that. Nor could he flush out Carter, who would leave the White House to make an appearance in Washington and then rush back without ever appearing with Ted. When Ted followed a Carter appearance at the Consumer Federation of America meeting before the Maine caucuses—the closest the two had come to an actual confrontation during the campaign to that point—he asked the audience with a wide grin, "Who was that man who just rushed out of here? He said he was double-parked, but some people say he was Jimmy Carter," and then he quipped that the president had to get back to "read a vital security document—the Portland, Maine, telephone directory." He also staged a mock debate, using a tape recorder of a press conference of Jimmy Carter's from 1978, following each of Carter's answers with, "Now for a comment from Senator Kennedy." But Ted wasn't going to get a real debate with Carter, and he blasted Carter, saying that if the president wouldn't debate, he should do what Harry Truman and Lyndon Johnson did: withdraw. But it was Kennedy who Carter thought should be withdrawing.

In thinking that, however, Jimmy Carter misunderstood Ted Kennedy again, as he had always misunderstood him, seeing him as an opportunist rather than a crusader. William Raspberry, in his accolades to the George-town speech, said some believed it didn't matter to Ted now whether he won or lost, that he had conceded the nomination to Carter and was now fighting for his place in history rather than for a place in the White House. "He has now laid out a platform that will enable us to look back, perhaps four years hence," wrote Raspberry, "and observe that he alone among the 1980 candidates had kept the liberal faith."

That is what Jimmy Carter couldn't understand: Ted Kennedy wasn't running for himself anymore, if he ever had. He was running for the fate of liberalism.

Now came Maine. The expectation, given all that had preceded them, was that Ted would lose the caucuses on February 10. But Ted, now unbound, was still energized after Georgetown. "He got his groove. You could feel it," said his son Patrick, who occasionally traveled with him. T. R. Reid of *The Washington Post* found him "more relaxed and humorous on the cam-paign trail," joking with voters and staffers and even reporters, and "put-ting in grueling days with a zeal that would seem to belie those who say his heart is not in this race for the presidency." And Ted told the reporters: "I have a sense, I have a feeling about this that's just a lot different from what you guys are writing." And Reid said that the new Kennedy strategy seemed to be to hold on until the inevitable decline in Carter's popularity occurred. Ted carpet-bombed the state, having his staff and even his fam-ily make so many calls to Maine voters that when Ethel Kennedy made an appearance, a woman began her question matter-of-factly during a Q and A session, "When your sister-in-law, Eunice Shriver, called me the other night to talk about the draft . . ." Ted himself, liberated, held a series of town meetings at which he hauled out charts to explain to voters his plans for wage and price controls and for gas rationing, which was an especially salient issue in the Northeast where oil prices were high, and the Ted Ken-nedy who spoke was the new/old Ted Kennedy—the one whose views, as Shrum put it, "weren't cushioned in caution." He had a "lot he wanted to say and plenty of time to say it." And unlike his previous appearances, where elected officials usually shunned him for fear of provoking the wrath of Carter, Maine governor Joe Brennan often accompanied him.

Carter was still hopeful that when Ted suffered another inevitable de-feat, he would withdraw. Two days before the Maine caucuses, Carter administration official William Albers—who had headed up Carter's campaign fundraising in 1976—wrote Hamilton Jordan that he had gotten wind of "disarray" in Ted's campaign, a dispute between young Carl Wagner and Paul Kirk, and heard a "whisper" that if Ted were to lose by ten points, he would drop out with Kirk's blessing, so long as it is "handled properly by us." But when caucus day came, Ted lost narrowly 44 to 40 percent, which was a moral victory since polls had shown Carter leading two to one just a week earlier. A Carter operative in New Hampshire, which was next on the schedule, told the *Times*, "The momentum this morning is clearly with Kennedy, but the results in Maine have shaken the complacency of our organization." Ted took the narrow loss and seemed inspired by it, delivering a scathing speech at the John F. Kennedy School of Government at Harvard—the "most strident attack yet on Carter," *Newsweek* called it—excoriating the president as the self-anointed "high priest of patriotism"; blaming him for the Soviet invasion of Afghanistan by not warning the Soviets of the consequences as they were preparing to invade; saying that the Iranian hostages might have come home if Carter had done what Kennedy suggested in his Georgetown speech, which was convene an international commission of inquiry; and once again chastising him for warmongering: "No president should be re-elected because he happened to be standing there when his foreign policy collapsed around him." Carter was furious, calling the speech "disgusting" and "disgraceful" and telling a press conference that Ted's remarks were "very damaging to our country," which was Carter's go-to criticism now to meet any criticism by Ted. But Ted, hearing Carter's anger on a car radio while campaigning in New Hampshire, joked, "I think we've got Jimmy Carter paying attention to us now, fellows."

The prospects for success were no better in New Hampshire than they had been in Maine, despite a poll that showed that if voters were asked whether they were more or less likely to vote for a candidate who held a series of particular positions—*Ted Kennedy*'s positions, though Ted's name was not attached to them—they would be more likely to vote for that candidate. It was a shaggy campaign in the state. When he arrived at an American Legion hall at seven-thirty p.m. and found only a few men drinking beer, he shook hands with them, went back to his car and laughed about it, then scrapped the last ninety minutes of his schedule. (He hadn't laughed

over similar disasters in Iowa.) Another day he simply stopped campaigning altogether and had dinner with Ted Jr. and Patrick in Manchester. But
this wasn't despondency. He was philosophical but upbeat. He enjoyed
being with his children, enjoyed having them ride with him in the old
school bus he used to take him from one campaign appearance to the
next. He expressed optimism. Playing duckpins in a church basement in
Berlin, New Hampshire, he threw a gutter ball, then knocked down seven
pins and said, "See that? The first one was Iowa—then the next seven in a
row." Still, just a week before the primary, he was forced to interrupt his
New Hampshire campaign to go back to Massachusetts to raise more
funds. Celebrating his forty-eighth birthday during the trip at the Boston
Harvard Club, he blew out the candles on his cake and said he wished for
a New Hampshire victory, even as his staff was saying that such a victory
would be impossible.

But, like Jimmy Carter, few in the press, especially the Kennedy haters
among them, of whom there were many, seemed to grasp that the campaign wasn't about impressing them or even the voters, that it wasn't
about winning. It was about him and the rudder he manned and about
keeping that rudder true. Garry Wills, one of those haters, said the press
was "incredulous" at Ted's door-to-door campaigning in New Hampshire.
"Why is he, how can he be so bad?" Wills would write. "He has lost all
sense of scale. In little rooms, he is too loud, in large halls too mumbly. He
seems to be talking to audiences somewhere else—mainly in the past.
When a Kennedy cannot do 'coffee' right, things are truly upside down."
And Wills averred that Ted was now "dazed" and "stumbling," so much
so that "some who do not witness the spectacle day by day think the press
is picking on him." But he said, in seeming contradiction, that the "regard" for him had actually been increasing—"along with pity." He called
the coverage a "set of multiple time lags": "When he seemed to be gaining,
he was losing; now in loss, he is subtly growing." And while Ted's manner
might have testified to his indifference to what the press thought of him
now that he had been liberated, Wills's account also testified to the difficulty of Ted's changing his press image, even if he had wanted to. T. R.
Reid, who did cover Ted daily, wrote, contrary to Wills's description, that
"one of the best concealed secrets of the current political season—a secret that has escaped the notice of politicians, pundits and, to date, voters—is that Edward M. Kennedy's drive for the White House has virtually
all the elements of a successful political campaign." Reid cited his new

stump speech in which he invoked the basis of his liberalism, which was the anguish of ordinary people. "Somewhere tonight a sick child will cry out in the night," Ted would say, "and his mother will lie in bed worrying whether her baby is $50 or $75 sick—because she has to find that money to get him treatment. Somewhere an elderly couple is living in fear—fear that some accident or illness will use up every penny they have saved. And our society ought to put some value on freeing people from that fear." And Reid noted that some of his sentences were never finished, not this time because Ted's voice would trail off into oblivion as in the past, but because his words were drowned out by the roar from his crowd.

But Ted Kennedy was fighting against his image now—not only the image of his incompetence as a candidate that had been amplified since the Mudd interview, but also the image of his liberalism, which many in the press and many among voters now found dated, a relic of the 1960s when America, particularly after John Kennedy's assassination, was searching for a form of moral redemption. By 1980, many actively scorned that redemption. Ted left New Hampshire briefly again near the end of the primary campaign there for a speech in Birmingham, Alabama, a speech he no doubt accepted precisely to face down the angry conservatism he so abhorred. What he found was an "ugly reminder," as *Time* called it, of the hostility to his family and to his beliefs: hecklers who interrupted his speech with shouts of "You're a murderer" and who waved signs, "How Can You Save the Country When You Couldn't Rescue Mary Jo?," and cheers when Ted, talking about handgun registration, said, "My family has been touched by violence." He lost New Hampshire later that week 47 to 37 percent, which was a smaller-than-expected margin. (Jerry Brown won just under 10 percent of the vote, prompting Brown's own campaign manager to tell Bob Shrum that Brown was only helping Carter and that the manager was going back home to California.) He lost even though the state was suffering from Carter's energy policies. He lost the Catholic vote—most likely because he favored federal financing of abortions for poor women if an abortion was medically necessary—the blue-collar vote, the vote of the largest cities—lost all his natural constituencies, the constituencies for whom he was fighting against Jimmy Carter's fiscal tightfistedness. The only group he carried was the young. Disconsolate, he wrote his pollster, Peter Hart: "There will be no more polls taken for my campaign. They always leak, and I have not benefited from them. That's it." He signed it, "Your favorite candidate."

• • •

Now, with another loss and no victories, and with his post-Georgetown buoyancy fading—Theodore White interviewed him that week at a restaurant on the Boston pier and said he listened to White "moodily," asking him what he should do—Ted regrouped yet again. Two days after the primary, his brain trust met at McLean, debated strategy for twelve hours—though not, this time, whether Ted would withdraw—and decided to spend ten of the next eighteen days in Illinois, for the primary there, to be held on March 19, after already having decided to forgo the Southern primaries, save for Florida, and appropriated $300,000 to three national television ads. But first, there was the Massachusetts primary—a contest in which he shouldn't have had to campaign but did. (He was actually scheduled to campaign in Florida instead but felt the need to return lest his support in his home state weaken.) So he went back to Massachusetts, and Ted, suffering from a cold and tired, wasn't particularly happy about it, and when he hit a General Electric factory gate one morning, the way he had when he first ran for the Senate in 1962, and the reporters following him kept repeating his famous line from that first campaign in response to the charge that he hadn't worked a day in his life—"Well, you haven't missed a thing"—Ted was in no mood for the jollity. He won easily, 66 percent to Carter's 29 percent, his first victory at long last, but a staffer said, "We got almost no goose out of Massachusetts." So the campaign trudged on.

He staked it now on Illinois. Chicago mayor Jane Byrne had been one of the few elected officials to support Ted at the outset, in fact even before the outset, pledging her delegates to him in October. ("I told the President I could support him, until I thought he couldn't win," she said in endorsing Ted.) She appeared at his launch at Faneuil Hall, and Chicago was one of his stops on his first campaign swing after his announcement. In the old days, in the days of Jack and Bobby, Mayor Daley, the city's boss, would have sealed the city and consequently the state for them; he had done so for Jack—the legend was that he had stolen the 1960 election—and he had been thought to be doing the same for Bobby, before Bobby's death, and he had been pressing Ted to accept the nomination in Bobby's stead in 1968. But Daley was gone, the great Democratic machine no longer working as efficiently—the election of Byrne, a bitter enemy of the Daleys, was proof of that—and Byrne's own popularity had nosedived with a transit strike and a pay holiday for teachers, so that Ted had neither the strength of the old machine nor the power of the new one, and many of the big pols refused to run as his delegates. As Elizabeth Drew observed, those pols "feared any challenge to the status quo, even if they hated Carter," which many of them did. But their reluctance to support Ted was based on more than their desire for "regular order," as Drew phrased it. One ward heeler, citing the familiar complaint, said, "Teddy's no Jack or Bobby." "He's in trouble," admitted George Dunne, president of the Cook County Board of Commissioners and a machine man. "And so are we."

The defining moment of the Illinois campaign—one of the defining moments of the entire campaign—was the St. Patrick's Day parade in Chicago, the day before the primary—an event, one reporter wrote, that "contained enough negative symbolism to summarize the state of his political fortunes, here as well as nationally." There was a heavy wet snow and a cruel knifing wind, and as Ted marched beside Mayor Byrne in the cold, the crowd booed both of them lustily, moving Ted to fall back, zigzagging down State Street, shaking hands, but really trying to escape association with Byrne, whose endorsement had turned toxic, while Joan gamely clung to him. "I remember being so embarrassed for Ted," she would later say. "My children couldn't believe it"—this from a city that had worshipped his brothers. The situation left an "ugly scar" on him, he told a friend. The next day he lost overwhelmingly, two to one—lost Roman Catholics two to one, lost Chicago two to one, lost the liberals for whom he had been the tribune two to one, lost labor two to one, lost Black people three to two, lost the voters who complained about inflation, even though Ted, red-faced and shouting, had made curbing inflation one of his central issues during the campaign, even though he had touted his wage and price controls, even though Carter had declared that he was willing to accept higher unemployment in order to bring down inflation. Instead of asking him about inflation, one television interviewer asked him six straight questions about his "character." Steve Smith told Arthur Schlesinger, Jr., of the loss of Illinois that it was a "blow in the stomach" for Ted.

Reporters who had briefly sung his praises were now writing his electoral epitaph. Sally Quinn of *The Washington Post* called it a "campaign out of Kafka by way of James Joyce" and wrote a Joycean reverie of the "awful deepdown torrent and the snow and the rain and the sleet and gray mournful Chicago sky and the towering buildings along the wide ugly avenue no and the hail of wet green paper shamrocks and the children in their bright green slickers no and the jeering nasty looks of the crowds as he walks from one side to the other and his anguished wife holding on to him for dear life no," and then elided into a vision of another Kennedy funeral, and ended with "him just standing there just watching no asking no no don't run no get out no leave it no please no please no." Tom Wicker, writing in *The New York Times*, saw the defeat as a political obituary not for Ted alone but for the very cause for which he was running, liberalism, which Wicker saw as anachronistic now in a country that had long turned from the moral strains Ted had tried so hard to invoke and resuscitate. "His rhetoric about compassion and minorities and activism seems more reminiscent of his brother Robert, dead these 12 years," Wicker said, "than a reflection of the political realities of the Eighties," a time in which the country's political compass pointed in a new direction. "Mr. Kennedy's strident, sometimes stirring calls for Humphrey-Hawkins full employment ('When we say full, we mean full'), improved health care, 'social justice' and 'economic democracy,' not only disturb some voters but sound like echoes from an honorable but largely forgotten past." Ted had recalibrated his campaign, but in doing so, he had only played into a problem that was proving as insurmountable as Carter's recent aura of leadership bestowed by the Iranian crisis and the Soviet invasion of Afghanistan, or even Ted's allegedly dubious character. He was running to save the nation's soul, just as Bobby had. But the nation didn't want its soul saved, and it certainly didn't want it saved by the least of the Kennedys. Instead, the voters seemed to want to keep humiliating him. "Advertising its and his own doom" was how Garry Wills bluntly assessed Kennedy's campaign and its knell for both Ted and for liberalism. But it was more than a political defeat; it was a defeat of the very things on which he had staked not just his campaign or even his career but his life and the values that sustained that life. "All campaigns involve mortification of the flesh," columnist George Will wrote after the Illinois primary, "but Kennedy's has involved spiritual mortification too." He had been amply mortified.

II

Illinois was the nadir, forcing Ted back to earth after the Georgetown boost. "Probably nowhere is the dizzyingly downward spiral of Sen. Edward Kennedy's presidential campaign more visible than here in Illinois," columnist David Broder pronounced, even before the results there had come in. Carter, who upbraided his staff because Ted got even sixteen delegates, once again called Democratic leaders to have them pressure Ted to leave the race, and by one account, Ted had even explored the possibility of Congressman Morris Udall, who had run against Carter in the primaries in 1976, taking over for Ted, but the party rules made that idea impossible. Meanwhile the campaign was running out of money, again, the unpaid staffers were leaving, including Ted's finance chairman, Martin Katz, and others were scaling back their workload, half the advance and scheduling staff were taken off the payroll, and those who remained had their salaries slashed. At the same time, Carter had been racking up victories in state after state: the Vermont caucuses the same day as Massachusetts, and Alabama, Florida, and Georgia on March 11. And then Illinois. What galled Ted and wounded him was not even so much the defeats as that, as Illinois demonstrated, dramatically and fatally for him, he was not carrying the liberal constituencies. Black voters were preferring Carter, despite the relationship those voters had had to his brothers and despite his own dedication to civil rights and to other causes that helped Black people and despite the fact that some early polling had given him a significant lead among Black people. Ted had originally thought he might even be competitive with Carter in the South because of Black voters, but they broke 68 percent for Carter in Florida, and six to one for Carter in Alabama, and eight to one for him in Georgia, where even the revered congressman and civil rights veteran John Lewis endorsed the president. One Georgia legislator explained Ted's dilemma. "People say the civil rights movement is dead," he said. "The movement is not dead. It is in government. And President Carter has brought a lot of blacks into the Federal Government and the courts at high levels," which was to say that patronage had begun to displace legislation in the Black consciousness. That was a battle Ted could not win against a sitting president. Nor was Ted carrying the Catholic vote, which had always been the property of the Kennedys, or the labor vote. The United Mine Workers union, against which Carter had threatened to invoke the Taft-Hartley Act to force them back to work after a series of wildcat strikes, was about to endorse Ted, when the president agreed to submit a bill that would gradually substitute coal for oil and gas. The Mine Workers wound up endorsing Carter. And one survey showed that even "very liberal" Democratic delegates to the convention were likely to support Carter over Ted if they had "strong partisan motivations," meaning that their loyalty to the party was greater than their loyalty to their cause, which was precisely the opposite of what Ted was counting on. In effect, Ted was sailing against the wind not only when it came to liberalism but when it came to the emphasis on issues over blind party loyalty.

Still, he trudged on.

Once again the dread loomed. The New York and Connecticut primaries came next, and Ted could hardly have felt more optimistic about them than he had about any of the previous primaries save Massachusetts. Patrick Caddell's polls showed Carter far ahead in New York—nineteen points ahead—but Caddell noticed something underneath those raw figures that concerned him. When he asked more probing questions than just who the voters favored, Caddell found that Ted actually made significant gains. Caddell and the Carter people were baffled, especially since the same polls showed more people viewed Kennedy unfavorably than favorably. Caddell finally concluded that now that Carter's renomination was a foregone conclusion, voters felt free to vent their frustrations against him. But the undercurrent couldn't be so easily waved away. Carter's own New York organizer Joel McCleary told Hamilton Jordan that "it doesn't feel good" and even felt Ted might have a chance to win.

But for Ted's campaign, there was no sense of imminent victory on the ground, only more humiliations of the sort to which Ted had become accustomed. At his first campaign stop after losing Illinois, the Forest Hills subway station in the borough of Queens at seven-thirty a.m., Ted, looking "tired but resolute," according to one reporter, nodded and tried shaking commuters' hands, but the press contingent outnumbered those commuters, and the commuters were in no mood to converse with Ted Kennedy, brushing past him, save for one woman who took out her autograph book to collect signatures from the reporters. At a campaign appearance in Harlem with five executives of the Harlem Chamber of Commerce, Ted waited patiently while the executives praised themselves but said not a word on behalf of Ted, and later that same day, Ted boarded a small plane for a rough ride through a storm to Syracuse for the endorsement of Representative James Hanley, only Hanley vamped for twenty minutes without giving that endorsement. And when a reporter asked point-blank whether Hanley intended to vote for Kennedy, the congressman "sputtered, coughed, cleared his throat, and finally said, 'I would have to say that I will keep that private.'" The crowd laughed, and Ted went up to Hanley, clamped his arm around the nervous congressman's shoulder, and said, "You can tell these guys, Jim. They won't tell anybody." And while Hanley continued to circle any endorsement, Ted and the reporters "howled with laughter," as one of them put it. Meanwhile Carter continued to run his ads pressing the character issue, showing him with Rosalynn and his daughter Amy and saying what he had been saying throughout, that you can't separate being a good husband and father from being a good president, or, in another ad, that even if you didn't agree with Carter, "You'll never find yourself wondering if he's telling the truth," of which there may be, he said, no more "useful quality in any person who becomes president."

Ted Kennedy had heretofore had little luck in his campaign. The Iranian hostages and the Soviet invasion had worked mightily to Carter's advantage. But he finally got a bit of luck of his own, and it came about through a mishap by Carter. On March 1 the United Nations voted on a Security Council resolution reprimanding Israel for building settlements on the West Bank territories, which Israel had occupied since the 1967 war. Typically, the United States voted to support its Middle Eastern ally, but this time the United States voted for the resolution. Carter immediately repudiated the vote, calling it a miscommunication between Washington and the UN, but it only underscored suspicions in the Jewish community that the Carter administration was less than wholeheartedly committed to Israel. (The United States had previously voted for General Assembly resolutions containing almost identical language with no outcry.) In the wake of the vote, New York mayor Ed Koch, a strong Carter supporter and Jewish, reviled a "gang of five," which included Secretary of State Cyrus Vance, for actively disdaining the interests of Israel, and Robert Strauss, the chairman of the Carter-Mondale campaign, told one group, "I think there are some goddamn Arabists over there," meaning the State Department, "and they ought to be fired." But Ted, turning the tables on Carter, leaped on the issue and kept hammering it before Jewish groups, leaving Carter to make abject apologies to the large Jewish voting bloc on the eve of the primary.

There was a seam now, an opening. Voters were beginning to lose patience with Carter—with the hostages still imprisoned in Iran four months after their capture (one poll showed that voters thought Carter's handling of the crisis now was unsuccessful); with the Soviets still in Afghanistan and the actions Carter had taken having no effect on them; with his clumsy handling of the UN vote; above all, with the economy, where inflation was galloping at nearly 14 percent and unemployment had jumped to just under 7 percent in April. "For weeks and months, Kennedy's campaign lingered on the hope that sooner or later Carter's balloon would burst—when the combination of hostages and inflation became too much," Hamilton Jordan would later write. "Maybe, I thought, it's finally happening," though Jordan also realized that for Carter's renomination to be jeopardized, Kennedy would have to win 60 percent of the remaining delegates, which was close to impossible. Ted had campaigned on Carter's lack of leadership, on Carter's missteps, on Carter's illiberalism, on Carter's bellicosity, on Carter's coziness with the oil industry and with the Middle Eastern oil states that were gouging Americans. But he hadn't focused almost exclusively on the economy, until New York—"Jimmynomics," he called the policies, which combined inflation with unemployment and low economic growth—the combination economists had labeled "stagflation." One reporter thought Ted had "found his stride" as a campaigner with the subject and with his new line, which he shouted at each stop, "Enough is enough." And even a Carter supporter was impressed. "Teddy was great the last few days," he observed.

Still, great as he might have been, even Ted doubted he was gaining momentum. As the New York primary campaign reached its climax, the crowds at Ted's appearances had grown larger, but a *Daily News* poll the final week had Carter leading Ted two to one, and another poll over the final weekend still had Carter comfortably ahead, 56 to 36 percent. Talking to *Washington Post* reporter T. R. Reid the last week of the campaign in the back of a limousine on the way to White Plains, Ted, in a candid mood, said his staff, expecting defeat, was debating once again whether he should leave the race and rely on the Senate as his megaphone. But Ted was reluctant to do so, reluctant to give up the race where he could deliver his message face-to-face. "My own sense is that you make a point, I mean, you know, if you can come personally as a candidate and tell people what you believe in in a way you can't on the Senate floor," he told Reid. And he felt that he could go to "any hall in the country and talk about health care and that I really feel that one," and he could get people "committed to it, they feel it, and nobody's going to say you're silly." And he said, "You can hang in." And he lamented too that Carter was already forcing the party rightward toward Reagan, that Carter's budget cuts were a Republican approach to problem-solving, and the "rich can invest their money at nineteen percent and fly by, but Jimmy's going to fight inflation with the poor," meaning squeezing the economy to bring inflation down. So certain was Ted that he faced another loss that the campaign booked a small hotel and dispensed with plans for a victory party. "We had those crying volunteer shots on the tube just about every Wednesday morning," one aide said, speaking of the morning after the string of Tuesday defeats, "and we figured, why do it again?" Paul Kirk spoke with Ted and told him, "Look, this is crazy. If we don't win in New York, we have to get out of this thing," and Kirk said Ted agreed. So Kirk rented a room at the Parker House hotel in Boston and had Barbara Souliotis book a plane to fly them there after the loss so Ted could make his withdrawal speech there. And the morning of the primary, also believing Ted was facing another defeat, Steve Smith called Shrum to his office and advised that he write a withdrawal speech, which Shrum said he wrote in an hour, and then, despondent about the campaign drawing to a close, he walked from 59th Street to the tip of Manhattan and back. But Shrum said that when he arrived back at his hotel after his glum walk, a staffer accosted him and told him to head to Steve and Jean's apartment on the Upper East Side. Shrum arrived to be told by Smith some astonishing news: that, after all the discouraging predictions and doomsday polls, Ted was actually winning the primary and was leading in neighboring Connecticut as well. Now Shrum had to draft a victory speech. Ted himself was incredulous. Nothing, nothing at all, had forecast this result. Ted had been whipping himself into enthusiasm, overcoming hopelessness with pure will. And now he had won New York. "Can you believe this?" he asked Shrum, not fully believing it himself.

Now that Ted Kennedy had won—won against all odds—there came the postmortems as to why he had won and not only won but won overwhelmingly, 59 to 41 percent. The most logical explanation was that Carter had suffered huge defections in the Jewish vote—38 percent of the primary vote—by his administration's support of the UN Security Council resolution against those Israeli settlements. Jews, who according to polling, had favored Carter by nine points before the UN resolution, voted four to one for Ted after it. But only 10 percent of the electorate said afterward that the resolution was the deciding factor, and Jews themselves, by 42 to 28 percent, listed inflation as a more important factor in their choice than support for Israel. So while Israel was a factor, it did not turn the election. Carter himself agreed with Caddell's earlier analysis that, as Carter put it, "whenever it seemed obvious that the ultimate contest with Kennedy would be decided in my favor, the people tended to use the primaries simply as a protest," which, he said, "delayed our final, inevitable victory," while some "titillated" voters just wanted to keep the contest going—neither of which, whether Carter realized it or not, seemed particularly favorable to him. As Caddell had said, if the race turned into Carter versus Carter, Carter would lose. Nor did Carter's analysis take into account something else that Caddell had detected in his polling: After months of having Carter bash his character, Kennedy was now considered just as "trustworthy" as Carter. (Caddell felt that personal morality didn't count as much in New York and Connecticut as in other states.) Nor did it take into account that a majority of New York voters agreed with the statement that Carter could not handle the presidency and with another statement that they would be better off with a new president. Nor did it take into account one more factor that was a complete reversal of Illinois: In both New York and Connecticut, which Ted won 47 to 41 percent, Ted carried the Catholic vote, the Black vote, and the Hispanic vote as well as the Jewish vote. More, he carried both working-class districts in Queens and more liberal districts in Manhattan, forging, by one account, the coalition that Bobby was supposed to have forged between blue-collar white people and minorities in 1968. Ted had tried to make the primaries a referendum on Carter—first on Carter's leadership and then on Carter's lack of commitment to the fundamental principles of the Democratic Party. He had failed. But in New York, where patriotism no longer seemed to shield Carter from the disasters of his foreign policy and where reflexive support for the president no longer seemed to shield him from the disasters of his economic policy, Ted had finally succeeded in—or Carter had failed to prevent him from—turning the focus from himself to the president. People might not have been voting for Ted or for the liberalism he represented, but they seemed, as even Caddell admitted, to be voting, at long last, against Jimmy Carter.

"You can hang in," Ted had told T. R. Reid about how he felt his passion about the issues would keep him in the race. Now he could. So he trudged on.

· · ·

Now the race seemed to have changed. Georgetown had provided a lift, however briefly, until Illinois sent Ted spiraling again. But New York had been a victory—an electoral victory rather than a moral one, even if the delegate haul was relatively small. "It put a little puff in our sails," Paul Kirk said. Carey Parker's metaphor was more muscular: "We felt as if we had pushed and pushed, and the whole dam just burst." Ted's old press secretary Dick Drayne said, "The President has been living in a house of cards, and it is finally collapsing." Money began flowing again. Volunteers began arriving again. The day after, Ted appeared in Mellon Square in Pittsburgh to kick off his campaign for the Pennsylvania primary, to be held on April 22, and fifteen thousand people crammed in to see him. A few weeks earlier no one would stop to shake his hand outside the Queens subway station, but now people filled the streets off the square—a larger crowd, just about every story made mention, than greeted the Pittsburgh Steeler Super Bowl winners earlier that winter. Then he headed to Wisconsin for the primary on April 1, where the campaign seemed reignited—crowded hotel lobbies, a second press plane, and, wrote *The New York Times*'s Drummond Ayres, the "teenage squeals and hoarse shouts from hard hats." Now Ted was suddenly riding a different story among the press, the story of a candidate gaining, which prompted them, out of their own narrative instincts, to keep his momentum going.

It was a narrative that Jimmy Carter's advisers felt the need to reverse as quickly as possible. By one report, Carter's campaign chiefs were now begging the White House for some good news to stem Ted's rise, and Carter answered with a three-day media "blitz," as *Newsweek* called it, that Carter was pushing right up until the morning of the primary, when he did something so unconscionable, in Ted's eyes, that Ted would feel freed from his self-imposed vow of silence on Iran. At roughly seven o'clock that morning, two hours before the Wisconsin polls were to open, Carter provided the good news his campaign so desperately wanted. He announced to the press that the latest statement from Iran on the hostages was "positive" and that he expected a breakthrough. Even then, by one report, Carter was so jittery that he phoned Caddell four times that day to make sure his lead was holding up. Carter's timely announcement was not necessarily true—nothing positive happened—but it might have been responsible for handing Carter a twenty-six-point victory, 56 to 30 percent, since one poll found that 36 percent of voters made up their minds on election day—a huge number. Carter also won 54 percent of those voters who said they were most concerned with fidelity to principle, though not even Ted's fiercest detractors could fault him on that score. He had remained faithful to a principle that seemed no longer popular.

Still, Ted trudged on.

But Jimmy Carter was right to feel jittery, even if his delegate lead seemed insurmountable. Ted had been gaining momentum as Carter lost it—lost it largely because the hostage crisis dragged on, despite Carter's hint of a resolution that turned out to be an empty hope, lost it because the economy continued to sink with Carter seeming to have no prescription for solving it, lost it because he fumbled the influx of 114,000 Cuban refugees that April and May, "boat people" they were called since they arrived in a flotilla, by using parole authority rather than a regularized process that had just been put into law in a bill that Ted had steered through Congress that March: the Refugee Act of 1980. This time the voters were becoming disenchanted with Carter, as they had earlier been disenchanted with Ted. And if Carter was jittery now, fearing he was losing his momentum, Ted was confident again. Again he hammered at Carter's economic policies—in the middle of the campaign, he introduced his wage and price control plan in the Senate—but his tone was lighter, a rapier rather than a bludgeon. A "traveling show that often seemed long on laughs and somewhat shorter on substance," T. R. Reid called the campaign, though what Ted was really doing was skewering Carter with sarcasm because his emphasis on policy prescriptions hadn't worked. On Carter's lifting the price controls on oil so that the companies would have more resources to invest in exploration, Ted pointed out that Mobil instead had used its profits to buy the Montgomery Ward department store chain. "How much oil do you think they'll find drilling in the aisles of Montgomery Ward's?" he asked the crowds. And of Carter's Rose Garden strategy, he said that he had seen some Carter supporters outside his rally and invited them in be-cause—he was shouting when he said it—"They don't have any rallies of their own to go to." At which point, Reid said, the crowds would roar. And of Carter's inability to address problems with successful solutions, Ted wrung his hands, like "Lady Macbeth," Reid said, and told the crowd that he was "tired of all this hand-wringing, hand-wringing" and advised that "if the politicians would stop this hand-wringing, the American people could go out and get the jobs done." Now that Ted was gaining steam,

Time too found a "dramatic improvement" in his campaign style and said that he "began to shine like the political star that he was supposed to be."

Jittery were Jimmy Carter and his men, so jittery that several of them advised him to concede Pennsylvania and move on. The campaign even released a poll showing Carter now three points behind Ted in Pennsylvania, which was designed to refocus attention on Ted and away from Carter, on the theory—a theory Carter continued to believe—that it was only because he was a sure winner that voters felt the license to attack him and vote against him. Instead, Caddell and Carter's media adviser, Gerald Rafshoon, hatched another plan. They would shoot man-in-the-street ads in which ordinary people, yet again, questioned Ted Kennedy's abilities and character. (While campaigning in the state, Ted had phoned the Kopechnes, as he occasionally did, and Mrs. Kopechne had told *The New York Times* that she was leaning toward Ted because Carter was too conservative.) "These spots are designed to remind people that they don't like Kennedy," Rafshoon said, as if that were a given, and listed the complaints: "He's too liberal." "Kennedy doesn't know what he's talking about." "I don't like his policy concerning our defenses." "I don't think he can deal with a crisis." But the very tactic was a concession that Carter was faltering. As columnist Mark Shields analyzed it, "Urging citizens to vote against the opponent rather than for him is the only strategy currently available to the President and his supporters." And Shields called Carter the political "remainderman": "He gets what's left over after his opponents have taken theirs by being the least acceptable alternative to the greatest number of voters." Caddell would say later that he realized the new ads would do "irreparable damage" to any relationship between Carter and Kennedy, should they later need Kennedy in the general election. "He'll never forgive us." But Caddell also would say this: "We'd have lost Pennsylvania by twenty points or more" had it not been for the ads. Just under half of Carter's supporters claimed that their opposition to Kennedy was the reason they supported the president, and nearly two-thirds of those supporters doubted Kennedy's character. Even many of those who said they were intending to vote for Ted were doing so, according to one report, for the very reason Carter had said they would: to issue a protest against Carter.

And yet Ted Kennedy won the Pennsylvania primary, albeit by a scant 9,800 votes and by less than 1 percent, largely by taking the most Democratic parts of the state and piling up a huge lead, 90,000 votes, in Philadelphia. Moreover, he assembled the same coalition he had constructed in New York—a traditionally Democratic coalition: Black people, Catholics, liberals (57 percent of them), and blue-collar conservatives. Carter, for his part, won small-town conservatives and Protestants—the segments of the Democratic Party that were most likely to defect to the Republicans in the fall. Moreover, those who voted for Ted, despite the talk of their registering a protest vote, were more likely to rank jobs and inflation as their most important issues than Carter voters. If they were trying to send Carter a message, the message was that he had not fixed the economy, which was precisely what Ted had been saying. Perhaps Carter's negative ads had worked in keeping the race as close as it was. But as pollster Lou Harris declared, "Carter is now falling and Kennedy is on the rise for the first time since he declared."

There was something else striking about Ted's narrow Pennsylvania victory: the message Ted drew from it. In scribbling notes for his victory speech that night, he wrote, "Not a victory for a candidate, but for a cause," which was why he said he stayed in the race. The columnists Robert Novak and Rowland Evans were astounded that Ted kept pushing the liberal line without making the "slightest concession to any doubt about the old liberal verity of economic health achieved through government spending. In a day when fealty to the 'balanced budget' is nearly universal among politicians, those words do not escape Kennedy's lips in Pennsylvania." And while they claimed that his philosophy lacked "rationality," which was also the new conventional political wisdom, "it has created a buoyantly self-confident Kennedy who sees not only successive victories, but an epidemic of defections by Carter delegates."

In his triumph, he was still manning the rudder true.

For Jimmy Carter, the fallback had always been the character issue. No matter that the hostages were not coming home soon, no matter that inflation was soaring along with an uptick in unemployment, no matter that the United States seemed feckless abroad and at home and that a sense of malaise seemed to grip the populace. No matter, because Ted Kennedy's character was questionable, which was why Carter staked a Pennsylvania victory on it. Caddell had said it: Character was the primary issue. Ted might not have fully appreciated how powerful this idea was, but he certainly anticipated that Carter would be deploying it against him, which was why he had recruited Joan, fragile as she was, into joining the campaign. Joan was to be his protection—her forbearance and forgiveness a sign of Ted's moral regeneration. But it was not an easy performance to pull off, precisely *because* Joan was fragile, and Ted might have had no business asking her to do so. Garry Wills would say that "Kennedy's task during the campaign was to produce Joan and protect her at the same time, and these were antithetical aims." He was right. She said that all summer after Ted asked her to think about his making the presidential run, she had "soul-searched" and finally concluded that she could maintain her sobriety while stumping for him—an almost heartbreaking admission. But she was under tremendous scrutiny from others to see if she really could. Marcia Chellis, her assistant, would write that Eunice arrived at Joan's Boston apartment the Tuesday after Thanksgiving, ostensibly to brief Joan, but really to make certain that she was in sufficient condition not to capsize Ted's campaign. Yet for all those concerns, Joan seemed almost jaunty, saying that she wanted to begin campaigning earlier but that Ted insisted she finish her master's degree first. "I know how hard you worked for it," she said he told her. And he told her, "I'm so proud of you." "I'm really starting to feel life all over again," she told one interviewer that December. "I feel younger now than I have in ten years," she told another. "I feel so much younger now than I did at thirty." "The result of this is that I feel I'm a brand-new person," she told yet another. "I have my old confidence back." Reporters noted that she looked better than she had, that she wore less makeup now, that her hair was shorter and more stylish. She said after going through her own "bout of hell," she had a "new appreciation for the tragedies Ted has had to go through in his life" and "greater admiration for him than ever before." And when, clearly being probed about the nature of her relationship to Ted, she was asked why she wasn't wearing her wedding ring, she said that she hadn't worn it in ten years because she kept having to take it off to play the piano. But she said this too: "You ask Ted Kennedy. I will never be number two again. We talked all about this."

But her actions belied her words. For all her professions of confidence, she was uncertain on the stump, vulnerable—an ongoing drama. Describing an appearance of Ted and Joan in Iowa, *New Yorker* reporter Elizabeth Drew wrote, "The members of the audience applaud her heartily, as if they had been pulling for her, and Kennedy himself leads the applause. She is treated as if she were a frail creature." (She was.) "Mrs. Kennedy's speeches have the wobbly uncertainty of a baby sparrow's maiden flight," wrote another reporter, T. R. Reid of *The Washington Post*, "and she seems as surprised as anyone when she succeeds on the stump. At Mundelein [College], she appeared astonished every time the audience interrupted her with applause—and it happened 25 times." And for all her vulnerability, or perhaps because of it, she gave another speech, this one a "passionate defense" of Ted's account of Chappaquiddick that struck reporters speechless, T. R. Reid said—the very reporters who had kept hounding Ted about Chappaquiddick throughout the campaign. "She answered with a faltering but obvious heartfelt defense of her husband that was so moving, nobody present could say a word when she finished. For a long minute, nobody asked her another question. Another minute. Finally, everybody just walked away; the press conference was over." And as Ted walked her back to her seat, he whispered to her, "Good. That was good," though Ted's approval, like that of the press, was condescending and even heartless.

And if Joan's actions belied her words about her newfound confidence, so did they belie her words about her relationship with Ted. They had not reunited. She was not number one. She was being used by Ted, which was something he did of almost no other individual. Reporters couldn't help but observe that they rarely spoke to each other, rarely even looked at each other. One reporter noted that during her very first campaign appearance, on a trip to her grandmother's ranch in Brooker, Florida, with Ted, the "two acted more like a pair of strangers on a blind date than husband and wife of twenty years." And the same reporter noted that during the Chicago St. Patrick's Day parade, Ted had been "oblivious" to Joan, even though she was clearly terrified by the hostile crowd and clung tenaciously to Ted, but then, he had always been oblivious to Joan. "His charm disappeared in her presence," said Marcia Chellis. And Chellis said that Joan complained to her that Ted would call and ask her to come or "I'll lose the election"—which seemed an unlikely thing for him to do—but that when she came, "he doesn't notice me or say I look nice or thank me, or ask my opinion on anything"—which seemed all too likely. But she told one reporter that Ted's lack of attention in public didn't matter. "That's just his style," she said. "Did you ever see Jack Kennedy kiss Jackie in public? Or Bobby kiss Ethel?" And she said that privately he would call her after seeing her on television and tell her how well she did. "And, of course, I'm just glowing at the other end of the phone." Even when they traveled together, early in the campaign, they stayed in separate suites, until the staff determined it would be better for them to stay together—better for the impression it gave since, when it came to Joan, Ted now cared only about the impression.

But in a campaign that was balky to begin with, Joan was always viewed as a mistake waiting to happen, and after Georgetown, the scrutiny, always intense, intensified. According to Rick Burke, Ted and his staff decided she needed a more decorous wardrobe, a more conservative one, and her psychiatrist, Dr. Hawthorne, was asked to inform her of the edict—yet another indication of Ted's near-cruelty to his wife. Marcia Chellis said that Joan was also assigned consultants to advise her on her manner and image, and the historian Doris Kearns Goodwin, a friend of the Kennedys, was assigned to coach her, but Joan erupted at the idea of being a "puppet" and not someone who was taken seriously. Still, Joan herself was concerned about her image, and she had sneaked away to get a face-lift in early January, then denied it when the *Boston Herald* broke the story. Larry Horowitz, who traveled with Ted during the campaign, felt that Joan was more hindrance than help, no matter how desperately she tried to help, and eventually, she traveled with Ted only two or three days a week, making her own appearances the rest of the time. She remained giddy. A "born-again politician," she called herself, no doubt remembering when she took Ted's place during the 1964 campaign, after the plane accident that left him flat on his back. She told another interviewer that "I just love my whole life," listing her degree, her children, her apartment, her music, and being married to Ted and campaigning for him as the reasons why. "I'm just having a wonderful time," she said. "And the Senator and I have a wonderful relationship. We are doing this together! I choose to be here helping him! I'm just so happy with myself. I love whatever I'm doing. It's all just so terrific—I'm terrific!" But the interviewer noted that she didn't seem as effusive as her words and that "there was no joy in her tone, no light in her eyes." Years later she would tell biographer Laurence Leamer, "The 1980 campaign was my high-water mark. I was sober. I was intent on proving to Ted and my family and to everybody that I was okay, that I was as good a campaigner as ever and that I was an asset to the campaign." One reporter observed that as the campaign wore on, Ted and Joan seemed more at ease with each other, gained more respect for each other, and one of Ted's aides told Drummond Ayres that the campaign had been good for the marriage and that Joan was even talking about returning to Washington after the campaign. But those dreams would turn out to be as insubstantial as dreams of an electoral victory. Joan Kennedy was a campaign prop.

III

After Pennsylvania, Jimmy Carter was foundering—a candidate almost certain to win the nomination but one who seemed to be limping into the convention. Good news, his staff had demanded during the Wisconsin primary, and Carter had delivered, even if the news of hostage negotiations had been false. Now, with the Michigan caucuses approaching on April 26, Jimmy Carter needed more good news, but it wasn't likely to come from Iran. It could come only through action. Over the vehement objections of his secretary of state, Cyrus Vance, but with the strong encouragement of his national security adviser, Zbigniew Brzezinski, Carter authorized planning for a military operation to free the Iranian hostages. A day before the caucuses he approved the plan: a desperate and dangerous rescue, sending eight helicopters into the desert with a small extraction team to go to the embassy and get out the fifty-two Americans held there. A daring plan. A highly complicated plan. A plan that would, if successful, have almost certainly sealed Carter's nomination victory and perhaps even his reelection. A plan that required perfect execution. But perfect execution was not to be. When the helicopters arrived at the first staging area in the black desert, where they were to be refueled, three of them were not operational, one due to a mechanical issue, a second due to a sandstorm, and a third due to a cracked rotor blade. Now, with only five helicopters, the field commanders advised Carter to abort the mission in the dead of night. He did so, and as the helicopters were evacuating, one of them hit a support craft, creating a fireball that destroyed both the helicopter and the craft and, worse, much worse, killing five airmen and three marines. (Ted and Joan would later visit the survivors in the San Antonio Army Hospital where they were recovering.) In the evacuation, the forces boarded another transport and left the helicopters behind in the desert. At one a.m., President Carter announced the failure of the mission. The Ayatollah Khomeini rejoiced and followed up by scattering the hostages to foil another rescue attempt.

A "debacle" was the consensus. Ted was asleep at his hotel in Detroit after a long day of campaigning, his only day campaigning in Michigan, while aides phoned Washington for details on the mission. He awoke at six a.m. and was briefed, but he decided to hold his fire and issued a statement expressing regret, which *Newsweek* called a "model of somber restraint." That evening Carter lost the Michigan caucuses to Ted by less than two points, though in a state where the economy was especially weak, the race had no doubt tightened because of the attempted rescue that once again rallied the country to the beleaguered president, and Ted won only one delegate more than Carter.

But the failed mission changed the campaign too. Secretary of State Vance had not been informed of the decision to launch the rescue mission—he was recovering from a bout of gout in Florida and had been left out of the loop by his own deputy, Warren Christopher—and was now so enraged that he tendered his resignation, further embarrassing the president. Damaged by the failure of the mission and by his secretary of state's resignation, Carter realized he could no longer hide in the Rose Garden. On April 30, five days after the mission and with the hostages no closer to release, he announced that the responsibilities that had kept him in the White House during the campaign were no longer so onerous that he couldn't hit the campaign trail. "Manageable enough" he called them, though the real reason, as one Carter aide admitted, was that the president needed to go out on the stump to thwart Ted. "He never thought the hostages would be held for so long," the aide said, "or he never would have painted himself into a corner the way he did." And if the failed mission pried Carter from the White House, it also pried Iran from the campaign narrative. Both Carter and the press, the first out of political necessity, the second quite possibly out of boredom since nothing now was likely to happen in Iran, deemphasized the hostage story. One study found that from April to June, the number of pieces on Iran on the nightly news of the three major broadcast networks dropped by a factor of five. The Iran story, which had so circumscribed Ted for most of the campaign after his San Francisco excoriation of the shah, now loosened its bonds around him. After the failed mission, he told one audience, without having to directly mention it, "I think the people are going to make some judgments on foreign policy. And they're going to consider whether we have a competent foreign policy," which was more than he had said since Georgetown. And Ted would later say that after the desert debacle, he felt the momentum building, and he felt even freer to raise the issues, the liberal issues, "which

I think were the core issues at the heart and soul of the Democratic Party."
And he felt that finally the "historic Democratic constituencies were responding to these themes."

A "death watch" was how Garry Wills said reporters described covering
Ted Kennedy's campaign before New York, meaning not the possibility of
assassination, which was always present, but the "certain dissipation of a
vast complex of hopes, the end of the entire Kennedy time in our national
life." And he attributed this to the fact that "Edward Kennedy has inherited a vast simulacra of power, not its reality." Wills was right in the sense
that even as Ted began to win primaries and caucuses, mathematically he
was virtually eliminated from winning the Democratic presidential nomination, and right also in the sense that Ted's power was only a shade of
that of his brothers, and that the Kennedy brand, in any case, was losing
its grip on the American imagination. And yet there was a resurgence in
April and May, a sense that Ted was finally gaining traction, and not just
for political reasons—the failings of Jimmy Carter would have crippled
him against any opponent—and not just because now that he had no
chance of winning, but because he had the appeal of the underdog, a
"subliminal mother instinct" for candidates in trouble, Jerry Brown's former press secretary called it, describing why the press kept Ted's candidacy alive now after having buried it for dead almost since it began. Ted
wasn't fooling himself about the politics of his situation, which were dire,
even though Jerry Brown had withdrawn, leaving it a two-man race.
"The Kennedys don't shit themselves." He knew he wasn't going to win.
(His aides called his only scenario for victory "sort of a Rube Goldberg
plan.") The political wisdom was for him to quit. UAW president Douglas
Fraser, one of those who was most responsible for pressuring Ted to get
into the race, announced in May that Ted should now withdraw because
it was "ridiculous" for him to think he had any chance of stopping Carter
and because staying in would be an act of "self-destruction" and would be
seen as handing the election to Reagan. And Fraser said that if he were to
continue, it would prompt people to ask, "Is he really interested in the
country, the party, the platform and the principle, or is he only interested
in promoting his own candidacy?" which was a very odd thing to say
about Ted Kennedy, whose candidacy was costing him so much in so
many ways. Quit. The party stalwarts were telling him to quit to save the
party from disaster in the fall. Quit. Many of his own advisers, including

his own brother-in-law, told him to quit. Quit. His closest friend, John Tunney, was telling him to quit. But Ted Kennedy would not quit, and Carey Parker said he couldn't recall a single meeting during the campaign that Parker didn't think was "positive," meaning Ted's attitude was positive. After Illinois, when things were at their bleakest, he told his administrative assistant Rick Burke repeatedly, "There's this thing inside of me; I've got to get the message across."

Carter and his advisers couldn't understand, and had never understood, and no one seemed to understand, why he kept running when he was facing certain defeat. But that was because they were thinking politically—thinking that when a candidate cannot win, he should concede, thinking that the real purpose of a campaign is victory. "He's trying to salvage his pride and family name," Carter's campaign chair, Robert Strauss, offered as an explanation, putting Ted's persistence solely on his hope for personal salvation. Nor could they understand why Ted fought harder now that he had no chance of winning, why he seemed more energized now that he had no chance of winning, why after enduring what *Time* described as a "series of bruising defeats that might have broken the spirit of many another politician," his spirit was not broken even though he had no chance of winning. Ted himself described what he had experienced as, "You're peering down into the grave as far as your political career and the hall of judgment and everything else. And then it gradually begins to come back around to what you'd believed and what you'd hoped," by which he clearly meant not his own personal popularity but the appeal of his message. And the reporters sensed it, and the public seemed to sense it—not the political tide changing, though it was slightly, but something else, something, in its way, larger than politics. Of what people were sensing, political activist and analyst Curtis Gans said in April, "There has been a certain nobility to the last two months of the Kennedy campaign," and he called him a "force, not a candidate." A fellow Kennedy called it "metaphysical."

Nobility had not been a word the press applied to Ted Kennedy during his campaign. He had been either a laughingstock or pathetic. But the narrative had changed there too—"from klutz to class," reporter Jeff Greenfield labeled the new media plotline for Ted—and not because Ted was winning some primaries now but because he persevered in the face of certain defeat. A "brave and determined campaigner" was how two media analysts described the coverage of Ted now, when just a month earlier he had been portrayed as hapless—CBS used the same footage for his bravery that had once signified his haplessness—even if the sudden change had been only the media following their own narrative prescription that, as the analysts said, was, "Frontrunners get worse press than challengers while the challengers survive." Now Ted was surviving—an intrepid survivor.

But he was more than surviving. Reporters noted that he seemed to be thriving, and the media found that even more commendable. The *Times*'s Drummond Ayres remarked on the "inner peace and self-confidence that he appears to have acquired in adversity." And Ayres said Ted left the impression of a "man who is thoroughly satisfied with the merit of his cause and the effort he has made to persuade others to join it. How else to explain his continued willingness to submit, with almost no complaints, to overwhelming defeats and intense scrutiny by the communications media?" T. R. Reid found his demeanor "happy, confident," and thought that in the "general hilarity of his entourage, there are unmistakable echoes of the Kennedy campaign before its slump." Columnist Colman McCarthy called him a "man unpracticed in contempt and unskilled in disdain," and he said that the reporters covering him, most of whom had slathered him in ridicule, "say they have yet to hear a churlish or self-pitying word from him." And McCarthy drew another conclusion from that: that Ted had the "kind of inbred character that hasn't been especially noticeable anywhere else this year"—this about a man whose character had been derided throughout. Anthony Lewis found the same equanimity, the same fortitude. "In adversity, Edward Kennedy is uncomplaining," Lewis wrote. "He exhibits none of the petulance of a George Bush, the resentment of a Gene McCarthy. To the contrary, he is good-humored, patient, never irritable with the press or unfriendly members of the public." Lewis said he seemed to have "internalized" the impending defeat and accepted it. His pollster, Peter Hart, called him a "different person" in June 1980 than he was in September 1979. "There was a whole period of time that he lost himself," Hart said. Now he had found himself. And Ted's sister Eunice recalled that even as the losses mounted, he had become ebullient. "He used to make a joke, 'Now in this pocket, tomorrow night, I'm ready with my statement if I win, and in this pocket, I'm ready with my statement if I lose.'" And she said, "Of course, he would lose," but before he went to bed, he would say, "Gosh, Euni, that was a good time.

I am sure we'll do well in the next one," knowing full well he probably wouldn't.

Why was he ebullient in the face of defeat? One of his aides told biographer Burton Hersh what others had said about Ted's reluctance to run in the first place: that Ted never really had confidence in his ability to be president—Ted would have vehemently denied that—and the "less he thought he could win, the better candidate he was." Others, like Anthony Lewis, thought it was that sense of liberation he felt when he no longer had to accommodate himself either to his brothers' style or to the conservative mood. The defeats, Lewis said, "made Edward Kennedy his own man" and his own "chief strategist." His close friend John Tunney, who was one of those advising Ted to quit, said he thought Ted was motivated by his desire "not to quit" because "he did not want to be a quitter." Gutting it out gave Ted a sense of pride and dignity and even that nobility. Ted himself said that it was more a matter of his hitting his stride, not of his changing. "I spent a long time in training. Now I'm coming into the playoffs and the Super Bowl," which, as Ted must have known, wasn't true.

But there was another answer, the answer he had given in his Georgetown speech, the answer William Raspberry had noted after that speech, the answer Ted kept repeating on the stump now, the answer that Carter and even onetime supporter Doug Fraser had disbelieved because it seemed so incongruous for a politician, so anomalous from what other politicians, including Carter, desired, which was victory, the answer that made his campaign, in the word of that Kennedy relative, metaphysical. Ted Kennedy persevered, Ted Kennedy was ebullient in that perseverance, because he was running not for his own success but for the success of a cause: to save liberalism, which, for Ted, was the repository of values that drove government to help those who would otherwise be neglected. And part of what made his campaign noble in the eyes of those who had scorned it was not only that he was fighting for a principle, despite what Douglas Fraser had said of him, but also that the principle he was fighting for, a rich moral principle, was largely seen as discredited, even by the head of his own party—a principle that had made him a pariah among the pols who thought liberalism was spent. The "Prince has been humbled," wrote left-wing activist Ronnie Dugger in Ted's defense, "but so have the poor, the sick and the old, who were already humble." In some ways, then, Ted was fighting a battle that was even more difficult, though

he would have argued more important, than his battle against Jimmy
Carter, who represented the rejection of liberalism and who sought to
transform the Democratic Party, in Ted's eyes, from a moral institution to
another self-interested political one. It wasn't simply ideological either,
not simply a matter of keeping liberalism alive. It was deeper—personally
deeper for him. "This is," Paul Kirk said, as Ted continued his quixotic
quest, "a campaign of the heart."

For Ted, the campaign meant keeping his hand on the tiller and the
rudder true. In April, in a speech before the American Society of Newspaper Editors, he derided Carter's "hurried effort" to "flee with the political
wind" and leave behind the "best traditions of the Democratic Party." He
called Carter's philosophy "alien to everything that I believe in this country and everything that my family has stood for and the Democratic Party
stands for." And he argued, "I am not appealing in this campaign solely
for a candidacy, or even for a program, but for a new social bond that can
temper the rancors and rivalries among us, a bond that can restore our
faith in shared enterprise and progress for all." "The moral issues of our
time are at risk in the period of the time of the 1980 election," he told the
congregants at a half-filled Black church in Washington in May. "Decent
quality health care for sick children is a moral issue. And when this administration cuts back on the school lunch program and the children go
hungry, I believe that is a moral issue." On moral issues—that was where
Jimmy Carter was failing—"failing the historical and traditional commitments to the Democratic Party," Ted said—despite Carter's frequent invocation of his personal morality. ("A man brings two things to a presidential
ballot," Carter's commercials pronounced, still flogging his moral superiority over Ted. "He brings his record, and he brings himself. Who he is is
frequently more important than what he's done," which was a sentiment
with which Ted could not have disagreed more. Ted brought his record.)
And Ted told *Time* that if he didn't speak up for the Democrats' liberal
traditions, his brothers' traditions, he wasn't sure that anyone else would.
Carter and other Democrats, trying to sail with the "prevailing wind" of
conservatism, were "wavering," he said, and he called Carter a "pale carbon copy" of Reagan. "I'm talking about issues that are important to me,"
he told T. R. Reid, "that I think ought to be the heart of the Democratic
Party." And he added: "So I'll keep going." Talking to columnist Lou Cannon, he said, "My deepest fears about the direction of this country have
really come true, and I'm pretty much convinced as to the importance of

the alternative policy"—*his* policy—"both being heard, debated, and hopefully—wishfully perhaps—acted on by the American people." And he thought the effort to have that debate "very much justified my campaign." (Cannon thought he sounded like Ronald Reagan when Reagan challenged Gerald Ford in 1976 and sought to restore conservatism to his party.) And when everyone seemed to be backing away from liberalism, Ted proudly embraced it. "I am a liberal," he told a group of Democratic Party leaders in Boston, decrying those who wanted to "replace positive action with negative reaction." And when he addressed the NAACP convention, he closed his address with a couplet from the Negro national anthem: "Facing the rising sun of our new day begun, let us march on 'til victory is won." As Super Tuesday approached, with a cluster of eight primaries, including California's, Colman McCarthy wrote, "Whether he wins or loses next Tuesday, Kennedy has pulled off one amazing achievement. He is a liberal who has not disenchanted other liberals."

That was Ted Kennedy's mission: "To help give the Democratic Party back its timeless truth," he told a group of senior citizens in Cincinnati that June. "He's fighting for the soul of the Democratic Party," his old press secretary Dick Drayne said. And another aide, as early as March, when everything seemed to be going wrong, believed that to Ted at least, the fight wasn't as quixotic as it might have seemed to everyone else. Said the aide, "He thinks he's going to be proven right."

And so he had trudged on.

Heading into Super Tuesday on June 3, the question wasn't whether Ted Kennedy would win those primaries, but whether he would finally drop out of the race when he didn't. There was talk of a rules fight at the convention that would free delegates from having to vote for the candidate to whom they were committed; the issue was freeing *Ted's* delegates, and Paul Kirk would not allow that issue to be discussed. And Peter Edelman, Ted's "issues man," was working on the platform, but Carter had not pledged to support it, and Ted wasn't sure how valuable liberalizing it would be if Carter simply disavowed it. Instead, Ted kept being asked about whether his crusade was about to end. To which he told one interviewer, "I learned many years ago from my father that if you start thinking about coming in second place, you're not going to come in first place." But he did say this: Were Carter to agree to debate him, Ted would withdraw if he lost on Super Tuesday. Carter dismissed the idea out of hand.

He had spent the campaign dodging Ted. He wasn't about to relent now. And an interviewer in Los Angeles told Ted that he sounded like an "idiot" insisting that Carter debate him, which triggered Ted to snarl, "Was John Kennedy an idiot for offering to debate Lyndon Johnson in 1960?" daring the interviewer to call his late brother an idiot.

Ted campaigned those last weeks as if his mission depended on it—an indefatigable campaign. He would typically start with an appearance in New York because, he said, the television stations there would hit New Jersey, one of the primary states. Then he would fly west, usually stopping in Ohio, another primary state, and occasionally touch down in South Dakota, yet another. Then he would fly on to California, where he would make several appearances, and then some days, board a plane late that night for a flight back to New Jersey and do the morning programs the next day before heading out again. When he wasn't crossing the country twice a day, he would crisscross it every three or four days, giving as many as fifteen interviews each day. By Super Tuesday, he had traveled fourteen thousand miles and looked the worse for wear. "The candidate's ruddy face is marked now by deep brown circles under the eyes," T. R. Reid wrote, "and as he limps from the pain of a bad back, his paunchy midriff pokes out over the waist of his crumpled blue suit. But somehow Kennedy keeps on handshaking and speechifying." Reporters still criticized the campaign for its disorganization, even after all these months—Ted would make last-minute changes in his schedule—but there was the residue of cheerfulness that had followed New York and Michigan, both his and that of those who now came to see him. When he insisted on making an appearance at a downtown Cleveland mall, four stories tall, even though he was behind schedule, the crowd was enormous and enthusiastic. "It did not look like a loser's crowd," Reid reported. But Ted closed the campaign—the entire primary campaign—on what Elizabeth Drew would call a sober note, with a speech at the University of California at Los Angeles, where he sounded the theme that had animated his run. Wearing glasses and reading the speech, he asked the crowd, "So we still have faith in our own best impulses and ideals?" And Drew said he invoked Franklin Roosevelt and his own brother, John Kennedy, and told the assemblage, "We have no magic solutions, but I do believe we can make meaningful progress on the basic questions of the quality of life in this country and move the country closer to the ideal of what I am committed to." And Drew noted this:

"Kennedy seems to actually believe what he is saying—a phenomenon that should not be noteworthy."

It would be the most joyous night of the long campaign in which there had been so little joy. Ted carried California easily, 45 to 38 percent, and New Jersey, 56 to 37 percent, and Rhode Island and South Dakota and New Mexico. Carter won Ohio, 51 to 44 percent (but lost the industrial areas of the state) and West Virginia and Montana, and while overall Carter had won twenty-four of thirty-four primaries and the majority of delegates, he had lost six of the eight most populous Northern states that, *Newsweek* noted, Democrats would need to win the fall election. Moreover, a *NYT/CBS* exit poll found that a minority of those Northern-state and California Democrats intended to vote for Carter in the fall. Ted had won the night, 2.6 million votes to Carter's 2.4 million, and while Carter won the nomination, he was damaged going into the election. In the final days of the primaries, Hamilton Jordan said a "casual friend" who was working in Ted's campaign phoned him and told him someone from Ted's brain trust wanted to speak with Jordan about easing Ted out of the race. (It was probably Paul Kirk.) The man met Jordan at Jordan's apartment and complained that Ted was on a "kamikaze mission," and that some of his advisers were simply determined to defeat Carter in the fall, Reagan notwithstanding. The brain truster said that Ted was likely to discontinue his race if Carter moved to the left or agreed to the debate that Ted had been demanding. Jordan said that neither of those things would happen. But they agreed to talk again after Super Tuesday. When they did, the man told Jordan, "Everybody here is up. The Senator has been in meetings all day today with staff and advisers and on the phone talking around the country. Everybody is telling him that he did great on Tuesday," and the man said Ted would not withdraw now. When Jordan asked what happened to the kamikaze mission, the man said that kamikazes usually changed a ship's direction. That boisterous night Ted yelled to his supporters, "Today, Democrats from coast to coast were unwilling to concede the nomination to Jimmy Carter. And neither am I." And he told them, "We are determined to move on to victory at the Convention and in the election next November."

That night before all the returns had come in, Carter, in an attempt to sue for peace, phoned Ted to wish him well, but also to say that Carter would win the nomination regardless of the outcome on Super Tuesday. He was told that Ted was resting—he was actually in the swimming pool—and couldn't be disturbed, and then rang him again at ten-thirty, when the returns had come in, but Ted was now on his way to his head-quarters and, in a bit of petulance of his own, didn't return the call until two-thirty the next afternoon, when Carter asked if he had had a nice rest, and Ted, picking up on the sarcasm, chuckled, though, by one account, Carter's men were not amused by Ted's disrespect.

When Ted declared on primary night that he was determined to move on to victory, he was operating on the unlikely principle that if he could only lure Carter into a debate, he could expose him. Not everyone in his inner circle was as sanguine as he. The morning after Super Tuesday, the brain trust and family assembled at McLean to discuss plans going for-ward. Kirk and Steve Smith, by one account, told him to be measured in his reaction to his success lest he close off a path to withdrawal. (Kirk in fact, by his own recollection, would tell Ted that it was time to fold.) Shrum and Parker, who had pushed Ted to embrace his liberalism and had kept pushing him to continue, thought he should take the fight to the conven-tion floor, though Carter already had sewn up the nomination, and the only way Ted could possibly reverse it was to get the convention to pass a resolution that the primary votes were not binding and the delegates were free to vote for whomever they liked. This was more than a long shot, but it gave Ted some small room to maneuver—very small. Despite his near-certain nomination victory, Carter was concerned that Ted had wounded him heading into the general election against Reagan. As Shrum recalled it, Ted argued that anyone who wanted to blame him for a subsequent Reagan victory would already have any ammunition they needed for doing so. And then, after several hours of debate among his advisers, Ted announced, "I'm not getting out under these circumstances," meaning not having had a debate on the issues, and phoned Carter to tell him so and ask that the two meet at the White House. By this account, Carter suggested the following week. Ted suggested the following day.

Now the two foes finally met, at four-thirty on the afternoon of June 5, for the first time since the campaign began—the same day, it turned out, that the Democratic Congress overrode Carter's veto of a bill that had re-jected a fee on oil imports he hoped to impose. It was a testy meeting, de-spite the opening cordialities and despite a note Ted would write to himself later that described it as "amiable." As Ted would later recall it, they sat in front of a fireplace with a vase of flowers between them, and Ted tried to set a "formal tone." He said he understood the delegate arithmetic—he didn't have enough delegates to win—but he believed that his supporters deserved a real discussion of the issues, which they had been denied because of Carter's refusal to debate. And Ted said he told Carter that "if we had a debate on economic issues and were able to make some progress through good-faith, constructive efforts on both our parts, then I would say that I would support the party's nominee," though there was no way the president could have accepted Ted's proposal. Carter complained that Ted had had a "lot of harsh words to say about me," and while he chalked up his own attacks to "campaign rhetoric," he said he had never attacked Ted personally—though, of course, he had, just by indirection. In fact, he had done little else in the campaign. Ted told Shrum afterward that Carter then asked if Ted would endorse him should Carter agree to debate, but Ted said he wanted Carter to outline an economic stimulus plan as well— the very sort of liberal plan that Carter had spent his presidency opposing. "Ambush" the president, Shrum had advised Ted by asking for the meeting and then bringing up the debate. But Jimmy Carter was not going to be ambushed and was not going to debate Ted Kennedy, saying that incumbent presidents never debated, that the differences between him and Ted were already clear, and that any debate could be conducted before the platform committee, where their respective representatives would lay out their positions. Relaying details of the meeting afterward to Jordan, Carter "looked irritated," Jordan said. "Nothing good" had happened, according to Carter. "He was nervous and kept rambling on about wanting to debate me, and that I should change my policies and stimulate the economy, and that he felt responsibility to his voters. And the party." But Carter concluded that Ted had little interest in the party. "Deep down, I suspect he'd rather see Reagan elected than me," Carter said, and he might have been right, since Ted might have thought that Carter's reelection would doom liberalism by snuffing it out within the Democratic Party, the only place it could survive, while Reagan's might have reinvigorated it. Carter offered a half-baked liberalism, in Ted's mind, if it was any liberalism at all. Reagan offered open warfare against liberalism, which drew the lines between the parties more starkly and gave Ted a bigger target to hit in his crusade to rouse those better angels. So Ted Kennedy would not withdraw from the race. Meeting the press afterward, Ted said, "I'm planning to be the nominee." Carter said Ted was acting "like a spoiled brat." And that was how the meeting ended.

And now, with the convention before him and a commitment to challenge Carter on the convention floor, Ted was fighting against all odds to bring his party home—home to what he saw as its timeless truth. For a man accustomed to a life of loneliness, it had been a long and lonely campaign for him—a campaign in which he had few allies, even within his own camp, with his brothers gone and his party against him and those who had initially encouraged him having largely abandoned him. The coming months promised to be even lonelier since his defeat was all but assured. During his time on the stump, a time, before his resurgence, of many humiliations and much abuse, he had shrunk into himself. "Impenetrable," some of his closest aides called him when he was not actively campaigning. Where he had once welcomed human contact, the handshaking and backslapping of retail politics, Drummond Ayres found him "elusive" now, unrevealing, almost as if he were shielding himself from the slings and arrows he knew were coming at him. "He eats many of his meals in the solitude of his hotel room, usually attended by only one aide," Drummond wrote. "He does not kiss babies, he visibly recoils from the hugs and tugs of the crowd and steadfastly refuses to model the hard hats and T-shirts given him by union officials and high school athletic teams." It was different when Patrick joined him. He would give him index cards on which Ted had written his talking points so that Patrick could follow along with the speech, and Ted told him to put stars next to the lines he thought were most effective. They were two companions on the road— Ted's only real companion. When Patrick wasn't there, Ted would retreat at the end of the day to his hotel room for those room service dinners with a young aide, Drummond said, presumably Rick Burke, while the rest of the staff ate in the hotel restaurant. "It's a lonely existence," a staffer told Ayres. "But it seems to be the way he wants it." A lonely existence in a long and lonely campaign.

"Everything but the Nomination"

TED KENNEDY'S "RUBE Goldberg" plan that was designed to get him the nomination he hadn't been able to win in the primaries was actually several plans, all of them equally unlikely. For one, he would finally get that debate with Jimmy Carter and demonstrate Carter's inadequacy. (In fact, Carter, so desperate to nudge Ted out of the race, finally conceded to a debate to be staged before the platform committee, only to retreat after two days of unrelenting lobbying by Vice President Mondale who, according to pollster Pat Caddell, went "absolutely berserk" at the prospect.) Or Ted would batter away at the platform, insisting on planks that would include his wage and price control policy, his gas rationing plan, controls on domestic oil prices, a new program, just introduced the week after Super Tuesday, that would appropriate $12 billion to job creation, and a reduction in the military budget, and by so doing, create a platform on which Carter could not stand, much less run, and thus convince the party of the error of its ways were it to renominate him. Or Ted would call for an "open" convention, a convention in which delegates would be released after the first ballot from their obligations to vote for the candidate who had won their state's primary or, depending upon how delegates were apportioned in that state, the district from which they were elected, and thus released, those delegates, Ted hoped, might turn to him as the true voice of the Democrats. All these plans were predicated on the idea that Democrats didn't really want Jimmy Carter; that, as Ted told Elizabeth Drew of *The New Yorker,* "those forces out there—the elderly, youth, church groups—have a synergistic effect on each other, and that moves this nation," presumably moving them toward him; that, as he told *Time,* there had been "very basic and fundamental changes in circumstances"

from the beginning of the primary season to its end, changes that had
resulted in his resurgence, and that Democrats were not "prepared to concede defeat" in the fall, which was what Ted insisted Carter's nomination
would bring.

During the two months between the end of the primaries and the Dem-
ocratic National Convention at Madison Square Garden in New York, Ted
Kennedy kept battling, traveling, speaking before liberal groups. He proposed his job creation plan before the American Federation of State,
County and Municipal Employees, and in mid-June, at the Americans for
Democratic Action convention, he continued to lacerate Carter, saying,
"If I stay in the race, it is because I have seen too many people trapped in
unemployment lines, strapped by inflation, left without health care and
limited by continuing discrimination. They cannot walk away from the
plight. . . . And I cannot walk away from this campaign because I believe
that their problems demand to be stated and debated." In a speech to the
NAACP early in July, despite his obvious fatigue, the crowd got him so
revved up that when he reached the climax, the point where he delivered
his liberal litany, he was "preaching," by Drummond Ayres's account,
pounding the lectern, "head and shoulders jerking and weaving," and
rousing the crowd to "Amens." At another meeting, this one of nineteen
labor leaders, the pressure for him to leave the race so as to preserve Carter's chances had lifted. "Nobody was pounding the table and pleading
with him to keep running," said one of them. "But when he said he was
still running, we all said we were going to be with him." Ted told T. R. Reid
that the campaign "feels good," and as if in evidence, he had lost fifteen
pounds during the postprimary period—his weight loss always a sign of
the seriousness of his intentions. But another reporter, Bill Stall of the *Los
Angeles Times*, following Ted that same week, found him "enervated" and
said that given his mood swings it was difficult to judge from one day to
the next just how seriously he took his chances of actually winning the
nomination.

Jimmy Carter, weary of Ted and exasperated with him, just wanted
him to stop, and short of agreeing to debate, he was willing to do almost
anything to coax him to do so. Don't be "confrontational," Speaker Tip
O'Neill had warned Carter before the June 5 meeting with Ted, and offered
to mediate between the two, if they needed it. Go easy on him, counseled
Richard Moe, Mondale's chief of staff and a senior adviser to Carter. Give
him five seats on the platform committee, have the president publicly

commend him, and ask liberal Arizona congressman Mo Udall to deliver
the keynote address. (Carter wrote on the memo that he agreed with
the prescription and did invite Udall to give the keynote.) In the event, the
seats on the platform committee were only window dressing. When the
committee met late that June, every one of Ted's eighteen planks was
beaten back by the Carter forces. "Democratic in name only," Ted called
the document and filed his own set of minority planks—part of his plan
to convince liberal delegates to abandon Carter.

But Carter's own plan was to pacify Ted without surrendering to him.
"Graciousness and conciliation," as Moe had put it, "coupled with firm-
ness and confidence." So on July 1 the president sent White House domestic adviser Stuart Eizenstat to Peter Edelman, Ted's domestic issues adviser,
to discuss the eighteen planks that were being contested. Eizenstat returned two weeks later with some accommodations on each of the planks.
But Edelman wasn't satisfied. He wanted more than compromises, which
indicated both Ted's new muscle-flexing and his commitment to his cause.
He wanted "significant" economic concessions from Carter, including, by
one account, a tax cut, the antirecession package, an industrial revitalization program, and being a politician, public acknowledgment of Ted's
role in wresting these concessions from Carter. By the same account, Carter sent Hamilton Jordan, his chief of staff, to meet with Paul Kirk and
several of the other Kennedy advisers at the Mayflower Hotel, where they
conferred over Cokes and ginger ales. Carter said that his own team recommended appeasing Ted with a small tax cut and a "moderate spending
program." Carter, apparently unwilling to bow to Kennedy, especially
when it came to economic prudence, told them he was not going to make
those concessions—"adamantly against it" was how he framed it—and
that was the end of the negotiations. Ted's speechwriter and campaign
aide, Bob Shrum, recalled it differently. He said that Carter's people were
willing to "concede almost anything" if Ted would make one concession
of his own: agree to drop a plank supporting gay rights. (No doubt Carter's advisers were concerned about the political fallout of such a plank.)
Shrum said Ted rejected the offer "outright."* So the stalemate continued.

But that was only the beginning of Ted Kennedy's fight. As one of his

---

*In another version, this one in *Time*, Carter campaign chair Robert Strauss said shortly
after the Carter-Ted meeting that they would agree to any platform concession that Ted
desired except for wage and price controls and gas rationing, and even on those, Carter
would give Ted the floor to make his case. "White House Face-Off," *Time*, June 16, 1980.

aides said, the platform that Carter had endorsed, a platform long on budget balancing and short on programs to aid the needy, "validates our contention that Carter is willing to throw the party and all it has stood for overboard if he thinks the political winds require it." Ted provided a sharp contrast. At the same appearance before AFSCME where he introduced his job creation plan, which was also during the week of the platform committee sessions, he said, "The jobless do not have seats on the committee of the Democratic convention, but my campaign does. The families without adequate health care and winter heat do not have floor passes . . . but my campaign does. The farmers who have lost their land do not have a place on the podium or microphone . . . but my campaign does. And from that place and that microphone, we will speak for all of them." A month later, at hearings before the Senate Labor Committee, he pressed assistant secretary of labor Ernest Green on the impact of the recession and asked when Carter would finally propose a job creation plan of his own. And to press the point, Ted brought witnesses from across the country—workers who had been hurt by the Carter economy. "You've heard about the New Rich," one of them testified "Well, we're the New Poor."

But it wasn't only the platform with which Ted hoped to contest Carter. He sought an alliance. A Republican congressman from rural Illinois, John Anderson, had been waging an independent campaign for the presidency in opposition both to the Republican nominee, Ronald Reagan, who had been chosen at the GOP convention in July, and to Carter, though Anderson's campaign was likely to draw more heavily from the latter than from the former since Anderson challenged conservative shibboleths. Looking like a small-town high school principal with neatly cropped snow-white hair and black horn-rimmed glasses and with a speaking delivery that was as clipped and modulated as Ted's was elongated and bellowing, Anderson had once believed in those shibboleths until becoming a born-again moderate who now attacked Carter's seeming ineptitude and Reagan's right-wing orthodoxy. He advocated for a fifty-cent-per-gallon gas tax, gun control, and choice on abortion, which had suddenly become a major issue among the Republicans, while also advocating for a 40 percent cut in Social Security payroll taxes as a way of stimulating the economy. Anderson won no primaries when he challenged Reagan—he came close in Massachusetts and Vermont—before launching his independent candidacy, but as an independent he had qualified to appear on every state ballot and was gaining momentum, especially on college campuses. One Gallup poll had him at 26 percent of the vote.

Ted and John Anderson did not agree on many issues, but they did agree on one thing: that neither of the leading candidates should be president. At the suggestion of an aide, Ted invited Anderson to his Senate office, where the two of them met for a half-hour and then emerged in a mist of mutual admiration, with Ted saying he admired Anderson's efforts to "reach a responsible solution to the concerns of millions of Americans," and Anderson saying that if the Democrats chose a candidate other than Jimmy Carter, "it would only be prudent . . . to reconsider what my position would be." Hamilton Jordan was steaming over the tactic. And then Ted extended another invitation—this one to Senate majority leader Robert Byrd to be his running mate. Ted must have known that Byrd, as staunch a Senate man as there had ever been, would never accept, but Byrd did something else: He vowed to work for an open convention where the delegates would be freed to vote their conscience after the first ballot.

An open convention. That was now Ted Kennedy's grail—his last and only hope of prying the nomination away from Jimmy Carter and rededicating his party to liberalism. And though Ted had always been a realist, he thought he still had a chance of turning the convention—a chance of winning a psychological battle against Carter that would become a political victory. His chance was no doubt based on polling shortly before the convention opened. A Gallup poll the first week of August showed Carter not only with the lowest approval rating of his presidency but also with the lowest approval rating ever recorded in the forty years of Gallup presidential surveys, 21 percent—lower than Richard Nixon's during Watergate—and a drop of forty points since December, when he was blasting Ted out of the competition by riding the Iran hostage situation. A Harris poll at the same time gave Reagan a lead of 53 to 26 percent over Carter, with John Anderson at 18 percent, but Carter actually ran third, behind Anderson, in a trial heat that asked voters to assume Anderson had a chance of winning. Equally important for Ted was a Gallup poll that showed Democrats now favoring Carter by just four points over Ted, 47 to 43 percent, down twenty-two points since mid-July. "Never before in the nearly 50 years of Gallup polls has an incumbent president entered a convention with less grass-roots support from his own party than will President Carter," Gallup reported, which said a great deal about how much

Democrats feared certain defeat and how much the country perceived Carter as weak and ineffectual.

The Democrats' fear of Ronald Reagan was real and deep, and it was warranted. Reagan was not the typical Republican presidential candidate who listed right but effectively subscribed to the old liberal consensus that accepted the New Deal. (Even Nixon had; only Barry Goldwater hadn't.) Reagan hadn't risen through the ranks of the traditional Republican political culture. He was a movie star—albeit primarily in B-movies—though it was precisely because he wasn't a real leading man that he could fashion himself as "Mr. Norm," as he had called himself in a *Photoplay* spread in the late 1940s. (Years later, when Warner Bros. head Jack Warner, who had been Reagan's boss, was told that Reagan was considering running for governor, Warner allegedly quipped, "No, Jimmy Stewart for governor. Ronald Reagan for best friend.") But even though Reagan was an actor by profession, he was actually a politician by temperament. (In fact, perhaps too much of a politician; his first wife, actress Jane Wyman, said that she had divorced him in part because he was always talking politics.) He had been the president of the Screen Actors Guild, the union for actors, and had weighed in on the fierce battles in the late 1940s and early '50s when Hollywood was being targeted by conservative congressmen, mostly Republicans, as a hotbed of Communist activity, and he testified before the House Un-American Activities Committee (HUAC), walking a thin line by defending Hollywood while attacking Communists, thereby offending neither his industry nor the public who hated Communists; ultimately, however, he sided with the producers when they imposed a blacklist against suspected Communists after ten of those suspected Communists made an obstreperous display when called before HUAC themselves. As one of Reagan's biographers, H. W. Brands, put it, "He didn't know it yet, but he had found the issue on which he would build his political career." That issue: He would stop socialism from taking over the country.

In embracing fear of a socialist takeover, Reagan had undergone a political conversion. He had been, he would say, an ardent supporter of Franklin Roosevelt. "A New Dealer to the core," he would call himself. "A near-hopeless hemophiliac liberal," he would call himself. And he would say that when he had seemed to shift rightward, he hadn't left the Democratic Party, the Democratic Party had left him. But Reagan *had* left the

Democrats—left them and then scorned them. It is difficult to say exactly what Reagan's Road to Damascus moment was: his involvement with SAG and anti-Communism ("I knew from the experience of hand-to-hand combat that America faced no more insidious or evil threat than that of Communism," he would write of that time in his autobiography); or his bitterness over high taxes, especially as his income had decreased while his movie career languished ("I'd always thought there was something inherently unfair toward actors in the tax system"); or his attribution of that career spiral to the Democrats' antitrust campaign against the film industry that broke up the studios' monopolies; or the influence of his Hollywood social circle, which included some of the most conservative members of the film community—among them Robert Taylor, Dick Powell, and George Murphy, who would later enter politics himself and be elected to the Senate. Reagan himself would attribute it, in part, to his "exposure to the business-as-usual attitude of many civil service bureaucrats during the war," and to his having had a "brief experience living in a country that promised the kind of womb-to-womb utopian benevolence a lot of these liberal friends wanted to bring to America." (He was speaking of his time filming a picture in postwar England under the Labor Party.) Whatever the sources, and it was probably a combination of things, by the early 1950s his conversion was complete, though he wouldn't officially change his party affiliation until 1962 because, he would say, Republicans felt it was more effective to have an avowed "Democrat" supporting Republican candidates.

His next job would testify to how complete the conversion was. In 1954, with his film career drying up, his agent, the powerful Lew Wasserman— a major Democratic contributor—landed Reagan a job as host of a Sunday-evening dramatic anthology program on CBS, *The General Electric Theater.* Along with his hosting duties, Reagan was to become a company "ambassador," spending ten weeks a year traveling the country, visiting GE plants, and delivering speeches that preached the gospel of American corporate capitalism and the dangers of government interference, high taxes, and unions. For Reagan, this wasn't just an obligation. It was a passion. One producer of his television show said, "He sounded as though he was running for something."

Whether Ronald Reagan knew it or not, he was. These speeches, deeply conservative in tone and substance—Reagan wrote them himself—were only a long, long rehearsal for the performance that would catapult him into the upper echelon of American politics. With Goldwater's presidential campaign foundering, several of Goldwater's well-heeled contributors recruited Reagan to deliver a half-hour speech on his behalf on the NBC television network on October 27, 1964, a week before the vote. Addressing the camera in front of a hand-selected studio audience of two hundred Goldwater supporters—it had been filmed in Phoenix earlier—Reagan gave a greatest hits of what liberals would see as conservative paranoia. He sounded alarums against encroaching socialism, illustrated with anecdotes about men and women who had been harmed by the government; against rising taxation and government redistribution ("We have so many people who can't see a fat man standing there beside a thin one without coming to the conclusion the fat man got that way by taking advantage of the thin one"), a swelling national debt, the threat of Communism ("We are at war with the most dangerous enemy that has ever faced mankind in his long climb from the swamp to the stars"), anti-intellectualism (the main issue of the election, he declared is "whether we believe in our capacity for self-government or whether we abandon the American revolution and confess that a little intellectual elite in a far-distant capital can plan our lives for us better than we can plan them ourselves"), centralized government (denouncing "those who would trade our freedom for the soup kitchen of the welfare state"), the failure of government programs and the concomitant scheming of those on the government dole (he related the story of a young woman, with six children and pregnant with a seventh, while her husband earned $250 a week, who was now seeking a divorce because she could get more money on welfare than her husband earned at work), even the failure of Social Security (Reagan claimed an individual investing the money from payroll taxes would do better than government "insurance" provided) and the way in which Medicare robs senior citizens of the right to control their healthcare, the harassment of business by government and by unions, and above all, the role of Democratic Party as a Trojan horse to smuggle socialism into America (he cited former New York governor and Democratic presidential candidate Al Smith, who had long ago accused his party's leaders, in Smith's case Franklin Roosevelt, of "taking the Party of Jefferson, Jackson, and Cleveland down the road under the banners of Marx, Lenin, and Stalin"). "Freedom has never been more fragile, so close to slipping from our grasp as it is at the moment," Reagan warned. This was Ronald Reagan's mantra, the issue on which, as his biographer H. W.

Brands said, he would base his career: *The socialist/Democratic government was about to strip away your freedoms if you didn't stop it.*

Formally, the address was called "A Time for Choosing," presumably, as Reagan articulated it, between freedom (Goldwater) and socialist enslavement (Johnson). Reagan himself called it simply "The Speech," and in retrospect it was one of the most important political addresses in modern American history. (Reagan, speaking personally, would call it "one of the most important milestones in my life.") Voters would repudiate Goldwater for making similar charges, and even mainstream Republicans kept their distance from what they regarded as the menagerie of fringe zealots who had seized the party with Goldwater's nomination. (Not incidentally, Reagan barely mentioned Goldwater in the speech, though its ostensible purpose was to promote his election.) But Reagan, with his actorly talents and his affable mien and his telegenic appearance, seemed anything but a zealot. If anything, his was a calming presence, and the Speech offered a preview of how he might perform and what he might do in electoral politics; the political columnists Rowland Evans and Robert Novak would later call Reagan's delivery "Goldwater's doctrine with John F. Kennedy's technique."

What followed was meteoric. The Republican donors who had recruited him to give the Speech immediately attempted to recruit him as the Republican gubernatorial candidate in California. After stumping the state for months to see if a candidacy was viable, he agreed to run and won the governorship over Democratic incumbent Pat Brown by nearly one million votes in 1966, which prompted Reagan prematurely to flirt with an informal presidential candidacy in 1968, declaring hopefully that he would accept the nomination if the convention offered it. (It didn't.) Having governed, despite his overwrought, bellicose rhetoric, largely as a moderate, having to find common cause with the Democratic legislature, he was easily reelected to the governorship in 1970, and six years later, now out of office, he excited conservatives by taking on the moderate Republican incumbent Gerald Ford—Reagan had once accused moderates of being "traitors" to the party, espousing the "same socialist goals of the opposition"—and narrowly lost on the convention floor.

For the next four years, he seemed to be the nominee-in-waiting. In 1980, once again vying for the presidency, Reagan had dispelled most of the doubts about him in his own party, which said a great deal about how the party had changed in the four years since nominating Ford. (Goldwater and Reagan had sprung from the red-baiting Senator Joseph McCarthy faction of Republicanism; now that faction, formerly disgraced, had taken over.) Facing his stiffest competition for the nomination from another comparative moderate, former Texas congressman and CIA director George H. W. Bush, Reagan marched triumphantly through the primaries and was greeted by the Republican convention in Detroit as the party's salvation and the nation's. The acceptance speech he delivered from the podium on July 17, before a cheering throng, still echoed the warnings that he had sounded in the Speech sixteen years earlier—"grave threats to our very existence," "a disintegrating economy," "a weakened defense," and the responsibility of Democrats for the "unprecedented calamity which has befallen us"—but it was light on the most controversial of his conservative prescriptions like the privatization of Social Security and the end of Medicare, which he had previously decried as "socialized medicine." Rather, it emphasized Jimmy Carter's shortcomings, especially Carter's pessimism and insistence on America's limits, which Reagan, like Ted Kennedy, threw back at him. "I will not stand by and watch this great country destroy itself under mediocre leadership that drifts from one crisis to the next," Reagan told the delegates. And he called for a "new beginning," one in which the federal government would have little place. He pledged a government whose "willingness to do good [was] balanced by the knowledge that government is never more dangerous than when our desire to have it help us blinds us to its great power to harm us," which was in direct contrast to how Ted Kennedy thought about government. In even greater contrast, Reagan said almost nothing about how government might serve the poor, the marginalized, or the vulnerable. (He mentioned the "needy" once.) Though Reagan was politic enough now to affirm his belief in Social Security, despite his previous attacks on it, he also declared that government was "overgrown and overweight." He called for a freeze on federal hiring and a 30 percent reduction in income tax rates over three years, his panacea for what ailed the American economy but that, Democrats well understood, was less a panacea than a way to starve the government programs that Reagan detested. He promised to beef up the military, even as he was instituting those tax cuts, despite the fact that Carter had already swelled the defense budget and was promising to increase it by 27 percent more in his second term. "We know only too well that war comes not when the forces of freedom are strong, but when they are weak." And he closed sheepishly if disingenuously, his voice wobbling and his eyes glistening, with what he said was a gamble—"I've been a little afraid to suggest what I'm going to suggest, I'm more afraid not to"—as if he might alienate his crowd with what he was about to say, though it was beyond unlikely he would: He suggested that they all join in a silent prayer for the nation.

It was easy to underestimate Ronald Reagan, and Jimmy Carter did. To Carter, Reagan was an actor, a lightweight, a simpleton, even a right-wing lunatic who had spent his political career firing salvoes at rioters, campus protesters ("cowardly little bums," he had called free speech marchers at the University of California at Santa Barbara), alleged welfare cheats, environmentalists, educators, proponents of public transit, budget busters, and government bureaucrats generally. It was easy to dismiss him and think that the American people would reject his dire prophecy of impending socialism and his prescriptions to save America from it, which were basically to cut taxes and scale back government. But in dismissing him, Carter was overlooking those qualities of Reagan's that had appealed to voters and that contrasted with Jimmy Carter's own deficiencies. It was true that Reagan was a rhetorical extremist, even if he hadn't governed as an extremist in California. But for many, it was less about what he said than about how he said it. Reagan was folksy. Longtime newspaperman Lou Cannon said that on meeting him for the first time, what he noticed most was that "everyone seemed to like him, the reporters included." No one would have said anything similar about Jimmy Carter. (They might have about Ted Kennedy.) And Reagan had something else from his acting days: a sense of the audience, which was how he thought of the electorate. At the end of his presidency, discussing with an aide how he had been demeaned by opponents as having become president only because he could deliver a speech well, Reagan admitted that that wasn't far from the mark—"because an actor knows two important things: to be honest in what he's doing and to be in touch with an audience." Reagan was nothing if not sincere. He believed in his jeremiads. "There are not two Ronald Reagans," his wife Nancy would say of him, meaning that what you saw was exactly who he was, which could not be said of every or even most politicians. And he did have the gift of making his audiences believe in his belief, whether they agreed with him or not.

And this was why Democrats were so terrified of him, not just because of his pronouncements, which were anathema to them, the negation of everything they held true, but also because were Reagan to win—and postconvention polls showed him with a 55 to 24 percent lead over Carter (NBC/AP poll) or a 61 to 33 percent lead (Harris poll)—the entire liberal enterprise that Franklin Roosevelt had launched in 1933 would be facing extinction. They were terrified because Reagan knew the audience in a way Jimmy Carter didn't, and that meant that Reagan, for all his deficiencies and for all the questions about his fitness for the presidency, *could* win. "Some people enter politics seeking power," one of Reagan's biographers would write of him. "Reagan wanted an audience. . . . He wanted a stage." And now he had them.

II

Ted Kennedy arrived in New York for the Democratic National Convention on August 8, riding a tide of encouragement, and "sounding as strident as he ever has," Elizabeth Drew wrote, so much so that he "seemed almost crazed, a caricature." Outside the Waldorf Astoria Hotel, where he would be staying, he greeted a large crowd by ripping into Carter. Peter Hart, his pollster, thought Ted now believed, with Carter's polls sinking, that he really could win the nomination if only he could get the delegates to change the rules and allow for an open convention. That might have seemed like another of Ted's pipe dreams, but now, with Carter facing likely defeat in the fall, others were also pulling on that pipe, including Senators Henry Jackson and Daniel Moynihan and, because of Ted's intervention, Robert Byrd. By one report, 60 percent of Democratic House members now favored an open convention, as did, by a *Washington Post* survey, 41 percent of the delegates. The same Gallup poll that brought Carter the bad news showed that 55 percent of Democrats wanted an open convention and 52 percent wanted a candidate other than Carter. Another poll put the number at 65 percent for to 31 percent against. Forty House Democrats had met before the convention to organize a Committee to Continue the Open Convention and raised $200,000 with the assistance of Hollywood movie executive Arnold Picker and opened an office on Capitol Hill. But they made no attempt to coordinate with Ted's campaign lest they be thought to be a stalking horse for him when they claimed not to want any particular candidate so much as they wanted to defeat Ronald Reagan and felt Carter couldn't do it. Meanwhile renowned Washington attorney Edward Bennett Williams joined forces with the House members, hoping to force an open convention, though there were rumors

Williams was working at the behest of, or at least in the interest of, Henry Jackson and Secretary of State Ed Muskie, who thought they might capture the nomination if Carter and Ted were to flag. (Williams publicly asked Ted to release his delegates before the rules fight.) And fearing anything that could stampede the convention against Carter, the president's aides refused to grant Ted a prime time speaking slot during the convention, and when Hamilton Jordan, during a heated negotiating session, threatened not to let Ted have any speaking time at all, Carl Wagner, Ted's field director, made his own threat: He would hand out cricket noisemakers to the delegates during Carter's acceptance speech. "Have you ever heard the sound of one thousand crickets chirping together?" he asked one of Carter's aides. In the end, the sides agreed to a prime time debate on the platform, at which Ted could speak, but only if he agreed to endorse the ticket. Paul Kirk would say that they had made no such agreement. "Nothing is certain in politics," he said. "Neither is President Carter's re-nomination."

Free the delegates. That was the rallying cry of all those who opposed Carter's renomination. And the open conventioneers had printed big buttons with robots on them and a red stripe slashed across, with the idea that delegates should not be robotically committed to a candidate when the situation had clearly changed. Even Paul Kirk, who had been one of the least enthusiastic of Ted's advisers and the one who pushed him hard to leave the race, now held a press conference before the convention on the Starlight Roof of the Waldorf at which he said that Ted would win the rules fight and would win the nomination. "I think we may be on the threshold of one of the major political stories of recent political history," he told the reporters, and said that Pennsylvania, Michigan, and Illinois were all "soft" on whether the convention should remain closed. And this time, when a reporter asked him if Ted was considering withdrawing, Kirk snapped, "You gotta be kidding." Carter, of course, had the votes, more than enough to coast to victory—but only if he could hold them, which is to say, only if they were not released in a rules fight. At one point, Carter even considered co-opting the open convention advocates by releasing his delegates, on the assumption that they would vote for him anyway. But by one report, his staff scotched the idea after they canvassed delegates. (Carter's delegate counter, Tom Donilon, thought the vote to free the delegates might come down to a few votes.) By another report, Carter delegates

were willing to vote for a rules change, but only if Ted removed himself
from contention first.

But Ted Kennedy was not about to remove himself. He would later say
that just before the convention began, he felt he had an "outside chance"
of changing the "faithful delegate" rule—Rule F3(c) that bound a delegate to the candidate who won the state or, in some states, the district in
which that delegate had run during the primary. Ted had been speaking
with delegates—"even in caucuses that had not had overwhelming Kennedy support"—and had received a "great reception" from Pennsylvania
delegates who were willing to defect from Carter and from Black delegates
in South Carolina and from delegates in Louisiana, who had turned on
Carter. But Ted said there was a problem: "All of them wanted to be the
ones who put us over. They didn't want to be the base group," the group
that would begin the avalanche to change the rule. And while Ted was
canvassing those delegates, Carter's forces, now fearing defections, were
going from hotel to hotel, trying to hold their troops, while Carter himself
and his wife Rosalynn, who were at the presidential retreat at Camp David,
were phoning delegates to keep them in line. Ted was to say that he was
only 130 votes short of rescinding the rule that would release the delegates, and he would also say that if he had gotten Carter to debate him,
he felt he could have lured those delegates by appealing to Democratic
core values. But he hadn't. Paul Kirk told him, "We just can't do it. We
can't put those numbers together." Ted tried to postpone the vote to the
second day of the convention to see if he could build support. He failed.
One reformer told Elizabeth Drew that it was the McGovern reforms after
the 1968 convention that did in the open convention campaign. He said
that those reforms turned delegates from party loyalists to candidate
loyalists—"it's a President-candidate convention"—and that while party
stalwarts might have opened up the convention to toss Carter aside and
increase their chances for a fall victory, Carter's own people wouldn't. The
vote for the rules change was held on Monday, as scheduled. Ted lost 1,936
to 1,390. Ted's supporters on the floor shouted, "No, no, no!" but, according to Elizabeth Drew, not very emotionally. They knew the odds, even if
Ted himself seemed to have forgotten them. Ted flashed Rick Burke a
"grim smile," though Burke said that "pain filled his eyes." The presidential hope, which had flickered for so long, had finally been extinguished.
Jimmy Carter, though all but certain to lose the general election, would be

nominated. Ted Kennedy, who had quickened pulses as the campaign proceeded, had been rejected and with him the last best hope of liberalism.

But even in that defeat, there was now some honor. Drummond Ayres of *The New York Times* called his behavior, "by almost everyone's measure," an "extraordinary personal and political performance." Ayres said what had often been said of Ted during the campaign, especially in his darkest days: "He never whined, never carped and somehow always came up with a laugh or self-deprecatory quip." Ted phoned President Carter at Camp David to tell him the news that he was withdrawing. Then, two hours after the vote, back at the Waldorf, Ted told Shrum, "That's it," and asked him to write a withdrawal statement, which Shrum did on a yellow legal pad, and which Ted then took to a press conference in the stifling ballroom on the eighteenth floor where he was joined by Joan, Kara, and Ted Jr., all of whom were shocked at Ted's sudden change of heart. (Paul Kirk had told reporters that Ted would not withdraw.) "I'm a realist," he said grimly, though he had allowed himself some unreality. "My name will not be placed in nomination." Supporters in the room shouted "No" again, as the supporters had on the convention floor. But he also said this: The "efforts for Democratic principles must and will continue." He spoke for only two minutes. Then he left for his room.

III

Even then, however, it wasn't entirely over. The campaign had been a crusade, a cause, Ted had said—to reassert the liberal values for which his party had so long stood and for which the Kennedys had stood and that, in Ted's view, Jimmy Carter seemed to have forsaken. The cause was simple: for government to dedicate itself to those who most needed it. He had lost, but the cause continued. There was still the platform over which to haggle—the platform over which to assert liberal values and what he had called the "timeless truth" of the party. The Kennedy and Carter forces had been negotiating over the platform since June, though what they were really negotiating was not the direction of the party but whether Ted would finally acquiesce in supporting Carter. By one report, just before the convention, Carter's aides trooped to Ted's suite at the Waldorf with a sheaf of concessions. Ted smiled. "This is getting to be the kind of platform that I welcome to run on," and he said that he would accept "additional concessions." One more he was said to have wrested was a commitment by the nominee to support the platform in writing. (Carter did not support the 1976 convention platform—the very platform of the party that had nominated him. If he had, Ted said, "I wouldn't be here.") Paul Kirk said that he and Jordan spent two days hammering out what he called a "peace agreement" that also included Tip O'Neill, who was chairing the convention and would be wielding the gavel for the platform vote. (Ted's office staff, Kirk said, thought Kirk's negotiations a betrayal; they wanted to press the fight on the platform.) But it wasn't to be that easy. Ted submitted a platform he titled, in what was clearly a jab at the nominee-to-be, "A Rededication to Democratic Principles," that included his massive jobs program, his wage and price freeze, his national health insurance plan, and abortion on demand. Carter agreed to allow votes on the jobs stimulus, the wage and price plan, and a plank that, in direct contradiction to Carter's policy, committed the nominee not to use unemployment to fight inflation. And Ted had not just submitted his platform. Kirk had wrested one more concession—a big one: Ted was going to speak in prime time on behalf of his platform before the vote, making him the first formal candidate to speak before the roll call since William Jennings Bryan delivered his Cross of Gold speech to the 1896 Democratic convention and wound up stampeding the delegates to nominate him.

There would be no nominating speech to place Ted's name in contention, no acceptance speech to take the nomination. Before he withdrew, when he still was fighting for delegates, he had asked Barbara Mikulski, the Maryland senator, to make that nominating speech, and she had bought a new dress for the occasion—$120 she had spent—and had her hair done and gone over the speech with Bob Shrum. "Coming now to the crescendo," she called her preparation to nominate Ted Kennedy. But then while she was at an event, she got called to the phone, and Ted had to break the news to her that he wouldn't be placed in nomination after all. But he told her that he was going to speak nevertheless, on Tuesday, for his platform planks, and asked if she would introduce him. Mikulski agreed, but she said that she had bought the dress for his nomination, and that "there will be another day for you." So she put it in the closet to await that day and wore another dress. (She would still have that nominating dress, unworn, thirty years later.) And then on Tuesday, she introduced Ted for his remarks on the platform.

Ted would later say that he had wanted to give a "good talk," but that he didn't have "any sense that the speech itself was going to be more than a good speech." Shrum and Carey Parker had written it in the back bedroom of Ted's Waldorf suite over the course of three days before the convention began, both of them writing in longhand, since there wasn't room for a typewriter table in the tight quarters, and Parker editing as they went. Shrum called it the acceptance speech that Ted would never have a chance to give. Ted had another, very specific idea of the speech—an idea that comported with what his entire campaign had been about. He wanted it to be a defense of liberalism at a time when it was under siege. Shrum said he originally stitched it together from other speeches. But when he showed a draft to Ted, Ted told him, "I'm not sure this does it." Shrum was furious. He threw his briefcase to the floor and charged out of the room, until Parker and John Douglas, one of Bobby's Justice aides and an old friend, who had been serving as an interceptor for Shrum, chased after him and told him to come back and apologize, which Shrum did. And then, as Shrum himself would tell it, he started over. It would be Shrum's and Parker's speech, but Ted would recruit many other hands: Douglas, Ted Sorensen, Richard Goodwin, and Arthur Schlesinger, Jr. And there would be a struggle—the same struggle with which he had begun his campaign: whether to be moderate and conciliatory, as one report put it, or strong and liberal. "At one point," Ted recalled of the suggested alterations to the speech, "I thought Shrummie was going to jump out the window."

Each night, when Ted returned to his hotel room, he conferred with his sisters there—all three of them—and they spent those evenings, over the weekend, working on the speech, laying it all out on the floor, while Ted was upstairs, and they would call up, "Look, Teddy, you have this part here." And they would redraft sections and edit and amend. And then they would do it again the following night. "Very good political sense" and "really good editors," he would say of them. And Ted sent a draft to Arthur Schlesinger, Jr., and Schlesinger thought it execrable—"a rambling attack on Reagan," he said, "that begged the question, If Reagan is so bad, why didn't Ted get out of the race earlier?" And Schlesinger began to draft an alternative version, with input from Richard Wade, an urban historian from the City University of New York and a political adviser, and then sent it on to Ted, though Schlesinger said he suspected that Shrum and Parker had intercepted it. Still Schlesinger got his revised draft to Steve Smith, who was no longer on speaking terms with Ted since the campaign had been so badly mismanaged, but Smith and Ted's nephew, Joseph Kennedy II, had both read the Parker-Shrum version and were angry. "If Ted gives that speech, I am not even going to the hall," Joe II said. This must have been Sunday because Schlesinger said that speech was already on the teleprompter by that point, and by that point Ted had made his own contributions—he insisted on Tennyson's *Ulysses* being quoted—and was rehearsing in his suite. Joe II and Steve Smith's reactions notwithstanding—Smith didn't like the speech either—Ted was "jovial" as he ran through the Shrum-Parker draft with all its many emendations, even chuckling over the last lines. He rehearsed it again at Madison Square Garden, twice on Monday and a third time on Tuesday. This would mark the true end of his campaign—his declaration of the political morality for which he had fought so hard.

Then came the night. And then came Mikulski. And then came Ted, who arrived on the podium with "McNamara's Band" playing, and the crowd reluctant to stop its cheers, clapping to the music, waving blue and white placards with KENNEDY written on them, and then breaking into a chant—"We want Ted! We want Ted! We want Ted!"—and only quieting when Ted began to speak over the bedlam. "Well, it worked out a little different than I had thought," he said, smiling. But then, turning solemn, his hair shaggy with gray tufts at his temples, and wearing a dark blue suit and monochromatic tie, he said he had come "not to argue as a candidate, but to affirm a cause," which he defined as the "cause of the common man and the common woman" and the "humble members of society—the farmers, mechanics, and laborers"—and he spoke with "a deep sense of urgency" about the "anguish and anxiety I have seen across America." He called the economic plank of the platform a "moral issue" and asked his party to pledge to help those common men and women in their economic distress. He said, "It is the glory and the greatness of our tradition to speak for those who have no voice, to remember those who are forgotten, to respond to the frustrations and fulfill the aspirations of all Americans seeking a better life in a better land." And he warned: "We dare not forsake that tradition." Then, voicing his deep concern that liberalism might be thrown on the ash heap, he asked that we not let the "great purposes of the Democratic Party become the bygone passages of history." And then he assailed the Republicans who, at their convention, invoked Franklin Roosevelt without also invoking his compassion. And he drew one of his loudest applause lines when he quoted Republican nominee

Ronald Reagan that "fascism was really the basis of the New Deal," and said that Reagan had no right to invoke Roosevelt. And here he loosened up, his grim visage breaking into a smile, and he waved at friends in the audience as the cheers cascaded. He called Republicans' promises a "voyage into the past." His own commitment, he said, was not to "outworn views" but to "old values that will never wear out." "Circumstances may change," he said, "but the work of compassion must continue." "The poor may be out of political fashion," he said, "but they are not without human needs. The middle class may be angry, but they have not lost the dream that all Americans can advance together." And he called for "new hope to an America uncertain about the present, but unsurpassed in its potential for the future." And he enumerated that new hope for Americans who so desperately needed it: for full employment, for reindustrialization of America's inner cities, for workplace safety, for clean air and water, for a stable noninflationary economy, for tax reform. And he decried the proposed Republican tax cut which, he said, would "redistribute income in the wrong direction." And then he called for national health insurance—his signature goal—and flashed his biggest smile. He talked of the differences that Democrats were willing to debate while the Republicans allowed no dissent at their convention, and he enumerated the heritage of his party and its hopes—things of which it could be proud, including the Equal Rights Amendment, which would put women and men on an equal standing, and "for the recognition at long last that our nation was made up of founding mothers as well as founding fathers."

It was the closing, however, that was most striking, most powerful. He invoked the words he had used at the Memphis convention ("often we sailed against the wind, but we kept our rudder true") and recalled his journey in the campaign, the miles he traveled (100,000 of them), the people he met ("What golden friends I had!"), and the memories he collected. And he recalled listening to those people, hearing their stories of struggle and suffering—Kenny DuBois in West Virginia, a glassblower with ten children who had just lost his job after thirty-five years; the grandmother in California who gave up her phone to pay her rent; the unemployed young workers, and the students who couldn't afford college, and the families who couldn't buy a home. He listened. And he said, restating the theme of his entire campaign: "Tonight, in their name, I have come here to speak for them. And for their sake, I ask you to stand with them. On their behalf, I ask you to restate and reaffirm the timeless truth of our party." He said that when the convention was over, when the signs came down and the cheering stopped and the bands no longer played, "May it be said of our campaign that we kept the faith. May it be said of our party in 1980 that we found the faith again." He quoted the lines from Tennyson that he and his brothers so loved—"I am a part of all I have met"—and then he ended his long campaign, the campaign he had begun with such promise and through which he had suffered so much defeat, ended it with words delivered so passionately and with such conviction that his eyes began to mist and he had to choke back the tears: "For me, a few hours ago, this campaign came to an end. For all those whose cares have been our concern, the work goes on, the cause endures, the hope still lives, and the dream shall never die."

And then the crowd exploded. As Joan mounted the podium and planted a kiss on Ted's cheek, the delegates waved their placards, they danced to Chuck Berry's "Johnny B. Goode," they cheered and, some with tears in their eyes not unlike Ted's, they celebrated the principles on which the Democratic Party had thrived and the moral mission the Democratic Party had purveyed at its best—the principles Ted Kennedy had just set forth in the thirty-five minutes he spoke. And the demonstration continued for nearly forty-five minutes afterward—in part for a man but more for his cause, even as the cause was fading.

It was a triumphant moment after a triumphant speech—perhaps the most triumphant speech of Ted Kennedy's career—the point at which he certified who he was politically and what he stood for, and the point at which he justified his campaign. Francis X. Clines in *The New York Times* said that for "Kennedy delegates, the successful speech had a special beauty," and those delegates finally felt that the "last of the Kennedy brothers had delivered a 'Kennedy speech,' well-paced, well-written, with the humor and a sense of history worthy of a candidate still in the fray." Even Arthur Schlesinger, Jr., who had hated the Parker-Shrum draft, was impressed by the presentation and called it an "enormous triumph." Watching it on television, *Washington Post* critic Tom Shales said that "one could suddenly feel the convention turning from a negative spectacle of acrimony and special pleading to a positive and even inspirational event. Kennedy turned its mood and personality from a chorus of 'we wants' to a bracing call to principle." And of the television coverage, Shales wrote, "Faces reflected awe and wonder and tears filled the eyes or dribbled down the cheeks. There was a montage of faces which Norman

Rockwell would have been proud to paint and which made the speech appear to be even more magnificent than it probably was." Ted had a "Sense of the Occasion," Theodore White would later write, "one of those mysterious intuitions that come to a political leader when he knows the moment and the mood will amplify words," and he called the peroration "one of the great convention passages of all time." NBC News anchor David Brinkley called the speech an incomparable moment in all the sixteen conventions he had covered, but he thought it was the context of the speech, all the things Ted had endured to be able to give it, and then, after enduring them, his having lost, that made it so. Ted himself agreed. He said it was less his rhetoric than the conviction that he expressed in the speech, his belief in the mission of the Democratic Party to help those who needed help, at a time when conviction was in such short supply, that gave the speech its unmistakable power. "The words have enormous impact because you've carried those words, and they've had meaning during the course of the campaign," Ted was to say. Those words meant something, they had "resonance," because "you've gone through it." And part of that context, a large part, was not just the campaign but the life of the man who had waged it. The speech had reflected that life: the bumps and bruises, the missteps and transgressions, that would end in absolution. As columnist Mark Shields wrote, "He had salvaged a failed campaign in an hour." And he had salvaged more.

There was still the platform to vote on that night, but the vote would be anticlimactic after Ted's speech. Bill Carrick remembered walking through the Mississippi delegation after the speech and asking Governor William Winter how his delegates would vote on Ted's planks. And he told Carrick, "We're all voting for the Kennedy plank," adding, "Son, that's the best speech I've heard in my life." So effective was the speech that the Carter forces knew instantly that they were not likely to win the platform votes. "We threw in the towel," Pat Caddell said. "We had to. Teddy had won the hearts of the convention with that speech."

But even as they knew they had lost the moral battle, Carter's men had to scramble to head off crushing political defeat on the planks themselves, so that it didn't seem as if the convention had repudiated its own candidate. Shortly after the speech, Robert Keefe, a special assistant to Democratic national chairman John White, ran into Carl Wagner at a hot dog stand and mentioned striking a deal. Keefe connected Wagner to Hamilton Jordan, who was sitting in a trailer in the Garden, and Wagner, who now had the upper hand after the speech, told Jordan he wanted a voice vote on the three planks most important to Ted: his jobs plan, his commitment to place the highest priority on unemployment over budget balancing and inflation, and his wage and price freeze. When Jordan and Keefe relayed that to Robert Strauss, Strauss was adamant that there be a tallied vote on the wage and price freeze, to which Carter was strongly opposed. As the negotiations continued, with the demonstration for Kennedy continuing on the floor, Keefe kept motioning the band to keep playing so as to head off a voice vote. Wagner finally capitulated on the wage and price freeze since Tip O'Neill, who wielded the gavel, was himself opposed and was unlikely to give the ayes the victory. Had a Kennedy supporter called for a point of order, Ted might have gotten his voice vote, but Keefe said facetiously that "we had seven deaf mutes answering the telephones" on the podium. With O'Neill unable to be heard above the din, Ted lost his wage and price freeze but won the other two and won a plank on the Equal Rights Amendment, which Carter opposed as well, though Carter did have enough delegates to vote down a plank on national healthcare. Jody Powell, Carter's press secretary, said it didn't make any difference what Ted had gotten in the platform; when Carter ran against Reagan, he would ignore the platform. Still, Ted aide Rick Stearns crowed, "After the June primaries, we realized the odds were virtually impossible—350 to 1. But in the last four days, we won everything but the nomination."

Ted Kennedy had withdrawn. Ted Kennedy had delivered the speech of his life. Ted Kennedy had won the hearts of the convention's delegates, so much so that there was a sense of remorse hanging over the convention rather than celebration—remorse that they were nominating the wrong man. But Ted Kennedy had not given his full-throated endorsement to Jimmy Carter, only a tepid endorsement expressing his confidence that the party would reunite and win in November. Speculation raged—in the Carter camp, nerves frayed—over whether Ted would, after Carter's acceptance speech, make the customary gesture of defeated candidates on the podium, Ted grasping Carter's hand and the two with hands clasped raising their arms in a show of unity. "We had all this tension going all the way through," Ted would recall, "and I had a very substantial group of supporters who said they would be very offended if, after all of this battle on the platform, if I even went on the stage with Carter." Ted himself was aggrieved as well. He believed that Carter made no effort to heal the deep wounds between them—no effort to coax Ted to the podium. Ted said he was there at the hotel all day Wednesday and all day Thursday, and that Carter could have invited him to visit with the Carters, to bring his family, to thank him for withdrawing. "They could have gotten all the pictures in the world at that place," Ted said. Ted said that would have been the "gracious" thing to do, what he said he would have done if the shoe were on the other foot. But Carter made no such gesture of peace. (The lack of graciousness, Ted said, extended to the nomination roll call rather than ask for acclamation. Since Ted had already conceded, the roll call was unnecessary, but Carter held it anyway, which, according to Ted, "many of my supporters thought was an unfriendly act, to rub it in.") And perhaps for those indignities and others, Shrum said that Ted was hesitant to raise Carter's hand on the podium, that he mulled over whether just to shake hands with Carter, and that he finally surrendered and practiced raising Shrum's hand.

For all his hesitation, though, Ted had agreed to appear on the podium, had agreed even to spend the day at Madison Square Garden before Carter's speech, but Carter and his men didn't want to risk having Ted divert attention from the president. So Ted stayed at the Waldorf, where he was told to wait until Carter finished the acceptance speech because the Carterites were worried cameras would cut away to Ted's departure while Carter was speaking, and then Ted was told to wait until after Mondale's nomination. And then Ted and his group were told to leave during the demonstration after Carter's speech, which was expected to last a while. But the Carter forces had stumbled once again. Carter, by Shrum's account, muffed the speech by referring to the late senator and vice president Hubert Humphrey as "Hubert Horatio Hornblower," the protagonist of the C. S. Forester naval novels, and was so flummoxed by the mistake that he rushed through the rest. (Ted was in the shower at the time.) Then Ted left his hotel on cue, but New York City mayor Ed Koch, an ardent Carter supporter despite his disappointment with Carter's UN vote over Israel, refused to provide a police escort, so Ted's limousine crawled through the traffic to the Garden—a forty-minute crawl. And then the demonstration that was supposed to last at least long enough for Ted to get to the Garden was much shorter than expected. Shrum and Kirk rode with Ted to the hall, and Ted was glum, irritable, more irritable when he heard a radio reporter scolding him for keeping Carter waiting and accusing him of being angry. "It was just, 'Let's get this thing over with,'" Kirk said. As Carter awaited Ted's arrival, Robert Strauss stalled by introducing a host of dignitaries and then lesser pols—a long, long list of them—sending Carter roaming across the stage, looking for hands to shake and backs to pat, trying to keep himself busy, then standing at the podium smiling as if he had no idea what to do with himself as the energy gradually dissipated from the hall. Even the balloons atop the Garden failed to fall on cue. "It's almost as if they are waiting for the nominee of the party to arrive," Ted Koppel of ABC News told viewers. "But, of course, they're waiting for the challenger, the loser!" And when Ted finally arrived with his Secret Service detail, twenty minutes after Carter had finished his speech, instead of his being escorted to the holding room, he was immediately hustled up to the podium, while Carter's handlers were yelling, "Come on up! You've got to run up! Everybody's worrying, wondering, 'Where the hell have you been?'" because they wanted their photo opportunity with Ted and Carter. By the time Ted reached the podium, it was jammed with people milling about. "You look at the picture of the podium," Ted would say, "there are thirty people there, and not just me and him." As the crowd chanted his name, Ted wandered the stage, he said looking for Carter in the mass— observers said instead that he "seemed to go to conspicuous lengths" to avoid meeting Carter—while Carter trailed after him like a puppy, until Rosalynn pulled Ted over, forming a line with Carter, Mondale, and Robert Strauss. "He's not going to do it," Kirk thought, watching Ted approach Carter. A "slow-motion political train wreck played out in front of tens of millions of viewers on television," Shrum said. "It looked like hell," a reporter told Strauss later. "It looked worse than hell," Strauss snapped. When Ted and Carter finally found each other in that line, Ted shook the president's hand perfunctorily but didn't raise it in a victory salute, his practice of the unity gesture notwithstanding. Carter would say that he suspected Ted had been drinking—"Everybody knew it"—which accounted for Ted's wandering aimlessly through the throng, though there is no evidence of that and though Ted wasn't aimless even when he had been drinking. Kirk believed that Ted just couldn't bring himself to raise Carter's hand, bearing "resentment" toward him, because "while he didn't have to be true to the Kennedy ideals, [he] wasn't even close to their spirit." Finally, Ted waved to the throng and quickly left "as if he had appeared at the wedding of his chauffeur," Theodore White would write.

There would be no unity. The wounds would remain unhealed as Carter limped into battle against Ronald Reagan.

For a campaign that had failed either to bring victory or to fulfill its political mission of liberalizing the Democratic Party, Ted Kennedy's ill-fated adventure nevertheless changed something in American politics. Its failure spoke to failings within the candidate himself, especially his perceived character flaws and his ineptitude, and to the bad luck of the Iranian hostage taking and the Soviet invasion of Afghanistan, which would now turn into Jimmy Carter's bad luck. As Drummond Ayres wrote of Ted, "Seldom in modern history has any candidate fallen so far or so fast." But its failure also spoke to something larger—to the end of an era in American politics, actually two eras. One was the Kennedy era. As Joseph Kraft observed, "The fact is that the Kennedy mystique represents a waning force. The young have no memory of Jack Kennedy and only the dimmest recollection of Bob. The hope they expressed vanished over the horizon of time. Their battle cries evoke less and less response." Ted had long drawn on those associations with his brothers; he had, in some people's eyes, based his entire political career on them. But these were now attenuated associations on which to draw, which, as Kraft also observed, represented a hole in American life that the Kennedys had once filled: a "reserve asset, a sign of resiliency, an augury of hope in a time of despair." And he saw this: "That hope now fades, along with many other blessings that made America what it was, and is ceasing to be." Though Ted briefly stirred those passions again in his convention speech, he failed to rouse them in the American people. Hope had faded, and Ted Kennedy symbolized it. The Kennedys were over.

The other era that ended with the campaign was the era of liberalism. "A big reason Senator Kennedy did not win," editorialized *The New York Times* after Ted's withdrawal, "is that many people feared his answers to social problems are too liberal, by which they mean, obsolete or too expensive or both." And the *Times* added, "One can regret the turn to conservatism in America; one can rail against it; one can work to reverse it. But through much of his campaign, the Senator pressed on as though it didn't exist." Obviously, this was because Ted Kennedy didn't want it to exist—because he held fast to the idea of a compassionate, big-hearted America, which was the America of his brothers. A Gallup poll on the eve of the campaign had found self-described conservatives outnumbered self-described liberals by twenty points, that 80 percent of the public thought the government wasted a great deal of money (up from 48 percent in 1964), and 70 percent thought taxes were too high (up from 47 percent in 1962). Ted could chide Jimmy Carter for talking about taxes and deficits and balanced budgets and forswearing social programs. He could call Carter out for his seeming lack of compassion. But it was the American people who had, at least by some polling, focused on lower taxes and forsworn social programs. It was the American people who had, after years of Republican hectoring, come to disdain liberalism, according to the prevailing narrative. Even Rick Stearns, one of Ted's campaign aides, had warned that Ted had to "become a leader in adapting the old notions of liberalism to a new time." He had made an effort to do so. And yet a close observer of the campaign would discover what nearly all the pundits had missed while being swept up in the conservative hyperbole. As one historian would later conclude, Ted had "not only revived the New Deal coalition, but also expanded it to include urban and suburban conservatives," and that he had drawn "divergent voting blocs"—not just liberals and minorities but those blue-collar white people who were angry at the decline in their living standard. Ted had been steadily gaining strength throughout the campaign, peaking at the convention. Had he won, he might have turned the narrative. But he lost, and his loss only confirmed the narrative. Liberalism was a spent force.

Because liberalism had been the ideology of hope, the way for government to serve the nation's citizens in need, its apparent demise signaled a larger malaise—the word often attributed to Jimmy Carter's July 1979 speech about the nation's dispirited condition. As America headed into the election, its mood was sour. The country seemed exhausted, spent. When Jimmy Carter ran for the presidency in 1976, shortly after the debacle in Vietnam and the Watergate scandals and the continuing faltering economy, the self-described "gonzo" journalist, Hunter S. Thompson, who had contempt for most politicians, saw in him the "promise, above all else, [of] a return to normalcy, a resurrection of the national self-esteem," and wrote gushingly that the "White House will be so overflowing with honesty, decency, justice, love and compassion that it might even glow in the dark." And Thompson described why Americans felt the need for resurrection, which basically came down to the missteps of the liberalism that had held out its own promises, only to break them:

"The underdogs of yesteryear have had their day, and they blew it. The reformers and radicals of the Sixties promised peace, but they turned out to be nothing but incompetent trouble-makers. Their plans that had looked so fine on paper led to chaos and disaster when hack politicians tried to implement them. The promise of Civil Rights turned into the nightmare of busing. The call for law and order led straight [to] Watergate. And the long struggle between the Hawks and the Doves caused violence in the streets and a military disaster in Vietnam. Nobody won, in the end, and when the dust finally settled, 'extremists' at both ends of the political spectrum were thoroughly discredited. And by the time the presidential campaign got under way, the high ground was all in the middle of the road."

In 1976 the middle was Jimmy Carter. But as it turned out, the middle didn't hold either. Carter did not restore normalcy or national self-esteem. He couldn't, given how much was collapsing around him, much if not most of it not of his own doing. Instead, Americans seemed to feel the nation spinning aimlessly, which *was* in large measure Carter's doing. He hadn't provided guidance or inspiration of the sort the nation so desperately needed. And though Carter, as Thompson observed, was no conventional liberal, which was after all, the reason for Ted Kennedy's presidential run, he was nevertheless, as a Democrat, identified with the failure of liberalism to provide direction—an identification that was probably far more responsible for liberalism's precipitous decline in the mid-1970s than Ted Kennedy's big government proposals.

A miasma. That was how Vice President Walter Mondale described the nation to Theodore White shortly after Ted Kennedy declared for the presidency in November 1979. "There's been this whole sea change of issues," Mondale told White. "In the early sixties you had a stable dollar, increasing employment. You could stimulate the economy, reduce taxes, the pie grew. . . . For twenty years there'd been this pent-up frustration to do something—for the Black people, for education, for the environment, for legal services. We passed the whole thing in the Eighty-Ninth Congress." And that was a result of liberalism. But Mondale, like Thompson, said that trouble followed—disappointments. There were "serious problems implementing them. There's waste. There's intrusion on private lives.

There's unanticipated costs." And to that was added inflation and the energy problem and the growth of the Soviet threat, which necessitated more money being spent on American defense. And then "to get a tight budget, you've got to cut all the programs we Democrats supported. The choices are just awful." And this was before the Iranian hostage situation.

America in 1980 was a country in a state of confusion as well as exhaustion and aimlessness: from Vietnam, from Watergate, from racial tensions and racial violence, from an unsteady economy (the so-called "misery index," the sum of unemployment and inflation, was above 20 percent throughout 1980), from stagnating wages after the wild growth in wages after World War II, from the energy crisis, and from rising crime rates (21,460 homicides nationally in 1979). The general tenor was that something was amiss, which had been the impulse for Carter's speech about America's spiritual destitution; in a survey taken a month before the election, when asked how they felt things were going in the country, 68 percent of the respondents answered "badly"—43 percent of them "pretty badly," 25 percent "very badly." And yet the nature of the dissatisfaction was almost existential, since in the same survey, 72 percent of respondents said that that state of the economy, which had been Jimmy Carter's biggest bugaboo, was actually "normal" or "good"—a surprising result given the "misery index." No one seemed to know how to solve whatever was ailing the nation, and no one, not even Carter, seemed to have faith that government could do so—a faith that was one of the very bases of modern liberalism. By another survey, people's trust in government, which had held steady in the mid-seventieth percentile throughout the Eisenhower, Kennedy, and Johnson administrations, had declined through Nixon's, Ford's, and Carter's, taking its sharpest dive in the last of these to less than 25 percent. As two veteran journalists, Jack Germond and Jules Witcover, who were covering the campaign, concluded, "If there was a single strain running through a variety of groups, it was the conviction that government in general, and the federal government in particular, was not doing anything to make people's lives better, despite the higher taxes most were paying," which struck at the very heart of liberalism.

And Ronald Reagan, who had spent his political career sowing distrust against the government, who had spent that career declaring that the federal government was actually averse to the interests of ordinary Americans and that those Americans would be better off if the government shrank into oblivion, was now poised to harvest what he had sown.

In this environment, Ted Kennedy was out of phase, as *The New York Times* had suggested after his defeat. He had waged his campaign promoting government as an engine for good and appealing to his fellow citizens' better angels, as he always had. But these were now hard sells. Americans were in no mood for government activism if they felt it primarily benefited Black Americans, which was how many white Americans had come to view the Great Society. And they were in no mood for moral exhortations of the sort that Ted Kennedy had routinely delivered to help the vulnerable. What Ronald Reagan was promoting, what Americans seemed to desire, was not compassion but a kind of moral retrenchment—an emphasis not on how one could serve one's fellow citizens but on how one could burnish one's own moral credentials: a "community of values," as Reagan called them, rather than a community of citizens. In fairness, Jimmy Carter did much the same thing.

And yet despite the cynicism engulfing the country, despite even his own loss, despite what seemed the certain impending victory of Ronald Reagan, Ted Kennedy was not despairing in the aftermath of his failed effort. By the end, Ted's campaign had gone through four stages: the fumbling beginning, in which he wrecked his chances almost before he announced; the post-Georgetown period, in which he stressed policy and liberal tradition and seemed to gain traction; the humiliating post-Illinois period, in which he almost seemed to luxuriate in his failure and in the irony of the campaign process and became loose and funny and philosophical; and the home stretch, in which he turned softer and more sober and seemed to win advocates through the sheer fortitude he displayed. In the end, a reporter noted at a session with the press at his McLean home, he and Joan "did not look or sound like people devastated by defeat." He "wolfed down" pastries. He replayed his campaign gaffes. He poked fun at himself. And he said that he could accept defeat because he had seen so many people who had been devastated by economic misfortune that the issues "took on a life of their own, expressed in human terms that I found very moving, very motivating." And he said he found that while defeat is not "pleasant," the "forces that have motivated me are much more significant than any particular outcome on a primary day." He said that he had learned "how to lose." But when asked if his father would have agreed that issues were more important than winning, he glanced at the ceiling, gave a "rueful" smile, and said, "If I told my father that . . . my father—I better not get into that."

He had learned how to lose, he said, and he almost seemed relieved by it. And Bill Moyers in an interview with him posited that voters might have felt they had to visit loss upon him, punish him for his "sins" and make him atone before they could make him president. Now they had. But in spite of the punishment, or because of it, Ted had emerged a "more contented man" at the end of the campaign than he had been at the beginning, as Drummond Ayres, who had covered him throughout, saw it. He was now the "undisputed leader of the party's liberal wing," if that leadership had ever been disputed, and he had succeeded by the end in turning his campaign into the crusade he had sought. There were those who felt the loss was preordained, that he didn't have the temperament to be president, that he was born to be a senator. Congressman Bill Delahunt would later toast him at a birthday celebration, saying that the "best thing that ever happened to the United States of America is that you lost in 1980." Steve Smith admitted to Arthur Schlesinger, Jr., a major admission, that he "does not understand Ted Kennedy," apparently not the way he understood his other brothers-in-law, Jack and Bobby, "that he does not think he will ever become President, that he had no sense of the way his staff used and abused him, but that his own political instincts none the less brought him to a kind of triumph in the end." And he thought, no doubt fastening on Ted's dream of winning, "Ted lacks the sense of political reality that his brothers had." Columnist Joseph Kraft came to the same conclusion about Ted's presidential prospects. "There is something deeply senatorial about Edward Kennedy," he wrote. "In mind, as in looks, he lacks tautness"—presumably the kind of tautness that Jack and Bobby had. But it was never tautness that Ted was promoting, nor was it political reality, though he had a dose of it. Those were the attributes of a pol. He was promoting his conviction, his compassion, his fortitude, and his endurance, which were the attributes of a moral leader, which was what he seemed to aspire to be. After the convention speech, Ted Sorensen, Jack Kennedy's aide-de-camp and speechwriter, wrote Ted to tell him that his campaign had been a "great personal victory—which overcame the doubters and nay-sayers who underestimated your ability to defy your detractors, adhere to your principles, and to accept defeat with grace instead of bitterness. . . . You emerged a winner . . . the conscience of the party, the hope of the nation." He had atoned.

IV

Jimmy Carter entered the general election campaign feeling that Ted Kennedy had inflicted serious damage on him, even though Hamilton Jordan's top assistant, Tom Donilon, had told Bob Shrum that Ted's challenge would "redeem the President's apparent weakness and strengthen him for the general election." For all the turmoil over the rules fight and the platform and the sense of Ted's moral victory, Carter did receive a substantial postconvention bump, actually a miraculous bump, and trailed Reagan by only a single percentage point in Gallup's first poll after New York: 39 to 38 percent with independent John Anderson getting 14 percent, which was up from Carter's preconvention deficit of fourteen points to Reagan. Robert Strauss, Carter's campaign chair, had predicted the polls would tighten, and he was right. "The President has serious political problems," Strauss admitted. "We all know that. But the President's problems are less serious than those of Ronald Reagan."

On the political front, one of Carter's biggest problems was unifying the party, which meant bringing Ted aboard and appeasing the liberals. It would have been difficult even if Carter hadn't treated the liberals so disdainfully, but he had. As E. J. Dionne, Jr., would later write, "Carter demonstrated that the politics of middle-class reform and the politics of New Dealism could run headlong into one another," and when it came to the old Democratic coalition, Carter "provided a model for how to alienate all its various wings simultaneously." Of course, this was especially true of Carter's relationship to Ted Kennedy. In June, after the primary season ended, Jordan had drafted a memo to Carter that listed the ways Ted had hurt him: He had made Carter seem political rather than presidential; he had alienated key Democratic constituencies from Carter; he had divided state parties that would have helped Carter if united. Carter had made few overtures to Ted before the convention or during it. He had felt too offended by Ted to do so. Now he had no choice. By one poll, 34 percent of Ted's primary voters so disliked Carter that they intended to vote for John Anderson, and 22 percent for Reagan. Carter needed those voters. Ted told the reporters at McLean in his postconvention interview that he intended to campaign for Carter, but he had added a proviso: "What I really do is going to depend on how much he encourages me to talk about the things I really believe in, and to show that he believes in them too," which was putting a significant onus on Carter. After the convention, Ted and Carter spoke by phone and agreed on a joint campaign appearance in Boston, and the two met in person at the White House on August 25, when Ted joined a congressional delegation, and the two exchanged pleasantries, including, Carter would write, the "need to be friends in the future." And Carter proposed a "modest," by his own estimate, jobs program and a rejection of any tax cut on the basis that "these stances might enable Kennedy and some of his supporters to accept my candidacy with more enthusiasm." But when Jordan met with Steve Smith at Ted's Senate office to discuss the details of Ted's contributions, Smith added another condition: that Carter help retire Ted's $1.7 million campaign debt. Jordan said he considered this "blackmail," but he had no choice but to agree, though as late as September, the Carter forces were attempting a quid pro quo in which Ted would enlist several of his prominent supporters—Rabbi Andrew Schindler of the Union of American Hebrew Congregations, Governor Joe Brennan of Maine, Raymond Harding of New York's Liberal Party—to help the Carter-Mondale effort, and for Ted to call for a Reagan-Carter debate without the participation of John Anderson, which Ted refused to do.

And as Carter and Reagan headed into the fall, it was neither a happy election campaign nor a spirited one. Seldom, if ever, had two more disliked candidates run for the presidency. Carter, as Strauss had noted, was beset by myriad problems from Iran to Afghanistan and the grain embargo and Olympic boycott that Carter had implemented in reaction to the Soviet invasion, to the energy crisis to the federal budget restraints to inflation and unemployment that had sent the economy into free fall, even to the eruption of the volcano Mount St. Helens in Washington state. Reagan, who had made an attempt, not unlike Ted's, to unseat a sitting president in 1976, for reasons, not unlike Ted's, to invigorate the party ideologically, had fought through the primaries over relative moderates and had emerged as the champion of the right-wing forces that had been trying to seize the party, and the country, at least since Barry Goldwater's nomination in 1964. Reagan had succeeded, and his party, unlike Carter's, was united. But Reagan had problems of his own, many of them emanating from his own policy prescriptions, including the privatization of Social Security, his doubts about air pollution, his opposition to unemployment insurance, which he called "vacation money for the lazy," and to health insurance subsidies much less a government healthcare program, and perhaps above all, his military aggressiveness, which prompted concerns about whether he was thirsting for war. And though the political narrative was that the country had turned sharply rightward, Reagan got support arguably in spite of his positions rather than because of them. *Too extreme* was the general consensus. Or as columnist George Will would later put it, "Americans are conservatives. What they want to conserve is the New Deal," without, Will might have added, expanding it.

One thing about Ronald Reagan, however, was not in dispute. Tall, tanned, handsome in a leathery, masculine way, gregarious, and self-deprecating, as Ted Kennedy was, Ronald Reagan radiated geniality as he had originally in "A Time for Choosing." He was not an easy target, especially not for Jimmy Carter, whose personal deficits were considerable in contrast to Reagan's. "There is no fun in Jimmy Carter," the *Times*'s Anthony Lewis would write during the campaign. "He has uplifted practically no one," neither charge of which could have been leveled at Reagan, who was both fun and, at least to his followers, inspiring. Carter had two lines of attack against his opponent. One was that Reagan was a trigger-happy warmonger, whose solutions to problems were military instead of diplomatic—basically the same line of attack that Lyndon Johnson had used against Barry Goldwater to such stunning effect in 1964. The second was that, as a former movie star, he lived within the nimbus of his dreams, which was not entirely false; Reagan often recited episodes as real when they were actually scenes from movies. Reagan's was a "world of tinsel and make-believe," Jimmy Carter had declared, in which "all problems have simple solutions. Simple—and wrong." But Carter had chosen the wrong points of attack himself. Reagan might have sounded like a saber-rattler, he might have believed fervently in American posturing, but unlike Barry Goldwater of the eternally grim visage, he had that geniality, that "aw shucks" way of cocking his head and giving a little grin that dispelled a sense of bellicosity. And while Reagan certainly presented simplistic answers to complicated problems, as Carter charged—government was, he thought, the source of so many of America's problems and limits on government were, he thought, the all-purpose cure—simplicity was hardly a detriment to him when Americans were searching for someone to provide simple solutions that Carter had not provided. Indeed, Ronald Reagan's great achievement might have been suggesting that America was a movie and that it would end happily, as movies typically did.

Still, it was a hard-fought campaign precisely because neither man had captured the public imagination, and neither was able to deliver a knockout punch or a dramatic moment. When either of them had soared in the polls, it was because the other had dipped. Carter refused to debate Reagan if John Anderson was included, and Reagan, believing, as Carter evidently did, that Anderson would still draw votes from Carter, insisted that he be, so that when the first debate was held on September 21, Carter was absent. But when the press complained that Carter in absentia was the loser of the debate, he conceded, against the wishes of Pat Caddell, to square off against Reagan, in part because Anderson's polling numbers had fallen below the threshold for inclusion. Caddell felt that Carter could only enhance Reagan's stature, and when the two met in Cleveland on October 28, a week before the election, Caddell proved right. Reagan came off as self-possessed, calm, self-deprecating, and—genial. When he closed by asking, "Are you better off than you were four years ago?" he posed the critical question for Carter's reelection, even though things had not been so good in 1976 either. But the Republican had turned the tables on the Democrat. As one analyst later observed of Reagan's ploy, "It has never before happened in modern times that the Republicans have been able to take the offensive on bread-and-butter economic issues," largely because the economy usually fared better under Democrats, despite Republicans' insistence that it hadn't. Now Reagan took that offensive. "He just got killed" was how Ted assessed Carter's debate performance to Shrum.

Economics, especially as they concerned poor Americans, had been Ted's territory. And as much as he might have resented Carter, he resented Reagan even more for seeming to disregard those Americans, for not wanting to relieve their distress, for refusing to think of government as an instrument of empowerment for them. So Ted did not sit out the campaign. Whether it was simply, as some speculated, Ted's way of fulfilling his end of the campaign debt bargain, he spoke on the president's behalf in New York in early October, appeared with him later that month in Boston, New Jersey, and Washington, D.C., and alone in Detroit, Wisconsin, and Texas. He taped commercials for Carter, produced by his own media adviser, David Sawyer, that were meant to appeal to Black people and Hispanics, and he held open the last week before the election, so that Carter could direct him where he was most needed. The one thing, however, he would not do was attack John Anderson.

But as the campaign moved into its final days, neither Ted Kennedy nor any Democrat could lure those aggrieved working-class white people into Carter's column. It was a close election heading into the last weekend, with Reagan having squandered his sizable lead by continuing to invite questions about his extremism. Carter astonishingly had regained what he had lost before his convention; the Gallup poll had Carter with an eight-point lead among registered voters and a three-point lead among likely voters. Other polls had the race a dead heat, as did Pat Caddell's own private polling. But as Reagan made his final campaign swing through the Midwest—Pennsylvania, Wisconsin, Michigan, and Ohio—his staff, who had grown edgy in those last weeks, finally relaxed. Their polling showed what the other polls did not: that Reagan was suddenly gaining. In the last thirty-six hours, Carter observed the same trend. He tried to remind voters that "our party had always represented the middle-class and working people of America," but those words rang hollow given Carter's lack of zeal in helping them. The public polls proved to be wrong. On election day, November 4, the first anniversary of the seizure of the American hostages in Iran, Reagan won a shocking victory, a landslide victory, 51 to 41 percent (John Anderson got 6.6 percent), and an even greater victory in the Electoral College, ten to one, where he carried forty-four states. It was an election in which the public hadn't seemed to want either candidate to win. But the man whom Mark Shields had called the "remainderman" did not get the remainder this time. Ronald Reagan, who had convinced enough voters that he was amiable and unthreatening enough, did.

Jimmy Carter would chalk up his defeat to the failure of the press to focus on substance and "to concentrate almost exclusively on who might debate whom, Reagan's 'blunders' and my 'meanness to my opponent.' " But the coverage in 1980 was no different than election coverage had ever been; issues always were obscured by drama. And he would blame Ted Kennedy for fracturing the party and wasting Carter's time with his convention tactics. As Larry Horowitz stated it, "Carter thinks he [Ted] elected Reagan. And Kennedy thinks he [Carter] turned the tide against the Democratic Party." ("Quite bitter" was how Theodore White described Carter's attitude toward Ted when he interviewed him six months after the election.) But if Ted Kennedy had cost Carter the election, the effects would have been apparent long before the final weekend of the campaign when Carter was still, by most polling, slightly ahead. Even as the pollsters were scratching their heads over how they had missed the result so badly, they came to a different conclusion than Carter's. Carter was the known quantity, Reagan the unknown one. Carter, as his low approval ratings illustrated, had botched the job. Reagan, as the trepidations about him illustrated, did not speak to the nation's distress. "If the election was in some important sense between anger at Jimmy Carter and fear of the great unknown which Ronald Reagan evoked, anger eventually won," wrote the political scientist Walter Dean Burnham. Clearly, many voters made up their minds on that last weekend, and "almost all of the undecideds moved to Reagan," Caddell told Carter—to Reagan, the unknown quantity, which meant that it wasn't so much that Reagan won as that Carter lost. (As evidence of the voters' disenchantment with their choices, participation in 1980 was the third lowest since the national party system first emerged in 1824.) Or as another political scientist, Leo Ribuffo, would put it, "Carter, the preeminent symbol of the crisis of confidence he had diagnosed, became its foremost victim."

A "wave election" historians would later call it, a conservative triumph, the way Franklin Roosevelt's landslide election in 1932 had created a Democratic wave that shifted the nation's political tectonic plates to the left. Even Ted would draw that conclusion. "He was more than a candidate at that time; he was a movement," Ted would say of Reagan. But it wasn't that simple. Nineteen-eighty was a wave only in retrospect. By one account, 38 percent of Reagan's voters said they chose him because they wanted a change; only 11 percent because he was conservative. He actually ran behind Gerald Ford's numbers in 1976 among Republicans and white-collar workers. And while there were definitely Democratic defections—Reagan took 28 percent of self-described Democrats, a very large percentage, and 8.5 percent more blue-collar workers than Ford had won in 1976, and 11 percent more Catholics, and even 19 percent more of those voters who considered unemployment a more serious problem than inflation, which was usually a Democratic constituency—these did not necessarily constitute a wholesale transformation in either party or ideology. One reason Carter lost was not that he was too liberal but that, as Ted Kennedy had argued all along, he might not have been liberal enough. He got fewer votes among liberals than he had in 1976—16 percent fewer liberal votes, the vast bulk of which went to John Anderson, whose main recommendation wasn't so much his politics (though many saw him as more liberal than Carter) as the fact that he wasn't Reagan or Carter, both of whom had earned the wrath of liberals. Examining that polling data, historian Timothy Stanley, who wrote a book on the 1980 contest between Carter and Kennedy, came to the conclusion that Ted Kennedy might actually have won the election against Reagan, his liberalism notwithstanding, or rather because of his liberalism: "The liberal bogeyman of U.S. politics, Edward Kennedy, was in fact quantifiably more popular than both Jimmy Carter and Ronald Reagan in 1980. . . . [Polls confirmed] that Edward Kennedy was denied the nomination by a series of historical accidents, and if these had not taken place, then it is conceivable that he could have defeated Jimmy Carter in the primaries and fought Ronald Reagan in the fall. Had he done so, it would have been on a platform that was supported by much of the American public—a platform of universal health care, massive federal job programs, and price/wage controls."

This was a charitable view of Ted's chances, given the bumpiness of his campaign, the stigma of Chappaquiddick, the animus he aroused in the press, the primary schedule that heavily favored Carter, the government largesse that Carter distributed to keep Democrats in line, and those historical "accidents," which are the sorts of things that can happen at any time in any campaign season, not to mention that however voters might have felt about healthcare or jobs programs or wage and price controls, there was undeniably that cultural tide that lifted conservativism, and there was the ugly reactionary populism that racial tensions had fueled. (Another statistic: Reagan beat Carter among white voters, 56 to 35 percent, while Carter won 90 percent of Black voters.) If there was a liberal undercurrent, it was a quiet one. Still, there was less anathema between Reagan and Kennedy voters than one might have thought. In fact, nearly one-third of those who voted for Ted in the primaries voted for Reagan in the general election, and one-half of blue-collar workers who voted for Ted voted for Reagan. In short, Stanley, at least, thought the pundits had gotten it wrong when they assumed Ted, for all his good intentions, was an anachronism.

Nor, by this view, would it have been just a matter of policy that made Ted Kennedy a viable candidate. Two years before Ted decided to challenge Carter, George Will attempted to understand why Ted seemed to retain his appeal in what was generally regarded as a conservative environment. He decided that it derived "less from what he is than from what he intimates. He is an intimation of political electricity, and the strength of his appeal in the summer of Proposition 13"—the California ballot initiative that slashed property taxes in what amounted to an anti-government revolt—"suggests a flaw in today's conservatism. Such conservatism neglects the craving for ennobling passions and enlarging public enterprises, a craving that great conservative statemen such as Disraeli and Bismarck and Churchill understood because they shared it. Kennedy, the legatee of the liberal party's tradition, is ascendant even in a conservative season because he is a thread of scarlet in an otherwise faded fabric of public life." By this reasoning, it wasn't ideology that Americans desired; it was inspiration, and not just inspiration, but passion, which certainly seemed a plausible conclusion as Ted Kennedy finally found his rhythm near his campaign's end and stirred the soul of his party if not of the entire country. Carter uplifted practically no one, Anthony Lewis had said, but Ted Kennedy did. And Will's analysis led to the same conclusion as Stanley's: that liberalism might have been pronounced dead by people who had a stake in its death, while it was still drawing breath. "What happened in 1980 was not an ideological tidal wave," Hamilton Jordan would say. "It was an expression of frustration with the Democratic Party and doubt that it could provide solutions to America's problems," which made it more about competence than about conservatism. The conservatism would actually come later. For now, people just wanted a vision—almost any vision, so long as it was clear. "One thing that is not working for Democrats is some basic, simple set of ideas of what this election is all about," pollster Peter Hart told the Democratic House and Senate campaign committees in March 1980. Reagan, for all the doubts about him, provided a vision. Carter hadn't.

When his fellow politicians had first courted Ted about running, they had done so not because Ted purveyed those ennobling passions or because Carter had betrayed liberalism but, more prosaically, because they feared Carter would take down the entire party. And now he had.* For the first time in twenty-six years—since 1954—the Democrats did not control

---

* A soloist to the very end, Carter, against the advice of his own staff, conceded the election to Reagan an hour before the polls closed on the West Coast, very likely costing his party, Tip O'Neill believed, several House seats, as those Western Democrats no longer saw a reason to vote. Jack Germond and Jules Witcover, *Blue Smoke and Mirrors: How Reagan Won and Why Carter Lost the 1980 Election* (New York: Viking Press, 1981), 314.

the Senate. But it wasn't just party control; it was liberal control. The Senate elected in 1958—the Senate in which the Democrats had gained twelve seats for an eleven-seat majority, the Senate that introduced the class of Phil Hart and Robert Byrd and Ed Muskie and Eugene McCarthy—had ushered in a long period of liberal hegemony. And that Senate was only strengthened by the LBJ landslide class of 1964 and by the post-Watergate class of 1974. Reagan had won only a bare majority of the vote, but the Democrats lost twelve Senate seats—the largest Senate swing since 1958—including those of the distinguished liberals Frank Church, George McGovern, Warren Magnuson, Gaylord Nelson, Birch Bayh, who had saved Ted's life, and John Culver, Ted's college friend, which might have spoken as much to Americans' wanting to throw out incumbents for their fecklessness as Americans' wanting to throw out liberals. Ted tried to mitigate the damage, telling Garry Wills that each of the twelve losers had been defeated by less than 4 percent of the vote. But the closeness of the races provided no mitigation and no solace. "It is almost not too much to say that an entire generation of older Democratic Senate liberals perished in the electoral earthquake of 1980," Walter Dean Burnham would write. Ted's fellow senator from Massachusetts, Paul Tsongas, put it both more simply and more devastatingly for the Democrats: "The New Deal died." And, he might have said, so did the liberals' expansive sense of public morality. In its place would arise the pinched Reagan morality of self-interest.

Ted Kennedy had prophesied all of this. It was why he had run in the first place. It was why he had kept running even when his money ran out and his chance to win had been extinguished and his closest advisers and friends urged him to quit. It was why he allowed himself to be humiliated again and again and again and to see the Kennedy brand tarnished. It was because he felt that everything was at stake, not for himself personally, whatever Jimmy Carter and his staff might have thought—Carter's press secretary Jody Powell had ascribed Ted's run to an "almost child-like self-centeredness"—but for the country. What was at stake, as far as Ted Kennedy was concerned, was its moral fiber.

And now, as the New Deal died, the era of Ronald Reagan was born; and even if the tectonic plates had not shifted before November 4, 1980, they would, as Ted Kennedy had feared, surely shift after.

NINE

Life After Disaster

I S T H E R E L I F E After Disaster?" *Time* magazine asked after Ronald Reagan's November landslide victory, speaking not of the country but of the Democratic Party. In the essay, Lance Morrow wrote that had Carter won, "Democrats might have been able to slide along in the self-delusion that their party remained, after all, the voice of the American majority, still something like the fractiously diverse pluralistic parade that Roosevelt organized. Now Democrats will have to face the truth: their party has been rusting and clunking along for years on only two or three cylinders. Unless they recover their partisan energies and intellectual vigor, the Democrats could enter a long historical passage of declining influence and relevance, becoming the political equivalent of some of the decaying cities of the Northeast, once flourishingly productive, the exuberant places where the modern Democratic Party originated." Ronald Reagan might not have captured the hearts and minds of the American people. He might not have converted the public into the antistatist, right-wing extremists of the sort who had championed Barry Goldwater. But the country that emerged from the election was different from the country it had been before the election. Ronald Reagan had changed the national conversation. He had seemed to make the Democrats irrelevant.

But if Ronald Reagan's election created a political shock wave, his victory was not so much the beginning of a new movement, as so many historians and journalists would later conclude, as it was the culmination of a movement that had been a long time aborning, at least since Richard Nixon's election in 1968. One of the movement's origins, ironically, derived not from the failures of liberalism but from its successes. As historian Eric Goldman put it, "New Dealism . . . found that it created a nation of the middle class." Modern liberalism, New Deal liberalism, was designed for the poor, the struggling, the marginalized, and it became the prevailing ideology in the 1930s because most Americans then were poor, struggling, and marginalized. But those who had benefited from the meliorations of the New Deal had, in the postwar period, found that their financial status had risen. When, during his 1968 presidential campaign, Hubert Humphrey, the most ardent of liberals, would be asked, "What happened to the wonderful liberal agenda you used to stand for?" he snapped, "I tell them, 'We passed it!' " (This was Mondale's remark to Theodore White too, only with the amendation that with success had also come problems.) Humphrey's answer wasn't entirely true. Ted Kennedy's Senate career testified to the fact that there was a lot more left to pass. But Humphrey wasn't entirely wrong either. Americans, even working-class Americans, saw less need for those government interventions, or at least new interventions, now that they had seemingly entered the middle class. And once the majority of white Americans felt they no longer needed government assistance—at least the most overt assistance, since there were many forms of more covert assistance, like the mortgage interest deduction, that Americans would have howled over losing—they began to complain about higher taxes and government waste and programs from which they felt they received no benefit. In effect, they believed they had outlasted liberalism. Indeed, by the 1980s, one might have asked not why liberalism was waning but why it had endured as long as it did when Americans weren't as consciously beholden to its ministrations as they once were.

Long before Ronald Reagan, Richard Nixon recognized this incipient working-class and middle-class dissatisfaction and provoked it. "Everybody talks about the Reagan Democrats who helped put the Republican Party over the top," Republican strategist Roger Stone told *The New Yorker*, "but they were really the Nixon Democrats. The exodus of working-class people from the Democratic Party was started by Nixon. The realignment was delayed by Watergate, but it was really Nixon who figured out how to win." "The predicate to the conservative revolution" was what pollster Stanley Greenberg would call Richard Nixon, in the same vein as Stone, though Greenberg added of Nixon, "he was not part of it. He fanned the flames, kept the country focused on disorder and race, and put forward a Republican face that was welcoming to the disaffected Catholics, blue-collar workers, and white Baptists of the Southern countryside," even as,

in terms of policy if not rhetoric, Nixon, as Greenberg noted, "helped legitimate the expansive, liberal state, from social spending to regulation."

Part of Nixon's success in getting those blue-collar Democrats to defect
to the Republican Party, Stone said, was that Nixon understood something that Democrats, who had continued Roosevelt's attack on "economic royalists," didn't: "The point that the Democrats missed was that
people who weren't rich wanted to be rich." Ronald Reagan would understand that too, and both Nixon and Reagan made the promise that if one
was willing to work hard, one *would* be rich. That was a large part of
American exceptionalism. But it was also a slap at those marginalized
Americans against whom the system militated. What Stone did not say,
however, really could not say, was that if Nixon understood the hopes and
dreams of working-class Americans, he also understood the obverse:
their seething anger toward those alleged slackers whom they felt were
undeserving of the American Dream, those who benefited from the redis-
tributive policies that liberals favored while most working-class white
Americans had, they believed, succeeded by their own lights.

And this was where race entered the picture. Richard Nixon, the king
of grievance and master of the dark arts of racial backlash, knew how to
arouse white Americans' resentments against Black Americans, and
those resentments would prove indispensable to the conservative drift
that would later carry Reagan to the White House and into a transformation of American politics—the Reagan Revolution, as it would be called.
And it *was* a revolution. During the moral crease of the mid-1960s, when
Congress passed the Civil Rights Act and the Voting Rights Act and the
Fair Housing Act, passed them with votes to spare, and for several years
thereafter, many Americans, *white* Americans, almost seemed to be exhilarated by a moral righteousness that undid the injustices of the past. A
Gallup poll in 1964 found that 58 percent of Americans approved of the
Civil Rights Act; another poll in 1965 found 74 percent supported the Vot-
ing Rights Act.

But these would be high-water marks, and the tide would soon turn.
For all the strides of racial progress, white Americans retained a certain
skepticism about Black Americans. Even at the time of the passage of the
Civil Rights and Voting Rights acts, 42 percent of white Americans
thought the Johnson administration was moving too fast on integration—
this after one hundred years of foot-dragging. And with this idea lurking
in the white American consciousness, it wasn't long before the backlash

arrived. Urban rioting, beginning with the Watts insurrection in Los Angeles in 1965, and increasing Black American militancy—"Burn, baby, burn!"—which Richard Nixon had exploited so skillfully in the 1968 campaign to terrify white Americans, undermined white support for civil rights, as if Black Americans' anger over the long, long denial of those rights made those Black Americans less deserving of them. (It seemed it was one thing for white Americans to bestow rights, another for Black Americans to demand them.) Already by 1972, according to one poll, 74 percent of white Americans agreed that "blacks should not push themselves" where they are not wanted, which seemed to contradict the advance of civil rights altogether.

And the backlash intensified throughout the 1970s, when white Americans discovered something else: that the cleansing of racial injustice eventually came with a price—a price that polling indicated white Americans were increasingly unwilling to pay. It was this price that turned Ted Kennedy's white ethnic Bostonians against him when a federal court ordered their children bused to Black schools and Black students bused to white schools in the furtherance of integration. (In a 1973 poll, only 19 percent of white Americans approved of busing to integrate schools.) It was this price that Americans felt they were paying when their taxes were used to fund antipoverty programs that many believed predominantly served Black people. (Nearly 60 percent of white Americans in the same poll felt that Black Americans should receive no special treatment from the government, and only 20 percent felt that government had an obligation to improve the living standard of Black Americans.) It was this price they felt they were paying when they believed they had sacrificed their own freedoms, especially the freedom to discriminate if they chose, for the rights of those of Black people, because many white people did not want to live among Black Americans. (This last had stalled what Congress ultimately passed in 1968 as the Fair Housing Act, which prevented discrimination in housing against Black Americans; when it finally passed, it was largely because of the momentum generated by Martin Luther King, Jr.'s, assassination.) And finally, it was the price they felt they were paying when they discovered that some of Black people's rights came at the expense of their own dreams. (Gallup polling in the late 1970s found only roughly 15 percent of white Americans supported affirmative action programs that redressed historic racial discrimination by giving Black Americans advantages in hiring and education.) As Theodore White would put it, "The American people were persuaded that the cost of equality had come to crush the promise of opportunity"— at least *white* opportunity.*

What White did not say was that Republicans were chief among the persuaders. Richard Nixon, the "predicate," had appreciated the political potential of the backlash, and he did all he could to engender it. (Barry Goldwater, after all, had won five states in the Deep South primarily because he opposed the civil rights actions that Johnson was promoting.) Nursing white antagonisms toward Black Americans—Republicans never seriously pondered the possibility that they might attract Black voters to a different coalition, instead ceding them to the Democrats—would be the basis for Nixon's Southern Strategy, which would become the Republican playbook after 1968, and while historians would focus their attention on Nixon's ability to attract white working-class voters who had previously been Democrats, the real challenge to the old and enduring New Deal coalition that Franklin Roosevelt had forged in 1932 was the Democrats' loss of the South after Lyndon Johnson's civil rights campaign, which was one reason Jimmy Carter won the Democratic nomination in 1976: He held the promise of restoring the South to the Democratic column, and he did.

Ronald Reagan certainly understood the political appeal of racism too. Asked by a reporter during Reagan's "unofficial" campaign for the 1968 Republican nomination whether he had any disagreements with George Wallace, Reagan, loath to alienate potential Southern delegates by attacking Wallace, answered, "He's been speaking a lot of things that I think the people of America are in agreement with," and said not a word about Wallace's racism. Twelve years later, in 1980, during his first campaign swing after he had received the nomination, he spoke before an enthusiastic all-white crowd of ten thousand at the Neshoba County Fair in Mississippi, a "traditional forum for the outpourings of segregationists," *The Washington Post* would report, and just miles from where three young civil rights workers had been killed by Klansmen in 1964, and delivered the message, "I believe in state's rights," which had historically been code words for racism.

---

*The extent to which this was a racial antagonism is indicated by polls that showed white people were, as two scholars of affirmative action put it, "significantly more likely to support the social and economic position of blacks and other minorities than of blacks alone." Charlotte Steeh and Maria Krysan, "Affirmative Action and the Public, 1970–1995," *Public Opinion Quarterly* 60, no. 1 (Spring 1996): 138.

That was about as overtly racist as Ronald Reagan would be—racism by code, racism by implication. Reagan was not a subtle man, but Republicans generally had come to understand that they could strip away much of the moral authority that had sustained liberalism, the moral authority associated with civil rights, but only if they did so by indirection, as Nixon and Reagan had done, lest they be lumped with George Wallace and drive off moderates. (As Nobel laureate economist and liberal *New York Times* columnist Paul Krugman bluntly put it years later, writing of the euphemisms behind conservative antigovernment and antitax sentiment: "Government is the problem because it takes your money and gives it to Those People," meaning, of course, Black people.) Interviewed in 1981 by a political scientist writing a book on the two-party system in the South, Lee Atwater, a young Republican political strategist and an aide to Ronald Reagan in the new administration, put it this way off the record: "You start out in 1954 by saying, 'Nigger, nigger, nigger.' By 1968 you can't say 'nigger'—that hurts you, backfires. So you say stuff like, uh, forced busing, states' rights, and all that stuff, and you're getting so abstract. Now, you're talking about cutting taxes, and all these things you're talking about are totally economic things and a byproduct of them is, blacks get hurt worse than whites. . . . 'We want to cut this,' is much more abstract than even the busing thing, uh, and a hell of a lot more abstract than 'Nigger, nigger.' "

So Republicans generally, and Ronald Reagan specifically, all seeking to destroy the Roosevelt coalition by peeling off the white working class and the South, learned to speak in abstractions to signal their racial position. Their white listeners heard, and their white listeners understood. Ronald Reagan, like Richard Nixon before him, made few blatantly racist appeals; his animus seemed to be reserved not for Black Americans, as Wallace's was, but for the government helping Black Americans. (The exception was his attacks on alleged welfare cheats, which were unmistakably racial.) Still, the Knights of the Ku Klux Klan endorsed his candidacy. They heard the abstractions, and they understood.

But there was more to the growing animus against liberalism than white disaffection with government or even racial backlash. As the conservative wind blew the country rightward throughout the 1970s, pundits who observed the new direction missed one of its most profound causes and what would be one of its most profound consequences, the latter of which would help fuel not only Ronald Reagan's new presidency but also the entire conservative enterprise: The country was undergoing a moral recalibration. Russell Kirk, the author of *The Conservative Mind* and one of the preeminent philosophers of modern conservatism, had drawn a line in modern politics between "all those who believe in some transcendent moral order, on the one side, and on the other side, all those who take this ephemeral existence of ours with a be-all and end-all—to be devoted chiefly to producing and consuming." Kirk intended that to be the divide between conservativism and liberalism—conservatives care about the whole man, liberals only about the material needs of man—but the longstanding dedication of the Republican Party, America's business party, to markets and production and tax cuts actually put it on the side of materialism rather than spirituality. (In order to merge the material and spiritual, some conservatives began to argue that capitalism actually was a form of benevolence.) Conservatives had little interest in the sort of public morality that promoted compassion to the vulnerable and that formed the basis of Ted Kennedy's Senate career. Barry Goldwater even began his foundational text on his philosophy, *The Conscience of a Conservative*, on the defensive, moaning that conservatives always felt the need to apologize for their presumed lack of compassion, then spent the rest of the book decrying every government action that was designed to help the poor and the vulnerable and even the working class. (He was adamantly opposed to labor unions.)

If Barry Goldwater didn't have much to say about public morality, except to condemn it, neither did Ronald Reagan. In Reagan's 1964 milestone address for Goldwater's presidential candidacy, "A Time for Choosing," he related his anecdote about the young mother who decided to go on welfare because it paid better than her husband's wages, and then said, "Yet anytime you and I question the schemes of do-gooders, we're denounced as being against their humanitarian goals," making Reagan's argument against government assistance the danger that the unscrupulous poor might take advantage of it. (This played right into the preconceptions of the newly aggrieved white reactionary populists.) The problem, and it was a problem the more astute conservative Republicans seemed to recognize, was that they had no humanitarian goals of their own. Their primary goals were punitive: to undo the New Deal and deny government assistance to the vulnerable.

A moral recalibration to discredit liberal morality had already been under way in conservative religious circles. Christian evangelicals, who faced the same problem of boasting a seeming moral rectitude but one devoid of empathy, met the challenge by inveighing against the ways in which the so-called secular liberal values of tolerance and compassion and charity had engendered what they considered a tidal wave of immorality, and when in 1979 several evangelical ministers, including an especially aggressive, self-promoting televangelist from Virginia named Jerry Falwell, formed a group to take back America from the liberals—they called their group the Moral Majority—he held a demonstration on the steps of the Capitol that April at which he declared that "the American people think this country is ready for a moral revolution."

What Falwell had in mind, however, was more of a moral *counterrevolution*. In founding the Moral Majority, he said his was a crusade against "abortion-on-demand, pornography, and sex and violence on television, and government intervention"—by which he apparently meant the intervention of the government against racial segregation. (He did not mention homosexuality, though it struck a particularly raw nerve and generated an especially deep anger among evangelicals.) But this was not just or even primarily a religious crusade; it was a political one. For Falwell would also say this: "If Christians do not master politicians, we will, most certainly, be mastered by those who do." And he left no doubt that those were the liberals he so detested. Jimmy Carter had disrupted attempts at a Christian-conservative-Republican alliance. He was a born-again Christian himself, and he did as much as any politician to inject religion into politics. But Carter soon disappointed those evangelical allies—it was his Internal Revenue Service that was threatening to take away the tax exemption for their schools on the basis that the schools were segregated—and they were soon looking for Republicans to join their cause and protect not only the country from liberal iniquities but also themselves from government action. This all seemed to comport with another of Russell Kirk's foundational ideas—that, as one scholar put it, "all political problems are really religious and social problems," and that a "transcendent moral order" was now the operative principle of conservatism, as Kirk himself described it. But this alleged moral bond might have been an excuse. A deeper bond might have been the one, as historian Sean Wilentz observed, between the racial attitudes of the new right and those of the evangelicals, who had been reinvigorated by *Brown v. Board of Education* to build their private academies in order to avoid school integration. What might have seemed like a moral bond, then, might have really been a matter of political convenience—a way to halt racial progress. And the evangelicals, having failed to do so themselves, decided that the best agent for doing so would be a prospective Republican president. It was in the guise of alleged liberal amorality that the Republicans and the religious right found common cause to fight tolerance.

Ronald Reagan was not necessarily a promising candidate for the mission. Although he hated liberals and would thwart civil rights, he cared little about religion. Charles Colson, one of Richard Nixon's henchmen during Watergate who would later attempt to redeem himself through his own devotion to born-again Christianity, said that when a reporter asked Reagan if *he* was born again, Reagan "shrugged, like the fellow had landed from Mars." Nor did Reagan, whose obsession was government overreach, buy into the evangelicals' moralizing. Among other things, as governor of California, he had signed a lenient "choice" law permitting abortions. But that was before he began running seriously for the presidency and that was before he saw the political benefits of joining forces with the evangelicals. Now, as a candidate in 1980, Reagan did not back away from the evangelicals' repudiation of public morality and social responsibility. Now he embraced it, touting personal morality and individual responsibility instead and making the same dire prophecies about the liberal threat to religious values that the evangelicals were making. He warned one televangelist that America could become Sodom and Gomorrah and asked whether this "might be the generation that sees Armageddon." The "traditional Judeo-Christian values based on the moral teaching of religion are undergoing what is perhaps their most serious challenge in our nation's history," he told a cheering throng of sixteen thousand evangelicals at a rally in Dallas during the campaign. Liberals, he said, had launched a "new and cynical attack . . . to remove from our public policy debate the voice of traditional morality." (He was right; liberalism did not promote the stern, censorious traditional morality of the sort that Reagan and the evangelicals advocated.) And he said, "If we have come to a time in the United States when the attempt to see traditional moral values reflected in public policy leaves one open to irresponsible charges"— presumably the charges that those moralists were without compassion or empathy—"then the structure of our free society is under attack and the foundation of our freedom is threatened." The crowd roared its approval.

Ronald Reagan had spent his political career sowing distrust of government and in doing so had managed to sow distrust both in New Deal liberalism and, collaterally and more significantly, in the sense of a large national community. In effect, he hoped to transform the country from an "us" to tens of millions of "me's." (As political historian Rick Perlstein would write, contrary to the conventional political wisdom, "Ronald Reagan is not a uniter. He is in essence a divider.") Now Reagan, more opportunistically, challenged something else: the alleged moral authority on which liberalism had rested and on which it had survived, if barely. That authority, which had been invested in the civil rights movement, had begun eroding under those assaults of Richard Nixon and the Republican right, who had used white backlash against civil rights to convince white Americans that Black people were just another interest group, no more deserving than anyone else, rather than a people who had suffered terrible injustices. (Given the persistence of racism among white Americans, in truth they didn't seem to need much convincing.) And it had eroded under the assaults that contended the poor were slackers who failed to take advantage of the opportunities afforded them (Reagan's charge that unemployment insurance was "vacation money for the lazy") or cheats (the story he persisted in telling about the Chicago woman who defrauded the government out of $150,000 and who was called the "welfare queen"). And it had eroded under the Democrats' own rightward tilt, Carter's tilt, in which segments of the party had abandoned liberalism for a tepid centrism rather than embrace it, as Ted had urged his party to do. And it had eroded under the Republican/evangelical emphasis on personal responsibility and on puritanical values—an emphasis that made Ted Kennedy, with his infidelities and his recklessness, particularly susceptible to attack and that, as he was the putative liberal leader, made liberalism susceptible too. Reagan wasn't the first to make charges against liberal values. He was, however, among the most effective to do so.

Without its moral authority, liberalism was no longer in a position to defend itself. At the time of Reagan's election, despite Jimmy Carter's fumbling, a majority of Americans still subscribed to liberal positions on a number of issues, if not specifically on racial ones: 60 percent favored handgun registration, 61 percent wanted passage of the Equal Rights Amendment that gave women the same rights as men, 56 percent upheld the right to an abortion. This might have led one to believe that it wasn't the substance of liberalism that had faltered so much as its aesthetics, which was why Ronald Reagan, the former movie star who lived by aesthetics, might have been so appropriate an adversary toward liberalism. Carter was right that Reagan offered simplicity: a handful of bromides like the power of hard work, the righteousness of individualism, the exhilaration of American exceptionalism, the idea that the best is yet to come, and panaceas like a beefed-up military and tax cuts and limited government.* In contrast, Democrats offered muddle—as demonstrated by the divide between Carter's centrism and Ted Kennedy's strenuous liberalism. One-time Bobby Kennedy aide and later member of the California Board of Regents Fred Dutton described the difference between California governor Pat Brown and Ronald Reagan, his 1966 opponent, by saying, "Pat had the grays, and Reagan had the blacks and whites," meaning those who saw the world without gradations. That hadn't changed in the fourteen years since their gubernatorial face-off. Reagan still had the black-and-white people, which scored points in a country in a state of confusion. And among the many assaults on it, that was also what happened to liberalism. It ceded its clarity to conservatism—its moral clarity. As Sean Wilentz summarized it, "Reagan had the excellent fortune to emerge as a presidential contender just as Democratic liberalism fell into intellectual confusion and political decay."

And so Ronald Reagan entered the presidency having worked hard to discredit both the federal government and public morality. The first, he said, would take away your freedoms. The second, he said, would destroy every value that you held dear, which played into the idea, also promoted by Richard Nixon, that liberals had contempt for ordinary people, at least ordinary white people; and those ordinary Americans repaid the contempt with contempt of their own. Americans didn't yet embrace Ronald Reagan. His victory was more the result of animus toward Jimmy Carter than of affection for the president-elect. Still, the campaign provided portents of a new direction for the country and a new form of moral discourse. Of the two battles Reagan waged, one against government and the other against public morality, the latter may in the long run have been the more consequential. By convincing millions of Americans that they had no civic obligations to fellow Americans in distress, Ronald Reagan helped strip away the last vestiges of liberalism's moral authority. And

---

* Republican pollster Richard Wirthlin found that Reagan voters in 1980 scored highest on such "values" as "respect for authority, individualism, and authoritarianism"—hardly liberal values. Rick Perlstein, *Reaganland: America's Right Turn, 1976–1980* (New York: Simon & Schuster, 2020), 674.

when he did, liberalism would have nothing left with which to rally the public to its cause or to the cause of those it supported. And neither would Ted Kennedy.

II

In the interregnum between Jimmy Carter's loss and the beginning of Ronald Reagan's presidency, Ted and Carter had not resolved their differences, and Carter was understandably embittered at and angry with Ted. But Ted, remarkably, had a favor to ask of the outgoing president. While Ted was campaigning, Stephen Breyer, his Judiciary Committee chief counsel, essentially ran the committee. (After the election, Republican Orrin Hatch told Ted, "We're so sorry to see you here. We loved Steve so much.") Ted had returned from the general election to the lame duck session of a Senate that was about to turn Republican, which meant he was losing his chairmanship, which meant that Breyer had no reason to stay. Breyer told Ted that he would prefer a judgeship, and it so happened that a seat was open on the First Circuit Court of Appeals, which served Massachusetts, among other states. Given the politics, with a new president coming in who could select his own judges, Breyer's appointment was unlikely, and in any case, as Breyer would later tell it, Ted was still eager to get Archibald Cox appointed to the bench, despite Carter's earlier rejection of him. But Carter still refused to nominate Cox, and Ted had great affection for Breyer, so he managed to get both Strom Thurmond, the ranking committee member, soon to be its chair, and Orrin Hatch, another committee member, to support Breyer's nomination. With those two on board, it seemed as if the Republicans would no longer be the obstacle.

But Carter owed nothing to Ted Kennedy, and Carter wasn't about to do him any favors. So Ted phoned Stu Eizenstat, Carter's domestic adviser, and asked if Eizenstat might approach Carter with the request since Eizenstat had worked with Breyer on deregulation and admired him. Eizenstat said he went to Carter with "more than mild trepidation," telling Carter that he would be doing a favor not for Kennedy but for Breyer, who was deserving of one. Carter agreed, no doubt thinking that the nomination would never be confirmed anyway, not realizing that Ted had already paved the way. But then Senator Robert Morgan, the West Virginia Democrat whose judicial nominee Ted had foiled due to blemishes on his record, decided to filibuster Breyer's nomination as payback against Ted. This proved to be not much more than a speed bump. Robert Byrd, the outgoing majority leader, told Ted he had the votes to invoke cloture. He did, and Breyer joined the bench. Eizenstat would later say that you couldn't find a better anecdote about Ted Kennedy's modus operandi than that one because Ted had to overcome Carter, Thurmond and the Senate Republicans, and the opposition of one of his own Senate Democrats, and to do it all in the waning days of the Senate.

That was Ted Kennedy at his most skillful. And he would need that skill now—now that Democrats controlled neither the Senate nor the presidency, now that the age of liberalism was ending.

There was another ending for Ted Kennedy late that January, the day after Ronald Reagan took office. After her separation from Ted, Joan had returned to the fold for Ted's presidential run. She had overcome her trepidations and anxieties, had soldiered on through the campaign, testifying to her husband's character, had allowed herself to be managed and manipulated, had even attended Reagan's inauguration with Ted. The next day, having spent inauguration morning over breakfast drafting a statement, the couple announced that they would be getting a divorce: "With regret, yet with respect and consideration for each other, we have agreed to terminate our marriage."

The possibility of divorce had been brewing for months. Shortly after Super Tuesday, as Marcia Chellis, Joan's assistant, would later write, Joan told her at the Boston apartment that she was considering divorcing Ted and that her psychiatrist had encouraged her to do so. She also said she would fight for Patrick's custody. And Chellis wrote that Joan continued to ponder divorce throughout the summer, vacillating, Chellis said, because at forty-four, she was worried about her future but had doubts whether, if she decided to stay with Ted, he would stop his womanizing. At one point, she came up to him while he was watching television or reading and asked cryptically, "How are you going to answer the questions?" And when Ted looked confused, she announced that she wanted a divorce. Ted didn't react. Instead, as Chellis told it, he said he was taking Patrick to Nantucket and would be returning on Friday, and when he arrived back in Hyannis, he invited his religious counselor, Father James English of the Georgetown Holy Trinity Church, to the compound to advise the couple. Joan told a slightly different version to Ted Kennedy's bi-

ographer Adam Clymer. She said that after the convention, Ted had asked
her to move back to Washington. But she told Clymer he did not say, "I
love you," or "I want you to come back," or "I'm going to be good," by
which, of course, she meant stop his philandering. He did tell her that "I
want to be married to you," but he added that "I could have all the freedom I wanted. I could carry on with my life. You could see anybody you
want to see." Joan believed that Ted did not want to divorce, even then,
even after their long separation, because of religion and family and children. (She didn't mention politics.) But those were not the terms that Joan
desired, and she said her psychiatrist had advised her against accepting
them. Still, she returned to McLean after the campaign, but she was uncertain whether to remain. And it was over the Christmas vacation, she
later said, on a skiing trip to Aspen, that she finally decided the marriage
was irretrievably broken. It was her decision, she said, not Ted's—a decision the campaign had fortified her to make. "I guess I felt like I could go it
alone," she said.

It hadn't been a real marriage for a long time, though Joan clearly
loved Ted; after the divorce announcement, she told *Ladies' Home Journal*
that she had never been in love with another man. Still, there had always
been more turbulence than tenderness. "Except for one visit to Hyannis
Port during the 1980 primaries when I'd sat in their bedroom and had coffee with them in the morning," Bob Shrum would say, "to me they seldom
looked comfortable together," which was what reporters had said during
their appearances on the campaign trail. And of the divorce announcement, Carl Wagner, Ted's campaign field officer, would say, "Rock bottom
is a good foundation to build on." Even Father James English, their religious counselor, would say that there had been "great strains in the marriage" and that they had been engaged in a "long and serious discussion
about their lives with one another" before the decision to divorce, and
while Joan had campaigned "very strenuously, genuinely," and would
have stayed with him had he won the presidency, "given the divergent
ways their lives have gone, both mutually felt they would probably be better friends if they no longer lived together." In the settlement, Joan would
keep her seven-room Boston apartment on Beacon Street that Ted had
bought shortly before their separation and the Squaw Island home. (Ted
would contest it bitterly, telling Joan she could buy another house in Os-
terville, near her "Republican friends," but eventually gave in.) Ted kept

the home in McLean. And Joan would receive a substantial financial settlement that was estimated at $4 million, after the terms were finally negotiated.

Now she was no longer a Kennedy, which might have been a blessing. Joan Kennedy wasn't built to endure the Kennedys. Asked once to describe herself in a single word, she had said, "Vulnerable," which was not a trait the Kennedys either admired or tolerated. But it was a sign of how much of the Kennedys she had internalized that years later she would protest, "They would all write about how vulnerable I was, and everybody felt sorry for me because I was in a marriage that wasn't good. If they only knew that I was so strong. I was stronger than anyone else just to be able to survive. It was very hard." And in an interview shortly after the divorce announcement, she came on with what the interviewer described as "bravado," saying, "I mean, my God, you are talking to, I think, one of the most fascinating women in this country. That's very immodest, I know, but that's the way it is. I have a very full life," though the boasts prompted the interviewer to say that Joan's "self-confidence and dogged positive thinking sound brittle, the forced rhetoric of a self-improvement campaign." At marriage's end, she was both vulnerable and strong, both a victim and a survivor. And while, given her proclivities to alcohol, Ted Kennedy hadn't destroyed her, he hadn't saved her either or showed much consideration to her. Rather, he had used her—used her politically in 1980—disregarded her feelings and showed her no particular sensitivity when she clearly needed it. "I regret my failings and accept responsibility for them and will leave it at that," he would write in his memoir. It was not enough.

III

Ronald Reagan's inaugural address, like Richard Nixon's, was a repudiation of the New Deal, which had been the bogeyman of the Republicans for nearly fifty years and the thing that Ronald Reagan was determined to slay, if, as Paul Tsongas had said, his election hadn't already slayed it. "In this present crisis, government is not the solution to our problem," Reagan said in that inaugural, repeating one of his favorite campaign applause lines, which was a direct assault on liberal dogma, "government is the problem. From time to time we've been tempted to believe that society has become too complex to be managed by self-rule, that government by an elite group is superior to government for, by, and of the people. But if no one among us is capable of governing himself, then who among us has the capacity to govern someone else?"

Despite the rhetoric, Ronald Reagan was no doctrinaire conservative like Russell Kirk or even Barry Goldwater. Ronald Reagan was no doctrinaire anything. Having come to politics through performance—as a spokesperson for General Electric, he had delivered those right-wing speeches that sold the GE party line against government, and sold it with conviction not unlike the conviction with which Ted Kennedy sold the liberal line—he was a political actor as he had been a movie actor. (*The Role of a Lifetime*, journalist Lou Cannon titled his book on Reagan's presidency.) He read lines and internalized them. His gift was for aesthetics, not ideology, for the way a movie could make an audience feel, not the way a politician could make a constituency feel, though he managed to bring the first—the feeling—to the second—the constituency. His chief criticism of Jimmy Carter, which was not very different from Ted Kennedy's criticism of him, was spiritual rather than political. "It seemed to me that America was losing faith in itself," Reagan would write of Carter's presidency in his memoir, something that Carter himself had said in his crisis of confidence speech. "Almost every day the president was sending a message to the American people that America had passed its prime, that Americans were going to have to get used to less in the future, that we should not have the same hopes for the future that we once had and that we had only ourselves to blame for it."*

For Reagan the antidote was not, as Carter had proposed, self-reflection. The antidote was uplift. The man who was tasked with undoing the New Deal cited Franklin Roosevelt as his inspiration. "Tell me the last time we had a leader we had a good deal of faith in," Reagan asked during a *60 Minutes* interview back when he was challenging Gerald Ford for the nomination. "Franklin Delano Roosevelt," he answered. "He took his case

---

*Providing an opening boost, it seemed serendipitous for Reagan, though clearly calculated by the Iranians, that the very day of his inauguration, Jimmy Carter reached agreement with Iran to free the hostages who had been held for 444 days. According to Kai Bird's biography of Carter, however, it wasn't as serendipitous as it looked. As Nixon had negotiated with the South Vietnamese during the 1968 election not to accept a North Vietnamese peace proposal, lest Hubert Humphrey benefit from it, Reagan's campaign manager, William Casey, encouraged the Iranians not to release the hostages before the election, telling them they would get a better deal from Reagan than from Carter. Kai Bird, *The Outsider: The Unfinished Presidency of Jimmy Carter* (New York: Crown, 2021), chap. 24.

to the people. When the New Deal started he was faced with a Congress that wouldn't go along. He went over their heads with the fireside chats. . . . And he enlightened the people." And Reagan said, "The greatest leader is not one who does the greatest things. He is the one who gets people to do the greatest things." Ted Kennedy might have thought that Ronald Reagan had no right to invoke the name of Franklin Roosevelt, but in Reagan's earlier days, the days before he turned rightward, he had been a Roosevelt Democrat, and even as a conservative, Reagan had deep affinities with Roosevelt, just not political ones. Reagan not only respected the performative aspects of Roosevelt's presidency; he also saw them as the quintessence of Roosevelt's presidency. In Reagan's view, a president's job was no different than a movie actor's job; it was to make people feel good. Conservatism had been gloomy. It had been hard, flinty, and mean-spirited. For all Russell Kirk's invocations of transcendence, conservatism had had a bleak and pessimistic view of human nature, seeing people as selfish, something that the novelist Ayn Rand, a kind of muse to many conservatives, tried to turn into a virtue: Selfishness led to progress. Reagan understood many, many things, but one of the things he understood best was that in order to succeed, he had to put a smile on conservatism; he had to give it what Franklin Roosevelt and John Kennedy had given to liberalism: a sense of optimism. Nixon had been angry. Reagan wasn't angry. He was suited to the task of undoing liberalism because he was genial. He made people feel good about themselves. A Massachusetts businessman named Norman Comins spoke for millions when he told a reporter at Reagan's inaugural, "Yes, I'm a Republican. But somehow it seems different to say that now. It feels good." Kill the New Deal, yes. But kill it with a broad, sunny smile.

Genial was Ronald Reagan. Even Ted Kennedy was susceptible to his charm, which was not unlike Ted Kennedy's own charm, and so very different from Jimmy Carter's off-putting smugness. Ted had had no personal relationship with Reagan as he had had with Richard Nixon. He had very little sense of the nonpublic man. Bobby had made two appearances with him—one on a global television program about American power, and another, most likely when Bobby was out campaigning for president in California—and Ted was impressed with how effectively Reagan spoke on those occasions. But there had been no other contact between Reagan and Ted—only the campaign barbs that had flown back and forth between them. And when, that December, in their last phone conversation,

Jimmy Carter asked Ted if he was looking forward to Reagan and his group, presumably a facetious question, no doubt a question Carter meant as a jab at Ted for having helped elect Reagan, Ted had answered without facetiousness: "Not one day sooner than they take office."

But Ted Kennedy, who had even extended an olive branch to Richard Nixon, was not one to create enmities. After Reagan's election but before his inauguration, Ted, clearly banking on his own charm, had asked Senator Paul Laxalt, a close friend of Reagan's, to set up a meeting with Reagan in the hope, Ted said, that "we can realize some areas we could constructively, productively work together on," and Laxalt had done so. Afterward, Ted had dinner with John Culver, who asked him how the meeting with Reagan had gone. "Well, if I ever had any reservations about my ability to be president of the United States," Ted said, "they have now been removed." Ted told Culver that he had prepared diligently with his staff to discuss four or five issues with which he had been deeply engaged and about which he hoped he might have a substantive discussion with the president-elect. But as Ted recounted it, "I'd start a subject, and Reagan would tell a joke. He was perfectly charming. He couldn't have been warmer or more delightful. But I couldn't get him to engage substantively on any one of those subjects where we might work together." They met again that March at a St. Patrick's Day luncheon at the Irish embassy where Reagan was "expansive and candid," telling stories about other world leaders, and where he confessed that he had no idea what he would be doing on any given day until he was handed an agenda, and again in June when Reagan awarded a posthumous Gold Medal to Bobby in the Rose Garden—something that Jimmy Carter had neglected to do—an event at which Reagan extolled Bobby with uncharacteristic encomia: "He roused the comfortable. He exposed the corrupt, remembered the forgotten, inspired his countrymen, and renewed and enriched the American conscience." Later that day the two discussed gun control measures and Northern Ireland. And later in the year, Reagan invited Ted and Rose to the White House after she had found some handwritten notes of Jack's about Notre Dame football in which he mentioned the Notre Dame legend George Gipp, whom Reagan had played in the film *Knute Rockne, All American*, and had them framed for the president. And Ted said Reagan and Nancy Reagan, the first lady, were "gracious" with their time. Whatever his expectations of the new president, Ted genuinely liked Reagan and appreciated his gestures. "He lit up a room, and he could summon laughter, intentionally or otherwise," Ted recalled. "In fact, sometimes it was hard to tell whether his whimsical side was intentional." (People had said the same thing about Ted's garbled syntax.) Ted cited a White House meeting of senators to discuss import quotas on shoes. Reagan didn't seem to know the names of any of the senators but Ted's, and asked him whether he was wearing Bostonians, a shoe manufacturer, after which Reagan expatiated for the next twenty minutes on the shoes his father had sold at his store. There was nothing said further about quotas.

It was almost impossible *not* to like Ronald Reagan. But that was Reagan the man. Politics was different. Politics was warfare. And in any case, Reagan had surrounded himself with hardcore conservatives whom it was very easy for a liberal like Ted Kennedy to dislike. Ted fully understood that there would be combat now, much fiercer combat than there had been with Nixon, who had seemed intent not on destroying liberalism so much as on preempting it. Ronald Reagan didn't want to preempt. Ronald Reagan wanted to end. How best to challenge Reagan on his assault on social programs? That was Ted's question. And now Ted had a decision to make—a big decision, a decision that would go a long way toward determining how he would fence with Reagan, a decision he himself would later call a defining one for his Senate career. With the Republican Senate takeover, Ted would lose his Judiciary chairmanship. He could remain as the ranking minority member and cross swords with Reagan on a host of issues from voting rights to abortion to gun control to judgeships. He could fight those battles, though he would likely lose most if not all of them. But he had another option. He could become the ranking member on the Labor and Health Committee and work on an entirely different set of issues: healthcare especially, but also labor issues like the minimum wage and job training programs and education issues and biomedical research—things that were much closer to people's daily lives. Ted was torn. He had his staff draw up separate plans of action for each committee so he would have a sense of what he might be able to accomplish on each.

But as he pondered the choice, he got a preview of what was in store for him and for the other liberals. That December, in the last days of the Carter administration, Ted brought a bill to the Senate floor—a bill that Birch Bayh had introduced before his defeat that fall—that would have toughened enforcement on the Fair Housing Act that had passed in 1968. The bill was under the jurisdiction of the Banking Committee, of which Ted was not a member, but he felt strongly about it and pressed it, even meeting with the incoming majority leader, Howard Baker. But Baker had no interest in fair housing, even though a handful of moderate Republicans had joined Ted's cause. It was the very last bill to be considered in the rump session before the Christmas recess and the installation of the new Senate. Republicans filibustered, and Ted lost a cloture vote, 54 to 43. Ted laid the defeat on a "small group of conservative Republicans who wanted to roll back the clock." But at least now he knew what he would be up against for the next two years and quite likely longer than that. Now he knew that Reagan and his Senate allies would be determined to dismantle the social programs and social advances for which liberals had fought so hard—programs and advances on which many Americans had come to rely. Now he knew.

To protect those programs, Ted made his decision: He would become the ranking minority member on Labor. It wasn't an easy decision. Judiciary was far more prestigious than Labor, far more active than Labor. Ted would say that fellow senators were so loath to join Labor that, when he later became chairman, he would have to beg them to come on, actually bribe them with the promise of some budget money. "Look, I'll guarantee you a staffer if you come on," he would tell freshmen. Most of the members, he would later say, were "waived on," meaning they had to obtain waivers to add a third committee because caucus rules limited them to two, and Labor was not one of their preferences. Kenneth Feinberg, who had been Ted's point man on deregulation and his administrative assistant and was now leaving Ted to earn money in the private sector for his family, was "stunned" by Ted's decision—"stunned that he would give up the majesty of the chairman of the Senate Judiciary Committee, which, you'll recall, was a driving force toward the Voting Rights Act and immigration reform." It seemed absurd for a Senate careerist, as Ted now seemed to be. But Feinberg came to appreciate that "Ted's instincts were absolutely right": "Why don't I go over to the committee that really matters, in terms of improving the day-to-day lives of the American people?" Feinberg imagined Ted telling himself. Ted himself said that he had chosen Labor finally because it had jurisdiction over the issues on which he had been campaigning in his bid for the presidency. They were "closer to the surface in my own psyche." Larry Horowitz, who would soon become Ted's administrative assistant, was not stunned. He said, "I never doubted for one second where he would go. I never doubted where his heart was." And he said that Ted made the choice for Labor because "he thought the

biggest assault would come from the Reagan administration" on those social issues.

That was Ted Kennedy's mission now. Someone had to stop Ronald
Reagan. Ted knew it would be a difficult charge. For all Reagan's pronouncements on the villainy of government, the conservative attack on
social programs was not frontal but stealthy. The conservatives didn't outright rescind those programs or defund them entirely. Instead, they
pushed them into "block grants" given to the states to use as they saw fit,
which was a backdoor way of starving the programs for funds and destroying their identities by lumping them together with other programs
and of ripping away their constituencies, those individuals and organizations who had fought for them, until the programs just withered away. Or
they created a budgetary gap that could, given the Republicans' commitments and priorities, be closed only by massive cuts to the social programs
that they so detested and that did not, in their minds, serve their white
middle-class constituents or their corporate donors. Reagan had sworn to
cut taxes by $280 billion—one of his most cherished pledges—while at
the same time adding $100 billion to the defense budget, and as a sop to
the business Republicans, he had also promised to balance the budget by
1984. That was the threat: money for tax cuts and money for defense and
the promise of a balanced budget, but no money for social programs. Ted,
still a realist despite his brief delusion about the nomination during the
convention, didn't fool himself that he could actually pass any legislation
through the Republican gauntlet. His hope was that he might be able to
hold the line against the most savage and unconscionable cuts. But he
couldn't do it alone, not in a Republican Senate.

He needed allies—especially Republican allies. And he had two. After
the election, Vermont moderate Robert Stafford called Connecticut moderate Lowell Weicker and convinced him to join the Labor Committee,
even though Weicker already had two major committee assignments.
Stafford made the same argument that had motivated Ted to move from
Judiciary to Labor: The social programs were in jeopardy from the new
president and his conservative Republican collaborators. (Orrin Hatch,
the conservative Utah senator who would now chair Labor, thought that
Ted had chosen Labor for more diabolical reasons: because he knew that
there were enough moderate Republicans on the committee to embarrass
the White House.) Now Ted had a bloc of three, with other Democrats on
the committee to join them—allies.

And if he needed allies, he also needed staff since Ted Kennedy knew as well as any senator the value of a powerful staff to move the Senate. Now there was a vacuum. Breyer and Feinberg had left, and without his chairmanship, Ted had lost both budget and staff positions, which put him at an enormous disadvantage. And because he had fewer staffers, he just didn't need staff. He needed an aggressive staff to wage the battles he was about to wage—most of them foreordained to be losing battles against Reagan. His present administrative assistant, Rick Burke, had risen from an intern—he had joined the staff as a student volunteer while at Georgetown—to a secretary to Ted's administrative assistant when Burke was only in his mid-twenties, a meteoric rise in an office where meritocracy ruled. But Burke was not a product of the meritocracy, and he was not the equal of David Burke, a predecessor, or Feinberg or Breyer or any of those luminaries who had been on Ted's staff. Most in the office considered him a lightweight—a "combination sycophant and mechanic who rose far above his ability," said one staffer. And the staffer said that he "tried to act like a chief of staff," but "nobody paid much attention to him." He even tried to institute a system in which he would sign off on every memo that went into The Bag, Ted's repository, but nobody paid any attention to that either. A "perfect enabler," Tom Oliphant of *The Boston Globe* called him. Others were even less charitable. "Devious and underhanded," Ken Feinberg said of him. "He had a cherubic face, always a smile, neatly attired," seemingly a "team player." And yet, Feinberg said, he was a "constant source of irritation," who harbored delusions of grandeur. Basically, he was an errand boy, perfectly capable of arranging Ted's schedule, and it was very likely that Ted kept him around because as much as Ted respected intelligence and achievement, he was comfortable with someone who was not Harvard and who was not an intellectual superstar, someone around him for whom he didn't have to be on his best behavior. Rick Burke made no demands on him. And yet as the staff shrank, Burke had to assume greater responsibilities, and as Tony Podesta, who coordinated Ted's campaign appearances in 1980, assessed Burke, something happened to him: "He cracked under the strain of all that was occurring and created this extraordinary, nutty fantasy." Early in 1981, Burke had become the target of death threats and even attempts on his life—a bullet was fired through the windshield of his BMW, and an intruder ran up the stairs of Burke's apartment one night and shoved a butcher knife through a sitting room door, while Burke said he was huddled inside a closet. Terrifying episodes. Forms of political terrorism against him. Except for one thing: None of them were true. Upon police investigation, it turned out that Burke had fabricated them—all of them. He resigned, citing the stresses of reorganizing the office, and said he was seeking treatment.

The man who would replace Rick Burke was like him in no respect other than his youth—he was only thirty-six—and in his enormous self-confidence, though in the replacement's case, it had been earned. Burke had come to the office with no accomplishments. Larry Horowitz was a Yale-trained doctor who had practiced and taught at Stanford. He had come to Ted as an adviser during the period when Ted was fighting for national health insurance, but he served other functions, including steering Ted to experimental treatments when Ted Jr. was diagnosed with cancer. Though he left for California in 1974, he had become so much a part of Ted's orbit that he would fly back each week to advise him and eventually stayed as staff director of the Health Subcommittee. When Ted made his presidential run, Horowitz traveled with him, at one point rescuing Patrick during a severe asthma attack on a flight from Wichita, Kansas. Horowitz was anything but an errand boy or a scheduler. He was "brilliant," said one staffer—"really, really smart"—and "he had the Senator's ear at every moment." "The Senator trusted and loved him," the same staffer said. And if Ted needed a warrior, Horowitz was that man. Horowitz was an inciter. He even looked like an inciter, not like one of the temperate Harvards: small and slender, with thick dark unruly curly hair, just a bit disheveled, palpably coiled with nervous energy. One staffer described his management style as: "Throw all the fish in the tank and let them fight it out. Let Judiciary fight with Labor for the Senator's time. Let foreign policy fight for domestic policy for the Senator's time. Just let them have it out." And the staffer said that the style increased Horowitz's power because the old spokes-in-a-wheel arrangement in which everyone had access to Ted at the center had yielded to Horowitz's arrangement in which most things flowed through him, and "he was the one who could resolve the conflicts"—even if he had helped foment them. "Machiavellian" was how more than one of Ted's staffers described him. He even reorganized the office physically, erecting barriers between the legislative assistants rather than the old open bullpen where everyone was talking and smoking and making phone calls and distracting one another.

But above all else, Horowitz, like the man he served, was impatient. "Larry Horowitz—your first comment was always, 'Would you please slow down?' Carey or Paul Kirk, who were in the famous group that wouldn't tell you if your coat was on fire, were monosyllabic," said Tom Oliphant of two of Ted's closest aides, though Oliphant also said that when you got to know them. "You can interpret a monosyllable as well as you could interpret a paragraph." But Larry Horowitz was not monosyllabic. One didn't have to interpret signs with Larry Horowitz. Larry Horowitz was loud, and Larry Horowitz was dynamic. When one of Ted's health aides, either Stan Jones or Lee Goldman or Phil Caper, suggested to Ted that he bring Horowitz back to the Health Committee after Horowitz had left for California, since Horowitz would know how to get them press for new initiatives they were planning toward the Food and Drug Administration, they joked that "this was an historic occasion" because while they knew he would be aggressive in pursuing Ted's agenda, none of them wanted to deal with the obstreperous, abrasive Horowitz, and they said that "this will just get him out of our hair. He'll work on FDA, we won't have to do anything with him because he's such an impossible son-of-a-bitch to work with."

But Larry Horowitz, the impossible son of a bitch, was precisely the kind of point man that Ted Kennedy needed as he girded once again for battle to save his liberal programs against the ongoing threats of Ronald Reagan and Reagan's conservative minions, even if, years later, he would joke that if it hadn't been for Horowitz, he might not have had to save them in the first place. "If you weren't so goddamned stubborn on national health insurance," Ted told him over a dinner, referring to the standoff with Richard Nixon when the two adversaries were so close to a bargain, "we wouldn't have had eight years of Ronald Reagan, [and] the country wouldn't be in this mess." But now, as far as Ted Kennedy was concerned, it was. And now, yet again, he felt he needed to rescue it.

IV

But Ted Kennedy did not relish the task as he often had in the past when he faced obstacles. He did not relish it because he fully appreciated how insurmountable these obstacles were likely to be. As Ronald Reagan took office, Ted was despondent. A "sense of pessimism," Carey Parker said, had settled over the office. "Senator Kennedy felt very strongly that he wanted to roll up his sleeves, get to work, and make sure the country didn't regress on the issues he cared about so deeply," but the energy he

usually displayed was missing. A "pretty oblique guy" was the way
Thomas Rollins, the chief minority counsel of the Labor Committee, described him at the time, by which he meant that he seemed remote,
directionless—not words usually attributed to Ted Kennedy. "He fulfilled
his duties," Rollins said, but he was "workmanlike rather than passionate." Rollins thought that for all Ted's equanimity after his presidential
defeat, he was "hugely stung" by the Democrats' loss of the Senate, giving
up his presidential aspirations, at least for the time being, only to find that
there was little for him to do in the chamber he so loved except to apply
brakes. "He seemed to be going through the motions," Rollins said, because Ted knew the Senate well enough, knew it very well, to understand
that "being in the minority is just a ridiculous job in the Senate." The minority had little or no budget. The minority had no staff. The minority did
not have the ability to hold hearings. The minority had no control over
which bills came to the floor and when. In short, the minority had no
power. Rollins had gone to the majority counsel to object to something
that the majority wanted to do. And the counsel said, "Oh, Tom. That's a
great point. Tell you what. Let's have a meeting of the committee, and
we'll count how many people are on our side of the committee and how
many are on your side of the committee, and we'll settle it that way." Ted
Kennedy had spent his seventeen years in the Senate rising in the ranks of
the Democratic majority—rising in the ranks of power—power the Democrats had held continuously since 1954. And now they and he had lost it.
And now the Republicans, who had chafed in the minority for all those
years, had their chance for revenge against the Democrats who had run
roughshod over them. And now Ted was fighting a rearguard action.

Stripped of power, Ted Kennedy, whose own sense of self-worth had
largely derived from his Senate power, was not only despondent, he was
also lost. Staffers and press noticed that he drank more now than he had
since before his presidential run, though he still didn't weave around the
Senate floor like Russell Long. "He seemed to have a pattern of drinking
like a fish," said *Time* writer Lance Morrow, "then sobering up for a while.
You'd see this funny sequence where he'd seem very dissipated, then relatively healthy. Most drunks, unless they clean up their act, have a long,
steady decline." Ted didn't sink, but he wasn't buoyed either. He became
philosophical. Tom Oliphant recalled the gathering with reporters at
McLean after the convention and Ted's soliloquy on the progressive Nebraska Republican senator George Norris, who had served from 1913 to

1943, and how Norris had been a staunch advocate of the New Deal, his Republicanism notwithstanding, and how Norris was the "legislative thread" that ran through the New Deal. And he talked of how, now that he had lost his chance at the presidency, a senator could have a tremendous impact on the direction of the country. But that was when he had reconciled himself to the Senate. Now that he had to reconcile himself to his own powerlessness in the Senate, Oliphant said he could tell that Ted was even considering leaving the chamber, not running for reelection. But the clearest sign of his disaffection might have been his weight. He had regained what he had lost after the convention. He didn't seem to care as much anymore.

He didn't care because he knew the odds were against him. "The American people to this day have this warm and fuzzy image of Ronald Reagan," one of Ted's moderate Republican allies, Lowell Weicker, would say years later. "Well, if he had been allowed to do what he wanted to do, believe me, they wouldn't have that warm and fuzzy image. He wanted to cut the safety net right out from under all the frail elements of our society, and that became pretty obvious even as the Senate was organizing." While Robert Stafford had recruited Weicker for the Labor Committee, he also encouraged him to use his seniority to chair the Health Subcommittee of the Appropriations Committee, through which all health authorizations passed. Reagan's men were furious at the gambit. So was Labor chairman Orrin Hatch. Ted, moderate Republicans Stafford, Weicker, and Mark Hatfield, and the remaining Democrats gave the liberal coalition a one-vote majority on Labor, which it exercised when Reagan tried pushing a $4 billion education appropriation into a block grant. And the new majority leader, Howard Baker, seeing those Republican defections, had little choice but to let the bill pass without the block grants. (Hatch took it personally; he would say that Ted took pleasure in thwarting him.) "Reagan's men now realize the committee will be a continuing problem," *Newsweek* commented after the victory. But that was precisely Ted Kennedy's lament. They would be a problem, a nuisance. Reagan was likely to win far more battles than he would lose.

Thomas Rollins, the Labor minority counsel, called this period the "darkness." Patrick Kennedy had another name for it: "political Siberia." Thinking back on it from his father's perspective, he said, "The best thing you could do was continue to articulate our core missions and keep the troops rallied and prepared for another day." William Carrick, who had been an official in Ted's presidential campaign, said of him, "It's one thing to be America's foremost liberal in a conservative age, and another to be America's foremost liberal in a conservative age and know how conservative it is." Reagan's was the most conservative age since the 1920s. (Reagan even kept a photo of Calvin Coolidge on the wall of the Cabinet Room.) "We had a new definition of 'winning,'" the minority leader, Robert Byrd, would say. "Winning now often meant moderating the extremes," which was the nuisance Ted had been on Labor. "Winning now meant sticking together and trying to do the right thing, even when we knew we would lose." And Byrd said he told his Democratic colleagues at their weekly Tuesday caucus meetings, "Let's go on the floor and offer this amendment because it's right. We won't win. But it's not so much how it will look today as how it will appear a year from now, when our position will have been proved right. That is what will count in the end." These were the words that now defined the operation of the congressional Democrats: *moderating, retreating, opposing, thwarting, holding the line.* They were fighting for moral victories now.

Reagan had the upper hand, and he used it skillfully. While he didn't see the need to preempt, as Nixon had, since the Democrats were no longer in control, neither did he see the need to polarize as Nixon had—what historian Rick Perlstein had called "positive polarization" because dividing America between the white middle and working class on the one side and the minorities and the poor on the other had redounded to Nixon's benefit. Reagan didn't feel he had to pit one group against another, in large part because minorities and their liberal allies had so little power that one didn't even have to appease them. Reagan could do whatever he wanted to do, so long as it didn't affect the white majority to which he was beholden. The poor and the minorities were at the mercy of the conservatives now. And there was little the liberals could do about it—so little that, as Bill Bradley, the basketball star turned U.S. senator, would bemoan, "Democrats lost not just their confidence, but some of their convictions. Indeed, beliefs about government of the previous twenty-six years were increasingly seen as the cause of the defeats. . . . Democrats began to believe that the voters' basic impulses went against them." Ted was to say that he never believed that the country had really lurched rightward, as the conventional wisdom had it, though he would sometimes talk as if it had. Rather, he said, as Jack used to say, that the country was basically conservative but open to progress; and the trick was talking conservative but voting liberal, though it was a trick that Ted himself never quite mastered. Those conservative words burned on his tongue.

Reagan was hardly great-hearted from the liberals' point of view. His compassion was highly restricted. He clearly felt that hard work was the answer to every personal difficulty and that adverse social conditions were merely an excuse for those who hadn't worked hard enough to succeed, which was no doubt a carryover from his Hollywood days. In American films, heroism was action, not compassion; heroism was taking care of things by oneself, not relying on anyone else. And Reagan was nothing if not an American hero in that movie mold. Speaker Tip O'Neill's criticism of Reagan was that he should have known better because he had come from the lower middle class himself, and his family, headed by an alcoholic father in Dixon, Illinois, had struggled. But then, O'Neill said, he went out to Hollywood "because he was a handsome guy with a great head of hair," and "he had allowed Hollywood to get the better of him." He had forgotten where he had come from. Reagan didn't see his cutting social programs on which the poor depended as cruelty. He saw it as promoting self-reliance, which was an easy sell to his own party and to white middle-class Americans who didn't depend on those social programs for their survival. Even his former campaign manager, John Sears, anticipated the revolution that was brewing in the Reagan administration and felt that it needed some pushback. Ralph Neas, a liberal activist who had come to Washington as a staffer for the Black senator Ed Brooke, Ted's onetime Republican Massachusetts colleague, had suffered from a near-fatal case of Guillain-Barré syndrome and after recovering had been offered a job with Sears's law firm, which he was going to take to earn some desperately needed money. Sears talked him out of it. He urged Neas instead to take a job he had been offered with the Leadership Conference on Civil Rights, an umbrella group working to advance liberal causes. "My friends are going to try to undo everything that your mentors and your friends have achieved over the last thirty or forty years," Sears told him. He said there was going to be an "epic confrontation." He said that Neas needed to be part of that confrontation. And Neas wound up taking the LCCR post.

An epic confrontation was what loomed that spring—a confrontation to shred the New Deal and Great Society safety nets. Ted called Reagan and his allies not conservatives but "neo-nihilists," whose "goal was to slash resources for domestic programs." But Ronald Reagan did not look or sound like a nihilist. Ronald Reagan was genial. As one historian put it, "Reagan believed in getting people to 'love you, not just believe in you,' in public and in private." And he quoted Reagan, "I think I gained that knowledge in show business, and out on the road I do my very best to establish a personal relationship with a crowd. It's easy for me, too, because truth of the matter is I do like people." He did. And people generally liked him too, so that when he proposed his huge tax cuts, there was mainly acclaim, and when he pushed vigorously for concomitant cuts in social programs, there was less resistance than one might have expected. "Lower taxes along with reduced federal spending, reduced regulation, and more military defense formed his center as president," pollster Stanley Greenberg would write. This was Reaganism or Reaganomics, as it came to be called. It was the opposite of the Keynesian economics, named after the British economist, John Maynard Keynes, that had dominated policy since the Great Depression: have the government spend to stimulate the economy in times when it was foundering. Reaganomics was what was called "supply side." Its theory was that one could pump up the economy, not through government spending, but by giving large tax cuts, especially to the wealthy, who would eventually put money into the economy because they would have more money to spend. Another name, one that detractors used, was "trickle-down economics," since the money would theoretically trickle down into the economy where it would benefit those who were not wealthy. And there was a moral component too. As one of its proponents described it, "A tax cut not only increases demand, but increases the incentive to produce. . . . With lower taxes, it is more attractive to invest and more attractive to work." The tax cuts would, conservatives said, actually *increase* tax revenues because with lower taxes people would theoretically be working that much harder. And if supply side was the antithesis of Keynesian economics, the morality on which it was predicated was the antithesis of the morality on which liberal economics had been predicated. One promoted the idea of individual responsibility and the spoils going to the chosen. The other promoted the idea of social responsibility with assistance going to those in need. The conservative point of view may have been best expressed by evangelist and Reagan supporter Jerry Falwell: Wealth was "God's way of blessing people who put Him first."

Tax cuts were the first battle. Reagan's entire revolution was based on cutting taxes, especially the tax rates that the wealthy paid, which would cut government funds and choke off those social programs. Liberals saw it, in effect, as a Rube Goldbergian contraption designed not so much to propel the economy as to end government activism. (Of course, conservatives saw it differently with trickle-down; lower taxes would allow the wealthy to spend more.) Reagan introduced his tax cut measure on February 18, a month after his inauguration. It called for 9 percent cuts in each of the following three years and a reduction of the top rates, the rates paid by the wealthiest Americans, of one-third, and a depreciation schedule for business that would halve corporate taxes. (To counter Reagan, Ted had introduced his own tax plan that provided greater relief to middle- and lower-class voters.) Reagan predicted a $500 billion surplus by 1984. But that surplus would not be provided solely by those increased revenues the tax cuts were supposed to spur. It was also provided by the cuts to social programs—$750 billion in cuts over the next five years. Meanwhile Reagan was increasing the military budget that Jimmy Carter had already increased by 12 percent during his presidency. Whether or not the numbers added up—and they didn't; there would be no surplus but instead a deficit of $2.6 *trillion* at the end of Reagan's presidency—the likable president had the Democrats over a barrel. And he gained an even greater advantage that March, when he was wounded in an assassination attempt by a disturbed young man named John Hinckley, just a month and a half after Reagan had introduced his tax and budget package. No one wanted to vote against tax cuts, even if the biggest chunk of them went toward the wealthiest Americans. And now no one was eager to vote against the new president who had narrowly escaped death. (One of the first nonfamily visitors he was allowed to see was Speaker O'Neill, who strode into the hospital room and planted a kiss on his forehead.) Reagan's polling skyrocketed on the eve of his first congressional battle. The Democrats—the Democrats who, as Bill Bradley had said, had come to doubt themselves and their principles—surrendered.

But not Ted Kennedy. "When everybody else was running for cover," Bob Shrum, now Ted's press secretary, would later write, "he absolutely refused to. He stood up on stuff that was very tough to stand up on." "Scorched-earth economics" he called the Reagan bill, and he warned his fellow Democrats, now in retreat, that "as Democrats we must be something other than warmed over Republicans." "Now is not the time for silence, delay and ambiguity," he told the Women's National Democratic Club, as the bill was making its way through Congress. "Real human beings suffer from illnesses as a result of unfair budget cuts. Real workers will be put out of work. The elderly on Social Security will be left next winter with a cruel choice between food on their tables and heat in their homes. Children will be born retarded because of cuts in protein for their mothers." He said the Republicans' priorities were "backward," and he spoke of a "religion of inaction," so unlike his own political religion, which was one of action to help those in need. Reagan had already gotten his budget through both houses of Congress in May—a budget with $37 billion in cuts to social programs—cuts so severe that when *The New York Times* reported the passage of the budget in the Senate, it said the budget "envisions the elimination and reduction of scores of agencies and social programs, many of which were created in the Great Society of President Lyndon B. Johnson." Ted had commandeered the floor for an entire week, opposing those cuts, and he was one of only twenty senators who voted against that budget, with Western and Southern Democrats now so terrified by the rightward tilt that they joined with Reagan in disemboweling the very programs their party had taken such pride in creating. (If one needed any sign of how much in retreat the Democrats were, one needed to look no further than the fact that even Minority Leader Byrd voted with Reagan.) Ted was the most fervent in opposing those cuts. "Anti-health, anti-education, anti-elderly, anti-poor and anti-middle class," he railed. To no avail. When Senator Donald Riegle proposed restoring just $1 billion to education, he was voted down overwhelmingly. Ted was among the eight senators who voted against the tax cut bill when it reached the Senate floor the following month. Even his own staff was cowed by the support for it. Horowitz told him it was "politically unwise" to oppose it. And Ted, in defiance, told a staff meeting "Well, why don't you guys have your discussion. But I'm voting against it."

There was a time when Ted Kennedy's fervor could have rallied his fellow liberals, a time when his appeal to the morality of helping the powerless might have headed off efforts to hurt them. But this was not that time. Ted was in the minority—within the Senate, and now even within his own party. A few liberal Democrats besides Ted pushed back, but they did so sheepishly. In the House, where Democrats still retained a majority, they called for tax rates pitched toward helping middle-class Americans, called for a corporate tax rate higher than the one for which the president had called, and called for "triggers" that would peg future tax cuts to certain economic benchmarks. But Reagan was on a roll, and he stood his ground. (The only area in which he was forced to retreat was a massive cut to Social Security; he lost the Senate vote 96 to 0.) The day before the scheduled tax cut vote, he delivered a national television address, with a chart behind him covered in red, to show the deficits the House Democrats' bill would bleed were it to be passed. And as for all the details, which had held up the passage as legislators tried to sneak their pet provisions into the bill, he quoted what a constituent had told his Southern Democratic congressman who offered to explain the minutiae: "Don't give me an essay. What I want to know is are you for 'em or agin 'em?" When the vote was taken, thirty-seven of the forty-seven Democrats in the Senate voted with the Republicans, and forty-eight Democrats in the House voted with their Republican colleagues—"boll weevils" they were called, because like the beetle that infested cotton, they were difficult to stop, and because they were a resurgence of the old "boll weevil" Southern Democrats who used to bedevil the liberal Democrats. The tax cuts passed overwhelmingly, 89 to 11 in the upper chamber, 238 to 195 in the House, with the Democratic majority rejecting its own party's substitute bill drafted by the Ways and Means Committee. A "great day for the aristocracy of the world," Tip O'Neill declared mournfully. Ted, no less mournful, said the bill "provides the juiciest possible plums for the favored few and the meagerest pittance for those who need help the most." Meanwhile the day after passage, *The New York Times* ran a picture on its front page of Reagan holding a doodle, a self-portrait, with a wide smile.

But Ted, even in his despondency, even in the darkness, even knowing that he would be defeated, took one last swipe at the bill. It still had to go to a House-Senate conference to resolve slight differences between the two chambers' versions. The conferees met for sixteen hours, through the night, reached an agreement at eight a.m. on Saturday, August 1, and the vote was set for later that day. By that time, nearly a quarter of the senators had left for the summer recess because the vote was considered pro forma. Ted, however, did not see it as pro forma. He said he had a provision he wanted removed: one that gave a break to oil companies by providing relief from the windfall profits tax that Ted had so vehemently supported. And now Ted insisted that the Senate defer action on the bill until August 3 so that he could submit a motion to return the bill to conference so the relief it gave to oil companies could be removed. The Senate reconvened at two p.m. that Monday afternoon, but Ted's motion didn't have a chance to carry. It failed by a vote of 55 to 20, only after, however, a two-hour debate in which he was excoriated for having stalled the vote and having brought the Senate back into an unnecessary session. "We are asking schoolchildren to pay more for their lunches," Ted declaimed to a near-empty Senate. "Should we be giving away billions of dollars to the oil companies?" Bob Dole, who was the sponsor of the oil relief bill, said that Ted should have shown up at the conference if he cared so much and called Ted's speech a "media event" and the "same old, tired liberal voices . . . knocking down the free enterprise system." Dole was right about those voices being tired. They had no effect. Ted himself said that "many colleagues whom I'd counted as reliably liberal began to move rightward from the issues we had championed together over the years"— among them, Joe Biden of Delaware, James Sasser of Tennessee, Paul Sarbanes of Maryland, and John Glenn of Ohio. Reagan signed the bill two days later, marking what Thomas Edsall of *The Washington Post* called the "completion of the basic foundation of the Republican economic strategy: deep cuts in domestic social programs combined with tax reductions largely benefiting corporations and the well-to-do." Ten days later Ted addressed an ironworkers' convention and assailed the bill, calling the tax cuts a "tree ripe with the richest plums for the wealthiest individuals and corporations, but . . . only bitter fruit for workers and the middle class." But his assault drew little response from the audience. Workers didn't care that "two-thirds of the tax cut goes to the rich," he lamented, "so long as they are getting their one-third."

And Ronald Reagan understood that too.

V

Was there life after disaster? Ted Kennedy didn't seem to know. "You're standing up and complaining about what these guys are doing all day, but you're not actually doing anything," recalled Tom Rollins of Ted's situation at the time. "You're being visibly left behind on all the presidential attentions." And Rollins said that Ted now made his way into policy discussions in "almost a mocking way," needling, sarcastic, because there was so little he could accomplish except to shake his head incredulously at the damage he thought was being done to the country's social fabric. Other than that, he was, as Carey Parker described it, "playing defense," forging alliances with moderate Republicans, especially those on the Budget Committee, to shield some of those social programs. As Stephen Breyer told it, Ted, looking for Republicans with whom he might be able to make a deal and get a majority, would tell his staff, "Work it out." But few moderate Republicans now were willing to work it out with him. He had always preached patience. A student of the chemistry of the Senate, he knew that most things happened incrementally there. But he could not even move the increments now. It was depressing work for him after what he had been accustomed to—"technical work," in Rollins's words, trying to put holds on administration bills. The senator who had once spoken boldly of sailing against the wind now told biographer Burton Hersh resignedly that he was "wading against the tide."

He was always searching for some way to ameliorate the worst of what he saw as the damage, even stealing moments with Reagan himself to try to move him. Carey Parker said he would show up at a White House bill signing with his cards—the index cards on which he would write his talking points—and grab a few minutes of the president's time to lobby him. Parker doubted anyone in the administration ever looked at the cards that Ted left with them, and his effect on Reagan was minimal at best. His effect on the Senate, the Senate that he had once commanded, was not much greater. He was even unable to conduct hearings of his own, since he was no longer a committee chairman. But Ted Kennedy, even in his despair, would not surrender. Instead, he came up with another, novel way to air his issues. It was hatched when he and Horowitz were musing on how to circumvent their powerlessness under the Republican majority. Horowitz said, "You know, it would be great if we could just get a room because then we could call them [hearings] 'forums,'" and they could do most of the things a committee hearing would do without the formal designation. Ted responded instantly that he could get a room. "I'm a senator. I can get a goddamned room." And so Ted began convening "forums" in the very same hearing room in which he had conducted his hearings—forums for which he selected subjects and invited witnesses and the press and at which he managed to get his issues into the public discussion just as he had done when he was a committee chairman. Even Republican senators appeared in order to gain the media exposure. A forum on the encouragement of the use of baby formula in developing countries where breast feeding had much better results landed prominently in *The New York Times* and thereby put a focus on the issue—one of the few areas in which he seemed to be able to apply pressure on the Reagan administration, which had put itself in the position of being the only government to oppose a World Health Organization voluntary code on the use of formula, arguing that it was an intrusion into individual freedom and free enterprise. Two U.S. Agency for International Development officials quit in protest, after testifying at Ted's forum, and both houses of Congress passed resolutions overwhelmingly urging the administration to adopt the code. "Nothing gave him more pleasure than to do little things like that," Horowitz said. But the operative word was still "little."

The "big" was yet to come. The Voting Rights Act of 1965 was arguably the single most important law in the history of the United States. Until that act, despite being given the constitutional right to vote by the Fifteenth Amendment, Black people in the South had been prevented from voting through various mechanisms, from bureaucratic impediments to bogus literacy tests that might require the registrant to recite the Constitution to the poll taxes that Ted had so vigorously opposed when the bill was first passed, to judicial blockades, to physical intimidation. In Mississippi in 1964, before the act's passage, 6 percent of the state's Black people voted. In 1969, five years after its passage, 59 percent voted. But the act, as morally inviolable as it was, was not politically inviolable. It had passed Congress overwhelmingly, with seventeen Democrats, all southerners, opposing it in the Senate, and only one Republican, John Tower of Texas, in opposition. But the Republican Party had changed since the passage of the act. Richard Nixon's Southern Strategy and his positive polarization had introduced an antipathy toward civil rights, and Ronald Reagan, genial though he might have seemed, was part of that antipathy, ostensibly ideological—the federal government shouldn't be telling states what to do—but largely political, since one of the best ways of winning white votes, especially in the South, was opposing the advancement of civil rights for Black people. The agent of Reagan's antagonism was, ironically, the man he selected to be the assistant attorney general for civil rights, William Bradford Reynolds. At least it would have been ironic before Nixon and then Reagan took the White House. Traditionally, the occupant of that position was the spearhead for civil rights. For Reagan, as for Nixon, the appointee was not a spearhead but a wall to block them. Specifically, Reynolds paid little attention to violations of the Voting Rights Act because he had little interest in remedies to discrimination.

As the act approached another extension, Reynolds's lack of interest in voting rights concerned Ted Kennedy and concerned him deeply. The Voting Rights Act had been extended in 1970 and 1975, the latter of which was a seven-year extension, to 1982. But in 1980 the Supreme Court heard a case, *Mobile v. Bolden,* in which it ruled that the at-large election for city commissioners in Mobile, Alabama—that is, an election not by district but citywide—was not unconstitutional even though the system effectively disenfranchised Black voters; the city had a white majority who could always outvote the Black minority. In his majority decision for the city, Justice Potter Stewart wrote that "action by a State that is racially neutral on its face violates the Fifteenth Amendment only if motivated by a discriminatory purpose." In short, the *effects* of discrimination were not sufficient to constitute a violation of section two of The Voting Rights Act, which prevented jurisdictions from abridging the voting rights of minorities. After *Mobile,* a plaintiff had to prove *intent* to discriminate. And the potential practical consequence of the decision was that jurisdictions wanting to curb Black voting could do so by holding at-large elections or gerrymandering or other techniques, so long as these appeared to be racially neutral in intention. As Ted put it, *Mobile* "paralyzed" enforcement of the Voting Rights Act. With the case hanging over the law, few cases were brought.

This was an "enormous change," Ted would say—one that effectively gutted much of the act. And Ted now feared that it was a precursor to eviscerating the act itself. He worried that the Reagan administration, which had no use for the Voting Rights Act to begin with, would use *Mobile* both to insert an intent provision into the extension and to justify extracting from the law one of its most important provisions, section five: that any modifications to state law in certain designated states, largely but not exclusively those of the South, had to be cleared by the Justice Department before they could be implemented to make sure they didn't curb the voting rights of Black people. He worried that the new Judiciary chair, Strom Thurmond, would do everything in his power to foil the extension of the act. And he feared that the longer he waited, the more momentum Reagan could build against any extension of the act. So he and Republican moderate Charles Mathias introduced an extension of the law in April 1981, more than a year before the law was to expire.

Given the new tenor of the Senate and of Washington, Ted was right to be concerned about opposition to the extension. The previous Voting

Rights Act extensions had sailed through the Senate, a testament to the consensus that had formed around the law and its purposes. Not this time. Ted and Mathias got only thirty co-sponsors for their proposed extension; he had expected more than fifty. This time President Reagan asked his attorney general, William French Smith, to study the act to see if it was the most effective means of securing voting rights and cited the provision that singled out southern states for special supervision as one that might need to be revised.* (The discrimination that bothered Reagan was discrimination against those Southern states, not discrimination against Black people.) This time the president said he favored mechanisms that would make it easier for states to opt out of the preclearance strictures. And this time Orrin Hatch, the new chairman of the Judiciary Subcommittee on the Constitution, had submitted a bill that wrote the *Mobile* intent decision into the act, just as Ted had feared. None of this boded well for the extension of the law as originally conceived.

Now arrayed across the battle line were the proponents of the discriminatory effects test, liberal Democrats with a few moderate Republican allies on one side, and proponents of intent, Southern Democrats and most Republicans on the other. The latter group's basic argument was that if the bill looked only to effects—that is, whether minorities were proportionately represented or not—then it was a "quota bill," setting up quotas for minority representation, and *quota* had become one of the dirtiest words for Republicans—a way, they said, of forcing democracy down the throats of Americans. And the stakes were high since the dispute was not only for voting rights, as important as they were, but also for every other area of civil rights. Intent clauses might be written into other civil rights legislation. But because Democrats still had their House majority, they were able to move the bill to passage with an "effects" clause in it. It passed on October 5, 1981, 389 to 24.

But the Senate was not the House, and not only because the Republicans now ran it. The chemistry of the Senate had changed. Along with so much else, the days of the Northern Democratic–moderate Republican coalition that had passed the Civil Rights Act and the first Voting Rights

*The cry that the Southern states were being discriminated against was an overstatement. Under section five, 340,000 requests had been filed with the Justice Department, and all but eight hundred had been approved, and of those eight hundred, a good many were forms of covert racism. "The Fate of America's Minority Rights May Rest On a Single Bill," *LAT*, May 31, 1981.

Act were gone. The Southern Democratic–conservative Republican coalition ruled now. By all rights, Ted should have lost this battle as he lost the budget and the tax cut battles, despite the history of interparty comity when it came to voting rights. He himself thought that there was a real prospect the extension would not pass this time, effectively killing voting rights. Unsurprisingly, the administration opposed the House bill with its "effects" provision and with another provision that continued the preclearance supervision for another ten years unless a jurisdiction could demonstrate good faith efforts to cure discrimination. Judiciary chair Thurmond opposed the bill, too, and so did the chair of the Constitutional Subcommittee, Orrin Hatch. The attorney general suggested modifications that were designed to make it more difficult to enforce—an "empty shell," Ted called the bill if Smith's modifications were adopted—prompting a bitter exchange at the hearing between Smith and Ted, in which Ted asserted that the administration faced a "crisis of confidence" in its commitment to civil rights, and Smith countered by saying that Ted was injecting politics into the debate, and that President Reagan "didn't have a discriminatory bone in his body"—a statement that was greeted with laughter by the audience.* To all that was added another impediment: Several Republicans were prepared to filibuster against it.

But there was something Ted and his allies still possessed that Ronald Reagan and his allies did not. And it was potent. Whatever Democrats had gained from civil rights legislation, which basically was more Black votes, they lost in the number of white people who fled the party—losing in fact nearly the entire South that had once been impregnably Democratic. But Democrats had not advanced civil rights for political reasons. And neither had the moderate Republicans who sided with them. Both those Democrats and Republicans, whatever other ulterior motives they might have harbored, had pushed for civil rights, finally, because it was simply the right thing to do, as Republican minority leader Everett Dirksen, a conservative, had said during that last day of debate on the Civil Rights Act in 1964. *The right thing to do.* The years since had eaten away at that moral

---

*This wasn't entirely true. When the United Nations voted to recognize Red China, and African nations that had voted for that recognition celebrated, an angry Reagan, in a phone call to President Nixon, made deeply racist comments about those African delegates. "To see those, those monkeys from those African countries damn them—they're still uncomfortable wearing shoes." Timothy Naftali, "Ronald Reagan's Long-Hidden Racist Conversation with Richard Nixon," *Atlantic*, July 30, 2019.

imperative, and that *was* politics—right-wing politics. The Reagan administration was not oblivious to the moral power of the Voting Rights Act, and it had never opposed *any* extension to it, only the extension that the House had passed with its "effects" test. But the Reagan administration also was hoping to strip out that test from the final bill by working on the straight, unmodified extension that Ted and Mathias had proposed in April—unmodified with effects. Hoping to counter the administration with a trick of their own, Ted proposed that he and Mathias reintroduce the bill on December 16, but that this time they introduce the House-passed version with its "effects" test and force the administration to wrestle with that. And because the courage of the House had had some effect on the Senate, and because many senators didn't want to be put in the position of seeming to turn back the clock on voting rights and, no doubt, then be attacked for it, Ted got sixty-one sponsors this time—one more than was needed to shut down the threatened filibuster by North Carolina conservative Jesse Helms. Reagan still opposed the bill, but he would soon be trapped between appeasing his white political base in the South and soothing moderate Republicans who favored securing voting rights for Black Americans.

That was Reagan's own doing because Ronald Reagan, in playing racial politics, had finally overplayed his hand. The previous September the Supreme Court had agreed to hear an appeal in a case filed by two religious educational institutions, Bob Jones University of Greenville, South Carolina, and Goldsboro Christian Schools in Goldsboro, North Carolina. The case involved the IRS decision to revoke tax-exempt status to those schools on the basis that they racially discriminated; Bob Jones had once denied entrance to any Black student, and then, having begun admitting Black people after the IRS decision, it prohibited interracial marriage or dating. (It was the revocation of tax exemption from religious schools clearly chartered for racial segregation that had stirred evangelicals against Jimmy Carter.) Bob Jones defended its policies as religiously based, insisting that the Bible demanded racial segregation and that the university could not be denied tax exemption because of its religious beliefs. Even Republicans had disagreed with the university's position. Through the Nixon, Ford, and Carter administrations, the IRS had not granted tax-exempt status, citing the school's discriminatory policies. But on January 8, 1982, shortly before the Court was to hear arguments in the case, the Reagan administration reversed the policy and granted Bob Jones its tax exemption. (The instigators seemed to be Treasury secretary Donald Regan and Attorney General Smith.) The administration then asked for the Supreme Court to vacate the case. The rationale for the change was one that Reagan had stated shortly after taking office and one that was purportedly based on conservative principle: that the "taxing power of the Government must not be used to regulate the economy or bring about social changes." But the real basis, unmistakably, was racial politics. "I don't think any Republican can do enough in their eyes," Orrin Hatch, who had inserted the provision in the Voting Rights extension explicitly calling for intent, complained, speaking of Black people. "Republicans start in a natural hole, with 85 percent of the blacks not willing to give us the benefit of the doubt." But there was a good reason for that, as the Bob Jones case illustrated. Ronald Reagan and the Republicans were now currying favor with racists.

But if Ted Kennedy had come to overestimate the power of moral authority, Ronald Reagan had underestimated it. The reversal of policy on Bob Jones raised an immediate outcry, and not just among liberals. Reagan, with his blatant racial appeal, had embarrassed members of his own party. And the administration had embarrassed itself. According to Ralph Neas, the civil rights activist who had been working with Ted to pass the extension with the effects test, after the Bob Jones decision, the extension forces suddenly gained new momentum, and Ted added four more co-sponsors to his bill almost as a way of showing their displeasure over the administration's action. Ted knew there would still be pushback from the White House and its allies. So the man who had felt so hopeless, the man who had resigned himself to fighting rearguard actions, decided to draw on the chemistry of the Senate that had once served him so well. As Neas would tell it, Ted called Bob Dole, the conservative Kansas senator. Dole was known for being tough and acerbic—a political hitman. But he was no racist, and Ted knew it. Ted also knew that just as Pete Domenici would want his name on the National Cancer Act, and Wilbur Mills would want to use national healthcare to advance his presidential prospects, which was why Ted had put their names on *his* bills, Bob Dole would not be at all averse to being regarded as the man who would be credited with "saving the Republican Party"—that was how a Dole aide phrased it—from its own racial hubris. Ted now offered a deal—a compromise he called it, though he later admitted it really wasn't much of one, just a "little sticker that permitted some of the other Republicans to come on." Since Dole wouldn't accede to the House's "effects" test, Ted said they could add a provision expressly denying that lack of proportional representation would, by itself, be proof of discrimination, but one that included discriminatory effects as a "circumstance" to be taken into account by a federal judge among the "totality of circumstances." That way, "effects" were sneaked into the bill. As for the argument over whether Southern states were being singled out for preclearance, another Republican sticking point—even though twenty-two states, not just the eleven states of the Confederacy, were subject to DOJ preclearance—Ted offered another concession, though it also wasn't much of one either: a twenty-five-year limit on the preclearance requirements. Dole was now placated and then went to the White House to see if he could get their backing and give them a way out of their own self-inflicted predicament. Neas said that Dole phoned him while he was negotiating there, and Neas said he told him, "This is your moment"—obviously Dole's moment to be a leader for civil rights. But Neas also warned him, "You either come on board or we have enough votes to override" a veto. By this time, Neas had been meeting every day in Ted's office or in Mathias's office, working with a dozen legislators, working sometimes for eighteen or nineteen hours a day to hammer out an agreement that would save the extension from the administration's efforts to weaken it, cripple it, even meeting with the arch-segregationist Strom Thurmond in Thurmond's office. And in the end, Dole came aboard and nearly every Republican came with him, and so did the administration, despite the continued efforts of a few die-hard Southern conservatives like Jesse Helms, who conducted a six-day filibuster, and his North Carolina compatriot, John East, who offered one weakening amendment after another. The extension passed the Senate on June 18, 85 to 8, with even Orrin Hatch finally voting for it.

It was "Dole's amendment," Dole's compromise, not Ted Kennedy's. It was Dole, not Ted Kennedy, who received the credit for gaining acceptance for the compromise, though Ted would say that "what he [Dole] did was virtually meaningless." Instead, Ted would say, "The House had really done it," because it was the House that had taken on the attempts to subvert the law. But Ralph Neas, who had worked so tirelessly for so long to save the extension, would credit Ted too. Ted had brought the stakeholders together, he said. Ted had recruited Dole and played on his vanity. Ted had worked out the compromise for all those months, from December through June. Ted had won the victory. And Neas felt, "If that battle had not been won . . . I'm not sure, whether it was a civil rights issue or some other kinds of issues, there would have been other victories [for the conservatives]. Because if you can't win on what is the heart and soul of civil rights, the voting rights act . . . you probably can't win on anything else. If you do win on that, you have a chance on everything subsequently. It was the first major social justice victory [against] the Reagan administration." And Neas called it a "defining moment"—both for the Reagan presidency and for Ted. Ted Kennedy had been resigned to those moral victories in the first year of the Reagan presidency, moral rather than political or legislative, resigned to being able to accomplish little against the conservative juggernaut. Now at last he had won a political victory because it was also a *moral* victory. "I do believe Senator Kennedy sensed that there was a national consensus behind certain kinds of values," Neas was to say. Voting rights was one of those values.

And Ted seemed to have learned something from that victory. He learned that consensus around those values could be his vehicle, perhaps his only vehicle, in battling Ronald Reagan, on behalf of those who thought the country had forsaken them. Ted Kennedy seemed to learn that it was with morality that he could combat the president who had a very different sense of what constituted morality.

VI

Ronald Reagan had an abundance of political gifts. He had that geniality. He had clarity and simplicity. He had no malice or arrogance or sense of retribution. He could communicate with the public so well that he was dubbed the Great Communicator. Perhaps above all, he knew what to communicate. He made no calls for sacrifice, no calls for social responsibility, no calls for government action to help those who needed help. He said the "nine most terrifying words in the English language" were, "I'm from the government, and I'm here to help." He believed that people were basically good, which was not a particularly conservative notion, and that all people should be self-reliant, which was. He would later learn how to lift the American spirit, which was a tonic after Jimmy Carter's presidency in which Carter seemed to indicate that presidents were helpless to do so. Ronald Reagan had many gifts. But there was one gift Ronald Reagan did not have. He could not rouse the moral passions of the nation, nor did he seem to want to. On issues like taxes and government overkill and

military strength, he was a powerful advocate. On issues like national responsibility and social assistance and peace—things that had seemingly
been discarded in the years since the presidency of Lyndon Johnson—he
chose not to be.

But Ted Kennedy did choose. He always had.

And while Ted understood and even admired, as one political practitio-
ner to another, those gifts of Ronald Reagan, he sensed in him that hole.
Ted Kennedy could not challenge Ronald Reagan's appeals to self-interest.
He could, however, challenge his lack of appeal to a larger interest. When
he was plotting whether to run against Jimmy Carter, Ted had received
that memo from Ted Sorensen, the most important sentence of which
might have been: "EMK's vision of the nation transcends a single administration; define country's purpose, articulate it, provide assurance to
people and nudge them beyond their personal concerns." Ronald Reagan
had many attributes and could do many things. But he could not nudge
people beyond their personal concerns. And Ted Kennedy could.

That was how one had to combat Ronald Reagan. One had to focus on
those issues that Reagan would never choose to embrace: moral issues
that spoke not to personal morality but to public morality, not to individual responsibility but to social responsibility.

And that was what led Ted to Randall Forsberg. Randall Forsberg—
"Randy" to everyone who knew her—had needed a movement. She had
come to realize that lobbying senators and congressmen was "fruitless,"
as she put it, "if you didn't have a movement." Otherwise the congressmen would "either say 'yes,' and do nothing, or say 'that's absurd.'" So
Randy Forsberg had built a movement—built it from scratch. She had
been born in Huntsville, Alabama, and grew up on Long Island outside
New York City, where her father was a stage and soap opera actor. After
graduating from Columbia University, she got a job in 1968 at the Stock-
holm International Peace Research Institute, an experience that led her
to pursue a doctorate in political science at MIT, where her main interest
was arms control. By one account, in 1979, having gotten her Ph.D., she
was giving a speech in Louisville, Kentucky, on arms control in which she
said that the way to stop the arms race between Washington and Moscow
was just to "stop it," adding, "Enough is enough." When she was asked by
people in the audience if she had ever written down her ideas, she was
prompted to write a brief manifesto titled, "The Call to Halt the Nuclear
Arms Race." The next year she founded the Institute for Defense and Dis-

armament Studies, which collected scholars to study ways to reduce arms. Her manifesto and her institute formed the basis of the movement that Randy Forsberg realized she needed if she were to make headway against the intransigence of the government. Forsberg's movement wasn't technical, as so many forays into arms control were. It didn't focus on the number of missiles and throw-weights and parity. "Enough is enough," Forsberg had said. Her movement was intended to "just stop it": to impose a freeze on the nuclear arsenals of both the United States and the Soviet Union. No more weapons.

And Forsberg had been right about needing a movement. The nuclear freeze movement she built when she was only thirty-nine, a grassroots movement, caught fire in part because Ronald Reagan seemed intent on accelerating the arms race rather than stopping it. (He called the Strategic Arms Limitation Treaty negotiated by Jimmy Carter with the Soviet Union but not ratified by the Senate an "appeasement"; as president, he called for increasing America's nuclear arsenal.) By early 1982, five hundred thousand people had signed a petition calling for a freeze, and another five hundred thousand Californians had signed a petition to put a nuclear freeze on the ballot in that state. Resolutions calling for a freeze had passed the legislatures in Connecticut, Oregon, and Massachusetts and in the statehouses of New York, Wisconsin, and Kansas. Referenda were planned for New Jersey, Michigan, and Delaware. *The Washington Post* reported that of 180 town meetings in Vermont in February, 159 voted to support a freeze. "It's sort of doubling every couple of months," a freeze organizer told syndicated columnist William Schneider that winter, speaking of the number of supporters. A Gallup poll put support at 60 percent, a *Time* poll at 70. "The most powerful, most spontaneous grassroot movement I have seen since I was elected to Congress," Representative Tim Wirth of Colorado told Schneider.

Ted Kennedy had a long-standing and deep interest in arms control. Part of it was an inheritance from his brother John, who had had an equally deep interest. In a speech at American University early in 1963, Jack Kennedy had announced a moratorium on nuclear testing, which led to the Nuclear Test Ban Treaty between the United States and the Soviet Union later that year. Ted had been affected by the speech—he called it "magnificent and would think so even if it hadn't been my brother"— and by the Cuban Missile Crisis, which had come right in the middle of his first Senate campaign. "My entrance into public life was in that shadow of that," he would say. After Jack's assassination, he picked up the baton. He called for a moratorium on nuclear weapons that were intended primarily as bargaining chips in negotiations; on weaponry that would disrupt mutually assured deterrence, namely defensive weapons; on a separation of arms control talks from summit talks so that more emphasis could be placed on them; and on a search for ways beyond Strategic Arms Limitation Talks to find areas of agreement between the United States and Russia. And as he did so often, he conducted his own rogue foreign policy, first discussing arms control with Soviet premier Leonid Brezhnev on a trip to Russia, and later, in 1980, sending John Tunney to the Soviet Union to discuss back channel arms control.

Randy Forsberg now offered another avenue. Forsberg's freeze movement was well under way when Ted began thinking about trying to advance it. He was on a ski vacation in the Berkshires during the Christmas recess and attended a town meeting on a wintry Monday morning at Mount Wachusett Community College in Gardner. A woman in a rose-colored hat and holding a child told Ted that she had skipped work just so she could come and ask him a question: "Why can't we have a nuclear freeze?" Ted said she asked it quietly and followed up with some facts, but what struck him was that the issue meant enough to her that she had stayed home from work to ask him to address it. And Ted said that at other community meetings he attended, he got the same question: Why not a freeze? And at a meeting of social workers in Craigville, near Hyannis, he got the same question: Why not a freeze? Ted himself worried that the movement might be faddish, and his staff was uncertain whether he should endorse it, debating whether its advocates appreciated the technical problems of arms control and whether it might not be too "far out." But Ted, who was in the darkness then, was in no mood to be cautious. He consulted with arms control experts and set up one of his salons at McLean to discuss the issue.

And now, after hedging, he finally told Horowitz, "No matter what you geniuses think, this is what I'm going to do." What he would do is support the freeze. Columnist David Broder talked about Ted having "seized" the "hottest new issue in American politics" after having been dismissed as a politician "whose time had come and gone." Others had gotten there before him. But they didn't do what he did, couldn't do what he did, which was amplify the issue. On March 10, 1982, he introduced a nuclear freeze resolution into the Senate, along with moderate Oregon Republican Mark

Hatfield—Hatfield was the fourth Republican he approached; the first three had declined—the kind of resolution that was being passed in state legislatures and town meetings—one that called on both the United States and the Soviet Union to cease production of nuclear weapons in a verifiable way and then begin more wide-ranging talks. Neither Ted nor Hatfield sat on the Foreign Relations Committee or the Armed Services Committee, and Ted would later admit that critics asked what they were doing introducing a resolution like this one or why they were holding hearings when they had no jurisdiction. But Ted said that when they conducted their hearing, there were probably fifty cameras present "because Hatfield and Kennedy were in that Senate Caucus Room." What they might have lacked in jurisdiction, they had made up in publicity. And what he did was have Shrum and Parker write a book on the nuclear freeze, not unlike the book on the antiballistic missile system with which he had promoted that issue. It sold 200,000 copies by June. But Ted was the beneficiary as much as the movement was. He had needed something to focus him, to ignite him. The movement did that. "The freeze has really energized him," an aide told the Los Angeles Times. "It's got his juices flowing full force." He was talking about it in every speech.

And yet despite the grassroots popularity of the nuclear freeze, it faced serious opposition. The defense community was opposed because the defense establishment was dedicated to an increase in weaponry. The arms control community was generally opposed as well, finding a freeze simplistic and preferring a more nuanced approach. (This was what had given rise to Forsberg's "Enough is enough.") Reagan was not pleased either, subscribing to the theory that one had to build up one's arsenal before one could build it down, but he appreciated that the freeze was gaining steam, so he didn't reject it outright. Instead, in his first prime time television press conference, he argued first that a freeze didn't go far enough to reduce weapons and then that a freeze was impractical until the United States had reached parity with the Soviet Union. Ted answered with a press conference of his own the next day in which he challenged the president, saying, "No one in authority, including President Reagan, would trade our deterrent forces for Soviet forces," and as for Reagan's declaration that we needed to build more nuclear weapons in order to have fewer weapons, he called it "voodoo arms control," after George Bush's criticism of Reagan's economic policies during the 1980 primaries as "voodoo economics." Seventeen television cameras broadcast Ted's rebuttal, which testified to the importance of the issue and to Ted's residual celebrity. The House resolution went to a vote in August, and despite Reagan's assertion that a freeze would impede his own efforts at arms control, it lost by only two votes, 204 to 202. Ted, who noted that the vote occurred on the anniversary of the bombing of Hiroshima, still claimed victory. "The nuclear freeze may have lost today in the House of Representatives," he said, "but it is winning day by day in the country, and I am confident that it will prevail at the polling places in November and beyond." Despite his winning the vote, Reagan was on the defensive. Now attempting to discredit the movement, he cited articles in *Reader's Digest*, which had called the freeze a KGB-inspired plot to weaken America's defenses, though this only spoke to the president's desperation. Ted hadn't won the battle—the resolution didn't make it to the Senate floor before the midterm elections—but by applying pressure to Reagan to talk about arms control negotiations, he had nevertheless won another moral victory, which might have been the only kind of victory Democrats could win against the new president.

But Democrats were hoping for more than moral victories, those that provided hope but not results, or *moral* victories, those based on moral principles. They were hoping for a political victory in the midterm elections after the economic slide of 1982. On the face of it, they had reasons to be hopeful. The initial impact of Reaganomics on the economy had been disastrous. The deficit that was supposed to be erased by 1984 had ballooned. Interest rates soared. The United States was in recession. The stock market was in decline. Worst of all, the unemployment rate was rising until it hit 10.8 percent in the very month of the midterms—the highest unemployment rate since World War II. "More families are more desperate now with less hope for the future than at any time since the Great Depression," Ted said that April. "And the President offers no compromise on the budget or the tax cut, no meaningful solution to unemployment and no hope for the nine-and-a-half-million unemployed."

But Ted was wrong. Reagan had had to adjust his tax cuts in the face of the situation, adjust them significantly, even as he calculated that the cuts to social programs were irreversible since there simply wasn't enough revenue to pay for them. In June, at another Democratic midterm convention, this time in Philadelphia, standing in front of a huge poster that read "Kennedy-Nuclear Freeze," Ted delivered yet another of his blistering liberal broadsides before a crowd of three thousand. "The dawn is near. Our hearts are bright," Ted said, though it was doubtful after the losses he had suffered to Reagan that he really believed that. "Our cause is right, and our day is coming again." And he insisted, as he always insisted, "We will be, as we have been before and at our best, an advocate for the average man and woman, a voice for the voiceless, a partisan for people who suffer and are weak." He spoke for forty minutes. His speech was interrupted by applause fifty times. Kennedy aide Harold Ickes told a reporter, "He needed that. Some of the party regulars were beginning to wonder if he was ever going to get started."

After nearly two years of setbacks, he was restarting, if slowly. In an interview with *People* magazine on his fiftieth birthday earlier that year, he puffed on a cigar and insisted that he wasn't slowing down, that his greatest satisfaction was the "opportunity to make some difference in improving the quality of the human condition," that from all his defeats "I've learned more about my own sense of values," that the "biggest drawback" to being a Kennedy was the "high standards being set by my brothers and being measured by those constantly," and that Ronald Reagan notwithstanding, his responsibility would continue to be to "speak for the middle-income family, for the working man and woman, for the elderly and for the very young." With the midterm elections, the Democrats had a chance to fulfill those promises. So did Ted, who was running for reelection against a Republican businessman named Ray Shamie. There was little chance of his losing. His own polls, late in 1981, put his favorable ratings at 77 percent among Independents, 77 percent among Catholics, 77 percent among low-income voters, 75 percent among retirees, and 77 percent among likely voters. Columnist Mark Shields, parsing those numbers, concluded, "After nearly 20 years of landslides, the emotional crush of the Massachusetts electorate on Sen. Edward Kennedy looks both hopeless and permanent," despite the fact that the "infatuation" was "short on logic and consistency." At the same time Ted was putting up those numbers, Ronald Reagan, who had failed to pull the country from its economic mire, had a favorable rating of 65 percent among prospective *Democratic* primary voters. *People liked Ronald Reagan.*

It was not a reassuring harbinger. Despite his overwhelming advantage, Ted ran a vigorous campaign, in large measure, it was assumed, because he was already the Democratic frontrunner for the 1984 nomination and had the right to challenge Reagan, and he needed not only a smashing victory but also one that would provide a theme for a general election. He commissioned ads that stressed his humanity rather than his politics— his sitting by Ted Jr.'s bedside when the boy lost his leg to cancer, or his walking his niece, Kathleen Kennedy, Bobby's eldest daughter, down the aisle at her wedding in her father's stead—with the line: Ted Kennedy "has been criticized for many things—but never a lack of compassion." Another tag line was, "He is no plaster saint." Asked why he had commissioned these ads, he answered, "I've been the target of radical right groups, and their assault on me has always been personal. It is important to recognize that the kind of distortion that has been written about in the press would also be continued in the media. . . . I hope this gives a dimension of where I am." One ad even featured his old childhood nursemaid Luella Hennessey Donovan. Ted would later say that he ran the ads reluctantly, exposing himself personally in a family where secrecy was the operative principle, though it was a way for him to test the approach before a possible run against Reagan: Ted's compassion against Reagan's self-reliance.

Still, the campaign wasn't just a precursor to another presidential run. Ted took Massachusetts seriously, and when the *Standard Times* of New Bedford published an editorial criticizing Ted for not doing more for their locality, this in light of the fact that Ted had always prided himself on delivering for his state, he sought out the editor and lacerated him, "red-faced and shaking," by one report, for thirty-five minutes. He closed his campaign at the home of an unemployed autoworker, telling voters, "There is no corner to be turned so long as we continue down the blind alley of Reaganomics." Ted won handily with just under 61 percent of the vote. Reagan lost twenty-five seats in the House and six governorships, but Republicans retained their control of the Senate, holding every one of their seats. Reagan's economic plan hadn't worked so far, prompting David Broder, one of the veteran Washington pundits, to observe that Reaganism was a "one-year phenomenon." But unaccountably to many liberals, Reagan wasn't getting the lion's share of the blame, and his seeming lack of compassion hadn't hurt him much. Reagan had been called the "Teflon president," after the chemical surface to which things didn't stick, because nothing seemed to stick to him.

And now the Democrats would remain in the Senate minority for at least two more years, while Ronald Reagan and the Republicans continued what Democrats saw as Reagan's assault on the nation's moral order.

• • •

Even with Reagan still firmly in control, even with the Democrats foundering, Ted was looking for ways of blocking him. After his nuclear freeze initiative, which he had taken without being a member of either of the committees that had jurisdiction, Foreign Affairs and Armed Services, Ted sought a way of blocking Reagan on issues of war and peace, which were becoming more and more prominent. Ordinarily, senators were not accorded the privilege of sitting on three of what were known as A committees—that is, the committees with the greatest influence and prestige. Ted already sat on Judiciary and Labor—two A committees. After the midterms, he asked to be assigned to Armed Services as well. By this point, Ted was entrenched enough that the caucus was not about to refuse him. But there was nevertheless some questioning of why Ted Kennedy was allowed three A committees when no one else was. As Ted's longtime aide Melody Miller put it, the answer was, "When you can put out as much as he does, you can be on three A committees." Armed Services allowed Ted to square off against the administration on a set of issues other than social issues, especially new weapons systems and disarmament treaties, though he had joined the committee not only so that he could take on what he perceived as Reagan's militarism but also so that he could fight for the ordinary troops as a member of the Armed Services Manpower Subcommittee.

But there was a general assumption that Ted had another motive in joining Armed Services—not just blocking Reagan but setting up Ted for opposing him in the next election. After the beating he had taken in 1980—a "brutalizing experience," Larry Horowitz called it, because it wasn't his stand on the issues that the voters had rejected, but Ted himself—the possibility of his running for the presidency again seemed unlikely, even though he had ended his campaign triumphantly with his convention address. But Ted had not been deterred by the defeat. He said that after the campaign he was already "looking down the line for '84" and was "gearing up." In 1980 his preparation had been haphazard, and he had begun his quest unprepared. He was determined not to make the same mistake again. He formed a group called the Fund for a Democratic Majority that raised millions of dollars for candidates in the upcoming 1982 midterms and for Ted's presidential reconnaissance. He worked to revise the party rules so that the "good faith" provision that had bound delegates to the candidate to whom they were pledged in the primary—

the rule that had helped thwart Ted at the convention—was eliminated. He reached out to former Carter supporters, to minority leaders, to women and gay activists. He sent four of his staffers to a meeting of Democratic state chairmen in New Orleans. And he was collecting chits that he would hope to cash in later. He had gone to Iowa, the first caucus state, the state that launched the presidential race, and at the annual Jefferson-Jackson Dinner there, a Democratic ritual, Ted, Carrick, and Horowitz held a private meeting with the popular former governor and senator Harold Hughes to secure his support. Hughes had declared for California senator Alan Cranston, but he asked how serious Ted's interest was. Ted answered that he was serious, but any announcement would be contingent on his family's approval. Hughes took that to mean he was running. Ted attended a fundraiser in New Hampshire for Dudley Dudley, one of the women who had spearheaded the Draft Kennedy movement in 1980, even though Dudley had decided Ted couldn't win and was looking for another candidate to support. He did a western swing and delivered what was called a "gracious" speech to the AFL-CIO. He stumped for other Democrats that fall, even though he had a campaign of his own, and made, by one account, twenty-five appearances on one three-day weekend. Bill Carrick said, "He was very definitely, very intensely, 'Okay, I'll do all that I have to do.'" And, Carrick said, he did.

But perhaps the most significant sign of his intentions was not the schedule he kept but the team he was building. He had kept Carrick on staff and added Jack English, another political adviser, this one from New York. He had media consultant Michael Kaye coach him on his speaking style, after Ted watched his performances from 1980 and was displeased. He adopted what David Broder called a "calmer speaking style—and with it has come a greater flow and continuity with words." He hired Pat Caddell, Jimmy Carter's old pollster, to conduct polls for him, and hired other pollsters in addition to Caddell to survey Iowa and Illinois—"expensive" polls by one report, and a "massive study" in Caddell's own description. He hired the veteran political operative John Sasso, who had helped organize Iowa for him against Carter and then joined the administration of Massachusetts governor Michael Dukakis, to run his New Hampshire campaign, and Tim Russert, Senator Daniel Moynihan's chief of staff, to serve as his press secretary. By one report, he even scheduled an interview with Roger Mudd as a way of acquitting himself on this second go-round. And he had those humanizing ads produced for his own Senate campaign but also to determine how successfully he could change his image else-where. To that end, he empaneled focus groups in other parts of the country to respond to the ads and had Caddell conduct polling in New Hampshire about the ads' effectiveness there since the Massachusetts market, in which the ads aired, also broadcast into that state where the first primary would be held. According to Caddell's private polling, the ads did work, and Ted's advisers told Martin Schram of *The Washington Post* that the change in attitude toward Ted "could be the biggest breakthrough any of the 1984 hopefuls achieved in this year's campaign." Ted surveyed the likely field and thought he could beat Walter Mondale, one of the putative frontrunners. "I mean genuinely no doubt," Horowitz said of Ted's feeling. (A Gallup poll that July had Ted leading Mondale two to one among Democrats, and both he and Mondale beating Reagan, albeit narrowly, while Caddell's own polls had Ted with wide leads in Iowa and New Hampshire against the Democratic field and also showed he could beat Reagan.) *The Washington Post* reported what was now one of the worst-kept secrets in Washington: that Ted was preparing for a run.

But Larry Horowitz, the new administrative assistant, said it was subtler than that. He said that Ted didn't want his defeat in 1980 to torpedo his leadership role in the Senate and define the rest of his career, and Horowitz himself felt that the only way to accomplish that was to do what Ted had so often done in the past: keep alive the prospect that he was a presidential candidate. A "process of restoration" was how Ted thought of his return to the Senate after his defeat, according to Horowitz, *restoration* being a word that was often attached to Ted Kennedy, though in regard to his brothers' legacy and not to himself, and Horowitz said that if it went well, if Ted did regain his power, he might then consider a presidential run. But Ted instructed Horowitz to proceed as if Ted were going to run. He told Carrick the same thing, again pending his family's approval. Over lunch with Tip O'Neill after the midterms, he said that he had made the decision to run, and O'Neill pledged his support, apologizing that he had felt "in a box" in 1980, given the fact that he was in the Democratic leadership, but he was in a box no longer. And so heading into and out of the midterm elections, Ted Kennedy seemed like a prospective presidential candidate. "Really raring to go," Milton Gwirtzman said. John Culver, after speaking with Ted, told Gwirtzman the same thing.

How much of the effort was a way to stop Reagan and how much a way to redeem himself—this for a man who was always searching for redemption—is impossible to say. As Carrick had observed, Ted seemed fiercely determined to take on the president. But he was enough of a realist to appreciate how difficult beating Reagan would be, the economic situation and his own polling notwithstanding. Horowitz said that Ted understood that Reagan would be well nigh unbeatable, that the economy would rebound, and in any case, though it "puzzled Ted," Ted fully appreciated that "there was some kind of a connection between Reagan and so many voters that it almost didn't matter what he said." He said the same thing to Bill Carrick: that Reagan was no Herbert Hoover and that the economy would recover. (It was already recovering.) He said it to Bob Shrum as well on a flight back from New Jersey where he campaigned for Democratic senatorial candidate Frank Lautenberg. There was just enormous goodwill toward Reagan, he said. And when Shrum wrote him a victory speech after his Senate reelection and included a hint of running against Reagan, Ted took it out. Shrum said he knew then that Ted wasn't going to challenge the president. Caddell said that for all the effort in preparing a campaign, he too knew Ted wasn't going to run. "You know how I knew he was [disinclined]?" Caddell told Adam Clymer. "When we discussed the stuff [polling data] we had on the [advertising] spots, he was very disinterested." His old administrative assistant Ed Martin was deeply pessimistic about his chances. Another old New Frontiersman told Ted that a run was inadvisable given the condition of the Democratic Party and Ted's own liberalism, and he said that when he delivered that verdict to Ted, he did not disagree. Horowitz was a constant naysayer, though he had prepared a sixty-page, single-spaced black binder laying out the pros and cons of a run and setting out a strategy—a "month-by-month battle plan" predicated on raising enough money early enough to deliver a "knockout," according to one adviser.

Even if seemingly less than fully committed, Ted Kennedy was ready for another run, *pending family approval.* That had always been his proviso to anyone with whom he spoke. Since his family had given their approval the last time, it might have seemed pro forma this time. But nothing with the Kennedy family was pro forma. No Kennedy ever made a decision unilaterally except for Bobby when he decided to run for president, and that unilateralism had been months and many meetings in the making before he finally disregarded most of the advice he was given. For six months, Ted had discussed with his children the prospects of running. Ted Jr., he said, was the main spokesperson, but he met with them separately and together a number of times and kept detailed memoranda of those discussions. He said all three of them were opposed; "adamant" was the word Gwirtzman had cited in those memoranda. And Ted recalled in particular one night when Patrick, then fifteen, came into his bedroom and addressed the possibility and was "all sort of teary-eyed." Ted broached the subject again during the last week of his Senate campaign, and Patrick, he said, hadn't changed his mind. But on election night, Ted raised the subject yet again, seemingly hoping for some reversal, and asked to discuss it with the children over Thanksgiving.

The family conclave, then, on whether to run would take place over Thanksgiving weekend at Hyannis, where members of the extended Kennedy clan gathered. Ted chartered a plane for his niece Kathleen and Horowitz to fly up from Washington. His sisters, Jean and Pat, were there, but not Eunice, who was intent on his running, and Steve Smith was there, who was intent on his *not* running, and so were several of the Kennedy cousins, two of Bobby's children, Kathleen and Joe II, to whom Ted was now paterfamilias, and all four of Jean Smith's children—"more than a few severely troubled kids," as Larry Horowitz described all those cousins. Patrick thought that Paul Kirk might have been there as well. The first session was held on an overcast Friday in the living room of Jackie's house, the room in which Jack had watched election returns on the night he won the presidency, with the family sitting in a circle. Caddell made a presentation, showing the ads of the last campaign, the ads that were meant to humanize Ted, and then showed how those ads had changed the opinions toward Ted of the people who had seen them—from 35 percent thinking him immoral to 52 percent thinking him moral; a change of fifteen points on the issue of trustworthiness and seventeen points on the issue of whether he would panic in a crisis.* Then Horowitz made a presentation, a long presentation, a three-hour presentation, laying out all the polling data and the focus group responses and the prospects of Ted's winning. Patrick said that Horowitz played "devil's advocate" and made the case against running—Horowitz would later say that he was "increasingly convinced" before the meeting that Ted wouldn't run "because of what I knew was going on in the family"—but Horowitz also told the group that while a race would be "very tough," it was "do-

---

* Caddell appeared according to Martin Schram's account in *The Washington Post*. In other accounts, Horowitz was the one who explained Caddell's polling and not Caddell himself.

able." Ted was, Horowitz said, "shockingly strong" in Iowa, the first caucus state and the one that often set the tone for the rest of the primary
campaign, as it had for Carter in 1980. Throughout, Ted pressed Horowitz
about his obligation to run. But when Horowitz finished his presentation,
Horowitz said that Joe Kennedy II spoke up. "Well, Teddy, we all know
what we feel," he told his uncle. "This is personal, not political. I don't
envy you for the next couple of days," meaning days of deliberation. Ted
said it was Ted Jr. who spoke, not Joe II, and that he said, "I'm not most
concerned about the poll data; I'm concerned about what it is going to do
to us." And there was a "strong consensus," according to a report by Tom
Oliphant, that this was not a "now-or-never proposition at all," and that
he could run another time. As Horowitz later described the aftermath, he
and Ted walked out onto the porch, and "he basically said to me, 'That's
it.'"

But it wasn't quite "it." Ted met one last time with his own three children at his Squaw Island home on Sunday. "We just sat down and we told
him," Patrick said at the time—told him that they didn't want him to run.
Kara and Ted Jr. prevailed upon him that with the divorce, Patrick especially needed his father. And Ted Jr. would say that Ted had essentially
been gone for three years, since 1979, when he was preparing to run
against Carter, and then ran against Carter, and then spent another year
retiring his campaign debt. "This man, I felt, is missing out on some important things he'd like to do. So was the family." Columnist Richard
Cohen, having spoken with Kennedy advisers, wrote of the decision, "On
one side, there was the presidency. They say the polls looked good. But on
the other side, there was a boy. . . . The presidency could wait. The boy
could not." Family won out over politics in large part because family for
the Kennedys would always win out over politics. Ted told his children he
would not run and only asked them not to tell anyone until he informed
his staff—the staff that had worked so hard to prepare for that nomination. "You should have seen Patrick sitting in this office after the press
conference, on that couch," Ted told *Newsweek*, speaking of the press conference at which he announced his decision. "If you could have seen him,
the look on his face, the way he was. There won't be any regrets."

But years later Patrick had a very different version of the events on that
Thanksgiving weekend. "It wasn't on the level," Patrick would say of his
father's preliminary campaign and then of his renunciation. He believed
that it was all an "exercise" because Ted was the liberal standard bearer

and because he had a campaign organization in place and because he was regarded as the "preeminent leader of the party"—basically, because he was expected to run. But Patrick felt that he never really wanted to run. "I think he was done after his 1982 re-election. I think he was tapped out." And he was looking for an excuse not to run—one that would help him "walk back all the people who were invested in him." Patrick said that he did not fear for his father's safety, which was one of the main reasons given for the decision not to run—certainly didn't fear for it the way Ted Jr. and Kara did, and that he actually enjoyed the 1980 campaign where he got to spend so much time traveling with his father. Whether Ted was looking for an excuse or not, he had made his decision. He phoned Tip O'Neill that Sunday to inform him—"My children and I have just enjoyed some of the most glorious days of our lives"—and then set up a meeting with his staff in his Washington office on Monday at eleven a.m. to give them a chance to change his mind. "I want to hear again why you folks think I should go," he asked them. They answered that the campaign was ready, the money was coming in, the nomination would likely be his. To which Ted told them, "I'd agree, if it were strictly a political judgment." But it wasn't. That night, by one account, he called Ethel and Eunice and Sargent Shriver, and on Tuesday morning he invited Horowitz, Shrum, and Carey Parker to McLean to break the news that his mind hadn't been changed. "Let's get it over with," he said and asked Shrum to draft a statement. Shrum had already done so. Horowitz said that he and Jack English then made calls to supporters from Ted's chair while Ted sat next to them on a couch. A few of those supporters actually stopped by the house to argue with Horowitz, whom they held responsible for Ted's decision. But Horowitz knew otherwise. Ted made the announcement in Room 4232 of the Dirksen Senate Office Building, crowded with family and retainers, in what one reporter called a "small and comparatively humble space"— that is, compared to the Caucus Room of the Russell Senate Office Building where Jack and Robert had launched their presidential campaigns with hoopla. He cited his family obligations and his pending divorce. And then he spent the rest of the day phoning some of his closest supporters to ask, Tom Oliphant wrote, for their indulgence.

Relieved. That was how many of those close to Ted described his feelings after he bowed out. John Tunney, his close friend, said that he had talked with Ted after his reelection—a "very specific conversation," he called it—in which Ted once again asserted that his goal was to be a "really great senator," and Tunney thought Ted felt "comfortable in that goal," that Ted felt he had achieved a "level of excellence" in the Senate, and that he didn't want to risk it all on a presidential campaign that would be problematic at best. Boston mayor Kevin White told columnist Joseph Kraft that even before he bowed out, Ted was not acting like a man who was going to run. "He's easy with himself," White said. "He's got time for chatter and for jokes. He isn't driven. He doesn't have a thing about the White House." For all that, Ted, however, made it seem as if bowing out were a sacrifice. He would write in his memoir, "I really felt this was the race for me" and that he saw it as a race "on my terms." And "I thought I had a good chance." Moreover, he did feel a moral duty to challenge Reagan, which was why he had pressed Horowitz during his presentation on that Friday after Thanksgiving. He saw no other candidate who could take on Reagan and stop what Reagan was doing to the country, which was hurt the poor and those in need. It was his obligation to protect them. But Ted was a realist, and Horowitz said that Ted had always thought beating Reagan would be a "very, very longshot"—and this was when Reagan was at his most unpopular. Now he had taken the pressure off himself. The renunciation stirred speculation. Columnist Ellen Goodman, a Bostonian herself, concluded, "Maybe the secret is that Ted Kennedy really doesn't want to run for the presidency. Maybe the secret is that he feels what a lot of us in his home state feel, what his kids feel. Maybe now he feels relieved." But it wasn't *his* relief he had been seeking when he abandoned the race. The night he had made his decision at Hyannis, he and his children ate dinner with Rose at the Big House. And looking at those children sitting at the table, Ted said, "I could clearly detect the relief in their minds and in their attitudes and general dispositions." With that relief, someone else would have to take on Ronald Reagan for the presidency, while Ted Kennedy resigned himself to taking on Reagan in the U.S. Senate.

TEN

"The Powerful Appeal of Our Most Decent Values"

N OW THEY WOULD be free of each other—free of the marriage that almost from the inception never quite worked, free of the anxieties that the marriage continually provoked: his of having to deal with Joan's alcoholism, hers of having to deal with Ted's infidelities. On a damp, chilly December afternoon, the air wet with drizzle, Ted, in his customary navy blue suit, arrived at the small Barnstable courthouse, five miles from Hyannis, accompanied by Paul Kirk and looking grim. Joan came breezing in, less grim, even relaxed, with three attorneys, her blond hair as loose as she seemed. She and Ted exchanged pleasantries, talking "almost affectionately" while they waited for the judge to arrive on the bench. At least that was one account. By another, Joan was hardly breezy. She was near tears, and Ted had to place his hand on her shoulder to calm her, and the court clerk said that when he did, she regained her composure. They were sworn in, the judge asked a few questions, and then the session ended. "So quickly?" Joan said in surprise. Then Ted whispered something in her ear, perhaps even kissing her ever so gently, though it was difficult to tell. Afterward she told the press that the settlement was "very generous." And with that their twenty-four-year marriage was over.

The divorce seemed to be part of a reckoning for Ted Kennedy. The losing campaign and the subsequent dismemberment of the liberals by Ronald Reagan had changed him, moved him to seek a kind of renewal—freedom from his personal responsibilities to Joan, freedom from his political responsibilities to carry the Democrats' presidential expectations. At least for the time being, he downsized his aspirations. "I think his career in the Senate was already an extraordinary one," Carey Parker would later say of this period, "but it became even more extraordinary once everyone got used to the fact that anything Senator Kennedy did was not done with one eye on the White House." "He found a form of liberation," journalist Jack Newfield, who had been both a friend and admirer of Bobby's, wrote of Ted, though this was something that was said every time he forswore the presidency. "He had nothing left to lose. The weight of the country's—and his family's—expectations was lifted from his shoulders. His motives were perceived as being less calculating and self-aggrandizing. He could settle into the Senate for the long march. He could become a patient and disciplined senator without feeling like a failure."

The problem was that patience and discipline hadn't counted for much in the first two years of the Reagan presidency. The president had largely done whatever he liked, and Ted had suffered despondency because of that. But once he gave up his presidential ambitions, at least his 1984 presidential ambitions, he began to readjust his Senate ones. "When the Republicans took over the Senate, I thought there would be less opportunity to shape policy," Ted told Tom Oliphant of *The Boston Globe*. "But with the loss of so many able and gifted Senate members, there has been an increasing vacuum." And Ted told Oliphant that he "welcomed the chance" to try to fill it, even though "I still feel frustration in terms of taking ideas and turning them into policies." To another *Globe* reporter, Ted was blunter. The "enormous vacuum" in the Senate, he said, made him even more aggressive against Reagan because so many of the most effective senators had been defeated, and he was left to carry more of the fight.

And it wasn't only the vacuum in the Senate that needed to be filled. There was a growing vacuum in the liberal ranks generally. Trade unions had been a vital advocate of the liberal agenda and a central engine of the rise of the working class into the ranks of the middle class. The Democratic Party had long relied on union funds and union foot soldiers. But union power had been declining for years, partly as a result of the unions' success, partly as a result of Republicans' success in passing right-to-work laws that didn't require employees to join unions even if the union negotiated the contract that benefited those employees. (Another factor was the perception of union corruption that Bobby Kennedy, as counsel to the Senate Rackets Committee investigating unions in the late 1950s, helped promulgate.) Reagan had taken dead aim at them too. Early in his administration, the union of the air traffic controllers—the Professional Air Traffic Controllers Organization or PATCO—threatened to strike after years of complaining of poor working conditions, overlong hours, and derisory pay. But because the controllers were federal employees, it was unlawful for them to strike. Though their job was both difficult and essential, Reagan would not relent—he said because it would be the equivalent of being blackmailed by terrorists, but also, almost certainly, because unions had long been a conservative bête noire, and his threat was a way to frighten unions generally. If the traffic controllers walked off the job, Reagan warned, they would not be coming back. They did walk off, and they weren't allowed back. Instead, Reagan filled in with a jerry-built crew of replacements. Fifty-seven percent of Americans, according to a Gallup poll, supported him. But it was as much a rebuke to unions as a cheer for Reagan. Just as most Americans didn't think they needed liberalism anymore, they didn't think they needed trade unions either. Reagan confirmed it.

But the vacuum Ted had referenced wasn't just a vacuum of personnel; it was a vacuum of principle and conviction. Before the 1982 midterm elections, Minority Leader Robert Byrd had appointed an economic task force to examine policy for the party's caucus. Ted and Senator Bill Bradley of New Jersey were among its members. But Bradley complained that Ted wanted "more government programs and fewer tax loopholes, and he remained unconcerned about the budget deficit or inflation," and said that there was no way to bridge the gap between a Ted Kennedy and a conservative like Russell Long—at least not with any clarity. "President Reagan had fused personality politics and political program," Bradley observed, "and the Democrats couldn't cope." (Of course, Bradley, a fiscal moderate, couldn't accept that Ted, too, had fused personality politics and political program; it was what the Kennedys were so adept at.) And Bradley came to another conclusion about the Democratic morass: "The failure to develop an alternative [to Reagan] was symptomatic of a larger problem: what did the Democrats believe?"

Ted Kennedy knew what he believed. And it was simple. He believed in government action to help the poor and middle class; he believed that curbing inflation and cutting budget deficits were less important goals than arresting rising unemployment; he believed in stimulating the economy through government expenditures; he believed in equality and all the instruments that helped achieve it; he believed in workers' rights, and strengthening unions, in women's rights and in the ERA, and in the rights of minorities; he believed that healthcare was a right to be ensured by the government; he believed that businesses should not be allowed to fleece the public, endanger workers and consumers, and despoil the environment, and that it was the government's job to regulate them; he believed that peace was best achieved not through costly weaponry but through prudent diplomacy. What he believed in was the traditional liberal litany—the one he had repeated, with only slight modifications, since entering politics twenty years earlier. But that litany was old now, fifty years old, out of fashion, and even though Ronald Reagan had barely won a majority of the vote, even though his policies had put the economy in free fall, at least in the first year of their implementation, even though he was eventually forced to rescind a large portion of his tax cuts—the largest tax *increase* in American history, some called it—to prevent a budgetary shortfall, even though the Democrats gained two dozen House seats in the 1982 midterm elections, the narrative of obsolescence that the Republicans and the media, not necessarily in conjunction or for the same reasons, both purveyed in the face of those facts was so powerful that, as Bill Bradley had said, even Democratic officeholders were now convinced by it. But that narrative had little to do with politics. It had to do with culture. Liberalism had been America's dominant ideology since Franklin Roosevelt, and its staleness might have been as punishing a blow as the erosion of its moral authority or its seeming to have outlived its usefulness, perhaps even more punishing since the media were keen on finding the next new thing and discarding the last old thing. And it was especially punishing to Ted Kennedy, perhaps the primary exemplar of liberalism in the age of Reagan as well as an old thing himself, politically speaking. "Ted has done much to embrace issues—wage and price controls, the nuclear freeze—that distinguish him from his brothers," Kenneth Auchincloss wrote in *Newsweek* a month after the midterms, providing a perfect example of the rise of political fashion. "But no matter what fresh cause he espouses, there is something backward-looking about his appeal. He is a Restoration"—that word again—"waiting to happen, the restoration of an era—the '60s—that many Americans look back on with some pain." Those who sought a restoration were thinking of the early 1960s, of the John Kennedy 1960s. But that era had passed, and the 1960s that most Americans recalled now were those that Auchincloss cited: the years of Vietnam and race riots and assassinations and student protests and chaos. And the chaos had been associated with Democrats.

It was a terrible affliction to have to overcome: the affliction of no longer being regarded as the party of the average American.

Ted Kennedy understood that the Republicans had successfully demonized the Democrats and turned them into the enemies of the white working class. But even as he was undergoing his reckoning and renewal, Ted Kennedy was not inclined to reinvent himself, his deregulation swoon notwithstanding. And it might not have done him any good if he had. Ronald Reagan seemed impregnable, at least legislatively impregnable. His popularity had languished before the midterms and hovered in the low forties in the year thereafter. And yet Reagan never had to endure the bashing that Jimmy Carter received, and the Republicans in Congress never turned on him the way the Democrats in Congress, most notably Ted, had turned on Carter. In Reagan's first two years, Ted had taken him on in the one area in which Ted felt Reagan was vulnerable: Reagan's moral vision. Ted had made some headway, especially with the Voting Rights Act extension, but not much. Reagan's domestic policies were antithetical to Ted's, arguably stony-hearted where Ted was derided by conservatives as a "bleeding heart," and yet Ted's moral arguments had not carried the day, which was one reason he had himself appointed to the Armed Services Committee, where he could intensify his role in foreign policy generally and arms control specifically and where the moral imperatives he stressed might get more traction because they wouldn't be muddled by domestic politics. He had returned to the nuclear freeze effort after the midterms and had gotten South Dakota Republican senator Larry Pressler to hold hearings on it and gotten Kansas senator Nancy Kassebaum, another Republican, to bring it to the floor. But he and Kassebaum lost the vote, 56 to 39, when they proposed it as a rider to a bill raising the national debt ceiling, and 58 to 40, when they introduced it as a procedural vote on the freeze itself, largely because Reagan had insisted the freeze would tie the hands of his arms negotiators. Still, as Ted's foreign policy adviser, Jan Kalicki, would say years later, "Ronald Reagan, who was a political figure to his fingertips, could see the power of that [the nuclear freeze movement]," and Kalicki felt it was a "major element" that would later lead Reagan to take a position to eliminate nuclear weapons entirely. And Kalicki called it a "reminder that this [Ted Kennedy] is not just a legislator; this is a political force."

He was not, however, the force he had been, in no small measure because morality was not what it had been. On the twentieth anniversary of
his brother John's assassination, Ted said, clearly thinking of his battle
with Reagan, "The only way we have seen important changes in our society is when we've been able to make the issue a moral issue and to bring
together the different elements in our society that can bring about change.
I'm talking about the religious community, the Catholics and Protestants
and Jews. I'm talking about the business community, the labor community, the political community, the idealism of the young people." Heading
into that anniversary, he had embarked on what might have been called a
compassion campaign. He traveled across the country on a six-day, six-
city swing, beginning in San Francisco, and talking about poverty, about
the marginalized, about the elderly, about those in need of healthcare.
On the day before his tour was to end, he spoke at the Holy Trinity Church
in the Georgetown section of Washington, Ted's own church, in a Mass
commemorating the anniversary of the assassination, before an
invitation-only group that included the Kennedy retainers (Sorensen and
Schlesinger) and Democratic nobles (Averell Harriman and Arthur Goldberg) and other dignitaries (Supreme Court justices Thurgood Marshall
and Byron White), and Ronald and Nancy Reagan. A "joyful affair," one
reporter called it, with reminiscences of the late president—joyful until
Ted spoke at the end of the ceremony. His call was solemn. It was a call to
the nation's better angels. In remembering his brother, he spoke of how
"he rejected the cold affliction of indifference and the comfortable erosion
of concern." He spoke of the "compassion" that was "at the center of his
soul." He spoke of the "powerful appeal of our most decent values." And
he said of those there that day, "All of us in this church may not gather all
together again, but to those who share the commitments, the compassion
and the high hopes of John Kennedy, there will never be a last assembly."
Afterward he shook hands with the president, then departed to Hyannis
for a private Mass with Jackie and Rose, who had remained behind there.
And then the next day, he resumed his tour, visiting Appalachian Kentucky, where the poverty was dire, prompting columnist Murray Kempton to write: "Did many of us much notice that, when the last fiddle and
bow of John F. Kennedy's threnody had been laid aside, Sen. Edward Kennedy went off at once to Little Mud, an eastern Kentucky mine patch, to
visit the cabins where pinto beans would be all too often the Thanksgiving
dinner? But then it has never been easy for most of us to recognize that

President Kennedy's best monument may well be the only one of his brothers left alive." A month later, putting his words into action, the late president's best monument proposed a $2.5 billion program to feed the hungry—one-twentieth of the increase President Reagan was seeking for defense. But Reagan said that there was no evidence of rampant hunger in America—which Ted lambasted as "Orwellian doublespeak." And the effort, like nearly every liberal effort in the Reagan years, expired.

Ronald Reagan's attempted moral recalibration against compassion and empathy in favor of personal responsibility had been designed largely to rip away the moral authority of liberalism that Ted Kennedy kept invoking in his sallies against conservatism and expose what Reagan and his conservative allies considered the moral anarchy underneath—an anarchy that harkened back to the race riots, student protests, sexual freedom, and religious hostility of the 1960s, which the right had always blamed on liberalism. (The war in Vietnam, an unmitigated disaster which did erode liberal morality, was not something Reagan mentioned because he had supported it vigorously; for Reagan, America could do no wrong.) "There's been a wave of humanism and hedonism in the land," he had told an interviewer as early as 1976, clearly attributing it to liberal attitudes, while lauding what he called "moral absolutes," meaning his own rigid values and those of the conservatives and evangelicals. Reagan's moral recalibration was then, in effect, a crusade against those he and his allies regarded as infidels. "Wherever possible," wrote one political scientist of Reagan's deployment of religion, "Reagan had to demonstrate that Republican versus Democrat meant good versus evil and that this was God's work." This was the Armageddon about which he had fretted to the televangelist.

Whether Reagan really believed his own prophecies or not—and like many actors, he might have internalized his "lines"—there was, of course, more than a little political expediency in the moral declamations of a previously unreligious man who claimed he had established a new relationship with God in a time of need and of a man who had not paid much attention to moral issues save for the issue of government overreach that obsessed him and that he framed in stark moral terms—issues like exorbitant taxation, the Supreme Court's decision to prohibit prayer in schools, the Equal Rights Amendment (which he saw as challenging family values), regulation of business, and welfare. But expedient as it might have been, his moral conversion had another aspect besides short-term political advantage against born-again Jimmy Carter. It was a smaller one in cultural terms—the terms by which Reagan had sought to change the entire tone of American morality—but a larger one in political terms: While he was provoking a moral recalibration of the country, Ronald Reagan was also fostering a wholesale political realignment of the sort that hadn't occurred since Roosevelt's New Deal. What Reagan saw was that Americans could now be arrayed across moral lines: those who supported the so-called traditional morality of personal responsibility against those who promoted a secular social morality.

Realignment had long been a Republican obsession. Richard Nixon had attempted to splinter the durable Democratic coalition by building a new coalition based on resentment and revenge among white Americans, particularly when it came to race, what he called the Silent Majority, and he might very well have succeeded had Watergate not derailed his plans. In Ronald Reagan's case, he was as much the recipient of the coalition as its engineer, since it is difficult to distinguish between whether he created a new coalition or the would-be members of that coalition created it for him to inherit. Whichever it was, in the end, his coalition would draw on the same resentments that Nixon's had—they ran deep, and they formed the foundation of the realignment—but Reagan's would also be built on something else: on moral wedge issues that would use the liberals' so-called tolerance and compassion against them as a way of drawing away traditionally Democratic constituencies. And it would prove a formidable force.

Reagan's was a coalition of people who had caught the rightward drift largely because of that moral antipathy toward liberals—like the evangelicals. And if it was a formidable force, it was also a large one. Forty percent of Americans identified themselves as "born again" Christians in 1978. But most of them did not identify as Republicans; 57 percent of evangelicals, according to a Gallup poll early in the 1980 campaign, called themselves Democrats, and 52 percent of those reported to Gallup that they intended to vote for Jimmy Carter. Then the disillusionment with Carter set in, particularly among the most aggressive of the evangelical leaders who thought him too liberal despite his pieties. At a White House breakfast meeting between Carter and seven ministers in January 1980, Jerry Falwell, placing a tape recorder on a table, challenged Carter to denounce gay marriage, while apparently declaring, in Carter's presence, his own fierce opposition to the ERA, the prohibition against school prayer, and abortion. Carter was appalled by their truculence but somehow thought that the breach between them and him was still bridgeable. Ronald Reagan didn't think it was, and Ronald Reagan pounced. This was why Reagan selected an evangelical, Representative Guy Vander Jagt of Michigan, to deliver the keynote address at the Republican National Convention and why he let evangelicals dictate the party's platform. ("It's right down the line an evangelical platform," said one delegate.) This was why Reagan ended his acceptance speech with that "spontaneous" prayer and ended his speeches with "God bless America." And this was why Reagan delivered at the National Affairs Briefing in Dallas what one reporter would later call "perhaps the most famous lines of the Age of Evangelism": "I know you can't endorse *me*. But . . . I want you to know that I endorse *you*." They did, however, endorse him. Carter had won the evangelical vote overwhelmingly in 1976. Reagan won two-thirds of it in 1980.

And there was another, even larger sector of the nation—roughly 25 percent of the electorate—that was also susceptible to Reagan's moral recalibration, even though these voters had long been a significant part of the Democratic coalition. Republicans, basically a party of white Protestants, had historically exerted little effort in trying to attract Catholic voters, viewing them suspiciously as having divided loyalties between Washington and Rome. Catholics repaid the suspicion by voting Democratic. As columnist Mark Shields would note, "Since 1860, Catholics have not made very good Republicans." They had in fact scarcely made Republicans at all, surrendering instead to the appeal of the Democrats who saw them as marginalized, disdained, while Republicans appealed to small-town Protestant America. But now finally the Republicans saw an opening to attract those Catholic voters, and Ronald Reagan was determined to take it.

The opening was abortion.

Neither party had previously shown much interest in abortion, and it wasn't an issue on which the two parties had faced off, though Carter had said he was personally opposed to abortion—"It is wrong"—and that he was opposed as well to the federal funding of abortions except in cases of incest, rape, or when the mother's life was endangered, and when he was asked at a press conference whether it was fair that a recent Supreme Court decision, *Beal v. Doe*, denied poor women access to federally funded abortions while wealthy women didn't need those funds, he answered coldly, "Well, as you know, there are many things in life that are not fair." (Still, the Democrats, under Ted Kennedy's prodding, endorsed a pro-choice plank in the 1980 platform.) Reagan had, if anything, been more amenable to abortion than Carter, having signed that generous abortion bill in 1967 on the basis that it would protect the life of the mother. But that was before the Supreme Court decision *Roe v. Wade*, which gave women a constitutional right to an abortion under certain circumstances and made the issue more visible, especially among Catholics. More to the point, that was before Reagan was a presidential candidate. Now Reagan, in a sudden change of heart, declared abortion a sin and said he would demand that a constitutional convention be convened to pass an anti-abortion amendment, despite the fact that, according to one poll, only 32 percent of Reagan's own voters supported a full ban on abortion and, according to Gallup poll in July 1980, 78 percent of Americans either favored legal abortion under any circumstances (25 percent) or under certain circumstances (53 percent).

But those weren't the voters, the vast majority to whom he was appealing now, and those weren't the voters who were appealing to him for his backing. It was the evangelicals and the Catholics, for whom abortion was a critical issue, even if it wasn't for most Americans, and whom he hoped to lure from the Democrats. And lure them he did. Carter had won 54 percent of the Catholic vote in 1976. He won only 40 percent in 1980. "The heart of the 'Reagan Democrats' along with Southerners," E. J. Dionne, Jr., would later call those Catholic defections. In the event, religion seemed to have done to the Catholics what race had done to the South and to much of the white working class: It had shaken them loose from the old Democratic coalition and melded them into a burgeoning new coalition—a conservative coalition.* And so in 1980 Reagan seemed to have

---

*The exact role that abortion played in the 1980 Catholic vote is difficult to determine. One study concluded that it was not significant and that the attitudes of Carter voters and Reagan voters on the issue were similar. Few voters named abortion as an important issue, and voters were confused on who stood where. But the study did not break down Catholic voters' attitudes. Donald Granberg and James Burlison, "The Abortion Issue in the 1980 Elections," *Family Planning Perspectives* 15, no. 5 (Sept.–Oct. 1983): 231. Another study came to a similar conclusion: "namely, that they [the data] do not support the interpretation that abortion attitudes had much effect on how voters differentiated between Republican and Democratic presidential candidates." But again, the study did not break out Catholic voters. The decline in Carter's Catholic vote suggests that abortion did play a significant role. Byron Daynes and Raymond Tatalovich, "Presidential Politics and Abortion,1972–1988," *Presidential Studies Quarterly* 22, no. 3 (Summer 1992): 556.

realized what Nixon had started. And by doing so, he had finally shifted the tectonic plates of American party politics—shifted them along with the tectonic plates of American morality, shifted them largely *because* he had shifted the plates of morality.

To demonize the liberal Democrats—that was the conservative strategy, now that they occupied the White House again. And Ted Kennedy's personal failings made him perfectly suited for the sort of moral demonization practiced by Reagan and the evangelicals. One not atypical right-wing screed, titled *Teddy Bare*, depicted him, in the words of *The Washington Post*, as "one of the prominent operators chosen by the Hidden Forces that are hurling the countries of Western Civilization toward the Animal Farm World willed by Lenin and his successors." (The Fairfax County Library in Maryland bought eighty-eight copies.) In truth, Ted was deeply religious, though seldom sanctimonious about it. Friends described him as a "religious policeman" while at Harvard, rousing his roommates during Lent to attend Mass at seven each morning, and rustling them to go to church for seven consecutive "first Fridays"—the first Friday of the month—because, as one of those friends, Richard Clasby, put it, "it's kind of an unwritten law that you're going to be really blessed" if you go. And it was Ted who pressured John Tunney to study Catholicism when both were in law school, despite the fact that Tunney had shown no previous interest in his Catholic roots. Even in later years, Ted practiced his religion faithfully, often getting up early in the morning before anyone else in the house, especially when he was at Hyannis, to attend Mass. Jack once joked to Eugene McCarthy's wife, Abigail, when he saw her missal, "That seems to be the thing now—Teddy carries one around that he can hardly lift with both hands." But it wasn't a "thing" for Ted Kennedy. It was how he lived his faith and, most likely, how he sought penance. When Rose reached a point where it was difficult for her to attend Mass, Ted invited a priest to the Big House and had Mass celebrated in the living room. Religion obviously informed his values; he said as much. "The teachings become inspiring," he would say. "You find out, do some of the things that these parables sort of go, you find out that this is enriching your life." And his religion was a source of strength. "You can get yourself in a downward spiral, the depression, negativism, loss," he would later say. But he would also say, "I've been lucky enough to be able, when I start down there . . . to see another side or know of another side that can try to catch you on the way." He called his faith "part of the eternal optimism" that buoyed him, even though he had admitted to having doubted his faith after his brothers' deaths. But he parted company with those "born-again" Christians who felt all one had to do was accept Jesus and "everything else is saved." The important element of Christianity for him was that Jesus's life was a "life of service," and that to serve Jesus, one had to be of service oneself. Religion was about doing, not accepting.

When it came to Catholic doctrine, whatever his personal morality, Ted did not subordinate his public morality, his politics, to his religion's dictates. Philip Lawler, the editor of *Catholic World News*, credited Ted with having accomplished two remarkable achievements—he became the "most influential opponent of Catholicism on key public issues," and he remained the "most visible Catholic legislator in Washington." But while remarkable, it wasn't easy. Abortion was particularly vexing for him. As a Catholic, Ted had opposed abortion on demand, and his 1970 Republican senatorial opponent, Charles Spaulding, actually had a more progressive position on abortion than Ted's. A friend thought his views were later affected by the fact that when Joan suffered her miscarriages, the priest refused to baptize the fetuses on the basis that they did not possess the characteristics of personhood since they had not yet been ensouled. He was certainly influenced by *Roe v. Wade* in which the Supreme Court, as part of the right of privacy, gave women a right to abortion under certain circumstances. Now it was no longer strictly a religious or moral issue but a constitutional one. Even so, he was not convinced. Melody Miller, his onetime aide, said that Ted made a point of gathering information after the decision from doctors and scientists and ordinary Americans he met and that his position changed from opposing abortion to believing in a woman's right to choose to abort, even while he remained personally opposed to abortion. But it was still an agonizing decision for him, and Harvard Law professor Laurence Tribe remembered "fights" between Ted and his sister Eunice, who was fiercely opposed to abortion, and Tribe said Ted would try to deflect her, "turn it into a source of some kind of family joke." "Euni, you're always saying that," he would reprimand her. Still, it was less a matter of constitutionality for him than a matter of morality, albeit a different morality than whether a fetus was a person or not; for him it was now the morality of whether poor women, often Black women, should be forced to bear a child against their will or desires. He fought Senator Dewey Bartlett of Oklahoma, who had introduced a bill banning

the use of Medicaid funds for abortion, arguing that while he was personally opposed to abortion, Bartlett's amendment would primarily affect
poor women who would not have access to one. The amendment failed,
54 to 36. And he fought a similar amendment, by Representative Henry
Hyde of Illinois, that would prohibit any federal funds from being used for
abortion, with the only exception being if the life of the mother was endangered. When Ted announced his opposition, the United States Catholic Conference called his health aide, Stan Jones, to set up a meeting. Ted
told Jones that he would take care of it himself and that there wouldn't be
a problem. "The next thing I knew," Jones was to recall, "I was invited to
dinner at his place," and Ted told Irish jokes and stories and "plied them
liberally with scotch, so liberally that the subject never came up." And
then, as Ted escorted his guests out the door, Jones looked at him in "total
disbelief," and Ted said, "I told you it wouldn't be a problem." In this case,
however, the Hyde amendment passed.*

But if Ted Kennedy often agonized at having to joust with his own
church, he had no compunctions whatsoever about jousting with the
evangelicals, nor in taking the fight to them. Sometime early in 1983, Ted
said, he received a plastic membership card from Jerry Falwell's Moral
Majority along with a fundraising appeal in the mail attacking "ultraliberals such as Ted Kennedy," and was so amused by it that he showed it to
a reporter at *The Washington Post*, who contacted the group's vice president and communications director, Cal Thomas, to ask facetiously if
Thomas would demand the card back. Thomas quipped that he wouldn't
because "we don't believe anyone is beyond redemption," then humor-
ously suggested that Ted come visit Falwell's Liberty Baptist College in
Lynchburg, Virginia—a response that the *Post* printed. Bob Shrum recalled that when Ted read Thomas's invitation, he smiled broadly and
said, "Why not?" A few days later Thomas received a call from Ted's
office—probably from Larry Horowitz—saying that the senator accepted
the offer. ("Divine intervention," Ted would call it.) Thomas was flummoxed. He hadn't really proffered an invitation. When he told Falwell, the

---

* While Ted supported choice, he also supported regulations on fetal research, on the basis
that such research invited unethical experiments, especially on the poor, and as one abortion historian put it of Kennedy's hesitation, on the basis that the research was a "medical
exploitation of people who could not defend themselves," thinking of the forced steriliza-
tion of Black women in the South. Mary Ziegler, *After Roe: The Lost History of the Abortion
Debate* (Cambridge, Mass.: Harvard University Press, 2015), 206–7.

minister turned "white as a sheet," and said that Ted was the "devil incar-
nate" to many of his followers. But Thomas convinced him of the public
relations value of a Kennedy visit. So Falwell sent his private jet for Ted
Kennedy and Kara Kennedy and Jean Kennedy Smith, and they all had
dinner at Jerry Falwell's home, and then Ted gave an address to five thousand students.

The speech he delivered that evening, October 3, 1983, in the Liberty
College gymnasium was not a gesture of conciliation but a challenge. He
challenged the name Moral Majority, which, he said, "in the minds of
many, seems to imply that only one set of public policies is moral and only
one majority can possibly be right." (Of course, that was exactly what Falwell believed.) He challenged another Christian organization, Christian
Voice, for compiling a "morality index" of legislators, which incorporates
"how they voted on Taiwan and Zimbabwe," issues that were morally
complex with large political dimensions. He challenged the intertwining
of religious principles with right-wing politics. "People of conscience
should be careful how they deal in the word of their Lord," he said. "In our
own history, religion has been falsely invoked to sanction prejudice and
even slavery, to condemn labor unions and public spending for the poor."
(Of course, this was exactly what the evangelicals had done.) He challenged the idea that Falwell was a "warmonger," as some liberals had accused him, or that liberals were "Soviet sympathizers," as the Moral
Majority had accused them. And he challenged his listeners to accept the
separation of church and state, two entities that the right was all too
eager to meld. "The separation of church and state can sometimes be
frustrating for women and men of deep religious faith," he told them.
"They may be tempted to misuse government in order to impose a value
which they cannot persuade others to accept. But once we succumb to
that temptation, we step onto a slippery slope where everyone's freedom is
at risk." And when he said that "we must never judge the fitness of individuals to govern on the basis of where they worship, whether they follow
Christ or Moses, whether they are born again or ungodly," he received a
single clap among the thousands in the audience. He had challenged
them, but the die of America had been cast, and the divisions now were
not just between Democrats and Republicans, or between liberals and
conservatives, or even between those who believed and those who didn't.
In the eyes of those evangelicals, this new postpolitical America, this
America of a religious crusade, was divided between good and evil. After

the speech, Falwell said to Ted, "You may have won a few souls tonight, but I'll get them back next Sunday."

He was right.

II

Despite what Ted Kennedy and other liberals viewed as the gaping moral lacunae in Ronald Reagan's domestic policies—economic policies that relied largely on draining social programs of funds; social policies that relied largely on turning the clock back to a white, Christian, rural America—those liberals had been neutered on that front. "It was very difficult to get much done domestically," Ted was to say years later of this time. But foreign policy was different. There Reagan had provided an opening. Reagan's campaign foreign policy adviser and later his United Nations ambassador, Jeane Kirkpatrick, encouraged Reagan to abandon Jimmy Carter's human rights campaign and embrace instead a policy that had America supporting authoritarian right-wing dictatorships, thus prioritizing anti-Communism over human rights. Kirkpatrick had justified the change in an influential essay in *Commentary* during the campaign, with the provocative title, "Dictatorships and Double Standards," on the questionable basis that right-wing dictators were more salvageable than left-wing ones: "Although there is no instance of a revolutionary 'socialist' or Communist society being democratized, right-wing autocracies sometimes evolve into democracies." Whatever the justification, this was not a particularly moral formulation for a foreign policy if one was looking, as Ted Kennedy was, for one. Moreover, Reagan wanted to flex America's muscles—to show the nation's military strength, which he believed was a predicate to dealing with the rest of the world, especially after Carter seemed to have backed away, in Reagan's view, from using that strength in favor of diplomacy. "America has never gotten in a war because we were too strong," he had said at his debate with Jimmy Carter in the 1980 campaign. When the prime minister of a tiny Caribbean island named Grenada and four of his cabinet secretaries were executed in a coup in October 1983, Reagan decided to invade to prevent the Soviet Union and its Cuban ally from strengthening a toehold they already had there. It was a minor operation, and a questionable one, and writer Joan Didion thought of it as a kind of performance rather than a real military assault. At a Medal of Honor ceremony afterward, Reagan gave the real reason for the invasion: to make a statement. "Our days of weakness are over," he intoned. "Our military forces are back on their feet and standing tall."

But our forces were not back on their feet, and they were not standing tall. The Middle East was a hornets' nest with Lebanon occupied by both Syrian troops and Israeli troops and harboring a force of Palestinian fighters. Hoping to keep the lid on the country until a settlement could be reached, Reagan sent a small detachment of Marines there and installed them at the Beirut airport both to be a presence and to train the Lebanese armed forces, even as Marines were being lost through sniper fire and rocket attacks. It was a tragically ill-fated decision. On October 23, the same weekend as the Grenada coup, two truck bombs detonated in the Beirut airport, killing 241 American servicemen, and fifty-eight French soldiers also bivouacked there, and wounding another 128, thirteen of whom later died and were included in the death toll. The man who was known for his clarity had sent in troops without a clear mission.

And Reagan was determined to leave a footprint in Central America, too, though the plan seemed no better articulated than the plan had been in Lebanon. The fear for Central America, as the fear had been in Grenada, was that several states were vulnerable to Soviet influence and could become Soviet proxies in the hemisphere, and the policy was that the United States would do everything it could to counteract that risk. As early as March 1981, scarcely a month after he had taken office, Reagan announced plans to provide an additional $25 million in aid to El Salvador, where the United States already had fifty-four military advisers to assist the government. Ted objected. He felt that that government was no gleaming democracy—it was a military dictatorship with a close relationship to right-wing death squads, so called because they roamed the country purportedly snuffing out left-wing guerrillas. (This was Kirkpatrick's policy in action.) That same month Ted introduced legislation to halt all military assistance to the country and remove the advisers.

Nicaragua was even more tangled. A left-wing coup in 1979, conducted by the Sandinista National Liberation Front—named for a Nicaraguan guerrilla leader of the 1920s—had displaced the dictator Anastasia Somoza DeBayle, whose family had ruled the country with an iron fist since 1936. (Somoza would blame Jimmy Carter for his ouster because Carter withdrew support for Somoza on the basis of human rights violations.) Sandinista leader Daniel Ortega Saavedra assumed power and enacted reforms, and Carter had provided financial aid. But Ortega was no democrat, and when Reagan took office, he and some members of his foreign policy team were suspicious of the left-wing junta—no one more suspicious than Reagan himself. Meanwhile the president had become enamored of a small, ragtag band of counterrevolutionaries based in Honduras—"Contras," they were called—contra to the Ortega government. He compared them to "our Founding Fathers and the brave men and women of the French Resistance," and funneled both financial aid and assistance to them from the CIA and the Defense Department to conduct covert operations to topple the Sandinista government.

Not everyone, however, was as enamored of the Contras as the president. Even some members of his own foreign policy team, including Secretary of State George Shultz and Defense secretary Caspar Weinberger, opposed further covert actions. To provide him with recommendations while his team argued, and to soothe a restive Congress, which was nervous over growing American military involvement in the region, Reagan appointed a special bipartisan commission in the summer of 1983 headed by former secretary of state Henry Kissinger. Kissinger submitted his report in January 1984. Asserting vital American security interests in the region and concerned about the development of those Soviet proxy states, the commission advised a heavy dose of economic aid—roughly $8 billion worth over four years—as well as a large increase in military aid, conditioning some of that aid, which was targeted for El Salvador, on progress in human rights, though Reagan had already vetoed a similar provision in an earlier aid bill. And the report "implicitly," as *The New York Times* put it, backed Reagan's policy of supporting the Contras and refusing to negotiate with the Sandinista government.

By this time, Ted, frustrated by his lack of success in turning back Reagan's domestic agenda, had already shifted his focus to foreign policy. He had hired a brilliant Harvard-trained attorney, Gregory Craig—Craig coincidentally had been on the defense team of Reagan's would-be assassin, John Hinckley—to become his foreign affairs adviser, and even before officially joining the staff, Craig made a tour of Central America, meeting with journalists and diplomats, including the U.S. ambassador to El Salvador, Thomas Pickering, and returning to report to Ted on what he had found. What he found was chaos. Craig said that Ted was intrigued and thought he should start talking more about what was going on in Central America on the Senate floor. Craig became a member of a group of House and Senate staffers who began to meet regularly on Central America. And now, with the Kissinger Commission report, which seemed to Ted to be an excuse to promote the administration's policy, he was fully engaged. And he was livid. He wrote a "counter-report," which he gave to columnist and editor Meg Greenfield of *The Washington Post*, and he wrote a *Post* op-ed attacking the Kissinger prescription as supporting the "forces of reaction and repression," and deploring the reliance of the Reagan administration on "more guns, more bullets, more soldiers." Unfazed, Reagan promptly endorsed Kissinger's report, citing its recommendations as the "morally right thing to do." Congressional Democrats, like Ted, worried that casting the Central American conflict in East-West terms, as Reagan and the commission had, would simply harden the sides, and they were distressed by the emphasis on military solutions without human rights assurances. And they were concerned about one more thing: that the administration was looking for cover to overthrow the Nicaraguan government. "The United States does not seek to destabilize or overthrow the government of Nicaragua," Reagan's chief of staff, James Baker, announced in trying to marshal support for the aid. In fact, overthrowing the Sandinista government was precisely what the administration was trying to do. Reagan would later admit as much. And Reagan, chafing at the restrictions, flatly decided to circumvent them.

Ted couldn't hold hearings because he was in the minority, and most in the Republican majority had no interest in airing the issues of Central America, which could have redounded against the administration. But what he had was the next best thing to hearings, his forums, and he and Republican senator David Durenberger, a moderate, now organized public forums to examine violence in Central America and to invite witnesses to discuss the situation there. Ted, however, wanted more than an airing of issues. He wanted a debate on the Senate floor. And the only way that was going to happen was for Ted to get the sponsors of the supplemental appropriations for Central America—the appropriations advocated by the Kissinger report—to agree to consider amendments to those appropriations. (He did.) Even then, according to Greg Craig, there wasn't a single other senator who was willing to carry the fight for those amendments. So Ted did, did it alone, which was something he seldom chose to do, preferring allies, even though it was near the end of the Senate session and he was heading off for a vacation himself, even though it would require him to stay on the floor hour after hour, even though he would be

Ted as a master of the Senate, chewing his cigar at a Judiciary Committee hearing. By the mid-1970s, the callow young man of whom little was expected had, through hard work, deference to his elder Senate colleagues, his natural sociability, and his understanding of both the chemistry of the institution and its physics—its parliamentary devices—graduated to the role of brilliant legislator and leader of the Senate's liberal contingent. *Bettmann/Getty Images*

Ted on a mission. With the Democrats back in the White House after the 1976 election that handed victory to Jimmy Carter, Ted once again pushed for national healthcare, driving a wedge between himself and the administration, which fretted about the effect of a major healthcare initiative on the budget. Here, before the Senate Finance Committee in July 1979, Ted explains his plan to (*left to right*) Senators Daniel Patrick Moynihan, Lloyd Bentsen, Robert Packwood, Abraham Ribicoff, and Committee Chairman Russell Long. Ted's frustration over what he saw as Carter's resistance to a healthcare program led him to challenge the president for the nomination. *AP Photo/ Charles Harrity*

The fatal stumble. On November 4, 1979, just before Ted was to announce his candidacy for president, the Columbia Broadcasting System aired a documentary, *Teddy*, in which Ted, interviewed by newsman Roger Mudd, was inarticulate to the point of incoherence, unable even to explain why he intended to run. Thus, before the campaign began, his performance punctured an air of invincibility. *CBS Photo Archive/Getty Images*

Announcing a presidential run. Ted is joined by his family: (*left to right*) wife Joan, daughter Kara, and sons Patrick and Ted Jr.—on November 7, 1979, at Boston's historic Faneuil Hall. He takes on incumbent Jimmy Carter, who Ted felt was insufficiently dedicated to liberal principles. *AP Photo*

On the stump. After a halting beginning, including losses in the Iowa caucuses and the New Hampshire primary that all but destroyed any hope for a victory, Ted's campaign nevertheless plunged ahead, and he became a better, more relaxed candidate even as his prospects diminished. Here, on June 3, 1980, he speaks at the Cleveland Arcade, with son Patrick to his left. *AP Photo/MBD*

The Democratic National Convention, August 12, 1980. At Madison Square Garden in New York City, where the Democrats convened to nominate their presidential candidate, Ted, having conceded, addresses the assembled delegates and delivers what was generally acknowledged to be the greatest speech of his career—one that, some observers believed, might have stampeded the convention had he not already lost. He concluded: "For all those whose cares have been our concern, the work goes on, the cause endures, the hope still lives, and the dream shall never die." *AP Photo/File*

The convention ends. After Jimmy Carter finishes his acceptance speech, and the pols and dignitaries crowd the podium, Carter searched for Kennedy to enact the traditional pose of winner and loser with arms raised in unity. Instead, Carter received only this perfunctory handshake, with Speaker of the House Tip O'Neill presiding, before Ted left the podium. Carter campaign chair Robert Strauss is at O'Neill's left and Rep. Charles Rangel is over Ted's shoulder. Carter would blame Ted's pettiness for Carter's loss to Ronald Reagan in November. *Bettmann/Getty Images*

Ted and new president Ronald Reagan sharing a laugh after Reagan awarded Ethel Kennedy, Robert Kennedy's widow, the Robert F. Kennedy Medal in the Rose Garden on June 5, 1981, in recognition of her husband's service to the nation. Ted found Reagan affable and difficult to dislike, but of Reagan's intellect and knowledge, he told his friend John Culver, "If I ever had any reservations about my ability to be president of the United States, they have now been removed." *AP Photo*

The conservative takeover. Reagan had forged a powerful alliance of political conservatives and religious fundamentalists—among the latter the Reverend Jerry Falwell (*right*), founder of the Liberty Baptist College in Lynchburg, Virginia (later Liberty University)— and of a fundamentalist political group called the Moral Majority. When Ted mistakenly received a fundraising appeal from the Moral Majority that invoked his name as one of the dangers to the country, Falwell initially joked to a reporter that they might want it back. Instead, he invited Ted to speak at the college. Ted accepted and on October 4, 1983, delivered an address to five thousand students in which he challenged their moral certitude. "You may have won a few souls tonight," Falwell joked to Ted afterward, despite the dead silence that greeted the speech, "but I'll get them back next Sunday." *AP Photo/Tim Wright*

Continuing the crusade. Ted with Rep. Carl Perkins to his left, in Floyd County, Kentucky, talks with reporters after visiting a poverty-stricken family during a nationwide tour in November 1983 to assess hunger in America. When Bobby made his tour of the South to draw attention to poverty and hunger, the nation was stirred. But Ted was sailing against the wind, and there was little inclination among his Senate colleagues to fight hunger when the nation's temper was conservative. *Imago*

Arms control. Ted meets with Soviet leader Leonid Brezhnev on September 9, 1978. Over the years, Ted was a conduit between the White House and the Kremlin. During the Reagan administration, he would become an invaluable go-between as Reagan sought to reach an arms elimination agreement with Russia. Ted's relationship with the Soviets was one, an aide said, "no non-president had ever had." Several years later, the new Soviet leader Mikhail Gorbachev told Ted that differences between the countries on nuclear weapons could be bridged, which created an opening for serious negotiations. *AP Photo*

Filling the void. Ted fully realized that Ronald Reagan would stymie almost any legislative effort he launched, and Ted would later describe this period as living "in the present tense, not despondently, because that is not my nature, but certainly with a sense of the void." One of the activities he resumed was painting, which was among the least damaging of those he pursued in his attempt to escape his personal sadness and political impotence. *CQ Archive/Getty Images*

Ted and fellow Judiciary Committee member Patrick Leahy meet Supreme Court nominee Robert Bork before confirmation hearings on September 15, 1987. Immediately upon the announcement of the nomination, Ted delivered a harangue against Bork, a doctrinaire conservative who had questioned civil rights, free speech, and even the right to contraception. Ted's attack helped set the tone for the hearings, and Bork was ultimately defeated—a loss that rankled conservatives for years to come. *Newscom*

Ted takes on Reagan. Unable to move the Republicans on most legislative issues, Ted instead moved to moral ones, which he hoped would put Reagan on the defensive. Among the most intensive of his efforts was one to impose sanctions on South Africa that would pressure the South African government to lift the policy of apartheid. Here he addresses an anti-apartheid rally on the Capitol steps on June 16, 1988. Reagan adamantly resisted the pressure, but Ted was able to enlist Republicans in the cause, using moral suasion. Ultimately, Reagan issued an executive order imposing some of the sanctions he had insisted he would never impose. It was one of the few victories Ted Kennedy would win over Ronald Reagan. *AP Photo/Charles Tasnadi*

Mandela comes to America. Released by the South African government after twenty-seven years of internment, Nelson Mandela arrives in America and visits Ted at the John F. Kennedy Presidential Library on June 23, 1990. At a speech later that day on the Boston Esplanade, Mandela thanked the citizens of Boston: "It was you who rallied around our cause at a time when we had to stand on our own by ourselves. And thus you became the conscience of American society," though he could really have been addressing Ted, who had led the fight against apartheid. *Imago*

Humiliation. Ted testifies at the rape trial of his nephew William Kennedy Smith in Palm Beach, Florida, on December 6, 1991. On Easter weekend, Ted, despondent after spending the evening reminiscing about his recently deceased brother-in-law Stephen Smith, roused his son Patrick and nephew Smith to go to a bar for drinks. The night eventually led to an encounter at the bar between Smith and a young woman, who would accuse Smith of taking her to the Kennedy Palm Beach estate and raping her. Ted was disgraced and humbled by his involvement. *Imago*

Another Supreme Court showdown. Law professor Anita Hill testifies at confirmation hearings for nominee Clarence Thomas on October 11, 1991. Hill, who had once worked for Thomas at the Office for Civil Rights, accused Thomas of sexual harassment. Before reluctantly going public, Hill had agreed to discuss her charges privately with Kennedy staffer Ricki Seidman, but Seidman instead handed her off to a staffer of Senator Howard Metzenbaum, presumably because Ted was compromised by the Palm Beach incident. *Universal History Archive/Getty Images*

"High tech lynching for uppity blacks." Thomas testifies that he is the victim of what amounts to a lynching, and the Republicans support him by impugning Hill. But Ted is largely silent throughout this portion of the hearings—a consequence, most assumed, of his reputation for drinking and womanizing, though Ted would later say he had worked hard to defeat the nomination and had not "muzzled myself," as one journalist had described Ted's performance. *Mark Reinstein/Getty Images*

Salvation. Ted and Vicki Reggie standing at the Hyannis Port compound shortly after their wedding. After a decade of personal aimlessness, Ted met Vicki, an attorney and the daughter of friends and longtime Kennedy supporters, then wooed her, and married her in July 1992. As he would describe it, his life suddenly had ballast and, more, true happiness. *AP Photo/Susan Walsh*

The battle of his political life. For his Senate reelection campaign in 1994, Ted faced young, handsome, wealthy, well-spoken Mitt Romney, who led Ted in the early polling. Ted turned the race with a series of ads accusing Romney, a venture capitalist, of buying companies only to fire workers, and with a brilliant debate performance—shown here—in which he challenged Romney to explain legislation he intended to propose. Romney fumbled, and Ted wound up trouncing him. *John Tlumacki/The Boston Globe via Getty Images*

browbeating his colleagues, many of whom didn't share his distaste for support of right-wing governments and assassination militias, so long as those governments and militias were fighting left-wing forces.

So that April, Ted Kennedy took to the Senate floor to oppose the new military aid, as he had previously taken to the floor for eight days to oppose budget cuts. He sat behind his desk lectern, sat no doubt because his back was aching, denouncing the policy—that lectern "littered with notes he regularly sent flying with a slam of the fist," as Eileen McNamara of *The Boston Globe* reported it. He said he had canceled everything else on his schedule for this debate, and he left the floor only to get a sandwich, otherwise staying at that lectern for hours, while Craig sat in a straight-back chair to his right and other aides sat on black leather couches against the wall. His office, McNamara said, was a "regular cottage industry" of his aides researching material for the debate and writing speeches on the fly and hopping the Capitol subway to get the material to him. He introduced one amendment after another to cut off aid or to hold off aid until after elections in El Salvador or to peg aid to those human rights benchmarks that even the Kissinger Commission report had recommended but that Reagan had dismissed. Roll call after roll call after roll call. And for each, he hectored his colleagues—asking them to look to their own morality and, by McNamara's report, "not winning many friends in the process." But Ted insisted that this was how the Senate worked. He said that at first Medicare had fallen short. HMOs had fallen short. The nuclear freeze had had only seventeen sponsors at the beginning but kept gaining more. And he even cited Robert Byrd and Senator Daniel Inouye successfully negotiating with Secretary of State Shultz to cut aid to El Salvador from $93 million to $62 million. And he told McNamara that winning wasn't even the objective. The objective was having a debate on Central America that had never been held even as the administration kept pouring more money and arms into the region.

But Ted was no more successful in blocking the administration in Central America than he had been in blocking its domestic budget cuts. After the days of debate in which Ted had taken the lead, the Senate voted 76 to 19 to give $61.8 million in military aid to El Salvador and $21 million to the Contras in Nicaragua. He and his handful of allies had submitted nearly four dozen amendments during those days of debate. Almost all had failed. "In my twenty-two years in the Senate," Ted lamented, "I have never seen a more shameful and dangerous piece of legislation. The Senate has voted for wider war in El Salvador, secret war in Nicaragua, the brink of war in Honduras, terrorism sponsored by the United States and the denial of justice for the victims of the death squads." And all because it was the "morally right thing to do," in President Reagan's words when he had asked for those funds.

But as the debates were winding down and the defeats were piling up, Joe Biden came across an alarming memo. It said that the CIA had been mining Nicaragua's harbor in Managua—an operation that had not been authorized by Congress. Biden showed the memo to Barry Goldwater, who was the chairman of the Senate Intelligence Committee. As Craig recalled it, Ted was away at the time, but Goldwater came to the Senate floor late one night, possibly inebriated, Craig felt, and fulminated about the mining. David Rogers of the *Wall Street Journal* picked it up and reported on it the next day. When Ted returned to Washington and Craig briefed him on the memo, Ted was furious yet again. "You know, we went through a whole week of debate on U.S. policy towards Central America," he snapped, "and this didn't come out at all." And he said that he was going to return to the Senate floor and "we're going to have a debate about mining the harbors in Nicaragua." And Ted introduced a nonbinding resolution to stop the mining. (To force the Senate's hand, Ted also introduced a resolution giving jurisdiction over disputes in Central America to the World Court, which he then withdrew in exchange for the vote on the mining resolution.) Ted's resolution passed, 84 to 12, with Majority Leader Howard Baker and Barry Goldwater among those in favor. "A first step to halt President Reagan's secret war in Nicaragua," Ted called it afterward. CIA director William Casey insisted that he had informed Goldwater—Goldwater insisted he hadn't—and that in any case it was the job of senators to ask the right questions to get the right answers.* But Ted had won. A "hideous embarrassment" to Reagan, liberal columnist Mary McGrory called it, and she called Ted a "one-man guerilla squad,

---

*That was Craig's account. Cynthia Arnson's account is more complicated. She writes that the CIA had slipped the mining past the Intelligence Committee, acting as if the Contras had planted the mines unilaterally, and Goldwater actually came to the CIA's defense. It was only when Goldwater learned that the CIA had actively participated that he exploded and said he and the committee hadn't been adequately briefed. Cynthia Arnson, *Crossroads: Congress, the Reagan Administration, and Central America* (New York: Pantheon, 1989), 158–62.

harassing his colleagues, making them squirm and blush while they vote for violence to Central America." And she said that Ted was going to "bring back every single amendment that went down so hard while the Senate was closing its eyes and saying aye to whatever Reagan wanted." After the debate and after Ted had left the floor, Craig said that Senator Richard Lugar, a foreign policy specialist and the chair of the Foreign Relations Committee, came up to him and asked him when Ted got interested in foreign policy. "This is all brand new," Lugar said, even though it wasn't entirely brand new. And Craig told him that there were people from Massachusetts in Central America and that the Catholic Church was heavily involved in the region—Ortega's minister of culture was a priest—but Craig admitted those weren't the reasons. The real reason, he said, was that Ted felt strongly about the injustices there and felt compelled to start that debate. And as a result, he "forced" the Senate to debate Central America when it had no inclination to do so.

And now they were forced to examine the morally right thing to do.

III

The only way to best Ronald Reagan was to defeat him at the ballot box, and that was not likely heading into the 1984 election. Before the 1982 midterms, the economy had been foundering and so was Reagan; the Democrats won the aggregate House vote by nearly twelve points and gained twenty-seven seats and a half-dozen governorships, though only a single Senate seat. Then things began to change. Before the 1984 presidential election, the economy righted itself, as Ted predicted it would. The growth rate was 7.2 percent, the inflation rate was down to 2 percent, and the unemployment rate 7.5 percent. How much of this could be attributed to Reagan was a complex matter. The tax cuts and trickle-down strategy of Reaganomics had not worked, and Reagan had had to capitulate with those tax increases. And, in fact, real wages were actually down 1.4 percent that fall from a year earlier. But Reagan's tax cuts and his massive defense spending *had* put money into the economy—the latter in the Keynesian government pump-priming way that Reagan disdained. That alone probably would not have revived the economy; it might only have fueled inflation. But the chairman of the Federal Reserve Board, Paul Volcker, a Carter appointee, was an inflation hawk. When Reagan's pump-priming met Volcker's tight money policies, the result, some economists felt, was a kind of happy marriage that along with other factors, like Reagan's active union bashing, fired up the economy without also firing up inflation, even if the largest benefits of that compromise did not go to ordinary working folks. In some respects, Reagan was a beneficiary of his own miscalculations and failures. He had asked voters in 1980 if they felt better off than they had in 1976. In 1984, he could have asked them if they felt better off than they had in 1982. The answer would certainly have been that they did, though Reagan would have been responsible in a rather perverse way.

By 1984, the mythology surrounding Ronald Reagan was already fully formed. He had rescued the country from its malaise. He had cured the crisis of confidence. He had invoked stern moralism and appeased the evangelicals, but he had also launched the country into the very sort of excess and materialism of which conservative Russell Kirk had disapproved, but of which not everyone disapproved. "It's morning in America," ran one of Reagan's most popular campaign ads in 1984, basically a trailer for the movie in which Reagan had been starring for the previous four years. "If we allow any Democrat to claim optimism or idealism as his issue," one Reagan aide warned at the beginning of the campaign, "we will lose the election." But there wasn't much danger of that. Having exited the race, Ted left the field to Colorado senator Gary Hart and former vice president Walter Mondale. He had visited Mondale at Mondale's house shortly after his renunciation, and they spent several hours discussing the next presidential election. "I don't think he said he'd endorse me," Mondale was to recall, "but he thought it [nomination] was mine and that he hoped I'd go on and be elected and so on." Mondale, benefiting from many of the same party mechanisms that had favored Carter four years earlier, won the primaries, though Hart, like Ted in 1980, was not willing to pull out, feeling aggrieved that, because of party rules, he had fewer delegates than the number to which he was entitled given his vote count. After the primaries, in late June, Ted and Horowitz flew to Mondale's home in Minnesota for the purpose of Ted's giving Mondale his endorsement and offered to mediate the dispute with Hart. Ted had already phoned Hart before arriving and discussed Hart's leaving the race, telling him that it was "essential" the Democrats win in the fall, but that he was sympathetic to Hart's complaint. (After his own 1980 campaign, how couldn't he be?) At Mondale's house, Ted presented the nominee with an agreement to change the rules for 1988, reducing the number of un-pledged delegates—so-called "superdelegates," who were party officials but not responsible to voters—and lowering the threshold needed to be awarded delegates. Mondale agreed. Then Ted phoned Hart again from Mondale's living room—it was well past midnight in Washington—and handed the receiver to Mondale and the two of them, Mondale and Hart, hashed out some final differences. The next day, at rallies in front of the Minnesota state capitol and the Farmers' Union Building, Ted, under a sun that had broken through the clouds, gave a ringing endorsement. "Boy, this Ted Kennedy is really something," Mondale quipped. "He has been in Minnesota for less than twelve hours and already the skies have parted, the sun is shining, and everything is beautiful." As to Mondale's distinct underdog status, Ted, referring to the 1948 presidential front-runner, who woke up having lost the election to Harry Truman, told the crowd, "Tell that to Tom Dewey."

He worked hard for Mondale, even though the cause seemed futile. At that same visit in which he mended fences between Mondale and Hart, he advised Mondale to choose a woman as his running mate just to "shake up the race," as Horowitz put it, which was precisely what Mondale did when he selected New York representative Geraldine Ferraro, the first woman on a major party national ticket. At the convention in San Francisco, Ted gave a spirited speech on Mondale's behalf, "jarring the rafters," said one reporter, and having the "whole hall on its feet—laughing, stomping and wildly waving thousands of small plastic American flags." He joked that "Ronald Reagan should not be the only senior citizen who does not have to worry about the cost of his medical costs." He ridiculed an idea purveyed by a deputy defense secretary that should nuclear war come, "Everybody's going to make it if there are enough shovels to go around." To which Ted said, "We have a better idea: Everybody's going to make it if the Reagan administration is no longer around." He put himself at Mondale's "disposal," as one Kennedy aide put it, raising money for him in New York and crossing the country to stump for him, going to Texas and Florida and California. He campaigned with Ferraro before a crowd of 25,000 in Boston's City Hall Plaza, in a drizzle, as the crowd chanted, "Ronald Reagan, he's no good, send him back to Hollywood."

Reagan would say that he thought it ironic that while Ted and Tip O'Neill and Mondale were "forever harping that I was the 'rich man's can-didate,' everywhere I went crowds of working men and working women roared with approval when I asked them if they thought they were better off than they had been four years earlier." And Reagan was right that he had built a sturdy coalition. He ascribed it in part to the Democrats'— "New Democrats," he called them—abandoning small government in the Jeffersonian tradition for a "conglomeration of blocs and special interest groups, each with narrow special agendas directed at grabbing more of the national wealth for their own interests," though the Democrats had been selling the idea of big government since the days of Franklin Roosevelt, when they were most successful, and Reagan's description of the Democrats as an interest group party could apply to any party, including and especially the Republicans. Reagan might very well have been aided by a Democratic Party in disarray, a party without a clear or persuasive message, a party out of fashion, but as one political scientist observed, it was just as likely that his victory coalition was a function of "race, religion, and negation," which was comprised of blue-collar white people, evangelicals, and Southerners. Reagan's triumph was smashing. He won 59 percent of the vote and every state but Mondale's native Minnesota. In declaring victory on election night, Reagan said, "You ain't seen nothing yet" and promised to devote his new term to limiting nuclear weapons, which was a sincere and abiding passion of Reagan's, and "lifting the weak and less fortunate," which was not.

And with that, the second term of Ronald Reagan began.

For Ted Kennedy, it was not likely to be very different than the first term. The Republicans did not take the House, but they did retain the Senate, so that Ted was still in the minority, still basically impotent. And that impotence had taken a toll on him, psychologically, even physically. He was no longer in robust health, and it wasn't only a matter of his gaining weight, the surest gauge of Ted Kennedy's misery. He had a basal cell cancer on his nose that first arose in 1979 and recurred in 1984. He had a tremor in his hands, which he attributed to his being excited or upset or angry, but which seemed to be a more permanent condition. He was hospitalized early in 1984 for an ulcer, which he attributed to his taking aspirin for the flu, but which also suggested that Ted was under greater stress than he revealed. And Reagan's first term had taken a toll politically—on Ted Kennedy and on his party. Ted's own Labor Committee counsel, Thomas Rollins, noted that there was "no clear agenda about what we wanted to get

done." He cited the conventional description of the primary battle between Mondale and Gary Hart as that between a traditional liberal and an
untraditional Democrat, one who didn't adhere to the old New Deal prescriptions. But Rollins saw the contrast differently, as "the old world in its
complete senescence and decline [Mondale], and the new world with only
a handful of weird new ideas and things that looked interesting but had
not been fleshed out [Hart]." And Rollins said, "There was no governing
set of principles. . . . Everybody was still trying to figure it out." Welfare
was under siege. National health insurance had made no progress, despite Ted's ongoing advocacy. Guaranteed full employment was still a pipe
dream. And if the party was torn between old and new, it was also torn
between individual ambitions, so that after the election, Senator Lawton
Chiles of Florida, a centrist with a Southern base, challenged Byrd, also
a centrist, for the minority leadership. Ted supported Byrd—he was grateful to Byrd for supporting his call to free the delegates at the 1980
convention—and Byrd won handily 37 to 11, but the contest showed the
party's fractiousness. The party was foundering. Ted Kennedy was foundering.

With his party seeming to teeter, Ted Kennedy had his own concerns
about whether his liberalism was still viable in the wake of Reagan's landslide victory. Speaking at Hofstra University on Long Island in New York
at a three-day conference on his brother's administration, he was in an
unusually reflective and self-critical mood. He said that Democrats could
not "blame the voters" or Reagan's superb television skills for their debacle. Instead, he said, the party had lost the "feeling of hope, the spirit of
change," those very things with which his brothers had infused the party
and with which Reagan had infused the Republicans. And he made what
Tom Oliphant called a startling confession: "We cannot deny the vote of
1984, which I also believe will be the verdict of history, that whatever the
wisdom of his policy, Ronald Reagan has restored the presidency as a vigorous, purposeful instrument of national leadership," which was a dig at
Carter, certainly, but a painful truth. Reagan *had* made it seem like morning in America. And Ted argued for the very thing for which he had criticized Carter and criticized him unrelentingly: "Those of us who care
about domestic progress must do more with less." Finally, he challenged
his party to serve the interests of minorities and the poor and the working class without becoming a party of special interests, which was the

accusation Reagan and the Republicans had increasingly leveled at Democrats—a criticism that seemed to contain at least a grain of racism. "We must understand that there is a difference between a party that cares about labor and a labor party," Ted said. "There is a difference between a party that cares about minorities without becoming a minority party. We are citizens first and constituencies second." Replacing old programs rather than adding new ones, tightening the nation's fiscal belt and relying on economic growth to raise the standard of living—these were Reagan positions, and now they were being declared by the man who had opposed Reagan for his lack of compassion, a man who was sniffing the wind. And Ted said something else: that he was considering running for the presidency again while forgoing another run for the Senate. The *Los Angeles Times* called the speech a "sharp break with the public perception of Kennedy as a die-hard and doctrinaire liberal."

But the speech was more. It was a sign of Ted Kennedy's deep and increasing disappointment over the direction of the country and of his and his party's inability to stop it. It was a sign of his frustration with wading against the tide rather than sailing against the wind. A few months later, in June, David Broder asked rhetorically whether Ted was moving toward the center in preparation for that 1988 presidential run, and Broder answered, "There is nothing subtle about it," citing Ted enjoying a handshake with the Reverend Jerry Falwell at a joint appearance at the National Religious Broadcasters convention the previous winter, and Ted's showing Broder, when he visited the senator's office, a framed enlargement of a letter Ted had received praising Ted for his work on behalf of servicemen and signed by Barry Goldwater. And yet Broder concluded, in seeming contradiction, that Ted was not really moving to the center, that he still held his belief in maintaining programs that help the poor, and that "if he is ever to become president, the country will have to come to him," adding that in his constancy, he was following the lead of Reagan, who never trimmed his sails.

Broder had written his analysis on the eve of another unusual event for Ted Kennedy. Ted was holding a fundraiser at his McLean home for the John F. Kennedy Library. And Horowitz had a brainstorm. He suggested that Ted invite the Reagans to attend. Ted told Horowitz that he was out of his mind. But Horowitz said that Ted wouldn't have to tender the invitation himself. Caroline, the late president's daughter, could do it, approach-

ing Reagan by saying, "I'd never ask you, but my father isn't here to do it."
Reagan accepted; he was, after all, a man of little or no personal malice.
The Reagans stood beside Ted in the receiving line, and at the end of the
evening, Ted presented the president with a token of appreciation: a small
brass statue of an American eagle, its wings spread, that had adorned
Jack Kennedy's Oval Office desk. That night, when the Reagans returned
to the White House, Nancy took the gift into their private quarters, but
the next morning she placed it on her husband's desk. *Newsweek* later reported that several old Jack Kennedy hands were disturbed that Ted had
given the eagle to Reagan, that "it was something of a symbol to a lot of
people," according to one of those hands. Meanwhile Reagan wrote in his
diary: "The whole family was most warm in their thanks. I wonder if
Teddy will still be able to blast me as he has?"

He was still able, but the blasts were still ineffective, and Ted was now
more willing to compromise because he seemed to have little choice. Deficits had become the political obsession. By 1985, "Reaganomics," Reagan's program of cutting taxes, which would lead, according to the theory
of trickle-down economics, to an actual increase in tax revenue (it didn't),
combined with Reagan's aggressive increase in defense spending, combined with an unwillingness of Democrats to slash spending on social issues, created a tax revenue shortfall, which Republicans refused to close
by raising taxes. The national debt, which Reagan had promised to retire,
had instead doubled in his four years, and the prospective deficit was the
largest in American history. Reagan could have raised taxes, as he had
done earlier, or cut the defense budget. He refused. The Democrats could
have conceded to Reagan's efforts to cut back social programs. They refused. Reagan's answer to the stalemate was to press Congress to give him
a long-cherished presidential prerogative—a "line item" veto that would
give the president the power selectively to veto individual appropriations
rather than be forced to veto an entire appropriations bill to achieve cuts.
Liberal Democrats had generally opposed a line-item veto on the basis that
it was a bald scheme for Republican presidents to kill social programs,
which was exactly what it was. Ronald Reagan was an especially vocal
advocate, while obdurate Democrats were just as vocal opponents. But
Ted Kennedy, who certainly appreciated the consequences of handing
Reagan a veto pen with which to sign a death sentence for individual so-

cial programs, bucked his fellow liberals and backed Reagan. During the Senate debate, he declared the budget process a "shambles," and the deficit "out of control," and said that "Congress has too much power over the purse, and the President has too little," which was what the Republicans had said. And to charges that Reagan would use that pen to "abolish programs that Democrats had been fighting to save and strengthen for the past four years," he said the president would lose his newfound power if he did so. (Some observers said that this was cleverness on Ted's part; what he really wanted was to place the responsibility for hurting vulnerable Americans squarely on the president.) The bill failed cloture by three votes. But the surprise in much of the media wasn't Reagan's defeat. The surprise was Ted Kennedy's support of Reagan.

Now, after the line-item veto failure and as the country faced an expanding deficit, there came a flurry of bills intended to close the revenue-spending gap, most of which would remove the onus from either the president or Congress. Among them, Republican senators Phil Gramm of Texas and Warren Rudman of New Hampshire and Democrat Fritz Hollings of South Carolina had crafted one that set a statutory budget ceiling that would, if Congress stayed under the ceiling, lead to a balanced budget by 1991. Ordinarily, a budget ceiling might not have meant much because it had always been flexible. In this case, however, if Congress and the administration failed to agree to hit targets within $10 billion of that ceiling, automatic across-the-board cuts would be triggered, chopping everything but Social Security, interest payments on the national debt, and a handful of entitlement programs designed for the poor. The effect of the bill was to mandate $36 billion in cuts over the next five years. Ronald Reagan wasn't pleased. He obviously didn't mind budget cutting; he was strongly in favor of it, except when it came to the defense budget. What he minded was taking the discretion out of the hands of the executive. The Democratic leadership opposed the bill as well, both because it imposed those steep spending cuts on programs it had fought for to aid the poor and because it took spending discretion out of Congress's hands. Democratic House majority leader Jim Wright called it an "act of legislative desperation," then voted for it. Columnist David Broder labeled it the "balanced-budget sham" that "deliberately invites chaos" by guaranteeing that the "deficit hot potato will be passed back and forth between President Reagan and Congress even more often than in the past five years."

The New York Times was more direct, calling it "balanced baloney" because the plan was "riddled with flaws from the height of the ceilings to the fact that there were no tax increases included."

Gramm-Rudman-Hollings might not have been the bill that Ronald Reagan desired, but it was a bill that demonstrated how much Ronald Reagan had changed the political debate. Jimmy Carter had earned the opprobrium of Reagan and of liberal Democrats by talking about limits— usually meaning limits in what government could do. Reagan's criticism of Carter was hypocrisy since what Carter called "limits," Reagan called "cuts"—cuts in social programs. But now it was the liberals who were conceding that government couldn't do everything and the American people shouldn't expect it to. "We have an elemental problem," Senator Daniel Patrick Moynihan of New York, a Democrat, told his fellow senators during the floor debate on the bill. "At this point Americans want more government than they are paying for. They need defense and they want the farm program. Shall we put it that way? They need defense and they want Amtrak. They need defense and they want student loans." But, Moynihan said, while you can cut just about everything, including those programs that serve the most vulnerable Americans, "do not devastate the defense system." It was Ronald Reagan's own argument, only now it was being made by a liberal Democrat. The issue was no longer how to save social programs from what liberals had always seen as the Republican meat-ax; the issue was how to cut them with the ax. This was fear. And this was surrender.

Ted Kennedy had seldom shown fear and almost never surrendered, and Gramm-Rudman-Hollings was precisely the kind of bill that he would have seemed likely not only to oppose but to oppose fiercely—a bill that seemed to take Ronald Reagan off the hot seat on which he had placed himself with his attempted economic sleight-of-hand, while the bill also mandated cuts in the programs that Ted Kennedy had spent his life enacting. (The line-item veto, on the other hand, had put Reagan on the hot seat.) But Ted Kennedy did not denounce Gramm-Rudman-Hollings, and he did not follow most of the Democratic leadership who did. Ted Kennedy supported the bill, which surprised even Hollings, who jokingly called the bill "Gramm-Kennedy" and told a reporter, who asked him about the opposition to the bill that Hollings had encountered, "Let him explain it," meaning Kennedy. "We are all crying 'fire' in the overcrowded

theater of the federal deficit," Ted said, even though he had always accused Republicans, who had long howled about deficits and the necessity
for cutting the budget, of using the deficit as an excuse for hurting the
poor. "We cannot continue to debate endlessly which fire extinguisher to
use while the fire itself rages on." He told another reporter that he voted
for the bill because of an "evolving understanding" that "there is not the
will in Congress to come to grips with tough decisions," adding, "The fact
is we are in the classical situation where we find out who is serious about
reducing the deficits and who isn't." In a debate with Republican Alan
Simpson, long after the bill's passage, he admitted that Gramm-Rudman-
Hollings was a "blunt weapon," but said it was the only way to put "backbone in the battle against the deficit." The bill passed the Senate 75 to 24,
with Ted joining twenty-one Democrats in support; twenty-two others
opposed it. As far as the president was concerned, Ronald Reagan hadn't
carried the day since he didn't like yielding power to Congress, and now
he was forced to do so. But he had carried the debate. It was all about how
to cut, not whether to cut, and half the cuts were to come out of domestic
programs.

But why did Ted Kennedy, the most vocal defender of those programs,
join the Republicans? One could take at face value that he thought it was
time to get serious about deficits, but Ted Kennedy had never been serious
about deficits; it was one of his major disagreements with Jimmy Carter,
who was serious. One could say that he was sniffing the wind and positioning himself for the next presidential campaign in a country that had
taken a hard right turn, but he had already made a decision not to run
and would announce it a few days after the vote. One could say that he felt
the provisions of the bill that spared Social Security from any cuts and
that divided the cuts between defense and domestic programs was the best
way of saving them from Reagan's chopping block, which was something
he said publicly; Reagan wouldn't be making those decisions anymore.
One could say that he liked the idea of putting Reagan and the Republicans on the spot, forcing them to defend what liberals thought were Reagan's failed economic policies that generated those giant deficits. One
could say that Ted believed, as many, many legal scholars and legislators
believed, that the bill was patently unconstitutional, delegating to the
comptroller general decision-making powers over the budget that were
designated to the president and that Ted wanted an exercise in which Republicans were forced not only to defend Reagan but to defend ending

those programs for the poor, even though or especially because there was nothing finally at stake. (The bill was in fact eventually found unconstitutional, and so after the "baloney" and the "sham" and the solemn declarations, Ted's included, that the time had finally come to address the deficit, it turned out to be much ado about nothing.)

But there was another possibility—a sadder one for Kennedy admirers and liberals generally: that Ted Kennedy, suffering defeat after defeat to Reagan and the Republicans and watching his programs ever-threatened and sometimes decimated, was feeling disempowered and lost. In the Senate debate on the bill, a debate that lasted nine hours, Ted Kennedy, who typically held the floor for long stretches when an issue moved him and often held it with passionate eloquence, spoke for only a few minutes and his remarks were perfunctory, saying that he was convinced the "only way to protect important Democratic programs that I care deeply about is to bring the budget under control—so that we can have a genuine debate about America's priorities" and closing with his conviction that the American people will see "the Democratic Party has the high ground" with the "twin essential principles of economic growth and social justice." But that was an empty conviction, given the nation's rightward turn—one with no force behind it. And so once again, Ted was wading against the tide rather than sailing against the wind.

And now he rambled across the nation, not in the service of any Senate committee but as a lone operator, clearly hoping to appeal to some moral grain that had survived the recalibration, clearly hoping to revive that morality. "He operates as a national senator," Larry Horowitz told *The New York Times* of this period, alluding to Ted's stature. But if he was a national senator, it was not, as it was previously, because his appeal was national but rather because he no longer had a base of support and had nowhere to go and no particular function to serve. The week after the Gramm-Rudman-Hollings vote, he toured farms in the Midwest, highlighting the plight of farmers who, he said, were making too little and paying too much and whose children were abandoning farming altogether—one farmer, quoting John Kennedy's inaugural address, "Ask not what your country can do for you but what you can do for your country," pleaded with him, "Senator, we're asking you to help agriculture"—and visiting food banks to underscore the plight of the hungry whom, he felt, Reagan had all but forgotten. And back in Washington, he was one of the fiercest critics of Reagan's nomination of Jefferson Sessions III, the U.S. attorney in Alabama, to the federal bench, calling Sessions a "throwback to a shameful period," a "disgrace," citing Sessions's prosecution of three Black civil rights activists for "voting fraud" (their crime was assisting elderly Black voters), which he claimed "alone should bar him from sitting on the bench" and calling the nomination "regrettable"—regrettable because of Sessions's obvious racism. (Sessions had also spoken favorably of the Ku Klux Klan until, he said, he heard that members smoked marijuana.) Still, for all the accusations against Sessions—he was said to have berated a white lawyer for working on civil rights issues and called a Black attorney "boy"—it took six months and nineteen hours of hearings for the Judiciary Committee finally to refuse to send the nomination to the floor, and when it did so, it was on a 9-to-9 vote. In a demonstration of how racism had already been normalized in the Reagan administration, Attorney General Edwin Meese called the rejection an "appalling surrender" to the politics of ideology. For Ted, it was a victory of morality—but it was one of the very few and a narrow one at that.

There was that one area, however, in which Ted Kennedy in a time of moral recalibration could still exercise some authority: foreign policy. Here it was not as simple for Reagan as cutting social programs that white Americans were convinced benefited only Black Americans and the indolent. Here the lines were not so clearly drawn since even within the administration itself there were intense disagreements over the direction American policy should take. And here above all, the Kennedy brand still retained a good deal of its potency. However much the Kennedys might have lost their aura in America, that aura glowed brightly in many places overseas. And so Ted Kennedy traveled. He embarked with his sisters, Jean and Pat, on a twelve-day tour of South America in January 1986, weeks after Gramm-Rudman-Hollings, ostensibly to celebrate his brother Jack's Alliance for Progress program, which had attempted to bolster the relationship between the United States and Latin America through massive economic aid, and to discuss the debt crisis, but really to encourage democratization. Here in South America the Kennedys represented democratic aspirations. "Most of these countries were in transitions, and you could see the wave of democracy coming," said one of Ted's foreign policy aides, Nancy Soderberg, "but they weren't there yet. So he felt putting the weight of a Kennedy behind the democracy movements there could help."

Soderberg said that Ted was an "icon" in most of those countries, and he had enormous influence, and she said that when she was walking through the slums of Rio de Janeiro, "You go into the homes and there are pictures of Jesus and President Kennedy—still." But that also made Ted Kennedy a threat to the governments that were resisting democracy, among which was the government of Chile. At the time, Chile was still under the brutal dictatorship of General Augusto Pinochet, who had come to power in 1973 in a coup in which the democratically elected socialist government of President Salvador Allende was ousted and Allende killed. Pinochet maintained power through repression, torture, and murder. In response, Ted had introduced and gotten passed a bill barring American military aid to Chile. (Nixon, on the other hand, had opposed any aid to the socialist Allende regime in hopes of making its economy "scream," as CIA director Richard Helms put it.) For Ted's opposition to his regime, Pinochet sought revenge. Ted was departing the American ambassador's residence in Buenos Aires, Argentina, for La Rioja, Chile, when, as Greg Craig recalled, an officer—he only later found out it was the CIA station chief—pulled him aside and told him that the Chilean military was organizing demonstrations against Ted in Santiago and intended to keep his party out of the airport there. When they arrived in Chile, the crowds, several hundred people who had been wrangled by the military, were raucous and angry. Some carried posters referencing Chappaquiddick and asking about Mary Jo Kopechne's "human rights." Opposition democratic leaders who had come to meet Ted were attacked with stones and eggs, and Ted's own motorcade was pelted with rocks and eggs too. The security detail would not guarantee their safety. Ted, his party, and the American ambassador were all trapped at the airport for over an hour. Ted felt that the press should be informed about the situation, and Craig took it upon himself to do so. The only escape route was via helicopter. So Ted was flown out. Banned from appearing at government sites, he posted himself at a downtown social club where mothers brought him photographs of their children whom the Pinochet government had "disappeared." That night he gave a speech in Santiago at a Spanish school. Craig called it a "Shrum special"—a beautiful speech, a poetic speech, one of the best and most moving speeches, he said, that Ted had ever given. "You have spoken out on behalf of those condemned to silence," he told his listeners, most of them in the opposition. "I have come to a country which has proven anew that the fire of freedom cannot be extinguished—even when the darkness descends, when dictators rule and law is lost, the flame still warms and moves millions of individual indomitable hearts. The spark still passes from soul to soul, connecting one person with another, across vast expanses of space and time, with each for a few moments or miles carrying and passing on freedom's torch, so that one day the light finally shines out again across the land." The crowd was moved—"ready to go," Craig said—a huge crowd, eight hundred strong. "The room was going to explode with people." As Adam Clymer reported it, a man then began to sing the "Internationale," which was associated with Allende. And the audience began joining him—"hesitantly" at first, Clymer wrote. And outside the auditorium, another crowd had gathered and sang "Chile Libre." And Ted and the ambassador drove through those demonstrators. And the next year, the "'No' Campaign" was launched—a campaign to encourage people to vote no in a plebiscite designed to extend Pinochet's power another eight years. And Ted organized a Committee to Support Free Elections in Chile, which he co-chaired with Senator Lugar and for which he got Jimmy Carter and Gerald Ford to serve as honorary co-chairs. Four years later he would return to Chile for the inauguration of a new president, and this time he received what *The Boston Globe* would call "rave reviews" for what he had helped accomplish in challenging Pinochet.

And that was a result of his residual moral authority.

It was Ronald Reagan's country now—in many ways an illiberal country. But Ted Kennedy kept pressing. He tried using moral authority yet again, this time to stop American support for the Contras in Nicaragua. His fellow Democrats chose him to introduce an amendment to ban aid to those Contras, but the effort failed. Reagan got $100 million approved, 53 to 47, in the Senate. Another bill sponsored by Ted to outlaw military aid failed. But Ted, searching for any kernel of victory, sent Craig to Nicaragua now with a mission. As Craig was to say of the situation there at the time, "The place was so polarized in Nicaragua, pro-contra and anti-contra, and the lines were so sharply drawn, that it was very difficult to have a substantive impact." Ted instead asked him to focus on a single issue: the Miskito Indians. According to Craig, the tribe had gotten embroiled in Nicaragua's messy internal politics when the CIA paid a group of Miskitos to assist the Contras, and the Sandinistas had retaliated against them. Ted, again with the help of Republican senator David Durenberger, had convened one of his forums to investigate and had several Miskistos flown up from a tiny village named Sumanbila to testify about how the Contras had forced some of the younger men in the village to join them. "Kidnapped" was how Craig put it. To extricate the Miskitos, Ted proposed and charged Craig with negotiating a separate peace between the Sandinistas and the Miskitos, so that both the CIA and the Managua government would leave them alone. Craig said the process took a year and a half, and that Ted invited a Miskito leader named Brooklyn Rivera to a dinner at McLean and was able to persuade him to pursue a separate peace with President Ortega. The two sides eventually reached agreement at the United Nations. Ted had, once again, led the effort. The Miskitos were henceforth left alone, which was another small victory, a single-handed victory.

But he still sought a bigger victory.

IV

Even as Ted Kennedy wandered the political desert, Ronald Reagan was morally vulnerable. And of all the areas in which Reagan's vulnerability was most evident, perhaps none was as glaring as South Africa, where a Black majority was ruled by and repressed by a white minority, denied nearly all its rights, and cruelly segregated by the policy of apartheid. Operating on the same principle that had sent Ted to South America—the principle that indigenous democrats needed to know that they had the support of other leaders—Bobby had made an epochal visit to South Africa in June 1966 where he was mobbed by Black South Africans, thousands of them, and where he stirred the Black majority with his speeches, even as the white South African government in Pretoria ignored his visit. "Each time a man stands up for an ideal, or acts to improve the lot of others, or strikes out against injustice," Bobby had told an audience at the University of Cape Town on June 6, in a passage that would be chiseled on the wall around his gravesite, "he sends forth a tiny ripple of hope, and crossing each other from a million different centers of energy and daring, those ripples build a current which can sweep down the mightiest walls of oppression and resistance." Robert Kennedy had given those Black South Africans hope, and he had fortified their courage. But in the nearly twenty years since that visit, little had changed in South Africa, though much had changed in America's attitude toward South Africa—much that had banked whatever fires Bobby Kennedy had helped manage to stoke. Ronald Reagan had no interest in feeding the hope and fortifying the courage of those Black South Africans. He had pursued a policy that he called "constructive engagement," which essentially meant leaving American businesses to operate in South Africa with impunity and letting the white minority government do as it pleased on the logic that the best way to influence that government was to avoid being confrontational. Almost everywhere South Africa had faded from the political radar.

But not for Ted Kennedy. In large measure because of his late brother's interest in the country, Ted had continued monitoring developments there. As early as 1969, he had submitted legislation to terminate sugar subsidies for South Africa, not because he expected the termination to have any real effect on changing apartheid—the subsidy amounted to only $19 million—but because he thought it would be a "significant moral gesture." But the Reagan administration's neglect of South African apartheid, its seeming willingness even to encourage the continuation of the policy by lifting embargoes on the country that Jimmy Carter had imposed, fired Ted's fury—a fury that virtually no one else in public office seemed to share. At the invitation of the president of the UN General Assembly, Joe Garba of Nigeria, Ted delivered an address on apartheid—a "very strong speech," Ted himself called it—before a crowded Assembly in September 1984. Whenever leaders of the South African Black community visited Washington, Ted made it a point to meet with them, even Oliver Tambo, the head of the African National Congress, a Black opposition party, the party of imprisoned freedom fighter Nelson Mandela, that South Africa had banned and the U.S. government had designated a terrorist organization. Tambo was a pariah. No other American official would take the political risk of meeting with him. Ted Kennedy did. That fall, when Bishop Desmond Tutu, another Black South African freedom fighter, was in the country, Ted and Greg Craig organized one of Ted's forums to discuss apartheid, though the forum had to be canceled at the last minute because Ted was needed on the Senate floor for the debate on Reagan's MX mobile missile system, which Ted vehemently opposed. Still, Ted lunched in his office with Tutu and Allan Boesak, another South African anti-apartheid activist, whom Ted had flown from South Africa expressly for the forum. Both, said Craig, made "eloquent and impassioned" arguments that the apartheid regime was gaining legitimacy and that something had to be done about it. When Ted asked Tutu what he could do to help, Tutu answered that he should visit South Africa as Bobby had done.

"You must come to visit us," Craig recalled Tutu saying, "because if you just come, the whole world will watch and where you go, the world will follow and whatever you see, the world will also see." Ted was reluctant to "disturb the particles," as he put it. He knew his trip would be compared to Bobby's, and he thought he needed to choose the appropriate time for fear he might set back the anti-apartheid movement rather than advance it. But Tutu was persuasive, and violence in South Africa was escalating, and the Reagan government had shown no signs of pressuring the white South African government to yield its power. He decided to go in December, but the trip had to be postponed. Several weeks after his visit to Ted's office, Tutu won the Nobel Peace Prize, and that December, he would be in Oslo to accept.

When Ted did go, a month later, it would not be as invigorating a visit as Bobby's had been, where the government had chosen neglect over confrontation. This time, the South African government, like the Chilean government, was determined to disrupt the trip. Ted arrived that evening, January 5, at Jan Smuts Airport to a demonstration of the Azanian People's Organization, which the security forces had let in—a Black group that promoted the idea only Black people should be fighting apartheid and that resented Ted's involvement. (Bishop Tutu's son was among those protesters.) But he was also greeted at the airport by Bishop Tutu, who called him the "foremost spokesman for social conscience and human rights" and the "foremost world spokesman on human dignity." The plan was for Ted to spend the night at Bishop Tutu's home in the Black township of Soweto, outside Johannesburg, even though it was illegal for white people to go there. Still, the government, realizing that it was responsible for Ted's safety, provided an escort. As Craig later told it, the caravan was about halfway through the forty-minute drive to Soweto, late at night, when their car was pulled over by the security detail, the leader of whom leaned into the car and told Ted and Tutu that a crowd of demonstrators was waiting for them outside Tutu's house and that they would be well advised to go to a hotel in Johannesburg instead. Ted had brought his children, Kara and Ted Jr., and Bobby's son Christopher and Bobby's eldest daughter, Kathleen, and Jean Smith and her son Stephen, all of whom rode in a bus behind him, and he directed the bus to take them and the accompanying journalists to the hotel while Ted and Bishop Tutu insisted on heading on to Tutu's home. When they arrived, there was no demonstration. (The security forces had clearly wanted to dissuade Ted from going to Soweto.) Instead, there was a crowd of well-wishers, many of them holding candles, to whom Ted said, "I give you the assurance that when I return to the United States, I will be a continuing force against apartheid and for human rights." And there was also a choir outside Tutu's home that night, from Tutu's own church, serenading Ted with soft songs, lullabies, really, to lull Ted to sleep—he slept in Tutu's own bed with the Nobel Prize on the nightstand—while Tutu sat up in a chair all night with the choir as they sang, until dawn when the choir disbanded, and Tutu caught an hour or two of rest.

When Ted had arrived at the airport, Tutu had said, "We want you to visit the ghettos in which we live. We want you to visit the resettlement camps to which our people are sent. We want you to be able to meet some of our people who lived under restriction." And that morning Ted Kennedy walked through the Soweto ghetto, as he had once walked through the refugee camps in Bangladesh. He walked through a hostel where six thousand workers, eight to a room, were housed. "One of the most distressing and despairing visits of any facility that I have made in my lifetime," he told the press. One man there told him that he had lived in the hostel for twenty years, getting to visit his family back in the Black homeland for only three weeks a year. Another said, "The worst part is the loneliness. Only when I am old will I be able to live with my wife and children." He visited a woman in her cramped home, who said that apartheid had each of them "by the throat" and that it "lets us breathe just enough so they can get another day's work out of us." At St. Pius X Church in Soweto, where Ted spoke, a man seeing Ted asked a fellow onlooker, "Please, madam. Who is that?" "That's Senator Kennedy of the United States," the woman answered. "Senator Kennedy of the brothers?" the man asked, for that was how they knew the Kennedys. One truck driver who met Ted outside the church said, "I have shaken the hand of a man I think can help us."

And yet there were those who were determined that he not help— among them, the South African government, which followed his every move and incited demonstrators to dog him, and the Reagan administration, whose ambassador to South Africa, Herman Nickel, derided the visit as a "whirlwind tour." But Ted was not cowed. He met with the minister of foreign affairs, Roelof Botha—a "very tense meeting," as Ted recalled. Botha warned that if Ted worked to impose economic sanctions on South Africa, he would only hurt the Black South Africans he was trying to help.

In Soweto, Ted said that when the question of sanctions arose, virtually everyone he spoke to, including the head of the miners' union, said to go ahead. As one told him, "We don't mind suffering if our children won't." And while Botha warned about imposing sanctions, Ted warned in return that unless South Africa accorded full citizenship and voting rights to its Black majority, it would reap the consequences. Ted said afterward that he didn't hear "anything that was very much encouraging." But that day, shortly before Ted was to speak before a white business group, a consortium of five business groups issued a statement calling for political reforms, including "meaningful political participation for blacks." One member was quick to say that Ted should not get credit for prompting the statement, then conceded that "he was truly the catalyst. We might have hemmed and hawed for two or three more months and eventually said half as much. He became a challenge to us: Why should an American tell us what is wrong with our society and how to fix it?"

During his meeting with Botha, Ted had made a request. He wanted to visit Nelson Mandela in his prison cell—Mandela who had been the face and the soul of the anti-apartheid movement and had paid dearly for it with his freedom. Botha took Ted aside and told him privately that the government would gladly let him see Mandela, but given how much Kennedy's own family had suffered from violence, he could see him only on the condition that Ted publicly oppose the use of any violence by Mandela's African National Congress in the furtherance of anti-apartheid. Ted refused the offer. He did, however, see Mandela's wife, Winnie, who had essentially been exiled to a remote area and restricted to a small shack under house arrest. Ted said her first words to him were, "How can you bring up children without a father?" Winnie Mandela was prohibited from being with more than one person at a time, and Ted had arrived with the son of Andrew Young, former U.S. ambassador to the United Nations. Winnie Mandela dismissed the threat. "If they jail me for it," she said, "it will make little difference. After all, this place where I live is just a slightly larger prison."

Bobby's trip had been triumphant because he was appealing to the aspirations of the Black majority, which was largely united. But if things had changed outside South Africa since that visit, they had changed inside too. There were factions now—the Azanian People's Organization that protested against Ted because he was white; and the Southwest African People's Organization, or SWAPO, which was a more militant group and one that pressed for immediate independence for Namibia and that was skeptical of any American involvement; and a group led by Zulu chief Gatsha Buthelezi, with whom Ted had met and who warned that Ted's sanctions would hurt Black people more than white people and told him, "It is no use doing things just in order to salve consciences." And to these there was added the ongoing South African government incitement of SWAPO especially, which intensified throughout the trip and which had protesters jeering Ted and disrupting his meetings. (Ted said that the government actually flew them in wherever Ted was to speak.) At one large rally in Cape Town, Allan Boesak introduced Ted, and immediately a group—Ted thought there were no more than one hundred of them out of the crowd of thousands—started to chant, so that Ted could not be heard. Ted told Boesak that he knew how to deal with hecklers. But Boesak said that he didn't know how to deal with *these* hecklers. So Boesak began a dance on the stage—"this enormously interesting and profoundly impressive dance," as Ted described it—and as he danced, Boesak began a recitation of the names of anti-apartheid heroes and casualties. And the crowd began repeating those names. And they got to their feet and began to move—a kind of shuffle. And the whole crowd was shuffling, dancing, and their chanting drowned out the chants of the protesters. And then Boesak stopped. And he said, "Now we'll hear from Senator Kennedy." And the crowd stopped its shuffling and its shaking, and a number of them encroached on those protesters, and Ted thought "they were going to tear them limb from limb." Terrified, those protesters ceased and remained silent through Ted's speech.

Ted had hoped to end the visit, as he had begun it, at St. Pius X Church, with a speech at the Regina Mundi Cathedral in Soweto. Shrum had written it, a speech that was meant to recapture the idealism with which Bobby had lifted the crowd at Cape Town. But this time there were two rival groups, one shouting "yes" to having Ted speak and the other "no" to having him speak. And Tutu asked the crowd to vote. And while the vote went to the ayes, Ted was afraid now that the South African police, with a large contingent there, were ready to wade into the crowd with their truncheons. He decided not to speak, decided that should there be any violence, the government and the press would blame him. He felt that the opposition to his speaking testified not to any particular animus toward him but to the extent to which Ronald Reagan's policies had led the Black freedom fighters to equate capitalism with repression and America with apartheid.

When it ended, the press was quick to label Ted's trip a failure. Even many Black South Africans were disappointed, citing a backlash among white moderates who objected to what one local newspaper called Ted's "arrogant talent to outrage," and a sense that the trip had further factionalized Black groups. Bobby had had to contend with none of those issues. Columnist Richard Cohen said there was "chortling" over the trip. He compared it unfavorably to Bobby's trip, where Bobby had been mobbed by Black people, white people, and those of mixed race. "Robert talked of human rights, and it seemed that people listened," Cohen wrote. But Cohen noted something too: that, as Ted himself had said, Reagan had "wrapped racial oppression, capitalism and the United States into one neat little package for every black to hate." Ted was a victim of that, even as he was trying, again almost single-handedly among American politicians, to fight injustice. And while Cohen said that the "pros fault his advance work and say he muddled his message," there was yet "another way to measure a politician, and that is by his willingness to go to the truth and tell us something we did not know before. Kennedy did that. He told us that American policy in South Africa is a failure. Any trip that teaches us that is a success."

But Ted Kennedy had not made the trip to educate. He had made the trip to bolster the freedom movement in South Africa and to rally the Senate to aid their cause. When he returned, he was "supercharged," he said. He testified without notes before the Foreign Relations Committee, notes being unnecessary since he had experienced during his trip that to which he would attest, and he brought his children with him to the hearing room. He called for sanctions—sanctions that would hurt South Africa, sanctions that would force South Africa to yield to its Black majority. While Ted might have been alone in focusing attention on South Africa, he was no longer alone, after his return, in wanting to pressure South Africa. For all the criticisms of it, the trip had had its intended effect. A number of senators were now proposing bills to impose sanctions. "South Africa is eventually going to be free," Ted said just a few weeks after the trip. "A continuation of policies will place the United States among the last allies of the basically white supremacist regime there and alienate a whole new generation of leaders." And when Reagan now insisted, as Botha had, that he was opposed to sanctions because they would hurt Black South Africans, Ted repeated what those miners had told him in Soweto: "They know they'll have to suffer even more, but they are prepared if it means a better life for their children."

With South Africa, Ted was engaged again—sailing against the wind. But he could not get sanctions through Congress single-handedly. He fully realized that even though he was working closely with Republican Lowell Weicker on legislation, it would be difficult to get a bipartisan sanctions bill through Congress—and any bill had to be bipartisan if it was to pass and then survive Reagan's veto—not only because the administration was strenuously opposed to one (Ted had had a heated debate with Ambassador Nickel) but also because the Black Caucus in the House, unshakably committed to punishing South Africa, was loath to compromise *its* bill that called for complete disinvestment by American companies in South Africa. Mickey Leland, the chairman of the caucus, invited Ted to speak to the group in the Whip Room on the third floor of the Capitol, but some of the members, fearing Ted might promote a watered-down bill, left. Ron Dellums, a California representative who had supported Ted's presidential bid and who had introduced the bill for the complete divestiture of any investments in South Africa, stayed and listened. But Ted was faced with finding a way of satisfying both the Republicans, who would have settled for a symbolic slap on the wrist, and the Black Caucus, who were in no mood to settle for symbolic gestures.

Republicans had their own needle to thread. In March Ted and Weicker had introduced a bill calling for four sanctions: barring bank loans, barring new investment by American corporations, barring the sale of computers to South Africa, and barring the importation of gold Krugerrand coins. But the president was unmovable. Republicans, appreciating the moral force behind the sanctions as well as their own president's hypocrisy in imposing total economic sanctions against the leftist government of Nicaragua but not even mild sanctions against the racist government of South Africa, wanted some bill, and the Foreign Relations Committee, while narrowly rejecting the Kennedy-Weicker bill, nine to seven, approved a bill retaining two of the sanctions: bank loans and computer sales. Meanwhile the Republican Senate leadership—Kansas senator Bob Dole was now majority leader after Howard Baker had decided not to seek reelection—had come up with a bill of its own that provided aid to Black

Africans and that would apply the so-called "Sullivan Principles," after Philadelphia clergyman Leon Sullivan, to South Africa—principles compelling American companies doing business there to push for equal justice for Black people and for an improvement in their living conditions. To appease their president, the bill also called for a two-year moratorium on any other action against South Africa. But Ronald Reagan still would not be appeased. When it came to apartheid, he was more than indifferent; he was actively supporting the South African government, despite new outbreaks of violence conducted by that government against its Black citizens. Tutu called him a racist.

Now Republicans were the ones who were frustrated with Reagan, and the ones who didn't want to be on the wrong side of racial history. As for the administration, its political concern was that the Republican Senate majority—the Democratic House had already passed the Black Caucus's bill—might pass a sanctions bill, most likely Dole's bill or Lugar's bill, forcing Reagan to veto it, which would put him squarely on the side of the repressive racist white South African government, even though he had kept denying he was sympathetic to it. As Richard Lugar told it, Secretary of State Shultz, a friend, phoned him and asked if he could come to Lugar's hideaway office in the Capitol. Shultz had come secretly on a Saturday and told Lugar that a bill wasn't necessary because the president was going to issue an executive order with everything in the Foreign Relations Committee's bill. But this was a secret promise, compelling Lugar and the others to trust a president who had shown little interest in dismantling apartheid. In July the Foreign Relations Committee's bill came to the floor, where it passed overwhelmingly, 80 to 12, with a few modifications, including the removal of the ban on Krugerrands. (Ted, again angry, convinced Dole to appoint conferees who would restore the ban on Krugerrands in conference.) It was one of the very few times the Republican Senate had repudiated the president. North Carolina senator Jesse Helms, a racial throwback, had threatened to filibuster it, delaying its passage. But Dole knew he had the votes. "We are going to pass this bill overwhelmingly," he said, in what could only be considered another challenge to Reagan, and which was an indication of how seriously congressional Republicans were now taking the issue.

Now the president was the one trapped by his own intransigence. With the Senate vote imminent, Reagan finally sprang his executive order—the one George Shultz had promised. Reagan ordered a ban on the sale of computers to security agencies in South Africa, loans to the government, excepting those that aided the poor, nuclear technology, and the Kruger- rand. He said that he hadn't abandoned his policy of "constructive en- gagement," only that he had amended it to "active constructive engagement." "America's view of apartheid is simple and straightfor- ward. We believe it is wrong," he said finally, although two weeks earlier he had told an interviewer that South Africa had "eliminated the segrega- tion that we once had in our own country," which was flatly and danger- ously false. "Too little, too late, and too involuntary," *New York Times* columnist Tom Wicker labeled Reagan's order, and he said that the Demo- crats, in pressuring Reagan to take some action or be embarrassed by a congressional rebuke, had wound up "saving Reagan from Reagan." With the executive order, the Republicans desisted from asking for a cloture vote. "I don't care when the president was converted, whether it was a minute ago," Bob Dole said of Reagan's sudden change of heart. But Ted, having finally forced Reagan to take a moral stand, called for one. He lost by seven votes. (Lugar, told by Dole, mistakenly, that he could stop the vote by physically taking the bill from the Senate floor, did just that.) And yet even having lost the vote, Ted had won. He had exposed Ronald Reagan's weakness. Reagan was a genial man, a likable man. He had inspired the country. But in sticking up for South Africa, he demonstrated what Ted had said he was not: He was not a moral leader.

But the South Africa victory, modest as it was, was not a personal triumph for Ted Kennedy, even though suspicions that he was ramping up, yet again, for a presidential run were circulating and that the sanctions fight was a way to promote that effort. Ted hadn't hidden his political inten- tions. Directly after his speech at Hofstra in March, he attended a Demo- cratic Party retreat in Shepherdstown, West Virginia, where, discussing his impending presidential decision, he called his desire to be president the "least well-kept secret in public life" and said, "Family considerations will always be important, but my children are older," and then he reminisced about Jack's 1960 campaign in West Virginia—an "emotional speech," by one account. His political action committee had 100,000 contributors and had raised $3 million, and he had contributed money to roughly two hundred candidates. His favorability rating had risen—to 55 percent. Bill Carrick was already talking to fundraisers and operatives, and Ted was scheduling speeches for the period after Christmas. And he commented to

Boston Globe columnist David Nyhan, while looking out on Nantucket Sound, that Florida has "softened up a little in the last six or eight months"—a prospective candidate's comment. That fall another columnist, Carl Rowan, meeting with Ted over lunch, left with the distinct impression that Ted was going to run, saying that Ted had indicated he felt he could "save both his party and the nation," and Rowan cited Ted's move slightly centerward as a sign. Even his move to the Labor Committee, Ted would later admit, was made with an eye not only to the Reagan agenda but to his own presidential chances: "I thought there was an important challenge now for new ideas recognizing the shortage and the limitation of funding."

But the South African trip, the trip that was viewed as a political trip, had begun to change his thinking about another run. "It bothered him that people in South Africa were saying, 'Senator, you're here because you're running for president. This is an issue you expect to use in your presidential campaign,'" Carey Parker said, and Ted was "genuinely offended by that." Ted thought long and hard about whether a presidential bid would actually undermine his efforts to end apartheid, and he said he had to decide whether to pursue an issue that he cared so deeply about or let political considerations dissuade him. He called that the "crescendo of my own thinking."

He hadn't reached the crescendo yet. The idea of a run hovered throughout the year as Ted was fighting for sanctions, but he did not instruct Horowitz to gear up for a campaign as he had in 1982, he did not commission polling, and he did not generally behave as if he were a candidate. Whether his heart had really been in a run in 1980 or in the 1982 run-up to 1984, Ted himself seemed to admit that it wasn't in a 1988 run. "You just don't decide you're going to run and announce you're going to run," he was to say, no doubt recalling 1979, when he had done exactly that. As he had in 1982, he planned to discuss a run with his family over Thanksgiving weekend at Hyannis. He actually had the discussion on November 16, 1985, twelve days before Thanksgiving. This time there were no objections, though no great enthusiasm either. He flew to Europe before Thanksgiving to sound out his sister, Jean Smith, who had always encouraged him to run. And then just before Thanksgiving, he and Horowitz had dinner at La Brasserie near Capitol Hill. As Horowitz later recounted it to Tom Oliphant, Ted was in one of his philosophical moods. "He asked me where the real opportunity for public service was for him, whether it was really as a presidential candidate for, in effect, three years and then possibly in the presidency, and where I thought he could make the greatest contribution." But Horowitz knew by dinner's end that Ted Kennedy would not be running for president in 1988 or perhaps ever. Ted said that he himself knew by the end of that Thanksgiving weekend. It was nearly two weeks later that Ted summoned Carey Parker and Bob Shrum to Hyannis and, sitting in an easy chair in the living room of the Big House, broke the news to them. Nursing a vodka, Shrum asked if Ted understood the implications: Were he to run, he would most likely be running against George H. W. Bush, Reagan's vice president and the putative Republican frontrunner, and that this would be his best chance to win. Winning was important now. He didn't want to embarrass himself. One Democratic strategist said that Ted had still wanted to be president and told advisers that "if we could demonstrate empirically that he could win the general election, he would run." But Ted, no matter how desperately he might have wanted to be president, knew there were no certainties and knew that his stock had not risen during the Reagan years. "I know and I don't want to run," Ted said evenly when Shrum talked about what Shrum saw as his favorable chances of victory. And he told Shrum and Parker what he had been telling himself: that if he were to run, everything he did would be viewed through that political prism. And he said something else—something Shrum said he had never heard him say before. He said, "Well, I realize this means I may never be president." He asked Parker and Shrum to write a withdrawal speech. (Shrum said that he and Horowitz wrote it.) Then they had a relaxed dinner—relaxed because the pressure was finally off. The next morning, having asked them to fly up from Washington, he informed Bill Carrick and Ranny Cooper, Ted's deputy chief of staff, in his Boston office. Carrick, Horowitz said, left the office "shaking." "He was almost apoplectic. He could not form words." Cooper drove everyone back to Hyannis to review the withdrawal script and supervise Ted's rehearsal, but she was shaken as well and drove off the road, puncturing a tire. The group had to take a cab to the Big House.

Ted himself seemed a bit shaken too by the realization that he had finally surrendered his presidential dreams, almost certainly forever—the dreams his father had schemed for him so many years ago and the dreams that had shaped so much of his adult life. He had asked the media consultant Michael Kaye to produce the brief filmed television address—Ted had requested and gotten five minutes from Channels 5 and 56 in Boston—

but Ted was jittery. "It was like he didn't want to say it," Horowitz recalled, "so it took ninety-seven takes, and it never did come out right. But that was that." He delivered it on December 19, in Charlestown at his cousin Joey Gargan's house, sitting in a high-backed chair next to a Christmas tree. "I have decided that the best way to advance the values that you and I share—peace on earth, economic growth at home, compassion to all Americans—is to be a United States Senator and not a candidate for president of the United States." He said, "The prospect is that the fog surrounding my political plans will cloud the far more fundamental challenge—to put aside complacency and the appeals to narrow interest—to care about one another, even the least among us." And he then told the public what he had admitted to Shrum: "I know that this decision means I may never be president, but the pursuit of the presidency is not my life. Public service is." Afterward he stopped by his Boston office to talk with the staff and spoke with his Washington office by speakerphone.

There would be great speculation about why Ted had made his decision when he finally seemed to have the field all to himself. Many discarded the idea Ted had offered, that he couldn't be a leader and a candidate simultaneously, that, given the cynicism about him, his motives would always be questioned, as his motive for withdrawing was itself questioned. At a press conference in Boston after his announcement had been televised, looking tanned and thin, he joked, "Well, here I don't go again," then griped, "People are more interested not in the substance of what I'm saying, but whether I'm moving to the left or the right, or my weight is up or down." (In fact, he had lost twenty pounds again, which had seemed a harbinger of another run.) One rumor was that he intended to get married, though Horowitz scotched that. There was no serious relationship. Horowitz said instead that there were serious family issues—he might have been referring to drug and alcohol problems among Bobby's children and Ted's own—that stopped a run, though Ted did not reference his family, except perfunctorily this time around when he had referenced them in the past. Ted himself might have suspected that his time had passed. He told Oliphant that the country "drifts between cycles of activism and relative passivity," and that right now the country was inclined toward the latter while he had always been inclined toward the former. A poll of state Democratic chairmen by *The Boston Globe* showed no great enthusiasm for a Ted run. "He's perceived as a candidate of the '60s who has not adjusted to the new political realities of the '80s," said one of them, referring obviously to the conservatism that Ted so vigorously battled. Liberal Massachusetts congressman Barney Frank said he was the "embodiment of all that the rightwing says is wrong with the Democratic party." But Ted didn't seem gun-shy, his liberalism notwithstanding, and it didn't seem a reason to abandon a race he might very well have won. (Associates would later say that Ted thought he could win the nomination but felt he would likely lose the election.) And while he certainly believed he could now be more successful in pursuing his agenda if he wasn't viewed as exploiting it for electoral gain, there might have been a deeper truth and a more personal reason for his withdrawal. Before his decision, he recalled something one of his University of Virginia law professors had said—"that we are really three individuals—what we are, what we think we are, and the way that we come across to people." Ted said that was certainly true of him. It is unclear precisely why he brought this up, though perhaps, he thought, it was time just to be who he is, which he could never be as a candidate. Bill Carrick, who had been so enraged about Ted's decision, would later say about that decision, "My sense of him is, he just got more inclined to let himself be himself."

It was over—finally—all the presidential expectations. He had been beholden to the inheritance of being president—his brothers' inheritance. He had spent much of his political career toggling between whether to run for the presidency or not, and nearly every move of his had been viewed, often cynically, through that lens. He would run. He was destined to run. But it was not Kennedy's era anymore—an era of government expansiveness and generosity. It was Ronald Reagan's—an era of government contraction and individual responsibility. Ted understood that the tectonic plates had shifted. Three months after his announcement, he told *The New York Times*'s Martin Tolchin that he was at ease with his decision. "I haven't regretted it one bit. I'm very happy with it, very comfortable with it. It's worked out just as I hoped it would." It had changed him. He had become more aggressive in the Democratic caucus now, one aide said. "More inclined to be himself," as Bill Carrick had said.

And now, freed from the expectation of pursuing the presidency, he was.

It was going to be different now—now that he was no longer a potential president, now that he had foreclosed the possibility of ever running for president. He had felt liberated the last time, but still, this was different because the prospect of 1988 had hovered then. Now no prospect hovered. "He knew very clearly that his status would be dramatically different after he withdrew in '85," Larry Horowitz would say. "He knew that was kind of the last time that people would look at him with a presidential look." He understood the trade-offs. He told biographer Burton Hersh, "When you're a presidential contender, you always get more attention here but less credibility. When you're not, you get more credibility but less attention." For years, he had parlayed his presidential prospects into power. Now he had to parlay the end of those prospects into a different kind of power—the kind of power that Richard Russell had when he lost his bid for the presidency in 1952, or that Robert Taft gained when he lost his presidential bid to Dwight Eisenhower that same year. A "reluctant grandee" was how another biographer, Theo Lippman, had predicted Ted's Senate future when he had declined to seek the 1976 nomination. He had been both an inside man and an outside man in the Senate. He still retained some of that outside power; he was, after all, a Kennedy, and that was a brand, if a tarnished one. "He operates as a national senator," Horowitz would tell *The New York Times* after Ted's renunciation, "and I think he always will." But he would have a gravity now among his colleagues that, however much they might have respected him, however much they might have thought him a workhorse, would be heavier than the weight he carried as a presidential contender. The very next day after his withdrawal, he flew on a chartered plane to West Virginia and the town of Albright, which had been devastated by a flood. The *Los Angeles Times* called the trip a vindication of his decision because no one doubted his motives now. "Ted Kennedy was in Albright, West Virginia, on Monday to let the people know that someone cares about them, that someone still is concerned about social justice in America," which was Ted's point all along.

He tried to make light of the fact that he would never be president. He joked at the Gridiron Club Dinner, an annual event at which politicians threw humorous barbs at one another and at themselves, "Frankly, I don't mind not being president. I just mind that someone else is." And he said: "I've decided it's better to make a long-range announcement of my plans: I will not be a candidate for president—in the year 2008—unless, of course, no one else in my family is running." He seemed more relaxed now. He lost weight, which was something he had done previously only when he was gearing up for a race. Representative Chester Atkins, the

Massachusetts Democratic chairman, thought he was a "much happier person, from what I can see," since his decision. Still, in less glib moments, Ted admitted to an emptiness. Years later, asked if he ever thought about another run for the presidency, he said, as he had said before, "I love the Senate and I think of myself as a Senate person, and that's where my ambition lies." But he also quoted poet Robert Browning, "If one's reach does not exceed one's grasp, then what is heaven for?" He had come to terms with being a senator—*only* a senator. "I've been around politics for a long time," he told one reporter. "There's enough work for a president." And then he paused and lit one of his little cigars. "And for a senator." "I don't think he didn't want to be president," Larry Horowitz was to say. "I think he wanted to be president. But he didn't think it was too bad, too shabby, so to speak, to be a first-rate senator." And Ted Sorensen, one of the keepers of the Kennedy myth, would say the same thing: Ted had learned that "he need not be president to fulfill his portion of the Kennedy legacy." And Ted himself talked of the process in the Senate, of how he once introduced a bill to fund Native American education and how that bill had passed and how Nixon then cut the funding and how he then worked to pass the bill again and got the funding restored. "You look back and see that you are achieving something after all," he said. "That gives you some satisfaction that you really don't get in the short term." And that now would be his legislative life—working for the long term.

The presidency for him was gone. In his Senate bathroom, he had hung a watercolor of the White House by Jamie Wyeth. In the painting, all the windows are dark—all but one. And Wyeth had inscribed the painting: "For Ted, How I wish that it were your light."

V

One of the main spurs to Ted deciding not to run for president had been his fear that by running he would be politicizing the South African sanctions in which he so firmly believed. The previous year Ronald Reagan had managed to short-circuit Congress and its sanctions with his executive order, thus allowing Republicans to render moot the bills they had passed imposing those sanctions so that no law reached the president's desk. But Ronald Reagan had no real interest in applying pressure to South Africa, most likely because his conservative base had no real interest in applying pressure to South Africa, preoccupied as it was with the supposed left-wing threat posed by the sympathies of the Black African National Congress. (The Reverend Jerry Falwell had made a visit to South Africa, but unlike Ted's visit, his was to express his support for the apartheid Pretoria government.) The situation in that country had not abated in the year since Ted had championed sanctions. Violence had intensified, but the Pretoria government remained intransigent. A commonwealth commission investigating a pathway to peace reported, "After more than 18 months of persistent unrest, upheaval and killings unprecedented in the country's history, the Government believes that it can contain the situation indefinitely by use of force." It tried. Meanwhile the Reagan administration watched and waited, primarily waited, it seemed, for opportunities to praise the South African government's baby steps.

But Ted Kennedy, along with many members of Congress, including some impatient Republicans, did not want to wait. In May, Ted and Lowell Weicker reintroduced their Comprehensive Anti-Apartheid Act, which now called for several new sanctions, including a prohibition on American deposits in South African banks. The Black Caucus in the House had grown even more impatient over the year of inaction. The next month the House passed a bill introduced by Ron Dellums that went further than Ted's—further even than Dellums's own bill the year before. The new bill called for a total trade embargo on South Africa and total disinvestment in South Africa by American companies. It passed unopposed, though only because some Republicans felt it would never get through the Senate. And now the Senate was put in the uncomfortable position of either passing the House bill, which seemed highly unlikely, doing nothing and surrendering to the administration and then accepting the consequences of inaction, or passing a bill of its own. Lugar, who had promoted a sanctions bill the previous year, before Reagan issued his executive order, now said he opposed a bill and thought the issue should be left to the president. This was no doubt capitulation. The administration had continued to press hard against sanctions, with Reagan delivering a speech on July 23, as the Senate was pondering its next move, saying that he abhorred apartheid and that he encouraged negotiations between Pretoria and leaders of the Black majority, but still giving the South African government kudos despite its violence and repression by comparing it favorably to Communist countries. "It's hard to think of a single country in the Soviet Bloc, or many in the United Nations, where political critics have the same freedom to be heard as did outspoken critics of the South African government," he said, ignoring the decades-long imprisonment of Nelson Mandela and the exile of dissident Oliver Tambo. At the same time, he slammed the "armed guerillas of the African National Congress." Bishop Tutu's response to Reagan was "The West, for my part, can go to hell." Meanwhile Reagan's director of communications, Patrick Buchanan, wrote an opinion piece in *The New York Times* railing against sanctions as likely to hurt Black Africans more than white people, the usual argument, but then revealing his real antipathy to sanctions: his sympathy for the Botha government. As for comparisons to sanctions of Nicaragua, which the administration had enforced, and those of South Africa, he wrote that South Africa has "not adopted as her ruling ideology the most odious form of tyranny over the mind of man," meaning Communism. Reagan had insisted he was motivated by a sincere desire to dismantle apartheid. But it was difficult not to see his motive as a mixture of racism and deranged anti-Communism— a now-familiar conservative blend—not to mention a favor to his business supporters. And it was difficult not to take his reluctance to sanction South Africa as anything but a failure of moral leadership. "Are the women of America prepared to give up all their jewelry?" asked Reagan's chief of staff, Donald Regan, referring to a ban on South African gold, as the debate raged.

Ted was outraged by Reagan's moral obtuseness. He called the administration's policy a "disgrace and an embarrassment" and declared that Congress needed to act to "put the U.S. back on the right side of history." And he warned of a bloodbath in South Africa if it didn't. To build support for his and Weicker's bill, that July Ted convened one of his forums, to which he invited former Australian prime minister Malcolm Fraser, a dogged conservative who had co-chaired the recent commonwealth commission that advocated sanctions, and former Nigerian head of state Olusegun Obasanjo. And then he hosted one of his issue dinners at McLean, this time inviting the Foreign Relations Committee chairman Richard Lugar, and the chairperson of the African Affairs Subcommittee Nancy Kassebaum, alongside Fraser and Obasanjo, hoping that by doing so he might bring Lugar and Kassebaum aboard. It was the first of several such dinners—basically a political courtship. Ted had sought to focus attention on South Africa. Now he had done just that. A *Time* cover asked: "If Not Now, When? If Not This, What?" Pressing for sanctions, *The New York Times* similarly opined, "Mr. Botha [the South African leader] cannot ignore a rebellion in Congress, no matter how much comfort he gets from his friend in the White House."

And now a rebellion was brewing. By this time, even the temperate Lugar was exasperated with the administration's lack of progress against apartheid, and reversing himself, he introduced his own set of mild sanctions, including revocation of landing rights for South African Airways and the freezing of bank accounts—sanctions that were toughened in committee and then voted out 15 to 2 on August 1. (One of the two nay votes, the segregationist Jesse Helms, had asked of Nelson Mandela, "Before we get his halo in place too securely, let's examine the guy.") The bill still wasn't strong enough for Ted. He had voted for the House version, which Senator Alan Cranston had introduced into the Senate and that had predictably failed, and then introduced his own tough sanctions bill, which Lugar, still hoping for a milder bill, managed to defeat narrowly, 51 to 48. Ted then, on August 15, removed several sanctions (among them, a ban on renewing bank loans) in a show of compromise but added several others (banning the importation of steel, iron, agricultural products and crude oil), and this time he won passage, 84 to 14. The Senate had taken its stand and taken it against the majority's own president.

But after more than a year of battles, the struggle still was not over. First, the Senate bill and the much more severe House bill had to be reconciled in conference, and neither side was likely to want to compromise. The House, and especially the Black representatives in it, had finally won their point, and they knew the Senate conferees were going to ask them to surrender it so that both Houses could pass a bill with a margin sufficient to override Reagan's veto. The only senator who had the credibility to make that request was Ted Kennedy. Ted and Greg Craig went over to the House and met with ten members of the Black Caucus. As Craig was to say, "Had it been any other senator trying to persuade them to give up what they'd won on the House side, it never would have happened." But Ted made the argument that the only way to pass a veto-proof bill was to pass a weakened bill, his own bill, and that if they did so, the Black representatives could win a real legislative victory, not just a moral victory. The House bill was Dellums's. Dellums had led the battle there, had debated a year earlier for hours on the floor, had succeeded not only in getting a bill passed but eventually in getting a tough bill passed that virtually terminated any economic relationship between the United States and South Africa. But Ron

Dellums trusted Ted Kennedy, and Dellums made a pitch to the caucus himself, and the caucus reluctantly agreed. When Ted had gone to speak with them, he thought "it wasn't going to happen"; he thought Reagan would win again. But now Dellums and the Black Caucus agreed to back Ted's bill, the Senate bill. And now Ted knew they were likely to win.

The second obstacle, the remaining obstacle, was Ronald Reagan. Reagan had been arguing so vigorously and unrelentingly against sanctions that he was now, as Senator Alan Simpson put it, "impaled on this thing." And no matter how vehemently he continued to insist that he only wanted to engage South Africa and that sanctions would inhibit engagement, especially when there was no effort whatsoever to engage the Sandinistas in Nicaragua, the vehemence with which he opposed sanctions, even though nearly every Senate Republican was now supporting them, betrayed that idea. The only plausible explanation for his stubborn opposition was that Ronald Reagan did not trust Black Africans as much as he trusted their white oppressors. Lugar, Dole, and Kassebaum even went to the White House to make a final plea for him to sign the bill. But Lugar would say that Reagan was unmoved. He told them he was going to veto it. And so impaled he was. The bill passed both houses of Congress easily. And then, on September 26, four hours before the bill would have become law had Reagan taken no action, he vetoed it. He tried to pressure Senate Republicans into upholding the veto, claiming that he didn't want to appear weak when he was heading to a summit meeting in Iceland with the new Soviet premier Mikhail Gorbachev. He wrote a letter to Bob Dole offering to impose new sanctions of his own and promised to appoint a Black ambassador to South Africa. But it was "a day late and a dollar short," according to Lugar's spokesperson. Lugar even said now that he would *lead* the override effort. Three days after the veto, the House overrode it, 313 to 83. And now it was the Senate's turn. Ted had invited several civil rights leaders, including Martin Luther King, Jr.'s, widow, Coretta Scott King, and the Reverend Jesse Jackson, who had been one of King's lieutenants before becoming a civil rights leader in his own right, and John Lewis, who had been one of the original Freedom Riders integrating bus stations and was a hero of the civil rights movement. They waited for the outcome in a meeting room down the hall from the Senate chamber.* And when Ted

---

*By another account, they had been sitting in the gallery. "Senate Rebuffs Reagan," *BG,* Oct. 3, 1986.

entered, after the Senate had voted 78 to 21 to override the veto, the room erupted with applause and hugs and congratulations, as Greg Craig recalled the scene. "A feel-good vote," Dole, who joined his president in upholding the veto, called it, scornfully, even though he had supported the legislation originally. Ted called it something else: "one of those moments that will live in our history." But while it was a moment for joy, it was not a moment for gloating. Just minutes into the celebration in that meeting room, Craig said that Ted spotted Treasury secretary James Baker watching from the doorway. Ted halted the congratulations, invited Baker into the room, and introduced him, one by one, to the celebrants.

Four years later, recently freed from prison, Nelson Mandela, the leader of the South African opposition, visited the United States and made an appearance before a joint session of Congress. Lugar recalled that afterward, at a luncheon in his honor in the Capitol, Mandela was asked to say a few words. Lugar said that Mandela reminisced about his years in prison and spoke of his sense that he had lost everything and of his terrible dread that no one would do anything to achieve justice in South Africa. And then he said, he got word that the U.S. Congress was acting. He said he didn't want to get his hopes up. British prime minister Margaret Thatcher had done nothing. The European Union had done next to nothing. Other nations and groups had done little or nothing. But, Lugar said, he told those congressmen and senators that "*you did act.*" And he told them, "You were decisive, and you mentioned me and my freedom." And he said this: "If you had not acted, there would be no relations between South Africa and the United States today." And Lugar said the tenor of the room changed abruptly because even though America had not let him down, it had come perilously close to doing so. And many years after that luncheon, Lowell Weicker, who had walked shoulder to shoulder with Ted in that long legislative crusade, who had been there when Ted was meeting those South African leaders whom no one else would meet, and who was with Ted when, as Weicker put it, he was "grinding away at this thing and making it happen"—Weicker said that "Ted, more so than anybody else in the world, and I mean that, can take credit for what happened in South Africa"—"one hundred percent of the credit," Weicker said. Ted Kennedy had been a ripple of hope and had helped build the current that, as Bobby had predicted, would "sweep down the mightiest walls of oppression and resistance."

ELEVEN

A New Man

W HEN TED KENNEDY decided not to run for president, he was liberated, as many noted, from the expectations that had burdened
him and from suspicions that every maneuver of his was politically inspired. Now he could act on his beliefs, not on his political advancement,
the latter charge of which had dogged him ever since he was promoted as
a candidate. The day after his announcement to surrender his presidential aspirations, flying on a charter plane to poverty-stricken communities
in Appalachia with *The Boston Globe*'s Tom Oliphant, he said, "You can't
be a national candidate without trying to build a national constituency. I
guess it's kind of self-evident. But it can be trying for someone like myself
who had tended to live on the cutting edge of social and foreign policy issues." He told Oliphant that there was an issue on that cutting edge that
he really wanted to raise now that he wasn't a candidate, now that his
motives weren't suspect, though he declined to tell him what it was. Oliphant said that Ted's staff later conceded to him that it was arms control,
and they told him that Ted had become reluctant to discuss it because, in
light of Reagan's military muscle-flexing, Ted thought he would look soft,
which was not something any candidate would likely survive. But Ted
Kennedy was no longer a presidential possibility, and now he could discuss arms control without undermining himself.

Of all the policy disagreements Ted had had with Ronald Reagan, arms
control was one of the most complex because Reagan's views on the issue
were complex—both belligerent and defensive. Reagan might have believed in the power of military might to ensure peace, and he was not
averse to characterizing America's enemies not just as our global adversaries but also, in the same vein of his attitude toward liberals, as morally

deficient; an "evil empire" was what he called the Soviet Union in an address before the National Association of Evangelicals early in 1983, once again deliberately merging politics and religion. Two weeks later, on March 23, almost as if to taunt the Russians, Reagan announced that he was launching a Strategic Defense Initiative—a program to investigate the feasibility of a high-tech system to shoot down incoming missiles, presumably Soviet ones. The announcement was made on impulse, with virtually no consultation with the Defense Department or the State Department or scientific advisers. (The germ may have been a 1940 film of his, *Murder in the Air,* in which he played a secret agent who foils a Communist plan to steal an "inertia projector" that can disable the navigation system of enemy aircraft.) In any case, Reagan had hatched the proposal on his own. "It kind of amuses me that everybody is so sure I must have heard about it, that I never thought of it myself," he boasted. "The truth is I did." His own advisers were incredulous at the idea—incredulous that America had the technology for such a system (it didn't), incredulous that such a system wouldn't destabilize the world order, not to mention that it violated a provision of the ABM treaty Richard Nixon had signed with the Soviets explicitly outlawing such a system, incredulous at the cost of the system. And many of them were incredulous that Reagan was abandoning the principle of Mutual Assured Destruction that had been the cornerstone of nuclear policy: the idea that the threat of retaliation was enough to prevent an attack. Reagan, who was dubious about arms control treaties with the Russians to begin with and thought they were a way for the Russians to con America, was not having any of it. To those worried about violating the treaty or destabilizing the World War II order, he later told reporters that he was willing to offer the system to the Soviets so that they would have the same defensive capability as America—an offer toward which his advisers were even more incredulous. Though Reagan had made no specific mention of space in his speech, Ted immediately derided the idea, with a presumed component of space-based antimissile weapons, calling the system "Star Wars," after the blockbuster science fiction film. The name stuck.

Ted's deeper concern was the possibility that the tension that had intensified between the United States and the Soviet Union since the invasion of Afghanistan might migrate to the two nations' nuclear policies, triggering a new arms race. It was that concern that had prompted him to send John Tunney to Russia in 1980, during his presidential campaign, to

speak with government officials there and see if there might be some accommodation. But that was during the Carter administration, which had
negotiated another arms limitation treaty with the Soviets, SALT II—
a treaty that, because of Soviet adventurism, the Senate had failed to rat-
ify. Ted distrusted Reagan when it came to Soviet relations because of the
strident anti-Communism on which Reagan had built his career and in
which he, his advisers, and his supporters so clearly believed, and Ted did
his best to court Secretary of State George Shultz, whom he regarded as a
reasonable man likely to restrain Reagan's more extreme effusions. Carey
Parker recalled a dinner honoring Shultz at which Ted teased that if a
Harvard man like Ted and a Princeton man like Shultz could get together,
then so could Reagan and Soviet premier Leonid Brezhnev. Someone in
the office, or possibly Ted himself, had found a small rare glasswork on
which a tiger, which was the Princeton mascot, was etched. Ted purchased it and presented it to Shultz, telling him that Shultz was the tiger
from Princeton who saw the world as it should be seen. And Parker said
that Shultz was touched by the gesture. And Parker said that Ted began to
deal extensively with Shultz on issues relating to the Soviet Union, while
Larry Horowitz dealt extensively with Jack Matlock, Jr., a special assistant
to the president who would later become the U.S. ambassador to the Soviet
Union.

There was a lot to deal with. If Reagan didn't trust the Soviets, they
didn't especially trust Reagan either, prompting Ted to open an informal
back channel with the Soviets, in the hope of opening a dialogue. In late
January 1984, during one of his visits to Moscow in his role as go-between,
Larry Horowitz received a message from Vadim Zagladin, deputy chief of
the Central Committee International Development, that he wanted relayed to the Reagan administration: The Soviets were open to discussing a
treaty to ban chemical weapons. As Jack Matlock later wrote, Ted "considered these matters above politics" and said he would be pleased to assist,
but would understand if the administration chose not to use his services.
They did use them. And Matlock felt that Ted had also, by cooperating
with the administration, sent his own message to the Soviets: "Reagan
was serious about negotiations." In the event, Horowitz continued to
serve as a liaison, while Matlock received permission from his superiors to
set up a meeting with Zagladin, which in turn, though not without fits
and starts, led to further contacts, which in turn led to negotiations in
Geneva on nuclear weapons, though not especially hopeful ones. During

those negotiations throughout 1985, Ted was part of a group of congressional observers attending the talks. "There seemed to be a feeling of
unity," President Reagan had noted after meeting over breakfast with
them before the group headed to Geneva, "even including Sen. Kennedy,"
he wrote. And now there was a new Soviet leader, Mikhail Gorbachev,
whom no one in the administration really knew and whom they were approaching cautiously. (Greg Craig said that he got a call from the CIA
while he was in Geneva because Ted was one of the only officials who had
met with Gorbachev's new foreign minister, Edvard Shevardnadze.)
Brezhnev, who had been frail and sickly when Ted visited him years earlier, in 1978, had died late in 1982. He was succeeded by Yuri Andropov,
the head of the KGB, or Soviet secret police, who had refused discussions
with Reagan.* Andropov died less than two years after assuming power
and was succeeded by Konstantin Chernenko, an apparatchik. But the
Soviet Union was a gerontocracy, its leadership old and ailing, and a little
more than a year later, in March 1985, Chernenko died as well. This time
the leadership passed to a younger Andropov ally, Gorbachev, a largely
unknown figure with a reputation, such as it was, as a relative reformer.
That presented a possible opening.

But it was unclear whether Reagan would take it. What made Reagan's views about arms control complex was that whatever distrust he
had toward the Soviets, however much he reviled their godlessness (and
he did), and however much many in his administration insisted that any
negotiations with them were futile, Reagan himself was dedicated not to
arms control but to arms elimination. As contradictory as it might have

---

*By one report, circulated in conservative circles and based on an alleged document from
the Soviet archives, Kennedy critics claimed that in May 1983, he again dispatched his
close friend, former law school roommate and Senate colleague John Tunney, to Russia to
convey a message to Andropov. According to an account of that memo, it said that Kennedy, who "is very troubled by the current state of Soviet-American relations," offered to
visit Moscow to provide assistance on positioning the Soviets on nuclear disarmament and
arrange American television interviews for Andropov to state his offers. Andropov in turn
would provide assistance to the Democratic Party in the 1984 election, which, Tunney was
purported to have said, might pit Kennedy against Reagan, though apparently nothing
was quoted directly from the memo to suggest this quid pro quo. Over and above the fact
that Tunney denied any such contact and that Max Kampelman, Reagan's arms negotia-
tor, said that Kennedy always worked in conjunction with the administration, the trouble
with the story was that Ted was not seriously considering a presidential run at the time,
and that there was nothing the Soviets could have done to help him, short of making some
peace offering—an action that would have benefited Reagan, not Kennedy. Peter Robinson, "Ted Kennedy's Soviet Gambit," Forbes, Aug. 28, 2009.

seemed to liberals, who castigated him as a warmonger, Ronald Reagan, largely with the encouragement of his wife, Nancy, wanted to rid the world of nuclear weapons, so much so that he was loath to negotiate any treaty that did not work toward total elimination. Nancy thought it would be his enduring legacy: the president who ensured peace. (Of course, there were undoubtedly political calculations: among them, that any treaty short of elimination would, he thought, benefit the Soviets and that Reagan was bargaining with the Soviets at a time of their vulnerability, and domestically, that the nuclear freeze movement had put pressure on Reagan.) For his part, Gorbachev was willing to talk with Reagan about an arms agreement. What both needed was a conduit. Ted Kennedy became a primary one. The Soviets respected Ted. Veteran diplomat Max Kampelman, who at the time served in the administration as ambassador and head of the U.S. delegation to the negotiations with the Soviet Union on nuclear and space arms in Geneva, said that Ted had developed a "special relationship" with the longtime Soviet ambassador to the United States Anatoly Dobrynin. Kampelman also believed that the Soviets had a fascination with the Kennedys and "thought they were powerful," which Ted himself had discovered in his meetings with Brezhnev, who received him, Ted believed, because Brezhnev clearly thought that Ted would become president. Larry Horowitz said the relationship between the Kennedys and the Soviets—he too called it a "special relationship"—was one that "no nonpresident has ever had," and Horowitz made frequent trips to Russia as Ted's representative, even arranging meetings between Ted and Andropov and then Chernenko, neither of whom lived to attend those meetings. But Kampelman also recalled that other members of the Reagan administration discouraged the president from using Ted in an intermediary role, suspecting a "self-aggrandizing effort," obviously meaning that Ted would exploit the contacts for his own political advantage. This might have been what Ted meant when he told Oliphant that his presidential aspirations had clouded one of his primary goals, which was arms control. Kampelman said that he intervened with Shultz to let Kennedy keep his channels with the Soviets open since the Reagan administration had virtually none of their own. And Ted did so, passing messages back and forth between the Reagan administration and the Soviets, and sending Larry Horowitz to Russia—four or five times that year, Horowitz said—to carry messages personally. As Kampelman summarized the results of these efforts, "I believe the negotiations were helped."

Reagan was a man who generally followed the script, and the script said that the Soviets were treacherous. But despite the best efforts of some of those in the administration, among them Secretary of Defense Caspar Weinberger, to discourage any further negotiations with the Soviets—Reagan would not be dissuaded given how much he prioritized the elimination of those weapons. While a new round of talks was already under way that year, the one to which Ted was an observer, Reagan flew to Geneva in November 1985 to hold one-on-one discussions with Gorbachev, primarily centered on nuclear arms, on the basis that Reagan and Gorbachev could personally come to terms on an agreement. And while the talks were largely cordial—Gorbachev was no more an ideologue than Reagan—there was nevertheless a sticking point: Gorbachev would not accept the militarization of space with Reagan's SDI or "Star Wars" system, and Reagan adamantly refused to give it up. Unless arms reduction was decoupled from "Star Wars," Reagan insisted, there could be no going forward. If it was, Gorbachev insisted, there could be no going forward. Reagan left Geneva with a deadlock.

But the personal diplomacy on which Reagan had placed such stock was not over—not quite yet. With Reagan's full approval—he and Ted met twice, Horowitz said, in preparation, and Reagan wrote in his diary that Ted "wanted to check in to make sure he wouldn't say anything there that would be at cross purposes with us"—Ted headed to Moscow in late January 1986, just weeks after Ted's latest presidential renunciation, to meet with Gorbachev and see if he could nudge the talks along. (Horowitz said that during one of those preparatory meetings, Reagan asked Ted specifically to find out if Gorbachev had been baptized. That would make a difference in finding common ground, Reagan believed.)

Ted wasn't particularly hopeful. Arms control was both massive and delicate, and the sides were intractable. But there was another issue close to Ted Kennedy's heart: convincing the Russian government to let dissidents emigrate. Twice before, in 1974 and 1978, he had met with Brezhnev, armed with lists of refuseniks. The second time, the Soviets conceded that eighteen of those refuseniks would be given favorable consideration due to Ted's intervention, though, by one account, only two were allowed to emigrate imminently. The others had to wait, in some cases wait years. Over those years, the number of émigrés had declined from over 51,000 in 1979 to 1,140 in 1984. So Ted accepted the invitation to Russia—it had been tendered by the Supreme Soviet, obviously hoping to get more traction on arms control with Ted than they could with Reagan—with one condition: that the Soviets take some action on a new list that Ted had brought of twenty-five dissident would-be émigrés.

Ted's meeting with Gorbachev was a long one—two and a half hours—and a tense one. Though a reformer, Gorbachev resented any American meddling on human rights, and Ted said that when he brought up the subject, Gorbachev detonated, shouting that Ted shouldn't lecture him on human rights. "It was like setting off a rocket. It was like he was watching my temperature go up." But then, after having chastised Ted, Gorbachev told him that he would allow twenty-five Jews and Anatoly Shcharansky, a noted refusenik who had been charged with treason and imprisoned for nine years, to leave the country, though six had already been repatriated. (Shcharansky had also been a translator for the Russian physicist, dissident, and Nobel laureate Andrei Sakharov, for whose emigration Ted had specifically asked Gorbachev; Gorbachev denied the request, but Ted, speaking later at the Soviet Academy of Sciences, lauded Sakharov and said, "The indispensable value of science is its ability to speak truth to power.") Then Gorbachev calmed. He told Ted how much he admired the Kennedy family—a trait of Soviet leaders—and how he had recently seen a film on John Kennedy in which he recalled the image of young John-John Kennedy saluting his father's casket, a famous image. And then finally came the discussion on arms limitation. Gorbachev stated the Soviet position, which was an agreement to eliminate intermediate-range missiles in exchange for a freeze on the British and French nuclear arsenals and a pledge not to move them to another country. And he reiterated that he too favored eliminating all missiles that could reach one another's territory. Differences between the United States and Russia could be "bridged," he told Ted. What he did not say, what startled Ted, was that the elimination of the intermediate-range missiles was still conditioned on the abandonment of the "Star Wars" defense system. He had now "de-linked" them, as Reagan had requested. And at meeting's end, Gorbachev pointed at Larry Horowitz, who had accompanied Ted, and said, "Let's keep your guy in touch with my guys—regularly." Horowitz said he and Ted took that injunction "very seriously." "We developed a coded telex system, and I made three, four, five visits a year, always in coordination with Reagan. Never was a secret from the administration." Ted told reporters that he left the meeting with a "real sense of hope that a breakthrough can be achieved in the reduction of intermediate-range nuclear forces," though Reagan wasted little time in rejecting Gorbachev's proposal on the British and French arsenals and later opted out of the SALT II treaty that Jimmy Carter had negotiated.* Ted called it the "worst mistake of his presidency," since the Soviets were slated to give up six hundred missiles under the agreement. As it so often was for Reagan, whose desire for nuclear arms elimination was at odds with his conservative demonization of the Soviet Union, he moved one step forward, only to move two steps back.

Nevertheless, it was a breakthrough, though even Ted's staffers thought Gorbachev was, as Horowitz put it, "playing" the White House, "telling them that a Democrat was getting full debriefings from the Soviets so the Reagan folks could not lie about what was going on." Carey Parker too thought Gorbachev was sticking it to Reagan and the conservatives. "Although the Soviets wouldn't tell the Reagan administration that they would acquiesce on a nuclear arms control agreement, or on an intermediate weapons treaty for Europe," Parker said, "they would tell it to Senator Kennedy, with the understanding that he would pass it along to Shultz. I think they felt that it showed the hardliners in the Reagan administration, 'You won't deal with us, but we can deal with the more reasonable people in your country.' That was unheard of. We were amazed. We thought the back channels would produce lesser information, and perhaps succeed in bringing out many of the dissidents, things like that," Parker was to say. "But to get an arms control agreement turned out to be one of Kennedy's major achievements." Still others thought that Gorbachev was using Ted to put the best face on the Soviet proposals, which was exactly what Ted did in an op-ed piece in *The Washington Post* after his return from Russia. "The Russians Are Ready to Bargain on Arms Control," it was titled. Before Ted left, the Soviets accorded him a rare privilege: He was allowed to tape a ten-minute television address to the Russian people. (Ronald Reagan had been given only five minutes at the end of the

---

*Later that year, with the talks still stalemated, Horowitz, who had left government by this time but who was still a courier for Ted, said that Dobrynin asked him to set up a working group that would coordinate with a Soviet working group to break the deadlock. Ted and Horowitz met with Reagan twice, and he was "delighted about the idea." But then Reagan's men insisted on appointing Richard Perle, a truculent and unbending anti-Communist, to the group. Gorbachev balked, saying that this would make the back channel group no different from the front channel one, and Reagan said he could name whomever he liked. And that ended the opportunity. Larry Horowitz int., May 29, 1992, H Folder, Box 3, Series 2, Clymer Papers, JFK Lib.

Geneva summit in November.) Ted used it to appeal for peace—"The greatest task of our time, the greatest human responsibility of all time, is to preserve and protect the world"—and while he said he opposed the "militarization of space," referring to Reagan's "Star Wars" missile defense system, he also said he supported the buildup of conventional American forces. It was an anodyne address that, save for the comment on missile defense, Reagan himself might have delivered, but it was a sign of deference to Ted that he seldom received during the Reagan presidency, when he was generally and largely accurately viewed as powerless.

But the speech had another effect. Coordinating with the Reagan administration—Ted would always go directly to the White House or the State Department after landing from his visits—he made certain the Soviets realized that the United States presented a united front: Reagan and Ted together, which left no doubt that it was Ronald Reagan's country now, not the Kennedys'.

When it came to health policy too, he was more driven than he had been while he was contemplating a presidential run. Of all the frustrations that Ted Kennedy endured during the Reagan administration, perhaps none was as grating as that over his signature cause: national health insurance. Since Reagan had taken office, the cause had languished. Ted tried to revive it after the 1980 election by asking the Committee for National Health Insurance, the old Committee of 100 that had helped pilot Ted's first heath insurance bill in 1969, to support his 1978 bill that included private insurers. One of Ted's old health advisers, Rashi Fein, who was now the head of the technical committee of the CNHI, recommended they decline because it was a compromise bill—the compromise Ted had offered to Carter—and it wasn't productive to support a compromise. "And that," Fein recalled, "was kind of the end" of Ted's relationship to CNHI. Now, with an administration in direct opposition to national health insurance, Ted was back to incrementalism—to fashioning a bill that at best could help some of the uninsured but could not provide universal coverage. Fein remembered a hearing for one of these incremental bills and the disappointment it engendered among those who still held out hope for a comprehensive bill. "During the testimony," Fein recalled of Ted, "he turned to the audience and said, 'There are those who would argue that a universal, comprehensive system is really the best approach, and I would not deny that. But that's not where we are politically, and I will not hold hostage those people who can be helped today because I want to argue for something bigger and better but which they can't have and wouldn't help them now.' "

The debate had changed. "For however important questions of efficiency have been," sociologist Paul Starr wrote in 1982, "questions of equity have always been the true moral basis of health insurance as a social movement. Today, however, health insurance seems less like a moral cause than an argument about economic management." Ted himself, who believed fervently in the moral justice of national health insurance, was arguing about economic management too because he felt he had no alternative. He proposed a bill early in 1984 to limit doctors' and hospitals' costs to Medicare payments as a way of saving Medicare when Republicans were threatening it by imposing large cuts. The following year, citing a rise in the number of uninsured, even though the economy had improved, he introduced a bill that required an employer mandate and private insurance—a significant retrenchment from the old Kennedy healthcare bills. It was reported out of committee—the first of Ted's health insurance bills to reach the floor—but went no further. The following year he introduced, along with Republicans David Durenberger and John Heinz and fellow Democrat Don Riegle, a bill that would require employers to continue insurance for laid-off workers and their dependents for four months and then allow those workers to pay premiums to maintain their insurance for another eighteen months or else the employers would face a tax penalty. Among the bill's other provisions, one required states to pay hospitals for charity or uncompensated care, and another provided insurance for those with preexisting conditions whom insurance companies typically would not cover, and he introduced two other bills that addressed uninsured children. These were increments, the best Ted thought he could get against an administration that seemed opposed to any assistance to those who needed health insurance—a reminder of Reagan's early opposition to Medicare as a long step on the road to socialism—but he couldn't get them either. As Representative Pete Stark, the chairman of the House Ways and Means Committee and the cosponsor of a bill with Ted to cover the indigent, put it, "Reagan's health policy is to cut virtually all federal programs that deal with health, welfare, or human services, or to turn the programs over to the states. Anybody who believes that this administration wants it any differently is, I think, politically naive." Ted did manage to steer through the Labor Committee and ultimately through the Senate the provision that allowed laid-off workers to buy insurance, but only because senators were preoccupied with other and bigger matters and only because he was able to get it thrown into a huge grab-bag bill, the Comprehensive Omnibus Budget Reconciliation Act or COBRA, that included everything from the Amtrak reauthorization to foreign fishing permits to agricultural funds to funds for public broadcasting. (When Hatch got wind of it, he threatened to stop it, and Ted had to find a state trooper in Iowa to go into the fields and get Senator Charles Grassley, a Republican supporter, off his tractor and fly back to vote.) Reagan signed it into law, and for decades thereafter COBRA, as Ted's provision became known, after the name of the act itself, allowed individuals to buy insurance when they were put out of work. But even Ted called it a "very modest step," and it didn't even merit mention in his memoir.

Modest steps were all he could accomplish now, even though he was unshackled from his presidential aspirations, even though he was a new man. He was stymied. There was only one way he could advance progressive legislation: He would have to help the Democrats win back the U.S. Senate.

Ronald Reagan seemed well situated to stave off that eventuality. He was still popular. Coming off of Jimmy Carter's bumpy presidency, Reagan had changed government significantly, perhaps for years, perhaps for a generation, perhaps longer. That June an assessment by Bernard Weinraub of Reagan's first six years, titled "The Reagan Legacy," in *The New York Times Magazine,* credited Reagan with having strengthened the presidency, having "totally eliminated for years to come any discussion of new social-welfare initiatives" and redirected the entire orientation of the government from activism to passivity, having reshaped the federal bench with conservatives who were likely to serve for decades, and having lifted the shadow of Vietnam and validated the use of American military might. (What Weinraub did not cite, since he was writing early in 1986, was Reagan's summit in October with Gorbachev in Reykyavik, Iceland, which led to another nuclear arms talk impasse but opened the door to further talks.) Perhaps, above all, Weinraub found, Reagan had managed to accomplish what his Republican predecessors had not. He had discredited liberalism, not just as an outworn set of policy prescriptions, which, after all, could theoretically be reversed by a successor (in fact, polls showed that liberal policies were still more popular than conservative ones), but as a cultural form of disdain for the preferences of ordinary Americans, the standard conservative criticism that liberals were elitists, that they had a different sense of morality than ordinary Americans, and that they thought they knew better than ordinary Americans, and Weinraub quoted a Reagan address at the Conservative Political Action Committee dinner, which neatly summarized the new conservative mythological view of liberalism: "The normal was portrayed as eccentric, and only the abnormal was worthy of emulation," said Reagan. "The irreverence was celebrated—but only irreverence about certain things. Irreverence toward, say, organized religion? Yes. Irreverence toward establishment liberalism? Not much of that. They celebrated their courage in taking on safe targets, and patted each other on the back for slinging stones at a confused Goliath who was too demoralized—and, really, too good—to fight back. But now, one simply senses it: the American people are no longer on the defensive."

But there were other parts to the legacy, less impressive parts: a ballooning deficit that required 40 percent of every income tax dollar to pay down the national debt (this from a president who promised to balance the budget by 1984) and that would weigh on the economy for years to come; a sluggish economy; an increasingly large federal government bureaucracy, thanks to the growth of the defense sector, despite his pledges— pledges central to his mission—to cut it (Weinraub quoted Senator Pat Moynihan, who praised Reagan's governing skills but lamented that he had "crippled the economy of the nation and this will be with us for the rest of the century"); and his legitimizing the intolerance of the religious right, which threatened to become as powerful a force in the post-Reagan Republican Party as labor had been to the Democratic Party. Pollster Patrick Caddell told Weinraub the evangelicals were a "monster" that might very well seize the party. And there was the assault on the poor, who bore the brunt of Reagan's budget cutting. Weinraub quoted Jack Meyers, a resident fellow of the conservative American Enterprise Institute, who admitted that the "cuts have, let's face it, caused a considerable amount of pain," raising the poverty rate and the rate of homelessness, which were things that troubled Ted Kennedy. If one of the major tests of a presidency was how the poor fared, then Reagan was a failure, which was what Ted had been saying all along. Still, for most Americans the positive "feel-good" of Reagan seemed to outweigh the negative and hurtful consequences of his policies, and the prospects for Democrats' recapturing the Senate in the 1986 midterms were not particularly good, despite the traditional midterm losses of the party in power.

At least, that was what the pundits had been predicting. Reagan barnstormed for the Republicans—25,000 miles and twenty-two states—trying to rub his popularity off on them. And Reagan did gain eight governorships and lost only five additional seats in the House, which was a negligible loss for a midterm. (In the last four midterm elections held in the sixth year of an incumbent's presidency, the out-party had gained at least forty-seven seats.) But the Senate was different. In the Senate, Ted Kennedy's Senate, the Republicans took a drubbing. Six of the twelve Republican senators who entered office with Ronald Reagan in 1980 lost; a seventh Republican seat, that of John East of North Carolina, who had committed suicide earlier that year, was also lost. The Democrats picked up eight seats in all, for a 55-to-45-seat majority. Some attributed it to the lack of a clear agenda in the second Reagan term. Some to the fact that Reagan had made himself the issue, thus detracting from the candidates, who seemed followers rather than leaders. Some to economic distress in several states that turned from Republican to Democrat. One Republican consultant conceded that the "country has a tiny bit of a sour stomach." What the victory constituted was hard to say. Republicans brushed it off, even though the Democrats now controlled both houses of Congress again. As columnist Russell Baker characterized it, "To conservatives, liberalism is like Count Dracula. They know it is dead, they keep telling everybody it is dead, but their secret terror is that the stake has not yet been driven through its heart." Democrats rejoiced. Moynihan called it a "new era" and said the Democrats had finally "exorcised the war, the riots and the rhetoric." Tip O'Neill, who was retiring from the House—Ted's nephew, Joe II, won the seat—declared, "If there was a Reagan Revolution, it's over."

But the triumph wasn't as clear as the Democrats might have thought. Pollsters Mark Penn and Douglas Schoen reported that while Senate Democrats might have won the votes, Reagan still seemed to have won the larger political battle. "Virtually every successful Democratic candidate for the Senate made it clear from the start," they wrote, "that he opposed wasteful spending on social programs, opposed using tax reform as a way to raise taxes and supported government policies to encourage economic growth and traditional American family values"—in short, the Reagan agenda. And the pollsters concluded that the election represented the "institutionalization of the anti–New Deal consensus in American political life."

But not for Ted Kennedy, who had campaigned vigorously for his fellow Democrats, and who had raised $3.5 million through his political action committee for them, and who had been waiting for this moment for six years—waiting anxiously to retake the initiative from Ronald Reagan and the conservatives. Not for Ted Kennedy.

II

"When we took the Senate back," his Labor Committee counsel, Tom Rollins, told biographer Burton Hersh, Ted "was transformed, a new man." During the campaign, when Reagan was stumping the country, he would adduce Ted as the danger the Republicans needed to stop, and he had warned that Ted, as Judiciary chair, would block Reagan's appointments to the bench. The day after the victory, Ted quipped, "Some people have said the President tried to make the election a referendum on Senator Kennedy. If that was the case, I'm pleased with the results." And Ted wasted no time in acting on those results. The night of the election, Rollins said that he got himself "lit up," he was so happy. He went home and collapsed in bed, and then was awakened by a phone call at six the next morning. It was Ted. "Tom, Tom. This is the Commander," he said, which, according to Rollins, was what he called himself when he was in a jolly mood. "I've decided I'm going to take that Labor thing," meaning the chairmanship of the Labor Committee. "We're going to have a press conference here in Boston at eleven. Can you remind me again of what a bunch of those things that we can do without spending any money?" Rollins said Ted was so giddy, he had forgotten the "bullet points of the briefing." Rollins briefed him on how they could circumvent Gramm-Rudman, the sequestration bill that handcuffed any new spending and that Ted himself had supported when Reagan was threatening those social programs. And Rollins said it was the first time he had heard that Ted was going over to take the Labor chairmanship, when he could have taken Judiciary, the more prestigious of the two committees.

There was a question in Ted's mind as to which he should take. When, after the Democrats lost the Senate in 1980, he deliberated whether to move to the Labor Committee as the ranking member, rather than stay as the ranking member on Judiciary, he had held a conference in his office discussing the pros and cons with the staff. Now he had a bigger decision to make, not just where he would be directing the bulk of his attention and energies, but where he would be spending the rest of his career, which made it a decision with implications not only for his current situation but also for his legacy. This time Ranny Cooper, his deputy administrative assistant, moderated the debate, which likely took place sometime after he had more or less made a decision on election night—Carey Parker would say Ted "felt that the Labor Committee was where he belonged"—and sometime before he would officially announce it, though the debate spoke to Ted's caution that he make the right decision and that he might change his mind. Cooper asked the staffers to present their case for whether Ted should take the Judiciary chairmanship, which Reagan obviously thought he would take to block those appointments, or the Labor chairmanship. Rollins, who worked for Ted on Labor, was to carry the case for that committee, but Cooper warned him not to "go negative" on Judiciary. Rollins said that his opening gambit was to ask Ted to recall the fights he waged in the Nixon administration against Supreme Court nominees Clement Haynsworth and G. Harrold Carswell—successful fights. Ted said that of course he remembered. And then Rollins asked him if he remembered who finally got the seat after they had failed. Ted didn't remember. And Rollins told him it was William Rehnquist, whom Ted had recently fought and fought hard after Reagan appointed him to chief justice. And then Rollins delivered the coup de grâce: "The point I'd like to make, Senator, in opening my case for the Labor Committee, is that a defeated nominee is a replaced nominee, but a public law is a thing of joy forever." Four days after the election, Ted officially announced his decision, calling it "an unusual opportunity to reverse the retreat of the past six years," though he made this proviso: that he was convinced that "new approaches can work without increased spending." In telling Joe Biden that Ted would be surrendering his position on Judiciary and that Biden would be chairman, he asked that Biden retain his staff. Biden said that if he got the job, he would fire the staff. Ted took Labor anyway.

He wanted Labor. He was energized by Labor. There were the battles he wanted to fight that he could fight through Labor, especially his long-running battle against the Republicans for national healthcare. And he couldn't wait to start. He convened his top staffers at Hyannis to lay out an agenda. Rollins "cranked out this book" with items to consider and sent it a week or two before the meeting to the senator and to Carey Parker and Ranny Cooper, who would be participating. "Big Hairy Ass Goals"— huge impossible goals—that was what Rollins laid out, having read a business advice book that recommended them. BHAGs because even though the goals were likely unachievable, at least in full, lesser goals were also likely to be unachievable, and Rollins's reasoning was that it was better to get 90 percent of the way to a BHAG than to a small one. The stumbling block, Rollins thought the first day of their meetings was not likely the goals but the senator. Rollins said that he had often found Ted to be in his incomprehensible mode; that "I couldn't make sense out of what he was saying half the time"; that he was "fairly certain" Ted "didn't know what was in memos that he had written notes on"; that he "just seemed kind of disconnected and dissolute," though Rollins also said that he never drank at work so Rollins couldn't attribute Ted's fogginess to that. (Of course, Rollins could have been wrong; having been in the wilderness for six long years, Ted might have cut loose without Rollins knowing it.) And Rollins worried that it might be a "fool's errand" going through the book and discussing the agenda given how distracted Ted often seemed.

But even though it was atypical for one of Ted's own staffers to discount him, Rollins certainly wasn't the first person to underestimate Ted Kennedy. Ted had been both infuriated with and frustrated by Reagan— with having, as Rollins himself said, to spend his time "throwing as much sand in the machinery as possible" to stop Reagan from dismantling social welfare programs. Ted had lost his edge as the losses mounted, with only a minor victory—the Voting Rights Act extension, South African sanctions—here and there. But as the "new man" ran through the briefing book, Rollins was shocked. He mused to himself, "Who gave this son of a bitch a bushel of smart pills?" Ted knew every detail. "He had examples going back fifteen years on subparagraphs I had written," Rollins would recall. "He could tell me who the key bastard was going to be on this and that provision, and who owned him back home; who was going to cause the problem on this or that issue." And Rollins said it went on like that for two days. Rollins's conclusion was that as soon as the Democrats retook the Senate, Ted decided not to have another drop to drink. But Rollins was likely wrong to attribute his fogginess to the possibility of drink— Ted was often foggy in conversation when he was perfectly sober—and his new clarity to abstinence. Ted Kennedy had spent six largely aimless years gearing down while Reagan had his way. It was the idea that he might get something accomplished that seemed to energize him and focus him and gear him up again, though it took a little time. (In fact, he had gone through these spurts after lulls before.) When Rollins said of him, "I think he decided, 'I'm back,'" he was right. Ted Kennedy was not a man to languish, which was what he had been doing. Ted Kennedy was a man to *do.* Now he felt he could.

Typically, chairmen waited until the State of the Union address to declare their plans for the session. Ted couldn't wait for that either. After having discussed the agenda at Hyannis, Ted and Rollins now strategized over how to advance it. While in the minority, Rollins had plotted, waiting for the day when they would be back in the majority. With Carey Parker's encouragement, he pored over polls and focus group data. He organized a binder titled "Must Do." Now that was not just a dream; it was a possibility. Having been exasperated by how catch-as-catch-can the staffers' responsibilities had been—one staffer might work on poverty issues and lighthouses because the senator was trying to get funds to refurbish old lighthouses—Rollins tried to systematize responsibilities by breaking the committee into six areas (he called them "task groups") and prioritized a piece of legislation for each: a BHAG. And Ted signed on. And rather than hire generalists, Rollins now hired specialists who could work on a specific piece of legislation and then leave once the legislative initiative was over. Big Hairy Ass Goals were what Ted introduced now: a Job Training Act; the Fair Labor Standards Act, which included a higher minimum wage; a welfare reform program that would pay bonuses to states if they saved federal funds through job training or enforcement of child support or if they managed to place a welfare recipient in a private sector job for a year; a program televising classes to schools taught by star university professors; and the health initiatives he had proposed that the Republicans had thwarted—from employer mandates, to risk pools to sell insurance, to a program for the working poor not covered by Medicaid, to funding research to cure acquired immune deficiency syndrome (AIDS), the disease that was ravaging the gay community. A "major player," *The Washington Post* called Ted, in the "counterattack against Reagan administration revisions of social programs."

He was a new man. And he was back.

One of the barometers of Ted's mood had always been his weight. He freely confessed that he struggled with weight, from the time he was a boy and had been nicknamed "Biscuits and Muffins" by his siblings, to the time schoolmates called him "Big Ed" or "Fat Ed," which was how he signed some of his own letters then. On his office wall, he had hung a framed letter from his sister Jean to their father, during his ambassadorship, in which she informed him that "Teddy now has to go on a diet. Miss Dunn has to get extra large size suits. Everybody looks skinny beside him." Senator Thad Cochran recalled that during the summer of 1962, while he was an instructor at the Naval Training School in nearby Newport, Rhode Island, a friend who had served as Ted and Joan's cook invited him to the compound, and Ted stood there and ate a "whole fistful" of chocolate chip cookies his friend had prepared. Ted's old campaign aide, Charlie Tretter, recalled how Ted would go to Brigham's restaurant where the "older women waitresses were just all over him with attention," and Ted would ask them for a hot fudge sundae with a request for a "little extra hot fudge," and then eat off the whipped cream and the fudge and ask if he might have a bit more hot fudge on top. Max Fine, who worked with Ted on health legislation, remembered flying with Ted and Ted poking his head through the first-class curtain to ask the stewardess for ice cream that was being served to those passengers. (They refused.) Thin had always meant that Ted was either preparing for a presidential run or feeling positively. During the first years of the Reagan administration, the barometer showed heavy weather. He would lose weight only to regain it, and his health suffered. But with the Democratic victory, Ted was exuberant. He lost twenty-five pounds, then, at least by one account, thirty-six pounds, trading four or five turkey club sandwiches for four or five cups of cottage cheese, said one of his aides, and betting his sister Jean, her husband Steve, and their son, Steve Jr., that he could outlose them, so that now the barometer forecast sunny weather.

As he waded into battle, however difficult he knew that battle would be, however much he had to concede that there was no money for most of his BHAGs, he led a new army. Larry Horowitz, who had given up medicine for politics, was now giving up politics for Wall Street so he could earn the kind of money he couldn't earn as an administrative assistant. Some staffers thought Horowitz, who had worked for Ted for sixteen years, had stayed that long only because he was hoping Ted would run in 1988 and that he would have a prominent position in the Kennedy administration, were Ted to win, and he almost certainly would have. But shortly after Ted begged off on making that race, Horowitz announced his departure, then stayed through a long transition. Horowitz had been brusque, abrasive, loud, opinionated, decisive, unyielding, and not easily intimidated. Melody Miller said that he would be no more deferential to Ted than he had been to anyone else. "You can't do that," he might snap at him. Or "That's the stupidest thing I ever heard." Carey Parker, who was as close to Ted in terms of policy and as respected by him as anyone on the staff, would handle disagreements diplomatically, Miller said. He might say, "I don't think that's wise." Or "You know, that's probably not the best way to go." Not Larry Horowitz. "You don't roll Larry Horowitz" was how Miller put it. He had been the perfect administrative assistant for a senator in the minority who had to compensate with raw energy and nerve for what he lacked in legislative power. Horowitz had kept Ted moving, kept Ted engaged. Horowitz had handled the tough jobs. He blasted the way for Ted. Ted always relied on his former aides and called upon them for assistance if needed, but he was seldom friends with them. He remained friends with Larry Horowitz.

But now Horowitz was gone, and with him his style of management. As Horowitz's replacement, Ted slotted Jim Wieghart, a veteran journalist and former editor of the *New York Daily News,* who had experience on Capitol Hill, and during the transition he named him and staffer Ranny Cooper as deputy administrative assistants. But Wieghart, as staffer Nancy Soderberg recalled, had been away from the Senate too long, and "he was just not up to the task," which was not a situation one wanted to be in while working in as competitive an office as Ted Kennedy's. Soderberg said that Cooper wanted the job and fought for it. "I don't know if she directly undermined Jim or if he did it to himself, but he was so clearly unqualified, and Ranny was so clearly qualified." Ted had not been especially comfortable around women, and he had been chauvinistic, which might be why Cooper hadn't gotten the position in the first place; there were still few women on staff, and none among the top advisers. But that chauvinism had gradually dissipated, and he had become more willing to hire women to his staff. "If you're good," Soderberg said, "Kennedy will work with you. And she was good." Ranny Cooper was no Larry Horowitz. She was almost the anti–Larry Horowitz. Horowitz had fomented tension and disorder; it reflected his personality. "A snake pit of staff dissension, self-loathing, territorialism, all this kind of nonsense" was how Tom Rollins described the Horowitz-run office. And then, Rollins said,

Cooper "parachutes in," and "all of a sudden there is smoothness across the waters." Order replaced disorder. The fight to advance legislation, by oiling the machine, replaced the fight against the administration, by throwing sand in the machine. Horowitz's had been a kind of guerrilla army. Cooper's was a well-drilled military force.

And Ted Kennedy was not only the general of that force but also, in some ways now, the general of all the Senate Democrats since, as one former aide to Senator Ed Muskie said of the new Senate, "More junior senators who were less well-versed on specific issues took over." Ted was always well versed. He began a tradition of delivering every January, usually to the National Press Club, a speech that the staff labeled the "agenda-setting" speech. As one staffer described it, "It was a major speech, and we would talk about it for weeks before he gave it, about what he wanted to say about how to drive the agenda for Democrats particularly." Parker and Shrum would usually draft it, and then Ted would send the text of the speech to the majority leader, when the Democrats were in power—Robert Byrd at that time—and the minority leader when they weren't, and the leader would send a copy to each Democratic senator. And the Democratic House leadership would get copies too. And the speech was usually heavily publicized and carried on C-SPAN. "It was," the staffer said, "a State of the Union à la Kennedy."

That agenda was the product now of even greater deliberation that overtook Ted's office. At eight a.m. each Monday, Tom Rollins would attend a meeting of all the heads of staff of all the Senate committees, so they would all know what every committee was doing, and then he would head directly to Ted's office for a ten a.m. staff meeting there, where Rollins briefed the aides and the senator, and where the staffers briefed each other. Though Rollins said that policy debates among the staff were now usually handled in memos placed in The Bag, those disputes that weren't resolved were debated at the meeting while Ted listened, the way it had been done previously for nearly all issues. "Then you might have a fight about whether we're going to do this or whether that policy is moving," Rollins said. Ted made the final decision. The logistics were determined by Ranny Cooper, either in that meeting or in a meeting with the principals involved but without Ted. Another staffer said, "Everybody got a say," and commented, "That was really one of the wonderful things about the process. We didn't have to defend turf. You didn't feel put down. If you were in those discussions, then you knew you were part of the decision-making circle. . . . You were there because you'd been around long enough to be respected." All the legislative objectives were written on a large three-and-a-half-foot chart with the way stations for progress written across: from introduction to finding co-sponsors to holding hearings to getting it through the subcommittee and then to markups and through the full committee and then to the floor for passage. Every piece of legislation Ted introduced was tracked this way on a weekly basis. Rollins called it "simple project management." And because Ted's staff was so good—by consensus, the Senate's best staff, if also the most arrogant—Ted, who was already spread thin, could delegate. One staffer said that rather than have Ted go out to meet with a fellow senator on a piece of legislation, the staffer would reach out to a staffer for another senator, and the two would try to find some accommodation before bringing Ted together with that other senator. But even when staffers were hammering out some sort of compromise, Ted wanted to be apprised constantly. "He'll drive me nuts sometimes," the staffer said, "calling every hour to find out how it's going." The one thing, however, that he didn't delegate was the management of his time. "*He* was his time manager," yet another staffer said. "Nobody else said, 'Senator, you're doing too much next week, we can't do it, you're supposed to be in Boston.' He would make the decisions about how he spent his time." And remarkably, for all the demands on his time and for all the causes to which he was now dedicated, he got it done. He always got it done.

As the members of the 100th Congress took their seats, Ted Kennedy was a Senate man again—a fully committed Senate man after his flirtations to take the White House. Paul Kirk, his onetime aide who had become the chairman of the Democratic National Committee, thought the rededication actually began after the 1980 presidential failure. That was when, Kirk said, "he really decided, The Senate is my public life, and I'm going to do everything I can to be the best that I can be." Carey Parker disagreed. "My sense is that if you had to pick a moment, it would be when he announced in 1985 that he would not be a candidate for president in 1988. He had become a respected leader in the Senate by then, and his colleagues recognized his national appeal and his leadership qualities, but until then, most of the senators felt that he was getting ready to run for the White House. People went along with him at that time because they thought he might become president, and they wanted to be on his good side. After '85, they went along with him because he was doing the things that needed to be done, and they admired him. He took a step up in their eyes."

But Ted Kennedy could not have taken that step up unless he felt he had a chance to advance rather than obstruct. He had entered the new year with that ambitious agenda—his BHAGs, as Tom Rollins defined them. The problem was that he wasn't going to get most of them through the Senate, much less signed by Reagan. Ted was obviously dedicated to national health insurance. But Rollins looked at the poll data, saw that while Americans thought anyone who worked full time should have health insurance, they didn't believe it was a right, as Ted had long insisted it was. And Rollins told Ted that if he kept pressing for a comprehensive universal bill, a bill that would insure everyone, he would make no headway. Ted countered that if he abandoned the initiative—*his* signature initiative—"we're going to get killed" by the stakeholders. To which Rollins rebutted that when Ted first introduced the bill, he had only nine co-sponsors, and it wasn't likely he would have more now. So Ted conceded the point—conceded it because he realized that the effort would block other efforts he wanted to pursue. And when the stakeholders came after him at a meeting in Boston and lambasted him for backing off his central cause, he repeated the arguments that Rollins had made and then asked them, "How many co-sponsors do you think I had on that thing?" And he answered, as Rollins had, "Nine. I got nine. All the work you do out there in the grassroots—nine." Rollins said, "He blew up at them. He said, 'We're never going to get this thing done this way. We've got a shot at getting millions of people insured.'" And so Ted pressed instead for his employer mandate and for a waiver of antitrust restrictions so that smaller businesses could join pools to provide insurance for their employees. He pushed for a increase in the minimum wage, even though the AFL-CIO fought him on it, preferring that wages be negotiated, and to win votes, he argued that it would help get people off welfare if they could earn a living wage, and that it might help them afford healthcare as well. When Rollins and he discussed prioritizing the minimum wage, Ted, who knew how slowly the Senate moved, looked at Rollins and said, "If we do this thing, it is going to take five years." And as Rollins was to recall, "It took five years." But it got passed.

It got passed. Ted Kennedy had always been a pragmatist, which wasn't necessarily at odds with his idealism. "The perfect is the enemy of the good," he had long said. Better to get 50 percent of something than 100 percent of nothing, he said. "If you can find a better way to skin the cat, I'm there," he said. But his six years in the wilderness, the six years in which he was only able to impede what he saw as Reagan's destruction rather than promote what he saw as positive good, had forced him to be even more pragmatic. Some doubters saw this as a concession from the preeminent liberal. They accused Ted of moderating his core beliefs, realizing the limitations and even the obsolescence of liberalism in the Reagan era and capitulating. Ted saw it not as moderation but as realism—an accommodation to the new America in which liberals had oversold their programs and failed to adjust them to conservative means, which they needed to do in order to achieve liberal ends. To win, he had to change. Speaking to conservative columnist George Will shortly after the beginning of the new congressional term, Ted sounded "mellow and a bit chastened," Will thought. He lamented that the "pragmatic tradition" of liberalism was being lost and told Will, "We weren't abandoning any programs that have failed." He admitted now—admitted for the first time— that when it came to healthcare, "Government cannot simply mandate that companies provide coverage," largely because small businesses couldn't pay for it, and he recommended that liberals look not to the federal government—where Reagan was unlikely to move on big issues—but to the statehouses and city halls. He criticized the ability of the Senate to move legislation because its committee system was antiquated and balkanized, scattering jurisdiction. But for all that, Ted told Will this, which he had clearly learned while in the wilderness: "Social change is a matter of shaping a river's path marginally, not by making a whole new channel." Ted had his list of great plans. But those plans would proceed slowly.

"Moderation, pragmatism, compromise"—those were the code words, one reporter wrote, in Ted's new domestic agenda. Compromise meant compromise with the Republicans. There had been a time when moderate Republicans and liberal Democrats made common cause on one side, and conservative Republicans and Southern Democrats made common cause on the other, crossing party lines for ideological ones, but even those ideological lines, except when it came to race, were once relatively thin. As one observer later put it, "The great age of bipartisanship wasn't a reflection of the gentlemanly character of an earlier generation of politicians. Rather, it reflected the subdued nature of political conflict in an era when the parties weren't that far apart on basic issues." But that had changed and changed markedly since Ted entered the Senate and even since Ted seemed to run it in the mid-1970s. One analyst traced what he called the "Senate's modern decline" to 1978 "with the election of a new wave of anti-government conservatives, and accelerated as Republicans became the majority party in 1981," and he quoted Senator Jesse Helms, the intractable North Carolina conservative and one of the very few men in the Senate with whom Ted Kennedy could not find common ground: "Others want to make waves; I wanted to drain the swamp." Republican Trent Lott, who would later become majority leader, said that the lack of comity was Republican revenge for the way *they* had been treated when they were in the minority. The Democrats, he would write, "simply rammed bills through, blind to the effect bad legislation might have on the future of the Senate. It was a nasty scene on the floor—devoid of courtesy and festering with hate." Republicans repaid the perceived hate with hate of their own. When he decided to leave the Senate in 1984, Majority Leader Howard Baker said that the institution "could not fight guerrilla war over every issue every time," which was what he believed the Senate had devolved to. Moreover, the president had accomplished what the conservatives had sought since Senator Joseph McCarthy accused Democrats of subversion: to demonize them so that political disagreements now had a moral dimension, which, in truth, they often *did* have as Republicans and Democrats debated who would be hurt by legislation. Ted might have been at the top of that list of demons, not because his Senate colleagues disliked him—even few Republicans did—but because the conservative activists who had commandeered the Republican Party detested him. "That's the way you would raise money," moderate Republican Lowell Weicker, who often worked with Ted, said. "Just yell the name 'Kennedy' to get people all fired up." Ted wasn't necessarily displeased. James Manley, Ted's onetime press secretary, said that Ted "loved the idea that Republicans were making money off him because he realized that as soon as they stop talking about you, that's a sure sign that you're losing your effectiveness," though he also enjoyed the irony of having Republican senatorial friends hailing him one moment and castigating him for public consumption the next.

Ted didn't have to be a legislative virtuoso when the Republicans were in the Senate majority because he could scarcely get anything done, other than save what programs he could from the fiscal guillotine. But now that he was back in the majority, now that he had an agenda, he had to use his resources again—to work the chemistry of the Senate, despite the fact that the Senate had undergone those changes. He could still work that chemistry. It was just his personality, his charm, and his infectious joyfulness. "He had that good laugh," onetime staffer John Podesta said. The liberal activist Ralph Neas said he had "this exuberance," and a way of "making stuff fun." And Neas said Ted knew how to "tease," which was a "very artful device." And he knew how to ingratiate himself. When he learned that poet Henry Longfellow, a Massachusetts icon, also had had a home in Mississippi, he sent Mississippi senator Trent Lott photographs of the two homes side by side in a frame and inscribed it: "We can work together. We have similar ancestry." These little courtesies had their effect, even on those like Lott who were likely to disagree with Ted on nearly everything. Parliamentarian Robert Dove said Ted was "loved"—that was the term he used. Loved. "In politics you don't have friends," Jack Kennedy used to say. "You have allies." And yet Ted had a knack for making those allies feel like friends.

But it was more than his outsize personality, more than his exuberance and joy and good humor, more than his consideration, that still, even in the newly embittered atmosphere of the Senate, captivated so many of his colleagues. He had a sensitivity to people that he had no doubt acquired from his own neediness of having been the least, of having been the Kennedy of whom so little was expected, and the one who most often exhibited his own fallibility. Even with his successes, Ted Kennedy knew weakness from having suffered so much of it himself. That was his empathy, which he had used to connect both to his constituents and to his colleagues. "Senator Kennedy was a people person," Michael Myers, a health staffer, recalled. "He loved people, and he could sense what was on their minds as he was conversing with them—a real master psychologist in a way. And that helped him in reaching across the aisle. He would know what his Republican colleagues were thinking. He was able to touch them in a way that few legislators could." "He had a good sense of how to get legislation passed," Senator George Mitchell, who would succeed Byrd as majority leader, said. "It wasn't so much this particular sentence in the bill or this technical language. It was in knowing his colleagues, understanding their views, what it was that moved them to take and hold positions." *What did they want?* That was the essential political question. Lyndon Johnson, his biographer Robert Caro said, could read men to get the answer to that question, could read them plainly. Ted Kennedy had been no great reader of men when he entered the Senate. But the years had honed that talent. And now he could. Now he needed to.

What did they want? Sometimes they wanted recognition or collegiality, and he would invite them to his McLean home for dinners. Some of these dinners were for Democrats only. Some were for Democrats and Republicans, particularly since the Labor Committee had some Republican moderates, like Weicker and Robert Stafford, with whom Ted collaborated. Some were for Republicans only. And Ted tended to every detail of these dinners, according to a staffer—from the menu, to the china and silverware, to the seating arrangements, to the nametags. "Tending to his relationships with other senators" was how the staffer described Ted's assiduousness.

Sometimes they wanted respect. Dan Quayle, a young freshman senator from Indiana, won office during Reagan's first presidential election. Quayle wanted to push a job training bill through the Labor Committee, which at that time was chaired by Republican Orrin Hatch, and Hatch was not receptive, preferring to wait to see what the administration might propose, if anything. "Completely disorganized," Quayle said of Hatch and felt that Hatch had a "whole lot of issues" before the committee that "he doesn't want to handle." The jobs bill stalled, and Quayle couldn't seem to move it. He was isolated. He had no allies on the committee. So Quayle had a staffer approach a staffer of Ted's to see if the two of them might work together on the bill. Quayle, however, had a condition: Any funds had to be channeled through the states. Ted accepted the condition. Quayle had disparaged Ted during his campaign, but the two now joined forces, which began a relationship—almost a friendship. And later, when Quayle ran for vice president on George H. W. Bush's ticket and often received scalding press during the campaign, Ted would leave him a message on his answering machine to buck his spirits.

Sometimes they wanted help. When Reagan, in his effort to disarm the federal government, decided that healthcare spending would be budgeted as block grants to the states, thus leaving spending discretion entirely to the states, Ted was concerned that the program of neighborhood healthcare centers, *his* program, would be doomed because the money for his centers would get lost among other health needs. Orrin Hatch, the ranking Republican of the Labor Committee, was concerned about something else: how he would apportion the money. So Ted made a proposal to Hatch:

that they announce a greater number of block grants and give them more specific targets, so that, in effect, they really weren't *block* grants at all; they were just grants. This way Hatch could say that he had actually increased the number of grants the president had asked for, even though the funds themselves hadn't increased, while Ted, to pacify conservative opposition and Hatch, could concede a victory to Reagan for having block-granted healthcare. But however the two of them characterized the deal, Ted got the money for his neighborhood health centers while Hatch got a way to apportion the funds as he had wanted to.

Sometimes they wanted an old-fashioned trade-off, which was how, as the Senate approached recess, Ted got Jesse Helms to lift a hold Helms had put on ten reauthorization bills for health issues. Biden had overheard Ted in the Senate cloakroom complaining about Helms's obstruction. He interjected that Helms wanted a judicial nominee approved. So Biden, the new Judiciary chair, agreed to sign off on the approval, and Helms signed off on the bills.

And sometimes, though more rarely now, it was the power of the moral argument, of senators wanting to vote their conscience if they could avoid the political consequences, as it had been in the Voting Rights Act extension and the South African sanctions—moral suasion.

That was Ted working the chemistry of the Senate as he always had. But now that Ted was back in the majority, he was also working the physics of the Senate—the Senate's rules and procedures and customs—with even greater diligence than he had in the past. The Democratic caucus met every Tuesday afternoon for lunch to discuss the party's agenda and how to advance it. And because Ted Kennedy was now a Senate veteran, because he was a Senate leader, "those moments were magical ones for him," as a staffer put it. "He could go in that room and stand up and provide a clear plan for how the Democrats should move forward on a particular issue"—the plan that he had gamed out in his staff meetings with his three-and-a-half-foot charts. He set the terms and talked them through. He also knew how to bargain. "He never started across the table [on legislation]," his son Patrick would say of his father's method, meaning the negotiating table. "He started by sitting down with them with lunch and coming over to their offices"—that is, ingratiating himself. That was chemistry. But then the physics kicked in. He would discuss not the ideas but the process of going forward. "I'd like to get one hundred percent of my stuff done. You'd like to get one hundred percent of yours," he would say. "If I got eighty, I'd be happy, and if you got eighty, you'd be happy." And they would begin their horse-trading to get that 80 percent. And he could horse-trade because, as John Podesta observed, he was a "master of detail" and had one of the "keenest senses" of legislation, despite the insults toward his intelligence that had been thrown his way. He always knew the "things he had to have and the things he could give up." Carey Parker observed the same gift: "If there's a reasonable chance of putting together a bipartisan compromise on legislation, he has a knack for figuring out what he can ask for and what he can get from the other side," and then he had the gift for selling that compromise to his own stakeholders, who were generally nowhere near as compromising as he was. And Ted knew *how* his fellow senators would vote, which was an essential skill when he headed to the floor. "There are forty guys who are against you no matter what," Tom Rollins would say. "There are forty guys who are with you no matter what. And then it's a fight over the twenty in the middle." But since a few of those, moderate Republicans, were likely to join Ted, and a few of those, Southern Democrats, were likely to oppose him, it came down to ten or twelve senators who might be influenced. "Then we would target all of our press resources just at those ten or twelve," Rollins said.

But there were occasions when it was neither chemistry nor physics but guile or passion or pressure that moved legislation. And Ted knew how to use these too. Ohio senator Howard Metzenbaum, a liberal Democrat, had introduced an amendment to the Omnibus Trade Act that required businesses to issue a six-month warning to employees when a plant was being closed so that the workers could prepare for the eventuality. The idea was that if management had ample notice, the folks on the factory floor should have notice too. Ted enthusiastically joined Metzenbaum's effort. Businesses strongly opposed it. Finally, Texas senator Lloyd Bentsen, a Democrat but a business conservative, convinced Metzenbaum to withdraw the amendment because it was likely to be filibustered. As soon as Rollins heard about the capitulation from Byrd's chief of staff, he phoned Metzenbaum's chief of staff and remonstrated with him to have the senator reinstate the amendment. (Rollins's suggestion was that Metzenbaum say he was inebriated at the time he pulled it, which, Rollins said, he did.) Now the bill went to the floor for debate. One of its opponents, Republican senator John Danforth of Missouri, argued that "this little provision" had kept the bill from "swimming to shore." He said it was as if there were a "barbell" on the back of this bill that was causing it to sink. Hearing that, Ted was incensed. Rollins said that Ted leaned over to him and said, "We have fifteen minutes before we miss the deadline for the evening news. What do I say that gets us on the evening news?" Rollins, who admitted he was as exercised as Ted, told him to mention how, if the opponents wanted to talk about barbells on backs, why didn't they talk about barbells on the backs of American workers who were trying to swim to prosperity? And Ted, now under a full head of steam, got up and hammered Danforth, "getting really wound up," Rollins said, an effect that Ted had tried to temper since his 1980 race when he was accused of being too hot for television. He was hot now. But the debate made the evening news as plotted, the bill passed, and Reagan let it become law. And that was passion.

There was another bill, this one proposed by Ted to prevent employers from using polygraph tests on their employees except in the case of the Department of Defense, where the tests could be used to determine possible breaches in security. Phil Gramm of Texas was the chief opponent of Ted's bill, and thinking he had outsmarted Ted, he offered an amendment that would permit the tests so long as an employer followed DOD procedures. Rollins quickly rifled through those DOD procedures and discovered that each request for a test had to be personally signed by the secretary of defense. So Ted got up and said that should Gramm's amendment pass, the secretary of defense would be signing off on every single polygraph test across the country, some two million of them, which was clearly ridiculous. The bill failed.

And that was guile.

The new man was succeeding. With chemistry and physics, passion and guile and pressure, the 100th Congress was an unusually productive one for Ted Kennedy, especially given that it was during a Republican administration. One observer would later call it the "best period he or almost any senator has ever had." Tom Rollins said that the first year after the midterms, 1987, "all we did was hearings and markups," but then there was a "tsunami of legislation." In that second session, the Senate worked for some ninety days. On eighty-six of those, Rollins said, Ted was on the floor moving legislation. Some forty-five bills that reached the floor through Ted's Labor Committee became law. "We owned the place," Rollins said. Among those laws were a Fair Housing Act that covered the disabled and families with children as well as race, which Ted had negotiated with Housing and Urban Development secretary Samuel Pierce; the Medicare Catastrophic Coverage Act, which was the first expansion of Medicare since its passage; the Working Retraining and Notification Act, the bill that Ted had pushed with Metzenbaum; and the AIDS amendments of 1988, which Ted had introduced and which provided increased funding for AIDS research and established a National Commission on AIDS. Most of the forty-five laws were not BHAGs; most were modest—the kinds of bills for which Ted could find Republican co-sponsors and the kind that weren't likely to infuriate Reagan and elicit a veto. They were bills that could be turned into law because they didn't threaten the conservative agenda.

But there was one major initiative, perhaps the biggest on Ted's docket in that 100th Congress—one that Ted introduced not to make incremental progress but rather to undo past damage. The bill, pointedly named the Civil Rights Restoration Act, originated with a case involving a small private Christian college in northwestern Pennsylvania named Grove City, after the town in which it was situated. Grove City College did not take federal funds on the grounds that it wanted to maintain its independence. But 140 of its students *did* take those funds as Basic Education Opportunity Grants—scholarships. That was the problem for Grove City College. Any institution of higher education that received federal funding had to comply with Title IX of the Educational Amendments Act of 1972, which prohibited discrimination by gender. (The provision had had its greatest impact on women's college athletics, which had seldom received the funding of men's athletics.) In 1976 the Department of Education asked for a certification of compliance from Grove City assuring the department that the school was not discriminating. Though there was no accusation that Grove City had discriminated on the basis of gender, the college refused to provide the certificate, arguing that *it* did not receive federal funds, the *students* did. The government felt differently and subsequently penalized Grove City by terminating the student grants. Grove City and several of the students sued. That suit wound its way through the federal courts, with the District Court of Western Pennsylvania ruling for the school, and the appeals court ruling for the government. The Reagan administration, given its close alliance with fundamentalist Christians and its negligence when it came to enforcing rules against gender discrimination, agreed with Grove City College, but trying to avoid an unnecessary confrontation and obviously assuming the Supreme Court would rule against the college, it asked the Court not to review the case. The Court ignored the request.

What worried Ted and his fellow liberals was that the issue wasn't about whether filing an "assurance of compliance" certification was necessary or even whether the government could terminate the scholarships. What worried them was that the issue was now whether a university that received federal funds could discriminate by gender in departments other than the one or ones that received the funds, in this case, Grove City College's financial aid office. Were Grove City to win, the consequences of the ruling would be far-reaching, basically allowing colleges to ignore Title IX or other legally mandated antidiscrimination provisions. On February 28, 1984, Justice Byron White, John Kennedy's friend and appointee, writing for a 6-to-3 majority, found that the government was within its rights to ask for a certificate of assurance and within its rights to terminate the students' scholarships since the college had not provided that certificate as required, though the majority also ruled that students could use their scholarships at another college if they so chose. This pleased the liberals, who wanted schools whose students accepted federal scholarship funds to be held to Title IX. But the most significant part of the ruling was this: that compliance was necessary only for the department that *directly benefited from the grants*, here the financial aid office, not for any other department of the university. In effect, though Grove City College had lost several of its arguments, the Court had ruled in its favor on what might have been the most substantive issue. Basically, any department at Grove City except its financial aid office could discriminate. The result was that women's athletic programs immediately lost Title IX protections, and colleges quickly began stripping them of funds.

Ted called the decision "absolutely extraordinary because one of the underlying tenets of the Civil Rights Acts of '64, '65, '68, and others was that we would not permit taxpayer money to be used in any way to support segregation in whatever form or shape it would be." Now the Court, by permitting gender discrimination in colleges and universities, was opening the door to other federally subsidized forms of discrimination, from race to disability to age. Ted acted almost immediately. In the spring of 1984, months after the decision, he introduced a bill reversing *Grove City* and applying the reversal to Title VI of the Civil Rights Act of 1964 on race, Section 504 of the Rehabilitation Act of 1973 on disability, and the

Age Discrimination Act of 1975 for age. Ted attracted a number of Republican co-sponsors, including Bob Dole. But the Reagan administration was wary, and the Reagan administration was divided. While the Education Department supported the bill as clarifying its authority, the Justice Department objected. The department's assistant attorney general for civil rights, William Bradford Reynolds, a longtime opponent of civil rights legislation, argued, "This bill has been portrayed as minor tinkering, a quick fix to overturn the *Grove City* decision, but it represents a monumental, drastic change in the civil rights enforcement landscape." President Reagan also weighed in, opposing the bill as an "intrusion" of the federal government. That June the House voted overwhelmingly for the bill, 375 to 32, and Ted had sixty-three senators signed on to it. But Orrin Hatch, the chairman of the Labor Committee, was vehemently opposed, saying, as Reagan did, that the bill would force the federal government into state and local jurisdiction. He threatened to filibuster, and when he called for a drafting session in committee, clearly intended to redraft Ted's bill and weaken it, Ted and the other committee liberals declared a boycott, telling reporters, "I have served in the Senate twenty-two years. I have seen obstructionist activities in civil rights legislation. I think I can see when it's coming." Majority Leader Howard Baker, who had come out in support of the bill, offered to mediate and met with proponents and opponents of the bill but had no success. Hatch said he was willing to compromise, but his compromise was to limit the bill to sex discrimination, which Ted and civil rights leaders vigorously opposed.

Ted was vehement. With the fall 1984 recess and the election barreling down on the Senate, and a spending bill delayed while Hatch and other conservatives tried to waylay Ted's bill with a filibuster, the Senate voted for cloture, which passed 92 to 4. (It might have been a sign of the moral force of the issue that twenty-three conservatives switched sides at the last minute, knowing they were going to lose and realizing that there was no reason for them to take a hit in opposing civil rights during an election year, though it may also have been that they were tired of Hatch stalling Senate business.) Ted called it a "major defeat for the enemies of civil rights" and tried attaching the bill to the spending measure, but Hatch objected and then bombarded the chamber with amendments and roll call votes to stall the proceedings. Meanwhile the president sat by, idly watching, while Ted said a "wink" from him would assure passage of the bill. "I think the Senate is beginning to look like a bunch of jackasses,"

Barry Goldwater complained. To which Senator Malcolm Wallop said, "We're already there." With the clock running out, and with Hatch submitting thirteen hundred amendments, Bob Packwood, the Republican sponsor of Ted's bill, after negotiating a compromise with Hatch—this one limiting the bill to educational institutions—and having that rejected by other supporters of the bill, finally surrendered "with a heavy heart." He made a motion to table the bill, which passed 53 to 45. Baker called it a "mark of courage," but Ted, who didn't see blocking civil rights as courage, was beyond anger. "Shame on the Senate," he thundered to his colleagues on the Senate floor. And he noted that "I quite frankly thought these battles had been fought in the 1960s," speaking of civil rights battles. Ted would resubmit the bill in successive sessions of Congress. But Ronald Reagan was no advocate for civil rights, and Ronald Reagan would not give that wink. Daniel Patrick Moynihan said it would not pass "so long as the present majority of the chamber is in place."

But now, in 1987, three years later, the Republicans were not the majority in the Senate. And now Ted had his chance. Saying the "lights went out on civil rights in 1981," meaning with Reagan's election, he wasted no time, reintroducing his bill early in January after the midterm elections. Ralph Neas, the head of the Leadership Conference on Civil Rights, who worked with Ted and lobbied for the bill, said Ted was tireless. He met with the LCCR or the AFL or the NAACP, sometimes until one or two in the morning, after Senate business. And Neas said that other senators would occasionally sit in on the meetings, and Ted would have his staffer Carolyn Osolinik painstakingly describe the bill to them, which Neas said was unheard of; staffers never described a bill to sitting senators. Conservatives still insisted that the bill was an example of federal overreach, and Reagan repeated the arguments he had made in 1984, even as he said that he now supported a nullification of the *Grove City* decision. Ted held hearings on the bill, and it was voted out of committee. And yet by the time the first session of Congress ended in December 1987, it hadn't reached the floor because the Senate, and especially its civil rights champions, had gotten diverted by another matter as important to them as the Civil Rights Restoration Act.

As the Senate grappled with that matter, the bill had to wait, but it had not been forgotten. When the second session of the 100th Congress convened in January, Ted's bill was the first order of business. Hatch was still as determined to stop its passage as he had been four years earlier, but he was in the minority now. Other conservatives argued that the bill would require religious institutions that accepted federal funds—colleges, universities, and hospitals—to permit abortions or risk discriminating against women. Reagan seized on this now to reverse himself and oppose the bill once again as he had opposed it in the past on the grounds of overreach, citing the bill's endangerment to religious liberty, even though it had been supported by most major denominations. (Of course, evangelical organizations fiercely opposed it.) Senator John Danforth introduced an amendment that provided an abortion exception to those institutions, and senators campaigning for president raced to the Senate to support the amendment—Dole from New Hampshire, Paul Simon from Texas, Vice President Bush in a four-car motorcade should his vote be needed to break a tie. The amendment passed, 56 to 39—Ted said he hoped the House would strip it out—and the amended bill cruised through the Senate, 75 to 14, with every Democrat voting for it. The House passed it a few weeks later, 315 to 98.

The only question now was whether Ronald Reagan would veto the bill as he had hinted he might, becoming the first president since Andrew Johnson in 1866 to veto a civil rights bill. Anticipating the veto, Ted called it a "kick in the teeth of civil rights." Reagan had proposed an alternative bill that excluded religiously affiliated educational institutions and would apply the old Grove City College rule to other religious organizations receiving federal funds. Ted called it a "sham." There would be no alternative on the floor. So Ronald Reagan vetoed Ted's bill. But as with the South African sanctions, Ted had something Ronald Reagan did not have, something that proved surprisingly powerful even then, even in the Reagan era: He had moral authority on his side. Reagan's arguments rang hollow. Federal "intrusion" to support the rights of Black Americans, the disabled, and women was not intrusion; it was the securing of human rights. The only reason for the veto was the antipathy of some conservatives, including those in the administration, toward Black people and women. But even most Republicans now did not want to be perceived as having halted a civil rights bill. Ted worked with Dole, a World War II veteran whose arm had been mangled in battle and who was particularly sensitive to discrimination against the disabled, often worked with him late into the night, and lined up enough votes to override the veto, though it meant accepting Danforth's abortion amendment. Strom Thurmond argued against the bill on the floor that "this is not a civil rights bill. This is an extension of federal authority." But that didn't hold. The Senate vote, at twelve-thirty on March 22, 1988, with a group of disabled spectators watching from the gallery, was 75 to 24, with twenty-one Republicans joining the Democrats. Three hours later, the House voted 292 to 133 to override.

The act was now law. And Ronald Reagan, who had beaten Ted Kennedy so many times in his presidency, had suffered a rare loss—a loss in a moral battle against Ted Kennedy.

III

The Civil Rights Restoration Act, after being passed by the Labor Committee in 1987, had been delayed going to the Senate floor due to something as momentous as the act itself: an impending change in the very institution whose decision the act was attempting to undo. That June 26, about a month after the committee vote on the act, Ralph Neas, the civil rights leader who worked frequently with Ted, was driving in his 1984 Renault on his way to work and listening to music on the car radio when during a break he heard the news that Supreme Court justice Lewis Powell would be resigning. Neas said his first thought was whom to call so that the liberal forces would be ready to leap to action when Reagan made his nomination. He phoned Benjamin Hooks, the executive director of the NAACP, first to discuss the need to develop a strategy, and then Nan Aron of the Alliance for Justice. Neas knew that progressive activists like him weren't going to like whomever Reagan nominated. And he felt that the progressive forces had to communicate that to Reagan, which they could only do through the media, since they had no direct influence on the president.

Beginning with Nixon, the Supreme Court had become a major point of contention between the liberals and Republican presidents and none more so than Reagan. Historian Sean Wilentz said that while conservatives stewed that Reagan hadn't done more to overturn *Roe v. Wade*, the 1973 Supreme Court decision that upheld the right to abortion, they missed Reagan's real if quieter accomplishment: waging a "pragmatic version of the culture wars" by reversing the "judicial decision-making bequeathed by the New Deal and the Great Society." Basically, Ronald Reagan packed the federal courts with intransigent conservatives devoted to overturning the decisions of the Warren Court, which had supported civil rights, affirmative action, privacy rights, freedom of speech, and a number of things that conservatives associated with liberalism. "A long-term strategy that was as comprehensive as it was deliberate," Wilentz would write of Reagan's Supreme Court nominees. And he would say of those judicial appointments, "Where competence or politics had once been the primary criteria, now ideology was." Administrations routinely had consulted with Congress on these appointments. The Reagan administration, Ted said, did not. Instead, they relied on what he called an "infrastructure"—hard-right groups like the Federalist Society and the Eagle Forum—to pressure Republican senators. "They were all in lockstep," Ted was to say of Reagan's judicial appointments. "They're in lockstep in terms of political power. They're pretty much in lockstep in terms of rolling back rights and liberties." And Ted was appalled, shouting at Attorney General Meese at a Judiciary hearing earlier that year that Reagan had appointed "racists to the federal courts" and that out of 291 appointments, only five were Black. "The most anti-civil rights administration I have ever seen," he boomed at Meese.

A year earlier, when Chief Justice Warren Burger stepped down and Reagan nominated Justice William Rehnquist to replace him, Ted led the fight against him. "Too extreme to be chief justice," Ted had said at the hearings and ran down a checklist that showed Rehnquist had voted against individual rights 77 percent of the time and was a lone dissenter in fifty-four cases. "Mainstream or too extreme?" Ted had asked at those hearings. He cited a memo that Rehnquist had written in 1952, while clerking for Justice Robert Jackson, in which Rehnquist upheld *Plessy v. Ferguson* and its "separate but equal" doctrine and opposed school desegregation (Rehnquist claimed he was merely stating Justice Jackson's feelings), and he noted Rehnquist's opposition to a public accommodations ordinance in Phoenix, where Rehnquist had practiced law, and his participation in "ballot security" measures in Phoenix where witnesses said he threatened minority voters outside polling stations. (Rehnquist denied it.) And Ted said, in a blistering attack that would prefigure an attack on another Supreme Court nominee the following year, "Imagine what America would be like if Mr. Rehnquist had been chief justice and his cramped and narrow view of the Constitution had prevailed in the critical years since World War II. The schools of America would still be segregated. Millions of citizens would be denied the right to vote under scandalous malapportionment laws. Women would be condemned as second-class

Americans. Courthouses would be closed to individual challengers against police brutality and executive abuse—even closed to the press. Government would embrace religion and the wall of separation between church and state would be in ruins. State and local majorities would tell us what we can read, whether to bear children, how to bring them up, what kinds of people we may become." It was not a legal argument Ted Kennedy made against William Rehnquist. Or an argument against his competence. It was a Senate argument: that the institution's responsibility to confirm nominees was more than a "rubber stamp." And it was a moral argument—an argument about the values that William Rehnquist applied to his decisions. When the nomination came to the floor, Ted again led the opposition, saying he should have never been confirmed in 1971, when Richard Nixon first appointed him to the Court—Ted had voted against him then—and that he showed a "persistent and appalling record of hostility against minorities." Reagan called Ted and two other fierce opponents, Howard Metzenbaum and Joe Biden, a "lynch mob." But the lynch mob did not get its man. Rehnquist was approved, 65 to 33. To fill the vacancy, Burger himself was replaced by a strong ideological conservative, Antonin Scalia, for whom Ted voted, he said, because he got a call from New York governor Mario Cuomo vouching for Scalia. "Don't worry about Scalia," Cuomo told Ted and apparently Joe Biden and others on the Judiciary Committee. "He's going to be OK. He's effectively one of us," by which Cuomo presumably meant an urban Catholic. He was confirmed easily.

The replacement of Lewis Powell, however, was even more important because it promised to tilt the balance of the Court. The Court was divided into factions. Burger, like Scalia, was a conservative. (Only time would tell how different those two conservatives were.) Powell was something else. He had been called by one judicial scholar the "single most influential member of the court," a moderate conservative but a nonideologue, the swing vote. And Ronald Reagan was not about to nominate another moderate to the vacancy. It was widely assumed that the nominee would be Robert Bork, a judge on the District of Columbia Court of Appeals, who had been solicitor general in the Nixon administration and a Yale Law professor, though Bork's central credential for a seat on the Court, as conservatives saw it, was not his experience but his record: He was among the most rabid of judicial ideologues, a "right-wing zealot," as one Reagan aide admiringly called him, who had opposed virtually all civil rights and any constitutional right to privacy—a position that pitted him against the Court in *Griswold v. Connecticut*, the decision that overturned a state ban on the use of contraceptives. When Reagan, as expected, did nominate Bork on July 1, Richard Viguerie, the direct mail impresario who had helped create the modern conservative movement, cheered, "Conservatives have waited over thirty years for this day," and he called it the "most exciting news for conservatives since President Reagan's reelection." Another conservative legal activist was even more effusive: "We have the opportunity to roll back thirty years of social and political activism by the Supreme Court." Robert Bork was that opportunity.

There was no cheering in the liberal ranks, only dread. Ted had fully expected the nomination too and was prepared for it. He had assigned his new Judiciary aide, Jeffrey Blattner, who had come to him from Harvard Law, to dig up information on Bork (Blattner called Harvard Law professor Laurence Tribe, who was in Europe at the time, for some ammunition), and then had the normally mild-mannered Carey Parker draft a speech that excoriated Bork in the same terms Ted had excoriated Rehnquist when he was nominated for chief justice. Ted pondered delivering it before the nomination was announced in the hopes that he might even head it off—Neas too had phoned White House communications director Thomas Griscom to warn him that if Bork were nominated, there would be vigorous opposition—but then reconsidered. Ted was familiar with Bork's antediluvian legal opinions that Bork justified on the grounds of "originalism"—the conservative idea that the only rights guaranteed in the Constitution were those rights that were expressly enumerated at the time of the document's drafting. But Ted also had a personal stake in wanting to beat back the nomination. After Attorney General Elliot Richardson had resigned rather than follow Richard Nixon's instruction to fire Special Prosecutor Archibald Cox, a friend of the Kennedy family, and after Richardson's deputy, William Ruckelshaus, had resigned as well rather than follow the order, Bork, the third in line as solicitor general, complied and fired Cox. (Bork would later defend himself, saying that he pressed Nixon to hire another special prosecutor and that if he had resigned, there would have been no leadership left in the Justice Department.) "The passion was because of Cox," Carey Parker was to say. "If the Cox issue hadn't been part of the case against Bork, I think the Senator probably would have waited, talked to a few constitutional law scholars, and made sure that we had the case against him together." But Archibald

Cox was involved, not just as a matter of Ted's personal loyalty to him, but as a matter of the raw injustice, as Ted saw it, of Cox's being fired to protect Nixon from being punished for his misdeeds.

Ted was angry, roaring angry, though he was also cagey, realizing that a scorching attack on Bork immediately, before Reagan and the conservatives had a chance to establish a defense for their nominee, would set a tone and fire up opposition. "The rhythms of these battles flow in favor of the nominees quite strenuously," he would later say. He hoped to change the rhythm. He had been told about the nomination during a break in a subcommittee hearing on housing while assistant attorney general William Bradford Reynolds, whom Ted had successfully opposed for promotion to deputy attorney general, was testifying. It was Attorney General Ed Meese who called him and spoke to him in an anteroom of the hearing room. Back at the hearing, when a comment was made about the upcoming nomination, Ted said, according to his aide Jeff Blattner, "Well, I think I may have something to say about that." And Blattner said Ted then walked directly from the hearing room to the Senate floor.

He did have something to say. But before he spoke, he phoned Archibald Cox to see if he could coax him to get involved, possibly testifying against Bork at the hearings. Cox demurred, saying that any involvement would seem like sour grapes. Then Ted phoned Harvard Law professor Paul Freund, a highly respected constitutionalist, to ask for his involvement. Freund was surprised to get a call from Ted and asked if he could think about it. Ted then asked Freund what he thought of Ted making a statement. Freund, who later said he was groping for an answer, told Ted he didn't see why not.

The speech that Ted Kennedy gave would be one of the most famous and important of his career, not for its eloquence or the loftiness of its ideas but for its intensity. He looked composed in a gray suit, rather than his customary blue one, and a red tie, and read the text while wearing steel-rimmed glasses. But as composed as he might have looked, he seethed. Blattner would call his speech "like biting into a jalapeno." Ted himself would later call the speech "red-hot" and say that he had wanted it to be that way—"immediate and fiery"—in order to "frame the debate." (It was delivered within a half-hour of the announcement.) And he said he was willing to make himself a "target" if it was a way to keep Bork off the Court.

For a speech that would cause such waves and be regarded as historic, for reasons both good and bad, depending on whether one supported Bork's nomination or opposed it, it was short, only a few minutes in duration. He began with the Cox firing, recalling how Richardson and Ruckelshaus had resigned out of principle rather than do the president's bidding. (Blattner said that this was the one passage that Ted wrote himself.) "The deed devolved on Solicitor General Robert Bork," Ted thundered, "who executed the unconscionable assignment that has become one of the darkest chapters for the rule of law in American history." And Ted went on, "That act—later ruled illegal by a Federal court—is sufficient, by itself, to disqualify Mr. Bork from this new position to which he has been nominated. The man who fired Archibald Cox does not deserve to sit on the Supreme Court of the United States." But Ted Kennedy did not stop there. He enumerated a few of Bork's "extremist" views: "He opposed the Public Accommodations Civil Rights Act of 1964. He opposed the one-man one-vote decision of the Supreme Court the same year. He has said that the First Amendment applies only to political speech, not literature or works of art or scientific expression." Yet it was the peroration for which the speech would be known—known as the "Robert Bork's America" speech because of that peroration: "Robert Bork's America is a land in which women would be forced into back-alley abortions, blacks would sit at segregated lunch counters, rogue police could break down citizens' doors in midnight raids, schoolchildren could not be taught about evolution, writers and artists would be censored at the whim of government, and the doors of the federal courts would be shut on the fingers of millions of citizens for whom the judiciary is often the only protector of the individual rights that are the heart of our democracy. America is a better and freer nation than Robert Bork thinks. Yet in the current delicate balance of the Supreme Court, his rigid ideology will tip the scales of justice against the kind of country America is and ought to be." Listening to it from a chair behind him, Blattner said to himself, "We better win this one."

Ted's colleagues were startled by his ferocity. Alan Simpson, a Wyoming Republican who had a cordial and largely joking relationship with Ted—Ted had assisted him when he first came to the Senate—thought Ted had engaged in "wretched excess" and approached him afterward to tell him so, but he said Ted "didn't even cock his head." Instead he barked, "This guy is a son of a bitch, and this is what he'll do." Some felt his vehemence had even tilted the battle to Bork. Alabama Democrat Richard

Shelby—he would later change parties—said, "With Senator Kennedy against him, that puts a lot of Southern Democrats in bed with Bork." Democrat Denis DeConcini of New Mexico felt that Ted had prejudged Bork and made it more difficult for DeConcini to vote against him. Even Laurence Tribe, whom Ted had phoned personally to ask if Bork was as bad as he thought he was—Tribe said he was; "He's extremely smart, but he will put his brains to use destroying the values that you care deeply about"—first cheered the speech, then wished Ted had found a more "nuanced way to say it," rather than leaving himself open to the charge of demonizing Bork. The administration was unruffled. William Bradford Reynolds, the assistant attorney general of the Civil Rights Division, with whom Ted had clashed continuously, said that the Reaganites viewed Ted as a "joke," a "non-player," which was a very odd way to characterize the man who had forced the administration to scale back its budget cuts, bow to South African sanctions, and take arms control more seriously, and who had foiled Reynolds's own advancement. Reynolds said they thought "Kennedy would get his headline, a snicker and a laugh."

But the administration couldn't have been further off. Those who understood the politics of the Bork opposition and Ted's call to arms were much closer to the mark. One liberal advocate called Ted's speech the "Paul Revere's ride" of the anti-Bork movement, which it was. And not just the movement. The new Judiciary chair, Joe Biden, had gone on record before Bork's nomination as saying that were Bork to get the nomination, Biden would vote for him and take the consequences from the liberals. "I'm not Ted Kennedy," he avowed. But Ted, with his mastery of the chemistry of the Senate, understood that the speech might apply pressure to Biden, and Biden later admitted that it had. He had come to oppose Bork, he said, in part to co-opt Ted. Senator Tom Daschle called the speech a "pivotal moment." "He caused the caucus to consider Bork in another light. More than any other speech, this changed the tone of that debate." And it was more than a pivotal moment for the Bork nomination, though that in itself would have made it a profoundly important speech, given how dramatically Bork would have changed the Court. Ethan Bronner, a *Boston Globe* reporter who wrote a book about the nomination fight, said it was a "landmark for judicial nominations." "Kennedy was saying," he wrote, "that no longer should the Senate content itself with examining a nominee's personal integrity and legal qualifications, as had been the custom—at least publicly for half a century. From now on the Senate and the nation should examine a nominee's vision of society." Conservatives would decry that new standard and decry the speech then and for decades thereafter as another kind of landmark: the speech that injected personal vitriol into the nomination process. The day Ted gave the speech, Senator Phil Gramm attacked Ted as a cheater, invoking Ted's having had a friend take a Spanish exam for him when Ted was a freshman at Harvard—"We know what cheaters think about this. Let's see what the A students think"—to which Ted replied evenly, "That was a low blow, Phil. But nice shot." One of the president's spokesmen remarked that after the speech, the president should have said, "Who is the swimmer from Chappaquiddick to be making such statements?" But that was precisely the point. There was a difference—a huge difference—between personal morality and civic morality, though Republicans seemed to believe that Ted's personal moral infractions disqualified him from speaking of civic morality. Ted had never argued that Bork was personally corrupt, only that he had no civic values, which was the only kind of values that mattered for a Supreme Court justice.

And so now the war began.

IV

For Ted Kennedy, it was the summer of Bork. It was the summer to mass all the opposition to stop the man who Ted Kennedy believed would turn back the clock and destroy the social progress the Supreme Court had advanced in the last fifty years. And Ted Kennedy was dogged that summer. Ted Kennedy released all the energy and anger that had been pent up in the six years during which he felt Ronald Reagan had slowly been dismantling America. "The guy goes in there and claws for his issues as if he were a first-term senator," a former staffer said of him at the time. It was a campaign now. The day after the nomination he phoned Tony Podesta, who had just, two days before, left his job as president of People for the American Way, a lobbying group established by the legendary television producer Norman Lear. Podesta was headed to Europe for a vacation, but now Ted was imploring him. "Tony, this guy Bork, we've got to stop him," Ted said. And he asked if Podesta would come to the office and discuss a plan. Podesta wound up spending the next several months of that summer in what he said were "round-the-clock meetings" with Ted and Jeff Blattner and Carolyn Osolinik, another of Ted's Judiciary aides, who were the point people. Podesta called it a "grass-roots political campaign to build a huge coalition of people to oppose Bork." (Meanwhile Ted asked People for the American Way to comb through Bork's articles, speeches, and decisions for material that could undermine his confirmation.) The "command center," as Ted called it, of the campaign was the compound at Hyannis Port. All that summer the compound buzzed. Ted was on the phone constantly. Podesta said he didn't know how much time Ted would commit, but Ted kept working the phones, and Podesta kept having to call Ted's Senate office in Washington to get more phone numbers of more people to call. And Ted brought people to Hyannis. In early August, he brought up twenty liberal activists with whom he coordinated the effort. He called in legal scholars, who worked with Blattner and Osolinik. He even brought in fellow senators. "This is the most important fight we've had in the Senate in years," he now told Podesta as a way to keep the energy from flagging, to keep the anti-Bork troops marching during the long Senate summer recess. "We need you to mobilize, to activate your people, to make this a top priority issue."

But grassroots energy wasn't enough. Near the outset, Ted told another leader, "This campaign can't be done on the back of an envelope," meaning that it had to be well organized, professional. And the professional activists had wasted little time mobilizing. The day after the nomination, Ralph Neas convened a meeting of his Leadership Conference on Civil Rights, his umbrella group of thirty progressive organizations, at the LCCR's office on DuPont Circle in Washington. Eighty people squeezed into the room. Neas was a firebrand—indefatigable, implacable, ferocious. He was a devout Catholic with the same sense of moral urgency and obligation to the less fortunate that Ted had; he had attended Notre Dame and then the University of Chicago Law School before heading to Capitol Hill, where he hoped he could be of assistance. When he had been stricken by that near-fatal bout of Guillain-Barré syndrome that paralyzed him and left him nearly blind, and then suddenly and miraculously recovered from it, largely it seemed on his faith rather than his doctors' medical know-how, his sense of obligation deepened. Ethan Bronner said it "added a cosmic dimension to his sense of destiny," and it made him even more of a dynamo. Alan Simpson had another name for him during the Bork campaign: a "monster." "Vicious," Simpson called him. Simpson had every reason to be concerned. The "monster" ran point for the activists. And while Neas's LCCR was meeting and strategizing, the Alliance

for Justice, another umbrella group of progressive forces, was also meeting, and Neas and the alliance's founder, Nan Aron, ultimately made
common cause. Five days later yet another group formed, Grassroots Task
Force, with the National Abortion Rights Action League head Kate Mi-
chaelman and the NAACP's Althea Simmons among the co-chairs. The
armies were massing.

Their weapon was pressure—public pressure on the Senate. Ted
worked those phones endlessly, Podesta making the calls, Ted taking over
to make the pitch, to rally opponents who would apply that pressure. He
phoned mayors all across the South, from New Orleans to Birmingham,
Alabama. He phoned all thirty members of the executive committee of
the AFL-CIO, and Ted said they turned their summer convention into an
anti-Bork organizing meeting. (Later in the summer he held a conference
call with forty state labor leaders.) He awakened the Reverend Joseph
Lowery, who was attending the Southern Christian Leadership Association convention, Martin Luther King's old organization, and asked him to
spread the word among the ministers there to work against Bork's nomination by going back to their congregations and preaching about him.
And Lowery did. And Ted personally phoned every Black minister in every
state where Ted was uncertain whether the Democratic senator would oppose Bork. *Personally.* "We spent hours sitting in his home dialing up anyone who would give us some influential flock who would be willing to call
their senators," Tony Podesta recalled. And then Ted wrote a letter to
6,200 Black leaders, asking them to "join me in actively opposing the
nomination." He called his fellow senators, and he even called their largest contributors, asking them to apply pressure, including a fundraiser for
Florida senator Lawton Chiles a day before a dinner for the senator. He got
Bill Taylor, another activist who had worked closely with People for the
American Way, to organize law professors, and Ted said that they ultimately got nineteen hundred to come out in opposition to Bork, which, he
claimed, was 40 percent of all legal academics. He called environmental
groups and got the Sierra Club Legal Defense to oppose Bork. Ethan Bronner said Ted sailed to the Maine summer home of Burke Marshall, the
former Bobby Kennedy Justice Department deputy, to convince him to testify against Bork. (He did.) And that was just Ted Kennedy himself.

The grassroots groups conducted their own letter-writing campaigns.
The Association of Community Organizations for Reform Now (ACORN)
sent four thousand letters in a week through churches in southern Loui-

siana alone; and by one account, the National Council of Senior Citizens, the American Association for Retired Persons, and Citizen Local had members in Florida inundating Senators Chiles and Graham with letters, while in Tennessee, by the same account, the NAACP, the AFL, Planned Parenthood, the Urban League, and local churches sent an anti-Bork petition to Senators James Sasser and Albert Gore. Interest groups, both liberal and conservative, had weighed in on Supreme Court nominations in the past, though Republicans made it seem as if this was unprecedented. What was unprecedented was the scale of the operation and the strength of the opposition. In all, an estimated three hundred organizations galvanized to oppose Bork.

But Ted had not wanted just a grassroots campaign, as he had warned early on. The American Federation of State, County and Municipal Employees ran radio and television advertisements. And People for the American Way produced an ad with actor Gregory Peck, who had played the righteous attorney Atticus Finch in the film version of the novel *To Kill a Mockingbird,* narrating about the dangers a Justice Bork would pose to America, doing so while a family of four ascended the steps of the Supreme Court and then stopped to gaze up at its columns. "The record shows that he has a strange idea of what justice is," Peck intoned of Bork, while Bork's photo appeared on the left side of the screen. "He defended poll taxes and literacy tests, which kept many Americans from voting. He opposed the civil rights act that ended 'whites only' signs at lunch counters. He doesn't believe the Constitution protects your right to privacy. And he thinks that freedom of speech does not apply to art and literature and music." Reagan's press secretary Marlin Fitzwater attacked the ad, which only wound up giving it more exposure. Other Republicans thought of the ad as blasphemy.

Ordinarily the White House would have fiercely defended Bork and counterattacked with a campaign and ads of its own. But the administration was preoccupied with another issue—heavily preoccupied because the fate of Reagan's legacy might rely on the outcome. The previous November it was reported that the administration, through the National Security Council, had been shipping arms to Iran in exchange for the release of hostages that Iranian proxies had taken in Lebanon. This was in direct contravention of Reagan's stated policy that he would not cooperate with terrorists. That would have been bad enough. But it was more complicated. A portion of the funds that the Iranians paid for the weaponry was diverted to the Contras in Nicaragua, Reagan's much-beloved "freedom fighters," who were trying to overthrow the Sandinista government there. Reagan had managed to maintain his funding of the Contras for two years, but after the revelation that the CIA had been involved in the mining of Managua's harbor, Congress was less cooperative and eventually passed a bill—an amendment to the budget—that severely restricted the administration's latitude, then finally passed another that ended that latitude altogether. But with Reagan's knowledge or not—it was never entirely clear—the NSC continued to fund the Contras, which added yet another transgression to the transgression of selling arms. A joint select committee of the House and Senate, both of which were now in Democratic hands, launched hearings the following May. Those hearings lasted for forty-one days and riveted the nation. But they and the aftermath also diverted the administration from the Bork battle. Bork was left to dangle throughout the summer while the nation and the administration focused on Iran and the Contras.

Still, for all the phone-calling and letter-writing and advertising and grassroots organizing that Ted and Neas and hundreds of others did that summer, there was one individual whose efforts did more to damage Robert Bork's Supreme Court prospects than anyone else. And that individual was Robert Bork. As Jeff Blattner, along with dozens of other researchers, scoured Bork's articles and speeches and opinions, a painstaking operation—Blattner said he gained thirty pounds that summer sitting reading through the material—and as Blattner spoke about Bork with legal scholars, he and they discovered that Bork was a proud reactionary who had applied his legal reasoning to halting the advance of just about every progressive right. In August 1963 he had written an article in *The New Republic* in which he argued that the Civil Rights Act, were it to be passed, would be unconstitutional, and he especially took exception to the public accommodation section of the bill, which would allow Black people access to hotels and restaurants and bus stations and other places from which they had historically been excluded or in which they had been segregated from white customers. "The principle of such legislation is that if I find your behavior ugly by my standards, moral or aesthetic, and if you prove stubborn about adopting my view of the situation," he argued, "I am justified in having the state coerce you into more righteous paths." He wrote that the principle "is itself a principle of unsurpassed ugliness," though the consequences of following Bork's logic would have ended the civil rights movement and denied civil rights to Black Americans. His argument against the *Griswold* decision was no less disturbing not only to liberals but to Americans generally: They had no right to contraception unless the state decided they did. (When Ted was being briefed by law professors, and they focused on the technicalities of constitutional law, Ted said, "Look, the masses are not going to rise up over the issue of congressional standing. But they will over freedom in the bedroom.") Bork had called *Brown v. Board of Education* wrongly decided too, but later changed his mind because he said the principle of "separate but equal" in *Plessy v. Ferguson* was untenable—separate had *physically* not led to equal facilities—and said the founders had not anticipated that contradiction, though why he made an originalist exception for *Brown* and not for other decisions he never explained. And while Bork's supporters adduced the power of precedent to parry arguments that he would radicalize the law, he had been caught on tape in a speech at Canisius College in 1985 in which he dismissed precedent as "not all that important," boasted that justices should not be bound by precedent, and in fact said it should be swept away when it conflicted with his own doctrine of originalism. All this was compiled by Blattner in a looseleaf binder. "The Book of Bork" it was called, though in truth there were many "Books of Bork," all tailored to individual senators, to the issues that had interested them over the years. Ted would send these out on a Friday with a handwritten note, and at least to the senators on the Judiciary Committee, he would send as many different "books" as necessary to address new issues that arose. As one of the coalition leaders would later say, "It was the 'Book of Bork' that beat Bork," but he added, "It was the campaign that forced the Senate to read the book."

The object of all this effort was a rumpled, portly sixty-year-old, his chin rimmed with whiskers so that he looked like a stern Scandinavian woodsman. It was not an inviting visage, and his was not an inviting presence. He had been born in Pittsburgh to a middle-class family, attended the private Hotchkiss School in Connecticut, and then the University of Chicago, from which he received both his bachelor's degree and his law degree. He was a dogmatist—first as a youthful socialist, then as a free-market conservative learning at the very center of free-market conservatism, the University of Chicago. When he practiced law, at the upscale firm of Kirkland and Ellis, he specialized in antitrust law, of which he was deeply skeptical, later writing a book about the benefits of monopoly. He would undergo one more conversion—this time from libertarian free-market conservative to social conservative. He was unquestionably brilliant, and he knew it. He was also known to be disarming and even charming, his cold and even inhumane vision of the law notwithstanding. And going into the hearings, Ted was concerned about that reputation, worried that Bork might talk and charm his way onto the Court. The White House felt he would. William Bradford Reynolds said, "Part of the mind-set is that all of this"—meaning the attacks on Bork—"is going to fall away when you have the candidate up there, and he's going to say what he's going to say."

The summer of Bork ended after the recess with the commencement of the hearings that September. Ted Kennedy had prepped for them exhaustively. He had Laurence Tribe, a brilliant constitutional scholar in his own right, play Bork. Tribe was not eager to enter the fight. But he agreed to come to Ted's Boston office before the hearings for what he called a "rehearsal." "What if Bork says this? What if Bork says that?" Ted was deadly serious. During one of these rehearsals, in a brisk exchange, a staffer laughed, and Ted glowered at him. "You can laugh. You're not going up against him tomorrow." Tribe met with Biden too—Tribe said he thought Biden was inspired by Ted to prepare himself, and Tribe wound up spending several days at Biden's house in Delaware, again with Tribe playing Bork, and even conducted a "murder board" session along with Duke University law professor Walter Dellinger—and he met with Howard Metzenbaum, and to all three he stressed that Bork's two greatest vulnerabilities were his position on privacy (that there was no penumbra of privacy in the Constitution) and his position on individual liberty (that individual liberties were almost always superseded by the state).

But Tribe wasn't the only resource. Ted held dinners at Hyannis with legal scholars that summer and several at McLean before the hearing. He also invited Cass Sunstein and Kathleen Sullivan, two outstanding legal minds, for what Tribe called "long, long dinners and conversations at McLean where we would go over all of the issues in great detail." And Ted met in his office with his fellow Judiciary Committee senators too—members-only meetings—with Biden, but also with Patrick Leahy and Alan Cranston and Metzenbaum. And for days before the hearing,

Blattner and Osolinik were at his side wherever he went—when he dedicated a senior citizens' home in the Bronx or when he spoke at a shipyard in Quincy—drilling him on Bork in every vagrant moment. And once the hearings began, Blattner said that he would arrive at McLean at seven a.m., and there Ted would be in his den, as Blattner described it, a "notebook open, a fire burning, wearing his reading glasses. Pages were folded over." And Blattner said that Ted's "intensity was unbelievably dazzling." And then after each session, Ted and Blattner and Osolinik would repair to his office to review the day's testimony and prepare for tomorrow's, staying there until three-thirty in the morning.

Even before the hearings began, there was jousting. On the eve of the hearings, Ted delivered a speech at Georgetown University Law Center where he once again charged Bork with "contempt for law, of searching for loopholes, of twisting clear language, of ignoring the intent of Congress." Reagan countered in the Rose Garden, calling Ted's remarks "irrational and totally unjustified." Ted also recruited former HEW secretary Joseph Califano to write an op-ed piece for *The New York Times* scheduled for the day before Bork's testimony, in which Califano argued that Bork's legal acumen was not the issue. The issue for each senator was whether Bork's philosophy of law comported with that of the senator. And Blattner said that Ted phoned Archibald Cox again from the anteroom of the Senate Caucus Room where the hearings were being held—a room Richard Ben Cramer had described as an "echoing temple of marble pilasters and an acre of tables for the nation's press," the room where the Iran-Contra hearings had just been held—to coax Cox to testify, but he continued to demur.

And now with the two sides girded for combat, the hearings began. Tom Korologos, a longtime Republican consultant who had prepared Bork for the hearing, said he was surprised by the "ferocity" of the opposition and surmised that "what it gets down to is that . . . they haven't had a big civil rights fight in a long time." Korologos wasn't wrong. This was a big fight. Ralph Neas laid out the stakes: "Without question, this is the most important legislative battle we have ever fought—because everything else we ever fought for is at stake."

Certainly, as far as Ted Kennedy was concerned, Neas was right. And because Joe Biden, the Judiciary chair, was running for the Democratic nomination for president, and because Biden had gotten himself entangled in a charge of plagiarism for a speech he had made, Ted assumed greater responsibility. He helped strategize, collaborating with Biden to set up the schedule for witnesses to maximize their cumulative effect, and he took a leading role in the questioning.

The most anticipated and dramatic scene might have been Ted's interrogation of Bork. Ted was ready, having prepared himself for months. But Bork was ready too. He had been preparing himself by a lifetime of legal argument. Ted was unsparing. He assailed Bork, getting "as close as you could get to punching the guy's lights out," Alan Simpson was to say. Ted's was not a legal argument with the kind of rhetorical gamesmanship that law professors might admire. This was political brawling where Ted Kennedy knew the outcome would have an effect far beyond law classes and courtrooms; it would affect every corner of the country and every person in the country, especially the poor and the marginalized for whom Ted had fought throughout his career. A litany of charges Ted threw at Bork: Bork said he was only applying "neutral principles," but Ted said there must be something wrong with principles that are "neutral in the face of discrimination because of race," or "neutral in the face of discrimination against women and in the face of gross invasions by the government of individual citizens' rights to privacy." A court must be fair, Ted said, but "Mr. Bork"—he never addressed him as Justice Bork, though he was a sitting judge—"has shown his bias against women and minorities and in favor of big business and Presidential power." Bork opposed the Court's ruling on one-man, one-vote—an issue that Ted had pioneered in the Senate along with Howard Baker—but in doing so, he "would allow majorities to write laws that give greater weight to some people's vote than others'." Mr. Bork asked to be judged on his jurisprudence, Ted said, but "again and again on the public record he's suggested that he's prepared to roll back the clock, return to more troubled times, uproot decades of settled law in order to write his own ideology into law." And Ted asked this: "Who is the real Robert Bork?"—the one who had opposed nearly every civil right and right to privacy, or the one who keeps trimming the sails of his past arguments? Ted had his own answer. He called Bork a "walking constitutional amendment." And then Bork had his turn for rebuttal against those charges:

"I have not asked that either the Congress nor the courts be neutral in the face of racial discrimination.

"I have upheld the laws that outlaw racial discrimination.

"I have consistently supported Brown against Board of Education in my writings long ago.

"I have never written a word hostile to women.

"I have never written a word hostile to privacy.

"I have complained about the reasoning of one Supreme Court case.

"I have never written a word or made a decision in which—from which you can infer that I am pro big-business at the expense of other people.

"And as far as Presidential power is concerned, I have very rarely dealt with that, but when I have it's on constitutional principles and upon occasion, as in the pocket-veto matter, you find me squarely opposing Presidential power." And he said this: "There is—I have no ideological agenda. And if I did it wouldn't do me any good because nobody else on that Court has an ideological agenda and I don't intend to be—I do not intend, if confirmed, to be the only person up there running around with a political agenda. In fact, nothing in my record suggests I have a political or ideological agenda," which was blatantly false, unless one defined legal philosophy itself as nonideological. Robert Bork might have been a brilliant legal mind. His was not a nonideological mind. And Robert Bork was not being truthful about his legal reckoning.

Conservatives castigated Ted. *New York Times* columnist and former Nixon speechwriter William Safire said Ted read from his script, prepared by his staff, punctuating it with "ah's" and "um's" as if he were mulling the questions himself. But pitting Ted's supposed lack of intelligence against Bork's brilliance, Safire said, Kennedy "is protected from having to think out loud. He makes short speeches containing a farrago of charges, concluding with a request for a rebuttal. When the Kennedy target—in this case a thoughtful, anti-activist judge being bespattered with charges of racism, sexism, hypocrisy, and dishonesty—responds ad lib in detail and with some eloquence, the Senator does not engage; it is not in his script. He says only, 'To move on.'" And to the moment when Ted sprang the Canisius speech on Bork—the speech Ted's staff had found in which Bork abjured precedence—Safire wrote that Ted was flummoxed when Bork said he was only joking—as if Bork had been joking. "Anti-intellectual" was the charge Safire threw at Ted. Not smart enough for Bork.

Except that the hearing room wasn't a law classroom, and Ted wasn't trying to score points with legal scholars—a large percentage of whom, that 40 percent, had come out against Bork anyway. He was trying to score political points to save the nation from what he perceived as the scourge of Robert Bork. Ted had been worried about Bork's performance— had expressed those concerns about his intellect and charm. But watching Bork in that witness chair, the worry had dissipated. (Biden too said that he knew within the first hour of Bork's testimony that he would fail.) Bork was brilliant but arrogant—full of himself. Ted could see that "he wasn't much of a listener. He was a talker, and he was confident about where he was and what he was doing." As he continued speaking, he continued digging a hole for himself, persisting in doubling down on his peculiar legal interpretations that made no room for civil rights or privacy rights, and Biden kept passing notes to Ted, keeping score, 12–0, 18–0, 24–0. "30–0 if he keeps on," read the final note Biden slipped to him.

Cold, bloodless, distant, superior—that was Robert Bork in the witness chair, a man who clearly delighted in legal gamesmanship but had no interest in the human or social consequences of the law or in justice, only in the decision-making process. Asked by Senator Paul Simon about a statement Bork had made that when a court adds to the rights of one person, it subtracts from the rights of another, Bork said it was a "matter of plain arithmetic," and that he had no quarrel with the redistribution of liberty—say, the freedom of slaves from the white slaveholder's rights to own them—*whenever the Constitution requires it or authorizes it.* Rights were always a matter of zero-sum, he said. But Bork always seemed to come down on the side of majoritarian rights against the rights of the vulnerable minority. When Howard Metzenbaum quizzed Bork on his decision in a case against the chemical manufacturer American Cyanamid in which Bork determined that Occupational Health Administration and Safety rules did not ban a company policy that required women to be surgically sterilized if they were to work in an area of a paint factory, Bork said nonchalantly, "They offered a choice to women; some of them, I guess, did not want to have children." (Two of the affected workers fired off telegrams to the committee immediately, saying that they had been put in the untenable position of getting sterilized or losing their jobs.) One of the most eloquent witnesses, former federal judge Shirley Hufstedler, thought that Bork was on a "quest of certitudes" and seemed to have found them, and in doing so, she said, he had tried to avoid "having to confront the grief and untidiness of the human condition," which was precisely why Ted Kennedy opposed him so strenuously. Asked by Senator Simpson why he wanted to be on the Court, Bork said it would be an "intellectual feast," as if judicial decision-making were a game, without his seeming to consider the effect the Court would have on ordinary people. Bork had fallen into the trap that Ted believed conservatives had long been springing for themselves and the one he had tried to exploit since Reagan's election—the trap of embracing dogma without acknowledging humanity. (Indeed, for Ted, conservative dogma usually seemed to be in the service of hurting the vulnerable.) "Scholarship devoid of moral content," Arlen Specter, a moderate Pennsylvania Republican, said of Bork's views when Specter announced his decision to vote against confirmation. "He misses the spirit of human rights in the Constitution."

As Ted Kennedy and Joe Biden both believed, Robert Bork had done himself no favors during his thirty-two hours of testimony and the twelve days of hearings—detailed hearings, scrupulous hearings, substantive hearings, even hearings largely and surprisingly devoid of partisanship as opposed to careful legal dissection, which was one reason Ted and Biden chose not to call those liberal advocates to testify, lest they turn the hearings into a right-left battle. Some worried Biden would use the hearing to advance his presidential candidacy. He didn't. Under duress from the charges of plagiarism leveled against him, he went directly from a press conference in which he tackled those charges and into the hearing room, and later, during the hearings, he bowed out of the presidential race and then again headed back into the hearing room, both of which won him plaudits for maintaining his objectivity and his focus as his presidential campaign collapsed around him. One legal reporter called the hearings "perhaps the deepest exploration of fundamental constitutional issues ever to capture the public limelight." Bork had had his chance to defend himself; the committee report was 480 pages long. But Bork's was a feckless defense. Polls showed that he was an unpopular choice, and the more people knew about his views, the less favorable they were toward him, though Republicans argued that that was just because his views had been so badly misrepresented. A poll commissioned by AFSCME found that 61 percent of Americans were less inclined to back Bork after being told about his position on *Griswold* and contraception, and more than half were less inclined after being informed of his decisions on the poll tax and

one-man one-vote.* A poll by Scripps-Howard found that even Southerners were evenly divided on Bork. And despite Richard Shelby's prediction,
Senate Southern Democrats, particularly those elected in 1986 with the
help of Black voters, had turned on Bork. (Even the longtime racist John
Stennis, who was retiring, rejected Bork.) The Judiciary Committee voted
9 to 5 against him, which made his confirmation unlikely, should it reach
the floor, and there was now doubt about that.

Among those doubters was Bork himself. Alan Simpson, one of Bork's
strongest advocates, said that Bork and his wife, a former nun with conservative views not dissimilar to her husband's, came into his office after
the hearings, and she was crying. She said she had never seen anything
like that. "How can they tear a person to bits?" she asked. And she asked
Simpson whether they should proceed with the nomination knowing full
well that Bork was likely to lose. Simpson asked Bork what he wanted to
do, but Bork said he was "puzzled" and asked what Simpson advised. And
Simpson told him that he was going before the Senate to join the debate
on the nomination and that about thirty-five of those senators, both Republicans and Democrats, would testify to Bork's worthiness and that
would go into the *Congressional Record* and that someday Bork could share
that with his grandchildren—show them that "you got screwed and that
you were an amazing man." Lloyd Cutler, Jimmy Carter's White House
counsel and possibly Bork's most avid supporter, harangued him for two
and a half hours not to withdraw. Bork didn't. Reagan pronounced himself happy with the decision. "Our efforts will be focused on setting the
record straight," he said.

But the floor debate did not stem the tide moving against Robert Bork,
even though Republicans had delayed the debate to try and turn it. (When
Ted spoke, Mrs. Bork left the gallery.) Ted told Blattner that he had spoken
with Senator David Pryor of Arkansas who told him, "When I run into
somebody back home and they say they are for Bork, I ask them why and
they can't give me a reason. If they say they are against Bork, and I ask
why, they give me a reason." And Ted told Blattner, "That's important."
Those senators opposing Bork knew the reason as well as their constituents did. They knew, as Ted had said at the outset in the speech for which

* As Republican supporters argued, these views of Bork's were not as simple as support for
poll taxes or against one-man one-vote. Bork was against the legal reasoning of the courts
in those decisions, though his own reasoning invariably upheld those very things—among
them a poll tax, majoritarian rule, segregation—that served the conservative mission.

he was reviled, the speech in which he was accused of exaggeration and character assassination, the speech that was said to have changed Supreme Court confirmations for generations, that Bork had little respect for civil rights or privacy or minorities or precedent or, above all, the morality of which Ted and Arlen Specter spoke, and that while most Republicans seemed to think the only thing that mattered was legal competence and that Bork's legal philosophy shouldn't have been subjected to scrutiny and that doing so was politicizing the process, and while they would keep on pressing those arguments for decades to come, they were disingenuous. However one felt about Bork, when Reagan nominated him, the president had politicized the process, which was why Ted reacted as he did. Supreme Court nominations hadn't been so politicized before Bork because, with few exceptions, like G. Harrold Carswell, the nominees were moderates and in the American mainstream.

Robert Bork, though he had what one critic called a "confirmation conversion" in which he walked back a few of his most egregious statements, was no moderate. The man who didn't believe in legal precedent was an extremist. The Senate voted on the nomination at two o'clock on the afternoon of October 23, and six Republicans joined the Democrats in defeating Bork, 58 to 42, only the fifth nominee to have been rejected in the twentieth century to that point—two of them, Haynsworth and Carswell, from Richard Nixon. (Bork and his wife, with the result foretold, were drinking cocktails at the Madison Hotel at the time.) Reagan had counted on Bork's intellect and his ideology to win. Instead, those were among the very things that cost him victory. "As America watched Bork," the *Washington Post* television critic Tom Shales wrote, "America learned to dislike Bork," and said that "he looked and talked like a man who would throw the book at you." Reagan had already engineered a social revolution. Neither the majority of the American people nor the majority of the Senate, however, seemed to want a constitutional revolution. Perhaps sensing that, Reagan had postponed that attempted revolution for seven years, lurking, waiting to strike. Now that he had, one reporter thought Bork's defeat testified to Reagan's waning power in the twilight of his presidency and to the realization that while people liked the president, they liked his conservatism less and his conservatism toward the Court even less than that. As Laurence Tribe put it, "The right wing lost the constitutional referendum of 1987." Jeff Blattner put it differently. The "Constitution won," he said. Seven years it had taken for Reagan to launch that

assault on the Supreme Court, seven years in which he had even appointed moderate Sandra Day O'Connor to the Court, most of those years
with Ted Kennedy wandering the political wilderness. Seven years of Ted
suffering a series of defeats with only a handful of victories. But with the
1986 midterm elections and the Democratic majority, Ted Kennedy had
become a new man in a new Senate. And now the new man had won
what was likely his most decisive and significant victory during the Reagan presidency.* And while conservatives would deplore Bork's defeat for
a generation and coin the word "Borking" to describe the process in which
someone had been treated with flagrant unfairness, Ted Kennedy, and the
forces he had helped marshal, and the millions those forces had marshaled, had stopped Ronald Reagan from, in Ted's view, ripping moral values from the Constitution—the values that had saved the most vulnerable
of Americans.

---

* Reagan had threatened to nominate another justice in the mold of Bork. But he first submitted the name of Douglas Ginsberg, who withdrew when it was revealed he had smoked
marijuana, and then Anthony Kennedy, who was more in the mold of Lewis Powell than
of Robert Bork.

TWELVE

"We Need the Results"

RONALD REAGAN, WHO had bolted from the gate when he became president and imposed his vision on the country—a country he had hoped to free from the shackles of the New Deal—shambled through the last year of that presidency without a vision of any kind. The Iran-Contra affair, in which Reagan had at first vehemently (and falsely) denied that the government traded arms for hostages, seemed to sabotage everything. Reagan's approval rating slipped precipitously with the revelation of the guns-for-hostages-for-money-for-Contras scheme—sixteen points in a single month—and his ratings remained low throughout the rest of his presidency, averaging fifty-three points in his final year, even after adjusting for a slight bump during the presidential campaign that fall. There was a sense that the administration's energy was spent, that it was time to move on, and in any case, America would have a new president in 1989 after Reagan retired to California. That presented Democrats with an opportunity to regain the initiative. In the Kennedy household, the winding down of the Reagan regime represented another kind of opportunity. When, in 1985, Tip O'Neill, the speaker of the House, announced he would not run for reelection the following year, Ted had immediately thought of having Ted Jr. compete for the seat, John F. Kennedy's old House seat, and even commissioned a poll that showed, according to one of Ted's political advisers, a "slam dunk for Ted [Jr.]." Patrick Caddell recalled Ted holding a meeting at the Big House with some fifty Kennedy retainers to discuss the race while Ted Jr. sat there morosely with, as Caddell described it, a "what-am-I-doing-here?" look in his eyes. Ted Jr. declined the opportunity to run—Bobby's son, Joe II, took it and won—and instead went to Yale's graduate school of forestry, gaining weight, growing a bushy beard, drinking, carousing, and doing everything he could to keep politics at bay. (He would tell *Newsweek* that his cousin wanted the seat more than he did.)

But there was another Kennedy in the family, a surprising one, who did have political aspirations. Two years after Ted Jr.'s decision, and with the 1988 elections approaching, it was Patrick, the Kennedy waif with his asthma and his freckles and his continuous bouts with drugs that sent him to rehabilitation in high school and his general sense of outsiderness, who decided to run for office, even though he was a twenty-one-year-old Providence College sophomore at the time. Earlier that year he had been diagnosed with a spinal tumor, which, he said, was actually a relief to his father since Ted believed he was complaining of pain in order to be medicated. He underwent a fourteen-hour operation, and a long recuperation, during which Ted visited him frequently. But despite those visits, Patrick would later admit that his decision to run for state representative in Rhode Island was motivated by his need for more attention from his father, and by a need for a "place in the world," and by a need for the camaraderie he hoped to find in the state legislature. And, not unlike his father when it came to political calculation, he knew that the incumbent in the district, a veteran "ward politician" Ted called him, named Jack Skeffington, was vulnerable. Ted was not enthusiastic about the idea; no doubt, he was worried about Patrick's fragility and his drug problems. But abetting his son's effort, he took Patrick to the home of retired senator John Pastore to introduce him, and Patrick won the endorsement of Pastore and Senator Claiborne Pell, and Ted recruited Tony Podesta, the activist who had helped him defeat the Bork confirmation, and Tony's brother John to assist Patrick, and he won the primary 1,324 to 1,009.

The main event that election year, of course, was the presidential contest. Vice President George H. W. Bush had beaten Senate minority leader Robert Dole for the Republican nomination, even though many of the more ardent conservatives worried that Bush was too establishment, too eastern, and not sufficiently right wing for their taste. The Democratic primary was more rough-and-tumble: Former Colorado senator Gary Hart, who had contested the 1984 nomination against Mondale, entered the race; so did Representative Richard Gephardt of Missouri; and Senators Al Gore of Tennessee and Paul Simon of Illinois; and the Reverend Jesse Jackson; and Governor Michael Dukakis of Ted's Massachusetts. (Several candidates, like Joe Biden, dropped out before the primaries, in

Biden's case, during the Bork hearing.) Ted supported Dukakis, not because he was especially close to him—he was closer to some of the others—but because Dukakis was Massachusetts. "He never hesitated," Dukakis would later say of the endorsement. " 'I'm with you.' He was a gutsy guy." And Dukakis won thirty primaries and emerged with the nomination. Just before speaking on Dukakis's behalf at the convention, Ted expressed no regrets about his not seeking the nomination himself, which almost surely would have been his. "It may be difficult to believe," he said, "but I find this job rewarding, satisfying. I'd said I'd like to be president, but I'm very satisfied with what I'm doing. I don't look over my shoulder."

Dukakis was the putative frontrunner as the general election began. He was the son of Greek immigrants, extremely bright and studious, a Harvard man the hard way, incorruptible, a liberal but no firebrand like Ted—a "post-liberal," Walter Shapiro of *Time* called him—a governor who had fired up Massachusetts's economy but, like Jimmy Carter, had emphasized competence rather than ideology, a colorless and uncharismatic figure and a straight arrow, not someone who was likely to rock the boat, maybe just tip it a bit, a candidate designed not to offend at a time when liberals were all too wary of offending. "The last man standing when the more impassioned Democratic contenders had fallen away," historian Sean Wilentz said of him. George H. W. Bush was, in many ways, like Dukakis: also smart, also a straight arrow, also inoffensive, less interested in ideology than in efficiency, even a war hero, which Dukakis was not. Neither man was going to appeal to the extremes of his party. But Dukakis thought that was an advantage—a way to ward off the charge of being too liberal. The people around Bush, who understood the fanaticism of the hard right, many of them being hard-right fanatics themselves, and the appeal of the Hollywood swagger of Reagan, knew Bush's seeming moderation wasn't an advantage, at least not in the post-Reagan Republican Party, and neither was his blandness. His war heroism notwithstanding, Bush, an eastern Ivy League elitist before he decamped to Texas and became an oilman, a man who even looked the part of eastern elitist, was labeled weak—a "wimp," said *Newsweek*, in a famous cover story. Ronald Reagan, the standard against which Bush would be measured, was no wimp. He had succeeded in portraying Democrats as abnormal, contemptuous, disdainful, haughty, irreligious—they made fun of religion, he had told that crowd at the Conservative Political Action

Committee in umbrage—and unpatriotic, not real Americans but actually at war with *real* Americans—Americans like Reagan and his conservative supporters. (There was a racial message here too: Democrats cozied up to Black people at the expense of white people, the zero-sum that Bork had talked about in his testimony.) Ted Kennedy had taken special exception to this because he knew the consequences, knew full well how fundamentally this view, a pernicious update on the postwar charge that Democrats were Communists or fellow travelers, could hurt the Democrats and change the country. "In this house, family, patriotism, and religion were assumed," he would later say, "and that was basically the philosophy that immigrants brought here." But then, Ted said, Ronald Reagan and his acolytes took these values—"core values in terms of the Democrats"—and "turned them on their head, so that he was the only one who was perceived to have them," and, Ted said, in the process, he "usurped them from a whole generation of political leadership."

And Ted identified what he saw as the cause: "The race issue was the overarching one that enabled him to do it." Richard Nixon had done his best to widen the racial divide by invoking law and order and thereby criminalizing Black people as a whole. Reagan had a different tactic. He invoked welfare fraud—the "welfare queen" who drove a Cadillac—and made it seem as if Black people were corrupt and indolent. The overt message of both was that Black people weren't like other Americans—white Americans who obeyed the law and worked hard. But there was that other message, a subtler but perhaps equally powerful message in each of these racial appeals, and one that changed the political calculus: that *because* Black people were unlawful and corrupt, the moral authority of those who advocated for them—liberals like Ted Kennedy—was nil. By this view, and it was clearly Reagan's view in his frequent expressions of contempt for welfare cheats, liberals might have been different from Reagan's so-called real Americans because they challenged nineteenth-century traditional values—this was Reagan's moral recalibration—but also because they supported Black people and the poor, supported values that went against everything in which his real Americans believed, and while liberals might have had the defense of moral authority in the past, the defense of the values of tolerance and charity and community, Reagan in his eight years had effectively stripped that authority from them. (Of course, conservatives insisted that Ted's moral authority had been discredited by the Chappaquiddick accident.) Basically, liberals had chosen the wrong side in the civil war that first Nixon and then Reagan had declared—the war that pitted white people against minorities, puritanical values against more humanistic ones.

George H. W. Bush was not a man with racial prejudices; nor was he a man who questioned the patriotism or values of his opponents, except when it was politically expedient, as it was in his presidential campaign. He was not a man who questioned much of anything. He was an old-fashioned conservative Republican, a scion of wealthy business Republicans—his father, Prescott Bush, had been a Wall Street banker before becoming a senator from Connecticut—and he played by the rules. But the election of 1988 was a rough game. Dukakis had a lead that swelled, after his postconvention bounce in July, to seventeen points. Bush's handlers, the closest of whom were not old-fashioned conservative Republicans, were taking no chances. It was going to be a difficult race, and one for which they borrowed the Reagan playbook to portray Dukakis as out of the mainstream, abnormal, not one of us. A memo after the convention from consultant Roger Ailes, later the power behind the conservative cable network Fox News, advised Bush that the "voter must know three things about Michael Dukakis. He will raise their taxes. He is opposed to the death penalty, even for drug kingpins and murderers. And he is an extreme liberal, even a pacifist on the subject of national defense." The last of these was the most important, though the suggestion of pacifism was absurd, but Bush was successful in conveying it: Michael Dukakis, the son of Greek immigrants, was not like *them*, the real Americans, because he believed in liberal causes, and he wouldn't stand up for America.

The election was fought on those grounds. Arthur Schlesinger, Jr., observed: "Bush's major theme so far is that Republicans are more patriotic than Democrats and that Dukakis is, heaven help us, a liberal." The novelist and essayist Joan Didion said that the rhetoric that dominated the campaign was not the "awareness of a new and different world," obviously a more diverse and modernizing world, "but nostalgia for an old one, and coded assurance that any evidence of ambiguity or change, of what George Bush called the 'deterioration of values'"—by liberals—"would be summarily dealt with by increased social control." Dukakis and Democrats, who had seen how effectively Reagan used this same tactic, ran scared, terrified of stating their principles, terrified of the label of outsider, which prompted *Time* to ask of these timorous men: "Is there a soul to the Democratic Party?" Years later Dukakis, whose big lead quickly evaporated, admitted his was a "lousy campaign." He said it had lacked three things: a "clear message"; a "carefully thought-out strategy for dealing with the Bush attack campaign"; and a "serious grassroots effort," and he complained that "I spent too much time listening to people who presumably knew more about getting elected to the presidency than I did, and who argued that it was all about money and media," even though it was really about articulating a vision. Dukakis took a battering. He carried only ten states, while Bush won 53.4 percent of the vote.

Ted had run that year too, against a handsome young Republican businessman named Joe Malone, who had been a Harvard football star and who had managed Ray Shamie's losing 1982 campaign against Ted. Malone had no better luck with his own campaign than he had had with Shamie's. Ted said the campaign effectively ended during a debate when Malone was asked which members of the Supreme Court he admired and why. Malone took a long pause and then a longer one. Ted said he could feel the "hook going deeper and deeper." And finally Malone offered that there were a lot of good Supreme Court justices. Ted won 65 percent of the vote. That night Patrick won his state legislature seat in Rhode Island. Weeks later Ted was relaxing in Hawaii after the election when Patrick called to invite him to the swearing-in. Ted flew fourteen hours and arrived only to be told that Patrick's advisers had decided Ted shouldn't be there, though it was really Patrick who had concluded that his father would only overshadow him. This was *his* moment. "I wanted to be seen as the neighborhood guy, my own guy, and not just a Kennedy." And Ted accepted the disinvitation with equanimity. He knew what it was like to have to escape the burdens of being a Kennedy. He knew very well.

That fall, his own victory notwithstanding, he was disappointed. The auguries had been good. Liberalism was on the rise again, he told Sidney Blumenthal of *The Washington Post* just before the Democratic convention. Something had "clicked," he said. "There's a consciousness. It's happening." But it was difficult to beat the racial politics and the politics of otherness and elitism, at least when it came to the presidency. Still, while Bush had won, the Republicans hadn't. Despite his landslide, the party picked up no Senate seats and lost two seats in the House. In a postmortem at the John F. Kennedy School of Government less than two weeks after Bush's victory, Ted blamed not liberalism for Dukakis's loss but rather

Dukakis's efforts to conceal his liberalism. Ted said this was an old Republican trick—to tar Democrats with the liberal label—and that Nixon had
tried it on Jack in 1960, but Jack had "embraced the 'liberal' label without
hesitation. He didn't run away from it. He welcomed it. He campaigned
proudly under its banner." And he chided Dukakis for promoting his competence. "Competence was not enough," Ted would later contend. "Ideology, which is about ideas, was missing, and our opponents filled the gap
with appeals to fear."

Democrats had once again run away from themselves. And they had
done so on the basis that Ronald Reagan had made liberalism that
"plague," as had been said, and that he had bolstered conservatism so
that it was now a given that the nation was conservative and that liberalism was dead, despite Tip O'Neill's declaration after the 1986 midterms
that the Reagan Revolution was over. Conservatives had beaten liberalism
on the basis that Reagan's had been a triumphant presidency, or so the
conventional wisdom went. According to that wisdom, he had been an
enormously popular president and a tremendously successful one. He had
nursed the economy back to health while trimming the government, and
he had strengthened America abroad by beefing up the military. And he
had changed the basic political conceptions of the last fifty years. Republicans had lusted to destroy the New Deal. As the conventional wisdom
went, Reagan finally had. And such, supposedly, would be his legacy. He
would enter history as the most consequential president since Roosevelt
because he was the one who had undone what Roosevelt did and freed the
nation from what Americans increasingly saw as the oppressive bonds of
liberal government.

How much of this was true was open to dispute. But it was certainly
not as true as conservatives contended. Contrary to the image, Reagan
had not been a particularly popular president, at least not during his presidency. His average rating as measured by the Gallup poll, 52.8 percent,
was lower than that of Dwight Eisenhower, John Kennedy, and Lyndon
Johnson. (It would be lower than that of George H. W. Bush and Bill Clinton too.) His economic statistics, which Republicans would tout for decades, were less than extraordinary, with allowance for the fact that he
had, like Jimmy Carter, inherited an economy in distress. The economy
did add 16.5 million jobs for a 16.5 percent increase, compared to Carter's
addition of 9.8 million jobs and a 10.9 percent increase, not inconsiderable numbers for Reagan, and unemployment dropped, but wages for

production and nonsupervisory employees declined throughout his presidency, forcing married couples in the middle quintile to work nine additional weeks each year to compensate; the deficit doubled from 2.5 percent of the economy during Carter's administration to 5 percent during Reagan's, saddling the nation with a huge national debt, despite Reagan's promises to balance the budget, and overall personal disposable savings actually fell; the budget of the federal government as a percentage of national income grew from 27.9 percent during Carter's term to 28.7 percent during Reagan's terms, despite Reagan's promise to cut the size of the government; income inequality rose dramatically, widening economic divisions, with the bottom quintile losing 7 percent in real family income, while the percentage of wealth held by the top one percent soared from 22 percent in the last year of Carter's presidency to 39 in the last year of Reagan's; tax revenues as a percentage of national income dropped only 0.4 percent from Carter's; and the poverty rate remained the same, while statistics aside, in cities across the country one could see familiar signs of an epidemic of homelessness: people sleeping over grates for warmth or on church steps because they had a better likelihood of not being rousted there, or living in cardboard boxes on street corners, or pushing shopping carts filled with their belongings down the sidewalk. Perhaps most surprisingly, given all the accolades accorded Reagan for his economic prowess after Carter's bumbling performance, economic growth during Reagan's terms was 3.5 percent, during Carter's term, 3.3 percent—a minuscule difference especially given the difference in perceptions of the two presidents. Reagan certainly deserved credit for the drop in the inflation rate, but Carter had appointed the inflation hawk Paul Volcker to the Federal Reserve—Reagan reappointed him—and Carter took the initial risk of raising the federal funds rate to push the economy into recession, which was what broke the inflationary spiral; Carter introduced deregulation (with Ted's help), which helped economic growth, whatever its other and less salutary consequences; and Carter fought the auto industry's efforts to be protected from foreign competition—competition that also brought down prices. Even if the policies that led to the results began in Carter's administration, the employment and inflation *results* occurred on Reagan's watch, and he got the credit, but in some ways it illustrated what one study by two respected economists determined: that economic success is a result more of "good luck" than of "good policies." In short, Ronald Reagan was no economic wizard. Conservative commentator

George Will put it this way: Liberals had practiced "tax and tax, spend and spend, elect and elect." Under Reagan, conservatives practiced "borrow and borrow, spend and spend, elect and elect."*

What is indisputable is Reagan's importance. Politically speaking, it was true that what Franklin Roosevelt had aligned, Ronald Reagan had realigned. He had broken the New Deal coalition of working-class white people and minorities, united by economic and social self-interest (the coalition of the South and the Northern cities had been broken long before) and forged a new coalition united by racial animosities, a distaste for big government, primarily taxes, and above all, as William Schneider, a political commentator, put it, a fear that "liberals will regain control of the federal government and use it, as they did in the past, as the instrument for carrying out their 'redistributionist' or 'reformist' or 'antimilitary' program." Yet "redistributionist" was another conservative euphemism. What Schneider would not say was that liberals might use the mechanisms of government to gain social and economic justice for minorities. Reagan's was a pure white coalition, a coalition of the angry white working class and the white upper classes, of the white South and the white West, of white Catholics and white evangelicals, of white conservatives and white reactionary populists—a broadening and ripening of the Nixon coalition, which seethed with the same fears, the same resentments— resentments against a changing America. And it was a coalition that altered the nation's political balance.

That was politics. But there was also the tone of the country—its feelings. Ronald Reagan was a consequential president because he changed the attitude toward government and the conceptualization of politics. Historians have written of an "Age of Reagan" or a "Reagan Revolution." America was a different place when he left office than it had been when he arrived. Whether it was a better place largely depended on whether one was a conservative or a liberal, white or Black, rural or urban. During the Great Depression, Franklin Roosevelt had induced the American people to trust that their government would help them. Ronald Reagan induced them to believe that government was their enemy. Distrust of government

---

*One of Reagan's true successes—the signing of an Intermediate-Range Nuclear Forces Treaty with the Soviet Union in 1987, which reduced both America's and Russia's nuclear arsenals, and his laying the groundwork for the Strategic Arms Reduction Treaty—were not touted by conservatives because these two accomplishments challenged conservative orthodoxy that peace could be achieved only through strength.

began long before Reagan—with Vietnam and Lyndon Johnson's duplicities about that war and with Watergate and Richard Nixon's duplicities
about his own administration—but as Ted would later assess it, Reagan
took the distrust he had helped engender and "used it cleverly, politically,
to both enhance his own regime politically and also to further undercut
that opportunity for government to be a force." (Twenty years later, Ted
was to say, "We have not recovered from that.") It wasn't just that Reagan
denounced government and attempted to shrink it. It was that Reagan
intentionally incapacitated government, encouraged gridlock, then
pointed to it to demonstrate that government *couldn't* work, that it was, in
the words of one political scientist a "mischievous force—a parliament of
whores living off the self-governing and otherwise perfectible market system."

As Ted observed, the attitude remained—it would remain for decades—
but Reagan didn't fully succeed in the substance. While government
needed to do a lot of bobbing and weaving, it survived Reagan's ax. In
part, it survived because the social programs he sought to starve were already entrenched. As Reagan's budget director David Stockman later
wrote sneeringly, "The Reaganites were, in the final analysis, just plain
welfare state politicians like everybody else." And he added, "The only
thing the Reagan administration could do about federal spending"—the
federal spending that ballooned during his presidency—"was fake." In
part, Reagan's plan to shrink government failed because some Democrats
fought hard to limit those cuts to social programs, most notably Ted Kennedy, and once they were back in the congressional majority, they fought
hard to restore those cuts. Reagan had tried to slash the food stamps program, Aid to Families with Dependent Children (welfare, as the Republicans called it), and Medicare and Medicaid. He had succeeded until he
failed. Welfare spending, as Sean Wilentz noted, was higher in 1989 than
it had been in 1980, which was Stockman's point. And when it came to
legislation like the Voting Rights Act extension or the South African sanctions or the Civil Rights Restoration Act, all of which the administration
sought to change or defeat, and all three of which efforts it failed to
achieve, including two veto overrides, Reagan was caught in a moral contradiction of promoting values that he and conservatives argued would
serve the public good, especially economically—values like greed, self-
interest, and materialism—but that clashed with powerful liberal values
like generosity, selflessness, and spirituality. "Self-aggrandizement wrapped

in the flag," Ted called conservative moralism during the 1988 election campaign. "The nobility of people's motives has been blurred." And while he said that he had been able to beat back the worst of those assaults on morality, as he construed it, "they were victories of not going backward, rather than going forward." Those were Ted Kennedy's small victories.

So the Reagan Revolution might have seemed like more of a revolution than it really was—at least when it came to the functioning of government. Government activism slowed—slowed appreciably. But it didn't stop. Laurence Tribe, the Harvard Law professor who had helped Ted defeat Robert Bork, said that Reagan had declared, " 'I'm going to dismantle FDR,' and the country said, 'No.' 'I'm going to dismantle Earl Warren [the Warren Court],' and the country said, 'No.' It basically said, 'We like your 'shining city on a hill' "—a frequent reference of Reagan's borrowed from John Winthrop—" 'we're happy to fight the Soviet Union and maybe even have some weird Star Wars program, and we like 'Morning in America,' " one of Reagan's commercial taglines in 1984, " 'but we don't like taking away the safety nets [of social programs] or the constitutional safety nets.' It was basically two referenda, and on each of them, Reagan lost."

What did the Reagan Revolution come down to then? In the final analysis, for all his strenuous efforts to shred the social safety net, for all his efforts to strengthen institutions that helped the white and the wealthy and to weaken those, like labor unions, that helped the working class, it was much more of a psychological revolution than a governmental one. One historian noted how "American sensibilities changed dramatically in the decade after 1975," and Reagan was in no small measure responsible. "Ideas of relativism and complex causation were replaced by simpler and more sinister versions of the enemies facing Americans and their nation. And the forces of evil arrayed against us were conceived in terms of conspiracy and clandestine manipulation," with political rhetoric "permeated by themes of external threat, national vulnerability, subversion, and internal decadence." In effect, he got Americans to think less complexly about their world, which, for a politician, was a gift.

Reagan's was a special gift. Having come from the movies, he had entered the presidency thinking of it as a movie. In the movie he envisioned, the country was endangered by a plethora of nefarious forces. But in the movie, and in the presidency, Reagan could rally his fellow Americans to vanquish the threats. Jimmy Carter had preached realism and called Reagan a fantasist. But people didn't generally go to the movies for realism.

They went for release, for catharsis. Reagan *was* a fantasist, and he provided that catharsis. As another historian analyzed it, rather than think of the Reagan Era as a new Golden Age, which was how conservatives typically did, or as a new and blighted Gilded Age, as liberals did, "it is more illuminating to speak of an Era of Good Feelings, when most Americans felt better about themselves and their country, thanks partially to Ronald Reagan." Governance mattered to Ronald Reagan. He had an agenda. But the agenda was subordinated to the script. He simplified the world. He restored faith. He rebuilt national self-confidence. He gave Americans a happy ending. But at some cost.

These are not insubstantial accomplishments. Franklin Roosevelt's revolution had a large psychological component too. And while Ronald Reagan wound up giving much more to conservatism than conservatism ever gave to him, the movement did pay him back by spinning a mythology around him, after he left office, that perpetuated the idea of his leadership as exemplary. Over the decades, Ronald Reagan, a genial man with a Manichean view of the world, would be lionized as a great one. Over the decades, he would be transformed into the hero of the national film. And those who had opposed him would be reduced to supernumeraries. In effect, through Reagan, conservatives seized the national narrative. Ted's assessment, naturally, was much harsher. Reagan "failed to meet the ultimate criteria of greatness," he would write in his memoir, citing Reagan's opposition to civil rights and to social programs that helped the poor. He "led the country in the wrong direction, sensing and playing to its worst impulses at a moment in history that called for a higher vision." Mario Cuomo, New York's Democratic governor, had an equally withering assessment: "At his worst, Reagan made the denial of compassion respectable." Of all the things Ronald Reagan did, that might have been the most significant and enduring.

But that was not the view that survived. That was not the view the conservatives grafted onto history.

II

George H. W. Bush was no Ronald Reagan, which was both his blessing and his curse. He didn't have a script and didn't need one. He had been in government nearly all his life, not only as the son of a senator but also as an elected member of the House, and as the U.S. ambassador to the United

Nations, and as chief of the liaison office to China, and as CIA director, and as vice president for eight years. He knew Washington. He understood how to use the levers of power there. But power had changed in those last eight years. Ronald Reagan had changed it. He had made the narrative in governance as important as governance itself. Bush had little tolerance or aptitude for what he called the "vision thing," which was the very thing that Reagan was so good at: telling the big story or laying out the big picture. Bush came to the presidency with a lot of things to do but with no narrative in which to place them. "Bush holds office," Ted scoffed after Bush had been in the White House for only five weeks, "but doesn't know what to do with it."

But Ted Kennedy knew what to do with *his* power. Tom Rollins had left during the election year, and so had Greg Craig, Ted's foreign policy adviser. Typically, a departing staff member recommended a replacement; that was how the Kennedy staff kept replenishing itself. Craig had recommended yet another Harvard graduate, one who had taken his law degree at Penn and then embarked on an odyssey through various government posts, including, on the recommendation of Archibald Cox, running the Massachusetts Anti-Corruption Commission, and working on Dukakis's presidential campaign. (A professional singer and actor, he had also taken a break to do musical theater, joining the national company of *My Fair Lady*.) When Nick Littlefield came to Ted's office expecting to work on foreign policy, Ranny Cooper, the administrative assistant, told him that the Labor counsel—Rollins—had also left, and Littlefield took that opening rather than Craig's, feeling, as Ted had done in joining Labor, that it was a place where he could "make sure the underdog got a chance."

At that moment, Littlefield would say, "Everything shifted for me." He met Ted for the first time on election night in 1988, and then again a month later at the Harvard Club in Boston, where Ted ran down his list of objectives. "We got to raise the minimum wage, we want to get healthcare for everybody, we want to do something about improving the schools," Ted said. Littlefield was writing this all down on a napkin and saying to himself, "Oh, my god!" In actuality, the Democratic Policy Committee, on which Ted sat, identified sixty-three items on its agenda for the first two years of the new Bush administration. In the Reagan administration, the lists had been shorter and nearly everything had been adversarial. Ted had had to push constantly, frustratingly, eking out his small victories and that handful of big ones. George Bush was not adversarial. George Bush was as much of a pragmatist as Ted Kennedy. Ted's job now was to pull as much legislation as he could to his Labor Committee, crafting bills so that taxes were never required because all bills relying directly on tax revenue went to the Finance Committee; instead, he looked to appropriations or user fees or, in the case of healthcare, employer mandates. And having pulled legislation to his committee, Ted then took those bills about which he cared most and sent them to the full committee rather than to subcommittees, as he had often done as chair of the Judiciary Committee, so that he could retain jurisdiction without having to make compromises with his fellow Democrats, knowing that he would later have to make compromises with the Republicans, and where he could expedite the process of drafting the bill. (Ted also kept half of the money appropriated to the majority for his own staffing and allocated the rest to the other Democratic senators on the committee.) It was a tight committee—not only tightly run, which it was, but tight in terms of the comity among the Democrats, while Republicans came and went because they were having to cast difficult votes, votes against liberal programs that the Republican caucus insisted on squeezing, but votes that they might have to defend in an election. For them, it was not worth the risk.

He was "onto the barricades," Ted would say then, and he was onto the barricades often, though not having to fight Bush so much as having to nudge him. Democrats would not always be happy with the collaboration, but Ted knew, from his dispiriting relationship with Reagan, what it was like to fight hard only to accomplish little, to have, as he had said, only "victories of not going backward." Paul Kirk said he knew that many times Ted's fellow Democrats would say to him, "What are you doing that for?" meaning working with Bush. "We need the issue." And Ted would say to them, "No. We need the results. That's what we need. We need the results." That first year he focused initially on the minimum wage, which the new Senate majority leader, George Mitchell of Maine, had placed fourth on the docket, S.4, a sign of its importance to the party. There hadn't been an increase in the statutory minimum wage since January 1, 1981, when the floor had been set at $3.35 an hour; there hadn't been a bill passed since 1977. Conservatives had adamantly opposed minimum wage increases—they had opposed the law when Franklin Roosevelt introduced it in 1938—on the basis that the market sets wages, not the government, and in an argument they hoped would appeal to workers, that a higher minimum wage would result in businesses firing workers or not hiring new ones, so that it became a matter, incongruously, of Republicans claiming to be fighting to save jobs. The liberal argument, even truer after Reagan had disemboweled labor unions, was that everyone was entitled to a living wage, and that workers often did not have the power to fight business.

There was no chance of Reagan ever signing a minimum wage increase, even if Ted could have gotten it through Congress. But George Bush was not averse, or at least he was not *as* averse. It would be very different working with Bush because Ted would now be working with him less over the bill itself than over the margins of the bill, haggling with the administration rather than butting heads with it—haggling because Bush was just as eager to use S.4 to demonstrate to the conservatives that he could be as tough as Reagan with the Democrats, as the Democrats were to use it to show not only that they cared about workers but also that Bush couldn't kick them around the way Reagan had. Ted had proposed a fifty-cent-a-year increase over three years that would eventually raise the minimum wage to $4.65 an hour. Bush insisted he would accept nothing higher than $4.25. But he also included another provision. He wanted a "training wage"—a subminimum wage to be paid for the first six months of a worker's hiring. Ted countered that such a wage would prompt businesses to fire older workers earning a higher wage and hire younger workers earning the new, lower one. He got his bill through his Labor Committee in early March. The House passed it later that month with only minor alterations—a $4.55-per-hour wage with a two-month training period. But now a veto hung over the bill, should the Senate pass it—a veto that, according to *The New York Times,* Bush actually welcomed as, in the words of Thomas Mann of the Brookings Institution, a "shot at showing macho by hanging tough." By one account, the administration was planning a veto "ceremony" to be staged at an economically distressed community just to rub it in. The differences involved were small; the political points were large. During the Senate debate that April, Ted argued that the Republican contention, advanced by its erstwhile ally, the Chamber of Commerce, that the minimum wage cost jobs was patently untrue, and the data showed it. In fact, employment had risen, he insisted, after a rise in the minimum wage. And Ted argued, and argued vehemently, something else: that while wages had largely been stagnant through the Reagan years, compensation for chief executives had skyrocketed—300 percent, 400 percent, 500 percent—as Republicans cried "crocodile tears" for the workers whose wages they were fighting against raising. After the debate, Bush countered by proposing a forty-five-cent-per-year increase over two years. But Ted wasn't ready for a full compromise yet. Ted's bill passed the Senate on May 17, 63 to 37, with Ted scaling back to the $4.55 in the House bill and reluctantly accepting a subminimum training wage, though limiting it to sixty days, as in the House bill, rather than the six months that Bush had called for. That same day, April 6, Bush threatened again to veto. When the House and Senate bills went to conference, were reconciled, and then were passed again, Bush made good on his threat, issuing the first veto of his presidency. (He signed it not in a distressed community but on Air Force One.) "We perceive it to be a forerunner of a number of issues that will follow," House minority leader Robert Michel said, indicating that Bush was going to keep flashing his toughness. Even so, Bush maintained he had compromised. "But with whom has the President compromised?" Ted asked. "Possibly with himself, but certainly not with Congress, for he has never once talked with us about the minimum wage. He has only talked at us."

But now came the difference between the last administration and the new one. Bush had to pacify the conservatives, but he was no extremist himself. Once Ted resubmitted his bill, the haggling began. Ted conceded to Bush's ceiling of $4.25 per hour to be achieved over two years, and to an exemption for small businesses with less than $500,000 in revenue. The administration conceded to a $3.61 training wage, over the $3.35 it had originally proposed, still to be paid for the first six months, but restricting the recipients to workers between sixteen and nineteen years old. The bill easily passed both the House and the Senate, 89 to 8 in the latter, with the vote being greeted by cheers by labor representatives awaiting the result in an antechamber. (Labor had opposed a raise in the minimum wage previously; now it was onboard.) Bush would sign it. Twelve years Ted Kennedy had waited to raise the minimum wage. And now it was finally done. "We need the results," he had said. He had one.

Now he was looking for another. Rosemary Kennedy, Ted's mentally handicapped older sister, had been the phantom of her famous family—the one who was scarcely mentioned and when she was, as a kind of accident. Rose spoke of what had happened to her—the lobotomy that Joe Kennedy had approved in 1941—euphemistically, saying that a "neurological disturbance or disease of some sort seemingly had overtaken her, and it was becoming progressively worse," which was why it was decided she "should undergo a certain form of neurosurgery." The form, noneuphemistically, was the lobotomy, leaving her "permanently incapacitated," in Rose's words. John Tunney, who was probably as close to Ted as anyone, said that there was "no clarity" from Ted, as Tunney put it, about Rosemary's condition. "I never asked, nor did he tell me exactly how much he could say or not say after her operation." Tunney never even knew whether she could talk. Ted said he had been close to Rosemary when he was a boy, that they would play together with a ball or chase each other in tag or "other children's games," because Rosemary "always seemed to be willing to spend more time with me than the others," meaning his other siblings. When she was sent off to the convent in Wisconsin, after her form of neurosurgery, Ted often visited her there, and Carey Parker would say that every time Ted returned from one of those visits, he would tell Parker, "We have to do this."

"This" was a law to assist the disabled. As president, John Kennedy, also moved by his sister's plight, had formed a federal agency, the Bureau of Handicapped, to investigate issues that affected them. But despite these efforts, they were largely left on the sidelines of society. Most of the early legal intervention was judicial, and most of it dealt with educating the handicapped. Ted had been one of the original co-sponsors of the Education for All Handicapped Children Act of 1975 that provided government assistance for court-mandated access to education by those who suffered disabilities. (By that time Ted Jr. had had his amputation, so Ted was especially sensitive to the issue.) Lowell Weicker, who was deeply involved in disability issues as well, would later say that Robert Stafford of Vermont and Ted "get the main credit here," though afterward Weicker would be responsible for amendments to the act that, among other things, lowered the age of the children to whom it applied. "The golden years of achievement," Weicker was to call that period from the 1970s to the '80s in terms of legislation. But education was relatively easy. Few could object to providing handicapped children with educational access, and even Ronald Reagan signed Weicker's amendments to the act without complaint.

What Weicker had in mind next, however, was more daunting and far more likely to raise objections: Weicker wanted to ensure that the disabled had the same rights as the able-bodied, which meant the same rights to access, not just in schools but in all public accommodations. At the time when the law was first being discussed, the only statute protecting the disabled was Section 504 of the Rehabilitation Act of 1973 that outlawed discrimination against them by any institution or program receiving federal funds; it was Ted's Civil Rights Restoration Act, undoing the Supreme Court's *Grove City* decision, that had applied Section 504 institution-wide, regardless of whether only one department of an institution received those funds. But Section 504, while it recognized the disabled as a class rather than divide them by their disabilities, was limited; it reached only institutions receiving those public funds. It did not reach restaurants, hospitals, theaters, office buildings, or public transportation facilities that did not receive federal funds. Moreover, the Reagan administration had worked hard to put restrictions on Section 504. Something needed to be done. Ted was not the only member of Congress for whom this issue was personal. Weicker had a son with Down syndrome. Senator Tom Harkin of Iowa had a deaf brother and a nephew who had been left a paraplegic after being sucked into a jet engine while he was serving on an aircraft carrier. Orrin Hatch's brother-in-law had survived polio but needed a breathing apparatus to get through the night. Bob Dole, the Senate minority leader, had his war injury that had forced him into two years of painful rehabilitation and would require him to hold his right arm, stiff and useless, at an angle, usually with a pen stuck in his clenched fingers to try to disguise the situation. In the House, Majority Whip Tony Coelho suffered from epilepsy and had been denied entry into a Catholic seminary because of it (his priest said epilepsy was still regarded as possession by the devil), and Representative Steny Hoyer's wife was an epileptic.

Though the disabled had many advocates, giving them a full array of rights would not be an easy crusade. Curing discrimination on the basis of disability required action and great expense to level the playing field—removing a physical barrier, building a ramp, providing an assistive listening device, buying an accessible vehicle for transportation. And the relief for discrimination could be costly too—back pay and penalties. Businesses, and the Chamber of Commerce that represented them, complained, fearing that the costs required to retrofit for the disabled would be prohibitive. The National Federation of Independent Business, the largest association of small businesses in America, objected on the same grounds. Both, however, appreciating the politics of opposing aid for the disabled, looked for accommodations. The National Association of Evangelicals was also opposed, and it sought no accommodations, arguing that the federal government had no right to tell them how to modify their churches to assist the handicapped. And, of course, with the business and religious right communities in opposition, there was Republican opposition as well. Weicker had been the shepherd for the bill, introducing it in April 1988, and he had asked Ted to be one of the co-sponsors with him—there were thirteen—since the two had worked together not only on legislation but also on the Special Olympics, the athletic competition for the disabled, that Ted's sister Eunice had founded. Weicker knew there was little chance of it being passed before the end of the congressional session, but he wanted the issue to be raised—raised so that he could submit a bill again in the new session. But Weicker, a liberal Republican, lost his reelection bid in 1988. And now Pat Wright, a disability activist, who had led a long and ultimately successful fight against the Reagan administration's attempts to amend and weaken both Section 504 and the Education for All Handicapped Children Act in the service of deregulation, asked Ted to champion Weicker's bill.

Weicker's had been an ambitious bill, perhaps too ambitious. It had in fact been drafted by an attorney at the National Council on Disability, an advocacy group, in an act of desperation after the Reagan administration failed to act on the recommendations of a panel on disability that Reagan himself had created. But the attorney had little sensitivity to the politics of it or to whether his bill could pass Congress. Ted said that Weicker had briefed him on the bill when he was first thinking of introducing it, and even Ted was a bit aghast at the scale. "He wanted to retrofit every railroad car, every tramway car, every [flight of] stairs, every elevator, every everything. The cost of this thing, even for a big spender, was out of sight, and I could see it wasn't going anyplace." But Ted said that Weicker was "so committed and so strong on it" that he worked with Weicker to try to get it into legislative shape. Though Ted had inherited the bill, he let Tom Harkin, with his deep personal stake, introduce it in the Senate and take the chairmanship of the Labor subcommittee that would hold hearings on it, and he let Harkin floor-manage the bill, effectively giving Harkin parentage of it. Harkin was to call it "one of the most generous, kindest things anyone has ever done for me." It wasn't entirely generosity, however. Harkin had told Ted of his interest in disability issues, and in order to lure Harkin, a solid liberal vote, away from accepting a position on John Glenn's Government Operations Committee, after Glenn had asked Harkin to join, Ted offered him the chairmanship of a new Subcommittee on the Handicapped. Even with Harkin's floor leadership, however, Ted still did a lot of the legislative heavy lifting. After Bush's election, at Ted's behest, Carolyn Osolinik said she took a "very hard look" at the Weicker-Harkin bill when it was about to be introduced and had her own concerns about it, chief among them what she called an "unreasonable threshold" up to which an employer or owner of a public accommodation would have to go to accommodate an individual with a disability: bankruptcy. Ted had told her long ago that "you can't start a legislative effort with something that's unreasonable because that's all that will ever be remembered." So Ted adjusted the bill accordingly—adjusted it so that it might make it through the Senate.

The bill's advocates knew this: that while there was dispute over the breadth of the bill and its cost, it was difficult to dispute the necessity of the bill. Among those who testified at the first hearing before Harkin's subcommittee that May was Joseph Danowsky, a legally blind young man, who despite his disability had been graduated from the University of Pennsylvania summa cum laude and was elected to Phi Beta Kappa, and who then attended Harvard Law School, only to find when he received his degree that of six hundred corporations he contacted for a job, not one made him an offer, due to his disability. Among those who testified was Mary DeSapio, a financial consultant and a vice president at Josephthal & Co. brokerage when she was diagnosed with breast cancer and had to undergo surgery, then returned to her job a month later to be told she was terminated immediately—*immediately*—because of her illness. Among those who testified was Dr. Mary Lynn Fletcher, the director of disability services in Lenoir, Tennessee, wheelchair-bound, who told the committee, "I live in agony from week to week as to how I shall be able to get my groceries or how I can get gas for my car," since the stations there were self-service. Among those who testified was Perry Tillman III of New Orleans, who lost the use of his legs during a helicopter crash while serving in Vietnam and who now couldn't get to the hearing in public transportation because there was no provision for his wheelchair, and he couldn't use the restroom outside the hearing room because there were no accommodations for his wheelchair, and whose own home was not wheelchair accessible, so his five-foot-two-inch mother had to carry him up the stairs.

There was no dispute about that necessity, but Ted and Harkin and Dole and Durenberger, the four who led the Senate fight, the latter two with some misgivings about the extent of the bill and the cost of compliance, still had to haggle. Ted had to haggle with the disability activists, who were a fractious group. Weicker had said that one of the things that had kept a disability act from advancing was that the "groups couldn't agree among themselves"; there were schisms among those who suffered from each particular disability and between the physically disabled and the mentally disabled and between factions of those groups and the victims of AIDS, who were bidding to be included in any bill for the rights of the disabled, even as they themselves questioned whether the idea of disability really fit them. Weicker and Ted had asked each of the groups to compromise in the service of finding what Weicker called a "common denominator"—a bill that would address the disabled as a single class. But Weicker said, "Everybody had their own nation; nobody wanted to give up whatever it was that they had fought for." And he would say that "Kennedy was key to that"—the key to bringing the groups together. And Ted was able to rally those groups. He had a disability staff person named Connie Garner, and Carey Parker said, "Sometimes he would call her and say, 'We have a difficult markup coming and we need your strong interest and support on this.' So she'd contact the disability community, and they'd send one hundred people in wheelchairs to the Capitol to support us." He had to haggle with other senators. Osolinik recalled talking to Ted in the Senate cloakroom, and he told her, "Well, we're going to have to give them two, and we're going to get two," speaking of trade-offs with the Republicans. And he asked her, "Which two do we *need*?" And then she said, he picked up the phone and called Attorney General Richard Thornburgh, who had been helping smooth the way for the bill with the administration because Thornburgh too had a personal interest in the bill, a deep personal interest. His wife had been killed in an automobile accident in 1960 after driving him to work, and his four-month-old son, Peter, was severely injured in that accident with multiple skull fractures that left him with mental impairments. When Harkin introduced the Americans with Disabilities Act (ADA), President Bush asked Thornburgh if he would be the administration point man, a role he said that he gladly assumed. And Ted would call him to see if he could get the administration to accept the modifications. Thornburgh, Ted said, "did it."

But above all, even with Thornburgh's devotion and assistance, Ted had to haggle with the administration that Thornburgh served and from whose loop Thornburgh was often excluded. Bush might have been a pragmatist, he might not have been opposed to what amounted to a civil rights act for the disabled, but he was nevertheless beholden to and frightened of the conservatives who largely disdained him, most of whom were nowhere near as inclined to pass such a bill as he was. Weicker had groused that Bush had said he supported the ADA while he was campaigning for president, then did nothing to advance it, which was not entirely true. Bush had in fact, after his election but before his inauguration, addressed a disabilities group and come out for the ADA. But some conservatives in his administration wanted to stop a bill, and Ted was concerned about how Bush would react to them. He would later say that the real question at the time was whether the liberals and their Republican allies could get Bush to "move," especially since the administration's negotiators did everything they possibly could to slow the process and keep the bill from getting to the floor.

It was a long bill, a difficult bill to hammer out, a bill with many parts and nuances. Carolyn Osolinik, who worked on it with Harkin's top aide, Robert Silverstein, even though she was attached to Judiciary and the bill was going through Labor, said that the Senate staffers and the administration representatives met as many as five times a week that spring, sometimes in meetings that lasted all day. Ted had wanted to craft a bill at the outset that would win the administration's approval. But those aides Bush had entrusted to negotiate the bill seemed to have little desire to give that approval. Instead, the administration's representatives kept haggling, as Bush always seemed to haggle, scrutinizing the bill line by line, foot-dragging, while the House Republicans refused to meet with the Democrats altogether, Osolinik felt, in order to put the brakes on a bill that might, in the Republicans' view, move too quickly to passage, and she was right. By April, she said, it became clear that neither the administration nor the House Republicans were going to cooperate. As one White House staffer described the administration's strategy, it was to "piss off Kennedy and wait till after the August recess," to slow everything down, while Ted, they believed, was hoping to move the bill through the Senate and then send it to the House as quickly as he could once the recess ended. The administration seemed to be prevailing. The bill that George Bush said he supported had stalled. If it stalled long enough, it would be held over until the next Congress, when all of them—the disability groups, the administration, the House and Senate—would have to start the entire legislative process all over again.

Ted Kennedy wanted results, *needed* results, and he tried to resuscitate the bill. But the biggest roadblock now was Bush's chief of staff, John Su-

nunu, one of those conservatives who seemed to have no interest in passing the ADA. (Sununu later told writer Lennard Davis, a historian of the
ADA, that he was only doing the bidding of White House counsel C. Boyden Gray, who was appeasing the business community.) That summer Ted
made an appointment to see Sununu in the West Wing of the White
House in an effort to convince him to push the legislation, and Ted said
that Sununu was "decent" to him but also "very abrupt." "Look," Sununu
said bluntly. "We're not going to support any social legislation. We're not
going to consider any such legislation during the sessions of Congress." It
was the Reagan administration all over again: appease the conservatives.
But just as Sununu was laying down his edict, Ted said he spotted the
president passing Sununu's office, and Ted asked him if he could have a
word. Ted explained to Bush why he was there, and he said that Bush told
him, "Well, that's of some interest to me, and I'll talk to John further
about it." But Bush also warned that he could make no promises given the
"program and the schedule."* That began, Ted said, a series of meetings
over the summer with people who supported the bill and were close to
Bush or to Sununu—the resuscitation.

But despite these discussions, despite the pressure placed on Sununu,
he kept trying to sabotage the legislation by picking on the staff members
who knew the most about it. Over the Fourth of July weekend, as Osolinik
was secretly working with administration negotiators and a few representatives of the disability community to narrow the differences—secretly to
keep Sununu and other opponents in the White House from torpedoing
those negotiations—Ted phoned her to say that Sununu had called him
and told him that the reason they hadn't been able to resolve their differences was Osolinik herself and that if Ted would fire her, they could reach
an agreement. Ted would never betray his staff, and he didn't then. But
Osolinik thought that it demonstrated the Bush forces didn't want tough
and knowledgeable negotiators across the table from them if, Osolinik
said, "they were going to get what the business community needed." Su-

* It is difficult to determine how involved Bush was or whether he was posturing. Tom Harkin told Bush biographer Jon Meacham that he too had talked with Bush that spring, presumably before Ted would, at a cordial get-together in the White House's private quarters,
and that Harkin, reluctantly, given the social occasion, told Bush about the problems with
Sununu. As Meacham reports it, Bush turned to Boyden Gray, his counsel, and said, "I
want you to take this over and get it done." But Sununu still resisted. Jon Meacham, *Destiny and Power: The American Odyssey of George Herbert Walker Bush* (New York: Random
House, 2015), 395.

nunu tried bullying the staff again at a big meeting on July 28, in Bob Dole's capacious minority leader's office at the Capitol where Ted, Dole, Harkin, Orrin Hatch, Senator David Durenberger, Thornburgh, Secretary of Transportation Samuel Skinner, and Senate staff members, including Osolinik, Harkin's staffer Bob Silverstein, and White House staffers, were in attendance—a summit, it seemed, to see if they could finally reach an agreement. Sununu tried to command the meeting. He kept asking how businesses could afford to comply, kept raising objections, kept throwing out hypotheticals. Silverstein, who had brought a stack of black binders—the provisions of the act—on a luggage cart, knew the bill as well as anyone and made mental rebuttals, but he dared not rebut Sununu verbally, even as Ted accused the White House chief of staff of "fly-specking" the bill. But finally Silverstein gathered his courage to challenge Sununu on one point. To which Sununu said, "Every time I say something, you always bring something up," which hadn't been true. And then he said: "I don't want to hear from you anymore." Osolinik recalled that after that "you could hear a pin drop." "An ugly moment," she called it. Harkin, whose staffer Silverstein was, said nothing, clearly not wanting to further infuriate Sununu, who was already plenty infuriated. Lennard Davis would report that Harkin shuffled papers nervously. And then, after an interminable silence, an "ugly" silence, Ted exploded. He slammed the table hard with his fist and leaped to his feet, leaning in to Sununu. Harkin said that he thought Ted was going to "grab him by the collar." Ted stuck his finger in Sununu's face and, shouting at him now, red-faced, which was how Ted flushed when he was angry, said, as Lennard Davis would recount it: "If you want to yell at anybody, you yell at me, or you yell at Senator Harkin. You don't go after the staff! You go after the big boys. You got something to say, you say it to me. You want to yell at me? You go right ahead and yell at me!" Sununu grumbled that they should make the staff leave the room. To which Ted countered that Sununu should go because he, after all, was staff too. And as Davis told it, Sununu slunk in his chair, his face drained—the bully finally confronted.

But if John Sununu had been confronted, he hadn't surrendered. The haggling, the foot-dragging, the fly-specking continued during several days of what Ted called "long, tough, hard bargaining," even though publicly the opponents, including business, still had to tread lightly for fear of seeming insensitive to the disabled. As the woman responsible for coordinating lobbying for the Chamber of Commerce admitted, "No politician can vote against the bill and survive." Sununu, however, was not voting against the bill—he was in no position to vote—just using delaying tactics against it. During another visit to the White House later that summer where Ted met again with Sununu—Ted made a point of bringing Osolinik—Sununu, who had been the governor of New Hampshire, kept throwing out more hypotheticals: "What's it going to mean in New Hampshire at the Sunapee Ski Resort?" Suppose a handicapped person came. He wanted to know if the resort owners would have to retrofit every chair on the ski lift. And when Ted answered that they would have to make a "reasonable accommodation," Sununu wanted to know exactly what a reasonable accommodation would be. "What about Keene, New Hampshire?" Sununu asked. Suppose a handicapped person came to a bookstore there. He wanted to know if the owner would have to put in steps if the store wasn't at street level. Suppose a blind person came into the store. He wanted to know whether the cashier would have to help that person with a book, and how long the cashier would have to help that person, and what would happen if that cashier had to leave the cash register unattended, and if there were customers who wanted to pay, how they would do so. Sununu's fallback position was that the law could apply to restaurants and hotels and theaters, but not to other private establishments. Ted and Harkin disagreed emphatically; Harkin argued that it made no sense that a disabled person could get a pastrami sandwich from a restaurant but not medications from a pharmacy. Still, the upshot of the meetings was that Ted, always conscientious, always compromising, went back to the committee and talked with Dole and talked with Hatch and made adjustments to the bill to find some common ground with the administration that clearly did not want the bill.*

By that point, however, Ted Kennedy was finished haggling. He had come to realize that the Bush administration wanted to subject every part of the bill to the Republican leadership's approval rather than seek compromise, which was always Ted's preferred way of doing business. (Of

---

*Dole had co-sponsored Weicker's bill but up to this point had not co-sponsored Harkin's, one scholar speculates, because he realized it was going to pass and wanted to wrest concessions, most likely that the enforcement could not place "undue hardship" on those expected to comply. Apparently, Dole wrested those concessions from Ted and signed on as a co-sponsor before the bill passed the committee. Ruth Colker, "The ADA's Journey Through Congress," *Wake Forest Law Review* 39 (Spring 2004): 12.

course, it was entirely possible Bush felt that between Thornburgh's advocacy for the disabled and Sununu's for business, the right bill would emerge—one that balanced those interests.) After the meeting with Sununu, Ted called another meeting, this one with the disability activists, and asked them what they felt were the most important provisions of the bill. They named access to transportation; access to buildings; access to medical care; access to shopping; and access to telecommunications. And with that answer, these now formed the basis of the act that Ted would propose to simplify. He simplified, too, the number of participants at the meetings—simplified it so that there would be fewer individuals to satisfy, fewer who could complain. At the beginning of the process, David Durenberger said that Ted had told him, "Drafting a bill like this was like playing the accordion. First you pull it open, fill it up with air, and then you squeeze it out." And now Ted was squeezing out the air. Armed with the list of provisions, he and Harkin and Durenberger met in Dole's office again, with their staffers, and they agreed on the fundamental issues and signed off on a bill. "This is the play," Ted would later recall of that meeting, meaning the best bill he could get. "And that's the way life is." He didn't get everything. But he got results.

And now came the markup of the bill on August 2—a massive bill. But because, by Senate rules, a committee cannot meet after the Senate has been in session for two hours until the chamber adjourns, and because opponents of the bill would not waive the rule as was customarily done, the markup had to be postponed until nine o'clock that evening. Late that night Ted and the other committee members went through the bill, slowly, while some of those members got tired and left. Strom Thurmond took out a book and began reading aloud. "I plan to read and read and read and read," he said, which would have brought the markup to a halt. So Ted got his disability staffer Connie Garner to contact Patrisha Wright, the fearless disability advocate who was legally blind herself, and that very night, late that night, Wright rustled up a band of the disabled, many of them arriving at the committee room in their wheelchairs, and at two a.m. the television cameras started arriving as well. Ted recalled there were two cameras at first, and then three, and then five and seven and nine. And then Strom Thurmond put down his book, and with the array of cameras keeping watch, the committee passed the bill. And now it headed, finally, to the Senate floor, where the disability activists had already identified senators who had a personal connection to disability and where Ted, Harkin, and Dole would approach them, talk to them, and try to win their support.

But there were a handful of Republicans still determined to prevent the Americans with Disabilities Act from passing, as there had been senators determined to stop the Civil Rights Act from passing. During the debate, Jesse Helms, the dogged racist from North Carolina who opposed any assistance to Black people or the poor or, in this case, the disabled, rose to ask Ted, "My brother owns a motel in North Carolina, and if there's a cross-dresser bringing children into it, and he's clearly going to molest them, can my brother keep them out or does the Americans with Disabilities Act bar him from discriminating?" And to sabotage the bill, Jesse Helms had gotten hold of the *Diagnostic and Statistical Manual of Mental Disorders*, and, using an old tactic, was reading through those disorders— a long process—in order to submit an amendment that excluded individuals with sexual aberrations (which he regarded as any deviations from heterosexual norms) from collecting damages under the act. (Helms's real aim was to make sure that homosexuals were not covered and to see if, since AIDS was perforce largely a homosexual problem, AIDS too could be excluded.)

Ted was worried by Helms's strategy—worried because only one day had been designated for debate, and he thought Helms's litany of disorders would take the air out of the legislative effort at this, its final hour. (The limited debate was intentional lest opponents to the bill gain time to challenge it. "It's a great lesson about not leaving things around the floor of the United States Senate," Ted would later say, meaning not prolonging debate.) As Helms was debating, Ted told Osolinik that "we have to resolve whatever issues there are tonight, because if this thing kicks over, we're going to lose it." Years later he would say, "I could just see this whole thing unraveling, gradually unraveling"—unraveling after all the months of work. Bush's congressional liaison, Bill Roper, a medical doctor, was outside the chamber when Ted expressed his concerns to him. Roper asked, "Will you take a third?" meaning a third of the disorders Helms was about to read. Ted had no choice but to agree—agree as a way of saving the bill. So Roper struck a bargain with Helms, whose amendment passed. (Among the "disorders" not included in the bill was, as Helms had hoped, homosexuality; AIDS, however, was included among the disabilities covered by the act.) Now Helms had been disarmed. And so had the evangelicals because Durenberger submitted an amendment exempting religious institutions and private clubs from the bill, and his amendment was approved. The bill, thus amended, passed the Senate on September 26, with only eight dissenters, all conservative Republicans, including Helms. Harkin, whose bill it was, delivered his remarks on the floor in sign language as a tribute to his brother. The House would follow several months later with its vote, and President Bush promised to sign it.

Though its passage received remarkably little attention in the press, given the magnitude of its jurisdiction—this was in some measure because the disability activists had tried their best to keep the process from being discussed in the media for fear it would only draw opposition—the ADA was landmark legislation. It covered more than forty million Americans, making it the most extensive civil rights act in history. The railings and ramps and "curbless" curbs and elevators and automatic doors and widened doorways to accommodate wheelchairs, and the technologies so that the deaf could see the dialogue when they attended a theater, and the lifts that were put on public transportation so that the disabled could use them, not to mention the legal rights that were now secured for the disabled—Ralph Neas of the Leadership Conference on Civil Rights called it the civil rights act of the disabled—these and thousands of other adjustments and modifications that would change the lives of the disabled and change the entire country, were there only because of the tenacity of those who worked for the passage of the Americans with Disabilities Act—above all, the disability community, which had drafted and pressured and lobbied. And Ted said on the day of that passage, "This legislation will go down as one of the most important accomplishments in the history of the Congress."

Senators, Ted included, were known for hyperbole. This was no hyperbole. And yet on the July day on the White House lawn where the president would sign the bill into law, that president chose not to honor all those who had worked for it. It was a bright warm day, and the lawn was a "sight to behold," recalled Bob Dole, who had been instrumental in gaining passage: people in wheelchairs, people with white canes, people with sight dogs, people on gurneys. Enormous crowds, three thousand people, celebrating, though some individuals who should have been there were missing. Among those who were not there was Lowell Weicker, who had first introduced the bill—absent because he had been invited by the White House and then was later disinvited. Among those who were not there was Ralph Neas, whose lobbying had moved the bill to passage. Among those who were not near the table was Tom Harkin, who introduced the bill, and floor-managed the bill, and along with Ted had argued for it and pushed for it and fought for it—he was kept far from that table because he would be running for reelection later in the year and the White House preferred not to give him a boost. Among those who were at the back of the gathering, far from the desk on which the law was signed, were Patrisha Wright, without whom there would have been no law; and Ted Kennedy, Jr., who, after his amputation, had become a disability activist in his own right and who had worked with Governor Dukakis to get the disabled employed; and among those far from the desk was Ted Kennedy, who had used his mastery of the chemistry and physics of the Senate to get the bill passed, and who had been given a seat nearer the table but chose instead to sit with his son and with Wright among the disabled who had lobbied for the bill and who had shouted in the halls of Congress for the bill and who had shown up at two in the morning at that committee room for the bill. *We need the results,* Ted Kennedy had said. That day, as George Bush signed the act, Ted Kennedy had a result—his first bill since Reagan's taking office that didn't prevent or scale back or undo or sanction or mitigate, the first bill that moved forward by guaranteeing new rights.

He had a result.

III

One reason why Jesse Helms and his fellow conservatives in the Senate and House had tried so hard to stop the bill was their suspicion that it was a Trojan horse, that its real objective was not helping the disabled but helping homosexuals, whom Helms openly and vocally detested. (For years, he had worked tirelessly to remove homosexuals from the protections of Section 504.) Ted and Harkin had both argued forcefully for the inclusion of HIV-positive individuals, those with a virulent and fatal illness that had been ravaging the gay community, and victims of acquired immune deficiency syndrome (AIDS), the last stage of the disease caused by HIV, in the ADA. Harkin went so far as to say that he hoped their inclusion would set a precedent for other legislation. The legislative record was clear: AIDS was covered by the act. It was one of the spurs for the act. But that was precisely Helms's fear. AIDS was a homosexual disease, he had said. Most victims—60 percent in 1990—had acquired the disease through homosexual activities. In the House, the Republican minority of the Energy and Commerce Committee had filed a report of its own, citing those statistics and calling the ADA a "homosexual rights bill in disguise." To help the disabled was one thing, though many of those conservatives were still wary of any expansion of civil rights. To help homosexuals was something else again.

As their efforts in Congress, or lack thereof, made clear, these conservatives had no sympathy for the plight of the AIDS victims. Indeed, during the Reagan administration, their antipathy to homosexuality had slowed the government's response to the AIDS epidemic—another case in which moralism defeated morality. Reagan himself seemed indifferent to the AIDS epidemic as he was indifferent to homosexuality itself. He was no homophobe;* it was hard to be homophobic in Hollywood where there was a great deal of homosexuality. But the evangelicals who supported him were homophobes. "AIDS is God's judgement on a society that does not live by His rules," the Reverend Jerry Falwell of the Moral Majority said. Whether as a nod to those supporters or whether he simply was uninterested, Reagan scarcely mentioned the AIDS epidemic in the first years of his presidency, even as the number of cases and the number of deaths soared. Ted Kennedy had had no particular interest in gay issues either, though no hostility to the gay community. A tough Bostonian himself, Eddie Martin, Ted's old administrative assistant, had warned him during his presidential campaign, "If you come out for gay rights, the steelworkers in Boston are not going to vote for you." Ted didn't seem to worry. During that campaign, he actively courted gay voters, attending a fundraiser in Los Angeles at which he pledged to support an executive order banning discrimination against gays in federal hiring, and he vividly recalled an encounter at that meeting with an activist named Forrest. "You have to be comfortable talking about these issues," Forrest advised him. "The community will understand"—Ted said "understand," but no doubt meant "sense"—"if you're nervous about talking about them, if you're uncomfortable talking about them." He said they would be watching Ted to see if he flinched when they shook his hand or slapped him on

* At least not publicly. Jesse Helms claimed that when he showed Reagan a comic book produced by the Gay Men's Health Crisis and depicting "safe sex"—a book that had been funded with a grant from the Centers for Disease Control—Reagan looked at a few pages, slapped it shut, and pounded his desk with his fist. William Link, *Righteous Warrior: Jesse Helms and the Rise of Modern Conservatism* (New York: St. Martin's Press, 2008), 349.

the back. Ted would recollect that incident as a way of gauging how far gay rights had come in the years since. Ted didn't flinch. Later he worked with Paul Tsongas, who had introduced a bill banning discrimination against gays in employment—one of only five co-sponsors. Though the bill never got a hearing, it was, Ted said, a "place-marker in the movement."

Then came AIDS. Ted said he did not take the lead on the issue because neither he nor anyone on his staff had any expertise in it. Few did. But Dr. Mathilde Krim, the wife of the film executive Arthur Krim, who was a major Democratic contributor, and herself an expert in and activist for AIDS, asked if she could brief Ted on the disease in New York in the hope that she could convince Ted to hold hearings on the issue. Ted agreed, but it was 1983, he was in the minority and couldn't hold hearings, and he still had no staff in the area. So Krim offered to finance two aides, Terry Beirn and Mike Iskowitz, to educate Ted, and she made a deal with Ted that if they proved valuable, he would then assume their salaries. (At least, that was how Ted remembered it. Iskowitz, a gay man and at the time a recent law school graduate, would tell author Lennard Davis that he had become haunted by AIDS, and during an internship in Washington, he followed Ted for weeks, "stalking him," he said, until he finally got a chance to speak to him and recommend that Ted should hire a staffer to deal exclusively with AIDS. "Well, that would be you," Ted told him. Whether Krim paid for him or not, Iskowitz didn't say and might not have known.) Ted later called Beirn and Iskowitz "superstars." With them on staff, he said he had two people who "understood it [AIDS], had thought about it, had felt about it, could write about it, think and explain it, and it just sort of jump-started this whole process here," by which Ted meant promoting legislation to deal with the AIDS crisis. "I wanted to get some things done," he would say.

But in 1983 it was not enough for Ted Kennedy to want to get some things done. He needed a Republican in a Republican-controlled Senate as an ally. And AIDS was not an easy sell to Republicans then, many of whom also held religious objections to homosexuality. Orrin Hatch, though a strict Mormon, was the likeliest candidate, first, because he was the chairman of the Labor Committee, which would be considering the legislation; second, because the Labor Committee had two moderate Republicans, Weicker and Stafford, who were likely to vote with the Democrats, which put pressure on Hatch; and third, because Hatch and Ted had had a good working relationship, despite their wide differences on policy. Some among the conservatives intimated that Ted had even cast a "spell" on Hatch or, as *The New York Times* reported it in an article on Hatch's seeming transformation, "managed to take possession of Mr. Hatch's political soul." Actually, it was just Ted's understanding of people—of what people wanted. Hatch wanted to be perceived as reasonable and able to reach across the aisle, even to Ted Kennedy. Hatch was certainly proud of the relationship, proud of being considered a legislator now rather than a rabid ideologue, and Ted, returning the favor but also working the chemistry of the Senate, took the opportunity to compliment him at every turn, even insisting that Hatch accompany him to the signing ceremony of the extension of the Voting Rights Act of 1984, which Hatch had opposed, because, said Ted, "You could have stopped it, Orrin, and you didn't." And whether under Ted's influence, or through what he himself called a new maturity, or whether, as some suspected, he was positioning himself for appointment to the Supreme Court, he almost sounded like Ted in explaining why he was more sympathetic to social legislation: "In a wealthy society such as ours, we should take care of the sick, the infirm, the disabled and the handicapped," though, true to his conservative instincts, he said that private charity was the best means to do so, government the worst.

Nevertheless, Ted had to lure Hatch to work for an AIDS bill. He had Hatch meet with Elizabeth Glaser, the wife of the television star Paul Michael Glaser; she had contracted AIDS while getting a contaminated transfusion during childbirth and had become an early AIDS activist; and with the film star Elizabeth Taylor, who had an interest in AIDS from her friendship to Rock Hudson, who had died of the disease. "I think they made an impact on him," Ted was to say later. But Tom Rollins believed that Ted had made an even greater impact on Hatch. The two of them had many conversations on AIDS, he said, and Rollins cited one in particular—a "big heart-to-heart"—he called it, where Ted told Hatch that AIDS was the "public health crisis of our generation" and that "we would be judged by how well we responded to this thing." And Ted then introduced his first AIDS bill, on April 21, 1986, a bill to increase funding for AIDS research and encourage large population centers to coordinate networks of health reviews to better conquer the disease. It was reported out of the Labor Committee two months later, and while it never reached the floor, it had Hatch's backing. And that was the beginning.

•   •   •

But only the beginning. After the 1986 midterm elections, Ted was in the majority and was the chairman of the Labor Committee, which would have jurisdiction over AIDS legislation. Now the issue was whether he could get more, whether he could he get an AIDS bill through the Senate. Four years of Reagan's presidency had passed before the president addressed AIDS directly, and then primarily to say that he thought his administration had provided adequate funding for research: $126 million. But that was only a beginning too. Gradually, Reagan acknowledged the crisis and began to discuss it, notably denying that it was a homosexual disease, which was the stigma that had prevented greater government action. And to further study the disease, in June 1987, he created the President's Commission on HIV Infection. Two months later, with the momentum for AIDS legislation finally building, Ted introduced his bill calling for $1 billion for AIDS research and education, adding 725 employees at the National Institutes of Health to work on AIDS, and $150 million for states and localities to deal with the epidemic. By this point, the urgency of the AIDS epidemic was such that there was near-unanimity about something having to be done, and Republicans and Democrats were working together; the conservative Hatch and the liberal Kennedy were the floor managers. But only *near* unanimity. When the bill reached the floor for debate that April, its primary adversary was Senator Jesse Helms.

Helms was a man of few good intentions. He had come to the Senate in 1973 from having delivered television editorials for the Capitol Broadcasting Company, where his targets were familiar ones for the far right: liberals, of course, and Black people and Communists, who were really no different from liberals in his view, and who had infested the civil rights movement, which he adamantly opposed, believing that the federal government had no right to tell states what to do (he included segregation among the things the government could not ameliorate) and the media and abortionists and homosexuals, the last of which was why he opposed Ted's bill. No one personified the far right as much as Jesse Helms, who was a hero of the movement. Helms looked like a bantam rooster and had the attitude of a bantam rooster. He was peppery, cocksure, unyielding, and argumentative, a man who did not abide by the courtesies of the "world's most exclusive club," where the words of debate could be snarling but the attitude was always polite, almost certainly the most conservative member of the Senate, and certainly the most openly and unapologetically racist and homophobic member, a throwback to Jim Crow—Helms came armed with what Thomas Rollins called a "batch of amendments" designed to undermine the AIDS assistance that Ted had proposed. Helms's batch included all sorts of things—including one to ban the government from providing fresh needles to drug addicts even though sharing needles had spread the disease; Ted said the amendment was so broadly written that it would have the "ludicrous and deadly effect of preventing the doctors from giving medicine to their patients"—but Helms's big amendment was one that prohibited the government from providing any funds that would encourage homosexual activity. Even though a similar amendment of Helms's had passed when attached to a spending bill the year before, proponents of AIDS education knew that it would hamstring efforts to control the disease since educating individuals on "safe sex" might be construed under Helms's amendment as encouraging homosexual activities.

Ted was enraged. So was Helms. Helms fulminated against homosexuals, called opponents of his amendment the "homosexual crowd," and practically dared senators who had voted for such a prohibition a year earlier to vote against it now, with the veiled threat that they would be tarred as homosexual advocates in an election campaign if they did. It was a mean encounter, bristling with anger and vituperation on both sides, the kind of encounter one seldom saw on the Senate floor, an encounter in which Ted shouted at Helms, "You distort and misrepresent!" when Helms reneged on a promise he had made to him privately, to which Helms shouted back, "Talk about misrepresentation! You have raised it to a fine art, Senator!" and Rollins said the two of them almost came to blows. And then Helms and Hatch, who had the look of a mortician, tall, thin, neat, and the solemn mien of one, Hatch, who was typically unflappable, got into a shouting match. To gut Helms's antihomosexual amendment, Hatch and Ted had proposed an amendment of their own: basically, that regardless of any other provision in the bill, nothing would prevent public health officials from conveying information to potential AIDS victims on how to avoid contact with the virus if doing so would advance public safety. Helms, knowing full well the effect of the amendment, had exploded. But now it was Hatch's turn to explode. He told Helms that he was a bishop in the Mormon church, that he had to counsel homosexuals, even though they are considered sinners by his church, and that he had to persuade them to change their behaviors. But, Hatch said, none of the men he counseled had chosen to be gay. And he said this: having counseled so many of them, he knew that many of them were of far higher character than members who served in this body. Ted's and Hatch's amendment carried, and the bill passed the Senate, 87 to 4. Reagan eventually signed it into law, the first comprehensive bill to deal with the AIDS crisis: the Health Omnibus Programs Extension, or HOPE.

HOPE provided funding for AIDS research and created a new structure for that research. It did not provide legal protections for AIDS victims. Ted introduced that bill later in 1988, but it went nowhere, which was one reason why Ted pushed so aggressively for the ADA, with its civil rights provisions for AIDS sufferers on the basis that they were disabled.* But AIDS sufferers needed other forms of support—medical, technical, above all, financial—especially for those who were poor and uninsured or underinsured. The federal government was now providing money for AIDS research; Ted had contributed mightily to that effort. It made no provisions for individuals suffering from the disease. That December 1988, after the passage of the ADA, Ted staged hearings across the country on healthcare, a four-day tour, traveling by chartered plane, a tour not unlike the hearings he had conducted when he was trying to gain passage of national health insurance. In New York, he focused on AIDS and drug abuse, which were connected since the latter often led to transmission of the former, and he looked at hospitals, which didn't have enough beds for the AIDS sufferers and drug addicts who might get AIDS. He flew to St. Louis, where he investigated health insurance for working men and women, and then to Los Angeles, where he looked at how the poor coped without health insurance, and then to Sparta, Georgia, where he examined healthcare in rural America, and where a woman named Joan Baity testified about her father having died and her mother suffering from Alzheimer's disease and her husband having divorced her, then told Ted, "Someway, somehow, I need some help." He listened, by one account, "head canted, mouth slightly ajar in concentration," asked a few questions, sat silently for a moment, then turned to the audience and said, "If we cannot try to deal with that kind of an issue and problem as a society,

---

*Helms had managed to defeat any AIDS bill that contained a confidentiality provision, which would have prevented health officers from reporting any individual who had contracted the disease. The fear was that without a confidentiality clause, individuals would not get tested, or those who did would be discriminated against.

and do it in a way that is fair and just, we have really to ask about our whole sense of humanity and decency." Ted spent the night with a farm family in Sparta and had the *Today* show there when he woke up and shared breakfast with his host family and discussed the need for health-care. While there, he also saw the effect of AIDS on a rural hospital. When he returned to Washington from his tour and talked with his two AIDS staffers, Terry Beirn and Mike Iskowitz, the three latched onto an idea. No one begrudged emergency aid to communities in extremis due to a natu-ral disaster—a flood, a hurricane, a tornado, a wildfire—regardless of the size of the deficit or the budgetary restraints. AIDS, they said, was like a natural disaster, and it was an emergency in many communities. So why not draft a bill with emergency funds for those communities struck hard-est by AIDS and for those individuals who couldn't afford medication or treatment or even food? Why not call it a form of "disaster relief"? Biern and Iskowitz thought they might be able to get $50 million. Ted asked for $600 million, half of which would be divided among the thirteen cities most affected by AIDS, the other half among states and localities based on the number of AIDS cases. (This was an addition of Orrin Hatch's.)

It was a different push this time, in 1990, than it had been in 1988, Reagan's last year in office. There was now greater sympathy for AIDS victims. There were still conservatives who were hostile to the idea of as-sisting individuals who were homosexual, chief among them Jesse Helms—still the "most vocal enemy of the gay rights movement," his bi-ographer called him—who had labeled AIDS a homosexual affliction. And Helms had questioned endlessly in debating AIDS legislation: Why help them? Why encourage them? Hadn't they done this to themselves? But the tide had been turning, not because there was any sudden affection among conservatives for homosexuals or a moral reawakening, but be-cause, as it spread, many of their constituents were affected by the dis-ease, and many of those victims were not gay, and there were political consequences for refusing to help the afflicted. Republican senator Connie Mack of Florida, a conservative, said he was affected when he visited a nursery at Jackson Memorial Hospital in Miami, and it was filled with newborns with AIDS who had contracted it from their infected mothers. Orrin Hatch, who co-sponsored the bill with Ted, was moved by the story of Ryan White, a teenage hemophiliac in Indiana, who had contracted AIDS from a contaminated transfusion and was prohibited from return-ing to school after he had been diagnosed, and Ted too believed that it was the story of Ryan White and of the Ray brothers, three young hemophiliacs in Florida who had also gotten AIDS from tainted blood, that turned Hatch into an advocate, however much Ted had proselytized him. Neither Ryan White nor the Ray brothers were gay. Former president Reagan was affected when he read a newspaper article about Elizabeth Glaser, who was not gay. And he would meet with Ryan White after Reagan had left the presidency.

President Bush had been no more tenacious in fighting AIDS than his predecessor had been. Fourteen months passed before he made his first remarks on the disease—this at a time when the Centers for Disease Control reported that 150,000 Americans had AIDS and 90,000 Americans had died. But when he did discuss it, three weeks after Ted and Hatch introduced their bill at a hearing at which the film star Elizabeth Taylor was the first witness, Bush said that he had friends who had died from AIDS, that those who suffered from the disease should be treated with "dignity, compassion, care, confidentiality, and without discrimination," and that he would be supporting the ADA, which was still wending its way through the House at that point, though he made no pledge to support Ted's new bill.

Now Ted seized the momentum. He had introduced the bill on March 7, 1990, as the Comprehensive AIDS Resources Emergency Act. A few weeks later Ryan White suffered a downturn and was hospitalized. On April 4, at a meeting of the Labor Committee, Ted or Hatch—it is unclear who—decided the committee should rename the bill the Ryan White Act. Part of this was good public relations since White had become the national face of AIDS. (Significantly, the face of AIDS couldn't be gay, given the politics of AIDS.) Part of it was a way of getting Senator Dan Coats, one of the hindrances to AIDS legislation, to support the bill since White was a popular constituent of his in Indiana. Part of it, no doubt, was common decency. A few days later, before another committee meeting, Ted phoned Ryan's hospital room for an update. Singer Elton John, who had befriended Ryan and was then keeping vigil, answered and informed Ted that Ryan was in a coma. Ted relayed that to the senators. Afterward, when Michael Iskowitz asked Ted how he thought this would affect the bill, Ted answered, "This one's for you, Ryan."

White's case—the ostracism he had suffered, the bullying he had had to endure with his classmates writing antigay slurs on his books and his locker, the fortitude he showed in the face of those abuses, and the way he continued to live as normal a life as he could after moving to a different community and enrolling in a different school—had a profound effect on the perception of AIDS. Senator Barbara Mikulski recalled a visit that Ryan White had made to Washington with his mother and how the media crowded him—"this frail little boy," she said—and how when Ryan and his mother were leaving the hearing, the media began jostling him, and how Ted, "big, bulky," then put his arm around him. And she said that moment became a metaphor to her. "It was just he protected him, and I was with him, and he said, 'Barbara, Barbara, get on the other side and grab Ryan's mother.'" And then he called on Senator Chris Dodd to come and provide a shield. And Mikulski said, "I was moved because he literally protected Ryan White. [And] he protected him legislatively." And Mikulski said she was sure that if he had gone into Ryan's school in Kokomo, Indiana, the school from which Ryan White had been barred, Ted "would have kicked down the goddamned door." Four days after the bill was renamed for him, Ryan White died.

And now Ted Kennedy had to protect Ryan White and those like him against the Jesse Helmses, only this protection was legislative. Helms was again threatening to introduce one amendment after another to sabotage the bill, and there was another threat: the threat of a filibuster. At the request of an AIDS activist named Thomas Sheridan, Ryan White's mother, Jeanne, agreed, a week after her son's death, to fly to Washington to lobby senators in the hope that proponents of the bill could get the required sixty-one votes needed to break the filibuster. Meanwhile Ted tried to reason with Helms. He even went to Helms's office, an extraordinary gesture given the animosity between the two men, to ask whether he really needed to offer all the amendments, presumably since the bill was likely to pass, and all Helms was doing was engaging in mischief. Helms said he would offer five or six. And when the floor debate began, he read from the Bible and insisted the bill promoted homosexuality and offered his amendments, one of which was that no one with AIDS could work at a salad bar. A "nasty time," Ted called it years later. But with Ryan White's death—the death of a young straight boy—the momentum had shifted decisively against Helms. The Senate passed the bill 95 to 4 on May 16. Hatch said he had to lobby Bush to sign it, presumably because of the money, but Bush did. Helms would oppose it again, on the same homophobic grounds, when it came up for reauthorization five years later, triggering another red-faced outburst from Ted, and again five years after that. But Helms would not win now. The Ryan White Act survived and saved untold lives, though Terry Beirn, Ted's brilliant young AIDS staffer, so instrumental in framing the act, would not be one of them. Beirn died at thirty-nine a year later—of acquired immune deficiency syndrome.

IV

Ted Kennedy worked. He worked as if to make up for the lost time of the Reagan administration. He worked because, as Nick Littlefield said, "Bush wasn't going to do big things"—he was far too concerned about the deficit—so "Kennedy was always on the lookout for little things, little bills he could get passed." It was a long, long list—the Older Workers Benefit Protection Act that undid Supreme Court rulings allowing employers to discriminate against older workers; the Excellence in Mathematics, Science and Engineering Act that provided grants to improve education in those areas; the Defense Economic Adjustment, Diversification, Conversion and Stabilization Act that assisted workers in getting retraining after cutbacks in the Defense budget; the Child Care and Development Block Grant Act that subsidized child care for poor families; bills on mammography quality and Alzheimer's research and lowering the cost of pharmaceuticals and a bill to fund, via user fees, expedited approvals of drug applications through the FDA—fifty-four bills in all that passed through Ted Kennedy's Labor Committee and became law in the first two years of the Bush administration. And there were those that passed not through the Labor Committee but through the Judiciary Committee, on which Ted also sat, like the Visual Artists Rights Act, which granted artists "moral" rights in their works that prevented individuals who owned the works or held the copyright in them from tampering with, mutilating, or destroying them—artist Ed Ruscha won a large settlement from someone who had painted over a mural of his—and through its Immigration Subcommittee, on which Ted still sat. Interest in immigration had resurfaced during the Carter administration with concerns that the border was too porous, and the House and Senate had created a Select Commission on Immigration and Refugee Policy to include four members from both the House and Senate Judiciary committees, four Cabinet members, and four members to be appointed by Carter. The commission's recommendations ultimately found their way into a bill introduced by Alan Simpson in the Senate, but immigration was a vexing issue, one with many different and opposing stakeholders, and the bill made its way through Congress very slowly, introduced each year and defeated each year. Even Ted was no champion of it. He was pleased that the bill provided amnesty for undocumented immigrants if they met certain conditions; Ted had been calling for an amnesty since 1980. He was less pleased that it included sanctions for employers who hired undocumented immigrants since he, and the Latino community, were certain this would prevent their being hired. As his aide Michael Myers, who worked on the legislation, recalled, Ted would tell him "over and over" that "if there's a possibility that discrimination can happen, it will happen." Still, Ted had gone through his routine of working with a Republican, in this case Simpson. "Ted and I would come to a loggerhead," Simpson would remember, "and I'd say, 'I can't go for that. Can you do this?' He'd say, 'Let me get back to you on Monday.'" Simpson said that Ted had to run any compromises by both his "legislative shop," that is, his aides who drafted the bills, and his "political shop," that is, the aides who worked with the activists and stakeholders. One day, Simpson said, Ted came back to him after they had discussed a compromise and told him that he couldn't do it politically. "I've got—I don't know—maybe eighty percent in one of these towns is Portuguese, and I can't do it." Simpson said Ted was "honest enough, but, you know, a political shop and a legislative shop? You don't see that often." But then no senator was as dedicated to getting results as Ted Kennedy, and none understood the process as well as Ted Kennedy. With so many stakeholders harboring so many objections, Simpson was resigned to his bill not passing yet again when 1986 arrived. And Ted, after all their dickering, finally decided not to support it because of the sanction provision against employers. But out of friendship to Simpson, he did not filibuster the bill, for which Simpson was grateful. To Simpson's surprise, the bill passed, and Ronald Reagan signed it.

But now, four years later, Congress was revisiting the immigration issue. At the time, 1990, there were two primary problems. In the twenty-five years since its passage, the quotas in Ted's 1965 Immigration Act had created a backlog of individuals waiting for family reunification, and Ted wanted to expand the number of visas beyond those stipulated in his old bill. On February 7, he introduced a bill to do just that. At the same time, there was the problem of providing visas for businesses that needed labor, and Alan Simpson, a business Republican, wanted to adjust the visas to meet the specific labor demands. Again, the two senators worked closely;

basically, they were now the Immigration Subcommittee since the third member, Paul Simon, left the legislation to them and engaged only to make sure they didn't move too far to the right, which was unlikely with Ted in any case. And Ted told his immigration aides, Jerry Tinker and Michael Myers, of his bargaining with Simpson, as he said of his bargaining with most senators, "Let's maximize where we agree and minimize where we disagree." Eventually, Simpson agreed to increase the number of immigrants permitted into the country to 700,000 and to increase the number of visas for family unification to 480,000, but restricted reunification to the immediate family. (Myers said that Simpson had a "heartache" about expanding visas to siblings.) Ted, for his part, agreed to new classes of work visas, especially those for skilled workers, that helped business. Ted wasn't especially enthusiastic about the bill, but he got that visa expansion and another provision that ended the exclusion of homosexuals. The bill passed, and Bush signed it.

George Bush did not sign many progressive bills. He was not an activist president. "Relax," he had told Ted, more as a warning than a reassurance, when the two of them met after Bush's election—relax because, as he apprised Ted, he wasn't going to pass any social legislation. (Sununu had told Ted the same thing.) Bush was far more interested in foreign policy, especially as the Soviet bloc began to crumble and the Cold War wound down. The Berlin Wall, the symbol of Cold War divisions, was opened in November 1989—*forced* open by a restless German populace. In the Soviet Union, reforms initiated by Mikhail Gorbachev had destabilized the Communist regime there. Across the Eastern bloc, citizens were emboldened, and autocratic governments were threatened by a democratic impulse. "It's spreading like wildfire through Eastern Europe," Bush had dictated to his journal. Ted, who had taken such an active role in foreign policy during Reagan's presidency, largely because the routes to major domestic policy changes were closed, and who was largely critical of Reagan's bellicosity, took a less active role during Bush's presidency and was far less critical of him. He did go to Germany three weeks after the wall fell, at a time when Europe was in convulsions, but he was careful not to upstage a meeting between Bush and Gorbachev. Instead, he met with Berlin mayor Willy Brandt, visited East Berlin and met with some activists there, and had his aides pass out postcards with a photo of Jack, Bobby, and himself, and then spoke from the portico of the Schöneberg Rathaus, the City Hall, where, after much deliberation, he uttered the famous words his late brother Jack had declared on that same portico: *"Ich bin ein Berliner."*

Though Ted wasn't indifferent to the epochal change in Europe and what it meant for the world, he also had an interest in the opportunity that the change afforded for this country. He saw the end of the Cold War as an economic boon—a way to revive liberalism, by which he meant the social programs that helped the poor and the marginalized. Two days before the wall fell, Ted was on the Senate floor, speaking to an empty chamber and promoting another raise in the minimum wage. As *Washington Post* reporter Rick Atkinson described it, Ted was droning, another perfunctory address, until he began talking about the big business leaders who opposed the effort. And then, warming to the argument, he shifted into what Atkinson called his "trademark bellow," reaching to his diaphragm, like an opera singer, to declaim: "If this body does not know where it stands on the simple, fundamental issue of justice for working people, we are in very difficult times." Atkinson saw this—Ted bellowing to an empty chamber—as a metaphor for "his long fall from grace, the fitting close to a disastrous decade."

The decade hadn't, however, been quite as disastrous as Atkinson thought—not when one looked at Ted's record of accomplishment and those fifty-four bills that passed through his Labor Committee. It was true, as Atkinson wrote, that "at least some of the blame for liberalism's decline may be laid at his door, and he has been unable to articulate a compelling vision of America's future acceptable to a majority of the Democratic Party, much less the American electorate." But Ted saw it differently. Ted felt there was a vision, even if Democrats hadn't promoted it, even if the country hadn't embraced it. It was the vision he had always presented. In a speech at Georgetown University the following April, he castigated his fellow Democrats as "timid," "muted," "befuddled," and asked them to use the "peace dividend" from the end of the Cold War to do what the Republicans would not do: invest in the social programs that George H. W. Bush had forsworn. It was a call to arms, a criticism of the "unnatural quiet coming from our party," and of the "kowtowing" to Bush's veto threats, and of "confining our own Democratic efforts to merely marginal improvements in Republican proposals"—something he himself had done—"or almost conceding a second term to President Bush." A few weeks later, when Rick Atkinson asked Ted what the Democratic message should be in what Atkinson called the "Reagan-Bush era," Ted answered,

"We ought to be in a more importantly and dramatic way focusing on the minimum standards of decency in terms of the quality of life for working men and women." And when Atkinson asked if he thought the Democrats could ride that message to the White House, Ted honestly replied, "There are some that would agree and some that would differ."

The 1990 midterms, however, would not be a referendum on a peace dividend or on liberal policies. Two other issues loomed. On August 1, the Iraqi armies of the dictator Saddam Hussein invaded neighboring Kuwait, using as justification that the Kuwaitis were taking oil that rightfully belonged to Iraq. The invasion was a clear violation of sovereignty. It also posed a threat to oil supplies on which the United States relied. Bush tried to rally the Arab states, most notably Saudi Arabia, against Hussein, but to no avail. And yet even as he negotiated and pressured, he told the press: "This will not stand. This will not stand, this aggression against Kuwait." Over the next several weeks, Bush did manage to arrange a coalition of thirty-five nations, including those timorous Middle Eastern countries. He war-planned for American troops to be sent to the Middle East, should it come to that. He addressed the country to assure his fellow Americans that there would be no appeasement. But what he did not do was ask for congressional approval to move militarily against Iraq. Congress passed resolutions supporting Bush to that point, commending his actions in working with the United Nations to impose sanctions on Iraq, and calling for the invasion to be resolved. The resolution passed the Senate on October 2, by a vote of 96 to 3. Ted was one of the three, saying that he was reminded of the Gulf of Tonkin resolution that served as a legal basis for the Vietnam War. Now the world waited.

As it waited, George Bush and the Congress were engaged in another war: the war against the swelling deficit. "Read my lips," Bush had declared in accepting the nomination at the Republican National Convention. "No new taxes." But the deficit was growing, a recession seemed in the offing, and a government shutdown was increasingly likely, which would have been disastrous at the very time when Bush was coping with the Iraq dispute and hoping to reassure markets. He needed a budget deal. And he reached one—cutting spending and raising taxes, thus violating his pledge: a deal that satisfied neither Democrats nor Republicans entirely, but that found a middle way—except that the hard-right Republicans were incensed by Bush's breaking the tax cut pledge (a betrayal of the great Reagan, they felt, despite Reagan's own tax increases), and the hard-left Democrats were furious over the spending cuts. "Nobody is particularly happy with me," Bush told his diary, but added, that I "don't want to be off in some ideological corner falling on my sword, and keeping the country from moving forward." Congress passed the deal. The midterms would provide the verdict.

But the verdict was inconclusive, just as the nation's attitude on going to war against Iraq and raising taxes to meet the deficit seemed inconclusive. Democrats gained seven seats in the House and one seat in the Senate—small gains for a midterm in which the president's party usually lost far more, but gains nonetheless. Now, with the election over and heading into 1991, the country braced for the possibility of war. But Ted Kennedy would be fighting another battle—this one a battle with himself.

THIRTEEN

The Undertow

TED KENNEDY WAS not wrestling with his inner demons quite yet. Now that Ronald Reagan was gone, he had been working, working as hard as he had ever worked, working, his aide Nick Littlefield said, to "change the focus of what government did again, to get it back to where it had been in the Great Society, and with Roosevelt and the New Deal." He had produced a prodigious amount of legislation, most of it minor, but some of it—the amendments to the Fair Labor Standards Act that increased the minimum wage, the Americans with Disabilities Act, the Ryan White Comprehensive AIDS Resources Emergency Care Act—was major, even life-changing legislation. One of his former aides said that he was relishing the battle again—the lonelier the better. "He would ask whether anybody else planned to vote against something," Jim Flug, his old Judiciary staffer said. "If there were five or six nay votes, he wouldn't be very excited. But if he was alone or almost alone, *that* excited him." He was in motion—always in motion. Rick Atkinson, in his article on Ted that April 1990 in *The Washington Post Magazine*, described him in the Senate cloakroom or on the floor as shuttling "between colleagues to lobby and subjects to discuss—'Durenberger: Chile, health,' or 'Specter: civil rights markup.'" A study by a political scientist determined that the kind of person most respected in the Senate was a senior member who led a committee, was a legislative specialist, was not "sycophantic" either to the president or to "ideologically extreme" interest groups, and didn't waste time with constituency mailings and travel and irrelevant floor speeches. Ted qualified on all counts, and in a poll of his Senate colleagues, the study placed him as the fifteenth most respected, though that ranking certainly was affected by conservative Republicans who thought

Ted too liberal and who disrespected him as a result. Still, Orrin Hatch, his friend and no liberal, called him "one of the great all-time senators."

But coming into 1991, legislation was not the nation's primary concern. War was.

On the foreign front, Ted was crossing swords with the administration on its creep toward a military intervention in Iraq after Saddam Hussein's invasion of neighboring Kuwait. Ted had been skeptical of President Bush's massing of troops—430,000 of them, the largest force since World War II—which had begun on November 8, the day of the 1990 midterm elections, a massing without congressional authorization, even as the president courted the United Nations and allies so that the United States would not seem to be taking unilateral action. Ted believed that the country should give sanctions an opportunity to work, saying that he had seen how effective sanctions could be with the pressure they exerted on South Africa; within four years, he said, Nelson Mandela was out of prison and South Africa had a new government.

But George H. W. Bush was impatient with sanctions. He had told Congress that he had the authority to go to war without congressional approval, and then on January 8, despite that assertion, he asked congressional leadership to support a UN resolution that set a January 15 deadline for Saddam to withdraw his troops, and he said that after that date, he felt empowered to send troops into battle, even though, privately, he fretted that he might be impeached were he to take such action. "We have not seen such arrogance in a president since Watergate," Ted said of Bush's claim. In a vigorous debate on January 11, a debate in which the Senate was gripped by what Illinois senator Paul Simon called a "grim mood here in Congress as I do not recall," Republicans invoked Munich and British prime minister Neville Chamberlain's capitulation to Adolf Hitler, said that if they didn't face down Hussein's aggression now, they would only embolden him, said that the threat of war would be the best way of ensuring peace, said that the president had been patient but that there was a limit to patience. Ted and many of his Democratic colleagues argued differently. "At this historic moment, it may well be that only Congress can stop this senseless march toward war," he said. "Let there be no mistake about the cost of war. We have arrayed an impressive international coalition against Iraq, but when the bullets start flying, ninety percent of the casualties will be Americans. It is hardly a surprise that so many other nations are willing to fight to the last American to achieve the goals of the United Nations. It is not their sons and daughters who will do the dying." And he noted the forty-five thousand body bags that the Pentagon had ordered sent to the Middle East. The final vote the next day was close, 52 to 47, with Ted in the minority. But George Bush got his blank check. And on January 16, American aircraft attacked Iraq. And the nation was at war.

While Ted was concerned about the toll the war would take on American servicemen and -women, he was also concerned about the toll it would take on his progressive agenda. Money sent to war was money denied to social programs. Even as the Senate was debating whether to go to war, Ted was holding hearings, the first hearings of the new legislative session, on the effects of the recession that had begun six months earlier, in part as a result of the Federal Reserve tightening money to stave off inflation. Ted opened the hearings declaring, "It is time for this administration to get as serious about fighting this recession as they are about fighting in the Persian Gulf." Three witnesses, all men who had lost their factory jobs, described their struggle to survive. But the senators seemed flummoxed. Senator Nancy Kassebaum, a Republican, said it was "difficult to know indeed what we can do." And it was a sign of how little the issue had captured public attention that C-SPAN, the public access cable station that regularly carried congressional activities, did not carry this one. Ted held hearings daily—on education, on healthcare, on children, on jobs, and he opened each hearing with a passionate speech. "Jobs, education, and healthcare," Nick Littlefield said, was the mantra. And Ted warned the administration that if it "continues to neglect our problems at home, refusing to act against this recession, then the Congress will have to take the lead and stand up for the people who are being hurt in this economy."

But the nation was preoccupied with war, and the war was going well, a virtual blitzkrieg against the Iraqis, and Bush's popularity was soaring, to 89 percent at the point of victory in Iraq at the end of February, despite the recession and a rising unemployment rate that was the highest in three years. There was little room for worrying about any of the issues that concerned Ted Kennedy. George Bush was unassailable. And so, after two years of working to regain his fighting spirit, Ted was right back where he had been with Ronald Reagan. For all his energy, for all his passion, he was impotent once again.

•   •   •

Watching him, one would not have detected that impotence, at least not from his outward demeanor. Outwardly, Ted Kennedy, at fifty-nine, was still jovial, seemingly lighthearted, ebullient, sociable, "effervescent," his friend John Tunney called him, and a "great person to have fun with." "If you want to find Ted Kennedy," said another close friend, Senator Chris Dodd, "listen for the laughter." He kept company with men of a similar disposition. Dodd was one. So was Claude Hooten, whom he had met when both were freshmen at Harvard. Another old college friend, John Culver, was one too; John Podesta said that Ted and Culver were "two giant characters, both physically and emotionally," and when they got together, "They'd be laughing and telling stories" and "their shirts"— probably meaning shirttails—"would come out, they'd be sweating." As much as he loved to laugh, he loved to sing. When the composer Marvin Hamlisch was visiting Ted's office to discuss rights for songwriters, Ted arranged to have a piano brought in, and Hamlisch played while Ted invited Nick Littlefield, who had been a professional singer before going to law school, to come in and sing along—a song from Hamlisch's show *They're Playing Our Song*. And Littlefield sang, and he said when he finished, he looked up and saw that the entire staff had gathered and was peering in through the door, and they burst into applause. And Littlefield said, "From then on, the Senator is very enthusiastic about my singing." When another senator was walking down the hall, Ted might stop him, invite him into the office, and have Littlefield sing. And when he threw an office party, Ted would invite Littlefield to the front of the room, and the two would belt out a duet. "He'll sing at the drop of a hat," Carey Parker said of Ted, who had once considered pursuing a career in opera. And now he had an accomplice. Ted loved to do impressions too. He could do a great impression of presidential adviser Clark Clifford and would drone on and on with Clifford's pomposities.

He was boisterous. He liked to throw parties—an annual party at Hyannis where singing was the main event; costume birthday parties at the McLean home, where one year he dressed as an Irish king and his girlfriend at the time as a queen, and his daughter Kara, sister Jean, and sister-in-law Ethel all dressed as Cleopatra, the latter arriving in a chariot, while the door was surrounded by a moat of dry ice; and his annual Christmas party—the "ultimate Christmas party," his aide Melody Miller called it. The Christmas parties, which were typically held in the Labor Committee hearing room, had begun as simple staff parties in the early

1970s, and Ted would usually make an obligatory appearance and stay for an hour or so to mingle with his aides and their families. But in 1976 Larry Horowitz, who was then a health staffer before ascending to administrative assistant, proposed that the attendees wear costumes. Horowitz himself appeared that year in a Rudolph the Red-Nosed Reindeer costume, with antlers and a bulbous red nose. The next year Ted suggested that he dress up too and came to the party as Santa Claus, which became his standard costume until the mid-1980s. In 1986 he arrived decked out as a lighthouse. And the next year, at the beginning of the Iran-Contra hearings, wearing a big blond wig, a flouncy blouse filled to capacity, and with reddened lips, he arrived as Fawn Hall, the secretary of Lieutenant Colonel Oliver North, a member of Reagan's National Security Council who had helped engineer the diversion of the proceeds from the Iranian arms sale to the Contras. (Joe Kennedy II in an Eisenhower jacket played North.) Ted sneaked through the back and entered from an anteroom, and when he made his appearance, the "roar was overwhelming," said Melody Miller. That moment began a new tradition. The following year, he came as Elvis Presley, and the year after that as Batman ("That's *Bat*-man," he told the guests, "not *Fat*man"), and the year after that as one of the two members of Milli Vanilli, a music duo that was discovered to have been lip-synching their songs while two other people actually sang them. By now, the party had turned into a full-fledged show, with skits and jokes and songs. Ted hired professional joke writers and rehearsed "quite a bit," over the course of a week, Carey Parker said.

And that was the familiar Ted Kennedy: the happiest man in the Senate, the liveliest man in the Senate, the most self-deprecating man in the Senate, the man who, as one of his cousins said, "walks in and lights up a room." *Outwardly.*

But there was also, within and obscured by the seeming exuberance, another Ted Kennedy—a Ted Kennedy few people could see because he chose to be opaque. "The most public of politicians," Rick Atkinson wrote, "is also one of the most difficult to know." "The most profound thing I said is not flattering," former Senate majority leader Howard Baker told an interviewer about Ted. "I served with him for eighteen years, and I still don't know him." A journalist who watched with him frequently said, "He had been trained to disjoin his inner feelings from the domain of public affairs. You could sense it when you were with him. His eyes revealed nothing. The man had venetian blinds on his soul." A friend and campaign contributor, Nancy Korman, chided him for being closed, for not revealing more of himself, for being too emotionally remote, for being overprogrammed—none of which could have been said of the political Ted Kennedy, but all of which seemed true for the personal Ted Kennedy. "You still stutter and stumble whenever you confront a question that has to do with your feelings," she wrote him in one of many notes addressing his emotional health. "You need to tell the world that you are very human, that you are crazy about your kids, that you love your work, that you have friends and that you will date in time." But Ted was a Kennedy, and the Kennedy pathology was, as one of his nephews had said, "secrecy." He seemed happiest in a crowd because then he could assume his political persona, which was authentic, and it was easier for him to function within that than having to cope with himself. He was uncomfortable with introspection—all Kennedys were—and more uncomfortable still with sharing his emotions. "He wasn't any good at talking about anything of a personal nature," his son Patrick would say. He was distrustful. "When Teddy is after advice from somebody he trusts completely," a "very close aide" told Burton Hersh, "he locks the door to his room and talks to himself."

And what one might not have seen outwardly was that this most extroverted of politicians, the man with a thousand friends, was still lonely, perhaps lonelier than he had ever been. He had been deeply alone in his marriage—"technically a marriage, but not really," Tom Oliphant would say—but he was deeply alone when it was over as well. "Anyone with two eyes" would have seen that, Oliphant said, but that meant people who looked closely, who could read him, which few could. Kara had married, Ted Jr. was away, Patrick was in college. "We just didn't have as much time to spend with him," Ted Jr. would say. "We didn't fulfill that need as we once had. We were hoping he would find a special person." "I think he was terribly lonely," John Culver recalled. "He'd go back to that big house alone." A *Time* report described a typical Ted Kennedy evening, with Ted "sitting in an armchair near the fire, a Scotch with lots of ice cubes resting nearby on the table. He talks with friends or puts a movie on the VCR." But alone. He had taken up painting again in the spring of 1991 when Congress offered lessons, and he enjoyed it, was actually good at it, but it was also clearly a way to fill time. Two friends went out to dinner with him one evening during this period and afterward watched him walk to his car. "And he turned around and waved," one said, "and he looked so lonely." An "extremely lonely man," Paul Kirk said of him, mentioning how he would go alone to pray at St. Joseph's Church on Capitol Hill.

But the loneliness was larger than the lack of companionship. It was historic—a loneliness so profound that it could never be ameliorated unless one could undo the past. The loss of his brothers haunted him, tormented him, isolated him, and according to Patrick, "he constantly was in a struggle to remain above it." But it was a losing struggle. Surrounded by their memorabilia in his home and his office, he told an interviewer haltingly, "I mean, the things that sort of catch you may, ah, in terms of . . . my brothers and family members, you're not quite sure when these things are going to come. You can pass different pictures, and, you know, walls, for a very considerable period of time, and then something will sort of catch it, you know, something will reawaken, ah, waken you," meaning awakening the memory. Melody Miller recalled attending a gathering at his home in McLean, and the song "Empty Tables, Empty Chairs" was playing, from *Les Misérables*, and Ted pulled himself away from the guests and went to the stereo and stood listening, and she said, "I remember watching his face, and seeing that there are moments when it all comes flooding back." Always the memories, and the brothers never far from his thoughts. "Occasionally, you'd be sitting around with the Senator," recalled a former aide, "and, like a stream of consciousness, he'd tell a story about an interaction with the President or with Bobby, and it's just in passing." But there were also times when he was so overcome by the mention of them that he would simply stop, even if he were giving a speech. And Melody Miller said that every time someone met him and shook his hand and said, "I loved your brothers so much, and I remember exactly where I was on November 22, 1963," the "wound opens." And every time, she said, he would stumble on a TV show or a picture or a voice on the radio, "you see his scar tissue get thinner and thinner, and finally, maybe, the wound can't heal." He visited their graves often and spontaneously. "Do you mind?" he asked two friends who had come to Washington. Do you mind if we go to Arlington Cemetery? And they went, and he wept. His sister Jean, telling a friend how much she missed Pat, who had died, and Eunice, who was sick, said she could finally appreciate "how lonely Teddy must have been through the years after losing all of his brothers." He was very lonely. And that August of 1990, he lost his brother-in-law, Stephen Smith, who was like a brother to him, to lung cancer. And he was lonelier still.

And if he was brutalized by the past, so was he weighted with the responsibilities of the present. As the last remaining male Kennedy of his generation, he had become surrogate father to Bobby's eleven children and Jack's two, as well as his own. He took those obligations very seriously and, by all accounts, performed them admirably. The "center of our lives" at Hyannis, his niece, Bobby's daughter Kerry Kennedy, said. "He took us sailing and taught us how to sail and he told us stories about politics, American history, our family. He was always very curious about what we were doing." And more, she said, "He gave us a sense of continuity. That sense of a role model, someone I could depend on, was very, very important." Ted was the one now who phoned Bobby's and Jack's children on their birthdays, because there was no father to do so, and, after they were married, their anniversaries; the one who attended their first communions and graduations; the one who gave them tongue-lashings when they misbehaved at school ("Believe me, he could scare you straight," Christopher Kennedy said); the one who, during the summers, rented a Winnebago and took that large brood to historic sites in Massachusetts, as his mother and grandfather Honey Fitz had shown him Boston sites when he was a boy—Herman Melville's home, the Norman Rockwell Museum and the Clark Museum, the Crane Paper Company, the furniture factories in Lee and Lenox, and Umpachene Falls where they would swim, and the Riverside Amusement Park in Springfield—and later on trips to Revolutionary War battlefields and Civil War battlefields, accompanied, his niece Kerry Kennedy said, by the "greatest historians in the country," Shelby Foote or David McCullough, who said that Ted had read every one of his books "in detail," as his brother Jack had taken *him* to battlefields with noted historians; and the one who, on those excursions, would look, by one account, like a "scoutmaster," in his "rumpled Bermuda shorts, sneakers and pullover shirt," stirring a pot of barbecue sauce and licking the splatter off his wrist because he was the Kennedy who was least self-conscious about how he looked or what he did; and the one who took them skiing and rafting and, of course, sailing, and when he won a race and got a trophy, he made replicas of it and gave one to each member of his crew; and the one who made sure to pull each of those nieces and nephews aside individually to give them his special attention because, as the man who drove that Winnebago, Ted's old friend Don Dowd, said, "he knew his role. He knew that basically they turned to him now"; and the one who usually took a few of them on his overseas trips, to Russia and

China and Ethiopia, where he was conducting a tour to study hunger; and the one who taught his nephew, Christopher Lawford, how to propel a cherry tomato from his mouth by pressing both cheeks; and the one who, when the children had a day off from school, would bring them to his office where they would help stamp passes or hide in his private inner sanctum when he left for a floor vote, and when he returned, he would bellow, "Fee, fi, fo, fum, I'm coming to get you"; and the one who, when they got older, brought them into his office over the summer, this time as interns, in part so that those nieces and nephews could see what their fathers, Jack and Bobby, had done, and where they would answer phones and open mail and file papers and hand out press releases, and where Ted would take them to his committee hearings with him or send them to lectures at the Library of Congress, and they would play on his Boston "Ted Sox" softball team. The children had a nickname for him, "The Grand Fromage": "The Big Cheese."

But if he was the paterfamilias, the man who served as the father now of them all, the one around whom they felt "chaos and laughter," as one nephew put it, he was also the great consoler, having had to learn so much about consolation for his own suffering. "My dad was unbelievable in moments of family crisis," Ted Jr. was to say. And there were many moments of crisis. Some of them were issues of misbehavior or adolescent turbulence. His niece Kathleen, the oldest of Bobby's eleven children, recalled being at the Putney School and having to leave dinner to use the only pay phone on the premises to talk with her uncle about her siblings' problems, "about what should be done and what we could do." And she said, "That's part of our lives," as if persistent trouble were part of the natural course of things. His office meetings were frequently interrupted by calls from family members needing his help, and he would almost always take the call, then ask his staff to leave the room. "Tremendous demands put on him that transcended his workload," one staffer said of these family responsibilities. He was the support, the morale booster, the person on whom everyone relied. His nephew Christopher Lawford said he could be "emotional and pragmatic at the same time," and that "just having him around made me feel better," which he attributed to the "fearless lust with which he embraced his own struggles"—so many struggles.

But there were serious crises, too, terrible crises that always seemed to plague the Kennedys, even if they were self-inflicted, as Ted's often were—crises that cast a pall that could not be lifted. In August 1973 Bobby's eldest son, twenty-year-old Joseph Kennedy II, was driving an open-top Toyota off-road vehicle on Nantucket heading toward the beach—one of his passengers said he was taking a shortcut—when he swerved to avoid a collision, and his vehicle flipped, injuring his eighteen-year-old brother, David, and David's girlfriend, Pamela Kelley—Kelley severely. She was paralyzed from the chest down. With Ted accompanying him to the courtroom, Joe II was convicted of negligent driving and fined $100 after a three-hour trial—despite his not-guilty plea, an investigating officer at the scene said Joe II had taken responsibility—and Milton Gwirtzman recalled seeing Joe II and Ted back at Hyannis Port, taking a "long, long" walk along the beach and Ted talking to him, doing what he had always done, which was give counsel. In 1983 Robert Kennedy, Jr., was arrested in South Dakota for heroin possession. In April 1984, during a visit to his grandmother, Rose, in Palm Beach over the Easter weekend, David Kennedy, twenty-eight, was found dead at the Brazilian Court Hotel from a combination of cocaine and prescription drugs. A woman who had met him at a bar shortly before his death said he told her that thinking of his late father, he could never find peace. "I've been full of pain. I am crying for help." At the wake at Hickory Hill, Ted and Patrick stood before the casket, and Ted recalled an incident shortly before the California primary in 1968 when Bobby and David were swimming in Malibu, and David got pulled out by the undertow and Bobby had rescued him. And Bobby had told Ted that there was an undertow in life and that David "seemed vulnerable to it." But the Kennedys, in that stoic bequest from old Joe Kennedy, never grieved—at least never "grieved properly, grieved openly, or were allowed to grieve," Ted's niece Maria Shriver said. And she said they would carry this grief around with them, which would then "pop out in a lot of different ways," sometimes as emotion, sometimes as rage, sometimes as intoxication or drug use. But not as grief, never as real grief. "They reacted like, 'Okay, that just happened. Let's go sailing. Let's go play football.'" That was the Kennedy way, as if it were the natural course of things.

And then there were the crises within Ted's own family, unrelenting crises, especially those of Patrick, who also was vulnerable to the undertow. At fifteen, he was, as he put it, "seriously impaired by depression. And I really did not want to feel that way." So on weekends, he would leave Andover, where he was attending school, and go out to nightclubs, occasionally with his sister Kara, who was at Tufts, and her boyfriend sneaking him in. "I didn't want anything but to be obliterated." He was. The summer after his cousin David's death, he was riding with his father in the blue 1972 Pontiac GTO, the car Ted had bought with John Tunney, when a pickup truck cut them off, and Patrick suffered a concussion, which left him with stretches of sleeplessness and memory loss and even deeper depression. Now he was in a spiral. In March 1986, he flew down to Palm Beach with two Andover classmates and promptly ran out of drugs. It was Larry Horowitz whom Ted asked to intervene—Horowitz had become a liaison between father and son—and Horowitz who arranged to fly Patrick back north, and Horowitz who put him into Spofford Hall, a treatment center in New Hampshire, for rehabilitation. When Patrick returned to Andover after ten days of treatment, Ted assigned him a live-in concierge—the same man who had tended to David Kennedy—to monitor him. "I felt like my dad wrote me off at that point," Patrick would later write. "I was just an enormous disappointment, like my mom." Still, he was graduated and was admitted to Georgetown because one of his Andover teachers interceded for him, but the summer before he was to matriculate, he began binge-drinking and downing caffeine. He lasted at Georgetown only a few weeks, moving back in with his father at McLean. It was Chris Dodd who recommended that Patrick attend Dodd's own alma mater, Providence, to which Ted acceded because Rhode Island was "great politically," he said, which gave Patrick some hope that his father hadn't given up on him. But there was a breach between them now, and Ted couldn't close it, even though he understood all too well the kind of pit into which Patrick had fallen, and the darkness that had overtaken him—understood it because he had been in that pit, might have still been in it, and he had been overtaken by that darkness. Ted couldn't address Patrick's fall, at least not directly. He couldn't talk about personal things, even with his own son. Patrick recalled one of those times when he was riddled with self-doubt, feeling, as he said, that he was a "loser" and wasn't measuring up to his father's standards or expectations of him, and Ted, the great consoler, couldn't verbalize any response to Patrick's torment. Instead, he took Patrick into his library at McLean, went to his wall of books there, pulled one from the shelf, and handed it to his son. It was a copy of *The Enemy Within,* Robert Kennedy's account of his fight against the labor rackets. It was inscribed: "To Teddy: Who has his own enemy within. Love, Bobby." And Patrick understood that it was his father's way of bridging the seeming chasm between them, a way of letting Patrick know that he had been there too—and that he had survived.

There was one other duty Ted Kennedy had to perform, and this too was a difficult one. He had to hold the family together even as it was spinning apart. This, as much as providing a paternal presence after Jack's and Bobby's deaths, was one of the main reasons for the trips and the phone calls and the appearances at graduations and weddings. *Keep the Kennedys together.* Over time this became more imperative, even as it became more arduous. Rose, the summer of her grandson David's death, suffered a stroke that left her debilitated and that served to remind the family that the forces that had kept it together were about to disappear. But it was more than uniting the family that obligated Ted, as important as that was. He also felt an obligation to maintain the sense of closeness among the extended Kennedys, the familial bonds that protected the Kennedys against the world by drawing them so tightly to one another—the bonds forged by old Joe Kennedy. This is what made the Kennedys the Kennedys: They were in love with one another. And Ted had to keep that love alive, had to instill in each of those nieces and nephews the sense of what it meant to be a Kennedy, had to, as he would later write, "ensure a continuum in this beautiful process, this precious tradition of the Kennedy family, regathering itself, replenishing its young with knowledge and love." And so he became, in his nephew Christopher Lawford's words, the "link between the future and the past," and the man whose "spirit and position" became "daily reminders of all that was great about our family." And Ted Kennedy, deep in his own melancholy, battling his own demons, had to present a resilient, optimistic face to his family to keep the Kennedys together and to keep them as their own refuge from the assaults of the world. Outwardly.

II

But the funk into which Ted Kennedy had fallen was not only the product of the burdens he bore, the memories that wracked him, or the loneliness he had to endure with his wife, his children, and his brothers gone. There was also the political anguish he felt. The Reagan years were largely years of fecklessness and torment, notwithstanding the respite after getting back in the Senate majority. The first two years of the Bush presidency were better—Ted was a new man in legislative vigor—but even so, he had had to pocket his national health insurance initiative, the project of his lifetime, and with the triumph of the war against Iraq, he knew that Bush would be in no mood to move on any social legislation or to compromise. After the initial burst of energy, Ted, by his own admission, "stopped looking forward to things." He believed in his friend Arthur Schlesinger, Jr.'s, theory of the cycles of history, a theory that conservatism and liberalism alternate every thirty years, and he bemoaned having spent nearly all his Senate tenure in a period of conservative ascendance. "He genuinely gets sick when the country doesn't go in the right direction in his view," Patrick told a reporter at the time. "He gets upset because, you know, he's trying to change it and he just feels as if he's run up against the wall sometimes." Ted had said that in his personal life, "I kept moving to avoid the tragedy behind me," and that the motivation had been a "blessing" as a senator where movement had led to action. That might have been the source of the energy about which everyone remarked—the restlessness that was not a particular Kennedy characteristic. He buzzed with nervous energy. "The man cannot stand still," author Richard Rhodes had written in an early profile. "He fingers his tie, pulls at his hair, buttons and unbuttons his coat, grits his teeth, moves to an aide, moves back to his desk, hikes over to consult another senator, stands in the aisle, drops to a chair. His office is piled with papers and documents and notes and supplies, the disarray of one who forever has more to do and more he wants to do than he can ever possibly get done even with the best of staffs and the best of intentions, the disarray of one who no longer cares to put up a front." Others too noted that Ted was fidgety, "as active as a third-base coach giving signs," said another reporter, "continually pulling at his ear, fiddling with his glasses, aligning the ends of his necktie, clicking his pen." A "man consigned to perpetual motion," said yet another interviewer. "He had as much energy in more areas of his life than anyone I have ever met," said Ralph Neas, the head of the Leadership Conference on Civil Rights, who often worked with Ted, and Neas wondered when he slept. House majority leader Richard Gephardt called him the "Energizer Bunny." His old administrative assistant, Dave Burke, described Ted's attitude as "I have to do work, work, work, work. Then I can have fun. And when I have fun, it's none of your business." And Burke felt that for Ted, "Work is the answer to a lot of things." But others felt—and Ted himself admitted—that work was not a way to win the right to let go. Nor was it even the way to prove himself, though there was a time when it had certainly served that function—to show his fellow senators his mettle. He had another reason. He was always running, as he told an interviewer, "to keep ahead of the darkness." "Keep moving," his son Patrick had said of Ted's work ethic. "If things aren't going well, just keep moving because they'll eventually change." But when there was no legislation to move, when the president told him that nothing would pass, or that if it did, he was more than willing to wield his veto pen, when the tide turned to the right and for all Ted's reassurances that it would soon turn back, it didn't, Ted could no more outrun his impotence as a senator than he could outrun his tragedies as a man. In the end, he couldn't outrun the darkness.

Instead, the darkness settled on him.

Ted Kennedy had always drunk, even though Joe Kennedy had forbade any liquor in his home but daiquiris, and even then only after 1956, and even then only a small glass. Now, with the political shadow over him, Ted drank more. On a flight from Boston to West Germany, Rick Atkinson reported that in one two-hour period Ted downed two Scotches, two vodkas, and three glasses of red wine, though Atkinson didn't notice any obvious effect on him. But others did. "One way Ted Kennedy differs from Jack and Bobby: he is the only one who seems to be affected by drink," Arthur Schlesinger observed. "JFK, of course, drank sparingly in the years I knew him well; RFK perhaps drank a little more but never showed it. Ted becomes a little high in an entirely merry way, lurches a little, his face grows a little flushed, and he wants to sing." His drinking was no secret. *Time* reported that "Kennedy's face sometimes looks flushed and mottled with the classic alcoholic signs of burst capillaries, puffiness and gin-roses of the drunk. Sometimes he simply looks like hell—fat, dissolute, aging, fuddled"—this of the man who had worked hard to lose weight and get himself back into shape. "He looked bad and felt bad" was how his friend Nancy Korman put it of this period. Even now, when he was drinking more heavily, he was never impaired for his Senate work, was never drunk on the floor or in committee or at hearings—"His head was always there," John A. Farrell, who covered Ted for *The Boston Globe*, said—though after a long lunch, he might return to the office a "little buzzed," as Rick Burke put it, if his afternoon schedule was light, and on those occasions, with Ted "feeling no pain," he would joke with the staff or on the phone with friends and, according to Burke, might even poke his head into the mailroom to say thank you with a "sloppy grin." Even so, those moments were infrequent, and he disdained those who were impaired when they were working. After an edgy union official showed up in his office for a meeting having taken a drink, presumably to calm his nerves, Ted told a staffer, "Hmm, martinis at lunch don't go over very well. You might tell him that." Even now he would abstain from alcohol from New Year's through his birthday on February 22. But when he wasn't working, when he was carousing, his restraint disappeared. Author Laurence Leamer described Rose's one hundredth birthday party, that July 1990, at Hyannis, where Ted and his sister Pat both got drunk, and Ted left with two young women for a sail. "He returned in time to say a good-bye to some of the guests," Leamer wrote, "attempting to kiss one woman on the mouth, a gesture that she found offensive, as did her husband."

In a man so squarely in the public eye, such behavior was reckless and led to speculation that it extended back at least to Chappaquiddick, when the rumor was that he was drunk as he drove off the narrow bridge. Tom Oliphant thought Ted's decline began later, on the twentieth anniversary of Jack's assassination in 1983, but Ted actually seemed to pull himself together before he fell apart again in the late 1980s and early '90s. Columnist Joseph Kraft thought that Ted's misbehavior was a way of testing the limits of his appeal by breaking the rules, even though he was fully aware he was hurting himself by doing so, and Kraft believed that survivor guilt or Ted's desire to prove that he wasn't as good as his brothers might have figured in to his need for self-punishment. One reporter suggested that Ted had a suicidal streak in politics—that he was always trying to kill the grander ambitions of his career: "The wild driving, the drinking, the womanizing—could they all be an elaborate, unconscious way of saying: Let this cup pass from me?" Some thought it was a form of self-medication for all the emotional and even physical pain he suffered. As one staffer asked of a reporter, "Can you imagine what's been going on inside him? Can you imagine? Some day his autopsy is going to show some scars that no one—not even us—realized were there."

Whatever the causes of Ted's drinking—and there were many possible stressors—Patrick, who would come to know a great deal about alcoholism and addiction, concluded, "My dad definitely had an alcohol problem," and Patrick said that anyone who denied it—and Ted himself vehemently denied it, despite the evidence—was "dissembling the truth because it's too painful to acknowledge." And Patrick distinguished between an alcoholic and a problem drinker and said that he had "difficulty" identifying his father as an alcoholic when Patrick had his mother, who was undoubtedly an alcoholic, as a standard of comparison. "My mother was the kind of alcoholic who could not function, period, who would be inebriated all day and would fall down." Ted was not, Patrick said, an alcoholic like that. Ted certainly didn't want to think of himself like that. He was contemptuous of what Joan had become. Ted was a problem drinker who could behave recklessly and contemptibly, but he could exercise at least a modicum of control. If he drank, he had problems. If he stopped, the problems stopped too. And Ted *could* stop. He did stop. And then he began again.

And with the recklessness of the drinking came the recklessness with the women, if by recklessness one meant numbers, which also dated back at least to Chappaquiddick when many assumed that he was driving off for a romantic tryst. There were a great many women when he was married. There were more after he was divorced. The *Boston Herald*, a conservative paper antagonistic to Ted, kept a running tally: Beverly Sassoon, the ex-wife of the hair stylist Vidal Sassoon, who "put a new curl in his romantic life"; Cindy Pease, whom he met when her brother fixed a sail on his boat; Charlotte Brewer, a vice president of marketing and sales at Filene's; Lacey Neuhas of Houston, a socialite and art dealer who had also dated Senator John Warner; a "gorgeous blonde" at Desiree's; an "unidentified leggy blonde"; a "new Kennedy blonde every 48 hours"; actress Angie Dickinson, who told the press, "I don't want to say too much because the press will have us running off together to Greece or something"; a girl named Stephanie Pinol, whom he allegedly took to St. Tropez; and another named Claudia Cummings. (The *Herald* left out Barbara Borin, a former Boston sportscaster who became the chairperson of the board of directors for the New Hampshire Commission on the Arts, but *The Washington Post* didn't.) Even his Senate colleagues would joke about it. Alabama senator Howell Heflin, poring over a picture of Ted leaning over a woman on a boat, quipped, "Well, Teddy, I see you've changed your position on offshore drilling." Patrick, speaking of the decade after the divorce, recalled being alone in the McLean house, with his bedroom nearest the driveway, and hearing cars come and go at night, the cars of his father's liaisons. Sometimes in his isolation, he would press the intercom late at night until Ted answered and then would hang up. But Patrick wasn't the only one isolated. So was Ted. Friends of Ted's, who appreciated his loneliness, now more than a decade of loneliness without Joan, longed for him to find true love, and so did Ted. "You know, it's wonderful when you find someone you're really in love with," he told his former press secretary and speechwriter Bob Shrum, over a dinner at which Ted advised him to marry his girlfriend. "I've always hoped that would someday happen to me."

The press assumed the worst. It tended to see a nearly sixty-year-old man, long divorced, and separated long before that, dating a series of women, not as a search for love or even for companionship, but as licentiousness, no doubt because the Kennedys were thought of as congenital womanizers. Even Ted's friend Nancy Korman tutted that "men over 50 who date women under are seen as immature and silly by most female Americans," and thinking of a possible presidential run in 1988—this was late in 1983, when he had already taken himself out of the 1984 race—she told him, "You are now old enough to have a grown-up social life. Give up the boys, the beer, and the playmates." But there was a period after his divorce where he did not go out, where he came home every night, and, when he did begin dating again, his romances were not all flings. Most weren't. Most of his girlfriends were, as Korman advised, serious women, professional women. And there were, Patrick said, "some great loves" and potential wives—women he dated for long periods. He had dated Suzana Maus, a beautiful Czech refugee who had emigrated to Switzerland after the Soviets ended the Prague Spring, and whom he had met on a trip to Geneva in 1988. He introduced her to one of his staffers, Terri Haddad Robinson, that summer, flying to Nantucket to do so, and Robinson, who said she hadn't seen him socialize with other women, found him "uncomfortable," though he was clearly smitten with her. Ted cared for Suzana's son—he took them all to a Neil Diamond concert—and had Robinson take her to George Washington's home Mount Vernon when Ted was occupied with work and couldn't. But, as Robinson put it, "there came a moment when he had to decide whether to go further in the relationship," which was complicated by the fact that she lived abroad. And with his issues with Patrick and his responsibilities to the larger Kennedy clan, the romance ended.

He dated Elizabeth Shannon, the widow of William Shannon, a former *New York Times* journalist whom Jimmy Carter had appointed ambassador to Ireland, and a friend of Ted's. (At the time of his death, Shannon had actually been writing a book about Ted with his cooperation, and they spent many hours together on it, with Ted reminiscing, and the two of them drinking tea and then Irish whiskey at workday's end.) As Elizabeth Shannon would later tell it, the day of or the day after her husband's funeral, which Ted attended, he came to the house and took Elizabeth and her three sons to the Ritz for dinner. And over the next year, while she was in mourning, he invited her to Hyannis. When her period of mourning ended, late in 1988, and after a memorial service for her husband at the Kennedy Library, Ted took her on a sail from Nantucket to Cape Cod— a cold sail on rough seas—and that was the beginning of a three-year relationship where she would come to Hyannis every other weekend during the summer and would fly down to Washington during the winter; she spent a Christmas at Palm Beach with Ted and his sister Jean and her husband Steve, who was wracked with his cancer then. "He couldn't have been a sweeter, kinder suitor," she would say of Ted. But it was not a romance destined to last. The Kennedys were, she said, a difficult family—an all-encroaching family. And Ted had to perform, almost as if he were on stage, even when he was at Hyannis, even, or especially, when he was with his oldest and dearest friends, who wanted the cheerful, companionable Teddy they remembered, not a mature one. And when she and Ted did sneak away by themselves—the best times, she said—there would always be people coming up to the table, "every three seconds," to praise him or berate him or just talk with him. But as much as she preferred being with him alone, she also thought that he liked being surrounded by people because "when you're alone, you can get a little introspective, and maybe that's not his best role." And there was the issue of Ted's drinking, which she thought set a bad example for her boys, the youngest of whom was fifteen when she and Ted started dating; and at that time, in the early 1990s, he was drinking a lot. And finally, there was this: "Although it was fun to go out with him and he was an eligible bachelor and a nice man and he'd been such a good friend of Bill's, I never fell in love with him." So that relationship faded too. But it wasn't only Elizabeth's decision. Teddy too would say of himself in this period, "I faced the fact that I no longer wanted to take that risk"—the risk of new commitments.

But trepidation and pain and loss and the weight of obligation were not what most outsiders saw. To those who hated the Kennedys, and there were many of those, the drinking and the womanizing were signs of privilege—the prerogatives of a wastrel who could do whatever he wanted without consequences, which had always been the detractors' narrative.

To those without antipathy, which applied to most in the press, they were signs of dissolution—of a man ravaged and coming apart. And to those who knew Ted and the Kennedys best, it was neither privilege nor dissolution. It was the undertow.

But it wasn't just the undertow that pulled Ted Kennedy out to sea and left him lonely and flailing. It was the scorn with which he was treated while he was in pain. After he had, through his years of hard legislative work, exorcised the view of him as the least of the Kennedys, his drinking and dating had made him once again an object of curiosity, gossip, and often derision as the no-account brother, and this was nowhere more true than in the capital, which could be a small and catty community. Henry Fairlie, writing in *The New Republic* just before Ted's presidential announcement in 1979, recounted a Washington dinner party Fairlie attended where, "for a full hour and a half, 14 talented and interesting men and women talked of nothing but the sexual activities of Edward Kennedy." Stories circulated of Ted's errant behavior: Ted and Chris Dodd smashing their autographed photos at La Colline; or Ted fighting a heckler at a Manhattan bar at two in the morning. After Ted battled Australian media magnate Rupert Murdoch on a bill that would have prohibited the Federal Communications Commission from changing its rule banning dual ownership of a paper and TV station in a market, or from extending a waiver it had granted to Murdoch, thus forcing Murdoch to sell either the *Boston Herald* or the *New York Post* or the television stations he owned in Boston or New York, Murdoch sent the *Herald* into battle against Ted. "The oldest juvenile delinquent," the paper called him in one column. "Was it something I said, Fat Boy?" opened another column by a snarky young conservative named Howie Carr. "Really, Sen. Kennedy, do you really believe that this newspaper employs the only people in the world to notice your periodic resemblance to the Goodyear Blimp?" However much they loved and appreciated him, even his nieces and nephews, by one account, had come to think of him as a "bit of a joke" for his errant ways. And one of his former press secretaries allegedly kept a card on his desk: "It is our duty never to comment on the endless gossip and speculation." Many of the reports were exaggerated. Many of them were apocryphal. Arthur Schlesinger, Jr., recounted a story that news anchorman Walter Cronkite's wife, Betty, had told him about a waiter who had spilled wine on her dress during Schlesinger's eightieth birthday party, and how Ted "gallantly" tried to remove the stain. "A few days later she ran into somebody who said, 'I hear that Ted Kennedy was very drunk at the Schlesinger party and spilled wine all over your dress.'"

And it wasn't only the Washington gossips or the media or the conservatives who now declared open season on Ted Kennedy. The Kopechnes, Mary Jo's parents, gave an interview from their home, where Mary Jo's picture hung over the piano and her stuffed animals were displayed in the corner, on the twentieth anniversary of their daughter's death, and this time they expressed anger, not forgiveness—anger that Ted had waited so long to report the accident. "He was worried about himself, not about Mary Jo," they told the *Ladies' Home Journal*. And they were angry at Mary Jo's fellow boiler room girls, too, whom they felt had been "shut up." "I think there was a big cover-up and that everybody was paid off," Mrs. Kopechne said. "The hearing, the inquest—it was all a farce. The Kennedys had the upper hand and it's been that way ever since."

But the Kopechnes aside, these were small shots—the usual volleys incited by the unrelenting interest in the Kennedy soap opera or the desire to make the Kennedys pay for their seeming blitheness or the unrelenting conservative campaign to damage the Kennedy legacy. The cannon blast came in February 1990. Michael Kelly was a gifted young neoconservative journalist who was making a reputation for himself by skewering politicians, especially liberal politicians, often in the most vicious and hyperbolic prose. What no doubt made Ted Kennedy an appealing target was that Kelly was also a fervent supporter of the war in Iraq, which Ted had just as fervently opposed. "Ted Kennedy on the Rocks," which was published in *GQ*, was arguably the single most important piece ever written about Ted Kennedy, and inarguably the most destructive. The gossip and innuendo about Ted had been scattered, disparate, consigned primarily to the tabloids and to Washington dinner tables, and it was just that: gossip and innuendo. No reputable newspaper, no respectable broadcast network, no acceptable magazine had ever presented documentation either about Kennedy's drinking or about his womanizing. Not one of these top-drawer publications or networks had ever given a credible, detailed, eyewitness, on-the-record account of Kennedy's alleged off-the-rails drunkenness or cited any woman whom he had molested or to whom he had given unwanted attention. Not one had ever published a photograph of Kennedy in a compromising position with a woman. As early as Chappaquiddick, a long *Time* piece referenced a photo of Kennedy "in the company" of a blonde on the yacht of Aristotle Onassis, but without showing the picture. In December 1979, during Kennedy's presidential race, a writer named Suzannah Lessard published a piece in *Washington Monthly* titled "Kennedy's Women Problem, Women's Kennedy Problem." The piece began with the assumption that Kennedy was a philanderer, without citing hard evidence, and moved from that to the idea that his philandering reflected an attitude toward women that, in spite of his championing of women's rights, should disqualify him for their support. Lessard had originally written the piece for *The New Republic*, but the magazine rejected it because, as *Chicago Tribune* reporter Jon Margolis would write, "like other accounts of Kennedy and women, this one offered no specifics but proceeded on the assumption that the rumors are correct, specifically rumors of 'a series of short involvements . . . lunch and a dalliance.'"

But Michael Kelly's *GQ* piece was different. Michael Kelly's accomplishment was to pull it all together in one big accusation and then find a reputable, or, at least, mainstream magazine to publish it. The Ted Kennedy he portrayed was physically a gargoyle: "Up close the face is a shock." And there followed a paragraph that described how the skin had gone from "red roses to gin blossoms"; how the "tracery of burst capillaries shines faintly through the scaly scarlet patches that cover the bloated, mottled cheeks"; how the nose is now "swollen and bulbous"; how the teeth are the "color of old piano keys"; and how the "eyes have yellowed too, and they are so bloodshot, it looks as if he's been weeping." (Kelly didn't seem to realize that it was possible Ted Kennedy was in a near-constant state of weeping.) And then came the anecdotes, one cascading after another, each one a condemnation of a man utterly out of control, not only a souse but a serial lecher: the story of Ted chasing a runway model during a fashion show; the story of the smashed photographs, only this one including a Mexican hat dance around the frames; the story of the fight in the Manhattan bar; two stories from La Brasserie—one in which Ted with Chris Dodd and "two young girls" as his companions grabbed a waitress when the girls went to the restroom and threw her on the table and then threw her on Dodd and then ground himself against her, another in which Ted was surprised while in flagrante with a blond date in a private upstairs room. "In Washington, it sometimes seems as if everyone knows someone who has slept with Kennedy, been invited to sleep with Kennedy, seen Kennedy drunk, been insulted by Kennedy," Kelly wrote. And it

might have *seemed* as if everyone did. And Kelly quoted Bill Thomas of
Roll Call, "He's off the reservation . . . out of control. . . . He has no compunctions whatsoever." The analysis for this behavior, Kelly reported, was
either that Ted, now that he no longer had presidential aspirations, could
do whatever he liked (the privilege theory) or that he was simply a case of
arrested development (the spoiled kid who never grew up theory). Of
course, it was also true that Ted Kennedy, having spent eight years being
thwarted by Ronald Reagan, had lost not only his political clout but also
whatever remained of his image as a great legislator and champion of the
underdog. In short, he was fair game.

By moving the story from the journalistic margins to the center, Kelly
seemed to provide the smoking gun that would confirm what Kennedy
haters and just plain Kennedy watchers had "sort of" known for years.
More, Kelly gave other respectable journals the license to report it. And
they did. The piece was explicitly cited in fourteen international publications, including the London *Sunday Times,* but it was no doubt implicitly
cited in dozens of articles, like Rick Atkinson's in *The Washington Post,*
that used its anecdotes as evidence of Ted Kennedy's waywardness without, apparently, Atkinson independently corroborating them. *Newsweek*
even published an article on Kelly's article, titled, "A Disintegrating
Teddy?"

But for all Kelly's purported reporting—he claimed to have interviewed seventy witnesses for the piece—the evidence he adduced was
scant. Neither of the principal waitresses involved in the two Brasserie
incidents had spoken to him, and another waitress had said that when
she saw Ted, "it was like he might have accidentally fallen" rather than
throwing himself on her fellow waitress. The only actual witnesses to
Ted's flagrant drunkenness and lechery whom Kelly cited by name were
two gossip columnists; a lobbyist, whom, by the man's own admission,
Kennedy once tried to get fired and whose date once ran off with
Kennedy; Howie Carr, the *Boston Herald* columnist notorious for hat-
ing Kennedy; Bill Thomas, the *Roll Call* columnist who told Kelly he
thought Kennedy was "mad . . . and has no compunctions whatsoever";
and the right-wing commentator John Podhoretz, who claimed to have
seen Kennedy pounding down a bottle of wine in record time, though
without a tale of how he behaved afterward. Ted Kennedy might have
been guilty of drunkenness, he might have been guilty of molesting waitresses, he might have been guilty of bellicosity and vandalism and

fraternity-boy hijinks. But Kelly hadn't proved any of it—not by most journalistic standards. It was still gossip and innuendo.

Even so, now it was widely reported gossip and innuendo, and now it was the new dominant Ted Kennedy narrative: Ted Kennedy as a stumblebum. Ted was devastated, his son Patrick said. An aide put it more mildly. "Quite upset," he said. And not long after Kelly's flaying, Rick Burke, the young, disgraced, deeply troubled former administrative assistant who had invented an assailant and a story of hiding in a closet that led to his dismissal, wrote a book in which he described Ted as not only a prodigious womanizer, who, especially for a man his age, would seem to have had time for little else—even Burke admitted to being amazed—but also as a drug addict, which would have been virtually impossible given the schedule he kept and the mental acuity his work demanded. Though Burke had been discredited, and though Ted fought the book's publication, Ted failed to stop it. With the narrative of his debauchery now in the public sphere despite all he had done to rehabilitate his reputation, he asked Tom Oliphant if he would go on the CNN program *Crossfire* and debate the book's publisher. Oliphant agreed, though not without joking to Ted, "What's in it for me?" Ted, who hadn't lost his sense of humor, roared with laughter. And Oliphant did appear, and he argued that if a man walked into a newsroom and made accusations of the sort Burke had made, the first thing a publisher would do was check the story with other sources and corroborating materials. Burke's story had no sources, no corroboration. But it was another blow to a man who had been warding off blows.

So he went to Hyannis Port and to the sea, the place to which he always retreated, the only place he could find relief. "He loved being in nature and kind of being humbled by nature," Patrick would say. "He loved big winds and big waves. It really allowed him to put his own inner turmoil into alignment with the world. He loved the feeling of awe that he got amongst great mountains and great oceans." He had always said that the sea was his metaphor. It was in fact many metaphors—among them, a metaphor for the turbulence of life and for its peace and tranquility, for the insignificance of personal problems, for the magnificence of God and the magnitude of nature, and for the need to keep the rudder true. It all began and ended with the sea. His Hyannis Port neighbor Melissa Ludtke said he would go out on his fifty-five-foot sloop, the *Curragh,* for four or five hours at a time, often with friends—Tunney and Culver and Claude Hooten would come to Hyannis every July—telling stories, singing, drinking, a "lot of laughing." (Watching that camaraderie among friends of forty years, Ludtke also said, taught her about friendship.) The best times were when the southwest winds would blow, which would roll the waves and rock the boat and let Ted hoist the sails to catch that wind. "He never wanted to come back in," she said. He treated the boat, one reporter observed, the "way a teenager nurses his first automobile," wiping a thumbprint off a chrome fitting or polishing the brass. And in August he would usually sail up the coast of Maine to visit Tunney and his friend Lee Fentress at Tenants Harbor or, when Fentress moved farther up the coast, to Islesboro, where Ted used to sail with Jack and Bobby. After the divorce, Ted kept a small apartment in Boston on Marlborough Street, off the square. But Fentress said he spent no more than five or six nights a year there because whenever he came to Boston, he headed immediately for the Cape, even if it meant having to drive back to Boston for a meeting. The Cape rejuvenated him.

But there was that other metaphor of the sea, the undertow, and the perils he could not escape. Ted would later write that his friends never confronted him about his excesses and that he never confronted himself about them either. "It was all part of my desire to escape, to keep moving, to avoid painful memories. And so I lived a string of years in the present tense, not despondently, because that's not my nature"—though even that was something of an avoidance—"but certainly with a sense of the void." And it wasn't true that no one confronted him. Some of them, as Elizabeth Shannon had said, enjoyed the raucous Ted Kennedy. Some of them, however, were afraid of confronting him, knowing that he didn't like being reprimanded about his personal conduct. Dave Burke told Burton Hersh that when he began to offer advice, Ted bristled and said, "If that's what we're going to talk about, why don't I lie down here on the couch? How much do you get for your services, doctor?" After the Kelly piece, with his drinking public and his behavior scrutinized, Ted was still defensive. He insisted he didn't have an alcohol problem. He told biographer Adam Clymer, "I have never felt I had a problem. I don't feel it now." And when John Culver finally broached the subject with him and warned him to cut his liquor consumption, Ted wasn't just sharp with him, as he had been with Dave Burke; he cut Culver off and refused to speak to him for four years—this to one of his closest friends since college.

And so, in his denial, he continued to be pulled down, though, as was often the case with Ted Kennedy, there was worse to come.

III

He had gone to Palm Beach at his sister Jean's request, and the time, the place, and the occasion couldn't have been more appropriate for a man in his condition. It was Easter weekend 1991, the time of resurrection. Now that Rose was too enfeebled to winter there, the Palm Beach estate had fallen into decrepitude. The once-grand house, Joe Kennedy's winter re-treat, was dark and musty, the beds unmade, the paint peeling, the gate weather-beaten, the surrounding wall crumbling—an image that mir-rored the family's demise. One visitor said, "If it was my house, I'd have it exterminated." And along with the aura of decay, it had an aura of death. Ted came to Palm Beach because Stephen Smith, his brother-in-law, had died the previous August, and Jean wanted her brother there to provide her company. As Ted was later to tell it, he, Jean, and William Barry, a former FBI agent who had protected Bobby and become a friend of the family, were sitting on the patio reminiscing, an "emotional conversa-tion," he called it, a "very draining conversation," a conversation about Steve. He would also describe it as a "haunting moment, a haunting time for me." Overwhelmed by grief, Ted decided to do what he typically did when he felt the undertow. He escaped. Earlier, he had seen Patrick, and Jean and Stephen's thirty-year-old son, William, pass by the glass win-dows entering onto the patio, and he asked them if they wanted to go out. Patrick and Ted left and wound up at a Palm Beach bistro called Ann'z at about 10:45, where they drank beers. Then, a little over an hour later, now also with Willie Smith, who had joined them, they moved on to Au Bar, described in *People* magazine as a "chichi nightspot where trust-fund idlers, obscure blue bloods, bejeweled society matrons and erstwhile ce-lebs like Roxanne Pulitzer go for gossip and $12 cheeseburgers." John A. Farrell, the *Boston Globe* reporter, described it more colorfully by citing a denizen who was "dressed with a double-breasted blue blazer and a beau-tiful white shirt and gorgeous tie, and he had this gray hair swept back." But "from the waist down, he was in a black skirt and stockings and high heels, and he was dancing." And Farrell delivered this judgment of the "weird place": "For Kennedy to have gotten anywhere near that scene was just awful, and he deserved everything he got." Ted, by one account, was a regular on the Palm Beach bar scene, and ordered a double Chivas Regal on the rocks, and sat with Patrick and Willie at a table near the dance floor. At the bar was Patricia Bowman, a twenty-nine-year-old single mother and the stepdaughter of Michael O'Neil, the former chairman of the General Tire and Rubber Company, and beside her was a friend, Anne Weatherly Mercer. Patrick got up to dance and met another young woman named Michele Cassone, who waitressed at a local restaurant, and he invited her back to the table. Willie returned to the table with Patricia Bowman, and after last call, at roughly three a.m., Patrick asked Cassone if she wanted to come back to the compound for a drink. She agreed, driving her Toyota while Patrick drove a white convertible. Ted returned home separately. And neither Patrick nor Ted saw Willie leave. He just "split," as Ted would put it.

On this much there was agreement. Then stories diverged. Back at the house, Patrick poured Cassone a white wine on the patio, overlooking the beach, and now, depending on the account, sat with Ted and talked idly about scuba diving and the importance of family, even though Ted was "very drunk," Cassone said. She and Patrick eventually went inside the house, to his bedroom, and again depending on the account, she said that Ted suddenly appeared in a long Oxford shirt but without pants and said nothing. She said she felt "weird" and told Patrick, "I'm out of here." So Patrick walked her to her car, and she left at about four a.m. But by another account, also Cassone's, after she told Patrick she was leaving, he convinced her to stay. They sat on the seawall where Ted, now with trousers, joined them and talked about the ocean and the importance of family. But she said that Ted was "making things sound strange"; she was no more detailed than that, other than to say, "It wasn't exactly innocent," and that "Patrick was getting edgy." So they left Ted behind, took a stroll on the beach, kissed—"innocent stuff"—and then she said it was time for her to go home. As Patrick walked her to her car, she asked him if his father embarrassed him. "Yeah, sometimes he embarrasses me," she said he answered. And then she drove off at between four-thirty and five a.m. And Ted and Patrick retired.

It was what happened between Willie Smith and Patricia Bowman that night, and what Ted was told about it, and what he then told police, where the stories got garbled. The next morning, Saturday, Ted hosted a lunch for a former girlfriend where the "mood was light," according to a guest quoted by *People,* and later that evening, he had drinks with friends at a restaurant called Chuck and Harold's. If Ted seemed agitated or nervous, no one noticed it. On Sunday he attended Mass at St. Edward's Roman Catholic Church and then went to lunch at Chuck and Harold's, where a diner said she overheard Ted telling his nephew, "You know, she's going to say it's rape," though Ted insisted that he was not with Smith then, and another diner would corroborate Ted's story, telling the police that Ted was dining not with Smith but with Patrick. It is uncertain exactly when Ted first heard that something had gone amiss between Smith and Bowman—something serious. Police arrived at the house at roughly one p.m. Easter Sunday afternoon and asked to speak to Ted—Ted would later say he didn't know they wanted to speak with him. William Barry, the former FBI agent, who would say that he was not apprised of what their inquiry was in reference to, told them that Ted was not home at the time, though, according to *Time* magazine, he "clearly" was, and the two, Ted and Barry, conferred in the kitchen after the police left. Ted later claimed that he was told nothing about a sexual assault—"I was never, never told that"—only that Barry might have mentioned that police wanted to ask him about an urn that might have been stolen from the house. An hour after their first visit, the police phoned the house again, and a housekeeper told them that Barry had driven Ted and Smith to the airport, even though he hadn't. (Whether this was a calculated effort to throw off the police, or whether the housekeeper really didn't know, is unclear.) It was only when Barry returned the police department's call, at 3:20, that he said he learned about an alleged sexual offense and told Ted after the call that the police wanted to speak with Willie. Still, Ted said the word *rape* was never used and that he thought it was about "sexual harassment." (Elsewhere, Ted said that Barry mentioned a "sexual battery.") In any case, Ted said he told Barry that "we ought to get to the bottom of this," and he called a friend, a Miami attorney named Marvin Rosen, whom he asked "to go down to the police station first thing in the morning and find out what this whole incident was about."* According to a deposition given by Pat-

---

*In another account, as reported in *The Washington Post*, Ted said he had phoned attorney Marvin Ross at 7:34 p.m. on Saturday night, not to ask his legal advice, only to wish him a happy holiday, but that Ross wasn't home, and that he then tried to reach him twice on Sunday but failed. "Ross" was likely a mistransmission of "Rosen," though that Ted was phoning him Saturday night, purportedly not knowing about any legal situation, seems implausible. "Kennedy Houseguest Saw '10 Seconds' of Incident," *WP,* May 15, 1991.

rick, he, his father, and Barry spoke on the beach seawall Sunday night about possible charges against Willie, and Patrick said, "I think you better talk to Willie because he had a guest who was a real weirdo and whacked out." And it was only then, Patrick said, that Barry told them the police were investigating a "complaint by a woman who was visiting the other night" and that "there was a sexual assault or battery." Later that night Willie phoned Ted and told him, "You know there's been some allegations against me," and he offered to tell Ted the "whole story." Ted told him to call Marvin Rosen instead. Ted returned to Washington on Monday and, in a divergence from his son's account, said it was only then that he heard about the rape allegation.

Smith's whole story, as he would later relate it in court, was that he met Patricia Bowman at Au Bar when she brushed against him. He testified that he bought her a drink, danced with her, and they kissed on the dance floor, then he brought her to his uncle's table. When, some hours later, he saw Ted and Patrick leave, he told her, "There goes my ride," and she offered to drive him home. At the Kennedy house, he invited her inside and then out onto the lawn where, he said, she began saying strange things: that she had been there before, that there was some bad family history. When Smith protested that he didn't understand, she snipped, "I didn't expect you to, Michael," and demanded that he show her his identification. He suggested that they go out for a swim, but she suggested instead that they walk down to the water, and Smith said he left to get a beach towel, then returned, and the two of them walked arm in arm. Smith believed they were going to have sex, and when he spread out the towel, they began necking, she unbuttoned his pants, she removed her underwear, and they stimulated each other until he ejaculated. Then they went for a swim. When he came back to the towel, they had intercourse, during which he accidentally called her "Kathy." She snapped then, Smith said, and ordered him to get off of her, which he said he did. He said he then jumped into the pool, swam a few laps, and got his clothes. By then she was in the house. He got her and walked her to her car, which was when she said, "You raped me, Michael," and told him she had called the police, though in fact she had called her friend Anne Mercer, with whom she had been at Au Bar earlier in the evening. Then she drove off but stopped, rolled down her window, apologized, and asked for his number. When he said he didn't remember it, she snapped again. "Tell it to Kathy," she said, and drove off. But she didn't leave the premises. When Smith went back into the house and ran into Patrick, she was in the kitchen. He took her into the den and asked if she wanted to talk, but she shook and cried and said that "Michael had raped her," though Smith took out his ID to show her his name. She stormed off again, but when Smith got to the living room, Anne Mercer was there with her boyfriend. To prove that they had been on the premises, Mercer and the boyfriend took an urn— the urn about which Ted expected the police to question him. (Bowman later testified that the boyfriend took the urn because "he thought she wanted him to.")

Patricia Bowman told a very different story.* At Au Bar, she had brushed against Smith on her way from the restroom, and the two struck up a conversation. In her telling, Smith had been nice, a gentleman. "I felt I could trust him," she said. In the café, they talked about her two-year-old daughter and about Smith's medical education, since he was finishing his fourth year at Georgetown Medical School. Then, after she agreed to drive him home, the two of them got to the Kennedy compound, and he gave her a chaste kiss and got out of the car. But instead of saying goodbye, he went to the driver's side of the car and asked her if she wanted to see the house. Even then she thought she was safe; there was, after all, a senator there, and she assumed there would be security. After taking her to the kitchen, he suggested the walk on the beach and a swim. But when they got to the lawn, and he began to disrobe, she would say that she had no desire to swim and that she got nervous and got up to leave, which was

---

*There would be a heated journalistic debate over whether to reveal Bowman's, the victim's, name. Ordinarily, rape victims were given anonymity as a form of protection. But when the supermarket tabloid the *Globe* named Bowman, she was "outed," and other media outlets considered whether to follow suit. NBC News was the first reputable news organization to break the self-enforced rule, on Tuesday, April 15, the day after the *Globe* story. *The New York Times* used her name the next day in an article that gave an account of her life—"She likes to drink and have fun with the ne'er-do-wells in café society," it quoted an acquaintance—on the basis that, as Alan Siegel, the *Times* assistant managing editor, told *The Washington Post*: "If we have a case against members of a very prominent family— with the senator himself involved in the evening's goings-on—there's an obligation to talk about the background of everyone involved." Howard Kurtz, "The Ethics of Identifying Rape Victims," *WP*, April 18, 1991. A *Times* article justified the use of Bowman's name and the account of her background by saying, "If the Senator's career is damaged beyond a point, for good reason or ill, it could affect important legislation, from national health insurance to refugee aid." Jonathan Kwitny, "Public Interest, Public Naming," *NYT*, May 8, 1991. Ted himself thought it "unfortunate for the victim." "Kennedy Faults Media for Identifying Woman," *NYT*, April 21, 1991.

when he grabbed her leg and began pulling at her clothes and lay on top of her and raped her. There was no mention of the mutual stimulation or the odd remarks he alleged she had made or the name "Kathy." She retreated to the house and to the pantry, she said, where she hid, then composed herself, got out, and phoned Anne Mercer to come and get her. When Smith confronted her before Mercer's arrival, and she told him he had raped her, she would say, "He looked at me, the calmest, smuggest, most arrogant man, and he said, 'No one will believe you.'"

But the Palm Beach police and prosecutors did believe her. William Kennedy Smith would be charged with sexual battery. And Ted Kennedy would be investigated for obstruction of justice.

And then the chaos descended. Though the story had no major import other than for the principals, and though Ted Kennedy, the only famous participant, was only very peripherally involved, and though the story was salacious and voyeuristic and basically tabloid fodder, hundreds of journalists, three hundred by one estimate, arrived in Palm Beach to report on it—the "greatest assemblage of journalists since Operation Desert Storm," wrote Margaret Carlson in *Time*, referencing the recent military campaign against Iraq, "reporters from as far away as Norway." She wrote that one tabloid had bid six figures for the alleged victim's story, while another tabloid reporter handed his business card to a hospital employee on the back of which he had written, "$500 for the name," meaning the name of the victim. Another reporter noted of his colleagues, "So many reporters are encamped on the alleged victim's front lawn that catering trucks deliver meals." Meg Greenfield in *Newsweek* decried the circus atmosphere even as she participated in it. "Do you get the sense that family and friends on both sides are attempting to get the truth of what happened and achieve a just outcome?" she asked. "Or do you get, as I do, a sense that the Palm Beach events have become a fee-generating, T-shirt manufacturing, media-hysterics' hustler's holiday?" The editor of the *National Enquirer* supermarket tabloid boasted, "The *Enquirer* is turning into the world of regular journalism. . . . We're the trailblazers." (He was right. The *Times* originally put the story on page twelve, the *Post* on page six. But that was before it turned into a tabloid sensation and migrated to the front pages.) Stephen Hess of the Brookings Institution agreed. "*The Washington Post* and other elite papers sent their reporters to Palm Beach after the same story. They were truly in the gutter with the tabloids this time." "It's gotten totally out of control," Palm Beach's police chief, Joseph Terlizzese, complained. "Since when do reputable publications publish rumor and gossip and go around interviewing half-drunk people?"

The answer was, when a Kennedy was involved. Though the media had become much more attuned to scandal, much more willing to scandal-monger—"junkyard journalism," one political scientist called it—and though they were locked into their own insatiable addiction, they were especially enthusiastic about a scandal involving the Kennedys, and Ted had done much to rouse that enthusiasm by generating so many scandals. "Of course the case would not have attracted such attention if a Kennedy had not been involved," wrote Dominick Dunne in *Vanity Fair*, the publication itself attesting to the mania. "But a Kennedy was involved, and the Kennedys are America's most famous theatrical family and have been for a half a century. They have outdone the Greeks for tragedy. They have outdone Hollywood for scandal. Love them, hate them, they are bigger than life, and they know instinctively how to play each scene in their continuing, mesmerizing saga." It was Chappaquiddick all over again.

Willie Smith might have been the protagonist or possibly antagonist of the Palm Beach melodrama. Ted Kennedy was the star. "It was the Senator's presence here that set off the avalanche of media coverage," reported *The Washington Post*, "and transformed a minor story into an epic saga." Almost all the coverage orbited Ted. What did he know, and when did he know it? Was he engaged in a cover-up to save his nephew? Had he lied to the police? Did his deposition contradict his public statements? Did his deposition contradict Patrick's deposition? What was he doing out at three a.m. to begin with? These were the questions—tabloid questions—that the respectable press now felt the license to ask since the tabloid press and the respectable press had gotten closer to convergence. "You hear something delicious, you can't confirm it yourself, and in some quarters of the press there's an attitude of just hoping that someone else will make the first move so you can get on the bandwagon," admitted *Newsweek* editor Richard Smith. In Palm Beach, everyone seemed to have hopped onto the bandwagon, including *Newsweek*. The Palm Beach episode was the magazine's cover story on April 29 with the tabloid headline "Unanswered Questions in Palm Beach." And there could be no doubt that if the respectable press had now lowered its standards and surrendered to scandal, Ted Kennedy had been the primary engine in driving that surrender. Ted Kennedy had provided the opportunity.

But it wasn't just the celebrity that prompted the frenzy. There was the story itself—not the story of the alleged rape, though that had its own titillations, but the bigger story, the story of the demise of the Kennedy family and of Ted Kennedy's contribution to that demise. The Palm Beach episode was almost immediately turned into a parable of power and privilege transmogrified into perdition, a parable with terrible implications for Ted. A "tar ball massive enough to stain the reputation of everyone involved in it," *Newsweek* called it. A "family fighting for its life," Dominick Dunne wrote in *Vanity Fair*. And Ted Kennedy was regarded as both the symbol and the source of his family's decline. "It would be sad enough if Ted Kennedy's demons had blighted only his own life," *Newsweek* began its first article on Palm Beach, accusing Ted of "presiding over a late-night drinking party." "Now they are eating his young—the third generation of Kennedys, already scarred with their own tragedies of drink, drugs and early death." *People* pronounced the episode the end of Ted: "In the long downward slope of Sen. Edward Kennedy's private life and public career, what happened at the family's Palm Beach, Fla., retreat last month may, in retrospect, mark the point at which sorry decline turned into free-fall." The problem was that Ted Kennedy had been in free-fall long before the Palm Beach episode, and Palm Beach was the result, not the cause. One piece, in *The New York Times*, even commented on the rustiness of the vaunted Kennedy response machine—the machine that supposedly kicked into action after the Chappaquiddick accident and that manipulated the justice system. But that was another of the Kennedy myths. The Kennedys suffered, none more than Ted, for being thought of as running a smooth and efficient operation that got them out of their scrapes, a conflation of John Kennedy's political machinery and the family's alleged machinery, when there was little efficiency, just a wealthy, hapless family stumbling and bumbling about.

And while the Palm Beach episode further sullied the entire Kennedy clan, raising the temperature on the long-simmering cynical backlash against the love that Americans had bestowed on them in more innocent times, as if those Americans had been fools to fall for that romance, it also wound up undoing over twenty years of public rehabilitation for Ted Kennedy, who was now fully disgraced. Lance Morrow, in a long essay in *Time* that attempted to plumb the hold Ted had on the American psyche, called him a "lightning rod with strange electricities still firing in the air around him—passions that are not always his responsibility but may emanate from psychic disturbances in the country itself." Though Morrow called him "one of the great lawmakers of the century," he said he "lives under a peculiar metaphysic": "He had to soldier on in the messy world after Camelot floated away into memory. Unlike his brothers, extinguished in their prime, Teddy would get older and coarser and lose some of the boyo's flashing charm. He would make mistakes—something that did not happen in Camelot—and he would pay for them." And Morrow noted too the "crack in life" that had been caused by Jack's and Bobby's deaths, after which the Kennedy myth fractured, and the "brief shining moment" gave way to "long, sordid aftermaths."

Mistakes he had made, though in Palm Beach that Easter weekend, Ted's sins—and they were frequently called that—consisted primarily of his exercising poor judgment in going out drinking with his nephew and son late at night on Good Friday, after a heartbreaking conversation, hardly a sin of the mortal variety, and then showing up in front of his son and the girl his son had taken home in a shirt without pants, though Ted insisted he was wearing a long nightshirt, not an ordinary Oxford. These were his offenses, while his nephew was being accused of rape—save one more. His crime, as *Newsweek* put it, was leading his nephews down the road to depravity, which was an irony. For most of his life, Ted Kennedy had been the beneficiary of his family, especially of his brothers, Jack and Bobby, whose aura and public affection he inherited. People read them into him. Now Ted, who had generally been able to control his drinking and who likely did not chase women half his age given his age-appropriate consorts, despite the new Michael Kelly–generated meme that he had, was having his nephew's behavior read back into him. Ted Kennedy had committed no crimes that night at Palm Beach. He hadn't even been particularly reckless, though his drinking was certainly an issue and he lacked judgment in imbibing, but that hardly merited the level of abuse slung at him. He had gone on a long melancholy binge, then returned to his home, perhaps tipsy, talked a bit with his son and the girl he had brought there, and apparently appeared in a nightshirt. These were the actions of a sad, self-abasing, emotionally bruised, even pathetic man, a man at the end of his tether, a self-destructive man who should have known better, but hardly a debauched one, and had it not been for the allegations against his nephew, or the memories of Chappaquiddick, which, in truth, it resembled not at all, or the meme of his unruliness, probably no one would have thought anything of it.

But he would not be forgiven for that mild transgression—"He deserved everything he got," John A. Farrell had said—in part, it seemed, because, as Morrow observed, he had betrayed the Kennedy image, in part because his reputation as a louche inebriate preceded him, and in part because there was a sense he had never paid in full for his alleged sins at Chappaquiddick. "Nobody suggests Senator Kennedy was present at the alleged attack," wrote conservative *New York Times* columnist William Safire, expressing this latter view. "The only sin charged to him was appearing in a T-shirt [Michelle Cassone had never said he was wearing only a T-shirt] elsewhere on the estate before the other woman and his son." And then: "In getting the full-court tabloid press, the Senator is serving his unsentenced sentence for slipping past the law on another night 22 years ago. But let's not confuse poetic justice with real justice: Ted Kennedy is being made to squirm for what he did not face then, not for what he did now." Richard Cohen of *The Washington Post* was more dismissive of the man but not of the charges: "Teddy may well be good for nothing." And Cohen then chastised Ted for waking up his nephew and son, making it sound as if they were children, and, like Safire, referred back to Chappaquiddick. "Well, you only get to leave the scene once in a public career." And always there was the sneer about the Kennedys feeling that they were not subject to ordinary rules of conduct, that they were above the law. "Surrounded by sycophants, Edward Kennedy thinks his name and title are license to do whatever he wants," wrote *Boston Globe* columnist Mike Barnicle, who had once been a Kennedy friend, "and apparently the only voice he hears in that dark lonely time before danger calls is the drink saying, 'Go ahead, you can get away with anything,' " which hardly described how Ted Kennedy really felt. And Barnicle too pronounced Ted politically dead. Margaret Carlson in *Time* was more brutal in laying out "rules" on how Kennedys behave when they get in trouble: "First, confine risky behavior to one of the vacation houses where the local police are malleable. Second, surround yourself with the best lawyers and investigators the combined trust funds can buy. Third, when finally cornered by the press, promise total cooperation and regret you cannot say more because it might impede the official investigation. Fourth, impede the official investigation."

But worse than the lashings he received for his alleged moral derelictions were the humiliations meted out to him for his being *sans* pants and drunk, though not, by anyone's description, an insensible drunk or an obnoxious drunk and not, except in the tabloid fantasies, a man who chased young women that night. Still, the humiliations came relentlessly because they could, because it was felt Ted Kennedy deserved them. The *New York Post*, a paper owned by Ted's sworn enemy Rupert Murdoch, ran daily headlines that first week: "Kennedy Mansion Sex Probe"; "Bachelors Party"; " 'I Want Justice,' " an alleged quote from the alleged victim; "Teddy's Sex Romp (Says Half-Nude Senator Chased Her Around Mansion)," which had no basis in fact whatsoever; and "WHERE WAS TEDDY?" when the alleged rape occurred. The *New York Post*'s Mike McAlary talked of "girls all over the place," and of the Senator "on the make"—neither of which was true—and then compared the Kennedy family that night to the Manson family who had brutally slaughtered innocent victims in Los Angeles in 1969. And worse perhaps even than the tabloid humiliations were the humiliations by the late-night comedians, whose ridicule turned Ted into a laughingstock—forever pantsless. Twenty years earlier Chappaquiddick had made Ted the butt of mordant jokes about his driving. Now Palm Beach made him the butt of skewering jokes about his recklessness. "How many other 59-year-old men still go to Florida for spring break?" quipped host Jay Leno on *The Tonight Show*. How is a solar eclipse like nightfall? Leno asked rhetorically on another program. The answer: "The temperature drops, the stars appear, flowers close up. And Ted Kennedy takes his pants off." Three weeks after the Palm Beach incident, David Letterman read a Top Ten List on the "Top Ten Good Things About Ted Kennedy," which included "Not the kind of person who snobbishly insists on wearing pants," "Still waiting to hear from the Palm Beach police," and "Holds high score on the Pac-Man machine at Au Bar."

But amid all the flagellation Ted Kennedy received for Palm Beach, and in all the derision he had to endure, there was one criticism that not only affected him and the other Kennedys but also struck at his life's mission to serve the powerless: that he lacked all moral credibility. This was where his carelessness was most costly, not just for him but for others he purported to serve. Again and again critics referred to the bifurcation between the tabloid celebrity Ted Kennedy and the legislative one. A front-page story in *The New York Times*, citing a speech that Ted had given at American University—a speech for which he received a standing ovation—called it "one more scene in the familiar morality play that has played out in Washington in recent days on the two images of Edward Kennedy: the powerful Senator who is caretaker of the family legacy, and the hard-drinking roue." Two Teds—always two Teds—with a foot in two worlds. *Boston Globe* columnist Ellen Goodman, after calling his behavior a "picture of conduct unbecoming," wrote, "What is breaking down in the Palm Beach aftershock is the careful cardboard barrier erected between the senator at work and Teddy at play." And she concluded, "He must have believed he could partition his life forever. It's the illusion of being in control." (She was right, though she didn't seem to realize the cost of tearing down the partition. As fellow *Globe* columnist David Nyhan wrote, "Take Teddy out of the Senate and what do you have?" and then enumerated Ted's legislative triumphs.) James Carroll, in a cover story for *The New Republic* titled "The End of the Dream," lacerated Ted, accusing him and those who supported him of accepting a dual morality: "The dualism in which we have engaged, applying separate moral standards to the private and public acts of Senator Edward Kennedy, has been wrong." Which is precisely what Ted's conservative opponents had been saying about him since Chappaquiddick: He talked about morality in his public life, but he was a moral bankrupt in his personal life. Could one really separate the two? Conservatives, self-servingly, said one couldn't. Liberals, self-servingly, said one could and that Ted had. But conservatives now prevailed—the media narrative was proof—and their argument effectively reduced Ted Kennedy's moral authority and effectively undermined liberalism generally yet again. "The sadness is that Ted's many virtues as a public man are being subverted and destroyed by many of his frailties as a private man," Arthur Schlesinger, Jr., wrote in his journal. That was Ted Kennedy's personal sadness. The greater sadness for liberalism and for those who believed in an active government to help those who needed help would be, as Garry Wills described it: "He is the Left to much of the Right, and his downfall would signal the permanent fall of the Left." Which meant that liberalism too was caught in the undertow.

FOURTEEN

Mea Culpa

I T WAS A harsh spring and a cruel summer. There were the criticisms and the taunts and the jokes and the political obituaries. Did he have an alcohol problem? Bryant Gumbel asked Ted point-blank on the *Today* show, and Ted stiffened in anger and embarrassment. There were the on-going investigations as the family braced for Willie Smith's trial, and the ongoing drips of information in the press, stories from other women who said that Smith had assaulted them, including a former girlfriend of Willie's own cousin, Max Kennedy, and one who said Willie had date-raped her, and an announcement from the prosecutor, Moira Lasch, that three women had come forward to tell stories, similar to Patricia Bowman's, of Willie Smith's conduct—that he was sweet, seemingly a gentleman, until he drank, and then he became a predator. There were the echoes and af-tershocks: Joan Kennedy being pulled over by police on 193, south of Bos-ton, the month after the Palm Beach episode, for weaving in traffic and then failing a sobriety test, and her then being ordered to an inpatient program; and later that summer, Michele Cassone, Patrick Kennedy's "date" the evening of the episode, overdosing and being turned over to mental health authorities, reportedly telling police that she wanted to end her life; and Ted Jr. and Patrick both sinking in drugs and alcohol.

But in that cruel and awful summer of agony and humiliation and reckoning, as Ted Kennedy was being pulled deeper by the undertow, he seemed to find, at long last, the hope of a rescue. He had known Edmund and Doris Reggie for years. Edmund had first met John Kennedy at the 1956 Democratic convention when Edmund, only twenty-nine, had sat in the Louisiana delegation. He was pledged to Tennessee governor Frank Clement for the vice-presidential nomination, but Clement had withdrawn, which, largely because the Louisiana delegation sat next to the Massachusetts delegation, got Reggie to thinking about John Kennedy, who was actively seeking the nomination. Reggie arranged to meet Jack and then had him address the entire delegation, which then pledged to Kennedy, infuriating the state's governor, Earl Long, who had pledged to Senator Estes Kefauver, primarily because Kefauver, who had conducted hearings on gambling, had skipped Louisiana in return for Long's support. Reggie's attraction to Jack, he would admit, was largely their shared Catholicism. (Reggie, his wife, and his secretary attended noon Mass every day for over thirty years.) But even though Jack didn't get the vice-presidential nomination that year—Kefauver did—Reggie and he kept in touch, and just before announcing for the presidency in 1960, Jack made a visit to Reggie's hometown, Crowley, and its annual International Rice Festival, where 135,000 people reportedly turned out, even though Crowley itself only had a population of 14,000. Reggie managed the state for Jack in the general election, and Jack carried it. And when Jack died, Reggie transferred his allegiance to Bobby, who had been scheduled to attend a reception at the Reggie house in Crowley the day after Martin Luther King, Jr.'s, assassination, and then, after Bobby's own assassination, Reggie transferred his allegiance to Ted. When Ted ran for the presidency in 1980, he received one vote after the call for acclamation had delivered all the other delegates to Jimmy Carter. It was Doris Reggie, who told her husband, "I could never vote for anyone but Teddy."

But it was more than allegiance. It became friendship. Ted began inviting the Reggies to McLean. Then the Reggies bought a house on Nantucket—Ted insisted they buy the house behind his in Hyannis, but Edmund said that knowing Teddy, "It would be one party from Memorial Day 'til Labor Day"—and Ted, one of their first visitors, brought them a pot of lobster stew as a housewarming gift. That was the first of many visits over many summers. When Ted bought his beloved schooner *Mya*, the first place he sailed was to Nantucket, where the Reggies said they christened the boat. (Edmund would recall Ted had a crew of "three beautiful girls.") Ted became the Reggies' New England guide. After the Reggies' move, and after they had a boat trailered up from Crowley, Ted told them that it was the wrong kind of boat, that he would buy them the proper boat, as a kind of broker, which he did, though Edmund joked with Ted about how much he "made on that deal." They called him "The Commander," the name he loved. On these visits, Ted, usually accompanied by a girlfriend, would typically go sailing or walking on the beach—Doris Reggie said that Ted had once stopped her from picking a wildflower because, he warned, "We don't pick wildflowers here. We let them go"—and he would spend the night in their home. Sometimes the Reggies' daughter Vicki, a Washington attorney, would be visiting them with her young children. (Ted knew her because she had interned in his office in the 1970s.) Vicki recalled one visit in particular, a picnic, just before the hearings for Supreme Court nominee Robert Bork, and Ted began talking about Bork, and Vicki said she found herself "in rapt attention," and that she hadn't seen this side of Ted Kennedy before, presumably meaning she had only seen the social, gregarious side of Ted. He promised to send her more information, making a note that he tucked in his pocket, and when he returned to Washington, he made good on that promise.

But then came the intervening years, the years that began Ted's personal decline, and the excessive drinking and carousing. And then came Palm Beach, when the darkness Ted had tried to outrun had overtaken him but where his own lack of self-control had overtaken him too. The Reggies had visited Washington—they were with Ted when he made that impromptu visit to Arlington Cemetery and his brothers' graves—and had invited him to Vicki's house in northwest Washington once or twice, but Ted hadn't gone. By this point, Vicki was divorced, living with her two young children, and still practicing law. That June, two and a half months after Palm Beach, the Reggies were celebrating their fortieth wedding anniversary and made a point of flying around the country to spend time with each of their children. They wound up in Washington and phoned Ted, without saying anything about their anniversary, to invite him to a cookout at Vicki's house: June 17. They told him to bring a date. But Ted, who had recently broken up with Palm Beach realtor Dragana Lickle, came alone carrying a bottle of fine wine. When he arrived, Vicki answered the door. "What's the matter?" she quipped. "Couldn't you get a date?" To which Ted riposted, "I thought *you* would be my date." "Dream on, Kennedy," he claims she answered. He assisted her in the kitchen, and for the rest of the evening, as Vicki would recall, "We just had that banter going on," but, she insisted, "just as friends." The Reggies had also invited John Culver, possibly to heal the breach that had opened between him and Ted after Culver's confronting Ted on his drinking, and Culver arrived with his young son because Culver's wife was away. "A delightful evening," Edmund Reggie called it, but added, "Nobody thought anything of it"—that is, nobody thought that it was anything but a friendly get-together. Culver's son began acting up, and Culver thought he might be coming down with something, so they left. And then it was just the Reggies and Vicki and Ted. *Nobody thought anything of it.* But Ted Kennedy did think something of it. "I had known Vicki before," he would say. "But this was the first time I really saw her." And at evening's end, as he recalled, "I hadn't felt that relaxed or lighthearted in a long time."

For a man who had been anguished by his marriage and by his wife's condition, Ted Kennedy had found a woman who couldn't have been more different from Joan Bennett Kennedy. Joan's parents were alcoholics who eventually divorced. Vicki Reggie's parents were deeply religious and deeply devoted to each other, and Vicki's was a blissful childhood in a large family of eight. Her mother's family owned the Bunny Bread baking company in New Orleans, which provided the Reggies with money, and her father was a judge and local banker, which provided them with status. "There was such a camaraderie of being at Vicki's house," a childhood friend remembered. The house had a jukebox, a pool table, a swimming pool, a pinball machine, and a "big movie theater with no adults and plenty of popcorn"—"everything to keep them home," Edmund would say. Victoria had grown up in Crowley—"How lucky we are to live here," the *Crowley Post-Signal* once enthused—and attended parochial schools there, where she was a straight A student, save for one B in physical education, right through high school, Notre Dame, where she put on a Daniel Boone costume and volunteered to be the mascot for her school's football team, the Pioneers. Edmund recalled taking her to the optometrist for an eye test when she was twelve, then bringing her back the next year. The doctor told Edmund that he had to change the eye chart. She had memorized the old one from the year before. Vicki was confident, assertive, ambitious, a go-getter, the class valedictorian. She attended Newcomb College, the women's sister school at Tulane University in New Orleans, where she majored in English, was president of Kappa Alpha Theta sorority there, and was elected to Phi Beta Kappa. (It was after she graduated that her father got her the internship in Ted's office; the family kept a photograph of her with Ted from that summer.) She studied law at Tulane, was named an editor of the law review, was selected for the Order of the Coif, the honorary legal fraternity, was graduated summa cum laude, and then clerked for Robert Sprecher of the U.S. Seventh Circuit Court of Appeals in Chicago, where she met and married a fellow attorney, Grier Raclin, in 1980. Vicki was driven. The couple moved to Washington, and Vicki joined the firm of Caplin & Drysdale, and then left for a firm that was later assumed by Keck, Mahin & Cate, specializing in tax law. "She eats a lot of salads at her desk," a colleague told *People* magazine, attesting to her work ethic.

That night at Vicki's house, Ted was smitten with her and asked her at evening's end if she would go out with him the following night. (By another account, he phoned her the next day.) She said she would, then wondered why she had agreed. "I mean, I wasn't expecting it at all," she would later say. She hadn't thought of it as a "romantic date." She had recently gone through a difficult divorce and wasn't looking for a relationship. "I never wanted to marry again," she would say, and, "I thought, 'Who could be a better person to go out to dinner with and not have to worry about a long-term commitment than Teddy?'" Ted was to say that he wasn't thinking of a relationship either. "I never thought I was going to get married. I think the people I had been very close to I had lost in my life, and I don't think I was ever prepared to think in those terms again." But Patrick felt that after Palm Beach, after the ridicule Ted was enduring and the gibes against him and the disgrace into which he had sunk, he must have been thinking of a path forward, possibly through a relationship. "I think there was a note of despair in his psyche," John Tunney would say of this period, "that maybe somehow 'I've gotten onto the wrong train and I'm heading down a road that's going to end up in catastrophe,'" either through assassination or self-destruction. "I think Vicki represented for him a way out, a way to suddenly have hope again that he could pull his life together. In a complete way." Seeing nothing to lose and seemingly not much to gain, Vicki agreed to a date and then another and another—"low key," she described those first dates, getting to know each other. They began going out regularly, to dinner, often with others, and Vicki told her mother, "Oh, Mom. We're just friends." But Ted was an ardent friend. He telephoned her, by his own admission, "a lot." He sent her flowers and notes. He left poems at her door. Still, Vicki took it slowly, discreetly. As Edmund would put it, "It didn't happen to her as fast as it happened to him." When friends visited from Crowley and asked if she was seeing anyone, she told them, "I can't talk about him. I can't even tell you his name." Still, all the Reggie children spoke with their parents daily, so Edmund and Doris knew every time Vicki was going out with Ted, and as Edmund said, "We could tell that it was developing."

It was a steady courtship, uneventful, save for a tiff late that summer when Ted sailed his *Mya* to Nantucket, where Vicki was visiting her parents, and then invited her to sail back with him to Hyannis to avoid an incoming storm, Hurricane Bob. Vicki, who was no sailor and didn't share Ted's love of the sea and was clearly unsettled by Ted trying to outrun the hurricane, declined the invitation, and Ted was hurt. He imposed what he would call "radio silence," not speaking to her for two weeks, while, he said, he tried to think of ways to break that silence. He was sitting at his desk shortly after Labor Day when his secretary buzzed him to say that Victoria Reggie was on the phone. He said it was the first time she had called *him*. And he would say that by the time the conversation ended, he invited himself to dinner at her home, and they entered a new phase of their relationship.

"Very old-fashioned" was how Vicki described what was becoming a courtship. Since her son, Curran, and her daughter, Caroline, were still young—eight and five respectively—Ted and Vicki didn't go out often. They developed a routine of Ted coming over for dinner and the two of them talking while they prepared it together. Often he would read the children to sleep, and then he and Vicki would talk during dinner, and talk afterward, "sit-in-the-parlor kind of talking," she called it, seldom about politics, mainly about family, about how her grandparents had come from Lebanon and his from Ireland, and about the affinities between those two experiences, and just generally about their lives. And she said that "there was a link that I think was almost familial," given the relationship between her father and Ted's brothers, "which was a comfort and something very good." And then, at about ten-thirty, Ted would go home. But he would come back again the next night, and they would talk again— more stories, more intimacies. He told her about his mother, and about his childhood, and about the difficult, painful times he had in school. They listened to opera together. He read "John Brown's Body" to her, a favorite of Jack's, and he would find the rhythm in the words—loving the poem, loving that rhythm. She said that they got "so close and connected" during that period. "Just friends," she had told her mother. But he was a close friend now, and Doris, who loved Ted but knew his proclivity for women, warned her daughter not to fall in love with him. A "lasting relationship was not going to happen," Doris said. And Vicki would reassure her again, "Don't worry. We're just friends." But they weren't just friends. Doris could hear it—hear the change in the tone of her daughter's voice. "I can hear it as if it's happening, that he was just winning her over." One night after they had established their routine, Ted phoned Vicki to say he would have to miss dinner because of Senate business. And Vicki thought, "Oh my. I really miss this person. Am I falling in love? You know, one of those revelations. I think that was probably it for me."

They had fallen in love, partly, no doubt, out of mutual need, but not only out of need. Ted said that Vicki "awakened these feelings, emotions, that I think had really been banked in my life, that I didn't think really existed there anymore." "It just wow, boom, happened, and I couldn't believe it" was how Vicki would later describe it. But she wondered and worried, as her mother had, about the future of a relationship. "Certainly, obviously, Mr. Bachelor couldn't have wanted to get married," she told herself. "And then I thought, 'Oh, my God, I'm so in love with this man, what am I going to do?' " She said hers was not a relationship with Senator Edward Kennedy. She never thought of him in those terms. "It was just about Vicki and Ted. It was really just two people. I loved him. I got to know him. I understood him, and he understood me, and he loved me. It was so—it was really powerful. It was really something else." And she said she described it to her friends as "jumping off a cliff and knowing that he'd be at the bottom to catch me." And Ted Kennedy, as she well knew, had fallen off his own cliff, and now was trying to claw his way back up.

II

The cliff was steep, and it was slippery. Ted had returned that fall to a new battle. Late that June, after the Supreme Court term, Justice Thurgood Marshall announced his retirement. Marshall was an icon. He had been the counsel for the NAACP and had argued *Brown v. Board of Education,* the landmark civil rights case desegregating schools, before the Supreme Court—the Court to which Lyndon Johnson would later appoint him as the first Black justice. George Bush, not unmindful of the Republican Party's seeming aversion to minorities, had wanted to appoint one when Justice William Brennan, Jr., announced his retirement a year earlier. But Bush's friend Senator Warren Rudman of New Hampshire, convinced him to appoint a justice on the First Circuit Court of Appeals, David Souter, who had been attorney general of New Hampshire and had sat on the New Hampshire Supreme Court, instead. Bush's chief of staff, John Sununu, also from New Hampshire, assured Bush that Souter was a reliable conservative, and after the Bork hearing, which still reverberated three years later, Souter had the additional advantage of having almost no paper trail with which liberals could tar him. Those were precisely the issues that concerned Ted about him. He thought that Souter would be a Sununu protégé. Before Souter's hearing, Ted met at Hyannis with Laurence Tribe, Kathleen Sullivan, Carey Parker, and Jeff Blattner, his judiciary aide, over a long dinner to discuss how to proceed when the nominee had so slight a judicial record to examine. Ted concluded that when you were faced with uncertainty, the Constitution was too important to leave to chance. You resolved your doubts not in favor of the nominee but in favor of the Constitution. Blattner, who called himself a "dove" on Souter, while Carolyn Osolinik, another of Ted's judiciary aides, considered herself a "hawk," argued that Ted could vote against Souter and, as he put it, "not necessarily tear down the walls of the temple" while doing so. Ted voted no. Souter was confirmed. He would become a reliable liberal vote, much to Ted's surprise and Bush's consternation. Bush would later call the appointment a "huge mistake."

But the man whom George Bush decided to appoint to the vacancy created by Thurgood Marshall's retirement, the man whom he had called the "best qualified for the job," when he clearly was not, was something else from either Thurgood Marshall or David Souter. Clarence Thomas, a forty-three-year-old appointed by Bush to the federal bench just the year before, was Black, like Marshall, which Bush clearly thought would make it more difficult for Democrats to deny him confirmation; in fact, he had been confirmed for his judgeship on the First Circuit Court of Appeals largely because William Coleman, one of the few prominent Black Republicans, had lobbied vigorously for him, and because Ted was working with Thomas's mentor, Senator John Danforth, on a civil rights bill at the time and chose not to oppose him. Thomas had been head of the Equal Employment Opportunity Commission (EEOC), charged with enforcing civil rights, but he was young and inexperienced—two members of the American Bar Association evaluation committee rated him "unqualified" and no member rated him "well-qualified"—and, like Souter, had left virtually no judicial paper trail, only the trail of his executive positions, vigorously opposed to civil rights, which made Ted suspicious. Not even Bush was certain of where Thomas would come down on issues before the Court. Because so little was known about him, Ted went to the White House with several Republican senators to get briefed by the president's counsel,

C. Boyden Gray, but Gray only handed them a sheet and a half of paper. Ted was livid. "Well, this isn't a briefing," he snapped, and asked to talk to the FBI. But George Bush didn't want anyone to know much about Clarence Thomas, so Gray pointed to the door. "Do you know what that is?" he asked Ted. Ted was perplexed. "That's the corner office," Gray said. "When you get to the corner office, then you can talk to our FBI." Ted told Gray that the meeting was over and stormed out. Nevertheless, he arranged to meet with Thomas "at length," Ted said, before the hearings scheduled for early September, and found him "vague." He refused to answer which justice or legal scholar exemplified his philosophy, and when Ted asked him about *Roe v. Wade*, the Supreme Court decision that had allowed abortion, Thomas said he hadn't made up his mind yet on that, which seemed disingenuous. Still, Ted said that he wouldn't make up his mind about Thomas until after the hearings, which might also have been disingenuous.

When Ronald Reagan nominated Robert Bork, Ted and the advocacy groups had been poised to strike and did—immediately. But Bork, with his long record of extremist views, was a fat target. Thomas posed a much more difficult one. For one thing, conservatives were ready this time, and even before Bush chose Thomas, one group, Citizens United, headed by a consultant named Floyd Brown, had a public relations campaign ready to go and aimed at opponents of a Bush nominee. In 1988 Brown had produced an ad supporting George Bush's presidential candidacy that featured a Black convict named William Horton ("Willie" in the ad) who had committed a rape while on furlough as part of a program in Massachusetts, Michael Dukakis's state. Liberals thought it a scurrilous ad, clearly a racist appeal. Now Brown produced another ad, this one preemptive, attacking the Democrats on the Judiciary Committee—specifically the Judiciary chair, Joe Biden, for plagiarizing a speech; Alan Cranston for involvement in a savings and loan scandal; and Ted Kennedy for cheating on his Spanish exam at Harvard, for the accident at Chappaquiddick, and for drinking at Palm Beach. By one account, Brown told another conservative consultant, "It's a battle between the values of Ted Kennedy versus the values of George Bush and whoever is George Bush's nominee."* Brown was right. But it wasn't only conservatives with whom liberals

---

*Bush and Sununu both pressed Brown to pull the ad, apparently fearing a backlash, but Brown insisted that conservatives were "bitter" about Bork, and he refused. "Bush Acts to Quiet Storm over TV Ad on Thomas," *NYT*, Sept. 6, 1991.

had to contend. Bush was also right in thinking Thomas's race would protect him. Though Thomas's judicial leanings were hazy, even while his political leanings were decidedly conservative, Black people were loath to challenge him the way they had challenged Bork, assuming that if he were defeated, Bush might appoint someone worse, and that appointee wouldn't be Black. And Black leaders were cautious, too, because they were afraid—afraid because racism was flaring. In Louisiana, David Duke, a white supremacist and former grand wizard of the Ku Klux Klan, was running as a Republican in the state's open gubernatorial primary after having come in second in the open senatorial primary in 1990. That same year Jesse Helms, in his reelection campaign, had used overtly racist ads against his Democratic opponent, Harvey Gantt, who was Black. One ad, showing a pair of white hands crumpling a notice informing the white man that he hadn't been hired—"You needed that job, and you were the best qualified. But they had to give it to a minority because of a racial quota," intoned a narrator—ended with a picture of Gantt juxtaposed with Ted while the narrator said that Gantt supported Ted's racial quota bill. And that bill played a role in Thomas's confirmation too. As he had done with the Civil Rights Restoration Act, Ted had been working for a year to pass a bill to undo another Supreme Court decision, this one making it more difficult for employees to sue for discrimination. Ted met with Black leaders about Thomas—among them Benjamin Hooks of the NAACP, Joseph Lowery of Martin Luther King's Southern Christian Leadership Conference, and John Jacob of the National Urban League—and Ted said "they all, to a person, indicated they couldn't in good conscience oppose him [Thomas]" because they thought it might affect the outcome of Ted's legislation, the Civil Rights Act of 1991, the passage of which was important to them." Ted himself had trepidations that opposing Thomas might harm his relationship with Danforth, Thomas's chief senatorial sponsor, with whom Ted was trying to gain passage for his bill, and so highly regarded a senator that he was known as "Saint Jack." So the forces that would likely have rallied to defeat Thomas didn't. Ralph Neas, the liberal activist who had organized progressives to defeat Bork, said that the Black activists with whom he had long worked and whom he tried to recruit to stop Thomas asked him who he rooted for when the all-white University of Kentucky basketball team played the all-Black Texas Western team for the NCAA championship in 1966, and they told him that Thomas was their Texas Western.

And there was one more factor that undermined the effort to defeat Clarence Thomas: Ted Kennedy, the man who had led the fight against Robert Bork, was chastened and damaged after Palm Beach and was not spoiling for another fight.

On the first day of Clarence Thomas's confirmation hearings, September 10, 1991, Ted Kennedy was virtually silent, while Clarence Thomas spoke a lot but revealed almost nothing other than that he grew up in poverty in rural Georgia outside Savannah, in a town named Pin Point, moved to live with his maternal grandparents, and then attended the College of the Holy Cross in Worcester, Massachusetts, and Yale Law School via the sort of affirmative action program that Thomas had vehemently denounced as the EEOC head. When challenged on some of the public statements he had made, opposing affirmative action, for example, Thomas parried that as a public official, he had been an advocate, but as a judge he had had to "shed the baggage of ideology," which some senators read as an obvious ploy to disguise his deep conservative convictions. "If you leave so much of this behind," Democratic senator Herb Kohl asked Thomas when he said he had basically stripped away his earlier self when he joined the bench, "what's left?" To which Thomas said what was left were his "underlying concerns and feelings about people being left out, about our society not addressing all the problems of people," which sounded like something Ted Kennedy could have said, though Clarence Thomas was no Ted Kennedy, either ideologically or emotionally. Kohl complained that Thomas had given them "much conversation, but not an answer."

Much conversation, but not an answer was a good description of the hearings in which Thomas obfuscated. Alabama senator Howell Heflin said Thomas was so successful in doing so that Heflin didn't know if Thomas was a "closet liberal, a conservative or an opportunist." But Heflin did know. Senator Paul Simon would later say that after one of Thomas's answers, Heflin, a large ungainly bear of a man whose appearance belied a reputation for intelligence and probity, turned to Simon and whispered, "He's lying." Still, for all the liberals' doubts about Thomas's real instincts, journalists Jane Mayer and Jill Abramson, who wrote an authoritative account of the Thomas hearings, said that the Democrats' "hearts really weren't in this fight." This time there were few fireworks of the sort that lit up the Bork hearings, only a group from the Black Caucus who opposed Thomas and said he had had two paths to success and had taken the easier one, the one in the Republican Party, where there were no Black people; several legal scholars who testified that he was undistinguished and unqualified; and supporters of *Roe v. Wade*, who testified that they were certain he would vote to overturn it. The hearings lasted eight sessions—Thomas spoke at five of them—over seventeen days, then dragged to their conclusion. Thomas hadn't especially acquitted himself with his evasions and his dubious promises to remember the people being left out. "A judge must not bring to his job, to the court, the baggage of preconceived notions, of ideology, and certainly not an agenda," he had said, which was almost certainly a prevarication. Thomas had a lot of baggage. In his concluding statement, after tangling with Thomas over his views of the Voting Rights Act, of civil rights laws and leaders ("You've trashed the leaders of the civil rights movement in many speeches, but now you emphasize your debt to them"), of the right to privacy, and even over Thomas's negative opinion of Justice Oliver Wendall Holmes, Jr., Ted compared Thomas's tepid testimony to his previous and much more strident public remarks and said, "The vanishing views of Judge Thomas have become a major issue in these hearings." He said he saw Thomas as a soldier in a "triple play against the role of Congress," in which Reagan and Bush had used "executive powers to rewrite statutes, persuaded the Supreme Court to disregard legislative history and congressional intent" to sustain those executive interpretations; and then "dared Congress to pass laws to correct interpretations in the face of a veto." And Ted ended by telling Thomas, "I continue to have major concerns about your nomination, and about your commitment to the fundamental rights and liberties at the heart of our Constitution and our democracy. This is no time to turn back." The committee divided seven to seven—Ted was in opposition, as was Heflin—and the nomination passed to the floor without a recommendation.

And that would have almost certainly resulted in Thomas's confirmation, given the unanimity of Republicans and enough Democratic defectors, especially from the South, who thought that were they to vote against him, their Black constituents might take electoral revenge on them. But that was not the end of it. Not at all.

After the hearings concluded, the Senate waited to vote. Danforth, Thomas's chief patron, had gotten the Senate to agree to a vote on October 8, largely to avoid the possibility of a filibuster against his protégé. But as the senators waited over what was to be just a matter of days, a new issue was gestating. According to Jane Mayer and Jill Abramson's account, when Bush announced Thomas's nomination back in July, a young Black attorney named Anita Hill, who had worked at the EEOC under Thomas, spoke with an old classmate from Yale Law School, now an FCC lawyer, named Gary Phillips and told Phillips why she had quit the EEOC. Phillips mentioned Hill's call during a bridge game, without explicitly using her name, and one of the bridge players passed on the information to Nan Aron, the head of the progressive group Alliance for Justice that had been active in the fight against Robert Bork. What the bridge player told Aron was that Hill left the EEOC because Thomas had sexually harassed her. Aron, no supporter of Thomas's nomination, passed the information on to Howard Metzenbaum's staff, since Metzenbaum was something of a firebrand and also no doubt because Ted seemed disinclined to fight, presumably because of his own situation over Palm Beach. As Mayer and Abramson would later tell it, an investigator on Metzenbaum's staff named Bonnie Goldstein began examining Thomas's travel records and found several trips to Oklahoma.* At the same time, Ricki Seidman, a staffer for Ted who had also heard about the sexual harassment allegation against Thomas, was also scouring travel records and found the Oklahoma trips, and the two women shared the information that August, which led inevitably to the unmasking of Anita Hill, a thirty-five-year-old Black attorney from rural Oklahoma, the daughter of farmers who had, like Thomas, graduated from Yale Law School and at the time of the hearings was a law professor at the University of Oklahoma. Metzenbaum's Labor Committee counsel, Gail Laster, a Black attorney and, like Thomas and Hill, a Yale Law graduate, phoned Hill, who was noncommittal about talking about the harassment accusation. Meanwhile Ricki Seidman had gotten permission from one of her superiors in Ted's office, most likely, Ranny Cooper, to phone Hill, which she did on September 5, five days before the hearings were to begin, and in the course of what Seidman said was a

---

*These trips, as it turned out, involved Charles Kothe, the dean of the Oral Roberts Law School, who was a close associate of Thomas's and a special assistant at the EEOC. Kothe had seen Thomas and Hill together in Tulsa, Hill's hometown, when Thomas invited Hill to join him when he was speaking at Oral Roberts. Kothe would later testify that Hill in her charges against Thomas must have been fantasizing about him. Jane Mayer and Jill Abramson, *Strange Justice: The Selling of Clarence Thomas* (New York: Houghton Mifflin, 1994), 112–13.

routine review of Thomas, she asked Hill about the harassment allegations. As a later statement from Kennedy's office put it, Hill "indicated she needed time to decide whether she was willing to discuss the issue." (By this time, Hill had also told a friend who was an attorney specializing in sexual harassment, though with no intention of going public with her charge.) Four days later, on the eve of the hearings, Hill agreed to speak about her charges privately with Seidman, but now Seidman, uncharacteristically for a Ted Kennedy staffer, handed her off to an attorney on Metzenbaum's Labor Committee staff, James Brudney, who had gone to law school with Hill. By one account, Brudney spoke to Hill the next day, the day the hearings opened, and, appreciating the explosiveness of her accusation, raced to the hearing room to discuss the story with Metzenbaum's Judiciary aides, Bill Corr and Chris Harvie. This was the beginning of a long deliberation over whether Hill would publicly testify against Thomas or would cooperate with the FBI instead. But Metzenbaum, the firebrand, retreated when he was informed of her story. He felt that Joe Biden, as committee chairman, should conduct any investigation, which was certainly not the way Ted would have operated had he been his usual self.

But Ted Kennedy was not his usual self. The reason Seidman had handed off Anita Hill rather than pursue the issue herself was that Ted had explicitly given orders that no one on his staff pursue the rumor, though the order had been secretly countermanded by a senior staffer, presumably Cooper, or Seidman wouldn't have made her call to Hill. Frustrated by Ted's withdrawal from the battle, his female staffers, according to Mayer and Abramson, waged their own fight. Ranny Cooper, Ted's administrative assistant, called Senator Patrick Leahy's chief of staff, Ellen Lovell, informing her of Hill's allegations. Lovell told Leahy's chief counsel, Ann Harkins, who believed that the committee had an obligation to investigate the charge, but the Kennedy staffers, honoring Ted's wishes up to a point, advised that she get in touch with Brudney. Meanwhile Carolyn Osolinik, one of Ted's Judiciary aides, was so cautious that she said when she heard of Anita Hill's accusation, "My first reaction was that we didn't know if it happened, and if it happened, we didn't know whether it would rise to the level of a Title VII [from the Civil Rights Act of 1964] employment harassment." And she called a friend, Susan Ross, a law professor at Georgetown, who specialized in women's employment issues and asked her advice. (Ross would later become one of Anita Hill's advisers.)

All this wariness, this handing off, this reluctance to be more forceful, was not because any one of those staffers thought Clarence Thomas wasn't guilty of the charges. It seemed to be more fallout from Palm Beach. As people close to Ted told Mayer and Abramson, "He feared his involvement on Hill's behalf could only be hurtful," presumably to the cause but also to Ted himself, given his own compromised situation as a presumed drunken lout and skirt chaser. And the two authors would conclude: "Had Kennedy, with his tenacious staff and his solid standing in the African-American community, played his customary aggressive role, the outcome of the confirmation hearings might have been different." But he was timorous—"paralyzed by embarrassment" was how Mayer and Abramson described him, which was no doubt accurate. Palm Beach had made him a laughingstock. He wasn't about to explore charges of sexual harassment when he himself was accused of inappropriate behavior. So first Metzenbaum and then Biden, who had neither the ties to the progressive activists that Ted had, nor Ted's skill in shaping the media narrative—a skill that served him well for legislative purposes if not for personal ones—nor Ted's tenacity, took the lead while Ted Kennedy shrank from the possible confrontation.

Suddenly, though, Hill's charges changed the entire process. As the hearings began, only Ted, Metzenbaum, Leahy, and finally Biden knew of Anita Hill or her allegations against Clarence Thomas, and it wasn't until September 12, two days into the hearings, that she spoke to the committee staff—privately. For the next seven days, she returned to silence, though the staff did contact a friend of hers to whom she had reported, at the time she worked at EEOC, her discomfort with Thomas. When Hill finally did speak again to the staff, she said that she had decided that she wanted all the committee members to hear her allegations, but she still hesitated to cooperate with the FBI, concerned about what "utility" such cooperation would have. It was only on September 23 that she advised the staff that she would submit a statement and *then* cooperate with the FBI, which she did. Biden would later say that all the committee members had read Hill's statement before the committee vote. But with the full Senate vote scheduled for October 8, the Republicans had no desire to investigate Hill's charges, and Biden and the ranking Republican on the Judiciary Committee, Strom Thurmond, agreed to keep the matter within the committee. In effect, they agreed that a vote would proceed without any consideration of Thomas's possible sexual harassment of Hill on the basis that Hill had asked that her statement be kept confidential.

So it was to be. But on October 6, that agreement blew up. National Public Radio ran a story on Hill's charges that included both an interview with Anita Hill and information from corroborating witnesses. The next day Hill announced at a press conference that she would testify if asked. Now, as much as the Republicans chafed at the prospect—Danforth took to the Senate floor and was so exercised and gesticulated so wildly that, by one account, his wristwatch flew off—the Republicans really had no alternative but to postpone the vote because Thomas would almost certainly lose with the charges hanging over him. Majority Leader George Mitchell canvassed his senators, and those who had intended to vote for Thomas's confirmation—some ten Democrats—told him that without a postponement to review Hill's story, they were prepared to vote against Thomas's confirmation—a shift that he conveyed to Minority Leader Bob Dole at four-thirty on Tuesday, October 8, just before the vote was to be taken.* Danforth checked with Thomas, who told Danforth that he was against any delay. But Thomas had no say now. Ted was adamant that the vote be postponed and that the hearings be resumed to review Hill's charge. Speaking on the Senate floor, after Hill held her press conference, and finally finding his voice, he said, "Any vote on the merits of this nomination today would be painfully premature. It is not a question of having the Senate train run on time, but whether we can stop the Senate train from running off the track." And he warned, "The Senate cannot sweep it under the rug or pretend that it is not staring us in the face. Nobody who saw Professor Hill speak yesterday [at her press conference] can dismiss her allegations out of hand. Anyone who paid attention to Judge Thomas's prior stereotype statements on women and work can see at a glance that his record raises serious questions about his sensitivity to discrimination against women in the workplace."

Having little choice, Republicans reluctantly conceded to three more

---

*The vote had already been set by unanimous consent, and any change would have required unanimous consent under Senate rules. The only way that Mitchell could gain that consent was to convince the Republicans that they would lose the confirmation vote, and the only way he could convince them that they would lose was to convince those senators who didn't want to be rushed into voting to agree to vote no if they were rushed. Hence the postponement.

days of hearings. And so now, on October 11, began the confrontation—
a confrontation even nastier and more fraught than the one between the
Democrats and Robert Bork four years earlier. But even though the Democrats controlled the Senate and the committee, as they had during Bork's
confirmation, the Republicans were not entirely powerless. Lest he and
the Democrats be viewed as trying to railroad Thomas, Biden allowed Republicans to exact some ground rules. Under the new rules, two senators
were to be designated for each side to conduct the questioning—Orrin
Hatch and Arlen Specter for the Republicans, Howell Heflin, a former
chief justice of the Alabama Supreme Court, and Patrick Leahy, a former
prosecutor, for the Democrats—which had the effect of removing some of
the more dogged inquisitors, including, had he been so inclined, Ted Kennedy. The witness list was pared. And there was one more concession—
a major concession. Biden permitted Thomas to choose when he wanted
to speak, and Thomas chose to speak first and then again after Anita Hill
had testified, essentially giving Thomas a rebuttal. This was a change
from normal legal procedure where a complainant would get the last
word, and it would be a tremendous advantage to Thomas. "There were a
number of people around town the first day who concluded that the Democrats had been taken for a ride on the scheduling," said a consultant
close to Ted. "A number of us screamed and yelled and the response came
back that there was a very strong feeling of the chairman [Biden] and the
Democrats that they had to give the impression of fairness."

Nor was that the only concession. Thomas read his statement that
morning of October 11 in the cavernous Senate Caucus Room, where so
much history had transpired, from the hearings on Pearl Harbor to the
Watergate hearings. He appeared, Senator Danforth at his side, in a state
of high dudgeon, the muscles in his cheeks clenched, his eyes focused
straight ahead, his visage grim. He detailed his relationship with Anita
Hill, to whom, he said, he had served as a guide and mentor. He decried
what had happened since her charges. "I have never in all my life felt such
hurt, such pain, such agony." He called the episode "Kafkaesque." He
said, "I will not allow myself to be further humiliated in order to be confirmed." (Actually, he would.) And he claimed to be a "victim of the process." He concluded that he would "not provide the rope for my own
lynching or for further humiliation." When he finished, Biden advised the
committee that their questions would be limited at that time to Thomas's
"general relationship" to Anita Hill since Hill had not released her state-

ment and was maintaining confidentiality until she read her statement before the committee. At that point, Hatch erupted, claiming that everyone knew what her statement was and saying that not allowing them to question Thomas on her charges at that time would be the "greatest travesty I've ever seen in any court of law," which prompted Ted to call for a recess, during which the committee met in his office across the hall and settled on yet another compromise: The hearings would recess for five minutes until Hill appeared, Hill would read her statement and testify, and then Thomas would return to testify.

And so began the three days—three volatile, tense, churlish, prosecutorial, unsenatorial days of hearings with Republicans and Democrats at loggerheads. Anita Hill testified that she had been introduced to Clarence Thomas by a mutual friend and that Thomas had said he was expecting a political appointment. When he did indeed get an appointment as assistant secretary of education for civil rights, he asked Hill to join him as his assistant, which she did, and when Thomas was transferred to the EEOC, Hill joined him again. It was while she was working there for roughly three months that she said Thomas asked her out the first time and then continued to do so even though she refused, with Thomas insisting to know why. Subsequently, she testified, Thomas "began to use work situations to discuss sex" and would turn business conversations "to a discussion of sexual matters," including, she said, his "sexual prowess" and the size of his organ. Distressed, and concerned that Thomas might use her refusals to damage her career, she took the job at Oral Roberts Law School. At a farewell dinner, Thomas warned her not to tell anyone of his "behavior." And that was the end of her association with Clarence Thomas, she said.

Or so she had thought. But now Anita Hill was fair game for Clarence Thomas's advocates. Arlen Specter, one of the key Republican votes against Robert Bork, and one of the chosen inquisitors, was especially severe on Hill. He challenged her memory, her veracity, her stability, her emotions, her fairness in bringing up charges of harassment so many years after the incidents. He called her a fantasist—Thomas's alleged romantic interest was a "product of fantasy," Specter said—and even a perjurer. He accused her of having embellished her FBI testimony in her committee statement. He accused and accused and accused. In truth, Hill had hesitated to come forward. In truth, she had balked at cooperating once the staffers found her. In truth, she had, on her own volition, taken a lie detector test and passed. And now, for hours, she had been subjected to the most intense questioning, the most personal questioning, questioning that doubted not only her truthfulness but her sanity. (She could have passed the lie detector test, said Republicans, because she was so deep into her delusions that she believed them.) Then at 7:40 that evening, after her inquisition, the committee recessed. But before it did, Thomas had notified the chairman that he wanted to return at nine o'clock to rebut Hill's testimony. "Her life will never be the same," Ted's Judiciary staffer Jeffrey Blattner had thought when Hill emerged. He was right.

When Thomas returned that evening, he was in a fighting mood—not only against Anita Hill but against the entire process. In a brief statement, he denied each and every one of Hill's charges. He called the hearing a "travesty." He said that "sleaze" and "dirt" were dug up on him by committee staff and then leaked to the media to be shown in prime time. He called it a "circus" and a "national disgrace." He was a "victim of the process," he said. He said this: "And from my standpoint as a black American, as far as I'm concerned, it is a high-tech lynching for uppity blacks who in any way deign to think for themselves, to do for themselves, to have different ideas, and it is a message that unless you kowtow to an old order, this is what will happen to you. You will be lynched, destroyed, caricatured by a committee of the U.S.—U.S. Senate, rather than hung from a tree." In short, he was saying that a Black person who was a conservative, a Black person who opposed civil rights and affirmative action, would be punished for doing so by the liberals. And thus did Clarence Thomas, who had been given the last word, transform an accusation of sexual harassment, which he was unlikely to win, into an issue of race, which he was likely to win.

Three days, but the last two days would be anticlimactic. Panels of witnesses appeared, alternating between those who supported Hill and those who supported Thomas and challenged her accusations, and the hearings ended on a Sunday, at 2:02 a.m., with the vote scheduled for the following Tuesday. But for all the thunder, one senator, flanking Biden on his left, had said little. Throughout, while Specter and Hatch and Heflin and Leahy dominated, Ted Kennedy had been largely silent—one of the committee's "invisible men," as *The Washington Post* labeled the senators who failed to speak up. His "liberal activism had been shut away behind a stony, embarrassed silence" was how Mayer and Abramson would later put it. When he interjected that Specter was putting words in Anita Hill's mouth, Specter acidly objected and said, "If Senator Kennedy has anything to say, let him participate in this hearing." In fact, he had spoken less than any other senator—only twice at length, in those three days: once to commend Anita Hill for her courage in speaking out and for the "dignity" with which she had conducted herself, and again, at greater length, after the committee relaxed its rule on the number of questioners, to upbraid the way the Republicans had treated Hill. This now was Ted's chance to erupt after his days of reticence. And now he finally did.

As supporters of Hill's came to the witness table, he warned his Republican colleagues, "I hope we are not going to hear any more comments, unworthy, unsubstantiated comments, unjustified comments about Professor Hill and perjury," obviously referring to Specter. "I hope we are not going to hear any more comments about Professor Hill being a tool of the advocacy groups. . . . I hope we are not going to hear any more about politics," he continued, since Hill had been a supporter of Robert Bork's nomination. "I hope we are not going to hear a lot more comments about fantasy stories picked out of books. . . . I hope we are going to clear this room of the dirt and innuendo." And he said this: "I hope we are not going to hear a lot more about racism as we consider this nominee. The fact is that these points of sexual harassment are made by an African American against an African American. The issue isn't discrimination and racism. It is about sexual harassment, and I hope we can keep our eye on that particular issue." It was his best moment, though one of his only moments.

Three days the hearings lasted. Three days, the first of which was dedicated primarily to an interrogation of a young Black woman by, as many commentators were quick to point out, fourteen elderly white men, many of whom declared that Thomas had been before this committee for his appeals court confirmation and had shown no trace of harassment. Three ugly, venomous days where the aim didn't seem to be to determine the truth but to salvage a nomination in trouble—to salvage it, said the liberals, so that the new justice could help turn back the social progress for which Ted Kennedy had fought so hard. (There was no time or inclination in those three days to call Angela Wright to testify, another woman who had worked for Thomas at EEOC, and who claimed to have been subjected to the same pressures and the same sexual remarks as Hill—testimony that might have been fatal to Thomas's confirmation.) The floor debate, though brief, given the scheduled vote, was also testy. When Ted, having summoned his courage, once again attacked Specter for his charges of perjury against Anita Hill—"There's no proof that Anita Hill perjured herself and shame on anyone who suggests that she has"—and bellowed, "Shame! Shame! Shame! Are we an old boys' club, insensitive at best, or something worse? Will we . . . tolerate any unsubstantial attack on a woman in order to rationalize a vote for this nominee?" Specter shot back, "We do not need characterizations like shame in this chamber from the Senator from Massachusetts," and when Ted repeated that she was being treated "shamefully," Orrin Hatch rose to Specter's defense and said, "Anybody who believes that, I know a bridge up in Massachusetts"— obviously referring to the bridge over Poucha Pond in Chappaquiddick— "that I'd be happy to sell them." Before the vote, Ted said, "There is a very strong likelihood that Professor Hill is telling the truth. In a case of this vast magnitude where so much is riding on our decision, the Senate should give the benefit of the doubt to the Supreme Court and the American people, not to Judge Clarence Thomas." But by Ted's reckoning, the Court and the people lost. Clarence Thomas was narrowly confirmed, 52 to 48—the narrowest Supreme Court confirmation vote in history. He had won a seat, but not a vindication.

And some who had opposed Clarence Thomas, and who now realized that he would, given his age, likely sit on the Court for decades, and likely, despite his attempts at disavowal, cast his votes to disembowel voting rights and civil rights and privacy rights, blamed Ted Kennedy for not opposing Thomas more vigorously, as he had opposed Robert Bork. While no senator emerged from the hearings unscathed—a Gallup poll found that half the public had less confidence in the Senate after the hearing than before—Ted Kennedy ranked lowest: Only 22 percent approved of him. Many in the media saw the hearings as another humiliation for Ted in the wake of the Palm Beach incident. Anna Quindlen of *The New York Times* took him to task for his passivity, especially in light of his forceful conclusion that the Republicans kept throwing out distractions on perjury or on race when the focus should have been narrowly on sexual harassment. "For just a moment," Quindlen wrote, "he was what he was always meant to be: Edward M. Kennedy: the liberal conscience of the Senate." But then, she lamented, he "lapsed back into a self-imposed silence, into the cat's cradle woven of the facts of Ted's private life," and she saw the hearings as proof that the "private life of a politician casts an indelible shadow over public affairs, sometimes to the detriment of the public." Liberal columnist Mary McGrory thought that Ted's "severe image problem" might have been the difference in the Thomas fight. Barbara Ehrenreich, writing in *Time,* said of Ted judging a sexual harassment charge against Thomas: "I have the greatest respect for Kennedy's stalwart liberalism and even for a few of his fellows on the Senate Judiciary Committee, but isn't this a little like asking Michael Milken"—a financier who had been found guilty of racketeering and securities fraud—"to monitor the SEC?" Others criticized his performance. Michael Kranish in *The Boston Globe* wrote that Ted "seems to be the most uncomfortable man these days as he questions Clarence Thomas, a black who broke out of poverty while rejecting Kennedy's political philosophy," and he quoted Harvard Law professor Charles Ogletree, one of Anita Hill's advisers and a Black person, as saying that Ted seemed unfocused when he questioned Thomas. "Kennedy in my view," Ogletree told Kranish, "did not hear Thomas's responses or understand them." Another columnist, Mark Shields, said the "most memorable visual" from the televised hearings—he was writing before the emergence of Anita Hill—was the "shaky and uncertain performance of Massachusetts Democrat Edward Kennedy whenever he read his questions to the nominee." And Shields, writing yet another Kennedy obituary, said the "powerful hold of the Kennedy legend on the imagination of the nation has been severed," and that the hearings "destroyed any last illusions that Kennedy still has the stature and moral power to deliver for the causes he believes in." Yet another columnist, David Nyhan, in Ted's own *Boston Globe,* did more than write an obituary. He compared Ted's performance to an assassination—a "tragedy in slow motion"—and wrote that after a "life of public gallantry, he is shunned as a private wastrel." And he said what Shields had said: "The plain fact is that Kennedy's personal reputation is at such low ebb, his moral authority has eroded."

And without moral authority, Ted Kennedy had nothing.

The assumption, of course, was that Palm Beach had silenced Ted at the first round of hearings and curbed him even more in the second round, the Anita Hill round, where his nephew's behavior at Palm Beach and Ted's own drinking and womanizing prevented him from challenging Clarence Thomas on sexual harassment, though Ted had never been accused of sexually harassing a woman, only of behaving like an overage fraternity boy, and even that charge had nothing to do with Palm Beach, where Ted had been a mournful drinker rather than a rambunctious one. (The more serious charge, of prevaricating to the police to protect his nephew, had nothing to do with Clarence Thomas either.) Ted largely denied that he had silenced himself because of his conduct at Palm Beach. He would argue that he questioned Thomas intensely in the first round and that he was more muted in the second only because of the rules, later abandoned, that placed the questioning in the hands of four senators and the chairman and ranking member. But even that initial rule, some felt, might have been directed at Ted Kennedy. As one of Ted's aides told Adam Clymer, "The idea that you have something, if true, that was as significant as that, and you would not have Senator Kennedy be one of those designees—it was really quite amazing," the implication being that the committee was nervous enough about Anita Hill without adding the baggage of Ted Kennedy to the situation. "And yet," said the aide, "I think that there was sort of a collective sigh of relief in the office when that decision was announced—from the guys." In discussing the matter of his restraint himself with Clymer seven years later, Ted discussed the Heflin-Leahy agreement again, and the fact that the Democrats thought the fight should be led by moderates (Leahy was considered a moderate at the time) and a Southerner to help attract other Southerners, and that his fight against Bork stigmatized him in waging a fight against Thomas, and that many Black people supported Thomas, thinking that he would moderate once he got on the Court. It was only when Clymer brought up the Palm Beach incident as a factor in Ted's relative withdrawal that Ted said, "Yeah, there is certainly some truth to that." He was more forthcoming in an interview with the Miller Center for an oral history project in 2007: "This is about the time, too, of the Florida trial of Willie Smith, and so I didn't ask questions in the second round," though he called it a "secondary factor." And while he denied the importance of Palm Beach again in his memoir, he did admit that "with all the background noise about Palm Beach and my bachelor lifestyle, I would have been the wrong person to lead the questioning in the second phase of the Thomas hearing" and admitted, too, that he realized he "disappointed" people because he was "unable to succeed in making a persuasive case against Thomas's confirmation." In the end, he was uncharacteristically quiet. In the end, Clarence Thomas was elevated to the Supreme Court, and for all Thomas's avowed dedication to being a new man and to thinking of the powerless and of those left behind when he adjudicated, he would be one of the most conservative justices in the history of the Court and one of the most averse to helping Black Americans.

III

There was another reason Ted Kennedy was reluctant to eviscerate Clarence Thomas the way he had eviscerated Robert Bork, and it had nothing to do with race or the ideology of each of the nominees. Ted knew and said publicly that Clarence Thomas would not be a voice for the poor and powerless—that he would not follow in the footsteps of Thurgood Marshall, which would have been cause enough for him to oppose the nominee. But the reason Ted held back was the Civil Rights Act of 1991, which in the mind of some Black activists, if not necessarily in the mind of Ted Kennedy, was even more important than a Supreme Court justice. At issue were job hiring requirements that served as subterfuges for favoring white employees over minorities and men over women, the way that literacy tests and poll taxes had disenfranchised Black voters, even though the tests and taxes applied to white and Black voters alike. Like the Civil Rights Restoration Act of 1987, which Ted had shepherded to passage, this new act was an undoing of several Supreme Court decisions that had the effect of preventing aggrieved employees from gaining redress for what they felt had been discrimination by their employers. In *Griggs v. Duke Power Co.* (1971) the Court had determined that hiring and promotion had to be based on a candidate's ability to do the particular job, and that even requirements that seemed on their face to be nondiscriminatory (for example, requiring a janitor to have a high school diploma) would nevertheless be discriminatory if the *effect* of the requirement was discriminatory—that is, if the requirements had a disparate impact on, in the *Griggs* case, Black employees. Under *Griggs*, employers bore the burden of proving that their job requirements were a "business necessity." But in 1989, in *Wards Cove Packing Co. v. Atonio*, a more conservative Court overturned *Griggs*. In the new case, a group of nonwhite workers for Wards Cove, an Alaskan fish-packing company, had sued the company, citing a violation of Title VII of the Civil Rights Act of 1964 on the basis that while they were disproportionately assigned unskilled jobs in the cannery, skilled workers at the company in noncannery jobs were disproportionately white. In a 5–4 decision, written by John Kennedy's appointment Justice Byron White, the conservatives on the Court ruled that the disproportion between nonwhite people and white people in unskilled and skilled jobs did not in and of itself prove the company had discriminated against those nonwhite people, thus eliminating the "disparate impact" test. Rather, shifting the burden of proof, the plaintiffs now had to show that the company's business practices resulted in the disparity, and the Court lowered the standard for the rationale of those practices from a "business necessity" in *Griggs* to a "business justification." For Black people, this was a major setback.

It was also the very sort of thing that had concerned Ted about the increasingly conservative Court, and no sooner had the decision been delivered than Ted had set to work to negate it. Ted and his new Judiciary counsel, Jeffrey Blattner, had sat in the President's Room in the Capitol, surrounded by the imposing frescoes of Constantino Brumidi, and as Blattner ran down a long list of Supreme Court decisions that had restricted the Civil Rights Act of 1964, including *Wards Cove,* he and Ted discussed what the provisions of a new civil rights act undoing *Wards Cove* might look like. Blattner remembered that at one point, Ted stopped the conversation and began scratching his chest, which was another tic of Ted's. He warned that the new bill should not become another "double breasting" bill, which labor had induced Ted to introduce in the early 1980s to stop the practice of a company running both a union and non-union shop—"double breasting"—and which, Ted told Blattner, had been so overloaded with provisions that it "sank like a stone." The bill that Blattner drafted in conjunction with the advocacy groups and that Ted introduced as the Civil Rights Act of 1990 was simply designed to reinstate the "disparate impact" standard for discrimination suits and to institute a new standard of "essential" to justify business practices. In addition, the act called for jury trials and punitive damages for discrimination as well as the normal remedies of back pay. Republicans were not entirely convinced. One conservative legal scholar carped, "The usual statement of the bill's high purpose is that it would make it easier for plaintiffs to win civil rights suits," and then added "whether the greater ease is in and of itself a good thing." Among the skeptical was the president. Bush had argued that the bill would not have the desired effect that Ted and its supporters advanced: to stop discrimination against Black people and women. Instead, employers would be so frightened of being subjected to suits for discrimination and of having to pay damages that they would preemptively discriminate *against white employees*—reverse discrimination. In effect, Bush said, the bill would impose quotas on business to avoid litigation. *Quotas*—it was among the dirtiest of words among Republicans. "It didn't make any difference what else was in the bill," Ted would later say. "If you could say it was a quota, you were going to be successful and halt it." Republicans said they favored equality of opportunity, making sure that everyone had the same starting point. But they did not believe in equality of results. The quota, they argued, was the engine of the latter. And Bush wanted, as Republicans had always wanted in civil rights actions, not just discriminatory effects but explicit intention to discriminate, which was nearly impossible to prove. And Bush wanted one more thing. The bill applied to racial discrimination and discrimination by sex, religion, national origin, or color. Bush wanted to restrict the bill to race alone.

Still, George Bush did not want to veto a civil rights bill, and that spring he had his chief of staff, John Sununu, and his White House counsel, C. Boyden Gray, negotiate with Ted as they had negotiated with him on the Americans with Disabilities Act. By July, Ted said that he and the White House were "dramatically closer." But that was wishful thinking. As with the ADA, Sununu kept balking. Finally, Majority Leader Mitchell called for a cloture vote on July 17. It passed, with eight Republicans joining all but one of the Democrats. The next day it passed the Senate, 65 to 34, and on August 3 the House, 227 to 154. Bush was still threatening to veto the bill. To placate him, the conference added two provisions. It specifically ruled out quotas, and it set a $150,000 ceiling on punitive damages. (In agreeing to the latter, Ted was excoriated by fellow Democrat, Representative Pat Schroder—he sat "red-faced," according to one report, as she upbraided him—but it was the only way, he said, he could pry away enough Republican and Southern votes to pass the bill.) And Ted had agreed to allow an employer to defend itself on the basis that a practice had, not an "essential relationship," but a "significant relationship to successful performance of the job." With these alterations, Ted believed he had the votes to override a Bush veto, should it come to that.

And it *would* come to that. Bush was in no mood to compromise, even when Ted attempted to win his support. After the conference report passed both houses in October, Bush phoned Republicans to get them to vote against it. Bush now, as promised, vetoed it. On October 22, the Senate voted, and Ted fell one vote short of an override, 66 to 34, with all fifty-five Democrats voting for the bill. The surprise was Republican senator Warren Rudman, whose vote Ted had thought he had. But afterward Rudman admitted, "When it came down to it, the administration was a mite unreasonable . . . but I didn't want to get into the position of overriding the President's veto." Bush claimed that Ted was the one who had reneged on the deal; that the president had sent a compromise bill to Congress and they wouldn't vote on it; that he was "strongly opposed to quotas" and that while he was opposed to discrimination in the workplace, "I will not accept quotas." The bill failed, and now it would have to wait until the next session of Congress.

When the new bill was introduced after the 1990 midterm elections, the national climate was different. Senator Richard Lugar claimed that Democrats had lost races in the elections because of the quota issue, which Republicans, like Helms, had promoted in campaign ads, and said, "If Democrats want to keep pushing the same old bill, bring it on." Ted, who appreciated the benefits of tenacity, did want to keep pushing the bill. That spring, 1991, the House had passed a bill similar to the 1990 bill, and Ted had introduced a Senate version. Once again Bush announced that he would veto it as a "quota bill." And Ted was stymied. If his bill was to avoid the same fate as the 1990 version, he would need Republican votes for an override, and he was not likely to corral those votes. But there was someone who could: Republican senator John Danforth—"St. Jack." As Danforth would recall it, he was walking with his assistant, Peter Leibold, around noon outside the Russell Senate Office Building, and Leibold, who, Danforth said, knew a lot about civil rights legislation, told him that he should weigh in. "You could find the center of this issue and get this done, get this passed," Leibold told him. Danforth, who had supported the new bill, said, "It immediately resonated." He made up his mind "on the spot." He had been looking for something because "I really didn't want to be a potted plant in the Senate." The something was the Civil Rights Act of 1991.

Part of Danforth's reasoning was that a bill would have a much better chance of being passed if it was sponsored by a Republican. So Danforth, fearing, as Ted had, that the same thing that happened to the 1990 bill would happen to the new one, began discussing a compromise with eight Republicans to see if they could meet some of Bush's objections and still attract some liberal Democrats as well. By one account, Danforth met with Ted for an hour, and Ted expressed what Danforth called "good will" over the prospect of a compromise bill. By another account that Danforth gave years later, he said he had a discussion with Ted—he believed it might have been on the Senate floor—about Ted's failure to gain passage for his bill, and said Ted was responsive to letting Danforth make an effort of his own. One reason, no doubt, was that this was late in the Senate session, in June, two months after the Palm Beach incident, and that Ted certainly realized that his chances of gaining passage, now that he had been made an object of derision, were not good.

In dealing with the bill, George Bush was walking a political and personal tightrope. Politically, for all his professions of sympathy for civil rights, he had, while a congressman campaigning for the Senate in Texas, voted against the Civil Rights Act of 1964, clearly a political decision, and he had political reasons for opposing the act of 1991 too—namely, that the quota idea was a potent war cry among conservatives and that his patrons in business were against a law that made filing discrimination suits any easier, which, of course, was the primary purpose of the act. But personally, Bush, despite his willingness to benefit from racist appeals, did not want to be labeled as a racist, especially as the Republican Party seemed to be increasingly congenial to racists. (David Duke, the former KKK grand wizard, had won his race for the Republican nomination for governor of Louisiana, and moderate Republicans raced to disassociate themselves from him.) These warring halves of Bush's, the political and the personal, seemed irreconcilable. Bush produced his own bill that eased discrimination suits, but it didn't go far enough even for Danforth. Meanwhile Danforth, who was interested only in passing a bill, which meant attracting both Democrats and Republicans, met with Sununu and Gray, without Ted, "long meetings with lots of 'wordsmithing,'" as Danforth put it, to see if they could reach some consensus, especially on a definition of business practices that would not, in the administration's mind, amount to the dreaded quotas. But Danforth was meeting the same resistance Ted had met the year before, and he groused, "It is not right for the Republican Party to use that issue," meaning quotas. By this point, Bush had recruited William Coleman, the Black former transportation secretary, who in turn recruited the CEO of AT&T, Robert Allen, who met with a group of businessmen to hammer out a bill that would be satisfactory to them. They brought an agreement to Danforth, who brought it to Ted, and Ted signed off on it. But Bush was deeply displeased, making the seemingly specious argument that disallowing a job requirement like a high school diploma for a janitorial job—an example that opponents of *Wards Cove* often adduced—would undermine his efforts to promote education. Danforth now was just as angry as Bush. "The President says he agrees with *Griggs*," the original Supreme Court decision that set up suits for disparate impact, he complained. "But he doesn't." And Danforth issued this warning: He had the votes to override a veto, and he would use them. Ted, who had been working with Danforth all along—Danforth even recalled the two of them discussing the bill "stark naked" in the Senate gym—added his voice to Danforth's, saying that he would help enact the bill.

And while all this was going on, something else happened that would affect the bill, the Court whose decisions were at issue in the bill, and Ted Kennedy personally: Bush nominated Clarence Thomas to replace Thurgood Marshall. Danforth was Clarence Thomas's patron, his chief advocate, the man who had spent much of the summer singing Thomas's praises to his fellow senators and rounding up votes for his confirmation, and the man who would sit beside him during his Senate testimony. In fact, Danforth introduced his own compromise bill, the one he and Ted had been working on since June, on September 25, during the first round of the Thomas hearings. This placed President Bush in the difficult position of either having to oppose the man who was doing more than any other senator to get Thomas on the Court or to concede to him, even though Bush continued to insist that Danforth's bill was a quota bill. By the same token, it put Ted Kennedy in the difficult position of having to oppose Danforth's protégé, even as Ted was working closely with Danforth to gain passage of a bill that meant so much to both of them. And for the civil rights advocacy groups, it put them in the difficult position of seeming to have to choose between a Supreme Court nominee about whom they were uncertain and a piece of legislation that would be a landmark in discrimination law. Because of John Danforth, one could not separate the Civil Rights Act of 1991 from the Clarence Thomas nomination, and those who thought Ted Kennedy insufficiently hard-nosed in his questioning of Thomas, those who thought he had left the battlefield, those who complained that Palm Beach had neutered him, failed to note how intertwined the nomination and the legislation were. "All this innuendo about Kennedy's own life could have been part of it," Danforth was to say about Ted's fade during the hearings. "But it could have been— I was Clarence Thomas's champion in the Senate and Kennedy had worked with me and was working with me and knew me. I think that entered into it, but I don't know."

And Danforth was a critical player not just for Ted or Bush or the civil rights advocates but for the Senate itself. Jeff Blattner recalled a sort of "pep rally" that the Republicans had organized shortly after Thomas's confirmation, to support the president's opposition to the Civil Rights Act of 1991. Danforth was not present because he was working on the legislation. But Alaska senator Ted Stevens, "one crusty son of a bitch," Blattner called him, rose and said to his colleagues, "You mean you're going to screw Jack Danforth after he just got your Supreme Court nominee confirmed? Well, not with my vote!" And Blattner said, "That was it." Within twenty-four hours, he said, Sununu and Gray were in Dole's office with Danforth and Ted and Senator Jim Jeffords and their staff members, and they got their compromise.

But Blattner made it sound simpler than it really was. Ted had met with Sununu and Gray all day on October 24, though apparently without a resolution. "We had deals many times," Sununu had said of his negotiations with Ted on the bill. "I had an agreement with Senator Kennedy, and Senator Kennedy after a while decided he didn't want to live up to the agreement," even though Ted was known for always keeping his word. And the administration said it had deals with Danforth too, but that Danforth had insisted on taking those deals to Ted, without whom he could not pass a bill, prompting Attorney General Thornburgh to snipe, "We did not know that Senator Kennedy was going to wield a veto power over that," meaning an agreement. As for the meeting in Dole's office, at which Dole pressed Danforth and the White House to reach agreement, it lasted twelve hours. And while Ted was part of the meeting, he wasn't in the meeting. He was "lurking" outside the door, Danforth would say, leaning on a railing because of his back, and Danforth would shuttle between Dole's office and Ted, checking with him every time a change was made, while Blattner and Osolinik were also going back and forth between Dole's office and Ted outside. By the time the session was through, a compromise had been reached that effectively reinstated *Griggs*, which was Ted's intention all along. In return, Ted agreed to an amendment that advised courts to look at a three-paragraph memo to determine congressional intent, which, again, was to reinstate *Griggs*. But for all the last-minute comity, how much of this was really compromise on the part of the administration and how much was capitulation was murky. Before the long meeting in Dole's office, Danforth had brought six Republicans to the White House, who told Sununu and Gray that they couldn't guarantee they would vote with the president to uphold a veto, and later that day Dole had Danforth speak to the Republican caucus, so the administration was on notice. Senate Republican whip Alan Simpson had warned the White House that Danforth had enough friendships in the Senate to override a veto. And Mayer and Abramson, who had written the account of the Clarence Thomas hearings, speculated that Bush knew he owed Danforth for getting Thomas through the Senate and that his signing the bill was payback, though the official position, as enunciated by Sununu, was that "it's a no-quota bill." And there was this irony: The Thomas-Hill confrontation had brought sexual harassment to the forefront, and the bill addressed remedies for sexual harassment, which put additional pressure on the president to sign a bill.

Given how strenuously the administration had resisted them, the final compromises were rather minor. The basic sticking points had been how business practices related to jobs that led to disparate impacts; who bore the burden of proof in showing that the practices met the standard; what kind and amount of damages a complainant could recover if the employer were found guilty of discrimination; whether the bill would cover discrimination only in hiring or on the job as well; and whether complainants, usually aggrieved white people in this instance, could sue on the basis of past consent decrees that had mandated quotas to remedy past discrimination. On each of these, the administration had largely caved to Danforth and Ted. (Danforth would say as much, telling reporters, while smiling, that the difference between the so-called quota bill and the new no-quota bill was a "lot of words" and "very technical formulations.") The standard for allowing an employer to defend itself for its businesses practices was now "job-related for the position in question and consistent with business necessity"—basically the sterner *Griggs* definition, though with a slight modification from "manifest relationship to the job in question" to the "consistent with business necessity," with "necessity" remaining undefined. The burden of proof would be on the employer—reversing *Wards Cove*. The bill would cover discrimination during employment as well as in hiring. Nonracial victims of intentional discrimination would be entitled to compensatory damages and even to punitive damages in some cases. But there would now be a cap on damages beyond back pay—a limit on which the administration had adamantly insisted and that Ted had just as adamantly resisted. In this case, Ted compromised, while promising he would introduce a bill in the next session to strip the limitations out of the bill. (In the event, he was not successful in doing so.) And finally, as for permitting claimants to sue on past consent decrees, the bill disallowed them from doing so if they had had "actual notice" at the time of the decree and "reasonable" time to object—which had been Ted's and Danforth's position.

Ted and Danforth had done it, though Danforth this time did most of the heavy lifting. Still, he could not have succeeded without Ted. "That's what's really great about Kennedy," Danforth would say years later. "He is a totally honorable politician because you can disagree with him, but he wants to get things done. When you make a deal with him, that's the deal," which was a refutation of Sununu's complaint. "So when the left wants to embellish this and add this and that, nope. He sticks with the deal. That's why you can deal with him."

But now Ted had to sell the deal to his fellow Democrats, which he did at a meeting the next day. And, a more difficult task, he had to sell it to the advocacy groups, who were unhappy about his concession to place a cap on damages, especially, coming just two weeks after the Thomas hearings, on damages for sexual harassment, which Danforth had told Ted was essential for Danforth's fellow Republicans to come aboard. Senator Tim Wirth, a Colorado Democrat, described women as "white hot" in anger over Ted's concession. Ted phoned Ralph Neas, the executive director of the Leadership Conference on Civil Rights, the next morning and asked him if he would come to the office and put it over with other advocates. But Neas begged off. Ted was the one with the authority, he would later say, not him. "Only one person could say, 'I've done as much as I could possibly do. Not everything we wanted, but it's a good compromise. We should support it.'" Only one person had that "moral authority," as Neas put it, with those groups: Ted Kennedy. That same day President Bush announced that he would sign the bill "enthusiastically" because, he said, it did not contain quotas, though the Civil Rights Act of 1990 hadn't contained quotas either. But Bush said more. Having stalled the bill for nearly two years over minor disagreements and having vetoed it once, he claimed credit for its passage. Ted said that the quotas on which Bush kept harping were a "phony charge," but Ted was gracious: "I think that President Bush deserves credit for rejecting at long last the advice of those who have been urging him to divide the nation over race." Danforth was slightly less gracious: "I believe the Republican Party has to be identified with civil rights, and that it's disastrous not to be." Bush seemed to have no deep emotional investment in the bill. He had clearly weighed the benefits of yelling "quotas," which roused his conservative base, against the benefits of passing a civil rights bill, which would appeal to moderates. (Neas claimed that a source in the administration had told him that White House counsel Boyden Gray had tried to convince Bush to use the signing ceremony to announce via executive order the end of affirmative action—giving with one hand and taking away with the other.) But in declaring himself enthusiastic about the bill, and in signing it after it had passed the Senate and House overwhelmingly—93 to 5 and 381 to 38, respectively—Bush was doing something else. The president of the United States, after more than a decade of Republican appeals to those who had little interest in advancing civil rights and to those who actively sought to reverse them, was trying to accrue some moral authority of his own.

IV

Ted Kennedy, his own moral authority in steep decline, sat at his Senate desk that morning and listened to the debate on the bill to which he had dedicated so much time and energy and the bill that he was floor-managing. Jeffrey Blattner, who was sitting next to him, said that as the debate droned on, Ted was reading. It was the text of a speech that he was to deliver that very evening, October 25, after the Civil Rights Act compromise, at the Political Institute of the John F. Kennedy School of Government at Harvard. Ted would later write in his memoir that after the Palm Beach episode, and after the beating he had taken in the media, he "needed to reestablish good faith with my constituents." Those constituents, who had stuck with him through his plane crash and long recuperation and the Chappaquiddick accident and his foundering presidential campaign, had finally lost patience with Palm Beach. A *Boston Herald* poll that August found that 62 percent of Massachusettsans felt he shouldn't run again in 1994. "What's different now is that people are beginning to wonder whether his personal life, which they did believe was his own, is in fact in some way impeding his ability to do a good job for them," commented one Democratic adviser, which was exactly what the pundits had concluded. He had often been in despair—after the cheating scandal, after his brothers' deaths, after Chappaquiddick. But this was different. This was humiliation—not just for himself but for the entire Kennedy legacy, and the Kennedy legacy, which certainly seemed to be negligible in comparison to the loss of a young woman's life, was not negligible to the Kennedys or to Ted. "He nearly took the whole thing down in flames," Patrick was to say. For his father, Patrick said, the worst wasn't cheating on an exam or Chappaquiddick or losing the presidency. The worst was "bringing discredit to the family name and the legacy." "White terror," Patrick called it. "Incomprehensible demoralization," he called it. "The core of the nuclear reactor," he called it. "I am going to be the final word" was how Patrick characterized his father's state of mind, "and it is going to be destruction."

Ted knew the consequences, and they corroded him. "It would not get better soon," he warned his staff. At best, it would be six to nine months before Palm Beach would begin to fade, and he would no longer be a joke or gossip fodder. Charles Tretter, who had been with him in his first campaign and had remained in touch with him, said of Ted in this period, "I think he was very disturbed. I think in some respects he thought his career was over." And Tretter would say, "with affection for him," that "he was not always the most pleasant person to be around." Tretter would banter with him as he had done in the old days, but Ted was unresponsive. "There was a lot of anger," and Tretter remembered "just talking with him and him almost being belligerent." And Tretter said, "The sense I had of it was that he was just willing himself to hold it together." Tretter recalled a Democratic State Committee dinner to which Barbara Souliotis, Ted's Boston office manager, had invited him because Ted wanted to be surrounded with people he knew. Tretter was seated next to him. "The thing that struck me," he said, "almost the entire night he either had the knife or the spoon or the fork in his hands, and he was just holding on to them. It was just—I don't know whether it was just a sense of something outside himself or whether it was the coldness of the silver-plate or the steel, whatever, but it was amazing." And Tretter noticed, "He wasn't just holding it; it was like he was clenching it. He was very uneasy that night, very uneasy." A Hyannis neighbor told biographer Lawrence Leamer about Ted's sailing out just before the hurricane—the trip that Vicki had begged off on. "I just couldn't believe it," the neighbor said. "The only thing I could think of is that the guy had a death wish. The guy wants to die."

In his humiliation and despair, the broken man, the man who had never sought counsel on his personal life, now did. "I don't really remember him ever talking about himself this way," one friend told *Newsweek*. An aide confided that "after Palm Beach, I think he really started to change. . . . It just seems that he resolved that he was going to change and began that process of change." But he didn't know quite how to tackle it. "It's frustrating," he told E. J. Dionne, Jr., of *The Washington Post*, late that summer. "Most of the political challenges of your life, you have some degree of ability—some ability to influence or control. . . . This particular incident is sort of outside your ability to try and come to grips with." Friends urged him to change his lifestyle—"settle down to a life style that matches your professional achievements," his self-appointed "Jewish mother," Nancy Korman, had told him. Others told him to curb his drinking, which seemed to lurch him out of control, and where, in the past, he had scorned them, put them in Coventry, as he had done to John Culver and even to his own children, now he listened sheepishly. Orrin Hatch, catching Ted at the Senate after Palm Beach, joked that he was going to have to send the Mormon Mission after him, and when Ted stared at the floor and said, "I'm just about ready for them," he took the chance, even though he knew about Ted's reaction to Culver, to give him advice, telling him, as Hatch recalled, that it was time for him "to grow up"; that he was the "leading liberal in the country, and you're acting like a good-time-Charlie playboy little teenage kid"; telling him he could "do a lot of good"; and telling him that he had to stop drinking. "His big Irish face got all red, his eyes kind of all teary-eyed," as Hatch told it later. "And he looked at the floor and he said, 'I know,' in the most mournful way you ever heard."

He knew. He knew his polling had slipped in Massachusetts, and though he and Vicki seldom talked politics in their courtship, looking grim, he mentioned over dinner that his poll numbers were "terrible"— down to 48 percent. To which Vicki quipped, "Boy, are you lucky. I've never gone out with anybody whose poll numbers are less than forty-seven. So we can still go out." And she said that they both laughed, and "that was end of that." But of course, it wasn't the end of it. "I want to address that," Ted told his old press secretary and speechwriter, Bob Shrum, of Palm Beach. "Not in detail. But people are troubled by things in my private life that I recognize I have to change." And he asked Shrum to write a speech to that effect, the speech he was reading in the Senate during the Civil Rights Act debate, a speech in which he would acknowledge his fallibility and his faults in a way that few if any politicians ever had, in a way that was confessional and self-abasing.

But as much as Ted might have realized he needed this kind of speech to clear the air and clear his name, to provide a defense against his near-silence during the Clarence Thomas–Anita Hill face-off, it was not all at his own instigation. It was his aides who pressed him to do it and who, by one account, debated over the words he would use to do it. So seven months after the Palm Beach incident, and ten days after Clarence Thomas's ascension to the Supreme Court, and a week before the beginning of his nephew Willie Smith's trial in Florida, he flew up to Boston one afternoon with Vicki and his press secretary Paul Donovan and, with his children in the audience, made an attempt to make amends for the disappointments he had visited upon his supporters. The Arco Forum at the John F. Kennedy School of Government was jammed, and crowds spilled over into adjoining rooms, where they could watch the speech on television; people had waited in line for hours, largely because there was a rumor that Ted was going to resign or announce that he would not run for reelection. The room was close and hot, the atmosphere less than joyous, though Ted was ostensibly there to celebrate the twenty-fifth anniversary of the Institute of Politics at the John F. Kennedy School of Government. He spoke purposefully, solemnly. He wore his trademark dark blue suit. He began with his familiar liberal assault. He accused the Bush administration of stoking racial tensions, and he called David Duke's campaign in Louisiana the "logical, inevitable and shameful extension of a politics that has increasingly appealed to our worst instincts." But even though the bulk of the speech was devoted to reciting Ted's liberal litany of causes, this was not a political speech, or one simply to vilify Republicans. This was a speech to address his own failings and explain his own reticence. "Some of the anger of recent days, the powerful public reaction to the final days of the Thomas hearings," he said, while the audience sat in rapt silence, "reflects the pain of a new idea still being born—the idea of a society where sex discrimination is ended, and sexual harassment is unacceptable." But he acknowledged his own near-silence during those hearings. "I am painfully aware that the criticism directed at me in recent months involves far more than honest disagreement with my positions or the usual criticism from the far right. It also involves the disappointment of friends and many others who rely on me to fight the good fight." He then looked up from the text and looked directly into the cameras facing him. "To them I say: I recognize my own shortcomings—the faults in the conduct of my private life. I realize that I alone am responsible for them, and I alone am the one who must confront them. Today, more than ever before, I believe that each of us must not only struggle to make a better world, but to make ourselves better too. And in this life, those endeavors are never finished." "I have been given many gifts," he continued, "not least, unlike my brothers, I have been given the length of years. And as I approach my sixtieth birthday, I am determined to give all that I have to advance the causes for which I have stood for almost a quarter of a century." And thanking the people of Massachusetts, he said, "I cannot promise you that I will fulfill every expectation, even my own. But I do pledge my commitment, unchanged and unwavering, to the core values that for two centuries have made this commonwealth a force for economic justice, for progress, and compassion. In short, I will continue the good fight." And he said: "Our day will come again, and we must keep the faith until it dawns. Individual faults and frailties are no excuse to give in—and no exemption from the common obligation to give of ourselves."

It was a brief speech—twenty-five minutes. He was interrupted seven times for applause, and he received a standing ovation at the end. And then he left the forum hastily.

"The speech speaks for itself," his press secretary Paul Donovan told reporters. Ted took Vicki out for what he called a "quiet dinner," and afterward he asked her to take a walk with him—a tour of his Boston, he would say: the Garden, the Common, Chestnut Street with its buildings designed by Charles Bulfinch, Louisburg Square on which he had once lived. And then they left for Hyannis.

But Ted would not escape so easily, with a few words of remorse. That evening the ABC program *Nightline* devoted its entire half-hour to Ted Kennedy's behavior. The host, Jeff Greenfield, cited the "stories of excessive drinking and womanizing," though there had really been only one story outside the tabloid press, Michael Kelly's in *GQ*, and a "run for the presidency in which he appeared clumsy, even inarticulate," as if this were a moral issue and not one of ineptitude. And then Greenfield introduced Michael Kelly to repeat his argument, which was the old conservative argument that Ted Kennedy, who had invoked political morality, could not do so because of his personal failings: "He has epitomized the framing of the dialogue in a good versus bad moral framework. Someone who does that and who has a semi-public life that strikes many people as immoral comes to represent, I think—he has come to represent—a kind of rank hypocrisy." In short, the charge of immorality aside, Kelly seemed to be saying that it was better not to work for the public good at all than to do so if one is personally flawed, which might have been a conservative argument too, but an odd one. In any case, Ted's alleged amorality in the eyes of his conservative detractors amounted to drinking too much and dating a lot, though his disregard for its consequences, his real moral failing, had caused many people to suffer and had seriously undermined his own political mission, as he himself admitted. Another conservative, Brent Bozell, said that Ted personified "personal corruption," though again, his corruption was drinking and dating. But none of this was about morality really. It was about politics—about silencing the voice of the preeminent liberal. And Greenfield closed by echoing Kelly and Bozell: "Ted Kennedy has a real problem serving as a public moral voice, because this is his public role. If he cannot do this, then what can he do?"

These were political attacks camouflaged as moral attacks. But others, much closer to Ted, made moral demands on him after the speech. Nancy Korman had been sitting in the rafters at Arco Forum and praised him. "It is never easy being vulnerable," she wrote him, "but unless one decides to express real feelings, there is no hope for real relationships." And yet she chided him too for his Falstaffian companions. "Your speech was a lot like going on a diet. It is a lot easier to make plans than to limit the calories. Believe me. You could begin by trading Chris [Dodd] and Claude [Hooten] for two sensible adults. That, of course, is the tip of the iceberg." And Patrick, who had not been told by his father in advance what the speech would contain, was less than impressed, both because he was convinced Ted hadn't given the speech voluntarily, but had done so at the insistence of his advisers, and because his father still would not admit to his lack of sobriety. "To me," Patrick would later write, "the speech reinforced the denial I had lived with most of my life."

There was one more ordeal. Willie Smith was finally going to trial for his alleged activities on the night at Palm Beach, and Ted would be testifying. For Smith, it had been a busy summer. He had hired private investigators to scrutinize his accuser and even her friend Anne Mercer, whose father had been convicted of perjury in a union pension fund scam. He had hired a public relations spokesperson, who had formerly worked for *The New York Times*. He had assembled an all-star defense team headed by former public defender Roy Black, whom *The New York Times* described as the "very top of the Southern Florida defense bar," and who was best known in Miami for defending two police officers who had killed Black citizens. Black worked the press all summer, issuing a twenty-four-page filing with the court asserting that Smith's accuser, Patricia Bowman, had a "long-standing psychological disorder," the result of abuse by her father when she was eight years old. (The Kennedys championed victims, but they could just as quickly victim-shame them when it was in their interest.) Meanwhile the prosecutor, Moira Lasch, had been working the press too, especially flogging the discovery of the other women who had accused Smith of attacking them. The "worst case of pretrial publicity that I've seen in the recent past," one legal scholar called it. When jury selection began, at the end of October, the main questions Black asked of those prospective jurors was how they felt about the Kennedys generally and about Ted Kennedy in particular. At one point, Black laid out what one reporter called "Ted's greatest hits"—his reputation as a womanizer, his drinking, Chappaquiddick, his less-than-forceful performance at the Clarence Thomas hearings—to gauge the juror pool's response to him and eliminate those who clearly detested him and, by extension, the Kennedys. At one point he asked, "Do you think the Senator really had his pants off?" And he asked them who they least respected among the Kennedys. The answer repeatedly was Ted. Ted was abashed. "My God! We're paying this guy," he complained to an adviser. But Black told the press, "I am not unconcerned or unembarrassed for the Senator, but I would be a fool to ignore the negative feelings people have about the Kennedys."

State of Florida v. William Kennedy Smith would be, *Newsweek* reported, the "most-watched legal proceeding in American history," with the Courtroom Television Network providing gavel-to-gavel coverage. *Newsweek* compared it to the Clarence Thomas–Anita Hill confrontation. Black, whose nickname was "The Professor" for his professorial manner and his bookish predilections, was a stern inquisitor. He eviscerated Anne Mercer when she admitted she had sold her story to a tabloid television show, and then he accused her of embellishing it to make it better. In five hours of cross-examination, he was more cautious with the alleged victim, Patricia Bowman, fastening on the apparent inconsistencies between her testimony and her police statement, though Bowman was unshaken and, at the conclusion of the examination, fired back, "Your client raped me!"

But if Willie Smith was on trial for rape, he was not the only defendant. All the Kennedys were on trial, the Kennedy legacy was on trial, and of course, Ted Kennedy was on trial, possibly the most vulnerable of those defendants. He had already testified over the summer before a grand jury that was determining whether William Barry, the family friend and security specialist, had obstructed justice. That, however, had been behind closed doors. For the Palm Beach trial, he would be testifying in the public glare, and there was a lot on the line. He prepared diligently. According to Melody Miller, Ted spent a full day in the conference room of Williams & Connolly with his administrative assistant Ranny Cooper; Carey Parker; Greg Craig, his former foreign policy aide; and Miller, and Miller said they were "throwing every question they could think of at him, including the kitchen sink." And Miller advised, as Nancy Korman always had, that Ted open up about how hard it was to be Ted Kennedy, that he "allow people to understand his emotions and what he felt, rather than just being stoic"—this for the man who had venetian blinds on his soul. And Cooper approached the testimony the way she might have approached a campaign, giving every staffer assignments, having them develop talking points, and having them present a gloss on his career. Miller's own assignment was to write what she called a "major memorandum" on his involvement with his family and his duties as paterfamilias—a "huge, big, long thing that backgrounded everybody and reminded everybody." And while Vicki denied that she played any role either in the mea culpa speech or in the Palm Beach testimony—"That just was not part of what was happening between us" or "We were in a cocoon"—and while she said that he would be preparing for his testimony and then call her to meet over lunch where they would talk about going to Sunday's Washington Redskins game or about what movie they should see or about Vicki's children, but never about Palm Beach, Greg Craig, who served as Ted's counsel in the trial, nevertheless said, "She had insights, ideas and opinions based on her training"—her legal training—"that had a lot to do with how he came out in the courtroom." And by this time, the changes in his life had begun to take hold as well—physical changes. He had curbed his drinking, though he hadn't stopped it. "You could stake out La Brasserie for the next five years, and you wouldn't catch him having after-dinner drinks," said an aide, which may or may not have been true, but if true reflected a new discipline. He lost twenty-five pounds—another measure of his rebound. And another aide, David Nexon, told Burton Hersh that despite the pressure Ted was under at the time—"rock bottom" was how he described his state—"he still had the same zest, worked the same hours."

• • •

As Dominick Dunne reported in *Vanity Fair*, when Ted arrived on December 6 at the Palm Beach County Courthouse—an arrival that, Dunne said, caused a "near riot"—"Everything about him in Palm Beach—hair, suit, tie—was in order. . . . There was no sense of walking toward his nephew's ignominy. He could have been going to another Kennedy wedding instead of being a witness at a rape trial. The imperial Kennedy had taken over. He entered the courtroom with the bailiff. He waved to Willie. He took the oath. He took the stand. His presence overpowered the court. The afternoon was his." Dunne was skeptical of the performance that Ted gave that afternoon and that Roy Black coaxed from him—teary-eyed, invoking his dead brothers and Stephen Smith as a surrogate brother, alluding to Bobby's assassination, talking about how close he felt to his now-widowed sister, Jean, and about his role as the family protector. A "masterly performance, reeking of bathos," Dunne called it, and surely some of it may have been. Others were more forgiving and more conscious of what the testimony signified—not an absolution but, as Robin Toner in *The New York Times*, put it, a "final, unavoidable collision between the private man and the public man, when the hard-drinking debauchee caught up with the influential Senator and attentive paterfamilias." He told his story—the story of how despondent he was after discussing his brother-in-law's death that night, the story of how he roused his son and nephew for companionship and because he felt he needed to talk to his son, the story of how they went out for late-night drinks and then returned home, the story of how he didn't see or hear anything that might have led him to suspect that his nephew had assaulted the young woman he had taken to the house. And he said in what might have been the saddest and greatest understatement of the trial, "I wish I'd gone for a long walk on the beach instead, but we went to Au Bar." He had testified for forty-five minutes—painful testimony. He was called as a prosecution witness, but he had clearly helped the defense. As Roy Black would later say of Ted's appearance, "Suddenly, it wasn't the Kennedys out carousing, but a sense of melancholy hanging over them that the jury saw." And after testifying, Ted gave what Toner described as a "sad smile and stiff wave" and hustled out to a white Lincoln.

After ten days and forty-five witnesses, the trial dragged to its conclusion, with Willie Smith testifying, calmly, gravely, a "boy-next-door performance," *Time* called it, not having to address the issue of the three other women—a doctor, a medical student, and a law student—who had also claimed to have been victims of his, because the judge had disallowed any mention of them or any testimony by them. (It was of no credit either to Willie Smith or to his uncle that the women had told the prosecution very similar stories and seemed entirely credible.) It took the six-person jury only seventy-seven minutes to find Smith not guilty. Roy Black would say that the prosecutor's major mistake was not appreciating the impact of Ted's testimony on the jury. "When he was testifying," Black told the press, "I was looking intently at them, and two or three of the jurors had tears in their eyes. When he came in and sat ten feet from them . . . they were looking at a piece of American history. They felt his charisma. They couldn't help but be impressed," though that charisma, which had traditionally been deployed in the service of those in need, was now being deployed to spare the family embarrassment and perhaps worse. For one of the few times in his life, Ted was sacrificing his public morality and sense of justice for his family. After the verdict, Smith exited the courthouse to a round of applause, made a brief statement—"My life was in their hands and I'm so grateful for the job they did and the seriousness with which they took it"—and then jumped into a wood-paneled station wagon. Ted would issue a statement too: that he "always believed that, after all the facts were in, that Will would be found innocent," which was exactly what a Kennedy would say of a family member. And he said, "My heart goes out to Will, who I love very much. If there's anything good that comes out of this whole long experience, it's the renewed closeness of our family and friends," which, again, prioritized the family over the pain one of its members might have caused. Still, one person close to the family told Dominick Dunne, "They'll stick by Willie through thick and thin, but when this is over, and they're alone, they'll beat the shit out of him." That night the family celebrated at the compound with pizza and beer, though Roy Black would say that the family had sat in a circle and held hands and said a prayer for the accuser, which was a vignette that seemed tailored for the media.

"If anything good comes of this," Ted had said. But while Willie Smith might have escaped conviction with his uncle's help, little good would come of a credible accusation of rape or of the public humiliation of Ted Kennedy. Two days after Ted's testimony, Patrick admitted publicly that he had abused drugs while a student at Phillips Andover Academy— forced to admit his drug use because the *National Enquirer* tabloid had paid one of Patrick's fellow patients at the Spofford Hall treatment center $10,000 for a story that was about to be published. Ted Jr., who had abused alcohol, would later say that after the Smith trial, he decided to check himself into the Institute of Living in Hartford, Connecticut, where—and this was a good thing—he met Dr. Katherine "Kiki" Gershman, a psychiatrist, with whom he would fall in love and whom he later married. "It took me a really long time to open up and trust Kiki," he would tell *The Boston Globe,* sounding very much like a Kennedy. "It was never easy for me to express my feelings," and he said that with Kiki, he learned "how to trust and to become vulnerable."

But Kennedys did not confess their frailties. Patrick would later say that Ted Jr.'s decision to get treatment for his alcoholism was a "great blow" to Ted, and Ted was "*not* happy" about it. Even after the Harvard apologia, which Patrick had felt was another denial rather than an honest reckoning, and even after the Palm Beach trial, where Ted got as close to revealing himself as he had ever done in public but did so in a performance that was, after all, intended to gain the acquittal of their cousin, the children remained concerned about their father's condition. "The whole world was talking about how he needed help," Patrick said. So on December 30, a few weeks after the end of the trial, they decided to confront him in his study at McLean, its windows looking out onto the Potomac, in what Patrick called a "quasi-intervention." They did so with great trepidation, knowing their father's sensitivity to personal criticism. As Patrick later described it, Ted sat in his favorite blue suede chair, and they told him of their concern about his drinking and about the effect they thought it was having on the family. Ted remained mute for a long time, just staring at them, but he was seething as he did so. "I've been seeing a priest," he finally told them. "But you wouldn't know that. If you had bothered to *ask* me rather than just *accusing* me, you would have known I'm trying to get help." And then he got up and left the room. Patrick later wrote him a note, and Ted responded with a six-page handwritten letter. "I get the message," he said, "the point has been made." But he went on to fume about the "ambush" they had staged and the imputation that his drinking had torn the family apart. "What in heaven's sake does anyone think has been on my mind day and night, in restless dreams and sleepless nights—My God, Our family." And Ted then did to his children what he had done to John Culver when Culver had had the temerity to tell him to stop drinking. He froze them out, told Patrick that when he visited Washington he should stay with his sister, and when at the Cape, with his mother, wouldn't talk to them for months, put them in the category, Patrick said, of "they just don't understand." No one, he felt, could understand his burdens, no one his pain, no one his humiliation.

Save possibly one person.

FIFTEEN

"Stability and Tranquility"

ONE PERSON COULD understand. Since June, thirty-eight-year-old Vicki Reggie had been the ballast in Ted Kennedy's life. Their courtship had continued through the Clarence Thomas hearings and the mea culpa speech and the Willie Smith trial, though it was less like a courtship now than a life. "We'd see the two of them together on Cape Cod," Vicki's brother, Denis, would say, "and you could see how devoted they were becoming to each other." Ted eased himself into the lives of Vicki's children, Curran and Caroline—let them "get used to him in our own time," according to Caroline. "He never forced himself upon us as 'I am this new person in your life and thou shalt accept me.'" Caroline said she was very shy as a child, a "little timid and wary of him," hiding behind her mother when he arrived at their house, but that "quickly wore off because he was so warm." By October, he was taking them trick-or-treating on Halloween, the way he had done with his own children, and Vicki said, "He loved it. He loved those kid things so much." And if Vicki had made him a part of her family, he was making her a part of his, which, given the Kennedy insularity, was no easy accomplishment. Ted and Vicki had dinner frequently with the Shrivers, who, she said, "were so sweet to me" and who, not realizing that she and Ted were a couple, tried to fix her up with their son Robert. She met Rosemary, Ted's older sister, who would come to Washington now for visits. She met Jean, who, like her sister Eunice, wondered if they were a couple. And they often dined out with each other's friends. Eventually, Edmund Reggie would say, Ted would lean over to him and tell him, "I love your daughter so much." "I knew this one was going to be it," Melody Miller said of Vicki, "because not only was Vicki a terrific, warm, and bright woman, but he also wasn't going to *not* be serious with her, with Judge Reggie being her father." That November 1991 Ted was at Vicki's house on a typical night, the two of them listening to *La Bohème*, when Ted asked her if she would like to see a new production at the Metropolitan Opera two months hence. Not long after that night, as Edmund Reggie would tell it, Ted sailed to the Reggies' Nantucket home on the *Mya* with a group of his friends—Reggie called them the "usual suspects"—and, since it was off-season, they went to a small pizza-and-burger joint named Fairgrounds. After dinner, Ted sent his friends back to the Cape on two planes he had chartered, even though Edmund said there was plenty of room at the house for all of them. Then Ted, Vicki, Edmund, and Doris headed back to the Reggie home. And it was that night, Edmund said, now that the usual suspects were gone, and now that Ted and the Reggies were alone, that Ted told Edmund and Doris he wanted to marry Vicki and that evening that he asked for their blessing.* Once Ted decided to ask for Vicki's hand, he called John Culver and John Tunney, who were overjoyed, and then began calling other friends with the news, concluding with Joan. And it was on January 14, 1992, at the Met, during the performance of *La Bohème* to which Ted had asked Vicki two months earlier, that he formally proposed to her, though the two of them decided to keep the engagement secret, even from their own children.

The secret didn't last long. The night Ted proposed, he introduced Vicki to his sister Pat, who assumed that Vicki was "another girlfriend of Teddy's," as Vicki put it. But after about thirty minutes, Vicki said that Pat "got it." This was the one. "She focused on me like a laser beam" and took Vicki to the ladies' room, where she asked Vicki to tell her about herself. And from Pat, the news spread to Eunice and Jean, even though neither Ted nor Vicki had told anyone yet. The sisters just knew. In February, at his sixtieth birthday celebration at McLean, the two appeared publicly—Ted dressed as Rhett Butler, Vicki as Scarlett O'Hara. That March Ted and Vicki told Curran and Caroline and Ted Jr., Kara, and Patrick—again with the intention of keeping the news within the family. But six-year-old Caroline told one of her classmates, who told her parents, who told Lois Romano of *The Washington Post*, which forced Ted to make the engagement

---

* At least that was how Reggie told it to the Miller Center for Edward Kennedy's Oral History Project. He told a different story to Jack Thomas of *The Boston Globe*, saying that Ted and Vicki had called him and Doris from McLean in March, and he asked for their blessing. The first story seems more likely since by March, Ted had already proposed. Jack Thomas, "Victoria Reggie: The Next Kennedy," *BG*, April 2, 1992.

public. "I've known her for many years," he announced. "We began dating last June, and she has brought enormous happiness into my life." Over Easter, Vicki, Ted, and Ted's children vacationed in St. Croix, where Pat had rented a home. Ted planted an engagement ring on the Buck Island coral reef where Vicki "discovered" it while the two went snorkeling. It was almost exactly a year from the Palm Beach episode that had nearly destroyed Ted's life. In that year, Vicki had become both atonement and salvation.

Ted and Vicki had proclaimed love for each other, and for anyone who saw them, it seemed deep, sincere, enduring. But, given Ted Kennedy's reputation, there were skeptics and even cynics. "Are you marrying her for politics?" friends asked Ted, meaning to rehabilitate his reputation in preparation for the 1994 senatorial race. Vicki thought it preposterous. "We had never discussed whether I even liked politics," she was to say, even though hers was a political family and even though some of her earliest memories were tallying delegate counts while listening to the convention on the radio. John Tunney saw the relationship as a transaction. "I think Vicki desperately needed a guy like Teddy," he would say, "because here she was divorced, her husband was not being very kind to her"—in Tunney's view—"and she was being marginalized, and she hated that. So all of a sudden, he [Ted] gave her the opportunity to be a very significant figure in history, and she gave him the opportunity to develop once again the characteristics of strength and leadership and what I would call a very positive interaction between his personal life and his public life." Patrick Kennedy, who often doubted his father's motives, was even more cynical. "So he's got this woman who's willing to stand by her man—the man that's repeatedly ridiculed as being this pathological womanizer, drunkard, running around with his shorts on." And he said that his father had what, in the world of recovery, would be known as a "moment of clarity" where he knew he had to change his life. "He didn't have time to go into some big kind of rehab." Instead, Patrick called it an "outside job," as opposed to changing himself from the inside. " 'Give me a few years, a breather, I'll get back to work hard. I'm not going to do the booze. I'm not going to go around dating when she's [Vicki] agreed to lock in with me. Boom. This thing is signed, sealed and delivered'" was how he characterized his father's thought process. "She was the right person at the right type of time" to secure Ted Kennedy's political survival. And Patrick believed, "She knew what the deal was."

There was certainly no question that Vicki would be a political boon to her husband, who needed a boon. She was tough and intelligent and knowledgeable and opinionated—an equal of his. And Ted was proud of her; he had confidence in her; he never had to worry about her public demeanor as he had worried about Joan's. That May, before they were married, he took her to the Garment Workers' convention in Florida. The delegates were shouting, "Ted! Ted! Ted!" When she was introduced to the crowd, Ted told her to get up and "say a few words." She demurred, but Ted insisted, encouraging her to tell "the story of such-and-such," as she recalled it. "Go on. They want to hear from you. They'd love to hear from you," he told her. And she said that he would do that to her all the time now. But if she was a political asset, a perfect political consort, she said that Ted had put it to her very differently when he talked about their partnership. When Ted asked her to marry him, he told her, "I want you to be a part of my life in every way. . . . I don't want to travel and have you not with me. I'm asking you to be with me all the time. . . . I don't want your life to be separate from my life." And Vicki said she told him that she wanted that too. Joan, whom he had married when both were so young and so fresh, had been an accessory. Vicki would be no accessory.

And had Ted simply been looking for a political asset, he did so with trepidation about forging a new life for himself. One of his aides, Terri Haddad Robinson, attended an engagement party that Eunice Shriver hosted for the couple at her Washington home, and Robinson said that Ted was "awkward . . . almost embarrassed . . . quite shy . . . a little clumsy," this of a man who was seldom embarrassed, shy, or clumsy. When he took the microphone, "He wasn't sure what to say." Melody Miller, his longtime staffer, recalled a similar case of nerves as they prepared for the wedding, and she gave him a pep talk, telling him how happy he was going to be and how this was the right thing to do. She said that Ted gave her a big hug and then confessed, "Actually, I'm really scared." And again she had to reassure him. "You're going to go forward, and this is going to make a huge difference in your life."

Theirs would not be an extravagant wedding like Ted and Joan's, not a Kennedy wedding, but a Ted and Vicki wedding. It was modest and sedate—held at the McLean home on July 3 with only their immediate families present—except for Patrick, whose flight from Providence had been grounded—and with the bride and groom's siblings and Ethel, Bobby's widow. There would be no church monarch officiating, as at the first wedding. (Ted had not yet formally received an annulment for his marriage to Joan, so his marriage to Vicki was not recognized by the church.) Judge A. David Mazzone of the U.S. District Court in Massachusetts presided. There was a string quartet playing Vivaldi, and an Irish singer named Maura O'Connell, and a reading of George Eliot and Elizabeth Barrett Browning that one of the family members had discovered in an anthology that belonged to Rose, who was obviously too weak to attend. Vicki wore a short white lace dress designed expressly for her in Atlanta— there was a minor crisis when the dress arrived and didn't fit because Vicki had lost weight, and the bridal consultant flew up to Washington, had it refitted, and then had it sent to New York for the retailoring and then back to Washington in the nick of time—and Ted wore a navy blue suit and gray tie. After exchanging vows in front of Ted's marble fireplace, the couple danced to their favorite song, "You'll Never Know," and the guests ate dinner under a tent—the meal included Louisiana lump crab salad—and Ted Jr. made a toast to the couple, and Ted gave his bride the gift of a painting he had done—of daffodils—and each guest was given a print of the painting captioned with a Wordsworth couplet: "And then my heart with pleasure fills / And dances with the daffodils." And then Ted and Vicki took a chartered plane to the Topnotch Resort in Stowe, Vermont, where they honeymooned. And so began the salvation. "He put it to rest," an aide would later say. "Whatever he was, he wasn't what the jokes said he was. He wasn't a fat, bumbling, stupid, drunken lout, and he will now receive the benefits of the exaggerated reaction—of being so completely vilified."

Whatever the skeptics might have thought of the marriage, Ted's life was different now. The undertow was no longer dragging him down. The marriage freed him, Ted would say, "from a lot of other kinds of distractions" and provided a "sort of single-mindedness that was, I think, not as evidenced in other phases [of his life]." She gave him "such a sense of stability and tranquility," he would say, "that I had almost begun to think of life in those terms—stable and tranquil. But never boring," when stability and tranquility had never been features of his life. "She has that wonderful quality of being able to share your whole life, your thoughts, your hopes, your dreams, your laughter, your tears, your disappointments, the exhilaration of happy moments, and brings an extraordinary zest to my life, and an extraordinary warmth and gentleness and great passion and fun," he would tell biographer Adam Clymer. And he told Clymer, "I had no idea of ever having a serious relationship like this in my life. And all of that went aside when I met her." His friends noticed a profound change. "He just seems more serene, relaxed, more at ease with himself," Senator James Sasser said. "More accessible than he's been before," observed another friend. "None of us had ever seen or known him that way, as a family man, a romantic man. He became much more of a complete human being after meeting Vicki." "A healthy relationship," Melody Miller said, recalling how the couple had gotten into a tiff when Vicki packed a big suitcase for a sail up the Maine coast and then how the two laughed about it as, Miller said, "normal married folks do." But he had never been a normal married folk—not with Joan. Ted and Vicki had "chemistry," Vicki's son Curran said. "A very special pairing." And Caroline would say of the marriage, "It's slightly scary, it's so good. They just love each other so much."

He was free, happy, serene, stable, tranquil. But Vicki changed him in other ways than bringing him a sense of contentment for perhaps the first time in his life. She domesticated him, knocked out the frat boy in him, which became a meme at the annual Christmas party when the couple came dressed as Beauty and the Beast, with Ted's headpiece sliding down, and Vicki readjusting it, and patting his cheek tenderly and saying, "Poor Beast." For a man whose weight constantly yoyoed, and whose temperament in any given period could be measured by whether he was heavy or thin, she put him on a diet, prompting Ted to complain that "when she was cooking for me when we were courting, I got the tenderloin with the bearnaise sauce and the broccoli with the hollandaise, and now I get the little scrod with—if I'm lucky—a little light lemon butter." He was back to eating fruit salad for lunch and quipped to a fellow passenger in an elevator who was eating a pizza, "You don't mind if I have a bite of that?" In the mornings now, he ran on a treadmill. He even drank less, not total abstinence—Ted would never do that—but in moderation. When he sailed, he no longer took his crew of eight or nine carousers. Instead, he would take his children and, now that he had become a grandfather, his grandchildren, and Vicki. "Just a different phase," his longtime Hyannis neighbor, Melissa Ludtke, would say. Though Ted had been religious, he and Vicki now regularly attended church, waiting while Curran and Caroline attended Sunday school. And then there was the issue of fidelity, which had damaged his first marriage and helped wreck Joan's self-confidence. Now, as his in-laws were to say, "his fidelity is beyond question."

It was a very different relationship from the one he had had with Joan, less dramatic, more loving, and more respectful. He would concede to Vicki. A great storyteller himself, he would often begin a story, only to stop and ask Vicki to tell it because he thought she could tell it better. He would sing with Vicki, to the point where Curran and Caroline couldn't get them to stop. He solicited her advice, including her political advice, and listened to it. She was never submissive. Vicki was "a bit volatile," Ted said, high strung. "I thought I was marrying Doris," Ted once joked, because, as Edmund put it, "Doris is a very placid kind of person." And Vicki interjected, "And you married Edmund." But he acceded to her. He loved to goad her, tease her, "torture her," as Caroline said lovingly, recalling a "fight" they had when Caroline wanted to go bungee jumping, and her mother said absolutely not, and Ted kept telling Caroline what a good idea that was, raising the ante, the argument running on and on until, Caroline said, "someone cracked."

And if it was a different relationship from the tortured one he had had with Joan, it was a very different home life, too, than the largely estranged one he had had with Joan. Vicki and her children moved into the McLean house, and Ted had kept his promise to his new wife that they would never be apart. For the first five years of their marriage, they spent every night together, and the first time they didn't was when Ted flew to Israel for the funeral of Premier Yitzhak Rabin, who had been assassinated by a right-wing zealot. Ted told Vicki that separation didn't really count because he couldn't sleep that night. "He loved home. He loved home," Vicki would say. "He wasn't a person who wanted to be on the cocktail party circuit. He wasn't looking to be at all the big parties in town or going to events. He'd stop by political things that he needed to do on the way home from the Senate. He'd do his little five- or ten-minute stop-by, do his little things, and then head for home." In the car he would dig through The Bag, as he always had, one of the constants in his life, but when he got home, he would have dinner at precisely seven-fifteen, an inheritance from his punctual father, where he would share Senate business with Caroline and Curran and ask about their day, then help the children with their homework, and then, when they were in bed, put on some music—Kenny G or Peter, Paul and Mary—sit down in that favorite blue suede chair in his study, and go back to The Bag. (The old issue dinners, to which he had invited experts, became less and less frequent and then gradually disappeared altogether because he preferred to spend that time with his stepchildren.) And then in the morning, after his treadmill and after breakfast with Curran and Caroline, he would pore over clippings—hundreds of them—that had been sent from the office, so that he could be on top of everything.

He had a new family now and a chance to do it differently than he had with his own children, who had grown up in turmoil. "If there was a textbook for an ideal stepparent, he could write it," Curran said. "He was completely fair, he deferred to Mom when need be, and fortunately for me, overruled her on occasion, but at no point did he ever try to supplant my father." But he nevertheless assumed a parental role, acting as a doting, involved father. He took Caroline to art classes when he was taking them, and when he did a painting for a charity auction, he asked her to help him and then signed both their names to it. When Caroline made her first communion, he gave her the rosary that Pope Pius had given him when he celebrated his first communion at the Vatican during his father's tenure as ambassador to the Court of St. James's. He played with them. A "pal," Curran called him, and vividly recalled Ted teaching him how to run routes in football, teaching him for hours, how to plant and square in, explaining the nuances to him, making sure he got it right, ribbing him when he dropped a pass. Caroline called him "childlike." He would hold diving competitions in the pool and handstand competitions in which he would participate, judging the handstands as if it were the Olympics, and, of course, always letting Caroline win, which was a very un-Kennedylike thing to do. And he would help her memorize poems for school and act them out with high drama. At night, when the homework was done and before he retired to his study and The Bag, he made a point of playing card games with Caroline and Curran—chess when they got older—each one separately for an hour. "Every night," Curran said. "There was never a question . . . just to spend a little time." And he would go to their sporting events, often cheering them on beside their father. And when they were old enough, he took them along on the Kennedy family trips to the Civil War battlefields with historian Shelby Foote or on camping trips.

And if he was a pal, he was also a support. Like his own children and his nieces and nephews, Curran and Caroline had his office number, and they could always reach him if they needed him. "Always calming" was how Curran described his stepfather's effect. "If you ever had any questions or any trouble, whatever it was, you always go to Ted first because he's the person to go to. He could talk to Mom in a way that no one else could." And when he gave advice, Curran said, it was never in the spirit of "take it or leave it." It was in the spirit of " 'I know what I'm talking about, and you should trust me.' And you did"—not because "you felt you had to" but because you just didn't doubt him. Years later, when he was in college, Curran got into a minor scrape and phoned home at two a.m. and explained the situation to his mother, who told him she was handing the phone to Teddy. "I can't tell you how relieved I was to hear those words." And Curran explained the situation to Ted, who told him to sit down and not move, and that Ted would call him back in six minutes, which he did. And then Ted said, "All right, here's what you're going to do—this, this, this. Good luck. Have a good night. I'm going back to bed." And Curran said it was just how relaxed Ted was that got him through it. "Whatever you're going through, he's been through that and worse." And Ted not only counseled them, he respected them. There was no children's table in the Ted Kennedy household as there had been in the Joe Kennedy household. Curran said that when he invited friends to dinner, Ted would ask their opinions of things, and when Ted had guests of his own, he would ask Curran's and Caroline's opinions. "It didn't really matter if you had no opinion. He just wanted you to have a chance to talk, and he always made time for everybody." And in that way, he began to repair both the boyhood indignities he had suffered and the suffering that his and Joan's relationship might have visited on their children.

Perhaps the hardest part of the relationship with Vicki early on was Hyannis Port, where Ted had so many memories, where he was so deeply entrenched, where the bonds of the Kennedy family were strongest, and where Vicki would have to fight all those issues. Vicki was a self-described "sports nut," who had happily attended Redskins games with Ted and even bought pay-per-view boxing matches, but she was not a sailor and didn't share her husband's love of the sea. Still, she made her concession as he had made his. They would sail up the Maine coast, as Ted had done every summer for decades, to visit the Fentresses or the Tunneys, who had a family island. But after the first few years of their marriage, John Tunney said, the annual sails stopped. "She wanted Teddy to have his fun in places where there was no history and where there were *their* friends, not he's there with *his* friends." Tunney said it made him sad, even angry, at first, but he came to accept the end of the tradition. "I realized that she had to do what she had to do, and he had to do what he had to do with her to make it work." And if Vicki wanted to create their own memories rather than have Ted wallow in his own memories, she gradually came to love the sea and sailing and created their memories on the water. He taught her to sail, buying her technical books on sailing so that she would know what to do in any situation. Eventually, he bought her a boat of her own, a twelve-and-a-half-foot blue Herreshoff, which they christened *La Bohème*, and which she would take out every day, while he followed her in an old motorboat they named *The Grand Fromage*, or in a dinghy, shouting instructions at her. And though she stayed within the breakwater at the beginning, as she got more experienced she became braver, and Ted stopped following her in the boat, though he would always watch her from their room in the Big House, and when she and Caroline, who often crewed, since Ted had taught her sailing too, got into some emergency and then reported it to him, Ted would say sagely, "I know." Vicki would join him for the annual Figawi—a chaotic race, Caroline called it— wearing a huge stopwatch on her wrist and calling out time—"Five minutes! Four minutes!"—and then "Thirty seconds" as the chaos reached its pinnacle. And sometimes, she would race without Ted but with Ted Jr. crewing for her as she barked orders, and Ted would beam in pride. And they would go on long sails now, ten-day sails—a "recipe for divorce," Curran would say, but not for them—and every anniversary, they would sail the *Mya*, Ted's beloved blue schooner, around Nantucket Sound or up from Sag Harbor. Caroline would recall an image of her mother from this time, "her face pointing into the wind and her eyes closed, and her hair is going back."

And during those summers, of course, the Kennedy cousins would descend, and Curran and Caroline would find themselves part of the horde, sailing and swimming and playing guerrilla tag or red light/green light on the vast lawn, the lawn that sloped down to the ocean, while the adults, including Ted, watched from the porch of the Big House, old Joe's house. And Caroline would say that from Ted and Vicki's room in that Big House, on the southeast corner, they could look down at the ocean and its dark waters, and on the table in that room he had tide charts, and right outside a wind meter. And Ted could not only look out on the ocean but watch from his room a pair of ospreys, huge-winged birds, their nest close to the house, and he would be obsessed with those ospreys. But it was different now on the Cape than it was when Ted was a boy, and more different still than when he had brought his own family there as a father. Joan said so. She noticed the change in him during a visit to the Squaw Island house, where he played with his grandchildren after marrying Vicki. "The man I used to know was always agitated," she would tell Adam Clymer, "in a hurry to do something." But now "he just sits there quietly." Serene and tranquil.

But serene and tranquil were not the Kennedy way, any more than open and confessional and tender and emotional and inclusive and willing to exhibit weakness and being a little out of control were the Kennedy way. The Kennedy way was energetic, competitive, strong, secretive, composed, stoic, insular—all the things that Joe and Rose had inculcated in their aesthetic object of a family. And Ted, the youngest and least of the Kennedys, had spent a lifetime trying to live up to that standard of self-possession that his father had demanded and that his brothers had achieved, had spent a lifetime in pursuit of being a Kennedy like his father and brothers and had often failed in the attempt, failed because Ted had never really been a Kennedy—at least, not a Kennedy like his brothers. He had always been a Fitzgerald, like his grandfather, more a hardy, affable mess of a man. And it was only now, having met Vicki and fallen in love with her, and only with her resisting the gravitational pull of the Kennedy family where in-laws could never really be Kennedys but would always be outsiders, and only with Vicki encouraging Ted to be Ted and not a Kennedy, and only with Ted now abjuring the Kennedy life for a different kind of life, a stable and tranquil life based not around the clan but around his partner, it was only then that Ted Kennedy, the man who had spent his life being a Kennedy, dedicated himself, consciously or not, to being something else—to being *not* a Kennedy but someone quite different. To being himself.

II

For the first time since 1968, a presidential election was pending in which Ted Kennedy had never been considered a potential candidate. He threw his support to his former junior senator from Massachusetts, Paul Tsongas, even though Tsongas was a deficit hawk who scolded his own party for its profligacy—the profligacy that Ted had encouraged to finance social programs. The frontrunner was the boyish young governor from Arkansas, only forty-six, a former Rhodes scholar and Yale Law School graduate. William Jefferson Clinton traced his political awakening to a brief handshake with President Kennedy when Clinton was a sixteen-year-old visiting Washington as part of a delegation of Boys Nation. Clinton had a Kennedy-esque flair. He radiated energy. Ted had first met him when Clinton hosted the healthcare symposium at the Democratic Midterm Convention in Memphis—the convention at which Ted had delivered his "against the wind" speech—and the incoming Arkansas governor felt that he and Ted had bonded then. Two years later, when the boy governor was defeated for reelection, he said that the very first call he received—the "very first person"—was from Ted Kennedy, who encouraged him to "hang in there." And when Clinton ran again two years later and this time won reelection, he said the very first person to call and offer congratulations was Ted Kennedy. And five years after that, he had contributed to the brief Ted was drafting in opposition to Robert Bork's Supreme Court nomination. Clinton said he had tried to beg off because Bork had been his constitutional law professor at Yale, but Ted made a "moral argument I could not back away from." But now that Clinton was running for president, Ted was suspicious. Clinton was a charter member of a group called the Democratic Leadership Council that argued that the Democratic Party had shifted too far leftward and needed to shift back if it was to win elections. "Too many of the people who used to vote for us, the very burdened middle class we are talking about, have not trusted us in national elections to defend our national interests abroad, to put their values into our social policy at home, or to take their tax money and spend it with discipline," Clinton had told a DLC gathering in May 1991. This was the very sort of rhetoric that Ted found so exasperating in Jimmy Carter—rhetoric that eviscerated the Democratic Party of the very values that had made it a party. The DLC called for a "New Social Contract" or, as Clinton would call it, a "New Covenant," of which Joan Didion wrote that it "talked not about what the Democratic Party should advocate but about what it 'must be seen to be advocating,' not about what might work but about what might have 'resonance,' about what 'resonates most clearly with the focus-group participants,'" whom it had empaneled. It was basically, in her eyes, a marketing plan rather than a political program. Ted worked hard for Tsongas—he phoned twenty-four labor leaders who had been supporting Senator Tom Harkin—and asked them to withhold support from Clinton after Harkin had withdrawn. But Clinton had the momentum and eventually the nomination. At the convention that July, a convention Didion described as "four days and four nights devoted to heralding the perfected 'centrism' of the Democratic Party," Ted delivered a perfunctory speech on Clinton's behalf.

Instead of campaigning vigorously for Clinton, Ted pushed the Democratic agenda by prodding George H. W. Bush, the incumbent who was standing for reelection, putting the man who had forsworn social programs on the defensive. In January, Ted got the Labor Committee to report out a national health insurance bill with cost controls and a mandate that employers could either provide insurance or pay into a fund that would subsidize it. That same week he proposed a government program providing $850 million to four thousand schools in poverty areas, which Bush parried with a $30 million alternative allowing poor children to attend private schools. But there weren't many parries. To most of Ted's initiatives, Bush responded with a series of vetoes. "They don't do anything but veto," Democratic senator Tim Wirth griped. But there was one issue that summer about which George Bush was cornered. A year earlier, on March 3, 1991, after a high-speed automobile chase, Los Angeles police savagely beat a Black man named Rodney King, claiming that King had resisted arrest and was violent. What the officers did not know was that the beating was videotaped by a neighbor, and that the video challenged their account. The following year the officers were brought to trial and were acquitted on April 29, the video evidence notwithstanding. The acquittal, as the assassination of Martin Luther King, Jr., had twenty-three years earlier, enraged the Black community and touched off days of rioting in South Central Los Angeles, resulting in sixty-three fatalities. At roughly the same time, Ted and Orrin Hatch talked about finding some legislative initiative on which they could cooperate. By this point, they had become the Senate's odd couple: the extremely conservative straitlaced Mormon and the extremely liberal boisterous Catholic. Hatch was especially susceptible to Ted's blandishments, chief of which might have been his thoughtfulness. Hatch had once admired a painting of Ted's, and that March the two of them were visiting the secretary of labor, Lynne Martin, at her office, with Ted carrying a large portfolio, which Hatch assumed contained charts for Ted to show the secretary. But when they arrived, Ted opened the portfolio and took out the painting Hatch had liked. Ted had inscribed it: "To Orrin, handle with care. If the paint comes off, the numbers will show. We'll leave the light on at the compound for you any time." And Martin brought in a cake. (Ted had known it was Hatch's birthday and informed Martin.) Later that spring, as the odd political couple were bruiting about ideas in an otherwise dormant legislative season, Ted invited Hatch and his staff to McLean for a dinner with Ted and his staff to see if they could settle on some legislation to advance. Ted was thinking of a new health bill—he and Hatch had worked closely on the Ryan White Act—but there was nothing they came up with that they felt had sufficient magnitude. Then they began talking about the impending summer and the possibility, after the Rodney King riots, of it being a long, hot one, and the fact that Bush had decimated a program that provided funds for summer jobs for poor teenagers, many of whom had been promised jobs and had expected them. Ted foresaw thousands of poor teenagers out on the streets with nothing to do. "Why don't we do something about it?" Ted asked Hatch. "Why don't you and I agree to put half a billion dollars into these summer jobs programs across the country?" They agreed that the very next day they would introduce a bill calling for an emergency supplemental appropriation of $600 million to provide 300,000 jobs that summer. In fact, though, they decided to ask for much more—for $5 billion to fortify the preschool Head Start program, to fund summer school, to provide job training, and finally to provide jobs themselves. Bush threatened to veto the bill, but with the summer tense, he struck a compromise with Ted and Hatch for a smaller bill, $1.9 billion.

Even as he suspected Clinton's dedication to liberalism and preferred provoking Bush to campaigning for Clinton, Ted still felt that Clinton would defeat George Bush. That March, before Clinton clinched the nomination, Nancy Soderberg, Ted's foreign policy aide, had been invited to join the Clinton campaign, and Soderberg was ready to decline on the basis that Clinton was too conservative for her taste and that he had no chance of winning. She said that she and Ted were riding the Capitol subway when she told him of her decision, and Ted looked at her and said, "You've got to do it. He's going to win." Soderberg called Ted a "hopeless romantic," and Ted said that while he might be a romantic, he was certain he was right and explained that Bush's numbers were still inflated because of the Gulf War and that eventually the election would come down to the economy and that would not be good for Bush, since the economy was slumping. *Clinton was going to win*, he insisted. And he turned out to be prophetic.

Bush's loss was catastrophic for the Republicans after they had easily won the past three presidential elections. In 1988 Bush had received 53 percent of the vote against Dukakis. In 1992, against Clinton, he received 37.4 percent of the vote. And while there was a third-party candidate, a plainspoken Texas businessman-populist named H. Ross Perot, who harped on deficits and received nearly 20 percent of the vote, half of his voters said they preferred Clinton to Bush. Even so, Clinton's vote share was virtually identical to that of Dukakis: 43 percent. The Democratic Party hadn't grown. The Republican Party had shrunk. And it had shrunk largely because the promise of the everlasting Reagan/Republican economic boom had been broken. "It was almost as if Reagan had set a trap with his supply-side profligacy," historian Sean Wilentz would write, "presiding over what looked like good times with the bill falling due when he left office." George H. W. Bush paid the bill with the loss of his presidency.

Bill Clinton, the new president, paid homage to the Kennedys, which ingratiated him with Ted. Clinton's wife, Hillary, also a Yale Law graduate, said that as long as she had known her husband, he had talked about "how President Kennedy inspired him and Senator Bobby Kennedy moved him." The day before his inauguration, Clinton and twenty of the Kennedys, including Ted, visited John and Bobby's gravesite at Arlington, where the president-elect knelt at each of the graves and placed a white rose on John's headstone. He would sit at John Kennedy's desk in the Oval Office, and he would invite the political historian Richard Reeves, who had written a book on John Kennedy's presidency, to the White House, where Reeves spent two hours discussing Kennedy's presidential style. He would, at Ted's urging, appoint Ted's sister Jean to be the U.S. ambassador to Ireland, even though Ted's old girlfriend, Elizabeth Shannon, whose late husband had once been ambassador, had asked him if he might put in a word for her. (Family, of course, won out.) And perhaps most of all, Clinton won Ted's allegiance, after Ted's months of doubts, by announcing that a national healthcare plan would be his top legislative priority. Interviewing Ted that March, Adam Clymer of *The New York Times* called this period a "singularly, calm, optimistic time in his life," and said his "enthusiasm for President Clinton's vision seems unbounded." This was political stability and tranquility. Clymer even noted that Ted compared the new president to President Kennedy, which was the highest accolade Ted could bestow. Overlooking Clinton's centrism, he said that for the first time since John Kennedy occupied the White House, he had a president with whom he seemed to be on the same page.

But as much as he might have impressed Ted Kennedy, Bill Clinton stumbled out of the gate. No sooner had he taken office than he was mired in controversy. He had promised during the campaign to sign an executive order lifting the ban on gays in the military, and he intended to make good on the promise, right at the outset of his presidency. But Clinton hadn't bothered to consult either with the military or with Congress, which Ted thought was a terrible miscalculation. Clinton said he had fully expected Republican opposition since they would see this as a traditional values issue in which discrimination against gays was justified. What he hadn't expected was the range or the degree of fury from the military and even from members of his own party. (Ted recounted how the Armed Services Committee met with Clinton, met with him for two and a half hours one evening, while Ted watched the clock because he and Vicki had tickets for the ballet to see Mikhail Baryshnikov, watched it while Robert Byrd, perhaps the Senate's most grandiloquent speaker, expatiated on how Julius Caesar and Marcus Aurelius had been sex slaves and returned to murder their oppressors, and then on something about Tiberius—a long disquisition at the end of which Clinton said, "Well, Bob, I'm very glad to get your views and I'm glad to get the views of everybody else here, but Moses went up the mountain and came back with the Ten Commandments and discriminating against gays wasn't one of them." When Ted finally joined Vicki at the ballet, he told her, "Just remember these names: Tiberius, Marcus Aurelius, Julius Caesar. I'll fill in the blanks later.") Thus, the first week of his presidency, which Clinton had hoped to dedicate to economic issues, was instead consumed by the issue of gays in the military. To stanch it, he conceded to a compromise suggested by the chairman of the Senate Armed Services Committee, Sam Nunn of Georgia, a conservative Democrat who was very close to the military community. Clinton agreed to postpone any executive order for six months while his defense secretary, Les Aspin, a former congressman, investigated the ramifications of allowing gays to serve openly. Until then, anyone professing to be gay or who was suspected of being gay would be discharged, which infuriated the gay community. "Normally, you just say the guy had a bad week," Minority Leader Dole cracked acerbically. "But he's only been there a week."

Ted Kennedy might have welcomed Bill Clinton's presidency as promising, but the Washington that Clinton entered was less receptive. The Republican Party had changed during its years of near-hegemony during the Reagan and Bush presidencies. The party of the business class, of small towns and rural America, of suburbanites and moderates, having been commandeered by political and religious extremists who challenged even George H. W. Bush's presidency as insufficiently conservative, had become increasingly accustomed to not having to make accommodations to the Democrats—become accustomed to thinking of the Democrats not only as powerless but as illegitimate. Clinton arrived in what was effectively a hostile environment, one in which Republicans were determined to see him fail. As far as the Senate was concerned, whether this new environment was the product of conservative intransigence or whether a more polarized environment in the Senate encouraged conservative intransigence, the Senate was a very different institution than it had been when Ronald Reagan took office—an institution transformed. As former majority leader Howard Baker put it, "These guys don't want to make a deal, they want to make their point." The old Senate of the 1950s, '60s, and '70s had been no lovefest—there had been bitter disputes and occasional lapses of decorum—but it was collegial. One usually entered the Senate with respect for the institution and a sense that one served the institution rather than the other way around. That was how Ted Kennedy had felt when he arrived—with a sense of awe and reverence. "A sacred place" was how Joe Biden thought of it when he got there, saying that thirty-five years later he still got "goose-bumps" when he emerged from Union Station and saw the Capitol dome. Being a senator meant rising to the standards of the Senate. Jeffrey Blattner, Ted's Judiciary aide, recalled Senator John McCain, a war hero known to have a hair-trigger temper, storming into the chamber while Ted was in the well floor-managing a bill, and fuming over some machination he felt Ted had pulled on him over an amendment. "Flying through the cloakroom doors" was how Blattner described McCain, "spittle flying out of his mouth, just barking mad, red rage." And Ted glanced up at the gallery, where the press was sitting, and then back at McCain and said evenly, "Act like a senator." And Blattner said, "You could just see McCain deflate."

Act like a senator. There was a way senators acted—a way they demonstrated respect not only for their institution but also for their colleagues. The "world's most exclusive club," the Senate had been called. Those club members acknowledged that and acknowledged what it meant to be members of that club. That was how Ted Kennedy, the most liberal of senators, managed to forge a working relationship with Judiciary chair

James Eastland, among the most conservative of senators and a bred-in-the-bone racist, or with John Stennis of the Armed Services Committee, with whom he worked on draft reform, also a conservative, also a racist, or with Orrin Hatch, a profoundly conservative Republican, or with Strom Thurmond, who was a Republican, a conservative, and a racist. Ted disagreed with these colleagues, disagreed with them vehemently on almost all matters. He fought them in the committee rooms. He fought them on the floor. On rare occasions, he castigated them. But he usually demonstrated respect for them because they were senators, and that was how senators generally treated one another, not because they deserved respect—Ted understood that—but because the institution conferred respect. One reporter cited what he called a "heated exchange" between Ted and Thurmond, who was the ranking member at the time on the Judiciary Committee Ted chaired, and when Ted gaveled the committee to adjournment, he threw his arm around Thurmond and joked, "C'mon, Strom. Let's go upstairs and I'll give you a few judges."

The institution required collegiality and encouraged it. At around twelve-thirty, senators would gather in the private Senate dining room on the first floor of the Capitol across from the main dining room—the "inner sanctum," this private room was called—and settle themselves around two large tables, one for Republicans and one for Democrats. But that division was organizational, not emotional or even, in most ways, political. The Southern bulls held court on their side, and according to Joe Biden, they held the dining room longer than they held the Senate, since their power faded in the latter as the liberals took over. But then Hubert Humphrey on the Democratic side and Jacob Javits on the Republican side and eventually, after Humphrey's death, Democrat Pat Moynihan held court, and it was in the dining room that the chatter and gossip and courtesies and pleasantries wafted, and as Chris Dodd would say, "It's awfully difficult to say crappy things about someone you just had lunch with." Or they would meet in the cocktail lounge in the evenings. Or they would meet in the Senate cloakroom. Or they would meet in the Senate gym or in the steam room, where Ted had hashed out the Civil Rights Act of 1991 with John Danforth. Or they would meet in the office of the secretary for the majority, Room S-309, at day's end for drinks. "There was just an open invitation on a bipartisan basis—repeat *bipartisan*," the secretary from 1965 to 1976, J. Stanley Kimmitt, would say. "Only senators. They knew that they should not bring staffers or anyone else." And the senators would fix their own drinks because Kimmitt wouldn't allow his staff to be used for that service. And Kimmitt said that the same thing happened on the Republican side, when Everett Dirksen was minority leader: bipartisan end-of-day get-togethers. Or they would have those summer picnics in front of the Capitol to which Ted had brought his children. They would meet. "In politics, there are no friends, only allies," Jack Kennedy had said. That had never been true for his youngest brother. But it hadn't really been true in the Senate either, where John Kennedy had been something of an aberration—a young man on the make. There *were* friends— friends across ideologies, friends across the aisle. Ted Kennedy had those friends.

And if senators were, by tradition, compelled to respect one another, and then found, by proximity, that they often became friends with one another, they were compelled to respect the process too. The Senate was not designed by the Founding Fathers to be efficient. It was designed expressly to be inefficient. It was a deliberative body—a careful body. The Senate slowed things down at best, stopped them at worst—the cooling saucer, as Washington had called it. Majority Leader George Mitchell said that the Founders had decided that the "best way to prevent bad things from happening was to prevent anything from happening," which accounted for the elaborate system of checks and balances in the Constitution but also for the Senate itself where it was "much easier to say 'no' to something than it is to enact something." The proof was in the rules of the Senate—rules like unanimous consent, which allowed a single senator to halt progress on legislation, or the filibuster, which allowed a minority to stall and defeat legislation. It also meant that to accomplish anything, there had to be some degree of collaboration, some way to overcome factionalization. While never a perfect institution, while an institution often riven by ideological and geographical divisions, despite its high-mindedness, it had more or less maintained some semblance of apoliticism—*some*. As Robert Byrd, not only the onetime majority leader but also the leading historian of the Senate, once gloated of his institution, "On great issues, the Senate has always been blessed with senators who were able to rise above the party and consider first and foremost the national interest."

But that had all changed over the fifteen years before Bill Clinton's presidency—changed completely. The collegiality nearly disappeared. Some attributed the new attitude among the newer crop of senators partly to the fact that a Senate seat was no longer the lifetime appointment it had effectively been for many senators in the past, but rather a job that one had to begin fighting to retain the moment one hit Washington. "Some of the newer senators," Ted's friend Lee Fentress would say, "they've really gotten farther than they ever thought they'd get in their lives, and they spend every waking moment of their lives trying to figure out how to stay there." And that fight to retain one's seat had a ripple effect that altered the very calendar of the Senate. When Howard Baker was majority leader, he revised the schedule from five days, Monday through Friday, to three days, Tuesday through Thursday, so that senators would have more time each week to spend at home in their states to lay the foundation for reelection. "It's ITT," Bob Dole would say. "In Tuesday, out Thursday." This made it much more difficult to form friendships—Ted said that most communication among senators was now by Blackberry or phone—and nearly impossible even to get to know a colleague. "You never get to know them, the real person," Bob Dole said. "You get to know the political persona, the person who comes to the floor and makes the speeches." The shortened schedule also made it much more difficult to get business done since there was now less time—Senator Tom Daschle, later a majority leader himself, said that Wednesday was the only day one could be certain all senators would be present—which Ted felt had been the real motive all along: to prevent the passage of legislation. Baker changed the schedule as another Republican means of disabling the Senate from acting, another means of demonstrating that government did not work.

And the need to spend most of one's time campaigning rather than legislating had yet another effect: The deliberative body became less deliberative. The great debates were now less great. The intensive, probing questions at Senate hearings, the sorts of questions for which Ted had become known, were less intensive, less probing when senators spent so much of their time scheming for reelection. The deep dives into issues became shallower. Senate business itself became less important, giving way to fundraising and profile-raising, which is to say that while being a Senate insider had once been the only way to advance in the institution, now being an outsider was the only way to advance politically. Everything became less substantive. Ted said that in the old days, the pre-Republican majority days, senators not only came to the floor, but "people listened to each other, and they took action," and he said, "That's nonexistent today."

Senators barely spent time in the Senate. "Ninety-five percent is done by staff, and people come what I call 'parachuting' into the Senate on Tuesdays to listen to the lunch discussion, go back to their office and see people, because we're so far behind," Ted was to say. "They're out the door for fundraisers every night—Tuesday, Wednesday. They want to be out of there Thursday night. We don't have serious votes on Friday. If we have a vote, it's at nine-thirty in the morning with no debate." "They vote and leave," William Hildenbrand, who had been secretary of the Senate, said. "Mice do that. When the bell rings, they know it's time to eat. That's the only time members come to the floor, pretty much unless they're managing a bill." And Hildenbrand said more. He said that it used to be that when a senator came to the floor, "he knew exactly what the vote was; he knew exactly what the issue was; he knew exactly what they were voting on." Now when members came to the floor, they have no more idea of what they are voting on "than they can fly."

Deliberative it had been in the old days, in the days when Ted Kennedy first came to the Senate. Slow it had been. He recalled a tax reform bill in the 1970s on which he had been a principal sponsor, and Russell Long, the Finance chair, said that they would do a title a week over a six-week period. "Everybody knew you had a chance to look at what those issues were and prepare the amendments," Ted said. "If you came in and said, 'I have one on Title IV,'" Long would say, "We'll put that off," or, "I'll table you right now." And in the old days, Ted said, leadership never permitted "stacked votes"—votes on a whole series of amendments at a single time. There was always a debate and then a vote on each bill. But after the Republican takeover, there were many stacked votes—"votearamas" they were called, particularly when the amendments pertained to the budget— votes without debate, one vote after another, hundreds of them, for hours on end. The "corruption of the Senate," Ted called it, and he said, "You lose the whole essence of what the Senate is, about your involvement in it, your relationship with people, and what the purpose is, which is the exchange of ideas." And Ted, once again, chalked it up to the Republican desire to destroy the comity of the Senate, to "paralyze" it, to make it ineffective when it had never been all that effective to begin with.

And while the Senate had never been a rapidly moving body, the paralysis was worsened by another device—a device that the Southerners had used to halt civil rights legislation and that Republicans now deployed to stop *any* progressive legislation: parliamentary nitpicking. "Floor debate has deteriorated into a never-ending series of points of order, procedural motions, appeals and waiver votes, punctuated by endless hours of time-killing quorum calls," Senator Nancy Kassebaum, a moderate Republican, lamented. "Serious policy deliberations are a rarity. 'Great debate' is only a memory, replaced by a preoccupation with procedure that makes it exceedingly difficult to transact even routine business." Citing just one example, every dollar spent was debated three times, she said—as a budget resolution, as an authorization bill, and as an appropriation—which meant that two-thirds of all Senate votes were on budgetary matters. It forced Ted, who thrived on substantive politics and meaty debate, to learn parliamentary jiujitsu. "He knows the game," Alan Simpson told a reporter. "Rules. Parliamentary procedure. Conference committees. Managing bills. Compromise. Markups." Ted knew how to work those rules; he had to learn how to work those rules—the physics of the Senate. But it gave him no great satisfaction. It was a concession to what the Senate—the Senate he had so loved—had become.

And the need to devote one's time to one's reelection, rather than to one's legislation, undermined the institution in yet another way. In the old days, when senators had been chosen by their party machines or organizations, they had been more or less beholden to them but also were able to rely on them for aid and assistance. Now every senator was an "independent contractor," in Howard Baker's words, "beholden to no one for fund raising, for media coverage, for policy analysis, for political standing or anything else." That led to another new and disturbing feature in the Senate: The Senate leadership, once so fearsome, now was impotent in light of the self-interest of the senators. "The guys you try to strike a deal with will say yes, but they can't deliver," Ted complained. "Okay, we'll go along," a leader might say. "The next day, they don't go along. He can't get the votes." "Personalistic, idiosyncratic, individualistic," and "steeped in anomie" was how two prominent political scientists and students of the modern Senate described the new institution of the Senate. "Owned lock, stock and barrel by private interests," Ted complained to Arthur Schlesinger, Jr., when he was contemplating running for president against Jimmy Carter, and when Schlesinger said it probably hadn't been any different when Ted entered the Senate, Ted disagreed, saying the "private interests are better organized now, and the mood of the country is more in their favor." And what *that* meant was that any institutional allegiance, the allegiance that had been so instrumental to making the Senate function, was effectively gone. One had allegiance to one's career, to one's patrons, who were often strongly ideological, and to one's party, in that order. The Senate didn't even figure into the calculation. The institution had fractured.

And that further weakened the already much-weakened committee system, the system under which the Senate had operated for years and years, the system under which power was apportioned, and the system under which things happened or, when the committee chairman chose, didn't happen. (Civil rights was for decades among the latter.) When Lyndon Johnson was majority leader, his power, said onetime Senate parliamentarian Robert Dove, was "getting things through." Dove said Johnson "worked miracles. But he didn't trample on the committees to do it." By the time Bill Clinton took office, the committees had sunk into near-irrelevancy, wracked by the greater turnover among senators (Eastland ran Judiciary for twenty-one years; Richard Russell, Armed Services for fourteen; John Stennis after him for twelve), the shortened work week, the increasing power of the presidency in comparison to Congress, the increasing power of outside interests, and both the centralization of power in the Senate leadership because senators no longer had the interest or the time to exert power the way the old Senate committee chairs had and at the same time the dissipation of that power as every senator worked for his or her own interests. When Florida senator Lawton Chiles got a "sunshine law" passed that opened up committee sessions to the press, and Alaska senator Mike Gravel got a resolution passed that allotted to every committee member a staff person with access to committee files and permission to attend hearings, according to J. Stanley Kimmitt, senators no longer needed to be invested in their committees. They could go to a session—and frequently sessions of committees were held simultaneously—ask questions, and leave. "That changed the whole tenor of the Senate," Kimmitt said. Again, it was every senator for himself.

And that sense of individualization, of caring more for one's own interests than for the institutional interests of the Senate, much less those of the country, only intensified with the introduction of television into the Senate chamber. That was probably one reason that Senate leadership had been so reluctant to introduce television into the chamber, unlike the House, which had done so in 1979. Baker and then Byrd and then Dole had all fought to get the Senate to agree to televise its proceedings, but even a resolution for a closed-circuit television system died in committee in the Ninety-fifth Congress, and it wasn't until four Congresses later that it finally reached cloture, and not until the summer of 1986 that broadcasts began. Now senators became personalities, which meant they drew power from television, not from the Senate. It also changed the measure of accomplishment from internal to external. In the past, showboats like Senator Joe McCarthy on the right or Senator Estes Kefauver on the left, who played to the press rather than to their colleagues, were disdained; they were Senate outsiders. But now television made it almost imperative to play to the press. That press corps had grown wildly, from 750 in the Senate Radio and Television Gallery in 1979 to 2,300 in 1987, but over the same period, two studies showed, the amount of government/political coverage had actually decreased. It became harder and harder to make government mediagenic, which meant it became more and more imperative to try. "What I learned over time is that nothing happens in Washington if it didn't happen in the press," Nick Littlefield, Ted's chief of staff for the Labor Committee, said. "It's as if it didn't happen. You can have the greatest hearing in the world, but if it's not reported in the press, it's as if it didn't happen." It was the press that created what Littlefield called a "sense of urgency, a sense of recognition, a sense of visibility," and Littlefield even suspected that it was his background as a performer that appealed to Ted because Littlefield's capacity for "staging" hearings and other legislative events made it easier for the office to deal with television. A "continuous plebiscite," Stephen Breyer, Ted's onetime aide, called the relationship between the legislator and television, as opposed to the ongoing, substantive legislative drudgery that had formerly occupied the Senate. Ted, his Roger Mudd interview notwithstanding, was adept at using television, which allowed him to retain his senatorial advantages. "No one has looked this senatorial since Claude Rains in *Mr. Smith Goes to Washington*," the *Washington Post* television critic Tom Shales wrote of Ted when television arrived on the Senate floor. But television's affinity for Ted went far beyond how telegenic he could be. His onetime Labor Committee chief counsel, Tom Rollins, said that after television came to the Senate, Ted would have Senate hearing videotapes edited and then have his interns send tapes to television stations in states whose senators might be recalcitrant on a certain issue, thus using the tapes to reach those senators' constituents who would then apply pressure to their representative.

But the single most powerful and transformative force in the Senate, a force that changed the institution so significantly that for all practical purposes, it ceased to function—no longer a saucer to cool the tea but a sink down which the tea ran—was a consequence of all these other changes: partisanship, the most intense, bitter, unshakable partisanship. What had once been mere political disagreements between Democrats and Republicans had, in the years since Ronald Reagan's presidency and under the pressures of ideological conservatism, taken on aspects of religious disagreements, in which compromise, conservatives seemed to feel, would be apostasy. The chasm had grown so wide, the arguments so heated, that the divide was nearly unbridgeable, the arguments uncoolable. "Combative" was how Carey Parker described the Senate after the conservative tide. "You don't see Republicans and Democrats wrapping their arms around each other nearly as much as you did before, when there was a sense they could work together," Parker said. Some argued that the new partisanship was stoked by the fact that the intense conservatism had sprouted outside traditional politics, as an activist movement, before commandeering the Republican Party with Reagan; others that it was a function of the fact that the geographical center of the Republican Party was no longer the Midwest and the Northeast, where there was a tradition of comity and compromise, but the South and West, where there was no such tradition. In some ways, no doubt, it was the result of the Republicans having been out of congressional power for so long that once they finally gained power, they saw an opportunity for revenge. (That was what Trent Lott had said.) And it was also certainly a product of the steady decline of party moderation, so that there was no countervailing force to strident ideology, especially as congressmen and senators came to view themselves as individualists. Back in the 1970s, Senator John Tower, who was head of the Republican policy committee, introduced a weekly Tuesday lunch for his caucus, in part to halt Senate business because none of the Republicans would be available on the floor, though it didn't stop Majority Leader Robert Byrd from scheduling votes at that time. When the Republicans took over, the new majority leader, Howard Baker, continued the tradition, which induced Byrd to begin holding his own Tuesday lunches that had a further polarizing effect. "They're like football teams meeting before a game. They just ramp each other up," said former Senate parliamentarian Robert Dove. "I hope you know you're coming back to the most segregated place in the country,"

California congresswoman Jane Harman said a congressman told her when she returned to Washington after an unsuccessful run for governor. Harman was perplexed. "What do you mean? There are thirty or forty African Americans and twenty Hispanics," she said. And he answered, "I'm talking about Republicans and Democrats. They don't talk to each other."

The old Senate had operated on a certain sense of trust. With intensified partisanship, that was largely gone now. "Political polarization—too much emphasis on which side of the aisle one sits, is not now and never had been, a good thing for the Senate," Robert Byrd would write. "I am talking about politics when it becomes gamesmanship or when it becomes mean-spirited or when it becomes overly manipulative, simply to gain advantage." And now the Senate had become all those things. "Everything is so closely calibrated," Ted would complain, "if there's a difference, it has to be exaggerated. That doesn't lend itself to positive outcomes when it comes to the national agenda." When Ted became Judiciary chair, he had reformed the old tradition of allowing a senator to submit a "blue slip" to derail a judicial nomination in his state, by now requiring anyone submitting a blue slip to come before the committee in closed session to lay out his objections. But Ted discovered that the opponents declined to appear. During the Clinton administration, he said, by which time he had vacated the Judiciary chair to Joe Biden, the old blue slip was reinstated, and 167 judges were not considered, either because the committee decided not to hold hearings or because they were blue slipped. It was the Republicans who stopped them. Ted later marveled, "It's amazing how the Republicans got away with that."

Nor was the hostility all political. The personal warmth that had once crossed party lines now could just as easily be personal antagonism. When Ted was promoting a national holiday to honor the late Martin Luther King, Jr., Jesse Helms vehemently opposed it, claiming that there were already too many national holidays, though really using that as a pretext for the fact that he was not about to celebrate a Black leader. But when Helms came to the Senate floor to debate Ted, as Ted's onetime aide Kenneth Feinberg recalled it, Helms brought up the fact that Robert Kennedy, while attorney general, had authorized wiretaps on King. Ted was apoplectic. "His voice cracking with rage," in Feinberg's recollection, Ted said that Robert Kennedy was not there to defend himself. And that kind of jab, which became more frequent now, like the personal jabs at Ted during the Clarence Thomas debate, the references to Ted's moral infirmities, created tensions that were not easily forgotten or soothed.

Ted managed to retain trust with some Republicans, which was his primary asset as an individual and consequently as a legislator. "A handshake with Ted and you take the risk," Alan Simpson said, adding that legislation typically failed because "you failed to trust." Ted knew enough never to double-cross and never to promise more than he could deliver. But he was now almost singular in that regard—a throwback, no doubt in part because he didn't have to worry about losing his seat, didn't have to run a continuous campaign, and was committed to the Senate traditions of fraternity, even across the aisle. He could focus on trying to get things done, which meant getting them done the old-fashioned way. But as skillful as he was, as trustworthy as he was, as bipartisan as he was when he needed a Republican to pass a bill, he was frustrated by what the Senate had devolved into. "If the Department of Health and Human Services said the glass was half-full, everyone on the committee said, 'It's half-full,'" Ted would later recall of how the Labor Committee had once operated. "I'd say, 'Let's fill it up.' Republicans would say, 'It's half-full. We're doing pretty well.' But no one disputed that the glass was there, or that it was half-full." But that had all changed. "Today you'd say, 'Even if the glass is there, it really isn't a glass, and I don't know whether there's water in it. And what do you care about that because I have another study that says the water is going to evaporate in the next two hours—all of this cockamamie kind of falsified information." He concluded that "Nothing has credibility" and that legislation had begun following the pattern of commercial advertising where facts were irrelevant.

Shortly after he came to work for Ted, Nick Littlefield said he got a call from Senator David Durenberger, a moderate Minnesota Republican, who asked Littlefield, the Labor Committee chief counsel, if he would drop by Durenberger's office, a highly unusual request from a senator to another senator's staffer. When Littlefield arrived, Durenberger said he was curious as to why Littlefield had given up a lucrative Washington law practice to work for Ted, and then answered the question himself: "I suppose you're one of those Kennedy people who really want to get things done in government. You're coming down here to get bills passed and get things done. That's what Kennedy's all about." And Littlefield said he was right. And then Durenberger set him straight. "Well, I want to tell you something, just so you have it in your mind," he said. "The Republicans on the committee and in the Senate come to Washington to make sure that you and Kennedy don't pass any laws. That's why they come to Washington. At the end of the day, if they can go home and say to their family or to their constituents that they stopped you from passing a law, that's going to make them really satisfied. That's their objective. I just wanted you to know that."

III

But Bill Clinton had a lot of bills he wanted passed. And so did Ted Kennedy—many of them bills that had been vetoed by Bush. And now the two, Clinton and Kennedy, worked in tandem to undo what Bush had done. Six days after Clinton's inauguration, Ted moved through the Labor Committee the Family Medical and Leave Act, which gave employees up to twelve weeks of unpaid leave for the birth of a child or a serious family illness. Ted said he had gotten the idea for the bill back in 1974 when he was making his Friday visits with Ted Jr. to Boston Children's Hospital for his son's chemotherapy, and he had listened to other parents in the waiting room complaining that they had lost their jobs because they had to take time off to care for a child with cancer. He had first drafted a bill in 1985, when it had no hope of surviving in the Reagan administration, and guided it through the Senate in 1990, while it passed the House. But President Bush had vetoed it on the flimsy grounds that the government should not be setting conditions for business. Two years later it passed Congress once again, and once again President Bush vetoed it. But President Clinton had made it a priority, and this time when it glided through Congress, the new president signed the bill in an elaborate Rose Garden ceremony on February 5. It was Clinton's first legislative achievement. In June, Ted steered through the Senate the National Institutes of Health Revitalization Act, which prioritized women's health, lifted Bush's ban on fetal tissue research, and reauthorized the National Cancer Institute and the National Heart, Lung, and Blood Institute. It was another bill that Bush had vetoed. During the Bush administration, Ted had pressed for a job training program, and a special commission had been empaneled to study the issue, ultimately reporting that job training led to higher wages. Ted began introducing legislation that addressed parts of the report, knowing full well that the Bush administration would not support that legislation but hoping that he could set an agenda. Now that Clinton had become president, those bills began moving through the Senate that fall. And also that fall Ted sponsored a bill to outlaw anti-abortion protesters from blocking access to abortion clinics. It was not especially popular with Republicans, who argued that it violated freedom of speech, but Ted compromised with Republican senator Bob Smith of New Hampshire to lower penalties for nonviolent protest, and it passed the Senate, 69 to 30. In addition, there were bills to provide student loans and to fund Head Start.

It was an audacious legislative beginning. But the most significant bill was one that had been gestating since early 1989, when Ted held one of his issue dinners at McLean. The topic that February night was national service, and one of the principal guests was Harris Wofford, John Kennedy's former civil rights adviser who was then the secretary of labor in Pennsylvania. As president, John Kennedy had introduced the Peace Corps, a kind of government-financed mission to send volunteers to developing countries. Ted's idea was to have a domestic Peace Corps, a program that would strengthen the nascent and poorly financed national service movement. Nick Littlefield recalled that evening as his first dinner as staff director, and he took notes assiduously. Once again, Ted had no illusions about getting the Bush administration to act. Instead, he tried to convince them to provide $75 million to establish a Commission on National and Community Service to study the issue. Then, Littlefield said, Ted campaigned hard for that appropriation. "He went to the House and literally went door-to-door," Littlefield said, when senators rarely ventured there, and never ventured there to talk to junior representatives. But Ted did. "We made a list of everyone who had served in the Peace Corps, and Kennedy went over to everyone in the House who had served in the Peace Corps and met with them one by one." They were "startled" that Ted would do this, but Ted told Littlefield, "That's how you do it." And Ted got his commission. But the commission was not the program. Now that Democrats held the presidency, he could convert those recommendations into legislation, and he did. The National and Community Service Trust Act, which set up AmeriCorps, Ted's and Bill Clinton's domestic Peace Corps, and provided education vouchers and loan forgiveness and job training in return for service, was enacted on September 21.

It had been a great year by most measures—a year in which the four years of legislative inaction of the Bush administration had been reversed. (Relax, we won't pass anything, Bush had told Ted. And now they had.) It had been a personal triumph too. Ted had needed redemption after Palm Beach. The legislative successes provided it—"some of the most exhilarating victories of his 30-year career," enthused one reporter that August, even before passage of the National and Community Service Trust Act. The man who seemed always to be making comebacks from personal tragedies or disasters had made another. Laying out his schedule on just one day that July, the reporter listed a breakfast with Secretary of Labor Robert Reich on job training; a floor debate on national service and a continuous shuttle from the Senate Republicans to the House Democrats on the student loan bill; a meeting at which he introduced MIT professor and air force secretary nominee Sheila Widnall, and Graham Allison, who had been nominated to be assistant secretary of defense, to the Armed Forces Committee; a hearing at Judiciary on the nomination of Louis Freeh as FBI director; then to the Labor Committee at ten p.m. to sing "Happy Birthday" to Nancy Kassebaum; and then back to his office at eleven to phone Republican senators in an attempt to stop a filibuster on the national service bill.

Littlefield, noting the pressure under which Ted had been working, given the scandal of the previous two years, observed that he "never changed his work habits during all the time he was so distracted, presumably, by all these things that were going on. He stayed in the Senate just as late at night; he was doing the legislative stuff just as aggressively, just as thoroughly. The dinners in his house were just as intense, just as frequent. He always had an amazing way of separating the personal distractions from the responsibilities as senator and as legislator." (This might not have technically been true—Ted did leave the office to be home for dinner with Vicki and the children, and the number of dinners did fall off over time—but the intensity hadn't slackened at all.) Majority Leader George Mitchell called him "tireless" and "one of the most productive and effective members the United States Senate had ever seen." When Mitchell listed the top legislative accomplishments at year's end, seven of the fourteen were, according to one analysis, attributable in whole or in part to Ted's efforts. "Kennedy is walking proof," editorialized *The Boston Globe*, "that productivity can still grow, even after three decades." Even Bill Clinton would say of Ted, "He's as good at what he does as Michael Jordan is at playing basketball," and added, "I mean, he can always see the opening." "The talk on the Hill is no longer of Kennedy's dissolute ways," wrote John A. Farrell in *The Boston Globe* that November after he had all but buried him over Palm Beach, "but of how the nation's premier liberal titan has cleaned up his private life, taken a new wife and—in a contract of mutual convenience—leased his legislative influence to the 'different kind of Democrats' in the White House."

Ted had been skeptical of Clinton, worried that he would be another trimmer as he thought Jimmy Carter had been, someone who would tack to the right and abandon liberal principles. But it was Ted who had moderated, saying that Clinton had taught him "to move beyond ideology," even though Ted had never been particularly ideological to begin with. "I don't think it is big government or small government," he told John A. Farrell. "It is better government." And he adduced job training as an example. "There's $20 billion there, 123 different programs. The challenge to the question isn't providing a lot of additional money. It's trying to pull all those together in a way that really works." On his job training bill, Ted had included a sunset provision that ended the program after a certain number of years, on the belief that if the program worked, local communities would pick it up and fund it. "This was a new model with which Kennedy was going to approach federal policymaking," Nick Littlefield would recall. "Let's try it. Let's create up-front seed money, and give the states, through a competition, the opportunity to compete for the money, to run school-to-work training programs, bringing businesses, communities, local governments, and schools into the process." If the programs took root, Littlefield said, it would be good. And if they didn't, "perhaps they weren't worth it in the first place." Whether this was just a practical way to outflank the Republicans, or whether Ted of necessity had become something of a centrist convert in more conservative times—he had long been sniffing the wind—he was looking now for ways to pass legislation in a conservative world. He was following Bill Clinton's playbook. And it worked.

But there was one issue that surmounted all others, both for Bill Clinton and for Ted Kennedy, and it was one that was difficult to moderate. Ted Kennedy had dedicated much of his political life to gaining passage of a health insurance bill that would protect the poor and the vulnerable. Bill Clinton had pledged in his acceptance speech at the Democratic National Convention to pass a national health insurance law. (Bush sneered that it was "socialized medicine.") While the Republicans held the presidency, such a law was impossible. Republicans thought national healthcare was a government incursion, not a service. At best, one could only nibble at the margins, which was what Ted had tried to do. During the Reagan administration, the debate that had blazed so hot during the Nixon, Ford, and Carter administrations had abated. Reagan had proposed "market solutions," though the object wasn't to bring insurance to those who needed it, so much as it was to keep the federal government out of healthcare and to cut federal spending. Ted instead proposed his employer mandate bill that provided minimal coverage with a $500 maximum deductible, and in announcing it, he made a point of saying, "It is not backdoor national health insurance." Ted mounted a campaign for the bill, sending his staff to speak to editorial boards, courting reporters, lobbying members of Congress. But there was no hope of passage. When Reagan finally conceded to signing an expansion of Medicare to include catastrophic illnesses—a bill that had passed both Houses easily—it was later repealed because seniors didn't want to pay for the benefits. Ted desisted in 1989 because yet another national commission—this one appointed by President Reagan in 1988 and dubbed the Pepper Commission, after its first chairman, longtime Florida Democratic congressman Claude Pepper— a commission on which Ted sat, was convened to explore healthcare reform in a bipartisan fashion. But once again, when the commission issued its report, essentially endorsing the sort of employer mandate that Ted had been proposing, there was no consensus, and though Ted signed off on the report, any progress was overwhelmed by the Gulf War. And so the yearly ritual resumed. Ted, along with Representative Henry Waxman, reintroduced his employer mandate bill, though this time with the addition of a Medicaid-like program to subsidize those who did not receive insurance through their employment and didn't qualify for either Medicaid or Medicare. It got out of committee, but it was derailed by business opposition. In 1991, after Harris Wofford won a special election to the Senate largely by campaigning on a healthcare initiative, Ted announced, "We are closer to enacting real reform than at any time since Medicare was enacted in 1965." Even a few moderate Republicans, beginning to fret over political fallout given their inaction on healthcare, began working on bills that created tax credits to allay health costs and regulate private insurance premiums. But despite Ted's optimism, the country wasn't any closer to enactment. That May, Ted, George Mitchell, John Rockefeller, and Don Riegle submitted yet again an employer mandate bill, this time with subsidies to small businesses and a national commission to set targets for health spending. Ted pushed it through his Labor Committee, but Mitchell didn't have the votes to bring it to the floor, so it expired as health-care had always expired. Why, even as the number of uninsured kept rising to nearly 20 percent of the population, there was no national healthcare in the United States, when every other industrialized country had national health insurance? asked one health historian. "The answer rests on the privileged status enjoyed by economic interests in American politics," he said. But one Republican strategist named Eddie Mahe had a more direct and truthful answer. Speaking of Ted, he said, "What we really oppose is his political philosophy, not his total lack of any morals. If he wants to diddle waitresses in the back rooms of bars, that's fine, as long as he doesn't get national health care passed." This was the Republican morality that healthcare was up against—the morality that forbade the government from helping those in distress.

Bill Clinton, himself not unmindful of the politics of health insurance, had a plan or, more accurately, a plan for a plan. Clinton would say that his commitment to national healthcare began when he moderated the de-bate between Jimmy Carter's secretary of health, education, and welfare, Joseph Califano, and Ted at the Democratic Midterm Convention in Mem-phis, when Ted was prodding Carter to advance national health insur-ance. Clinton, then thirty-two and the governor-elect of Arkansas, recalled Ted's impassioned account of Ted Jr.'s long recovery from his can-cer and Ted saying how "wrong it was that his son had done well because of the good fortunes of his family, but that other families didn't." "I prom-ised myself that day," Clinton said, "that if I ever got a chance to give health care to more Americans and keep more young children like his son alive, I would do it."

Now that time had come. And now Ted and George Mitchell had their bill, the bill that they had introduced during the Bush administration, a bill they had worked on for three years, a bill for which they had gotten the support of forty-five Democratic senators, who had sent a joint letter to the president-elect essentially saying, as Nick Littlefield put it, "The bill is ready. We've been working on it for three years. But we couldn't do it with a Republican president. We can do it with you. So now let's go." In early December 1992, Ted and Vicki attended a dinner hosted by *Washington Post* publisher Katharine Graham at Graham's home, in honor of the president-elect. Vicki sat at Clinton's table, and he began to expatiate about healthcare—"very specific," Vicki said. And he told his tablemates that "if he couldn't get healthcare reform, he didn't deserve to be president," which led Vicki to believe that this was a "deep commitment" of his. Two days later Ted attended a luncheon with Clinton and eighteen other senators, and the president-elect discussed national service and healthcare—the first formal meeting between Ted and Clinton—and Ted left saying, "I think we're off to a good start." And it *was* a good start. Clinton had appointed the veteran health policy expert Stuart Altman and the chief of staff of the Pepper Commission, Judy Feder, to his transition team precisely to develop a health insurance plan, and they had settled on a plan very much like Mitchell's and Kennedy's—a play-or-pay plan, meaning that employers either provided insurance or paid a penalty that would be used to provide insurance. Ted himself had made the same proposal to Clinton, and also promoted John Chafee's bill, which Bob Dole supported, that called for individual mandates.

But Clinton was more of a moderate than Ted had bargained for and less of a healthcare enthusiast. On January 11, shortly before the inauguration, the president-to-be was pondering policy at a retreat at the governor's mansion in Little Rock, and Altman and Feder presented their plan. Clinton was less than enthused, arguing, as Jimmy Carter had, that the plan was too expensive and he wasn't sure an employer mandate was politically viable. Instead, he had decided to scrap Ted's plan and Altman's and Feder's similar plan and start from scratch—this after Democrats had been working for years to craft a bill that they thought might have a chance of passage. As Altman told it, when he raised his hand during the meeting and protested that Americans were unlikely to want to see their entire healthcare system reinvented, he sealed his fate with the new administration. Instead of Altman and Feder, and instead of the Democrats who had worked so long and hard on healthcare heading the campaign to pass it, five days after his inauguration Clinton named his wife, Hillary Clinton, and business consultant Ira Magaziner to lead a Task Force to Reform Health Care. Feder would later say that for all Clinton's professions of wanting a healthcare plan, he was focused not on the moral underpinnings of such a plan but, like Jimmy Carter, on the economic consequences of not cutting health costs, since Clinton was dedicated to trimming the deficit, and worried about promoting a program that would swell the budget. According to Carey Parker, Ted knew that he wasn't going to get his comprehensive Medicare for All plan because he was realistic enough to realize that it would never get through Congress against the fierce Republican opposition. But the employer mandate program, with its role for private insurers, was something else. By nixing the plan and steering the administration toward something like managed competition with health maintenance organizations, Clinton had emboldened his own critics who, as Parker put it, "seized on Clinton and his so-called Third Way"—a moderate path between liberalism and conservatism—to undercut the liberals. Still, Ted, who had long lamented letting the moment pass when he might have struck a healthcare deal with Richard Nixon, was hopeful. That February, he told Adam Clymer, who was researching a biography of him, that he thought the odds of getting health insurance through Congress were good, and he said that Majority Leader Mitchell had been dispatching senators to talk to their colleagues and solicit their input and put them on task forces, comparing this initiative to what Franklin Roosevelt had done in the early days of the New Deal to develop programs.

But if Ted had miscalculated Bill Clinton's moderation, he also miscalculated Clinton's priorities. Ted had hoped to hit the ground running with a healthcare plan. Clinton, as Ted's health aide, David Nexon, would recall, had said in so many words, "It was the economy, stupid, and don't forget health care." Instead of leading with healthcare, Clinton led with the Deficit Reduction Act, which effectively stalled any healthcare bill because Clinton's economic advisers thought that it would be unseemly to pretend to cut the deficit at the same time that the president was proposing health insurance that was likely to be costly. "Kick the health-care can down the road and complete the rest of the economic plan" was how Clinton himself would later put it. Most of the initial energy, then, the energy that fired up an administration, was devoted to the economy, to cutting the deficit in order to rally the bond market, and most of the energy was eventually drained by the economy. Clinton's plan passed in August by a single vote in the House and by a tiebreaker cast by Vice President Albert Gore in the Senate; not a single Republican voted for it. (More, it stirred resentments among Democrats who felt compelled to vote for a BTU tax on energy, which was unpopular.) While the president was focused on deficit reduction, his wife was focused on healthcare. But the momentum for health insurance was already being lost, and the longer Hillary Clinton and Ira Magaziner took to reinvent American healthcare, the more time they gave to opponents to mount a campaign against them, and the more the energy of proponents was dissipated.

They took a long time. The task force began meeting that winter, shortly after Clinton's inauguration, but it wasn't a single task force. Hillary Clinton and Magaziner had invited policy experts from around the country, nearly seven hundred of them, then divided them into thirty-five groups, each with a separate responsibility. It was an unwieldy process, more than unwieldy. Among the most expert legislators on health policy were those who had been working for years on various insurance bills, but the Clintons sidetracked them in the interest of their desire to redo health-care from the ground up. As Rashi Fein, one of the leading health policy experts in the nation, would say, "They didn't talk to [Daniel] Rosten-kowski," who was the chairman of the House Ways and Means Commit-tee and one of the most powerful Democrats in the House. "They didn't talk to [Daniel Patrick] Moynihan, the chairman of the powerful Senate Finance Committee," and a skeptic toward health insurance, who pre-ferred that the administration work first on welfare reform. (One White House aide had sneeringly said that they were going to "roll" Moynihan on healthcare, and the comment got back to Moynihan, which only steeled his opposition.) "They didn't talk to—it's a long list of Carter peo-ple," Fein said. "They didn't talk to me. I think they really believed that they didn't want to talk to anybody. They wanted to have their task forces." Rostenkowski had warned Clinton about appointing Hillary to lead the effort because he said it needed politicians—people with "dirt underneath their fingernails," rather than academicians. And even when Hillary and Magaziner did solicit legislators, they did so perfunctorily. "There's a dif-ference," Judy Feder was to say, "between consulting, where you are really dealing with members and developing strategy together and getting them on board, and inviting staff to come to your meetings," and she said that Hillary and Magaziner never really consulted with legislators and staff in a serious way, which "angered" them. But perhaps worst of all, while they at least made some nods to Democrats, they didn't talk to Republicans, which was something the Democratic congressional leadership had ex-pressly advised Clinton to do. George Mitchell, recalling an early meeting with President-elect Clinton, said that neither House speaker Thomas Foley, nor Majority Leader Richard Gephardt, nor Mitchell himself had told Clinton that they "could do this without Republicans. My whole effort was to the contrary." "The Republicans complain that they're not allowed in the room," Nick Littlefield would remember. "They're not even allowed to talk to Magaziner. They don't know what he's doing." And he called the idea that the Clintons could simply erect a whole new health-care system without the input of those politicians as the "hubris of the Clintons."

And there was more hubris. Hillary Clinton and Ira Magaziner held hundreds of meetings with those task force members, but they banned the press, which led to accusations that the process was being conducted in secret—"We had the perception of secrecy in which there were no secrets," Chris Jennings, a senior policy adviser on health to the president, was to say—and which ultimately led to the shutdown of all the task forces on the grounds that they had violated the Federal Advisory Committee Act, calling for open meetings. But the whole process, the seeming secretiveness of it, the insularity of it, the arrogance of it, seemed to frustrate and exhaust the very Democrats Clinton needed to pass healthcare, much less the Republicans. "Whoever is interested, come to these meetings," George Mitchell had told his caucus, but eventually the only ones who showed up were Mitchell himself, Tom Daschle, Harry Reid on occasion, and Ted.

Though the Clintons had abandoned Ted's plan and proceeded to promulgate their own in a way that violated every legislative precept of Ted's, including the exclusion of Republicans, which was something Ted himself never did, Ted Kennedy was nevertheless doing everything he could to assist Hillary Clinton in devising a plan that could pass Congress. As Chris Jennings put it, Ted and Bill Clinton both thought that "this was the last opportunity to pass health care reform in their lifetimes." As early as April, Ted convened a seven-hundred-person, all-day conference at the Tufts School of Medicine, outside Boston, to discuss recommendations of Massachusetts officials for health reform. After that, Jennings said, Ted "went a little bit underground," while Hillary Clinton continued to hammer out a plan. But Jennings admitted that Ted only seemed to retreat. It was a tactic so that he wouldn't seem to be directing the process and so that the bill wouldn't seem to be *his* bill, which might incite Republicans to oppose it. "The best of all things would be it's quiet," Jennings would say. "It's real, and it's acknowledged in the White House, but it's quiet, and no one else knows about it." In fact, even though Jay Rockefeller, who had co-chaired the Pepper Commission, seemed more involved in the day-today business of fashioning the new plan, Ted was deeply if invisibly involved in the deliberations—as deeply involved as anyone. In some ways, he compensated for Hillary Clinton's own political deficiencies. By her own account, she met frequently with Ted and "came to appreciate his style of talking with people about an issue that he's working on and really working through in his own mind and trying to gauge where others of his colleagues are so that what might sound like it would be a sort of wandering discussion, I soon understood was really filled with all sorts of hints and forward movements, and tactical retreats, as he was gauging who he was talking to and where they were." In short, Ted was demonstrating the chemistry of the Senate at which he was so proficient.

That was about the politics of healthcare. For the substance, Ted directed his staff, especially his top health staffer, David Nexon, to work closely with Clinton and Magaziner, even as the staffs of other senators hung back, waiting to see what Clinton came up with. As Nexon would put it of Kennedy, "At one point, his whole health staff"—roughly ten of them—"was essentially working two jobs: one for him and one for Magaziner and the task force." Jennings said that Ted's staff had "unprecedented access to that process, and they were more involved than any one member of any congressional staff." Judy Feder said that Nexon was "everywhere" and "was involved in everything." In those first months, Magaziner would bring in members of the task force to meet with the president and vice president for hours, and Nexon was there for those discussions. Nexon later said he spent 90 percent of his time at the White House in this period. "Relentless" was how Jennings described Ted and his staff. Jennings suspected that even though Ted was working behind the scenes, he eventually wanted credit if a bill passed—though this might have been a misimpression, since it was not the Kennedy way to take credit if it meant threatening passage, and in this case, Clinton clearly wanted credit—and that Nexon's collaboration was a way not only to establish that credit but to craft the ultimate bill in such a way that Ted's Labor Committee would get jurisdiction over it and that would give him, as the Labor chair, his own crack at the bill. Jennings said that Ted's staffers called him continuously, and that Ted himself called Jennings three to five times every week or would come over to the Old Executive Office Building in the course of the next six to eight months, until the drafting of the bill was finally completed in September. He even talked healthcare directly with the Clintons during a sail, when the first couple visited Jackie Kennedy at Martha's

Vineyard. At the same time, as a plan was coming together that summer, Magaziner was meeting frequently with Nexon—met with him "more than probably any other staffer on Capitol Hill," Jennings said—and "relied on David quite a bit."

And now, after nearly nine months of deliberation, and after Clinton won the narrowest possible passage of his deficit reduction program in August, came the long-awaited introduction of the plan: the Health Security Act. Hillary met with the Democratic leadership on September 9 to give them a preview of the bill and, according to Littlefield, had "them all eating out of her hand," even receiving a standing ovation before she spoke. As Hillary recalled it, Ted came into the session late, while she was answering questions, then sat down and at one point tipped back his chair and interjected that if they would all just look at page fifty-seven of Hillary's explanatory booklet, they would understand—meaning, Hillary thought, that he had absorbed the entire health plan in all its complexity. Her message was that as much as many of them, Ted included, had pined for a single-payer, government-run system, the idea had never been politically feasible. More, she said that the Democrats should be careful not to promote the bill as a way to aid to the uninsured, which would surely not move Republicans, but as a way to help small businesses cover health costs for their employees. It was a complicated bill, a jerry-rigged bill, a bill that sought a third way between private insurance and government insurance, a bill that sought to split the differences between Democrats and Republicans, a bill that was meant to have a little something for everyone but not everything for anyone, a bill that was so compromised, as Hillary's suggestion on how to sell it indicated, that it seemed designed less to address the healthcare problem than to address the political problem of how to get healthcare passed in Congress by appeasing the very Republicans who had not been privy to the process of its creation. It ran 1,342 pages. The basics were that employers were required to insure their employees and pay 80 percent of the cost—which was not dissimilar to Ted's own modified plan—and it required the self-employed to buy insurance. Private insurers were proscribed from rejecting any enrollee, whether or not he or she had a preexisting condition, which had usually made him or her ineligible for private insurance. And it set a cap of $3,000 for out-of-pocket expenses.

But that was where the simplicity ended. It laid out three types of coverage: a low-cost health maintenance organization; a provider preferred organization, which limited the insured to doctors within the organization but allowed them to visit doctors outside if they were willing to pay to do so; and a high-cost plan, which allowed the insured to visit any doctor of their choice but set higher deductibles and co-pays. The most Rube Goldbergian component of the bill, intended to cut costs and to pacify Republicans by incorporating a large role for private insurers, set up "regional health alliances," essentially large insurance groups, to contract with private insurers. Employees in firms of less than five thousand workers would have to join one of these alliances, as would the self-employed and Medicaid recipients, though the government would subsidize employers who joined an alliance as well as families up to 150 percent of the poverty line. It also mandated limited increases in private insurance premiums to hold down expenses. And the whole thing was said to cost no more than $100 billion.

The rollout came at a speech before a joint session of Congress and a national television audience on September 22, 1993, the same day Clinton had signed Ted's AmeriCorps bill into law, and with Hillary sitting proudly in the gallery where Clinton saluted her. He called his effort a "new chapter in the American story," the most sweeping change in social policy since the Social Security Act of 1935, and he called healthcare "our most urgent priority," and he said this was a "magic moment" at which all sides had conceded something needed to be done, and that doing something was an "ethical imperative." He described the dire condition of healthcare in America: the thirty-seven million uninsured; the small businessman whose premiums had risen so high that he could no longer afford them (that businessman's insurer said that two of his employees were too old; they happened to be his mother and father); the small businesses that even had to declare bankruptcy because they couldn't afford health insurance; the Americans who were only a pink slip away from losing their insurance; the nurses and doctors who spent hours and hours, up to twenty-five hours each week, filling out paperwork; the doctors who had to receive approval for tests from a bureaucrat in an office hundreds of miles away; the cutbacks in government budgets to pay for the skyrocketing health costs; the restrictions of healthcare plans that no longer allowed the insured to choose their doctors; the huge disparity in costs for the very same procedure in the very same state; the willingness of insurers to cast out the insured when they got ill; the pharmaceutical companies that charged exorbitant prices for their drugs; the families who had to choose between healthcare and food. "This is our chance," he said in closing. "This is our journey. And when our work is done, we will know that we answered the call of history and met the challenge of our time." It was a stirring speech; he was interrupted thirty-five times in fifty-three minutes. It was an optimistic speech. It was a speech that challenged Congress to act. When Clinton mounted the rostrum, Ted, who was sitting with Senator Harris Wofford, called the president the "coolest person I've ever seen" and noted how nervous he would be if he were giving the "speech of my life," as Clinton was. (In fact, the teleprompter had been inadvertently loaded with Clinton's February speech on the budget, so that for the first seven minutes, he was speaking from memory—until the proper text was loaded.) But while marveling at the president's cool, Ted told an aide something else: "I've waited all my political life to hear a president utter those words from this place."

Now, at long last, he had heard those words.

But not everyone joined the chorus. When Clinton finished, the Republicans would have at it, and they did not greet it with any enthusiasm. Governor Carroll Campbell, Jr., of South Carolina, who delivered the Republican response to Clinton, called it a "giant social experiment devised by theorists who had never met a payroll," which was one of the kindest things said about it. Clinton had tried to induce the minority leader, Bob Dole, to join him in drafting the bill. He declined, saying that Clinton would have his input once the bill was introduced. It had been introduced too late in the session to secure passage then, but Ted, realizing how much opposition would mount to the bill from the AMA and the pharmaceutical industry and Republicans and, above all, insurers, scheduled hearings for the following week. ("They are very well financed and have tremendous financial interest in preserving the status quo," he said.) Hillary was the first to testify in the Senate Caucus Room, which, she remarked, was the place where both John and Robert Kennedy had launched their presidential campaigns, and she told Ted, "You have added your own stamp to our history in this room, and your name has been attached to every piece of health legislation that has passed through Congress." Ted returned the favor. He had prepared her for her testimony, sharing with her his understanding of the chemistry of the Senate. As Chris Jennings observed, "She was a rock star, and he was like a proud father." By this time, Bill Clinton's favorability rating had risen from 36 percent earlier in the year to 56 percent after the speech. Ted was feeling optimistic.

But no one knew better than Ted Kennedy that the hurdles of remaking the healthcare system were high, and they were treacherous. Even before Clinton's speech, the Health Insurance Association of America, a trade organization headed by a former Republican congressman, had financed a series of television commercials featuring a couple named Harry and Louise who sat at their kitchen table and lamented a "government-run" healthcare plan "designed by government bureaucrats" and encouraged viewers to call their congresspersons to oppose the Clinton bill. That had come as no surprise. The insurance industry had always vigorously and self-servingly opposed healthcare reform. But there were other hurdles in the Senate itself. As early as the previous March, with Republicans unlikely to sign on to any reform bill and likely to filibuster the Clinton bill, Ted had approached Clinton with the idea of using budget reconciliation to pass the upcoming plan. Reconciliation, a process created by the Congressional Budget Act of 1974, permitted bills dealing with tax and spending and deficits within the budget resolution to be passed by a simple majority vote in the Senate rather than be subject to a filibuster. The object was to expedite the approval of the budget. Submitting the new health bill, which clearly dealt with taxes and spending and even deficits, under reconciliation would obviously allow the Democrats, who held the Senate majority, to steer the legislation around the assumed Republican opposition and filibuster. Clinton authorized Ted to discuss the prospect with Robert Byrd. Jay Rockefeller, who was deeply involved in the healthcare bill, and George Mitchell also petitioned Byrd. Byrd held the key. He was no longer majority leader, but he occupied a sacred role in the Senate chamber. A brilliant parliamentarian and a stickler for process, he had essentially become the policeman of budget reconciliation, the authority to whom anyone seeking reconciliation had to plead— a position so elevated that bills proposed for reconciliation had to survive what had become known as the "Byrd Rule," which said: Provisions of a bill that are nonbudgetary do not qualify for reconciliation. Most health policy in the 1980s had been achieved through reconciliation, or the bills wouldn't have passed at all. But that spring, on Clinton's healthcare plan, which had yet to be even formulated, Byrd had spoken. It did not, he said, qualify as a budgetary bill, though he also said that it was hard for him to refuse Ted when Ted asked him. Byrd's decision might have been enough to doom the project before it had even been introduced because now the bill would require Republican votes for a supermajority to avoid the filibuster. Sunk it, Ted thought.

But there was yet another hurdle—this one on jurisdiction. Ted had watched the process carefully because he had wanted to ensure that his Labor Committee had jurisdiction. He and Vicki had even invited Magaziner to Hyannis Port that summer and went to Great Island with him and his family for a picnic. It wasn't entirely a social visit. "It was all to find out what was in that task force," Ted would later say. "We found out what we needed to find out, which was whether we were going to get squeezed out in terms of jurisdiction." Ted believed that since the bill was going to have a major employer mandate component, his Labor Committee should get jurisdiction. Magaziner was not averse. He realized that having Ted get jurisdiction would be a tremendous advantage in gaining passage, and he was, Ted said, "helpful in making sure we had a foothold in that." But even Ted realized that Magaziner had to "maintain his security of the plan," meaning not letting out the details quite yet, lest anyone think he had made a deal with Ted, and Ted himself had to be discreet. The problem, not an insubstantial one, was Pat Moynihan, the senator who chaired the Finance Committee, and the one whom the administration hoped to circumvent, and the one who had no particular affection for the Clintons or for healthcare reform itself. "He hated the Clintons and he hated health care reform" was how Jennings put it less delicately. But Moynihan wasn't too fond of Ted Kennedy either, since he and Ted frequently crossed swords over jurisdiction, especially on matters like Medicare and Medicaid expansion, where both the Finance and Labor committees could make jurisdictional claims. (Other members of Finance were no more enamored of Ted.) On the Clinton healthcare plan, the two had tangled not so much because they were fighting for jurisdiction, though they were, as because Moynihan was fighting to kill the bill entirely and Ted was fighting to save it. "He couldn't have been more counterproductive," Jennings said of Moynihan. "He really undermined the effort." "Completely uncooperative," Ted agreed of Moynihan.

Ted had spent four years fighting with a Democratic president, Jimmy Carter, urging him to put financial muscle behind health insurance. Now that he had a president who was willing to do so, he found some of his fellow Democrats in Congress preventing him. Hillary Clinton and Ira Magaziner had written the bill in such a way—with the emphasis on the employer mandate and a deemphasis on any tax subsidies—as to get a referral to Labor rather than Finance. But it was no done deal. As Tom Daschle would put it, Ted was "in his prime at that time. He had the seniority; he had the clout; he had the respect. But unfortunately, he didn't have the committee assignment." Majority Leader Mitchell was sympathetic to the bill and also wanted it steered to Labor where Ted could push it, but Mitchell realized that Moynihan would erupt if he were circumvented. So Mitchell, who had been a federal judge, decided to ask both committees to submit memoranda on why they should have jurisdiction, and then he and his chief aide, John Hilley, would make a determination. The plan didn't work. The Senate parliamentarian stepped in and decided that Labor should take the bill since the employer mandate was not a tax, but Moynihan, as Nick Littlefield described it, "pitched a fit" and blocked the referral by refusing to separate that key element from the rest of the bill. Mitchell appointed Daschle, the chairman of the Policy Committee, to see if he could coordinate the two committees, but Daschle soon found that there was no rapprochement between Ted and Moynihan, or really between the majority of the Democratic caucus, who backed Clinton's plan, and Moynihan, who was determined to sink it. Now Mitchell was forced to hold the bill at his desk because of Moynihan's objection. Former Senate parliamentarian Robert Dove, who was working for Minority Leader Dole at that point, suggested they invoke Rule 14, which would allow a bill to bypass the committees and go directly to the floor. But by then there was, Dove said, a "huge fight" between Ted and Moynihan, and nothing reached the floor that year because there was no single bill to reach the floor. Unbowed, Ted was eager to call the committee to meet over the Christmas holiday. Mitchell, fearful of escalating the dispute with Moynihan, urged him to wait. Instead, informally, Ted invited some Democratic senators to scrutinize the bill with his staff every morning at eight a.m. before the Senate went into session. Still, the delay took its toll. Support for the bill, which polls showed had risen to 56 percent in late September, after its introduction, with only 24 percent in opposition, had steadily fallen until, by early December, only 46 percent supported it, while 43 percent were opposed—a bare plurality. The television campaign against it had clearly worked. Moreover, Republicans had marshaled their legislative forces against it. That December William Kristol, former vice president Dan Quayle's chief of staff, who had formed an organization named the Project for the Republican Future, had written a four-page memorandum to the congressional Republicans, setting out a strategy for defeating Clinton's bill, which he labeled a "*political* threat" to the Republican Party, and urged his fellow partisans to "adopt an aggressive and uncompromised counterstrategy designed to delegitimize the proposal and defeat its partisan purpose"—as if Democrats had only proposed healthcare to gain votes. Republicans had decided they were not about to hand Clinton a legislative victory. So the bill languished until the next session— languished and, in languishing, lost what little momentum it had had.

IV

It was the last chance, Ted thought, of getting health insurance through Congress, and he was not about to surrender. It was the "big enchilada" of his career, he told a reporter, while hedging over the possibility it would actually happen. "I don't even let myself think about that yet. I believe it will happen, but there's too much more to be done." At his State of the Union address that January, Clinton waved a pen and threatened, "If you send me legislation that does not guarantee every American private health insurance that can never be taken away, you will force me to take this pen, veto the legislation, and we'll come right back here and start over again," which prompted Democrats in attendance to cheer. But this was bold talk. The intervening months had not been kind to the plan. "In '93, the opposition was pretty well in disarray," Ted told Adam Clymer a few years later, "and I think most of them were sort of looking out after their own particular specialties and special areas of interest. By the time you get back to '94, and the time it had taken"—since January 1993 from the beginning of the process and September from the introduction of the bill—"I think the basic core interests in opposition had been able to galvanize and had begun to consolidate." And Ted added this ominous analysis: "The opposition was not going to let anything—with Clinton's name—of substance get through that session of Congress."

Ted plowed ahead anyway. What he had done with fellow Democrats— having his staff go over the bill with them—he did with selected Republicans that winter, in the hopes that he might once again work the chemistry of the Senate. One told David Broder and Haynes Johnson that the sessions were "exhilarating and promising." Then on May 9 Ted introduced his own version of the Clinton bill and spent six weeks marking it up section by section—marking it up as quickly as he could, despite the bill's length because, he said, "Time is not our friend"—as if he had had full authority over it, but without any of the taxing provisions that would have given Finance jurisdiction, and then reported it out favorably that June, 11 to 6, with Vermont Republican Jim Jeffords joining the Democrats. It was, however, a pyrrhic victory. Even though Nancy Kassebaum, the ranking Republican, had actively participated in the markup and would later express admiration for Ted's efforts "to achieve some success in getting people together," the Republicans, all of them but a handful of moderates, had come to the same conclusion that William Kristol had come to: that passing the bill, or any bill, would only abet Bill Clinton. Kassebaum herself, who was no dyed-in-the-wool conservative but a pragmatist, recalled being out in Kansas with her ill mother and seeing the "Harry and Louise" ads on television and thinking, " 'This is really going to be a trouble-maker.' Because I related. I don't want to be on hold, trying to push one, two, three or four," referring to an ad that highlighted the likely waiting time on the phone. "Nobody wants that." And she said, "What killed it"—meaning Clinton's health reform—"was the 'Harry and Louise' ads."

But it wasn't only the Republicans or the insurance industry who were threatening the bill and with whom Ted had to contend. There was still one other nemesis: Pat Moynihan, who had declared at the start of the year that there was no healthcare crisis to begin with. Moynihan's Finance Committee was wrestling with the tax provisions of the plan and meeting resistance from both Republicans and more conservative Democrats, though there were suspicions that Moynihan was not terribly disturbed by their intransigence. Bob Dole, who also sat on the Finance Committee, was no more enthusiastic. Dole was gearing up for a presidential run, and though he had been a pragmatist himself and seemed willing to work with the Democrats for a bill, he couldn't afford to alienate the conservatives in his party, which had made him less pragmatic. By one account, by the time that Moynihan and Dole got through with the bill in committee, Magaziner wrote a memo to Bill Clinton saying that if it passed in that form, it would "potentially hurt many middle-class Americans," and Magaziner was so distressed by that eventuality, he now backed off his own plan in favor of something less comprehensive. Meanwhile Moynihan had come to the conclusion, whether as a way to waylay the bill once and for all or because he sincerely believed it, that despite the Democrats' majority, they could not get a bill passed without a supermajority that could invoke cloture on a filibuster, and that in order to get one, they had to make a deal with Republicans at the outset. Moynihan's top staffer, Lawrence O'Donnell, and Dole's, Sheila Burke, who had been a nurse, had, Burke said, "many conversations in a dark room about, 'Can we get these two guys' "—Moynihan and Dole—" 'together? Was there any opportunity?' " Ted disagreed with the approach, thinking it a capitulation. He had recently beaten back Republican filibuster threats on the National Service Corps and on education reform. He felt he could do it again. Of course, Ted had been wooing Republicans all along, as he typically did. An aide described Ted's modus operandi as "start left, move to the center with enough votes so that you can get on the bill, push and push until the other side has to come to you." He had done that in the Labor Committee by modifying the Clinton bill to have Congress decide which health benefits would be available, subject to review by an independent commission that would determine if there were funds to pay for the benefits. He called it, "One small step for health care, one giant step for bipartisanship." And he had made other concessions as well: to exempt small businesses with five employees or fewer; to enable individuals to opt out of the regional alliances; to allow individuals to participate in the Federal Employees Health Benefit Plan; to require individuals to get coverage; and to make provisions for mental health—the latter three all Republican ideas. But those concessions notwithstanding, this time it was different. This time he didn't bring Republicans aboard. This time Republicans and Democratic moderates decided that they might be able to strike a better deal with Moynihan than with Ted—meaning a deal for a less comprehensive, more private-insurance-friendly bill. Ted didn't want to compromise the bill any more than he needed to, before he needed to. When Clinton debated strategy—tailoring the bill to attract Republicans or holding firm and then later negotiating compromises—Ted strongly endorsed the latter, saying that even if the Republicans filibustered the bill, the public would rally to Clinton. Hillary agreed, and she and Magaziner even began listing the compromises they felt comfortable making should they need to do so. But not yet—even though the Republicans were largely inflexible, and even though Moynihan was undermining any hope of keeping the Democrats united. Not yet. Nick Littlefield told David Broder and Haynes Johnson of Moynihan's declaration that he wasn't going to have a bill unless a deal was struck with Dole, "You have essentially given the ball game away to the other side."

Ted knew. He was frustrated. He asked Jeff Blattner, his former aide, if Blattner might reach out to Republicans John Danforth and John Chafee—Blattner had worked with both on civil rights—to see if he might engage them on the healthcare fight. (Chafee had already proposed a bill of his own in December, so he wasn't completely opposed to healthcare reform.) Blattner tried and said that he couldn't "pin them down" and that he had a "terrible sense of foreboding" about the prospects of the bill about which Ted cared so much. He told Ted, "You've got to make a deal. This thing is coming unglued." (In an interview with "aide B," almost certainly Blattner, conducted by Adam Clymer, he was more direct: "We're going to lose," he said he told Ted.) And Blattner said that Ted turned on him, spoke to him sharply, which wasn't customary. "We are going to have this debate on the floor of the Senate," he yelled. "We are going to take this to the American people."

But even though one poll that June found 61 percent of Americans favoring a federal guarantee for healthcare, the problems persisted. The bill was very complicated—those 1,342 pages—and every small change might have large repercussions. Ted told Adam Clymer shortly after the effort that he knew how to write a comprehensive health insurance bill because he had done so in the past. "But now people will say, 'Well, we want carve-outs for small business.' So, okay, we carve out something for small business . . . thinking those are mom and pop stores. But what if you carve out that small business, and it is eight people working in the biotech [sector], all making a hundred thousand? They get exempt from coverage." And then, if you try to distinguish between individuals making the minimum wage and those making higher wages, which would be fair, "suddenly you are developing a bureaucracy." And there was another issue—this one generated by the bureaucracy. Bills were "scored" by the nonpartisan Congressional Budget Office as to their costs. In the case of the Clinton plan, this would have serious political ramifications, since if the regional alliances that the bill established to help people afford insurance were regarded as government appendices, the cost of those alliances would be included as part of the federal budget, whereas if they were regarded as private entities, their cost would not—which would mean the overall "score" of the bill would be much better. Ted got word that the CBO head, Robert Reischauer, had made the former determination, which would have put another stake in the heart of the bill, and Ted, furious, phoned Reischauer at nine a.m. that morning, yelling at him "at the top of his lungs" for a half-hour, according to Broder and Johnson, telling him that Clinton had been elected to enact a healthcare plan and that no "minor staff official" should get in his way. Reischauer admitted to being shaken by the dressing-down. But it didn't change the outcome. Even though the CBO ultimately determined that the plan would bring health costs down in the long run, it would raise them in the short run. And then, to add to the difficulties, when Moynihan's Finance Committee finally finished its markup on the bill, Moynihan announced they would be voting on a new bill—this one fashioned by John Chafee and conservative Louisiana Democrat John Breaux—that would cover 95 percent of the uninsured but not, as Clinton had so boldly promised in his State of the Union, *all* the uninsured. Clinton, fearing that nothing would pass, hinted that he would finally accept less-than-universal coverage, which prompted Ted to tell him and Hillary not to make those sort of statements because it undermined his own dealmaking.

But that dealmaking had already hit a stalemate. David Broder said he spoke to Ted and wrote that he was getting "more and more frantic to figure out how to get it moving," even pressing Mitchell again to bring the bill to the floor without Finance's referral. Mitchell said he didn't see any way he could do that. In July, Ted, at a loss for what to do—which was a rarity for him—and getting desperate, tried firing up the troops. He met nearly every night with liberal activists in the Labor Committee hearing room—doctors, nurses, hospital workers, the disabled, labor—one hundred at a time, telling them, with, one attendee said, "more emotion than anybody else," that "this is something we have to do. People are counting on us. This is our moment in history."

Ted Kennedy was not the only one who was frustrated and frantic. So was George Mitchell. Mitchell, who had forgone an appointment to the Supreme Court just to pass the healthcare bill and who had announced his intention to retire effective at the end of the Congress, said that he had had bipartisan conversations earlier that year, especially with John Chafee, and that he felt he and Ted and Chafee might agree on a compromise bill. But as Chris Jennings put it, the Republicans now "smelled blood," and they wouldn't allow a compromise even with their own bill—Chafee's bill. "The whole focus shifted to the right, and the Republicans moved to the right," Mitchell was to say, blaming, as Kassebaum did, the "Harry and Louise" ads. Still, Mitchell hadn't given up either. He wanted to bring something to the floor. On August 2 he submitted a bill of his own, closer to the Finance Committee bill—a form of capitulation—than to Ted's, a bill that would cover 95 percent of Americans, as the Finance Committee bill did, but contained a trigger that if that goal were not achieved by 2004, a more comprehensive plan would kick in. To skirt the problem of financing, Mitchell's bill called for subsidies that would be funded by the elimination of Medicaid, cuts to Medicare, and an increase in tobacco taxes. "Very good and very clever," Ted called it, years later. At the time, he was simply looking for a way, any way, to keep health-care alive. Later that week, in a morose mood at a breakfast with health-care reporters at the National Press Club, Ted said that the problems were largely the Republican refusal to give Clinton anything. Asked if there was anything now that they might wrest from the Republicans, Ted said maybe they could have gotten coverage for children, but asked, "Could you have taken children if we had dropped everything else?" (In fact, the Republicans refused even that.)

"He's devastated," one visitor said of Ted. But even then, even with the handwriting on the wall, Ted would not admit defeat. He kept fighting—fighting in the face of near-certain defeat. He instructed his aides to write a new health bill—one that Chafee, who was one of the only cooperating Republicans, might sign off on. He attended a meeting on July 27 with Clinton that Rockefeller and Daschle had requested, asking Clinton to "rally the troops" before floor consideration. They felt that Mitchell's im-pending retirement made him less tenacious than they desired, and they wanted assurance from Clinton that the president would continue to fight. More, they wanted to know what the administration could provide in terms of "ammunition" to fire back at the Republicans. And Ted told the president that he was working on a floor strategy. The day before Mitchell submitted his new bill, Ted held a rally at Faneuil Hall in Boston, along with Hillary Clinton, and two other guests, a woman and her daughter, the latter afflicted with Hodgkin's lymphoma, who had been re-jected by insurers—a rally where folksinger Peter Yarrow of Peter, Paul and Mary, sang "Health care belongs to you and me," to the tune of Woody Guthrie's "This Land Is Your Land," and where a four-day bus caravan set out for Washington. And every night now Ted sat up writing notes to his fellow senators, encouraging them to keep up the fight, or entertaining activists, or asking who he should call in the morning. Chris Jennings said no other senator was doing that. "The guy was incredible. That's who he was. And you wanted to do things for him."

And he kept fighting. There was no August recess that year—only a three-week break before Labor Day—and Ted worked through the summer, worked with everyone, trying to find some way of reviving the flagging healthcare effort, even as his Senate reelection campaign was beginning in Massachusetts. Chafee hadn't given up either, and he had formed what he called the "mainstream group," or the "mainstream coalition," a group of roughly twenty moderate Democrats and Republicans, to give one last push to see if *they* could hammer out a bill. (By this time, Dole had peeled off. "Chafee was prepared to go too far, farther than he was prepared to go," Dole's chief of staff, Sheila Burke, said of her boss. And she said the question was again: "Do you want to give Clinton the win?") Ted was no moderate, but he reluctantly joined the meetings, hoping that there would be a bill for the Senate to vote on, joined them in Chafee's small Capitol hideaway office with the senators, often a rotating group of them, sitting at a big table in the middle of the room and the staffers huddled around the sides of the room—"packing the room to the gills," John Danforth, one of the mainstreamers, said—or in Chafee's or Mitchell's office in the Hart Senate Office Building, often late at night, sometimes around the clock, often in the oppressive summer heat, meeting after meeting after meeting, and Chafee would announce, "All right, now we've got this," and then, according to Danforth, someone else would "breeze" into the room and raise the same point again and would undo it. "Keep the process going," Nick Littlefield, who attended many of these meetings, kept saying. *Keep the process going.*

But the process was gasping, and Ted himself had come to feel that the mainstreamers had made too many compromises—Chafee's bill, which had no employer mandate, covered only 92 percent of Americans—even as he continued to encourage their efforts. The Health Care Express Bus Tour, which was meant to buck up the senators, had been targeted by conservative radio host Rush Limbaugh, and it arrived in Washington having been pelted with eggs and fruit, its riders tired and "bedraggled," as Chris Jennings described them. They could only pretend that healthcare reform was going to be passed. The Democratic caucus was equally dispirited. On August 18, the Democratic senators met to discuss the Mitchell bill. Some were mildly critical of its backing off of universal care. Bob Kerrey of Nebraska, a moderate who had reluctantly cast the tie vote for Clinton's deficit reduction plan, delivered what Broder and Johnson called a "blistering attack," saying that the Democrats were on the "cusp of a major political disaster" unless they endorsed Chafee's mainstream bill. And then he stormed out. But Ted was blistering too—only he was furious over the foot-dragging of the mainstream group. "Here it is," he yelled. "We are waiting for the mainstream group. We are taking hits. How long does it take to find out about cost containment?" He called the long deliberations of Chafee's group the "self-destruction of all of us because the mainstream group can't make up their minds." A "wall-shaking, unprecedented moment," Lawrence O'Donnell, Moynihan's chief of staff, called it. And when Kerrey, out in the hall, heard it, he returned to the room, full of fury, and, pointing directly at Ted, shouted that if the Mitchell bill went to the floor now, it would lose. Defeat hung in the air. When leadership decided that Thursday that they wouldn't be working through the weekend, Ted had another explosion, berating those leaders at a private meeting for their "complete abdication." *Keep the process going.*

Now the question was whether Mitchell would bring the bill up for a vote. Chafee had given up on reaching any accommodation on his own bill and knew that there wouldn't be the votes for cloture if he had, given most of his fellow Republicans' hostility to any bill. Ted was not hopeful, but he wanted a vote on a bill anyway, a "dramatic vote," Carey Parker called it, so that those senators who voted against it would be identified and would have to explain why they denied healthcare to their constituents. "They defeated it without getting their hands caught," Ted complained. Mitchell disagreed. He didn't see the benefit in it. He told Ted that he felt it would be "devastating" to bring it to the floor only to see it defeated. In the end, the Republicans wouldn't have allowed a vote anyway. They filibustered the motion to bring the bill to the floor, not the bill itself, and there were not enough votes for cloture. As a result, the Clinton healthcare reform was never debated in the Senate.

So came the end. Chafee and Mitchell met with the mainstream group, and Mitchell told them he didn't have the votes for cloture, and that there was nothing else to do. That night Nick Littlefield went to Chafee's office and told his aide, Christy Ferguson, who was downcast, that Ted would somehow find those votes. But Ferguson knew better. "Look, do you understand what's happened?" she told him. "Do you understand how stupid you people have been?" Chris Jennings, who had been the point man for the Clinton plan, recalled being in Mitchell's office after the two of them tried numerous ways to modify the employer mandate so that Republicans would accept it. "Chris, it's over," Mitchell said. "It's over." Jennings described it as being like a parent telling a sad child that he or she is not going to make the team. Ted, speaking on the Senate floor, said that they had been within "striking distance" of a bipartisan compromise, meaning a compromise with Chafee and the mainstream group, and then it had fallen apart. On September 26, almost a year to the day since Clinton introduced his Health Security Act, Mitchell pronounced the bill dead, saying that Republicans would not sign on to it. And *The New York Times* quoted a gleeful Senator Robert Packwood, generally considered a moderate Republican and one who had even submitted a bill of his own, as saying to a Republican strategy session, "We've killed health reform. Now we've got to make sure our fingerprints aren't on it."

It died the death of a thousand cuts: from the right wing's two-decade drumbeat that had driven confidence in government to just 20 percent of Americans in 1994; from Clinton's initial concentration on the deficit and the subsequent delays that allowed opposition to build; from the idea to start from scratch rather than introduce a bill that had already gone through the committee process; from the realization by Republicans that health reform was a Democratic issue and that Clinton would be the likely beneficiary of any law; from the ambition to craft a bill that could satisfy both Republicans and Democrats with both a private insurance component and a public one that only made the bill enormously complex and opaque to most Americans; from, as Judy Feder would say, the fact that it was the product of a "policy process in which a proposal was worked out on paper, but they hadn't begun to work the politics," which meant the involvement of Congress and especially of Republicans; from the disarray of the Democrats, especially that fomented by Pat Moynihan; from the fact that 85 percent of Americans already had insurance, and many of them might not have been inclined, as Ted was, to help the other 15 percent, or nearly 40 million Americans; from the distraction of the North American Free Trade Agreement at the beginning of the process that consumed the attention of labor activists and divided Democrats; from the unwillingness of Robert Byrd to allow the bill to be passed under budget reconciliation; from the skirmish between Ted and Moynihan over whose committee would have jurisdiction; from the clash between the overreach of liberals, who wanted a comprehensive, universal plan, and the underreach of conservatives, who wanted no plan at all; from the impatience of legislators who wanted to leave Washington for their fall campaigns; and perhaps, above all, from the vehement opposition of the insurance and medical industries that provided so much financial support to congressmen and senators. Minnesota Senator Paul Wellstone, who had submitted a single-payer bill of his own, asked, "What killed health care?" and answered, "I think the unholy mix of money, power and politics. Communication technology became the main weapon—just an all-out ad campaign that spread fear throughout the country." (He was no doubt thinking of "Harry and Louise.") "It was very effective. And the second part is the unprecedented giving of money from the health industry to senators and representatives at the very time we were considering this legislation. And that money was not given out of the goodness of anybody's heart. It was to buy time and buy access."

A thousand cuts, and now the bill was dead, and with it the hopes of Ted Kennedy for his most cherished goal. The Clinton presidency had begun with Ted's feeling political stability and tranquility matching the personal stability and tranquility he felt with Vicki. The healthcare battle was a harbinger of turbulence to come.

SIXTEEN

"The Battle of His Political Life"

WHILE TED KENNEDY had been preoccupied with the Health Security Act, in the hope not only of gaining passage of national health insurance, his dream, but also, politically, of giving a boost to his upcoming Senate campaign with its passage, he had largely neglected that campaign. Ted had never worried about reelection. He was a Kennedy in Massachusetts. He assumed he would win, and in the past Republicans had scarcely mounted a challenge against him. A *Boston Globe*/WBZ poll that July showed him with a huge lead over his prospective Republican opponents—twenty-six points over one; thirty over another. He launched an early television ad blitz that month, but then decided not to air any ads during August because, Carey Parker said, he felt he was comfortably ahead and didn't need to do so. He was so unconcerned that instead of a seasoned political professional, he put his young nephew, Michael Kennedy, one of Bobby's sons, in nominal charge of the campaign as Kennedys had traditionally done because working on a campaign was a way for them to gain experience, especially when the result was not in doubt.

But there were signs that this campaign might be different. The episode in Palm Beach had eroded Ted's popularity, and though it had largely rebounded with Vicki's help, some trepidations lingered. *The Boston Globe*, citing a poll in which Ted's favorability rating was just 41 percent, reported as early as March 1993 that the Democratic establishment was "jittery" about Ted's upcoming reelection campaign. In response, Ted quipped, "If the polls had been right in 1979, I would have been president and beaten Ronald Reagan." But the summer before the campaign, there were new ominous signs. Another *Globe* poll showed that 52 percent of Massachusettsans thought it was "time to give someone else a chance," and *Newsweek* quoted political experts who said 35 to 40 percent of the state's voters were now "Kennedy haters." Similarly, the *Globe* poll that showed Ted coasting to victory also showed something less promising: that voters were evenly split, 45 to 45 percent, when asked if it was time for a new senator. His campaign manager Michael Kennedy noted a "nastiness out on the street." He said voters were telling him, "I have been with him every time, not this time. He is a bum, throw him out." Vicki too noted "ugly moments" where voters refused to shake Ted's hand. "They were angry—a lot of anger out there."

Ted recognized those auguries. He discovered that older voters seemed to take his accomplishments for granted and that many younger voters didn't know who he was. The *Globe* reported one student who attended a commencement at which Ted spoke, asking, "Kennedy. He's in the State House, right?" He admitted that voters said he had "lost his touch" or that his "politics is out," meaning outmoded. He referenced articles that said "I was gone," meaning he was likely to lose. And he *had been* gone, literally, a good deal of the time over the previous ten to fifteen years. He had become a world statesman, had visited Ethiopia, Chile, Argentina, Bangladesh, India, the Middle East, and the Soviet Union several times to discuss arms limitation and to gain the release of refuseniks. And as a national senator, he also traveled the country frequently to hold hearings and campaign for fellow Democrats. "And all that time," he said, "I was away from Massachusetts," which served to disengage him from his own constituents. And there was a mood he and Vicki detected too that was a portent, a post-Reagan mood, a mood exacerbated by the House minority whip Newt Gingrich, an ambitious conservative ideologue who was determined to eviscerate government—a "whole different anti-government, government-is-the-problem sort of thing that was very palpable out there," Vicki would say. And, seeing this turn in attitude, she would tell Ted, "Well, maybe we really are out of it," meaning that Ted was no longer connected to the national mood and that his politics were, indeed, out of fashion, as much as Ted continued to think that the mood might change.

And the Republicans sensed this weakness too. The Republican National Senatorial Committee, headed by another antigovernment zealot, Senator Phil Gramm of Texas, had pegged Ted's race as one of the five priority contests, and candidates were auditioning for the chance to take him on: among them, Bush transportation secretary Andrew Card, state consumer affairs secretary Gloria Larson, Massachusetts businessman and former gubernatorial contender John Lakian, former talk show host Janet Jeghelian, and Governor William Weld. But the leading contender was a tall, slim, handsome, lantern-jawed investment banker, himself the son of a former governor, George Romney of Michigan. Mitt Romney was "right out of central casting," Ted's old administrative assistant, David Burke, said. Fifteen years younger than Ted, Romney, at forty-seven, was what *Time* magazine called, in a "particularly vicious irony," the "mirror image of the veteran Senator's former self," whose "life mocks Kennedy's controversial past." Romney was an upright Mormon, a teetotaler, a father of five, devoted to his first and only wife. He was Teddy without the flaws, it seemed. Ted would say of Romney that he ran with a "Mr. Clean image, whose hard work had blessed him with a fortune"—though his father had been the millionaire head of American Motors before becoming governor—"and who was now going to 'give something back' by bringing good honest business principles to the messy game of politics." Romney had read the national mood, too, even in a traditionally liberal state like Massachusetts. When he announced his candidacy that February, he said that he opposed giving welfare to any mother who was already on welfare and had had another child. Ted was livid. "He was rich—and he wasn't prepared to keep his Senate seat by taking the food out of the mouths of poor children," Bob Shrum, who was advising Ted, said. But Shrum told him to hold his peace. "If that was the price," Ted answered indignantly, "well, they"—the poor—"needed the help a lot more than he needed the Senate."

Shrum advised Ted to be circumspect because he realized Romney would be formidable, and Ted's liberalism could be a liability. Politics aside, Ted was already an object of ridicule. At a Republican debate before Romney's announcement, businessman Lakian joked that were Lakian to win, his victory would attract tourists; they could visit Woods Hole, where he lived, and then Chappaquiddick. Talk show host Janet Jeghelian said that Ted "certainly knows a good deal about women, but perhaps not running against them." These were jesters. Romney, however, was a real candidate, the first real candidate Ted had faced since Ed McCormack in the 1962 primary and George Lodge in the general election that year, and while Ted remained confident into the summer, his fortunes were sagging. Gerard Doherty, Ted's old political mentor, saw the signals as early as June. He thought there were "rogues," old Democrats who had turned on

Ted—one who whispered to the press that Ted was no Robert Kennedy, another a former state senator who wrote a piece himself saying that it was time for Ted to go. "Very early these things kept popping up." Doherty said he sent a memo to Ted and then got a call from Vicki, who had read it and who asked him to talk to the staff and tell them the trouble they were in. Doherty would say that an old political hand had once told him, "The best thing you can do is sweat in public," by which he meant work doggedly to win votes, even if it meant going door to door. And now with the possibility of Ted Kennedy facing defeat, Doherty was advising that Ted sweat in public.

After his complacency, Ted was already sweating. As early as June, by one report in *The Boston Globe*, he had visited 125 cities and towns in Massachusetts, had built a war chest of $5 million, and had signed up 4,570 volunteers—fifteen times as many, according to the *Globe*, as in his last campaign. But as the general campaign approached, Ted was tied up with the Health Security Act, and Romney was building momentum. By the time Ted was able to campaign in September, Romney had trounced John Lakian in the Republican primary. More than the victory, primary night itself was an omen. Ted ran in his primary unopposed, but he had flown in from Washington nonetheless where he had been working tirelessly on Clinton's healthcare plan. As Vicki recalled it, the "victory" party was held in a dark room; Ted scarcely knew the people there; he hadn't been campaigning because he hadn't needed to, so he wasn't in his campaign groove; he had broken his foot somehow; he was tired; and while Romney was "like this big rocket"—Romney even called himself a "rocket" of change in his victory speech—Ted was "not feeling exhilarated," and the whole scene was, in Vicki's word, "flat." "It was a bad night," Vicki concluded, "and was a total contrast with Romney's." And now Ted knew—knew what he was up against. A poll the previous week showed Ted and Romney dead even. The polling agency, Opinion Dynamics, called it "not fatal but bad" for Ted. Later that month Ted was riding from the House side of the Capitol to the Senate side with Rhode Island senator Claiborne Pell after a conference on an education bill, and Ted turned to Pell and said, "Claiborne, you don't know what it's like out there this year," and then conceded, "I may lose." To Patrick, who was running for a seat in the House from the first district of Rhode Island, he half-joked, "If you get elected, make sure you don't forget me. I may need a job."

As if the political climate weren't bad enough, there were new per-

sonal issues. Joan had become disgruntled over her divorce settlement—
the settlement she had previously described as "generous"—and wanted
to reopen it, though without telling Ted. (By one account, she had met Ted
twice in May to discuss it, then let it drop before picking it up again months
later.) He learned about it when a reporter from the *Boston Herald* phoned
him just before the primary. Rumors swirled that Joan was unhappy over
Ted's seeking an annulment of their marriage on the grounds that neither had been mature enough to understand the commitments of a relationship, or that she had chosen to pressure him during the campaign to
get a better settlement. She would tell biographer Laurence Leamer that
she was contesting the original agreement on the grounds that Ted had
more assets than he had revealed and that she had not gotten what press
reports said she had gotten: $4 million, the Squaw Island home, and her
Beacon Street apartment. It was only when the children interceded that
Joan agreed to defer the issue until after the election. And then that October, in the midst of the campaign, Rick Burke, Ted's former administrative
assistant, who had had to resign after a mental breakdown, resurfaced,
this time bringing charges before the Senate Ethics Committee of sexual
harassment by Ted of women staffers and apparently accusing him of
drug abuse as well. In acquitting Ted, the committee took the unusual
step of not only denying the charges but also of publicly rebuking Burke:
"Contrary to statements attributed to Mr. Burke, the committee did not
receive complaints by women who claimed to have been sexually harassed
by Sen. Kennedy." Burke appealed to the conservative watchdog Accu-
racy in Media, but to no avail. As for the drug charges, Thomas Quinn,
who had headed Ted's Secret Service detail when he ran for president in
late 1979 through the November election the following year, said, "There
is no way" Burke's story was true. "I would have known. If there was any
illegal activity going on with a Secret Service protectee, the service is
going to take action." Nevertheless, the stain was on Ted's record.

It didn't help his reelection chances either that he had tied his fortunes
to Bill Clinton's. Clinton had had a series of successes in his first two years,
and Ted was involved in many of them, from the Family and Medical
Leave Act; to the National and Community Service Trust Act; to the Elementary and Secondary Education Act reauthorization, which dispensed
$60 billion of aid to schools and set in motion a number of reforms, in-
cluding lengthening the school day and year, reducing the size of classes,
and encouraging teacher development; to the National Skills Standards

Board that set national standards for vocational training and allowed workers to transfer their certificates from one state to another; to the Goals 2000: Educate America Act, which, among other things, incorporated the Safe Schools Act to prevent violence in schools. "I worked hard . . . to demonstrate to the people of my state that I was a force they could rely on," he told *The Boston Globe*. But he had also voted for Clinton's North American Free Trade Agreement (NAFTA), which removed trade barriers between the United States and Canada and between the United States and Mexico, and which labor had strenuously opposed, fearing that jobs would flow across the border where workers were paid less. "The strengths of the agreement are bittersweet," Ted said, saying he knew "why business is salivating over NAFTA and labor is spitting at it." Yet he said he felt it might actually save jobs. And then there was the Health Security Act, which had ended up going nowhere and fomenting both frustration and resentment among voters—frustration and resentment that Ted, having been identified so closely with it, was now reaping.

With Clinton's popularity falling, there were reasons for Ted to want not to be bound too closely to the president, but he couldn't have extricated himself even if he had wanted to, and there were real advantages in his not doing so—just not electoral advantages. Ted had come to like the Clintons and admire them. And he had come to trust them. "Clinton was a charmer on almost anything," Carey Parker would say, "and the Senator wanted to be able to work with him," adding that Ted was "very much on the Clinton team, and we weren't likely to second-guess most of his judgments." By the same token, and one source of Ted's trust, the Clintons admired Ted's legislative acumen—admired it and needed it—making the relationship mutually advantageous. "He's a real pro," Hillary Clinton said of Ted. "He really knows how to make Washington work," and the "President and I respect his judgment." He wasn't "part of the hand-wringing crowd," she said. "He is pragmatic and effective." And because he was effective, the Clintons would do what they could to accommodate Ted, and Ted, for his part, was not reluctant to ask them. When Byron White, John Kennedy's lone Supreme Court appointment, announced in March 1993 that he would be retiring from the Court after its current term, Ted wanted Clinton to appoint his old mentor and Harvard constitutional law professor, Laurence Tribe, but Clinton was worried that Tribe, a brilliant but outspoken liberal, would get "Borked" by the conservatives, and even though Ted told Clinton that he had done a Senate nose count and that Tribe could be confirmed, Clinton chose not to pick a fight. Ted had a fallback: Stephen Breyer, Ted's former aide who had gone on, with Ted's sponsorship, to be appointed a federal appeals court judge—the lone Carter nominee who had gotten confirmation after Carter and the Democrats lost the 1980 election. Ted wasn't reluctant to press Breyer's case. Ted told Breyer to prepare a "big book" on himself— "Everything I'd ever done," Breyer said—and Breyer sent it to Carey Parker, who doubtless passed it on to Ted, who sent it to Clinton. By one account, Clinton had already decided to name his interior secretary, Bruce Babbitt, to the vacancy, but Western governors pleaded with Clinton to leave Babbitt in the Cabinet because they needed his advocacy on environmental issues there. So once again Breyer became an alternative. But that week Breyer was struck by a car while riding his bicycle in Cambridge—an accident so serious that he had broken two ribs and was hospitalized. Just after the accident, White House aides went to his bedside for an eight-hour interview and came away unimpressed. (Breyer was aching and groggy and in no condition to fence with those aides.) Even so, he left the hospital and went to Washington to meet with Clinton himself that Friday, still light-headed. Clinton too was unimpressed. According to one White House official, he found Breyer professorial, too intellectual, "and a little too eager." Clinton's attorney general, Janet Reno, had been pushing another federal appeals court judge, Ruth Bader Ginsburg, who had made a name for herself in women's jurisprudence, and the following Sunday, two days after his Breyer meeting, Clinton met with her. This time Clinton was captivated—by her personal story and her work for women's rights, which had been compared to Thurgood Marshall's work for civil rights; and by what he considered her judicial temperament. (Breyer's nomination was also endangered by the revelation that he had failed to pay Social Security taxes for a cleaning woman.) "Kind of fell in love with Ruth Ginsburg," Clinton aide John Podesta said of the president. Clinton phoned Breyer the evening of his Ginsburg interview to tell him that he was going to nominate her.

Breyer seemed to have lost his chance. After Clinton's announcement, Ted stood on the White House driveway outside the entrance to the West Wing and graciously told the press how wonderful the nomination of Ginsburg was and how much of a trailblazer Ginsburg was and that even though he was disappointed that Breyer was not selected, there would be, he said, other vacancies. "Just unbelievably effusive" was how John A.

Farrell described Ted's comments. And when Farrell, walking with Ted back to Ted's car, pressed him that he had to be a "little bit pissed" about Clinton's bypassing Breyer, Ted told him evenly, "No. We didn't get it this time. A really masterful politician always has a long game." Ted even attended Ginsburg's swearing-in. Not long afterward Farrell interviewed Mack McLarty, Clinton's chief of staff, who told Farrell, "Your Senator piled up an amazing amount of good will with the way he took that," meaning Clinton's decision not to appoint Breyer, and called Ted "very mature, very constructive, very gracious."

This was Ted Kennedy working the chemistry of the presidency. And it was to pay off, as his understanding of the chemistry of the Senate had so often paid off. The following April Harry Blackmun announced his intention to resign from the Court at the end of its current session, and once again Ted kicked into action. Clinton wanted to name Senate majority leader George Mitchell, a former federal judge, to the vacancy, but Mitchell was invested in the healthcare battle and thought that if he left, they would lose any chance at passage. While Clinton was enamored of Judge Richard Arnold, the chief judge of the Eighth Circuit Court of Appeals, Ted now pushed Breyer—"really pushed for Breyer," John Podesta said. But Clinton harbored doubts. Ted's former aide Jeffrey Blattner said that Breyer had given a speech to the American College of Trial Lawyers, of which Blattner's father-in-law happened to be president, and the father-in-law told Blattner that Breyer had been very effective. Blattner happened to mention that to Breyer, who then asked if Blattner might get him a videotape of the speech, which Breyer gave to a district court judge, Rick Stearns, who had been Clinton's roommate at Oxford when Clinton was studying on his Rhodes scholarship there. Stearns sent it to a friend, Susan Brophy, who was a legislative aide to Clinton, and Clinton watched the tape, which, Blattner said, "resuscitated Breyer in Clinton's eyes." Ted lobbied for Breyer with Clinton every chance he had. Ken Feinberg recalled attending a meeting on healthcare between Clinton and Ted that spring, four days before Clinton made his announcement, and as soon as the press left, Ted turned the conversation to the nomination. (Meanwhile Judge Arnold had undergone treatment for cancer, which discouraged Clinton from nominating him.) But even as he continued to press Breyer's case, Ted was concerned. He had heard that Ginsburg had gotten the nomination the year before because Pat Moynihan, who was a Ginsburg supporter, had spoken to Clinton the morning of the announcement, and

Ted told Nick Littlefield, "If we ever have another chance, I want to be the last person to see Clinton before he makes the announcement." So Ted determined where Clinton was going to be that morning—it turned out he would be delivering a speech before a group of educators at the Hyatt Hotel on Capitol Hill—and Ted got himself an invitation to speak there as well, then followed Clinton out into the hallway afterward and said to him, "I hope it's going to be Breyer. He's the right guy." And it was.

As Ted began his campaign, his fortunes and those of the president to whom he was tied were sinking—both of them plummeting downward after the failure of the Health Security Act and labor's anger over NAFTA. Still, that September the president attended a fundraiser at Ted's McLean home. He sang Ted's praises, listing his legislative accomplishments in just the last two years, which were impressive. He argued that Ted "made enemies in his life because he has fought for things" and said "the things he has fought for are things that would help people who are very different from him," clearly drawing a contrast between Ted and his opponent, Mitt Romney, whose battles, Clinton implied, were on the side of business. "Ninety-five percent of the people that would have been given the things that he was given in life," he said, speaking of Ted, "never would have spent their life trying to get all that for everybody else in the country. . . . They wouldn't have put themselves on the line day in and day out, year in and year out." But then Clinton addressed the political situation in which "we're going through big changes and the future is not clear." He compared the nation's crisis to a personal crisis where those changes were also met by a combination of hope and fear. "It's almost as if we have a scale inside us," he told those contributors, "with blind justice holding it, and hope is one side and fear is the other. And each day it may take a little different balance."

Hope and fear—those were the dueling twins that Ted Kennedy had often confronted in his political crusades, and now he sensed that the balance was tipping toward fear, and he seemed powerless to stop it. Romney, so handsome, so well-groomed, so stalwart, so articulate, a businessman who scorned government without sliding too far right, seemed impregnable, an aesthetic icon of success, Ted anything but. The race was called a real-life version of *The Last Hurrah,* the novel about an old Irish Boston pol, the sort of man Ted had confronted back in 1962 and the sort of man Ted now was, fighting off a younger, newer pol. One reporter said of Ted,

"He looked bad. He sounded bad. And in that way he was vulnerable." A "homeless man in a $1000 suit" was how one article described him. He had begun wearing contact lenses—he made a point of knowing every one of his staffers who wore lenses too in case he needed contact lens solution—and had stopped smoking his thin black cigars, the Alhambra Mahaba Regaliz cigarillos from the Philippines, after Stephen Smith's death from lung cancer—Smith had made him promise—but it didn't change the affect of a man in decline. "Pudgy, silver-haired and a bit dissolute looking," reported *Newsweek*. "Pudgy" was charitable. He had always been able to lose weight before a campaign. But this time, despite Vicki's rebukes, he couldn't. The food was just too good, he admitted to Adam Clymer during the campaign, and the diet on which Vicki had put him made him irritable. It was, Vicki said, the heaviest he had ever been, which got tongues to wagging: "Oh, he's heavy, he must not be doing well." Or "Oh, he's old." To complete the picture, he had a jagged scar on his nose from basal cancer surgery he had undergone in 1982. One article in *The Boston Globe*, titled "Kennedy Outliving Family Charisma," cited the dissonance between a film of Ted shown at the Massachusetts Democratic Convention that June and his appearance in person. "On the screen in Worcester, Kennedy was handsome and imposing, his words dramatic and forceful," the article went. "But then reality stripped back the curtain from the Oz machine. On the podium, the senior senator seemed an epigone of his video image. Even his speech, a flat, windy, partly recycled effort delivered with an occasional grandfatherly quaver, emphasized the difference." It concluded: "Beefy, thick-featured, red-faced, with an unruly shock of white hair, he has arrived in the autumn of a hard life the antithesis of his brothers' image." All this about the man who had once been regarded as the most athletic of the Kennedys, the handsomest of the Kennedys. But then, his brothers never aged out of their images. "We have no template for aging Kennedys," George Colt wrote in *Life* at the beginning of the campaign. Neither did Ted.

II

Desperate, serious, alarmed, losing, out of date—those were the words that rattled through the Kennedy campaign when Ted finally returned from the healthcare battle to take on Mitt Romney. Martin Nolan, a veteran political reporter at *The Boston Globe*, said the "well-oiled Kennedy machine" was "sputtering in a campaign of quarrelsome turmoil," and quoted an adviser who said, "The senator has received a very serious reality check." That reality check hit on September 18, with polls now showing Ted running behind Romney, when his brain trust—among them, Vicki and his father-in-law, Edmund Reggie; consultants Bob Shrum and Shrum's partner, Tad Devine; pollster Tom Kiley; John Sasso, who had managed Michael Dukakis's campaign; and Ted's campaign manager, Michael Kennedy—met at his Marlborough Street apartment. A "very pivotal and important meeting," Tad Devine called it. The group was disheartened. "Looking into the abyss" was how one participant described the mood. Nothing had been going right, and on one matter, the attendees agreed: Things needed to be shaken up and shaken up significantly. Ted had hoped to get by on the cheap. Now he knew he couldn't. He had to commit to spend whatever it took, and the feeling was that it would take at least $10 million. And the approach had to change. Shrum's ads had been promoting Ted's work for his constituents—his past successes. "He's been called the most effective senator" was the keynote of those ads, and the tagline was, "Making a difference for Massachusetts. Kennedy in the Senate." Vicki thought the ads "pedestrian," not forceful enough, and said that they were ceding the race to Romney who came across as "Mr. New." "Vintage 1970," one campaigner mocked Ted's ads, while another described them as telling viewers, "An icon we have the privilege of voting for." Shrum and Devine countered that they didn't want to make too big a claim for Ted as one of the great senators without first laying the groundwork. But now there was a consensus that the ads had to do something else, something more than say what Ted had done. They just didn't know what yet. They only knew this: They could no longer just promote Ted. They had to take on Romney, go on the offensive, strip away his shining armor.

And while they pondered how to do that, the media were arriving— "all drawn to a quiet Boston borough to see for themselves if the rumors are true. Could Ted Kennedy really be on the brink of defeat?"

And there was yet another problem—a major problem. Ted Kennedy had never had to worry about funding his campaigns, in part because he was wealthy, and in part because he didn't need to spend exorbitantly except for his primary against Ed McCormack. Joe Kennedy had set up each of his children with a $10 million trust, which had been managed by Ted's brother-in-law, Steve Smith. According to a *New York Times* article, when he ran for president in 1980, Ted had another roughly $8 million in a blind trust and held a 13 percent interest in the Merchandise Mart in Chicago, the world's largest commercial building, which his father had owned. He also held several thousand acres of land in Florida and small oil leases in the South, and he owned a portion of a large stock portfolio of $100 million. The *Times* concluded that Ted's personal wealth was in the vicinity of $20 million, which was certainly enough to fund any election campaign. But Mitt Romney was wealthy too; as early as July he had an $8 million war chest, and an official of the National Republican Senatorial Committee declared, "Romney will not be outspent" and that "he will spend dollar for dollar what Kennedy will spend," promising that "for the first time, we will have a competitive race with Kennedy." To keep up, as Ted had pledged he would—he and Romney were each spending, by one report, between $300,000 and $400,000 a week on television ads alone—Ted raised $8 million, but by October he had already spent $6 million of it, and he put up his McLean house as collateral to the Bank of Boston for another $2 million to help finance the campaign and spare himself having to dun his supporters. "He's taking the race very seriously," his new chief of staff, Paul Donovan, told *Newsweek*. As Gerard Doherty might have said, he was now sweating in public.

And Ted Kennedy, who had decided to change the direction of his campaign, now needed soldiers in the trenches to help him. Michael Kennedy, who might have been up to the task of running a typical Ted Kennedy campaign, was not up to the task of running this atypical one where Ted's back was against the wall, and the office was manned, observed Dave Burke, by "people who the last time Ted Kennedy and I worked together were in pre-nursery school or something," and he added, "They gave him no comfort or assurance at all." Burke, Ted's old administrative assistant, said that Ted would be out campaigning in his car and talking to headquarters, with all these young people he doesn't really know, and "he's getting frightened." It was clear he needed reinforcements, campaign veterans, people who had worked for him in the past and were committed to him. And so now the call went out. Burke remembered getting a phone call from Milton Gwirtzman, the brilliant attorney and counselor who had helped Ted when he first arrived in the Senate and written some of his best speeches. Burke had left Ted's office in 1970 and had had a distinguished career since as the president of news at CBS and executive vice president at ABC, as the secretary to New York governor Hugh Carey, and as an adviser to the Dreyfus Fund, where he had just overseen a merger of Dreyfus and Mellon. Burke was semiretired when Gwirtzman, with whom he hadn't spoken in years, said, "You know, Teddy's in some trouble up here," and asked if Burke might give Ted a call himself. Burke did, and after a few pleasantries—they hadn't talked either in quite some time— offered his assistance, to which Ted said, "To get a call like this makes my day." Burke thought he had fulfilled his obligation. But Ted called him back the next day. Burke figured Ted might ask for a financial contribu- tion or, with Burke's television experience, some help on that end. But instead Ted made an odd request: He asked Burke if he would ride in the car with him, essentially be what was called a "body man"—the fellow who accompanied the candidate. Burke's wife, who was not, Burke said, Ted's "biggest fan," was aghast that her husband would consider some- thing she thought demeaning. But loyalty to Ted Kennedy ran deep. Burke agreed, went up to Boston, and spent the rest of the campaign sitting in the back of the car with a yellow pad and a Pentel marker, writing and passing notes to Ted in the front seat. And Vicki would say, "What a differ- ence it made."

More were called, and more came. Dukakis aides Charles Baker, John Sasso, and Jack Corrigan had already joined the campaign. Ted asked his old chief of staff Ranny Cooper, who had left his office in January 1992 and joined Weber Shandwick Public Affairs, if she would take a leave to help organize his campaign, and she couldn't refuse him any more than Burke could. That first night after she came aboard, Ted told Vicki, "I'm going to sleep tonight because Ranny's going to be worrying about it," meaning his campaign, "and I don't have to anymore." When Bob Shrum released the first ads touting Ted's legislative achievements, Carey Parker, Ted's longtime legislative aide, stepped in and provided twenty-six pages of corroboration—"We need some back-up with this shit, all right?" Shrum's partner, Tad Devine had asked—and sent it out to the press. Paul Kirk came aboard. And Ted's current chief of staff, Paul Donovan, took a leave of absence from the Senate office. So did Ted's press secretary Pam Hughes. David Broder, walking into Ted's headquarters, remarked that it was "like reliving my whole life" since "everybody I had ever known in any Kennedy campaign, going back to 1960, was at a desk and on a phone there." And others came too: Jesse Jackson, the Black leader; Martin Lu- ther King III; Bobby Kennedy, Jr.; and Ted Jr., who traveled together to colleges and got students to register to vote and wound up adding tens of thousands to the rolls. Did he think he could lose? Vicki asked him one night when things were looking bleak. "Well, I could," Ted answered. "But I won't, because I know what I have to do and I'm going to do it."

But for all that, it did not get better. Romney was a Mormon in a heavily Catholic state, and reporters wondered whether Ted would attempt to exploit that. John A. Farrell recalled asking Ted early that year if Romney's religion would be an issue, and Ted saying that his brother Jack had laid religion to rest once and for all as a political detriment when his Catholicism was under scrutiny during his 1960 presidential campaign, and he spoke before the Greater Houston Ministerial Convention and said that a man's religion had no bearing on his ability to govern. Farrell said he wrote a piece quoting Ted but also warning that a test might come. The test came, Farrell would later say, because Ted was "desperate." As the campaign geared up, Ted had remained mum about Romney's Mormonism, but his nephew, Bobby's eldest son, Joseph Kennedy II, who now represented Tip O'Neill's old district in the House, did not. He criticized the Mormon religion for its treatment of Black people and women—Black people hadn't been eligible for the priesthood before 1978 and women still weren't—and said that Romney, who had been a lay leader himself and not just a church member, was open to criticism, while Romney rebutted that Kennedy's remarks were an intrusion into religion. (Questions were also raised about whether Romney had condemned homosexuality as a "perversity," had told an unmarried pregnant woman that she would be excommunicated if she didn't give the baby up for adoption, and had a woman removed from a church position because women weren't allowed to hold such positions.) Ted waffled, saying at first that the discrimination was a legitimate issue and then retreated, saying "religion should not be an issue in this campaign." But the damage, which was the specter of religious intolerance on the Kennedys' part, had been raised.

Now, as Tad Devine described it, "We were in the bunker on this." Joe Kennedy issued an apology in both a letter to the *Globe* and a twenty-minute phone call with Romney, who had played up the issue and even invoked John Kennedy at a press conference that Devine called "brilliant." But Ted had not apologized, refused to apologize, even though, during a conference call with Devine, Shrum, John Sasso, and Paul Donovan, his advisers all but ordered him to retract his statement so that they could get on with the campaign. Ted was livid. "Are you guys telling me I've got to put my tail between my legs and go out there?" he asked. (In another interview, Devine said Ted used a less polite word than "guys.") And Shrum told him, "That's exactly what we're telling you." And Ted swallowed his pride, made a statement that Devine called "pitch perfect," and as Devine put it, "It was all over." And the campaign continued.

Of all those who answered the call to save Ted's campaign, the single most important might have been the person closest to him: his wife. Vicki, who had never been on the campaign trail before they wed, hadn't known whether she would take to retail politics or even whether she wanted to. She hadn't married Ted for that, though many still believed that Ted had married her for that. A "cynical marriage of convenience" was how many saw it, according to John A. Farrell. Even she would joke, when Ted got imperious, that the only reason he married her was to raise his poll numbers. She was certainly an asset. Paul Donovan admitted that at Ranny Cooper's instigation they had worked at rehabilitating the perception of Ted as louche by featuring long interviews up at Hyannis with Vicki, both on television and in the Boston newspapers, and Ted's early television ads had the two of them nuzzling. When two *Boston Globe* reporters asked Ted about charges that he was exploiting his marriage to polish his tarnished image, he replied that his "life now is one of enormous happiness with the woman I love and is a time of enormous personal strength and gratitude and joy," and he thought that his constituents "sort of feel that." "You can talk about it," he said, "but you can't effectively fool them about it." She had accompanied Ted in 1992 when he campaigned throughout Massachusetts for his fellow Democrats, and by the time his own 1994 campaign rolled around, he recruited her to do events while he was in Washington. But she was more than a surrogate, which was what Joan had been. "She was very much involved in every kind of decision," Ted was to say. "As a strategist and tactician, she was excellent. . . . She can listen to me talk to people and talk with their parents and then go in that other room and write a talk . . . and it will be as good a speech as you'll ever see in your life." By the spring, she was sitting in on all the strategy meetings, and by the summer, she was appearing with him whenever he campaigned, taking notes when he gave interviews and giving his staff feedback on his appearances. Michael Kennedy said that Ted could be rough with that staff. So Vicki served as an intermediary. "She can express it," meaning criticism, "without it being taken in a personal way and soften the criticism." And in the fall, she got her own daytime schedule while Ted was off with his, and then the two would connect every evening and appear jointly at events and then "trade stories" afterward, as Ted put it. "You couldn't watch Ted and Vicki without realizing," John A. Farrell said, citing Bill and Hillary Clinton as well, "that the rich are very different from you and me, and that marriages at that level still owe a little bit of something back to the sixteenth century, when kings married their daughters off to rivals to get another province and stop the war. . . . Hillary Clinton could be both madly in love with Bill Clinton, furious at him for his weaknesses, devoted to the political causes they both share and devoted to maintaining the investment of twenty years of politics." And Farrell said that he "always looked at Vicki and Ted and sort of felt the same thing." They were bound both personally and politically, in love with each other but also in love with the political life they now led together.

But even with Vicki tempering Ted's image, as the campaign moved into its last month, the contest was still basically a dead heat, and Romney ramped up his attacks on Ted, accusing him, in a series of ads, of being soft on crime and favoring welfare for irresponsible citizens. "The steady beating of the Romney drums had done their damage," *The Boston Globe* reported. And Ted had yet to find his stride, it said. "Bloated and mottled, Kennedy looked bad and at times sounded worse on the campaign trail." Perhaps the most alarming sign of just how close the race was came when Michael Kennedy met with ten Black clergymen at the Charles Street AME Church in Roxbury, and one of them told him that he would not "put all his eggs in one basket." "If Mitt Romney pulled a stunning upset and won the campaign," he said, "and all the black clergy are at home sitting with Kennedy, then what does he [Romney] owe to the black community? Absolutely nothing." This was close to heresy when it came to the long-standing relationship between the Black community and the Kennedys. The September 18 meeting at the Marlborough Street apartment had established the need for a new strategy. What it hadn't done was establish what that strategy should be. Romney had few vulnerabilities. He was running as a successful businessman who would bring those skills to government. But as Romney seemed to be succeeding, Vicki thought he must have at least one weakness in his business dealings. Romney boasted of the thousands of jobs he had created in Massachusetts as a venture capitalist. Some of Ted's strategists remarked of Romney's career at Bain Capital, a private investment firm, "Oh, well, he had a business record, and he just took over companies, and there's really nothing there," but Vicki, who had worked in corporate law and who knew what could happen when venture capitalists gobbled a company, countered, "Well, wait. Of course, there is." She said there were different ways to take over companies, different ways to handle the employees of the companies that were overtaken, choices that new ownership made, things like downsizing and layoffs, and she encouraged them to look at what Bain had done when it assumed control of a company. At her urging, the campaign hired the Investigative Group, a corporate investigations firm headed by former Watergate counsel Terry Lenzner. "She was key," Shrum said of Vicki.

And as it turned out, there *was* a weakness. The weakness the Kennedy campaign found was AMPAD—the American Pad and Paper Company, which manufactured office supplies. AMPAD had been founded in 1888 in Holyoke, where it claimed to have invented the yellow legal pad, and one hundred years later, when it was purchased by the Mead Corporation, it had extended to thirteen factories across the United States. But in 1992 Bain Capital, Mitt Romney's company, took over AMPAD and moved its headquarters from Holyoke to Texas. At one of AMPAD's subsidiary's factories, an SCM plant in Marion, Indiana, Bain took precisely the sorts of actions about which Vicki Kennedy had warned. It downsized the workforce by one-fifth or 350 employees; it cut wages; it reduced the health insurance plan; and it eliminated the retirement plan entirely. On September 1 the International Paper Workers, Local 154, struck the plant. Bain answered by hiring replacements. Early in September, Mark Brooks, the union's special projects director, contacted a researcher at Ted's campaign, Caitlin Sherman, who spent the next several weeks collecting information about the strike and then informed Michael Kennedy about the situation. Michael Kennedy told Tad Devine, who decided to take a trip to Marion with a cinematographer and soundman to shoot footage of the disgruntled workers. He also hired a man to run a teleprompter, assuming that the workers' complaints would have to be scripted. But when he sat down with ten discharged employees who had been enlisted from the union hall, Devine realized they didn't need a teleprompter. All one had to do is ask them, "If you had to say one thing to Mitt Romney, what would you say?" and "the floodgates opened up." One couple said they lost their health insurance because of Romney. Another young worker in a navy blue baseball cap asked Romney where the ten thousand jobs were that he

One of the most collegial of senators, Ted mans the phones here with Republican Senator Orrin Hatch in Ted's hideaway in June 1997 to promote their Children's Health Insurance Plan, providing insurance for children whose parents did not qualify for Medicaid but were too poor to afford private insurance. Ted and Hatch worked together on a number of issues, demonstrating that a liberal Democrat and conservative Republican could find common cause, or at least Ted could find it with them, even though Hatch once pronounced that he had come to the Senate with the express goal of stopping Ted Kennedy. *CQ Archive/ Getty Images*

The two-decade crusade for raising the minimum wage: Ted had fought long and hard for an increase in the minimum wage, gaining victories in 1989 and again in 1997. Here, he advocates at a rally on March 8, 2005, for the first increase in eight years. *Win McNamee/Getty Images*

Impeachment. Ted meets here with reporters in his office in January 1999 to discuss William Jefferson Clinton's impeachment. Ted had advised Clinton and bucked his flagging spirits, but he also worked with Republican senator Phil Gramm to devise rules for the Senate trial. *David Hume Kennerly/Getty Images*

"A great promise of things to come." Ted watches as (*left to right*) Patrick, Douglas Kennedy, Ted Jr., and Maxwell Kennedy carry the coffin with the remains of John Kennedy Jr. to Woods Hole, where later a boat would take his ashes to be scattered at sea alongside his wife's. Both Kennedys were killed in a plane crash on their way to the wedding of John's cousin Rory on Martha's Vineyard. John was the Kennedy prince. And now, with his death, the dynasty seemed over. *The Boston Globe/Getty Images*

Standing behind President George W. Bush on January 8, 2002, at Hamilton High School in Hamilton, Ohio, (*left to right*) Rep. George Miller, Ted, Education Secretary Rod Paige, Senator Judd Gregg (R-New Hampshire) and Rep. John Boehner watch Bush sign into law his No Child Left Behind initiative, which set standards for schools in poor and minority areas. Bush had forcefully recruited Ted as a backer of the bill, but Ted later felt betrayed when Bush refused to fully fund the program. He would be betrayed again when Bush reneged on a deal for a Medicare prescription drug plan. *AP Photo/Ron Edmonds, File*

Ted and his beloved Portuguese water dog Splash. Ted took him everywhere, including to the White House. And when, a year later in 2001, he acquired another Portuguese, Sunny, he took *both* of them everywhere. He would say that his idea of a perfect day was "sailing on the *Mya* with Vicki at my side and my dogs, Splash and Sunny, at my feet." *Douglas Graham/Getty Images*

Ted in his office in 2002. The office was yet another tool of his, basically a Kennedy museum, and the tours he conducted there for freshmen senators and other dignitaries were a form of ingratiation. The year before, he had had the office redecorated, with one wall dedicated to memorabilia and photographs of his brother John, another wall to Bobby, and another to parents Rose and Joe. In the reception area hung the Andy Warhol portrait of Ted, lithographs of which had helped finance his presidential campaign in 1980. On another wall was a chart of all 355 senators with whom Ted had served. *David Hume*

The house in the Kalorama section of Washington. Ted and Vicki moved in in 1999. "A warm welcoming house," Vicki called it, which comported with how Ted then viewed his life— happy and comfortable—though the structure's white façade and colonnades gave it the effect of the house he had never achieved: The White House. *The Washington Post/Getty Images*

The Iraq War. Ted sits in the Senate press gallery talking to reporters as the debate on October 10, 2002, over the resolution of whether to empower President Bush to take military action against Iraq proceeds on the television behind him. Ted was one of only twenty-three senators to oppose it, and he continued to be an unrelenting critic of the war, pressing the administration to use diplomacy rather than arms. *Scott J. Ferrell/Getty Images*

The futility of immigration reform. Partly as a political bequest from his brother John, who promoted immigration reform, Ted became the Senate's leader on immigration, but he was to face far more failure than success. Here, on November 7, 2007, he is consoled by an unidentified fellow senator after a press conference calling for the Senate to reach a compromise. He had fought for two years and had wrangled Republicans to join him, but in the end, conservative opposition and President Bush's timidity sunk his bill. *Philip Scott Andrews/Getty Images*

Hope. Convinced by his niece Caroline Kennedy Schlossberg that Barack Obama was a torchbearer for her father's idealism, Ted announces his endorsement of Obama at a rally at American University on January 28, 2008, and helps turn the primary race toward Obama. Obama, Caroline, and Patrick listen. *Chip Somodevilla/Getty Images*

The diagnosis. On May 21, 2008, Vicki, Ted, and Splash walk the grounds at the Hyannis Port compound after Ted is diagnosed with incurable brain cancer. *AP Photo/Steven Senne*

On his porch of the Big House at Hyannis overlooking the ocean and reading, the day after the diagnosis. *The Boston Globe/Getty Images*

Determined not to let the disease dictate its terms to him, Ted had a "secret goal." He spent weeks preparing to address the Democratic National Convention in Denver and, overcoming both cancer and kidney stones, delivered a short, stirring speech that roused the delegates and left them teary, knowing that this would be his last convention. *Chip Somodevilla/Getty Images*

Ted returns to the Senate on November 17, 2008, after months away battling his cancer. He arrives at the Senate Office Building with Vicki, Sunny, and Splash to continue to push his agenda. *Tom Williams/Getty Images*

The cause of his life. Even though he was struggling with incurable cancer, Ted kept fighting to enact a national healthcare plan after the November 2008 election. Here he meets on November 19 with the Senate Finance Committee to strategize: (*left to right*) Mike Enzi (R-Wyoming), Charles Grassley (R-Iowa), Max Baucus (D-Montana), and Chris Dodd (D-Connecticut). In effect, Ted pressured the new president to propose a plan. *Mark Wilson/Getty Images*

Fighting on. Ted unsteadily returns once again to Washington on March 4, 2009, to attend a healthcare summit at the White House convened by President Obama. A "magic moment," Obama would call Ted's entrance, as the guests applauded. And Ted left them a warning: "I'm looking forward to being a foot soldier in this undertaking. And this time we will not fail." *Jim Watson/Getty Images*

His last legislation. On April 21, 2009, at the SEED Charter School in Washington, Barack Obama hands Ted a pen after signing the "Edward M. Kennedy Serve America Act," which tripled the size of AmeriCorps. It was appropriate that the law was one of public service to help the vulnerable. Between Obama and Ted are House Speaker Nancy Pelosi, Sen. Orrin Hatch, and Vicki. *Pool/Getty Images*

His marker and gravestone at Arlington National Cemetery are alongside the graves of his brothers, John and Robert. *James Talalay/Alamy Stock Photo, WENN Rights Ltd./Alamy Stock Photo*

said he had created. Another woman said he had taken away not only their jobs but their dignity. Yet another middle-aged woman said that workers now had to ask the foreman to use the restroom. Another woman in a white sweater said Romney had "basically cut our throats." With the campaign moving into its final month, there was little time. Devine took the tapes with him on a plane to Washington, then trained to an editing room in Philadelphia the same day, and two days later, two long days, he sent five new ads to Shrum—"some of the best ads they ever made," Shrum said. They tested them immediately with a hundred-person focus group in a suburban hotel, and they scored well. The only obstacle, they feared, might be winning Ted Kennedy's approval. Ted had never run negative advertising before. He had never had to. But Ted did not need convincing. He recognized how dire his situation was. "He leaped right in," Devine said, already strategizing. He told Shrum and Devine that he didn't want to start with the ads about Romney costing those workers their jobs, but with another ad excoriating Romney for giving health insurance to foreign workers of his companies while denying it to American workers. *Then* move on to the jobs ads. The ads were on the air within a week.

Ted was now on the offensive. He charged Romney with making $11 million from Bain's takeover of the Staples office supply company, while slashing health benefits to its workers; of having no minorities at Bain and only one woman in the firm's top echelon, which enabled Ted to challenge Romney on women's issues; and most effectively, he charged Romney with being insensitive to the plight of ordinary working people. And now Mitt Romney was finally on the defensive. "This is not fantasy land," he rebutted. "This is the real world and in the real world, there is nothing wrong with companies trying to compete, trying to stay alive, trying to make money." It was a Republican argument, an argument for the sanctity of business, but it wasn't an argument that would appeal to discharged workers, and try as he might to salvage his businessman credentials and savage Ted—"continuous distortions," Romney called the ads—he now only dug himself into a deeper hole. "It seems that words were put in people's mouths," a Romney spokesman charged of the new ads. But *The Boston Globe,* itself skeptical, sent a reporter to Indiana and discovered that the workers hadn't been coached. "What I said was from the heart," a fifty-three-year-old mother of three, Sharon Alter, who had worked at the Marion plant for thirty years before being fired by Bain, told him. And worse, a number of those fired workers headed to Massachu-

setts in a van, not to help Ted but to confront Bain. Romney, however, refused to meet with them for three days—a refusal that now became a
headline and a deeper hole. "And that's when the bottom drops out of
Romney," Devine recalled. "His unfavorable [rating] starts going up in almost a straight line." Romney's negatives rose to 31 percent and his positives sank to 40 percent, Shrum said, while Ted's positives rose to 57
percent, though he still had negatives of 38 percent.

The whole race began to turn. Devine remembered sitting with Ted on
a plane and showing him the latest polling data—that data that revealed
Romney's soaring negatives. "And Ted just reveled in it," he said. "He
loved the politics." Now, on the attack, he was energized. And Romney
still had no rebuttal. He accused Ted of making a profit off a building
owned in a blind trust by JPK Enterprises, Joe Kennedy's old holding company, by leasing it to the government, but Ted had only a 0.04 percent interest in the building and had forgone any profit from his share precisely
to avoid a conflict of interest. And Romney attacked Ted for failing to halt
the closing of shipyards in Massachusetts, though those closings had occurred in Republican administrations. And he complained feebly that
Ted, "by virtue of those slick ads," had created the "impression that I am
somebody who doesn't care about people," which was exactly the impression Ted had wanted to create and did. Meanwhile Ted was doing what he
did best—meeting voters on the stump. "Nothing works for me like being
out with people," he told *Life* magazine's George Colt, "feeling their sense
of injustice, their sense of hope." But it was his own sense of hope he was
feeling now too—the growing sense that he might be able to pull out a
victory after all, that the old warhorse could still beat a young comer.

III

Yet even as Ted had seemed to right his campaign, there was still one possible chink in his armor—one opening that could undo all that the ads
had done. Romney, beginning to flail, demanded debates. Two had already
been scheduled, but Romney now wanted two more and these without
moderators. Lincoln-Douglas-style debates, he called them, with the candidates questioning each other. Ted had been hesitant to debate. Romney
was articulate, Ted not, and more, the physical contrast between the two
wouldn't redound to Ted's benefit. Reading both the politics and the aesthetics of it, Ted had adamantly opposed any debates, even though *The*

Boston Globe, the *Boston Herald,* and the Boston affiliates of ABC, CBS, and NBC had requested them and had gone so far as to take out ads demanding them. Ted protested to his advisers that he couldn't do it, wasn't up to doing it. Dave Burke, who had joined the campaign by then, was equally adamant that Ted had to debate and threatened to quit if Ted didn't. "I'd like *you* to sit in the back of that car every day, fifteen microphones through the windows, yelling at you, 'Why won't you debate?' And an atomic bomb falls on San Francisco. 'Why won't you debate?' Russia declares war on the United States. 'Senator, why won't you debate?'" "It's going to be endless, and he's going to be demeaned, and he'll get smaller by the day," Burke told Ted's braintrust during a conference call. And so finally, reluctantly, Ted agreed to those two debates, now with one half of each devoted to the Lincoln-Douglas format, to be held on October 25 and October 27, shortly before the election: the first in Faneuil Hall, and the second at Holyoke Community College.

The complexion of the campaign changed then, Dave Burke said. Once Ted decided he would debate Romney, once he overcame his trepidations and committed, he was "liberated and every strength he has came out." He had been testy through most of the campaign, uncertain, worried. Now, Burke said, "he was wonderful to be with, and it was fun again." "Let's kick ass"—that was the new tenor. "It got good. It really got good." He was back in training. The staff organized mock debates with Shrum serving as moderator; the Dukakis aides, John Sasso and Jack Corrigan, and Ted's own legislative assistant Carey Parker were the questioners; and a business partner of Ranny Cooper's, Dave Smith, played Romney. Shrum had once taught debate, and as Dave Burke put it, "He's never seen a jugular vein he hasn't attacked." And Shrum coached Ted that at some point in the debate, Romney would mention the profit Ted allegedly made on that Washington building, and he had an answer. And Shrum said they would discuss healthcare, and that when they did, Ted was to go after Romney, "without ever stopping again," asking him, "What kind of a bill would you [write]?" And "How would you get it written?" And "What subcommittees would you go before and what committees would you go on to push that bill?" *Don't let Romney catch his breath.* And the staff prepared too. That year Democratic gubernatorial candidate Mark Roosevelt had debated Governor William Weld at Faneuil Hall, and Paul Kirk recalled thinking that Roosevelt, who was short, looked fine behind the small podiums that had been provided, but that Weld, who was tall and slender, looked awkward towering over his podium. Kirk knew that Ted was likely to look ridiculous too behind a tiny podium since he was now so wide of girth. So during the debate negotiations, he suggested that the two sides visit Faneuil and take a look at those podiums and said that Romney was likely to dwarf them. Romney's negotiators said Kirk could get whatever podium he wanted, which was how Kirk and Ted's old aide, Eddie Martin, managed to hide Ted behind a huge podium. And then there was the matter of Ted's perspiration. Before the debate, Gerard Doherty had run into an acquaintance who offered him a tip. "That place is awful hot," the tipster said of Faneuil Hall. "Your friend the mayor runs the place." So the man said, "Turn the air conditioning on the night before and make it the coldest place next to hell so that Kennedy's not going to sweat in public." And so the candidate who had been sweating to show how much he wanted to win reelection did not sweat on television during the debate.

Ted was ready. "The expectation was that Romney would do very well," Shrum would say, and he cited a "non-well-wisher" who asked him, "Did you come to see your guy destroyed?" But two days before the debate, Ted was brushing his teeth and turned to Vicki, "apropos of nothing," and told her, "I'm ready, you know." And Vicki said, "Yeah, I know," because "I did. I knew. You could just see it." *He was ready.*

And the afternoon of the debate, the debate that he knew could make or break his reelection chances, he and Vicki went to the John F. Kennedy Presidential Library, and he pulled up a chair out on the water side of the building and took out his thick briefing book and sat there, "just absorbing whatever inspiration he could invoke from his brother," Paul Kirk said. And then that night he and Vicki and Dave Burke were in the van on their way to the venue, Ted sitting in front still poring over his briefing books. Burke tried to break the tension and keep him loose—the most important thing they had learned in the campaign, he told Ted, was that the Roy Rogers restaurant on the Mass Turnpike didn't serve fried chicken until eleven a.m. The van's windows were steaming up on that hot and muggy fall night, steaming up in part because Ted was exuding such nervous energy. And the state police led the van toward the Hall, and when it pulled in, there were blue lights flashing, and a group of Teamsters and a group from the Carpenters Union were chanting his name and holding Ted Kennedy signs and, as Dave Burke recalled, were "ready to beat off anybody with a Romney sign." And the van crept through the crowds, huge crowds—a "mad scene," the police called it—with Ted rolling down the window and pumping his fist. And when he disembarked, those crowds enveloped him, and he was hot and his face florid, but he was hugging those supporters as he entered the hall. And Gerard Doherty, who had been there at the very beginning, at the very first debate with Ed McCormack, told him this: that he had done so well back then that all he had to do was be himself.

And then the moment arrived, under the glowering white marble bust of John Adams and under George Peter Alexander Healy's enormous painting of Daniel Webster, pictured in Ted's beloved Senate, replying to South Carolina senator Robert Hayne during a debate on the future of the Union—Romney thin, young, dark-haired; Ted fat, old, white-haired. (One of Romney's ads had shown Ted struggling to lower himself onto a park bench.) Three million Bay Staters were watching the face-off. The candidates sparred over why the race was so close when Ted had been in the Senate thirty-two years and had never faced a real contest. (Ted said it was about job uncertainty and anxiety, Romney because he was promising economic reinvigoration through the private sector.) They sparred over attack ads, with Ted saying that he would have thought Romney would be more interested in what to do for working families than in advertisements. They sparred over whether Romney had provided health insurance for his employees and whether Ted had provided it for part-time employees of the Merchandise Mart. They sparred. And Ted did not back down. The man who was so concerned about his inability to perform had gained confidence. He was steady now, forceful, fluid, composed, cogent, perhaps, above all, authoritative—in complete control. And Mitt Romney walked into his punches. As Shrum had anticipated, Romney brought up the profit that Ted had allegedly made by renting that Washington building to the government, and Ted counterpunched with a line he had used to good effect in an earlier debate: "Mr. Romney, the Kennedys are not in public service to make money. We have paid too high a price." Ted brought up healthcare, his signature issue, and, again following Shrum's advice, asked what plan Romney endorsed. And Romney walked right into another punch. Romney would *show* Ted the plan. "It isn't a question of showing *me* your paper," Ted bellowed, feigning high dudgeon. "It's a question of showing all the people in here that are watching the program your paper." And then Ted matter-of-factly, like a professor drilling a student, asked Romney the cost of his program. Romney didn't know. And

Ted asked him how the tax incentives in his program would impact the budget. Romney couldn't say, fumbling that he would have to go through it piece by piece if he were to provide that information. "That's what you have to do as a legislator," Ted said, as if flunking the student. And Shrum, who had been pacing throughout, knew at that point that Ted had scored his knockout. But it wasn't over. Ted asked Romney, who had professed to be a moderate, how he felt about the fact that if the Republicans were to win the Senate, Jesse Helms would chair the Foreign Relations Committee, and Orrin Hatch the Judiciary Committee, and Strom Thurmond the Armed Services Committee—all extreme conservatives. And Romney brushed it off, saying that he was not a partisan and that no one in Massachusetts really cared who ran those committees. To which Ted said that Romney would have to toe the Republican line—Bob Dole would *make* him toe the Republican line—because that was how the Senate was run. And when Romney, thinking he had gotten the better of Ted, snapped, "Is that the way you run your committee?" Ted, without hesitation, replied, "You bet I do!" because, he said, that was how things got done in the Senate. And finally Romney opened his last question to Ted by saying, "Women," to ask about the glass ceiling and the treatment of women. And again, Shrum felt shivers of relief. No one in the Senate had a stronger record on women's rights than Ted did now, and by bringing up the issue, Romney was only giving Ted an opportunity to expatiate on all the legislation he had passed to serve women's rights. "It was like pitching a slow ball over the plate to Babe Ruth," Shrum would tell biographer Burton Hersh. Gerard Doherty would use another analogy. "There are some people who, when the circumstances are mediocre, they can be mediocre," he observed. "But if it's do-or-die, they can catch the ball." Ted Kennedy caught the ball. And David Burke had another analogy still: "He may have been right out of central casting, but Romney had a glass jaw. He'd never been in a fight where someone could be as mean to him as he had been to others." "He killed him," Burke said of Ted. Ted said he knew as he stood there that his prospects had improved, and "you could feel in the room that the crowd was feeling that way too."

The "bigfeet" political reporters, as Richard Ben Cramer called them, were in attendance—R. W. Apple of *The New York Times,* David Broder of *The Washington Post,* Terence Smith of CBS among them—to witness what they thought might very well be an execution and the end of Ted Kennedy. But there would be no execution that night. Ted won. "Romney won points for earnestness and sincerity," Martin Nolan wrote in his post-mortem in the *Globe*, "but Kennedy won the expectations game by not showing up a stuttering wreck." This, however, understated Ted's accomplishment, as even Nolan would say. "The incumbent took his thirty-two years of experience, supposedly a set of handcuffs and leg irons, and fashioned them into cudgels to cuff about his rookie opponent." A WBZ poll showed that 40 percent of viewers thought Ted had won, only 24 percent Romney, and from a tight race, he now held a twenty-point lead over Romney. The next day Joe Kennedy II reported to Ted that "people were crossing the street to shake his hand, congratulating him on the great debate." Joe II would later tell Adam Clymer of the 1994 race, "People say the ads won it, or the money won it, or this. The fact is Teddy won that campaign at that first debate and in the first ten minutes of that debate."

But another *Boston Globe* veteran political reporter, Robert Healy, the man who had broken Ted's Harvard cheating scandal in 1962, thought the debate had larger ramifications than just seeming to ensure Ted's Senate reelection. He saw the battle between the young businessman and the quintessential liberal, the heir to his brothers' liberalism, as a battle for the future, even the very survival of liberalism. An "event that comes down the road but once in a decade," he wrote. The event, he continued, was "tied to the notion that Romney would destroy Kennedy and the old progressive who had fought consistently for liberal programs would come crashing down." And he asked: "If Ted Kennedy could not defeat Mitt Romney in Massachusetts, where else could a liberal politician survive?" But Ted Kennedy did not come crashing down. Ted Kennedy had defeated Mitt Romney and had not only saved liberalism to fight on, Healy thought, but also exposed the weaknesses of conservatism. "How does a Republican candidate running in a state where he must attract Democratic and independent votes square the bankrupt policies of Reaganomics, which resulted in one of the worst recessions since the '30s and changed the entire job structure of the nation, made millionaires out of venture capitalists who went to jail and still kept their great fortunes, and sent the bill to the public for one of the largest financial scandals of our government—the savings and loan crisis?" Healy asked in what was the question the liberals themselves had been asking. And the answer was: He couldn't.

By the second debate, two days later and less than two weeks before election day, the contest seemed over. "Ted Kennedy is one debate hour away from almost certain reelection," the director of the WBZ poll that had given Ted the twenty-point lead said, and he explained that Ted's lead was "across the board with virtually every group." This time the debate, in a town hall format with ordinary citizens asking the questions, was described as "anti-climactic." Ted was more subdued, "off stride," by one account, save when he explained to Romney that his prescriptions for welfare reform had already been enacted. Romney, realizing now that his bid was certain to fail after such soaring expectations, was snippy, and after Ted, thinking of his brothers' assassinations, answered a question about crime by saying his family had experienced crime, Romney cracked, "We heard that before. That's the last resort each time." It was a cruel rejoinder—the rejoinder of a man desperately hoping to land a punch. After this one, Ted emerged with a twenty-two-point lead. And Romney was not going to overcome it.

Ted spent election day out on the hustings, even handing out coffee at a New Bedford polling place, while Romney spent his day voting in Belmont, accompanied by his father, the former Michigan governor and one-time presidential aspirant George Romney, and watching his sons play football on the lawn. At ten that evening, with the expected defeat now certain, Romney took to the podium at the Westin Hotel and acknowledged that across the country, the "tide of change is rising," but not yet in Massachusetts, where he had spent $7 million, $3 million of it his own money, and where, as his campaign manager was to gripe, Ted brought in "all those former aides and consultants" and turned the race into an "onslaught." (Ted won 58.1 to 41 percent.) Ted delivered his victory speech an hour later at the Park Plaza Hotel, calling his win one for "those who believe we should have a voice and a vote and a fighter in the United States Senate," and thanking Vicki, the "love of my life" who has "made such a difference to me." "I may not be the youngest," he closed. "Eventually I'll be the thinnest. But I'm going to be the fightingest candidate that you ever had, and I won't let you down." Of the victory, Carey Parker would say, "Inevitably, the voters will choose the real thing."

It had been a terrifying campaign for him—a campaign in which Romney had seemed the preordained victor. The "battle of his political life," Adam Clymer wrote in *The New York Times*. And Ted had had to fight as he had never fought before, calling in reinforcements, running negative ads, staying on the attack, sweating in public. But in a time when Republicans had further succeeded in discrediting government, in a time when they had derailed healthcare and made Congress and the president both look incapacitated, Ted didn't abandon his faith in liberalism but instead embraced it. "The '60s liberal agenda hasn't worked," Romney told voters. To which Ted said, "I stand for the idea that public service can make a difference in the lives of people. I reject the laissez-faire notion that all government has to do is get out of the way, and kind, caring, generous, unselfish, wealthy private interests and power will see to it that prosperity trickles down to ordinary people." Ted had won on that basis before, even as the country took its alleged rightward swing. But it was different this time because now he wasn't coasting on his brothers' legacy; he was rising on his own. "It was the first election he knew was a personal victory," one of his campaign aides, Charles Baker, was to say, "not one he got because he was Edward Kennedy, Brother of . . . He hadn't let down his family or staff or all the people who believed in him. It was probably his most fulfilling victory ever." *His own victory.* And the same note was sounded that Thanksgiving, when Ted invited some friends to join his family. And the day after Thanksgiving, he was to recall, when Vicki had made turkey gumbo and turkey tetrazzini, and the guests toasted Ted for his victory, he said modestly that his family had won, not he, which had been his customary response, his customary feeling. But Vicki wouldn't have it. "Bullshit!" she said. "You know, Teddy, if you had lost, it would've been you that lost. It wouldn't have been your family that lost. You would've lost." And she said, "You won. You won! Not your family. You." And Ted made an admission years later in his memoir that "it was something he needed to hear—perhaps one I'd yearned to hear." "Outliving Family Charisma," the *Globe* had bitingly titled a piece on him earlier that year. Now he had. But in doing so, he had finally established himself as himself. The man who had been learning how *not* to be a Kennedy, despite his deep and abiding love for his family, had proved himself at the ballot box. Vicki was right. *He* won, no one else.

IV

But if his was a victory for himself, it was because it was a triumph of his life in politics—not of ideology or promises or history but of the things he had accomplished for the people of Massachusetts and of the things he was. The "Senate's last great liberal lion rarely mentions the causes of social and economic justice around which he has built one of the most impressive legislative records in American history," *The Economist* noted that fall. "Instead, he talks pork. At stop after stop, he recounts the cash he has delivered to the state (a point illustrated with mock blow-ups of federal cheques) and suggests that without him in Washington, the local economy will suffer." And to the notion that if Ted were to lose, the liberal era would lose along with him, *The Economist* said, "Judging from his timid conduct on the campaign trail, it already has." This was not, however, timidity; it was what Ted Kennedy did. It was good politics, obviously, but also love for his state and its people. He delivered. He delivered $17 million for a prison at Fort Devens. He delivered for a defense training center that would provide several hundred jobs after a defense accounting center for Southbridge had fallen through and President Clinton awarded that consolation prize since Ted had worked so tirelessly on healthcare. He delivered billions of dollars for the "Big Dig" that put a highway artery underneath central Boston. "To me, the sublime trick in Washington is not to do anything in the Appropriations Subcommittee, not to do anything in the Appropriations Committee, not to do anything when the bill in on the floor," said reporter John A. Farrell, "but somehow, either because you're in the conference committee or somebody else is on the conference committee who owes you a favor, out of nowhere the bill comes out to be voted on in three hours at the end of a session—bing, bang—and the next day you wake up and find out that there has been $20 million inserted in there for Boston University, and you sort of say, 'Where the hell did that come from?' It was Teddy pulling a favor at the last minute." Even though he was, by all rights, a national senator, he never forgot Massachusetts. His Labor Committee chief counsel, Thomas Rollins, once asked Ted how he managed to work on massive national programs that were not directly connected to the state. "He said, 'The first thing you always do is take care of your base. Massachusetts, number one. Massachusetts, first. If there is something we can do for Massachusetts, we are there for Massachusetts, and they understand they are first." And with that understanding, he continued, "They'll let you go do that other stuff."

And over all those years, in thousands of ways, he demonstrated to those constituents that he belonged to Massachusetts as Mitt Romney, a relative newcomer and a venture capitalist to boot, never could. Ted was one of them, shouting to a group of construction workers when he was driving by, "Listen, you fellows go take the rest of the day off. Tell 'em the Senator said it was OK." One of them, telling a woman at the Dimrock Community Health Center in Roxbury who explained her problems in getting child care and asked him if he knew what it was like to be unemployed, "Oh, I do. Some people think I've never had a job." One of them, when Romney staged a campaign event in Dorchester where houses were boarded up and called it "Kennedy country," and Ted's office got Mayor Thomas Menino to go to the area and decry Romney for insulting the neighborhood. Always one of them.

And more, much more, there were all those kindnesses over those thirty-two years in the Senate, tens of thousands of them—the letters, the phone calls out of the blue to people who had suffered a loss or cherished a victory, the home visits. And people remembered. "He was the best politician I ever met," Tad Devine would say. "Kennedy was great because he loved people and he loved politics," which was why it must have been so disheartening to him when, early in the campaign, the people no longer seemed to love him back, when they turned on him. But he had that long reserve of good feeling on which to draw, and eventually they remembered, and eventually they forgave him in large part because they did love him and in large part because he was right about his opponent and the Republicans: Mitt Romney might not have been a bad man or the callous, unfeeling one that Ted portrayed him as being, but he would never be as big-hearted or as feeling as their now-overweight, bumptious senator, never a man who could speak to the needs of his constituents as movingly as he spoke to the needs of his own pocketbook, never one of them. Asked at the first debate to describe his failings, Ted fumbled and rambled—he said the question surprised him—then settled on all the ways he had managed to disappoint people, and then he turned to Vicki, who, he said, had saved him. Romney spoke about how he took a day each week from his work to help people, a self-aggrandizing answer, before being reminded that it was his *failings* he was being asked about—to which Romney revised his answer to say that he never felt he had helped people enough—a saccharine answer even if a true one. Ted had many failings, but his constituents forgave him because when the father of a man from Allston-Brighton who had worked years ago in his campaigns died, Ted Kennedy suddenly appeared at the wake in their house—the kind of a house that had a picture of the pope and John Kennedy hanging on the wall—and sat down next to the widow at her kitchen table and took her hand and stayed with her for four and a half hours. They forgave him because when the daughter of Don Dowd, a man who had been with Ted as everything from a campaign aide to a driver, suddenly died, Ted got on a plane from

Washington, even though there was an important vote in the Senate later that day, and flew up to Hartford, then was driven to West Springfield, visited the family, and flew back again. They forgave him because when a woman whose young nephew had Hodgkin's disease and was taking an experimental drug and then suddenly had the drug withdrawn, and whose only hope, she felt, was Ted Kennedy—when that woman phoned Gerard Doherty, whom she knew, and asked him if he might ask for Ted's assistance, which he did, and then later found out that Ted was discussing the FDA budget with a bureaucrat in Ted's office, and he told the bureaucrat that he would love to help solve their budget problems but that there was this boy he had to see first and . . . the bureaucrat reinstituted the experimental therapy. They forgave him because after Ken Jones of Wenham lost his son when terrorists planted a bomb on Pan Am Flight 103 and it exploded over Lockerbie, Scotland, Ted assigned a staff member to handle the problems and then met personally with the families ("It wasn't like he was looking at his watch," Jones said) and talked about his own losses with them to help them with theirs, and then would call Jones ("Ken, this is Ted—Ted Kennedy") or send him notes, "at a time when caring mattered."

They always forgave him. And they forgave him on election day in 1994.

The rest of the country was not so forgiving. Ted had won. And Patrick had won his House seat—he and Ted were hardly on speaking terms at the time, and Patrick hadn't sought his father's blessing to run—and Patrick would take his oath in January wearing a pinstripe suit that Ted had bought him for Christmas, accompanied by Ted, who called himself the "proudest father in America," and with Joan and Kara and Kara's infant daughter looking on in the gallery, while tears welled in Patrick's eyes. (Their estrangement would end when Ted showed up at the White House only to find his son meeting with the president.) But while Ted and Patrick won, their fellow Democrats had taken a drubbing. Ted had been focused on his own race, and as Carey Parker recalled, "He was as surprised and appalled as anyone to wake up and find out that he was no longer the chairman of his committee. It was a thunderbolt." On November 8, Democrats lost fifty-four seats in the House, including that of Speaker Thomas Foley, and Republicans gained a majority there for the first time since 1954. Democrats lost every contested governorship—eleven. And Republicans won eight seats in the Senate, which gave them control there as well. A "tide election" was the indisputable outcome—the worst election loss Democrats had suffered since 1946, even worse than 1980, where they had at least retained the House. "We got the living daylights beat out of us" was how Bill Clinton characterized the defeat.

Democrats had lost because the North American Free Trade Act, which Ted had reluctantly supported, angered labor. They had lost because the National Rifle Association, which had unsuccessfully opposed a Clinton-backed ban on assault weapons, and the Christian Coalition, which reviled Democrats as un-Christian, had been especially active in ginning up the Republican base. They had lost because Clinton's economic plan included a gas tax and a tax on Social Security for upper-income Americans, which allowed Republicans to yet again denounce Democrats as "tax and spend." They had lost because of a scandal in the House about a bank there that provided free loans to members and that took down one of the chamber's most powerful Democrats, Dan Rostenkowski, the chairman of the Ways and Means Committee. They had lost because of the failure of healthcare—an enormous stain on the idea of active government—and because, as Clinton himself admitted, he kept pushing for some compromise rather than hold the bill until after the election and look for a bipartisan solution when election fevers had broken. Instead, the Democratic defeat left Americans, most of whom wanted some form of health reform, feeling lost, disappointed, and frustrated, and they didn't blame the Republicans, who had vowed to stop any reform, but Clinton, who had promised and pushed it. They had lost, Clinton believed, because of poor messaging that failed to tout all of his accomplishments. They had lost because of a new media ecology in which radio talk show hosts spent hours upon hours each day demonizing Democrats to a receptive audience, inciting conservatives. And they had lost because the fifty-one-year-old Republican House minority whip, Newt Gingrich, a no-holds-barred ideologue and opportunist, had, as Clinton conceded, "proved to be a better politician than I was." Gingrich had announced with great fanfare late that September—the same day that George Mitchell threw in the towel on passing a healthcare bill—a "Contract with America," which was a promise of structural reforms including term limits; a list of legislative initiatives, including an amendment to the Constitution that would require a balanced budget; a crime bill that would strengthen sentencing, broaden the death penalty, and authorize more funds for building prisons; welfare reform that would terminate recipients after two years; a reduction in funding to the United Nations and a proscription against putting American troops in UN peacekeeping missions; a moratorium on federal regulations; and the weakening of product liability laws and punitive damages. Whether the Contract actually changed votes—it came late in the campaign, and most Americans had no idea what was in it—it changed the political contours of midterm elections by making each House race a subset of a larger race against the Democrats, a national race using a single national message. As Bill Clinton would put it, "The nationalization of midterm elections was Newt Gingrich's major contribution to modern electioneering." Tip O'Neill had famously said that "all politics is local." Now they weren't.

But there was more to the loss than messaging. Ted had won in a liberal state by pushing the effectiveness of government and by relying on his own goodwill. For years, the ongoing conservative attacks on government had destroyed any faith in its effectiveness; by the 1994 midterms, Americans' belief that government did "what is right" either "most of the time" or "always" had plummeted to a historically low point of less than 20 percent. And there was no goodwill on which to fall back. Ted, during the debate, had spoken of anxiety. Americans, particularly white Americans, were anxious not just about the economy but about the direction of the culture. Asked by Arthur Schlesinger, Jr., why Southern white males felt such antipathy to Bill Clinton, who was one of them, Hodding Carter, a progressive Democrat who had grown up in Mississippi, told him, "They look back with longing at the good old days—the days when abortion was in the back alley, gays were in the closet, women were in the kitchen, blacks were in the back of the bus and condoms were under the counter." That was an America that Democratic liberals had not only threatened and tried to transform; it was an America that conservative Republicans were promising to restore. Black people were especially reviled. A report by pollster Stanley Greenberg, commissioned by the Michigan Democratic Party in 1985, found that Democratic defectors to the Republican Party "express a profound distaste for blacks, a sentiment that pervades almost everything about government and politics. Blacks constitute the explanation for their vulnerability, and for most everything that has gone wrong in their lives." Writing after the 1994 debacle, Greenberg attributed it to something else: Bill Clinton's abandonment of the middle class, though, again, it seemed only the white middle class whom he thought Clinton had abandoned. He had promised, Greenberg said, a middle-class tax cut and not delivered on the promise, so that while taxes rose on the middle class in his first term, incomes remained static. It was yet again an election of resentments, in a country that had been living within its resentments for a long time. Liberalism presented itself as being about hope—about all the things that could be accomplished. But there was little hope in America, little faith that anything could change for the better.

Once again, the pundits wrote obituaries for liberalism. And Republicans gloated, no one more than Newt Gingrich, who said that he was now prepared, as Joe Klein of *Newsweek* put it, to "dismantle the welfare-state bureaucracy brick by brick," and boasted, "I am a transformational figure. I'm a much tougher partisan than they've seen . . . much more intense, much more persistent, much more willing to take risks to get it done." "Open warfare against the Democrats," the new Senate minority leader, Tom Daschle, called Gingrich's declaration. Partisanship might have grown in Congress during the Republican years. Comity might have diminished. Compromises, the lifeblood of Ted Kennedy's politics, might have become much harder to broker. The Republicans would just as soon filibuster as find a middle way, and filibuster was exactly what they had threatened to do to Clinton's healthcare plan, even though a few rogue Republican moderates, like Chafee and Danforth, had still held out hope for some agreement. But, as Daschle was to say, despite the very real divisions that had developed in the Senate and perhaps with misplaced optimism, "a sense of decency and decorum still ruled the public debate." But that was before Newt Gingrich. With Gingrich's victory, with Gingrich's ascendency, since he was rewarded as the architect of the party's victory with the speakership of the House, decency and decorum were gone. "Our differences, according to them, were no longer political. They were moral," Daschle lamented, though this had actually been true for a long time. "We Democrats were not only wrong or misguided, now we were 'evil.'" And Daschle said that this was "unprecedented in American politics"—though it wasn't entirely unprecedented; again, the Republicans had been heading in that direction since Nixon. It would make the 1994 midterms, in the assessment of journalist James Traub, the "most consequential non-presidential election of the twentieth century"—the election that not only ended the congressional hegemony of Democrats that had begun with Franklin Roosevelt, but that also ended the norms of congressional politics altogether.

No Republican now dared cross Gingrich and his army of rabid conservative politicos. According to Nick Littlefield, ten days after the election, Republicans in the House distributed questionnaires to their staffers to guarantee that any new hires would commit themselves to a series of ideological litmus tests: no abortion, with the only exception being rape; no racial preferences for hiring; prayer in schools; a ban on gays in the military; and denial that individuals had a right to healthcare. The belligerence and uniformity that Gingrich imposed upon the House soon descended upon the Senate as well. When, a few months later, Senator Mark Hatfield, the new chair of the Finance Committee, voted against the balanced budget amendment, the Republican conference decided to have committee chairs chosen by the caucus by secret ballot.

But it wasn't just war against political norms that Gingrich was promising to wage. "Put simply," the political columnist E. J. Dionne, Jr., would say of the new Republican cadre, "they legitimized war on the state." Gingrich would institute a "starve the beast" mentality, Carey Parker said. "They wanted to reduce the role of government, and they felt the most effective way to do it was to reduce discretionary spending in a range of programs. They wouldn't try to repeal the program, but they could cut the budget, and sometimes severely cut it in a number of programs." And nothing was sacrosanct, not even Medicare, which was often called the "third rail in American politics" because any politician who touched it was likely to be electrocuted. Gingrich would touch it. In the House, which Gingrich now ruled, the majority could stop any legislation. In the Senate, the filibuster, which had been used sparingly in the past, would become the tool of obstruction so that nothing could be done, and government would be made even more impotent. And it wasn't only the norms and the state that Gingrich was pledged to battle and destroy. It was the culture that he felt had given rise to the liberalism he so detested. "Counterculture McGovernicks," he labeled Bill and Hillary Clinton after George McGovern, the 1972 Democratic presidential candidate who had been elevated by the Democratic left. Elitists, he branded them, in what had increasingly become the conservative club used to wallop Democrats, the idea being that the only real Americans were rural and small-town and white and conservative—also an old idea. As historian Steve Gillon concisely put it of Gingrich, "His mandate, he declared, was to uproot the permissive 1960s culture, and the elites who supported it, and replace it with a new culture that stressed moral character"—the same morality Reagan and his evangelical allies had trumpeted, not the tolerant, compassionate morality one usually thought of when one invoked the word, but the strident, intolerant moralism that had come to replace it. "The core of his argument," Bill Clinton was to write of Gingrich, echoing Daschle, was "not just that his ideas were better than ours; he said that his *values* were better than ours because Democrats were weak on family, work, welfare, crime, and defense, and because, being crippled by the self-indulgent sixties, we couldn't draw distinctions between right and wrong." Gingrich, who abhorred moral relativism, which he saw as one of the cardinal sins of liberals and who had dubbed himself a "transformational figure," was going to transform the politics of America, the government of America, and finally the values of America. It was an agenda more ambitious even than that of Ronald Reagan, a grand, fiery, ferocious culmination of Nixon's positive polarization but without the liberal policy preemption with which Nixon hoped to circumvent Ted Kennedy and his liberal allies, and of Reagan's political realignment and moral recalibration but without the genial Reagan's politesse that had camouflaged his aggression and tempered his assault. Newt Gingrich would not preempt and would not temper. Newt Gingrich had one last, overarching ambition—the conservatives' long-standing ambition: He would drive a stake through the heart of liberalism once and for all.

SEVENTEEN

Stiffening Their Spines

BILL CLINTON WAS bereft at the midterm election results. "I was profoundly distressed," he would later write in his memoir, "far more than I ever let on in public." Hillary Clinton seemed beyond bereft. Weeping, she told a Clinton political adviser, Dick Morris, "I don't know which direction is up or down. Everything I thought was right was wrong." Among liberals, there was an all-too-familiar sense of despair, panic, and worst of all, retreat. Democrats had long flirted with abandoning the principles that had built the modern party, and many had come to feel that a vigorous, activist government was outmoded and no longer appealed to the electorate. The midterms, with a sense of déjà vu, seemed an awful confirmation of their fears. The Clintons had never been seen as ardent liberals to begin with; to those on the left, they were centrists and temporizers. Bill Clinton was always searching for accommodation, no doubt because he thought he needed to—his Third Way split the difference between liberals and conservatives—but the idea that he might now move further right shook the old liberal establishment. Senator John Kerry once told Bob Shrum, "The only thing the Clintons care about is themselves and power," and power now seemed to rest with coming to terms with the right.

When it came to the midterms, Ted was no less frustrated than the Clintons and no less concerned about the possible effects of the elections than his fellow fervent leftist. As Nick Littlefield recalled, "Immediately upon getting back to Washington, we were beginning to hear from other Democrats, 'Oh, my god. We have to change everything. We have to be more like the Republicans. We have to abandon our advocacy of the working people in face of tax cuts and smaller government.'" Some Democrats, in the wake of defeat, decided to abandon politics altogether. "There were senators who were thinking, 'I'm going to retire in a couple of years. This isn't a place I want to be anymore,'" Carey Parker said. But Ted Kennedy never considered retreat. On the contrary, his own come-from-behind victory had revitalized him, friends and family said, "allowed him to reconnect with his reasons for believing in public service," as one reporter put it. He began meeting with his staff as soon as the elections were over, and as Littlefield told it, he was girding for battle again. Ted told them, "I just got reelected by standing up for what Democrats have always believed in," and he spent the time between the elections and the seating of the new Congress in January in "full throttle," according to Littlefield, "persuading people to stand up against the Republicans and defend against Gingrich, and also laying the groundwork to go forward with his own positive agenda around health care and the minimum wage." But even as he tried to rouse the liberal forces, Ted was not blind to the fact that the midterms had been an earthquake, that they had shaken Democratic faith, that they had shown it wasn't enough for Democrats to plow forward and that they had to regroup around something. The question was what they could regroup around. So he also spent that interim doing what he had often done when he waded into legislative combat: He conducted what Littlefield called a "meetings tour," really a revival of his old issues dinners, in which he sat down with leading liberal politicians, academics, historians, and policy experts to examine the reasons for Gingrich's success and to find a way forward from it. Why had liberals, who had fought so hard for the workingman and -woman and for the poor and the dispossessed, failed to convince their fellow Americans that the government was working for them, not against them? And more plainly and practically: How did one save the Democratic Party from Newt Gingrich?

To beat Newt Gingrich, or at least impede him—that was now the mission, as it had been with Nixon, Reagan, and Bush. But because Gingrich had already beaten the Democrats politically, Ted knew he had to beat him with ideas. So now, the Sunday after Thanksgiving, Ted began an intense investigation to find those ideas—the ideas around which Democrats could regroup. (Actually, he was hoping to reformulate the traditional liberal ideas.) He met first with historians Alan Brinkley of Columbia University, and Doris Kearns Goodwin, and with Robert Kuttner, the editor of *The American Prospect*, a progressive journal, at a hotel in downtown Boston. Goodwin said the problem was that the Republicans had come to own traditional values and personal responsibility and had sullied Democrats as indulgent and profligate. Democrats needed to change that narrative, though she also felt that this would not be easy since conservatives had the more effective messaging with their radio talk shows. Brinkley argued that there was a gap between the perception that government is corrupt and the things that government managed to accomplish, and Democrats had to close that gap. Kuttner said the primary issue was the lack of faith that working families had in government, and that Democrats had to "rub the faces of the Republicans" in the fact that "Democratic programs were designed to help working people and Republican programs weren't." But everyone agreed on this: that Clinton now might be frightened to fight for liberalism. "What people find most troubling about Clinton is that they don't know if there's anything he'd go to the mat or fight to the death for," Brinkley told Ted. And with Clinton's tenacity in doubt, Brinkley said, Ted had to "keep the spirits of the Democrats up. The Democratic base is at a moment when it is dying to be energized." Ted was the hope. Ted was the cheerleader.

He kept meeting. He met with Robert Coles, the Harvard psychologist, who told Ted that "Republicans cultivate groups for middle-class Americans to hate." He called it the "politics of envy and resentment and hate" and said he had heard it "in the homes of people who have nothing to gain from Republicans and everything to gain from Democrats," but they "hate the liberal elite, Harvard and the *Boston Globe.*" (Coles, of course, was a member of that elite.) He met with Michael Sandel, a young Harvard political philosopher, who told him that once the New Deal had passed, the dominant issues of political life were no longer programs but values—community, citizenship, a sense of belonging, and the feeling that Americans were losing control of their lives. And Sandel felt that Republicans had learned how to tap into those fears and frustrations and Democrats hadn't. That had to change. He met with economists George Perry of the Brookings Institution, and Robert Reischauer, the former head of the Congressional Budget Office, and this time it was Ted asking them why, when the economy was rising and business profits were high, ordinary Americans hadn't benefited. And he met with the legendary economist John Kenneth Galbraith, a longtime Kennedy adviser, at Galbraith's Victorian home in Cambridge, and Galbraith spent an hour talking about voter turnout and economic inequality and inflation and globalization and the so-called "burden" of the government, as conservatives liked to call government activism, and Littlefield remembered Galbraith saying sarcastically, "Government is always a burden when it's helping people with health care or education, but it's never a burden when it's spending money on defense contracts or shoring up the oil industry." He met with pollster Robert Blendon, who told him that Clinton's healthcare plan had failed because people were frightened by too much reform all at once and because people with healthcare didn't believe that there were people with jobs who didn't have it, and they were less inclined to support the uninsured who were unemployed. Littlefield said that Ted reached out to "everybody he had talked to over his career who was around, who could be reached"—between fifty and one hundred people, at breakfasts, lunches, dinners, at his house and at hotels and in offices— reached out to them to learn how to parry Newt Gingrich.

And having met with those experts, Ted met with his Senate colleagues—with Tom Daschle, who had just beaten Ted's closest friend in the chamber, Chris Dodd, for the Democratic leadership (by a single vote), and with House minority leader Richard Gephardt, and with other Democratic members of the House—"taking their temperature," Littlefield said, letting them know that he had not lost faith, laying down his marker, asking them to join him in challenging the Republican agenda. Daschle said Ted had told him that when Daschle went to see the president to discuss the legislative agenda, he should say, "We work with you, not for you," and that the congressional Democrats and the president could work together on a legislative program. But Ted did more than rally those legislators. He invigorated them and stiffened their spines. "They needed to see that people like Kennedy would not simply stand their old ground and say nothing," Carey Parker recalled, "but would instead say, 'We'll find a new way forward that will bring us closer to our goals. We won't give up or give in. Eventually we'll find a solution to these problems, and if we have to compromise now in order to do it, so be it.'" And Parker said of Ted's approach, "We won't treat this period as just an interregnum in which we wait until we regain the majority. We can show the country that our principles and our ideals are still the direction we need to move in." But Ted Kennedy understood this too: It wasn't about legislation; it was about the kinds of feelings that propelled legislation. Those feelings had changed. Asked by Adam Clymer near the end of his Senate campaign what he worried about most, Ted said, "The breakdown in the community of caring." He told Clymer that he had spent most of the past thirty years fighting for individual rights and liberties, but he acknowledged that there had been an unintended consequence of that fight: "people are focused on themselves and their own individual rights and their own individual liberties," and they had lost a sense of common good and common purpose. "We have to get back in touch with our sense of community," he told Clymer. Without that, there was no hope of beating Newt Gingrich and the conservatives, no hope of restoring liberalism. We had to learn to be good again, to be selfless, to be moral.

Of all the people who Ted thought needed their spines stiffened, the most important was the president of the United States. "I don't think he was concerned that Clinton would jump onboard the Gingrich ship," Carey Parker said. "The question was, 'How far do we have to move to compromise?' " But Nick Littlefield read it differently. He thought that Ted believed Clinton was ready to cave to the Republicans to save his political skin, and Ted wanted to do everything he possibly could to talk him out of it. Clinton was scheduled to make a brief radio address on December 15, his first since the election, an address in which it was assumed that he would deliver his response to the Republican victory, and Ted wanted to speak with him before he did to head him off from making concessions. But Ted didn't go directly to Clinton; he felt, as he had when he approached the president over the Breyer nomination, that the last person who spoke to Clinton before he made a decision had the greatest effect on him because Clinton was likely to change his mind. In the meantime, Ted prepared. Having completed his "meetings tour," he now met with administration officials to get a bead on what Clinton might do either to appease Gingrich or to challenge him and to lobby them to support his own policies. The director of the Office of Management and Budget, Alice Rivlin, told him that Clinton was now leaning toward deficit reduction and a middle-class tax cut, which would likely mean cutting social programs to pay for it, and transferring power to the states, which left Ted less than enthused, but she also told Ted to impress upon Clinton how much budget austerity had cost Jimmy Carter in his standing with his own party and how Ted had won by not conceding to the Republicans. Chief of Staff Leon Panetta listened patiently and approvingly as Ted told him Clinton should not touch Medicare, even though Gingrich was making it a whipping boy. Vice President

Albert Gore, and George Stephanopoulos, who was a senior adviser to the president, and deputy White House chief of staff Harold Ickes, who was a former Kennedy aide, and Secretary of Labor Robert Reich—Ted spoke with them many times late that November and early that December to urge them to urge the president to hold the line. What he came away with from all these meetings was a read on Clinton that he would use to try to sway him. The read was that even though Ted, on his "meetings tour," had solicited ideas about how to confront the Republicans, Clinton, understandably given that he would be running in two years, would be far more interested in politics than in ideas. Ted had to convince Clinton that it was good *politics* to promote the liberal agenda, and that Democrats had lost, as Ted had often said of past defeats, not because they were too liberal but because they had run away from their liberalism, while Ted had won by embracing his. It was, Littlefield was to say, an assiduous preparation for a detailed presentation. Ted and his staff worked on it for weeks, realizing it was the only chance they might have to guide Clinton's agenda—the only and last chance to stiffen the president's spine.

The meeting, which Littlefield would call "one of the most unforgettable moments" in the ten years he spent on Ted's staff, occurred not in the Oval Office, where meetings were usually held, but in Clinton's private office in his residence, an overstuffed room with the aura of history, on the night of December 13, two days before Clinton's radio address. Clinton, Chief of Staff Panetta, deputy chief of staff Ickes, director of legislative affairs Pat Griffin, Littlefield, and Ted sat around a coffee table. Ted had brought a three-page outline—a "fighting document," one reporter would later call it. But before Ted could even begin his presentation, Clinton said that he knew what Ted was going to say: that the administration should "stick with the working family themes"—the themes that Ted had used so effectively in his own campaign. Clinton was right. Fight for working families, Ted told Clinton. Lay out policies to show the commitment to working families: no cuts to Medicare (the Republicans were threatening cuts); a new healthcare proposal that would be targeted to children (moderate Republicans like John Chafee had already told Ted any healthcare plans were unlikely to pass); no cuts to education (the Republicans were threatening cuts and had vowed to disband the Department of Education, a longtime goal); a raise in the minimum wage (Republicans had talked about indexing capital gains to inflation for stockholders but had vehemently opposed raising the minimum wage for ordinary citizens); new funding for food stamps (Republicans wanted to cut the program) and aid to children (Gingrich had cited the Boys Town orphanage as a solution to welfare). He told him to think of the budget he was about to propose as a political weapon aimed at Republicans who were willing to strip away anything that benefited ordinary Americans and poor Americans. Reveal Republicans for the extremists they were and emphasize that every dollar taken from a social program was a dollar taken by Republicans. And Ted reiterated the political point: He had done this in his own campaign and won. Not doing so, he argued, would alienate the base of the Democratic Party—Rivlin's suggestion. "Hard to head into 1996," he told Clinton, clearly hoping to strike a nerve, "without enthusiastic support of our base." But Clinton, about whom the liberals had been so concerned, was as adept as Ted at political disarmament. Rather than stonewall him or challenge him, he engaged him, even embroidering upon some of Ted's proposals—why not make college expenses tax deductible? he asked— engaged him for over an hour, despite the fact that Clinton was supposed to be attending a Christmas party.

And now, in the two days after the meeting, Ted Kennedy waited— waited for the speech that would set the direction of Clinton's next two years and waited to see if his presentation, for which he had spent a month in preparation, had had any effect on the man whose spine needed stiffening.

Ted and his staff huddled in Ted's office, listening as Clinton spoke. The president began by decrying how wages had remained stagnant even as the economy had grown and jobs had been added: "Economic statistics are moving up, most of our living standards aren't." And to meet that situation, he proposed what he called a "Middle-Class Bill of Rights," in contrast to Gingrich's Contract with America—a bill of rights that proposed a tax deduction for college tuition (the idea he had raised with Ted at their meeting two days earlier), a tax cut for the parents of all children under thirteen, an expansion of Individual Retirement Accounts so that the middle class would benefit, and funding for job training programs that would be given as vouchers so that individuals could choose training for themselves. And he extended an olive branch to the Republicans, asking them to "put aside the politics of personal destruction and demonization." It wasn't everything for which Ted Kennedy had asked. But it allayed his deepest fears. He would not be fighting alone, and he would not be fighting against his own administration, as he had had to do so often with Jimmy Carter. Ted had been told he was the hope of liberalism. And now, after the Democrats' stunning defeat, he was also something else: He was hopeful.

II

If the last remnants of the old political order had fallen with the midterm elections, the Kennedy dynastic family order also fell as the new Congress was being installed. The Kennedys had been the product of Joe and Rose—of his sense of muscular competition and stoicism and her sense of aesthetics and decorum. Both the virtues and vices of the family were endowed by them and passed from generation to generation, even as the two of them had faded. Joe Kennedy's stroke in 1961 had rendered him not only mute but also ghostly for nearly a decade before he died. It cost him his role as the family regent. But Rose Kennedy had endured as the matriarch, after she passed into her nineties and after a series of "pencil strokes" in the late 1970s robbed her of her lucidity. Though she was well into her dotage, Ted honored her position—honored it despite the fact that she had been a distant mother, a largely uncaring mother, a mother who would rather gallivant around Europe and buy clothes than look after her children, a mother who was still scolding her senator son for lapses in grammar when he was into his fifties. Those who saw them together in her later years remarked on their relationship, which was not the typical relationship of son to mother. Barbara Gibson, who had worked as Rose's secretary from 1974 to 1977, called their relationship "flirtatious," and wrote, "She always wanted him to see her as special." When her daughters paid her a visit, Gibson said, Rose was perfectly satisfied wearing a nightgown or pajamas. But when Ted visited her, "She would put on one of her colorful suits from Courrèges, add a matching wide-brimmed hat, and modify her voice so it was girlish." And Gibson wrote, "They were more like close friends who knew how to make each other laugh than mother and son." Rita Dallas, Joe's nurse, observed that "Teddy was always open and spontaneous with his mother." Her other children never teased her. Teddy would, grabbing her around the waist "in a hearty bear hug," and then laugh, "How's my girl? Havin' any fun?" And Dallas said that Rose would giggle.

And Ted was the child who visited her most after her husband's death when she was usually alone in Palm Beach or the Cape, and he doted on her when he did. A family friend told biographer Burton Hersh that the "first thing he would do at Hyannis Port was put down his briefcase"—the ever-present Bag—"and go to her room." And the friend said that you would then hear his "booming voice": *"Hello, Muthah, we're here for the weekend."* His father-in-law Edmund Reggie recalled that before Ted married Vicki, he would visit them on Nantucket and drink and dance and carouse. But then the time would come, usually midafternoon, when he would depart for Hyannis because he said he had to play the piano for his mother. (Actually, he hired a musician to play.) Elizabeth Shannon, whom Ted dated in the 1980s, said that on Saturdays at Hyannis in the summer, at precisely six o'clock—because the family had been bequeathed that punctuality by Joe Kennedy—everyone would congregate in the living room of the Big House, all of them well dressed, and then Rose, also well dressed and well coiffed, and with makeup and jewelry, would be brought down from upstairs in the elevator and wheeled in, and they would all drink (now that Joe was gone), and Ted would hold her hand and sing to her, old Irish songs and songs from her youth. She loved to sing, too. They sang "Sweet Rosie O'Grady," which must have reminded her of herself, and Ted would later recall that when she finished, "her voice would lilt and her eyes would flash, and she would ask if we would like to hear it one more time. And we always would." Or they would sing "Sweet Adeline," the song her father, Honey Fitz, had sung on the campaign trail and that Ted had adopted as his own. And Ted would sit next to her and tell her that he had seen some old friends of hers—friends from forty years past—and they had told him how beautiful she had looked at that party and how they wished he would take them to the party—fantasies he spun for her. And she would smile and snap out of her dementia and tell him, "Well, you'll have your hands full." During holidays, Ted and Eunice would wheel her around and fabricate quotes that she had allegedly said to maintain the image of the old, feisty Rose Kennedy who had become legendary with her son's presidency: "I'm like old wine—they don't bring me out very often, but I'm well-preserved." And on Sundays, he would invite a priest to the home to celebrate Mass.

But there was another side to their relationship, less tender, more tense. "Ambivalent," Elizabeth Shannon would call Ted's feelings toward his mother, and though she didn't say it, Rose's to him. Harvard Law professor Laurence Tribe recalled visiting the family at a time when Rose was still sentient and being "struck by what a complicated role he played" in it, meaning Ted. He said that Rose was "merciless with him, joking in various ways, making fun of him." And later, after a few drinks, Ted would open up, this time less jokingly. "Mom, you always left me behind." "Family tensions" was how Tribe described them. She was always admonishing Ted, correcting his grammar, telling him how to pronounce *nuclear*, schooling him in when to use *whom* and when *who*, reproaching him for applauding during the State of the Union address or for using the word *ass*. ("You will be pleased to know that I have taken your last admonition to heart and have used the word 'ass' only once," he wrote her back.) But in a reproach of his own, he had framed one of his mother's report cards from tenth grade in which she got a C– in algebra—and which he had circled in red—and wrote, "What happened, mother?" During those visits to the Big House, he would also bring along videotapes and news clips to show her what he was doing—still trying to win her respect, still trying to prove he was not the least.

Hard, tough, demanding she was, and remote. "Indomitable for all her days," Ted would say of her. The world had not conformed to her wishes, largely because her husband was not the kind of man to abide by her strictures, mostly religious, and because he was not the kind of man to be faithful. And it did not conform to her wishes for another reason: Fate had taken her three eldest sons, and her second-eldest daughter, and had impaired her eldest daughter. As a result, she had undergone a kind of "self-hypnosis," as her ghostwriter put it, which allowed her to deny the tragedies that didn't comport with her vision. She lived within her dreams and within her faith, and when Ted was to say of her that "she was ambitious not for our success, but for our souls," he was speaking less of her interest in her children's spiritual life than in their hard, dogmatic religious life. But as cold and aloof and prudish as she was, she was the last binding force in the Kennedy family. And they gathered that cold, windy, dark afternoon of January 22, at the compound in Hyannis to bid farewell to their 104-year-old matriarch, who lay dying of pneumonia. Ted called her death an "even more heartbreaking blow than I could have anticipated," and said he felt as if the "legs had been knocked out from under me." It was all Ted now—Ted alone at the head of the family.

He eulogized her at St. Stephen's, the church in which she had been baptized. (He received communion because the church had finally annulled his marriage to Joan, she said on the basis that he had never intended to be faithful to her.) He said that his father was the "spark" of the Kennedy family, but his mother was the "light," and that if he was their "greatest fan," she was their "greatest teacher." He said, "As she did all our lives, whether it was when I walked back home through the rain from school as a child, or when a President who was her son came back to Hyannis Port, she will be ready to welcome the rest of us home someday." And he said, "She is home. And at this moment she is happily present at a heavenly table with both of her Joes, with Jack and Kathleen, with Bobby and David."

Ted Kennedy returned from his mother's funeral to the funereal mood of the Democrats in Washington. He had delivered his annual agenda-setting speech before the National Press Club on January 11 and sounded publicly the same message he had sounded to his fellow Democrats and to his Democratic president: Democrats must stick to their principles. Once again referencing his own recent victory in which "I ran as a Democrat in belief as well as name," he said. "If Democrats run for cover, if we become carbon copies of the opposition and try to act like Republicans, we will lose—and deserve to lose." And he encouraged Democrats "not to turn our back on the Clinton administration." (Senator David Boren of Oklahoma had been suggesting that Clinton not run for the presidency in 1996 unless his popularity recovered.) And he still believed that Democrats could achieve something, despite the Republican obstacles. He said that healthcare reform was at the top of his list and lamented his party's efforts in 1994 when "we engaged in a search for a phantom compromise that our opponents never intended to achieve."

And yet even as he talked to his fellow Democrats and tried to boost their spirits and stiffen their spines, he was trying to make good on his own legislative promises by speaking to potential Republican allies. The House, he knew, was hopeless—the hot tea that the Senate was designed to cool, now boiling. But the Senate still had a few Republican moderates with whom he hoped he could do business. Shortly after the election, he had called Nancy Kassebaum in Kansas, who would now be replacing him as the Labor chair, to congratulate her, and then met with her when they had both returned to Washington. Kassebaum wanted to push job training and asked for Ted's help. Ted wanted to push healthcare reform, not the massive bill that Clinton had proposed—he knew that kind of reform was dead—but something incremental, something bipartisan, and he asked for Kassebaum's help. And he met with Jim Jeffords, the moderate Republican from Vermont who had often voted with him in committee and against his fellow Republicans and was now the second-ranking member on Labor, and they discussed the agenda for the upcoming session. Ted pressed for the minimum wage raise and for some kind of health-care reform. But Jeffords warned Ted that the Republican caucus was engaged in a civil war of its own between moderate conservatives like the now-majority leader Bob Dole, and New Rightists of the Gingrich stripe, fierce ideologues, and that Dole had actually tried to stop Phil Gramm and Trent Lott, two of those New Rightists, from getting on the Finance Committee, where they could exercise their power over the purse, but Jeffords said, "It was a losing game for Dole." Lott was elected whip by one vote over Alan Simpson, a moderate and a frequent collaborator with Ted. Not all Democrats were happy with Ted's discussions with the opposition. Richard Gephardt, now the House minority leader, said that members complained to him about Ted's outreach, despite the fact that Ted was the one who warned Democrats not to surrender and that Ted's liberal bona fides were impeccable, and Gephardt said he told them that they had to help Ted, that Ted was doing the right thing. In fact, he was doing the only thing if he hoped to pass legislation.

No longer in the majority but still with the chemistry of the Senate to wield—that was how Ted saw his role now. Chris Jennings, the Clinton health adviser who had worked with Ted on the Health Security Act, said of this period, "That's when you see Kennedy taking over. Because Kennedy is not the raging liberal at this point"—though his liberalism was still intact—"he was the raging legislator." He was the senator who wanted to cut a deal. "So he's captured all the Democrats, and if he cut a deal with a few Republicans, he's got a deal," Jennings said. "The dynamic was fascinating to watch."

But now the question was: Would there still be Republicans willing to cut deals with him in the Gingrich Congress, where Democrats were no longer opponents but mortal enemies?

He would begin with the minimum wage. It was the simplest proposal, the one with the fewest moving parts, the one with the greatest public support, and he had gotten a raise in the past with Republican help. Years ago, Carey Parker said, Ted had adopted a strategy when it came to the minimum wage. He would introduce a "substantial increase" but would phase it in over a three-year period, so that it seemed far less substantial, and he would do that once or twice a decade. As Parker said, it usually resulted in a fierce battle with the Republicans, who saw a legislated minimum wage increase as an incursion on business prerogatives and who always insisted that it would cost low-wage workers their jobs since businesses would fire them rather than pay them. But in the end, Ted would take his big charts to the Senate floor—he loved charts, particularly after television arrived in the Senate—to illustrate how wages had actually declined after inflation, and he worked out one of his compromises that would reduce the increase, and Republicans would agree and, as Parker put it, "sigh in relief" that "we don't have to do that again for four or five more years." Which was how Ted had won the last increase, during the Bush administration. Ted had already discussed a new increase with Clinton, but Clinton had vacillated, fearing that the Republicans would attack him as antibusiness if he proposed one. Ted forged ahead anyway. He introduced his bill on January 11, the same day that he spoke before the National Press Club, lacing into timorous liberals while telling his party to stop blaming Clinton for the midterm defeat and support the president instead. Whether that was what had changed Clinton's mind, when Ted brought up the minimum wage during a condolence call Clinton made after Rose's death, Clinton said that he intended to include the issue in his State of the Union, telling Ted, by one account, that he thought he could use it as a bargaining chip with the Republicans to give them something they wanted.

Now that he had Clinton onboard, Ted needed to bring his fellow legislators aboard. Having just returned from his mother's funeral, he arrived at a breakfast meeting of the Democratic congressional leadership in Room H-201 on the House side of the Capitol on January 31, in the middle of a heated debate over whether the minimum wage was relevant at a time of Republican dominance, and he was not happy with what he heard. Senator John Kerry was balking. "I'm not sure we can do this right now," he said. "It's a Republican era. This is a poor person's program." *A poor person's program.* Kerry's remark detonated Ted—detonated him into an eight-minute diatribe with Ted shouting "about who were we if we didn't do this," as Nick Littlefield recalled it, and "If you're not for raising the minimum wage, you don't deserve to call yourself a Democrat." His voice at full volume, Ted said, "If there is one cause the Democrats should stand for it is improving the wages of working people." He said, "We can't do much about wages generally, but raising the minimum wage is something we can do." He asked if the caucus was afraid of the National Restaurant Association or the National Federation of Independent Businesses, which had always opposed raising the minimum wage because those businesses often paid their employees the minimum. H-201 was a small room, windowless, packed with the leadership huddled around a table—such were the indignities of defeat; the majority assigned rooms—and after Ted's attack, Littlefield said, the "air is sucked out of the room, and there's sort of silence for a moment, and then everyone says, 'Whewww!'" The tension finally broke—Richard Durbin cracked a joke, "Well, I guess we now understand how Ted feels about this"—and, Littlefield said, everyone was "extremely solicitous" afterward—if Ted heightened tension, he also could ease it by joking and slapping colleagues on the back—because they knew "where those eruptions come from." Ted often exploded when Democrats seemed to shrink from what he saw as their mission and when he felt the need to remind them of it. His face often reddened, and his voice often bellowed. But they knew that Ted Kennedy was only angry because of his conviction. He was only angry because he was passionate to get things done. It wasn't about power. It was about moral fervor.

And, save for the Reagan years, when so much seemed not just difficult but hopeless, he was even more passionate if the odds were against him, as they were now. It wasn't only that most Republicans were likely to fight any increase; it was that the Democratic senators were not enthusiastic about it either, as Ted had discovered at the leadership meeting, and House Democrats thought that any big increase was impossible to pass. Meanwhile, now that Republicans had effectively disempowered unions, labor was pressing, and pressing hard, for a $1.50 increase over three years, which was Ted's original position too. But the day after his explosion at the leadership meeting, Ted met with Daschle, who told him that after canvassing his own caucus, Senator John Breaux, a Louisiana conservative, was calling for a fifty-cent/twenty-five cent increase over two years, and Daschle thought he might be able to get consensus on fifty/fifty. So Ted once again became a go-between, a kind of fixer, to see if he could find common ground. Littlefield said that over the following week, Ted literally went door to door, meeting with every single Democratic senator, soliciting their advice and trying to gain their commitment. "He kibitzed with senators on the floor during votes, telephoned each member of the Labor

Committee, rallied staff—his own and staff of other senators—and met with labor groups and others in the minimum wage coalition," which was a group Ted had formed in 1989 during the last minimum wage raise and had summoned again in November after the election. And once again he went to the House side, the side where senators rarely went but where Ted Kennedy had gone before, putting aside senatorial pride, and met with the congressmen too, because pride meant nothing when he had a cause to carry.

Then came the bargaining. Clinton had proposed a seventy-five-cent increase spread over three years. Ted had now backed off his $1.50 in favor of fifty/fifty. At a meeting on welfare reform that same week, Ted talked with Clinton advisers and pulled Clinton himself aside to argue for his bill, and Clinton said that he could live with fifty/fifty. But now, according to Littlefield, David Bonior, the Democratic House whip, said that he wasn't sure the more conservative members of his caucus would go along and proposed forty-five/forty-five instead, a small decrease, but the same settlement to which Bush had agreed during the last negotiations. Now Ted began bouncing among the stakeholders—from Lane Kirkland, the president of the AFL-CIO, and Tom Donahue, the AFL's treasurer, both of whom contested anything less than $1.50 but whom Ted felt were movable and would eventually sign on; to each Democrat on the Labor Committee; to Daschle and Gephardt, to whom he said that the forty-five/forty-five agreement seemed the appropriate compromise and one he believed he might get Republicans to support because of that 1989 settlement. On February 3, Bill Clinton, surrounded by congressional Democrats in the Rose Garden, introduced a formal proposal for the ninety-cent, two-year minimum wage increase. And on February 13, Ted submitted his bill with the new figures.

But there were no Republicans at that Rose Garden meeting. Though Ted Kennedy had won the support of his own caucus, he needed to win a lot more support to make his bill into law. What he had learned long ago from past legislative initiatives—and from the Bork confirmation hearings—was that while he was building a coalition within the Senate, he needed to build a coalition outside it as well that could and would apply pressure. He had reassembled the minimum wage coalition from 1989 to do precisely that. He created a steering committee that included Lane Kirkland and Marian Edelman of the Children's Defense Fund and John Mack of the Urban League and Arthur Flemming, the former Republican secretary of Health, Education and Welfare. To head it, Ted coaxed the former executive director of the Americans for Democratic Action, Leon Scholl, who had performed the same function in 1989. As Littlefield described it, after Ted introduced his bill, he and the committee met every Monday morning at eleven o'clock all through the year, organizing the campaign, making sure that ordinary citizens were making their voices heard, tracking votes. And Ted had learned that he needed a media campaign as well. He could no longer hold hearings since he was no longer the committee chair, but he fell back on his old device, his forums, which were hearings in disguise, and at which he invited citizens to testify to how they had been affected by past increases in the minimum wage, and he held press conferences, and public sessions at which public officials—Cabinet officers, senators and congressmen, and members of the minimum wage coalition—explained why a raise was necessary. And to keep pressure on his Senate colleagues and to assess where the bill stood, Ted had another idea. Rather than hold a vote on his bill, for which he was afraid he hadn't yet won sufficient support, he attached a sense of the Senate resolution— a nonbinding resolution—to a Defense Appropriations bill that July. That would allow senators to express their position on the minimum wage without being forced to vote for the minimum wage bill itself. He lost 49 to 48, but he won four Republican votes and kept every Democrat.* "We were jubilant," Littlefield would recall. When Ted submitted another sense of the Senate resolution in October as an amendment to the budget—actually Ted let John Kerry, who was up for reelection in 1996, formally introduce it, despite Kerry's previous doubts—the Senate parliamentarian ruled that it was not germane (Ted knew he would) and a point of order was raised, and the vote whether to set aside the point of order carried 51 to 48, with two more Republicans joining the Democrats. And now Ted knew he had a majority if he could just coax them to stick together when he finally asked for a vote on the bill itself.

All of which proved that even without the power of his committee chairmanship and the perks of the majority, he could still be a raging legislator.

---

*Bob Kerrey actually voted against the resolution, but only because he thought he was voting on whether to table the resolution.

III

But that was the Senate. The new House was under the control of Newt
Gingrich, and Gingrich had vowed not compromise but revolution. Tall,
prematurely gray, paunchy, a bit unkempt, like a stereotypical bumptious
professor, which was what he had been before he entered politics, and also
vainglorious, pompous, self-regarding, windy, and intellectually preten-
tious, with an unshakable belief in his own destiny and an unslakable
thirst for power, Gingrich understood the revolution that Ronald Reagan
had begun as well as anyone. But Gingrich felt Reagan had missed an opportunity to finish it. Reagan and Bush, he said, had blinked when they
agreed to tax increases after swelling deficits. "I will not blink," he asserted. Gingrich had been born in Harrisburg, Pennsylvania, to a teenage
mother whose marriage to Gingrich's abusive father lasted all of three
days before she left him. Newt was conceived in those three days. She re-
married when Newt was three—to a career soldier, Robert Gingrich—
and the family traveled from one of his stepfather's postings to another,
across the United States and across Europe, before settling in Fort Ben-
ning in Georgia. Growing up in an army family with a strict religious upbringing and then moving to the South, where his moral and religious
values were reinforced, he lived in a Manichean world, a world endangered by mortal threats, and he set his mission as fighting to protect it.
While so many others of his generation wrestled with the social tumult of
the 1960s, Gingrich resisted it, seeing in it only the pernicious. He seemed
to live against his times. He got married when he was a freshman at Emory
University—his wife, whom he started dating when he was sixteen, had
been his high school geometry teacher—and had two children over the
next four years.

But if Gingrich was an absolutist and moralist who clung to tradition,
he wasn't a reactionary—at least not yet. As a history professor at West
Georgia College, he was antiestablishment, both left and right establishments, and when he decided to run for Congress against a conservative
Democratic incumbent, he ran as a moderate Republican who embraced
racial harmony. It was only after he lost twice to the incumbent that, out
of opportunism and the belief that he could never win in Georgia with a
message of racial harmony, he began to move rightward. "America needs
to return to moral values" was emblazoned on his campaign brochures.
At the same time that he boasted of his moralism, he proclaimed his eco-

nomic populism, attaching himself to the tax revolt that had begun in California with Proposition 13, which gutted property taxes, and to the plan promoted by Delaware senator William Roth and New York congressman Jack Kemp that proposed reducing income taxes, especially on the wealthy, on the theory that those tax savings would then be reinvested in the economy. (This was the trickle-down economics that opponents had derided when Reagan signed on to the theory.) It was Gingrich's first political pivot.

But there was to be another. Gingrich was reelected to his seat from his suburban Georgia district in the Ronald Reagan wave of 1980, and he enthusiastically supported Reagan. Reagan had succeeded in passing massive tax cuts in his first year, but the recession persisted, unemployment rose along with Reagan's unfavorable rating, and the Democrats gained seats in the House in the 1982 midterms. Now Gingrich was concerned—concerned the same way that Ted Kennedy would be concerned about Bill Clinton after the disastrous 1994 midterms that brought Gingrich to the speakership: Gingrich was afraid that Reagan would compromise with the Democrats, that he would prove to be insufficiently conservative for the ambitious Gingrich. (Reagan *did* compromise by signing tax increases and *was* insufficiently conservative for Gingrich.) In a demonstration less of his ideological purity than of his hubris and ambition, Gingrich thought he could take Reaganism farther and faster than Reagan himself. "Gingrich is Reaganism at warp speed," the conservative tax opponent Grover Norquist said approvingly. Now Gingrich set out to complete the revolution. As his second wife would say of him, "He has to be historic to justify his life." And that was the second pivot. Gingrich out-Reaganed Ronald Reagan. Richard Nixon had advised him that if he was going to topple the Republican establishment, he needed Young Turks. So, aided by a group of young conservative disciples, mainly freshmen congressmen who were even more zealous and significantly more ideological than he, Gingrich, in the words of historian Steve Gillon, merged the "moralistic rhetoric of the New Right and the mystical conservative faith in tax cuts into a powerful ideological weapon." (Gillon left out only the ambition.) As a result, he created a cult within the Republican Party—no one within the party was more averse to the centrist George H. W. Bush than Gingrich—and then, when he got power, led the assault on what he labeled Democratic corruption and indecency. (Gingrich had advanced his career by leading a crusade that forced out Democratic speaker Jim

Wright on ethics charges for Wright's having sold bulk copies of a book he had written as a way of circumventing campaign contribution laws.) Ted Kennedy had lived his life invested in the morality of politics. Newt Gingrich lived his invested in the politics of morality.

Now that the Republicans had chosen him speaker, Gingrich took the fight to the Democrats and to their president, and it wasn't too much to say that it was a fight for the political soul of the country and perhaps even its moral soul. "If they could cut funding for Medicare, Medicaid, education, and the environment, middle-class Americans would see fewer benefits from their tax dollars," Clinton would write in his memoir, "feel more resentful paying taxes, and become even more receptive to their appeals for tax cuts and their strategy of waging campaigns on divisive social and cultural issues like abortion, gay rights, and guns." But nothing was more critical to conservatives than to prevent government assistance to those who needed it. To dismantle the welfare state: that was Gingrich's promise with his Contract with America, which he rammed through the House in less than one hundred days—the anti–One Hundred Days to Roosevelt's famous legislative successes in his first term. But the Senate, that cooling saucer, was a different institution, even in this time of hyperpartisanship. In the Senate, while the minority couldn't pass legislation, there were nevertheless mechanisms that permitted it to slow and even halt the process. The Senate required unanimous consent—literally *every* senator's agreement—on procedures and certain issues, and all bills, save budget reconciliation, which needed only a majority to pass, were subject to a filibuster, which could be broken only by a "supermajority" of sixty senators. That meant forty-one votes could foil any piece of legislation. The Democrats had forty-seven seats. If those forty-seven held together, they could defeat anything but budget reconciliation. The problem, in a diverse caucus where so many Democrats were already spooked by the last midterms and where so many feared their own obsolescence, was getting them to hold together. Ted Kennedy continued throughout the year, 1995, to remind those Democrats of their traditions and their promises— remind them of what separated them from Republicans. That nudging was part of his much-vaunted chemistry. But Ted Kennedy needed to rely on the physics of the Senate too, its rules and procedures, if he was to stymie the Republican revolution that threatened to undo everything in which he believed.

Republicans had long targeted the National Labor Relations Act, passed during the New Deal to empower labor unions and workers against business. Business and its Republican allies searched for ways to undermine the law, and based on a footnote to a 1938 Supreme Court decision, *National Labor Relations Board v. Mackay,* businesses had claimed the right to replace striking workers with permanent employees, which would obviously undermine the very intention of the NLRA, essentially removing the strike as a weapon. Reagan relied on that footnote when he replaced the striking air traffic controllers. But Democrats and their labor allies were determined to rewrite that footnote, and when attempts at legislation failed, Bill Clinton signed an executive order prohibiting companies seeking to do business with the government from hiring permanent replacements for strikers. And now, with their congressional majorities, the Republicans sought to rescind that order legislatively. Nancy Kassebaum, the new Labor chair, brought it to the floor herself on March 14. Ted took the floor the next day to argue against it, calling it an "assault on working families," and then, under the rules of unanimous consent, made his objection to bring it to a vote. Cloture failed by two votes, and Ted won. And he would win yet again when the Republicans proposed a deregulation bill that would, in the name of preventing government interference, dramatically reduce worker safety protections, environmental protections, and food inspection and rules. Dole could muster only forty-eight votes for cloture. The Republicans' effort failed. The Democrats' spines had stiffened.

Then came the assault on government spending. In every session of Congress, emergencies arose—most often, natural disasters or military contingencies—that required additional funding that had not been included in the original budget. In 1990, rather than try to find places in the budget to pay for these supplemental emergency funds, President Bush, the congressional Republicans, and the Democrats had reached a budget understanding that allowed these funds to be appropriated separately from the budget. And that agreement had worked successfully ever since. But the Gingrich Republicans, seeing this as additional spending, introduced a different plan. On the pretense that they were controlling spending, they demanded that all emergency funding be offset by funds already authorized in the previous year's budget, and not incidentally, they proposed carving those offsets from social programs. Democrats knew that the new explanation was a ruse. The Republicans' real aim had nothing to do with paying for emergencies and using budget constraints to do so; their aim was to defund social programs that had already been funded in order to help pay for Gingrich's promised tax cut, and to get it done without having to wait for the new budget. (Indeed, the Appropriations Committee voted $13.5 billion in cuts to those social programs, which, Nick Littlefield said, was more than twice the emergency funds appropriation.) Ted was furious, especially over the cuts to education. But the only way he could stop them was to keep the Democrats united so that Majority Leader Dole couldn't get cloture. Once again, he rallied the forces by talking to senators whose own pet programs were likely to be affected, and trying to win their support.

That was easy. But there were those terrified conservatives and moderates in the Democratic caucus—terrified that if they voted against cutting the budget, they would be vulnerable when they faced a Republican opponent who would label them "tax and spend" Democrats. Ted needed a strategy, and he and Majority Leader Daschle developed one. They fastened on those education cuts, which they calculated would not be popular. To hold wavering Democrats, then, they decided to offer an amendment to restore the cuts to education, since it would be difficult for any Democrat to oppose it, and possibly, Ted thought, a few Republicans as well. But Dole, who controlled which bills went to the floor and when, kept postponing the vote on their amendment, clearly fearful that he might lose. At this point, in early April 1995, Bob Dole couldn't afford a loss; he was about to announce his candidacy for the presidency. So now Dole, to save face, offered a compromise. He would restore between $500 million and $700 million of the education funds to be lost to the rescission—that is, the revocation of funds that had already been appropriated. Daschle, working with Ted, told Dole it was not enough. They needed $800 million. The only problem now, as Littlefield would recall, was that at a caucus meeting, other senators wanted *their* funding restored as well. Ted argued with them that the restoration of the education cuts was a victory, if not a total one, and certainly better than the rescission bill in the House. And they needed victories—demonstrations that they would not allow the Republicans free rein. In the event, the amendment passed 99 to 0. Even then, however, the bill didn't become law. At conference, where the differences between the House and Senate versions of the bill were reconciled, the cuts to education turned out to be much steeper than in the Senate bill. Bill Clinton vetoed it on May 17, at Ted's urging and with Ted's assurance that he had the votes to sustain the veto. It was only after those cuts had been restored that Clinton signed the bill, on July 27.

And Ted Kennedy had beaten back the Gingrich revolution again.

IV

All those challenges were ways for the newly emboldened Republicans to flex their muscles and demonstrate that Democratic rule was over, even with a Democratic president in the White House. But those were preliminaries. Now that March, and throughout the rest of 1995, came the big battle—the battle for which both sides had been bracing, the battle that would determine the shape of American government for years to come, perhaps for decades. The big battle was the battle over the new budget, the budget that funded the government, which was where Republicans could finally slash social programs, as they had promised, and kill the welfare state. The first salient was to pass a balanced budget amendment that would constitutionally obligate Congress to spend no more than the tax revenues the government took in—anathema to many but not all Democrats, who saw it not as a way to cut the deficit but as a ploy, once again, to strangle social programs to death, even as the Republicans passed tax cuts for the wealthiest Americans. The amendment passed the House but failed by a single vote in the Senate—another embarrassment to Dole. It was the second part of the plan, however, that was most terrifying to liberal Democrats because Republicans had the votes to pass it: to impose massive cuts on social programs while, at the same time, enacting that massive tax cut, which would make social spending impossible in any case—in short, achieving the same ends as the balanced budget amendment but by different means. Republicans had attempted this slash-and-tax cut gambit for years, but there had been enough moderates in the Republican caucus at the time, and Democrats had been unified enough, and most of those programs, from Social Security to Medicare to clean air regulations to educational benefits to job training, had been popular enough to save them from extinction. Not now—not now that Republicans felt the midterm elections had disabled Clinton and empowered them. The cuts that Gingrich proposed were massive; on Ted's Labor Committee alone, nearly all the health, education, and workers' programs were axed by 25 percent—programs whose appropriations had usually risen each year. In the House, Democrats were helpless to stop the destruction, and the cuts passed. In the Senate, the budgetary process was more complicated, and Democrats were less helpless, but only if they stuck together, which was Ted Kennedy's mission.

What made the process complicated was that in order to pass a budget, first, a budget resolution had to be passed that set the parameters for the overall budget and provided instructions for how those parameters were to be met if new taxes and changes in laws were required. Then the resolution had to be sent to the individual Senate committees, which would make appropriations within those parameters for programs under their jurisdiction. Those recommendations would then be sent to the Budget Committees, which would shape them into the budget and, if new taxes or modifications in tax law were required, into a budget reconciliation bill. That was simple enough. It was the third stage that was more problematic for Ted and the Democrats. Entitlement programs—that is, programs like Social Security and Medicare and Medicaid, which under the law *guaranteed* benefits to groups of qualified Americans, like the elderly and the poor and the disabled—were outside the normal budgetary process. If Republicans wanted to cut them—and they desperately did, more desperately than anything—they had to change the laws that provided those guarantees.

And that was where the budget reconciliation bill came in. Reconciliation meant reconciling the budget with the law by changing the law—in this case, the laws that established those entitlement guarantees: the laws, for example, that had set up Social Security, Medicare, and Medicaid. And what made this problematic was that because of the agreement in 1974 to make it easier to cut the deficit, the reconciliation bill required only a majority vote and limited debate to twenty hours, so that the Democrats in the minority could not filibuster it. At all three stages, any differences between the House bill and the Senate bill had to be resolved in conference. The budget resolution was not submitted to the president; it was for Congress's guidance only. But the appropriations bills and the budget reconciliation bills *were* submitted, which meant that Clinton could veto the budget reconciliation. There was, however, a danger in doing so, and Newt Gingrich was well aware of it. If Clinton were to veto the budget, the very thing that paid the government's bills, he would effectively be shutting down the government because there would be no funds to run it. (The Republicans had their own poison pill to swallow: not passing an increase in the debt ceiling, which would make the government default on its obligations—something that had not happened in the history of the country.) Gingrich assumed that Clinton wouldn't risk the political consequences of shutting down government offices and furloughing government employees. He knew that presidents didn't shut down the government. It was bad politics to do so—worse than bad. In effect, Gingrich was blackmailing Clinton to agree to eviscerate the welfare state.

And when it came to cutting social programs, Newt Gingrich had two particular targets in mind: He wanted to squeeze Medicare and Medicaid, two of the most popular government programs and two of the largest, the first providing healthcare to the elderly, the second to the poor, including poor children, and to the disabled. Gingrich's budget called for $270 billion in cuts over seven years to Medicare and the virtual elimination of Medicaid by cutting its funds by $163 billion and by turning it into a block grant program to be run by the states and thus effectively removing it as an entitlement. (The Republicans claimed that they weren't actually cutting Medicare but rather slowing its growth, which was a semantic distinction rather than a real one; given the fact that the growth was mandated by law, slowing it amounted to cutting benefits.) Cutting Medicare had been one of the few taboos of American politics, that "third rail," and although Republicans had always salivated at the prospect, they had also been circumspect about actually doing it. But Newt Gingrich, the would-be historic figure, was seldom circumspect, especially as he was flush with his new power. Republican pollster Linda DiVall had advised party leaders never to talk about "cuts" in Medicare, but rather about "saving" Medicare from insolvency by reducing benefits and raising patient contributions. In short, saving Medicare by destroying it. There was a reason, though, that Medicare was the "third rail" of American politics: No one, least of all those senior citizens who relied on it, wanted to see it cut. While other social programs, including Medicaid, might not be sacrosanct, and while Republicans might gain political traction by promising tax cuts and budget cuts that made them seem like responsible financial stewards, Medicare *was* sacrosanct. And that was where Ted Kennedy thought Newt Gingrich let his hubris get the better of him. Gingrich didn't just want to cut it. He proposed those $270 billion in cuts, which just happened to be roughly the same amount as the tax cuts Gingrich was proposing, $245 billion, pitched disproportionately to the wealthy. It enabled Democrats to tie the first to the second, insisting that Republicans were cutting healthcare to seniors in order to provide tax relief to the rich. "This is a budget that Marie Antoinette would love," Ted roared on the Senate floor. " 'Let them eat cake.' And it is Medicare that is being sent to the guillotine."

Still, the Republicans had their majority, which meant they had the votes, especially as those terrorized Democrats had convinced themselves that voting against spending cuts and tax cuts could be political suicide. So now Ted Kennedy, who was in a state of fury rather than panic, felt he had to find another way to prevent Newt Gingrich from devastating Medicare.

The problem, though, wasn't just Newt Gingrich. In June, Gingrich had muscled his budget, with all those cuts and with the elimination of Medicaid, through the House, and then it passed the Senate. The only way to stop him now was a presidential veto, which would require a two-thirds majority in each chamber to override. And that made Bill Clinton the problem too—a problem because Ted was never sure if Clinton, whose liberal instincts were nowhere as strong as Ted's, and who was often accused of bowing to the last person to whom he spoke, and who fancied himself a "New Democrat" rather than a "tax and spend" Democrat, and who was desperate to be liked, whatever it took, and who embraced a "Third Way" or "triangulation" that allowed him to steer a path between liberals and conservatives and hold himself aloof from his congressional party, and who was always searching for compromises, even if, unlike Ted's compromises, they might actually compromise principles—Ted wasn't sure if Bill Clinton would screw his courage to the sticking place when it came to Medicare cuts, much less shut down the government over those cuts. Ted thought he had stiffened Clinton's spine earlier in the year when he got Clinton to support the minimum wage raise, and when the Republicans had introduced their Medicare and Medicaid cuts, he, Daschle, and the White House had devised that joint strategy to hammer away at the Republicans and ask how they could take money from seniors, the poor, and the disabled while they were giving money away to the wealthy. They had been united. They had made an effective argument. They had seemed to win their point. But now that the budget had passed both houses of Congress, Ted wasn't sure.

Ted Kennedy and Bill Clinton had a close but complicated relationship. Littlefield called Clinton a "Kennedy junkie," and he was doubtless a John Kennedy wannabe: a dynamic young leader to stir the nation. And Ted genuinely liked him. Nearly everybody did, even Newt Gingrich, who, for all his heated rhetoric, loved to banter with the president and intellectually joust with him, which distressed some of Gingrich's more ideological colleagues. George Stephanopoulos, a Clinton aide, called Ted and Clinton's congeniality "more of a peer relationship" because "being a Kennedy cancels out being president, so they just deal with each other." Ted was always respectful to the office his brother had occupied. He always called Clinton "Mr. President," never Bill, and while they could be informal with each other, theirs was neither a social relationship nor a friendship but a political relationship. "His big thing was," Clinton adviser Chris Jennings would say of Ted, " 'I need Clinton to play the role of president for me. And his role of president is to find priorities that I want and to message them well and, importantly, to put them in the budget. All three of those things.' " And Ted stayed on Clinton, phoned him, and went to the White House frequently and worked on him to make sure he didn't retreat. When it came to the budget, Jennings said that most senators had no idea when it would be finalized. Ted knew—knew that submissions had to be made by November, and he made them. There were many submissions. "He never cared about the budget adding up," Jennings said. "That was our problem." He would just say, "I *need* it in the budget." And Jennings said more. He said that most senators visiting the White House were just awestruck and glad to be there, but not Ted Kennedy. Every time Ted came to the White House, he would come with an agenda: not only those budget requests but a long list of requests he had written out on three-by-five index cards, and sometimes he would hand the card to Clinton or to a top aide, and Clinton would tell Jennings or whichever aide happened to be there, "Do it!" whether it was a major piece of legislation or a constituent service for a local Massachusetts hospital.

Ted liked Bill Clinton and respected him—respected his political instincts, even though they were not congruent with his. Carey Parker was to say that Ted "loves to go before liberal, Democratic crowds and give them the red meat they want. That's where his heart is." But he also understood that Democrats in this Republican environment had, in Parker's words, "to come up with incremental steps to reach" liberal goals, "which was basically what we saw as Clinton's Third Way. 'We're on the right path. We can't take the giant steps we were proposing before.' " But the question, always the question with Bill Clinton, Parker said, was, "How far do we have to move to compromise?" And would Clinton go too far?

Clinton had the same respect for Ted—respect for his political instincts and his political skills. "He has what he has because people know that he shoots straight with them," Clinton would say of Ted. "They trust him to do that, and they know that he believes in what he's doing, and he believes in the way he's doing it." Clinton called it the "secret of his survival." And Clinton said that "we're very close" and that he talked to him often, and "I seek his counsel a lot." Clinton's staff secretary at the time, John Podesta, agreed that "Kennedy could find a path through, find a compromise, always worked harder than anybody else, always was better prepared than anyone else," and when he came to the White House, though he brought his "wish list," as Jennings called it, he also asked Clinton, "How are we going to get this done?" And he did get things done. Stephanopoulos said Ted was a "key player in every major piece of legislation that made the difference [for Clinton] between being reelected and not," and he said that Clinton was usually attentive to him because a "Democrat can't win if you lose Kennedy."

But now, late that spring, as Gingrich was plowing forward on his Medicare and Medicaid cuts and having slashed and burned his way through the budget, Ted thought Clinton might capitulate just to prevent Gingrich and the Republicans from co-opting him on having cut the deficit and gaining a political advantage. The effect, Ted knew, would be to rob the Democrats of their most potent issue and, worse, jeopardize Medicare. More specifically, Clinton was going to present his own revised budget that June—his first budget had been rejected unanimously as presidential budgets often were—and it was rumored he would include a proposal for a balanced budget schedule—the idea that liberals so dreaded. (A "debacle," Secretary of Labor Robert Reich had called the idea in a meeting with Clinton.) Ted monitored Clinton closely, speaking frequently with Stephanopoulos, who said that Ted "insisted on having a very, very, very clear difference on Medicare" with the Republicans. Clinton's advisers knew how persuasive—and how dogged—Ted could be and did their best to keep Ted away from Clinton before he presented his budget. But Ted could not be headed. On June 7, Clinton hosted a ceremony in the Rose Garden honoring high schools that had combated drugs. As Littlefield described it, Ted had wheedled an invitation to the event and sat in the front row because he knew that if Clinton saw him, the president wouldn't be able to resist talking to him. He was right. After the signing, Ted joined Clinton on a stroll to the Oval Office—Clinton's advisers were stewing—

and Ted spent the next forty-five minutes badgering him on the budget, arguing that if he abandoned liberalism, liberals would abandon him, while Clinton countered that the best way to check the Republicans was to offer a balanced budget proposal of his own, albeit a softer one. (It happened to be the same day that Clinton signed his first veto—of a Republican bill cutting $16.4 billion in spending. "This is old politics. It is wrong," Clinton said of the cuts in social programs.) Ted left his meeting having won a week's postponement in Clinton's announcement.

But the delay was only that. Clinton had been listening to conservative adviser Dick Morris, who kept pushing triangulation as a way to seize the middle ground from the Republicans and to keep from becoming too entangled and too closely identified with liberal Democratic legislators, and Clinton himself felt that from the moment the Republicans had proposed their budget, all he had done was attack rather than lead with ideas of his own. It was from Morris's advice, and from Clinton's own desire to try to find what was being called a "grand compromise" with the Republicans, that Clinton, against the wishes of most of his other advisers and against Ted's wishes, finally decided to propose a balanced budget, though in ten years rather than the seven the Republicans had passed, as well as a middle-class tax cut. These would have almost certainly required some reductions in social programs. (The Republican budget called for cuts of one *trillion* dollars over seven years.) But Clinton now offered something more and, as far as Ted was concerned, worse. On June 13, in a televised address, he proposed a $124 billion cut in Medicare, which he saw as a reasonable counterproposal and compromise to the Republicans' much larger cut, and a $54 billion cut in Medicaid, though he rejected the block grants and instead proposed a per capita cap on benefits, which would preserve the program and allow it to grow but also rein in what he saw as out-of-control costs. He called it a "turning point for us." Ted saw it differently. He saw it as a turning back.

Most Democrats were incensed. "I think the President *wanted* a pretty sound chorus of Democratic anger," Representative George Miller, the co-chairman of the House Democratic Policy Group, griped, meaning that Clinton welcomed the liberals' protests as a way of further centering himself on the political spectrum and proving that he wasn't the left-winger the Republicans accused him of being. At Clinton's instruction, Daschle formed a working group to lay out a balanced budget, but the ranking committee members were skeptical. "We don't need a balanced budget,"

Ernest Hollings of South Carolina remonstrated. "We can't get to a balanced budget proposal of our own without jiggling the funds. It's poppycock. I don't see why we should waste our energy." But Ted held his fire, no doubt realizing that Clinton was exercising damage control against the Republicans, and perhaps hoping to keep his lines of communication to Clinton open so that he could continue to try to influence him, especially since Clinton held the veto pen. He said that he agreed with the "President's direction and where he's trying to go with the country," and he told his Senate colleagues, "We need to try to be close to where the President comes out with his plan." They needed to protect Medicare, Medicaid, welfare, and education, and they could do so only if they could find additional funds elsewhere to cut—in defense and corporate welfare, and in reducing the tax cuts—and only if they had the president's support. But at another meeting, when Daschle announced that there would be sessions the next morning to work on a Democratic budget, Ted was incredulous. "Am I hearing right?" he asked. "We are discussing cutting Medicare more?"

Ted had largely set the Democratic strategy against Gingrich's dismantling of the government. He had seized first on the education cuts during the rescission bill and then on the Medicare cuts during the budget battle, and he kept at it, day after day, blasting away at Republican overreach, denouncing the Republican budget for cutting the heart out of social programs, and Republicans, seemingly blinded by their own power, played into the Democrats' hands. "I deeply resent the fact that when I am sixty-five," Republican House majority leader Dick Armey said, apparently oblivious to the import of his remarks, "I must enroll in Medicare. It's part of a government that teaches dependence, and a program I would have no part of in a free world," which was certainly not how most Americans felt, but was certainly how most House Republicans felt. Over the next several months, though, as Dole and Gingrich and Clinton negotiated to find some compromise between the Republicans' budget and Clinton's and avoid a government shutdown, congressional Democrats, including Ted Kennedy, were largely sidelined, which rattled their nerves. Ted's primary function was more presidential spine stiffening. That October he invited strategists to his house to discuss what the Democrats and their president should do—whether to make a deal or eschew one, though Ted, not believing that the Republicans were likely to compromise on their primary mission, preferred the latter course. As Littlefield described the deliberations, there was little agreement. Some argued that Clinton should veto the reconciliation bill, and then, having shown his mettle, he could negotiate from strength. Others felt that Clinton should sign the bill, then use it as a target in his presidential reelection campaign, telling voters how the Republicans had failed them. Others believed that having no reconciliation bill would confirm voters' belief that the government was paralyzed. And Democratic pollster Celinda Lake believed that holding firm against the Republicans was the best strategy since, as her polls showed, Republicans were already being blamed for the huge cuts to social programs. Littlefield said that another group of strategists meeting with Ted a few days later tackled another problem—not what to do but how to frame a narrative to put the Republicans on the defensive. And here there was a consensus. American workers felt that they had been excluded from the country's economic gains. The economy rose, but their wages stagnated. And the strategists argued that Ted had to repeat again and again and again this story: Republicans had turned their backs on the working class, while Democrats had the backs of the working class. He had to promote it to gain public support that would strengthen Clinton's resolve.

As the Republicans pushed their reconciliation bill, Ted Kennedy's was arguably the loudest voice of Democratic resistance. During a Senate debate on an amendment to yet another Republican bill—this one cutting student loans that Ted's amendment would restore—he shouted in a speech that Littlefield called "one of his strongest to date," "Republicans are being found guilty beyond a reasonable doubt of hurting senior citizens on Medicare; guilty of hurting helpless elderly patients in nursing homes; guilty of punishing innocent children on welfare; guilty of closing college doors to the sons and daughters of working families; guilty of pandering to polluters and endangering the environment; guilty of massive giveaways to powerful special interest groups; guilty of taxing low-income workers; guilty of taxing hard-pressed college students—all to give tax breaks to the millionaires." And he added in what was a wishful if not certain prediction, "This bill will be dead on arrival at the White House, and we ought to bury it right here in the Senate."

But the bill wasn't buried. After a session that lasted from nine o'clock in the morning to midnight, and after a record thirty-nine roll call votes, the reconciliation bill finally passed the Senate on October 28, 52 to 47, and the Republicans there rejoiced. It passed with most of its draconian cuts intact, including those to Medicare and Medicaid. It passed with a provision that ended federal assistance to children on welfare. It passed with stricter eligibility requirements for the Earned Income Tax Credit, which was a benefit for low- and moderate-income families. It passed with its promise to balance the budget in seven years. Many Democrats left the floor afterward somber. Ted stayed. Dole called it the "most historic moment in my memory in the Congress of the United States," presumably because this was the bill that was supposed to transform the federal government and dispossess it of the legacies of Franklin Roosevelt and Lyndon Johnson, the bill that would finally free Americans from government assistance. But at the time it passed, it was generally understood on both sides of the aisle that it would never become law and that liberalism wasn't quite dead yet, as Gingrich had boasted. Everyone knew that Clinton had decided to veto the bill and begin another round of negotiations to improve it and reduce its harm, as he saw it—veto it, even though doing so would result in that government shutdown or, as it had become known, a "train wreck."

Gingrich had always assumed that a veto and subsequent shutdown were impossibilities, believing, as Ted had, that Clinton was all too eager to compromise, but also that Clinton was operating from a position of weakness after the midterm thrashing he took, and believing that those same midterms had given Gingrich and his fellow Republicans unassailable power. And yet Newt Gingrich, the self-described transformational figure, turned out to be wrong on all three counts. Clinton did look for some middle ground, but under immense pressure from his own congressional party, among them Ted Kennedy, he was not willing to sacrifice every social program to find it. And Clinton was no longer in a position of weakness, but one of strength, both because the Democrats, with Ted taking a leading role, had changed the narrative and turned the Republicans from deficit fighters to Medicare fighters in the public's mind, and because whatever power Gingrich had won, he and his fellow Republicans had managed to squander in the year since the election. Liberal programs survived in part because many of them were popular, despite the Republican antagonism to them, but they had also survived because Republicans, especially Newt Gingrich, proved to be inept and bumbling and had a vastly inflated notion of how much the public favored their radical course.

And while Gingrich's popularity was sinking, Clinton's had rebounded, in part because of an impressive and highly presidential performance in Oklahoma City that April, after domestic antigovernment terrorists bombed the federal building in that city and killed 168 people, among them nineteen children in a daycare center there. Clinton went to Oklahoma City to help heal the national wound, but there was no denying that the attack, as *The New York Times* reported, was the result of a "virulent hatred of the Federal Government," which forced Newt Gingrich to defend his own attacks on the government as having in no way provoked the violence. And Clinton didn't make it any easier on the Republicans when he condemned "promoters of paranoia" for creating the climate of hate— all of which helped give the conservatives' decades-long warnings about liberal government and their glee over dismantling government a new sinister cast. "The full political significance of Oklahoma City would not become clear for months and even decades," historian Sean Wilentz was to write. "But by piercing through the antigovernment animus that underlay the tragedy, Clinton helped shift the political mood. The shift would dramatically alter the dynamics of his presidency." Moreover, Newt Gingrich, who had been a political master, as Clinton said, in taking voter frustrations and turning them into a victory, was much less adept as a legislative tactician. Gingrich had been the match, but the freshmen conservatives and their fellow ideologues were the gasoline, and Gingrich could not control the conflagration. The man who had thought Ronald Reagan insufficiently tenacious was now considered by his own caucus as too eager to strike a deal with Clinton in order to salvage his own endangered political aspirations—so much so that the hard-nosed and ideologically unbudgeable majority leader Dick Armey now was appointed to "chaperone" Gingrich to the White House whenever he negotiated with Clinton. Gingrich had had to choose between his caucus and the public. Now he was losing both. As early as June, polls showed that in a head-to-head presidential contest, Clinton would trounce Gingrich. And Gingrich further damaged his standing when he admitted that he had toughened his budget bill because Clinton hadn't invited him to the front of Air Force One when an American delegation was traveling with the president to Israel for Yitzhak Rabin's funeral. With that admission, the press excoriated Gingrich as petulant and infantile—the entire front page of *New York Daily News* featured a cartoon of Gingrich in a diaper and holding a baby bottle and was headlined: "Cry Baby"—and accused him of putting his own ego ahead of the nation's interests. (It was an example of how he used his political power to compensate for his personal deficiencies.) And if Gingrich was foundering, so were the Republicans. Not surprisingly, polls also showed that Americans by a two-to-one margin did not want large cuts to Medicare, and by the time of the passage of the reconciliation bill, 61 percent wanted Clinton to veto it.

The train crashed on November 13 when Clinton, without having yet received the budget reconciliation act, vetoed a continuing resolution to keep the government open because Republicans had insisted on attaching, among other provisions, an increase in the Medicare Part B premium to it, and he vetoed as well a debt-limit rise, without which, Republicans had threatened, the government would be thrown into default—a tactic they were using, opponents said, to try to extort Clinton into signing their budget. The shutdown lasted only six days, when a revised continuing resolution was passed to keep the government funded while negotiations continued. But the sides once again failed to reach agreement, and now Republicans were insisting that Clinton not only back their seven-year balanced budget proposal, which he had reluctantly done, but also accept the Congressional Budget Office forecasts, which were always more conservative than the White House's own Office of Management and Budget figures, meaning larger cuts. Republicans were unyielding. They told Clinton he could either accept their budget or accept the consequences, which Dick Armey, Gingrich's chaperone, assured Clinton during an Oval Office visit would be the end of his presidency. Clinton, the great compromiser who had become exasperated by the Republican's unwillingness to find a compromise, said he would never sign that budget, and if they wanted it, "You'll have to get someone else to sit in this chair!" Finally, on December 6, invoking the word *values* repeatedly to underscore what was at stake, which he felt were the moral values of the American government, Clinton vetoed the Budget Reconciliation Act, the Republicans' revolutionary blueprint that had been the center of partisan warfare for the better part of the year, and with a bit of dramatic flair, he signed the veto with the same pen with which Lyndon Johnson had signed the Medicare and Medicaid bills in 1965. "With this, the Republican budget is dead," Stephanopoulos declared, "the Contract with America is dead." With no budget and no continuing resolution, on December 16, the government was shut down again—another train wreck. Here too the public sided with Clinton against the Republicans, who were perceived as intransigent. Polling showed that roughly half of Americans blamed Republicans for the shutdown and only 25 percent the president. Gingrich received even lower grades; his approval ratings, which had stood at just under 40 percent before the shutdown, plummeted to under 30 percent after it.

Meanwhile Ted continued to tell the White House to hold firm, and he did so publicly on the Senate floor, even when Clinton reached an agreement on January 6 for another continuing resolution that would keep the government open until the end of the month. (The resolution, Ted complained, contained floors but also ceilings for funding that amounted to cuts.) But Clinton, who had once seemed too eager to deal, was now resolute. He had refused to surrender, partly in principle and partly, almost certainly, because it was proving good politics to blame Republicans for the shutdown, which had the added benefit of shoring up the support of the congressional Democrats. Republicans now realized that Clinton had outwitted them and that they were fighting a losing battle. Though Clinton announced in his State of the Union address, "The era of big government is over," seeming to give the Republicans at least a rhetorical victory in declaring the old liberal shibboleths obsolete, that had more to do with Clinton's political posturing than with a real retreat. The retreat was the Republicans'. They agreed to another continuing resolution, but when it came to the big issues over which the parties had been squabbling, Republicans restored most of the cuts, and Clinton, under tremendous pressure from the liberals, especially Ted, backed off from the balanced budget, postponed consideration of the cuts to Medicare and Medicaid until after the next election, and reached a budget agreement that was far more favorable to the Democrats than to the majority Republicans.

And so the great revolution to overturn liberalism fizzled. The Contract with America that Newt Gingrich had announced with such fanfare on the Capitol steps nearly eighteen months earlier was unfulfilled. While all ten of its planks had passed the Republican House, only three of its minor provisions were ever enacted, and all its major targets survived, notably Medicare and Medicaid. Newt Gingrich had been both thwarted and discredited. During the budget impasse, only 29 percent of Americans approved of his job as speaker. More important, the Republicans and the conservative movement had also been discredited. They had overplayed their hand and paid a price. Fifty-four percent of Americans thought Bill Clinton was concerned about doing what was best for them and for their families; only 36 percent felt similarly about the Republican Congress. By the time the budget battle was over, even Bob Dole, who had been one of the chief Republican negotiators and a prospective Republican presidential nominee, was running away from his own party's intransigence, having seen his own poll numbers drop. Not with politics but with ideas, Ted had said at the outset, referring to how Democrats could beat back the Republicans. In the end, however, it was both politics and ideas, especially the idea that the Republicans were snatching away programs that Americans wanted and needed. And in the end, there was something else Ted and the Democrats took to their fight: a dose of morality about hurting the Americans who were most imperiled, which still, it turned out, had residual power in the country.

The president had stopped the Republican onslaught, stopped it with his vetoes, but so had the Senate, the saucer. And in the Senate, where the liberals had carried the fight, the most influential of them, the one who had contributed most to bolstering their resolve, was Ted Kennedy. "There were things he was just not willing to compromise, and that was the message that he was sending to people at this point too," recalled Kennedy staffer Melody Barnes. "We have a firm sense of who we are and where we want to go and what we want to accomplish." And he reminded his fellow Democrats, whose nerves were jangled and who were fearful of defeat, not only what they had stood for, but also what they could accomplish. "We can work with the system that's been given to us to try and achieve what we want to achieve," Barnes said, quoting Ted's belief. "They had the votes to jam it through the House," Carey Parker told Burton Hersh of the Republican budget, "but then it got to the Senate, and I think Kennedy played a major role in developing arguments about what Republican cuts in medicine would do, what Republican cuts in education would do, the unfairness of the Republican tax plan."

That August, as the budget battle heated up, Paul Kirk told Nick Littlefield, "When you get the Republican crowd so intensive and so mean-spirited, you need a clear and compelling voice out there, and that's Senator Kennedy's role." The voice of the Democratic resistance would arrive every Friday afternoon in the Senate with his charts that showed how the Republican cuts would affect average Americans. "He'd talk for two hours about that stuff," Nick Littlefield told Burton Hersh. And he would declaim every time the Republicans proposed another bill to disembowel government programs that he felt helped the working class and the poor—passionate speeches, heartfelt speeches, speeches both eloquent and angry, his voice rising in indignation. And even after Clinton sidelined him, he kept the pressure on. A *Boston Globe* reporter following him one morning that October—his piece was titled "Sen. Kennedy's Salvage Mission"—found him on *CBS This Morning* blasting Republican cuts to student loans; and then on the Senate floor decrying the attempt to eliminate one of his personal achievements, national service; and then at two strategy sessions to plot how to save Medicare; and then at a rally of the United Food and Commercial Workers on the steps of the Capitol. And he kept the pressure on the president in those face-to-face meetings too. Tom Daschle, who shared Ted's doubts about Clinton's resolve, recalled the "many times there was a real concern about the direction of the Clinton administration," and said that when there was, the "conversation would start with Teddy and expand then to the caucus." And then Daschle and Ted would ask to meet Clinton and try to coordinate the presidential and senatorial efforts with the caucus behind them. "Teddy was always the benchmark by which many of the issues were defined," Daschle would say, "and that benchmark was extremely important as we tried to find consensus with the Clinton administration."

Ted had been the spine-stiffener, the spirit, the voice, the strategist, the propulsion, the chief narrative changer, the benchmark, and ultimately the heart of the resistance that had succeeded in stopping the Gingrich revolution. And Bill Clinton had been, despite Ted's doubts, the executioner. "Democrats came out way ahead after this long, contentious and difficult year," Nick Littlefield would say. "The Republicans were blamed for the shutdown, and the misguided notion that the public would welcome the Republican shutdown turned out to be as far from the truth as anything could be. They were forever tarred with extremism, with recklessness, with irrational and threatening conduct, and it alienated large numbers of Americans from constituencies across the spectrum." But Littlefield obviously had his liberal bias. Mississippi Republican senator Thad Cochran, whose biases were much different from Littlefield's, put it more succinctly but no less depressingly for his party. The Republicans came into the 1994 midterm elections, he said, needing to make "sharp, clear distinctions, or we're not going to be able to win the majorities that we need to govern." So they made those distinctions, and they got their majority. "And it wasn't any great shakes," Cochran concluded simply. "We weren't able to get much done."

EIGHTEEN

Running the Senate

W E WEREN'T ABLE to get much done" was an understatement. That year Newt Gingrich's House passed 396 bills and the Senate 322, including the Budget Reconciliation Act, but Clinton signed only sixty-six of them into law. The bills were largely for show—part of the demonstration of how Republicans were trying to make good on their promise to revolutionize the government by dismantling it. But the revolution really wasn't about trying to get bills passed. Ted would later say that what the Republicans were trying to promulgate had more to do with values than with legislation. Gingrich himself had said the same thing—a "cultural revolution," he had called his campaign, "with societal and political consequences that ultimately change the government." "If you read the Gingrich revolution," Ted told an interviewer, "the commitments are all about the individual, myself, and against the government. There's nothing about common humanity, nothing about the common good in this. This country was founded on the basis of the common good and Judeo-Christian ideals," which was also the lament he had made to Adam Clymer during the midterm elections when he complained about the direction in which the country seemed to be heading. Clinton would say the same thing in his State of the Union address that January after the long budget battle. Though the era of big government might be over, as Clinton declared in the speech, he also said, "We can't go back to the era of fending for yourself. We have to go forward to the era of working together as a community, as a team, as one America, with all of us reaching across these lines that divide us—the division, the discrimination, the rancor—we have to reach across it to find common ground. We have to work together if we want America to work."

The budget impasse had preoccupied both Congress and the president in 1995 and led to little. *We weren't able to get much done.* But 1996 was an election year—a year in which Majority Leader Bob Dole was the Republican presidential favorite—which meant that gridlock wouldn't do for Dole. He needed achievements to prove his leadership, so long as Bill Clinton didn't also get credit. Similarly, Bill Clinton, after a year of saying no, needed to show that he could also say yes, so long as Republicans didn't also get credit. (There were many congressional Democrats who preferred not moving legislation for that very reason.) As for Ted Kennedy, the raging legislator had suffered through most of that year, spending his time toughening his caucus's and his president's resolve and protecting cherished programs from the Republican ax, but passing almost nothing. This year was going to be different. Even though major legislation seldom passed in election years, this year there was legislation on the docket, legislation that had been stalled during the budget battle, legislation like the minimum wage bill, which Ted had been positioning with his sense of the Senate resolutions before the budget fight overwhelmed everything else, and a healthcare bill that he had been working on with Nancy Kassebaum, modest but important, and a tax reform bill, and a welfare reform bill that Bill Clinton had proposed, to make good on his campaign promise to "end welfare as we know it." If 1995 had been trench warfare, 1996, with the Republicans no longer quite as emboldened, was shaping up to be a game of chess.

And few senators were more skilled at playing legislative chess than Ted Kennedy. Though Ted had been manning the legislative gates, making sure that harmful bills didn't pass, he had also been sounding the call that Democrats needn't only be defensive; they could still take the offense, the Republican congressional majorities notwithstanding. Ted Kennedy had sat and watched Dole and the Senate conservatives abet Newt Gingrich's plan, watched them try again and again to destroy the achievements of the New Deal and Great Society—"The President has to realize that Lyndon Johnson's Great Society has failed," Newt Gingrich said when Clinton vetoed Gingrich's budget—watched the Senate pass those bills that Bill Clinton ultimately vetoed. He watched and he seethed and he denounced and he declaimed. By one account, he was "rushing from crisis to crisis, trying to save programs and policies he has created and nurtured over the years," and he was "working himself into a lather wherever he goes—in committee, on the floor, on the steps of the Capitol." During a committee meeting in which $10.1 billion in cuts to student loans were being considered, he shouted so loudly and so angrily while sitting next to Nancy Kassebaum that she stopped and said she would continue only "if Senator Kennedy would stop yelling in my ear." Kassebaum called his outburst "demagoguery," but if it was, it was also fury over the attempt and over his impotence to stop it.

But that was 1995. In 1996 he was eager to play offense again, just as he had encouraged the caucus to do. Playing offense, however, required another narrative—a different narrative than the one he had purveyed against the Republicans: the narrative that had turned their revolution against them by telling Americans how the Republicans wanted to sabotage the very programs that had helped them. A "new big idea," Nick Littlefield, his Labor Committee chief of staff, called it, and Littlefield said that Ted huddled with him and Carey Parker and Bob Shrum, his former aide, and deliberated over what narrative would work positively rather than negatively and could reenergize the Democrats. What they finally seized on was something Ted had heard repeatedly during his "meetings tour" after the midterm defeat. The economy was rising; Clinton had bragged about job creation and economic growth. But ordinary Americans didn't feel they were benefiting. They suffered from a "quiet depression," Ted said, and the economy had to be tweaked to help them climb out from it. It was an argument against the affliction of growing economic inequality, one that he felt would appeal to the disaffection and frustration he had sensed when he was running. "The Rising Tide: How to Make It Lift More Boats," he titled his annual agenda-setting speech, this time at the Center for National Policy, and he cited those rising economic indicators while also saying that "appearances are deceiving" and that the alleged prosperity was "uneven, uncertain, and inequitable." Moreover, income inequality was "economically unjustified, socially dangerous, historically unprecedented"—and he would add another phrase—"morally unacceptable." This was about values, he said. America needed values that helped its citizens benefit from a growing economy, and he cited in particular two of his pet projects, the minimum wage, which had been lost in the budget battle, and the healthcare proposal that he and Nancy Kassebaum had been working on, which would let workers take their health insurance from one job to another. Closing the income gap and restoring "true progress" to the country were, he said, the "defining mission of the Democratic Party." And with the Republicans chastened, Ted Kennedy was ready to pursue that mission.

There was another meeting early that year, on March 26, this one at the Capitol, this one between Clinton aides and congressional staffers, including Littlefield, and this one dedicated to determining how the Democrats in the Senate and House could best help Bill Clinton in his upcoming re-election campaign. Clinton was not inclined to embrace Ted Kennedy's "new big idea." Heading into his campaign, he wanted to tout his achievements, not identify where they had fallen short. As Nick Littlefield recollected, George Stephanopoulos and the Clinton aides had in mind not a new narrative but a plan. Bob Dole was the likely Republican nominee, but Bob Dole was also the Senate majority leader, and as such, Bob Dole could be bound to the Senate, forced to do its business, made to engage with his Democratic antagonists rather than be out on the stump campaigning. "Make him seem to be the 'legislator-in-chief,'" Littlefield said Stephanopoulos told them, "responding to pressures from his party, responding to questions from the press, generally bogged down in the muddle and gridlock on the floor. Create votes on new issues each week that will cause Dole to take unpopular positions. Make him vote on assault weapons, where he'll have to vote to repeal the assault weapons ban," which was a bill that Clinton had pushed and passed. "Make him vote on family and medical leave again and again." In effect, Stephanopoulos was proposing that the Senate Democrats use Dole's leadership position and his positions on issues against him. "Let Dole be Dole," which was to say, let Bob Dole be the fellow vainly trying to pacify his own extremist caucus by halting the Democrats' agenda.

Ted Kennedy had no particular animus against Bob Dole. Conservative though he was, Dole was no flamethrower like Newt Gingrich, and though he was personally ambitious, he was not without principles. One could reason with him and bargain with him, and Ted often did. "We had times we couldn't move," Dole would say of his relationship to Ted, then added that "in most cases we'd reach some agreement." But as Dole all but wrapped up the nomination that March with a victory in the South Carolina primary, and headed back to the Senate from the campaign trail, he had a difficult task ahead of him. He had both to demonstrate his leadership capabilities to the electorate and to prove his conservative bona fides to his increasingly conservative party, even though he didn't share many of its more extreme positions. Dole was an old-fashioned conservative in a party that had been so radicalized that when Dole went to Arizona to pick up a presidential endorsement from Barry Goldwater, the father of conservative Republicanism, Goldwater reviled the New Right as the people who had "ruined our party" and said, "We're the new liberals of the Republican Party." But Dole had no choice but to move right, no choice but to buckle to Gingrich and his crew, no choice but to be obstructive toward social legislation. And that was something for which Ted Kennedy, who was now eager to pass bills and pursue what he had called the "defining mission" of the Democratic Party, had little tolerance. "That was our moment," Stephanopoulos would say of Dole's return to the Senate that March, and he said this: "Who better to have on your side on the floor than a man who's been in the Senate for thirty-five years?" If Bob Dole was to be stuck in the Senate trying to do Senate business instead of campaigning, if the Democrats were to embarrass him by forcing votes on bills that provided assistance to working and poor Americans, bills that he couldn't support given his caucus, if he was to be made to seem obdurate and uncompromising and extreme, if he was to be hounded and taunted and thwarted, then Ted Kennedy, a master legislator, was the perfect adversary. The Republicans, Dole included, had wasted a year trying to destroy the welfare state. Now, the Democrats felt, came retribution.

If this session was to be chess, Ted Kennedy was the chess master—the senator who understood the nuances of the Senate as well as anyone sitting there, including Bob Dole, who was a pretty good chess player himself. And Ted had his own plan. Ted had fought for the minimum wage. Republicans had opposed it, though they argued, justifiably, that if Democrats had wanted it so badly, they could have passed it in 1993 or 1994 when they had the majority; instead, they had opted to concentrate on Clinton's failed health reform. Ted had accepted a compromise in the amount of the increase. Republicans had rejected it. Ted had twice called for a nonbinding sense of the Senate resolution to support a minimum wage raise and got a handful of Republicans to support it, adding up, the second time, to a Senate majority. Still Republicans would not bring it to the floor. For Bill Clinton, making the Republicans commit to a minimum wage raise or making them oppose it might have been politics. For Ted, it was politics but also morals. The minimum wage, then $4.25, was at a forty-year low in purchasing power. While the poverty level for a family of four was $15,150, the minimum wage before Ted's proposed increase was only $8,500 a year. The raise would affect thirteen million Americans who made the minimum wage, and while Republicans insisted that these Americans were largely teenagers, Democrats countered that three-quarters of them were adults and that most of those were women. And Ted argued on the Senate floor that the increase, roughly $1,800 a year, would lead to "two years of college tuition, nine months of groceries, eight months of utilities for working families." At a time when the salaries of CEOs were skyrocketing, he called his proposed increase a "small, modest step to try to do something for working families, families that work forty hours a week, fifty-two weeks of the year, trying to make it."

But Bob Dole, who had voted for the minimum wage increases in the past, was now determined to block its passage because politically he felt he had to. And that locked Dole and Ted into their arcane parliamentary maneuvering—the legislative chess match.* Since, as a member of the minority, he had no power to introduce a minimum wage bill on his own and have it sent to the floor, Ted sought to attach a minimum wage increase amendment to a piece of legislation that would put the onus on Dole either to let there be a vote or to pull the bill to prevent a vote, which meant that the underlying bill, the bill that was being amended, wouldn't be voted upon either. (By Senate rules, amendments needn't have anything to do with the bill being amended.) Dole had to be vigilant, and Ted's tactic forced him to race to the floor to pull a bill every time Ted feinted at an amendment, or forced him to call for a quorum, which delayed business, or forced him to ask for a recess to confer with the Senate parliamentarian to examine his options to stop Ted's amendment from being considered and voted upon, often filling up the amendment tree by recognizing other amendments first so that Ted couldn't file his amendment, which was a majority leader's prerogative. Of course, Ted had his preroga-

---

*The amendment process in the Senate is highly complex and would fill, and has filled, a small book. Amendments made by committee are a fairly simple matter. They are voted up or down. Amendments made on the floor are a different matter. They are subject to other rules, and these are not so simple. Amendments are filed on "trees." These amendment "trees" are branches off the original bills, but there is a limit to the number of amendments on the tree, which allows the tree to be "filled" in order to block other amendments, and since the majority leader has first recognition, he can choose which amendments will fill the tree. This is the kind of jousting in which Dole and Ted were engaged. See Christopher Davis, "The Amending Process in the Senate," Congressional Research Office, Sept. 16, 2015, for a thorough explanation of the amendment process.

tives too. He could threaten to filibuster the underlying bill if he could get forty other Democrats to join him, and if it was a bill about which Republicans cared, this would not be an idle threat. So in those first months after Dole's return, months he had hoped to devote to burnishing his legislative credentials in preparation for his presidential run, he was instead entangled with Ted Kennedy in an ongoing game of highly technical parliamentary maneuvers, trying to fend off a debate or a vote on the minimum wage bill, when he would have much preferred to have been out campaigning to defeat Bill Clinton. And all this time, while the chess match continued, Ted was rousing the activists—that spring a rally on the Capitol steps was organized under the banner "America Needs a Raise"—and calling press conferences to underscore how Bob Dole, the presumptive Republican presidential nominee, wouldn't even allow a minimum wage bill to come to a vote, even though polls showed that an overwhelming percentage of Americans favored the increase, press conferences that accused Bob Dole of holding up Senate business.

"Little legislative traps," *Boston Globe* reporter John A. Farrell called Ted's gambit. And Bob Dole kept falling into those traps. "He's having just a royal, riotous good time with the minimum wage," Alan Simpson said of Ted. "He's just playing it like a violin." Dole was obviously not oblivious to what Ted was doing to him. As a Senate veteran himself, he understood it and understood the gamesmanship of it. One afternoon Ted was on the floor—"for a very long time," said his former press secretary Scott Ferson—and yelling, his face reddening, about Dole's inability to govern, and then afterward he went over to Dole and calmly discussed with him a bill on national parks. (Ferson might even have been referring to the minimum wage, which would be attached to a national parks bill.) Dole knew the trap and knew he had been trapped. "We used to think he was running the Senate, even though they had others who had the title," Dole would say years later. " 'Well, what's Kennedy got in store for us this week?' 'He's not the leader,'" Dole would quote his fellow Republicans as insisting. "I would say, 'Well, OK, maybe not on paper.'" But Ted Kennedy was now running the Senate where it counted: on the floor. And Bob Dole knew it.

By this point, as important as the passage of the minimum wage was to Ted as a substantive matter to improve the lives of ordinary Americans, it was also hostage to presidential politics—to Bill Clinton's desire to occupy Dole and embarrass him and to Dole's desire to show Republicans he was up to the task of halting Democrats. For nearly a month, Dole was able to prevent the minimum wage bill from coming to a vote by deploying his own tactics. But on the very day when Dole was winning the California primary and locking up the Republican nomination for good, Ted, who was sitting in his office during a briefing, phoned the secretary of the minority, Marty Paone, to check what was happening on the floor and to see whether he might find a bill for his amendment, and Paone told him that, because of an oversight by Dole's deputy, Mississippi senator Trent Lott, the last slot on the second amendment tree had not yet been filled. Now Ted had his chance. He bolted out of his office and to the floor, got John Kerry to file an amendment, and then Ted filed a motion to recommit, which was how Ted finally managed to get his minimum wage amendment attached to a bill—in this case, the bill on creating national parks, which both Democrats and Republicans wanted passed and one that Dole would have a difficult time pulling. Dole was blindsided. He had been in Russell, Kansas, his hometown, and as soon as he arrived back in Washington and heard what Ted had done, he raced to the floor himself and attempted to quash it through a series of his own parliamentary maneuvers that would end with a cloture vote on the amendment. But now at least, the bill was under consideration, even if it was only consideration to stop it from going forward, and Ted used the opportunity on the floor to quote Bob Dole from three previous occasions when Dole had enthusiastically supported a minimum wage increase, then asked, "Where is *that* Bob Dole?" Dole's vehement, politically inspired opposition to the bill also allowed Ted to tie him to the highly unpopular Newt Gingrich and paint him as one of the New Rightists, even though Dole was anything but. "Speaker Gingrich and Senator Dole make a remarkable couple," Ted said on the Senate floor when he was fighting for Dole to allow his amendment to come to a vote. "It is like Bonnie and Clyde writing the Republican platform. Newt Gingrich wants to repeal the ban on assault weapons, and Bob Dole wants to block any increases in the minimum wage. Democrats do not share those appalling priorities and neither do the vast majority of the American people." And though the cloture vote ultimately failed, Ted's minimum wage amendment received fifty-five votes this time—all forty-seven Senate Democrats and eight Republicans.

Dole was flummoxed. He held up any new vote on the actual bill for weeks, even making a deal with Ted that he would bring the amendment up in June, then breaking his promise. And by making certain that the minimum wage would not come up for a vote, Dole effectively shut down the Senate for six weeks, from March 22 through May 7, not allowing any business to proceed, lest Ted Kennedy attach his amendment to another bill—Ted had said he would offer an amendment on any bill he could—and force a vote on it. Dole, for his part, sought to outfox Ted by tying the Senate into procedural knots—filling the tree with his own amendments, then amending the amendment, then tabling the amendments, then re-committing the bill to committee, then readopting the amendments, then filling the tree again, then going to cloture—convoluted maneuvers, highly complex maneuvers, illogical maneuvers, all designed expressly for one thing: to delay action and prevent Ted Kennedy from submitting his minimum wage bill, even though the maneuvers also had that effect of stopping the Senate from doing anything at the very time Dole wanted to exhibit his ability to get things done. And Dole did more. He offered to allow a vote on the minimum wage but only if it was packaged with a se-ries of antiunion "poison pills," including a national right-to-work law that Ted could never have permitted to pass and that Clinton would have vetoed in any case, even if it meant vetoing the minimum wage increase itself. But Ted, normally so impatient, was patient now. He knew that time was on his side and not on Dole's—knew that momentum was building for the bill and that the minimum wage would eventually pass and that holding it up was only wounding Dole politically. Dole knew it too—restive moderate Republicans in the House were now pushing for a minimum wage bill they supported—saying on the floor that "sooner or later the issue will be debated and voted on, directly or indirectly, but not today, not tomorrow and not next week." "Dole threw up his hands because he couldn't deal with Kennedy and his legislation and still be a Republican," Littlefield recalled. "He couldn't stop these bills, and the Republicans were saying, 'What's wrong with you? You can't stop these bills. You're the ma-jority leader. Why can't you do anything?' "

But Bob Dole, the majority leader with all the power, was no longer running the Senate. As he had conceded, Ted Kennedy was. Dole had been beaten by the chess master, and finally, exhausted, he surrendered. On May 15, his eyes welling with tears and his voice choked with emotion, Bob Dole announced in a crowded room at the Hart Senate Office Build-ing that he would be resigning his Senate seat and leaving the Congress he so loved, loved as much as Ted did, "probably something that he loved more than anything else in his life," John Farrell would say, and in which he had served for thirty-five years, leaving it to wage his presidential campaign. He had kept his own counsel on the decision, telling almost no one before the announcement. The press speculated that he was resigning because it was the only way he could distance himself from Newt Gingrich and the other congressional Republicans who were now political anathema to most Americans and whose association with him burdened his already slim presidential chances. But there was another legislator who had prompted his decision—Ted Kennedy—and another reason—the minimum wage bill that Dole seemed unable either to escape or to destroy. As Dole's campaign manager, Scott Reed, would later tell Elsa Walsh of *The New Yorker* of Ted's minimum wage campaign, "It was the perfect vehicle for portraying Republicans as mean, white, and male." And he added, "They just smoked us on minimum wage to the point where we just caved." That had been Clinton's strategy, and it had worked: to frustrate Bob Dole and disempower him. Ted, however, had his own misgivings about driving Bob Dole from the Senate. "I felt sort of sad, you know," he later confessed to a reporter. "I had a lot of respect for Dole." Ted knew that the old Bob Dole would have compromised on the minimum wage bill, would have struck some deal with Ted. And he knew that the new Bob Dole, circumscribed by Newt Gingrich and the New Rightists, couldn't.

II

But Bob Dole wasn't driven from the Senate just because of the minimum wage. All the time that Ted Kennedy, the man who ran the Senate, was working on his minimum wage bill and playing legislative chess against Bob Dole, he was also working on his other goal: healthcare. Throughout 1993 and 1994, when the Senate was considering Bill Clinton's ill-fated Health Security Act, Ted, as the Labor chair, had sat next to Nancy Kassebaum, the ranking Republican, through forty-five hearings and fifteen day-long executive sessions, and for a month during the markup of the Clinton bill. Though they did not always agree—Kassebaum was another moderate Kansas conservative like Dole—she and Ted had come to know and trust each other. (Their offices also happened to be across the hall from each other in the Russell Building, and Ted had given her the Kennedy treatment, the treatment he often gave fellow senators, inviting her to his office, showing her mementoes of his brothers, discussing political history.) After the 1994 midterms, Ted had made that congratulatory call to Kassebaum and then sounded her out about bills on which they could collaborate. He brought up two areas on which they had previously agreed: insurance portability, that is, letting employees take their health insurance from one job to another to prevent what was known as "job lock" or locking an employee into a job for fear of losing insurance if he or she left; and preventing insurers from excluding coverage for those with preexisting conditions, which had kept some of the sickest individuals from getting insurance. Kassebaum would say that she had already been thinking about portability herself when a Senate staffer—not one of her own—confessed to her that she wanted to leave her job but had a daughter to care for and needed insurance. That was the catalyst. In March 1995 the Labor Committee held hearings on health reform, and by July, Ted and Kassebaum submitted their bill, the modesty of which was suggested by the fact that it ran only forty-four pages, as opposed to the 1,342 pages of Clinton's Health Security Act, and that seven Republican co-sponsors had signed on. The bill did nothing for the roughly forty million uninsured, and it did nothing to regulate premiums. Still, the Government Accounting Office calculated that it would affect twenty-five million Americans—Americans who had lost their jobs or changed jobs and would otherwise be forced to buy insurance themselves under Ted's COBRA plan. What Kennedy-Kassebaum, as the bill was labeled in the press, did was permit those workers to take their insurance to their new jobs, and where one of the impediments to doing so had been any previous condition or illness, under this bill, the worker would be covered if he or she had been continuously employed for twelve months under his or her previous employer's group plan. For new workers, coverage for preexisting conditions would begin after twelve months of continuous employment. This was its most important provision and the one that frightened insurers.

A modest bill. A bipartisan bill. A bill with thirty-eight sponsors. A popular bill. A bill that the deputy director of the conservative Heritage Foundation had called the "lowest common denominator politically," which he meant as a compliment. A bill for which Ted Kennedy almost felt he had to apologize since its concerns were so narrow compared to the comprehensive plans he had introduced in the past and Clinton's plan the previous year. A bill that was reported unanimously out of the Labor Committee that August. But for all that, it would never reach a vote.

Under Senate rules, conservative Republicans, who remained anonymous, placed secret "holds" on the bill, meaning that it could not be taken up. Democrats suspected that the subversion of the bill was done at the bidding of insurance companies, which feared it. In any case, Kennedy-Kassebaum was dead in that session. When Bill Clinton, at Ted's urging, decided to mention in his State of the Union address his hope that the bill would be revived in the next session of Congress, Kassebaum got wind of it a half-hour before and fretted that it would sink the bill again by marshaling Republican opposition.

But Clinton's remarks didn't marshal opposition. They changed the nature of the opposition. At the time, in late winter and spring of 1996, Bob Dole was still majority leader, and the Senate was still stuck on the minimum wage bill. Meanwhile both Ted and Kassebaum, fearing that Dole would bury their bill the way he had tried to bury the minimum wage bill, made the same threat that Ted had made on minimum wage: They would attach a Kennedy-Kassebaum amendment to every piece of legislation unless Dole scheduled a vote. Ted said that he dogged Dole. Every time Dole came to the floor to discuss the day's agenda, Ted would ask him to yield, which he was obligated to do under Senate rules. And then Ted would ask, "Why aren't we taking up this bill? It's bipartisan. Why aren't we doing this?" And Ted said, "I just kept after him and after him and after him on this," until Dole, at wit's end, finally capitulated. Wanting to avoid yet another stalemate and hoping to deliver something, Dole decided to call up Kennedy-Kassebaum on April 18, not because he necessarily favored the bill, despite the fact, as Ted would point out, that he had introduced an even stronger bill of his own the previous year, but because he seemed to see it as an opportunity both to advance health reform, for which he could take credit in his presidential campaign, and, because of an addition of his own to the bill, to provide a windfall to the insurance industry, which would help support that campaign. Given the high partisanship in the Senate during a presidential election year in which the majority leader was a candidate, Ted and Kassebaum had taken measures to protect their bill from a conservative onslaught. As Littlefield would later describe it, Ted, borrowing a page from Everett Dirksen, who, back in 1965, had extracted a vow from a bipartisan group of senators not to amend the Voting Rights Act, brought his bipartisan group together and elicited a similar promise from each of them that no one would submit an amendment to the Health Insurance Portability and Accountability Act

(HIPAA), as Kennedy-Kassebaum was legislatively known. The bill would stay as drafted by committee.

At least that was the commitment of those who had drafted it. But Bob Dole and his conservative allies had other plans. As Dole had done with the minimum wage bill, he decided to attach what amounted to a "poison pill" amendment that Democrats would not support, and over which Clinton had threatened to veto the bill were it attached. The pill was the "Medical Savings Account" (MSA), and it had already passed Gingrich's House in that chamber's version of the bill. The idea of MSAs was to permit individuals or their employers to contribute to tax-free accounts, not unlike Individual Retirement Accounts, from which the individual could withdraw funds to pay for health expenses—withdrawals that would also be taxable. By law, the accounts would be coupled to low-cost high-deductible health insurance policies—withdrawals could be used to pay for the deductibles—and any growth in the account would be tax free. This was more an investment than real health insurance, but Republicans embraced the idea ostensibly because it removed government from healthcare, including government regulation, and left healthcare management up to personal responsibility. (The Republican House Ways and Means Committee had considered it the previous year as an option to help undercut Medicare itself.) But there also seemed to be an ulterior motive. A major Republican contributor from Indiana, J. Patrick Rooney, head of the Golden Rule Insurance Company, had pushed the idea of MSAs because he realized that Golden Rule, which specialized in individual and small business insurance, would benefit from high-deductible policies. A "payoff to the Golden Rule Insurance Company," Representative Pete Stark, a California Democrat, called Dole's bill. But where Republicans saw a profit, Democrats saw a problem: MSAs would pull the healthiest individuals, the individuals that the market needed to sustain itself, out of the insurance pool and leave the market to the sickest individuals, those who desperately needed insurance and couldn't afford high deductibles and didn't have money to invest in MSAs. Moreover, MSAs would be a boon to the wealthiest individuals who could contribute to them. What MSAs threatened, then, was to raise the premiums on all those left in the conventional insurance system. "Healthy and wealthy" was how liberals labeled the MSA-insured.

Once again Dole seemed to be trapped, only this time he had done it to himself. He didn't have enough votes to pass his MSA amendment, even though he kept pressing his caucus to do so, and yet as Kevin Kearnes, the chairman of the Business Coalition for Affordable Health Care and a Dole supporter, said, "Senator Dole needs to include medical savings accounts to put his stamp on this legislation," lest Bill Clinton get the credit if it were to pass. At the same time, Dole had offended Kassebaum, the junior senator from Dole's own state of Kansas. She told Ted, "This is very bad of Bob," and promised to resist it. Ted was more direct. He told reporters that the amendment would "certainly sink the bill." As Dole had promised, on April 18, Kennedy-Kassebaum was debated, acrimoniously, all day and into the night until just before midnight. Ted, true to his word that he would not allow any significant amendment to the bill, even voted against one offered jointly by Pete Domenici, a Republican whose daughter suffered from schizophrenia, and Democrat Paul Wellstone, who had a deep interest in mental health, to include mental health parity in the bill—that is, to cover mental health in the same way physical health was covered—even though Ted was in favor of the substance of their amendment. At the conclusion of the debate, Kassebaum offered her amendment to strike Dole's amendment on MSAs, and though Dole held up the roll call to try and rustle votes, four Republicans joined Kassebaum to pass her amendment, 52 to 47. Dole had miscalculated, and Dole had lost. The bill passed 100 to 0, with Dole now claiming credit for it, saying that the passage "could very well restore the faith of the American public that the work of Congress is not just a series of stalemates," though it was Dole who had tried to make it so. Ted again praised the bill but lamented its limitations. And Kassebaum may have issued the most accurate benediction when she said, "This legislation isn't exciting, but then again good government often isn't."

But Bob Dole, his resignation still a month away, wasn't done quite yet. The bill that had passed the House still included MSAs. So now the Senate and House conferees had to sit down and reconcile the two bills before sending a single bill back to their respective chambers for a final vote. Trent Lott, Dole's deputy, had assumed some of his duties as Dole prepared to campaign, and Lott, with Dole's input, had chosen the Senate conferees. Typically and logically, those selections supported the Senate version of the bill. This time, however, Dole and Lott chose conferees who had supported Dole's MSAs, despite the fact that the Senate had rejected them, and Dole and Lott even excluded Nancy Kassebaum, whose bill it was, from the conference. Livid, Ted refused to grant unanimous consent on those choices. Lott protested. But Ted, clearly distrusting Dole, demanded that those who had been most involved with the legislation negotiate a pre-compromise before going to the House. Lott and Dole had no choice but to agree, since they would have needed to invoke cloture to get their selections approved, and they didn't have the votes. Ted had beaten them again. He ran the Senate.

At conference, however, the House Republican conferees not only insisted on their MSAs but also insisted that any individual who wanted an MSA should be able to get one, which would have had a devastating effect on the conventional insurance market. Now the conferees were at a standoff. Trying desperately to reach some compromise and save her bill, Kassebaum shuttled among the House Republicans, Dole, and Ted, fielding new proposals, but Ted found none of them acceptable, and the Republicans would not yield, offering only a slight limitation on MSAs that would have included not everyone but would have restricted enrollment to the self-employed and the employees of small businesses—an aggregate of thirty million people. Ted knew an enrollment that large would drain the conventional insurance pool. And after all he and Kassebaum had gone through to get the bill passed without MSAs, Ted was concerned that it might actually wind up being voted down in the Senate or vetoed, though he was equally worried that Clinton, yet again, might make a concession and accept MSAs in order to win passage. Moreover, some House Democrats, believing it was even better to run on the slogan of a "do-nothing" Republican Congress than on a "do-something" Democratic minority, were becoming less than enthusiastic about passing Kennedy-Kassebaum.

And still nothing was getting done. Throughout June, even after Dole decamped for the campaign, Republicans and Democrats played legislative tennis now, going back and forth on both MSAs and on the minimum wage. Ted took to the Senate floor prepared to unleash an attack on the "far right" House Republicans who were threatening the HIPAA bill by holding out for MSAs, but Kassebaum scolded him, "Now, Ted, don't get too wound up." And Ted told a reporter that he listened to her advice and then "I get wound up." Wound up, Ted Kennedy was—wound up to pass a piece of legislation that only the insurance industry could oppose. Dispirited by her negotiating, which had led to no movement, Kassebaum thought that this time they were not going to succeed. "We might as well recognize it's going to fail," she told Ted, advising them to strike a deal to allow MSAs but limit them to businesses with fifty employees or more. Ted disagreed. He wasn't willing to surrender yet. He organized a briefing in his office on MSAs, conducted by Littlefield—"This is going to be a long one, so take your coats off," Littlefield warned—and Ted leaned back in his wingback chair with his feet up on his coffee table while Littlefield grilled experts to give Ted ammunition to defeat MSAs once again, and Ted even jokingly chided Littlefield when he fumbled an answer of his own. "That's in the briefing sheet. I'm surprised you didn't pick it up, Nick. Page three!" Ted was girding for another round. He had been told that Clinton, too, thought it best for Ted to compromise so that Clinton wouldn't have to veto a bill he very much wanted to tout on the campaign trail, but Clinton had gotten wind of Ted's dissatisfaction and phoned him. As Littlefield later reported their conversation, Ted said that his briefings had convinced him that the number of MSA enrollees could be no higher than 500,000 if conventional health insurance was to survive and that consumer protections would have to be in place and that it could be only a pilot program, not a permanent program, and that there had to be a sunset provision to end it. Clinton said glumly, "I guess they don't want me to get this bill." But Clinton also told Ted this: "I'm calling to tell you let's get this thing done. I've told the Republicans, 'If you get Kennedy, you get it all done.'"

And now Bill Clinton had made Ted Kennedy the Democrat responsible for finding a way to achieve HIPAA, if there was to be a way. Meanwhile, with the minimum wage bill still to be voted on and Kennedy-Kassebaum hung up in conference, Bob Dole left the Senate empty-handed.

Ted, Nancy Kassebaum, and Bill Clinton weren't the only ones frustrated by the lack of progress. Trent Lott had assumed the position of majority leader from Dole, and while Dole had searched in futility for a way to burnish his legislative credentials and also to prove his conservative faith to his caucus, Lott also wanted to get something done, both because he needed some accomplishment to prove to his caucus that he could get a deal and because the Republicans needed one as they headed into the election. Ted, Daschle, and Lott met on June 25 to discuss some way forward on HIPAA, at which Ted reiterated that any MSA program had to address the size (so that it wouldn't damage health insurance), the sunset provisions (so that the program could be terminated if unsuccessful), and the consumer protections (so that enrollees would not be at the mercy of the insurance companies). And while the discussion led to Lott suggesting another meeting, Lott told Ted later on the floor that he had spoken with Dennis Hastert, who headed the House Republican health task force, and with William Archer, the chairman of the House Ways and Means Committee, and told them what Clinton had told Ted: If they wanted a deal, they had to make it with Ted Kennedy.

But the ongoing fight over Kennedy-Kassebaum had stalled Ted Kennedy's other pet bill: the raise in the minimum wage. It had been stuck in the Senate as Ted tried to get a vote, a clean vote, without Dole's antilabor provisions, even as Dole tried to prevent any vote. But now with Dole gone, and a few new provisions added to the bill to help small businesses whom Republicans had claimed would be hit by the increase, it finally—after two years of Ted's efforts, and after months of his relentless dunning of his Senate colleagues, and with the August recess hard upon them so that the legislators could leave Washington for their own campaigns—was headed toward that vote. On June 25, the same day Daschle, Ted, and Lott spoke about MSAs, Lott agreed to bring the minimum wage bill up for a vote on July 9, provided that Republicans were allowed to offer an amendment that would delay implementation and limit the number of workers eligible for the increase. Ted was amenable (knowing how to read the temperature of the Senate, he obviously believed they would be defeated), and with that, he finally got his minimum wage vote, raising that wage from $4.25 an hour to $5.15 an hour. The debate began on July 8 and continued the following day. On July 9 Ted took the floor one last time to make his case. He cited the lack of purchasing power in the current minimum wage. He cited the millions of people, working poor, who would be lifted out of poverty and put on their way to realizing the American Dream. He cited how a vote for his amendment to the Small Business Job Protection Act—the underlying bill helping businesses that Trent Lott had chosen to have amended—would be a vote "in a spirit of generosity that extends a helping hand, not the back of your hand, to all those who need and deserve this help." And he cited Tonya Outlaw of Windsor, North Carolina, a young mother of two who had taken a job at a daycare center at $4.25 an hour because it was the only way she could afford daycare for her children, but who could not afford insurance or medicine for her daughters, or coats for them for the winter. And he cited Alvin Vance, a sanitation worker, who earned $4.25 an hour and worked fifty hours a week and walked seven miles to and from work, unless he managed to catch a ride with a friend, because he couldn't afford a car, and who had no insurance and lived in what Ted called a "shack" because he took home only $200 a week. And Ted said, "It is time for him to get a living minimum wage."

And then at two-fifteen that afternoon came the vote so long delayed—first on the Lott-Bond amendment to exempt businesses with revenues of under $500,000 from the minimum wage and to enact other exemptions that some Democrats claimed would undermine the entire minimum wage structure. It failed 52 to 46. And minutes later, without fanfare, Lott called the long-stalled Kennedy amendment—stalled for eighteen months from the time that Ted first promoted it—to a vote. It passed 74 to 24. And now it was over.* "They need our help," Ted said at the conclusion of the roll call, speaking of those working poor for whom he had fought. "And today they received it."

But that was only the minimum wage. There was still Kennedy-Kassebaum to resolve—still the gridlock over the MSA provision that Ted feared would gut conventional health insurance. As Littlefield would recall it, on July 22, Lott told Ted that he would be appointing conferees both on the minimum wage and on Kennedy-Kassebaum (a new set of conferees) and that he would be calling the latter up for a vote shortly. Lott was clearly trying to force Ted's hand with the recess approaching, forcing him to make some accommodation, and this time Lott succeeded. Again, by Littlefield's account, Lott told Daschle that Ted could resolve the disagreements with the House if he met with Bill Archer, the Ways and Means chairman, who had been insisting on MSAs. Obviously wanting to move the legislation on which he had labored for two years, Ted phoned Archer, suggested that their staffs get together to look at solutions, and that the two of them meet personally. Littlefield said that Ted did not go into that meeting unprepared. He did his usual due diligence. He didn't know Archer, a staunch conservative, personally, but he talked to many who did, and he collected information hoping that he could work his chemistry on him. Among the things he learned was that Archer's mother, to whom Archer was devoted, had been fascinated by Ted's mother, and he learned as well that Archer's district was home to the

---

*There would be one more hurdle. Senator Don Nickles, a Republican, said he would refuse unanimous consent to the conferees on the Small Business Job Protection Act, of which the minimum wage was a provision, unless Ted lifted his refusal to approve the conferees on HIPAA. This, however, was a small hurdle given what the legislation had been through.

gymnastics coach Bela Karolyi, who was currently with the U.S. women's team in Atlanta for the Olympic Games. So Ted brought Archer a copy of Rose's memoir, which Ted autographed, and he boned up on gymnastics so that he could discuss the subject with Archer, and in doing so, he tried to create what he hoped would be an environment more conducive for an unwavering liberal and an equally unwavering conservative to hammer out their differences. As the point of no return drew near, they met a second time, on July 31, with the clock ticking before the Senate would recess on August 2. And under that pressure, at six-thirty p.m., they arrived at a solution. Ted would accept MSAs, but only as a pilot program, which would have to be reauthorized, and only with a cap of 750,000 enrollees. And now this was done too.

Ted had outlasted Bob Dole, and though Lott was no less conservative than Dole—he was more—and though he complained, as Dole had, that Ted was "calling the shots" and that "Ted Kennedy is the problem" when it came to passing legislation, Lott was also more amenable to compromise now than Dole had been, especially with the month-long recess and the election campaign upon him, and he would even claim to have steered Kennedy-Kassebaum through the Senate himself as part of a deal he had struck with Clinton to move legislation. The bill was reconciled in conference, where Ted squared off against his son Patrick on the mental health parity addition—Ted held to his promise to exclude any amendments, including one like this that he would otherwise have supported, while Patrick was one of its foremost advocates—and without the mental health parity provision, it passed the Senate on August 2, without a single vote in opposition—a year to the day since it had been voted out of the Labor Committee. It passed the House by an equally wide margin, 421 to 2. A half-hour later, on the very next vote, the Senate passed the reconciled version of the minimum wage bill—the bill that had barely made it to the floor—by 76 to 22. In victory, Ted, uncharacteristically, was not generous toward the Republicans, chalking up the passage of Kennedy-Kassebaum not to their cooperation but to their fear. "Republicans have decided they need to pass Democratic initiatives before the election because their own record is too empty and too shameful to run on," he said, and he called the bill a "transparent insurance policy for endangered Republican candidates." (And if ungenerous, he was also incorrigible. At a press conference celebrating the passage of the minimum wage outside the Russell Office Building, he whispered conspiratorially to Representative George

Miller, "I'm introducing a new bill to increase the minimum wage again.") Now, after the bills had passed both houses of Congress, they awaited Bill Clinton's signature to become law—one, an unexciting law, as Kassebaum had said, and a small one, as Ted had said, but still arguably the most significant new healthcare reform since Medicare in 1965; the other, the first minimum wage increase in five years. Ted called it a "doubleheader victory" for two bills that had had "nine lives" and "needed all of them," and he told *The New York Times*'s Adam Clymer that it was the most satisfying day of his thirty-two years in the Senate because both bills represented something "very tangible" in bettering people's lives.

They weren't all victories. Bill Clinton in his bid for reelection sought to co-opt Republicans on their own issues, which was why Ted and his fellow liberals were always so wary of Clinton. The president had bought in to the Republican idea that the country was fundamentally conservative—an idea Ted had pushed hard against, even though he harbored his own doubts about the liberal hold on Americans. For years, Republicans had clubbed Democrats on welfare, had called welfare recipients irresponsible, lazy, and worse, chiselers—this had been Ronald Reagan's main gambit in tackling welfare—and had done their best to cut welfare funding, even though most of those recipients, two-thirds of them, were children under sixteen years of age, and even though the average welfare family, which Republicans had often characterized as an unmarried woman with a dozen offspring, was no larger than the average nonwelfare family. "Stopping the insanity of entitlement programs," Senator John Ashcroft had said the morning that welfare reform legislation was being voted upon, which reflected exactly how most Republicans viewed assistance to the poor: insanity. Clinton had made that campaign promise to "end welfare as we know it," and in September 1995, with Gingrich and his fellow House Republican leaders looking on, the Senate passed a welfare reform bill, 87 to 12—a "revolutionary step," Dole called it. Revolutionary it was. It ended the federal Aid to Families with Dependent Children program, which had guaranteed assistance to the poor, blockgranted funds to states, and slashed funding, though the most revolutionary provisions were forcing able-bodied recipients off welfare after two years and placing a five-year lifetime cap for anyone on welfare. Ted was one of the twelve senators voting against it, railing against the bill as "legislative child abuse," and in a long, impassioned speech on the floor, he denounced the bill as breaking America's promise to its poor children. "This bill is not about moving American families from welfare to work," he shouted. "It is about cutting off assistance to millions of poor, hungry, homeless, and disabled children." The House bill was even more draconian, denying benefits to teenage mothers and their children altogether.

Republicans thought they had Clinton in a vise, and that he would feel politically bound to sign a tough bill or veto it. He chose the latter. Clinton vetoed the Republicans' welfare reform measures twice—once as part of the budget reconciliation and a second time when Republicans, just to force Clinton to veto it, separated it out for a vote. But in 1996 it rose from the ashes, passed the Senate again on August 1, a day before the passage of Kennedy-Kassebaum and the minimum wage, and with an impending election and with most Americans antagonistic to welfare, Clinton decided to sign it into law, despite having called it, by one report, a "decent welfare bill wrapped in a sack of shit." A few Democrats, notably Pat Moynihan, who as an academic had been an expert in welfare, were enraged. Ted, though opposed, was philosophical, understanding that Clinton would bow to the politics. "He knows where I'm coming from," he said.

And Ted and Clinton were at loggerheads again when Clinton felt the need to co-opt Republicans on family values. The Defense of Marriage Act (DOMA) had been introduced by Republicans Bob Barr in the House and Don Nickles in the Senate. Though it had little legislative purpose—the House Judiciary Committee justified it as expressing a "moral disapproval of homosexuality"—it did have an electoral purpose, which was to pacify conservatives and especially the religious right. It defined marriage as a union between a man and a woman for the purposes of federal law, and it allowed states to deny recognition of same-sex marriages that had been sanctioned in other states. The gay community was understandably outraged. So was Ted Kennedy. DOMA arrived in the Senate during Ted's legislative campaign and shortly before the presidential election. Ted had no illusions about stopping it. He knew that there was too much homophobia in Congress and in the nation to do so. He assailed the bill as a "mean-spirited form of Republican gay-bashing cynically calculated to try to inflame the public eight weeks before the November 5 election." "We were not going to sit around and debate what was going to happen with the Defense of Marriage Act," his aide Melody Barnes recalled. Instead, Ted began working on a hate crime bill and on the Employment Non-

Discrimination Act that barred employer discrimination against gays. The latter bill came up for a vote on the same day as DOMA, September 10. It failed by a single vote—a "very emotional" vote, Barnes called it. Afterward Ted and Barnes walked out of the Senate chamber, and "there were wall-to-wall people," she said—gay activists and civil rights activists and labor activists—in the reception area, "standing on tables and benches." And when Ted appeared, they gave him an ovation in appreciation for what he had done. Then Ted and Barnes walked back to the office, and Barnes said that she and other staffers were "feeling really bad" at the loss and wondered how they might have won that extra vote. (Barnes said that she came to realize, "The Republicans weren't going to give us that vote.") But Ted was not dispirited. DOMA had passed the Senate 84 to 14, including 32 to 14 among Democrats. By comparison, he saw his narrow loss on job discrimination, with eight Republicans joining the Democrats in support, not as a defeat but as a victory. And that night they rounded up the activists and held a party in his office and on the balcony that ran outside the office, as a way of thanking all those who had worked so hard and "to celebrate something incredible that had been done," as Barnes put it.

III

As the legislators headed off to their campaigns that summer, Bill Clinton was comfortably ahead of Bob Dole in the polls and all but certain to win reelection. (At the time that the minimum wage and HIPAA bills passed, he had a twenty-three-point lead over Dole in the Gallup poll.) Clinton had snatched victory from the jaws of defeat—defeat being a Republican Congress that had been elected two years earlier with the intention of destroying liberalism and Clinton along with it. But Bill Clinton had co-opted them, taken their issues and made them his own, with a crime bill that put 100,000 more police on the streets and welfare reform and what Ted regarded as the legalized homophobia of DOMA, and he had outwitted them by pressing those elements of the Democratic agenda for which the Republicans, arrogantly and foolishly, had thought Americans shared their disdain, like the Kennedy-Kassebaum health reform and the minimum wage raise and federal funding for education, and resisting a Republican attempt to take the teeth out of FDA regulation as a sop to big pharmaceutical companies. Clinton was riding high. Newt Gingrich had lost his revolution with the budget stalemate and the government shutdown, which had turned not only ordinary Americans against him but also many moderate Republican legislators who realized how much of an electoral albatross he was. And by tying his fate to Gingrich's, Bob Dole sealed his own fate.

But as much credit as Clinton was given for his phoenix-like rise, and as much discredit as Gingrich and Dole had been given by Democrats for assisting it, Ted Kennedy had emerged from the legislative session as a Democratic hero and, in some quarters, as the man who had saved Bill Clinton's presidency. Almost single-handedly, Ted Kennedy had destroyed Bob Dole's campaign before it had even begun. "It was he who identified the minimum wage increase as a key issue of both principle and politics," Nick Littlefield was to say. "It was Senator Kennedy who forged a consensus among sometimes reluctant Democrats both on the substance of the bill and on the importance of making it a priority. It was Senator Kennedy who put together the coalition and the press strategy that made the issue salient to the public. It was he who relentlessly kept the issue alive with his knowledge of Senate procedures and willingness to go to the mat for what he believed." Littlefield could have said the same things about Kennedy-Kassebaum. In a chamber in which Ted Kennedy had little power on paper, as Bob Dole had said, he had bested the Republicans at their own game and rescued liberalism too by forging coalitions that supported his legislation. Democrats knew. "Virtually as effective in the minority as he is in the majority," Bill Clinton told Elsa Walsh, "and you can hardly say that about anybody." On Ted Kennedy's most satisfying day in the Senate, August 2, his double-header day, he was showered with praise—"precisely what being a U.S. Senator is all about and why it is so important for people to be able to make a difference in the lives of our fellow citizens," John Kerry said of him. Minority Leader Tom Daschle, who had been instrumental in helping Ted, commended him as a "professional's professional" and pointed to "his dedication, his intelligence, his integrity, his willingness to compromise and work with Senators from both sides of the aisle on both sides of the issues." Even Bob Dole and Trent Lott had conceded that Ted Kennedy ran the Senate.

And now, so too, did the media—the very media that had ridiculed Ted in 1991 after the Palm Beach episode, that had buried him and then written his political obituary, calling him an embarrassment, a lush, and a womanizer who would have a hard time keeping his Senate seat, that had talked of "Ted Kennedy on the Rocks," like one of his schooners run aground. Ted had been devastated. He had abased himself at his Harvard mea culpa. He had become even more guarded with the press, more nervous, "curiously lacking in self-confidence, even socially awkward . . . as if years of being judged have made him wary," a reporter noted of a man who had typically been outgoing and gregarious and usually unguarded. His longtime staffer Melody Miller talked of a new emotionalism he exhibited, a sensitivity, saying his "scar tissue is so frayed" that it had worn away at the old Kennedy stoicism and left him raw. But in a life that was defined by defeats, particularly those self-inflicted ones, and then by near-miraculous rehabilitations, he had risen once again by demonstrating his mastery of the Senate. "Big Man in Congress: Kennedy, of All People," Adam Clymer wrote in an admiring New York Times piece that August, which observed, "Probably not since Senator Everett Dirksen and Representative William McCulloch provided a critical balance in getting civil rights bills passed in the 1960's has any member of the Congressional minority influenced the agenda as much as Edward M. Kennedy has this year," and he quoted Tom Daschle, "I don't know anybody who contributed more" to the session's Democratic successes. The "consistent figure in every task force at every meeting," Daschle said of Ted. Ross Baker, a professor of political science at Rutgers University, told Clymer that for Ted "to have had an influence to varying degrees on important aspects of public policy over nearly 40 years ranks with the Henry Clays and Daniel Websters." (Ted's father-in-law loved to tell the story of how he mentioned to Ted that a writer had called Ted and Webster the two greatest senators in history, and that Ted drolly quipped, "What did Webster do?") Lloyd Grove wrote an equally admiring and much longer profile in The Washington Post, describing Ted "with the whitening mane and the mottled face of a man who's been to hell and back," which Ted had been. "The blue-gray eyes are rimmed in red. The famous face—almost as iconic on the American landscape as the faces on Mount Rushmore—is coarse and blotchy. The senator's pale hands are perpetually in motion—tickling the air, worrying his shirt collar, or scuttling around his richly tailored navy suit like disoriented crabs." An older Ted Kennedy, Grove had painted, a seeming wreckage of the Ted Kennedy who had entered the Senate thirty-two years earlier with strength and youth and beauty—and yet Grove was impressed by what Ted had managed to accomplish against the odds. "Despite being out on the leftward wing of the minority party, Kennedy is somehow still formidable—more, perhaps, than ever," Grove found, calling him the "minority party's most visible strategist." And there were more, many more accolades: "Ted Kennedy, a new man [yet again]. The Ted Kennedy walking the halls is a far cry from the one two years ago. He's trimmer, more focused and on a roll," wrote the *Los Angeles Times*, clearly seeing a different Ted physically than Grove; "Kennedy, An Unlikely Star of the 104th Congress," in the *Chicago Tribune;* "Climbing Back Atop the Hill," in *Newsday;* "Senate Icon Shows Off Skill," in the *Christian Science Monitor.* Columnist E. J. Dionne, Jr., told *PBS NewsHour,* as Congress was about to recess for the campaign, "This is not the Republican Contract with America. It's Ted Kennedy's Contract with America." And Elsa Walsh titled her long Kennedy profile in *The New Yorker* four months after the 1996 election, "Kennedy's Hidden Campaign," attributing Bill Clinton's reelection victory to Ted Kennedy's strategy of defending liberalism and to Ted's legislative successes—*his* campaign. Trent Lott would later boast that the legislation that passed in that session was the result of a "truce" that Clinton adviser Dick Morris had arranged between Lott and Gingrich on the one side and Clinton on the other and that Democrats were deeply resentful of it. "In the end, it didn't matter," Lott would write. "With Morris's help, Clinton, Newt Gingrich and I engineered all the changes. The Senate Democrats were like a fifth wheel. We didn't need them." But this was revisionist history and blatantly false. Ted Kennedy, not Bob Dole or Trent Lott or Newt Gingrich, was the main player in that Congress—and Ted Kennedy was the victor.

Satisfying, Ted had called those victories, and coming after his Massachusetts reelection during the horrible midterms of 1994, when Democrats had gone down to humiliating defeat, he had, as a survivor, assumed a new role: At sixty-five, he was an elder statesman. His friend John Tunney said, "I'll talk to him and ask how things are going. 'Well, I got this done and I got this done,' and he loves talking about this stuff . . . about what he's accomplishing on a day-to-day basis." And Tunney said Ted was thinking now of his legacy as well. "He loves history. He reads a lot of books on history," and he was seeing himself, Tunney said, not just in the context of the Kennedy legacy, comparing himself to his brothers, "but more than the family, of the Senate as well." David Burke, his old administrative assistant, found him different, and more confident about his work, more substantive, deeper, able to speak knowledgably about any issue, and with an understanding of the Senate. "He had no doubt about himself and the issues of the day facing our nation," Burke said. "He was a truly grown-up senior citizen." Milton Gwirtzman noted the same thing in how Ted operated at hearings. He used to be deferential to witnesses. He was deferential no longer. He was in command. The "lion of the Senate," some called him now in an acknowledgment both of his age and of his stature. Ted himself told Elsa Walsh it was an "enormously different phase to me in my life, not one you could have sort of anticipated or expected or described, but it has been a very real one and it's been a wonderful one."

Longevity had helped make him an elder statesman, but many senators had been in the chamber a long time without receiving the kind of respect Ted had earned from his colleagues, even if it was only respect for the preternatural ability he had to get his way; nor did they have the power he exercised, even in that Republican Senate where comity was in short supply and the Republicans were on a political search-and-destroy mission. Republicans publicly reviled Kennedy, and many of the most ideological reviled him privately as well. "Ted Kennedy is still the man in American politics Republicans love to hate," the late Republican National chairman Lee Atwater had said. Another Republican operative called him "utterly shameless, brazen and indifferent to what should be his internal conscience." Another conservative wrote, "No one in America has more liberal guilt than Ted Kennedy. It oozes out of him. In word, deed, and lifestyle, the Massachusetts Democrat symbolizes the worst aspects of limousine liberalism, liberal guilt and all."

But these were not Senate colleagues, without whom Ted could have accomplished nothing. In the Senate, among most of his fellow legislators, the feelings were different because Ted Kennedy was not shameless or brazen, was not dripping with liberal guilt—Elsa Walsh called Ted's liberalism a "political religion, of a kind not otherwise found in politics today," which was not a description of someone wracked with political guilt, whatever personal guilt he might have suffered—and he was not an inflexible ideologue, no matter how much he might have believed in the causes he pursued. In the Senate, he was one of them. "What really makes the Senate work—as our heroes knew profoundly," former majority leader Howard Baker once wrote, "is an understanding of human nature, an appreciation of the hearts as well as the minds, the frailties as well as the strengths, of one's colleagues and one's constituents." That described Ted Kennedy. The standard of senatorial power had always been Lyndon Johnson, as chronicled by Robert Caro in his classic *Master of the Senate.*

Men feared Lyndon Johnson, feared his power to manipulate and his power to deny. Ted Kennedy had become a master of the Senate, perhaps *the* master of the Senate, but even as he gained power and exercised it, he was no Lyndon Johnson. No one feared Ted Kennedy, save for the fear they might have had that he would beat them tactically or through the force of his commitment. Johnson was a backslapper, an arm-twister, both an intimidator and a wheedler—whatever the task required. Ted Kennedy was none of these, save an occasional backslapper, and that was less a manipulation than a genuine expression of his sociability toward his colleagues. Lyndon Johnson used those tactics—whatever it took— because he was in a hurry to get out of the Senate and into the presidency he coveted. Ted Kennedy was in no hurry and that might have been one source of his appeal to his colleagues. He had long ago given up his dreams of the presidency and had opted for a lifetime in the Senate, and he used his social skills over time, slowly and deliberately, to accrue a different kind of power than Johnson's—not the hard power of senatorial muscle but the soft power of congeniality and eventually even of legislative integrity of the sort Ted had so admired in Phil Hart, the conscience of the Senate and one of his mentors. Ted understood people not because, like Lyndon Johnson, he could read their hearts and minds and use it against them. He understood people because he was so intimate with his own fallibility.

And so at sixty-five, when he had become the "lion of the Senate," he didn't roar, but he nonetheless ran the Senate in the 104th Congress. He ran it even though he was in the minority and the Republicans controlled everything, and even though Majority Leader Bob Dole and then Trent Lott were determined to get their way and stop Bill Clinton from getting his, and even though, one might have added, he had disgraced himself just a few years earlier and been something of a pariah. That was what prompted some to marvel and ask: How had Kennedy managed to redeem himself and seize that power? The young Ted Kennedy had relied on the deference he had cultivated as the youngest and least impressive of his impressive family to ingratiate himself with his Senate colleagues. He had no arrogance. The older Ted Kennedy no longer needed to be deferential. He could have rested on his laurels—in those times when he had had laurels. He could have used his seniority and stature to cow colleagues, as solons of the past, like Richard Russell, the most powerful senator in the chamber in the 1950s, had done. But Ted Kennedy's power was a function less of his seniority or of his status than of his constancy—political, yes, his politics hadn't changed in his thirty-five years in the Senate—but even more, his personal constancy. The respect he received, the awe he could engender as a senior senator, wasn't a matter of how much Ted Kennedy had changed or even grown during his long time in the Senate as of how much he hadn't changed.

Tactics changed, the institution itself changed, the motives of many of its members changed, the antagonisms sharpened. But he was the same man he had always been, with the same acute sense of the chemistry of the Senate and the same personal tools to work it.

The older Ted Kennedy *still* never personalized his legislative battles. "He could give the most partisan speech he'd ever heard on the floor," John McCain quoted Bob Dole, "and then come into the cloakroom and convince you that he wasn't talking about you." And he never took the brickbats personally either. Ted would throw his arm around a Republican colleague and say, "I know about those letters you send out to blast people as being a Kennedy liberal," and the colleague would say, "Yes, but we don't want you ever to be defeated. We need you to raise money." And said Senator Patrick Leahy, a Ted ally, "Ted was okay with that." While there were those across the aisle, albeit few in number, who thought him an enemy, *he* had no enemies, with the possible exception of Jesse Helms; he had only opponents, and the Republicans knew and appreciated that.

And the older Ted Kennedy, though slower of step and bigger of girth, *still* had his drive, his ambition to get things done that impressed his fellow legislators and pushed them to keep up with him—their sense of not wanting to disappoint him being both a source of his power and a consequence of it. "Once he started to see that the Rose Garden"—meaning a presidential bill signing—"was coming into focus," Representative George Miller was to recall, "boy, you'd better get your stuff done quickly, because that's about to leave the station, and then, once he said, 'This is it,' you lost your ability to get your remaining things in the bill." And Miller said of Ted's pressure, "There weren't many people who could do that. Maybe the Speaker of the House or the leader of the Senate. . . . This is a tough thing to do around here, because it's hard to get that kind of deference. But he was a Kennedy, Ted Kennedy. He was a lion of the Senate." And his colleagues did defer to him as he had once deferred to them. And it wasn't only that Ted was getting things done, but that he invited those colleagues to join him, among them almost always a Republican colleague, which meant that *they* were getting things done too—a power derived from mutuality. In 1995 and 1996, 145 Black churches were destroyed by fire in an arson wave. Ted recruited North Carolina Republican Duncan Faircloth, one of the most conservative members of the Senate, to join him in introducing the Church Arson Prevention Act, which made it a federal crime to damage church property or inhibit the right to worship and extended penalties for doing so. It passed the Senate 98 to 0. Yet at the same time, Ted would read a fundraising letter that had been sent over Faircloth's signature, excoriating Ted for "quietly" working to kill a national right-to-work law—a letter Ted would read aloud at union rallies and tell the crowd, "We're going to kill it. But we're not going to do it quietly," and then tear it up and toss the pieces in the air.

And though he was now an elder statesman himself and might have coasted, Ted Kennedy *still* prepared for his legislative battles as painstakingly as he had when he was proving himself as a young senator—preparation that made him so effective on the Senate floor, more effective than any other senator on that floor, where reputations were made and lost. He still never went into battle unarmed, and he never went into battle without a clear strategy. "He studies the subject, learns it well," Senator Joe Lieberman told the *Christian Science Monitor* in that laudatory profile calling Ted a "Senate icon." When he came to the floor, he was fully briefed. The "best briefed senator down there," his onetime press secretary, James Manley, said. And though he had reviewed the issues in his office with his staff and at night rummaging through The Bag in his study and could always talk knowledgably about them, he created a system when he was floor-managing a bill by which he was able to discredit opposing arguments as soon as they were delivered. He would have his staff bring him a big accordion file filled with folders with his talking points, and as he sat there listening to the debate, listening to the opponent's attack on his position, he would tell his staffer—a "substance staffer," the person was called—that he was going to have to respond and then had him or her pull the appropriate rebuttal from that file and provide him with the answers he needed point by point. (When Tom Rollins, who had been a debater, served as chief counsel to the Labor Committee, he even hired two former national debate champions to prepare briefing materials for Ted, and Rollins would say, "We were ready for floor debate. We were *wired* for floor debate.") No senator was better, as his aide James Manley would say, at "give-and-take on the floor," because "nine times out of ten he knew more than anyone else trying to challenge him on the floor," and because "it wasn't so easy to go down and try and sandbag Senator Kennedy."

Those charges earlier in his career that he was a puppet of his staff were discredited by now, which was power too. His briefing books were "legendary," James Manley said, for their annotations and underlinings—*Ted*'s annotations, *Ted*'s underlinings—and staffers knew how assiduous he was in examining their arguments. When he was being briefed on the effect on employment after the implementation of the last minimum wage raise, a staffer was showing him charts on how employment eventually rose, but Ted noticed that employment had actually decreased as the raise was being phased in and angrily—angrily because he knew he might have to defend this in the floor debate—asked the staffer to explain. "We passed it in '89. The first year is '90, and the second year is '91. It's going down," Ted snarled. "We were in the middle of a recession," his staffer answered. "Well, you can say that. If I was the opponent, I'd say that in 1990, when you first put in the increase, employment went down," Ted bristled. And before he left for the floor, he told the staffer, "We'll have more answers than we have now." And his floor speeches were just as meticulously prepared as his debates. "When Kennedy got up to speak," Bob Dole was to say, "—I don't know whether that was the first time he'd read the speech, maybe the second or third—he could rely on it being accurate. I assume they made mistakes, but it was just a given that when you were going up against Kennedy, you'd better have some good staff work, because he's got it, and he's got resources where he can get it from Harvard or wherever it comes from."

And the older Ted Kennedy *still* knew how to use the Senate floor not only as a platform but also as an informational and social hub where he could learn and where he could ingratiate as he had done as a young senator. Most senators arrived on the floor to vote and then left. Ted Kennedy arrived with an agenda—"Who do I need to talk to? Who do I need to persuade to vote a certain way?" Melody Barnes would recall—and he didn't leave immediately. He loved the Senate floor; he was "most comfortable" on the Senate floor, according to James Manley; "such a home to him that he can't make any mistakes on the Senate floor," Dave Burke would say. He had learned how to "read" the Senate floor, sitting at his desk with his staff nearby, surveying the scene, watching closely the action there and calculating his tactical maneuvers. He had a red folder on the desk outside his office—the "floor folder" it was called—and staffers who had an issue that they wanted him to discuss with a fellow senator would put a card in the folder, just as they put their memos in The Bag, and Ted would take those cards, which had become so familiar to his colleagues during his years in the Senate, to the floor and talk to those senators, sometimes walking the floor and hunting for them, zeroing in on them, then clapping his hand on their back and taking them aside to a desk or into the cloakroom, his hand remaining on that back all the while, and after the chat, handing them the card with the points on why that senator should vote a certain way. And Carey Parker would say that he never had to look at those cards, that he knew the issues so well—as Dave Burke had also remarked—he could talk extemporaneously about them, and that would often surprise the senator to whom he was talking, the "degree to which he is familiar with some rather esoteric details of the particular legislation they're working on." Parker said that during the "vote-a-rama"—the day at the end of a session of Congress when there is a rush of business before the recess, and amendments to appropriations bills are "stacked," one after another in rapid succession—a process that didn't lend itself obviously to deliberation—Ted would be at his best, collaring colleagues ("He'll find five Democrats and three Republicans and talk to each one about a separate issue on a pending bill") and talking over the bills with them at breakneck speed, which was, Parker said, "remarkable to behold." A "master at it," Parker called him.

And if Ted Kennedy knew how to use the floor to his advantage during debates and during votes, he *still* knew how to use the floor—that floor where reputations were won and lost—during speeches to build his status among his fellow senators. He made "great speeches," Senate parliamentarian Robert Dove said, "well-thought-out speeches." Loud and dramatic speeches. Ted could be histrionic. Though he could have moved up nearer the front of the chamber as his seniority increased, he had elected to stay in his brother Jack's old Senate seat in the back row just off the cloakroom, a seat among the freshmen, a friendly cabal, the better to socialize, the better to spot who was coming onto the floor and who was leaving it. But because he seldom went to the well of the chamber, the area just in front of the dais, where many of the senators chose to speak, Ted often had to declaim. "It was usually very passionate. It was usually red-faced. It was usually exhortation," Martin Tolchin, who covered the Senate for *The New York Times*, recollected. "He was angry . . . very, very emotional." *Bel-*

lowed was the word that was often used to describe his speeches. "When I'd see Kennedy get up in the back, I knew we were in for something," Bob Dole said. "Then he'd start screaming and shouting, and I knew this must be more than I thought." "One had the impression that he could have been heard without public address system, or maybe even outside the chamber," Senator Richard Lugar said, adding, "I can't remember what he had to say, but it was very impressive." (In fact, Ted seldom used the amplification system.) Once, after Nancy Kassebaum chided him for his volume, he returned from the Thanksgiving recess and told her that his sister Eunice had also complained about his volume at the dinner table. Another Republican Senate colleague, Mike Enzi, said of Ted's floor speeches, "His blood pressure goes up and up, and he gets louder and louder and louder." But Enzi also said that Ted would tell him, "On this one, I've got to rant a little bit, and I'd be a little more than comfortable if you'd leave the floor." Barack Obama would later describe Ted Kennedy speaking on the Senate floor: "The argument would unspool—the face reddening, the voice rising—building to a crescendo like a revivalist sermon, no matter how mundane the issue at hand. And then the speech would end, and he would become the old avuncular Teddy again, wandering down the aisle to check on the roll call or sit next to a colleague, his hand on their shoulder or forearm, whispering in their ear or breaking into a hearty laugh—the kind that made you not care that he was probably softening you up for some future vote he might need."

"Theatrics," many of his colleagues called these performances where Ted would be assailing the Republicans in those booming tones of his and then clapping that arm around them afterward and asking, as Orrin Hatch remembered, "How was that, Orrin?" as if it *were* a performance. And even James Manley would say that one of his "most memorable experiences" was watching Ted on the floor one Friday afternoon, delivering what Manley called a "stem-winder"—the "full pounding and the roar and the whole ball of wax"—a speech so thunderous that Manley said his ears were ringing, and he was literally driven out of the chamber. And when it was over, the two of them walked together to the elevator, and Ted smiled at him, as if to say, "We did good. That was fun." And for Ted Kennedy it was fun—part of the fun of being in the Senate.

But there was little real power to be derived from fun, and his fellow senators knew this of him: It wasn't all performance, and it wasn't all fun. Ted

Kennedy reddened and pounded and thundered because, after all those years in the Senate, thirty-five years, he still cared—"he really cared," as Senate parliamentarian Robert Dove said of those speeches. "You could tell that." And this might have been the greatest source of his power: that for all his personal foibles, Ted Kennedy had the moral authority of one who still cared sincerely and passionately. Lyndon Johnson, the last great master of the Senate, seldom wielded moral authority. Senators were afraid of him because of what he could do to them, the multitude of ways that he could help and hurt them; it was only later, as president, that Johnson invoked moral authority and invoked it often, only later that he *felt* it. Ted Kennedy always invoked morality—in every piece of legislation he proposed, in every debate in which he engaged, and in every speech he gave. His was the voice of the powerless, as he liked to say. While there might have been some political benefit in doing so when he had his eyes on the presidency and he wanted to rally the liberals in his party and the minorities who voted Democratic, there was no benefit once he forsook his presidential ambitions, and less benefit still when most of the country forsook its concern for the powerless and marginalized and stressed aspiration and success instead. Republicans had a different idea of moral authority. It was about personal responsibility and freedom from government and about religious dogma and helping business, presumably because business was self-actualizing and people in need were not. Republicans had come to see the morality that Ted Kennedy promoted as a weakness, a deficiency, a lack of strength. *Bleeding heart* had long been the derogatory term for those who cared. But theirs was not a moral argument; it was essentially a political one—an appeal to those who were self-sufficient. Ted Kennedy was *all* moral argument. And whether one agreed with him or not, this too was true: His opponents might have dismissed his moral vigor, but they recognized it, still recognized it after all of Ted's foibles, and it cowed them. John McCain said that Ted had a kind of majesty in the Senate—something that not even Lyndon Johnson had. And McCain recalled that once Ted was offering an amendment when Trent Lott used parliamentary maneuvers to delay it by adjourning the Senate. And Ted, this time leaving his back desk for the well, stood and thundered in that well, even though he had no right to speak now: "How long? How long, how long, how long, how long will we wait to give the American people what they deserve?" And McCain said that Ted's fellow senators, most of whom were still on the floor after a vote, were aghast, stunned by the force of his declamation. "And when we came back from recess, guess what?" McCain said. "We took up Ted's issue." And McCain said this: "It was tremendous. It was good."

And there was another form of moral authority too that still empowered Ted Kennedy among his fellow senators—not the loud, emphatic one that Ted had used to subdue those senators on the floor but a much softer form of authority, the one he had used in defeating Mitt Romney in his Senate reelection, when so many in Massachusetts were reminded of the deeds that Ted Kennedy had done for them. The best-prepared senator, the hardest-working and most driven senator, the most knowledgeable senator, the most tactically acute senator, the most sociable senator, the most trustworthy senator (Ted's word was always good, his colleagues said), the most generous senator when it came to parceling out credit, was still also the kindest and most thoughtful senator, which was something that no one would have said of Lyndon Johnson. Ted Kennedy was the senator who sent Robert Byrd's beloved wife roses for her birthday, and when she turned seventy, he sent seventy roses to her in West Virginia. He was the senator who took the train up to Joe Biden's Delaware home unannounced after Biden suffered an aneurysm, arriving with a painting of an Irish stag under his arm as a gift and a bathing suit for jumping into the Biden pool, and who stayed for six hours encouraging Biden. The two men hadn't been close, but Biden would say that "something changed once I was under attack" and that "Teddy has a strong streak of loyalty" and that "when you are down, when you are in jeopardy, he not only helps you, he jumps in on all fours." Ted Kennedy was the senator who phoned Republican Gordon Smith when Smith's son committed suicide to share his own sorrows with him and commiserate with Smith in his grief. Ted Kennedy was the senator who when Phil Hart was dying of cancer visited him often and then rounded up the votes to name the new Senate office building after him while he was still alive to receive the honor, and he was the senator who would visit former senator Frank Church in the hospital when Church was succumbing to cancer and tell him what was going on in the Senate and read to him at his bedside. Ted Kennedy was the senator who sent little gifts to his colleagues—a pair of training pants with Irish Mist on the back when Mike Enzi's first grandchild was born, or a cane that Joe Kennedy and Jack Kennedy had used, when he heard that Senator John Warner had wrenched his knee—the cane that he had also loaned to Barry Goldwater. Ted Kennedy was the senator who, when George Mitchell was in electoral trouble and Pat Moynihan quipped snarkily at the Democratic caucus that "even Mitchell is only twenty-four points behind," came up to Mitchell afterward—the first one who did, Mitchell said—and put his arm around Mitchell's shoulder and told him, "We believe in you. We have confidence in you. We think you can win. Don't get down as a result of this." Ted Kennedy was the senator who sent thank you notes—always the thank you notes—since no courtesy, however small, ever went unremarked upon. (As one staffer said, "His mother trained him well.") "When people ask about him, one word that comes to mind is 'thoughtful,'" Representative Nancy Pelosi, later the speaker of the House, was to say of him. "He was so thoughtful, always calling people to see how they were, to congratulate them, wish them well, or, if they were sick or whatever."

Thoughtful he was, and the thoughtfulness was pervasive, no more a performance than his most passionate speeches and no less sincere. When Bill Clinton had nominated Nancy Soderberg, Ted's former foreign policy adviser, to the United Nations and Republicans blocked it by falsely accusing her of funneling Chinese money to the campaign, Ted phoned her unsolicited and asked how she was doing, and when she burst into tears, he spoke to her for a half-hour and "just told me about all the horrible things that have happened to him," Soderberg recollected, from the Harvard cheating scandal to Ed McCormack sniping at his first Senate election debate, "If your name was Edward Moore," "and he just said, 'You think everyone is staring at you, and it's going to be horrible,' and then I would go into a campaign with a bunch of women who couldn't pay their bills and they didn't care about all that stuff. Just get through it. No one's going to remember it in six months." When a young translator during a hearing kept garbling the translation and the audience started laughing, Ted told him what a good job he was doing and how much he appreciated the man's efforts. When he and Jan Kalicki, one of his first foreign policy advisers, were walking from the Senate Office Building to the Capitol and Kalicki, focused on his papers, looked up to see that Ted was no longer at his side, he found him kneeling beside a boy in a wheelchair, talking to him. "And there was no camera or other people to say, 'Oh, isn't that amazing, what he's doing?'" Whenever he passed a Capitol policeman, he would ask, "Hey, how are you doing?" "He just liked people," said John McCain, who had witnessed that gregariousness of Ted's with those policemen. When Michael Johnson, the young man who sold newspapers to the senators, earned an A in school, he said Ted gave him a dollar for each one. And when Ted entered the Capitol elevator, where the operator had Down syndrome, Ted would always get into a conversation with him and pull a coupon out of his pocket for an ice cream cone because he knew the young man liked sweets.

And in the final analysis, this was, more than anything else, why Ted Kennedy became the master of the Senate in that 104th Congress when he had passed his legislation against those overwhelming odds and prevented Republicans from passing some of theirs. It was because he still exuded moral authority, and he still exuded it because he still exuded personal decency. Though he was an astute and adept politician, he was the master because he was also a good and kind man who believed fervently in compassion, both legislatively and personally. He was the master because his colleagues knew that Ted Kennedy, for all his flaws, or perhaps because of them, really cared about them and about others. And there was tremendous power in that—enough power to rule the Senate.

NINETEEN

Endings and Epilogues

THE 1996 PRESIDENTIAL campaign was anticlimactic. With the Republicans having once again overplayed their hand—and with Newt Gingrich's seeming arrogance permeating the entire party—they and their candidate Bob Dole were on the defensive throughout. Ted, speaking at the Democratic National Convention late in August, cited an attack on Clinton delivered by Texas Republican senator Kay Bailey Hutchison at the Republican convention, and retaliated in prime Ted Kennedy style against what he called the "radical wish list of the education-cutting, environment-trashing, Medicare-slashing, choice-denying, tolerance-repudiating, assault rifle-coddling, government-closing, tax loophole-granting, minimum wage-opposing Republican majority." And of attacks leveled on Hillary Clinton by Gingrich and by the savage conservative radio talk-show host Rush Limbaugh, who now seemed to be the voice of the party, he cited the defense of admirers of Eleanor Roosevelt against *her* critics: "We love her for the enemies she has made." That November, Clinton won easily with 49 percent of the vote to 40.7 percent for Dole and 8.4 percent for H. Ross Perot, the Texas businessman who ran as an independent as he had four years earlier. Ted played a major role in that victory. Elsa Walsh in *The New Yorker* would say that the "message of the Clinton reelection campaign—of the more than eighty-five million dollars' worth of ads that were paid for by the Clinton campaign and Democratic fund-raising efforts—was defined and driven by Edward Kennedy." Ted was still a bête noire among most Republicans, who tried to blacken other liberal candidates by pointing to their association with him: Alabama Democratic senatorial candidate Roger Bedford, who had been a Ted delegate in 1980 and whom Republicans labeled "way too liberal for

Alabama"; Senator Max Cleland in Georgia, who had been gravely wounded in an ordnance accident in the military that cost him his legs and an arm, but who had written Ted in 1992, during Ted's doldrums, "Hang in there! Millions of your fans in this country and around the world are pulling for you in your reelection campaign"; Senator Max Baucus in Montana, who voted with Ted 71 percent of the time, which Republicans clearly saw as inexcusable. And while Clinton was easily reelected, in part by following the Kennedy playbook, Republican objections notwithstanding, Republicans maintained their majorities in both houses of Congress, in some measure, no doubt, by laying into that playbook, too, the playbook of government activism, which meant another two years, at least, of the legislative slog that had marked the previous two years.

Even Bill Clinton's overwhelming victory came with its caveats. After the failure of his healthcare plan in 1994, he entered 1996 with a series of small initiatives rather than large ones; the "Small Deal," *Newsweek* labeled it, and attributed his win in part to his having changed the subject "from grand to homelier concerns that didn't require swollen bureaucrats and red ink." On the other hand, the Democratic pollster Stanley Greenberg concluded that Clinton had won largely because of his support for "Medicare, education and the environment," big Democratic issues, rather than for welfare reform and cutting the deficit, Republican-driven issues, much less his "small deal." In short, by embracing liberalism tentatively while co-opting conservativism, Clinton had managed to hold the middle, but he had muddled the message. A victory for the "vital center," Clinton had called it in his victory speech at Little Rock, borrowing Arthur Schlesinger, Jr.'s, term, though Schlesinger himself pointed out that there was a difference between a "vital center" and a "dead center." Bob Shrum had another verdict. He called Clinton's win a "victory without a mandate."

The "dead center" or the "Third Way" or "triangulation" or a "victory without a mandate" did not particularly appeal to Ted Kennedy, who had hoped that a win might move Clinton further leftward. He told biographer Burton Hersh shortly after the election that he was once again deeply concerned about Clinton's direction, especially since George Stephanopoulos and Leon Panetta, two of Ted's liberal allies, had left the administration, to be replaced by centrist New Democrats. It was no time, he felt, for retrenchment. "What has been developing in America since 1972 is an enormous [economic] disparity, with close to sixty-five percent of Americans losing ground," he told Hersh. "So that's the overarching issue as we go into the next century. Is the system going to work for a few, or should it work for everybody?" which had become liberal boilerplate. But it wasn't boilerplate for Bill Clinton. He quickly set to work trying to find some accommodation with the Republicans to cut the deficit while at the same time cutting taxes, especially for the wealthy, and slowing Medicare growth. The "repairer of the breach" was how he now saw himself, according to one of his speechwriters. Assembling his economic team that November, Clinton said his highest priority was a balanced budget bill, which was one of Gingrich's highest priorities too, but one that held little appeal for liberal Democrats, who saw it as the Republicans did: a way to starve government. But Clinton was no ideologue. He was a survivor. Like the election itself, Clinton's legislative wish list constituted, as Shrum described it, a "strategy of personal presidential survival," but while he would rescue himself by yielding to his Republican opponents, Shrum thought that he had "built no lasting foundation for a Democratic comeback," meaning a liberal comeback, and seemed to have no interest in one. He had capitulated to the very people he had defeated.

Even before his inauguration, Bill Clinton and Newt Gingrich began bargaining, and later in the year, that August, they finally struck their long-delayed budget deal—a balanced budget deal. Clinton and Gingrich were suddenly in partnership—Clinton because he was protecting his flanks, particularly his right flank, and Gingrich because he had been "shell shocked," as Republican congressman Joe Scarborough put it, speaking for many in the party, from the government shutdown that had driven his popularity into the ground, and he was now looking for a rapprochement with Clinton to save himself. He got it. John Harris, a Clinton biographer, noted the irony for Clinton that a "man who had run on a 'putting the people first' platform had retained the support of those people by following Wall Street's economic policies." (The bill had the largest tax cuts since Reagan's in 1981, including a reduction in the estate tax and an 8 percent cut in capital gains taxes, both of which went almost exclusively to the wealthy.) And Harris wrote, "So be it, Clinton decided." On the day of the balanced budget bill's and the tax cuts' passage, Clinton called the bills the "achievement of a generation and a triumph for every American."

But this was not Ted Kennedy's way of thinking. Ted Kennedy had opposed the bills as they were being negotiated. "Are the wealthy corporations being asked to give up any of the massive subsidies they receive under the current spending and tax laws?" he questioned. And yet in the end, even though a few liberals, including House minority leader Richard Gephardt, opposed them as being against the party's principles—Ted's principles—Ted voted for both the balanced budget and the tax cuts, compromising those principles. Ted did so despite his abhorrence for the balanced budget because he had a powerful reason to support the bills—one that was both substantive and political, which is to say the only way he could achieve the substantive was through the political. The reason was that tucked inside the budget was one of Ted Kennedy's most cherished goals, and without that budget, it would not have been realized. Inside that budget was a major new healthcare program.

Since the demise of Clinton's Health Security Act, health reform had been in a death spiral. Republicans had tried ceaselessly to defund Medicare and eliminate Medicaid, and even the modest Kennedy-Kassebaum bill had had to weather those Republican efforts to halt it with MSAs. Ted realized that there would be no comprehensive or universal health insurance for the foreseeable future. That was a lost cause—lost because Trent Lott, disturbed by Bob Dole's inability to prevent Republicans from working across the aisle and then by Lott's having to make concessions himself to help the Republicans in the election, was determined not to let that happen again on his watch. Lott's opposition to bipartisanship was so implacable that he had rebuked Jim Jeffords, the moderate new chairman of the Senate Labor Committee—Nancy Kassebaum had decided not to stand for reelection in 1996—for collaborating with Ted on a bill that set standards for managed care plans, a bill known generally as the "Patients' Bill of Rights," on the basis, said Lott's spokesperson, that the majority leader was "very suspicious of those who might be using well-intentioned legislation to move the ball on national health care," even though there was no possibility of that. Ted responded by releasing a memo that had been drafted by the Health Insurance Association of America, a health insurance lobbying group, citing a concerted effort to stop any healthcare bill from passage. In truth, for all Lott's worries, Ted had become even more of an incrementalist than he had been. He had no choice. In the majority, Ted had had a staff of one hundred, all working to advance Ted's legislation. In the minority, it was less than half that number across all his committees and his office. On the Health Subcommittee, where he was still the ranking member, he had three full-time staffers and five fellows and a group of interns who came and went, and they divided a long list of health issues, but in the minority, he was fighting mostly rearguard actions now, like his defense of the FDA since Gingrich and his fellow Republicans were intent on pulling its regulatory teeth. Ted had beaten back their efforts in 1995 and 1996, and as they intensified their efforts in the first year of Clinton's second term, he fought even more vigorously to prevent them. Ted had twenty objections to Gingrich's reform bill that had already passed committee. "Kennedy went to the mat on this," his health adviser, David Nexon, recalled. "By delaying and arguing and blustering and negotiating and mounting a major PR campaign and writing inflammatory letters to *The New York Times*," Nexon said, he was able to get compromises on all but two of those twenty provisions. "And the question was whether to keep fighting or declare victory and go home." Kennedy kept fighting. One of those issues was the regulation of cosmetics and whether the federal government should regulate them or whether that task should devolve to the states, where regulation was likely to be lax, and the other was lifting FDA limits on approval of medical devices for a purpose other than the one for which the device was originally intended. Ted took to the floor with the charts he loved so much and began a long speech—a speech that lasted three days, a speech for which, Nexon said, the staff sat at the back of the chamber devising ways to keep him going, a speech that threatened to be a filibuster. The bill passed, 98 to 2 with all Ted's changes but the last two. But Ted Kennedy *still* was not finished. Ted kept fighting. In conference, he won two more compromises—one that allowed states to regulate cosmetics unless the FDA issued regulations of its own, because, it was said, the cosmetics companies realized that Ted had done more harm to them through his negative publicity than they would have gained from the relaxed regulation; and the other that allowed the FDA to test medical devices if it found a "reasonable likelihood" that a device would be used for a purpose that could have a harmful effect. He had fought and he had won.

But those were relatively small concerns, incremental concerns—health at the margins. There were bigger concerns, and one in particular. If Ted had accepted the fact that large-scale health reform was finished for the foreseeable future, there was yet one reform worth fighting for, one that Republicans could only reject at their peril, one that was, Ted felt, morally unassailable: Ted Kennedy wanted to provide healthcare for children, and not just poor children for whom Medicaid already provided healthcare, but children of the working poor and the lower middle class whose parents could not afford insurance but were not poor enough to qualify for Medicaid. Denying healthcare to those who needed it on the pretext that private insurance could do the job more efficiently than government had been the Republican talking point since Medicare, which even Bob Dole had voted against in 1965, along with sixteen other Republicans, though demonstrably the market had not provided that care. Denying healthcare to children was something else again. When Lyndon Johnson signed a bill early in 1966 extending the enrollment period for seniors in Medicare, he discussed another initiative as a bookend to Medicare: to insure all children under six years of age. "I want to be remembered as the one who spent his whole life trying to get more people . . . to have medicine and have attention, nursing, hospital and doctors' care when they need it," Johnson said, and he cited the Declaration of Independence and its line that "all men are created equal" as applying to healthcare, but he said, "They are not equal if they don't have a chance . . . for a doctor to take care of their teeth or their eyes when they are little." Much as he wanted to, Johnson had failed to provide that chance. Now Ted Kennedy, who had wanted to be remembered as the senator who provided comprehensive healthcare, would try.

Ted had proposed a child healthcare bill on the last day of the Senate before the 1996 midterms, opting for block grants to the states to be paid for by the federal government and with unlimited enrollment, but he let John Kerry introduce it because Kerry was in a fierce reelection campaign against Republican governor Bill Weld and needed the help. It couldn't pass then. Ted knew it wouldn't. He wanted to put the item on the agenda only so it would be ready for the next session of Congress. Two days before the election, as Nick Littlefield was to tell it, Ted and Littlefield flew up to Massachusetts to confer with Dr. Barry Zuckerman, the head of pediatrics at Boston Medical Center, and with State Representative John McDonough, who had worked with Zuckerman in passing a state bill to insure children, which was funded by a tobacco tax, and Ted convinced Minority Leader Daschle to include the initiative in Daschle's annual list of ten legislative priorities. The problem was finding a Republican cosponsor in a Republican-led chamber. With Lott's injunction not to assist Ted, Ted nevertheless met with a series of Republican moderates—Jim Jeffords, John Chafee, Christopher Bond, Arlen Specter, Maine senators Olympia Snowe and Susan Collins—but none of them, clearly believing that there would be no Republican support for such a program, would commit to a bill providing health insurance for children. None of them. As Littlefield would tell it, Ted then approached Orrin Hatch, more conservative than any of those to whom Ted had spoken, and a fiscal hawk. Moreover, Hatch was proud of saying that he had entered politics expressly to fight Ted Kennedy. "I thought he stood for everything I did not. I thought someone had to take him on, and I just didn't see anyone that was doing it."

But Hatch had, of political necessity, been forced to change his mind. When he assumed the chair of the Labor Committee after Reagan's 1980 landslide victory that also turned the Senate, he realized that the Republican moderates on the committee were likely to vote with Ted and against the conservative Republicans and thus give Ted the upper hand, and Hatch appealed to Ted to work with him. Ted told him that there were certain things he just could not do, but there were others he could. "And he bent over backwards to do it," Hatch would later say. And Ted, needing Hatch too, subjected him to the Kennedy treatment. When Hatch was embroiled in a scandal involving the Bank of Credit and Commerce International, he said that Ted was the only senator who called him to offer support. When Hatch's grandson developed an infection after being operated on for colitis, Ted arranged to have his medical experts at Massachusetts General Hospital advise Hatch's grandson's doctors in Utah. And beyond the gestures of kindness, it turned out that Hatch, for all his initial animosity, had more in common with Ted Kennedy than he had thought and that he had some religious and moral convictions that overrode his political ones, especially when it came to children. Having formed a legislative bond, Hatch and Ted had worked together previously on AIDS bills, including the Ryan White Act, and on the summer jobs program for teenagers, and Ted believed that as a strict Mormon, Hatch would be amenable to a tobacco tax—Mormons were forbidden to smoke—that would not only raise money to fund the children's insurance, as in Massachusetts, but also discourage teenagers from smoking. Still, Hatch vacillated. He didn't want to be on the wrong side of his caucus any more than those other senators with whom Ted had spoken had. But Ted was persistent, and Ted knew how to play the moral card. According to Littlefield, as Hatch was deliberating, Ted tracked down Hatch's chief health staffer, Patricia Knight, who was on a tour of Poland with a group of Harvard professors—tracked her down in a cabin in a remote rural village—and phoned her in the middle of the night to encourage her to press the case for Hatch to join him in providing health insurance for ten million uninsured children. And in February, Hatch authorized his staff to meet with Ted's to see if they could find some accommodation.

Though they were now allies, they were not of one mind, and their negotiations proved difficult. The staffs met in Hatch's office, not Ted's, which was one of those concessions Ted made when he needed to get something done; he never invoked his seniority, deferring instead to Hatch's chairmanship. And Ted even came to Hatch's office himself to negotiate—another concession to show his respect and his eagerness to get something done. Over the years, however, the two of them had developed a working style, loose and amiable, and Littlefield described the Hatch-Kennedy conferences as a kind of routine in which Hatch, a songwriter and vocalist, would play a CD of one of his "patriotic or religious" songs on his massive sound system, and then the two would engage in "friendly teasing," and then Hatch would protest that Ted was about to be "taking him to the cleaners," and only then, with Hatch sitting in a wingback chair in front of his desk, and Ted in another wingback next to him, and their staffs sitting across the room facing them, would they begin the legislative minuet over the compromises that each felt duty-bound to make. Hatch insisted any children's insurance program must be state-run and not open-ended (which meant that not all children would be insured, which was Ted's goal), and with a private insurance component (something on which Republicans always insisted), and that the proposed tobacco tax of seventy-five cents a package had to be reduced, presumably because Hatch couldn't get that past his fellow Republicans who took large contributions from the tobacco industry. And Ted made another compromise on which Hatch had insisted. Ted had wanted the standard of coverage for his bill to be the same standard as Medicaid, which included extensive prenatal care and preventative care. Hatch refused, saying that states could be compelled to offer some services but not all the services Medicaid offered. Ted pushed back by appealing to Hatch's conscience: "But, Orrin, there are so many children in Utah who can never see a doctor!" But Hatch was adamant. And with those points in mind, the staffs once again collaborated to find a bill that both their senators could support.

And even as they conferred, one more issue arose—this one an issue of time. Ted had discovered that the conventions of the Children's Welfare Fund, headed by Marian Wright Edelman, a fierce advocate who was married to former Bobby Kennedy aide Peter Edelman, and of the Child Welfare League of America were to be held simultaneously in Washington on March 11, 1997, and he thought those would be the perfect venues at which to announce the bill. The problem was that the conventions were only a week away, and Ted and Hatch had not yet resolved their disagreements. So now the staffs worked furiously as the senators sent letters back and forth hashing out the bill. But the coup de grâce came during the final meeting in Hatch's office between Ted and Hatch. Earlier in the negotiations, after Hatch played one of his songs at the beginning of a meeting, Ted had told Littlefield, the onetime Broadway singer, that he should learn a song and surprise Hatch and sing it. So Littlefield learned "The Girl That I Marry," from Irving Berlin's *Annie Get Your Gun,* and when he and Ted arrived at Hatch's office, Ted announced that Nick was going to sing to Hatch's aide, Patricia Knight. As Littlefield later told it, "Hatch is ecstatic. Kennedy is ecstatic." So once again, before they arrived for their final meeting to work out the details, Ted asked Littlefield to prepare a song, only this time he asked him to learn one of Hatch's own compositions, "Freedom's Light," and then sing it. Littlefield did. Hatch was surprised and moved, even though he knew he was being flattered. "Nice move, Teddy," Hatch said. By that point, Hatch had decided to soften his stance. He was now willing to fund $18 billion for the program. Ted thought $25 billion was necessary over five years, but he countered with a $30 billion bill, $20 billion for the health component and $10 for deficit reduction, which he knew the Republicans would demand, and with a raise in the tobacco tax—David Nexon hastily calculated that forty-one cents would do it—to pay for it all. They shook hands, and when Ted left the room and turned the corner down the hallway, Littlefield recalled, "We high-fived each other and whooped with joy." And then came the two conventions and the rollout and "thunderous" cheers from the attendees.

But the enthusiasm was short-lived because there was an impediment—a huge impediment. Lyndon Johnson had had to fight the Southern bulls to pass his meager Civil Rights Act of 1957 so that he could demonstrate to Northern Democrats that he was no racist Southerner himself. Later Johnson, as president, and his liberal allies had had to face those same bulls and their Southern successors to pass the Civil Rights Act of 1964 and the Voting Rights Act of 1965. It was understood that this bloc, hard, obdurate, was dedicated to stopping any advance on civil rights on the transparent pretext that they were not racists, though they were, but rather supporters of states' rights dedicated to resisting federal incursions on those rights. For decades, they had won that fight, had stopped the Senate from accomplishing all but the smallest advances in racial progress. And in the end, they failed because history had passed them by. But there was no such acknowledgment of the Republican conservatives in the Senate who had been just as hostile to and just as obstructive of any social legislation, even a minimum wage increase, which was hardly revolutionary, or HIPAA, which was designed only to let workers take their health insurance with them to a new job, even if they had preexisting conditions, or now to insurance for uninsured children. Those Southern bulls had been marginalized, berated for being on the wrong side of history, even humiliated, forced finally to surrender their power. But there was no such marginalization, humiliation, or surrender, no claim that the men who obstructed bills that gave poor Americans the right to a living wage or the right for healthcare for them and their children, were just as morally culpable as those Southern bulls who had denied the right to Black people to eat in restaurants and to lodge in hotels and to use public accommodations and transportation and to vote without having to overcome absurd obstacles. They suffered no rebuke, which was a dramatic illustration of how American politics and American values had changed in that time. These new obstructionists opposed with impunity.

No money for poor children. This was what Ted Kennedy had been up against and was still up against. The majority of the Republican caucus was determined to stop the Hatch-Kennedy bill, which Hatch's staffer Patricia Knight—the woman whom Ted had called in the middle of that dark Polish night—had cleverly labeled the Children's Health Insurance and Lower Deficit Act of 1997: CHILD. Republicans and conservatives were appalled at what they saw as Hatch's perfidy. The *National Review* called him a "latter-day liberal," the Americans for Tax Reform assailed him by saying they never thought he would do something this "extreme," and Paul Weyrich of the Free Congress Foundation said that Hatch lacked a "solid philosophy" and accused him of talking about "constitutional government and judicial restraint while he pimps for Clinton."

With the idea generating so much hostility on the right, an old question remained: Could Ted and Hatch even find Republican co-sponsors? That was Hatch's assignment, and he assured Ted that he had found a handful. But Trent Lott warned, "A Kennedy big-government program is not going to be enacted," and Ted didn't need Lott's warning to know how difficult it would be—he knew from his own experience in the 104th Congress—to get around the Republicans, who were much more committed to balancing the budget as a way of stopping government than they were in providing health insurance to children, even though Ted and Hatch's bill was deficit neutral, which is to say that the funds came from the tobacco tax and that the program would be fully paid for without raiding the federal treasury. And it was not only the Senate that had to pass the bill, though that seemed difficult enough. While Hatch was searching for co-sponsors who would be willing to buck their own leadership, Ted had to find a Republican who would introduce the bill in the House, where Newt Gingrich still held sway. It was, Littlefield said, Ken Duberstein, Ronald Reagan's former chief of staff and a friend of Ted's, who directed him to Republican Bill Thomas, the chairman of the Ways and Means Committee, and Thomas who directed him to Nancy Johnson, a moderate Republican who sat on the committee, and who finally agreed to offer it in the House. In short, it came through Ted's friendship with Republicans.

And Ted didn't only have Trent Lott and the Republican caucus and the Republican House with which to contend. Once again he had his own president. Early in 1996 Ted had pressed the White House for his children's insurance bill, but as Clinton's healthcare adviser, Chris Jennings, put it, Clinton was determined to balance the budget, another co-optation of the Republicans, and that seemed to outweigh any other priority. (In this, Clinton was behaving toward the Republicans very much the way Richard Nixon had behaved toward Ted.) Ted used his moral suasion. Jennings said that Ted and Littlefield and David Nexon were calling Clinton and Hillary at this time and telling them repeatedly, "You gotta do kids. You gotta do kids." But the choice ultimately came down to Kennedy-Kassebaum or the children's insurance, and the first won because it was so much smaller than children's insurance and it came at little or no cost to the government. So Ted had to do what he had often done—push the administration from the outside with his advocacy groups, led by Marian Edelman's Children's Defense Fund and the American Cancer Society, even as the Republicans, financed by tobacco money, were applying pressure of their own against the bill. Ted's advocates were fierce. They lobbied legislators in their districts, held meetings, and with a gift of $100,000 from the film mogul Lew Wasserman, took out advertisements on the back page of *Congress Daily*, which was read by most of those legislators— ads that juxtaposed a young boy named Joey with Joe Camel, the cartoon mascot of Camel cigarettes who promoted tobacco. And legislators were asked to choose between them: Joey or Joe Camel?

But Republicans were unbending. Lott, having seen Ted outfox Dole on the minimum wage and HIPAA, was not going to bring Hatch-Kennedy to the floor for a vote, especially since momentum seemed to be building for it. An NBC/*Wall Street Journal* poll found 72 percent in favor of the bill. Ted realized that the only way he might achieve passage for the bill was by including it in the budget resolution where, by Senate rules, it required only a majority vote and could not be filibustered and where it was almost certain to be passed since Clinton and Lott and Gingrich had worked out their balanced budget agreement and no one was eager to vote against it. Ted felt this might be the only chance for its passage. It was Robert Byrd's refusal to allow this tactic for the Clinton healthcare bill that had resulted in its defeat. Byrd, however, had argued then that the healthcare bill was not germane to setting the budgetary goals for which budget reconcilia- tion was designed. Ted argued that the rule didn't apply to his and Hatch's bill. Adding the child insurance bill as an amendment to the budget reso- lution would not change the budgetary goals; it would simply rearrange funding and maintain deficit neutrality since the program was being fi- nanced by tobacco taxes. Clinton had already bargained with Lott to in- clude $16 billion in the budget for Ted and Hatch's children's insurance. But Lott, who was opposed to any insurance program, warned Clinton that if Ted's amendment were attached, with its increase in spending, deficit neutral or not, the Republicans would sink the entire bill for which Clinton had worked since the government shutdown. Clinton couldn't af- ford that. He urged Ted to accept the $16 billion instead of the $20 for which he and Hatch were asking—which was already for Ted a compro- mise. And Ted was feeling pressure from his own advocates too—Marian Edelman, he said, had been "cool" to the bill—who were afraid that CHILD might draw money from other programs and that Ted's concession to allow CHILD to offer less than full coverage and to award the federal money as block grants to the states would be a Trojan horse to eliminate Medicaid altogether and turn it into a block-grant program, which had been one of the Republicans' long-cherished dreams. Chris Jennings,

Clinton's health adviser, said that Clinton was worried about the same thing—that the Republicans would somehow use CHILD to undermine Medicaid.

Buffeted by all these forces, and with the vehement opposition of his own president, Ted was still determined to offer the bill as an amendment and convinced Hatch to join him—the liberal-conservative odd couple against their own president and majority leader, respectively. They did so on May 21. Hatch took the floor first, asking his colleagues for whom they stood: Joey the boy or Joe Camel? He argued that the ten million uninsured children were not just the poor, for whom he knew his fellow Republicans had little sympathy. "Who are the Hatch-Kennedy kids?" Hatch asked. "I will tell you who they are. They are, in large part, the children of good, hardworking families who make too much for Medicaid and not enough to buy their own health insurance," and he said that 88 percent of the uninsured children came from families in which one parent was employed. And then, after Hatch's long plea, Ted took the floor. "Our plan has broad bipartisan support—because healthcare for children is not a Republican issue or a Democratic issue," Ted said. "It is a human issue. Six former Secretaries of the Department of Health and Human Services and four former Surgeon Generals have endorsed the plan. These leaders served under Presidents Nixon, Ford, Carter, Reagan, and Bush. They all understand the importance of health insurance for children and decisive action to reduce smoking. They all understand that health care for children is an issue that should transcend political party and ideology." But, of course, it wasn't really bipartisan. Hatch had only wrangled a handful of Republican moderates. Lott was firmly opposed, and Littlefield thought that his opposition was personal. Lott had seen Ted run the Senate the year before, had seen him run Bob Dole out of the Senate, and Ted Kennedy was not going to run *his* Senate. Pete Domenici, the Budget Committee chair who had crafted the final agreement, was just as firmly opposed, speaking for most of his caucus when he asserted, "There can be no more frontal attack and violation of this agreement than this amendment. Now let me make it clear. It says that the tax cut to the American people is reduced by $30 billion. And it says we will spend $20 billion of that. So we are going to reduce the tax cut and spend more money. And we already cover the children in this agreement." (It didn't, however, cover them in full.) Tobacco senators argued that the bill punished the tobacco industry and even claimed that doing so would hurt the children of the tobacco states by taking money out of their parents' pockets. Others argued that the tobacco tax was not included in the amendment—Ted couldn't do so because it would not qualify for the budget resolution had he done so—and that the Senate could wind up with a different source of funding. Others simply argued that $16 billion was sufficient. Nearly all those Republicans argued, however, against the amendment, against funding a program to insure those uninsured children—nearly all of them. And not only the Republicans. There was that other opponent: the president. Bill Clinton was terrified. The night before the vote, Ted had phoned Vice President Al Gore and the president to encourage their support. Neither returned his call. In fact, Clinton, still trying desperately to salvage his balanced budget—which Lott said again on the floor that he would defeat were the Hatch-Kennedy amendment attached to it—was pressing Democrats to oppose Hatch-Kennedy. Nine senators Clinton had allegedly contacted, though other reports said he had his aides and Cabinet secretaries call as many as fifteen, and as Littlefield would recount it, five of them decided to vote against the amendment because the president had essentially told them that they had to or Lott would pull the balanced budget bill.

It was another long debate that lasted into the evening and another contentious debate in the long series of contentious debates in which Ted Kennedy had participated throughout his career. Ted pushed back. "Let us not lose sight of what the issue is before the Senate this afternoon," he declared. "Will we support the Hatch-Kennedy bill that will provide the resources to insure the sons and daughters of working families in this country? That is the issue. You can talk about other kinds of issues all you want, but every American understands this one. When you come right down to it, this is the issue." Daschle stood with Ted, and Ted had even been told that Vice President Gore was heading to the Senate floor in case there was a tie that needed to be broken. (The White House denied that, and when asked about it, Ted said, seeming to acknowledge the support and then what he saw as the White House's betrayal, "Yes, yes. I can only bite my tongue so long.") Ted had fought hard, and so did Hatch, but standing against both the Republican leadership and the president, they had little chance for victory and could only promise, as Ted had done with the minimum wage bill and Kennedy-Kassebaum, that he would keep attaching it to every subsequent piece of legislation. Clinton's press secretary Mike McCurry told reporters that the White House "applauded" the efforts of Ted and Hatch, but that was precisely why they felt the subject should be excluded from the budget resolution and eventually be voted upon as a freestanding bill. "The President is not about to see all that hard work go down the drain," meaning the hard work of a budget compromise, "and he has very clearly been told by the majority that this amendment is a deal-buster." Hatch-Kennedy failed, 53 to 47, and Ted was incensed. (Other reports listed the vote as 55 to 45.) As he saw it, the Senate—and the president—had decided it was more important to balance the budget than to save children's lives.

But it had failed only at being included in the budget resolution. Ted had another plan. He would try to have it included in the budget *reconciliation,* which was the bill that incorporated all the instructions and changes in the budget resolution. To do so, however, he needed to have the bill considered by the Finance Committee, since it had jurisdiction over tax matters, and the tobacco excise was a tax. Ted did not sit on the Finance Committee, which was headed by a conservative from Delaware, William Roth, who had made a reputation as a deficit hawk. But Orrin Hatch did. Ted worried, however, that Hatch might surrender to his fellow Republicans, and he sought to stiffen Hatch's resolve with a typical Ted ploy. Hatch had complained to him that he could not get a recording company to release an album of his religious songs. Ted, picking up on Hatch's problem, immediately phoned his nephew, Bobby Shriver, an agent, who quickly arranged a distribution deal. In the meantime, Hatch brought the bill to the committee, where, on June 18, it was subjected to a long and tortuous negotiation that again lasted into the night—a negotiation to which Ted Kennedy was not privy. Now it was Orrin Hatch trying to save the bill. And the salvation was complicated. Jay Rockefeller, a West Virginia Democrat who was as deeply invested in healthcare as Ted Kennedy, and John Chafee, the Rhode Island Republican who had battled for years to find some compromise on healthcare, had introduced a bill of their own that would expand Medicaid and provide funds for children who were eligible but had not yet enrolled. Hatch and Ted had both supported that bill, not seeing it as mutually exclusive with their own, but recognizing that it was unlikely the Senate would pass one children's health bill, much less two. (Rockefeller would remain miffed at Ted—"hate him" was how Chris Jennings put it—for what he perceived as Ted's bill undermining his; Ted clearly felt Chafee-Rockefeller wouldn't pass.) Still, the two bills had to be consolidated in committee. That was the first hurdle, which was settled by giving states an option to cover those children either in Medicaid or in CHILD. Now the negotiations got down to details. As Littlefield described it, the bargaining was hard, and it wasn't in Ted's or Hatch's favor. The tobacco tax was too high. So Hatch reluctantly agreed to lower it—lower it considerably—from forty-three cents, which Ted's staff had calculated would raise the requisite $30 billion—to twenty cents. The money should be dedicated, said Roth and ranking member Pat Moynihan, who had little interest in health reform and who had helped tank the Clinton Health Security Act, not just to children's insurance but to infrastructure. Now Hatch was livid. As Littlefield told it, he gave an "impassioned" speech during markup, warning that he and Ted would "clean their clocks" on the Senate floor if they passed the infrastructure component. But Hatch had little beyond threats. The committee settled on the twenty-cent excise tax and a division of the $15 billion it would raise over five years between the insurance ($8 billion) and infrastructure, corporate welfare, and tax breaks (the remaining $7 billion).

Ted was enraged by the surrender. He phoned Hatch and "laid into him," Ted later said, telling him he was "selling out" and calling it a betrayal akin to Benedict Arnold's. Ted would say that Hatch never forgot that conversation. The next day Ted, who hated conflict with an ally, appeared at Hatch's office to apologize for his tirade. Hatch defended himself. He said that while he made concessions—concessions he had had no choice but to make under the circumstances—the budget resolution that had passed the House on June 12 included the $16 billion that Clinton had negotiated with Lott, though as a block grant and without a provision that it would be used exclusively for children's insurance. Hatch argued that that money was already allocated. The $8 billion that he had wrested from the Finance Committee would be *in addition* to the $16 billion, thus providing $24 billion over five years for children's insurance, which was more than that for which he and Ted had originally asked. Hatch was right, Kennedy wrong. On June 25 the Senate passed the Balanced Budget Act with the $16 billion, and two days later it passed the Revenue Reconciliation Act with the $8 billion. Though Ted hadn't realized it after the markup, Hatch had actually snookered the Finance Committee and done an end-run around his Republican colleagues.

At least his *Senate* Republican colleagues. There was still Newt Gingrich and the House Republicans to deal with and the conference between the House and the Senate, and Bill Clinton, whose threat of a veto would be the only real leverage that the Democrats had. Ted lobbied. He got Marian Wright Edelman to energize her advocates again while Hatch lobbied his moderate Senate colleagues and Lott to support the bill for fear of the political repercussions of not doing so. *No money for children's health.* That was the rallying cry. And Ted lobbied one more individual—an important one: Hillary Clinton. Hillary, who had become a supporter of the bill, was indispensable in trying to win her husband's support. Meanwhile Bill Clinton, knowing that he had run afoul of Ted and not wanting Ted's antipathy, had Gore and Clinton's Health and Human Services secretary Donna Shalala call him to apologize and promise to support him going forward.

But Ted was unconvinced by Clinton's professions of support. In yet another attempt at spine-stiffening, he met with Bill Clinton on July 22 before the White House negotiations with the Republican House over the final contours of the budget bill. It was another tense meeting, by one report. Ted was distressed by Clinton's abandonment and by the balanced budget generally. But now Ted had Hillary on his side and Clinton's remorse to draw on, and Clinton headed into the negotiations with Dick Armey and Phil Gramm saying that funding CHILD—which Republicans would insist on renaming State Children's Health Insurance Program or SCHIP, to emphasize the state role and to remove any trace of Ted's involvement, lest it be called Hatch-Kennedy—would be a priority and thus, as Chris Jennings put it, "making Kennedy very happy." By the time the negotiations were over, even Gingrich had come to see the futility of opposing children's insurance, and not only did Ted and Hatch get their $24 billion, but the program was also authorized for ten years, not just five, though another tobacco tax reduction, this time down to fifteen cents per package, now necessitated taking funds from general revenue.

There were those, particularly on the left, who thought CHIP—the S had been dropped—was actually a step backward; that it undermined Medicaid, as Rockefeller and even Bill Clinton feared; that its block grants meant it was not an entitlement program in which all eligible children would be covered, as Medicaid was, but a program in which states would determine who qualified, which meant that there would be waiting lists in some states; that its reliance on private insurance permitted insurers to provide less adequate coverage than Medicaid; and that the need to have it reauthorized, unlike Medicaid, made it vulnerable. One skeptical scholar said of CHIP, "It can be understood as a victory, not for the new ground it broke in child health policy, but for using the cause of children to advance the politics of policy retrenchment for the poor." Much of that might have been true. None of it, however, took into account the political realities of the Republican Congress. Ted Kennedy always took what he could get. "The perfect is the enemy of the good." "Eighty percent is better than nothing." For all its faults, CHIP, in just two years increased the number of children enrolled from 38 to 49 percent of those eligible, and many states added a provision allowing those working poor parents, who made incomes of up to 200 percent of the poverty line, to be covered as well.

Nick Littlefield thought CHIP a kind of conclusion. "If the defeat of comprehensive health reform in 1994 was the prologue to the Republican revolution, the children's health legislation was its epilogue . . . a clear sign that even with Republicans still in control of Congress the tide was beginning to turn, at least temporarily, back to a more progressive view of government as an engine of social justice."

II

An epilogue, perhaps, but Republicans were not yet ready to close the book. Though Gingrich and the New Right had concluded the balanced budget agreement with Clinton that provided tax cuts while, at Clinton's insistence, holding the line on many of the endangered social programs, the Republicans tried to revive their so-called revolution. "[There] were guys in our caucus who were always just out to screw Bill," Alan Simpson, onetime assistant Senate majority leader, was to say, and he insisted that his fellow Republicans were wasting their time, "talking about how to craft a piece of legislation that would blow up under Bill Clinton's nose." Clinton seemed to keep co-opting them, and eventually, after so many defeats, the Republicans seemed to give up trying to outwit Clinton politically.

But there was another way. Newt Gingrich knew the value of political scandal-mongering. He had made his reputation forcing House speaker Jim Wright from office by exposing the scheme in which Wright sold his donors books he had written in order to raise money. Now the Clintons became the Republicans' next Jim Wright. They besieged Clinton with a series of investigations on alleged improprieties under the rubric "Whitewater," named after the Whitewater Development Corporation, in which the Clintons had invested to develop property in their native Arkansas along the White Water River. It was a poor investment. They had actually taken a loss, and they were not implicated in any wrongdoing.* But the object of Republican efforts seemed less to get justice than to bedevil the Clintons and sully them, and after special prosecutor Robert Fiske, a Republican, cleared the Clintons, a new independent counsel, Kenneth Starr, a conservative Republican aligned with the far right, was appointed under a new law, one signed by Clinton, and Starr was no Robert Fiske. He conducted his probe as if he were Inspector Javert and the Clintons Jean Valjean. (At the time of his investigation, Starr was, among other things, representing tobacco companies that were fighting the administration's attempts to have the FDA regulate the marketing of cigarettes to teenagers.) Whitewater was to provide a wormhole through which Starr and his Republican allies hoped to find something, anything, to tarnish the Clintons, especially since Clinton's popularity was rising and all but overshadowed Gingrich's grand scheme.

Given the resentment that the Republicans felt toward Bill Clinton, despite his relative moderation, or possibly because of it, and given their relentless determination to bring him down and with him the whole Democratic Party, Clinton should have put himself beyond reproach. But he hadn't. He had had a well-earned reputation as a womanizer, and Gingrich, a sanctimonious moralist, despite his own affairs—he informed his wife that he was leaving her while she was in the hospital recovering from cancer—understood how to wield moralism for his political benefit. So began a long skein of scandal. The Republicans found a young clerical worker at the Arkansas Industrial Development Commission, Paula Jones, who had accused Clinton of sexual harassment, which, after Jones's advisers sought unsuccessfully to get the story publicized in the mainstream media, presumably to harm Clinton, led to her filing a civil suit against him. The charges then allowed Ken Starr, who had been given wide purview by Clinton's own attorney general, Janet Reno, to add Jones's complaint to the Whitewater investigation, which allowed him to pry into Clinton's other alleged infidelities, which ultimately led to an-

---

* After intensive digging, reporter Michael Isikoff would conclude: "No evidence ever surfaced that Clinton took an active interest in Jim McDougal's [it was McDougal's machinations with his Madison Guaranty Savings and Loans that had allegedly involved the Clintons] Byzantine dealings—or that he personally benefited." Yet this was the trigger for the entire investigation. Michael Isikoff, *Uncovering Clinton: A Reporter's Story* (New York: Crown, 1999), 382.

other young woman, Monica Lewinsky, a twenty-two-year-old White House intern with whom Bill Clinton had had an alleged affair. This in turn led to Clinton's denials—false denials—that he had had a relationship with Lewinsky, one that began during the government shutdown, and to various efforts to hide the relationship, that included, Starr claimed, witness tampering, perjury (in the Jones sexual harassment case and in grand jury testimony), and obstruction of justice. That led to Starr's charges that Clinton had betrayed his "constitutional duty to faithfully execute the laws" of the nation. And *that* led to an impeachment inquiry. Such was the long, torturous road to the Republican dream to remove Bill Clinton from office. "I have sinned," Clinton would finally admit months later. But he insisted that he had done nothing illegal, and his defenders insisted that his transgression was personal and moral and not legal.

Clinton was no paranoiac, like Richard Nixon. Success, not suspicion, had led to his humiliation. "It is a Clinton pattern to get into trouble when he is doing better," his secretary of commerce, Mickey Kantor, would say, without also saying that it was his success that drove the Republicans to try to damage him. The Whitewater investigation had been crawling until the revelation about Monica Lewinsky broke publicly in *The Washington Post* on January 21, 1998—it had broken on the conservative website *The Drudge Report* two days earlier—with the additional information that Ken Starr was investigating whether Clinton had asked her to lie under oath in the Jones case. Ted said he was watching television with Vicki that morning when he learned of it for the first time and that Vicki had told him that if it was true, the Republicans were going to try to impeach Clinton. Ted admitted that the atmosphere was now "poisonous." Ted had closed 1997 by parting with tradition and delivering his annual speech at the National Press Club laying out his legislative initiatives for the coming year in December rather than January. He called again for a minimum wage increase; an increase on the cigarette tax, this time to fund research; a Patients' Bill of Rights to assist those in managed care systems; a GI Bill of Rights for students; a reduction in the Social Security payroll tax; what he called "genuine" tax reform; campaign finance reform; and his annual plea for national health insurance with an employer mandate. "Often the great advances in America have come as a result of crisis," he said. "In this unusual time of peace and prosperity, our capacity to act has never been greater. We need to resist temptation to complacency or self-congratulation. . . . Let's direct the tide, not just ride it." But there would be little legislative success in 1998. Even after a judge in April dismissed Paula Jones's harassment claims, which had been the spur for Lewinsky's outing, the Lewinsky affair overshadowed everything. This would not be the year of accomplishment. This would be the year of scandal.

It was to be another politically vicious year, riddled with divisiveness and full of distractions—Clinton's from the Lewinsky matter, the Republicans from Clinton's attempts to govern. Clinton left no doubt that he felt Starr was a conservative operative and not an objective officer of the court. The crescendo came on August 17, when Clinton testified before the grand jury about the Lewinsky relationship as, Clinton would later write, Starr's "interrogators did their best to turn the videotape into a pornographic home movie, asking me questions designed to humiliate me and to so disgust the Congress and the American people that they would demand my resignation, after which he might be able to indict me." That night, at ten o'clock, he addressed the nation in a televised address and delivered a mea culpa. Ted, who knew a great deal about personal transgression and public abasement, probably as much as any officeholder, and who, Clinton adviser John Podesta said, understood "better than most the emotional toll on Clinton," phoned the president immediately afterward to tell him that Ted would stand behind him, as much, Ted would later write, to protect the presidency as to protect Clinton himself. Clinton, Ted believed, had been under "assault" from the Republicans from the time he entered office. "I felt that this kind of attempt to delegitimize a president was dangerous for our democracy."

Still, Clinton's emotional toll mattered to Ted too. When Clinton made a visit to Worcester, Massachusetts, nine days after his public confession, Ted found him "functioning on all cylinders, focused on policy, talking about getting things done," though Ted thought that "the president may have been a bit in denial, not quite ready to deal yet with the depth of his problems and the direction in which things were moving," which was toward impeachment, since Starr was an inexorable opponent and since Republicans controlled the House, where articles of impeachment would be voted upon. Ted showed him polls indicating that 77 percent of Americans thought Congress should not be focused on his private life and tried to lift his spirits, but Clinton was perplexed, even "polling" his luncheon guests as to what he should do. When Ted offered assistance, Clinton asked him to speak with Robert Byrd, whose status in the Senate and whose knowledge of Senate history, including the impeachment trial of

Andrew Johnson, could help guide Clinton, and whose condemnation, should it come, would almost certainly doom him. Ted came to Byrd with his own suggestion: that rather than having the Senate Democrats defend Clinton, they should focus their attention on the procedures for trying him, if the House voted to impeach. Ted himself believed that while Clinton might have sinned—as Ted had done himself—he hadn't committed impeachable offenses. Ted had lunch with his old mentor and Harvard political science professor, Sam Beer, who concurred, after reviewing the long history of impeachment with Ted: The only grounds for impeachment that tradition and the Founding Fathers had countenanced was the abuse of power, not personal conduct. And Ted consulted legal scholars, who agreed with Beer, and he talked to Senate colleagues with the question, again, not of how adamantly they should defend Clinton, but of whether his actions, however deplorable, warranted expulsion.

And now they waited for the inevitable.

III

It was a vicious year, which had become the political disposition in the Gingrich era, a divisive and partisan year, a year given over to squabbling over Bill Clinton's sexual conduct while little else got done—the kind of year that Ted Kennedy, the raging legislator, detested. Clinton, now blocked on the domestic front, turned to foreign affairs, and so did Ted, just as he had done when he was stymied by Ronald Reagan. And for him, there was one conspicuous matter: Ireland. Ted Kennedy was the Irish-American politician par excellence, the very quintessence of the Irish-American politician, which was highly advantageous in Massachusetts but came with its own set of perils. Irish-American politicians had largely kept their distance from Irish politics, especially the politics of Northern Ireland, because they were complex and seemingly vexed, and because Britain was an American ally with a wintry attitude toward the Irish Republic, and politicians were loath to cross that ally, and because the issue of the Irish Republican Army, the IRA, and its political arm, Sinn Fein, which did not rule out the use of violence to unite the two Irelands, forced a choice for those Irish-Americans between rapprochement between Northern Ireland and the Republic of Ireland and between their love of Ireland and their hatred of violence. Ted had kept his distance too, despite Jack Kennedy's invocation of his Irishness and his wildly successful trip to

Ireland, and when Ted did engage, he trod lightly. When he spoke in March 1970 in Dublin at the College Historical Society at Trinity, a speech on which he labored, he took a moderate tack, praising Edmund Burke, famous for his condemnation of the violence of the French Revolution, also a moderate, "not because he lacked passion or conviction, but because he combined an acute sense of human limitation with a deep reverence for the moral values essential to human liberation," which was very much in the spirit of Ted Kennedy. "To him, a lifetime of thought and action," Ted said of Burke, "consumed by the slow labor of improving the human condition was more valuable than all the rhetoric of destruction and impossible visions." But the following year, when Ted was visiting Europe to study national healthcare plans, an Irish woman accosted him in London and asked why he had been so vocal about the National Guard troops in Ohio attacking students protesting the invasion of Cambodia and said nothing about Protestant paramilitary troops in Northern Ireland attacking Catholics. Ted was shaken. When he returned to the United States, he spoke with Representative Hugh Carey of New York, who had been to Belfast and witnessed the abuse of Catholics there. Agitated by his own experience and Carey's, Ted asked Senator Abraham Ribicoff if he could co-sponsor Ribicoff's resolution calling for an immediate British withdrawal from Northern Ireland and for the unification of the two Irelands. The British were incensed by his interference in what they saw as their affairs. When, on the Senate floor, he compared the situation in Northern Ireland to Vietnam, British prime minister Edward Heath called his remarks an "ignorant outburst." Still, when Heath suspended the Northern Irish parliament, Stormont, after the Bloody Sunday massacre early in 1972, in which British soldiers gunned down twenty-eight Catholic protesters, there were reports he had been influenced by Ted's attacks. And now Ted was in the middle of the Irish mire.

It was a deep mire, and he would be stuck there for decades, as the "troubles" violence in Northern Ireland continued to escalate, and as his own rhetoric escalated over the indignities he felt the British visited upon the Catholics. But something happened and someone arose that caused Ted to reevaluate. In November the following year in Bonn, he met with John Hume, a Catholic member of Parliament from a Northern Ireland constituency—he had phoned Hume requesting the meeting—and it was Hume, Ted said, who "began the great education of Edward Kennedy" and "outlined a pathway that would offer the opportunity to help resolve the differences"—a peaceful pathway for a joint settlement between Catholic and Protestant, Republican and Unionist. Amid all the distrust and acrimony in Northern Ireland, Hume believed that the two sides could be brought together. And Ted and Hume now became allies in finding some way to end the violence.

It was not an easy sell either to the Congress or to the president. Ted and Tip O'Neill, then speaker of the House, began an annual St. Patrick's Day lunch, which they intended to use to provide a voice in Congress for peace and reconciliation, and to which they invited the president. And Ted, who had previously waffled, now came out forcefully, condemning the violence and brutality of both the British and the IRA, which won him few adherents either in Ireland or among the Irish-American faithful who had despaired that anything but armed resistance could solve the troubles. By this time, in early 1977, John Hume—the "most passionate, articulate, knowledgeable" person about the Irish situation, in Ted's words—had taken a fellowship to study at Harvard's Center for International Relations, and Ted organized meetings between Hume and Tip O'Neill and Hume and Hugh Carey, both of whom, Ted said, supported unification but were less avid about stopping IRA violence. Those meetings, he said, had a "quite dramatic effect" that convinced them, as Hume had convinced Ted, to disengage from the IRA and find another path to reconciliation. And now, that March, Ted joined forces again with Tip O'Neill and also with Hugh Carey and Senator Pat Moynihan—the Four Horsemen, they called themselves—to issue a statement on St. Patrick's Day drafted by Carey Parker in conjunction with John Hume that declared a commitment to a peaceful resolution and an "appeal to all those organizations engaged in violence"—they were clearly thinking of American organizations helping to finance the IRA—"to renounce their campaign of death and destruction and return to the path of life and peace." A "historic break with Irish-American tradition," Ted would call it, and he said that it was "welcomed with relief by both the British and Irish governments." And now Ted and the other Horsemen began pressing the Carter administration to get involved, where previous administrations had left the Irish imbroglio to the British. Secretary of State Cyrus Vance rejected Ted's suggestions to provide aid to Northern Ireland in return for the beginning of a peace process, but the Horsemen did get the administration to issue a statement recognizing minority rights in Northern Ireland. The Four Horsemen's statement had changed the policy of Irish

Americans toward Ireland. Carter's statement had changed the policy of the American government toward Ireland. America had finally acknowledged a stake in the outcome of Northern Ireland's troubles.

But Ted, who had taken so much fire from the British government, now was taking fire from the IRA and its supporters. Under John Hume's tutelage, he had become a "constitutional nationalist" and wound up leading a group of twenty-four senators, congressmen, and governors that also supported constitutional nationalism under the name the Friends of Ireland, and that promoted supporting Hume's Social Democratic and Labour Party rather than Sinn Fein as a potential partner with the Protestant Unionist Party. And Hume would say, "There are many men, women and children who are alive today, I am convinced, because of the political courage and concern of these men," meaning the Four Horsemen. Ted continued to push, urging British prime minister Margaret Thatcher to "implement reforms" after a hunger strike by Catholic prisoners in April 1981 staged to protest their treatment by the British, and the Horsemen sent her a telegram accusing her of "intransigence." He met with William Clark, Reagan's national security adviser, to push President Reagan to become more fully engaged in the Irish situation, and Reagan attended the St. Patrick's Day lunches where the mood was generally light, but where Irish guests would sometimes indirectly raise the issue of Northern Ireland. He pushed for the appointment of an envoy to investigate Northern Ireland and report on a possible way forward to peace. Ted said that Reagan was seemingly not interested, apparently concerned that he would be trespassing on Thatcher's authority, but when Thatcher visited Reagan at Camp David, he did express his concern over Northern Ireland and urged her to move forward. And still Ted pushed. He met with the Irish prime minister, Garrett Fitzgerald, who came to Hyannis to discuss ways in which the Irish Republic could play a role in resolving the stalemate in Northern Ireland. (Later that year Fitzgerald did reach an Anglo-Irish Agreement with Thatcher that gave the republic an advisory role in determining the future of Northern Ireland, which was something the Protestant Unionists vehemently opposed.)

He pushed, but progress was slow. Throughout, however, Ted remained in contact with John Hume, and Hume told Ted that he had been meeting secretly with the leader of Sinn Fein, Gerry Adams. Hume was urging Adams to forgo violence, to meet with all the parties, including the Protestant Unionists, in a conference to be hosted by the republic, and to try to reach a settlement that would, in any case, be voted upon both by the republic and by Northern Ireland. Adams had always been persona non grata in America because he would not disavow the use of violence. Now he was clearly reaching out to Americans, but the question became: To whom could he reach out in order to convince the White House, which was now occupied by Bill Clinton, that he had had a change of heart? Ted Kennedy became that conduit, though a reluctant one, since he still didn't entirely trust the IRA himself. Niall O'Dowd, editor of the *Irish Voice* and a supporter of Adams's, had set up a channel through Ted's aide on Irish affairs, Trina Vargo, and through Vargo to Nancy Soderberg, Vargo's predecessor, who now worked in the National Security Council in the Clinton administration. O'Dowd was looking to get Adams a visa to come to America, and resistance was stiff since Adams was still identified with violence. "You had to get Kennedy onboard," Vargo would say. "It was an absolute must to make it happen," because people knew that Ted would not endorse a visa unless he was convinced that Adams no longer embraced violence. In effect, Ted would be vouching for Adams. By one account, O'Dowd met with Vargo in July 1993 and promised that he would pass on to her any intelligence he got, presumably from Adams himself, which was the very best source of intelligence into the IRA. O'Dowd talked to Vargo daily during that period, and she in turn talked to Soderberg, until Soderberg finally began talking to O'Dowd herself, and then decided at last to talk to Adams herself, avoiding all the middlemen.

But after twenty-three years of involvement in the complexities of Irish politics, Ted Kennedy hadn't become a convert yet. He had, however, pushed Clinton hard to appoint his sister, Jean Smith, to the ambassadorship to Ireland, which Clinton did, and Jean *had* become a convert. Once there she was convinced that Adams had personally renounced violence, though he had yet to do so publicly. But there was another matter. Irish prime minister Albert Reynolds had persuaded Adams that he should now go to America to dissuade American supporters of the IRA, who had provided them with guns and with money for weapons, though Reynolds surely understood that gaining Adams admission to America would raise his standing among the Northern Irish Catholics. Hume was persuaded, too, that Adams should come to America and tamp down the more extremist elements among Irish Americans, since he had begun negotiations with Adams that would lead to Adams's joining discussions on the future of Northern Ireland were he to renounce violence. Those negotiations had resulted in a declaration on December 15, 1993, memorializing Hume's offer.

Still, Adams did not renounce violence publicly or publicly embrace the declaration. So any visit to America was in abeyance. Two weeks later Ted and Vicki and Patrick were celebrating New Year's Eve in Dublin with Jean. Ted hadn't come to talk politics; he had come to keep his widowed sister company. But Jean had Gerry Adams on her mind. According to Taoiseach Reynolds, Ted and Vicki and Jean met at his apartment in Ballsbridge and spent the night discussing Adams's situation. Ted recalled it differently. He said that almost as soon as he arrived in Dublin, he was shuttled to meetings, and then he attended a dinner with Jean and Reynolds and a group of about ten—all talking about Gerry Adams and his visa—the visa he would need to acquire if he was to visit America. Reynolds would say that Jean had a "job with Ted to convince him—a big job," and that Ted harbored grave doubts about Adams's sincerity. "We were constantly, quietly watching for signs from the IRA," Trina Vargo, Ted's Ireland specialist, would say of Ted's monitoring of Adams's state of mind. Ted would say it was Reynolds himself who allayed those doubts, telling Ted that a "new day was possible" if Adams got his visa; that it would have a big impact on the IRA if Adams's claims were taken seriously; and that he himself was privy to British intelligence and that the negotiations between Hume and Adams were genuine. With those reassurances from Reynolds and Hume, Ted now believed that Adams's acceptance into the political process might very well lead to a solution. And Ted would say, "I left Ireland completely convinced that Adams should be able to get his visa."

But others were not convinced, and they were the ones who would make the final decision. The British government, which did not make the decision but exercised great influence on those in the American government who did, and which believed that Adams was a terrorist, was unalterably opposed, seeing the visa as bending to pressure. And so was the State Department, which would have to issue the visa. The sense was that Adams's appearance would only harden the British resolve and that the American Irish would still insist that the British leave Northern Ireland, no matter what Adams told them, and that, in any case, the visa would damage America's relationship to Britain. The FBI and CIA agreed with that assessment. Clinton, whose final decision it was, told Taoiseach Reynolds that he would consider a visa if Adams received a speaking invitation (he soon did, to a peace conference in New York) and then asked Soderberg and NSC adviser Anthony Lake to make their own assessment. By this point, Soderberg had come to the same conclusion as her former boss: Adams was sincere, and the visa would give him status with Sinn Fein and the IRA that he could use to good effect. And Ted himself did one last thing. He asked to meet with Clinton, who listened carefully to Ted's arguments.

Still, Ted never knew with Clinton whether he had carried the point, and he was afraid when he heard that the State Department intended to ask Adams in a pre-visa interview to renounce violence. "Out of hand" was how he described the process and told Tony Lake so. Ted threatened to offer an amendment to the State Department authorization bill, then on the Senate floor, asking that the visa be granted, and he let both Vice President Gore and Clinton's chief of staff, Mack McLarty, know from the floor that he had the votes. (This was a bluff, since Ted really wasn't sure he had the votes and because he thought it was unlikely he could carry the House.) In the end, however, under pressure from Ted, whom he did not want to disappoint, and with the support of the NSC, and with Adams finally condemning attacks on innocent civilians, Clinton granted the visa, without which, Ted was certain, the peace process could not advance. And in January 1994 Gerry Adams finally came to America for a brief visit—a forty-eight-hour visit. The British tabloids were especially venomous toward Clinton. "See what the Brits are saying about me?" he told Ted. To which Ted said, "Don't worry about it. That's what the Brits have been saying about the Kennedys for years."

And now the process was moving slowly toward its goal. Seven months after Adams's visit, the IRA declared a ceasefire, and Adams was issued another visa to come to America, on September 24, and this time Ted and Vicki, who had kept their distance from him on the first visit, met him at Boston's Logan Airport. Of course, it couldn't be lost on the more politically astute that Adams was visiting during Ted's reelection campaign against Mitt Romney and that he could provide Ted with a much-needed boost among Irish Massachusettsans. Nevertheless, Trina Vargo, knowing how clever Adams could be, had another concern. She worried that he would greet Ted with a hug, and that Ted would instinctively hug back, which would seem to be Ted's endorsement of Adams—an endorsement that Ted was not yet ready to give. But Vicki said of Ted, "Trina, he's Irish. They barely hug their wives."

Whether the airport appearance was an endorsement or not, it seemed like one. One member of NORAID, an organization dedicated to raising funds for the IRA, said, "If the Sinn Fein leader is good enough for Kennedy, he was good enough for everybody else." Whether he was good enough for Bill Clinton was still an issue. Adams insisted that he should be given the same privileges as John Hume and the Protestant Unionists, who had received a meeting at the White House, but Clinton had promised British prime minister John Major that there would be no such meeting—yet. At a fundraiser at his house, Ted approached Clinton directly to argue for a meeting, only to be told it was impossible. Niall O'Dowd, publisher of the *Irish Voice*, who had opened the channels to Adams, negotiated with Nancy Soderberg and Anthony Lake to see if Al Gore might at least *call* Adams so Adams would have some token of recognition from his visit, and Ted made an "angry" call to Lake to press the case. Finally, after all the pressure, Gore called Adams—Adams was staying at Bobby's old house, Hickory Hill, in Virginia—spoke to him for five minutes, and told him that the ban against Sinn Fein was lifted. But it was not all one-sided, not all Ted pressing the Clinton administration. He had warned Adams, too, that he could not be a "democratic" politician and still have a "private army," and during one visit, he took him aside in the corridor and told him that while he had "every kind of opportunity in terms of the future," he had to "get out of that shadow of criminality" and that he "cannot have a blind eye to these thugs and the criminal element in the North," meaning, of course, the thugs of the IRA.

Things changed then—changed for the better. "There was a several-year period of a lot of quiet conversations and activities and appeals to important leaders for an opportunity for a change and new direction," Ted would later say. He followed the situation closely. "I gave him about three memos a day on the issue," Trina Vargo said. Now also more deeply interested in Northern Ireland, Clinton appointed former Senate majority leader George Mitchell as his special adviser to Northern Ireland, and it was Mitchell who helped guide a process over three years that led, at long, long last, to an accord between the parties of Northern Ireland, Protestant and Catholic, and between Great Britain and Ireland. Clinton met with the parties on St. Patrick's Day in Northern Ireland, citing his role as "basically to keep reassuring and pushing all the parties into the framework George Mitchell was constructing." Less than a month later, on Good Friday 1998, with Clinton staying up most of the night making calls to close the deal—the final one at five a.m. with Gerry Adams—the agreement was reached. "One of the happiest days of my presidency," Clinton would call it, and he rightly claimed that "my first visa to Gerry Adams and the subsequent intense engagement of the White House made a difference." But it was Ted Kennedy who had convinced Bill Clinton to give Gerry Adams that visa and Ted Kennedy who had worked for years to reach the accord.

And in the vicious, ugly year of stagnation, this was an epilogue too—to thirty years of violence.

III

Came September, and Ted said that Bill Clinton's mood "seemed privately to plummet" as Starr delivered to the House his report containing eleven allegations of wrongdoing, and as the eventuality of the Republican House voting for articles of impeachment neared. Ted said he met with Clinton nearly every day during the crisis and spoke to him frequently on the phone, though Clinton "didn't seem to be able to confront the ultimate cause" of his situation: that he had disappointed those who believed in him. (Ted well knew that cause from his own experience in having disappointed so many himself.) Mostly, Clinton said that Ted provided spiritual counsel. "His advice is always simple. It's just sort of get up and go to work, just keep going, and remember why you wanted the job in the first place." But that was not always enough, given the gravity of the circumstance facing the president. At one point, they discussed a plan hatched by Louisiana senator John Breaux, a conservative Democrat, to enlist thirty-five senators to sign a letter endorsing the view of prominent legal scholars that Clinton's conduct had not risen to impeachable offenses, but Ted said he couldn't find those thirty-five and that Minority Leader Daschle had said that he would need fifty-one in any case to avoid a trial. Robert Byrd was apoplectic at the scheme and said it would amount to jury tampering, though Clinton argued that the Republicans had launched a conspiracy to destroy both his presidency and the Democrats, and that they were just prolonging the process in the hopes that they could drive down his poll numbers.

All this was interrupted by the 1998 midterm elections, which would clearly be viewed as a referendum on Clinton. The Gallup poll showed that Clinton's favorability rating had actually increased substantially that January, since the charges of his having had an affair with Lewinsky and lying about it, jumping 5.6 percent that quarter over the previous quarter, even though, already in February and long before he made his public confession, 63 percent of Americans thought he had had sexual relations with Lewinsky. At the time of the November midterms, his rating stood at 66 percent. The impending impeachment, then, had made Clinton more popular rather than less. The election results bore that out. The Democrats picked up five seats in the House, the first time a president had gained seats in his sixth year of office since James Monroe in 1822. Republicans were aghast. One Republican representative, likening it to the *Titanic* hitting an iceberg, called for new leadership. Above all, it was a stunning rebuke for Newt Gingrich—so stunning, in fact, that Gingrich, now ostracized by members of his own party for yet another example of his overreach, announced his intention to resign the next day when Representative Robert Livingston declared that he would challenge Gingrich for the speakership and, with a veiled stab at "Newt Gingrich, my dear friend," hinted that he would be more focused on the "day-to-day business of the House of Representatives" than on "inspirational speeches." Gingrich complained about the criticism. "The ones you see on TV are hateful," he said. "I am willing to lead, but I won't allow cannibalism." Rather than be eaten, he left.

And so Newt Gingrich, the self-proclaimed transformational figure who promised to destroy the Democratic Party lock, stock, and barrel and in attempting to do so was as responsible as any single figure for returning American politics into the blood sport it had been in the nineteenth century; the bloviator who, despite his boasting, self-regard, and self-puffery, had accomplished virtually nothing of significance; the vainglorious opportunist who had always put his own ego above his nation's and even his own party's interests; the egotist who shut down the government on a whim and on the infantile pettiness of not getting a better seat on Air Force One—this man, who had begun his assault on government with such bombast, ended his reign of terror with a whimper.

The Republicans had miscalculated badly in thinking that Americans wanted Clinton taken down in favor of their revolution. One Clinton biographer would analyze Clinton's midterm victory this way: "The president's success since 1995 has been based on the fact that the electorate was less partisan in nature than it had been in decades. The capital, by contrast, was more partisan than it had been in decades. America was yearning for an age of moderation. Washington was governing in an age of extremes." Given Gingrich's own dreadful poll numbers, which had never recovered since the government shutdown, and the midterm election results, there seemed truth in the fact that Americans were tired of the unceasing partisan and ideological warfare that Republicans had waged. Bill Clinton was no ideologue. He was, often to Ted Kennedy's consternation, a moderate, which now seemed the public's preference. As far as impeachment was concerned, the midterms rendered a verdict on that too. "No matter how many mentions of 'perjury' and 'rule of law' and 'constitutional obligation' got pumped into the noise, the possibility of dallying and lying about it continued to be understood by and regarded as irrelevant to the survival of the nation by a majority of the nation's citizens," Joan Didion would write. And Didion said this was another epilogue—not for the political revolution that Gingrich had hoped to engineer, but for the cultural one. Conservatives, perplexed that Clinton seemed to maintain public support amid the charges of sexual improprieties, argued that, in Didion's words, the "citizens were incapable of understanding momentous events"—namely, Clinton's alleged transgressions—"because they had succumbed to the lures of hedonism, materialism, false modernity, 'radical individualism' itself." (This alleged moral torpor of Clinton's, of course, had been the charge leveled at Ted Kennedy too after Chappaquiddick and again after Palm Beach.) At least that was what the conservatives had been banking on in thinking Clinton would be driven from office. But it seemed it was the conservatives who were incapable of understanding—incapable of understanding that Americans could make distinctions between personal and political conduct, and between what had become known as the "politics of personal destruction" and constitutional high crimes and misdemeanors. None of this dissuaded the Republicans from pursuing the impeachment, and on December 19, with narrow majorities in the House, they did so—even after their prospective new leader, Robert Livingston, stepped down when *Hustler* magazine announced revelations of extramarital affairs of his own.

Now came the Senate trial. The Senate Democrats met on January 6 in the Lyndon Johnson Room of the Capitol to discuss strategy. In his meetings and phone calls with Ted, Clinton had been defiant. He told Ted that he would not be driven from office, that he would deliver a blistering State of the Union address that would show the nation he was continuing to conduct its business, and that *he* now, not the Republicans, could drag out the process to illustrate that he would not resign. But Ted was not looking to save Bill Clinton, as much as he personally liked him and as much as he thought Clinton had been the victim of a partisan crusade. He was looking to save the Senate from the disgrace it would incur if it did not hold a fair trial. Ted argued that they had to have a bipartisan proceeding, but he also argued that if the Republicans insisted on making it partisan rather than judicial, the Democrats should ask for a test vote and get it over with. The Senate as a whole met to discuss procedures on January 8, 1999, five days after Gingrich's resignation, in the old Supreme Court chamber in the bowels of the Capitol, an ornate room decorated with red French brocade, and to add to the solemnity, the senators, according to Majority Leader Trent Lott, generally wore dark suits. Daschle and Lott had agreed in advance to let three members of each caucus present their suggestions. Byrd spoke first, calling for his beloved chamber to "restore some order to the anger which has overtaken this country and the chaos which threatens this city," as Ted remembered it. But the anger did not subside. The sticking point that divided the caucuses was whether witnesses would be called, to which Democrats were opposed, fearing the witnesses, almost certainly including Monica Lewinsky, would be used simply to embarrass and humiliate the president, or whether the House managers would lay out the case themselves. Lott said the last of the six to speak was Phil Gramm—Ted recalled Gramm was third—who invoked the words of Daniel Webster during the debate over the Compromise of 1850 ("I wish to speak today, not as á Massachusetts man, nor as a Northern man, but as an American and a member of the Senate of the United States") and who recommended that rather than spend time deliberating over the process in partisan bickering, they just commence the trial with the House making its case, and only then would the Senate decide whether witnesses were necessary.

The debate, lasting two hours, was tense. Carey Parker said that "senators were practically at each others' throats." But Ted was looking for a fair and dignified process that would allow Clinton to make his defense. So Ted, who seldom agreed with the conservative and partisan Gramm, promptly agreed with him this time. "A defining moment," Parker called it. Ted would say, "You could hear the bitterness and the tensions begin to expire." Lott would recall that he hustled Ted, Gramm, the Senate's chief lawyer Tom Griffith, his own legal adviser Mike Wallace, and Lott's chief of staff Dave Hoppe, as well as, Ted said, a few other senators—*New York Times* reporter Peter Baker would say Joe Lieberman and Slade Gorton were among the conferees—to a conference room where they spent the next two hours, according to Lott, converting that verbal agreement into a formal one. According to Ted's aide Melody Barnes, it took the entire day, "going back and forth, in and out of these meetings, and then up in the Senator's hideaway." And in Barnes's version, Ted consulted with his Judiciary staff and with Carey Parker and with Vicki, who was also in the hideaway. And then he left the hideaway, which was up a stairway above the Senate floor, and talked with the press—"I have never seen so much press in my life"—who pumped him with questions about the measures on which they had agreed, and Barnes said she thought Ted was "really proud" of having hammered out a deal with Gramm, with whom, by Ted's own admission, he had had neither a political nor a personal relationship. It passed 100 to 0. Now the rules were set.

With a vote of two-thirds of the Senate required to convict and expel the president, votes the Republicans did not have, the result was a foregone conclusion. Still, Ted was active, protecting Clinton, protecting the Senate process. When he wasn't on the floor, he spent his time in his hideaway, decorated with Kennedy memorabilia, where he would meet with his staff during the breaks and tell his press secretary Jim Manley to "bring some folks over," meaning reporters, and Manley would bring in ten or fifteen of them, and Ted would hold court, giving his version of the events transpiring on the floor below. His sisters Eunice and Jean would be there every day of the trial, and so would Vicki, who would participate in the briefings that he received from his Judiciary staff. As for the witnesses, over whom the parties had nearly come to blows, Lewinsky and others testified in closed-door sessions, but not publicly.* The trial was brief, be-

---

*One footnote to the proceedings: At a Democratic Party caucus on January 25 to discuss procedures, Senator Patty Murray insisted that Monica Lewinsky should not be called to the Senate floor as a witness, and that were she to be called, "This is going to be ninety white men leering at her as she's being asked about her sex life." At which point Ted's close friend and former fellow carouser Chris Dodd interjected, "Why is everyone looking at Kennedy?" which drew a hearty laugh from the participants. Peter Baker, *The Breach: Inside the Impeachment and Trial of William Jefferson Clinton* (New York: Scribner, 2000), 358.

ginning on January 31 and ending on February 12, and in the end, Clinton was acquitted of all the charges. Republicans had been determined to drive him from office, he said. But he would not be driven from office, nor did the public want to see him driven out. The week in December that the House voted its articles of impeachment, his approval rating stood at 73 percent. The week of his acquittal, it stood at 68.

But the trial too was an epilogue. In the middle of the impeachment preparations, Clinton delivered the State of the Union address he had promised Ted he would deliver—an aggressive presidency-saving address full of new initiatives, many of them, as a biographer put it, explicitly meant to "challenge his party's orthodoxies," almost as if to prove that he had never been the liberal government activist the conservatives had accused him of being. Few were passed. The impeachment had sapped the energy from any legislative agenda, and while Clinton remained popular, he was sapped too. Gingrich was gone. But Clinton was neutered.

IV

There was to be one more epilogue that summer—this one of almost unbearable agony. Through all the personal strife, through all the tragedy, through all the electoral and legislative effort that consumed most of his life, through his new marriage and the commitment to his new family, Ted Kennedy had remained the paterfamilias—the Grand Fromage of the Kennedy clan. He was, however, a very different patriarch than the one his father had been—yet another late-life adjustment to his being not more of a Kennedy, but less of one. He was a patriarch without imperiousness. "Rank didn't matter," one reporter noted of Ted's personal sense of democracy, saying that he engaged in the same obscene banter with Jay Rockefeller as he had with his old driver, the crusty Boston Irishman Jack Crimmins. He and Senator Dale Bumpers had even proposed a bill to eliminate first-class air travel. (It was soundly defeated.) He once told his civil rights adviser Bob Bates that Black people ought to block the runways at National Airport to change things, presumably because inconveniencing the rich and powerful was a good tactic. He preferred to drive his old blue Pontiac convertible—"old shit cans" was how one reporter described the Kennedy cars—with a light built into the back seat. When he dined with family, he made it a point, Doris Reggie, his mother-in-law, said, of telling everyone afterward to pick up his or her plate and take it into the kitchen.

"Our housekeeper was so impressed. She just couldn't believe that he would care that much about lessening her load." And if he was less than imperious, he was also surprisingly unworldly given his life experience. When an aide recruited him for the Comedy Central charity, Comic Relief, the aide said Ted had never heard of the event's hosts, the famous comedians Billy Crystal, Whoopi Goldberg, and Robin Williams.

He bore his responsibility comfortably, too, though it was a heavy responsibility. He was the keeper of the Kennedy flame, the man who maintained the legacy, even as he had occasionally tarnished it, the chief adviser and consultant to his many nephews and nieces, not to mention his own sons and daughter, the one who ministered to them when they were in jeopardy, which they often were as the next generation spun away from the traditions and the decorum of the previous one, and the chief consoler when they sought consolation, which was so often and so tragically necessary. Being Kennedys had come with great benefits, but it had also taken a great toll on all of them. Ted Jr., who suffered his own bouts of drug and alcohol abuse before getting treatment in 1991 and reaching sobriety, probably spoke for many Kennedys of his generation when he complained of having to be cautious, reticent, closed off. "It was never very easy for me to express my feelings. I think it's a consequence of growing up in my family and having people prying and feeling like somebody's always trying to get something from you." And he said, "Then I realized this is no real way to live a life."

But for all the struggles of the generation—Joe Kennedy II's misadventures that had caused the paralysis of a young woman; David Kennedy's fatal drug overdose in Palm Beach; William Kennedy Smith's alleged rape for which he stood trial and was acquitted; the death of Joe II's and David's brother Michael when he slammed into a fir tree in Aspen while heading down a mountain during a game of "ski football" on New Year's Eve 1997, which prompted *Newsweek* to comment that the Kennedy legacy had been "reduced from mythology to mere celebrity"—the family had always had its prince, the handsome young man designated to carry the Kennedy name and charisma forward and possibly even its political fortunes someday without also seeming to carry its burdens. The nation had known John Kennedy, Jr., the late president's son, since his birth, just weeks after his father's election in 1960. It had watched him cavort as a toddler under his father's desk in the Oval Office, and it had watched him salute his father's passing casket on what was also John Jr.'s third birthday. It had watched him grow up into an effortlessly charming and self-effacing celebrity whose name and romances filled tabloids and gossip columns, though as a celebrity, his manner was as informal as his uncle's. It had watched him attend law school and then launch a magazine, *George*, that merged politics and popular culture as the Kennedy family itself had done. It had watched him marry a beautiful young woman, Carolyn Bessette, forming one of America's most handsome couples. "American Son," an author called him, and he was. In some ways, he was America's promise, too, to bring luster again to the Kennedys, whose luster had dulled since the high days of John and Bobby.

Determined to keep the flame alive, that July Fourth, Ted, who had been reading about family reunions, decided to hold a Kennedy reunion at Hyannis. A "command performance," his longtime aide and family friend Melody Miller called it, with Kennedys assembling from across the country. Even Rosemary appeared from her retreat in Wisconsin. Miller said that Ted set up a big tent and had face painters for the children, now the fourth generation of Kennedys, and the surviving Kennedy sisters conducted tours of the Big House and explained the family's history, and there was a big sail, in a rented boat because Ted's own boat *Mya* could not begin to accommodate the crowd, and at the end of the day, they gathered for a group photo. In the front row of that photo were John Jr. and his wife, Carolyn.

And they gathered again, less than two weeks later that summer, again at Hyannis, this time for the marriage of Bobby's youngest child, daughter Rory Kennedy. Ted had been in high spirits that week. In a year of legislative fizzle, he had challenged the Republicans on a long-standing issue of his, a Patients' Bill of Rights, which would permit individuals much wider latitude in appealing insurers' restrictions on which doctors they could see, on whether they could go the emergency room without preauthorization, on whether insurers could override doctors' decisions, including matters like the length of a hospital stay, on whether HMOs would be subject to malpractice suits, and on other medical concerns that had yielded to the insurers' financial ones. Lobbied by a group called the Health Benefits Coalition that had organized five hundred meetings with members of Congress and inundated them with thirty thousand phone calls, Republicans were strongly opposed—they had killed a similar bill the year before on a narrow procedural vote, with Ted saying, "Today, the Republicans paid off the special interests"—but Ted after the midterms reintroduced his bill, which the Republicans, clearly fretting over the politics of opposing something most Americans desired, had countered with a bill in name only that stripped out nearly all of Ted's provisions. Even with its teeth pulled, it was only because Ted had held up the Senate for four days, with speeches so impassioned that even his colleagues, by one account, began "ribbing him for his enthusiasm on the floor," that Trent Lott brought the Republican bill to a vote. It passed, with Ted in opposition, and Clinton threatened a veto. Nevertheless Ted had, by one report, achieved a public relations victory in getting the Republicans on record as opposing the Patients' Bill of Rights. Then he left the floor and headed to a convention for the homeless at which he was to deliver a speech on mental health. He arrived forty-five minutes late (delayed by a television interview), arrived to an ovation, read the speech as best he could (the makeup from the interview had run into his eyes so that he had to extemporize the conclusion), and then left for Hyannis and his niece's wedding.

It was Joe II who delivered the news to Ted. John Jr., only thirty-six years old, had been flying up from New Jersey with Carolyn and her sister Lauren, piloting his own small single-engine plane, a Piper-Saratoga, with a scheduled stop in Martha's Vineyard to drop off Lauren before the short hop to Hyannis. He never arrived. The following afternoon a visitor to the Vineyard pulled a black overnight bag from the water at Philbin Beach with a business card in a clear plastic baggage tag—"Lauren G. Bessette, Morgan Stanley Dean Witter. Vice President"—and called the police. They appeared with a three-wheel buggy that contained an aqua duffel and a plane wheel they had already fished from the water, while divers down the beach, searching for wreckage, pulled out an airplane seat and a landing gear and a toiletry bag. "The world stands motionless and hearts are heavy with sadness," read a note a visitor left at the Kennedy gravesite at Arlington National Cemetery.

There was a search mission. President Clinton, who was in regular touch with the family, instructed naval vessels to keep looking. It took five days to find the plane and the bodies. During that time, Ted had flown to Long Island to console Caroline, John's sister, thirteen years to the day since he had given her away at her wedding. When he returned, a helicopter took him, Ted Jr., and Patrick from Hyannis to the Coast Guard station on Martha's Vineyard, and a cutter then took them to the crash site, and they boarded a navy salvage ship, the USS *Grasp*, where they waited hours for the bodies to be lifted and where they identified them. Two days later

John Jr.'s ashes were scattered at sea off Martha's Vineyard from the deck of the USS *Briscoe* with Ted and sixteen family members aboard. "We are tied to the ocean," John Jr.'s father had once said. "When we go back to the sea, whether it is to sail or to watch it, we are going back from whence we came."

The next day Ted, so practiced in eulogies, delivered another—this time at St. Thomas More Church, where John Jr.'s mother had worshipped on the Upper East Side of Manhattan, and hundreds, many in tears, looked on from behind the cordons as the mourners arrived. Ted had been deep in grief. "He was so deep inside himself that he just shut down," Patrick would say of his father when they recovered the bodies. "He couldn't comprehend what we were witnessing; it was too much, so raw." "I have never seen him as shaken," his nephew Douglas Kennedy said. "It affected him in a way that I have never seen before." And a Barnstable police sergeant who kept watch during the recovery reported, "He was very low-key, very somber. He sat on the front porch a lot, looking out to sea." Ted spoke of his nephew before a small congregation of invited guests that included the president and the first lady. (Ted had wanted a large public ceremony; Caroline a small private one.) He talked of how his nephew belonged "to the American family" and how "the whole world knew his name before he did." He talked of "his amazing grace" and how "he accepted who he was, but he cared more about what he should and could become." He talked about his nephew's love for his young wife and his love for helping those who needed help, whom he helped quietly, privately. He talked, and his voice cracked as it had during similar sad moments. And he said of his nephew, "He had only just begun. There was in him a great promise of things to come." And now that promise was gone and with it so many hopes to which the family and its patriarch had clung.

TWENTY

The Charm Offensive/The War Offensive

FOUR DAYS AFTER scattering his nephew's ashes at sea, Ted Kennedy returned, as he had from John's death and Bobby's death and from Chappaquiddick and from Palm Beach, to the Senate, *his* Senate, where he promptly went back to work to escape the pain, casting two procedural votes that very evening and making plans to submit a bill on prescription drug coverage. "The fold," he called the chamber at a Senate luncheon the next day, as in "back in the fold," and he said he was happy to be "back in the Senate family," though his colleagues told the press that they would have understood had he taken time off. He returned enhanced by tragedy. He was the man, in the words of *People* magazine, "who carries the clan"—the Kennedy clan—"on his shoulders." "We grew up to think of my father and uncle as saints," *People* quoted Douglas Kennedy, one of Bobby's sons. "But it is really Teddy who had stood up to the great challenges and lived it." *People* called Ted "The Torchbearer." *The Washington Post* wrote similarly of him, as the Kennedy who was "supposed to be the kid brother, the engaging and rambunctious boyo," but it noted that "a 35-year family catalogue of death and transfiguration cast him against type" and converted him into "the tragic hero, the flawed, self-destructive protagonist who flees frantically from death only to encounter it repeatedly in some unexpected place and form."

Enhanced he was, but also emptied. Tragedy engulfed him, tragedy hollowed him. Nearly every noon now, he attended Mass at St. Joseph's Church, near the Capitol. And at a Senate prayer breakfast that fall—the breakfasts that John had advised he attend to curry favor with his elders when Ted first came to the Senate thirty-seven years earlier—he spoke solemnly, haltingly, agonizingly of the tragedies his family had endured and of his faith, which had not been a "loud and boisterous faith" but a "faith of patience, pathos, endurance and grace." He told his colleagues that his faith had often been shaken, as it was, he thought, for anyone who was "awake to the brokenness of the world and of our lives." But he told them one learned that "God plays no favorites; that we all suffer, that we all die," and that for all our torments and our anger at God for them, "if we are lucky, we all come home to God in the end." And he spoke now of sitting at family gatherings, surrounded by his children and grandchildren and nieces and nephews, and how "tears come to my eyes" both at the marvel of them and at the healing power of family itself—"that to be held in the arms of a loving family redeems even the most numbing pain."

That he was in the arms of a loving family now, there was no question. He and Vicki had become their own family, no longer an adjunct of the Kennedy family, no longer even an adjunct of Ted Kennedy's own earlier and tormented personal history. They had separated themselves from that life to further the new one they had forged together. Early in 1997 they had decided to sell the McLean home, the home that Ted had bought in 1968 in hopes of rehabilitating his relationship with Joan, the home that sat on 6.5 acres overlooking the Potomac and just down the road from Bobby's, and the sale would be another marker in Ted's own detachment from being a Kennedy and becoming his own man. The reason he gave for the sale was that he and Vicki wanted to be closer to his stepchildren Curran and Caroline's private school in Washington, and Vicki wanted to be closer to her work since she had continued to practice law. The McLean home was on the market for only three weeks before a Hong Kong industrialist bought it for just under $6 million, nearly $1 million over the asking price. That began a long transition. It wasn't until the summer of 1999 that they bought a new house, for $2.775 million, at 2416 Tracy Place N.W. in Washington in the quiet, leafy Kalorama neighborhood, near Embassy Row, where Woodrow Wilson and William Howard Taft had lived after their presidencies and Franklin Roosevelt before his— "quite possibly the most affluent section of Washington, D.C.," said one observer—and several months more before they finally made the move in September 1999. ("We saw it in the morning and put in a bid that evening," Ted would tell *Architectural Digest*.) The Kalorama house was a large (nine thousand square feet) white "mansion," as some called it, with a long portico and colonnades that almost gave it the affect of the White

House, but it was without the amenities of the McLean house—that house's forty-foot-long swimming pool and the tennis court on which Ted had so loved to host those morning doubles games. "Cape Cod on the Potomac," Ted had called his old home because it was perched on a bluff over the river, approximating, as much as he was able to approximate it there, the ocean, and because he had decorated it with antiques from Cape Cod and even beams salvaged from New England barns.

The new house would be no Cape Cod home, though Ted had a painting of the Hyannis compound hanging in the entranceway—a painting he had done himself—and other still lifes he had done of New England on walls throughout. It was the kind of home that would befit a senator—decorous, ornate, formal, overstuffed—with the only real departure a gym across from the master bedroom decorated with cartoons of Ted, including a few that vilified him. Though it was his and Vicki's home, there were ghosts he could not escape; in a gallery on the second floor that ran the length of the house, he had installed, as he had at his other homes, a veritable museum to his family, especially to John and Bobby, with photos of Ted with his brothers, and a framed note from Jack scribbled during a meeting of the National Security Council in 1963: "Teddy's house on Sunday." And presiding over the sitting room was an oil portrait of old Joe Kennedy and one of Rose up the staircase in a wide-brimmed hat. Still, for all the Kennedy presence and for all the home's formality, so different from the demeanor of its occupants, the decorator, Josepha Faley, said that the main instruction she received from Ted and Vicki was to make it "calm." "A warm welcoming house," Vicki would say—"fireplaces and candles are our thing"—which, after a lifetime of turbulence and tragedy, comported with how Ted Kennedy now saw this chapter of his life. Dignified, calm.

It was a complete life now, a happy life—"years in which my love for Vicki and my Senate work deepened," he would write—save for a domestic hole that Ted Kennedy had long wanted to fill. Ted had always loved dogs, though his peripatetic childhood—from Hyannis to Palm Beach and back, from one school to another to another to another—had prevented him from having one. (It is likely that Rose was too fussy to have permitted one in the house anyway.) When he was at law school at the University of Virginia, his roommate John Tunney said they adopted two German shepherds—"He loved those dogs," Tunney would say—and that the dogs mated and Tunney took one of the puppies, but presumably because Ted got married to Joan soon after, he didn't take one of them himself, and when Patrick was born, the child suffered from severe asthma, which precluded Ted getting a dog. Shortly after the family moved to Kalorama, his stepdaughter Caroline begged him for a dog, but Ted once again reluctantly refused, telling her that Patrick would be visiting them. By one account, Caroline, however, had gotten wind that Patrick had been around some dogs without suffering ill effects, which she said negated Ted's excuse. With that prod, Vicki and Ted conducted some research of their own—"believe me, they researched it," Caroline would say—and discovered that Portuguese water dogs, big sweet fluffy dogs, were hypoallergenic.

And now Ted was launched. He apparently consulted a noted dog trainer in the Washington area, Dawn Sylvia, who directed him to Art and Martha Stern, who bred Portuguese water dogs in northern Virginia. As Art Stern would recall it, Vicki phoned them the Saturday of President's Day Weekend 2000, three days before Ted's birthday, and, without identifying herself, said that she and her husband were interested in buying a dog but that her husband was very busy and asked if they might stop by that afternoon and look at puppies. (Martha Stern was astonished when she opened the door and saw that Ted Kennedy was the busy husband.) Vicki and Ted were sitting in the Sterns' kitchen when Martha brought in a four-year-old woolly black dog of theirs, Splash, just to acquaint the Kennedys with the breed. Splash bounded across the living room and jumped on the arm of Ted's chair and, as Caroline would recount it, her stepfather immediately had "visions of sugarplums dancing in his head with the dog." Ted was "smitten," Art Stern would say. The Kennedys left without bothering to look at the puppies, and several days later either Vicki or Ted—Stern couldn't remember—phoned to ask if they might buy him. Splash had been a champion, and though the condition of his hips precluded him from being a stud, the dog was not for sale. But Ted was persistent and the Sterns relented, and two weeks later Splash joined the Kennedy family. Now Ted finally had his dog.

Smitten he was. Ted took Splash with him everywhere. He took him to his Senate office. Sharon Waxman, who would become Ted's national security advisor, recalled that when she was waiting to be interviewed by Ted, she shared the waiting room with Splash, unattended, and she grew increasingly uncomfortable as Splash grew increasingly "antsy," barking, even squatting at one point when Waxman was sure he would be relieving himself, and she prayed that someone would enter the room and take him away—which eventually happened. Ted took him to committee meetings. Representative George Miller recalled a conference on a bill in a room just off the Senate entrance where Paul Wellstone lost patience with the deliberations and declared that they were all wrong—"You're completely wrong"—his voice rising in anger. And Wellstone stood up and pointed at Ted—at which point, Miller said, Splash charged across the room, jumped up, and growled at Wellstone. Ted broke the tension, quipping to Wellstone, "I told you your ideas were no good, and even he knows it." Ted took him to markups, where Splash would sit under the table at Ted's feet and, in another example of Ted Kennedy's legislative brilliance, sometimes lightened the mood and made opponents more receptive. He took him to the White House and once even into the Oval Office for a signing ceremony, on a religious liberties bill that Ted had worked out with Orrin Hatch, where the presidential staffers were "freaking out," according to one witness, because Splash started barking. So Ted went over to Splash and said, "Splash, relax. I'm just talking to people. Behave." Thirty seconds later Splash was barking again, and Ted had a staffer take him out of the room. And when Clinton arrived and asked if there had been a dog in the office, everyone, including Ted, shrugged with, the witness said, "that guilty kind of look."

But Splash was *his* dog, not the family's dog. So just over a year later, in May 2001, Vicki phoned Martha Stern to complain that Ted had monopolized Splash, and that the dog that was supposed to be *their* dog wasn't. And Vicki and Caroline got another dog from the Sterns, a puppy named Sunny—black with a white bib. But the situation was no different than it had been with Splash. Now Ted took both dogs to his office, where there were always water bowls and tennis balls, until Sunny and Splash were "part of the landscape there," as one White House staffer would say, and he would take both dogs to a patch of grass outside the Russell Office Building—they sometimes tore at the shrubbery outside the building too, ignoring Ted's reprimands—or to a field near the FDR Memorial and, as Mark Leibovich observed, swat them tennis balls with a racket, yelling happily, "Now whaddya want, now whaddya want?" and when they fetched the balls back to him, he would pat them on the head lightly with the racket and tell them they were "good boys." Ted Kennedy loved those dogs. (He would later write a children's book in Splash's voice titled *The Senator and Me: A Dog's Eye View of Washington, D.C.*) And he would say this: that his idea of perfect happiness was "sailing on the *Mya* with Vicki at my side and my dogs, Splash and Sunny, at my feet."

There were to be few legislative achievements that fall. Ted continued to work on the Patients' Bill of Rights and on a hate crimes bill with protections for sexual orientation and gender ("One elephant too much for this boa constrictor," commented Republican senator Judd Gregg on helping halt the bill), on a jobs program for people with disabilities, and on funding for after-school programs to reduce teenage crime—a program to which Republicans, having mocked a similar program a few years earlier as "midnight basketball," were once again opposed, preferring funds be given for law enforcement over crime prevention. And once 1999 slipped into 2000, the last year of Bill Clinton's presidency and an election year, Congress ground to a halt as it braced for the fall, neither side wanting to give the other anything on which to campaign. The leading Democratic contenders for the nomination were Vice President Al Gore, and New Jersey senator Bill Bradley, a former Rhodes scholar from Princeton who had been both a college and a professional basketball star. The morning before a New Hampshire debate between the two, Ted endorsed Gore—the call had come from Bob Shrum, who worried that Gore might lose there—largely, Ted said, because Gore had fought for healthcare reform and Bradley had not, and Shrum would say that when Ted arrived and headed a large rally in a barn where he compared the Kennedys' commitment to public service to that of the Gores, "Gore seemed to catch the charisma gene," and Shrum said Gore might have lost there were it not for Ted's intervention. Later that June, when Tad Devine, who had helped guide Ted's 1994 Senate campaign and who was now running Gore's campaign, slotted Ted and his niece Caroline to speak at the convention in prime time, and Ted phoned him to express thanks for his doing so, Devine said, "Senator, it wasn't me who got you that speech. You know who did? You did when you won New Hampshire for Gore." And Devine said that Ted "roared" with laughter.

Ted had had his difficulties with the last two Democratic presidents, Jimmy Carter and Bill Clinton. He had no such problems with the Democratic nominee, Al Gore. Shrum, who had written Ted's speeches in the past, was now writing Gore's, including Gore's acceptance speech, which touched on many of the same themes as Ted's. "The people versus the powerful," Gore had announced in that speech as one of the hallmarks of his campaign—a line that Ted himself had used. But populism wasn't the main issue of the 2000 presidential campaign. Once again morality was. Bill Clinton's behavior with Monica Lewinsky had given the Republicans another opening to discuss one of their favorite subjects dating back to the 1960s, and a subject that Newt Gingrich had flogged continually to advance his revolution: the liberals'—and Democrats'—alleged moral turpitude. As Joan Didion described the process by which moralism entered politics, "America, in this apocalyptic telling, has been from its inception until the 1960s a deeply religious nation. During the 1960s, through the efforts of what Robert H. Bork called the 'intellectual' class and that class's enforcement arm, the judiciary, headed by the Supreme Court of the United States, the nation and its citizens had been inexplicably and destructively 'secularized,' and were accordingly in need of 'transformation,' of 'moral and intellectual rearmament,' or 'renewed respect for moral authority.' " It followed that Republicans would redeem the nation from its secular sins and from the elitists who promoted them. (Jimmy Carter had injected religion and moralism into politics too, but his idea was that Americans weren't the primary sinners; a failing government was. And in any case, Carter's beliefs, heavily influenced by theologian Reinhold Niebuhr, were complicated.)

Now the Republican presidential candidate, Texas governor George W. Bush, eldest son of former president George H. W. Bush, a born-again Christian and reformed alcoholic, took up the cause. It made no difference that Al Gore was no wanton like Bill Clinton or that Gore had tried to put distance between himself and the popular president he served, even selecting for his vice-presidential nominee Connecticut senator Joseph Lieberman, an Orthodox Jew and moralist who had been quick to condemn Clinton. Clinton himself had told Gore, "Al, there's not a single person in this country that thinks you messed around with Monica Lewinsky." Gore, however, was tainted by his association with Clinton and by his association with his own party. It didn't help Gore that he was waging a populist campaign, a Ted Kennedy campaign, while both Republicans and a good deal of the media insisted on floating the idea that Americans were risk averse, that they no longer had any tolerance for large governmental change or for social change, and that Gore was simply too extreme for the American he sought to represent—a theme sounded so insistently that it nearly became a self-fulfilling prophecy. Nor did it help that the Republicans and their media engine managed to malign him with false charges of mendacity (an alleged lie that he had claimed to have "invented" the Internet, though he hadn't made such a claim) and inauthenticity, which was always a charge leveled against men of intellect.

Still, it was a close election—none had ever been closer. Gore had Clinton's popularity going for him, even if he also had that moral miasma going against him, and a booming economy in which Bill Clinton had achieved what no president in recent memory had: a budget surplus. Though Al Gore narrowly won the popular vote, given the vicissitudes of American presidential selection process and its Electoral College, in which there are actually fifty separate elections to determine the outcome and not one large one, the election came down to contested votes in a single state—the state of Florida—where the candidates were separated, depending on the count (and there would be a recount) by mere hundreds or thousands of those votes. Whoever won there would win the presidency. So now began the jousting between Republicans and Democrats, for which the stakes were the future of the country—jousting over which votes would be counted in which counties and precincts, and which not; over which would be *recounted* by hand and which not; over who would determine how and when those votes would be recounted, state election officials, who were Republicans, or the Florida State Supreme Court, and who would determine when the recount would end; over whether manual recounts should be counted in the final vote totals; over whether the Supreme Court should hear a suit, brought by Bush, to have the recounts declared unconstitutional; over whether 14,000 disputed ballots should be counted; over whether 25,000 absentee ballots in Seminole and Martin counties should be disqualified or included, as had been ruled by the Florida Supreme Court. Over 100 million votes were cast nationally, and Al Gore won a plurality of them. But there were only five votes that really counted: the five votes of the conservative justices of the Supreme Court, who ordered the manual recounts to stop. With the recounts stopped and the disputed ballots excluded, Bush's margin was 527 votes. And so Florida's electoral votes went to George W. Bush. In the end, five weeks after the election, with the results having been in abeyance during that time as the country held its breath, those five justices, all Republican appointees, elected George W. Bush the president of the United States. "I have waited for thirty long years to see my country in a position to pull together, and build a future of our dreams," Clinton had told one gathering, during the campaign. "We dare not blow that chance." But from the Democrats' reckoning, the nation *had* blown its chance. The nation was divided and fractious, with a conservative minority president and an opposition party that felt the ideologues had stolen the election from them. Newt Gingrich might not have won his revolution. But the election proved that he did successfully stoke political hostilities.

What had Bill Clinton accomplished in his eight years? By the standards of peace and prosperity, by which most administrations were measured, he had achieved a great deal. Across the globe, he had kept America out of war, had helped broker peace in the former Yugoslavia and in Northern Ireland, and had come closer than any previous president to brokering peace in the intractable Middle East where only a sudden, late change of heart by Palestinian leader Yasser Arafat during negotiations conducted by Clinton derailed a truce. Domestically, the economy was booming, with sustained growth, growth that was much higher, 4 percent per year, than that during the Reagan years that Republicans had celebrated as a new American golden age, and more significantly, real median family income rose 2.2 percent a year from 1995 to 2000. There was full employment, and a record 22.7 million jobs were created. The ratio of debt to gross national product fell 14 percent in the course of his administration, and the government had that budget surplus not just in the last year of Clinton's administration but in the last four years. Inflation fell too. And so did the poverty rate. Though his fellow Democrats were not always enthused about it, Clinton also cut taxes on capital gains and small businesses. And even when it came to government spending as a percentage of GNP, a Republican bogeyman, Clinton cut it by three points. For all his personal failings, Americans seemed to appreciate him. He left office with an approval rating of 66 percent, higher than Reagan's, which attested to just how successful he had been as a commander in chief and steward of the economy.

But legacies are not built solely on peace or prosperity. Clinton, as many, including Ted, had complained, had no governing principles, no idea around which to rally the country, no inspirational summons to be the repairer that he had claimed he wanted to be. He was improvisational and expedient, compromising not just when he felt he had to, as Ted so often did, but before he had to. He was clever, always managing to outfox and co-opt the Republican ideologues and leaving them stupefied, which was an achievement, since they controlled both houses of Congress through his last six years, but he was not a bold leader or a courageous one—a man of decidedly liberal instincts, but one who always seemed to leave his allies wondering how hard he would fight for them and always left Ted wanting to get in that last word lest someone else come along and convince Clinton to do otherwise. He managed the country as successfully as any of his recent predecessors, but he did not lead it to some higher aspiration, as his idol, John Kennedy, had attempted to do, or change it in any fundamental way, as Lyndon Johnson and Ronald Reagan had done. And while he had left it better off than he had found it materially, it was more fractured spiritually and politically than he had found it. Ted's benediction was this: "We fell short of our most ambitious goals during the Clinton years," especially, he might have said, national health insurance, "but we accomplished a lot, including portable health insurance; the largest increase in health insurance for children since the creation of Medicaid; and an increase in the minimum wage." Of course, those were all Ted Kennedy's initiatives, but Clinton had finally supported all of them, without which they would not likely have passed. Bill Clinton had talked grandly of building a bridge to the twenty-first century. Instead, for all the good he did, he built a bridge to George W. Bush.

II

George W. Bush was not supposed to be his father's successor. His younger brother, Jeb Bush, a man much more in his father's image of the aristocratic blueblood Republican establishment with its moderate conservatism and its decorous manners, was supposed to take that baton. George was the wayward son, the Texas hell-raiser, a self-described "boozy kid," a wiseacre, jocular in a frat boy sort of way, ostensibly unserious. (Liberal Texas columnist Molly Ivins would later take to calling him "Shrub.") When a professor at Harvard Business School, where Bush matriculated, told the students to consider a profession in politics as well as business and said one of them could be president someday, Bush grinned and made a Nixon victory sign, arms thrust in the air, fingers in Vs, at the preposterousness of it, since, like Ted Kennedy, he knew he was regarded as the least of his family. But for all that, George had something that his younger brother Jeb didn't have, even something his father didn't. He had impressive social skills—the kind of preternatural social skills that Ted Kennedy had. He possessed a raw, puerile charm. He liked to tease and goad, to hang colorful nicknames on people, to ingratiate himself by his informality and sense of personal democracy, again, not unlike Ted Kennedy's. He was a man without airs unless they were the airs of a faux Texas cowboy. People enjoyed being around him. People felt comfortable around him. (One of the memes during the presidential campaign was which candidate you would rather have a beer with, and the conclusion was George W. Bush.) And George W. Bush had something else. *He knew it.* He knew the power of that puerile charm of his, knew how to work it. It was his political talent. He might not have been an expert reader of men, like Lyndon Johnson, or a man who could slaver them with kindness and understanding, as Ted did, but he could be *likable,* and when he mounted a charm offensive, he was difficult to resist. Even Ted would later say so: "I like Bush personally. He has an excellent sense of humor, and I can communicate with him." And he would call him a "professional friend." Before the election, Ted had scarcely known him, though he had known his grandfather, Senator Prescott Bush, from the time that Jack had arranged for the elder Bush to appear at Ted's Student Legal Forum at the University of Virginia, and Ted and the former senator had remained friendly. George W. and Ted had met the preceding July at the funeral of Republican senator Paul Coverdell, and George had approached Ted and said, presumably jokingly, "I've heard of you. I understand what you do, you do very well." Now that he was president, however, it behooved Bush to stage one of his charm offensives. Ted had won reelection easily. His opponent was an unknown, Jack E. Robinson III, a Black Republican trading off the name of the baseball immortal, and according to *The Washington Post,* on the day Robinson announced his candidacy, he also released a profile that listed sexual misconduct, drunken driving, plagiarism, and three failures of the bar exam. The *Boston Herald* reported that a blind date had called him "Jack the Tongue," which led to the headline "The Tongue Refuses to Admit When He's Licked." Robinson wasn't even a Massachusetts resident, and the Republicans promptly withdrew support. Ted won 73 percent of the vote.

With Ted returning to the Senate, George W. Bush knew he had to make an accommodation with him. Bush phoned Ted in late December as a courtesy, and the two spoke for fifteen minutes. Members of the transition team reached out to him as well, sounding him out about nominees for secretary of labor, and Bush's chief of staff, Andrew Card, a former

Massachusetts legislator who had once considered running against Ted, called him in the Caribbean, where Ted was vacationing. They missed connection, but Ted returned the call and left a message. Bush called him ten minutes later. It was a nascent charm offensive from a professional charmer. But Ted was not blind to Bush's manipulations—they were many of his own tactics—and he was not inclined to surrender. He was especially upset when Bush nominated recently defeated senator John Ashcroft for attorney general. Ashcroft was the personification of the Republican religious moralist—a man whose strict and antediluvian religious views led him to oppose civil rights, women's rights, and gay rights, and it was widely thought that Bush chose him for justice as a "message appointment" to reward the evangelicals who had supported his candidacy. Ted was angry not only because he thought Ashcroft was a rabid ideologue, but also because he feared that it was a step toward Bush appointing him to the first Supreme Court vacancy. The election, in which the Republicans had lost four seats, had divided the new Senate right down the middle: fifty-fifty. In effect, since Vice President Gore was the tiebreaker, that gave the Democrats power until inauguration day, when Dick Cheney would be installed as vice president and become the tiebreaking vote in his position as president of the Senate.

Ted Kennedy decided to use that interregnal power to try to defeat the confirmation of John Ashcroft, who, with his sense of overweening rectitude and his unbending certitude, might have been as close to an antithesis to Ted Kennedy as any public figure save Jesse Helms, to whom Ashcroft bore many similarities. As Ted's aide Melody Barnes recalled, "Senator Kennedy was really adamant." He felt, "We need to start moving confirmation hearings forward *now*." And she said that he conveyed that to his fellow Democrats on Judiciary. Meanwhile he had his staff gathering information on Ashcroft and drafting white papers. And they strategized, going down the list of senators and assessing what each had said about Ashcroft and who would be voting with them and who against. And Ted would say that they would go to visit a senator to make their case, and he would make an appointment and go to that senator's office and spend forty-five minutes to an hour discussing why Ashcroft was unfit to be attorney general, how he had led the fight against school desegregation in his native Missouri, how he had spoken at Bob Jones University, the Christian college where interracial dating had been forbidden (Ashcroft claimed he wasn't familiar with Bob Jones's policies), how Ashcroft had granted an interview to a white supremacist magazine that had even celebrated John Wilkes Booth for having assassinated Abraham Lincoln. (Ashcroft claimed he hadn't known the magazine's orientation.) And Ted would spend his evenings at home in his study with his staff, seven days a week, preparing for the confirmation hearings, poring over the material, and bringing in experts. And when it came to the hearings, Ted attacked. (Even *The Boston Globe* noted how different he was now, how much more aggressive, than he had been nine years earlier, after the Palm Beach episode, when he sat nearly silent during the Clarence Thomas hearings while his Republican colleagues flayed Thomas's accuser Anita Hill.) And when Senator Jon Kyl said Ted distorted Ashcroft's views, Ted, not bowed this time, declared, "I don't retreat. I don't retreat on any of those matters." And then Ted snatched off his glasses and pointed his finger and said that Ashcroft's answers were "wrong. Plain simple wrong."

By January's end, only Ashcroft of the Bush Cabinet nominees remained to be confirmed, and Ted had done everything he could to deny him. (Barnes claimed that he indeed changed some of his colleagues' votes.) The debate was prolonged, ranging over several days. The debate was bitter, with Republicans and Democrats squaring off in a largely partisan battle. And the debate was prophetic, foretelling how the Bush administration, for all Bush's professions, not unlike those of Nixon or Bill Clinton, to be a "uniter and not a divider," would be one of the most ideological and divisive in American history. Ashcroft, Democrats argued, had had a "confirmation conversion," by which they meant the rigid conservative moralist suddenly seemed to moderate his views, including declaring his acceptance of *Roe v. Wade*, the case that folded a right to an abortion under the right to privacy, as settled law—this of a man who Chris Dodd, Ted's closest Senate friend, said on the floor had "throughout his career plunged so decisively into the most divisive issues of our time: civil rights, women's rights, equal rights and gun safety," all of which Ashcroft had fiercely opposed. After a morning of long detailed addresses, Ted spoke second to last. He was unsparing. Ashcroft, as Missouri attorney general, had fought desegregation and fought it tenaciously, and he scolded Ashcroft defender Orrin Hatch for "expressing outrage about the fact that desegregation can be expensive without [his] being outraged by the injustice being done to the African-American children in St. Louis." If desegregation was expensive, Ted argued, then Ashcroft's foot-dragging and resistance had helped make it so. Ted moved on to Ashcroft's opposition to

Black judges, singling out his fight against Ronnie White, a justice on the Missouri Supreme Court whom Bill Clinton had nominated to the federal bench. It was Ashcroft who led the opposition, accusing White of being an "activist with a slant toward criminals" and someone who provided opportunities for the guilty to "escape punishment," as if White were a defense attorney rather than a judge, since White had overturned several death penalty sentences. Ted called Ashcroft's smears on White the "ugliest thing that has happened to a nominee in all my years in the Senate." White was not confirmed. And Ted went on to cite Ashcroft's opposition while a senator to the appointment of Dr. David Satcher to be surgeon general on the bogus charge that Satcher had, in following medical protocols in AIDS research, somehow acted unethically, though Satcher's real offense, Ted hinted, was that he was Black; and to Bill Lann Lee, whom Clinton had nominated to assistant attorney general for civil rights, this time on the grounds that Ashcroft distrusted Lee's promise to enforce a Supreme Court decision that forbade quotas on race (Lee was Asian); and to James Hormel, nominated by Clinton to the ambassadorship of Luxembourg, on the basis that Hormel was homosexual and Ashcroft had denounced homosexuality as a "sin." (Ashcroft wouldn't even grant him the courtesy of meeting him and answering Ashcroft's questions.) And he cited Ashcroft's reversal—this one not a confirmation conversion but an electoral contribution conversion—on a concealed-gun referendum in Missouri when the National Rifle Association contributed $400,000 to his unsuccessful Senate reelection campaign.

The Republicans in rebuttal said they didn't recognize the man the Democrats were assailing as racist and homophobic. They called Ashcroft a good man, a man of honesty and integrity, a man of courage, a man of high values, a deeply religious man. And that had followed the prevailing narrative of modern Republicanism: Democrats had forsaken moral values or, at least, the values Republicans perceived as moral. "I'd have to say that as I have listened to this organized campaign against John Ashcroft," Phil Gramm said, in a familiar Republican barb, "I sometimes wonder if there's not an effort to make the love of traditional values a hate crime in America." Ashcroft was eventually confirmed, 58 to 42, with eight Democrats, including Chris Dodd, joining the Republicans, but Ted and the opposition had served notice to the new president that, as *The New York Times* editorialized, "He should think twice about sending any more right-wing nominees." However, George W. Bush, who had not won the popular vote and who was leading a country that was highly polarized, George W. Bush, who 51 percent of Americans in a CBS poll said was not legitimately elected, would not heed that warning. His was to be a very conservative administration.

And yet even as Ted Kennedy was leading the assault against George Bush's nominee for attorney general, Bush was conducting a charm offensive for the man who was likely to be one of his greatest congressional foes. His first week in office, the new president invited Ted to the White House. "You know your way around here," Bush told him and, pointing at his desk in the Oval Office, asked Ted if he recognized it. It had been John Kennedy's. And the very day of Ashcroft's confirmation, as if to show he harbored no hard feelings, Bush invited Ted to the White House for an informal dinner of hamburgers and ribs and a screening of the film *Thirteen Days*, which dramatized the Cuban Missile Crisis. "I don't know about you," Bush told Ted that evening, "but I like to surprise people. Let's show them Washington can still get things done." Ted and Bush spent four hours together on that occasion, and Ted would write Bush one of his thank you notes, citing how "gracious" Bush and his wife, Laura, had been, and saying that he too had "every intention of getting things done, particularly in education and health care." And while Bush was plying his social skills on other Senate Democrats in an effort to woo them, even attending the Senate Democrats' retreat, Ted seemed, one reporter observed, to be Bush's main target. Five times Ted appeared at the White House in those first two weeks, sometimes bringing Sunny and Splash with him. Bush's press secretary Ari Fleischer joked that he had to remind people that Bush "also has friends who aren't Democrats."

But George W. Bush wasn't just extending an olive branch as a way of showing his bonhomie or even of uniting the country. He obviously had a motive. No less than Ted Kennedy, Bush wanted to move legislation, and in a divided Senate, he clearly thought it wise to ingratiate himself with Ted, who was susceptible to ingratiation. George H. W. Bush, realizing that the Republican drumbeat against legislation designed to help the poor and the working class was politically disadvantageous, had introduced the concept of "compassionate conservatism"—conservatism with a kinder, gentler face. That had largely been abandoned with the Gingrich revolution, where there was conservatism in abundance but very little compassion. George W. Bush, however, had revived the idea during his campaign, fastening on one particular issue where he thought it might have traction: education. Again, Republicans had shown very little interest in education, much less in educational equality. It had long been a goal of the party to disband the Department of Education, and Republicans had opposed nearly every educational reform, including Lyndon Johnson's Elementary and Secondary Education Act, targeted to poor and minority schools in the interest of closing the achievement gap. But George W. Bush, under prodding from his wife Laura, a former school librarian, had instituted educational reforms as governor of Texas, and he had promised in his campaign to do the same for the rest of the country. "The soft bigotry of low expectations," he had singled out as one of the problems with American education when it came to the poor and minorities. Bush wanted to fix it, both as a political matter—unlike his fellow Republicans, he fully understood that this was good politics—but also as a personal one. He believed in it. But there was also a philosophical component that was not so generous or big-hearted. Educational reform had been largely a liberal effort, and for liberals the engine was affirmative action, which was anathema to conservatives. As one scholar put it, with his new educational initiative, "Bush and his advisers thought they could hammer the final nails into the coffin of affirmative action by offering minorities a new route to socioeconomic achievement," in which they used standardized testing as their guide. And the scholar added this motive: "Minority voters, blacks and Hispanics, would then reward Bush's 'tough love' Republican Party with their votes, thus ensuring that Bush would become the architect of that which he and Karl Rove [Bush's chief political adviser] most ardently desired: a permanent and multicultural Republican majority." It had been Richard Nixon's dream, then Ronald Reagan's. Now it was George W. Bush's.

And that was why he unleashed his charm on Ted Kennedy—because he knew that he would not have the full support of his own party in these kinds of efforts and that he could use the influence of Kennedy to abet his plan. Ted was sympathetic. Bobby had had a major hand in fashioning the original Elementary and Secondary Education Act, which made education yet another Kennedy legacy. And Ted, working with Republican senator Lamar Alexander, had fought for standards in education in 1988, 1989, and 1990; later, in the Clinton administration, the two introduced the Goals 2000 program, which proposed standards-based reforms. "Higher standards, testing, rewarding incentives for schools that do well and punishing schools that don't do well, publicizing the results, smaller class size—all of this is Kennedy's agenda for fifteen or twenty years," his former aide Nick Littlefield said. But for all Ted's involvement in educational reform and for all Bush's early courtship of him, Ted was not invited to an education summit in Austin, Texas, on December 21, during the interregnum. As Bush's domestic policy adviser and later secretary of education, Margaret Spellings, put it, "Ted Kennedy was public enemy number one for Republicans, and somebody, Judd Gregg [the second-ranking member on the Labor Committee] or the staff or somebody had decided that we weren't going to invite Ted Kennedy to the meeting."

George W. Bush, however, whose political instincts were keen, was no Kennedy hater. He appreciated Ted's usefulness. On Inauguration Day, Alan Simpson, a friend of both Ted's and Bush's, took Ted to meet him and told Bush, "He is an ornery S.O.B., but you can do business with him." Bush knew he could. That was why Ted Kennedy was invited to the White House on January 23, when Bush made his comments about Ted knowing his way around the Oval Office and recognizing his brother's desk; Ted had come as part of a small group with whom Bush could discuss education, and Bush made a point of taking him aside and asking him to emphasize their agreements rather than their disagreements, while Ted told him, "I want to help you do this," meaning education reform. And that was why Bush invited Ted to that White House screening of *Thirteen Days*. And that was why Ted Kennedy was in the White House five times that first week; Bush hosted five days of educational events with Ted, and John Boehner, the chair of the House Education Committee; and Jim Jeffords, the chair of the Labor Committee, now renamed the Health, Education, Labor and Pensions Committee, or HELP, which oversaw educational issues; and George Miller, the ranking member of the House Education Committee. The "Big Four," Margaret Spellings called them. And they would be the point men for Bush's program—none more so than Ted Kennedy.

Bush called his plan No Child Left Behind. The basic premise was that public schools were lacking accountability. NCLB would provide an annual assessment of every student based on state standards and determined by testing. That data would be broken down into demographic clusters, and analyzed and published, and schools would be expected to show what was called "annual yearly progress" in order to receive federal funds. Those schools that failed to achieve sufficient AYP would then be subject to certain corrective actions, all the way up to closing the school. But the most important provision was that having identified which schools were underperforming, the act provided federal funding to help those schools, particularly schools in poor areas, close the gap between them and more affluent schools. Lyndon Johnson had intended his 1965 landmark Elementary and Secondary Education Act to use the federal government to compensate for inequities in school funding. Now finally it would. Bush introduced the act in a Rose Garden ceremony on January 23, after his meeting with the Big Four, and though Ted pointed to "some areas of difference," he also cited "overwhelming areas of agreement" and expressed his support. The week after the rollout, the Big Four piled into a van with the president and went from school to school in Washington. "A mating dance" was how Spellings described it, to develop trust, since it had been some time since Democrats and Republicans had trusted each other. At one stop, at a largely Black school in Washington, Bush questioned the principal about accountability, and Ted, impressed, told George Miller, "I don't think we need any more hearings. We can work together on this." And the mating dance was over almost before it began.

But not all Democrats were convinced of Bush's sincerity. Minority Leader Daschle said that even before Bush took office, there was a rumor that Ted was willing to cut a deal with Bush on education, and Daschle warned Ted to be careful in bargaining with Bush. Paul Wellstone of Minnesota, a fervent liberal, was especially suspicious. He said that Bush would not commit sufficient resources to the policy. In effect, it was just testing and punishment, and he challenged Ted's support of it at a caucus meeting. Ted was affronted. He argued that they would eventually get the resources, but they had to establish accountability first—Ted's familiar the "perfect is the enemy of the good"—and he assured Wellstone, "We can't ask for it now, but, believe me, we'll get that funding." Knowing Republican retrenchment, Wellstone was skeptical as well as suspicious. "We'll never get it," he countered. "We'll never get it." "The two of them got into a terrible screaming match," Daschle said. "They just both lost control of their emotions and it was an extremely volatile meeting." Daschle ultimately sided with Ted—"to the chagrin and outrage of Paul." At the full caucus, Ted's position, with Daschle's support, carried. And now the Democrats had signed on to NCLB.

By that point, Ted had fallen for Bush's pitch. Bush had introduced Ted to his education adviser, Dallas Democrat Sandy Kress, who had sat on that city's school board—Kress said that when Bush introduced him to Ted that January and told Ted that Kress had been chairman of the Dallas County Democratic Party, Bush stretched out "De-mo-*crat-ic*" so that it took him ten seconds to say it—and he was clearly hoping that Kress would entice Ted to cooperate. Ted and Kress met a dozen times with each other and another dozen with staff, and by one account, they spoke daily on the phone. A "sweet talker," Ted called Kress. *Washington Post* reporter Dana Milbank called Kress "Bush's Democratic Weapon." But it didn't take much now to woo Ted Kennedy. He hated inaction. And Ted's staff knew it. If Bush's sincerity was in doubt, as many Democrats said, education seemed like a good place to test it; there weren't likely to be too many other places. "We need to work with this president," Michael Myers, one of Ted's staffers, told him, and advised that Ted take Bush "at his word and try to work on it." Carey Parker, Ted's alter ego, agreed with Myers that "we could work well on this issue with President Bush," though Ted and his advisers knew that Bush needed Ted Kennedy more than Ted Kennedy needed George Bush.

They negotiated. Parker said that the negotiations took a "good deal of time that first year, ironing out the details" with the administration. Most of those negotiations were conducted in Ted's Capitol hideaway office, looking out on the Mall, around the rough-hewn green table that his children had had fashioned from an old boat rudder and given him as a gift. It was, as Ted's negotiations typically were, a tedious process—twice a week over four or five months, Judd Gregg would say of those hideaway meetings, where they "pounded out the language almost sentence by sentence, core idea by core idea." "Always bipartisan," Gregg would say, with "no personal rancor." And then they handed it over to the staff to draft the agreements.

But it wasn't only hashing out a bill with Republicans that occupied Ted Kennedy. He also spent time, Carey Parker said, "trying to reassure skeptical Democratic colleagues" who doubted "anything the Bush administration was attempting to do"—skeptical because, while Bush, like Nixon before him, talked about accommodation and bringing the nation together, his actions like Nixon's usually belied the talk. George Miller, with whom Ted worked closely, said that despite the Democrats' trepidations, "I think his"—Ted's—"conscience was clear. His sense of, *Was this liberal or conservative or what have you?*, really was nothing, that this data would speak for itself. It would tell us what these schools have been doing or not doing, and how they've been treating their kids." The biggest disagreement between the Democrats and the administration was over vouchers for private schools. Republicans had encouraged the idea of privatizing education, which they justified as choice, but they also knew that taking money from public schools to support private ones was a way of disempowering the teachers' unions, which were closely allied with the Democrats. Ted got Bush to abandon those vouchers. "We can't have vouchers," he said he told Bush point-blank, and Bush said, "OK. I'll take the vouchers out, but I'm going to offer them on the DC approach," by which he meant a pilot program in Washington. To which Ted said, "That's fine. We'll fight it there, and we'll go on to the other issues." While Bush surrendered on vouchers, Ted surrendered on school construction, smaller class size, and the prohibition of any funds for private education—he agreed to funds for private tutoring and after-school programs—and in return gained larger block grants to states, lower regulations, and more rigorous testing. Ted and Sandy Kress had also made another agreement, this one in Ted's office: that failing schools be required to provide transportation to students to go to better schools. And Kress wrested one last concession himself: a seven-state, twenty-five-district pilot program allowing those states and districts to do whatever they chose to raise the AYP.

Many Democrats—Wellstone among them—made a charge that had often been made of Ted: that he had been so eager to make a deal, he had given up too much. Carey Parker would later admit that Ted "loves to go to the White House for a meeting with senior education officials and the education leaders from the House and Senate in both parties." And that he also "loves the charm that President Bush can turn on in a meeting," and that he "likes to reciprocate" with his own charm. But when it came to criticism that he was gulled by Bush, he was unmoved. To a group of education lobbyists who were trying to derail the bill on the basis that Ted had made too many compromises, Ted exploded. "Kennedy just read us the riot act," a lobbyist said of that meeting. "You may not have noticed," Ted told them, "but we don't control the White House, the Senate or the House. I'm doing my best, but I'm not going to let you stop this." He told a reporter that Bush "gets the reform, and we get the additional resources." And he asserted once again, as he had done in the caucus, that while Bush had only asked for a $4 billion increase in education spending, the Finance Committee would provide much more. He would see to that. So

Ted and New Hampshire Republican Judd Gregg introduced NCLB in the Senate. And now Ted and George W. Bush were partners.

Tax cuts were something else. In his campaign, Bush had promised substantial tax cuts, which, since Reagan and the forswearing of Keynesian economics, had become the Republicans' all-purpose economic panacea, whether the economy was in distress or whether it was booming, as it was at the time of Bush's inauguration. Democrats had long viewed these tax cuts suspiciously, not as a way to rev the economy, in this case an economy that hardly needed revving, but as a way to enrich the already-wealthy at the expense of the poor and needy whose programs those taxes funded. (Depending on the calculation, the richest one percent of Americans would get 22 to 45 percent of the benefits from Bush's tax cut.) But to oppose tax cuts was a treacherous position politically, and some Democrats, realizing that they would have a large target on their backs if they voted against them, felt the need to surrender. No one wanted to pay more taxes, even if tax cuts had demonstrably not achieved what Republicans claimed they would achieve. Reagan and George H. W. Bush had both had to backtrack on their tax cut pledges when those cuts led to massive deficits. George W. Bush, however, had an advantage his father didn't have. He had those budget surpluses, courtesy of Bill Clinton, and while Democrats wanted to see those surpluses given to social programs and infrastructure repair or, in the case of Democratic moderates and Bill Clinton himself, to deficit reduction, George W. Bush wanted to see them go to tax cuts instead. The surplus is the people's money, Bush was fond of saying, not the government's, though Democrats rebutted that government efforts benefited the people. As Jim Jeffords would say, "Every dollar in tax cuts is a dollar unavailable for education." And those cuts were steep— a proposed $1.6 *trillion* in cuts over ten years, though crafted so that the biggest hits would come later, thus camouflaging the effect on the deficit. Bush's plan would reduce the top marginal tax rate, which Reagan had already reduced, from 39 to 33 percent, and would eliminate the inheritance tax, which Democrats had seen as democratic in purpose, but which Republicans had cleverly named the "death tax." Though the economy was already beginning to lose its head of steam in the first months of the new administration, and though Secretary of the Treasury Paul O'Neill, fearing the consequences of a tax cut under circumstances in which tax revenue declined and the deficit ballooned, remonstrated with Bush and

Cheney that there should be a mechanism in the bill for the tax cuts to be reduced should the surplus shrink, Bush was having none of it. Even in the eyes of members of Bush's own administration, politics had always been more important than economic prudence, and on March 8 Bush submitted his tax cut bill to a Congress that could hardly afford to reject it.

Democrats tried their best to trim it—in April, the Senate voted to slash $448 billion from it—and to slow its progress. They countered with a plan of their own with $900 billion of tax relief pitched to the middle class. They attached amendments to the bill that prolonged the debate on it, and Ted managed to extend it further with dilatory parliamentary maneuvers, all of which had some effect. The House approved Bush's full $1.6 trillion; the Senate only $1.35 trillion. Bush realized that time was not on his side and that the tax cuts needed to be passed as quickly as possible before public sentiment changed. On May 22, the day before the final vote, the debate raged through the night, and cots were set up off the chamber for senators who wanted to nap, as some did, newspapers spread over their faces. A "football game," Senator Bob Graham called the battle. Ted had two grievances against it: the traditional Democratic one that the fruits went to the wealthiest Americans and another, more personal, that Bush, in his haste to get the bill passed, had all but ignored No Child Left Behind. "The Republican position could not be clearer," he declaimed on the Senate floor. "Education can wait while we rush to give away hundreds of billions of dollars in tax breaks for the wealthy. In Republican priorities, the needs of the wealthiest taxpayers for new tax breaks rank far higher than the needs of America's school children." And Ted said he would offer an amendment to postpone the lowering of the top marginal tax rate until education was fully funded as the Senate had already voted to do in the extension of the Elementary and Secondary Education Act.

But there was no heading it off. The tax cuts passed the Senate 62 to 38, with twelve Democrats voting with the Republicans, and two Republicans, Lincoln Chafee and John McCain, both deficit hawks who worried about the effect of the cuts, voting against it. And so, in one fell swoop, the surplus for which Bill Clinton had proselytized and for which he had worked throughout his two terms, the surplus that was supposed to help retire the deficit, the surplus that even Republicans had professed to want, was gone, and with it any hope as well for the social programs that Ted had so dearly wanted. Instead, the wealthy got a payoff.

As he celebrated his congressional victory, there was, however, a price for George W. Bush to pay for his cuts—one he hadn't foreseen. Republican Jim Jeffords was a strong proponent of special education, and Jeffords had asked Bush for a $200 billion appropriation for the Individuals with Disabilities Education Act, which had been passed in 1975 and had yet to be fully funded. If the government was able to afford a huge tax cut, Jeffords argued, it could afford to fund IDEA. The administration thought he had lost his mind in making such a request at the very time it was pushing its tax cuts, and in any case, now that Bush had launched his charm offensive on Ted, he didn't feel he needed Jeffords, even though Jeffords was the chair of HELP. (In time, Judd Gregg replaced Jeffords as one of the Big Four.) Senator Chuck Hagel, a Republican, warned Bush's chief of staff, Andrew Card, that there might be a "Jeffords problem" brewing and that Jeffords should be issued an invitation to the White House to nip it, but Card and Bush, in their arrogance, refused to issue one. Jeffords had never been a member in good standing of the conservative coven into which the Republican Party had been transformed. He had endorsed John Anderson in the 1980 presidential race, had, as a member of the House, voted against Ronald Reagan's tax cuts, the only House Republican to do so, and had voted against the articles of impeachment in Bill Clinton's Senate trial. He was called, sneeringly by his party faithful, "Bill Clinton's favorite Republican." A "loose cannon," Trent Lott said of him, and claimed that he kept blackmailing his party for his vote in exchange for more money for his programs. Bob Dole had liked Jeffords—Jeffords had supported his presidential bid in 1988 against George H. W. Bush—and Dole indulged him when other Republicans wouldn't. But the new Senate, split fifty-fifty between Democrats and Republicans, was not like the old Senate where the Republican majority allowed senators more independence. One Republican told *The New York Times* that the Bush administration's attitude was, "If you're a Republican in a 50–50 Senate, there must be absolute party loyalty." Jeffords wasn't that kind of loyalist. As the tax cut vote neared, rumors wafted through Washington that Jeffords was aggrieved and was thinking of leaving the Republican fold. Bush and Cheney finally acted and invited him to the White House to discuss his complaints the day before the tax vote. But it was too late. On May 24, the day after the vote, Jeffords declared himself an independent. He would later write, "I felt that if I did not make the switch, important lasting policies and appointments would be made that would drastically change the history of our nation." Declaring his independence in and of itself wouldn't have changed the balance of power in the Senate. But Jeffords, in a final nose-thumbing at the famously charming president, decided that he would caucus with the Democrats. And so, on June 6, the Democrats once again took control of the Senate, with Tom Daschle assuming the role of majority leader, and Ted Kennedy replacing Jeffords himself as the chairman of HELP. (Jeffords took the chair of the Environment and Public Works Committee.)

Now George W. Bush had lost his Senate majority, in effect because the education president, as Bush liked to think of himself, had refused a request to fully fund special education.

Ted Kennedy, at last back in the majority after having to fight from the outside, was reenergized yet again, though he was nearing seventy, had regained whatever weight he had lost under Vicki's discipline, and walked now with that lumbering bearish gait, a long distance from the swift pace of the trim, athletic young Ted Kennedy. His legislative energy, however, was undiminished. A week after Jeffords's defection, Ted guided NCLB through the Senate, after it had been nudged aside by Bush's tax cuts. Meanwhile the new majority whip, Harry Reid of Nevada, also energized by the Democrats' good fortune, began pushing for another minimum wage increase, a Medicare drug benefit, campaign finance reform, and new energy policies. Ted focused his immediate attention on one of his longtime initiatives: the Patients' Bill of Rights, which would help level the playing field between the insured and their insurers and restore medical decisions to doctors rather than bureaucrats. Ted had fought for the bill in the previous Congress, only to see Republicans gut it and pass a weak bill of their own while narrowly rejecting his, 51 to 48. In the new Senate, Ted had worked with John McCain on a bill, but Bush, already feeling empowered enough to welch on his promises of bipartisanship, threatened to veto it—it contained an option for patients to sue insurers, something that was anathema to Republicans—and rather than negotiate with Ted and McCain, the administration recommended that the two of them work with Tennessee senator Bill Frist, himself a doctor, who was drafting a bill of his own with a much more restrictive lawsuit provision. "Bipartisan talk is fine," Ted told *The Boston Globe,* referring to Bush. "But just bipartisan talk without action is not going to help the children that need to see specialists and the women that need the kind of clinical trials because of breast cancer, the kinds of needs which are out there for American families. What we need is action."

But action was difficult. It was difficult because there were those in the Democratic caucus who still distrusted Ted and worried that he might compromise with Bush on the Patients' Bill of Rights as he had on NCLB. So Ted pulled Senator John Edwards of North Carolina, a former plaintiffs' trial lawyer who had won large settlements in personal injury cases, into the negotiations to protect Ted from those charges. And it was difficult because powerful opponents outside the Senate wanted no part of leveling that playing field. "I think we underestimated the cloud of special interests," John McCain was to say. "Colleagues who had come up from both sides of the aisle who had said, 'I'm with you. You can count on me,' a few days later said, 'Well, I've got some real questions about this provision,' or 'I have some concerns.' " "A lot of press conferences, a lot of outreach, a lot of secret meetings [with McCain and Edwards] that didn't end up on his schedule," Ted's press secretary James Manley would say of Ted's work on the Patients' Bill of Rights that spring. In those secret meetings, in the President's Room in the Capitol every morning at eight o'clock, Manley said, the three plotted strategy for the floor debate to come that June.

Bush had cagily not pushed a bill of his own, but instead endorsed the bill drafted by Frist, Jim Jeffords, and Louisiana Democrat John Breaux and introduced in May that contained the limitations on lawsuits and that required anyone who did sue to exhaust all appeals and even then to sue only in federal court with a strict ceiling on damages. Ted, McCain, and Edwards's bill had no such requirement, no such restriction to federal courts, and no such ceiling on damages, though they did make a concession to allow states that had passed their own patients' bill of rights to gain exemption from the federal bill. As the two bills butted against each other, there was a difference from Ted's earlier efforts to pass a Patients' Bill of Rights, and it was a major one: The Democrats controlled the Senate, which meant that they controlled the agenda, which meant that they were not on the defensive, as they had been when Republicans kept hurling questions at them. Now the Republicans were the ones on the defensive. Majority Leader Daschle, using his prerogatives, said that he would keep the bill on the floor until it got a vote, hoping to achieve that before the Fourth of July recess.

Two weeks of debate there would be—two weeks during which George W. Bush threatened to veto the Kennedy-McCain-Edwards bill on the basis that it would fuel lawsuits and that the lawsuits would raise premiums, though Republicans had never seemed to be concerned with rising premiums in the past. Two weeks during which Republicans accused the legislation of doing nothing to help the uninsured, though Republicans had never seemed to be concerned with the uninsured in all the many years that Ted Kennedy had offered legislation that would insure every American or in 1993 and 1994 when Bill Clinton had offered such legislation. Two weeks during which some Republicans argued that the legislation would usurp states' rights and during which others, including the president, argued that federal rules for lawsuits should usurp state rules and that, in any case, HMOs should be allowed to require patients to go to arbitration rather than to court. Two weeks during which Bush would seem to offer a compromise and then pull it back when it had been accepted. For the truth was that the Bush administration didn't really seem to want *any* Patients' Bill of Rights, and the Democrats and their few Republican moderate allies didn't want to pass a bill that protected insurers rather than the insured. But this time, the Republicans could not delay, as they had when Ted had pushed for the minimum wage or Kennedy-Kassebaum because this time Republicans did not control the Senate. After those two weeks, on June 29, Daschle called the vote, and the Kennedy-McCain-Edwards bill passed, 59 to 36, with nine Republicans joining the Democrats.

Still, as Ted Kennedy knew all too well from his time in the minority during the Clinton years, there were impediments to seeing his bill into law. One impediment was the Republican-controlled House, which had passed its own bill, so that the two would have to be reconciled. The other was George W. Bush, who continued to insist that the Senate bill would generate a surfeit of lawsuits and who continued to threaten to veto it, even though Bush must have realized that doing so was not good politics. As far as the House went, Georgia Republican Charles Norwood, a dentist, had declared when Frist, Jeffords, and Breaux introduced their Bush-backed bill, "If it is brought up in the House, I will personally exhaust every effort to defeat it," adding, "This bill protects health maintenance organizations, not patients." Instead, Norwood had proposed a bipartisan bill similar to Ted's. But for all Norwood's bold talk, once the bills were passed, Bush began to apply pressure, and Norwood surrendered by agreeing to Bush's demand that damages be capped and that employers be buffered from liability unless they directly participated in a health decision. Norwood's allies, by one account, were "stunned." He had not bothered to consult with them when he cut his deal with the White House. "The bottom line and the goal is, we want to change the law," Norwood said in his defense. "And the last time I looked, that's pretty difficult to do without the presidential signature." Ted said that Norwood's deal made the rights in the bill "unenforceable." But Ted himself was in an uncomfortable position. He would either have to see the Patient's Bill of Rights yet again thwarted or try to reach some accommodation with the administration himself. To that end, Nick Calio, Bush's legislative affairs director, hosted a series of meetings—"innumerable meetings," Calio said—with a "large group of senators," but he said that they were "leading nowhere fast." So he approached Ted with the idea that a smaller group could perhaps reach a compromise, and he said they did, only to find that when the issues were given over to the staffs for finalization, "gridlock set in." When Calio ran into Ted one day at the Capitol and Ted told him that he felt "things were really moving along well," Calio said that he disagreed, that in fact things were not moving along, and Ted said he would look into it. When he called Calio later that afternoon, he had a proposal: that Calio and the deputy White House chief of staff for policy, Joshua Bolten, join Ted and McCain at Ted's house for a Sunday breakfast. And Calio said that was exactly what they did for the next five or six Sundays—sit down on the couches, talk, eat breakfast, retreat again to the couches and talk some more, basically about how to overcome Bush's opposition to the lawsuit provisions in the bill and the unlimited damages. Three weeks into the discussions, Ted told Calio that he wanted to bring Edwards in too, though Calio was hesitant, given Edwards's background as a trial lawyer. But Ted needed Edwards for his caucus. So the breakfasts continued, which was Ted Kennedy's way when he wanted to get something done: patient, courteous, "professional," Calio said. But in the end, the distance between the sides was too great. And in the end, the House and Senate couldn't reconcile. "If they had been willing to hold the HMOs and the insurance industry accountable, we could have gotten legislation," Ted said, after having accepted defeat. But they weren't, so he didn't.

Bush had promised bipartisanship—a "uniter not a divider"—and he had romanced Ted Kennedy in part to provide at least the illusion of that bipartisanship, realizing that Ted would likely "bend over backwards," as Orrin Hatch had once said of him, if he felt he could score a legislative victory. But as the tax cuts and the Patients' Bill of Rights illustrated, while Bush was charming and congenial, he was still a hardcore conservative who was not willing to make major compromises, and his ambitions were seemingly no different from those of Reagan and Gingrich. "A radicalized form of Reaganism," historian Sean Wilentz would call Bush's first eight months in office. "He spurned bipartisanship," Wilentz said. "He also undertook initiatives aimed at undoing that fundamental structure of American government and diplomacy built up over the previous half century and more." And Wilentz would conclude that Bush was no conservative at all, despite his pretense at being a compassionate one like his father, but rather a "radical." And Wilentz would say that Bush "represented the culmination of political trends that had marked the entire age of Reagan, even before Reagan himself was finally elected president, going back to Richard Nixon"—trends that disputed the power of Congress and that looked toward an augmentation of executive power. Newt Gingrich had wanted to conduct a revolution through policy and through culture. George W. Bush, more genial than Gingrich but equally driven, understood that he could revolutionize the government by changing the dynamics of power.

All that in his first eight months.

III

The morning of September 11, Ted Kennedy was in his office in the Russell building with Judd Gregg, awaiting the arrival of First Lady Laura Bush. Mrs. Bush, the former school librarian, was to testify on early education, in the Senate Caucus Room across the hallway from Ted's office, before Ted's HELP Committee. As Ted and Gregg waited, a staffer told Ted that Vicki had phoned him with a piece of breaking news: An airplane had crashed into the World Trade Center at the southern tip of Manhattan. Ted assumed it was a small plane that had veered off course—an unfortunate accident. Minutes later Vicki phoned again with another report and with the suggestion that it might be terrorism. Now the mood changed. Ted and Gregg saw Laura Bush coming down the corridor and intercepted her and brought her into the office with them. Ted's chief of staff, Mary Beth Cahill, said she passed him a note after the second plane had slammed into the Towers of the World Trade Center. Ted phoned Vicki, who urged him to leave, but Ted said he needed to stay with Mrs. Bush, and that, in any case, he was safe since the Secret Service was there to protect the first lady. "Well, they can't stop a plane," Vicki told him, and informed him that the Pentagon had been hit as well and that from their home, she could see the smoke rising across the Potomac River. Ted and Gregg escorted Mrs. Bush across the hallway to the Caucus Room, which was jammed with people awaiting the hearing. Ted announced that the hearing had been canceled, and Mrs. Bush made a brief statement. And then the three of them—Ted, Gregg, and Mrs. Bush—returned to Ted's office. It is unclear how long they spent there until the Secret Service hustled Mrs. Bush back down the corridor to the east elevators before deciding, "We'd better hold," and heading into Judd Gregg's office, where the three of them awaited instructions and where Mrs. Bush attempted to reach the president, who was in Florida, making an appearance at a grammar school in an attempt to boost No Child Left Behind, and then to contact her two daughters. But the phone lines were busy. It took her another twenty minutes to a half-hour to get through, during which time, depending on the account, they either watched the news or deliberately stayed away from television. Meanwhile, back in Ted's office, Carey Parker said he watched the smoke rising from the Pentagon while officers rounded up senators to take them to safety. Ted's national security adviser, Sharon Waxman, saw the smoke too from the balcony that ran outside Ted's office—"not a little smoke; it was a plume of smoke"—and decided to evacuate to the grassy square outside the building. When she called into the office later that morning, Carey Parker, eternally calm, was still sitting at his desk, though Parker did say that he eventually joined the evacuees in the park until police told them all, at about four o'clock, to go home because they wouldn't be allowed back into the building that day. While Waxman was leaving, Ted waited for Mrs. Bush to be led away and then headed to his car to go home. The streets were jammed with traffic, bumper to bumper, and Ted phoned Vicki from the car to tell her he was going to take the Metro. But Vicki, terrified that the Metro might be bombed, told him to stay in his car. As he inched his way home, Vicki's daughter Caroline managed to get through to her mother and, hysterical, insisted that her mother pick her up from school immediately. So Vicki now got into her car and inched her way to the school and picked up Caroline and a friend and brought them home and then waited for Ted. "A pretty traumatic day," Vicki would call it. She could have been speaking for the entire country.

It was a day of doom—a day in which the images of the Towers crumpling and of the white ash drifting down on Wall Street like snow and of the survivors walking zombie-like down the streets, searching for safety, burned their way into the American consciousness. (Later there would be a defining image: of a man falling from the towers, having jumped with no other way out.) The nation was rattled. The nation was confused. Terrorists, dispatched by Saudi radical Osama bin Laden, had hijacked two commercial airliners and flown them into the World Trade Center, and flown another into the Pentagon, while on a fourth plane, the passengers attempted to overtake the gunmen, and the plane crashed into the Pennsylvania countryside, outside Shanksville, sparing Washington another target and an even larger loss of life, though everyone on the plane perished. Two thousand, nine hundred and seventy-seven people died on the planes and in the buildings that day. The nation was stricken. Many compared the attacks to that by the Japanese on Pearl Harbor on December 7, 1941, and now there were two days that would live in infamy. Ted urged Tom Daschle to bring the Senate back into session that night as a show of strength. But Daschle declined. The nation needed healing.

In the days following the tragedy, while Americans tried to make sense of it all, Ted took it upon himself to phone the families of each of the 187 victims from Massachusetts—long calls, personal calls, calls in which, as he so often did, he shared his own losses, anything but perfunctory calls. To one of those mourners, whose husband had been lost on American Flight 11, the plane that had crashed in Pennsylvania, he told her how heroic her husband had been, and she told Ted that he had survived so many tragedies and that "I hope I can survive this as you have done." "It was as if Kennedy was personally holding my hand," she would later tell her son. And to another of the grieving, he sent a letter that his own father, clearly drawing on his own grief, had sent to a friend who had lost a son: "Whenever one of your loved ones goes out of your life, you think what he might have done for a few more years, and you wonder what you are going to do with the rest of yours. Then one day, because there is a world to be lived in, you find yourself part of it, trying to accomplish something—something he did not have the time to do. And, perhaps, that is the reason for it all. I hope so."*

---

*There was another note. Ted had vigorously opposed Bush's nomination of Ted Olson, a founding member of the conservative Federalist Society, to solicitor general. Olson's wife, Barbara, also an attorney, died in the plane that crashed into the Pentagon on 9/11. Ted Olson received what was called a "deluge" of condolences, and according to former Bush speechwriter David Frum, whose wife had volunteered to field the notes and letters, Ted sent

And as the grief continued, Ted's efforts continued. He met with those Massachusetts widows and widowers and mothers and fathers and siblings and children as a group at the Park Plaza Hotel in Boston, both to console them but also to help them. He got the Massachusetts Bar Association to provide free legal advice to them. He got representatives from the Social Security Administration and the Red Cross and even the FBI to provide assistance to them. And when one of the family members complained that she was so overcome with grief she could barely get out of bed in the morning and yet she had twenty phone numbers to call twenty different people at various agencies for various forms of help, and she asked him, "Is it too much for someone to be a helper for each of us?" Ted took action. He was going to arrange to have a group of student volunteers help, but over dinner with Nick Littlefield, his former aide, Littlefield suggested that Ted find social workers to do this job. And Ted did, assigning a social worker to each family. But the assistance didn't end then. Every four months he would invite the grieving to a get-together at Pier 4, where they could eat hors d'oeuvres and drink wine and beer and discuss their situations. "They've just run out of steam," Ted would say of them. "They have such terrible troubles." And Ted convinced Daschle to assign Ted's old chief of staff, Kenneth Feinberg, as the special master of the 9/11 Victim Compensation Fund to determine aid to those who needed it. And still Ted did not forget them. He never forgot them. Years later he would still be helping and comforting them.

9/11 changed everything. The week before the attacks, George W. Bush had the lowest approval rating of his young presidency, 51 percent, lower than any modern president at that point in his presidency save for Gerald Ford, whose pardon of Richard Nixon had punctured his popularity. The following week, as the nation in its distress rallied around the president, his rating soared to 86 percent. It was as if the country were at war, which, in a manner of speaking, it now was, only not against state actors but against bands of terrorists. Ted Kennedy did his best to maintain normalcy. Because of an anthrax scare at the Hart Senate Building targeting senators—an envelope addressed to Daschle contained anthrax spores—

---

a handwritten note "so elegant and decent, so eloquent and fascinatingly written in so beautiful a hand as to revolutionize one's opinion of the man who wrote it." Quoted in Tobin Harshaw, "Kennedy, Bork and the Politics of Judicial Destruction," *NYT*, Aug. 28, 2009.

and forcing them to vacate the premises while the building was decontaminated, Ted, though his own office was in Russell, began working in his Capitol hideaway while, by one account, six aides in the cramped quarters juggled laptops and cellphones. The most immediate business for Ted was No Child Left Behind, which, having already been usurped earlier in the summer by Bush's tax cuts, was now at risk of being usurped by 9/11. Ted, much to the chagrin of many of his fellow Democrats, had negotiated hard and worked hard for its passage that spring, both in the Senate and outside the Senate, where he hoped to put pressure on the chamber. Press secretary James Manley said that as with the Patients' Bill of Rights, there were "dozens of press conferences, aggressive press outreach, background briefings by staff for reporters, briefings by Senator Kennedy and Congressman [George] Miller [Ted's Democratic House ally] for reporters at key times." And at the end of a markup, Manley said, he would usher a group of reporters into the room or outside the hearing room and have Ted expatiate on the bill for five or ten minutes. For the floor debate in June, Ted was no less diligent. His aide Michael Myers said that the staffers would go to Ted's house in the morning and run through the bill for two hours, then return in the afternoon for another two hours and invite experts to explain sections of the bill. It ran eight hundred to nine hundred pages, a massive bill, but Myers said that Ted read every single word, making extensive notations. He even found a discrepancy between one page that set the effective date as October 1, and another page that set it as January 1. Manley called Ted's briefing books on the legislation "legendary"—"dog-eared," and "heavily underlined," and, again, annotated, and "carefully tabbed," so he could find whatever he needed to access during the debate. With all that effort, he had won passage in the Senate in June, but then came the August recess and then came 9/11, and NCLB, allegedly George W. Bush's top priority and his hallmark legislation, stalled while Congress debated what to do about terrorism.

That fall Ted Kennedy and George Miller seemed to be the only ones who really cared about education reform. Bush was preoccupied with 9/11, and liberals were still dubious about Bush's commitment to education, especially his commitment to fund the bill. Miller said that when he and Ted had met with Bush in the Oval Office to discuss the bill in the spring, Ted emphasized that the reforms would be expensive and that the president had to "put up the money." Ted was "just emphatic." And Miller said that Bush responded on more than one occasion, "You four"—

meaning Ted, Miller, Gregg, and Boehner—"get me the reforms, and I'll get you the resources." But that was before 9/11, before the drift had set in. George Miller recalled getting a call from Bush to come to the Oval Office, and he and Ted did. And Bush asked them, "Is there any chance we can get this done? It would be important to the nation to see the Congress work, to see agreement." It might have been another ploy, another tactic for Bush to get his way, but Miller said, "Obviously it resonated." Still, the issue of funding scared the liberals. When Miller complained to Ted that he was having trouble with his caucus, Ted told him, "You've just got to get Congressman [John] Boehner"—the Republican chair of the Education Committee—"to give you the money." And when Miller said he was still having trouble convincing the Democrats, Ted himself told Boehner, "It's just money. Put up the money. We're going to get these changes"—the testing and the standards and the carrots and sticks to enforce them—"we're going to get you your accountability. We're going to get you your test scores. We're going to get you your reporting. Put up the money." Whether or not Bush was really going to get them that money, he was determined to keep Ted's cooperation, and as a way of ensuring that, in November, by executive order, he renamed the Justice Department building the Robert F. Kennedy Building. As *Time* put it of Bush's efforts to break down Ted's resistance, "Bush hasn't won Ted over yet, but throw in the Washington Monument, and they might just get a deal."

Meanwhile the bill was stalled in a House-Senate conference, which dragged on for five months, much of the speed dictated by Ted, who kept insisting on adequate funding that the Republicans were loath to provide. The administration had proposed a $685 million increase in the education budget. The Senate Appropriations Committee had proposed a $4 billion increase, and Ted himself had asked for $8 billion. But the House Republicans were proposing nothing at all. And the legislation might have died, as so many other bills expired in the Republican House, had not George W. Bush, who had not passed a single piece of major legislation in that first year outside his tax cuts and who wanted NCLB as a political marker, pressured the congressional Republicans to make a deal. Even then, there was uncertainty. By one report, Ted got a call from a staffer at his home at six-thirty a.m. on November 30 informing him that the progress they had been making in their negotiations was about to be undone by a disagreement that had erupted among the aides to Ted, Miller, Gregg, and Boehner. The point at issue was whether religious and community groups hiring staff for after-school programs were subject to civil rights laws. Ted headed to the Capitol—the Senate offices were still closed due to the anthrax scare—and met with the other members of the Big Four at eight a.m., where Boehner and Gregg, after much back-and-forth, seemed to solve the issue, only to have it flare again when the staff attorneys disagreed on the language. This time it took a thirty-six-hour conference call to re-solve the last details, which testified to how badly the players wanted this bill to pass.

And then finally it was done. "There were two moments," Bush educa-tion adviser Sandy Kress, the former Democrat, would recall. "One when Kennedy said, 'I think we have a deal. I think we're going to make it on the substance.' And when Kennedy laid out conditions on the final policies and on the money and they got to an agreement on that, we knew we were home free." The liberals were still unconvinced, particularly Paul Wellstone, who had fought it, and even Majority Leader Daschle won-dered whether it was worth passing the bill so late in the session—December. But when the twelve senators who had helped draft the legislation met across from Daschle's office to discuss whether to proceed, the moderates joined with Ted in arguing that they had won enough con-cessions from the Republicans to endorse the bill, and Daschle once again concurred. The conferees had agreed to a $22.6 billion appropriation for Title I of the Education Act, the section that directs money to schools as determined by their poverty rates—not as much as Ted had wanted but enough that he was willing to accept it, prompting one senator to label Ted a "New Democrat," the designation for the Clintonian moderates with whom the liberals had so often sparred, though Senator Evan Bayh said Ted "protested vigorously" at being called that. *The Economist* had an-other analysis in saluting what it saw as another example of Ted's legisla-tive acumen: "Yesterday's libertine has become today's King of the Hill." And it reported that Ted had trained his dog Splash to bark whenever Paul Wellstone, who still opposed the bill, raised his voice against it. It passed the Senate the following week, 87 to 10.

George W. Bush was elated. He signed the bill into law in January at Hamilton High School in Ohio, in John Boehner's district, with Ted loom-ing behind him, white-haired and large. It was just under a year after Bush had first discussed it. "The folks at Crawford Coffee Shop would be somewhat in shock when I told them I actually like the fellow," Bush said to the audience, speaking of Ted and the coffee shop in Crawford, Texas, where he had a ranch. "He is a fabulous United States senator. When he's against you, it's tough. When he's with you, it's a great experience." And Ted told the crowd, "President Bush was there every step of the way," which wasn't entirely true. Then after the signing, Bush, Ted, Judd Gregg, George Miller, and Boehner embarked on another victory lap, a flight across the country, that included a stop at the Boston Latin School, Joseph Kennedy's alma mater. In New Hampshire, Judd Gregg joined Ted on the stage and lavished praise on him similar to Bush's. "The way I see it is if Ted Kennedy can come to New Hampshire to be on this stage with President Bush and myself, then this must be the year the Red Sox win the World Series"—the team that had not won the championship since 1918.

It was a big victory—"likely the most significant social policy initiative of the Bush years," a historian was to say. *Washington Post* political reporter David Broder said it "may well be the most important piece of federal education legislation in 35 years."

"The bill lays a solid foundation for a stronger, better and fairer America in the future," Ted had proclaimed at its passage.* But the celebrations were premature. Appropriations were just a suggestion. It was the budget that would turn the suggestion into a reality. And after all the haggling over funding—five months of haggling—and after Ted had seemingly wrested an agreement from the Republicans to appropriate more than $20 billion to back NCLB, George W. Bush, the self-declared education president, did not put the money he had promised into his budget when he submitted it the very next month, or very much money at all. The federal education budget had increased an average of 13.4 percent from 1996 to 2002. In 2003 the increase was 2.3 percent. There would be arguments over how much of a cut it was, but there was no argument that Bush had reneged on providing adequate funding. "It's expensive," Ted had said, but Bush had reassured him. Now Bush blamed it on the war on terror. There was no money for education. Ted Kennedy felt betrayed. "I remember the Senator saying that this had never happened in his entire career," said Melody Miller, "that he had been lied to, and that they'd gone back on

---

*The eventual success or failure of the law would be a matter of fierce debate. Conservatives would bemoan federal interference in local education. Liberals, and especially liberal allies in the teachers' union, would bemoan what they saw as punitive testing. Many states were allowed waivers that had the effect of neutralizing the law. In any case, it was never the landmark it was intended to be. See Kevin Carey, "Requiem of a Failed Education Policy: The Long Slow Death of No Child Left Behind," *New Republic*, July 13, 2012.

a handshake. How was he ever supposed to work with them again?" For Ted, a man's word was sacred. It was one of his own gifts, part of his legislative chemistry, that Ted Kennedy could always be trusted, and in turn, his colleagues had felt duty-bound to *be* trusted by him. George W. Bush could not be trusted. "A spectacular broken promise of the Republican administration and Congress," Ted would call it in his memoir. Paul Wellstone had predicted this outcome, and Ted had rebutted him—testily. But Wellstone had been right, and Ted had to apologize. And Ted and George Miller held a joint press conference the day after Bush released his budget, lamenting the inadequacy of the resources and specifically criticizing an administration plan to provide a tax credit for students who sought to move from a poorly performing school to a better one—a plan that would cost $4 billion over ten years that Miller and Ted thought could be better spent on helping Title I students, those poor students, in repairing schools or making classes smaller. But there was even more. Bush and his coterie seemed to take a certain delight in having tricked Ted Kennedy. They gloated over Ted's surrender, saying that Ted had been around a long time, and they figured he would have known better—known better than to trust their promises. Bush had gulled him because Ted had trusted Bush.

IV

That fall and winter the effect of 9/11 still hung over the country like the smoke and dust that had hung over lower Manhattan that terrible day. George W. Bush had rallied the country. He had gone to ground zero of the attack in lower Manhattan, the ruins still smoldering, three days after 9/11, grabbed a bullhorn, and told the rescuers, "I can hear you! The rest of the world hears you! And the people—and the people who knocked these buildings down will hear all of us soon." It was war, Bush told America, but he acknowledged it would be a different kind of war—cyberwar, financial war, a war of intelligence and clandestine actions. "We had to uncover the terrorists' plots," he would later say. "We had to track their movement and disrupt their operations. We had to cut off their money and deprive them of their safe havens. And we had to do it all under the threat of another attack. The terrorists had made our home front a battleground. Putting America on a war footing was one of the most important decisions of my presidency." On September 14, the same day Bush visited ground zero, Congress voted him authority "to use all necessary and appropriate force" against the terrorists and any group or nation that had aided them. The vote was unanimous in the Senate; there was one "no" vote in the House. In short order, Congress authorized the creation of a new department to coordinate safety, the Department of Homeland Security. A Patriot Act, to allow stepped-up surveillance against possible enemies foreign and domestic, easily passed both houses of Congress too that October. Only Senator Russ Feingold, a Wisconsin Democrat, voted against it in the upper chamber.

Ted took no particular leadership role on these issues, and he didn't equate the resolution to grant Bush power to pursue America's enemies with the Gulf of Tonkin resolution that Lyndon Johnson had used to justify the escalation of the Vietnam War. Ted said that the day after 9/11 the CIA had briefed senators that the terrorist group Al Qaeda was responsible for the attacks. No one had mentioned any state actor, including Saddam Hussein, the leader of Iraq, against whom George H. W. Bush had waged war in 1991 when Hussein invaded neighboring Kuwait. Sharon Waxman, Ted's senior national security adviser, who had helped draft the force resolution in Tom Daschle's office, said, "Kennedy supported the resolution. There was no question about it." Ted thought that the international response to the attacks was heartening: Go after Al Qaeda and its mastermind Osama bin Laden in Afghanistan, which was where they had trained and were presently headquartered. On October 7, Bush did exactly that—launching air attacks on Afghanistan, then under the rule of a fundamentalist Islamic group that called itself Taliban.

Ted Kennedy left the military options to others. His initial interest was on immigration, which was an issue he had helped steer since the landmark 1965 Immigration and Nationalization Act loosened the immigration restrictions that had practically forbidden immigration. In the wake of 9/11, with border security suddenly paramount, many legislators, including some liberals, wanted to shut down programs, like the foreign-student-visa program, that enabled foreigners to come to the United States. At the time of the attacks, Ted was working on comprehensive immigration reform; he had held a hearing before the Immigration Subcommittee, of which he was still chairman, on the matter on September 7, and on September 11 his staff was meeting to discuss the bill when the planes plowed into the Towers. Ted feared the long-term consequences of closing down immigration, and he and Republican senator Sam Brownback of

Kansas instead argued against the wholesale shuttering of programs and for a careful analysis of loopholes in the immigration law that might be closed by better policing and coordination among authorities. Ted and Brownback introduced their bill that fall. California Democrat Dianne Feinstein and her Republican partner, John Kyl, introduced a bill of their own that was much more draconian. As Ted's immigration specialist, Esther Olavarria, described it, Ted, Brownback, Feinstein, and Kyl got together, as Ted did so often when his approach conflicted with another, and resolved the differences in their two bills. And while civil libertarians had some criticisms of the bill—the sharing of information between law enforcement and government agencies like the State Department and the Immigration and Naturalization Service that might result in the targeting of certain immigrant communities; the possibility that provisions in the bill might be used to create a national identification system; a border perimeter system that could prevent individuals from seeking asylum; heightened scrutiny of visas from state sponsors of terrorism, which could be used arbitrarily; and the establishment of terrorist "lookout committees" in each embassy to identify possible terrorist groups, which could have a chilling effect on free speech—the bill was eventually passed, 97 to 0 in the Senate, and signed into law by President Bush the following May. It was Ted's signal contribution to national security after 9/11. But he would soon have other concerns about the effects of 9/11.

Afghanistan, which had harbored Bin Laden and Al Qaeda, had been the target. Attack Al Qaeda safe havens from the air, attack Taliban forces from the ground with the assistance of native Afghan fighters. That was what the use-of-force resolution that had been passed by Congress and supported by Ted Kennedy had envisioned. But that was not solely where the Bush administration was focusing its energies. As early as September 15, at a meeting of Bush's "war council" at the presidential retreat of Camp David, in rural Maryland, where Bush's advisers were discussing the next moves, deputy defense secretary Paul Wolfowitz, as Bush himself would recall it, made a suggestion: Why not confront Saddam Hussein and Iraq as well as the Taliban? Donald Rumsfeld, the secretary of defense, quickly seconded the idea. "Dealing with Iraq would show a major commitment to antiterrorism," he said. Secretary of State Colin Powell disagreed, saying it would seem like a "bait and switch," and that the

United States risked losing the support of the United Nations and NATO. He didn't rule out doing it at some time in the future, but, again as Bush remembered it, Powell said, "We should not do it now because we don't have linkage to this event," meaning any linkage between Iraq and 9/11. And so Afghanistan remained the primary theater of war in those first months after 9/11. But the idea had been planted, the idea had been given consideration, the idea was left to percolate. *Why not confront Saddam Hussein in Iraq?*

It didn't percolate long. Bush would say that after war planning for Afghanistan, he turned to Iraq, but he seemed inclined to side with Powell. "Unless I received definitive evidence tying Saddam Hussein to the 9/11 plot," he would write in his memoir, "I would work to resolve the Iraq problem diplomatically." But Bush had not received definitive evidence of Saddam's involvement in 9/11, and he did not attempt to resolve the problem diplomatically. Rather, the truth was that George W. Bush and his advisers seemed to see 9/11 as an opportunity—an opportunity to take down Saddam Hussein, whom Bush's father had not taken down in the 1991 Gulf War, even though America had decisively beaten Saddam and forced his retreat from Kuwait, and even though Saddam had agreed to abandon his biological and nuclear weapons. (The psychological origins of this obsession, son redeeming father, or son exceeding father, were a pundit's delight.) Saddam had not attacked America. He had not trained or encouraged the 9/11 hijackers. He had not harbored them. But George W. Bush was convinced that Saddam, after expelling weapons inspectors in 1998, had breached his arms agreement and had weapons of mass destruction in his arsenal and might use them, and *that* became the link to 9/11—namely, that Hussein could potentially be a bad actor. As Bush would later put it, "Before 9/11, Saddam was a problem America might have been able to manage." But now, Bush said, "I could only imagine the destruction possible if an enemy dictator passed his WMD to terrorists."

Imagine it was all George W. Bush could do, but his imagination was sufficient. "We would confront the threat from Iraq, one way or another," he wrote in his memoir—a decision that some critics would compare to searching for lost keys in a spot with better lighting, even though the keys weren't lost in that spot. One administration official told *The New York Times*'s Peter Baker that the only reason Bush fastened on Iraq was that "we were looking for somebody's ass to kick," and the official said, "Afghanistan was too easy."* As the State of the Union approached, Bush was ginning up for the next phase in the war on terror. "Provide a justification for war," Michael Gerson, Bush's chief speechwriter, told David Frum, another speechwriter. And Frum would later write in a cynical observation with enormous consequences: "Bush needed something to assert, something that made clear that September 11 and Saddam Hussein were linked after all and that for the safety of the world, Saddam Hussein must be defeated rather than deterred." And in that State of the Union, Frum provided the "something" that Gerson had requested. He coined a term—the "axis of evil"—to yoke North Korea, Iran, and Iraq, all of them "arming to threaten the peace of the world." And he had the president declare, "The price of indifference would be catastrophe." George W. Bush would not court catastrophe. And so, from Paul Wolfowitz's suggestion to Donald Rumsfeld's enthusiasm to the endorsement of the rest of the administration, especially Vice President Dick Cheney, who was a perfervid war hawk, to George W. Bush's new triumphalism, America was ramping up to a preemptive war to stop a nation that had had nothing whatsoever to do with 9/11 in order to keep it from propagating another 9/11. "The 'axis of evil' speech was not a declaration of war, and there were still plenty of ways to avoid an armed showdown," *New York Times* reporter Peter Baker would write, "but it set Bush and Cheney on a course that would dominate the rest of their time in office." It was just a matter now of when.

Bush's decision had come quickly. The selling of the decision took nearly a year, and much of that year, 2002, was devoted to convincing the American people that Saddam Hussein had worked with Al Qaeda and was an imminent threat to world peace. It was a strange strategy. In times of crisis, most presidents provided reassurance. Bush provided instead a sense of dread. There was a pall over the country. George W. Bush intensified it. One poll showed 77 percent of Americans favored going to war against Iraq. In another, 72 percent believed that Saddam had been involved in the 9/11 attacks, though the only evidence of cooperation was

---

*It would turn out that Afghanistan wasn't so easy after all. In 2019 *The Washington Post* would uncover a trove of documents that indicated the United States' effort there was hopelessly bungled—that Americans had no understanding of the country and no plan going forward, that the infusion of money only corrupted officials, that Afghan troops could not be adequately trained, and that officials lied about the progress being made there. See "A Secret History of the War," *WP,* Dec. 9, 2019.

the president's own saber-rattling. Ted Kennedy had been supportive of the actions against Afghanistan that had led to the toppling of the Taliban and the installation of a new government. But he was deeply suspicious of Bush's sudden pivot to Iraq. Already Bush was tossing aside decades of deterrence and containment for a new and more aggressive posture in which America acted preemptively against perceived threats. That summer Bush had made a bellicose speech at West Point, a speech, *The New York Times* reported, that "seemed aimed at preparing Americans for a potential war against Iraq," and a speech in which Bush pointedly told the cadets, "We must take the battle to the enemy." Ted, fearful of what Bush's speech portended, conferred with former president Bill Clinton. Clinton had recently spoken at a labor conference outside London and had talked with British prime minister Tony Blair, and Clinton reassured Ted that for all Bush's rhetoric, Blair had convinced Bush to go to the United Nations before taking any unilateral action and that, in Clinton's words, the UN "would put some common sense into the two of them." Ted heard similar news from Gordon Brown, the chancellor to the exchequer, who visited Hyannis that same summer. Bush was hot for war. The world would cool him down.

But Ted was not pacified. Cheney gave a speech at the Veterans of Foreign Wars convention in Nashville, which he intended as a rebuttal to a *Wall Street Journal* op-ed piece by Brent Scowcroft, a close friend of George H. W. Bush and his former national security adviser. It was titled, "Don't Attack Saddam." But Cheney and Bush had every intention of attacking Saddam, and Cheney told the delegates that there was no doubt whatsoever that Saddam had weapons of mass destruction (even though there were serious doubts) and that he intended to use them (more serious doubts still) and that he would have nuclear weapons shortly, which meant, essentially, that any diplomatic maneuvers were fated to fail. This was even too much for George W. Bush. And yet Ted was deeply concerned that "something big was coming," as his national security adviser, Sharon Waxman, put it. He phoned her the Friday of Labor Day weekend and said that he might want to give a speech encouraging the approach to the UN and questioning whether the nation really faced a threat from Iraq, ostensibly in an attempt to try to change public opinion and head off the confrontation that the administration seemed certain to engineer. And he asked Waxman if she could deliver a draft by Tuesday, which sent her into a paroxysm of anger and panic—anger because she felt Ted was asking the impossible, panic because every source of information she might have contacted would have left for the holiday. One hadn't. She called a friend, Don Mitchell, who worked on the Senate Intelligence Committee, and asked if he might have documents to support Ted's view, and Mitchell sent her an Intelligence Committee report that quoted CIA director George Tenet to the effect that Saddam was not a threat and Bin Laden and Al Qaeda were—statements Tenet had made before the administration's decision to target Saddam.

By the end of summer, the administration was already preparing a congressional resolution to authorize war against Iraq. "Doing nothing is not an option," Bush said on September 4. But when Ted, at a Senate hearing, asked Secretary of Defense Rumsfeld to provide evidence of Saddam's hostile intentions, Rumsfeld refused to do so. On September 12, Bush spoke at the UN General Assembly and attacked Saddam relentlessly and made a threat that the United States would try to work with the UN, but if the UN failed to act, the United States would, rendering the UN irrelevant. Two weeks later Ted was the loudest voice during hearings at the Armed Services Committee at which John Shalikashvili, former chairman of the Joint Chiefs of Staff; General Wes Clark, former head of the Supreme Allied Command of Europe; General Joseph Hoar, former commander in chief of U.S. Central Command; General William Nash, who had commanded the First Armored Division in Bosnia; and General Thomas McInerney, who had held various posts at the Pentagon, testified, and they were, Ted would recall, "virtually unanimous in cautioning against going to war," which, Ted said, "had a very important impact on me." (Actually General McInerney was a dissenting voice.) Asked by Ted what urban warfare in Baghdad might look like, General Hoar said that it would look like the "last fifteen minutes" of *Saving Private Ryan,* Steven Spielberg's brutal, bloody film about D-Day and its aftermath.

But the administration wasn't listening. Later that week, on September 27, Bush cited newly declassified intelligence that he said showed Iraq's "longstanding and continuing ties to terrorist organizations," and he claimed that "there were Al Qaeda terrorists in Iraq." Though these seemed like fabricated charges, cooked up to promote war, Bush was nonetheless clearly winning the publicity battle, which infuriated Ted. The world was poised for war. Even American allies were being bullied into complying with Bush's push toward war. In Congress, Democrats too were loath to challenge the president, and many of those who feared

Bush's apparent eagerness to go to war still bought into his argument that Saddam was an imminent threat and had conspired with Al Qaeda. Ted was not among those. He felt that Bush was being disingenuous, and he felt that while there might be legitimate disagreements over the degree of the threat Saddam posed, any connection between Saddam and Al Qaeda was invented, and that, in any case, Bush had already made the decision to take the country to war, evidence or none. But few would challenge Bush's assumptions. Sharon Waxman said that there was a "void" when it came to opposition.

Moving into that void, Ted took the tiller and held it almost single-handedly. Realizing that he was once again sailing against the wind, he nevertheless delivered a speech on September 27 at Johns Hopkins School of Advanced International Studies that *The Boston Globe* called "impassioned" and the "most sweeping criticism yet from any Democratic Congressional leader of President Bush's request for approval to take military action against Iraq." Ted called for Bush to work with the UN to get weapons inspectors back into Iraq, and only then, if Iraq were to resist, did he believe military action should be contemplated. "War should be a last resort, not a first response," he said. "In launching a war against Iraq now, the United States may precipitate the very threat that we are intent on preventing—weapons of mass destruction in the hands of terrorists." Republicans were incensed. House majority whip Tom DeLay accused Ted of "subcontracting our national security to the United Nations" and claimed that Ted's argument was predicated on a "benign view of Saddam's relationship with terrorist organizations," as if the relationship were an established fact. Ted was under no illusion that any war resolution—the most prominent was one being promoted by the administration allowing Bush to take military action against Iraq without any preconditions—wouldn't pass Congress easily. He predicted it would receive seventy-five to eighty votes in the Senate.

George W. Bush was not patient. He was in a race to war, and he wanted a vote on his resolution even before the Armed Services Committee finished its hearings and heard from Tommy Franks, the commander in chief of Central Command. Ted was just as resolute as Bush was hasty. "Every day we were tracking," Waxman said of everything that was going on in the Senate regarding Iraq. One staffer was assigned to follow the debates at the UN and then send the information to be put in The Bag each night. Anything that was happening on the floor or in committee would go into The Bag too. Any television report went into The Bag. Waxman had file drawers filled with Iraq memos, and Ted studied them, had to know them "from the ground up," she said, because he was largely operating alone—one of the few congressional voices raised against war. And every utterance in every speech he made had to be footnoted and cross-referenced just in case some journalist wanted to check the data. (The briefing books were six inches thick and all tabbed by subject.) "He just had an insatiable appetite for information," Waxman said, and she was so tenacious about finding and then writing down every possible argument against intervention that she developed tendinitis in her hand. And Waxman said this: "He wasn't giving these speeches and arguing against the war and introducing legislation and writing op-eds because he likes to see his name in print." He was doing it because he was still hopeful that he might be able to change policy—that he might influence public opinion enough to dissuade Bush from following through on his chosen course: war.

But as the debate and the vote neared early that October, Ted, knowing full well the consequences of voting against giving Bush the power to attack Iraq and wondering whether he might be committing political suicide by voting to deny him that power, a power that the country and the Congress were all too willing to give the president, was still indecisive over exactly what to do. Dave Burke, his former administrative assistant, said that the two of them met, and while Burke admitted he might have had a "glass of wine too much," he "berated him endlessly about his indecision," "berated him up one side of my kitchen and down the other." And Burke asked him directly, without allowing Ted to equivocate: "What are you going to do? And don't give me the double-talk about it, Senator." Though he was still uncertain, Ted didn't double-talk. He solicited advice. He had briefings with former secretary of defense William Perry, who told him that the real peril was North Korea, which was producing uranium that might find its way into the hands of terrorists to make nuclear weapons. Iraq was not that kind of threat. He spoke daily to his friend William vanden Heuvel, a former diplomat from whom he often sought advice, and Vanden Heuvel said that Ted very well understood the danger of the United States waging a preemptive war against Iraq and understood the war hysteria that was seizing the country and thought it was "deliberately provoked" by Bush's political adviser, Karl Rove, in the interest of political gain. Vanden Heuvel said that Ted believed Rove had soothed Republican concerns about the 2002 midterm elections by assuring them that the Republicans would have a "war to help them through it." In short, war was good politics. Vanden Heuvel told Ted that he was "strongly opposed" to war unless it was channeled through the UN, and Ted agreed, seeming to hope that the UN, like the Senate, would be the saucer that would cool the tea. And Ted asked Vanden Heuvel to meet with Tom Daschle, who was disposed toward voting for a war resolution, and try to talk him out of it. Ted spoke with his former foreign policy adviser Gregory Craig as well, but Craig said that while Ted was soliciting advice, it was clear that he had "already made up his mind." His hearings and private discussions with the military had convinced him to vote against the resolution. And Ted, relying on Thomas Aquinas and Saint Augustine, devised a checklist of conditions for a "just war" and determined that Bush's imminent war on Iraq met none of them.

Robert Byrd had similar concerns and also opposed a war resolution, and according to Ted's close friend Lee Fentress, Byrd asked Ted to lead the Senate fight against the resolution. Ted demurred. He thought that he was too much of a target and that the Republicans would easily dismiss him, presumably as too liberal and too partisan. Byrd, now the grand old man of the Senate, was less easily dismissed. So the two worked together. Ted said they met in Byrd's office the Friday before the vote—Ted, Byrd, and three or four other senators who were opposed to the resolution. They conceded that they had only eight votes on their side. They knew they had no chance of winning, but they worked their colleagues, and by Monday the group had doubled in size, with Michigan senator Carl Levin, and California's Barbara Boxer, and New Jersey's John Corzine among those joining them. The debate over the resolution a week later on October 4 was "somber," as *The Washington Post* described it. The senators acknowledged the gravity of their responsibility, one after another calling it, as Senator Jim Bunning did, "one of the most important—if not the most important—that I or any of my colleagues will ever take in Congress." It was a cautious debate, a surprisingly even-tempered debate given the stakes, a debate in which every senator, including Ted Kennedy, seemed eager to bash Saddam Hussein, and in which the real disagreement was not over whether to stop Saddam—that was a given—but on how best to do it. Carl Levin, the chairman of the Armed Services Committee, had

introduced his own resolution countering the one that Senators Lieberman, McCain, and Warner had drafted for the administration, calling for
multilateral action through the UN and asking for the UN to press for unlimited access for weapons inspectors and for the use of force only if Saddam were to refuse—basically the policy that Ted had endorsed. Byrd
spoke forcefully, urging the Congress to delay its vote until after the midterm elections, as George H. W. had done before launching air attacks on
Iraq in the first Gulf War, saying of the senators, "Let them make a decision when they are not distracted by politics, by an election," and he urged
the voters, "Let them hear you." Ted spoke at length, admitting that Saddam was a "serious danger," a "tyrant," and that "his pursuit of lethal
weapons of mass destruction cannot be tolerated." But like Levin, he objected to a "unilateral, preemptive American strike and an immediate
war." And in a colloquy with Byrd, he cited the likely bloodshed of such a
war and the enormous cost in both treasure and lives—issues that had
scarcely been discussed. And he raised an issue that supporters of the impending war had not raised: the "immense post-war commitment that
will be required to create a stable Iraq." Afghanistan was easy, said the
administration. Ted was certain that Iraq would not be easy.

But none of this mattered. Bush, Cheney, and others had whipped the
country into war frenzy. Saddam had to be stopped because, as administration spokesmen, including national security adviser Condoleezza Rice,
now said, "We don't want the smoking gun to be a mushroom cloud." The
resolution came to a vote a week later, on October 11, at 12:50 a.m. The
Senate, 77 to 23, authorized George W. Bush to go to war unilaterally if he
so chose, the twenty-three votes against constituting a small moral victory for Ted, given how high war fever was running and how much courage it took to vote against it. Most of the Democrats, 58 percent of them,
voted in favor. Liberals—including Hillary Clinton, who had been elected
to the Senate from New York, Joe Biden, and Majority Leader Daschle—
expressed their reservations and then voted for it. So did Democratic majority leader Richard Gephardt in the House, which passed it 296 to 133,
where Patrick Kennedy voted for it. Ted waylaid his junior senator, John
Kerry, before the vote and implored him to vote no, "passionately contending," said Robert Shrum, "that even if it [a yes vote] looked like good politics now, siding with Bush was wrong on the merits—and even politically."
But Kerry voted with Bush anyway. "I have been in the Senate fifty years,

and I never thought I'd find a Senate which lacked the backbone to stand up against this stampede, this rush to war," Robert Byrd lamented. President Bush reacted differently, betraying his insistence that he hadn't yet decided to go to war: "The days of Iraq acting as an outlaw state are coming to an end." And now war was inevitable—war between the United States and Iraq, war between Ted Kennedy and George Bush.

TWENTY-ONE

"A Fraud Cooked Up in Texas"

FOR TED KENNEDY, legislative war was brewing against an administration that he felt had no scruples—an administration he would have to fight tooth and nail. But first came the midterms. George W. Bush used them, as expected, to hype the impending war against Iraq and build support for Republican candidates. He crossed the country delivering what amounted to a pro-war stump speech, twenty times, assailing Saddam Hussein, insisting yet again that Saddam had weapons of mass destruction and would use them (had already used them on his own people), tying Saddam to terrorism (Saddam would have "liked nothing more than to provide the arsenal and the training grounds for these cold-blooded killers" and "We know that he's had connections to Al Qaeda"), and sneering that the United Nations would just be an "ineffective debating society" unless it found the "backbone necessary to assume its responsibilities," which were to support Bush's effort against Saddam. Senate majority leader Tom Daschle would later say that Bush's message was that the "security of our country would be determined by the outcome of the November elections," and clearly Bush was telling voters that only Republicans eager for war could provide it. The previous January Ted had told *The Boston Globe* that 9/11 had created a "different wave, a different feeling" in the country; that people had been "shocked to a great extent"; and that to "pretend we've just got business as usual misses the whole thing." And he said that he thought the politicians who could "break through and talk about something different and do it in a different way"—the politicians who could somehow circumvent 9/11—were the ones who "are going to be elected."

But Ted was wrong. There was no circumventing 9/11, no breaking

through. Nine/eleven dominated everything, and Bush, who had benefited greatly from 9/11, talked about little else for good reason. If the midterm elections of 2002 were a referendum on Bush and his war fever, he
won that referendum. He gained eight more seats in the House, and two
seats in the Senate, which turned that chamber from Democratic to Republican once again. (Prior to Bush, only Franklin Roosevelt in 1934 had
won seats in both houses in a midterm.) One of those lost Democratic
seats had belonged to Paul Wellstone, the ardent and feisty liberal who
died in a plane crash while on the campaign trail. Majority Leader Daschle said he received a call the night of Wellstone's death from Ted, who
related a conversation he had had with the historian David McCullough,
who told him that the Adamses had always answered the call of duty, and
that had been the basis of their greatness. Ted now told Daschle that former vice president Walter Mondale, who had been a Minnesota senator
like Wellstone, would no doubt answer the call and run, so that Democrats could retain the seat. Mondale did answer and run, but he lost the
election. And now Daschle said he was "consumed" by a question: "Had
the world changed so drastically in these monumental two years that the
very practice of politics as we had come to know it was altered?"

For Ted Kennedy, the election was soon eclipsed by another in the long
series of Kennedy crises. Ted's forty-two-year-old daughter Kara had been
plagued by shoulder pain, apparently from a stenosis. But an X-ray just
before Christmas at Johns Hopkins Hospital in Baltimore revealed something else—something much worse. It revealed that Kara, a heavy smoker,
had lung cancer. That very afternoon, Ted and Kara discussed the prognosis with a medical team there, but Ted said he found those discussions
"very unsatisfactory." (The doctors told her that she had less than a year
to live.) He left immediately and consulted other experts, including Dr.
David Sugarbaker, the chief of thoracic surgery at Brigham and Women's
Hospital in Boston, who recommended a lobectomy, the removal of part
of the lung. Joan would say of Ted, "He really saved her life." Kara had
been the most self-sufficient of Ted's three children, the one who asked for
the least from him, and Melody Miller, Ted's longtime staffer and family
counsel, said she thought that Kara "felt a little left behind and left out,"
and that Ted often said, "I have to reach out to Kara. I have to make sure
she's involved in this or taken care of in that." And with Kara, as with Ted
Jr. and Patrick, Ted had to assume the role of mother too, since Joan was

so often disabled by alcohol, but he couldn't replicate the mother-daughter relationship, and it seemed to bother him. "When Kara got lung cancer," Melody Miller said, "he was just devastated; everybody was devastated." Ted had gotten her past the death sentence. Now came the chemotherapy and radiation, and as he had done with Ted Jr.'s cancer, Ted got up every morning, this time with Vicki, and the two of them would accompany Kara to the treatments and when Ted left for his Senate duties, Vicki and Kara would watch videos and talk, and Melody Miller said that "they really bonded through the crisis." And afterward at noon, Ted would go to St. Joseph's, where he had prayed after John Jr.'s death, and celebrate Mass and pray now for his daughter's recovery, and he did so every day. And he would rally Kara, buoy her spirits, fortify her faith, and let her know that she would beat her illness as he had beaten every calamity he had suffered.

Ted Kennedy was not often helpless—he prided himself on not being helpless—but he was helpless now. George W. Bush had only strengthened his hand in the midterms, and the war Bush so desperately seemed to want was increasingly inevitable. At his annual speech to the National Press Club that January, Ted lit in to Bush on his Iraq policy and on his tax cuts and on Bush's claim that he couldn't afford NCLB now because of the costs of terrorism, of which Ted said, "We cannot say it is wartime for the rest of America but still peacetime for the rich," and Ted pointed out that not a single incumbent who had opposed those cuts had been defeated. "The lesson of 2002 is clear," he said. "We will not succeed if we fail to stand up and speak out." Two days later, at Harvard's Kennedy School of Government, he attacked Bush's Iraq policy in stronger terms, calling it a "chip-on-the-shoulder foreign policy," and saying, "If this were a court of law, the administration's case for war would be laughed out of the courtroom." But his was still a lonely voice as the administration continued to beat the war drums publicly and to plan for war privately. The Iraqis, under pressure from UN Resolution 1441 that Secretary of State Colin Powell had shepherded through the Security Council after the election, decided to let weapons inspectors back into the country, but that did not deter Bush from his warpath. Rather, he feared that the inspectors might find no evidence of weapons of mass destruction or that Saddam would not be in full compliance but would be fooling those inspectors, and in either case, the war might be postponed. Indeed, the inspectors had asked for more time to complete the job.

But George W. Bush had no time. He ignored facts, abjured evidence, preferring to make up his own, and in his State of the Union address, he said categorically that Saddam had weapons of mass destruction. Bush, however, wasn't fully trusted, even by many of his fellow Americans or by the international community. His secretary of state, Colin Powell, a former general, a man of unimpeachable integrity, a man with no ideological predisposition, unlike the hawkish Vice President Dick Cheney or Secretary of Defense Donald Rumsfeld, was tasked with going before the recalcitrant United Nations to lay out the case for the WMDs that Saddam was supposed to have. And on February 5, Powell made that case and made it convincingly, even if the evidence on which he relied was cherry-picked and faulty—convincingly because Powell was spending his reputation on a case he knew was less than airtight. (When Joe Biden, then the chairman of the Foreign Relations Committee and a friend of Powell's, warned him before the UN appearance to "stick to what we know" and not buy into the administration's fabrications, Powell told him, "Joe, someday when you're retired and I'm retired, I'll tell you about all the pressure I've been put under over here.") Nevertheless, after Powell's indictment, 63 percent of Americans, according to a Gallup poll, were willing to go to war to remove Saddam from power. Even Ted was impressed, and Sharon Waxman thought it might have been the only time he "wavered," the only time he might have thought that he could be wrong on Iraq and WMD—wrong because he had such respect for Powell and couldn't imagine Powell lying for the administration to take the country to war. Writing in *The Boston Globe* three days later, he acknowledged Powell's "strong presentation," but he still questioned the plan, asking whether an invasion would divert us from Al Qaeda, whether the cost in lives would be too high, whether we could win the peace if there were massive civilian casualties and Iraqis were displaced from their homes, and whether Americans might be greeted not as liberators but as occupiers, which might trigger terrorism there against our troops. These were serious questions, but not questions the administration wanted to ask. Instead, Bush insisted that the Iraqis would welcome American soldiers and that America would rebuild the nation it might have to devastate in ousting Saddam. And while Bush was talking to people who gave him the rosiest view of the outcome of war, Ted had gone up to Boston and met with strategic thinkers from Harvard and MIT at the Charles Hotel in Cambridge to see what they thought of a possible invasion, and their prophecies were far less rosy.

Ted Kennedy needed to know. He had Sharon Waxman compile a list of experts to whom he could speak—twenty-seven pages' worth of experts. He consulted with Congressional Research Service analyst Ken Katzman, who had worked for the CIA and knew Iran and Iraq and was concerned about the rush to war. He talked with a series of retired generals: Eric Shinseki, Joseph Hoar, John Abizaid, Wesley Clark. He met with Jimmy Carter's former national security adviser, Zbigniew Brzezinski, and with George H. W. Bush's, Brent Scowcroft, who had written the *Wall Street Journal* editorial in 2002 that had already warned against going to war in Iraq, and with Clinton's, Anthony Lake, and with Clinton's secretary of state, Madeleine Albright. He spoke with former CIA director John Deutch over breakfast up in Massachusetts. He spoke with the heads of nongovernmental agencies, like David Albright of the Institute for Science and International Security, and Ken Bacon of Refugees International. He spoke with diplomats like Prince Zeid Al-Hussein of Jordan. They met in restaurants, two or three at a time, where the dinner would begin promptly at seven o'clock, as it always had at Joseph Kennedy's house, and end promptly at ten. Other times they met in his office. Sometimes they met surreptitiously at out-of-the-way places because the individuals—Shinseki or Scowcroft or Brzezinski—didn't want it known that they were talking to Ted Kennedy. And before each session, Carey Parker would brief Ted, challenge him, play devil's advocate, so that Ted knew the arguments he might encounter and could engage the experts. And at one point, early on, Waxman suggested that they go up to the United Nations to talk to the "internationals," and they did, including meeting with Secretary General Kofi Annan, but Waxman told Ted, "If you really want people to be honest, let's get out of the building," and he invited a number of the permanent UN representatives to a private discussion at the UN Association. He did all this to learn, to understand, to internalize, and he wanted to learn, understand, and internalize for one aim: to see if he was right in trying to stop the rush to war. "The pace was relentless," Waxman was to say. "It was every day. I'd be talking to him about any issue, and he just couldn't get enough of Iraq. Every second. He was seized." And he came away convinced: *He needed to stop the war.*

"Why weren't there more against the war?" Ted would later ask himself. He said that he and Robert Byrd were virtually the only ones in the Senate who actively and publicly and continuously opposed the march to war, and he felt that Bush, cynically, was using the prospect of war to distract the country from a sagging economy and a lack of any other legislative victories, and he said that Bush's poll numbers rebounded with the prospect of war, though that wasn't entirely true. His numbers only soared—thirteen points—once Americans were finally engaged in combat. Byrd, as vehemently against the coming war as Ted was, took to the Internet, posting comments on *Huffington Post* and other websites, which, Ted's press secretary James Manley said, got Ted excited by the Internet, too, and by the idea of him and Byrd, "two old bulls," eighty-five year-old Byrd and seventy-year-old Ted, taking on the administration and, as Manley put it, "leading the charge one last time."

Stop the war. Early in March, at the annual meeting of the United Methodist Church's General Board on Church and Society, Ted made another sally against the impending war, calling war planning "unnecessary" and reiterating yet again that "Al Qaeda, not Iraq, is the most imminent threat to our national security." But the administration was not listening to criticism. It hadn't listened to the reports from Hans Blix, the head of the UN weapons inspectors, or Mohamed El Baradei, the director general of the International Atomic Energy Agency, which had been charged with finding out whether Iraq had revived its nuclear weapons program, both of whom found no evidence of WMDs or of a program to produce them. It didn't listen to American allies who cautioned against jumping into war or to public protests around the world. Instead, Americans had come to revile those allies. It didn't listen to army chief of staff Eric Shinseki, one of Ted's experts, who told the Armed Services Committee that it would take hundreds of thousands of American troops to occupy Iraq after a victory. It didn't listen to a personal envoy from Pope John Paul II sent to dissuade them. The administration didn't listen. And on March 19, George W. Bush announced to the nation that "coalition forces" were striking Iraq. Ted Kennedy had failed—failed to convince his fellow Americans or his fellow senators that war was misguided.

The initial attack and campaign was brief. By April 9, American troops had taken Baghdad and driven Saddam out. On May 1, Bush declared "Mission Accomplished," on the aircraft carrier USS *Abraham Lincoln,* onto which he had landed wearing a flight suit, which might have been the perfect image for a war fueled by hawkish ideology and machismo about "kicking ass" and "making Saddam toast," rather than by careful tactical planning or about diplomacy, which the conservatives seemed to think was unmanly. The president's vaunt, however, was premature. The mission was far from accomplished. The mission had really only just begun, because now American troops had to occupy Iraq, calm its internal warring factions, and begin a rebuilding effort that included both infrastructure and, more dauntingly, government. Still, most Americans were giddy. Ted Kennedy was not. He knew what now lay in store. He had predicted it. "It was gross incompetence," he would later say of the Bush policy, which was based on "the ideology of rosy scenarios, blank checks provided for funding with no accountability, distortions and misrepresentations, failure to accurately and truthfully characterize the circumstances in Iraq, and denial that Iraq had slipped into a civil war." In July, in a speech before the Johns Hopkins School of Advanced International Studies, where he had made one of his first attacks on Bush's seeming war lust, Ted called American troops "police officers in a shooting gallery" and condemned the intelligence that had gotten us into war as "shoddy," "hyped," even "false." He promised to introduce an amendment to the defense appropriation bill that would compel the administration to devise a plan to rebuild Iraq, and he called for a UN resolution that would set up a UN peacekeeping force.

But there was to be no plan, only improvisation, and there was to be no UN force, only American soldiers desperately trying to maintain order amid near-total chaos. When, in September, Bush asked for an additional $87 billion for the war effort, Democrats adduced a poll showing that most Americans opposed the supplemental appropriation, and Ted wanted to push back. He asked if there was a forum where he could have what amounted to a media megaphone, and his Boston office director, Barbara Souliotis, suggested he speak with Associated Press reporter Edward Bell. When they met up in Massachusetts, Bell asked Ted to talk about Iraq, and Ted, clearly boiling mad, thinking, no doubt, of the awful costs of the Vietnam War that he had so haltingly opposed, now obliged, opening up to Bell, speaking his mind, telling him that the entire war had been a "fraud cooked up in Texas" for the purpose of promoting Bush's political fortunes. "There was no imminent threat," he said of Iraq. Rather, Bush and his advisers had met in Texas, settled on going to war against Iraq, told the Republicans in January about the decision, and said it "was going to be good politically," as Ted put it, which was a damning charge to make publicly and was only partly true: Bush seemingly had decided to go to war against Iraq almost as soon as he took office, but his motives were far more complicated than only political ones. Furthermore, Ted questioned where the money for the war was actually going, and he cited a Congressional Budget Office report that found that only $2.5 billion of the $4 billion being spent on Iraq each month was being spent on Iraq, while the rest, he claimed, was being doled out to foreign political leaders, "bribing them to send troops" to Iraq, which was nearly as incendiary a comment as his charge that the war had been "cooked up" to help Bush's political fortunes.

Ted, who was seldom incautious, had been incautious. Even Waxman said to herself, "My god! What did he just say?" Ted was visiting Framingham to discuss base closings when his staff came up to him and told him that his comments were all over the wire and that the press was going to ask for some proof—this from the man who had always instructed his staff to annotate everything he said about Iraq. Ted's "proof" in this case were articles he had read describing how the war planning was done before there was any evidence of Saddam's involvement in 9/11 or any danger he posed, but Ted admitted, "I would have had a difficult time putting my finger on it."* Meanwhile the Republicans expressed outrage. Bush himself called the remarks "uncivil." Tom DeLay, the House whip, said that Democrats had "spewed more hateful rhetoric at President Bush than they ever did at Saddam Hussein" and called Ted's charge "hate speech." John Warner, normally temperate, asked people to "stop to think of the reaction of a young wife surrounded by small children, not knowing from day to day whether her husband will survive another day's engagement in Afghanistan or Iraq. And they hear that this whole thing has been a fraud perpetrated upon his family and was made up in Texas. I find that very painful." But that was precisely Ted Kennedy's point: that innocent men and women might be sacrificing their lives for a threat that didn't exist. The anger was still boiling when Ted returned to the Senate

---

*Eventually, Ted did get that evidence. Former secretary of the treasury Paul O'Neill cooperated with journalist Ron Suskind on a book and told Suskind that the plan to attack Saddam Hussein was in the works before 9/11, and Richard Haass, who headed the Council on Foreign Relations, said publicly that Condoleezza Rice had told him the decision to go to war had been made in August in Texas. See EMK int., Dec. 9, 2003, Miller Center, UVA.

the next week, but he was hardly contrite, calling the "administration's rationale [for war] . . . built on a quicksand of false assumptions." And that only further provoked the Republicans, which, again, was what Ted Kennedy wanted to do: to have a real reckoning on why Americans were fighting and losing their lives in Iraq when Iraq hadn't attacked us.

And while some Republicans were firing back at Ted, others were trying to change him. Bush's chief of staff, Andrew Card, phoned Ted and implored, "You don't have to get this kind of intense," to which Ted riposted, "Well, you don't have to get us involved in war," though in another account, Ted recalled that he said the war was tough, "bad things are happening" in Iraq, and the administration had to expect criticism. He delivered more on the eve of the vote for the $87 billion supplemental appropriation, calling the war "mindless, senseless and reckless." "The American people were told Saddam Hussein was building nuclear weapons. He was not. We were told he had stockpiles of other weapons of mass destruction. He did not. We were told he was involved in 9/11. He was not. We were told Iraq was attracting terrorists from Al Qaeda. It was not. We were told our soldiers would be viewed as liberators. They are not. We were told Iraq could pay for its own reconstruction. It cannot. We were told the war would make America safer. It has not." And then five weeks later, Ted was heading to Texas A&M University to receive the George H. W. Bush Award for Excellence in Public Service, though Ted asked Alan Simpson to ask the former president if he wanted to retract the award, given Ted's criticism of his son, and Bush said no. After Ted returned to Washington, however, the senior Bush wrote him, saying, as Card had, that Ted had been too hard on George W. Bush. Ted said he thought a long time about how he would respond, then decided instead to phone him, tell him that he understood his feelings, appreciated the letter, and would give it some thought.

But as sensitive as Ted Kennedy was to people's feelings, and he was very sensitive, he couldn't retreat on Iraq, which he felt was a disaster based on those false premises. It was not the feelings of those in the administration about which he cared, but the feelings of those who had lost loved ones in combat. Ted was at Arlington National Cemetery on a cold, gray November day when Brian and Alma Hart of Bedford, Massachusetts, were burying their twenty-year-old son, Army Private 1st Class John Hart, who had been killed in Iraq. Before the burial, Brian Hart, a fundamentalist Christian and a Republican and, before his son's death, a strong advocate of the war, asked if he could speak with Ted Kennedy. (Hart's relatives warned him not to meet with the perfidious Kennedy.) They spoke so long—thirty minutes—that the ceremony was delayed. Hart told Ted that John had called him repeatedly to complain about the inadequacy of the matériel. "This is how it's going to be," his son had told him on one of those calls. "We're going to be riding down some road when we're ambushed from the side." John Hart died because the Humvee in which he was riding was not armored. And Ted Kennedy promised Brian Hart he would act. Ted pressured the Defense Department to provide those armored Humvees that American troops needed, and when Brian Hart later expressed his thanks, Ted thanked him instead for bringing the issue to his attention and told the Harts that he knew what they were going through because his mother had been a Gold Star mother. And a year later, on the morning of the anniversary of John Hart's death, Ted and Vicki were at Arlington again with the Harts, and it was for the Harts and those who suffered losses as they did that Ted continued to fight against the war.

And earlier that year yet another casualty spoke as profoundly as anything to Ted Kennedy's heart and to his compassion. No journalist had likely hurt Ted Kennedy as deeply as Michael Kelly, who had made his reputation on the GQ piece "Ted Kennedy on the Rocks"—the piece that savaged Ted and portrayed him as an out-of-control drunkard and a reckless womanizer and a man lacking in all moral scruple. And Kelly had not only written that piece, dripping with contempt, he had ridden that piece, had flogged that piece, had appeared on Nightline the day that Ted issued his mea culpa at Harvard in 1991, to revile Ted Kennedy again. If there was anyone for whom Ted Kennedy's detestation would have been fully justified, it would have been Michael Kelly, the conservative who turned ideology into character assassination, not only against Ted Kennedy but later against Bill Clinton and Al Gore and any Democrat who had the temerity to work for the powerless regardless of their own individual failings. Kelly was a strong supporter of George W. Bush's war, the war Ted had felt was without basis, and he had gone to Iraq in March, shortly after the invasion, to travel with the Third Infantry Division and tell their story. He was in a Humvee that April when it came under fire, and the driver took evasive action, which led to the vehicle flipping into a canal. Both Kelly and the driver were killed. At the time, Kelly and his wife and his two young sons were living in Massachusetts, so he was a constituent of Ted

Kennedy's. By one account, Ted phoned his widow that night to ask if there was anything he could do for her. She said there was. She suspected that she would have a difficult time getting her husband's body back from Iraq. Ted told her to consider it done. And it was.

II

"They blew it," one Democratic official said of George W. Bush and his minions and their relationship to Ted Kennedy. "They came into office, and they started to work together on a number of issues, and then they completely dissed him." The relationship had been ruptured with the administration's decision not to fund No Child Left Behind after Bush had personally enticed Ted to join him in promoting the bill and after fellow Democrats had warned Ted to be wary of Bush. It had been further damaged by the Iraq War and the ongoing sniping between Ted and the administration. But Bush, with such well-honed social instincts, was no Newt Gingrich, out to run roughshod over his opponents. He was wily. He understood Ted Kennedy, understood Ted's need to further legislation, especially since the war had pushed aside everything else, and Bush, having fooled Ted once and even gloated about it, obviously felt he could fool him again by doing to Ted what Ted had often done to gain allies: bait them.

The bait this time was a Medicare prescription drug plan. Medicare had had no drug plan, even though many seniors had a difficult time affording their prescriptions. Ted had taken on the challenge and fought for a plan that would expand Medicare by having the federal government provide a drug benefit. The cost was $594 billion, and for three years Ted had proposed it, 80 percent coverage with a $200 deductible and a cap of $3,000, and for three years it had failed in the Senate, though only by one vote, 50 to 49, in that third year, 2002, after weeks of debate and after the Democrats had compromised on a $390 billion bill that would be means-tested so that seniors who could afford their drugs would not receive the benefit. Republicans, however, would not budge. They wanted no federal expansion whatsoever, but instead proposed a plan that went through private insurers. "How many of us are willing to face our constituents . . . knowing that we have secure coverage for seventy-five percent of our drug costs," meaning Congress's own health plan, "but we reject proposals that do even less for our fellow citizens?" Ted asked after that defeat. In January, when Bush was planning to attack Iraq, Ted made a speech at the Kennedy School of Government, excoriating not only the impending war but also Bush's unwillingness to support a real prescription drug program, not a private program, and called Medicare a "solemn promise between the government and the people, not just a potential profit center for HMOs and the insurance industry."

But Bush lured Ted Kennedy with a blandishment that Ted had a difficult time resisting. Ted had always expressed regret that he had not accepted Richard Nixon's national health insurance compromise in 1974, when Nixon was fighting for his political life after Watergate and needed a legislative win. That had been the last, best chance for Ted's cherished program until the Clinton plan, which also failed. After the 2002 midterms, Bush once again proposed a drug benefit plan, realizing that it was good politics to do so, neutralizing an issue that the Democrats had owned, though, as with NCLB, there was seemingly an ulterior motive as well. While Bush's plan provided $400 billion for drugs, it had a kicker: As with previous Republican plans, once again, the drugs had to be purchased through private health insurance. And he had another provision: that those who remained in traditional Medicare would not get the benefit but would receive only a catastrophic drug benefit that triggered if their costs rose above $5,500. Democrats saw right through the scheme. Bush's idea was to privatize Medicare, long a Republican goal, and thus destroy it. Bush would later say as much: By reforming Medicare, he would "create an opportunity to expand Medicare Plus Choice, later renamed Medicare Advantage, which allowed seniors to obtain all their health care through flexible, affordable private insurance plans." In short, end Medicare. Ted desperately wanted a drug benefit, but he was having no part of that. Instead, on June 3, he and Max Baucus—by other accounts, John Breaux was also involved—struck a compromise with Republican Charles Grassley, the Finance Committee chairman, that they would permit the private drug benefit, but only if Medicare provided the same benefits, thus making the private plan compete against Medicare. Bush compromised on that issue. He seemed to have no choice. Two weeks later, on June 18, Bush invited a group of Republican and Democratic senators to the White House to show their support of the bill, and Bush pressured them to pass it by the July Fourth recess. While some Democrats balked, Ted, always searching for some compromise, pushed ahead. The bill passed the Senate later that month with thirty-five Democrats in support, and it was widely thought that it would not have passed had Ted Kennedy not endorsed it, since the size of the vote belied the doubts about it, and many supported it grudgingly. Jay Rockefeller called it a "pathetic bill," a "dangerous bill," also "cruel, misleading, cynical, calculating, political in its formulations." Ted batted down some Republican efforts to weaken the bill. When twenty senators "huddled in the well," by one account, to challenge a Republican attempt to means-test Medicare, Ted headed to his seat and began pulling out his familiar charts and threatening to filibuster the bill if the means test passed. It failed by a voice vote.

But the House, yet again, was a different matter. Democrats there were still concerned about introducing a private insurance component into Medicare and worried that, despite Bush's apparent compromise, it was a Trojan horse expressly designed to wreck Medicare, which was exactly what it was and what Ted Kennedy should have seen it was. Meanwhile conservatives were still worried about cost. In the House, only nine Democrats voted for the bill, which passed by a single vote, 216 to 215, and then only because Speaker Dennis Hastert held up the roll call for forty minutes while he strong-armed two of his members, Jo Ann Emerson of Missouri and C. L. "Butch" Otter of Idaho, to vote for it, with Emerson even crying when she cast her vote. It finally passed at two-thirty in the morning. Afterward a few House Democrats wore black armbands to mourn the death of Medicare. But Ted was not downcast. Thinking he had removed its worst provisions, he called the bill the "greatest action in a generation to mend the broken promise of Medicare," though he added it was only a "down payment" for a more robust commitment to seniors. And now it was headed to a conference to reconcile the Senate and House bills. But the Republicans were taking no chances. As the leadership had done on the Kennedy-Kassebaum conference, where they excluded Kassebaum from conferring on her own bill, this time they excluded every Senate Democrat but the conservatives Baucus and Breaux and every single House Democrat. Even then, even with the opponents sidelined, the sides could not find common ground, and so the Republican leadership took over, circumventing even the House Republican, Bill Thomas, who had been conducting the negotiations and who was not happy about his own party's tactics. Part of the issue, again, was the cost, estimated at that $400 billion over ten years, though Bush insisted that as many as half of Medicare enrollees would leave the program for private insurance and take the drug benefit with them. Another issue was the difference between the benefits in the two bills. The Senate provided half of all drug costs up to $4,500 after a $275 deductible and then 90 percent of costs over $3,700, while the House bill had what was called a "donut hole"—coverage up to $2,000 and then the "hole" that would force seniors to pay all the drug costs between $2,000 and $3,500. And the Senate bill had Medicare pick up drug benefits in any region where there were two or fewer private health plans doing so. The House bill had no such provision. (The House bill also included the Medical Savings Accounts that had practically sabotaged Kennedy-Kassebaum, and the means test that Ted had stripped from the Senate version.) Bush had thought he could pacify conservatives with the private component and liberals with the benefit itself. Instead, he had seemed to alienate both.

The negotiations dragged on until November, during which time Ted continued to say that "reasonable compromises make sense," and that "obstruction for the sake of obstruction is the quickest way to political defeat," which had long been Ted Kennedy's legislative bromides. That was exactly what George W. Bush had been counting on: Ted Kennedy's willingness to compromise in order to get something done. But Ted, the great compromiser, was losing patience. He had assumed that the things to which he had objected would be jettisoned. That was how business had always been done in Congress—through the goodwill of legislators on both sides to give a little in order to achieve a lot. But Republicans would not give a little. Ted told the press that the bill was on "life support" and the negotiations were in "free fall" because House Republicans were insisting on provisions that called for private competition for Medicare and for cuts in Medicare if the program grew faster than Congress was anticipating. And there was worse to come. By the time the bill emerged from conference, it had the MSAs that Ted had once fought so fiercely to defeat, and a provision that put private insurers in direct competition with Medicare, which Ted felt would pull out the healthiest seniors and leave to Medicare the sickest. This seemed to have been the Republican plan all along. "It is the beginning . . . of privatizing Medicare," Ted now said, which was what opponents had been saying all along. And he added, "Next is social security." Having been excluded, Ted had been waiting in his Capitol hideaway for the conference to announce its agreement. Once it did, late at night, Ted had his press secretary James Manley put out a statement that he would now oppose the bill, and he had Manley race down the hallway to find Robert Pear of *The New York Times*, who was on deadline, so that Ted could get his objections out in public. As Manley would later put it, "Let's face it, he was behind the eight ball a little bit" for having supported the bill in the first place, "and he had to get out of it."

Ted knew Bush had rolled him, just as Bush had rolled him on NCLB—charmed into thinking that he could make accommodation with the Republican president when the president really had no intention of accommodating him. Ted Kennedy, the great legislator who seldom miscalculated, had miscalculated badly once again. "When you're dealing with President Bush, you don't think you're dealing with an ideologue," Carey Parker would say. "He seems to be willing to listen to what you're talking about." But that was an act, a very accomplished act, and now Ted saw through it. He had been playing by old rules that no longer obtained; he had been relying on his own instincts, which worked only when he was dealing with people of honor who subscribed to a sense of political morality; he had relied on trust, but he had finally, sadly, and angrily come to realize that one couldn't trust George W. Bush, that beneath all that Texas bonhomie was a tough ideologue who was anything but a uniter. Seeing how he had been outwitted, Ted now raged against the bill. He went on *Face the Nation* and called the bill—the bill he had helped steer through the Senate and that probably wouldn't have made it through the Senate without him—"basically a slush fund" for insurance and pharmaceutical companies. And even as he decried the bill, critics said that Ted Kennedy, a master of the Senate, should have known better, that having been fooled on NCLB, he shouldn't have allowed himself to be fooled again. Representative Barney Frank and Hillary Clinton, who had opposed the bill at the outset, said Ted had "made a mistake" in giving Bush his support. He had. But even then, with his back against the wall, he worked with Connecticut senator Joe Lieberman to see if they could improve the bill, take out the privatization, but the American Association for Retired Persons (AARP), ostensibly a nonpartisan group, had come out in favor of the bill and was running advertisements to support it. That endorsement gave the bill the momentum it needed, and at a rally organized by the Alliance for Retired Americans, which was affiliated with the American Federation of Labor, Ted said, "We're here to say, 'President Bush, keep your hands off our Medicare,'" and he added, "I want them to hear it all the way downtown at the headquarters of the AARP." But Ted knew the odds were against him, and he said that between the House-Senate conference and AARP, "Virtually overnight we were isolated."

It wasn't quite over. The House was divided, with the Democrats nearly unanimous in their opposition and many Republicans objecting to the price tag. The morning of the House vote on the bill, November 22, the anniversary of John Kennedy's assassination, Ted and other members of the Kennedy family laid white roses on John's grave and then attended Mass—a juxtaposition of the legacy that Ted was trying to uphold and that the new Congress was trying to destroy. The vote later that evening promised to be close, given the number of Democrats fiercely opposed to privatizing Medicare and the number of conservatives opposed to a $400 billion government giveaway, even if that money was being given away to insurers and pharmaceutical companies. "Give this bill a fair vote in the House," Ted said later that day, by which he meant a vote without White House pressure and horse-trading, "and I'll drop my filibuster in the Senate." But it would not be a fair vote. Bush had flown back from a state visit to England to lobby for it, even phoning Republican congressmen from Air Force One, and his HHS secretary, Tommy Thompson, went to the House floor to buttonhole conservatives who objected to the bill and convince them otherwise. Speaker Hastert, as he had done in the original vote back in June, pressured flagging Republicans too. As the votes were tallied and members watched the numbers projected on a scoreboard in the back of the chamber, it stalled at 216 to 218 against, and it looked as if, after all those months and all those conferences and all those debates and all that arm-twisting, the bill might not pass after all, handing Bush a major defeat. But then Speaker Hastert did something—something that violated all House norms: Though the roll call began at three a.m., and though votes usually took the allotted fifteen minutes, he stretched that roll call for another three hours while he bargained and arm-twisted some more to see if he could get the votes he needed to put it over the top. "This vote has been held longer than any I can remember," complained Democratic whip Steny Hoyer, a comment that Republicans greeted with hissing and yells of "Give it up!" Hoyer was right. It was the longest roll call in House history. By one account, during those three hours, Hastert told Bush's lobbyist, David Hobbs, that he had to get the president on the phone and have him twist some arms himself, but it was four forty-five a.m., and Bush had gone to bed. When Hobbs finally awakened him, Hobbs corralled recalcitrant Republicans one by one and handed them the phone so Bush could pressure or charm them. By this same account, Representative Trent Franks of Arizona told Hobbs that he *and* a group of conservatives who had voted against the bill wanted to talk to Bush, and so the group gathered around a phone in a room off the House chamber, and Franks handed Bush an ultimatum—a quid pro quo. Franks said that he and his fellow conservatives thought the bill was another government expansion, but if Bush would promise to appoint Supreme Court justices who would overturn *Roe v. Wade*, the president could get his prescription drug bill. Bush vacillated and haggled for a while—he didn't want to make a commitment that might go public—but Franks kept pushing back, and finally, said one participant, Bush told Franks, "I tell you what. I think I'm going to make that commitment. You know I'm a man of my word." (Hobbs and Hastert would deny Bush said it.) And so Trent Franks and a few fellow conservatives switched their votes, and Hastert finally carried the bill, 220 to 215, just as dawn was breaking. Democratic House leader Nancy Pelosi compared the tactic to the Bush win in Florida, where the Republicans had pulled all stops to prevent votes from being recounted. They had won then by breaking the political norms. They won again.

The next day it moved to the Senate, and Ted Kennedy was ready to fight. When the bill reached the floor, he filibustered as he had said he would, even though Daschle was against that tactic, and twenty-two Democrats joined him, but the Republicans forced a cloture vote and won. Then Ted and Daschle, who, despite his lack of enthusiasm for the filibuster, was a vehement opponent of the bill, raised a point of order that the bill exceeded the $400 billion appropriated for it in the budget resolution. This time the vote was 58 to 39 to suspend the budget rules, but that was two fewer votes than the sixty it needed, which seemed, yet again, to be the end of the prescription drug benefit. But Republican Trent Lott and Democrat Ron Wyden, both of whom had opposed the bill, though on different grounds, now changed their votes. Lott, while he was walking up to the well to cast his vote, was intercepted by Majority Leader Bill Frist, who had replaced Lott when Bush forced him out. (Lott had praised Strom Thurmond at a testimonial and seemed to endorse Thurmond's past racism by saying the country would have been better off if Thurmond's independent presidential race in 1948, promising segregation, had been successful, which gave Bush the occasion to oust him for the more compliant Frist.) Frist and the White House aides on the floor begged him to change his vote, even as, Lott said, he was shaking his head no. But he did. And with those switches, that parliamentary avenue was foreclosed. The bill passed a short time later, 54 to 44, with Ted and Lott both voting against it. Ted left the floor fuming and brushing off the condolences of his fellow Democrats.

But Ted Kennedy did not go down gently. Citing the administration's perfidy on NCLB, he said he had been misled on one bill and, speaking of the Medicare prescription drug benefit, "strong-armed" on the other. He called the deceivers and strong-armers the "most ideologically-driven administration I've ever seen." And he swore he would fight back. At a rally of opponents on the Capitol steps, he shouted of Bush and the Republicans, "You sold us out!" And he said, "We're going to go all out to repeal what you've done." But many in his party thought that Ted was really the one at fault for allowing Bush to sell him out both on NCLB and on the Medicare bill, and those critics said that there would have been no Medicare bill if Ted hadn't endorsed it in June, handing Republicans the chance to take that bill and turn it into a death knell for Medicare. "A 40-ton chunk of falling sandstone, and Kennedy was Wile E. Coyote," wrote E. J. Dionne, Jr., in *The Washington Post*, comparing Ted Kennedy to the hapless victim in the Road Runner cartoons. Among those who were critical of Ted was Tom Daschle, who doubted his steadfastness even after Bush had made his intentions clear on Medicare. "He and I opposed the drug bill together, but for the longest time, I was reasonably certain he was going to cut a deal." But then, Daschle said, "Ted felt there were questions of good faith with regard to how they were negotiating, and he thought he had some understandings that didn't ultimately come about," and "he backed away from the deal." In short, he had come to his senses. By then, however, it was too late.

Still, Ted was defensive rather than contrite when he should have accepted responsibility. "When the President of the United States looks you in the eye and says the resources will be there," he said of NCLB, "I believe it," which was all the more reason he shouldn't have believed Bush on Medicare. When it came to Medicare, Ted claimed he had been working for a drug benefit since 1978 when he first sponsored a bill with Strom Thurmond, and when he saw a new chance, he leaped at it—exactly what Bush was anticipating. But "Republicans controlled the House, they controlled the Senate, and they controlled the presidency. And they used that power in an abusive way," seeing that they could "ram this thing through rather than work out the historical give-and-take of the legislative process." Give-and-take was the Kennedy way, the very basis of his legislative modus operandi. "Too ready to compromise," his own staffer Michael Myers said was how some people characterized his determination to "fill out his legacy," which a prescription drug benefit would have helped do. That, however, had not only been a modus operandi but also, to many, a legislative virtue of his. "The key to his legacy," *Time* would later write in naming him one of the ten best senators, "is not that he is determined to stick up for his principles. It's that he's willing to compromise on them." But compromise assumed the presence of a partner. Now, Thomas Mann of the Brookings Institution said, after Ted had been hoodwinked on Medicare, the rise of partisanship was such that it was suddenly Ted who was the anachronism, Ted who didn't understand how the new Senate functioned, a Senate in which there were few partners and in which no one's word could be trusted. Dionne thought the Medicare House-Senate conference and the long-delayed House vote "proves that Republicans are ruthless and determined and that Democrats are divided and hapless." And Dionne said, as Mann had, that "Republicans have changed the rules in Washington, but some Democrats"—he could have been referring to Ted—"still pretend to be living in the old days." Ted had reluctantly come to the same conclusion, which meant having to abandon the very methods that had made him a master of the Senate and for which he had been amply praised just a few years earlier. He told reporters, as he left the floor after the Medicare vote, that he would henceforth insist on bills being "pre-conferenced" before passage, and said that from now on he would be asking himself, "Do we pass this or not pass this? Will it get hijacked in conference?" And he admitted that although he was tired and frustrated, "If I made up my mind that there's no need to try, I wouldn't remain in the Senate."

He was still steaming when Bush signed the bill early that December, inviting only two Democrats, Baucus and Breaux, to the ceremony while calling the law an example of bipartisanship. The same day Ted addressed another rally of several hundred retirees crammed into the Senate hearing room and asked them, "Who do you trust? The HMO-coddling, drug-company-loving, Medicare-destroying, Social-Security-hating Bush administration? Or do you trust Democrats who created Medicare and will fight with you to defend it every day and every week of every year?" And to reporters he fumed that the law was the "most antisenior, antidisabled, anti-Medicare, antifamily, antiworker" piece of legislation in American history. "They call it a signing ceremony," he said. "But they're quietly gloating that it's a funeral ceremony for Medicare." To him, it had been yet another fraud—a terrible fraud—this one cooked up in the White House.

III

After forty-two years in the Senate, Ted Kennedy was not naïve about how the institution worked. But George W. Bush and the Republicans, he felt, had changed everything, and NCLB, the Iraq War, and the Medicare prescription drug benefit had shocked Ted into realizing that the chemistry of the Senate on which he had relied for decades, even in the dark ages of Newt Gingrich, no longer functioned as it had. An article in *The Boston Globe*, titled "On Hill, Relations Take Turn for the Worse," reported that the Beltway consensus was "things are as bad as they have been on Capitol Hill," and it quoted the congressional scholar Norman Ornstein: "It has changed, much for the worse." (Of course it had been changing for a long time.) Another piece, this one in *The Washington Post*, came to the same conclusion: Democrats had been duped by the Republicans largely because Democrats still believed in the sanctity of congressional institutions, especially the Senate, and because they still believed in at least the vestiges of senatorial courtesy—the courtesy on which Ted Kennedy had based his entire legislative career. "We never imagined they would not include all the conferees," Daschle lamented, speaking of how the Republicans had frozen the Democrats out of the negotiations on the prescription drug benefit, something that just wasn't done until recently. "Our mistake was that we didn't insist on inclusion" before bills were sent to conference for final drafting—what Ted had also said. But the reason Daschle hadn't insisted was that Democrats had never had to insist before—before George W. Bush decided that while he liked the appearance of comity and the rhetoric of comity, he eschewed actual comity. Ted too said Democrats "probably should have done more" to protest the conference, though he was condemning himself in saying so, and said that they would be "much more resolute" in the future, and that the Republicans' tactics would eventually "backfire on them." These were bold words, but words without much force behind them. The Republicans now ran everything.

After the Medicare disaster, the hostility of Democrats toward the Bush administration intensified, but perhaps none of them was as hostile as the man who had lent the adminstration his status and then felt he had been betrayed: Ted Kennedy. "Personally burned and injured by the failure of No Child Left Behind and especially Medicare," said his close friend Chris Dodd. Ted, who had made regular visits to Bush, stopped coming to the White House, and he and the president seldom spoke on the phone now. Though Bush persisted in citing Ted's work on NCLB as evidence of bipartisanship, on the first anniversary of the law, Ted didn't appear in the East Room for a ceremony, but instead sent a letter to Secretary of Education Roderick Paige calling the law for which he had fought, "greatly imperiled" due to a $6 billion shortfall in funding. He gave a series of speeches early in 2004, including one at the liberal Center for American Progress, in which he excoriated the administration, labeling it "breathtakingly arrogant," "dishonest," "vindictive and mean-spirited," and another at the Brookings Institution, in which he compared Bush to Richard Nixon, claiming that he had "created the largest credibility gap" since Nixon, and saying more: that Bush had "broken the basic bond of trust with the American people," which might have been a projection of the trust Bush had broken with him. Stripping away Bush's patina of amiability and compatibility, he said that "truth is the first casualty of policy" in his administration and cited the tax cuts to the wealthiest Americans and Bush's lies about the drug benefit, calling it a "triumph of right-wing ideology-making as moderate reform." (He didn't mention then the president's lies about Iraq.) Bush had posed as compassionate. Ted thought that was a lie too. "We had endless trouble prying out funds for urgent liberal programs," Carey Parker was to recall. "These programs deserved more than just the back of the hand or the argument that, 'We need to keep the deficits under control'"—this from an administration that lost the Clinton surplus through its huge tax cuts to the wealthy. Ted had worked with Bush because he so desperately wanted to get things done— too desperately. But that was over now as well. "We're doing absolutely nothing in the United States Senate that's relevant to anybody's life," he said at the time, and cited a class-action bill that "has no relevance except to keep workers at Wal-Mart from being able to bring their cases," and a bankruptcy bill that "just makes bankruptcy courts collecting agents for credit card companies." A bill to raise the minimum wage once again, one of Ted's pet projects, had been stalled by Republicans for months. When Ted attempted to add it to a welfare reauthorization bill and then to the class-action lawsuit reform bill, and the Republicans couldn't get cloture, they pulled those bills rather than let the Senate vote on them. He called

those months of legislative wheel spinning "five months of having absolutely nothing to do with anything that anybody, any family, is concerned
about." A "non-functioning institution" was what he said the Senate, the
Senate he so loved, had become under Bush and the Republicans, and
rather than push legislation of their own, Democrats had become primarily obstructions to bills that Republicans were eager to pass—one preventing lawsuits against gun manufacturers, another preventing them
against HMOs—by threatening to filibuster. It was Reagan all over again.
Democrats couldn't even get votes on their amendments to bills like a renewal of welfare reform or a trade bill because the Republican leadership
wouldn't allow it unless Democrats agreed to send those bills to conference, which, after the Medicare drug benefit debacle, Democrats refused
to do.

Ted Kennedy was stymied. The man who in the past had worked the
Senate so brilliantly, even when Republicans controlled it, could not work
it under George W. Bush. "Can you believe what those bastards are doing
now?" he would vent to his aide Michael Myers when he let his guard
down and permitted Myers to see behind his facade of being the optimistic
"liberal warrior," as Myers put it. "Can you believe what timid people we
have in our own party who won't stand up and fight for anything?" And
there were times when, Myers felt, Ted's frustrations were so great, his
rage at Bush so overwhelming, that even Ted thought, "Is it worth being
here? Should I be trying to do something else in order to make real progress on issues?" And Myers said Ted would wax nostalgic, saying he
"misses the day in which there was a group of very competent, progressive senators who went to the floor together and battled the battles together, and they were a team. I think he misses having those old friends."

Ted would have understood the conservative passion to undo liberal
policies. He had been fighting it his entire political life. But the complaint,
even among some of those within the administration, was not that Bush,
as conservative as he was, had a conservative agenda he was determined
to promote, as Newt Gingrich had. It was that Bush had allowed everything to be politicized, even his war, so that policy was always subordinated to politics. Everything was a function of whether it would help the
president's reelection chances and the chances of strengthening the Republican Party, with little or no regard for the American people. John Dilulio, Jr., an academic who became the director of the White House Office
of Faith-Based and Community Initiatives and who chafed at this focus,

told *Esquire* early in the administration, "There is no precedent in any modern White House for what is going on in this one: a complete lack of policy apparatus. What you've got is everything, and I mean everything, being run by the political arm. It's the reign of the Mayberry Machiavellis," he said, referring to the cracker barrel hometown of the protagonist of *The Andy Griffith Show*, where everything, Dilulio said, was simplified. And Dilulio admitted that Karl Rove, Bush's chief political adviser, whom most of Bush's officials felt the need to pacify, was "maybe the single most powerful person in the modern, post-Hoover era ever to occupy a political adviser post near the Oval Office." (Dilulio eventually resigned.) Another senior administration official made the same charge: "They," meaning the other officials, "relished the 'us versus them' thing": Republicans versus Democrats. And the antagonism wasn't just about making sure that whatever was done legislatively benefited the president's political chances and hurt the Democrats'. It could be as petty as telling the surgeon general, David Carmona, that he could not attend the Special Olympics because it was sponsored by the Kennedy family. "Why would you want to help those people?" a White House aide asked him.

All this political obsessiveness, this narrow focus on seeing policy only in terms of politics, was the antithesis of how Ted Kennedy viewed the political process, the antithesis of his faith in the chemistry of the Senate and the goodwill that bound its members. "It's basically a result of understanding how the institution is working and how things get done and to know that intuitively," he told *The Boston Globe Magazine* of his way of doing business. "The other stuff is just part of the deal. If you don't learn it, you might as well not bother serving in the Senate," and he cited how he and Orrin Hatch could argue fiercely on fetal cell transplantation, which conservatives opposed, and then the two could work together on the Religious Freedom Restoration Act, which protected certain religious rights. "You can just be an advocate," Ted said, "and there's nothing wrong with that, or you can be an accommodator, and you're going to be a leader if you do that." Ted had always been an accommodator. But now there was no accommodation, there was no compromise. Accommodation and compromise were critical to the chemistry of the Senate, for which Bush and the Republicans had little use.

But if they had little use for the chemistry of the Senate, they had little use for the physics of the Senate either—for the traditional procedures of the Senate that Ted had mastered. Republicans were proposing what

Trent Lott called a "nuclear option"—that is, changing the Senate rules so that Bush's judicial nominees would need only a majority and not the sixty votes needed to break a filibuster. (The consideration of such a drastic move came because out of more than two hundred of Bush's judicial nominees, Democrats had filibustered ten, which Republicans stewed was ten too many.) Ted called it an "aggressive way of imposing will, by effectively removing the Parliamentarian, who is supposedly called according to Senate rules and precedents, and substituting this prescribed format." "That's radical," he said. "What we have is a radical regime, not a conservative regime." And it wasn't only the Senate that Bush and the Republicans were undermining, Ted asserted. They were doing it in agency after agency—the FBI, the intelligence services, the Environmental Protection Agency—"putting people who don't believe in the programs and are really committed to undermining them into key positions in the administration." Though Ted Kennedy, when it came to protecting some cherished program or advancing some cherished idea like healthcare, could be fearsome, he loved comity. The Bush administration, he concluded, loved tension—loved it because, he said, "They think it's politically helpful": "division for political purposes." (It was an even more unrestrained version of Richard Nixon's positive polarization.) Ted would say that the administration would further inflame "emotional kinds of issues," things like flag burning, on which, he said, the Senate would waste six or seven weeks, or gay marriage, neither of which, he felt, was a significant issue in the country. "It's about the politics of division, the politics of fear, frustration. . . . It's not the politics of unity, of bringing the country together to deal with central challenges." He hadn't even felt that way about Ronald Reagan, who, however misguided Ted might have thought him, seemed to believe sincerely that his conservatism served the country. But Ted felt that way about George W. Bush—felt that Bush put his own political interests above those of the nation. It was like having Newt Gingrich in the White House. And that he could not abide.

Meanwhile there was the war—the war that Ted Kennedy had so fervently opposed, the war in which so many Americans and Iraqis were dying, the war that he felt was destabilizing the Middle East, but the war that still had the support of the majority of Americans, some 55 percent by a Pew Research poll. That January, as that war approached its first anniversary, with still no evidence of weapons of mass destruction but before public or political opinion had begun to turn against it, Ted spoke to the Center for American Progress, seizing once again on former Treasury secretary Paul O'Neill's recollection that the administration had already been focused on ousting Saddam Hussein before 9/11. "The agenda was clear," he told the audience. "Find a way to end Saddam's regime," and he called it a "war of choice, not of necessity," as if it were a "product they were rolling out," which was the analogy Andrew Card had used in discussing the ramp up to the war. Ted accused Bush of being abetted by a "congressional majority willing to pursue ideology at any price, even at the price of distorting the truth," and he said that the war "could well become one of the worst blunders in more than two centuries of American policy." To which House Republican majority leader Tom DeLay snapped that Ted had "insulted the president's patriotism, accused the Republican Party of treason, and resurrected the weak and indecisive foreign policy of Jimmy Carter and Michael Dukakis." In another speech that March—a "gutsy speech," Sharon Waxman called it, because it continued to challenge the administration's credibility when nearly everyone was afraid to do so—this one before the Council on Foreign Relations, he again accused the administration of altering the "state of facts and the evidence of the threats we faced from Iraq," and he lambasted CIA director George Tenet for backtracking by saying that his recommendations to the president had contained caveats and disagreements among analysts, and that he had never described Saddam as an "imminent threat." The administration's rebuttal, issued by Senator John Kyl, was that Saddam had been removed from power and "what was said before is not important," meaning that any lies that had led to the war—Saddam's alleged alliance with Al Qaeda or his possession of WMD—should be disregarded. On the war's first anniversary, later that month, Ted appeared on *Meet the Press*, and in a combative interview not only called the war ideological yet again, but also said that it had isolated America from the rest of world—more than at any time since World War II. When the moderator, Tim Russert, invoking the conventional wisdom at the time, pressed Ted to say that the war had been worth it, Ted countered that we should never have taken our eye off Al Qaeda and diverted attention to Iraq. In yet another address, the following month, at the Brookings Institution, he called Iraq "Bush's Vietnam."

It was not popular for Ted Kennedy to be making these statements at the time he did, when the war was popular. Sharon Waxman said that even people in his own office questioned why he was doing so, and others outside the office, Democratic officials included, were not sympathetic, especially of his speech before the Council of Foreign Relations, in which he attacked the foreign policy establishment that had largely supported the war and continued its support. "What? Is he crazy?" "Why is he doing this?" "Why is he saying this?" "Why doesn't he just go along with the party?" "What are you doing? Don't make us vote on that." Those are the comments that Waxman said rained down upon her as she fielded phone calls in the office. There was little to be gained in any political sense from making the speeches he made, which was why the Democrats were so terrified when he did, and why nearly every other politician, including the liberals, either supported the war or were wary of criticizing it. But James Manley, his press secretary, said that to Ted Kennedy, the war wasn't just another issue, and his opposition wasn't ideological. It was personal. Manley said that Ted became especially engaged when he met the Harts and attended their son's funeral at Arlington and heard taps played eight or nine times in those forty-five minutes and worked with the Harts to ensure that the Humvees would henceforth be shielded in armor, which, had they been so shielded, would have saved John Hart's life. Sharon Waxman too said she was struck by "how personal it was for him," which was why she believed he was so "passionate" and "intensely focused" on trying to stop it. And she thought it might have had something to do with Ted's early support for the Vietnam War and a sense that he had waited too long to oppose it, which he had. "I felt the Vietnam War was always in the room," Waxman said. One reporter interviewing Ted at the time noted how easily he cried now—this man who seldom revealed his emotions and who choked them back even at the funerals of his brothers and his nephews. The reporter said he had cried at a photo of his schooner *Mya* having run aground by a sailor who had hypothermia and lost his way, and he cried when he spoke of Private John Hart. At one point, much to the consternation of several of his staffers, he decided to go to the Senate floor and read the names of every Massachusetts serviceman and -woman who had died in Iraq. Those who opposed it thought that the families of those servicemen and women might think he was politicizing their deaths. But Ted had no desire to politicize. And he sat in his office carefully poring over those names, making sure that the pronunciation of each was correct before he went to the floor where he read the names slowly, deliberately. (He wanted the Senate chaplain to open each Senate session by reading the names of those who had died the previous day, but the Democratic leadership nixed it.) And he would say now that his vote against the war was the single most important of his Senate career, even though there were members of his staff who disputed it, who went through his votes and found others that were arguably more important, like his vote for the Civil Rights Act of 1964. But Ted continued to insist otherwise. And he did all this, as Manley and Waxman said, because he cared so deeply and because he still believed in the power of persuasion, still believed that even though the Congress and the nation were behind the president, he could change that. "Senator Kennedy is the most hopeful person," Sharon Waxman would recall of this time, even though he wasn't so hopeful privately. "He's always looking for the way to change the debate. He always believes it can be changed. He always believes public opinion can be moved. That's why he does what he does. He wasn't giving these speeches and arguing against the war and introducing legislation and writing op-eds because he likes to see his name in print. It's because he's always very hopeful that it will change the policy. He always hoped, 'If we get this report, that law changed, this piece of information, maybe it will change things.' " And he did—slowly. "I long ago stopped paying attention to Ted Kennedy," columnist Richard Cohen, a bitter Kennedy antagonist, wrote that September, "but now I find him a typhoon of common sense and intelligent indignation. He has not lost the gift of outrage." And as the war continued, the outrage only grew.

IV

Avoid discussing the war. That was the counsel that most Democrats kept as the 2004 presidential election neared. "The Democrats were convinced that they could win the election if they kept the focus on domestic issues," said William vanden Heuvel, Ted's friend and quondam counselor. "They didn't want to give the Republicans the argument that they were undermining the president in the exercise of foreign affairs." And Vanden Heuvel said that the Republicans had exactly the opposite approach: "Make the war an issue" that "overwhelmed the Democratic advantage on domestic issues." Ted thought otherwise. Ted thought, according to Vanden Heuvel, "I don't care what the polls show. Politically, this is going to be the overwhelming issue, and we've got to make it now." Already former Vermont governor Howard Dean was waging an antiwar campaign in his bid for the Democratic nomination, calling for greater involvement of the United Nations in transitioning Iraq to democracy.

But Ted had another candidate to whom he was beholden: the junior senator from Massachusetts, John Kerry. Their relationship went as far back as Ted's 1962 Senate campaign, when Kerry was a new high school graduate and got to accompany Ted on the stump because Eddie Martin, Ted's press secretary then, felt Kerry deserved a reward for working so hard on the menial tasks he had been assigned. Their real acquaintance-ship began nine years later when Kerry, a decorated Vietnam veteran and a leader of the Vietnam Vets Against the War, was encamping on the Mall with other protesters and Ted came down to the site with his friend John Culver and sat and talked with the veterans and listened to their complaints—"the first person to dare to do that," Kerry would later say, "because a lot of them," meaning congressmen and senators, "were un-sure," meaning afraid. And Kerry said that Ted returned the next day, and the day after that, this time with John Tunney. "It was a breakthrough moment," Kerry said, and other senators soon followed. And Kerry testi-fied before the Foreign Relations Committee, and Ted managed to get one hundred war protesters admitted to the hearing. And eventually, Kerry entered politics, becoming lieutenant governor of Massachusetts and, in 1985, senator, taking the office right next to Ted's.

Theirs was a cordial relationship if not, at the beginning, necessarily a close one. The staffs perceived each other as rivals, *Boston Globe* reporter John Farrell said, because Kerry saw Ted as a rival, and Ted's staff thought the Kerry staff was not "properly submissive to their guy," as Farrell put it. Kerry was ambitious—Farrell said that the first time he met him, Kerry pulled out a yellow legal pad on which he had written out his political philosophy in what was, in Farrell's words, "clearly . . . a precursor to a presidential run"—but it was hard to match Ted Kennedy's record. Oc-casionally the two had little tiffs. At one point, when Kerry parked in a handicap spot, one of Ted's staffers called the newspapers to report it, and when the 2004 Democratic National Convention was awarded to Boston, Ted was miffed that Kerry spoke at the announcement as if he had done it. And along with the rivalry came a tension over Kerry's rightward drift in the 1990s when, like so many liberals, he thought he would doom his political prospects if he were too liberal. So Kerry gave a speech at Yale challenging affirmative action, he supported educational reforms that took aim at teachers' tenure, and he had the blowup with Ted over the Clinton healthcare bill. But for all that, Kerry was still a Bay Stater, and Ted had a deep affection for his home state and anyone tied to it. (He had supported Paul Tsongas, too, even though Tsongas was a deficit hawk.) And Ted did his best to help Kerry, especially in 1996, when he was locked in a tough reelection campaign against Governor William Weld, and Ted let Kerry put his own name on the Children's Health Insurance Program bill that he and Orrin Hatch had negotiated, so that Kerry, who had little interest in legislation, could have a bill to point to. And beyond politics, there was the typical Ted Kennedy personal touch; when Kerry's father passed away, and Kerry was mourning at Nantucket, Ted, whom Kerry had once called the "master of the personal gesture," and Vicki sailed there to provide solace.

Whatever chill had existed between the two Massachusetts senators had long ago thawed. As early as January 2003, Ted announced that he would be supporting Kerry for the Democratic presidential nomination, and Kerry was now speaking warmly of the Kennedys. (Kerry would also tell *Newsweek* that he had studied Ted, trying to learn what had made him so successful, and had determined from those studies that it was "the people" who were the fundament of politics, not the policies one espoused.) And when Bob Shrum, Ted's old press secretary and speechwriter who was now a coveted political consultant, was debating whether to work for Kerry or for the handsome young North Carolina senator John Edwards, with whom Ted had worked on the Patients' Bill of Rights and whom Ted genuinely liked, Shrum said that Ted made an "impassioned" plea for Kerry, one that was anything but "pro forma." And Ted Kennedy's support mattered. Kerry was trailing badly in Iowa, the first of the states to ballot for the nomination, in this case a caucus rather than a primary. And Shrum, who had joined the Kerry campaign, called Ted, as he had done four years earlier for Al Gore's campaign, and asked him to ride to the rescue. Ted arrived even earlier than he had been requested to do, in September 2003, four months before the caucuses, because, his aides told the press, he was eager to reassert liberal values that Bush had done his best to destroy. Shrum called those first appearances in eastern Iowa a "magnet for Iowa Democrats," and said that a "lot of them didn't arrive at a rally as Kerry supporters, but a lot more of them were when they left." Ted returned in January, and he was in good form, teasing the voters about their rejection of him in 1980—"Are you going to make up with

me?"—joking that he could be in Boston watching the New England Pa-
triots against the Tennessee Titans, but instead he had told himself, "I
want to be in Dubuque, Iowa, and I want to see every one of you show up
at those caucuses, or I'll never forgive you"—telling the crowds that he
wanted to talk to them about a "bold, handsome, intelligent leader—
a man who should not only be president, but who should wind up on
Mt. Rushmore," and then delivering the punchline, "But enough about
me." And Kerry himself was "revved up," as Tad Devine, one of his campaign consultants, put it, saying that he had been asked how it felt to be
living in the shadow of Ted Kennedy, how it felt to know that Kerry's own
legislative record would never match Ted's, and whether he was jealous of
having to follow a living legend—"And it was Ted Kennedy who asked me
that." Ted would howl with laughter.

Before Ted Kennedy arrived in Iowa, it was Howard Dean who was attracting thousands and Kerry just hundreds. But Ted changed that. Ted
had loaned his chief of staff, Mary Beth Cahill, to Kerry as his campaign
manager, and Cahill said that Ted was exuberant during those two weeks
he spent in Iowa in January stumping for Kerry, even asking her for more
time there. One Democrat said of Ted, "It was like going back and doing
his own victory lap." Devine said that Ted could "campaign for you by
showing up, or he can campaign for you by going all the way, and he went
all the way for Kerry. He flipped the switch." And Kerry himself would say,
"He worked his heart out for me . . . and he made the difference in Iowa."
Dean, who had won the endorsement of Al Gore, slid to third in the caucus voting, slipping behind John Edwards. Kerry, who had trailed by
twenty-three points just two weeks before the voting, won easily with 37
percent of the vote and propelled his candidacy, which had once seemed
dead in the water. But it wasn't only his affection for Kerry that motivated
Ted. It was his distaste for George W. Bush and the way Bush had con-
nived the nation into war. And as he cheered Kerry, he also lacerated
Bush, saying that the Democrats had to beat him and that Kerry could,
though the political seers were dubious. And on the plane back from Iowa
to Washington, Ted told Shrum, "I think everybody's wrong about this
thing. I think you've got a chance."

In some ways, too, the campaign had the sense of a valedictory for Ted
Kennedy. He was seventy-two. He looked it. One reporter, Charles Pierce,
said of him, "See how he's not gone all gut-fat but rather squashed with

that Irish hunch that makes the old ones look bowed and slowed as if their lives collapse inward like stars, all the extraneous material consumed until there's nothing left but the invisible gravity of the core. See how his right hand quivers until he covers it with his left, a gentle movement that he camouflages by looking at his watch." And Pierce noted how Ted's speech sounded like an "AM radio stuck on scan, chopped to bits by throat-clearing and by pauses that are long enough to be considered tactical." Mark Leibovich, writing in *The Washington Post* that summer, said, "He looks all of his 72 years—jarringly so, given that the country met him as a young man and little brother. He wears his mileage plainly: His purply-red cheeks have gone puffy, his hair a bright white. He suffers from chronic back pain, hunches and grimaces while he walks, and his breathing is labored after just minimal exertion." He was a relic of other and better political times, a husk, and one got the sense he knew it, which was one reason, no doubt, he was fighting so hard for Kerry—fighting to restore liberalism before he faded. At a clambake over Memorial Day weekend, to which Ted had invited one hundred journalists—"to catch up with each other well before the convention," read the invitation—reporter Joan Vennochi of *The Boston Globe* found an "eeriness" to Ted as he laid his arm on a shoulder and pointed out Bobby's house and Jack's house, and looked out "to the twinkling lights on a small island off in the distance," and said, "The view has been the same my whole life." And Vennochi wrote, almost certainly accurately, that "he has probably spoken those words countless times to others—and, one imagines, whispers them countless times to himself. Everything looks the same, but everything is different. A beauteous but creepy movie lot is all that is left of Camelot by the sea. Most of the people who gave it life and fame are dead. The new generation can never match the magic, real and invented, of the past." The only vestige was Ted Kennedy, and he too now belonged to the past.

The convention in Boston seemed like yet another valedictory—an early farewell. Ted had worked hard to get the convention to Boston, in part because he knew it would be good for the local economy, in part because he knew it would be good for Kerry, in part because he felt it would just be good for Boston generally. The main competition was New York, heavy competition, but Ted and Boston mayor Thomas Menino raised the funds and convinced the Democratic National Committee that the city could pull it off, and Boston won. It was not, however, an especially festive convention for Ted Kennedy, one of those boisterous affairs in which he needled the Republicans and rallied his own party with his bellowing insults and entreaties. Ted was not boisterous. He was determined to defeat George W. Bush, who had endangered so many of the things in which Ted believed and who had engendered the sense that a certain kind of civility, Ted Kennedy's kind of civility, was ending, never to be recovered. Ted had had virtually nothing to do with Bush since what he regarded as the Medicare con, except for a brief encounter at a St. Patrick's Day reception at which Bush had commented that Ted looked as if he had lost weight, and Ted had said, "Yeah, I've been out campaigning," to which Bush told him he shouldn't lose any more weight. Ted had spent the year reviling Bush, accusing him of lies, accusing him of concocting data to justify war, accusing him of ascribing threats to intelligence reports that those reports didn't contain. "Iraq. Jobs. Medicare. Schools," he had said at the Center for American Progress the previous April. "Issue after issue. Mislead. Deceive. Make up the needed facts. Smear the character of any critic." Bush campaign spokesman Steve Schmidt answered him then by calling Ted "Kerry's lead hatchet man."

But Ted, who could certainly be a hatchet man when it suited him, was not engaging in the typical and reflexive barb-throwing that marked campaign combat. Nor was he attacking Bush out of the personal betrayal he felt on NCLB, the Medicare drug benefit, and the Iraq War. His anger at the president went deeper. It went to the very essence of how he viewed the political system and political ethics. Because of what he considered George W. Bush's mortal threats to political comity, including his threat to trust, he saw the campaign as a matter of political survival, which was why he had become more involved in Kerry's election than in any other presidential campaign save his brothers' and his own. The "most important election of my lifetime," Ted called it, and Patrick told Mark Leibovich of his father's commitment to Kerry, "This is like oxygen for him." He conferred with Kerry frequently. He invited labor leaders to his home to meet Kerry over dinner. He offered to fundraise for Kerry, and he arrived unannounced at a Kerry gathering, delivering what a reporter called a "stem-winder while perspiring." He advised Kerry. "Above and beyond what I would have ever expected," Kerry said. "Impossible to quantify," he said of Ted's assistance, and called him "one of the smartest strategists

I've ever been around and one of the smartest hands there is at actually getting things done." By one account, it was Ted who encouraged Kerry to select John Edwards as his running mate.

So when Ted took the convention stage at 8:05 at the Fleet Center on July 27, the second day of the conclave, before a roaring crowd that included ninety members of the Kennedy family, he was not in his usual festive, jocular convention mood. Earlier that day, at Harvard Square, Ted had called Bush's decision to invade Iraq the "greatest fall from grace, the greatest blunder, in American foreign policy." Now he delivered a scorching speech, a "fiery attack," *The New York Times* called it, a speech with little of Ted's usual levity. He compared Bush to King George III and said that like King George, who was turned out by the American colonists, George W. Bush needed to be turned out and could be, but only "if we all work together, only if we all reach out together, only if we all come together for the common good." He had seen many elections, he told the delegates. But "never before have I seen a contrast so sharp or consequences so profound as in the choice we will make for president in 2004. So much of the progress we have achieved has been turned back. So much of the goodwill America once enjoyed in the world has been lost. But we are a hopeful nation, and our values and our optimism are still burning bright." And Ted said that while America was a covenant, George W. Bush and the Republicans had broken that covenant with their political enmity. "In our own time, there are those who seek to divide us. One community against another. Urban against rural. City against suburb. Whites against blacks. Men against women. Straights against gays. Americans against Americans. In these challenging times for our country, in these fateful times for the world, America needs a genuine leader—not a divider who only claims to be a uniter." Fixing on what he saw as the Republicans' obsession with political power and their belief that politics was a zero-sum game, he said, "We have seen how they rule—they divide and try to conquer. They know the power of the people is weakened when our house is divided. They believe they can't win, unless the rest of us lose. We reject that shameful view."

But within the very real anger that Ted displayed, the very real hostility he felt toward an administration that he believed had no scruples, there was another unmistakable element to the speech—a poignant subtext. The *Times* called it a "near farewell," and Ted himself alluded to it when he said jokingly of his upcoming reelection in 2006 that he intended to stay in the Senate "until I get the hang of it." Some felt that he wouldn't be standing for reelection two years hence, when he would be seventy-four, that this appearance was a last performance. In an editorial on his speech, *The Boston Globe* cited Ted's call for unity—"All of us are connected. Our fates are intertwined"—but also noted that Ted was now "passing the torch" to John Kerry and saw in that the end of an era. And there was more poignance, albeit within a celebration, when Ted left the Fleet Center directly after his address for a tribute at Boston's Symphony Hall before two thousand friends and supporters, and the Boston Pops, cellist Yo-Yo Ma and Bono of U2 performing—a "celebration of all the things he's meant for the party and country," his former administrative assistant Dave Burke, who was organizing it, called it. Ted, having donned a white jacket handed him by the actor and fellow Bostonian Ben Affleck, conducted the Pops in John Philip Sousa's "The Stars and Stripes Forever," "going bananas," by one account, to urge the trombones to go louder, and turning to the audience at the end and smiling broadly. And later he came back to the stage to sing "Sweet Adeline," with a barbershop quartet from New Hampshire, which took him back to the days when he accompanied his grandfather, Honey Fitz, on his rounds of Boston—took him back to his political beginnings, as he neared what most believed would be his political curtain call.

It was to be another brutal campaign. Ted had warned Kerry not to vote for the war authorization in 2002 when Kerry was torn about it. "I think you vote the substance, then the politics of it," Ted would later say of his advice to Kerry, and the substance, Ted had felt, was that the war was wrong. And even politically, Ted had surmised that if Kerry voted to authorize the war and it went well, he wouldn't harvest any credit, but if he voted against it, and it went poorly—as Ted ultimately felt it had—he would harvest that credit. But Kerry had played politics with the war, had voted, along with nearly every other senator, to give Bush war authority, and when the war went south, when Americans were not greeted as liberators, as Ted had predicted they would not be, when casualties rose—849 Americans dead in 2004—when reports of human rights violations by American soldiers and CIA officers against detainees at the Abu Ghraib prison facility headlined the news that April, when chaos descended on Iraq, when the price tag for the operation continued to rise, and when the war seemed to have no end in sight, Kerry was caught in the accusation that he had "flip-flopped" on the war, supporting the authorization before turning on it by voting against increased funding. Meanwhile a group of conservative Republicans who called themselves the Swift Boat Veterans for Truth took dead aim at one of Kerry's perceived assets, his résumé as a decorated war hero in Vietnam, by producing a series of television commercials that attacked Kerry for turning on the Vietnam War and testifying in Congress against it back in 1971, and they challenged accounts of his service as a Swift Boat commander in Vietnam for which he had won a Purple Heart and Silver Star. As Kerry would later describe the assault on him, "Money, lies and television—and more money—are a toxic combination." Because Kerry had agreed to use public funding for his campaign and had tapped those funds during his primary efforts and consequently would have to hold funds in reserve for the general election, he didn't have the resources to mount a counterattack. Nor did he prepare a big speech to rebut the charges. He recalled Ted's advice to him on an earlier occasion when he was under attack, "If you're explaining, you're losing." So the attacks largely went unanswered, and the damage was done, and it was severe. And yet again the Republicans deployed one of their most effective tactics, one that incorporated Ted, who had campaigned vigorously for Kerry, by pasting the now-pernicious label of "liberal" on Kerry and his fellow Democrats, which was largely a code word for being sensitive to minorities and the poor and out of touch with conservative sensibilities, namely using government to help those in need and preferring diplomacy to military action. When the *National Journal* rated Kerry as more liberal than Ted himself—in large part, the *Journal* admitted, because Kerry had missed a number of votes while campaigning—Bush cracked that Ted was now the "conservative senator from Massachusetts," which was intended as another jab at Kerry. "The label is a badge of honor," Ted riposted. "In this election, liberals stand for a safer America, more jobs, better schools, and affordable health care for all our people. Republicans can't compete with that." But this was a status quo election—an election against change. Kerry, a Catholic, didn't even carry the Catholic vote, in part because Bishop Raymond Leo Burke of St. Louis had announced that Kerry could not receive communion in his diocese because Kerry supported a woman's right to choose to have an abortion, which triggered other conservative clerics to oppose his candidacy and the media to attend every Mass that Kerry attended to see if he would be allowed to receive communion. Kerry called it the "wafer watch." (Ted faced a similar backlash and a threat of being denied communion, which infuriated Vicki, and which forced Ted to find churches that would be willing to grant him communion.)

Still, polls predicted a close election, surprising for a contest in which there was a wartime president who kept invoking American security. When Ted voted at Hyannis the morning of election day, he said he had a sense that the "momentum was with John." He and Vicki took a sail afterward, then drove to Providence to see Patrick, and then went on to Boston where they watched returns at their pied-à-terre on Marlborough Street surrounded by a coterie of aides and friends with what Ted said was growing confidence. When former Clinton campaign adviser James Carville came on television and said that Kerry had to carry Ohio to win, Ted phoned a political friend there, Tim Hagan, who assured him that it was looking good. But as Bush began accumulating states and electoral votes, Ted made another call to Hagan, and this time his prognosis was less optimistic. "I think we've lost it," he said. When their guests left, Ted suggested to Vicki that they visit the Kerrys at their Louisburg Square apartment. By Kerry's own account, he awakened early that morning and, before a small group in his kitchen, a group that included Ted and Vicki, placed a call to his lawyers on the ground in Ohio where there had been long lines in Black precincts and where thunderstorms threatened to hold down turnout. In Ted's account, he and Vicki arrived at two-thirty a.m., and the Kerrys' assistant woke the candidate and his wife Theresa because she said that Kerry would be upset if he knew Ted and Vicki had come to see him and he hadn't greeted them, and Kerry lamented to Ted, "There are so many things I wanted to do for this country."

Ted too was devastated. The "most important election," he had called it—the election, he hoped, that could end the tragic war that he said had been "cooked up" in Texas, and the election that he hoped could restore a sense of unity and civility to the country. Now he knew the war would continue and, with it, the bloodshed. Now he knew the divisions he thought Bush had intentionally exploited would remain. And now he knew his dreams for what he considered a better, kinder, more just America would further recede until they threatened to disappear altogether.

TWENTY-TWO

"The Moral Challenge of Doing the Right Thing"

D EMOCRATS HAD BECOME accustomed to postmortems, to self-reflection, to soul-searching and ultimately breast-beating and hand-wringing, and they were doing so again, even though theirs had not been a landslide defeat. George W. Bush won with a bare majority, 50.7 percent of the vote, and 286 electoral votes, just sixteen over the minimum. Had Kerry taken Ohio, which he lost by 118,000 votes, he would have been president, which was why the Ohio ballots had been watched so closely that night and why Democrats bemoaned the dearth of voting machines in minority areas in that state. "I was furious about the voting system," John Kerry would later write of the Ohio situation, "the extraordinary discrepancy between the ease of Republicans voting and the purposeful hurdles placed in front of Democrats by a partisan secretary of state." In the Senate, the Republicans had a net gain of four seats, and among the casualties was Democratic minority leader Tom Daschle of South Dakota, now a reliable Republican state; in the House the gain was three. There was no gain among governorships. All of which indicated what the polls themselves had indicated: that, for all the ongoing talk about how conservative Americans had become, Bush had no more completed the Reagan Revolution than Gingrich had, and the country was now essentially divided equally between Democrats and Republicans. As for the meaning of the election results, the outcome seemed to have turned on the war and the idea that a nation did not abandon its commander in chief when its soldiers were in combat, even if the commander in chief had chosen no good reason to place them in harm's way, as Ted Kennedy believed George W. Bush had done. Bush's campaign advisers had emphasized this to him: If it's about national security, we win.

But many Democrats, and many pundits, did not see it that way. They blamed the Republicans' superior ability to get out the vote, as abetted by the National Rifle Association and evangelicals. They blamed the Democrats' inability to frame an antiterrorism policy. They blamed a cultural shift that some felt had made the country more conservative, despite the closeness of the election—something Democrats themselves had been saying since at least Ronald Reagan's presidency. And they blamed the Democrats' having ceded moral issues to the Republicans—not the moral issues in which Democrats believed, helping those in need, but the moral issues that Republicans had long emphasized, punishing those who transgressed traditional moral values and punishing those who had been left behind by the American system because their personal values were deemed wanting. As the theologian and religious activist Jim Wallis would put it, after the election Democrats were accused of losing the "moral values voters" in the country and of being the party of "secularists" hostile to faith and religion—a charge that had been leveled against Democrats at least since Newt Gingrich. Ted took this analysis seriously—took it seriously because he had based his political career on moral values and clearly felt that political morality was more than a matter of winning elections, though that was certainly important; it was a matter of restoring the nation's soul, as Bobby had wanted to do. Wallis, who had not taken any active role in the election, said that in that electoral aftermath of defeat and despondency, the very first Democrat to phone him was Ted Kennedy, who invited Wallis to his Kalorama home to discuss how to change the moral debate that the Republicans had been winning. That night Ted, Vicki, and Wallis talked for about ninety minutes—a "very thoughtful conversation," Wallis later called it, "about the relationship between faith, morality, and politics," not a partisan discussion, he said, about how the Democrats could win back those so-called "moral values voters," but a discussion of how the nation could confront the great moral issues that faced it. And Wallis said something that would not often be said of Ted, despite his deep religiosity, or of Vicki: "Their own deep Catholic faith was evident and their articulation of it very impressive."

Ted did not spend the postelection period in despair. He thought about how to actualize those moral values about which he and Jim Wallis had spoken. Peter Edelman, Bobby's old aide and the husband of the activist Marian Wright Edelman, recalled being asked by Ted to the office that December, before the new Congress was seated, to discuss how Ted might

tackle poverty. The Russell Office Building was deserted, save for Ted, Edelman, and a few of Ted's staffers. And he and Ted spent the next two hours
on that cold, gray winter day wrestling with the issue. "He pushed back,
probed, asked question after question," Edelman remembered. And just
before Christmas that month, while Ted was pondering policies to help the
helpless, he visited with wounded soldiers, casualties of the Iraq War, at
the Walter Reed Army Medical Center—another reminder of the human
cost of the administration's failures and of its political ruthlessness.

There was a lot to push back against. Bush began the new year push-
ing for personal savings accounts to replace parts of Social Security—
analogous to Republican attempts for MSAs to replace Medicare. Or as
journalist Robert Draper put it plainly, "privatizing social security." When
Montana Democrat Max Baucus, whom Bush had invited to the White
House to discuss the new effort, balked, then told Chief of Staff Andrew
Card that he couldn't sell privatization to his caucus, Card was dismissive.
"This is where we're going," Card said peremptorily. And as Draper would
describe Card's thinking, "He figured they didn't need Baucus anyway. No
Child Left Behind, tax cuts, the Patriot Act, Homeland Security, authorization to invade Iraq, Medicare prescription drugs, supplemental war
funding—the White House had always gotten what it wanted. And that
was before November 2004." Before November 2004, George W. Bush had
felt the need to present himself as cordial, amenable, a uniter. Now he
didn't. The postelection Bush had shed the mask. He was arrogant, smug,
and boastful—daring the Democrats to oppose him. "I've got political capital," he said chippily, ignoring the closeness of the election, particularly
close for an incumbent. "And I intend to spend it."

And it didn't end there. In January, Bush asked Congress to cap malpractice awards, a longtime Republican goal and one that put him
squarely at odds with Ted Kennedy, who called the proposal "nothing but
a shameful shield for drug companies and HMOs who hurt people through
negligence." And when Bush submitted his new budget of $2.6 trillion, it
contained the largest cuts for social programs since Ronald Reagan's
budgets—slashing one percent in all domestic programs not related to
national security, with the Iraq War adduced as the reason—though not
even Reagan had wielded an ax with that severity. It was conservatism finally untethered from basic moral values. When Ted delivered his annual
address before the National Press Club, he decided to fasten on the values
he had discussed in that conversation with Jim Wallis. Ted had told Wallis

that "faith guides and sustains me," but that he had perhaps been loath to discuss it for fear, as Wallis said Ted put it, of being "sectarian." Now, at a moment when he was concerned that moral values had been co-opted and things in which he believed were being discarded, he thought he might have to be more "explicit" about his own religious and moral values. And Ted had consulted, too, with George Lakoff, a linguist and cognitive scientist at the University of California, Berkeley, who had insisted that it wasn't enough to be right on the issues—one had to frame the issues in such a way as to tap the psychological and emotional depths in people. In his previous annual agenda-setting speeches, Ted had usually provided a list of initiatives he hoped to advance, and he did so again in his National Press Club address: Medicare for all, paid sick leave, guaranteed college education for those finishing high school. But this time Ted, melding Wallis and Lakoff, sought something deeper—not just a list, but an appeal to the political morality on which he believed liberalism was predicated. "No doubt, we must do a better job of looking within ourselves and speaking out for the principles we believe in and for the values that are the foundation," he said. "America needs to hear more, not less, about those values." And he said that had been one of the failings of liberals—not addressing the moral authority that underlay liberalism. "We were remiss in not talking about them more directly, about the fundamental ideals that guide the progressive policy, and then pointing out that, unlike the Republicans, we believe our values unite instead of divide." He offered a "progressive vision—a vision rooted in our basic values of opportunity, fairness, tolerance and respect for each other, the north star of the Democratic Party, fairness and justice." He spoke of "deep conscience," and about how liberals had to fight for this vision—a "vision not just of the country we can become, but of the country we *must* become, an America that embraces the values and aspirations of our people now and for coming generations." In an interview with *Boston Globe* reporter Eileen McNamara a few days later, he regretted the Democrats' past reticence to speak out for moral values of "equal opportunity and social justice," of their occupying "some tepid middle ground," and thought that if they had been more forceful in asserting their moral values, they would have won the debate. He told McNamara of a recent visit to Wisconsin to see his sister Rosemary shortly before her death that January and how a nun there told him of a meeting to oppose the nomination of Bush's White House counsel, Alberto Gonzales, as attorney general, from which Ted deduced that there is a "lot of energy there we need to tap into"—obviously moral energy to challenge the political energy of George W. Bush. Now he had to tap that moral energy himself.

When Ted Kennedy spoke of asserting moral values, he was speaking of values of opportunity and justice. But one large issue continued to loom over everything: the Iraq War. The war had sapped the treasury, cost thousands of American lives and tens of thousands of Iraqi lives, had thrown the Middle East into chaos, had divided America, and had done more: Like the Vietnam War, it had corroded the country's own moral values, beginning with preemptive warfare and continuing with the administration's sanction of torture against detainees in contravention of the Geneva Conventions on the treatment of prisoners of war. And there was still, two years later, no end in sight. That February 55 percent of Americans, by the Pew Research poll, still felt that our troops should stay in Iraq until the situation had stabilized. Ted was not among them. His staff, which had been reticent, was already pressuring him now to step up his opposition to the war. Michael Myers said that it was he who convinced Ted to take the dramatic step of discussing withdrawal. In January, a day after thirty-seven Americans had been killed in Iraq, in a speech before the Johns Hopkins School of Advanced International Studies, where he had first expressed his opposition to the war, Ted did. Comparing Iraq once again to Vietnam and noting that the number of troops in Iraq at the time was equivalent to the number of troops in Vietnam in 1965, he announced, "We need a political military strategy that gets us out of this country, where they take responsibility for their own future. We broke it, but they have to fix it." And he said that the United States should suggest a timeframe for withdrawal, roughly eighteen months hence. He made the argument again ten days later on *Meet the Press*, asking, "Why can't we expect that we can train their troops in four months, eight months, twelve months, fifteen months?" and asking, too, "Why can't they defend their own country?" "The Senate went crazy," Ted's senior national security adviser, Sharon Waxman, said of the reaction to the speech. She said she was receiving phone calls from staffers of other senators terrified that Ted might submit a resolution forcing them to vote on withdrawal. Waxman said she advised Ted to draft the resolution in such a way as to give them a way out. But Ted was adamant. He didn't want to give them a way out. It was no time for trimming.

But as Ted was calling for withdrawal—again, a largely lone voice—there was another concern. Waxman said that near the beginning of the war, she met a government official at a coffee shop who had just returned from Iraq, and he told her that while the administration had rushed to war, it had no plan there. Puzzled, Waxman asked him, "What do you mean by that?" The official said plainly, "There are no documents, there's no strategy, there's no one in charge, there's no clear direction." And when she asked to see an organizational and planning chart, he took out a napkin and drew a sketch, and Waxman recalled, "It was nothing." Now, in the spring of 2005, two years into the war, she said that Ted waited for the administration to present a postwar reconstruction plan. And when they finally submitted one, again, there was nothing—just five or six pages—what Waxman called a "power point essentially": "Begin military operations. Begin reconstruction. Continue reconstruction." Ted was incensed. Speaking to a member of the Black Caucus, he threw the plan into the air so that the pages fluttered to the floor and said it wasn't worth the paper it was written on. So on his own volition, Ted went to the RAND Corporation, the strategic global think tank, to ask researchers there if they would undertake a comprehensive withdrawal plan and a postwar reconstruction plan, and when they agreed to do so if Ted could get them the funding to finance the research, Ted did. Basically, he was doing what he felt the Bush administration should have done before it even invaded Iraq. But even as public opinion began to turn against the war that summer, most Democrats were wary of criticizing the administration, including Hillary Clinton, Joe Biden, and the new Senate Democratic leader, Harry Reid of Nevada—wary that they would seem to be contradicting the commander in chief and being labeled unpatriotic. Meanwhile Bush's favorability numbers, though sinking steadily through 2005 and hitting 40 percent that summer, were still higher than that of congressional Democrats.

And the war continued with no clear objective or plan.

II

It was not much better on the domestic front. Bush had begun the year with his announcement that he would introduce those private savings accounts that would essentially compete with Social Security, and he made it his chief policy initiative of 2005. He insisted, as Republicans often did, that the Social Security trust fund system would soon go bank-rupt—it wouldn't—and that his pet private accounts, which allowed indi-viduals to invest their Social Security benefits in the stock market, could save it, and he waved off warnings that Social Security, along with Medi-care, was the "third rail" of politics and that anyone who touched it was likely to be electrocuted. Bush, however, was a dedicated conservative, and in practice that meant what it had long meant for conservatives: un-doing the New Deal. What better way to undo the New Deal than to undo Social Security, which was the very foundation of the New Deal welfare state and government activism? In all this, Bush was encouraged by his political adviser, Karl Rove. And Bush was not only determined to under-mine Social Security in the guise of saving it. He was determined to do it quickly, complaining that his tax cuts and No Child Left Behind had taken too long because he had followed the niceties of legislative cooperation. Now that he was reelected, the new unleashed Bush felt he didn't have to respect those niceties—the very basis on which the Senate operated. He had no interest in securing Democratic participation. As it turned out, Democrats themselves had little interest in participating, seeing the effort for what it was. Democrats, even the moderates, might have cowered in the past over Bush's initiatives, but they were not about to let Social Secu-rity be privatized. They argued that it was an *insurance* system to help se-nior citizens, not an *investment* system that would put their money at risk if the markets fell. And seniors themselves were concerned. Bush took off on a sixty-day speaking tour to sell his so-called reform. But as Robert Draper would put it, when Bush was finished, "his Social Security initia-tive was less popular than when he had begun." And Draper added, "Bush himself was less popular as well." In his seeming postelection arrogance, he had thrown Democrats a lifeline. They grabbed it. And Bush's top leg-islative priority foundered.

But Democrats had not blunted the threats of the newly emboldened and newly defiant George W. Bush. That summer, there arose a new one. Su-preme Court justice Sandra Day O'Connor, whom Ronald Reagan had ap-pointed, announced her retirement, creating the first Court vacancy since 1994. That July, Bush appointed District of Columbia Circuit Court judge John Roberts, Jr., who had a long pedigree as a Republican official, includ-ing serving as deputy solicitor general in the George H. W. Bush adminis-tration, as O'Connor's replacement. (Roberts's appointment to the circuit court had been stalled by Democrats in opposition.) When Chief Justice William Rehnquist, for whom Roberts had once clerked, died early in September, Bush now nominated him to be Rehnquist's replacement. Much to the conservatives' consternation, the Court had long been one of the primary engines of social change—something they had worked to alter, though not always successfully. They looked for young appointees, who would hold their seats for decades, and for demonstrably conservative appointees, who had been vetted by the Federalist Society, a legal group dedicated to de-liberalizing the courts. Ted, even as he had been excoriated by conservatives for having torpedoed Robert Bork's nomination, continued to work hard to protect the bench from those he saw as right-wing extremists. He called Bush's federal court nominees "Neanderthals" and led filibusters against the most conservative of them, though it still amounted to only six of Bush's 172 appointments at the time. He led the charge against the nomination of Charles W. Pickering to the Fifth Circuit Court of Appeals, a man whose record on racial issues had gained the attention and earned the scorn of civil rights groups. Bush appointed him to the bench twice, and both times he faced a filibuster, and then he gave him a recess appointment, before Pickering finally decided to withdraw his name when his recess appointment ended.* In another instance, Ted wrote an op-ed in *The Washington Post* against William Haynes, a nominee to the Fourth Circuit Court of Appeals, who had been the general counsel for the Defense Department where he had advocated denying captives in the war on terror the status of "prisoners of war," which would have qualified them for protections under the Geneva Conventions; planned military tribunals for the accused rather than submit them to civil justice; and called for the imprisonment of American citizens without judicial review. "Nominations do not get much worse than this," Ted wrote. Ted didn't see his opposition as essentially political. He saw it as the antithesis of political—that it was the Republicans who were politicizing the courts, especially on civil rights cases, and that they were relying not on legal precedent to make their determinations but on partisan advan-

*Ted worked closely, as he had in the past, with liberal advocacy groups. Memos from 2001 to 2003 showed that Ted's staffers were in contact with those groups, discussing filibusters. One memo, from Elaine Jones of the NAACP Legal Defense and Education Fund, asked the Judiciary Committee to postpone consideration of any nominees to the Sixth Circuit until the Supreme Court had rendered its decision on a case on affirmative action concerning the University of Michigan. "Judge Feud Turns to Memos," *BG*, Jan. 4, 2004.

tage, and he complained that on issue after issue, "It isn't the career jurists who are making the judgments; it's the political operatives in the
Justice Department" who were then being upheld by Republican-
appointed justices. He believed deeply that the moral values he had promoted and that had been memorialized in law—progressive law—were
not a matter of politics. They were woven into the essence of America.
"The idea that we want to go back and re-fight these battles—getting a
minimum wage or helping disabled people—is a failure to understand
what this country is about," he would say of his opposition to Bush's
nominees. "You could say that America is a living force more than a land.
It's an idea, a continuum, and you either understand that or you don't."

Yet Ted was being disingenuous. The issues were certainly entangled
in values—conservatives had very different values, especially when it
came to minority rights, than liberals had—but the issues were political
as well, which was why the fights over judicial nominations became so
vitriolic. There was so much at stake—namely, the entire direction of the
country. The Court, Ted would say, had, under a conservative majority,
"undermined the work of a generation in our committee," meaning the
Judiciary Committee. The only weapon the Democratic minority had to
halt appointments was the filibuster, which they had used sparingly but to
good effect. The Republicans, however, had a weapon of their own: that
so-called "nuclear option," which Trent Lott had threatened to use
earlier—excluding judicial nominees from the filibuster by subjecting
them to a majority vote only—a rule change they could inflict by a majority vote. Republicans knew how titanic a change this would be for the Senate, and they knew too that it could come back to haunt them when
Democrats regained the majority, as they inevitably would, and could
confirm their own nominees. To avoid the catastrophe, a group of seven
Republicans and seven Democrats reached an informal agreement—
"fragile" was how *The New York Times* described it—that Democrats would
deploy the filibuster only in "extraordinary" circumstances and hold their
fire if the Republicans would forgo the nuclear option. Jeffrey Blattner,
Ted's former Judiciary aide, called the deal an "abdication," though he
said he had warned Ted that using the filibuster excessively could have
negative consequences, even as he conceded that there were instances,
like the Bork nomination, where one had to set the terms of the debate at
the very outset. Ted nevertheless agreed with the Democratic leadership

to support the agreement, saying that the disputes over judicial nominees had become a "distraction" and had held up Senate business.

None of that applied, however, to John Roberts, the nominee for chief justice. A year earlier, amid all the discussion of a nuclear option, Ted had been concerned about what a Supreme Court nomination might portend for the Senate. Hoping to head off a senatorial bloodbath, he called Senator John Danforth—who later left the Senate to become United Nations ambassador—telling Danforth, who was highly respected among his colleagues, that he expected a "big blowup" and asked Danforth, a Republican, if he had any ideas on how to avoid that. Danforth, in what amounted to an admission that Supreme Court nominations were now hopelessly politicized, said he didn't. So Ted braced for the blowup, even as Minority Leader Harry Reid, anticipating a possible vacancy, with Rehnquist suffering from cancer, asked Ted to head up research into potential Supreme Court nominees. The product of that research was, like so much that Ted Kennedy did, deliberate and detailed. In February—with his former communications director Stephanie Cutter, who had served in the same capacity for John Kerry's presidential campaign, returning to manage the Supreme Court operation—he assigned twenty of his staffers to scrutinize the biographies, speeches, and writings of probable Bush nominees, which he compiled into two dozen three-ring binders. He discussed strategy with liberal advocacy groups. He read debates from the Constitutional Convention to his fellow Democratic senators. And he invited the biographer Robert Caro to inform those members of the duties of the Senate when it came to judicial confirmation.

The Senate had historically been timid when it came to rejecting Supreme Court nominees, and it was Ted who in the past had helped stiffen his colleagues' spines, orchestrating opposition to Nixon appointees Clement Haynsworth and G. Harrold Carswell and particularly to Reagan appointee Robert Bork, though Ted often voted against even the less contentious nominees of Republican presidents, like David Souter, believing, as he did, that those nominees were more likely to be ideologues and partisans than fair legal scholars. The Senate, he had always insisted, had not only a right but also an obligation *not* to rubber-stamp presidential nominees, and in setting standards for his own decision on whether to confirm, he appealed to the old liberal consensus of the 1960s, when Republicans and Democrats more or less agreed on ends if not means, and he invoked the notion that a Supreme Court justice should unite the country rather than divide it. "The American people deserve to know whether nominees would roll back civil rights laws or uphold the rights of the disabled, the elderly and minorities," he declared after Roberts's nomination. "The American people are entitled to know if a nominee respects women's rights to equal treatment in our society and to privacy in making reproductive decisions." Ted had told reporters in his hideaway that he and the White House had discussed possible nominees who were centrist in their approach. Roberts, he felt, was not one of them. But neither was Roberts a Robert Bork or an Antonin Scalia. Those Republican nominees had clearly not defended civil rights or the rights of the disabled or the right of a woman to have an abortion. John Roberts was a more enigmatic nominee. Young at fifty, attractive, extremely smart, affable, and agreeable, the very personification of the rich Ivy League conservative elitist, he insisted that he was no ideologue, just a legal umpire who called balls and strikes, though Ted expressed "real and serious reasons to be deeply concerned" about his record, and opened his questioning at Roberts's confirmation hearing, just a month after Hurricane Katrina devastated New Orleans, with his main interest: "Today we want to find out how you view the Constitution and our ability to protect the most vulnerable. Do you believe that Congress has the power to pass laws aimed at eliminating discrimination in our society, or do you believe that our hands are tied, that the elected representatives of the people of the United States are without the power to pass laws aimed at righting wrongs, ending injustice, eliminating the inequalities that we have just witnessed so dramatically and tragically in New Orleans? The American people want to know where you stand." And Ted began walking Roberts through each piece of major civil rights legislation, then asking if Roberts believed in its constitutionality, pausing at length on the Voting Rights Act of 1965, Roberts's view of which, during a time when he was working for the Reagan administration, Ted said he found "narrow and cramped, and perhaps even meanspirited." Roberts denied it and said the argument at the time was whether intent or effects should govern the application of the law. (Ted had been one of the strongest advocates for effects, Roberts an advocate—Ted would call him an "architect"—for intent.) Ted asked if Roberts recanted his memos for the Reagan administration expressing antipathy for affirmative action. Roberts said he had a distaste for quotas but not for affirmative action itself. Ted asked if Roberts was still willing to allow colleges to accept federal aid if they discriminated against women. Roberts asserted that he had never felt that way and that Ted had distorted his position. In the end, Roberts kept his composure and was confirmed easily, 78 to 22, with Ted among those in opposition.

But George W. Bush's remaking of the Supreme Court had just begun. Since Roberts had originally been nominated to replace Sandra Day O'Connor before Chief Justice Rehnquist's death prompted Bush to pull that nomination and resubmit him to replace Rehnquist, there was still O'Connor's vacancy to fill. In nominating Roberts, *New York Times* correspondent Peter Baker would write, Bush, who saw his own Iraq War as a way to erase his father's unwillingness to oust Saddam Hussein during the Iraq War of 1991, and his tax cuts as a corrective for the tax increases that his father instituted to lower the deficit, was now performing another act of filial erasure. He was "exorcising the ghost of the David Souter nomination"—the alleged conservative who turned out to be a liberal. And when Bush ran into Representative Trent Franks, to whom he had promised during the Medicare drug benefit roll call that he would nominate judges who opposed *Roe v. Wade* in exchange for Franks's vote, and Franks said he had liked the Roberts selection, Bush told him, "Well, I am just getting started."

He was. For O'Connor's seat, Bush first tapped his White House counsel and a longtime associate from Texas, Harriet Miers, in large part because Laura Bush had impressed upon him the need to appoint a woman. But almost immediately Miers faced a series of land mines, primarily from conservatives who feared that she might be insufficiently conservative, and from others who thought her ill-prepared to sit on the court. Eventually, on the eve of her hearings and under enormous pressure, she asked the president to withdraw her nomination lest she embarrass him. Relieved, Bush now tapped Samuel Alito, like Roberts a justice of the court of appeals, in Alito's case, the Third District. But that was where the similarity ended. Ted had waffled on Roberts. His aide Melody Barnes said that he didn't make a final decision on him until he took a "hard look" at his record, though Ted, in truth, seems to have made up his mind fairly early. Roberts was cautious, cool, seemingly reasonable—a closet ideologue. Alito was something else. Armed with the threat of the nuclear option, Bush seemed to feel that he could nominate someone whom Ted at least perceived as a right-wing judicial extremist and a member of the Federalist Society. Ordinarily, Democrats would have been outraged by the Alito

nomination. But by this time, the Democratic caucus seemed fatigued—
too tired to rouse itself to oppose Alito strenuously and too fearful of Republican retaliation if they did so. Not Ted Kennedy. Ted was adamantly
opposed to him. Even before Alito's confirmation hearing that January,
Ted wrote an op-ed for *The Washington Post* titled "Alito's Credibility Problem," in which he cited Alito's statement, when seeking a job from Reagan attorney general Edwin Meese, that his legal philosophy was shaped
by "deep disagreement with the Warren Court decisions," those liberal
decisions that Ted thought had moved the country forward; Alito's objection to "usurpation by the judiciary" of executive power; his membership
in the Concerned Alumni of Princeton, Alito's alma mater, which was
dedicated, Ted believed, to decreasing the number of women and minorities at the university (a membership, Ted wrote, Alito failed to recall during his confirmation hearings for the Third Circuit and which, Ted would
later say, had been mysteriously expunged from Alito's record); his failure
to recuse himself from cases that involved a company in which he held
mutual funds; and his declaration before the Federalist Society that he
believed in what was known as a "unitary executive," meaning an executive basically unrestrained by legislative or judicial checks. An "all-
powerful presidency," Ted called Alito's position, which was a popular
conservative position, during the hearings, when Ted asked him if he
thought the president would have to abide by an antitorture law initiated
by Senator John McCain, a former prisoner of war, were it to pass.

Ted understood that stopping Alito's ascension to the Court would be
difficult. There was no grassroots groundswell as there had been against
Robert Bork. Moreover, the nomination had been sent to the floor by the
Judiciary Committee on a straight party vote, the first since Louis Brandeis
faced the Senate in 1916, and Republicans had fifty-five votes in the Senate, not one of which was likely to go against Alito. The only alternative
was a filibuster, and Harry Reid was opposed to one. Ted said he didn't
care. At the end of the hearings, he had gone up to Boston to give a speech
at Faneuil Hall and was greeted with a standing ovation, he said, when he
broached the idea of a filibuster. He knew times had changed since Bork.
"I had difficulty understanding whether people were really involved in
this battle," he would later say. Now he knew. When he returned to Washington, he told the Democratic caucus—"strongly," Ted admitted—that
he was now prepared to filibuster and asked if there were any among
them who wanted to join him. John Kerry said he was willing to do so,

then huddled with Reid after lunch, and then met again with Ted late that day, only this time he asked, "Is this really the best [thing to do]?" Ted brushed aside Kerry's vacillation. He was going to filibuster no matter what. (Ted said that Kerry then headed off to the Davos World Economic Forum meeting in Switzerland and announced that he would now *lead* the filibuster.) Meanwhile Ted met with Reid the next day, a Friday, to tell him his plan to filibuster Alito's confirmation. Reid reluctantly agreed, but not before reaching an accommodation with the Republicans: They would allow a cloture vote on Monday after Ted had made his argument against Alito, and if he didn't get cloture, which required sixty votes, the nomination would be voted on the following day, Tuesday. Ted tried to "build the case" that weekend, as he put it—build it to save the Court from right-wing ideologues. He manned the phones, calling colleagues, urging them to vote against Alito. He rallied nearly half the caucus, but Reid, he said, was concerned that Ted might convince enough senators to embarrass Reid after his deal with the majority. Reid needn't have worried. It was a sign of the new times that Ted couldn't muster the numbers, and the filibuster effort failed. Cloture was invoked 72 to 25, and Alito was confirmed the next day, 58 to 42, the closest vote since Clarence Thomas's narrow confirmation.

For Ted Kennedy, the defeat was a galling one personally, a painful demonstration of how impotent the Democrats had become in the face of an especially uncompromising conservative intransigence, and a difficult one politically, given that he knew the new Court would redraw the lines of civic discourse. The Court would now lurch even further rightward. Sandra Day O'Connor had been a moderate conservative. Alito would be a rabid one. And John Roberts, for all his professions of commitment to precedent and to civil rights generally and the Voting Rights Act specifically, would later vote to gut Section Five of the Voting Rights Act, which had required certain jurisdictions to gain federal approval for any voting change lest the change be deemed discriminatory. Again, Ted would lament not so much the conservative direction of the Court, though that certainly distressed him, as something else he had deeply feared when he had pondered the possibility of Bush's appointments: the extreme politicization of the Court. The Court was now dominated, he would remark ruefully, by "people who have been in the political operation of the Republican machine." The recent justices, Rehnquist, Antonin Scalia, Clarence Thomas, and even O'Connor, had worked in Republican administrations, doing what Ted felt was political bidding, and the newer justices, Roberts and Alito, had both been, in his view, Republican functionaries and had "strong ties" to the Republicans. There was, he believed, no longer the pretense of the Court as a legal institution. It was now, he felt, just another arm of a political party that had little interest in equality or justice or democracy or the interests of anyone who needed the government's help. To him, the Court had lost its moral values, and there was nothing he could do about it.

III

In opposition, sailing against the wind, Ted Kennedy now made little headway. But there was one issue on which he felt he might be able to make common cause with the president, who now disdained bipartisanship and common causes. Karl Rove, George W. Bush's political mastermind, the man whom John Dilulio had called the most important political adviser since the days of Herbert Hoover, had, like so many before him, that goal of creating a permanent, unassailable Republican majority, even as he appreciated the demographic difficulties of achieving it. The Latino vote was growing, and it was going overwhelmingly to the Democrats. Rove recognized that Republicans needed to pry those votes from the opposition and said that doing so was "our mission and our goal." And to achieve that goal, Rove and Bush felt they needed to enact immigration reform. The problem was that congressional Republicans had absolutely no interest in such reform. "Doing something good for someone who has broken the law" was how House majority leader Tom DeLay described any effort at legalization for undocumented immigrants. The Republicans' only interest was in increased border security, which was not a likely road to increasing the Republicans' portion of that Latino vote.

Ted Kennedy had been interested in immigration reform since his early days in the Senate when, to fulfill John Kennedy's dream of loosening immigration restrictions, he sponsored the Immigration and Nationality Act of 1965 that rewrote the exclusionary immigration laws of the 1920s and liberalized immigration to the United States. (Of course, his interest in the inequities of immigration had arisen much earlier, on his trips through Boston with his grandfather, Honey Fitz, when he saw the "No Irish Need Apply" signs.) While it was landmark legislation, many observers, and not only conservatives, felt that this had been one of the great disservices that Ted Kennedy had done to America. Otis Graham, a professor of history at the University of North Carolina–Wilmington, writing in the *Christian Science Monitor,* called it "perhaps the single most nation-changing measure of the era," and that Ted's assurances it would not "upset the ethnic mix of our society," were almost immediately debunked. Four hundred thousand immigrants entered the nation shortly after passage, Graham said. That number doubled by 1980, and these were, he contended, less skilled and educated than previous immigrants, namely those from northern and western Europe who had previously been given priority. And Graham, who called himself a "former" liberal, attributed much of the decline in the support of liberalism to this influx. The journalist Theodore White had made a similar charge, saying the act was "noble" and "revolutionary," but "probably the most thoughtless of the many acts of the Great Society" by conceiving of America as "being open to the world."

Though some of this animosity was a reaction against non-European immigration and sprang from the idea that America should be a largely white Anglo-Saxon country, Ted himself realized that immigration needed to be reformed, both because the number of immigrants entering the country had gotten out of hand and because many of them had entered illegally and had no pathway to citizenship, even if they had resided here for years. Ted bristled at the injustice and inhumanity of that. But instead of comprehensive reform, Congress had acted in a piecemeal fashion: a migrant worker health bill to protect farmworkers from pesticides; a refugee bill in the aftermath of the Vietnam War that led to one million Vietnamese immigrants; a bill that divided refugees from immigrants, giving the former privileges over the latter. Alan Simpson, who headed the Immigration Subcommittee during the years of Republican majority in the Senate, took the lead on immigration reform during the Reagan administration and, along with Democratic representative Romano Mazzoli, pushed the Simpson-Mazzoli Act, which made it a crime to hire illegal immigrants knowingly, but which also provided that any immigrant who had entered this country before January 1, 1982, and had remained here continuously—Ted had earlier proposed and the Judiciary Committee had rejected a bill with the same safeguards for those who had entered the country before January 1, 1977—could stay so long as they paid back taxes and a fine, passed a background check showing that they had not committed crimes, and demonstrated a knowledge of the country. The bill took five years to debate and two years to work its way through Congress—Ted voted against it on the grounds that employer sanctions might harm Hispanic workers—but Ronald Reagan signed it at the Statue of Liberty on November 6, 1986. In effect, Reagan was admitting that amnesty was the price to be paid for fixing a broken immigration system that had allowed millions of undocumented aliens into the country.

But Simpson-Mazzoli did not repair the system. Instead, it exacerbated many of its faults. "Many businesses found it impossible to continue if they no longer had access to illegal immigrants," Carey Parker recalled. "They said, 'It will be a nightmare if you try to shut off the only avenue we have to the workforce we need.'" Almost as a form of penance for the unintended consequences of the Immigration Act of 1965, Ted attempted some fixes of his own, particularly the imbalance that the 1965 law had generated between Asian immigrants, who had risen from 8 percent of the total in 1965 to 45 percent of the total in 1986, and European immigrants, who had declined from 50 percent to 10 percent in that time. To restore balance, in 1988, he sponsored a bill that would prioritize education, mastery of English, and occupational skills, all of which favored Europeans, over the "chain migration"—migration of those with family ties to the United States—that had taken precedence in the 1965 bill. It easily passed the Senate, but it stalled in the House where it was converted into an Irish immigration bill to permit more nurses to enter the country. In June 1989 Ted joined forces with Alan Simpson to make another attempt to reform immigration and increase the number of skilled workers admitted to the country and further redress the imbalance between Asia and Europe "without departing," Ted said, "from any of the basic goals of fairness established in the 1965 reforms." The bill set a limit of 700,000 immigrants for each of the first three years and 675,000 thereafter, which was Simpson's provision, while excluding a provision favoring English-speaking immigrants, at Ted's insistence. A "very good bill," Ted called it, after much negotiating with Simpson, "and it got even better on the floor of the Senate," where provisions to provide amnesty for people seeking asylum were added. It passed the Senate, but Simpson was concerned that the bill would be liberalized by the House. So Ted agreed to "pre-conference" the bill, not allowing any further amendments in the Senate and refusing any alterations in the conference with the House. When they got to the House on the other side of the Capitol, Simpson recalled, Representative Jack Brooks, the chairman of the House Judiciary Committee, was waiting for Ted and Simpson with a cigar in his hand, and sitting there and tapping his cigar, he told Ted, "We're here for you. We're going to help you all we can." And Brooks began going through the bill and stripping out what he considered the more restrictive provisions. "Well, we're not going to have any of that part right there," Brooks, a Texan in the swaggering Lyndon Johnson mold, said, expecting Ted's agreement, but Ted told him that Simpson and he had reached an agreement of their own and that the bill would not be changed. Simpson said Brooks's "jaw flew open" in apparent astonishment. Long sessions followed in the Capitol with the House conferees, and "it looked like the legislation was going to fall apart," Simpson said. But he and Ted kept their pact, and the bill finally passed and was signed by George H. W. Bush. There would be subsequent bills and subsequent jockeying over border security and quotas and national identity cards and an attempt to nationalize California Proposition 187 that required anyone seeking government assistance to prove his or her citizenship, but any real reform had run into obstacles, from Republicans demanding greater limitations and from Democrats demanding fewer, and little of consequence happened. Immigration was just too fraught.

Still, Ted Kennedy, who had caused many of the problems with his own 1965 bill, would not give up. He had resumed working on reform even before 9/11 and drafted a bill with Senator Sam Brownback, a conservative Republican, but according to Ted's immigration staffer Esther Olavarria, Brownback was up for reelection in 2002 and decided to leave the Immigration Subcommittee because immigration was not a winning issue in Brownback's Kansas. After the 2002 midterm elections, Ted had met with Tom Daschle and Republican senator Chuck Hagel of Nebraska to draft a bipartisan piece of legislation, one that would attract both labor support and business support—the first worried about cheap workers who would undermine American workers' wages, the second about attracting workers for less-than-desirable jobs. But John Sweeney, the president of the AFL, canvassed other labor leaders and decided it was not the right time for immigration reform, so Ted desisted rather than pursue legislation that was unlikely to advance. Ted's retreat, however, created a vacuum. That January 2003 George W. Bush decided to fill the vacuum with a speech of his own about immigration reform. He proposed a guest worker program awarding temporary visas—good for three years and then renewable for an indeterminate period—to millions of immigrants if employers could show that Americans were not available for the jobs these immigrants would fill. To satisfy conservatives, Bush was explicit that there was no amnesty in his proposal for those who had entered the country illegally. "We must make our immigration laws more rational and more humane," he told a cheering crowd in the White House East Room, "and I believe we can do so without jeopardizing the livelihoods of American citizens."

George W. Bush was disingenuous about many things, perhaps most things, frequently looking only to the political benefit he could gain. He was not so about immigration reform, even though he was not unmindful of the political gain there as well. In his memoir, he would recall tenderly Paula Rendon, a Mexican immigrant who had come to the Bushes when George was thirteen, to be the family caretaker and eventually a "second mother," as George put it, to him and his siblings. "As governor and as president," he would write, "I had Paula in mind when I spoke about immigration reform." And Bush would say, "Family values don't stop at the Rio Grande." Still, Bush's was not a generous proposal; it was aimed more at business needs than at what liberals saw as the human needs of the immigrants. In any case, Bush left the details vague lest he rouse opposition. Shortly after the president's proposal, Frank Sharry, executive director of the National Immigration Forum, an immigrant advocacy group, and others from the immigrant activist community urged Ted to introduce a bill of his own rather than leave the field to Bush and the Republicans. Ted obviously was no innocent when it came to legislation. He thought the prospect of gaining passage, given the chasm that divided most Republicans and most Democrats, was wide, even with the president's new initiative, but he offered to broach the subject with the Democratic caucus and with Sweeney of the AFL-CIO. Bush, meanwhile, had backed away from presenting a full plan. So Ted, along with Representatives Luis Gutierrez and Robert Menendez in the House, and Hillary Clinton and Russ Feingold in the Senate, introduced the Safe, Orderly, and Legal Visas Enforcement Act (SOLVE), which would have provided 350,000 work visas to immigrants and would have legalized undocumented immigrants who had lived in the country for five years and agreed to pay fines and taxes and learn English—the amnesty that Bush had expressly forsworn—and allow members of their immediate families under the age of twenty-one to emigrate if they hadn't already done so, creating "family unification," which Ted had regarded as a central tenet of immigration reform. As Sharry described the attempt, "We wanted to counterbalance kind of a left-leaning version of comprehensive immigration reform against the right-leaning principles of Bush."

Ted Kennedy was not the only one seeking some kind of immigration reform. John McCain, who represented a border state, Arizona, and who was interested in immigration rights as well as border security, had introduced a bill of his own that year, which, like Bush's proposal, permitted temporary workers' visas and contained protections for immigrants and provisions for family reunification. Ted and McCain both sat on the Armed Services Committee, and while, as McCain said, they disagreed on some issues, they shared a deep commitment to the men and women of the military, through which they developed a relationship on how to best serve those men and women. After the 2000 election, when the Senate was evenly divided between Republicans and Democrats, and Ted waged a campaign to get McCain to switch parties—unsuccessfully—the relationship strengthened. That relationship eventually extended to other issues beyond the military; Ted and McCain had worked closely on the Patients' Bill of Rights and on campaign finance reform, on which McCain had led the charge. McCain said that "cynical" Democrats were practically forced to support the bill after Ted had publicly endorsed it. Ted said that McCain approached him late in 2004 and mentioned in "casual conversation" that they might be able to reconcile their two immigration bills creating a single bipartisan bill, no matter who won the presidency in November. Frank Sharry called it a "match made in Heaven." Ted's staff met with McCain's staff, and they hammered out an agreement between Ted's bill, which was roughly one hundred pages long, and McCain's, which was a dozen pages long. And when it came before the Judiciary Committee, Ted said that a "very strong nucleus of Republicans and a very strong nucleus of Democrats" met every morning and then again during the day, reviewing their common ground. "That was a classic example of Ted Kennedy," McCain would say, "because he had to take [liberal] positions that in no way impacted the whole principle and effort for immigration reform, but at the same time, he realized that in order to get a sufficient number of votes, he had to make a concession." The unions had been vehemently opposed to a temporary worker program, fearing the competition to unionized workers. Ted, though he was personally opposed to those programs himself, supported them now for what McCain called the "greater good." "Ted was very aware people die in the desert every day, people are exploited, young women are mistreated, and have no recourse," McCain said, and he said of Ted that "everything about his humanitarian spirit was appealed to, and that's why he made it such a high priority and the reason why we kept going back at it." That meant he wound up casting votes against things in which he believed. Their bill passed the committee and passed the Senate, only to die in the House with the support neither of the unions nor of the president, who had abandoned the effort.

And then came the presidential election and Bush's victory, and Social Security privatization took precedence over other domestic issues, and immigration was all but forgotten—again.

Forgotten by the administration, but not by Ted Kennedy or John McCain. Bush spent most of 2005 fighting for his Social Security privatization—and losing the fight. ("One of the greatest disappointments of my presidency," Bush would call it, blaming "rigid Democratic opposition.") Ted spent a good deal of 2005 in that rigid opposition, parrying the Social Security effort, speaking out against the Iraq War, which was going very badly and rapidly losing public support, and trying to keep John Roberts and Samuel Alito from sitting on the Supreme Court. But he was also committed to taking another crack at an immigration reform bill, hoping that it might be one of the few areas in which the administration, now flailing, might cooperate. So that January, after the election, Ted's staffers met again with McCain's and Jeff Flake's, a Republican representative from Arizona, and those of Jim Kolbe, another Republican representative from Arizona, and of Luis Gutierrez, to fashion a new bill that Frank Sharry would describe as "center-left." Ted's staff drove the effort. "McCain didn't sweat the details," Sharry said of the bill, "Flake is a libertarian for whom less is more, and Kolbe was, 'I'll go along for the ride.'" It was introduced on May 12 and immediately it hit a wall. John Kyl, the junior senator from Arizona, and Texas senator John Cornyn announced their own bill that would create a new Social Security card, machine-readable, that every American would have to present upon applying for a job, would fund the hiring of ten thousand additional Homeland Security agents to hunt down illegal immigrants and another one thousand to investigate immigrant fraud, and finally would require any undocumented immigrant who wanted to apply for a temporary worker visa to leave the country before doing so—some ten million to twelve million individuals.

Opponents derisively called it "Report to deport," and McCain, who sat next to Kyl during a Judiciary Committee hearing, told him that anyone who thought workers were going to abide by that was living in a "fantasy land." On the House side, Republicans were pushing what Tom DeLay called the "toughest border security bill we can get," and wound up passing a punitive bill sponsored by Wisconsin Republican James Sensenbrenner, the House Judiciary Committee chairman, that would have thrown illegal immigrants in jail. Throughout the year Ted, McCain, Colorado Democratic senator Ken Salazar, and South Carolina Republican senator Lindsey Graham, a close friend of McCain's, continued to meet outside the Capitol with the National Immigration Forum, trying desperately to build support for some version of McCain-Kennedy as a way to short-circuit the Sensenbrenner bill, which was popular among Republicans. But the senators were all caught in a vise—accused by their own partisans of compromising with the opposition too much, while the opposition thought they hadn't compromised enough. So nothing happened—again.

The dilemma was that while everyone seemed to want an immigration reform bill, if only for political reasons—either a generous bill to appeal to Hispanic voters or a punitive one to appeal to anti-immigrant voters—the sides just didn't share the same objectives or want the same bill. Now, heading into 2006, a clutter of bills arrived: McCain-Kennedy again, which contained the workers' visa program with protections for undocumented immigrants and, at Ted's insistence, a pathway to citizenship; a bill submitted by Judiciary chair Arlen Specter during the markup of McCain-Kennedy that Ted called a reintroduction of a stern bill that Newt Gingrich had supported, one with provisions eliminating so-called Title II protections for undocumented aliens like giving wide latitude to the discretion of judges in how to handle those aliens' petitions to stay, and allowing appeals for deportation, and putting limits on detention, that Specter promised to moderate in conjunction with the American Bar Association (instead, Ted said, Specter never talked to the ABA and "stiffed us"), and one provision that provided temporary workers' visas but no real path to citizenship since the number of green cards would not increase; and a bill submitted, with White House encouragement, by Majority Leader Frist, a "Chamber of Commerce" bill, Ted called it, that protected employers hiring undocumented workers but stripped away most protections for those workers themselves and emphasized border security over reform. Supporters of reform knew that Frist's bill was essentially a threat, not a serious proposal. The Judiciary Committee had spent three weeks that March wrestling to come up with some compromise that would satisfy Democrats' desire for fair treatment of immigrants, and Republicans' desire not to reward illegality and to prioritize border security (the Republican-led House had already passed the punitive Sensenbrenner bill to build a wall to keep out immigrants and to criminalize anyone who entered the country illegally, but with no provision for a guest worker program, much less a path to citizenship), and Frist, who was no friend of reform, said that if the members didn't come up with a bill by midnight on March 27, he would bring his own punitive bill to the floor. Ted, even as he said that he would filibuster Frist's bill, tried to maintain an optimistic front, saying that he didn't underestimate the difficulties of hammering out a bill, but there was "at least a pathway."

It was, however, a narrow pathway. With Frist's deadline looming, Ted did what he had always done when he was trying to pass legislation— press his Democratic colleagues, court Republican allies, and rally interest groups. And the interest groups responded. On March 25, two days before Frist's ultimatum would take effect, half a million supporters of reform marched in Los Angeles, many wearing white shirts and carrying American and Mexican flags. (Opponents of reform cited this as an example of dual loyalties.) Tens of thousands of others gathered in Denver, Phoenix, Detroit, Dallas, Atlanta, Chicago (100,000 of them there), and on the Boston Common. A "nation-shaking event," *The Boston Globe* called the rallies, intended to remind the Senate of what was at stake. Meanwhile that Sunday morning in Washington, the day before Frist's deadline, dozens of religious leaders rallied outside the Capitol, many of them wearing handcuffs as a protest against a provision of the Sensenbrenner bill, this one making it a crime to provide aid to illegal immigrants. And when the Judiciary members returned from lunch later that afternoon and passed the group, the clergymen hummed the civil rights anthem "We Shall Overcome."

The clock was ticking. Frank Sharry and his staff from the National Immigration Forum, along with the other immigration advocacy groups, were working with Ted and his staff "day and night," Sharry recalled, even as they realized that the more amendments Republicans added at the markup of Ted and McCain's bill, the worse the bill got for immigrants. Still, the advocacy groups wanted to force a vote in Judiciary, believing that they could win—it would be a close vote either way—and in any case realizing that if Specter ran out of time, Frist would introduce his tough border security bill and they would probably lose everything. Heading into the deliberations that morning, as the Judiciary members raced the clock, Kyl and Sam Brownback, the latter of whom had worked with Ted on immigration reform early on, had had a blowup in which Brownback meticulously destroyed Kyl's arguments against a guest worker program— "It's in the Bible," Brownback had told Frank Sharry, when asked why a conservative like him supported liberalized immigration, and Brownback referred to scripture that called for "welcoming the stranger"—while Ted aggressively lobbied California senator Dianne Feinstein, who was being pressured to vote against the bill, both by anti-immigrant forces in her state who were unshakably opposed to helping immigrants and by unions who feared the competition of immigrant labor, and to vote for it, by agribusiness interests that wanted immigrant labor. ("She had 500,000 good reasons," activists would say, pointing to the march in Los Angeles, though Ted's and Feinstein's staffs actually worked out a plan three days before the Judiciary meeting to provide a pathway to citizenship for undocumented agricultural workers in order to get her vote.) After all the conferences and jockeying and compromises, when Specter finally brought down the gavel at six o'clock, after a whole day of markups but before Frist's deadline, McCain-Kennedy, with some added enforcement provisions, had passed 12 to 6, to the applause and cheers of the winning senators and their tired staffers. Now the bill would head to the floor. Still, however, a great deal of enmity lingered. Shortly after the vote, Bill Frist, who by one account had planted stories in the conservative *Washington Free Beacon* that Specter had lost control of the process and that Frist himself would take control of it, got off an elevator and ran into Specter, and the majority leader was steaming over his defeat. But Specter was in no mood for conciliation. "So much for your border enforcement bill," he snarled at Frist. "I just gave you a comprehensive bill. And you're going to the floor tomorrow. Good luck with that."

Now it seemed as if the forces of border protection without immigrant protection had been beaten back, and Ted and McCain seemed victorious. "Ted Kennedy hasn't won yet, but he's closing in," *Time* magazine reported after the bill reached the floor, adding that "to the surprise of everyone in Washington," Ted had managed to get a vote for a bill that would "make citizens of millions of illegal immigrants," given a provision, Ted's provision, allowing illegal immigrants who had been employed in this country for five years, had learned English, and had no criminal record to apply for work visas and then, after five more years, for citizenship itself. "There's one negotiation left and only one," Ted told *Time*, while sitting on a windowsill under the Capitol dome. "The President." But Bush had been keeping his distance from the fray, caught between wanting those Hispanic votes and not wanting to repel those anti-immigrant voters, and realizing that he would be in a vise himself if he supported a guest worker program without a means to gain citizenship, or a means to gain citizenship without a strict border protection policy. That week, at a meeting on education at the White House, despite their now-chilly relationship, Bush pulled Ted aside and told him, "We want to try and work this out," which Ted took to mean that Bush would finally weigh in on the side of his and McCain's bill, though Bush still was hedging on any path to citizenship. And so now the sides tried to work it out.

But nothing might have so demonstrated the new dysfunction of the Senate and the politicization of the entire legislative process, even when there was some bipartisan agreement on wanting to reach a compromise, or the new challenge of trying to appease two diametrically opposed constituencies, or the intractability of immigration itself, than the immigration reform bill. In years past, before the Gingrich revolution, the bill would likely have moved through the Senate, been amended, and then faced a conference with the House where differences would be reconciled, and it would then have passed both houses and be signed by the president into law. That was in years past. Now the bill faced an obstacle course. Most Republicans were still fiercely opposed to McCain-Kennedy, which they saw as an "amnesty" bill—"amnesty" being the Republican taboo. So Republicans Chuck Hagel and Mel Martinez struck a compromise of their own that, like McCain-Kennedy, still allowed a pathway to citizenship, though a more difficult one, and only for those who had been here for five years or more. Those who had been here between two and five years were required to leave the country and reapply for a green card— some 2.8 million people—while those who had been here less than two years would be forced to leave altogether. With those new measures, the bill attracted fifteen Republicans who had not supported McCain-Kennedy as modified by Arlen Specter. One of them was Bill Frist. John McCain and Ted Kennedy, usually amenable to compromise, agreed to the deal too, though Ted did so only reluctantly, and only after McCain himself and

Lindsey Graham abandoned McCain-Kennedy, and only by wresting a concession to reduce the number of worker visas and expand the number of green cards so that more immigrants could be on the road to citizenship.

But the agreement didn't last long. A few hours later, under pressure from the more truculent members of his caucus, Frist withdrew his support and called again for those enforcement amendments. And now it was Minority Leader Reid who reacted. Reid—who came from the hardscrabble Nevada mining town of Searchlight, notable for "hard rocks and inhospitable soil," he said, where bordellos outnumbered churches—was soft-spoken, his voice dry as dust and so modulated there were times it was nearly inaudible, and his manner recessive. Some Senate leaders intimidate. Rough though his upbringing was, Harry Reid, more in the mold of former Senate majority leader Mike Mansfield, did not intimidate. But he did calculate, and he calculated that the Republican amendments would effectively turn the bill from reform to enforcement—at least that was the argument he made initially—and rather than accept that, he decided he would use every device at his disposal to stop the bill from advancing. That night, Thursday, April 6, at Reid's office, Ted met with Reid; Charles Schumer, the New York senator who chaired the Democratic Senatorial Campaign Committee; and Richard Durbin, the Illinois senator and Senate minority whip, where he argued strenuously for Reid to let the bill proceed, saying that they could beat back the Republican amendments and could gain passage of McCain-Kennedy. Reid countered that even if they beat back the amendments, Frist could take the bill to conference and strip out Ted's provisions, as Republicans had done previously, leaving just the punitive measures, though there were also suspicions that Reid was just as eager to deny Bush and the Republicans any victory so close to the midterm elections as he was to help desperate immigrants. (This would be Ted's assessment.) When the senators returned to the floor the next day, the Republicans, as Reid had warned they would, offered a flurry of amendments to drastically reduce the number of immigrants eligible for citizenship, while Kyl and Cornyn, who were unalterably opposed to any reform, offered amendments that Reid said would gut the bill altogether. It was an indication of how much politics dictated policy that when Ted and McCain began collaborating, Cornyn had actually worked out an amendment with Ted on a plan for temporary workers. But then, Ted said, Cornyn went back to Texas and disowned it, and when he returned to the Senate, he offered the bill with Kyl. "This is a bullshit amendment," McCain snapped at Cornyn. "And we don't want any more of your bullshit amendments. You're going to sink the Republican Party. You're going to antagonize all the Hispanics, and your amendments are all bullshit." Ted said he was shocked to hear McCain address Cornyn that way, and both men turned red. But Cornyn would not be deterred. He submitted his amendment anyway.

But now it wasn't only conservative Republicans who wanted to waylay the bill. Harry Reid seemed determined to do so as well, expressing the concerns he had shared at the meeting in his office: concerns that the temporary worker program might harm labor, which opposed it; concerns that Republicans would gain a political advantage from passing a reform bill, if they could do so; concerns, perhaps above all, that any bill that passed, given the hostility conservatives had toward a route to citizenship for undocumented immigrants, would do much more harm than good. So Reid, deploying parliamentary maneuvers, prevented the Republicans from attaching their amendments, then insisted that—since the House bill, which was purely punitive, and the Senate bill (essentially McCain's and Ted's bill) were so far apart, and since the Republican Senate leadership had taken to excluding Democrats from conferences, as they did on the Medicare drug benefit negotiations—the entire Judiciary Committee be appointed as conferees to protect the McCain-Kennedy bill from House Republican depredations. (There's a "foul odor that's coming out of the U.S. Senate," Republican representative Dana Rohrabacher said of the compromise bill, in an illustration of what Reid thought Democrats were up against.)

And now it was Frist's turn again. Frist was appalled and angry both at Reid's parliamentary maneuvering and at his demand for conferees. Frist had proposed a new compromise that day that would offer a pathway to citizenship for illegals, but only if they worked *eleven* years, and he asked that it be committed to Judiciary for a vote. Reid objected, realizing that this could be a retreat from the more liberal McCain-Kennedy bill, and instead called for a cloture vote on that bill. When the roll was called, only thirty-eight Democrats—and not a single Republican—voted to end debate out of the sixty senators needed. Even McCain, feeling that Reid had overstepped his bounds, did not vote for cloture for his own bill. But Frist's bill, which had gotten a mild endorsement from Bush, couldn't get enough Republican votes either. The Senate then went on a two-week recess for

Easter, and that seemed to be the end of immigration reform before the 2006 midterm elections. "Politics got in front of policy on this issue," Ted told reporters, meaning not just Republican politics, but the politics of his own Democratic leadership. "I'm disappointed, not discouraged. I think we came a long way. I've been around long enough not to let me get too optimistic too soon on this sort of thing." But as the senators headed for home, optimism was in short supply. A great deal of energy had been expended. But once again, nothing had been accomplished.

Ted Kennedy had been around long enough, as he said, and had suffered enough defeats in his Senate career, even when the finish line was in sight, to understand how difficult it was to gain passage of complex and politically intractable legislation, as immigration reform clearly was, though he might have underestimated just *how* difficult it was. Still, he refused to give up, especially since Bush had afforded so few opportunities to pass anything else that was meaningful and because he appreciated how significant a new law permitting undocumented immigrants to become citizens could be. "We're starting to feel our own mortality," his close friend former Tennessee senator Jim Sasser, would say, "and it becomes more important to get something done than to make partisan points." And Sasser said of Ted, "If he doesn't get it done now and make a compromise with the Republicans and maybe alienate some of his own leadership, it won't get done." And Sasser explicitly cited the immigration reform bill, which Ted was pushing at the time Sasser spoke, even as Reid kept pushing against it. But Harry Reid wasn't the only one doubting Ted. Just as Ted had fretted that Bill Clinton might be too eager for a bargain with the Republicans, Ted's fellow Democrats had increasingly been afraid that his instincts for compromise would give away too much, as they felt he had on No Child Left Behind and the disastrous Medicare drug benefit plan. Michael Myers, Ted's staffer, said that Ted felt he could be a stronger advocate for immigration reform "if there's a sense that we've got it under control, and we've taken strong steps to make sure that fraud is at a minimum [and] we're letting in the people we want to let in and kicking out the people we want out"—in short, if he showed that he was for enforcement too, which was precisely why the Democrats were nervous about his efforts. "Just about everyone in the caucus is worried that without safeguards that this is headed into an unfair, unbalanced bill," one liberal senator told *The New York Times*, speaking of his concern over where Ted might lead them. But for Ted Kennedy, as Sasser had said, this was not just a matter of morality now, as important as morality was to Ted; it was a matter of mortality—of his legacy. He wanted to be the one to gain immigration reform, especially, one might have suspected, because of his own 1965 bill that had been a source of immigration problems in the first place.

And reform wasn't dead quite yet. Reform advocates wouldn't let it die. Shortly before the recess ended, more than one hundred thousand people marched past the White House to the National Mall in sight of the Capitol, some of them having wrapped themselves in American flags, some waving WE ARE AMERICA placards, many of them speaking English and Spanish, and all of them demanding immigration reform. "This debate goes to the heart of who we are as Americans," Ted told the crowd at a rally that day. "Some in Congress want to turn America away from its true spirit. . . . They say you should report to deport," alluding to the provision in the Hagel-Martinez compromise. "I say, 'Report to become American citizens.'" He told reporters later that listening to the crowd that afternoon, he heard the echoes of the civil rights movement, and he said of the grassroots movement that had organized similar rallies in 150 cities that day, April 10, "There is too much velocity to deny it."

But George W. Bush seemed to be denying it. One of the obstacles to reform had been the unwillingness of the president to promote reform, despite his promise to Ted to do so. (At a White House luncheon for Irish prime minister Brian Ahern on St. Patrick's Day, which Ted attended, Bush glanced over at Ted and winked when Ahern mentioned immigration.) "The president . . . has to get involved in immigration right now," Arlen Specter said when he returned from the recess. Harry Reid and Ted made the same pleas: Bush had to get involved, or congressional Republicans would not budge. For his part, Bush blamed Reid for scuttling reform by not allowing amendments—though the president didn't say that those conservative Republican amendments were largely dedicated to scuttling any real reform as well. But with reform in a state of hibernation after the collapse of McCain-Kennedy in April, and with immigration advocates holding their marches and threatening an economic boycott on May 1, there was, as Ted had said, too much velocity to deny it. And now, late that April, George W. Bush finally addressed, albeit tentatively, the issue he had been loath to address, notwithstanding that his press secretary called it a "top priority." Speaking to the Orange County Business Council in Irvine, south of Los Angeles, Bush declared that deportation was not the answer—hardly a bold statement, but one that Ted seized upon to say that the president supported his and McCain's bill—and Bush said that he would finally be meeting with supporters of the Senate bill, including Ted, in a few days. The president didn't move with alacrity, though; nor did he make any endorsement of legislation or lay out any specifics. As Bush often did, he preferred to have Congress take the lead, letting him husband his political capital. But political capital was what was at stake. The only reason that immigration reform still had any life left was that with the midterm elections breathing down on them, every legislator and the president had something to gain from passing a bill, depending on the bill they passed.

Bush, though hesitant, knew it. He knew too that his administration had done next to nothing legislatively that year—the immigration debate had been postponed by debates on supplementary funding for the Iraq War and hurricane relief, neither of which redounded to Bush's benefit—and his popularity continued to sink. After Frist and Reid agreed to restart the Senate debate and name members to the conference committee on May 11, George W. Bush finally made a national address on immigration—his first in two years. Speaking on television from the Oval Office the evening of May 15, he said, "We cannot build a unified country by inciting people to anger or playing on anyone's fears or exploiting the issue of immigration for political gain." Bush now would try to split the difference. To pacify the conservatives in his own party, he proposed six thousand new border patrol agents, drawn from the National Guard, and an increase in the number of beds at detention centers. And to enforce violations of employment of illegals, he called for digitized security cards. To pacify the remaining moderates in his party and the Democrats, and businesses with a need for labor, he proposed a guest worker program. But while he hinted that there might be a path to citizenship for those who had been in this country longer than five years, as the Hagel-Martinez compromise did, so long as they went to the back of the line, he explicitly rejected amnesty. Even so, Ted praised Bush's "courage," which was a sign of how badly Ted wanted legislation; there was very little courage involved. Others were not so generous. Undocumented immigrants told *New York Times* reporters Ralph Blumenthal and Monica Davey that they were afraid the border would be militarized, afraid of identification cards, afraid of being driven deeper into an underground economy. "I have been working really hard. I have learned English. I pay taxes. I am not here in the country to bring problems," said one of them, a young man named José, who worked at a social services agency in Chicago. On the other side, conservatives told the reporters they strongly opposed any leniency toward illegal immigrants. "I don't like the idea that money can buy citizenship," one said, adding that in any case she didn't think there were any jobs in the country that Americans themselves couldn't do. And so the legislative wrangling continued.

It continued into late May, with the pressure for a deal in the Senate escalating. Two days after Bush's speech, the Senate agreed to add three hundred miles of new border fencing to the bill, seventy miles of fortifications, and seven hundred miles of barriers, and a new provision that any guest worker needed a sponsor promising employment. Ted opposed the latter, saying that it would put immigrants at the mercy of employers. But he wanted the bill, *a* bill, so he kept pushing. Meanwhile Harry Reid, who still had mixed feelings about the bill, was meeting with immigration activists who were pressing him for one, telling them that he was only trying to protect them, since the House would never agree to the guest worker provisions in the Senate bill, much less the citizenship provisions. "You don't know how this place works," Reid told them. "We'll lose control of the process. If we don't have enough protections, this is a fool's errand." But Reid, revealing his other motive, had also told them this: "You want a good deal. I want a good election." On the floor, as the debate continued, tempers flared and chaos erupted. Frank Sharry of the National Immigration Forum called it "out of control." "All the Republican senators came and started yelling at Harry Reid, and he was, you know, 'I object,'" while McCain's staffers were calling the activists and telling them, "You gotta let these guys vote. We can win these votes," and Ted, Sharry said, was immobilized, caught between his and the activists' desire for compromise—"All we need is for you to say yes to cutting the best deal possible," Sharry said they told Ted—and the desire of his leadership not to give the Republicans either an advantage on gaining passage of a bill or a knife with which to savage the bill.

By this time, conservative Republican senators were marshaling their amendments to sabotage the bill while the moderates and establishment Republicans were scurrying to find some palatable bill, and most Democrats were searching for a compromise while their own leadership was skeptical of any such compromise. As the Senate debate continued that May, Ted invited a half-dozen of the immigration activists to his hideaway to take their temperature. Once again they pressed him to make some deal. After they spoke, Ted was "pensive," Frank Sharry, one of those activists, recalled. He gazed downward, silent, for "what seemed an eternity," according to Sharry, though it was probably only thirty seconds, and he thought Ted was "thinking through . . . the moral challenge of doing the right thing versus go along with my colleagues who have some legitimate policy concerns." And then Ted lifted his head and looked at Ken Salazar, the freshman Colorado senator who had been working on immigration reform and had proposed an amendment making English a "unifying" language as a way to defuse some of the Republican opposition since Republicans had been demanding a provision that English be designated the "national language." Ted had invited Salazar to the meeting, and he asked Salazar what he thought. Salazar said, "Well, Ted, if we can do something to help our people, I think we should." And Ted, who was clearly hoping for a nudge, pondered a moment and declared, "I think you're onto something." And he turned to his aide Michael Myers and told him, "Let's get to a deal." And that was that.

To get to a deal, a small bipartisan group, mostly of Judiciary Committee members, met at eight-thirty every morning in the President's Room off the Senate chamber before that day's floor debate to discuss amendments and how they might defeat the most noxious of them: Kennedy, Salazar, Dick Durbin, Joseph Lieberman of Connecticut, and Barack Obama of Illinois on the Democratic side, and McCain, Lindsey Graham, Mel Martinez, Chuck Hagel, Sam Brownback, and Mike DeWine of Ohio on the Republican side. "Very spirited discussions," McCain said of those deliberations. "Ted would say to Democrats and I would say to Republicans, 'You've got to vote against this amendment, even though, if it was "stand-alone," you would vote for it.'" Usually, Ted would issue his instructions with humor, McCain said. But "sometimes he would speak as sternly to a senator as I have ever seen one senator talk to another senator in front of a group of senators." McCain recalled one session where Obama, who frequently followed the labor position, brought up an objection, and Ted just snapped. "Why don't you pitch in and help instead of making demands every morning?" McCain said the outburst stopped the conversation dead, but McCain suspected that while Ted was trying to earn points with the Republicans in the room, he was also trying to teach Obama, of whom he had spoken highly to McCain, on how to legislate effectively. Meanwhile McCain served as the go-between connecting Majority Leader Frist and Minority Leader Reid—one on one phone, the other on another—negotiating how many amendments they would permit and who the conferees would be, though there was a good deal of theater in the process. Frist wasn't particularly keen on getting a bill into law and was confident the House Republicans would stop that from happening while allowing him and the president to declare a victory in the Senate; Reid had all those old trepidations, while not wanting it to seem as if he had been the one to sink an agreement so that Democrats would take the blame. During the final day of debate, May 25, ten days after Bush's address, Ted and McCain worked earnestly to beat back a series of amendments—Jeff Bingaman's to put a cap on the total number of immigrants (it passed 51 to 47); Jeff Sessions's to deny any undocumented immigrant from taking the Earned Income Tax Credit, which was designed to give relief to the poor, even if those immigrants had legal status and had paid their taxes (it failed overwhelmingly, 60 to 37); and another by John Ensign of Nevada to deny illegal immigrants tax credits, including their own tax refunds, or Social Security benefits (it passed 50 to 47). Ted would call the Sessions and Ensign amendments "absolutely punitive, mean-spirited, and basically racist." And then came the final pronouncements before the final vote. Harry Reid, labeling it Part 2, after the failure of Part 1 in April, called the bill a "blockbuster," comparing it to the big films of that early summer, *The Da Vinci Code* and *Mission: Impossible III*, and he praised Judiciary chair Arlen Specter and Ted for their "yeoman's work to sort through all of the hurt feelings that people have in offering amendments and not getting the votes they wanted when they wanted them." McCain spoke movingly of how this bill was not just a matter of policy; it was a "matter of life and death for many living along the border." And then Ted spoke, calling the Comprehensive Immigration Reform Act of 2006 the "most far-reaching immigration reform in our history." "Wisdom in immigration policy doesn't just happen," he said. "It is a choice between a future of progress as a nation of immigrants or a future defined by high walls and long fences." Ted understood the odds. But he closed: "I'm optimistic we can resolve our differences again."

And so finally the Comprehensive Immigration Reform Act, the blockbuster, came to a vote, and it passed 62 to 36.

It seemed like a victory. Ted boasted, "I can't wait until we get on the Lou Dobbs show," referring to a nativist television host fiercely opposed to immigration reform. Though conservatives railed against the bill, saying, as Jeff Sessions did, that it would repeat the mistakes of the failed 1986 bill, which granted amnesty but did not stanch the tide of illegal immigration, and that it needed to be "pulled down," both Republicans and Democrats, many of them for their own political reasons rather than for moral ones, sought some middle ground. What had begun as a tense, sometimes rancorous fight between two diametrically opposed positions—virtually no immigration versus a pathway to citizenship for illegal immigrants—turned into an act of legislative horse-trading that, after the polarizing battle of April, was a throwback to the days before Newt Gingrich, when Republicans and Democrats sometimes worked in concert. Harry Reid said that he had been in Congress for twenty-four years and in the Senate for twenty, and that "this is the way it used to be. This is the way it should be in the future. I have every hope and every belief that we can make it that way." For at least ten years, Republicans and Democrats had been at loggerheads, abandoning the chemistry of the Senate that Ted so loved. Now, for two weeks, they weren't.

But that, again, was just the Senate, and even that was a bit of wishful thinking, given how many Republicans opposed the bill. Reid warned of "dark clouds forming on the horizon," by which he meant the House and its determination to block the Senate bill from becoming law. (Sessions said, probably truthfully, that many Republicans were voting for the act because they knew the House would never agree to its provisions.) Just as immigration activists applied pressure to the Democrats to pass a bill, conservative activists applied pressure to Republicans not to pass one. Talk radio, which had become an increasingly powerful force in Republican politics, was especially averse to any pathway to citizenship, and by one account, after Bush's May 15 speech, the hostility only intensified. At the same time, a group of enraged citizens formed what they called the Minutemen with ad hoc efforts to patrol the border and keep illegal immigrants out. One group, devoted to border security, organized a campaign to send bricks to their congressmen—an estimated ten thousand bricks. (By the same token, Cecilia Muñoz of the National Council of La Raza, an immigration advocacy group, said that the Minutemen, talk radio, and the Sensenbrenner bill were what roused the immigration activists to hold their marches.) None of this boded well for the eventual passage of a comprehensive reform bill. Bush had sent his political mastermind, Karl Rove, to the House on two occasions to make the case for passage, but Rove made little headway. Arlen Specter argued, as he had earlier, that the only hope for the House to relent was for Bush to get more deeply and personally involved, but Bush's fortunes, with the war and Hurricane Katrina, which devastated New Orleans and the rescue operation of which Bush had managed to bungle badly, continued to plummet, and though Specter said the president had told him privately that he was in favor of the Senate bill, when he finally did get involved that June, making several appearances out west to highlight immigration, he seemed far more concerned about not riling his conservative base and far more enthused about border protection and security than about the comprehensive act the Senate had passed. "Suicide for some of our members" was how the communications director for Thomas Reynolds, the head of the Republican Congressional Campaign Committee, described the bill. Then late that June, Speaker Dennis Hastert told Bush that he intended to hold more hearings on the House bill, Sensenbrenner's draconian bill, that summer, which was effectively a death knell for reform. There would be no immigration bill in 2006. Once again it had all been for naught.

IV

The Democrats might have acclimated themselves to losing midterm elections, to being in the minority, to being told that the country was unalterably conservative now and that Democrats were out of touch. But the first two years of George W. Bush's second term had not gone well for him. His Social Security privatization campaign, his major initiative, never got off the ground, despite his sixty-cities-in-sixty-days cavalcade. Immigration reform, his major initiative of 2006, had failed and failed in large measure because Bush was reluctant to push it, and when he finally did, he waffled on the legalization portion. The disaster of Hurricane Katrina in New Orleans, which flooded the city and displaced most of the city's Black population, still stalked him. And above all, the Iraq War, the war the United States was supposed to win handily before democratizing the Middle East, had gone terribly wrong, with divisions between Sunni and Shia Muslims splitting Iraq, and Bush's only answer was to say repeatedly that he would let the commanders set the troop levels, even as his advisers were hoping to change strategy and reduce forces. By the time he had a change of heart and looked to devise a new policy, in August, it was too late. Bush himself would confess that the summer of 2006 was the "worst period of my presidency" and that he "thought about the war constantly." And he confessed as well, "If Iraq split along sectarian lines, our mission would be doomed. We could be looking at a repeat of Vietnam," which was what Ted had been saying since the inception of the war. Bush's approval rating, which had reached a high of 90 percent after 9/11 and hit 71 percent shortly after the invasion of Iraq, had declined to 31 percent in May 2006, just as he was trying to pass immigration reform, and remained mired in the thirties and low forties throughout the year, which was especially threatening to his own party since the midterm elections were looming. (His low approval rating was one reason why Republicans felt they could ignore him on immigration with impunity.) Republican candidates kept their distance. "We had people who didn't want him to land at the airport," White House political director Susan Taylor would tell *Times* reporter Peter Baker. One candidate, Charlie Crist of Florida, who was running to succeed Bush's brother Jeb for governor, stood the president up at a campaign appearance.

Bush tried to seem unbowed. He took to the campaign trail assailing Democrats for looking for a way, now, to get out of Iraq, while Bush said that he was looking for a way to win. But the handwriting was on the wall. Ken Mehlman, the chairman of the Republican National Committee, told him the weekend before the elections that the Republicans were likely to lose enough seats to put the House majority in jeopardy. He was right. Republicans lost thirty seats, which gave the Democrats a 233-to-202 majority. In the Senate, where the Republicans had had an eleven-seat edge, six Republican incumbents lost, and Democrats regained control by virtue of having two independents, Bernie Sanders of Vermont and Joe Lieberman, who had lost the Democratic primary and then run as an independent, caucus with them, giving them a 51-to-49-seat margin. Overall, Democrats won 52 percent of the aggregate vote.

Republicans had been casualties of the war they so vigorously supported, even as 56 percent of the electorate disapproved of it; of congressional inaction, which was partly a result of Bush's inaction—62 percent of those voters who decried Congress blamed Republicans, not Democrats—and of an energized coalition that Bush had antagonized. "Remember the revenge of the angry white men that powered Newt Gingrich and company into office?" pollster Andrew Kohut asked shortly after the midterms. "Well, plenty of angry voters propelled the Democrats to victory this November, but they were female, liberal and secular." (There was also a Republican lobbying scandal, which hurt the party.) But

Matt Bai of *The New York Times* suggested another cause for the Republican defeat: arrogance. Though he posed as a Texas cowboy and an ordinary Joe, George W. Bush, Bai observed, was, in his second term, perceived as being too arrogant to listen as the country was unraveling. "Ruling parties and presidencies are almost never felled by issues alone," Bai wrote. "Rather, it is the more general perception of a creeping chaos—the sense that leaders no longer have a firm grasp on events or the credibility to unite disparate constituencies—that causes political powers to come undone." Now George W. Bush, who presided over an unraveling, was undone.

Among the victors was Ted Kennedy. Clearly sensing Bush's vulnerability and a chance for Democrats to retake the Senate, he entered his own election year more determined than he had been since the Romney contest in 1994. He had raised millions of dollars—already $4.7 million by the beginning of the year. He had shed, by his own estimate, thirty or forty pounds in 2004 and planned to lose another ten pounds in 2006, the usual sign of his electoral focus. "That makes a big difference in people's minds," he said laughingly of his past weight issues. "You're really not interested in them; it's a bowl of spaghetti or something." He had dispatched two of his grandnephews, Joe Kennedy II's sons, Matthew and Joe III, around the state as campaign managers, and he said, "Their presence helped people know that I take the election seriously. 'Kennedy is in Washington, but he does obviously care about our Greek celebration of our church, because one of his nephews is here.'" And when Republican state executive director Tim O'Brien admitted, "Finding someone to run against a Kennedy in Massachusetts is a difficult task," Ted warned Republicans, who had held out the possibility of luring a candidate by having him think of a run as a "stepping stone," that he considered "everything is fair game" against any contender. The man they found was Kenneth Chase, an agreeable forty-four-year-old owner of an after-school program. Ted and Chase debated on October 10, mainly agreeing—on a bilateral treaty on nuclear arms with North Korea; on the need for energy independence; on the mistake of the Iraq War. Their only real disagreement was over immigration, where Chase stressed enforcement. When he went to Barnstable Town Hall with Sunny and Splash to cast his vote on November 7, Ted lumbered up the stairs and, when asked if he would run again, used his well-worn joke, "I'm to stay until I get the hang of it." Ted won handily with 70 percent of the vote.

And now began a new session of Congress with a new list of priorities—the priorities that George W. Bush and the Republicans had dashed.

There was so much unfinished business to do now that the Democrats held both houses of Congress. Ted Kennedy was sworn in for his eighth full term, his ninth overall, that January, returning to his office for a small celebration before excusing himself to pay a courtesy call on Robert Byrd, who had also been sworn in that day. At a bigger celebration later that day, attended by hundreds of legislators, union leaders, and liberal activists, *The Boston Globe* reported that his supporters "acted as though the Massachusetts Democrat had been crowned king." And the *Globe* added, "In political terms, he had." Previous Kennedy swearing-in parties, the *Globe* said, had been like Irish wakes, beclouded by gloom and the prophecy that Democrats would once again be thwarted. But not now. Not with the Democrats triumphant and George W. Bush on the ropes.

Bush was shell-shocked. Now that he had to cope with a Democratic Congress, the man who had tried to steamroll Congress, the man whose party had excluded Democrats from House-Senate conferences, the man who had conned Democrats, especially Ted Kennedy, into cooperating with him, only to betray them and then brag about it, asked for bipartisan cooperation at a press conference. Ted called it the "most ambivalent press conference because he was combative and kind of arrogant in one sense and sort of conceding in the other sense." But Ted said that "there was no sense of alteration or change or sort of willingness to embrace the new paradigm. When we watched that, it sort of looked like we were in for a period of continued confusion, when they're really not sure where they want to go." As if to demonstrate that, Bush announced at the press conference that he had accepted the resignation of Defense Secretary Donald Rumsfeld, one of the chief architects of the Iraq War, who had recently been recommending the drawdown in troops there, though Bush announced no new policy.

If George W. Bush was shambling, Ted Kennedy himself was spirited. House Democrats declared a hundred-hour legislative offensive to push bills through, as a way of demonstrating how feckless the Republican House had been, and Ted spoke eagerly of what he hoped to accomplish in the Senate: "trying to get the minimum wage right away . . . and if they want to filibuster it, it sort of puts people in the place where they should be"—that is, forced to vote against a very popular idea; ethics reform to police the nexus between legislators and lobbyists that had hurt the Republicans; a new healthcare initiative he introduced with Representative John Dingell that would extend Medicare to some individuals under sixty-five; a bill to protect gay rights and another to include assaults against gays in hate crime legislation, which he introduced with Republican Gordon Smith; an expansion of the FDA; reform of student loans to move privately subsidized loans into government-funded Pell grants; and a reauthorization of the Head Start program for preschool children, which had been surviving year-by-year with appropriations rather than by long-term support, and which he introduced with Republican Mike Enzi. In 2006 before the midterms, he had proposed a rise in the minimum wage from $5.15 to $7.25, the first such rise since 1994—a full-time minimum wage worker had received a yearly income of $10,712 in 2006, which was $6,000 less than the poverty level—and attached it to an appropriations bill to better its prospects, but it lost narrowly, 51 to 47. When he tried again, the Senate Republicans called for a unanimous consent provision that required sixty votes rather than a majority, so he lost again.

But Democrats had made the minimum wage increase one of their top priorities during the midterms, and Ted, who had always been the champion of the minimum wage increase, bolted from the gate that January. The House passed the increase on January 10, and at the insistence of the chairman of the Ways and Means Committee, Charles Rangel, had a "clean" bill—that is, one without one of the provisions that Republicans and the president had sought: tax breaks for employers to offset wage increases. "This is the day for the people who empty the bedpans, change the bed linens, sweep the floors and do the hardest work of America," said one House Democrat. Meanwhile the Senate, where the Democratic majority was only two thin votes and where sixty votes would be required to attain cloture, turned down the House bill, and Republicans demanded that any increase be paired with $8.3 billion in tax breaks to restaurants and other small businesses that they said would be adversely affected by the rise through higher wages. Ted was not pleased. "Why can't we do just one thing for minimum-wage workers, no strings attached, no giveaways for the powerful?" he asked. But most Senate Republicans were in no mood for any minimum wage increase, much less one that didn't include those tax breaks. To slow the bill, they introduced a series of amendments and demanded votes on them—everything from restrictions on employment of immigrants to wages for farm workers to a healthcare plan for small businesses meant to sink the bill. Ted was enraged once again. He took the floor, as he often did, armed with charts that showed how inflation had sapped the 1994 increase, and he thundered once again: "What is it that the Republican leadership has against working families? What really gets [into] our Republican friends that they just can't stand hard-working Americans?" He labeled their attitude "hostility" rather than "indifference." Ted Kennedy was not above using parliamentary techniques himself to slow or derail legislation; he was a master of them. But he had done so to prevent what he saw as harm to his constituents—the powerless and poor and marginalized. The Republicans, he felt, did so precisely to inflict harm on those constituents.

But Republicans would not relent. Not even the House majority was immune to Republican pressure. After holding steadfastly against any tax breaks, it added $1.3 billion of them to its bill in order to get to sixty votes in the Senate for cloture. Since the Senate bill offset much of its breaks with new taxes on the wealthy, including executive compensation, the Chamber of Commerce gave grudging approval to the House bill, which also gave Republicans cover. After what was described as a "bruising debate," the Senate finally passed Ted's bill overwhelmingly, 94 to 3, with the provisions that Ted had so lamented. George Bush reluctantly signed it, and Ted Kennedy had won a major victory—his first in some time.

Still, for all the promises of bipartisanship, neither side was especially amenable. Bush introduced his budget in early February with deep cuts in social programs, including $100 billion in Medicare and a limitation on the number of children who would qualify for one of Ted Kennedy's signature achievements, the Children's Health Insurance Program (CHIP). Given the giant tax cuts that Bush had pushed through his Republican Congress and the huge bill for his Iraq War, Ted, who, with the Democratic victory, had returned as chairman of the Health, Education, Labor and Pensions Committee, was irate at the poorest having to bear the cost of what he regarded as the president's folly, but "fortunately," he said, "the new Congress is determined to change course—and will."

Ted had some reason for confidence. Already in March, just two months into the new congressional session, Ted wrote in a *Washington Post* op-ed of Congress's dynamism, "Rome wasn't built in a day, but if this new Congress had been its architect, it might have been." He called the results in just sixty-six days "remarkable." "In my forty-five years in Congress, I have never seen the Senate turn so rapidly from stalemate toward real progress." The ethics reform bill had passed, the minimum wage bill had passed, a new bill to help credit card consumers had passed, and Congress had held hearings on derelictions of care at the Walter Reed Hospital and on attorneys general whom the administration had fired for political reasons.

But there was more to be done—one issue especially, an issue with, for Ted Kennedy, large moral implications as well as those implications for his legacy.

V

The failure of immigration reform in 2006 had galled Ted Kennedy, and now that the Democrats had the upper hand in Congress, he wanted to revisit the issue. Shortly after the midterm elections, he was already meeting with John McCain and Arlen Specter to fashion a new bill and organized a meeting with twelve senators, both Democrats and Republicans, to see if they could find a way forward. "The dynamics are right," Ted told *The Boston Globe,* and even Tom Tancredo, a Colorado Republican and one of the fiercest leaders of the anti-immigration movement in the House, conceded that comprehensive immigration reform was virtually inevitable. It had taken three Congresses to pass civil rights legislation, Ted told *The Boston Globe*'s Susan Milligan, and he expected the same fortune for immigration. And Ted would not give up because, as he said at a press conference early that year, immigration reform, like civil rights, was a "moral issue" for him, and morality drove his legislation. By February, he and McCain had finished drafting a bill nearly identical to the McCain-Kennedy bill a year earlier, the primary difference being a provision that increased border enforcement—a concession to the Republicans—but still including a citizenship pathway for the roughly twelve million undocumented immigrants in the country. In introducing the bill early that March, Ted claimed that Bush had told him at a private White House meeting on January 8 that he was committed to supporting a "comprehensive" bill, which Ted took to mean a bill with the citizenship provision in it—if one could trust the president.

The bill wasn't just legislative routine. It had, as McCain had said, real-life consequences. That March, Homeland Security had sent Immigration and Customs Enforcement officers on raids of businesses employing undocumented aliens—one of them a defense contractor in New Bedford,

Massachusetts, in which agents rounded up some three hundred undocumented immigrants. Ted headed up there and went to a church basement to meet families that had been disrupted by the raids, and he was both astonished and angered by what he found. Mothers had been dragged off and separated from their children without the government providing any care for those children. One father said his two children were so traumatized by their mother's incarceration they had been unable to sleep since, and he asked Ted if he might take them to see her, at a facility in Dartmouth, which Ted did. Ted said that the children of nursing mothers had been taken away to hospitals while their mothers were in detention. Others in the roundup had been deported, even though some of them had actually been American citizens with foreign names. "Gestapo-like," Ted called the raids, and said he protested to Homeland Security secretary Michael Chertoff, who, Ted complained, didn't seem to care. And Ted said that immigration attorneys had asked him plaintively, "Can't you do something?"

He would try. But this time Ted and John McCain would not be working shoulder to shoulder as they had in 2006. McCain was preparing to run for the Republican nomination for president, and he was suddenly cautious not to offend his partisans, most of whom still regarded any reform other than border security as dreaded amnesty, and McCain now objected to a provision in their previous bill that required guest workers to receive the prevailing wage in the industry in which they worked. McCain, the war hero who had spent years in a Vietnamese prison camp, had seemed, in many ways, irreplaceable in battering moderate Republicans into compliance by his own moral example. But Ted nonetheless convened a group of senators who had expressed interest in the issue—Lindsey Graham, Mel Martinez, John Kyl, and Trent Lott, on the Republican side, and Dianne Feinstein and Ken Salazar on the Democratic—and Ted had each of them at that first meeting relate how their parents had come to America—Ted, of course, spoke of his own family's Irish immigrant history, which had been the impulse for his interest in immigration—to establish a bond among the senators. Working his old chemistry, the chemistry that had been lost in the last session, he invited some of them to his Capitol hideaway to ingratiate himself and to describe what was at stake. Lindsey Graham said that Ted told him he equated his immigration bill with the Civil Rights Act and showed Graham memorabilia of his brothers. ("You could just see how his eyes lit up when he talked about his brothers.") The negotiations were long—ten or eleven meetings every week, Ted would say, held in the vice president's office on the second floor of the Dirksen building. Every senator was welcome, but many of those who had worked with Ted and John McCain on the 2006 bill had fallen away, frustrated or skeptical of making any progress, or fearful, as McCain was, of damaging their bona fides with their party's rank and file. A few, like Robert Menendez and Majority Whip Dick Durbin, were primarily interested in their own narrower provisions—in Menendez's case, retaining chain migration, which allowed family members to get priority; in Durbin's, passing the Development, Relief, and Education for Alien Minors Act (DREAM), which would provide a pathway to citizenship for those minors who had been brought to this country by their undocumented parents. The most unusual of the new participants was Arizona senator John Kyl, who, along with John Cornyn, had introduced one of the most punitive amendments to the 2006 bill but was now being pressured by his agricultural constituents to support a guest worker program. (Occasionally Cornyn came to the deliberations too, Ted said, to "disrupt" any possible compromise between the Democrats and Republicans and to try and peel Kyl away.) And there were other participants, these from the White House: Homeland Security secretary Michael Chertoff, and Commerce secretary Carlos Gutierrez, and deputy chief of staff for policy Joel Kaplan, and with them, their attorneys, all of whom were there, in Ted's words, "upholding Republican positions," though Graham would say that for a long time they were wary of whether Ted was serious and were monitors more than facilitators. The group called themselves the "grand bargainers."

The bargaining, however, was slower and more deliberate than it was grand. Bush, for all his continued professions of wanting a reform bill, largely stayed out of the deliberations, appearing at a border fence in Yuma, Arizona, to promote a bill but only convincing immigration activists yet again that he was far more interested in security than in what they believed was justice, especially when an internal document leaked to the press that showed the administration considering stricter rules for immigration and significantly larger fines—up to $20,000—for the undocumented. Patrick Leahy, the new Judiciary chair, said what Arlen Specter, his predecessor, had said a year earlier: "The president has got to be personally involved. He cannot just send up Cabinet members and ask them to speak with a few members of the president's party and think that's going to get them through." No matter how many times legislators had told Bush that, he had remained largely disengaged—wanting legislation but not willing to risk the opprobrium his support would incite from the right wing.

Still, Ted pushed forward. "There were times he blew up," Lindsey Graham would say of Ted, "and I had to calm him down. There were times I blew up, and he calmed me down." When asked if there were moments when Ted rescued what seemed to be a futile process, Graham said there were "112 moments." Now, after three months of efforts, the "grand bargainers" faced a deadline like the one Bill Frist had imposed during the last negotiation. Harry Reid, citing other legislative priorities, demanded a bill by Wednesday, May 16, which, at Ted's request, Reid extended by a day. If no bill was forthcoming, Reid said, he would have to move on. With the pressure intensifying as the deadline neared, negotiations continued through the weekend. Few pieces of legislation had so many different stakeholders. Few pieces of legislation triggered such acrimony. Kyl, who had wanted no reform whatsoever in 2006, had reached agreement with Ted on a system that awarded points to prospective immigrants, giving priority to those with education and skills and to those who filled economic needs, like Kyl's agricultural guest workers, in exchange for a process to legalize the twelve million undocumented workers—essentially amnesty. But Bob Menendez wanted a family priority system instead that allowed relatives to obtain green cards and wanted those green cards rather than a provisional guest worker program. Ted tried to broker a truce, assuring Kyl that he would get the temporary guest worker program he so badly wanted for those agricultural constituents of his. "We'll take care of you," Ted told Kyl. "You have to stay with this thing." But if Ted pacified Kyl, he couldn't pacify Menendez, who threatened to vote against the bill. (Ted agreed with Menendez, but this was an instance where the greater good was the path to citizenship.) Leahy, as Judiciary chair, was angry over Bush's attempt to politicize the U.S. attorneys by replacing those who would not do his bidding and was not inclined to help Bush get a bill passed. Even labor was divided between those, like the AFL-CIO, that believed the unions should be putting more of their money into campaigns and were less likely to support immigration, which, once again, they thought might cost their members jobs, and those, like the Service Employees International Union and the Hotel Employees and Restaurant Employees International Union, that wanted to emphasize organizing at the grassroots level and were pro-immigration reform because they hoped to bring legalized immigrants who filled those jobs into the movement. And then there was the major schism—the schism between conservative Republicans who wanted no bill whatsoever, and liberal Democrats, like Ted, who were willing to do nearly anything to get a bill passed, in Ted's case, again, not because there was any political gain for him in doing so—in fact, given the skepticism of liberals, there was a great deal of trust to lose—but because he wanted to rise to the moral challenge of doing the right thing. Helping immigrants was, to him, the right thing—the thing he had consistently compared to civil rights, the great movement of his lifetime.*

The bargaining continued right up to Reid's deadline and even past it. Though Ted and Kyl reached agreement on Wednesday at noon, and though Ted held a press conference to announce the agreement, with Kyl and Feinstein and Republicans Arlen Specter, Saxby Chambliss, Johnny Isakson, and Lindsey Graham, and though Graham declared the bill the "last best chance to pass immigration reform on our terms"—Republican terms—Ted admitted the so-called "grand compromise" was an overstatement, and that there were yet a few issues to iron out before taking the bill to the floor. Always obstructionist, Cornyn had come armed with four new amendments, of which Ted's top immigration aide, Esther Olavarria, told Ted, "Every one of them is bad, just bad." But Ted knew that rejecting them outright might torpedo the compromise, which already was fragile, so he told Cornyn that he could have a vote on two of his amendments—he could pick which ones—but not all four. Cornyn agreed. ("You're going to take these two amendments," Ted remorsefully told Olavarria, who had tears in her eyes, "or this thing isn't going to happen.") On Wednesday night, while the negotiations continued and the group was reaching exhaustion, Ted by one account looked at them and said, "Let's shoot for ten o'clock tomorrow morning," Thursday, in the Rules Committee room. At eight o'clock the next morning, Ted called Graham in despair. "This thing is coming apart," he told him, and the only hope was that they could pull it together at that final ten o'clock session. But when ten o'clock rolled around, there was a floor vote on another issue, and only Ted and Cornyn, who, again, wanted to wreck the bargain,

---

*Ted would say that three issues brought out the "worst in terms of the functions of the Senate": civil rights, gay rights, and immigration. Of the last, he said, it starts out "reasonably sanitized," and then "it basically deteriorates into racist amendments and racism on the floor of the Senate." EMK int., Oct. 8, 2007, Miller Center, UVA.

showed up to the immigration reform meeting. This time Cornyn arrived with yet another amendment, which was a portent of obstacles to come. So now Ted suggested that everyone convene again in the vice president's room after the vote, but this too turned out to be another portent. Leahy showed up, telling Ted that his state, Vermont, had all different kinds of farmers, and he wanted to scrutinize the bill to see how it would treat those farmers, and he explicitly said that he was "going to just take my time to go through it," even though Reid was pressuring them to get this done as quickly as possible. Then McCain, who had been absent for most of the negotiations, appeared with Chertoff and Specter, and Cornyn told them that he wanted to offer up a few more amendments, and McCain just exploded, telling Cornyn, "We're sick and tired of you," and Cornyn fled the room. And now Ted told them that if they didn't reach some agreement then and there, at that very moment, the bill would fail. With that hanging over them, Ted asked if there were any more amendments to be offered. There weren't. And so now the bill, SB 1348, went to the floor. Ted celebrated afterward by meeting with the members of families who had been terrified by the raid in New Bedford the previous March. "When I told them the bill would make them safe and secure, you should have seen the look in their eyes," he would tell the press. "They knew they didn't have to be scared."

It was a hodgepodge of a bill—all 380 pages of it. Kyl got his guest worker program for four hundred thousand migrants who would receive two-year visas renewable three times, though each worker was required to leave the country for a year after the visa expired, and the program would be initiated only once border controls were in place. Those controls included the 370 miles of fence and fortifications that had been in the 2006 bill, eighteen thousand new border agents, seventy radar stations, enough funds to house 27,500 undocumented detaineess, and new identification cards. Kyl also got his point system. Ted got what was called a "Z visa," which would allow any immigrant who was in the country prior to January 1, 2007, to stay and work, provided the individual had no criminal record, had a job, took English and civics lessons, and paid a $5,000 fine. After eight years, a Z visa holder could return to his or her native country and apply for permanent legal residency. Bush, who had played no role in the negotiations but who wanted credit for a bill, insisted that the bill was "without amnesty." But whatever the president called it, the Z visa was a form of amnesty, albeit hard-earned amnesty, and that was

Ted's triumph—the core of all his efforts. "This is not the architecture of an immigration bill I would initially have liked to see," he said after the bargain was announced. "But we're not dealing with that. This is a legislative process." Ted got his half a loaf or his 80 percent or his good without getting the perfect.

That, however, was just the grand bargain. Now the Senate had to approve the bargain. SB 1348 reached the floor on May 21, and a resolution to begin debate passed easily 69 to 23. But that, like so much else in the immigration reform legislation, was misleading. The bill was not only a hodgepodge; it was fragile. Already the bill's opponents were submitting amendments designed to sink it: One by Oklahoma Republican James Inhofe to make English the nation's official language; another by Democrat Byron Dorgan to eliminate the guest worker program altogether, which would have lost Kyl and almost certainly ended any possibility of passage; a third by Cornyn to require immigrants to pay a surtax to fund any health and education benefits. One amendment would have permitted local police to pick up immigrants if they suspected they had committed a crime—just *suspected* it. Ted said he was standing in the Senate well with Bob Menendez as the amendment was being submitted when a page ran breathlessly up to Menendez and said, "Senator Martinez," mistaking him for the Florida Republican, another Hispanic. "Here's a note for you. Call your office," which prompted Menendez to erupt, "We all look alike don't we?" and then give a speech on the floor ripping the amendment. Ted and Kyl had reached another agreement before taking the bill to the floor—this one to beat back any and all amendments that would substantially change the bill. And Ted also wrangled the bipartisan coalition— the grand bargainers—to meet every day during the debate, as he and McCain had met in 2006, to join forces to detect threats to the bill and to ward off other amendments.

On the floor, it was Ted Kennedy's show. Because of the time pressures and because of Patrick Leahy's reluctance to embrace the bill, it had not gone through the Judiciary Committee for markup and approval. (Ted would later say that if it had been subjected to only three days of Judiciary markups, the delay, which he would have used to build support, and the imprimatur might have made a difference.) Not having been sent to the floor by Judiciary meant both that it didn't have the seal of Judiciary approval and that it was at the mercy of everyone on the floor. Ted orchestrated. He called for votes, he parried objections, he smoothed ruffled feathers, he parceled out time, he questioned his fellow senators and drew out issues, and perhaps above all, he beat back amendments, even those of his fellow Democrats, even those of which he would have approved if they had not threatened the passage of the bill. He was a master of the Senate on those four days of debate late that May, summoning every tool at his disposal—chemical, parliamentary, and moral. And he was nudging the bill, the most important immigration reform in twenty years, as it was generally called, ever closer to passage.

And then came the Memorial Day recess.

While the senators were home, listening to their constituents, the antagonists to immigration reform, especially conservative talk radio and the conservative Fox News cable network, who had commandeered the Republican Party and all but driven the moderates out, seized the debate. Now Republicans were terrified. Jeff Sessions, one of the most obdurate opponents of the bill, said that its supporters had been trying to hurry it through "before Rush Limbaugh," the popular right-wing radio host, "could tell the American people what was in it." The "Kennedy-Bush Amnesty Bill," Republicans had taken to calling it. Meanwhile, Democrats had been hearing from the immigration reform advocates who were pressing provisions of their own. When the Senate reconvened on June 6, after the recess, twenty-one amendments were awaiting votes, including one to sunset the guest worker program, and another, Menendez's old amendment, to have Homeland Security consider previously filed applications for family-based immigration (the "chain migration" issue again), and yet another, from Menendez and Chris Dodd, to double the number of green cards for the parents of American citizens. Kyl said that if either passed, he would try to quash the bill himself, and admitted, "I know that we've got a tough week ahead of us."

It was to be a very tough week. Reid had scheduled a cloture vote to end debate on June 7, a Thursday, which would mean that all the amendments would have to be voted upon by then, and Ted knew that without the opportunity to submit their amendments, even or especially those Republicans whose amendments were intended as "poison pills," the bill would not get cloture and would die, which seemed to be Harry Reid's intention. It was hard to read the majority leader's motives in moving to kill the bill, as he had tried to kill it the previous year, because they were likely mixed. Part of it, he claimed, was wanting to get the Senate in motion again after the bill had stalled its business. Part of it was that Reid was a tough partisan himself who, he admitted, didn't want to give the Republicans a victory among immigrants and employers if the bill should pass, nor one among the Republicans' own dogged rank and file if they managed to defeat it. Part of it was that he might have thought it a waste of time since Republicans really had no interest in immigration reform. And part of it, no doubt, was Reid's genuine fear, as he had said repeatedly, that the bill, as it was likely to be amended, was inadequate and would wind up hurting undocumented immigrants more than it would help them were it to pass.

Whatever the reasons for Reid's dagger, Ted was livid. When he complained to Reid that Reid hadn't let even their Republican allies vote on some of the amendments and that now, having angered them, the Democrats would almost certainly lose the cloture vote to end debate and thus lose any chance of passing the bill, the majority leader told him he had "filled the tree," meaning he had filled the amendment tree, leaving little room for more of the Republicans' amendments before a vote. As Ted would later put it, the "atmosphere had been polluted" by Reid. *The New York Times* called Ted's plea the "last gasp for immigration," and it seemed to have failed. Now neither Reid nor the Republicans hoping to stop the bill made any pretense of working seriously on the legislation. Ted said that the amendments were hustled through that Wednesday night past midnight with little time apportioned for debate. "When they do that, when they don't take their two hours on one amendment," he would later say, "it means they've given up. . . . Our people were off in their hideaways drinking wine." Just past midnight, the Senate voted to approve the amendment from Byron Dorgan, a labor-backed amendment, to sunset the guest worker program, with four conservative Republicans switching their votes to gain its passage, and the bill was effectively killed.* ("I've been trying to kill it since the beginning," said Republican Jim Bunning, one of those who switched.) Ted, who felt that Reid had encouraged Dorgan to submit the amendment, himself was sensing apprehension from the bill's supporters, but he was still not ready to give up, even as the amendments made the bill progressively more conservative. "Hope is a

---

*Young senator Barack Obama had co-sponsored the Dorgan amendment, obviously at the behest of labor in an attempt to kill the bill, which prompted another angry outburst from Ted, accusing Obama "at length," John McCain would say, of "bad faith," though Obama defended himself by saying that he had never agreed to Ted's ground rules of voting against any amendments that might jeopardize the bill. John McCain and Mark Salter, *The Restless Wave* (New York: Simon & Schuster, 2018), 225–26.

powerful thing," he told the press, "and it will not be deterred." At seven p.m. the next day, June 7, with the cloture vote imminent, Ted went to Reid's office and made one final appeal to delay it, saying that if Republicans had the opportunity to amend the bill, even if the amendments were beaten back, Ted felt he could still carry it. Reid countered that the Republicans would only stall the bill anyway with all their amendments if he let them. Ted's Republican allies had said they thought they could reduce the number of amendments down to six or eight and that they should proceed with votes. But Reid, who had never been enthusiastic about the bill to begin with, thought the debate would be too protracted. So at seven-thirty that evening, the cloture vote proceeded. It failed, 45 for to 50 against. The measure of how Republicans had retreated was that only one of them voted for cloture, and even Kyl, who co-sponsored the bill, voted against it. "This place is a very chemical place," Ted told a group of reformers by way of explaining how a bill that seemed to be heading toward passage now suddenly couldn't get a vote to end debate. "There's a rhythm to this place. There's an ebb and flow in terms [of] when things are possible. . . . You have to have a lot of patience." But patience was in short supply. Reid blamed Bush for not pushing more aggressively for the bill, even though Bush's influence among his own party was now minimal and might even have backfired. "The headlines are going to be 'The President Fails Again,'" Reid said, insisting, wrongly, that this had never been a Democratic bill but a George W. Bush bill, but also giving another reason why he seemed determined to stop it. (It was actually a Ted Kennedy bill.) And now Harry Reid pulled the bill, saying that he hoped to resubmit it at a later date if there were an agreement to limit amendments and debate—which, by Senate rules, would require either unanimous consent or a five-day waiting period. That made its resurrection unlikely.

But George W. Bush did care about immigration, and he badly needed a political victory. Reid, after blaming him, sent him a letter asking him to intensify his involvement, and just days after Reid pulled the bill, Bush announced that he would be attending the weekly Republican policy lunch to push for immigration reform—a highly unusual visit. As he flew back on Air Force One from a summit in England before the meeting, he phoned senators, including Kyl, Ken Salazar, and Ted, and discussed the effort to whittle the number of amendments to the bill so that Reid would bring it back to the floor. (Reid was considering relenting only because he was under tremendous pressure of his own—"inundated," as *The New York*

Times put it, "with telephone calls, letters, faxes and e-mails" from "groups as diverse as the National Restaurant Association, the National Council of La Raza, the New England Apple Council and the business software company Oracle" asking him to reconsider putting the bill up for a vote.) After Bush's meeting with the Republican caucus, the White House made Ted an offer: three days of debate and a limit of twenty-one amendments. So eager was Ted to revive the bill that he accepted, even though the new bill, now SB 1649, contained provisions for security measures that SB 1348 had not contained. Though SB 1649 restored the guest worker program, Frank Sharry, the immigration activist, thought that Ted had conceded points that didn't have to be conceded and that "made it harder on the left and didn't pick up any votes on the right." Sharry was right. No one on the left was particularly happy about the new bill. Labor was against it. Latinos were against it because it prioritized skills over families. Most liberals were now against it. "We were holding on by our fingernails," said Sharry, who supported the bill because it included legalization and a path to citizenship.

It was the last chance, but with nearly all the Republicans unalterably opposed to anything but border security, with liberal Democrats feeling that the bill had been compromised beyond the point of usefulness, with Harry Reid disinclined to push the bill and more inclined to kill it, that chance was slipping away. Ted said that Reid and Minority Leader Mitch McConnell sat down with him and discussed how they might reach an agreement to get the bill to a vote, which Ted, perhaps wishfully, still thought he might win. Neither leader, however, seemed to have much interest to push it, and they might have only been humoring Ted. McConnell, Ted would recall, sat there "nodding and nodding, and leaving, and having absolutely no intention of doing anything but sinking the bill." Even for Ted the bill was now "right at the border in terms of my own support," but he felt that if he could steer it through the Senate and if it got through the Democratic House, he could negotiate with Bush, who needed this bill far more than Ted did, to adjust the bill to make it more acceptable for liberals. But Ted was taking a risk. "I want you to know," Cecilia Muñoz of the National Council of La Raza told Ted as the end of debate neared, "that out there in this city there are five hundred mimeograph machines all ready to say, 'Kennedy sold us out.'" And Ted told her, "Well, make sure they spell Salazar right," referring to his close ally, Ken Salazar. That seemed to calm them. "One more crack," Ted said the activists gave him at passage.

Ted, however, was nearly alone in his hopefulness—only Bush also seemed to think the bill was still alive—and even Ted's hope was diminishing. Ted asked to meet Bush personally to plead his case and see if the president might still get Republicans to budge, but Homeland secretary Chertoff and White House chief of staff Joshua Bolten refused, forcing Ted to deal with them instead. "Unless you move toward a compromise," he said he told them, "this is where we're headed," which would be another dead end. "I'm just giving you the straight scoop on it." On June 28, Reid brought up the bill for another cloture vote. Ted took to the floor once again, this time without notes, and spoke passionately of the weight of the moment—"perhaps the most important vote we have had here on the issue over the period of the last three years," and he said "outside of the issue of the war in Iraq, this is front and center of our country." He decried the "voices of fear" that had opposed the bill to bring twelve million undocumented immigrants out of the shadows and said that those opponents had proposed nothing to tackle the problem except punitive measures. And after other senators spoke, he took the floor one last time, one last desperate time, looking "deflated" and "exhausted," Frank Sharry said, his shoulders sagging. And he made one last appeal—this time to the institution. "It was in this Chamber a number of years ago that we knocked down the great walls of discrimination on the basis of race, that we knocked down the walls of discrimination on the basis of religion," he declaimed. "We knocked them down regarding national origin, we knocked them down with regard to gender, we knocked them down with regard to disability. Here in this Senate we were part of the march for progress. Today, we are called on again in that exact same way. This issue is of the historical and momentous importance that those judgments and those decisions were. When the Senate was called upon, it brought out its best instincts, values, and its best traditions. We saw this Nation move forward. Who among us would retreat on any of those commitments? Who among us would say no to that great march for progress that we had in this Nation? The question is: Is it alive? Is it continuing? Is it ongoing?" And he closed: "This is the place. Now is the time. This is the vote."

This is the vote.

And so came the vote that would determine, as Ted Kennedy saw it, whether the 110th Senate would make its moral mark as those earlier Senates had—whether it would do the right thing. Emotions ran high. The Capitol switchboard was flooded that day, mainly from opponents who had been incited by talk radio. Some senators had received death threats. Others had their home addresses posted by opponents. Bush pushed back. He phoned Republicans to urge them to vote for cloture, but to no avail. Republicans were no longer receptive. Though McConnell and Reid had reached a tentative agreement to vote on a limited number of amendments, when Senators David Vitter, Jeff Sessions, and Jim DeMint, all conservative Republicans and all vehemently opposed to the bill, attacked Reid, McConnell simply left the floor and left the agreement. "Intense" jockeying for votes was how *The Washington Post* described the scene that morning before eleven o'clock, when the roll was finally called. And when the vote was taken, cloture failed, 46 ayes to 53 nays. "The bill now dies," proclaimed Dianne Feinstein, one of its authors. The last best chance was gone.

Ted sat at his desk in the back row, dejected. All those years of bargaining had failed. The "voices of fear," as Ted had called them, those on talk radio and in nativist circles, had won. Some colleagues stopped by to console him. Republican Mel Martinez, one of the supporters of the bill, approached and extended his hand. "Thank you, my friend," Ted said. And then later that day, Ted had his office call all the advocates with whom he had worked to gain passage and invited them to a dinner. It was, as it so often had been in the past, even in defeat, even in as stinging a defeat as this one, a celebratory dinner. Ted hugged everyone. "There were lots of tears," Cecilia Muñoz would recall. "But he was also—it's hard to describe—he was relishing the fight. The message he was sending was, 'OK. We are not done. You know, it didn't work out this time, but we are not done.'" And she said he told "war stories" that night about what had happened during the negotiations between himself and McCain and the White House in 2006. And he told them about the twelve hours that he had spent locked in a room with other senators back in 1964 when they were negotiating the Civil Rights Act, and he taught them that they had to see this effort through the "arc of history." Muñoz said that he would later send her a note: "We didn't complete the journey, but we'll get there."

We'll get there.

TWENTY-THREE

Hope

T HE "PERCEPTION OF a creeping chaos—the sense that leaders no longer have a firm grasp on events or the credibility to unite disparate constituencies." That was how *The New York Times*'s Matt Bai identified the reason "political powers come undone" and why George W. Bush's party lost the 2006 midterms. In the year since, the sense of chaos had not abated. The demise of the immigration reform bill was Ted Kennedy's failure, his failure to recognize just how many forces were arrayed against it and how strong those forces were, but it was also George W. Bush's failure—his failure to convince the members of his own party to support the cause and to support their leader, as legislators typically did. Bush had been more successful on the Iraq War, but only somewhat. When, after the midterms, he fired Defense secretary Donald Rumsfeld and then, later, decided to reverse policy in Iraq by not drawing down troops but by pouring more in—a "surge," it was called—Republicans rallied to him, though even that was more likely because the alternative, to admit the miscalculation of the war and embrace what so many Democrats, like Ted Kennedy, had been saying about it, would have been politically catastrophic. Ted submitted a bill early in 2007 that would have capped the troop level at its number at the time, 132,000, and required the president to get approval from both houses of Congress for his surge, and said, "Congress must no longer follow [the president] deeper into the quagmire in Iraq." But where he had once been a lone voice in opposition, his was now increasingly the voice of many Americans who had grown weary of the war. And while Ted fought the way the war was being prosecuted, he also fought to permit those in Iraq who had assisted American forces there to gain admission to the United States under special immigrant status—at a hearing Ted convened, one Iraqi told the senators that those who aided the United States were considered "traitors and infidels" in their own country—and Ted suggested raising the cap from fifty to five hundred, and permitting refugees to be processed in-country, where it was more expeditious, rather than outside the borders. "This was all done quietly," Ted's senior foreign policy adviser, Sharon Waxman, said, for fear, presumably, of rousing conservatives who might oppose it, though Ted complained that of two million Iraqi refugees, only 466 had been admitted into the United States, and that while the administration was spending $8 billion a month on the war, it had budgeted only $20 million in the entire year to assist refugees. Republicans, and even many Democrats, might not have been ready to abandon the war effort— that December 2007 the Senate voted 75 to 25 to provide Bush with $70 billion of unrestricted funds for the war and voted down bills to withdraw troops—but it had carried in large part because it was attached to an omnibus budget bill that Bush threatened to veto if he didn't get his way. "When is enough enough?" Ted asked during the floor debate. Bush won, but he paid a price. Throughout 2007 and into 2008, his approval ratings in the Gallup poll never hit as high as 40 percent.

Moreover, heading into an election year, when legislators were usually reluctant to do anything that might upset the status quo, Bush's agenda largely ground to a halt. There would be no further effort on immigration reform. After the reform bill died that June, it was Ted Kennedy, not George W. Bush, who worked with Immigration and Customs Enforcement on a set of protocols on how to treat undocumented immigrants rounded up during raids who were either pregnant or nursing infants or had children for whom to care—the issues that had so disturbed him during the raids of March 2007 in New Bedford. On the sixth anniversary of the passage of No Child Left Behind, Bush's signature legislation, the law still had yet to be fully funded, even though Congress typically increased whatever the administration proposed. "If you were to give the Act a grade," Carey Parker said, "you might give the mandates," which were the standards proposed by the bill, "an A or A–, but give the funding only a C, and that left a lot of schools shortchanged"—usually the poor schools, Ted would say, and he criticized the act himself for failing to reward schools that had made incremental progress, for encouraging teachers to gear their work to a test, for not involving parents sufficiently, and for ignoring dropouts.

And there was another issue, one very dear to Ted, on which he and the president were at odds. They butted heads on the State Children's Health Insurance Program (SCHIP), which Ted had introduced in 1997 with Orrin Hatch, and which provided healthcare for children who were above the poverty line and thus didn't qualify for Medicaid, but whose parents didn't earn enough to provide health insurance. Late in 2007, both the House and the Senate passed bills increasing the funding so that SCHIP could add roughly six million more children to the four million already covered. The bill, with a price tag of $35 billion, to be paid for entirely by a sixty-one-cent increase per package on cigarettes, sailed through the Senate by a 67-to-29 vote, in a rare bipartisan agreement. And that should have settled the matter. But George W. Bush was no compassionate conservative, despite his rhetoric. His legislative failures and low approval ratings sent him scrambling back to the safety of his party and to its ideology. Bush now threatened to veto the bill, prompting Ted to say of Bush, "With each coming day, he reveals ever more clearly that the values of his administration are out of touch with those of the average American." And then Bush made good on his threat, and when the bill passed Congress again with slight modifications—almost a way for the Democrats to bait the president—he vetoed it again, saying that it would lure children from private coverage they could afford and that it was too expensive, and he called it socialized medicine, the familiar charge that Republicans had leveled at every healthcare reform, including Medicare, though Ted countered, "This is all a matter of priorities: the cost of Iraq, $333 million a day; the cost of SCHIP, $19 million a day." Still, Republicans, even those who had voted for the bill, sustained the vetoes, setting up a potent political issue by branding the party as anti–children's healthcare. (Moreover all four of the party's leading presidential aspirants for 2008 supported Bush's veto.) A $1 million ad campaign, sponsored by a coalition supporting the bill, showed a group of young children and then a baby while an announcer intoned, "George Bush just vetoed Abby," and asked why he prioritized war over children's healthcare.

And to the growing sense of creeping chaos that was now enveloping the administration and the country—the mounting casualties of the Iraq War and the seeming endlessness of it as well as the expense of it, the legislative paralysis, the retrenchment of social programs, the widening gulf between Republicans and Democrats that recalled that of the Gingrich era—was added one more crisis: As the country had headed into recession during the father's administration, so that December did it head into recession during the son's. By the middle of that month, only 32 percent of Americans approved of the president's performance, 65 percent did not.

And amid all that, the Republicans were about to head into a presidential election year.

Given Bush's unpopularity and the problems dogging the Republicans who were saddled with both a badly managed war and an economic downturn, 2008 had portents of being a milestone election for Democrats. Ted Kennedy had been looking forward to it eagerly. No sooner had the 2006 midterms ended than he began pressing John Kerry to make a decision about whether he would be a candidate again, and Ted told *The Boston Globe* that he couldn't wait "indefinitely," lavishly praising two early possible contenders, Senators Hillary Clinton of New York, former president Clinton's wife, and Barack Obama of Illinois, a brilliant, Harvard Law–educated attorney with whom Ted had worked on immigration reform and whom he respected and admired despite disagreements. "Formidable figures," he called them, and said they were "ringing the bells [of the party faithful] because they're talking about what people were, I think, concerned about during the course of the election," referring to the midterms. Ted had a close relationship to Hillary Clinton. She had been one of the liberals in her husband's more centrist and tentative administration—someone to whom Ted would appeal when he tried to get Bill Clinton to endorse one of Ted's liberal initiatives. When she arrived in the Senate in 2001, she said that Ted helped her get a seat on his HELP Committee and gave her advice, which was primarily the advice he had received when he entered the Senate: Do your work and be deferential. "I'm really trying to absorb and learn as much as I can from him," she said at the time. And Ted could have been talking of his own early Senate days when he told *The Boston Globe*, "I don't think she'll ever be just another senator, but I think she'll understand what's necessary to be done in order to gain respect in the Senate," adding, "There may be grudging respect, but I think they'll give it to her."

But Hillary Clinton did not follow Ted Kennedy's advice—at least not all of it. He and Wyoming senator Mike Enzi, a Republican, had decided to introduce a bill on information technology. Hillary called Ted and said that she and Bill Frist, the majority leader, were also working on an IT bill, and when Ted protested that she was trespassing onto his territory, she said that Frist would call up their bill before Ted's. Hillary, however, was tangling with the wrong senator, even if her co-sponsor was the nominal leader of the Senate. Ted met with Enzi who said immediately, "That's not going to happen, Ted. If Bill Frist calls that bill up, I'll publicly oppose it on the floor of the United States Senate, and I've told him that." And then Ted received a call from Hillary Clinton, who had obviously been told of the reprimand, with a request: "Ted, could you put our bill as an amendment to yours when you report out yours? And could I be, then, a principal co-sponsor?" And Ted said he would and she could—that the bill would be "Enzi-Kennedy-Frist-Clinton." And that was how Hillary Clinton got a lesson on how the Senate operated and on how Ted Kennedy functioned there.

Barack Obama was cocky, too, but he also understood the status of Ted Kennedy within the institution, and he appreciated the fact that it was better to be a protégé of Ted's than to stand apart from him. "The thing is, even though he never technically ran the Senate," Obama would later say, echoing what Bob Dole had said, "it often felt like Teddy did. It was his arena. That's why if you came to the Senate hoping to be a great senator someday, he was who you went to see first. I know that's who I went to see first, because rather than lord over it, Teddy sought to mentor others to better navigate it. Rather than go it alone, he sought cooperation." Still, though Ted did his best to mentor Obama—there was the McCain story of Ted upbraiding Obama for not being more cooperative on immigration reform—the two men had not been especially close during Obama's first eighteen months. "Collegial" was how one reporter described their relationship—this of a senator who typically sought to be more than collegial, to be a friend. John McCain said that he never saw a "lot of personal relationship between the two of them." But, by one account, the relationship took a turn when Obama met with Ted in 2006 to ask his advice about whether the young Illinois senator should run for the Democratic presidential nomination. They met in Ted's office, "with the shades drawn and a soft light," Obama would recall, and Ted began telling stories, taking off on tangents as he often did, before settling on the purpose of the visit: Obama's presidential ambitions. By one account, Ted told him, "Your time only comes once, and this is your time." Vicki Kennedy, obviously hearing about it from her husband, described the meeting slightly differently. She said that Ted told Obama, "The brass ring doesn't come around that often, and you'll end up taking votes that you wish you hadn't taken the longer you stay here," which could have been a small lament of his own for how long he had been in the Senate and how often he had been stymied there. But in Vicki's account, he did tell Obama this: "Go for it." And once Obama decided to try to grab the brass ring, he began calling Ted more frequently to draw on his experience. By Obama's own account, Ted was more expansive and told him, "The power to inspire is rare. Moments like this are rare. You think you may not be ready, that you'll do it at a more convenient time. But you don't choose the time. The time chooses you. Either you seize what may turn out to be the only chance you have, or you decide you're willing to live with the knowledge that the chance has passed you by." Ted knew whereof he spoke.

Barack Obama was an unusual presidential aspirant. He was young—forty-six, the age of Bobby Kennedy when he ran for president. He had been in the Senate only two years after being in the Illinois state legislature for eleven, and before that had been a community organizer, which was not a typical way station toward the presidency. But something else about Barack Obama distinguished him from nearly every other presidential contender in American history. Barack Obama was Black. His father was Kenyan, his mother a white woman from rural Kansas, and Obama himself grew up largely in Hawaii, where his mother attended university, then lived with her in Indonesia, after she divorced Obama's father and married an Indonesian graduate student she had met at the University of Hawaii, and then Obama returned to Hawaii for high school. He was an exceptional student—at Harvard Law he would be president of the *Law Review*—as well as charismatic. Tall and thin and dignified and a masterful speaker like one of his political forebears in his adopted state, he would be called "Lincolnesque" when he ran for office in Illinois. He was also recognized as a political comer. Though only a senatorial candidate at the time, he was chosen to deliver the keynote address at the 2004 Democratic National Convention and made a powerful and eloquent affirmation of America that raised his stock even higher—so high that two years later he could consider what would otherwise have seemed an improbable presidential run.

Inspiring, Obama was called, and among those who were inspired was Caroline Kennedy Schlossberg, John Kennedy's daughter and Ted's niece. As early as Christmas 2006, Caroline said that her children were talking about Obama, and one of their friends was working for him. Caroline said that she attended events at which Obama spoke that spring and met him on Martha's Vineyard that summer. And she said that she and her children had begun talking up Obama to her uncle. But Ted had differences with Obama, even as he had expressed admiration for him. Obama had apparently made a comment at an AFL-CIO meeting in June 2003 at which he criticized Ted for having lent support to Bush's Medicare drug benefit plan—an issue that had become sensitive for Ted when he felt Bush had betrayed him. "We've got to call up Ted Kennedy and say, 'Ted, you're getting a little old now, and you've been a fighter for us before,'" Obama was supposed to have said. "'I don't know what's happening now. Get some spine and stand up to Republicans.'" Ted had a clipping of the remark and showed it to Illinois senior senator and majority whip Dick Durbin, and Durbin, by this account, phoned Obama, who insisted he hadn't said it—Durbin had actually seen a video—and Obama then went to Ted's office to offer an apology. Moreover, Ted was still miffed over Obama's behavior on the immigration reform bill, when he felt the young senator had reneged on his promise—the promise Obama said he hadn't made—not to back liberal amendments that might imperil the bill's passage.

But Ted Kennedy had his issues with Hillary Clinton as well. Once she declared her candidacy, he found her campaign unnecessarily abrasive, and he was offended by Bill Clinton's alluding to a Southern Strategy for Hillary and suggesting that were he to gain the nomination, the Black Obama would be at an electoral disadvantage because of his race. Ted was particularly troubled by Clinton's comment, to rebut those who compared Obama to young John Kennedy, that Lyndon Johnson was the one responsible for the Civil Rights Act of 1964, despite the work of John Kennedy and Dr. Martin Luther King, Jr., before Johnson. "Dr. King's dream began to be realized," Clinton said, "when President Johnson passed the Civil Rights Act. It took a president to get it done." Ted took that as a personal affront—an insult to his late brother. So Ted was caught between two candidates who had some very real assets but about whom he had some personal concerns. And to resolve his uncertainty, Ted said he had one quality for which he was looking. "I was waiting to see who was capable of lifting up and inspiring our nation to move forward, to our highest and best ideals, before I decided to endorse anyone," explaining why he was refraining from making an endorsement during the early primaries in late 2007 and early 2008. But sitting with Vicki and watching Obama's victory speech on January 3 where he won the Iowa caucuses, Ted said that he and Vicki "knew that he had the capacity to inspire."

It was a sign of the weight that Ted Kennedy's endorsement was perceived to carry that Clinton supporters and Obama supporters, including some from his former staffers, barraged him with phone calls to lend his voice to their candidate. One of those supporters was the former majority leader Tom Daschle, who was working with Obama to "monitor and generally nudge, persuade, or just suggest to my former colleagues that they ought to look at Senator Obama." Daschle said he would occasionally call Ted during that time and that he detected Ted's irritation at the pressure the Clintons had been applying to him. Other pressure was coming from within his own family, and it was far more persuasive to him. Caroline was ready to declare for Obama, seeing in him, she said, the same qualities that her father had had, especially the quality to inspire that Ted prized so highly. ("I'm looking for someone who can inspire," Ted told Tim Russert, the moderator of *Meet the Press* late that January, as he was on the verge of making a decision, once again citing inspiration as his primary criterion.) The South Carolina primary was to be held on January 26, a Saturday. By that point, Gregory Craig, Ted's old foreign policy adviser, had gone to work for the Obama campaign and had been up to Iowa and then New Hampshire for the primary there and then to South Carolina, and Craig was distressed by what he regarded as the Clintons' innuendoes in that state against Craig's candidate—that Obama's campaign had strongarmed voters in the Nevada primaries; that Obama had dissembled about his opposition to the Iraq War; that Jesse Jackson, another Black candidate, had also won the South Carolina primaries, hinting that white people like Hillary Clinton would have a difficult time winning there—so distressed that he decided to write Ted a letter explaining why he was supporting Obama and why Ted should too. (Craig had cleared the idea with Vicki.) No sooner had Craig's law office delivered the letter to Ted's home than Craig received a call from Ted, who said that he had scheduled a phone call with Bill Clinton and asked if Craig might prepare a series of talking points on the things the Clintons had done that Craig considered "off base" and "over the line." Craig said it took him only a few minutes to compile a list. Meanwhile Craig got a call from Caroline Kennedy—Ted had asked if he could show Craig's letter to her—who told him, "I'm thinking of doing something," that is, endorsing Obama, and Craig and Caroline spoke for about forty-five minutes.

Ted's call with Bill Clinton was "difficult," as Evan Thomas of *News-week* described it. Ted enumerated what he saw as the Clintons' errors of judgment—no doubt the Craig list—and Bill Clinton was defensive. "Well, they started it," he said. "Well, I don't think that's true," Ted responded. But Ted might have been looking for excuses. By that time, he had made his decision: He would endorse Obama. When a colleague asked him why, Ted answered simply, "Caroline." Caroline had already decided to write an op-ed for *The New York Times* scheduled for Sunday, January 27, the day after the South Carolina primary, in which she announced her choice and laid out the reasons why, and she had informed the Obama campaign earlier that week. That Wednesday, January 23, Ted called Daschle in an attempt to get in touch with Obama, and Ted and the candidate spoke early Thursday morning, at eight o'clock, while Obama was campaigning in Dillon, South Carolina. "Listen, pal," Ted said he told him when they finally connected. "Is there room on that train of yours for an old—" And Ted said that before he could finish his sentence, Obama burst out laughing. And Ted told him what he had felt about him: that he could inspire the nation. Caroline's op-ed appeared three days later, invoking her father's presidency—"A President Like My Father," it was titled—and summoning the heyday of the liberal consensus when the country seemed to be headed in the right direction by the liberals' assessment. "We need a change in leadership in this country," she wrote, "just as we did in 1960." Writing of Obama, but clearly recalling her father too, she said, "I want a president who understands that his responsibility is to articulate a vision and encourage others to achieve it; who holds himself and those around him to the highest ethical standards; who appeals to the hopes of those who can still believe in the American Dream, and those around the world who still believe in the American ideal; and who can lift our spirits, and make us believe again that our country needs every one of us to get involved." When Hillary Clinton's campaign manager, Patty Solis Doyle, read the essay, she reportedly said, "Oh, my God. We're done."

It was change that Caroline, and subsequently Ted Kennedy, were endorsing as well as inspiration—a new generation of leadership. Yet even as he had decided to back Obama, but before he had announced it, Ted suffered a pang of his own political mortality. Laurence Tribe, Ted's quondam constitutional adviser and Obama's onetime law professor at Harvard, called Ted in this period and asked to meet with him. Ted was appearing at a fundraiser for Dick Durbin at the Parker House Hotel in

Boston, and he and Tribe met in a large empty ballroom. Tribe launched into his appeal for Obama, but Tribe said Ted immediately cut him off and revealed that he was about to endorse Obama. But then Ted told Tribe, "You know, Barack is very much in favor of turning the page," by which he meant turning the political page. And Tribe recalled that Ted made an "interesting" comment, though *poignant* might have been a more apt description. "That means turning the page on people like you and me," he mused. And Tribe realized that as impressed as Ted was by Obama and as enthusiastic as he seemed to be over a change in the nation's course, Ted recognized that Obama would be ushering in a "new period of history" and that Ted himself belonged to the old one.

The pending endorsement, which was to come that Monday, January 28, was an event at which the old generation passed the torch to the next. Bob Shrum had come to Ted's house that Thursday after Ted's phone call to Obama to help draft a speech to be delivered at American University, and Ranny Cooper, Ted's old administrative assistant, was there too, and Greg Craig arrived with a bottle of champagne and a bouquet of balloons, and Ted took him aside and asked a favor. Patrick had already endorsed Hillary Clinton. Would Craig have a word with him? And Craig met Patrick at the Mayflower Hotel over breakfast and explained why he was supporting Obama over Hillary and why he was so excited about it and what he thought it would mean to the country. Ted had, no doubt, meant for Craig simply to ease Patrick into his father's decision, though Craig would laugh that he got Patrick to reconsider.

It was an unusual speech Ted Kennedy delivered that Monday afternoon, just before one o'clock before a cheering, festive crowd of thousands in the American University gymnasium, Patrick Kennedy now among them, sitting behind his father, and Ted standing at a wooden podium with a blue sign on its front, "Change You Can Believe In," his body thick, his hair snow white, reading the speech through glasses with flesh-colored plastic rims—unusual in how fervent his endorsement was; unusual in how, as *The New York Times* observed, "deeply personal" it was for a political speech; unusual in that he did something that he seldom did now, which was invoke the memory of his late brother, John Kennedy; unusual in that the speech was less about the failings of George W. Bush and his party or even about the promise of Barack Obama—though he gave Obama fulsome praise as someone who could and did "connect with people from every walk of life," and who could and did "appeal to the better angels of our nature," and who could and did have the capacity to "close the book on the old politics" of division that pitted one group against another and would unite the nation, and who could and did generate "new hope that our greatest days as a nation are still ahead"—than it was about a force of change that was rippling through the country. "I feel change is in the air," he said with his trademark quaver. He said, "The world is changing. The old ways will not do." He exhorted the crowd that they could "replace the politics of fear with the politics of hope," but only if they had the "courage to choose change." He quoted Martin Luther King about the "fierce urgency of now," and he recalled how former president Harry Truman advised John Kennedy to wait his turn because he was too young to run for president and how John answered him: "It's time for a new generation of leadership." And the crowd, largely students, chanted, "Yes we can. Yes we can. Yes we can." And throughout, Barack Obama, the object of the effusion, sitting behind Ted and next to Caroline, listened intently, still, his left index finger resting lengthwise on his nose or his chin resting on his fist, seeming to understand the enormity of it—the enormity of the Kennedys handing their legacy to him. But what might have been the most unusual thing about the speech was the very aspect that Ted had reflected upon when he met Laurence Tribe in that empty hotel ballroom a week earlier: Ted was himself turning a page and celebrating a new generation, and in so doing, he knew he might have been writing his own political epitaph.

But Ted Kennedy did not seem like a man on the wane. His endorsement had been coveted. Barack Obama had been the upstart, the rookie, the darling of the elites, as some analyzed it. One even compared his coalition to the old George McGovern coalition of 1972—"educated, upper income liberal voters; Blacks; and the young"—that had failed so disastrously then. Ted's endorsement had given the imprimatur of full-throated blue-collar liberalism to Barack Obama, of whom one Democratic strategist said that he "has had the Starbucks vote throughout the campaign," alluding to the educated professional class that allegedly bought its coffee at the upscale Starbucks chain, and that "Ted Kennedy can now help with the Dunkin' Donuts vote, and that's what he needs to round out his candidacy—to be able to appeal to classic Democrats." (In point of fact, Ted Kennedy did have plebeian tastes; he loved Dunkin' Donuts.) Obama understood the implications of the old Democrat endorsing the new. He told *Time* of Ted, "Nobody's better than him," and called him the "heart and soul of the Democratic Party—the belief in civil rights, the belief in opportunity for all people, in upward mobility, in caring for the least of these." And Obama, admitting that the public was still getting to know him, thought, "Their vision of this day will make them give me a closer look." "Bamalot," the *New York Post* headlined its coverage, melding the Kennedy aura with Obama's, and quoting Obama's speech that afternoon that he had been too young to remember John or Robert Kennedy's campaigns, but "in the stories I heard growing up, I saw how my grandparents and mother spoke about them, and about that period of our nation's life—as a time of great hope and achievement." *The CBS Evening News* led that night with the endorsement. "It was a moment packed with political significance," reporter Jeff Greenfield said. "The torch has been passed." Even though it had been forty-five years since a Kennedy sat in the White House, anchorman Brian Williams opened the story on *NBC Nightly News* with the "Kennedy name still has the power to grab the attention of millions of Americans," and correspondent Lee Cowan followed, "A nod from the Kennedy camp would put a whole new trajectory to his campaign," speaking of the Obama campaign, and the "endorsement brought the Kennedy mystique to this campaign." On ABC's *Nightline* that evening, David Wright said that the "audacity of hope had its rendezvous with destiny," combining the title of Obama's memoir with a line from John Kennedy's inaugural address that Kennedy himself had borrowed from Franklin Roosevelt. Obama would later have another take of the importance of that endorsement. He said that it had "added poetry to our campaign."

New York Times columnist David Brooks, writing the next morning, recognized that in all the rhetoric about change, there was also a strain of nostalgia that united the young Obama and the old Kennedy—a coming-together of generations. Once his own presidential ambitions had been dashed, Brooks wrote, Kennedy had embraced the Senate and "served that institution with more distinction than anyone else now living." But he could do so, Brooks believed, because "culture really does have rhythms." And the "respect for institutions that was prevalent during the early 60s"—the JFK era—"is prevalent with the young again today," and those young people cheering Obama, and Ted, were aware that they functioned not as "self-made individualists" but as "parts of networks, webs

and communities." And what they promised was a reversion to civic virtue like that Ted extolled from his brothers' days. "There was something
important and memorable," Brooks concluded, "about the way
75-year-old Kennedy communed and bonded with a rapturous crowd
half a century his junior.

"The old guy stole the show."

All of which suggested that Ted Kennedy wasn't finished quite yet,
even if he feared he might be. He was still trying to revive the moral commitment that he felt had once stirred the nation and to restore the moral
authority that had once energized the Democratic Party before the Republicans managed to tarnish it by posing liberal support for minorities
and immigrants and the poor as a danger to traditional white America
and by denigrating government activism on their behalf as a danger to
individual liberty. And this time, many, indeed a whole generation, seemed
to be listening. This time, Ted hoped, the moral authority could carry the
party to victory and the nation to its better angels.

Barack Obama, however, still had a nomination to win, and the race was
still neck and neck. After the endorsement, Ted Kennedy headed west to
stump for Obama in several of the twenty-three states that were about to
cast their primary votes in what was known as Super Tuesday—"hot, hot,
hot on the trail" was how Mark Leibovich described Ted's campaigning in
The New York Times. "Are you glad to see me, Santa Fe?" Ted shouted to a
crowd at a rally at a community college there. And they shouted back,
"Yes." The crowds were large, "raucous," said the *Times*. In East Los Angeles, the crowds screamed, "Teddy! Teddy!" And when Ted, attempting to
speak in Spanish, mangled the sentence with his thick Boston accent, and
the crowd laughed affectionately, he joked, "There may be some who don't
understand my Spanish. It's a Castillo accent." He was swarmed by fans,
reaching for him, asking for his autograph, as they had for Bobby's forty
years earlier, and security men had to push them back. "It's like when
Tony Bennett suddenly became hip again after the kids discovered him,"
one of Ted's former campaign aides and a Democratic consultant, Bill
Carrick, said, comparing Ted to the old singer whose career had been revived. Ted himself acknowledged a "special kind of feeling this time," and
Patrick observed that the campaign seemed "more personal" to Ted than
some others had been. "It's like an opportunity for him to connect with
the touchstone of his brothers' legacy," which was the point Brooks had

made. Again and again in his speeches, he referred to the past, to the sixties, to his brothers, and to Martin Luther King and Cesar Chavez, and to the Voting Rights Act and the Civil Rights Act, and to laws that ended discrimination. It was Jack and Bobby all over again, only with Obama as the centerpiece. And while Ted could be solemn in recounting those liberal triumphs, solemn in talking about John and Bobby, he was also enjoying his campaign swing immensely. "Pretend we're love birds," Vicki said as a photographer took their pictures while they boarded a charter plane in Albuquerque. "Yes, love birds, love birds," Ted said. And as the love birds crossed the country for Obama, Ted called the campaigning "fun, sheer fun."

And after Obama won thirteen states on Super Tuesday while Hillary Clinton won ten, Ted returned to his Senate to vote on a $158 billion stimulus package to help ease the recession that was now roiling the economy. Hillary was on the floor and in a chipper mood after her respectable showing. Ted was cautious. The Clintons were not pleased with his endorsement of Obama. He had been bombarded with angry calls from their supporters. Lindsey Graham, then traveling with his friend John McCain on the campaign trail, phoned Ted and asked if he could have his hideaway office in the Capitol, and when Ted asked, "Why?" Graham said, "Because the Clintons are going to have you murdered." Ted hated confrontation, unless it was to move legislation. He was apprehensive. But he approached Hillary, who was speaking to Dianne Feinstein at the time and made a few self-deprecating remarks, since Hillary had carried Massachusetts, which prompted Obama to chime in, "Maybe, Hillary, I should have let him endorse you," and when Ted spotted John Kerry, Ted joked, "Well, I'm not too good on the endorsing. I endorsed Kerry, too, and look what happened to him."

And now, with some of the tension relieved, he and Vicki, exhilarated, headed back to the campaign trail.

II

Ted Kennedy, who had been an athlete in his youth, had ceased to pay particular attention to his health. He was always in a battle with his weight and usually lost. His back ached from the days of his airplane accident, and where once he had sprinted through the halls of Congress, at seventy-five he ambled, his arms swinging stiffly, his body pitched forward and listing slightly from side to side, that gait that had been described as an Irish cop's, but stepping lightly, one last vestige of the grace he once had, as if he were afraid to dirty the carpet. It was an old man's walk. He seldom visited the doctor, and Vicki said that one day, in the hope of getting him to make an appointment, she told him that his doctor had called and had set up an appointment for him. But Ted knew she was, as Vicki put it, "lying through my teeth," and acted incredulous that his doctor would do such a thing on his own volition and said sarcastically, "How kind of him." When, in October 2007, he had surgery to clean his left carotid artery—a "very high-grade blockage," it was called, that was discovered during magnetic resonance imaging he routinely underwent to check on his spine—it was his first serious hospitalization since his plane crash in 1964 that had necessitated those routine spinal MRIs. His legislative pace, though, never slackened. Three days after the surgery, he was back on the Senate floor. Nor did his determination to help others fight illness slacken. Early that May, he chaired a Senate hearing on cancer, with the cyclist Lance Armstrong and the wife of Senator John Edwards, Elizabeth Edwards, both of whom had fought cancer, and he declared that it was time for new weapons to battle the disease on which he had helped declare war in 1971 with the National Cancer Act. He was all too familiar with cancer. After the hearing, he choked up with emotion when he recalled to the press Ted Jr.'s bout with bone cancer that had cost him one leg, and Kara's bout with lung cancer, and though he didn't mention it then, his brother-in-law Stephen Smith's losing battle with cancer had devastated Ted.

There was, however, to be one more encounter. Ten days later, on the morning of May 17, a morning dark with clouds and damp with rain, a little before eight o'clock, Ted was at his Hyannis home, having coffee with Vicki in the sun room, and then got up to take Sunny and Splash on their morning walk. (By some news accounts, he had already returned from a walk and from hitting tennis balls to the dogs. By his own account, in his memoir, he was preparing to take them.) As Ted himself would describe it, he arose from the table and "meandered" through the living room of the Big House, his father's and mother's old house and now, after Rose's death, his. He passed the piano at which his mother had so often sat to play and at which he had so often sung to her accompaniment. At that moment, he suddenly felt "disoriented." He said he told himself that he just needed some fresh air and headed for the porch that overlooked Nantucket Sound, Ted's beloved sea. But he never made it to the porch. Instead, feeling unsteady, hazy, he stopped at the dining room and lowered himself into a chair.

And then he blacked out.

He would later learn that their household assistant, Judy Campbell, discovered him in that chair and that she called out to Vicki and that Vicki ran in from the sun room and told Campbell to phone 911 and Ted's physician, Dr. Larry Ronan. And then Vicki knelt beside him and cradled his head and kissed him and whispered, "You're going to be all okay." And then a Hyannis police officer who said he had been an army medic arrived—within four minutes—and then, almost immediately thereafter, the paramedics did and then they took him to Cape Cod Hospital—by one account, Ted suffered a second seizure en route—while Vicki phoned his doctors, who arranged for a helicopter to airlift him from Barnstable Municipal Airport, just minutes from the hospital, to Massachusetts General Hospital in Boston. And Vicki phoned family members and told them they should come. And then Vicki rode with the Hyannis fire chief on the half-hour ride to Boston. By yet another account, it was during the short flight that he had another seizure, either his second or third. His father-in-law, Edmund Reggie, told *The New York Times* of the seizure, "I would think that's bad, but they said it was good. He moved all his limbs, head, neck, everything. They said it was a good sign he was not subject to a stroke." By the afternoon, the sedation had worn off, and Ted was joking with his family and friends—Ted Jr., Kara, and Patrick had all rushed to the hospital, as had Caroline and his nephew Joseph II, and his stepchildren, Curran and Caroline, and John Kerry and Kerry's wife, Theresa—and they watched the Red Sox play the Milwaukee Brewers on television and ate chowder brought in from Legal Seafood, one of Ted's favorite restaurants, and Ted was already asking when he could return home. The next morning Barack Obama, who was campaigning in Oregon, called to wish Ted well and told the press afterward that he had expected Ted to be groggy but instead he "sounded like the Ted Kennedy we all know and love," and Ted joked with Obama about how this was what happened when you had an "old politician going out there on the road" and that the "old lion needed to catch his breath." George Bush called too and told Vicki, "Take care of my friend." The rest of the day, Ted watched baseball and some films his family had rented—*The Great Debaters, Best in Show,* a few Fred Astaire and Ginger Rogers movies. Meanwhile his doctors performed a battery of tests, and he had a brain biopsy as doctors investigated what might have caused the seizure.

The news of the seizure hit Washington like a "small earthquake," *Time* reported, not, it said, because of the narrow political concern for how it might affect the Senate's balance of power, but because of the larger concern of how it might create a moral vacuum in Ted's absence— the absence of the man for whom the encomium had now become nearly obligatory: "one of the greatest legislators in the history of the country." Outside Mass General, the media, dozens of them, congregated, with rows of microphones and cameras, and long snakes of wires. Edmund Reggie quipped of his son-in-law, "I said a lot of people do things to get their name in the newspaper, but not quite that." Ted himself seemed unflappable. There were no subsequent seizures. He was soon up and walking around the hospital, his usual gregarious self.

But the test results that arrived on Monday and were announced on Tuesday afternoon brought a dark mood that settled over the nation like a storm cloud. Though many of those tests, his doctors, Dr. Lee Schwamm, the vice chairman of neurology at Mass General, and Dr. Larry Ronan, Ted's own primary care physician, reported, had proved inconclusive, "preliminary results from a biopsy of the brain identified the cause of the seizure as a malignant glioma in the left parietal lobe. The usual course of treatment includes some combinations of various forms of radiation and chemotherapy. Decisions regarding the best form of treatment for Sen. Kennedy will be determined after further testing and analysis." It was unemotional language, clinical language, language without affect, language that belied the gravity of the prognosis, especially with its upbeat conclusion that he "remains in good spirits and full of energy." What the doctors had said was that Edward M. Kennedy had brain cancer, an aggressive form, an incurable form—what NBC science reporter Robert Bazell called "one of the worst kinds of cancer diagnoses you can get." A death sentence.

A "very pessimistic prognosis" was how Vicki would later describe what she and Ted heard that morning. One of his doctors told him that he had only two to four months to live. Vicki said that Ted "wouldn't accept it" and "it just didn't compute with him." And Vicki issued an email that day calling the "last several days" a "rollercoaster" and calling the diagnosis a "real curveball." And yet putting the best possible spin on it, she said, "This is only the first inning" and that Ted "is leading us all, as usual, with his calm approach to getting the best information possible." Meanwhile he is "making me crazy (and making me laugh) by pushing to race in the Figawi this weekend"—an annual sailing competition from Hyannis to Nantucket in which he had raced every year since his early adulthood. She added that Ted was in "fighting form, and ready to take this on." Though it might have sounded like one, this was not a gloss for public consumption. Ted *was* in fighting form. He advised his staff to go back to work, while, an associate said, Ted was "plotting his course of treatment as if he were mapping a strategy to enact a piece of legislation, peppering his doctors with questions and planning to reach out to other specialists before determining a course of action." As for whether he had pondered retirement, a friend said, "It's not even an option." Another confidant, his old administrative assistant, Larry Horowitz, who was also a medical doctor, said that while Ted accepted the inevitability of the outcome, "It's nothing compared to the feelings he had when people told him his children had cancer." John Tunney, who spoke to Ted after the diagnosis, said that while those who loved him were "having a very difficult time addressing this new reality," Ted "knows that cancer can be beaten because he's seen it in his own family time and again," and was "very positive in his conversations about the future and how he will address the cancer. When you talk to him, you just feel better." But even as he girded for the battle of his life—and *for* his life—and even as he faced it with equanimity and even levity, Vicki said that after the diagnosis, he put his affairs in order, presumably meaning settling all legal issues pertaining to death.

The news of the seizure had been a storm cloud hanging over the country, pregnant with threat and impending grief. The news of the diagnosis was the storm. The effect was profound. The effect was devastating. At the weekly Senate luncheon of the Democratic caucus that day— where John Kerry announced the diagnosis—there was stunned silence. "Ted Kennedy spent his life caring for those in need," Majority Whip Dick Durbin said. "Now it's time for those who love Ted and his family to care for them and to join in prayer to give them strength." At the Republican luncheon, Senator John Warner said his colleagues interrupted their business to pray for the man whom so many of them had berated in their campaigns. When Robert Byrd heard the news on the Senate floor, he wept and then looked at Ted's empty desk and said, "My dear friend, I love you," and, wiping his eyes with a tissue, repeated, "Thank God for you,

Ted. Thank God for you." One after another his colleagues called him a "fighter" and a "lion"—the "last lion in the Senate," John McCain said, "because he remains the single most effective member of the Senate." Frank Lautenberg said he "makes the Senate the place that it is." Patrick Leahy said that in his thirty-four years in the Senate, he had a hard time remembering a day "I've felt this sadly," and former senator Bob Kerrey, in expressing his own sadness, said of Ted that "he's the one politician who brings tears to my eyes when he speaks." Harry Reid said, "He's not just the patriarch of the Kennedy family; he's the patriarch of our family," meaning, of course, the Senate itself. And he was.

Those were his colleagues. Even members of the press, normally reserved, normally cynical about politicians, were neither reserved nor cynical about Ted Kennedy that day. Carl Hulse of *The New York Times*, citing how Congress struggled with "why the mere thought of a Senate without Mr. Kennedy was so unsettling" and asking "what about the idea of Mr. Kennedy never again thundering from the floor, lumbering down the hallway or joking in the corridor," was so "disturbing to lawmakers, no matter their party," concluded that Ted Kennedy, "love him or loathe him, personifies stability and continuity"—a "sense of reassurance that political tumult is transitory while serious achievement is not." And Hulse noted, too, that "few are willing to take the risks that Mr. Kennedy has in attacking the big topics of the day, hammering away at the injustices he sees, leaving him red-faced and shouting on the floor"—in short, his moral courage and his moral outrage. And columnist Bob Herbert, also in the *Times*, wrote of how many old friends had called Herbert "who just wanted to talk, to express their sadness and revisit the memories of years now stretched into decades for which Jack, Bob and Ted are still the touchstones." "I'll tell you, man, this Teddy thing has hit me hard," said an old high school pal of Herbert's. "The brothers meant a lot. They were inspirational. I don't care what anybody says." On *NBC Nightly News* the evening of the diagnosis, anchorman Brian Williams said the report "made a lot of Americans think about our past and his future." And then there were the ordinary Americans—overwhelming Ted's office phones with their calls, so many that other senators loaned their staff to help field them, and sending eleven thousand emails to his office by midday.

His was a stricken nation, but Bob Herbert ended his column reminding readers that while this was being called "Senator Kennedy's toughest fight . . . this is a guy who has experienced every kind of horror, who went down in a plane, who had to fight back after Chappaquiddick, who had had two kids stricken with cancer and on and on. So who knows?

"All I know is that the show's not over until the curtain comes down, the lights go out, and everybody has left the theater. We're not there yet. Hang in there, Ted."

The fight would continue that Wednesday morning when he left Mass Gen and returned home to Hyannis and to the sea with Vicki and Sunny and Splash, a white bandage on the back of his head where the biopsy had been, crowds waving to him as his black Chevrolet Suburban cruised down Route 3, one of those supporters hanging a "Get Well" banner on an overpass. (A picture of him leaving the hospital and waving to well-wishers was on the front page of *The New York Times* the next morning.) "Remarkably quickly" was how his doctors said he had recovered from the procedures he had undergone, which was why they had decided to release him earlier than planned—days earlier. And having arrived home, less than an hour later he and Vicki and the dogs boarded the *Mya*, Ted's blue fifty-foot schooner, and headed out to sea, Ted wearing a red City Year jacket—City Year being a public service organization for young people—with his name embroidered on the front. Since his hospitalization, this was where he had wanted to be, he said, on those waters. And when, two hours later, he returned to the dock, "shuffling," as one reporter put it, to the black Suburban, he said, "It was wonderful to be on the water. It's all it takes," and remarked, "It's nature. It's the closest thing to nature . . . sort of an aspect of life—some place you grew up on, learned to swim on, learned to sail on," though what he was really saying was that the sea had given him so much in his life and now he returned to savor that place and those memories. A metaphor, it had been, of the churn and constant evolution of life. Now he called it an "*affirmation* of life."

He had not been accustomed to slowing down, but now he had to. He had been scheduled the Saturday following his seizure to give the commencement address at Wesleyan University from which his stepdaughter Caroline would be graduating that day, but he had to bow out and asked Barack Obama if he would fill in. "Considering what he's done for me and for our country," Obama said, "there's nothing I wouldn't do for him." And Obama's speech, while summoning the hope that the country could unify after its divisions and encouraging the new generation to assume the challenge, was also a tribute to the Kennedys generally and to Ted specifically—to all the battles he had fought, from providing healthcare for children to creating family leave for parents to raising the minimum wage to allowing people to retain their health insurance when they changed jobs—and he said, with Vicki in attendance, "I have a feeling that Ted Kennedy is not done just yet." Some of those graduates had stenciled the word HOPE and an outline of Obama's face on their mortarboards. It was thought Ted would miss the Figawi Regatta that weekend, —the race he had begged Vicki to sail after his seizure but before his diagnosis—and *The Boston Globe* reported his *Mya* sitting idly in the harbor that Saturday, its sails furled, and Ted slowly, haltingly, making his way down the dock with Sunny and Splash and a small band of friends, waving to photographers, the *Globe* said, but looking tired and holding on to a railing as he made his way to the boat for a leisurely sail as the racers he longed to join were headed to Nantucket. But that Monday, Memorial Day, he took a ferry to Nantucket and then surprised the press by helming the *Mya* in the race's last leg, back to Hyannis, a southern wind in her sails now, a two-hour trip, with Vicki and Chris Dodd and Ted Jr. and Ted Jr.'s wife, Kiki, and Patrick and Ted's stepdaughter Caroline on board, and wearing a blue windbreaker and a Boston Red Sox hat, he told the reporters afterward that "it couldn't be a more beautiful day," and one crew member told the *Boston Herald* that Ted had been in a "great mood" and Ted himself hastened to add, "I think we ended up in the front part of the fleet." (Actually, the *Mya* had come in second in division three in the Nantucket-to-Hyannis leg.)

Despite the grim prognosis, the certain sentence of death, he was a Kennedy and Kennedys were stoic. They did not surrender, Joe Kennedy would not let them surrender, and Ted Kennedy refused to surrender. "We were taught never to give up, never to passively accept fate, but to exhaust every last ounce of will and hope in the face of any challenge," he would write in his memoir. And citing the similarly grim prognoses for Ted Jr. and Kara, he wrote, "I would live on for as long as I could. And in electing to live on, I would offer myself as an example to those struggling with the unacceptable news that there is no hope." "Live each day to the fullest," Vicki would later say of their attitude, "but be very realistic also, not bury our heads in the sand, not be Pollyanna." And yet she said it was not just Kennedy stoicism or Kennedy courage that Ted was expressing; Ted would not let his optimism waver, even in the face of the diagnosis, even in the face of realism: "We never even felt that this was a man who was dying." "Life is a bowl of cherries," he told his old Senate colleague Alan Simpson when Simpson phoned him shortly after the diagnosis, and Simpson would send him cards in "exceedingly bad taste," by Simpson's own admission, and Vicki said they made him laugh. And though Ted loved the Senate and thought of it as his second family, he said that he became very close to Phil Hart, the conscience of the Senate, a man whom Ted tried to emulate, when Hart was dying from cancer—closer, he said, than when the two had been colleagues on the Senate floor—and that Hart was one of the first to choose to stay home with his family after his diagnosis rather than come to the Senate. Now Ted chose to do the same—to stay at Hyannis with Vicki, to stay near the sea.

But not just to rest. To fight. Four days after the Figawi, Ted asked Larry Horowitz if Horowitz might convene a group of doctors to discuss treatment options for him just as Horowitz had done when Ted Jr. was diagnosed. It was Ted's way—to brief himself with experts, as he briefed himself on legislation, and to be the best-informed man in the room, though this time there was an obvious difference: They were providing him information on his very survival. *Save Ted Kennedy's life*—that was the mission, as difficult, even impossible, as it might have seemed. "My role is to reach out to everybody everywhere," Horowitz told *The Boston Globe*—to Mass Gen, to Brigham, anywhere across the country—and he said that he had already had "dozens of discussions" with experts at the National Institutes of Health, the FDA, research hospitals, and pharmaceutical companies. (It was Horowitz who, years ago, had pointed Ted to the experimental treatment that Ted Jr. had undergone to save his life.) The experts Horowitz collected met on May 30 at Mass Gen, and Lawrence Altman, the medical correspondent of *The New York Times* and a doctor himself, said that it was a remarkable gathering for two reasons: because it demonstrated the ability of someone with resources to gather this esteemed group; and because it demonstrated Ted's efficiency in bringing together some of the biggest authorities on cancer, a dozen of them from around the country, in one place, while others participated by phone. "Horowitz is trying to organize all the flying objects" was how Gerard Doherty, Ted's onetime political adviser from the days of his 1962 run and a longtime friend, described the effort. The experts debated. Some recommended surgery to remove the tumor. At least two, by the account of one of the participants, disagreed, and Dr. Raymond Sawaya, the chair-

man of neurosurgery at the Baylor College of Medicine and the MD Anderson Cancer Center in Houston, said that the tumor had spread over too
large an area now for it to be removed successfully. Ted nevertheless made
the decision: surgery. There was, however, a problem. He was scheduled to
receive an honorary degree—this one important to him, this one from
Harvard, this one from the institution at which he had embarrassed himself as a freshman—just six days after the consultation, but doctors advised him that it would be imprudent to wait that long for the surgery. So
Ted personally phoned Harvard president Dr. Drew Gilpin Faust to ask if
he could reschedule. (At the ceremony, when she told the graduates and
guests that Ted would receive his honorary degree at a future time, the
crowd stood and applauded.)

The doctors at Mass Gen had agreed with Dr. Sawaya's assessment
that the surgery was likely to be futile, but Ted had made up his mind. He
arranged to fly to Duke University where that Monday, June 2, he underwent a three-and-a-half-hour operation. (Lest his legislative initiatives
wither during his recovery, on his way to the airport he phoned his close
friend Chris Dodd and asked him to take his place in promoting a mental
health parity bill that would give mental health sufferers the same insurance benefits as those who suffered from physical illnesses, and he called
Barbara Mikulski to ask her to take his place on the conference for the reauthorization of the Higher Education Act that provided funds to help
poor students afford a college education.) Dr. Allan Friedman, the surgeon and co-director of the Brain Tumor Center at Duke University Medical Center, declared the operation "successful" and said it had
"accomplished our goals." Ted, who was awake through most of the procedure because surgeons in this type of operation probe the brain to make
certain that they have not impaired the patient's ability to function, told
Vicki afterward that he felt "like a million bucks." There was still hope,
however vague, however small, though not hope for recovery—hope for
postponing the inevitable. Doctors not involved in the surgery told *The
New York Times* that the fact the tumor was operable was a "good sign."
"Better than anyone expected" was Patrick's assessment afterward. Ted's
stepdaughter, Caroline Raclin, who later worked with patients who had
undergone brain surgery and would see them the next day and the day
after that, said that "they don't get up and walk; they're not able to, that's
it." But Ted, she said, "got up and walked, you know?" And she added,
"He's just disciplined. It's creepy. 'I'm going to do this, and I am going to

get better.' " One account had him up and walking the hospital hallways the very next day. And Patrick said that Ted talked about getting back to the Senate so that he could work on healthcare legislation should Barack Obama win the election. "That is what he is talking and thinking about," Patrick told reporters. "It adds a great deal of poignancy to his recovery. . . . He has to recover so that he can get health care for the millions of people who don't have access to the care that we do."

Still, this was wishful thinking—*Kennedy* thinking. His senior counsel, Kathy Kruse, and a staffer from his Boston office, Tom Crohan, and the office director, Barbara Souliotis had all gone down to Duke Medical Center in Durham during Ted's hospitalization, and Souliotis admitted it was nerve-wracking because "we just didn't know what the result of the operation was going to be." They wouldn't know even after the surgery, since Ted would still need chemotherapy and radiation treatments when he returned to Hyannis. He stayed in Durham for five days and then flew back north on June 8, with the doctors issuing a statement that they are "pleased with his progress since surgery." Throughout Ted's medical crisis, the Democratic nomination was still being contested, and on the same day that Ted was released, Hillary Clinton announced that she would be withdrawing from the presidential race and endorsing Barack Obama. Obama would be the Democratic nominee.

And now, with Ted back in Hyannis, began the recuperation. He was prepared to "do battle," Patrick said when the family gathered there the following Sunday to celebrate Father's Day. Visitors came—Chris Dodd and friends from Harvard and some from his days at Virginia Law—but Patrick said everyone appreciated that Ted needed "moments of quiet"— "space and time to recover where he doesn't have to be 'on,' " this for a man who had spent most of his life being "on." It would be a tranquil summer. He would sail virtually every day, and he would rest. Ted Jr. set up an office next door, in Jack's old house, and he and his family stayed there throughout the summer. Kara too brought her two children to spend the summer at Hyannis. His sister Jean rented a house nearby, and his sister Eunice and Bobby's widow Ethel had their homes there, and the Kennedy cousins and now their children too congregated at the compound. And Vicki managed everything. "She basically put my uncle, who had always carried our entire family on his shoulders," Ted's nephew Joe II would recall, "she put him on hers, and she just carried him." And though Ted suffered fatigue, when he could, he worked the phones to his colleagues because he couldn't let his Senate business drift. He and Patrick worked together on the mental health parity bill, and Ted was drafting a national service act that would provide a way for individuals to give back to the country through public commitment. And there was always national health, which he believed would have a new chance were Obama to win the presidency, and which he hoped to launch as soon as Obama took office. And while he was focused on the nation's business, in his own distress, he also thought of the distress of others, as he had so often done in the past. Tom Daschle's brother was suffering from the same kind of cancer—a glioma—that Ted had, and Daschle phoned Ted and Vicki, who connected him with their doctors. And while Daschle's brother underwent the same regimen as Ted did, up in Boston at Mass Gen, the Kennedys loaned the family their apartment there throughout the course of the treatments. And when Robert Novak, the conservative political columnist who had often taken aim at Ted, was also diagnosed with glioma, Ted and Vicki phoned him—as Ted had phoned Michael Kelly's widow—recommending Dr. Friedman at Duke, who wound up operating on Novak as he had operated on Ted.

"The news is really all positive and encouraging," Vicki wrote in an email to the Kennedy family and to Ted's close friends early that July. "My incredibly strong and resilient husband is handling the treatment very well. The only side-effect is fatigue, and that word has never been in Teddy's vocabulary before. But he's learning to cope with it." She wrote that he exercised every morning and then took the ninety-minute drive to Mass Gen for treatments—targeted proton-beam radiation—and on the drive back he made phone calls to friends and his fellow politicians. And when they returned to the Cape, he sailed, Vicki said. "I have drawn the line at thunderstorms," she wrote, "but other than that, he's out on the water just about every day." And she added something else: He was "still pushing all the issues he cares about." Ted described his cancer, she said, as a "bear." She, however, told those friends and family that she was "betting on the lion" to beat the bear. But Joan Kennedy, who had seen Ted over July 4 at a family celebration, was less optimistic. She said the gathering was somber. "It was like [he] was their real—like their father," she said, speaking of all his nieces and nephews, so many of whom had no father now. And there was the dread of what seemed inevitable: the loss of that father.

. . .

The Senate returned that July for a month to tackle unfinished business, one piece of which was a Democratic effort to prevent the Bush administration from slicing 10.6 percent from doctors' fees in Medicare; and a Democratic bill that would allow a 1.1 percent increase in those fees to be offset by a cut in payments to private insurers in the Medicare Advantage program, a private opt-out program, which was one of the sticking points—a sticking point because Republicans wanted to encourage private healthcare and discourage Medicare. Even the American Medical Association, which had opposed nearly every healthcare reform, including, initially Medicare itself, backed the Democratic plan, and doctors throughout the country complained that they could no longer afford to accept Medicare patients with the fees continuing to drop. Some said they couldn't afford to practice at all. Democrats had fallen one vote short of cloture on June 26, just before the July 4th recess. And now, as the bill came up for another vote on July 9, Majority Leader Harry Reid needed every single Democrat to get to sixty. He had told Ted that, given the danger of Ted's catching an infection while his immune system was compromised by the treatments, he would ask him to return to Washington only if he absolutely needed Ted's vote. And now he did. Ted and Reid spoke several times that week, and there was a debate among Ted's family and staff, according to one account, over whether he should go. Ted ended it. "I'll be there," he told Reid.

Republicans had not been forewarned, lest they mount a defense. And Vice President Dick Cheney had met Republican senators at their regular Tuesday luncheon, warning them that the president was going to veto the bill should any of them decide to join the Democrats and vote for cloture. The vote came later that afternoon at four o'clock while Ted waited in Reid's office. And then, at four-fifteen, as the roll call was being taken, Ted suddenly, surprisingly, arrived on the floor through the front of the chamber, flanked by a praetorian guard of his close friends Chris Dodd and John Kerry, and his son Patrick, and the Democratic presidential nominee, Barack Obama, while Vicki and his niece Caroline and members of his staff sat in the gallery, beaming. His white mane of hair was in disarray, and his face was bloated by steroids. (Ted himself would have another explanation for his weight: He ate a lot of previously forbidden, locally produced Four Seas ice cream that summer: "I may be the only patient in the history of Massachusetts General who went through both chemotherapy and radiation and *gained* weight!") But he was steady. Debbie Stabenow of Michigan bolted up the aisle to hug him. Patrick Leahy put his arm around him. And then, once the Senate realized what was happening, realized that Ted Kennedy had come back to them, lumbering up the aisle to the clerks at the dais where his vote would be recorded, other senators and their staff, Republicans and Democrats alike, rose and began applauding, and by one account, "spectators rained down applause from the galleries." For many, their eyes welled with tears. Some of his colleagues slapped him on the back. Some shook his hand. A few—Patty Murray of Washington and Amy Klobuchar of Minnesota—kissed his cheek. Minority Leader Mitch McConnell smiled at him. And around him the mob of senators swelled. "It was like an emotional depth-charge had been dropped in the Senate," Patrick would recall. "Everybody turned to watch it explode." And then, as the commotion subsided, Ted banged on the table with his hand—partly to steady himself, Patrick would say—raised his arms, his palms open, "like a preacher receiving a blessing," wrote one reporter, and Ted shouted, "Aye," and with his arms still raised, gave a "thumbs-up" sign. And then he was crowded once again by well-wishers. The cloture carried 69 to 30, with nine Republicans switching their votes, presumably because they knew they had already lost. And Ted Kennedy had once again beaten back a Republican effort to subvert one of his social programs. "I love this place," he told reporters afterward.

III

All that summer, since the day he decided upon his surgery in early June, Ted Kennedy had harbored a "secret goal," as he called it—harbored it through the six weeks of radiation and chemotherapy, harbored it as he recuperated at Hyannis, harbored it as he gradually began to regain his strength. Ted Kennedy's goal, his "mission" that he said had "stayed in the forefront of my mind" as he underwent those treatments, was to address the Democratic National Convention that would nominate Barack Obama in August in Denver. He had his old staffer and speechwriter Bob Shrum come up to Hyannis to help draft the address, though the mission remained a secret for fear that he might not be able to fulfill it. "Things are day to day," a source said on the eve of the convention, while his spokesperson Melissa Wagoner said an appearance would be "extremely unlikely." Patrick said, "If anything, it'd be an eleventh-hour call," but said that if his father felt up to it and the doctors approved, "he might be able to pull it off." Vicki was opposed to his going, and another spokesperson said, "He's truly humbled by the outpouring of support and wouldn't miss it for anything in the world," yet added that while he might appear at the convention, he would not be speaking. Instead of a personal appearance, in mid-July, the documentarians Ken Burns and Mark Herzog shot a short film about Ted in which he delivered some remarks that would be shown during the proceedings.

But even amid the secrecy, Ted overruled Vicki and flew into Denver late Sunday evening, August 24, the day before the convention opened, and went directly to a hospital for what was called a precautionary examination, given the ongoing concern about his immune system. (Patrick said he had actually gone because of abdominal pain.) And yet now, once he was in Denver, the speech he so desperately wanted to deliver was endangered. He had survived the flight, but once he had settled into an apartment that had been rented for him, he felt a stabbing pain and was taken back to the hospital, where he was diagnosed with kidney stones, which were often collateral to chemotherapy. Now, Ted would later recall, his concern was that the medication, strong medication that he would take to alleviate the pain, would prevent him from speaking. Vicki, who, Ted said, was usually "unflappable" at times of crisis, began crying since it now seemed as if all Ted's preparation would be in vain, his desperate desire to speak thwarted. Nevertheless, after all those weeks of fixating on making an appearance, Ted was not about to let kidney stones stop his speech. He said he made an agreement with the doctor to give him only as much pain medication as he might need to get him through the day and that would be purged from his system by the time of the speech. But a nurse hadn't received the instruction and gave him the larger dosage. Vicki suggested that he go out on the stage and wave, but Ted insisted that he hadn't come to Denver to wave. He arranged to cut the speech should he suffer from drowsiness from the medication, and the shorter version was put on the teleprompter, though because the surgery had impaired his eyesight, he had had to memorize the speech. He took a nap, then awoke to see if he could walk. He could. Still, it was "touch and go," as Caroline would describe it, whether he would be up to speaking or not.

But it was not touch and go as far as Ted himself was concerned. On his left hand he wore an ACE bandage from which a medical tube protruded from the intravenous solutions he had been given. And backstage, uncharacteristically silent, he sat on a golf cart that had taken him from his car to the Pepsi Center auditorium, not looking like a man about to deliver a rousing address. And yet despite the cancer and the kidney stones and the medication and his general infirmity, he was ready. He had been ready for weeks. "He knew it all along," Caroline would say. "There was no way he was not going to do it." It was Caroline who introduced him, telling the crowd that she had come to "pay tribute to two men who have changed my life and the life of this country." Speaking of Obama, she said that never had anyone "inspired me the way people tell me my father inspired them. But I do now: Barack Obama. And I know someone else who's been inspired all over again by Senator Obama. In our family, he's known as Uncle Teddy." And then Caroline segued from the nominee to her uncle. "More than any senator of his generation, or perhaps any generation, Teddy has made life better for people in this country and around the world. For forty-six years, he had been so much more than just a senator for the people of Massachusetts; he's been a senator for all who believe in a dream that's never died." And she recounted a few of the many achievements of her uncle Teddy. They played the film that Ken Burns and Mark Herzog had made—"He feels a moral obligation to do everything possible to make this a better world," Vicki says in the film—and when it ended, the lights came up.

And then at seven-thirty Mountain Time, Ted took the stage, walking gingerly—he was called a lion, but he moved like an old circus bear—steered by Vicki in a bright pink jacket and black skirt, who kissed him tenderly and retreated as he stood in his trademark blue suit at the lectern, bathed in cheers, even as some in the crowd, including some in his own family up in the gallery, wiped away their tears. "My fellow Democrats, my fellow Americans, it is wonderful to be here. And nothing, nothing is going to keep me away from this special gathering tonight," he opened, his voice steady. He talked of how so many of them had been with him in the "happiest days and the hardest days," "in victory and defeat," but "we have never lost our belief that we are all called to a better country and a newer world." And he pledged then that "I will be there next January on the floor of the United States Senate when we begin to write the next great chapter of American progress." And the crowd began chanting "Teddy" and waving blue placards with KENNEDY lettered in white. He spoke of hope. And he concluded: "If we set our compass true, we will reach our destination. Not merely victory for our party, but renewal for our nation. And this November the torch will be passed to a new generation of Americans." And echoing his great speech from an earlier convention, he concluded, "The work begins anew. The hope rises again. And the dream lives on." And when he finished, the crowd leaped to its feet, and the band played "Still the One," and Ted lumbered in his rolling gait over to the dignitaries on one side of the stage to shake their hands, and then he walked across the stage, bent, halting, and embraced his family and they him, and then he departed, leaving the stage empty. "Triumphant," Adam Nagourney of *The New York Times* would call the appearance, writing that "every sentence was greeted by loud applause," and that while Ted spoke slowly, he was "firm and energetic," and sounded "very much like the man who had enraptured the party's convention 28 years ago," referring to his speech at the 1980 convention when he caused the convention to stampede and overshadowed the nominee, Jimmy Carter. It wasn't a long speech—scarcely seven minutes—and even then, Patrick would say, his father stopped to wave during the cheer lines, which Patrick realized was his father's way of gathering his energy for the next rhetorical assault. The triumph was that he was able to deliver it at all. When, four years earlier, Ted spoke at the Boston convention that nominated John Kerry, it had seemed like a last hurrah. (Ted's white shock of hair even resembled that of Spencer Tracy who played the aging pol in the film *The Last Hurrah*.) Now some reporters used the same term, a "last hurrah," only this time everyone knew this really would be the last hurrah for Ted Kennedy. And while the crowd cheered, these were cheers not of joy but rather of tribute, tinged with pathos. When Ted Kennedy left that empty stage, everyone knew that he would never be returning. Everyone knew that this was the end of a deep friendship and of a political era.

The Senate reconvened after Labor Day for a five-week session before recessing again for the campaign, and Ted Kennedy wanted to be there, but his doctors advised against it, and at the convention he had reset his return for January when he hoped Barack Obama would be inaugurated. Many of those dog days of summer he spent resting, sailing, and receiving accolades. The Mexican government had announced in July that it would award Ted the Aguila Azteca, the highest honor the government could bestow upon a foreigner, which it gave him for his championing of migrants and for his work on immigration reform. Later that month President Michelle Bachelet of Chile made a special trip to Hyannis to award him the Order of the Merit of Chile for his support of that country while it was ensnared in the dictatorship of General Augusto Pinochet. (Ted had made that brave trip to the country in 1986, even as Pinochet hired goons to protest the visit and harass Ted.) Ted and President Bachelet took a golf cart from the Big House and down the long slanting lawn to a rose bush where they both made brief remarks. President Bachelet called him "one of the true friends of Chile," and said that he was "there for us when human rights were being massively and systematically violated, when crime and death was around our country." And Ted, who had nearly toppled while walking across the thick grass and who had a patch on his head, quoted the great Chilean poet Pablo Neruda that a person could cut off a flower but not deny spring, which seemed to be as much a personal reference as a comment about the Chile's emergence from the horrors of the Pinochet regime.

But it was not like Ted Kennedy to bask in glory, any more than it was like Ted Kennedy to retreat from battle. In those first weeks of September, Melody Miller, his longtime staffer, said that he was on the phone every afternoon with his office and videoconferenced with senators—he had what his stepson Curran called a "giant camera" in his room—and induced them to introduce legislation with his co-sponsorship. (He announced that he and his old partner, Orrin Hatch, would be introducing the Serve America Act to recruit Americans to perform public service.) "He's getting people to drop things in the hopper," Miller said, speaking of bills. "He is talking to various folks about strategic planning for health insurance should Obama win, so that we'll have all of the groundwork laid between the House and the Senate staff people who will handle the legislative path of this." And she said he would "hit the ground running when Obama comes in." The staff, always regarded as the best in the Senate, if also the most arrogant, picked up the slack for the things that Ted could not do from Hyannis. And even his former staffers, feeling the imminence of his decline and the need for comfort, had, as Ted's former foreign policy aide Nancy Soderberg put it, begun "regrouping now because Kennedy is so sick, and having dinner and keeping in touch and reminiscing." And she said that they would look around the table at the array of talent and say to themselves, "God, this is a great group. It's really extraordinary," and they would attribute it to Ted—to Ted Kennedy who always knew how to "attract real talent and keep it."

But the sense of pride and gratitude wasn't only about the job and the legislation and the way Ted Kennedy had enabled them to make a differ-ence and change the nation. He meant more to them than that. It was about how he had taught them to live. Tom Rollins, who nearly twenty years earlier had been the chief counsel of the old Senate Labor Commit-tee, wrote Ted in this period: "I know you're hearing from everybody about how you're the greatest senator ever, which of course you are. I was there. I watched you do it. And I know you're hearing from everybody about the impact of your legislation, and you know all that. You've been there." But then Rollins recalled something else. He recalled one day when he was with Ted at Dulles airport after the senator had arrived on a long transcontinental flight and was waiting for yet another flight, and Ted called Patrick, who was just a boy then, and he said, "Hey, what do you mean, 'Who is this?' It's your loving da." And Rollins recalled think-ing, "Your loving da?" Given the way Rollins was raised, more formally, less emotionally, he said to himself, "If those words came out, that meant dad needed to be taken to a hospital." And he remembered thinking, "What would it be like to say that to a kid? What would it be like for your kid to hear you say that about him?" And when Rollins wrote Ted, he wrote that "I just want to tell you what you did to my life and what you've done to the lives of my children. I learned how to be a loving parent from you." And Rollins closed: "My debt to you in inestimable. I shall honor and love you all the days of my life." And Ted, even as he knew he had little time left, even though he and Rollins had scarcely talked in twenty years, took that time to write him a letter back, thanking *him* "for making me proud and touching my heart."

Ted had seemed strong and healthy that summer. Despite his unsteadi-ness, he had spoken "forcefully," wrote one reporter, and he "showed few signs of his illness" at the press conference with President Bachelet. But the illness always lurked. Two days after President Bachelet's visit, at roughly five o'clock in the evening, Ted said he was feeling unwell and was rushed by ambulance to Cape Cod Hospital. A "mild seizure," as the result of a change in medication, was the diagnosis. Ted insisted on returning home by eight that night to watch a presidential debate between Obama and the Repub-lican candidate, Ted's old legislative partner John McCain. But in a con-test about which he so desperately cared, all he could do was watch.

It erupted in the middle of the presidential campaign. George W. Bush, in his ongoing efforts to undermine what he saw as government interference in the economy and what he deplored as dependence upon the government, had stressed turning the country into what some conservatives had come to call an "ownership society"—that is, a society that did its best to remove government from personal decisions. Most of his efforts—the Medical Savings Accounts, the privatization of Social Security, the attempts at vouchers in No Child Left Behind—had failed. One, however, had succeeded: programs that encouraged individuals seeking to buy a home. Under Bush, homeownership rose to just under 70 percent of Americans, and housing prices rose too. Lenders were only too glad to provide subprime mortgages—another name for low-grade mortgages—to people who, under previous market conditions, might not otherwise have qualified for a mortgage but who, under a housing boom, did. Some 20 percent of mortgages in 2007 were of the subprime variety. And so long as the housing boom continued, there was no problem.

But the boom didn't continue, and neither did the rising value of mortgage-backed securities. As George W. Bush would describe the situation in his memoir, "Together, the global pool of cash, easy monetary policy, booming housing market, insatiable appetite for mortgage-backed assets, complexity of Wall Street financial engineering, and leverage of financial institutions created a house of cards. The precarious structure was fated to collapse as soon as the underlying card—the nonstop growth of housing prices—was pulled out."

And so, seemingly without warning, one by one, the cards fell: first the investment house Bear Stearns; then government-sponsored enterprises and mortgage lenders Fannie Mae and Freddie Mac; then Lehman Brothers, which announced a $3.9 billion loss and five days later filed for bankruptcy; then the brokerage house Merrill Lynch; then the insurance company American International Group, which the government, fearing an even greater collapse, bailed out in return for 80 percent of the company. One by one. "Wall Street got drunk, and we got the hangover" was how Bush himself described the subprime binge and its aftereffects. The entire American economy was teetering. The worst economic disaster since the Great Depression, it was called. Republicans had always ballyhooed their economic stewardship, notwithstanding the fact that Democrats had been far more successful in guiding the economy, and that even Reagan's much-vaunted economy, to which Republican successors pointed triumphantly, was overrated when measured by most metrics. Now a Republican administration was charged with saving the country from an economic collapse it hadn't foreseen, and George W. Bush was charged with the double dose of an unpopular war and a catastrophic recession. The primary remedy, as devised by Treasury secretary Henry Paulson, was to seek a $700 billion appropriation so that the government could buy up the bad subprime mortgages and mortgage-backed securities—basically a bailout of those who had gambled and lost—in an initiative called the Troubled Asset Relief Program (TARP), which, after failing to become law once, largely because of Republican unwillingness to back it, despite the imminent economic collapse, finally passed Congress on October 3.

If the collapse shook the entire economic system, it shook the political system as well. Republicans hadn't begun the fall race in an especially strong position, given the president's unpopularity. When they lost a congressional seat in Mississippi that May in a special election, Republican representative Tom Davis warned in a memorandum, "The political atmosphere facing House Republicans this November is the worst since Watergate." And the recession and bailout—the Dow Jones Industrial Average fell 777 points the day the latter passed—didn't help matters for John McCain. Writing in *Rolling Stone*, Matt Taibbi cast the 2008 presidential election as very much like all recent elections in which conservatives put liberals on the defensive: "It's not about the war, or the economy, or the faltering Republican brand, or any of that: This is about hate and fear . . . the seemingly endless quest to crush the mythical leftist revolution, which for some reason has spent most of the last half-century cleverly disguised as a bunch of ineffectual bourgeois New Yorkers sitting around watching Stanley Kubrick movies and eating whole foods while conservatives took over the world."

But Bush's disasters had changed that mechanism, and most observers would see it differently. Conservatism had once again overplayed its hand. In the 2006 midterms, *before* the recession, Republicans had lost independents by 18 percent; had gotten less than 30 percent of the Hispanic vote; had lost the suburban vote for the first time since 1992; and had been crushed by Democrats in the contest for the under-thirty vote. McCain, sensing the backlash, initially played down his conservatism, but that only served to attract the opprobrium of conservative zealots like the radio host Rush Limbaugh, who called McCain's "embrace of a radical environmental agenda" a sign that the Republican Party was "abandoning those things and those people that made it victorious." But when McCain selected Alaska governor Sarah Palin as his running mate, a woman who pandered to the most strident and extremist wing of the party, a woman who divided the country between "real Americans" (conservatives) and un-Americans (liberals), a woman with little governmental experience, a woman McCain barely knew, he tied himself to the very policies that now seemed discredited. (Bush wanted to campaign for McCain; he said he was never asked.) Writing in *The New Republic,* Hillary Clinton's former press secretary Howard Wolfson noted, in contrast to Taibbi, how different this election was from recent ones because the old Nixonian labels on which McCain via Palin finally relied no longer worked: "John McCain, raised in Nixonland, calls Senator Obama a socialist, trots out a plumber to stoke class and cultural resentments,* and employs his Vice President to question Obama's patriotism by linking him to terrorists. Nixonland 101—and if its rules still applied, Senator Obama would be in trouble. But they don't." George Packer, writing in *The New Yorker,* made a similar argument: that Obama didn't seem to fear conservatism the way Democratic candidates typically did because conservatism had lost its potency. "By the end of the campaign, Obama wasn't just running against broken politics, or even against the Bush Presidency," Packer wrote. "He had the anti-government philosophy of the entire Age of Reagan in his sights."

It had been a long time, since even before Ronald Reagan, that Democrats had been bold enough, confident enough, to talk that way—to talk about a moral vision. A very long time. But even as Barack Obama's stock and that of the Democratic Party rose, Ted Kennedy, the moral compass of that party, wasn't able to participate in the campaign designed to elect his chosen candidate.

The combination of the war and the recession and the administration's incompetence over Hurricane Katrina seemed to have sealed the Republi-

---

*The plumber was Joe Wurzelbacher, who confronted Obama during an appearance in Toledo, Ohio, telling him that his tax plan would burden the plumbing company Wurzelbacher intended to start. (Obama said that it would cost him more only if the company made more than $250,000 a year.) McCain adopted the would-be plumber, under the moniker, "Joe the Plumber," and he became a meme in the campaign for the ordinary Joe who allegedly would be harmed by Democratic tax policies.

cans' electoral fate, though the foundation for that fate had been laid long before the election with the Republicans' hawkish foreign policy that punished Saddam Hussein for Osama bin Laden's crimes, and with Bush's privatization push and no-look regulation of the financial industry that led to the housing tailspin, and with the administration's lack of interest in effective governance, the consequences of which were the tragedies of Katrina, largely among the Black community, and with its disdain for any Americans but the Republican base. Barack Obama won the presidency on November 4 by seven points with 52.9 percent of the vote. Democrats gained eight seats in the Senate and twenty-one in the House—a humiliating defeat for the Republicans. Premortems had anticipated a Republican loss. Now as the postmortems that examined that loss rolled in, they called it not just a change of power or even a repudiation of one party for another. It was an "inflection point," analyst Michael Barone called it, in which public sentiment finally shifted against conservatism; or more positively, a "swing to the left," as *Newsweek* portrayed it, citing a Pew poll that showed Americans now much more likely to embrace liberal policies and values; or a "political milestone," as Nicholas Kristof called it in *The New York Times*, in which the working class no longer voted like stockbrokers; or a "ratification of an essential change in the nature of the country," as Joe Klein called it in *Time*, or a "realignment" election like the elections of 1932 and 1980 that had changed the basic political coalitions. George Packer, in another *New Yorker* piece, this one titled "The Fall of Conservatism," wrote that the nomination of John McCain—the "least conservative, least divisive Republican in the race"—already showed "how little life is left in the movement that Goldwater began, Nixon brought into power, Ronald Reagan gave mass appeal, Newt Gingrich radicalized, Tom DeLay criminalized, and Bush allowed to break into pieces." As Packer analyzed it, the disparate factions of conservatism— "libertarians, evangelicals, neoconservatives, Wall Street, working-class traditionalists"—had been held together by Reagan and the Cold War. Now he asked, "Without the Gipper and the Evil Empire, what was the organizing principle?" (The organizing principle, borrowed from the old anti-Communist playbook, which always had a liberal page, seemed to be that liberals were the new Communists, an evil fifth column that posed an existential threat to the American way.) Stanley Greenberg said the Republicans appeared "increasingly as an aging, monochromatic, regional party in the grip of its evangelical base." Ron Brownstein in the *National Journal* argued that the Republican Party had long been a regional party, a Southern party, which was how Richard Nixon had devised it after Lyndon Johnson lost the South to racial animosity with his civil rights campaign, and that "Republican strength in the South has both compensated for and masked the extent of the GOP's decline elsewhere." And Brownstein noted that the party over the past five presidential elections had won a smaller share of the Electoral College votes outside the South than in any other five-election span in the party's history. (Obama beat McCain by fourteen points outside the South.) Others said that the Republicans were victims of their own success. Bush speechwriter Michael Gerson, in an essay, "How My Party Lost Its Way," said that the "Republican coalition of the 1980s was built around a series of issues—reducing high marginal tax rates, reforming welfare, fighting crime." And now, just as Hubert Humphrey had once attributed the demise of liberalism to the fact that it had passed its agenda, Gerson said, "The success of this agenda has made it less compelling." Representative Tom Davis, who had been sounding the warning of an impending Republican decline for several years, agreed with Gerson but with an emendation: "With the heavy lifting out of the way, we indulged in more trivial pursuits, and this led to trouble." By *trivial* he meant issues like stem cell research, which Bush had thwarted, school prayer, and opposition to gay marriage, and by *trouble* he meant the party's lack of interest in minorities, the young, and the urban—growing cohorts of the country. "Not so long ago, it was easy to paint the Democrats as extremists," Davis said. "Now, they say, we are the extremists, and voters agree." Thomas Frank, in the *Wall Street Journal*, put it more bluntly: "What had been contained to the movement's feverish fringes," he wrote, speaking of conservatism, "moved to center stage." Others blamed George W. Bush personally and his arrogance. Writing before the election, Evan Thomas in *Newsweek* cited the Republican verities— "lower taxes, stronger defense, conservative social values" (he failed to mention one of those verities: racial antagonism)—and said Bush had squandered the voters' trust in them. "He seemed to be saying, 'I'm taking care of this, you have to trust me.'" And those who didn't were "scorned as ditherers or cowards." Ron Brownstein added that Bush had further divided the country and would call the election a "final grade on Bush's bruising and polarizing political strategy," in which he governed "more by mobilizing his base than by reaching out to voters and interests beyond it." His guiding principle, Brownstein wrote, was "deepen, not broaden." In the end, it shattered his party.

But there was another side to the election—the side that Ted Kennedy had long wished for: not just the decline of conservatism, but the revival of liberalism. In Chicago's Grant Park the night of Obama's election, where he would make his victory speech, tens of thousands gathered, many of them cheering, many crying tears of joy. Peter Beinart in *Time* contrasted it to a scene in the same park in August 1968 during the Democratic National Convention, when Vietnam war protesters were attacked by police and chaos ensued, as well as an eventual Democratic electoral defeat to Richard Nixon. For Beinart, the "distance between those two Grant Park scenes says a lot about how American liberalism fell, and why in the Obama era it could become once again America's ruling creed." It fell, he said, "because Americans who had once associated it with order came to associate it with disorder instead." As he characterized it, "racial freedom came to mean riots and crime; sexual freedom came to mean divorce; and cultural freedom came to mean disrespect for family, church and flag." And Nixon and Reagan took full advantage by "promising a new order: not economic but cultural, not the taming of the market but the taming of the street." But now, after the economic disorder of the housing collapse, Obama could restore the order that Beinart felt had sustained liberalism in its good times.

There were other interpretations, many interpretations, of what Obama's victory meant for liberalism: "You're really talking about a new deal," Democratic representative Barney Frank predicted, foreseeing a "new era of government restraint of the banking and financial services industry," akin to what Franklin Roosevelt enacted after the Great Depression; a "momentous moment" that heralded "generational change," "geographic realignment," and "racial progress," editorialized *The Washington Post*; a "new majority" of the center-left that would only get stronger from demography, one that was young, diverse, female, secular, tolerant, and well-educated, as opposed to Karl Rove's so-called "permanent majority" of evangelicals and the "country-club establishment," Stanley Greenberg thought; a new liberal appeal to the most affluent voters, who typically chose the Republicans, observed pollster Mark Penn in *Politico*; also a new Democratic majority of a postindustrial society, which indicated a reversal of the politics of resentment, said John Judis in *The New Republic* (by the same token, Obama lost the white working-class vote to McCain by 18 percent, though that cohort had declined 15 percent since 1988); the end of the myth of an "irrepressible moral conflict pitting a 'real America'"—Sarah Palin's term—"against some pale imitation," wrote E. J. Dionne, Jr., also in *The New Republic;* and a "new kind of politics: more decentralized, entrepreneurial and grassroots," opined *The Boston Globe* in a postelection editorial. Perhaps most important, Obama's election seemed to be less a political touchstone than a cultural and even moral one. "His election in and of itself displays how dramatically America has moved to transcend the division of its past," Laurence Tribe, the Harvard Law professor, observed in *Forbes* of Obama. Republicans had spent decades working to open those divisions—Nixon's "positive polarization," as Rick Perlstein had called it. Now Barack Obama had given hope, to those Americans who wanted an end to those divisions, that he could close them.

And there was still one more inescapable component to Barack Obama's election: race. As *Time* reported, when the contest was called for Obama, "there was a rush of noise, of horns honking and kids shouting and strangers hugging in the streets. People danced in Harlem and wept at Ebenezer Baptist Church and lit candles at Dr. King's grave. More than a thousand people shouted 'Yes we can!' outside the White House, where a century ago it was considered scandalous for a President to invite a black hero to lunch." "Remember this day," Nancy Gibbs went on to write. "We now get to imagine, at least for a while, that the election of Obama has not just turned a page in our politics, but also tossed out the whole book so we can start over." In *Newsweek,* Anna Quindlen said that Black people who had lived through the murders of Martin Luther King, Jr., and Medgar Evers and Malcolm X, "never thought they would see the day" when this could happen. "They wept, some of them, and so did I." A "moment so powerful and so obvious that its symbolism needs no commentary," said John Harris in *Politico.* He called it the "Obama Revolution." "Let cynics sleep," Marc Ginsberg, a former ambassador who had also been a Ted Kennedy staffer, said in the *Huffington Post.* "Let them discount the magnitude of this moment. Let them deny the righteousness of this cause. It does not matter. They are small in mind and do not deserve to share in it if they do not succumb to it."

The magnitude of the moment had a special gravity for the Kennedys. Nearly three years earlier, at the funeral of Martin Luther King, Jr.'s, widow, Coretta Scott King, Ethel Kennedy had whispered to Obama, "The torch is being passed to you." And Obama told one of his aides, "A chill went up my spine," and he said that to bear that legacy was "pretty intimidating." With so little time left, Ted Kennedy appreciated the magnitude of handing his family's legacy to the new president, too—to a man at last deserving of it, he felt. "We lost our way," he would write in his memoir, of what happened to liberalism after the Vietnam war. "It would take time for the voters to endorse those values again." With Obama, he believed, Americans finally had. And Ted said: "I rejoice in having lived to see it happen."

TWENTY-FOUR

Return to the Sea

Though he hadn't been physically capable of campaigning for Barack Obama in the general election, Ted Kennedy now had an errand. Thirteen days after Barack Obama's victory, Ted arrived back in Washington for the first time since his July appearance, accompanied by Vicki and Sunny and Splash, and, "beaming," made his way past a large banner, "Welcome Back, Senator!" through the Russell Caucus Room to a staff meeting, while a "roar of applause," as one reporter put it, from one hundred of his aides greeted him. (They had also ordered a lunch from Legal Seafoods.) He walked tentatively, using his father's old black cane—the cane he had loaned to Barry Goldwater and then later to Chris Dodd and John Warner when they were infirm from surgery—and he looked thinner than he had the last time he came to the Capitol. Still, one reporter called him "remarkably spry for a man battling malignant glioma." "I feel fine," he told the press outside, though his voice had a slight quiver when he said it. "I'm looking forward, particularly, to working with Barack Obama on health care." He asked the reporters if they had said hello to his dogs—"They missed you too," he said—and told the press that Sunny and Splash were "trying to decide which one is going to be top dog."

The healthcare bill for which Ted Kennedy had fought for most of his political life, the bill that would provide insurance for forty-five million uninsured Americans, was not a pipe dream now, and he was determined that it not be so. But he also knew that the Democrats would have to act quickly lest they allow opposition to build as it had before Bill Clinton introduced his healthcare bill in 1993, and that they had to use the momentum of a new administration to pass it. Earlier in the year, even before the outcome of the Democratic nomination had been determined, Ted was having what John Podesta, Bill Clinton's former White House counsel, called "tactical discussions" with Democratic activists over whether Ted should hold hearings rather than propose his old single-payer Medicare-style bill, just to give a Democratic president room to maneuver and propose a less comprehensive plan, since Podesta said that Ted conceded a Medicare for All bill would never pass Congress. "He was thinking, 'How do you set the table for big change?' " Podesta said. The basis of Ted's planning was a program instituted in 2006 in Massachusetts, one to which he had devoted a great deal of time and energy, dubbed "Romneycare" after the state's then-governor and Ted's onetime senatorial opponent, Republican Mitt Romney, who was apparently hoping to use the achievement in a likely bid for the Republican presidential nomination in 2008 but also to cut state spending on emergency care for uninsured Massachusettsans.

The basis of Romneycare harkened back to Richard Nixon's 1971 plan—the plan he had devised to co-opt Ted Kennedy. It had employer-mandated health insurance, meaning that large businesses were obligated to provide health insurance for their employees; subsidies for those who were unable to afford insurance or were not provided it; penalties for those who refused to buy it; and no exceptions for those who had preexisting conditions. It was a conservative plan compared to Medicare for All—an idea hatched by the right-wing think tank the Heritage Foundation. In effect, it was a Republican plan, initiated by a Republican governor, though Ted, seizing the moment, had supported it and convinced fellow Democrats in the state legislature to support it. And at a celebration at Faneuil Hall in Boston on April 12, 2006, where a fife and drum corps marched into the room, and at a desk high on a platform and flanked by signs declaring, "Making History in Healthcare"—the desk at which Romney would sign the bill into law—and with buttons distributed bearing the same slogan, Ted joined Romney in announcing its implementation. (The hall had also been the scene of Romney's disastrous 1994 debate with Ted, which prompted Romney to say that coming to the hall for him was like the "*Titanic* returning to visit the iceberg.") Ted, borrowing the term used for the Battle of Concord that began the Revolutionary War, called it the "shot heard round the world on health care in America," since it was the first attempt at statewide health insurance.

That was two years earlier. Now Ted Kennedy wanted to nationalize what had been done in his home state—a plan that he hoped might attract Republican support. After it seemed Obama had clinched the nomination but before Ted's seizure in May, and in anticipation of Obama's election, Ted had convened a meeting of medical experts to help craft a bill, and he had John McDonough, the former state legislator and now a public health academic who had been one of the architects of Romneycare, form a team out of the group. "He was like a professor," one attendee said of Ted at that meeting. "He encouraged people to disagree or pile on or take a different slant on what someone had said." When the cancer was diagnosed, that effort evaporated.

But only that particular effort. Three weeks after his surgery, his staff, at Ted's instruction, organized the first of what would be fifteen meetings that summer and into the fall of other Senate staffers and of healthcare stakeholders to discuss a national health insurance program—members of Obama's Senate staff attended these meetings—and to lay the political groundwork for a program. As one participant put it, Ted the legislator was trying to "build a fair amount of consensus among his Senate colleagues, House colleagues and the Obama campaign"—bipartisan consensus. On September 18, Ted himself teleconferenced with members of his HELP Committee from his Hyannis home, and divided the committee into three working groups: One, headed by Barbara Mikulski, was assigned the task of improving the quality of care; another, by Tom Harkin of Iowa, of improving prevention; and a third, by Hillary Clinton, of examining the issue of insurance coverage itself. It was Ted's way of "empowering us to carry a lot of the day-to-day work while he maintains focus on the strategy and internal politics," Mikulski said at the time. Working on those internal politics, the following Tuesday, September 23, he teleconferenced with key senators, both Republicans and Democrats, to discuss areas of consensus. And because Ted was unable to manage the details himself, over the course of those fifteen meetings—several times a week in the Senate conference room in the Dirksen building—he asked the labor union officials; healthcare lobbyists from the American Medical Association and the Federation of American Hospitals and the America's Health Insurance Plans; corporate representatives from the Chamber of Commerce, the Business Roundtable, and the National Federation of Independent Business; and advocates from groups like Families USA and Consumers Union and the American Association of Retired Persons, to work with his staff to iron out details. They called themselves the "Workhorse Group."

Ted Kennedy knew he was in a race, and not only a race against time, though there was certainly that to consider. No doubt one of the reasons he returned to Washington that November was not only to announce he was working on a healthcare bill but also, in doing so, to put pressure on President-elect Obama, should he decide to retreat from the battlefield and prioritize another issue, namely the economic recovery, as many of Obama's advisers were urging him to do and as Bill Clinton had done in 1993. "We're hopeful this will be a prime item on the agenda," Ted had told reporters that day, and when one asked whether he expected Obama to sign a healthcare bill early in his term, Ted bluntly said, "Well, yes. He's stated that." But there was another race—a race to beat Ted to the issue. Hillary Clinton, whom Ted had appointed to head one of his HELP task forces, now asked Ted if she could head a subcommittee to shepherd the bill, assuming that Ted couldn't, but he declined, obviously feeling that he could. (This was before Obama appointed her secretary of state.) And Ron Wyden, an Oregon Democrat, submitted a bill along with Utah Republican Robert Bennett. And there was one more contender—a serious contender who wanted to put his name on national healthcare: Max Baucus, of whom his top healthcare aide said, "He wanted to do something big, and he thought this was the time." (Obama would write of him dismissively, "In three decades as a senator he had yet to spearhead the passage of any major legislation.") Before his illness, Ted had already been meeting with Baucus, the chairman of the Finance Committee, which, because any health bill required tax revenues and because that was the province of Finance, would have ultimate jurisdiction, to see if they could agree to a single bill—one for which Baucus might win conservative votes and Ted liberal votes, making it a marriage of political necessity. Baucus worked with Ted, but he did not defer to him. Baucus and the ranking Republican on Finance, Charles Grassley, had been collaborating throughout the year on finding some compromise to which they could both agree. After Ted's diagnosis, Baucus and his staff held a bipartisan healthcare summit of their own on June 16 at the Library of Congress with three hundred attendees, and the implication was clear that Ted Kennedy, whose cause of a lifetime this was, was being shunted aside. Ted, Baucus, Grassley, Chris Dodd, whom Ted had delegated to lead the effort on healthcare in his absence, and a handful of other senators from HELP and Finance met in mid-November to discuss strategy. Ted, looking to the urgency of getting something done quickly, argued that they should push to get any healthcare bill through reconciliation—the process by which the Senate could pass revenue and spending bills that were considered germane to the budget by a majority vote without the necessary sixty votes to break a filibuster. Ted had wanted the Clinton healthcare plan to be passed by reconciliation; Senator Byrd, a stickler for Senate rules, had refused to permit it because he said the bill was not strictly a budgetary one but included massive changes to healthcare. It was that decision that effectively prevented Clinton's plan from being passed since Republicans could, and did, block it. When the senators reconvened a week later, and just weeks after Obama's election, they ruled out reconciliation. And so now any bill would need sixty votes to pass, which would only prolong the process in endless attempts at compromise, at a time when Ted Kennedy had no time. Later that same month, November, Baucus took the lead once again, proposing an eighty-nine-page health "white paper" of his own that he labeled "A Call to Action," which laid down a general plan similar to Romneycare. Baucus said that Ted phoned him and was "very complimentary." And Ted also issued a statement saying Baucus's plan provided "thoughtful recommendations for reform."

But despite his comity and compliments, Ted Kennedy was not about to leave the battle to Max Baucus. His illness notwithstanding, he soldiered on, marshaling his strength, Susan Milligan and Lisa Wangsness of *The Boston Globe* would write, for those meetings with White House staff and with his Senate colleagues, phoning Mikulski at least weekly, and Kent Conrad, the chairman of the Budget Committee, at Conrad's home on evenings and weekends to discuss the bill, and inviting Nancy-Ann DeParle, Obama's healthcare liaison, to his Kalorama house for further discussions—and all this while his staff and the lobbyists, the Workhorses, were meeting and forging ahead, tending to the minutiae. And while Baucus might have seized the initiative, Ted Kennedy remained the moral force behind the effort. "Very significant," Senator Mike Enzi, the ranking Republican on HELP who had often worked with Ted, said of Ted's return to Washington that November, and Arlen Specter, another Republican, noted that Ted's "personal situation" would add weight to the healthcare campaign. "People are very sympathetic." "We're carrying it out in his absence, but this is his doing," a Kennedy aide said. "This is Senator Kennedy at the helm." And Karen Ignagni, the president of America's Health Insurance Plans, the primary insurance lobbying group, said of Ted: "His presence is felt."

Ted's presence was felt. But now, with the concern that Ted Kennedy might not be able to construct and guide the bill—might not live to do so—some of the stakeholders started working on their own in a kind of mad scramble. The Pharmaceutical Research and Manufacturers of America (PhRMA), a lobbying group for the drug industry, reached out to Ron Pollack of Families USA, an advocacy group. At the same time, the Service Employees International Union (SEIU), which had worked with Ted to fashion a bill, was meeting with Karen Ignagni, and they invited PhRMA and Nancy DeParle to their discussions, working around the Workhorses. And, by one account, Baucus held negotiations in his office with PhRMA and with Nancy DeParle and with the chief executive officers of a half dozen drug companies to find an agreement on savings. Which meant that Ted Kennedy, powerless to fight back in his customary way, *rendered* powerless, was now sidelined from enacting what he had always called the "cause of my life," even as his life was ebbing.

Meanwhile, as his time was running out, Ted Kennedy had other issues to which to attend, personal issues, notably one involving his son Patrick, the young congressman from Rhode Island. There was no doubt that Ted Kennedy loved Patrick, and that Patrick loved him. The "North Star by which I navigated my life," Patrick would say of his father. But Patrick would also say this of the man who showed such compassion for those marginalized Americans in need, but so little compassion for those in his own family who were also in need: "He didn't always respect me, and he didn't understand the chronic mental condition I struggled with. He often said that all I needed was a 'good swift kick in the ass.'" Ted neither grasped nor wanted to grasp Patrick's ongoing battle with drugs and mental illness. (He hadn't with Joan either.) That sort of battle did not conform to the Kennedy brand, which was why Patrick insisted on being admitted to the medical department at Mayo Clinic, shortly after Christmas in 2005 and just eight months after an earlier hospitalization there, rather than the mental health department, when he checked himself in for one of his periodic attempts at rehabilitation. A physical illness was acceptable for a Kennedy. Mental illness was not. In any case, Patrick had successfully hidden his illness and his addictions for years. But at two-thirty a.m. on May 4, 2006, in a period in which his father was embroiled in his effort to pass an immigration bill, Patrick rammed his 1997 Mustang into a security barrier at First and C Street S.E. in Washington and narrowly missed hitting a Capitol Police car. The police escorted him home without arrest, handing him only three driving citations, but the accident was widely reported, and the next morning Ted, having seen photos on television, phoned Patrick to say that he didn't know why the media were making so much of this: "It looked to me like it was only a little fendah bendah." In truth, Patrick had taken an Ambien to get to sleep and Phenergan, a painkiller that had been prescribed after a mishap in his office when he was hit with a hammer head during a demonstration of a new protective gel, and, drug-addled, he said he had no memory of what led up to the accident or the accident itself, only that he thought he was racing to the Capitol for a vote. It might have seemed as if he had escaped scrutiny again. And yet his was a different kind of escape. When the story broke—though it was originally reported as a combination of a sleeping pill and an antinausea drug, which was in fact the primary prescribed use of Phenergan—and with it, the news that Patrick suffered from bipolar disorder and that he was a binge drinker and that he had previously spent time in drug rehab, he said he actually felt an "overwhelming sense of relief" and that he had "waited for this day my entire life." His illness, he said, had created a sense of isolation, and he said he had been "seeking out self-destructive, exhilarating, risky situations that would take me out of the anguish of being all alone." (It was a description that might very well have fit his father as well.) Now he no longer had to. Now everyone knew.

But if the admission of his addiction and illness was a liberation for Patrick, it was not a liberation for his father, who seemed to vacillate between relief that Patrick had faced his demons and embarrassment that Patrick's battle with those demons had gone public. On the way to National Airport, after Patrick decided to check himself back into Mayo Clinic in the wake of the accident, he stopped at his father's home. Ted, sitting on the porch, told him, "You did a good job today. You're doing the right thing." That was the relief. Patrick spent his next twenty-eight days in treatment at Mayo, then returned to undergo cognitive behavior therapy, which, he said, focused on the here and now rather than on the past, and on coping strategies—which, though he might not have realized it, was essentially what his father had been doing as well, without formal therapy: learning to live *against* the past and not from it, learning how *not* to be a Kennedy because the burdens of being one were too great. "Sometimes I think that each of us in our many different ways have struggled with the same realization," Patrick's cousin, Tim Shriver, wrote him while Patrick was at Mayo "—that no matter what we do, we cannot achieve the greatness we are expected to attain." Patrick said he also made a discovery while at Mayo, this time in the inpatient mental health section: "I tearfully admitted that I had always felt the most emotional connection to my father when he was drinking. When he wasn't, he seemed more intense and difficult to bond with." "He was not comfortable around me," Patrick would say of his father. And though father and son tried to bridge the chasm between them—which was the chasm between what a Kennedy was supposed to be and what a Kennedy, or any individual, actually was—and though the two met every Wednesday for lunch during the Bush administration in Ted's Capitol hideaway, Patrick came to realize that it was not a truly intimate form of intimacy, and that his father never asked about him personally. Ted's professed admiration for his son's courage in making the admission brought them no closer and might have even widened the breach. That was the embarrassment. When, later that year, Patrick told *The New York Times* about his bouts with mental illness, his father, he said, was "livid" and called the article a "disaster." "Save that stuff for your shrink," he told Patrick, "not a reporter."

And yet Ted Kennedy was deeply sympathetic to mental illness in others, and he had long worked to pass a mental health parity bill that would have forced insurance companies to treat mental illness exactly the way they treated physical illness. Working with Pete Domenici, a Republican whose daughter suffered from schizophrenia, and with Paul Wellstone, a Minnesota Democrat whose brother suffered from mental illness, he got an amendment to Kennedy-Kassebaum, the health insurance portability legislation, that included a limited form of mental health parity—Patrick thought it too great a compromise—but in the end, Ted pulled back, fearing that opposition to the provision from the insurance industry would threaten the entire bill. Stripped from the bill, the mental parity provision passed as stand-alone legislation and was signed into law by Bill Clinton, though the bill did little—its only "parity" was assuring that any group insurance plan already offering mental health benefits place a cap on those benefits that was no lower than the cap on physical health benefits—and one analyst said the law was "so toothless that it will have zero effect on the bottom lines of companies." Moreover, substance abuse was not included among the mental illnesses covered. Even Wellstone disowned his own bill.

But the idea of a more expansive parity bill, one that would close the loopholes, was kept alive, largely because Domenici and Wellstone would not let it die in the Senate, and Patrick Kennedy would not let it die in the House. When Wellstone was killed in the plane crash in 2002, while campaigning for reelection, Ted took up the cause, and, as Carey Parker recalled, "Over a period of five or six years, Senator Kennedy, working with Senators Domenici and Gordon Smith [an Oregon Republican] and a few other Republican senators, got it to the point where we could go to House members who shared our commitment and emphasize to them: We can make this happen. We need your help." It was routinely submitted. It routinely failed—blocked by the pressures of a recalcitrant insurance lobby—so in 2004, Ted, Domenici, and Wyoming Republican Mike Enzi, the ranking Republican on Ted's HELP Committee, decided to disarm the opposition by enlisting the insurers themselves and giving them veto power over the language of any bill. And now it slowly began to gain momentum as the stakeholders gained each other's trust.

But only slowly—three years. In 2007 it was on the docket once again, and this time, Ted and Patrick worked in concert, if not always in lockstep. (The undertow kept pulling too as a reminder of why the bill was necessary. That year Kara checked herself into rehabilitation, meaning that all three of Ted's children had wrestled with drug and alcohol abuse.) The insurance industry had come to realize, as Carey Parker would put it, "the need to accept the importance of the principle of parity, and the only question was how to achieve it." In September 2007, after over two years of meetings with those stakeholders, including insurers, Ted and Domenici won passage of S558, but it was, Patrick felt, a pyrrhic victory. The bill did not specify the illnesses covered, and Patrick thought his father yet again had made too many concessions to the insurance companies. "The bill was written by members of the insurance industry," he said, which was true. Moreover, Patrick said that Ted and Domenici had "pre-conferenced" their bill, meaning that the House and Senate conferees had already determined they would not disagree in order to gain passage. But Patrick threw up a roadblock. Despite the pre-conference, Patrick pressed for a more specific and comprehensive bill, one that included coverage for every condition listed in the American Psychiatric Association's *Diagnostic and Statistical Manual for Mental Disorders*—Ted's and Domenici's did not cover treatment for addiction or any "non-biological" mental illness—to which both insurers and businesses objected as an onerous mandate, and Patrick held hearings for his bill and spoke passionately on the House floor on its behalf, in a direct challenge to his father. Ted, who wanted his bill to pass, was miffed that Patrick's House bill now included illnesses like alcoholism—whether this was a legislative decision or a matter of personal sensitivity on Ted's part was impossible to determine— a provision that, he was convinced, would prevent it from becoming law. And Patrick said that as he worked for his bill, his father did something rare: That March, as the bill was coming up for a vote, he came to the House floor during the debate and sat there watching for an hour. And afterward he pulled his son aside and said, "You keep this up. I think we can get a better bill," which was also rare: an admission that Ted, the master of the Senate now, might have been wrong—too acquiescent to the insurers—and that his son might have had a better understanding of how to manage the bill. In the end, Patrick got coverage for treatment for addiction, but his bill never reached a Senate vote.

By this time, however, Ted had suffered his seizure and received his diagnosis, which reopened the breach between father and son. Patrick said that Vicki restricted his access to Ted—"He needs time alone," or "It's too much," or "I'll let you know when he's better," she would tell him—and when she saw him at a healthcare function and realized that Patrick had suffered a relapse, she told him, "You're not healthy. You're uncomfortable to be with," and Patrick said it became even harder for him to reach Ted on the phone. But Patrick Kennedy needed to reach his father, if only for the sake of their legislation. Time was running out—for Ted himself and for Ted's bill. The pre-election Congress would be meeting for only a few days in October before adjourning for the campaign, and while Patrick and his House partner, Republican representative James Ramstad, a recovering alcoholic himself, and Ted's staff and Domenici had come to an agreement, there was other Senate business, primarily the Troubled Asset Relief Program (TARP), the $700 billion stimulus package to bail out wounded financial institutions and rescue the faltering economy, that was likely to push the Mental Health Parity and Addiction Equity Act aside because, as Carey Parker put it, "there was concern all the way along that there wasn't enough impetus behind it to get it to the finish line on its own." That was the case even though, Parker said, the Republicans wanted to pass the bill for the sake of Domenici, who was retiring after six terms in the Senate, and nearly everyone in the Senate wanted to pass it for the sake of Ted, whose chief legislative priority it was that year. A revision of Patrick's bill had already passed the House overwhelmingly on September 23. When Patrick finally got through to his father, then convalescing at Hyannis, Ted agreed to call Chris Dodd, who had taken over most of the legislative heavy lifting for his friend, and to call Majority Leader Reid and Reid's deputy, Dick Durbin, to see if they could advance the bill in the Senate in spite of the TARP delay. And Patrick said that sort of offer from his father was rare too. According to Patrick, it was Chris Dodd who came up with the idea of attaching the Mental Health Parity Act to the must-pass bill that had been delaying its consideration: TARP. When TARP passed the Senate on October 3, 74 to 25, with both presidential candidates, Barack Obama and John McCain, in support, so did the Mental Health Parity Act, Wellstone's act and Domenici's act—it was named for them—and the Kennedys' act, both Ted's and Patrick's. That same day George W. Bush, who had opposed the bill when it was a stand-alone, signed it into law. And quietly, the long fight, a twelve-year fight to treat mental illness the way that physical illnesses were treated, was finally over.

But because the act was part of the omnibus bill, there was no official signing ceremony for the Mental Health Parity Act itself, no opportunity to honor Ted Kennedy and Pete Domenici. Carey Parker said that Ted's office got a call from the White House a week or so after Bush signed TARP and invited Ted to a special reception scheduled for November 21 when Ted had returned to Washington. The four principals—Ted, Domenici, Patrick, who had just returned from another stay at the Mayo Clinic, and James Ramstad—arrived at the Oval Office together, and George W. Bush, now a lame-duck president, staged a small signing ceremony for them, as if the bill had been passed separately. Photos were taken as if it had been a real signing too, and pleasantries were exchanged. Bush sat at John Kennedy's old desk, and Ted joked about young people having to respect their elders, meaning Patrick, and Patrick quipped to the president, "You know, it's pretty tough to follow your father in public life," to which Bush said, "Boy, don't I know it." And then George W. Bush, who had been an adversary of Ted's, a man who Ted felt had betrayed him, took his arm and, with Ted leaning on his cane, escorted him slowly, slowly down the hallway and out through the Rose Garden and to Ted's car—a journey, Carey Parker would say, of about seventy-five yards. And Ted slid into the car, and the two men shook hands and said goodbye, and that was the end of their relationship.

• • •

That Thanksgiving, a week after his appearance in Washington and five days after his visit with the president, Ted Kennedy returned once again to the sea. The Friday after the holiday, he and Vicki invited one hundred friends and family to Hyannis Port—a group that Mike Barnicle, a long-time Kennedy watcher, called the "ultimate safety net." Sitting in a straight-back chair next to his mother's piano in the parlor of the Big House, Ted did one of the things he loved to do. He sang—"tunes that were popular when the ghosts were still alive, still there in the house," Barnicle would write. He sang "Some Enchanted Evening," one of his favorites, as his blue eyes "sparkled" with life, and "sitting, smiling," he mouthed the lyrics to songs that others sang, and the sound of those songs, recalled Barnicle,"spilled out past the porch, into a night made lighter by a full moon whose bright glare bounded off the dark waters of Nantucket Sound." And Ted Kennedy was happy.

But there were still stains, many of them, still attempts at redemption for those sins of his, and one of the most humiliating of those stains was his cheating scandal at Harvard—humiliating because he had besmirched himself at an institution so closely identified with his family, whose honor was so important to them and to him. Harvard had offered him an honorary degree the previous spring, when Ted, about to undergo his brain surgery, had asked the University's president, Drew Gilpin Faust, if he might receive the degree at a later time. The postponement was an even rarer honor than the degree itself. Harvard seldom granted honorary degrees outside the spring commencement. By one account, among those exceptions were George Washington, Winston Churchill, and Nelson Mandela. Now Ted Kennedy would join them. Held on December 1, four days after Thanksgiving, at the Sanders Theater in Memorial Hall, it was a special ceremony, like the signing ceremony of the Mental Health Parity Act—special not only because it was being held at all, or because he received an ovation so enthusiastic that he couldn't quiet it, or because Supreme Court justice Stephen Breyer, Ted's onetime staffer, would speak, or because Vice President-elect Joe Biden was in attendance, or because the cellist Yo-Yo Ma would play a George Gershwin prelude for him, or because Ted, who was seen in public only infrequently now, had to be steered off the stage by Vicki, so eager was he to stay, but above all because Ted could now, in some small way, expunge the guilt of his old scandal. Presi-

dent Faust, in awarding the degree, said it was for Ted's "lifelong commitment to public service," but she pointed out in particular how he had
"worked tirelessly on behalf of society's most vulnerable members" and
"made their dreams his own." In his own remarks, made while he stood at
the podium without his cane, his suit now hanging loosely from his frame,
and read in a "strong, sure voice," wrote one reporter, he called Harvard,
which his father had entered exactly one hundred years ago that past September, a "second home" and thanked it for the things he had learned
there, but he saved his most reverent comments for the new president,
Barack Obama, who offered the "possibility of hope," and he called this a
"turning point in history." And he said this: "We know the future will out-
last all of us, but I believe that all of us will live on in the future we make."

And as he thought of redemptions and unfinished business and reconcili-
ations that fall, he also thought of legacy, which was something so precious to the Kennedys and to this Kennedy especially. On the day Ted
appeared at the White House, Barack Obama had announced that his
presidential rival, Hillary Clinton, would be his designee for secretary of
state, which meant that New York would have a senatorial vacancy, to be
filled by the governor, David Paterson. Ted had a candidate: his fifty-one-
year-old niece Caroline Kennedy-Schlossberg. By one report, Ted had let
Paterson know that should he select Caroline, her contacts and connections would give her special attention in the Senate when she was promoting the state's interests. Another report said he had called Chuck Schumer,
New York's senior senator, and Robert Menendez, the New Jersey senator
and head of the Democratic Senatorial Campaign Committee, with the
message that Caroline could run in the special election two years hence
and in an election two years later to a term of her own and would have
ample resources to do so. (Ted's aides denied he had made those calls, or
that he had spoken to Governor Paterson.) Yet another report had Michael Myers, the staff counsel of Ted's HELP Committee, contacting union
officials and urging them to support Caroline's candidacy. One said, "I
think they know enough to know that in New York, you will need the support of labor. And there is no one who is a bigger friend of labor than Ted
Kennedy." By December 15 the notoriously shy Caroline was said to be
campaigning for herself, calling Governor Paterson to tell him of her interest in the seat and speaking to a number of New York state officials to
declare her candidacy, while planning a statewide tour. But even as she

was gearing up to campaign for the job, her effort was beginning to fizzle. Other aspirants with deeper roots in New York politics, like state attorney general Andrew Cuomo, son of the former governor Mario Cuomo, mounted a quiet counterattack; the press expressed concerns that she was short on government experience; the governor was said to be chafing over the idea that her appointment was a foregone conclusion; and she was less than articulate—another victim of the high expectations placed on a Kennedy. Ted saw her as his political heir—they had become very close, closer still with the Obama endorsement—but that bequest wasn't Ted Kennedy's to give. On January 21 she left the race, leaving the impression, it was said, that Ted's illness was one reason why, which infuriated Ted's aides and friends, who felt that, one staffer said, "it makes him look like he's at death's door." But Ted, by the same report, didn't blame Caroline because she hadn't made any statement to that effect. It was said she really withdrew because she had concluded that Paterson wasn't going to select her anyway. There would be no heir.

II

Ted Kennedy had been in training—"serious training," Vicki said— exercising every day, counting his steps, training to have the stamina to attend the inauguration of Barack Obama, to whom he had passed the torch. He had attended the swearing-in ceremony at the Senate, walking, as was the custom, his junior senator and friend, John Kerry, down the center aisle, for Kerry to take the oath, and then accompanying the whip, Dick Durbin of Illinois, because Durbin, another friend, had no fellow Illinoisan to escort him—the other Illinois senator now being the president-elect. And then Ted sat in his seat—the same seat he had occupied as a young freshman senator, the seat at the very rear of the chamber where those freshman sat before working their way forward with seniority, the seat that Ted chose to stay in despite his forty-six years in the Senate, the seat nearest the cloakroom where he could make his observations of who arrived and left the floor, the seat from which he could chat up his colleagues as he did that morning. Senators marveled, by one report, at how well he looked, much as he had before his seizure, the only difference being his silver-headed cane that he used to steady himself. "He really looked good," John Kerry said. "Fit" and "robust," Barbara Mikulski said. "Relaxed," wrote a reporter, who said his presence seemed to buoy his colleagues. Missouri senator Claire McCaskill hugged him. Robert Byrd, his old friend, now ninety-one years old, before being wheeled down the aisle in a chair by his junior senator, Jay Rockefeller, stopped at Ted's desk and took Ted's hand and brought it up to his cheek. And then Ted, having mixed with his Senate family, left for the House chamber to attend Patrick's swearing in.

And then two weeks later, in the bitter chill of the capital, he attended Barack Obama's inauguration, wearing a heavy black coat and a light blue silk scarf and a black felt fedora and balanced on his cane. He was ebullient, reminiscing with Democratic Party official Donna Brazile about Bobby's 1968 presidential campaign and saying how Obama's inauguration, from a campaign built on the same promise as Bobby's, was a fulfillment of Bobby's effort. It was an uplifting day for him. "It's a great day," he repeatedly told the guests who approached him. The crowd, estimated at 1.8 million, filled the National Mall, which was opened to inaugural spectators for the first time. And as Obama finished taking his oath, administered by Chief Justice John Roberts, against whose confirmation the new president had voted, Ted, sitting two rows behind the new president, just a seat to the right away from the new vice president, Joe Biden, smiled broadly, his face bright, and Harry Reid, the Senate majority leader, embraced him, while Patrick, who had checked himself out of Mayo to accompany his father to the event, beamed behind him. And as Obama stood, erect and tall, waiting to be introduced by Dianne Feinstein, to deliver his inaugural address, Ted stood just feet away, no longer erect but hunched slightly, gazing at him proudly. And then, after the speech, the dignitaries retired to the old House chamber in the Capitol for a luncheon in the new president's honor.

Ted arrived in what Massachusetts representative William Delahunt called a "very happy, jocular mood." Barack Obama made a point of going to Ted's table and giving him a gentle hug. And during lunch, Senator Daniel Inouye, a tablemate of Ted's and a longtime Senate colleague, said Ted was upbeat, "regaling us with a few jokes." But all the serious training he had undergone proved insufficient for the rigors of that happy day. As Ted was finishing his meal—of pheasant and fish stew—Inouye would recall, "All of a sudden, he slumped his head like he was going into a seizure," and Inouye said, "His teeth were clenched." He collapsed, but he was still conscious, muttering, "I'm cold. I'm cold," and then he seized up. Before Ted could receive medical attention, Obama returned to Ted's table to comfort him, and then Ted was placed in a wheelchair and taken to an anteroom, where he was attended to by a physician and then, with Vicki beside him, placed on a stretcher and taken to an ambulance outside. "*Oh God, don't let this happen today,*" John Kerry prayed to himself. "A lot of us were making the cross in there," Patrick Leahy said, and Norah O'Donnell of NBC reported that the once-festive mood was now "remarkably different." Obama, addressing the group, called Ted a "warrior for justice" and said that a "part of me is with him." Another report had Robert Byrd also suffering a collapse, but Byrd later said he was just overcome with emotion at Ted's spell and had to leave. Orrin Hatch observed that Ted was smiling as he left, and Ted's close friend Chris Dodd said Ted shouted from the stretcher that he didn't need any help. "When he bellows," Dodd said, "he's usually in pretty good shape." Later Patrick said that Ted uttered his signature phrase of incredulity in times of distress, "I caahn't believe it," but this time it had a comic inflection. (Ted Kennedy, always considerate, phoned Vice President Biden the next day to apologize to him for frightening Biden's fifteen-year-old granddaughter, who had seen the seizure. "I'm so sorry I upset your granddaughter," Biden said Ted told him.)

Ted's plan had been to stay in Washington after the inauguration to work on healthcare. (After his diagnosis, Harry Reid had loaned him a hideaway on the second floor of the Capitol to shorten his walk to the Senate chamber, now just thirty feet away.) But because of the brutal winter weather in Washington and his compromised condition, he went instead to Florida to recuperate. Vicki had found a house on Biscayne Bay in Miami—a "perfect spot," Ted's longtime friend Lee Fentress, who visited him there, said, a "quiet, private place," where he could see the Miami skyline to the west and the ocean to the east, and where there was a slip for his beloved *Mya* so that he could sail every day. Ted spent most of the winter in the house, but when Barack Obama's stimulus package was being voted on early that February, and every vote was needed, Ted returned to the Senate for the third time since his diagnosis. (He had phoned Harry Reid and said, "Kennedy, reporting for duty.") Kerry escorted him onto the floor for the vote, where he was once again greeted with hugs from his fellow senators—"People were walking on eggshells when they saw him," Senator Ben Nelson said of Ted's earlier visits, which was only partially true, but now "people treat him in a normal way"—and where his vote proved necessary for cloture, which passed with no votes to spare, 61 to 36. "Here comes my hero," California senator Barbara Boxer announced when she saw him, and said how "selfless" of him it was to come when he was so ill. Then just two minutes after his arrival and after signaling his "aye," he ambled through the exit and to a parlor where Vicki and several aides awaited him, and he donned his blue scarf and his coat and disappeared into an elevator and returned to Florida.

It was there two weeks later that he celebrated his seventy-seventh birthday with a small group of friends, who spent the evening singing songs—Nick Littlefield, Ted's onetime chief of staff for HELP, and the onetime professional singer, was among the guests and sang duets with Ted—and Vicki had arranged for one of the stars of the Broadway show *Mamma Mia!* to perform. And the next morning Ted and his guests celebrated Mass in the house with a young local priest, and when the service ended, Ted began asking questions of him, asking whether the apostles might have been more inquisitive, might have wanted to know more, had they had the kind of information that people now had, and Ted, in his probing, cited scripture by heart and left the young priest at a loss for words.

Now there was always the issue of time—how little there might be left and how much still needed to be done. "His Time Is Now," *Newsweek* titled an article on him that March, which needed no explanation, and speaking to Mark Leibovich, the *New York Times* national political correspondent, in a five-minute phone conversation just before Ted's birthday—the only formal interview he had given since his diagnosis—he said, "I have to pace myself," which was not something Ted Kennedy had ever done in his career because his pace had always been breakneck. Lee Fentress said that while Ted was in high spirits in Miami, it was clear his condition was deteriorating. He moved more slowly. He would focus and then lose focus. And when Ted was in Washington for the stimulus vote and a reporter asked him how he was feeling, Ted answered without his customary optimism, "Some days are better than others." But he was back in Washington again, a few weeks after the stimulus vote, to attend to business, Senate business, telling his colleagues, many of whom now wore blue silicone "Tedstrong" bracelets, that the "cancer is in its cage," even though it was not. He was there in part for a public celebration of his birthday at the Kennedy Center, where comedian Bill Cosby served as the master of ceremonies, and actress Lauren Bacall and singers Bernadette Peters and James Taylor performed, and composer and Boston Pops conductor John Williams led the orchestra. Current and former senators, current and former staffers, current and former Cabinet secretaries attended, Caroline gave him the Profiles in Courage award, and the guests sang "Happy Birthday," with President Obama belting it out at center stage and waving his hands as if leading the orchestra while Ted smiled from the balcony and gave him a thumbs-up. As the evening wound down, Broadway star Brian Stokes Mitchell sang another of Ted's favorite songs, "The Impossible Dream," which had many in the audience crying, realizing the implications now, and as a group of performers sang, "The Best Is Yet to Come," President Obama went to Ted's box. It was a joyous occasion, but everyone knew that for that night's honoree the best was not yet to come. Everyone knew this was a public goodbye, and as Barbara Souliotis would recall, it was "probably the last time that many of the Senator's friends saw him."

But Ted Kennedy had not come back to Washington solely to be celebrated. He came to pass legislation. One of his missions this time was the passage of the National Service Act, which he and his quondam partner Orrin Hatch had introduced in September 2008—his first piece of major legislation since his diagnosis. Ted had been one of the chief co-sponsors of the National Community Service Act in 1990 creating a demonstration project that ultimately led to AmeriCorps, a kind of domestic Peace Corps to bring volunteers into distressed American communities as the Peace Corps, a brainchild of John Kennedy, brought American volunteers into distressed developing countries. The new bill, which was to be funded over five years at a cost of $5 billion, was an expansion and reorganization of AmeriCorps. It originally called for a corps of 175,000 Americans, baby boomers as well as young people, or actually a series of specialized corps in specific areas, to perform public service, for which they would be paid a modest salary and for which their employers would receive tax benefits. Ted and Hatch reintroduced it in the newly seated Senate on January 16, Ted's first piece of legislation in the Obama administration. Obama supported it, even singling it out in his first address to a joint session of Congress, and it passed the House 321 to 105, with seventy Republicans voting for it. With Barbara Mikulski having taken Ted's place as its spearhead, it passed a cloture vote, 74 to 14, though Ted did not speak on its behalf. When it passed the Senate, it was renamed the Ted Kennedy Serve America Act.

It was a bill very much in the tradition of Ted Kennedy's past legislative efforts—a bill dedicated to service and to helping those in need; a bill that built on his family's own legacy, in this case John F. Kennedy's Peace

Corps, and on other Americans' legacies, including George H. W. Bush's Freedom Corps and Bill Clinton's support of AmeriCorps; and a bill that, even as partisan divisions continued to widen and Republicans fought Obama at every juncture, recruited Republicans to join Democrats in drafting the bill and attracted a large bipartisan coalition in voting for it. With former first lady Rosalynn Carter, former secretary of state Colin Powell, and former president Bill Clinton in attendance, President Obama signed the bill into law on April 21 at the SEED Charter School in Washington, which served disadvantaged students, citing the "spirit of the man for whom this bill is named" and a family that "has made an immeasurable difference in the lives of countless families." Ted spoke too, his voice quavering slightly, once again comparing Obama to his brother John as "another young president" who "has challenged another generation to give back to this nation" and comparing the day to one thirty-three years earlier when he welcomed his brother's first group of Peace Corps volunteers back from their assignments. It was a legislative triumph, but also a personal one. As Joe Biden had once said, people didn't want to disappoint Ted Kennedy. And as Ted faced the end of his life, they were determined they wouldn't.

Nor did Ted Kennedy want to disappoint the people for whom he worked or fail the causes for which he had labored. For years, he had submitted a bill to have the FDA regulate tobacco by, among other things, banning harmful additives, ordering stronger warning labels, and restricting sales to teenagers, and to have the FDA oversee tobacco advertising. For years, with most of the tobacco industry and more recently the Bush administration in opposition, he had not succeeded. But now Barack Obama was president, and the House passed a bill that April that Ted introduced in the Senate with Chris Dodd carrying the battle while Ted convalesced, and as Ted would say after the 79-to-17 vote, "Miracles still happen. The United States Senate has finally said 'no' to Big Tobacco." And it was Ted Kennedy who had pulled off that miracle.

But with time running out, Ted Kennedy had one last mission, and one last challenge. This was the errand for which he had returned to Washington despite his illness: to achieve the cause of his lifetime. Since 1969 he had worked for national health insurance, doggedly, year after year, bill after bill, defeat after defeat. (Obama said that when he met Ted in the

White House before they entered the East Room on the day of the signing of the National Service Act, Ted told him, "This is the time. Don't let it slip away.") Twice he had come close—first, with Richard Nixon, who wanted a national health insurance bill to co-opt the Democrats generally and Ted Kennedy specifically, but the Democrats had refused compromise and so had Ted, waiting for Nixon's demise after the Watergate imbroglio and then for a Democratic successor to Nixon, and the chance was lost in the waiting; and again with the Clinton healthcare plan, which was too complex and faced too great opposition from Republicans who didn't want to hand Clinton a victory, even if it would also have been a victory for the American people. Now as Ted Kennedy was dying, Barack Obama offered him a third chance, a last chance, and Ted Kennedy—who, his old administrative assistant Larry Horowitz said, needed goals to sustain him in his illness, like the goal to sail in the Figawi; the goal to speak at the convention; the goal to attend the inauguration—had another goal, a big goal, one of the biggest goals: to pass, at long last, national healthcare. *His cause. His bill.* "That's what keeps him going," Horowitz said. Ted understood all too well why the Clinton plan had failed. Putting aside that most Republicans seemed to have little interest in a healthcare bill, it had failed in large measure because Clinton had waited too long to introduce it—the September after his inauguration—and because it had gotten hung up in jurisdictional disputes, primarily the dispute between Ted's Labor Committee (later HELP), whose chairman—Ted—desperately wanted a bill, and Pat Moynihan's Finance Committee, whose chairman seemed determined to do everything he could to stop one, with both proposing different measures. Ted had tried to address both those issues long before the election, which was why he convened what would become his Workhorse Group and why he invited to those meetings staffers from any committee that might claim jurisdiction and why he worked closely with Max Baucus (so as not to repeat his friction with Moynihan) and why he met regularly with both Republicans and Democrats—the HELP Committee held meetings throughout the summer, meeting separately with various stakeholders—and why he kept bringing the interested parties all together to hammer out their differences and why, perhaps above all, he hoped to get a single bill on which all could agree. "Move very early," his aide Michael Myers said Ted had advised Obama on how to achieve a healthcare package. And "work from one bill." And to focus his energies, Ted decided to step down from the Judiciary Committee—the committee to which

James Eastland had assigned him when Ted first came to the Senate, the committee on which he had sat for forty-six years, and the committee he had once chaired. Now he was all in on healthcare, and despite his illness, despite his fatigue, he would spend hours on the phone each day pushing for a united effort. "This is the opportunity of a lifetime," he said in announcing his decision to leave Judiciary, "and I intend to make the most of it." "He's working tirelessly," Ron Pollack of Families USA said, one of those with whom Ted was working. And another activist, Adrienne Hahn of Consumers Union, said, "Kennedy is really seizing the moment. He's making things happen."

Now the issue was whether the new president would *let* things happen. Obama was tackling the economic meltdown, crafting his stimulus package to resuscitate the economy (the bill that Ted would return to vote on in February), and overseeing a number of other initiatives to rescue the country from the disaster he had inherited and pull it back from the brink. Though he had promised to push healthcare during the campaign, he had been vague about the details, and once elected, he had yet to announce that commitment. Ralph Neas, the liberal activist who had worked so closely with Ted on so many issues over so many years, said that going into Obama's State of the Union address, members of the administration who wanted a healthcare plan were lobbying Neas to lobby the administration. "Everyone was on red alert," Neas recalled, about keeping the pressure on the new president. Ted was among the most active of those lobbying Obama, making calls in support of Tom Daschle's appointment as secretary of Health and Human Services because he knew that Daschle, understanding the Senate as well as he did, would be an effective advocate, though, once appointed, Daschle had been forced to withdraw over a controversy on non-payment of taxes, which only upped Ted's pressure on the administration to prioritize healthcare, even as he knew it would be more difficult to achieve without Daschle. He and Baucus sent a joint letter to Obama encouraging him to make the fight. Ted also had his Workhorse Group, roughly twenty strong, continue to meet after the inauguration to provide a politically viable bill that Obama could back—not a single-payer plan, though most Democrats supported one, but a plan using private insurance—a national Romneycare. ("While there was some diversity of views," David Bowen, the director of the health staff of HELP, wrote Ted, "the sense of the room is that an individual obligation to purchase insurance should be part of reform if that obligation is coupled

with effective mechanisms to make coverage meaningful and affordable.")
As *Newsweek* reported, "Kennedy is squeezing every bit of influence he
can out of his life, and the limited time he has left," and it quoted Ralph
Neas, who paraphrased the exhortation of the old Notre Dame football
coach Knute Rockne to "Win one for the Gipper": "It's win one for Teddy."

Obama didn't make his decision until March, when he convened a
healthcare summit at which he expressed his full commitment to pass a
healthcare reform law. "There is a moral component to this," the president said, "that we can't leave behind," before moving on to address costs.
On his trip to Washington from Florida that March, Ted had celebrated his
birthday and watched passage of his Serve America Act. But there was
another purpose to the trip—a larger purpose: Its primary purpose was to
attend Obama's summit. Ted was still undergoing chemotherapy, and his
aide Michael Myers noted, as Ted himself had, "There were good days and
bad days." But, Myers said, "On that day I think he felt the moment, and
the juices were flowing, and there was nothing that was going to keep him
from the White House on that March day." And Myers said that the summit took a lot of staff work, but the "real question" was whether Ted Kennedy would be able to attend. And when he did—when he entered the
East Room of the White House that afternoon of March 4 after morning
"breakout sessions" to discuss various facets of healthcare—"it was a
magic moment." The audience of 150 legislators and business people and
union leaders and advocates broke into applause, and Obama, citing the
fact that the day before Great Britain had announced it would award Ted
an honorary knighthood, said, "That's the kind of greeting a knight deserves." "Teddy's walk was unsteady that day," Obama would recall in his
memoir, "his suit barely fit after all the weight he'd lost, and despite his
cheerful demeanor, his pinched, cloudy eyes showed the strain it took just
to hold himself upright." And yet, Obama said, he had insisted on coming
to advance his dream. But if Ted Kennedy was the spirit of the summit, it
was Obama's warnings on the consequences of failing to pass healthcare
that were the crux of the summit: "The status quo is the one option that's
not on the table," he said, clearly addressing the Republicans, "and those
who seek to block any reform at all, any reform at any costs, will not prevail this time around." When Obama introduced Ted, the senator who
had spent his legislative career as a general for national health insurance,
said, "I'm looking forward to being a foot soldier in this undertaking."
And he added emphatically, "And this time we will not fail."

• • •

Ted Kennedy wasted little time in making good on his declaration. The very next day after the summit, Ted and his health aide David Bowen met with Baucus and his health aide Elizabeth Fowler over lunch for two hours at Ted's Kalorama home where Ted gave them the grand tour, the way he would always ingratiate himself, whether at his home or his office or his hideaway, by showing guests mementoes of his family. But one observer said that there seemed to be another motive now. Ted was more pensive than he had been—"wistful" when he spoke of healthcare, said one of the guests. "There was a sense of urgency in Kennedy's voice," the invitee said. "You could just sense how committed he was to getting this done, no matter what happened to him." And in strategizing with Baucus over what was achievable, and in their agreeing that the Senate would have to take the initiative because the White House still seemed to be laying back, he was also finally handing Baucus the reins. He gathered his HELP Committee in his new Capitol hideaway, still working with Mikulski on quality care, Harkin on prevention, and now Senator Jeff Bingaman of New Mexico, who had replaced Hillary Clinton, on expanding coverage. "I was impressed by how eager he was," Senator Bob Casey said, "how up to speed he was." "He's impatient," his friend John Kerry said. "He wants to get this done. He's pushing people. He's pushing the process. He's not sitting around worrying about himself." *The Boston Globe* called him the "man at the center." And while HELP continued to work on its bill, Ted met regularly with Baucus that April, still trying to fashion a bill, a single bill, that both of them could support. Baucus's chief of staff, John Selib, said the two senators' collaboration was a throwback to the days before the crippling partisanship. "There are very few institutionalists left in the Senate, very few members who remember the Russell Longs and the way deals were made in the Senate for a long time. Ted Kennedy and Max Baucus are two of those folks." By this time, some members of HELP and the Finance committee were meeting jointly—roughly eight senators—to work out the jurisdictional issues that had hampered the Clinton effort in 1993. When Ted was finally able to make an appearance, Mike Enzi, the ranking HELP Republican, warned his staff that it was going to be an interesting meeting because of the jurisdiction discussion; Ted wouldn't want to yield. But as soon as the meeting began, Ted said that Baucus and Finance would be in charge. Enzi, who had worked with Ted on healthcare reform for years and with whom he had set up ten basic principles for health reform, was shocked that Ted had surrendered without a fight, which he would have never done in the past, and Enzi said he thought the bill might have been totally different had Ted held fast. But Ted gave the HELP reins to Chris Dodd, who was far less willing to compromise than either Ted or Baucus. "Take it or leave it" was how Enzi described Dodd's approach. And when the meeting ended that day, Ted left slowly out a side door to avoid the press. And Enzi said he realized then, as Ted was exiting, just how sick Ted Kennedy was. It was the last time Enzi would see him.

By late April, Ted and Baucus announced jointly that they expected to have compatible bills by June—bills so similar that they could be "quickly merged into a single bill for consideration on the Senate floor." But Ted was not as compliant as Enzi might have thought. Despite Obama's personal intervention—he had Baucus to the White House and spoke to Ted on the phone—the two institutionalists could not reach agreement, even as they professed to keep working toward one. Ted wanted a public option to compete with private insurance plans, albeit a modest one that would force the government not to undercut the rates of private insurance, which made it an option in name only. Even so, the Republicans were immovably opposed to any option, saying that it would drive private insurance out of business because private insurers would never be able to compete with the government. Ted typically sought bipartisan agreements as a legislative necessity, but Baucus had always been willing to go farther than Ted—too far, many liberal Democrats felt, which was why Baucus, as Finance Committee chairman, might have had power but far less weight in the Senate. (Liberal senators called him "Bad Max" for having worked with Republicans on Bush's tax cuts and joined the conference on Bush's Medicare prescription drug benefit, which most Democrats abhorred.) Baucus bent over backward to accommodate his Republican members. But there would be no accommodation. His efforts only served to divide the Democrats on Finance from those on HELP.

But that did not stop Ted Kennedy from moving ahead, though he had delegated much of the cause to Baucus and Dodd, and though he had returned to Hyannis for treatment—returned with a clear foreboding that this time he might never see Washington again or see the end of his long, long battle for healthcare reform. With that in mind, he wrote a farewell letter to the president he so admired—a "few final words to you to express my gratitude for your repeated personal kindnesses to me—and one last time to salute your leadership in giving our country back its future and its truth." And thanking President Obama and the First Lady Michelle Obama, he wrote, "You helped make these difficult months a happy time in my life." "When I thought of all the years, all the battles, and all the memories of my long public life, I felt confident in these closing days that while I will not be there when it happens, you will be the President who at long last signs into law the health care reform that is the great unfinished business of our society," and he said that "in the past year, the prospect of victory sustained me—and the work of achieving it summoned my energy and determination." He said he was confident that despite the struggles to come—"there always have been" those struggles—"I learned that you will not yield to calls to retreat," and that "you have reminded all of us that it [healthcare reform] concerns more than material things; that what we face is above all a moral issue; that at stake are not just the details of policy, but fundamental principles of social justice and the character of our country." He wrote that he had entered public life "with a President who inspired a generation and the world," and he leaves as "another young President inspires another generation."*

Ever conscious of how little time he had, Ted Kennedy, back in Hyannis, made his final push for the cause of his lifetime. "If this were easy, we would have done it a long time ago," he would tell his staff repeatedly. After all the months of meeting and discussing and listening and compromising, he had given up on getting agreement among his colleagues on a single bill, and by late May, his staff had drafted a summary of a plan. (He previewed it in an op-ed in *The Boston Globe*.) A few weeks later there was a rough draft of the bill itself. Though it was 170 pages long, Ted's spokesperson called it a "draft of a draft" and said that it was subject to further revisions as discussions continued, but it was the first real proposal. (Baucus's early "Call to Action" had laid out broad principles, and his actual bill was still being negotiated.) Its primary features were the ones Ted had started out with: an employer mandate to provide insurance, a private insurance component, subsidies for individuals up to 500 percent of the poverty level, prohibition of denial of coverage for individuals with preex-

---

*By one account, and by Obama's own, Vicki did not deliver the letter to the president until September 3, 2009, a week after Ted's death. EMK, "It Was the Cause of My Life," *WP*, March 24, 2010; Barack Obama, *A Promised Land* (New York: Crown, 2021), 410–11.

isting conditions, and coverage of children up to twenty-six years old on their parents' policies. "Senator Kennedy is on the cusp of achieving his dream," Senator Ron Wyden said when the plan was released.

But nothing was settled yet. It was still a race between HELP and Finance, between Ted and Max Baucus, as to which bill would emerge and who would author it. *The New York Times* reported that the "run-up to major health care legislation is now a full-on frenzy" and cited a "marathon meeting" in Ted's hideaway on Monday, June 8, the day before the HELP Committee was to reveal its bill. Though Ted was still back in Massachusetts, he had been on the phone with Obama and had met with Dodd that Sunday—a "very productive meeting," Ted's spokesperson said—and Dodd reported that he was "getting indications every day that the Senator will get back here as quickly as he can," adding that Ted brought a "spirit," a "dynamic that is hard to quantify." Ted's old legislative partner, Orrin Hatch, went further: "He is the only guy who can bring us together, temper the demands of liberal advocacy groups and steer people toward a pragmatic solution." The HELP Committee unveiled its plan in the Caucus Room of the Russell Senate Office Building, one of the most ornate legislative chambers, the place, Ted noted in a statement issued to the press, as he so often did when he used the room to launch an initiative, where his brothers had announced their presidential candidacies and where so much Senate history had transpired. But Hatch might have been right: Ted Kennedy seemed to be the indispensable man, but Ted Kennedy wasn't there. Though Ted had guided the HELP bill—a bill that Hatch derided as "partisan," for which he blamed Ted's staff—only Ted might have been able to forge a consensus around *a* bill, and while he remained in Massachusetts, legislators flailed. House Democrats unveiled a bill of their own, much like Ted's but with a tougher public option to buy insurance through the government, which Ted had finally abandoned as a concession to Republicans because they had already said they would never support it, and Baucus, at the same time, was trying to assemble a group of three Republicans (Enzi, Charles Grassley of Iowa, and Olympia Snowe of Maine) and three Democrats (himself, Jeff Bingaman and Kent Conrad) for a bipartisan bill—an effort that stalled and that prompted the administration to threaten Baucus that he either make some progress or it would draft a bill of its own.

And *still* Ted Kennedy would not give up. He would phone Michael Myers several times a day, keeping tabs, asking him, "What are people thinking? What are they saying in the cloakroom? What's the atmo-sphere?" Myers said Ted was worried that it was taking longer than he expected, and with his feel for the chemistry of the Senate, he needed to know "what the psychology was at the moment and what was possible." And though, as one report put it, he had "hours of sharpness followed by hours of weakness," he kept working the phones—with the White House, with his colleagues—orchestrating as best he could and monitoring when he couldn't orchestrate. He remained optimistic. By summer, Michael Myers said, Ted felt that so many committees were engaged in the Afford-able Care Act, as the healthcare reform effort would be known, that Ted told him, "We had crossed a point of no return, that we could get this done." House speaker Nancy Pelosi said that Ted would call her and ask her hopefully, "We're going to get a bill?" And Pelosi would answer reas-suringly, "We are going to get a bill." "*When* are we going to get it?" Ted wanted to know. And Pelosi would answer, "We're going to get it when we do." And she said that Ted would laugh then and say, as if he were trying to buck up his own spirits, "We're going to get it." And Pelosi would con-cur with him. But then Ted would call her again for confirmation, saying less as a question than as an assertion: "It's going to happen." And that summer, as he rested at Hyannis, she would convey messages to him: "Tell him it's going to happen." That July, in what were characterized as "near-marathon" sessions, with Chris Dodd conferring with Ted constantly by phone, HELP marked up their bill, fending off most Republican amend-ments—798 of them—that were intended to sink it. (In the end, Dodd restored the public option and set fees on employers for employees who they had not covered, which cut roughly $400 billion from the cost over ten years.) And on July 14, while Ted watched from his home on C-SPAN, HELP voted along straight party lines to send its bill to the Senate floor, where it would still have to be reconciled with the Finance bill—the bill for which Baucus was still trying to attract Republican votes. But it had made it out of committee. And now, with his bill on the floor, Ted wrote a cover story for *Newsweek*, urging the Senate to pass healthcare reform—a piece with special poignance given Ted's commitment to seeing the issue through, and given his condition that would almost certainly prevent him from doing so: "It has never been merely a question of policy; it goes to the heart of my belief in a just society. Now the issue has more meaning for me—and more urgency—than ever before." Much, much more urgency.

III

And so Ted Kennedy rested at Hyannis, the "place he associated with his parents and siblings," Vicki would say; "the last place they were all together," she said; "the place he had the happiest memories"; "the place of joy in the summer when he had that nomadic school lifestyle"; "the place he learned to sail"; and the place that was simply "home." "He just loved home," Vicki said. And now he had come home to die. "I have good days and not-so-good days," he would write in the memoir he was dictating at the time, in what was now a refrain. "But more than a year after my diagnosis, I have not yet spent a day in bed. . . . I look forward to going outside every day, rain or shine, to breathe fresh air. I tire more easily than before and need extra rest, and sometimes I use one word when I mean another. Still, I continue to sail, as much as the weather allows. And I pray." His stepson Curran said that throughout his illness, he never complained, and despite an agony that required medical aides to manage his pain, he never let anyone see the pain he must have endured. Instead, he tried to lighten the mood for everyone else. "You know, all of us would get pensive or depressed," his stepdaughter Caroline would say, "and he would be the one to think of something funny." And then at dinner, with Ted at the head of the table, the table from which he had been exiled as a young boy, and with Vicki to his right and her daughter Caroline next to her, and Kara, who visited her father often that summer, on Ted's left, and Ted's sister Jean next to her, they would break into show tunes, and it got to the point where it could no longer be spontaneous but each had to prepare a performance, though Jean had no repertoire, only one act; she recited "The White Cliffs of Dover" every evening.

His old friends visited, one by one: Claude Hooten and John Culver and Tim Hannan from his Harvard days. John Tunney came up to the Cape in August and spent three or four hours with him alone, talking, over the course of two days, which, Tunney said, was a violation of the restrictions that had been laid down for visitations. But "Teddy wanted it, and I wanted it." By this time, Ted didn't talk as much as he had, and he was garbling words sometimes, as he admitted, and was sometimes confused. Patrick said that his father had once called him "Splash," the "name of his absolute most beloved dog." As the summer wore on, Chris Dodd, who was in his own bout with prostate cancer, said that at times Ted could barely speak at all. But Tunney said that he and Ted could communicate "in ways that were impossible in a more public setting." John Kerry visited him, and the two of them sat on the porch of the Big House, reminiscing and talking about sailing and about contemporary politics, though this might have been Kerry's exaggeration, given Ted's condition. And as he got up to leave, Kerry said he did something he had never done before with Ted, who eschewed intimacy and whose meetings typically ended with a vigorous handshake or a "thump on the back." This time Kerry hugged him—"close"—and "held on for a moment, as did he." Ted asked Barbara Souliotis, his longtime Boston chief of staff, to visit that summer too. "I had the sense that he was saying goodbye, but never saying it." And Gerard Doherty, his old campaign manager from Ted's first Senate contest, came. "Toward the end, it would be an understatement to say he wasn't himself," Doherty recalled. "He was a quick study, and he knew better than anybody that he wasn't functioning well."

And the family came. Jean, who had rented a house on the Cape the previous summer, rented a house again, "for weeks and weeks," Caroline Raclin said, "and when that expired, or whatever, she stayed at the house"—"always there," Caroline said. Jean was the second youngest, and she and Ted had "paired off," as Ted's niece, Maria Shriver put it, and "they became very close." Jean, she said, was a political animal like her younger brother. She had many of the same political connections and acquaintances as he did, she was politically active like her brother, and she and Ted shared that political enthusiasm. But they shared a special bond outside politics too. They had a private sense of humor. They loved speaking in faux British accents, and that summer they would banter continually and "just crack each other up," Ted's stepdaughter Caroline said: "Oh, Teddy, what are you doing over there, sitting in your chair?" "Oh, I'm just looking at you, you ugly thing!"

And that summer they soon had another bond—the tragic bond of survivors as the last two Kennedys of their generation. Joe Jr., Jack, Kathleen, Bobby, Rosemary, who had died surrounded by her sisters and Ted at a Wisconsin hospital, and Pat were all gone. Only Eunice, Ted, and Jean remained, but Eunice had suffered a stroke in 2005 and had been in poor health since. Ted, who had always taken his family duties seriously, was attentive to her, her daughter Maria said, "very involved in her care," calling her, visiting her, checking in with her doctors, pressing, successfully, to get a building at the National Institutes of Health named in her honor. "He really tried to make her happy." That summer, as Ted was declining, his sister Eunice was declining too at her nearby home in Hyannis. She suffered another stroke in August, and Ted, despite his condition, would be taken to his sister's home almost every day, and the two of them would sit on her back patio looking out at Nantucket Sound. On August 8, after yet another stroke, she was taken to Cape Cod Hospital where she languished and then died at two a.m. the morning of August 11. "She understood deeply the lesson our mother and father taught us," said a statement issued in Ted's name, "—much is expected of those to whom much has been given."

In that summer of imminent mortality, the children came, and with them their children. Kara was there again most of the summer, and Ted Jr., who would take his ailing father sailing, was there for virtually all of the summer, and Patrick, who had suffered another relapse that June, returned to Hyannis in July to be with his father. Patrick would call those weeks a "big gift"—a "chance for us to bond together and share a special time together," and a "chance to tell him how much we love him. And him to be there to hear it." They talked a lot, Ted and Patrick, out on the porch of the Big House, something they had seldom done before. And sometimes Ted would go out in the motorboat with his friend and physician, Dr. Larry Ronan, and Patrick would go along with them, and Patrick said that Ted would brace himself on Patrick's shoulders, which "I took as some form of what could be our last hug. And then we would just cruise around the bay." But on one of these excursions, Patrick said that he and his father were talking, leaning into each other, their heads nearly touching, and Ted told him, "You know you don't have to run for public office anymore. You can do what makes you happy"—which was Ted's permission for his son to escape from the Kennedy imprisonment that had confined so many in the family, his permission for his son to live his own life. And it was their reconciliation.

And if Ted had his friends and his family, he also had the sea, even though he struggled to the dock; Chris Dodd said he had traded his cane for a wheelchair and had to take a golf cart to get to his *Mya*. "The sea does something," his father-in-law, Edmund Reggie, said of him. "It restores him. It calms him. I don't know how much thinking he does out there. I don't know how much un-interruption allows him to see himself maybe as he can't on land, but it is the beginning and the end." And Reggie told his daughter that she had to understand the "pecking order of your husband's life": First, the Senate. Then *Mya.* Then Splash. Then Sunny. And then you."* First the Senate. Then the sea. (Of course, this wasn't true; he loved and adored Vicki.) Always, always he returned to the sea for succor and solace. In the past, he would talk of how the wind came in off the sea and blew up to the house—"in an emotional way," Nick Littlefield recalled—and what it felt like when it did, and what the sea smelled like and what it sounded like from the house. And now, he would sit on the porch, he wrote in his memoir as his days diminished, passing "many contented hours," in his green-cushioned wicker chair, a hot mug of tea on a table beside him, while he gazed past the expanse of lawn at the sea and the "diving osprey, the gulls that can be suspended in midair as they fly against the wind." Sometimes he would sit with Patrick, sometimes with Jean—there were two particular spots on that porch he liked— usually silent as the summer passed. And he wrote, "I love the reflection of the setting sun on the wooden masts of *Mya;* the rising moon; the beauty of a rainbow after a storm."

But it was not just the solace of the sea Ted Kennedy sought and loved. It was the metaphor of the sea he so often invoked that he also loved. Ted Jr. said his father thought of calling his memoir *Perseverance,* which certainly described the life of the least of the Kennedys. (Ted would use it as the title of the last chapter.) He opted instead for the nautical title *True Compass,* which described how he had tried to guide his life, his wanderings off course notwithstanding (he called Vicki his "true compass"), and he used an epigraph from Eugene O'Neill's *Long Day's Journey into Night,* a story of an imperious father, a distant and broken mother, their lost boys, and unrealized dreams: "I lay on the bowsprit, facing astern, with the water foaming into spume under me . . . I become drunk with the beauty and singing rhythm of it, and for a moment I lost myself—actually lost my life. I was set free! . . I dissolved in the sea . . . I belonged, without past or future, within peace and unity and a wild joy, within something greater than my own life, or the life of Man, to Life itself! To God, if you want to put it that way." *Something greater than my own life.* That was

---

*The previous December, Ted and Vicki had gotten another puppy from the Sterns, who had bred Splash and Sunny: Cappy. And in April, they had gifted the Obamas with a Portuguese water dog whom the Sterns had bred but who had been returned to them by the owner—a friend of Vicki's—because the dog did not get along with her other dog. The Obamas named him Bo. Art Stern int. by author.

what, at the end, the sea signified to a man who had spent most of his life searching for a larger purpose to redeem him.

He would not live to see the publication of his memoir, though he was always, since his diagnosis, recalling events and telling Vicki, "Remind me, Vicki, to put that in the book," and though he and Vicki would read parts of it to each other. He would not live to see the passage of a national healthcare bill, though he was still strategizing about that passage, and sent a letter to Massachusetts governor Deval Patrick, state senate president Therese Murray, and state house speaker Robert DeLeo, a "poignant acknowledgment of his mortality," one reporter called it, asking them to amend the state succession law that called for a special election within five months to fill a Senate vacancy. He asked them for a new law that would permit the governor to make an interim appointment until the election, so that the commonwealth would have "two voices speaking for the needs of its citizens and two votes in the Senate during the approximately five months between a vacancy and an election." In writing them, however, Ted wasn't thinking generally of representation. He was thinking of the impending vote on the Affordable Care Act, since without his vote and without Robert Byrd's—and Byrd was also in failing health—the Democrats would have only fifty-eight votes, counting independents Joe Lieberman and Bernie Sanders, who caucused with the Democrats—two short of cloture. And he was thinking of Vicki, too, whom he wanted Deval Patrick to appoint to his seat when he was gone. When the press assumed that the letter was a signal of Ted's imminent death, John Kerry parried truthfully that Ted had been thinking about the issue of succession since the early summer—he had actually written the request in a flurry of letter-writing in July—and, less truthfully, that Ted was still "fully engaged" in the healthcare debate and that "if Harry Reid required sixty votes tomorrow, Ted Kennedy would be on the plane and down in the Senate to vote."

But Ted Kennedy wouldn't be getting on any plane now. Barack Obama awarded him the Presidential Medal of Freedom, the nation's highest civilian honor and one inaugurated by John Kennedy, on August 12 along with other honorees, physicist Stephen Hawking, former Supreme Court justice Sandra Day O'Connor, actor Sidney Poitier, and the late congressman Jack Kemp. But Patrick had to accept the award in his father's stead. After the ceremony, the president took Patrick into the Oval Office, shut the door, and asked about Ted. To which Patrick said that his father could still understand what was going on and was kept apprised of things, but that he was frustrated in not being able to participate in the healthcare battle, even as, during the summer congressional recess, legislators returned home to town halls where Republicans, having no interest in passing any healthcare reform whatsoever, instead instigated people to sabotage it by making ridiculous claims against it like calling a proposal for end-of-life counseling a call for the creation of "death panels."* (By this point, even Grassley, who had worked so closely with Baucus, was castigating health reform as a "government takeover.") Ted could still speak. He would phone friends and tell them, "I'm still here," and "Every day is a gift." To others, he said, "I had a wonderful life." And he was still engaged enough that when John Kerry was convalescing from hip surgery early that August, Ted called to wish him well. At that same time, Vicki invited several friends to the house—Nick Littlefield and Lee Fentress and Vince Wolfington, a Hyannis Port neighbor, and their wives, and there was a piano player, and, as always, they sang, though Ted was clearly failing. Still, Fentress said, "The last couple of times you'd see him and look at him, he would look at you and not say anything, but there was a message in his penetrating eyes," which Fentress read as Ted's deep sense of friendship. He was still fully sentient, those around him said, but he was no longer mobile, and as days passed, he had greater difficulty speaking. And he had even given up his daily sails after going out in the *Mya* on August 16, a hot, breezy Sunday afternoon. It was the last time he would be out on the sea. Later that week, by one account, Ted Jr. and Kara drove him around Hyannis Port. It was the last time he would do that too.

After fifteen months, when, at the time of his diagnosis, he was only given a few months to live, night descended rapidly and quietly. "The end was so quick," his stepson Curran would say. "You'd talk to him, and he can't remember a name. Well, names haven't always been his strong suit, so it's hard to remember he's sick. It's hard to accept that there was a problem because he used pronouns with no antecedents"—the familiar Kennedy-speak—"but he's been doing that since I've known him." That was just Ted Kennedy wrestling with the English language. But, Curran

*Obama, fearing that the ACA was losing steam, met with his staff that August—a meeting at which his chief of staff Rahm Emanuel and Vice President Biden both counseled him to cut a deal with Republicans to cover only women and children. But Obama rejected their advice. He said he "felt lucky." Jonathan Cohn, "How They Did It," *New Republic*, June 10, 2010.

said, "there were times that he had a bad day, and it was really difficult. I didn't want to see him like that." Even as his condition deteriorated, Ted still began each day, by one account, reading the newspapers and drinking a cup of coffee on the porch with Sunny and Splash. And he continued to work on his memoir, fine-tuning it. "I've got to get it right for history," he said. He flagged but never surrendered. His stepdaughter Caroline recalled that one of Ted's favorite phrases, when he was coaxing his stepchildren to do something challenging, was "ruff-tuff-'em," as in "Don't you want to be a ruff-tuff-'em?" And she said that one of her last conversations with her stepfather, as he was soldiering on through his cancer, was her whispering in his ear, "You're a ruff-tuff-'em," which he was.

He was thinking of his legacy. He had long thought of his legacy—something with which he could match his brothers, something that would have made them proud. *He wanted to know that he mattered,* Melody Miller had said. And he had an appetite, a voraciousness, for greatness—for leaving behind a sense of great accomplishment—that had been born largely from his sense of insufficiency. (His former aide and longtime friend Nick Littlefield said that long before Ted's illness, he and Ted jokingly used to grade the introductions he got on the basis of how effusive they were; the "greatest senator in the last half of the twentieth century" or "since the War" rated a C, the "greatest senator of the century" a B, the "greatest senator of all time" an A.) For decades he had written a precise account of everything he did, keeping a diary and recording notes after every meeting he had. His friend Lee Fentress recalled that after a visit to Mexican president José López Portillo on which Fentress had accompanied Ted nearly forty years earlier, Ted took out his recorder and then recited "every detail of that meeting": "where they sat in the room, the president, where he sat, what he wore, who was there, what they discussed, a picture in the room." "Ever was his eye on history," Fentress said. And in the interests of history, Ted had spoken with Bill Clinton and with Clinton advisers and with advisers to George H. W. Bush about an oral history project, and he had asked Fentress to canvass the country to find an appropriate repository for that project, which wound up at the Miller Center for Public Affairs at the University of Virginia, where there were extensive oral histories of recent presidents—hundreds of interviews for each of them. Before his illness, he would meet with the oral historians, usually on Fridays, and talk with them for hours, recounting his life, nearly two dozen times. And he would use his diaries and recordings and oral histories for his memoir. And long before his diagnosis, he hatched plans for a memorial, an Edward M. Kennedy Institute for the U.S. Senate, to be housed in Dorchester near the University of Massachusetts on the same spit of land where the John F. Kennedy Presidential Library stood— a "salute to him and the institution he loves at a place he loves," one of his fundraisers said of the institute, and a place where schoolchildren and prospective legislators and even current legislators could learn about the Senate in hopes of their gaining greater understanding of the Senate and improving its operation, and that effort had accelerated after his diagnosis. Paul Kirk, Ted's onetime aide and longtime friend and the former chairman of the Democratic National Committee, called the institute the "single most important thing, other than family and health, that Senator Kennedy is focused on."

And if he was thinking of his legacy, he was also thinking of his soul. Father Mark Hession of Our Lady of Victory in Centerville would frequently come to the house to celebrate Mass there because Ted couldn't go to church, but now, as Ted weakened, Hession said that Ted and Vicki ruminated on the Gospel According to St. Luke, which was often called the Gospel of the Poor, in which Luke said, "Blessed are the poor," and in which he declared: "When you hold a banquet, invite the poor, the crippled, the lame, the blind; blessed indeed will you be because of their inability to repay you. For you will be repaid at the resurrection of the righteous." When Barack Obama was heading to the Vatican for an audience with Pope Benedict XVI in July, Ted sent the president a sealed letter and asked if he would hand-deliver it to His Holiness. Obama did, behind closed doors in the papal library, and asked the pope to pray for Ted, and then phoned Ted afterward to tell him he had done so and spoke with him for ten minutes. For a man who had often been at odds with his own church, it was a plea for a papal blessing as Ted was dying—what Tom Oliphant, who had covered Ted for years for *The Boston Globe*, called the note of a "penitent on a deathbed seeking a prayer from his priest." Citing the gift of faith that had been given him by his mother, he wrote that it had "sustained and nurtured and provided solace to me in the darkest hours. I know I have been an imperfect human being, but with the help of my faith I have tried to right my past." And in hopes of salvation, he wrote of his efforts to serve his fellow man: "I want you to know, your Holiness, that in my 50 years of elected office I have done my best to champion the rights of the poor and open doors of economic opportunity. I've worked to welcome the immigrant, to fight discrimination and expand access to health care and education. I've opposed the death penalty and fought to end war. Those are the issues that have motivated me and have been the focus of my work as a U.S. Senator." He cited yet again his efforts to achieve healthcare for all. These were the accomplishments for which he wanted to be remembered—his accomplishments which he hoped had served God. And he asked the pope to pray for him.

As that summer of grace wore on, he was ready for the end—less troubled, less roiled by doubt, less insecure about his standing, happier possibly than he had ever been. "Melancholic" was how his son Patrick had described him through much of his life, dark and brooding, though Ted never showed that publicly where he was gregarious and ebullient and convivial. Now he seemed to have expunged the darkness and become the man he often pretended to be. "A man in full," the political columnist Richard Reeves had called him when he last saw him, which was Labor Day of 2007 at Cape Cod—"singing and laughing hugely through one of those parody songs that folks compose for friends' birthdays." "He was free at last," Reeves thought watching Ted then. "He had the right job and the right wife. He was free of the presidential ambitions forced on him by others, especially by his dead brothers. He was free of being a Kennedy. He was what he was meant to be, a great senator. The great senators stand for something, and they stay a long time and get things done. He had a mission, making health care an American right, and too many friends to count." Reeves titled the column, "A Publicly Moral Man."

But Ted Kennedy's sense of well-being now was more than joy or freedom—much more. It was not so much a matter of what happened outside him as of what happened inside. Ted—indeed, all the Kennedys—had suppressed his feelings in the interest of fitting the Kennedy mold as designed by Joe Kennedy. There was no room in that mold for overt displays of affection or bursts of emotion, no room for intimacy or confession or doubt or failure or introspection—a suppression that Ted had borne all his life as an enormous weight. But over the years, Vicki had lifted that weight. Vicki had enabled him to look within himself and get in touch with himself. And in that last year, as he worked on his memoir, he would say that he never would have embarked on it—embarked on revealing himself—had it not been for Vicki: "had she not helped me to talk more openly about feelings that had long since been shut away." And in those last months, when they would read passages of the memoir to each other, Ted Kennedy, finally, finally, was not just a man in full, but a man whole—a man no longer entrapped in an image and a man no longer at odds with his inner self. He had not so much escaped from himself as he had accepted himself, which might have been his greatest personal triumph.

He had been bracing for his death for more than a year, and he did not act like a man in fear of it. Rather, he was at ease with his mortality, perhaps in some measure because as a Kennedy he was intimate with death. John Kerry said that when he and Ted had met a few weeks earlier, "Ted seemed incredibly peaceful" with "no hint of anger or rebellion against his fate." Vicki told Kerry that Ted had never had any bitterness about his illness, and Kerry said that Ted had told him that he felt it important that he provide an example for others of how to die, which was living life to the fullest and without regrets. "There were a lot of happy moments at the end," Mark Leibovich of *The New York Times* would write. "There was a lot of frankness, a lot of hugging, a lot of emotion." He spent his last days in repose, watching James Bond movies as he had at the hospital when he had suffered his seizure, and the television program *24*, and eating bowls of mocha chip and butter crunch ice creams, which were mixed together. No one knew exactly how much time he had left, only that there was not much, and Barbara Souliotis drove down to Hyannis on Tuesday morning, August 25, and met at a local hotel with Vicki and Paul Kirk and Ted's onetime administrative assistant Ranny Cooper to discuss what needed to be done when the time came. And then Souliotis headed back to Boston. But when she reached Andover, she received an email from Vicki. Ted had taken a sudden turn for the worse. He didn't look good, she wrote. The family now gathered at the Big House, all but Patrick, who was filling in for his father at a rally for the United Farm Workers union in Santa Rosa, California, where the farm workers shouted, "Viva Kennedy" in Ted's honor, and the Reverend Patrick Tarrant, a young priest from Our Lady of Victory, arrived that evening to administer the last rites. "He was ready to go," Vicki had told Vice President Biden that morning. Now it had, at long last, come. The water and the sky at Hyannis that night merged, gray and bleak, solid, without any visible horizon, almost, John Kerry would recall, as if the sky "seemed to be in mourning." At eleven-thirty p.m., on August 25, a year to the day since he had taken the stage at the Democratic National Convention in Denver, now surrounded by his family, in a room that looked out onto the sea, the same room in which his parents had died, Ted Kennedy, who had lived his life at first catching the wind and then sailing against it and struggling against the undertow but keeping his rudder true, who had lived owning his fallibility, who had lived serving those who had not had the good fortune of birth he had, who had lived working the instruments of power for the public weal, who had lived trying to outrace himself and his family expectations, who had lived with sin and with the hope for redemption, who had lived with trial, turbulence, and tragedy, and with drama, dread, and darkness, but who had lived throughout it all, whatever his personal failings, as a publicly moral man, in Richard Reeves's words, slipped into eternity—the last of his brothers, the first of his brothers.

A "peaceful departure," it was called.

ACKNOWLEDGMENTS

A lengthy biography like this one is necessarily a long journey—in my case, a nearly twelve-year and ultimately two-book journey. In truth, I had never thought of this biography as two books. I wrote it (them) with the intention that it (they) would be a single book, albeit a very long one, and I wrote them consecutively, without pause. But as the biography kept growing, it became obvious to Crown, my publisher, and to me that the story needed to be divided in two, if only because few readers would have been able to lift, much less read, a single volume of that heft. Thankfully, the story split neatly, with the rise of liberalism and its subsequent demise each constituting a separate volume. I felt I was, to paraphrase a quotation from *Catching the Wind*, on the *right* side of destiny. But if the book split in two almost spontaneously, there are, because I wrote both volumes without pause and because those same individuals and institutions who provided me with their assistance and encouragement for *Catching the Wind* also did so for *Against the Wind*, no two sets of acknowledgments. I apologize for largely repeating here the thanks I have already given in *Catching the Wind*, but I can justify the repetition on the basis that the gratitude I feel may only be adequately expressed by doubling it.

While my long journey was largely a happy and fulfilling one, it was not without its treacherous stretches, for which it helped to have had support. I was very fortunate in that regard. As I explained in the acknowledgments to *Catching the Wind*, the IRS hounded me and threatened me for back taxes, as it so often hounds and threatens writers and artists, few of whom get paid on a regular basis, and were it not for the extraordinary efforts of my son-in-law Braden Beard, a brilliant and fearless attorney, who got the Justice Department, which does the IRS's dirty work, to temporarily desist while I continued writing, I could not have finished these two volumes, collected my advance, and paid my obligation. So once again my first debt of gratitude, an enormous debt, much larger than anything I owed the IRS, goes to him. I can only hope the books will repay it, as I hope my success in overcoming my own financial difficulties may encourage others to persist and overcome theirs.

I owe thanks again to the esteemed editor John Glusman, who set me on this wonderful journey and suggested the subject of Ted Kennedy to me after I had proposed another political subject through which I had also hoped to examine the tortuous course of American politics generally and American liberalism specifically. John subsequently left Crown to become the editor in chief at W. W. Norton, but I have never forgotten his encouragement and his faith in this project, and those helped sustain me during that journey.

My journey also took me to several institutions that provided much-needed support. So again: The Woodrow Wilson International Center for Scholars in Washington awarded me a public policy scholarship and lent me a young researcher named Nick Lewis, who found books and articles for me and joined me in explorations of the National Archives, where the archivists were kind enough to let us loose to pore over the records of Ted Kennedy's Senate committees. As I wrote in the acknowledgments to *Catching the Wind,* Nick and I were like prospectors panning to find a gold nugget, and occasionally we did. I also owe a large debt of gratitude to the Shorenstein Center on Media, Politics and Public Policy at the Harvard Kennedy School of Government, which awarded me a fellowship and the gift of a semester in Boston. While working on a paper there examining the relationship between Ted Kennedy and the press, I roamed Harvard, Ted Kennedy's alma mater, and used its facilities, retraced Ted's steps in Boston, and absorbed, as best I could, the sense of that city that meant so much to him. I drew upon the kindness of the Shorenstein staff and the brilliance of its then-director, Alex Jones, and of its faculty, in particular Richard Parker and Thomas Patterson, the first of whom was always open to share his vast knowledge and sharp insights, the second of whom gave me an invaluable crash course in quantitative research. The center also introduced me to Alexi White, my research assistant there, and an exceptional one, who helped me hone the ideas of this book and provided informed and brilliant contributions. Like the fellowship itself, he was a gift. Once again, I owe a large debt as well to the Starr Center for the Study of the American Experience at Washington College in Chestertown,

Maryland, where I was the Patrick Henry Writing Fellow, so named because as a fellow I was housed in a dwelling that once belonged to Patrick Henry. I am especially grateful to the center's director, Adam Goodheart, a great historian in his own right, and a wonderful colleague, and to Jenifer Emley, then the program coordinator, who somehow managed to listen to me expatiate on Ted Kennedy while concealing the boredom I know she must have sometimes, perhaps often, felt. The center gave me the opportunity to work, uninterrupted, morning to night, seven days a week in the best possible surroundings, and it gave me friendship and fellowship too that made my stop there an especially rewarding one.

My journey also took me, virtually, by correspondence, and in person, to many archives, libraries, museums, and repositories where I was blessed by the assistance of many librarians, scholars, and docents. Again, at the John F. Kennedy Presidential Library, I owe debts to Stephen Plotkin and Maryrose Grossman for their generous work on my behalf. At the Senate Historical Office, I was the beneficiary of the kindnesses of the former Senate historian Donald Ritchie, who unfailingly answered my questions and, as I acknowledged in *Catching the Wind,* took me on an unforgettable tour of the Capitol, including a visit to Senator Kennedy's hideaway, which gave me a sense of how the senator navigated those hallowed halls. At the National Archives, my debt extends to the entire staff who generously gave me access to the Senate records to which I alluded earlier. And at the Miller Center at the University of Virginia, the home of the Edward Kennedy Oral History Project, which I used extensively for both volumes, I am indebted to Barbara Perry, Robert Martin, Marc Selverstone, and Brian Balogh, who fielded many questions from me over the years and deflected many requests as I waited—again waited years—for the oral histories to be transcribed and released. Once again, the librarians at the Amagansett Free Library, in the community of Amagansett, New York, where I lived for twenty-six years, were a great resource to me: Francine Lane, Corrine Page, Meaghan Pease, and Anne Jones. There was literally never a book they couldn't find for me, and I made hundreds of requests to them. The librarians at the Topsham Public Library, in my new hometown of Topsham, Maine, have been no less diligent, though they have been on the journey with me for only a short time. Still, I thank them.

Long ago, on another journey, I was fortunate enough to meet Robert

Reeves, who, first as the chairman of the Creative Writing and Literature Program, and now as the associate provost of the Southampton Graduate Arts Program of the State University of New York at Stony Brook, where I have taught for over a decade, has extended to me more kindnesses than I can count and has extended to me his friendship, which I treasure. Once again I also thank my colleagues at Stony Brook, a group as supportive as it is illustrious. And as before, I thank my students, who, through their own enthusiasms and their probing questions and their spirited class discussions and their energy, have continued to stoke my own passion for writing, have helped me clarify my thoughts, and have kept me, I like to believe, young, at least in spirit.

Once again, I have had some great companions on this journey, though I have never met any of them save through their words. They are the Edward Kennedy biographers who went before me and whose work has informed my own, and I owe them an enormous debt of gratitude: among them James MacGregor Burns, Peter Canellos, Lester David, Burton Hersh, Max Lerner, Murray Levin and T. A. Repak, and Theo Lippman, Jr. Special gratitude is due to the late Adam Clymer for donating his notes and interview transcripts to the Kennedy Presidential Library, where they are available to scholars and where they proved indispensable for these books. As I said in *Catching the Wind*, I have stood on the shoulders of all these men, and whether they knew it or not, they supported me through the long years and the long journey.

And on that long journey of mine, I have had wonderful friends who have not only supported me but, once again, have also sustained me. Bill Moyers is as close to being our national conscience as any other figure, and he has been a moral lodestar to me. I had the great good fortune to work with him for two years writing a column for his BillMoyers.com website—two of the most satisfying years of my life. And as I wrote this book, which is as much about political morality as it is about the figure who, I felt, exuded it, Bill was never far from my thoughts. We meet few great men in our lives. One of them is a friend of mine. Two other indispensable friends are my film and television agent, Deborah Miller, who provided me with more encouragement than anyone I know, and her husband, Sandy Lakoff, the Dickson professor emeritus of political science at the University of California at San Diego, a man knowledgeable and brilliant and generous, who read every chapter with a scrutiny an author only dreams of and whose eye, as I wrote in my first acknowledgments, kept me from errors of fact while his wisdom kept me from errors of judgment. They are family to me. And again, thanks to Bob Bookman, my *other* film and television agent and a legend in Hollywood, who out of his kindness and big heart called me years ago, though he didn't know me personally, to offer assistance after reading my essay on my financial tribulations in *The Atlantic*. He has been my friend ever since. And then there is Elizabeth Bassine, a friend of nearly thirty years, who read the early chapters of *Catching the Wind*, even as her eyesight was failing; and Elaine Grove, a dog-walking compatriot who spent many mornings over many years hearing me talk about Ted Kennedy far more than she would have liked, I am sure; and Inda Eaton, another dear friend and listener; and Annemarie McCoy, yet another longtime friend who bailed me out of many a technical snafu; and Kevin Abernathy, yet *another* dear dog-walking friend and one of the gentlest souls I know, who also let me discuss the book as I was writing it and at least did a great job of feigning interest. My friend and fellow biographer—and a world-class one—Bob Spitz provided the encouragement that only a fellow biographer and sufferer can provide. Once again, I owe another enormous debt to Ian Lynch, an outstanding young man who became my research assistant in the final stages of my work, and who proofed the notes and organized the bibliography and read the manuscript and became another indispensable friend on the journey. I am a less-than-trusting soul when it comes to my books. I like to do nearly everything myself. But I trusted Ian, which is the highest compliment I can pay him. I would be remiss if I did not thank—and thank profusely—my accountant Gary Orkin, who has always been there for me, going above and beyond what accountants normally do and always reassuring me that I would have the resources to finish the book. I did, and he was largely responsible. And there are my two oldest friends, Patrick Cosgrove and Craig Hoffman, whom I have known for more decades than any of us would want to admit, and who have always been steadfast supporters and consolers and more, much more. I know how fortunate I am to have friends like these.

Years ago, after I had started the book and my literary agent, Elaine Markson, passed away, my journey took me to my new literary agent, Joy Harris, for whom superlatives are inadequate. Joy has been a relentless advocate for the book and helped me in countless ways, not the least of which was making sure I had the financial wherewithal to finish it (them). Her associate, Adam Reed, has been another great support. Adam always looked after the logistics of the project, which is a largely thankless task, but not thankless from me. In the acknowledgments of *Catching the Wind*, I called my gratitude to Joy and Adam "boundless." I still have yet to reach the boundaries.

At Crown, my publisher, where the journey began and has now ended, I received the kind of support that books seldom get: respect for the book as a book to be read and not as another product to be sold. Christopher Brand designed the beautiful jacket for *Against the Wind* as he did for *Catching the Wind*; the two jackets are mated, and there is a lovely interplay between them, which reflects what I was hoping to do with the content of the books, once they became books, plural. Fritz Metsch once again provided the clean, elegant interior design. Regardless of its content, for which I am wholly responsible (or guilty as the case may be), they are responsible for making it an aesthetic object, which is a true bonus for an author. Dennis Ambrose, the production editor, as I wrote in *Catching the Wind*, shepherded the manuscript to printed text with such concern and devotion and examined the book assiduously, the way Ted Kennedy examined legislation. As I said of *Catching the Wind* and that is equally true of *Against the Wind*, he made the book better. Lydia Morgan and Katie Berry did the sorts of things that seldom get recognition, the little things that are absolutely necessary to get a book to print. Let me give recognition here. They made the journey so much easier.

My erstwhile traveling partner and often my guide on the long last stretch of my journey, the writing phase, was my editor, Kevin Doughten. Kevin inherited this book when it outlasted two previous editors, John Glusman, acknowledged earlier, and Rachel Klayman, who showed the book nothing but respect when it was in her custody. There was no reason, certainly no emotional reason, for Kevin to be invested in the book—a book he hadn't signed and had only been assigned, and one by an author, no less, he had never met. No reason, and yet from the outset of our relationship, he did something remarkable: he lavished attention on the book, giving it the most careful of reads, asking questions constantly that forced me to rethink passages and to refine, discussing the book with me in what would amount to hours upon hours of conversation, and even doing something beyond remarkable, something unheard of in this market where the object generally is to make books shorter and thus more salable. He would ask me to elaborate—actually make the book longer when he thought it necessary. There is an idea afoot that editors no longer edit books; they acquire them. Kevin is an editor—an honest-to-god editor. And he is an advocate, which is something every book needs. No one championed these books more than he. Finally, to me, he is something more than a great editor and an ardent advocate. He is a dear friend and collaborator. I cannot imagine the journey without him, and he certainly deserves a second round of accolades for this second volume, though these are insufficient thanks.

When the journey of *Catching the Wind* ended, there was one group of individuals who could not be acknowledged then. They were the luminaries who kindly read the book and, I am happy to say, provided enthusiastic "blurbs" for it. Typically, these are friends lending their imprimatur, and typically there is a good bit of logrolling in the process. But these were not friends of mine; I did not know any of them personally, nor had I ever blurbed their books. They were people to whom I had asked Kevin to send the book because I sincerely respected them and hoped they might respect the book. It is no small thing when you don't have a personal relationship with an author to have that author read a manuscript, especially a long one like *Catching the Wind*. I am more than grateful that Kai Bird, Douglas Brinkley, Walter Isaacson, Jon Meacham, and Sean Wilentz, my all-star team, as I regard them, did.

Above all, before the journey, during the journey, and now after the journey, there is my family about whom, yet again, truly no words are adequate to express my appreciation and, more, my love. My daughters, Laurel and Tänne, my daughter-in-law Shoshanna Fine, my son-in-law Braden Beard, without whose work, as I said, this book would not exist, and my four grandchildren—Sadie, Oren, and the twins, Kaya and Theo—are the true blessings of my life, who make everything worthwhile. The thought of the last four and of the world they will inherit, and the hope that Ted Kennedy's life might provide them with a guidepost to make the world better, helped fuel the engine that drove these books and that kept me going on the journey. And lastly, there is Christina.

I repeat here what I wrote at the end of the acknowledgments in volume one. It goes without saying that no one acknowledged here is responsible for any errors of fact or judgment or infelicity of prose. Those acknowledged are blameless for everything except the support and encouragement they provided a writer in need and one so deeply appreciative of them.

NOTES

INTRODUCTION: A COUNTERVAILING WIND

xv   **"Garbage Mouth":** J. Anthony Lukas, *Common Ground: A Turbulent Decade in the Lives of Three American Families* (New York: Knopf, 1985), 452.

xv   **Races shouldn't mingle:** Ibid., 453.

xvi   **Palladino had led another:** See *Catching the Wind*, Chapter 17.

xvi   **"jungle bunnies":** Ibid., 137.

xvi   **"First among his":** Ronald Formisano, *Boston Against Busing: Race, Class and Ethnicity in the 1960s and 1970s* (Chapel Hill: Univ. of North Carolina Press, 1991), 181.

xvi   **"at the top of her lungs":** EMK int., May 30, 2007, Miller Center, UVA.

xvi   **accused of punching:** Lukas, *Common Ground*, 137.

xix   **"From roughly 1963":** Godfrey Hodgson, *America in Our Time: From World War II to Nixon* (New York: Vintage Books, 1978), 368.

xxii–xxiii   **"To permit the thought":** Rick Perlstein, *The Invisible Bridge: The Fall of Nixon and the Rise of Reagan* (New York: Simon & Schuster, 2014), 154–55.

xxiii   **"like a banshee":** Formisano, *Boston Against Busing*, 181.

xxiv   **"Sure we're racists":** Ibid., 135.

xxiv   **"Beginning in the mid-60s":** Thomas Edsall, "Why Trump Still Has Millions of Americans in His Grip," *NYT*, May 5, 2021.

xxiv   **"tapped a much broader":** Lukas, *Common Ground*, 135.

xxv   **"Pixie's pugnacious":** Formisano, *Boston Against Busing*, 183.

xxv   **"Kennedys look down":** Ibid.

xxvii   **"simple moral principle":** Franklin D. Roosevelt, acceptance speech at Democratic National Convention, Chicago, July 2, 1932, www.presidency.ucsb.edu/documents/address-accepting-the -presidential-nomination-the-democratic-national-convention-Chicago-1.

xxvii   **"we are confronted":** Sen. Everett Dirksen, "The Civil Rights Bill," June 10, 1964, https://www .senate.gov/artandhistory/history/resources/pdf/DirksenCivilRights.pdf.

ONE: A MAN OF THE SENATE

4   **commissioning polls:** Milton Gwirtzman int., Apr. 3, 1993, G Folder, Box 3, Series 2, Clymer Papers, JFK Lib.

4   **still a student:** Richard Burke with William Hoffer and Marilyn Hoffer, *The Senator: My Ten Years with Ted Kennedy* (New York: St. Martin's Press, 1992), 52.

5   **"somber and silent":** Arthur Schlesinger, Jr., *Journals: 1952–2000*, ed. Andrew Schlesinger and Stephen Schlesinger (New York: Penguin Press, 2007), 410.

5   **"The hard truth is":** Tom Wicker, "Kennedy Frees Democrats," *NYT*, Sept. 24, 1974.

5   **"He is unwilling":** Gwirtzman int.

6   **"The eras that shaped":** Edward Kennedy, *True Compass* (New York: Twelve, 2009), 343–44.

6   **"Teddy is the one":** "Ready for Teddy?" *Newsweek*, June 2, 1975.

6   **"bottom of the list":** Jonathan Alter, *The Very Best: Jimmy Carter, A Life* (New York: Simon & Schuster, 2020), 212.

7   **"would do nothing":** Ibid., 106.

7 **"white trash dingbat"**: Hunter Thompson, *The Great Shark Hunt: Gonzo Papers, Volume One* (New York: Simon & Schuster, 1979), 455.

7 **"The time for racial"**: Alter, *Very Best*, 167.

8 **"Puzzlingly changeable"**: EMK, *True Compass*, 353.

8 **"mood in the car"**: Thompson, *Great Shark Hunt*, 467.

8 **"push Kennedy around"**: Hunter Thompson int., CBC, 1977, quoted in Jon Ward, *Camelot's End: Kennedy vs. Carter and the Fight That Broke the Democratic Party* (New York: Twelve, 2019), 88.

9 **talk to Kennedy**: Eleanor Clift, "Prophetic Game Plan," *Newsweek*, May 10, 1976.

9 **"Behind the reflex"**: Robert Shrum, *No Excuses: Concessions of a Serial Campaigner* (New York: Simon & Schuster, 2007), 64–65.

9 **"wasn't in his DNA"**: Alter, *Very Best*, 37.

9 **"Clearly the most conservative"**: E. J. Dionne, Jr., *Why Americans Hate Politics* (New York: Simon & Schuster, 1991), 127.

9 **"They chose to be miners"**: Shrum, *No Excuses*, 67.

9 **He talked of honesty**: Alter, *Very Best*, 226.

9 **"I still don't have"**: "Kennedy on Carter," *WP*, May 26, 1976.

10 **"Aching to be president"**: David Broder, "Kennedy, O'Neill Trip on Language Barrier," *WP*, July 29, 1975.

10 **accept a genuine draft**: "I Know I Cannot Run Now," *Time*, May 31, 1976.

10 **"I'm glad I don't have"**: Adam Clymer, *Edward M. Kennedy: A Biography* (New York: Harper Perennial, 2000), 247.

10 **"highly uncertain"**: Schlesinger, *Journals*, 414–15.

10 **"He wanted to be separated"**: EMK int., Mar. 28, 2008, Miller Center, UVA.

10 **"I want to make that clear"**: "Kennedy Almost an Afterthought at Convention," *LAT*, July 16, 1976.

10 **invitation had come too late**: "Kennedy Invited Too Late to Unity Night," *BG*, July 17, 1976.

11 **"Their triumph was one"**: Peter Goldman, "Jimmycrats," *Newsweek*, July 26, 1976.

11 **"To be frank, Jimmy Carter"**: Quoted in John A. Farrell, *Tip O'Neill and the Democratic Century* (Boston: Little, Brown, 2001), 442.

11 **Carter refused, Ted believed**: EMK, *True Compass*, 352.

11 **Carter could have had**: Gerard Doherty int., Oct. 10, 2005, Miller Center, UVA.

12 **deviated from the plan**: Timothy Stanley, *Kennedy vs. Carter: The 1980 Battle for the Democratic Party's Soul* (Lawrence: Univ. Press of Kansas, 2010), 23.

12 **endorsed national health**: Stuart Auerbach, "Health Insurance: The Debate Has Shifted," *WP*, Apr. 3, 1976.

12 **"talked his way around"**: EMK int., Mar. 28, 2008, Miller Center, UVA.

12 **"no ideology, no central"**: Shrum, *No Excuses*, 62–63.

12 **"as good and honest"**: Alter, *Very Best*, 218–19.

13 **"The Carter river"**: Goldman, "Jimmycrats."

13 **Carter received fewer votes**: Stanley, 29.

13 **"Well, this busing thing"**: Theo Lippman, *Senator Ted Kennedy: The Career Behind the Image* (New York: Norton, 1976), 257.

13 **"historical anomaly"**: Alter, *Very Best*, 281.

14 **"as antiquated and anachronistic"**: Sean Wilentz, *The Age of Reagan: A History 1974–2008* (New York: HarperCollins, 2008), 83.

14 **McGovern was so distrustful**: Schlesinger, *Journals*, 506.

14 **"you can make a connection"**: Ibid., 421.

14 **"Kennedy senses problems"**: Memo: Caddell to Carter, Dec. 10, 1976, Box 49, UAW Coll., Papers of Douglas Fraser, Walter Reuther Lib., Wayne State Univ., quoted in Stanley, 25–26.

15 **"There was a certain sadness"**: Schlesinger, *Journals*, 415–16.

15 **"I can't sit around"**: "I Know I Cannot Run Now."

16 **"great crusade"**: Quoted in Theo Lippman, *Senator Ted Kennedy: The Career Behind the Image* (New York: Norton, 1976), 272.

16 **"presidential senator"**: James MacGregor Burns, *Edward Kennedy and the Camelot Legacy* (New York: Norton, 1976), 248.

16 **received a thousand**: Ibid., 237; Burke with Hoffer and Hoffer, *Senator*, 4.

16 **accosted continuously**: Richard Rhodes, "Things as They Are, Things That Never Were," *Audience*, Nov.–Dec. 1971.

17 **"it affected to some"**: Gwirtzman int.

18 **"free senator"**: Joseph Alsop, "Kennedy's Experiment," *WP,* Sept. 27, 1974.

18 **"verbose sterility"**: Ibid.

18 **"it's possible for individuals"**: John Tunney int., Mar. 6, 1995, T Folder, Box 5, Series 2, Clymer Papers, JFK Lib.

19 **"Well, I do"**: Robert Dove, Senate parliamentarian, int. by author.

19 **never any animosity**: Charles Mathias int., Mar. 10, 2006, Miller Center, UVA.

19 **"old days"**: James Eastland int., n.d., James O Eastland Papers, J. D. Williams Lib., Univ. of Mississippi.

19 **"went in to have"**: "Remembering Ted Kennedy," *National Journal,* Sept. 5, 2009.

20 **"you could really take"**: Quoted in Lippman, *Senator Kennedy,* 272.

20 **to flag his disapproval**: EMK to Eastland, May 1970, Folder 6–7, Box 6, Subseries 18, Series 1, James O. Eastland Papers, J. D. Williams Lib., Univ. of Mississippi.

20 **"roared with anger"**: "Senate Voter Registration Bill Blocked," *LAT,* Mar. 10, 1972.

20 **"I was deeply touched"**: EMK to Eastland, May 1978, Folder 6–7, Box 6, Subseries 18, Series 1, James O. Eastland Papers, J. D. Williams Lib., Univ. of Mississippi.

21 **"I thought they were going"**: Kilvert Dun Gifford int., July 13, 2005, Miller Center, UVA.

21 **"couple of pops"**: Ibid.

22 **"He was a young, good-looking"**: Walter Mondale int., Mar. 20, 2006, Miller Center, UVA.

22 **"He is intelligent in the sense"**: "Ted Kennedy Acquires Humility from Rebuff," *LAT,* Aug. 11, 1963.

22 **"gap remains between"**: Schlesinger, *Journals,* 236–37.

22 **"takes in everything you"**: Burton Hersh, *The Education of Edward Kennedy: A Family Biography* (New York: Morrow, 1972), 102.

22 **"The dumbest of the three"**: Quoted in Burns, *Edward Kennedy,* 299.

23 **"The impression is abroad"**: Richard Reeves, "Teddy or Not," *New York,* Apr. 22, 1974.

23 **"bright, but he's not"**: Lawrence Tribe int., Apr. 27, 2009, Miller Center, UVA.

23 **"There is some force"**: Charles Haar int., Oct. 10. 2005, Miller Center, UVA.

24 **"Too many blue suits"**: Robert Bates int., May 8, 2007, Miller Center, UVA.

24 **political intelligence**: Ibid.

24 **"Very intelligent"**: Eastland int.

25 **"closet of unused verbs"**: Rick Atkinson, "Why Ted Kennedy Can't Stand Still," *WP Magazine,* Apr. 29, 1990.

25 **"Better in amphitheaters"**: Martin Schram, "Running for Office in Massachusetts, Kennedy Stumps the Whole Country," *WP,* Oct. 26, 1982.

25 **"A personal dialect"**: Atkinson, "Why Kennedy Can't."

25 **"biggest thing you have"**: Thomas Rollins int., May 14, 2009, Miller Center, UVA.

26 **"inarticulate and lacking"**: Edward Brooke, *Bridging the Divide: My Life* (New Brunswick, N.J.: Rutgers Univ. Press, 2007), 252.

26 **"One of the loudest"**: Sheila Burke int., July 27, 2007, Miller Center, UVA.

26 **"wrong at the top"**: EMK, *True Compass,* 478.

26 **"Dear Ted"**: Alan Simpson int., May 10, 2006, Miller Center, UVA.

26 **speech therapist**: Milton Gwirtzman int., Apr. 3, 1991, G Folder, Box 5, Series 2, Clymer Papers, JFK Lib.

27 **"music of that speech"**: EMK int., Nov. 11, 1998, EMK Interviews 1997–99 Folder, Box 5, Series 2, Clymer Papers, JFK Lib.; William Honan, *Ted Kennedy: Profile of a Survivor* (New York: Quadrangle Books, 1972); Hersh, *Education,* 255.

27 **"little bit inarticulate"**: Betty Taymor int., July 8, 2005, Miller Center, UVA.

27 **"more than one person"**: Burns, *Edward Kennedy,* 336.

27 **"tendency at times"**: John Tunney int., Mar. 6, 1995, T Folder, Box 5, Series 2, Clymer Papers, JFK Lib.

27 **"very, very smart businessman"**: Ted Sorensen int., June 17, 1996, S Folder, Box 5, Series 2, Clymer Papers, JFK Lib.

27 **"sense that he knows"**: John Danforth int., Oct. 25, 2005, Miller Center, UVA.

27 **"fog machine"**: Thomas Oliphant int. by author.

27 **"Whenever we came close"**: Christopher Lawford, *Symptoms of Withdrawal: A Memoir of Snapshots and Redemption* (New York: Morrow, 2005), 379.

28 **childhood of half-sentences**: Shrum, *No Excuses,* 80–81.

28   "Always having to live": Honan, 139.

28   "He was never a wunderkind": Robert Shriver III int., Jan. 29, 2010, Miller Center, UVA.

28   "This amazing capacity": Dun Gifford int.

28   "He always operated": Quoted in Peter Canellos, *Last Lion: The Fall and Rise of Ted Kennedy* (New York: Simon & Schuster, 2009), 201.

28   "make them love him": Carey Parker int., Oct. 6, 2008, Miller Center, UVA.

29   "Some people who": William Weaver, Jr., "By His Deeds . . . ," *Esquire*, Feb. 1972.

29   "He can keep one hundred": Carey Parker int., Nov. 17, 2008, Miller Center, UVA.

29   "we will work harder": "Kennedy Funeral Service," CNN, August 29, 2009.

29   "One of the hardest-working men": Eastland int.

30   "We would be talking": David Boies int., Sept. 23, 2008, Miller Center, UVA.

30   "I am just getting used": Burton Hersh, *The Shadow President: Ted Kennedy in Opposition* (South Royalton, Vt.: Steerforth Press, 1997), 17.

30   "This guy worked our tails": Stan Jones int., Nov. 11, 1993, I–J Folder, Box 4, Series 2, Clymer Papers, JFK Lib.

30   "He would grind through": Rollins int.

30   "presidential schedule": Melody Miller int., July 15, 2008, Miller Center, UVA.

31   "There was never a moment": Lee Fentress int., Oct. 16, 2009, Miller Center, UVA.

31   five of those cards: Lippman, *Senator Kennedy*, 145.

31   "Energy pours out of him": Burns, *Edward Kennedy*, 246.

31   soak his aching back: Burke with Hoffer and Hoffer, *Senator*, 63.

31   "He'd want to go home": James Manley int., Sept. 28, 2009, Miller Center, UVA.

31   "if somebody didn't show up": Miller int.

32   "His battery never seemed": Rollins int.

32   "The liberal intelligentsia": Carey Parker int., Sept. 22, 2008, Miller Center, UVA.

32   also invite members: Carolyn Osolinik int., Mar. 27, 2007, Miller Center, UVA.

32   "That approach won't work": Kenneth Feinberg int., July 8, 2008, Miller Center, UVA.

32   "Kennedy was very sensitive": Osolinik int.

33   "plenty of back-up reading": Nick Littlefield int., May 3, 2008, Miller Center, UVA; Steven Breyer int., July 26, 1997, B Folder, Box 3, Series 2, Clymer Papers, JFK Lib.

33   "enormous amount of material": Littlefield int.

33   "Want more on that": Thomas Susman int., May 23, 2007, Miller Center, UVA; Michael Myers int., Aug. 28, 2006, Miller Center, UVA.

33   "then he can make a decision": Breyer int.

33   "Not a details man": "A Hell of a Senator," *Economist*, Aug. 29, 2009.

33   "If you watch Kennedy": Robert Dole int., May 15, 2006, Miller Center, UVA.

34   "The Bag": Doris Reggie ints., May 15, 2006, and Dec. 16, 2008, Miller Center, UVA.

34   "Must do": EMK, *True Compass*, 298; Littlefield int.

34   "sitting on that briefcase": Dun Gifford int.

34   "Whenever he had a spare": Burke with Hoffer and Hoffer, *Senator*, 7.

34   "You'd walk in through": Melissa Ludtke int. by author.

35   "you sit down on the airplane": Timothy Hannan int., May 7, 2009, Miller Center, UVA.

35   "drives the day": Myers int.

35   "You'd always say, *The Bag* would be leaving": Scott Ferson quoted in Martha Bebinger, "Kennedy Remembered as Senate's Hardest Worker," WBUR, Aug. 26, 2008, wbur.org/2009/08/26/kennedy-tributes.

35   annotated by the senator: Atkinson, "Why Kennedy Can't."

35   Was it better to submit: Ibid.

35   "all kinds of stunts": Ibid.

35   "mad dash": Mark Schneider quoted in "Remembering Ted Kennedy."

36   If he left a checkmark: Dun Gifford int.

36   "I'm angry" and you'd better: Leroy Goldman int., May 5, 2007, Miller Center, UVA.

36   "You'd get a memo back": Rollins int.

36   "ultimate translator": Mark Schneider int., Feb. 2, 2009, Miller Center, UVA.

36   "I was there too long": "Remembering Ted Kennedy."

36   "You worked for Kennedy": Manley int.

36   "He took his standard": Paul Donovan int., Nov. 14, 1998, D Folder, Box 3, Series 2, Clymer Papers, JFK Lib.

37 **"On any given day"**: Richard Reeves, "A Publicly Moral Man," *USA Today*, Aug. 27, 2009.

37 **"My real bias"**: Thomas Oliphant, "The Lion at Rest," *Democracy*, no. 15 (Winter 2010): 101, https://democracyjournal.org/magazine/15/the-lion-at-rest/.

37 **"I was astonished"**: James Sasser int., May 25, 2006, Miller Center, UVA.

37 **"Nobody works harder"**: Lowell Weicker int., June 19, 2008, Miller Center, UVA.

37 **"He's a leader"**: Eastland int.

37 simply **"Ted"**: Burns, *Edward Kennedy*, 141.

38 **"never permits ideology"**: Clayton Fritchey, "Who Belongs to the Senate's Inner Club?" *Harper's*, May 1967, 108.

38 **"The true and ultimate"**: William S. White, *Citadel: The Story of the U.S. Senate* (New York: Harper & Bros., 1957), 179.

38 **"to sit around forever"**: Martin Tolchin int. by author.

39 **reforms he implemented**: Nelson Polsby, "Goodbye to the Inner Club," in *Congressional Behavior*, ed. Nelson Polsby (New York: Random House, 1971), 107–9.

39 **adopting many**: Robert Byrd, *The Senate: 1789–1989: Addresses on the History of the United States Senate* (Washington, D.C.: U.S. Govt. Printing Office, 1988), 4:258–59.

40 **"very insider process"**: Edward Kennedy int., March 23, 2005. Miller Center, UVA.

41 **"The only reason"**: Dick Clark int. by author.

42 **"We had the most"**: EMK int., Mar. 23, 2005, Miller Center, UVA.

42 **photo in *The New York Times:*** "Drive to Reform Rules in Congress Shifts to Senate," *NYT*, Jan. 18, 1975.

42 **"The End of an Oligarchy"**: *NYT*, Jan. 1, 1975.

42 **put himself on the firing line**: Clark int.

42 **"Kennedy utterly dominated"**: "A Quiet Revolt Under Way in Senate," *WP*, Jan. 26, 1975.

43 **the Refugee subcommittees**: Lippman, *Senator Kennedy*, 267–68.

43 **proposed a resolution to give**: Dove, int.

43 **"Always looking for the best"**: James Wechsler, memo, n.d., Re: Conversation with Ted Kennedy, Kennedy, Edward M. 1968–71 Folder, Box 37, Joseph Rauh, Jr. Papers, Library of Congress.

43 **"ablest, most gifted"**: EMK int., Oct. 9, 1995, EMK Interviews 1996–99 Folder, Box 5, Series 2, Clymer Papers, JFK Lib.

44 **fewer than two hundred**: Rochelle Jones, *The Private World of Congress* (New York: Free Press, 1979), 135–36.

44 **number of staffers**: "An Army of Experts Storms Capitol Hill," *Time*, Jan. 23, 1978; Jones, *Private World*, 136.

44 **streamline the system**: Byrd, *Senate*, 4:260–62.

44 **"if you weren't up to speed"**: EMK int., June 3, 2005, Miller Center, UVA.

44 **"packed like sardines"**: Dun Gifford int.

44 **"Too crowded"**: Robert Bates int., July 26, 2007, Miller Center, UVA.

45 **Ted would invite them**: Susman int.

45 **"all of us in stitches"**: Miller int.

45 **typical senator had around twenty**: Susan Webb Hammond and Hamilton Fox, Jr., "The Growth of Congressional Staffs," *Proceedings of the Academy of Political Science* 32, no. 1 (1975): 113.

45 **cost of $500,000**: Burns, *Edward Kennedy*, 244; Lippman, *Senator Kennedy*, 266.

45 **"So much staff"**: EMK int., June 3, 2005, Miller Center, UVA.

45 **organization as a circle**: Lippman, *Senator Kennedy*, 261.

46 **"the schedule, what appearances"**: Paul Kirk, Jr., int., Nov. 23, 2005, Miller Center, UVA.

46 **"everything else"**: Ed Martin int., Apr. 20, 2005, Miller Center, UVA.

46 **staff director for**: Nick Littlefield int., Feb. 14, 2009, Miller Center, UVA.

47 **"What the hell is this bill"**: Dun Gifford int.

48 **"You just had the dynamic"**: Kirk, Jr., int.

48 **"He's a leader in the"**: Sharon Waxman int., Dec. 19, 2008, Miller Center, UVA.

48 **"instantly close and connected"**: Jan Kalicki int., Mar. 18, 2009, Miller Center, UVA.

48 **"I probably wouldn't have"**: Parker int., Sept. 22, 2008.

48 **"to be under the radar"**: Martin int.

48 **"there was a crisis"**: Littlefield int., May 3, 2008.

49 **"great writer and a great thinker"**: Martin int.

49 **"The highest caliber staff"**: John McCain int., Oct. 16, 2009, Miller Center, UVA.

49 **"It wasn't the blue-blood type"**: Susman int.

50   "Judiciary had very large": Ibid.
50   "A very limited way": EMK int., Oct. 9, 1995.
50   "Teddy doesn't demand": Doherty int.
50   "Just put you in the pot": Dun Gifford int.
51   "He wanted new ideas": Carey Parker int., Oct. 27, 2008, Miller Center, UVA.
51   "We would go to him": Stan Jones int., Sept. 14, 2007, Miller Center, UVA.
51   "When Kennedy got up": Dole int.
51   "You don't just serve": Warren Weaver, Jr., "By His Deeds . . ." *Esquire*, Feb. 1972.
51   "digest that, condense": Parker int., Oct. 6, 2008.
51   "One of those uncommon": Shrum, *No Excuses*, 82.
52   "extremely helpful": Parker int., Sept. 22, 2008.
52   Kennedy *loved* those sessions: Ibid.
52   "Like a shark": Atkinson, "Why Kennedy Can't."
52   "We have a limited amount": Stephen Breyer int., June 17, 2008, Miller Center, UVA.
52   "Oftentimes people would just": Donovan int.
52   "Get me an energy program": Reeves, "Teddy or Not."
52   "He just laughed as he": Burke with Hoffer and Hoffer, *Senator*, 35.
53   "It's okay. Paddle away": Stan Jones int.
53   "Ride 'em hard": Quoted in Atkinson, "Why Kennedy Can't."
53   "Brusque and imperious": Myra MacPherson, "Senator Kennedy: Alone with the Legacy," *WP*, June 4, 1978; Reeves, "Teddy or Not."
53   "bellowing at him": MacPherson, "Senator Kennedy."
53   explode at anyone who did: Quoted in Hersh, *Education*, 193.
53   "Snitty": Atkinson, "Why Kennedy Can't."
53   "Very nervous and upset": Philip Caper int., Mar. 20, 2007, Miller Center, UVA.
53   "What do you mean you": Atkinson, "Why Kennedy Can't."
54   "Heaven help you if you": "The Kennedy Challenge," *Time*, Nov. 5, 1979.
54   "Forgiving": Caper int.
54   "You blow up, you realize": Rollins int.
54   "Fall all over himself": Atkinson, "Why Kennedy Can't."
54   "He never lost his temper": Roger Wolfson, "A Former Counsel to Ted Kennedy on Kennedy," *Huffington Post*, Aug. 26, 2009.
54   "If you screwed up": Bates int., May 8, 2007.
54   "Peace": Ibid.
54   "semi-whiney": Oliphant int.
54   "He could really laugh": Anne Strauss int., Apr. 10, 2008, Miller Center, UVA.
54   "I'll thank you to let me": Atkinson, "Why Kennedy Can't."
55   "Rarely, as I discovered": D. A. Pollack, "Reflections on Working for Senator Edward Kennedy," *Community Mental Health Journal* 46, no. 2 (April 2010): 103–11.
55   photographs taken with his staff: Miller int.
55   "jovial and light-hearted": Wolfson.
55   "brisk approach": "The Kennedy Challenge," *Time*, Nov. 5, 1979.
56   "How are you?": Nance Lyons int., May 9, 2008, Miller Center, UVA.
56   "What I loved about": Ibid.
56   "everybody wants to be": Bates int.
57   "We're trying to do something": Dun Gifford int.
57   "It's a bill; it's a hearing": Feinberg int.
57   "Very smart, very ideological": Danforth int.
57   "Kennedy staff people get": Atkinson, "Why Kennedy Can't."
57   pecking order was much: Hammond and Fox, 122.
57   "most aggressive": Ralph Neas int. by author.
58   "Believe me": Oliphant int.
58   "His press person and I end up": Leroy Goldman int.
58   "Tremendous staff competition": Hersh, *Shadow President*, 16.
58   "closest thing to being a clerk": Neas int.
58   "inspired in them a degree": McCain int.
58   "public image of his being": Bates int.
58–59 "It was very sexist at that time": Ibid.

59 "legislative correspondent's": Strauss int.

59 "It was horrific": Lyons int.

59 assumed she was there to serve: Ibid.

59 notified of a raise on a Post-it Note: Strauss int.

59 "shaking in his boots": Ibid.

60 "No way," he said: Barbara Souliotis int., Nov. 9, 2009, Miller Center, UVA.

60 "Very male chauvinistic": Ibid.

60 "not willing, pretty much": Lyons int.

60 likely have invited gossip: Garry Wills, *The Kennedy Imprisonment: A Meditation on Power* (Boston: Houghton Mifflin, 2002), 57.

TWO: THE CHEMISTRY OF THE SENATE

62 could read men: Robert Caro, *Master of the Senate* (New York: Knopf, 2002), 136.

62 not infrequently sputtered: Ranny Cooper quoted in Nick Littlefield int., May 3, 2008, Miller Center, UVA.

63 succumbed to the charm: Samuel Patterson, "Party Leadership in the US Senate," *Legislative Studies Quarterly* 14 (Aug. 1989): 393–413; Barbara Sinclair, "Senate Styles and Senate Decision-Making, 1955–1980," *The Journal of Politics* 48 (Nov. 1986): 877–908.

64 "We don't need your kind": Martin Tolchin int. by author.

64 open-door policy: "Senators Launch Open-Door Policy," *WP*, March 13, 1955.

64 "just up and go home": Joe Biden, *Promises to Keep: On Life and Politics* (New York: Random House, 2007), 112–13.

64 "Senators would have get-togethers": Ernest Hollings and Kirk Victor, *Making Government Work* (Columbia: Univ. of South Carolina Press, 2008), 170–71.

65 "helped senators listen": EMK, *True Compass* (New York: Twelve, 2009), 486.

65 "thousand little": John Farrell int., July 13, 2006, Miller Center, UVA.

65 ask after him or her: Elsa Walsh, "Kennedy's Hidden Campaign," *New Yorker*, Mar. 31, 1997, 68.

65 "very soulful": Nick Littlefield int., Feb. 14, 2009, Miller Center, UVA.

66 Ted wrote a tribute: Howard Shuman oral history, Senate Historical Office.

66 "Never expect any": Tip O'Neill with William Novak, *Man of the House: The Life and Political Memoirs of Tip O'Neill* (New York: Random House, 1987), 83.

66 "If you don't get a thank you": Tom Glynn, deputy secretary of labor, quoted in Martha Bebinger, "Kennedy Remembered as Senate's Hardest Worker," WBUR, Aug. 26, 2009.

66 "as far as he was concerned": Thomas Oliphant int. by author.

66 "Very willing to embrace": John A. Farrell int., July 13, 2006, Miller Center, UVA.

67 they cemented a relationship: Michael Myers int., Aug. 28, 2006, Miller Center, UVA.

67 the first person: "Remembering Ted Kennedy," *National Journal*, Sept. 5, 2009.

67 "These people of mine": Alan Simpson int., May 10, 2006, Miller Center, UVA.

67 "If he had done it a thousand": Mark Leibovich, "The Kennedy Factor," *WP*, July 13, 2004.

67 "extensions of the old ego": "RHIP on Capitol Hill," *Washington Star*, Apr. 25, 1971.

67 "My older brother said": Jimmy Breslin, "What Does Ford Stand For? For Status Quo," *LAT*, July 15, 1975.

67 "LBJ Ranch East": Carl Hulse, "For Power, Prestige and Office Space," *NYT*, July 2, 2010.

67 windows gave out: Rick Atkinson, "Why Ted Kennedy Can't Stand Still," *WP Magazine*, Apr. 29, 1990.

68 "Elegant": Ralph Neas int. by author.

68 "tactic": John McCain int., Oct. 16, 2009, Miller Center, UVA.

68 "museum": Ibid.

68 photograph on his desk: Breslin, "What Does Ford Stand For?"

68 phoned him every day: Joe Biden, memorial remarks, MSNBC, Aug. 26, 2009.

68 "regular trips": Biden, *Promises*, 85.

69 "precinct organizer": Barbara Mikulski int., Sept. 26, 2006, Miller Center, UVA.

69 "In politics, you don't": William Shannon, *The American Irish: A Political and Social Portrait* (reprint Amherst: Univ. of Mass. Press, 2003), 402.

69 friends you haven't met: Carey Parker int., Nov. 17, 2008, Miller Center, UVA.

69 "If you're Teddy": Kilvert Dun Gifford int., July 13, 2005, Miller Center, UVA.

69 "We always knew": Patrick Leahy int., Aug. 5, 2009, Miller Center, UVA.

69 **"Leavin' early today"**: William Honan, *Ted Kennedy: Profile of a Survivor* (New York: Quadrangle Books, 1972), 168.

70 **"played him like a Stradivarius"**: William vanden Heuvel int., July 19, 2005, Miller Center, UVA.

70 **"It was always with"**: Patrick Kennedy int. by author.

70 **"He doesn't have any enemies"**: Carey Parker int., Oct. 6, 2008, Miller Center, UVA.

70 **"Most politicians, I'm sorry to say"**: Ted Sorensen int., May 19, 2005, Miller Center, UVA.

70 **"whereas in this racket"**: Oliphant int.

70 **"Ted doesn't have a mean"**: Quoted in Jack Newfield, "The Senate's Fighting Liberal," *Nation*, Mar. 25, 2002.

70 **"He'd get really mad"**: John Podesta int. by author.

71 **"He's not a bully"**: Quoted in Peter Canellos, *Last Lion: The Fall and Rise of Ted Kennedy* (New York: Simon & Schuster, 2009), 314.

71 **"He was Lyndon Johnson"**: Oliphant int.

71 **"Did I read that right?"**: John Tunney int., May 3, 2007, Miller Center, UVA.

71 **"He is not a mean-spirited"**: James Sasser int., May 2, 2006, Miller Center, UVA.

71 **"hogging good issues"**: Walter Mondale int., Mar. 20, 2006, Miller Center, UVA.

72 **"He would just do something"**: Robert Bates int., May 8, 2007, Miller Center, UVA.

72 **"He's the biggest thief"**: Theo Lippman, *Senator Ted Kennedy: The Career Behind the Image* (New York: Norton, 1976), 233–34.

72 **"If you would like it"**: Stephen Breyer int., Sept. 28, 2008, Miller Center, UVA.

72 **"He is willing to do"**: Carolyn Osolinik int., Mar. 27, 2007, Miller Center, UVA.

73 **"one of the least successful"**: Francis Valeo oral history, Senate Historical Office.

73 **asked Alabama governor**: EMK int., Apr. 12, 1996, EMK Interviews 1996–99 Folder, Box 5, Series 2, Clymer Papers, JFK Lib.

73 **"only man who can"**: Michael O'Brien, *Philip Hart: The Conscience of the Senate* (East Lansing: Michigan State Univ. Press, 1995), 200.

73 **"I want you to tell me"**: Charles Ludlam oral history, 40–41, Senate Historical Office.

74 **"easy"**: John Danforth int., Oct. 25, 2005, Miller Center, UVA.

74 **"If he has the votes"**: Orrin Hatch int., Feb. 27, 1992, H Folder, Box 3, Series 2, Clymer Papers, JFK Lib.

74 **"He comes at you like"**: Dun Gifford int.

74 **"He never made it"**: *CBS Evening News*, Aug. 26, 2009.

75 **"some rich, powerful"**: Stan Jones int., Sept. 14, 2007, Miller Center, UVA; Melody Miller int., Aug. 16, 2006, Miller Center, UVA.

75 **"I can stand up"**: Richard Rhodes, "Things as They Are, Things That Never Were," *Audience*, Nov.–Dec. 1971, 91.

75 **"I don't think you"**: William Hildenbrand oral history, 76, Senate Historical Center.

75 **"I can teach it flat"**: Adam Clymer, "After Three Decades Working in Senate, Kennedy Gets a Turn for His Agenda," *NYT*, Mar. 8, 1993.

76 **"He'd start [legislative] fights by"**: Podesta int.

76 **"I can't imagine how many"**: Quoted in Canellos, *Last Lion*, 315.

76 **"Let's get half a loaf"**: Kenneth Feinberg quoted in "The Kennedy Network," *National Journal*, Jan. 10, 2009.

76 **"The perfect is the enemy"**: Kenneth Feinberg int., July 8, 2008, Miller Center, UVA.

76 **"Yes, we settle for"**: Quoted in James MacGregor Burns, *Edward Kennedy and the Camelot Legacy* (New York: Norton, 1976), 250.

76 **"art of the do-able"**: Thomas Daschle with Michael D'Orso, *Like No Other Time: The 107th Congress and the Two Years That Changed America* (New York: Crown, 2003), 97–98.

76 **"We leave out what"**: Quoted in "Kennedy Set for Major Health Care Push," *USA Today*, Nov. 21, 2008.

76 **"I don't think there's"**: Paul Kirk, Jr., int., June 20, 2007, Miller Center, UVA.

77 **"How can we go against"**: Larry Horowitz int., May 29, 1992, H Folder, Box 3, Series 2, Clymer Papers, JFK Lib.

77 **"You've got to get me"**: Stan Jones int., Nov. 11, 1993, I-J Folder, Box 4, Series 2, Clymer Papers, JFK Lib.

77 **"He has this idea to"**: Quoted in Oliphant int.

77 **"When the wooing was"**: Ibid.

77 "thing that makes him": Dale Bumpers int., May 20, 1998, B Folder, Box 3, Series 2, Clymer Papers, JFK Lib.

77 "some senators have": Charles Ferris int., Apr. 10, 1992, F Folder, Box 3, Series 2, Clymer Papers, JFK Lib.

77 "consensus go-to guy": "Kennedy the Pragmatist," *National Journal*, Dec. 1, 2008.

78 "A handshake with Ted": Quoted in John A. Farrell, "Comeback Kid Rising from the Ashes," *BG Magazine*, Nov. 21, 1993.

78 "I never had him back": Carl Hulse, "Kennedy: A Little Like Everyone, A Lot Like No One," *NYT*, May 22, 2008.

78 "Ted always keeps his word": Newfield, "Senate's Fighting Liberal."

78 "manipulation and conniving": Breyer int.

78 "all the interest groups": Littlefield int., May 3, 2008.

79 "He and his staff were among": Podesta int.

79 "no one [in Ted's office]": Thomas Rollins int., Apr. 22, 2009, Miller Center, UVA.

79 "A huge magnetic grid": Quoted in Burton Hersh, *The Education of Edward Kennedy: A Family Biography* (New York: Morrow, 1972), 213–14.

80 "Kennedy went to bat": Quoted in "Remembering Ted Kennedy."

81 "if he was in the mood": James Manley int., Sept. 28, 2009, Miller Center, UVA.

81 "innate caution": James Manley int., Sept. 28, 2009, Miller Center, UVA.

81 "They had very, very explicit": Oliphant int.

81 "He'd just charm the hell": Manley int.

81 "They adored him": Tolchin int.

82 "imperial pretensions": Henry Fairlie, *The Kennedy Promise: The Politics of Expectation* (Garden City, N.Y.: Doubleday, 1973), 278.

82 "There are a lot of serious": EMK int., Mar. 23, 2005, Miller Center, UVA.

83 "weak senator": Bill Stall, "In the Senate, An Ability to Compromise," *LAT*, Dec. 18, 1979.

83 "I thought at the time": Charles Mathias int., Mar. 10, 2006, Miller Center, UVA.

83 marveled that Ted: Robert Dole int., May 15, 2006, Miller Center, UVA.

83 "best-prepared person": George Miller int., Oct. 13, 2009, Miller Center, UVA.

83 his aides to the side: Stall, "In the Senate."

83 "had a wonderful way": George Miller int.

84 "not making a lot of headway": Quoted by Melody Miller int., July 15, 2008, Miller Center, UVA.

84 "heavy lifting": Atkinson, "Why Kennedy Can't."

84 "vaulted ceilings looked": Simpson int.

85 "dawned on me that this guy": Oliphant int.

85 "much more active": Sinclair, 878.

85 "hyperactives": Ibid.

85 "This is a goal line": Parker int., Nov. 17, 2008.

86 "He knew it perfectly": David Boies int., Sept. 23, 2008, Miller Center, UVA.

86 "A master of detail": Podesta int.

86 "How to bring them": Boies int.

86 "I think you have a good": Parker int., Oct. 6, 2008; Nov. 17, 2008.

86 "If we could change": David Burke int., Apr. 9, 2008, Miller Center, UVA.

87 floor sessions were substitutes: Tunney int.

87 "extraordinarily good": Leahy int.

87 votaramas could tackle: Parker int., Nov. 17, 2008.

87 "so hesitant to be discourteous": Burke int.

87 once castigated John Kerry: Robert Shrum, *No Excuses: Concessions of a Serial Campaigner* (New York: Simon & Schuster, 2007), 264.

87 "What I remember most": Quoted in "Remembering Ted Kennedy."

88 "cut loose": "When Carter Goes Down, I Go Up," *Time*, Aug. 21, 1978.

88 "caring, compassionate": Hatch int.

88 "everybody knew the Senator": Jan Kalicki int., Mar. 18, 2009, Miller Center, UVA.

88 "He's a fighter": Quoted in Lippman, *Senator Kennedy*, 143.

89 "You must decide whether": James Abourezk, *Advise and Dissent: Memoirs of an Ex-Senator* (Lincoln: Univ. of Nebraska Press, 2013), 103.

89 "There isn't anybody that's": Bumpers int.

89 **"Sometimes you have politicians"**: Charles Pierce, "Kennedy Unbound After 40 Years in the US Senate," *BG Magazine*, Jan. 5, 2003.

89 **"The power of his personality"**: Richard Burke with William Hoffer and Marilyn Hoffer, *The Senator: My Ten Years with Ted Kennedy* (New York: St. Martin's Press, 1992), 109.

89 **"he's just one of those"**: Quoted in Pierce, "Kennedy Unbound."

89 **"would all be infinitely better off"**: Bumpers int.

89 **"physical love of the place"**: EMK, *True Compass*, 482.

89 **"It's like a fix every day to go"**: Dole int.

90 **"People didn't want to feel"**: "Kennedy Memorial Service," CNN, Aug. 28, 2009.

THREE: "A SPECIAL PLACE IN HIS ANIMUS"

91 **set the tone for his presidency**: Jimmy Carter, *Keeping Faith: Memoirs of a President* (New York: Bantam paperback rep., 1982), 19–20.

91 **"natural extension of the change"**: Sean Wilentz, *The Age of Reagan: A History, 1974–2008* (New York: HarperCollins, 2008), 77.

91 **"He lacked a unifying political"**: Hamilton Jordan, *Crisis: The Last Year of the Carter Presidency* (New York: G. P. Putnam, 1982), 316–17.

92 **"No ideology, no central"**: Robert Shrum, *No Excuses: Concessions of a Serial Campaigner* (New York: Simon & Schuster, 2007), 62–63.

92 **"His entire national career"**: James Abourezk, *Advise and Dissent: Memoirs of an Ex-Senator* (Lincoln: Univ. of Nebraska Press, 2013), 145.

92 **"last progressive"**: Leo Ribuffo, "From Carter to Clinton: The Latest Crisis of American Liberalism," *American Studies International* 35, no. 2 (June 1997): 4–29.

92 **"achieving maximum bureaucratic"**: Carter, *Keeping Faith*, 66.

92 **"We have learned that more is not"**: Timothy Stanley, *Kennedy vs. Carter: The 1980 Battle for the Democratic Party's Soul* (Lawrence: Univ. of Kansas Press, 2010), 9.

92 **"Republican in Democrat clothing"**: Quoted in T. A. Repak, *Edward Kennedy: The Myth of Leadership* (Boston: Houghton Mifflin, 1980), 30.

92 **"In some ways, dealing with limits"**: Carter, *Keeping Faith*, 20–21.

92 **"His mind seems managerial"**: Arthur Schlesinger, Jr., *Journals: 1952–2000*, ed. Andrew Schlesinger and Stephen Schlesinger (New York: Penguin Press, 2007), 423.

93 **"if we don't figure out some way"**: Jordan, *Crisis*, 329.

93 **"as antiquated and anachronistic a group"**: Quoted in Wilentz, *Age of Reagan*, 83.

93 **"fights with the Democratic party's"**: Carter, *Keeping Faith*, 65.

93 **early opponent of the Vietnam War**: Leo Ribuffo, "Jimmy Carter and the Ironies of American Liberalism," *Gettysburg Review* (Autumn 1988): 741.

93 **"baffled"**: EMK, *True Compass* (New York: Twelve, 2009), 352.

93 **"Carter had a way of making me"**: Joe Biden, *Promises to Keep: On Life and Politics* (New York: Random House, 2007), 131.

94 **"He was bent uneasily forward"**: Ibid.

94 **"They were parochial"**: John A. Farrell, *Tip O'Neill and the Democratic Century* (Boston: Little, Brown, 2001), 446.

94 **"I did not get as big"**: Stanley, *Kennedy vs. Carter*, 43, 45.

94 **"In contrast, when you read"**: EMK, *True Compass*, 361.

94 **Carter felt aggrieved**: Carter, *Keeping Faith*, 71.

94 **"Once policy was set"**: Ernest Hollings with Kirk Victor, *Making Government Work* (Columbia: Univ. of South Carolina Press, 2008), 181.

95 **"I think he had simply"**: EMK, *True Compass*, 353.

95 **openly antagonistic to them**: Robert Novak and Rowland Evans, "The Showdowns That Bolstered Carter," *WP*, Aug. 2, 1978.

95 **"Actually working against us"**: Tip O'Neill with William Novak, *Man of the House: The Life and Political Memoirs of Tip O'Neill* (New York: Random House, 1987), 308.

95 **"moral zeal"**: O'Neill with Novak, 314.

95 **"You told me to play tennis"**: Kai Bird, *The Outlier: The Unfinished Presidency of Jimmy Carter* (New York: Crown, 2021), 311.

95 **"much more liberal"**: Carter, *Keeping Faith*, 73.

96 **"almost every policy"**: Shrum, *No Excuses*, 64–65.

96 **Carter assured Ted that he had:** Frank Moore to Carter, memo, Oct. 19, 1977, Name file: Kennedy, Edward, Jimmy Carter Papers, Jimmy Carter Lib.; "Kennedy Joins Carter Attack on Energy Bill," UPI, Oct. 20, 1977.

96 **campaign for human rights:** Burton Hersh, *The Shadow President: Ted Kennedy in Opposition* (South Royalton, Vt.: Steerforth Press, 1997), 28; EMK to Carter, Sept. 3, 1977, Aug. 77–Sept. 77, Name file: Kennedy, Edward, Jimmy Carter Papers, Jimmy Carter Lib.

96 **"reserved a special place":** EMK, *True Compass* 352.

96 **"there was something he didn't":** William vanden Heuvel int., Dec. 7, 2006, Miller Center, UVA.

96 **"When the Senator walks into":** Charles Haar int., Oct. 10, 2005, Miller Center, UVA.

97 **one of the primary lures:** Leonard Woodcock int., Feb. 12, 1996, V–Z Folder, Box 5, Series 2, Clymer Papers, JFK Lib.

97 **"not very important":** "Health Insurance, The Debate Has Shifted," *WP*, Apr. 3, 1976.

97 **"day after day":** Max Fine int. by author.

98 **"talked his way around":** EMK int., Mar. 28, 2008, Miller Center, UVA.

98 **"Bet on what you think":** EMK, *True Compass*, 358.

98 **"basically deregulation":** EMK int., Oct. 14, 2005, Miller Center, UVA.

98 **prioritized small changes:** Stuart Altman and David Schachtman, *Power, Politics and Universal Health Care: The Inside Story of a Century-Long Battle* (Amherst, N.Y.: Prometheus Books, 2011), 213.

98 **"pipeline":** Carey Parker int., Oct. 13, 2008, Miller Center, UVA.

98 **"as for most elected Democrats":** Joseph Califano, Jr., *Governing America: An Insider's Report from the White House and the Cabinet* (New York: Simon & Schuster, 1981), 92–93.

98 **demonstrate to Ted that he:** Ibid., 94.

98 **Jones declined:** Stan Jones int., Mar. 9, 2007, Miller Center, UVA.

99 **"phase in":** Jill Quadagno, *One Nation, Uninsured: Why the U.S. Has No National Health Insurance* (New York: Oxford Univ. Press, 2005), 129–30.

99 **"We already have a program":** Califano, *Governing*, 97–98.

99 **"If we're not going to move":** Larry Horowitz int., May 29, 1992, H Folder, Box 3, Series 2, Clymer Papers, JFK Lib.

99 **"rousing":** Califano, *Governing*, 98; "Kennedy Chides Carter on Lack of Health Reform," *LAT*, May 17, 1977; Horowitz int.

100 **"committed to the phasing-in":** "Carter Pledges Action on National Health Insurance," *LAT*, May 18, 1977; "The Road Show Goes West," *Time*, May 30, 1977; "Carter Renews Vow for U.S. Health Plan," *NYT*, May 18, 1977.

100 **That led to meetings:** David Blumenthal and James Morone, *The Heart of Power: Health and Politics in the Oval Office* (Berkeley: Univ. of California Press, 2009), 265–66.

101 **"Creeping incrementalism":** Fine int.

101 **"He's equivocating":** EMK, *True Compass*, 359.

101 **UAW leadership had even met:** EMK int., Mar. 28, 2008, Miller Center, UVA.

101 **"Voices were raised":** Fine int.

101 **advised Carter to drop health reform:** Califano, *Governing*, 99–100.

101 **"Where are you going to get":** Blumenthal and Morone, *Heart of Power*, 265.

102 **"It was only a matter of time":** Califano, *Governing*, 89.

102 **"with great care":** Jan Kalicki int., Mar. 18, 2009, Miller Center, UVA.

103 **called for the withdrawal:** Parker int.

103 **"most forthright and detailed":** "Kennedy Calls for Diplomatic Split with Taiwan," *NYT*, Aug. 16, 1977.

103 **"blatant challenge to Carter":** Jerome Cohen, "Ted Kennedy's Role in Restoring Diplomatic Relations with China," *New York University Journal of Legislation and Public Policy* 14 (2011): 347, 353.

103 **"part of a larger view":** Kalicki int.

103 **"hard-won":** Cohen, 354.

104 **Deng would meet with:** Parker int.

104 **expectorating into a large:** Kalicki int.

104 **explained to China the deep:** Adam Clymer, *Edward M. Kennedy: A Biography* (New York: Harper Perennial, 2000), 261–64.

104 **"People would have expected":** Kalicki int.

105 **"defense articles":** H.R. 2479, Taiwan Relations Act, 96th Cong., https://www.congress.gov/bill/96th-congress/house-bill/2479

105   "I did not believe he would": Hersh, *Shadow President*, 29.

105   pacify both the left: Wilentz, *Age of Reagan*, 108–9.

106   Ted's intercession with Brezhnev: Robert Bernstein to EMK, Mar. 28, 1974; Goldberg to EMK, Mar. 19, 1974, Box 4, Soviet Jewry Cases, Senate Refugee Subcommittee, Center for Legislative Archives, National Archives.

106   sit in front of the fire: EMK, *True Compass*, 339.

106   "defensive": EMK int., Mar. 27, 1998, EMK Interviews 1997–99 Folder, Box 5, Series 2, Clymer Papers, JFK Lib.

106   informed Ted that Rostropovich: Ibid.

106   compiled lists of émigrés: George Abrams int., June 17, 1992, A Folder, Box 3, Series 2, Clymer Papers, JFK Lib.

107   exchanged letters with Brezhnev: Jimmy Carter int., May 15, 1998, C Folder, Box 3, Series 2, Clymer Papers, JFK Lib.

107   "a series of rather blunt": Kalicki int.; EMK, *True Compass*, 363–64.

107   "intense": By another account, this meeting occurred at night. See Kalicki int.; Peter Canellos, *Last Lion: The Fall and Rise of Ted Kennedy* (New York: Simon & Schuster, 2009), 202–4.

107   "The impression was inescapable": "Kennedy Gets Russ Pledges to Act on Some Emigres," *LAT*, Sept. 12, 1978.

107   "He said to me once": Abrams int.

108   "Government cannot eliminate poverty": Jimmy Carter, State of the Union, Jan. 19, 1978, https://www.presidency.ucsb.edu/documents/the-state-the-union-address-delivered-before -joint-session-the-congress-1

108   "The character of this recovery": Thomas Supel, "The US Economy in 1977 and 1978," *Federal Reserve Bank of Minneapolis Quarterly Review* 2, no. 1 (Winter 1978): 1.

108   "lean and tight": Carter, State of the Union.

108   made the same promise: Carter int.

108   lobbying Carter's vice president: "Health Insurance Bill: '78 Introduction Seen as a Gesture," *WP*, Jan. 6, 1978.

109   "The part that I knew": Rashi Fein int., Mar. 21, 2007, Miller Center, UVA.

109   "forward and backward": Ibid.

110   not enough time: Eizenstat to Carter, Jan. 19, 1978, Jan. 1978–Mar. 1978, Name file: Kennedy, Edward, Jimmy Carter Papers, Jimmy Carter Lib.

110   "There is little stomach": Califano, *Governing*, 102.

110   "Kennedy is wrong": Ibid.; "Kennedy Seeking Compromise on U.S. Health Plan," *WP*, Mar. 28, 1978.

111   "no plan will significantly": Alan Derickson, *Health Security for All: Dreams of Universal Health Care in America* (Baltimore: Johns Hopkins Univ. Press, 2005), 149.

111   Ted's plan was dismissed: "White House Gets Health Plans Memo," *WP*, Apr. 6, 1978.

111   "agonizing": Califano, *Governing*, 102.

112   "It is one thing": Blumenthal and Morone, *Heart of Power*, 268.

112   "made the point that": Califano, *Governing*, 106–7.

112   "series of meetings": Onek to Eizenstat, memo, Apr. 26, 1978, Subj: NHI, Apr. 1978–July 1978, Name file: Kennedy, Edward, Jimmy Carter Papers, Jimmy Carter Lib.

113   approval rating had dropped: "Presidential Job Approval," American Presidency Project, n.d., https://www.presidency.ucsb.edu/statistics/data/presidential-job-approval.

113   "upstage": "The Talk About Teddy," *Newsweek*, May 8, 1978.

114   "for real or not on this": "Health Insurance Tide is Rising," *WP*, May 15, 1978.

114   "important educational experience": "Carter's Health Plan Faces Snag," *LAT*, May 20, 1978.

114   "pretty close": "Carter's Health Plan: Difficult Choices Ahead," *LAT*, June 5, 1978.

114   "rupture": Eizenstat and Onek to Carter, memo, June 2, 1978, Box 92, Office of Staff Sec., Staff Offices, Jimmy Carter Papers, Jimmy Carter Lib.

115   "how politically untenable": EMK, *True Compass*, 359–60.

115   "Opponents would pick it off": Bird, *Outlier*, 307.

115   healthcare now seemed back: Califano, *Governing*, 112–16; "Health Insurance Struggle Continues," *WP*, June 28, 1978.

116   worked until midnight: Horowitz int.

116   "From the minute we walked": Larry Horowitz int., June 23, 1995, H folder, Interviews, Box 3, Series 2, Clymer Papers, JFK Lib.

116   "I want to work": Edward Kennedy int., March 28, 2008, Miller Center, UVA.

116   "It will doom health care": Stuart Eizenstat, *President Carter: The White House Years* (New York: Thomas Dunne Books, 2018), 828.

116   "I'm facing serious problems": Ibid.

116   "fingers tightly clasped": EMK int., Mar. 28, 2008.

117   "My own sense was": Hersh, *Shadow President*, 27.

117   "That bastard": Califano, *Governing*, 117.

117   would never have betrayed: Carter, *Keeping Faith*, 87.

117   "misread the mood of the people": Jack Nelson, "Kennedy Splits with Carter on Health Policy," *LAT*, July 29, 1978.

118   "It was a tragedy": Carter, *Keeping Faith*, 87.

118   flew out in February: Horowitz int., June 23, 1995.

118   "struggled for months": Carter, *Keeping Faith*, 86.

118   A phase-in, he felt, would never: EMK int., Oct. 14, 2005.

118   reducing inflation was more important: "Carter Links Health Care Proposal to Inflation," *LAT*, July 30, 1978.

119   "We looked prudent and careful": Califano, *Governing*, 119.

119   "A great political story": David Broder, "The Carter-Kennedy Split," *WP*, Aug. 9, 1978.

119   "It certainly didn't help": Nelson, "Kennedy Splits with Carter."

119   "heated": Jimmy Carter, *White House Diary* (New York: Farrar, Straus & Giroux, 2010), 183.

120   "The President and his economic": Califano, *Governing*, 118.

120   "We had a big victory": "Liberals Alive and Kicking," *Newsweek*, Oct. 30, 1978.

120   "Taxes, taxes, taxes!": "The Tax-Slashing Campaign," *Time*, Oct. 23, 1978.

120   "cry against bigness in all forms": "Why Kennedy Doesn't Want to Run," *WP*, Aug. 20, 1978.

120   desired increases in healthcare: "Wishing More for Less," *Time*, Oct. 23, 1978.

120   "transitional": "Teddy on Tour," *Newsweek*, Dec. 11, 1978.

121   "anti-inflation, anti-regulation": Eizenstat to Carter, May 31, 1978, Box 88, File 6.1.78, Staff Secretary File, Jimmy Carter Papers, Jimmy Carter Lib.

121   under 40 percent: E. J. Dionne, Jr., *Why Americans Hate Politics* (New York: Simon & Schuster, 1991), 136.

121   Carter suspected: Carter int.

121   "starve": EMK, *True Compass*, 363.

121   "thereby placing": Schlesinger, *Journals*, 453–54.

122   "You will hear a lot": "Mr. Scrooge's Budget," *Newsweek*, Dec. 25, 1978.

122   written by Max Fine: Fine int.

122   "He wanted to stir the pot": Horowitz int., May 29, 1992.

122   "lukewarm": "Jimmy vs. The Liberals," *Newsweek*, Dec. 18, 1978.

122   "This is the orneriest": Myra MacPherson, "Closing Scenes from a Kennedy Marriage," *WP*, Jan. 22, 1981.

122   would have been a Republican: "Kennedy Presses for Health Plan," Dec. 10, 1978; Warren Weaver, Jr., "Democrats Prod Congress to Act on Health Insurance Legislation," Dec. 11, 1978; Hedrick Smith, "The Message of Memphis," *NYT*, Dec. 11, 1978.

122   "There could be few more": Martha Bebinger, "Kennedy Remembered as Senate's Hardest-Working Man," *WBUR*, Aug. 26, 2009; Califano, *Governing*, 121–23.

123   "startled": Horowitz int., May 29, 1992.

123   "stem-winding speech": Weaver, "Democrats Prod Congress."

123   "winged it quite a bit": Horowitz int.

123   "mysteriously appeared": McPherson, "Closing Scenes."

123   "surge": Fine int.

124   "The stage literally trembled": Califano, *Governing*, 121–23.

124   "God, in His infinite wisdom": David Broder, "Kennedy Exposed a 'Gaping' Carter Weakness," *WP*, Dec. 13, 1978.

124   "The son of a bitch is going": Patrick Caddell int., Jan. 1, 1998, C Folder, Box 3, Series 2, Clymer Papers, JFK Lib.

124   "If Kennedy would run": MacPherson, "Closing Scenes."

125   "basic and fundamental in determining": Adam Clymer, "Carter's Clash with Kennedy," *NYT*, Dec. 13, 1978.

125   "public mood is behind": Jack Nelson, "Carter Downplays His Differences with Kennedy," *LAT*, Dec. 13, 1978.

125   **"This is not a war":** Nelson; Caddell int.
125   **dismissed the warning:** Stanley, *Kennedy vs. Carter*, 86–87.
125   **"throwing down the gauntlet":** Carter int.

FOUR: SNIFFING THE WIND

126   **showed Ted with huge leads:** "Kennedy Would Defeat Ford or Reagan," *WP,* May 28, 1978.
126   **led him by double digits:** "Carter's Popularity Leaps After Summit," *LAT,* Oct. 6, 1978.
127   **"Being a liberal today":** "A Cautious Senate Begins," *Time,* Jan. 29. 1979.
127   **"lot of Democrats":** Ibid.
128   **looking into antitrust laws:** "Kennedy Plans Probe of Economic Denominators," *WP,* Apr. 8, 1978.
129   **won his chairmanship:** David Boies int., Sept. 23, 2008, Miller Center, UVA.
129   **committee to which one-fifth:** Betty Koed, *Committee on the Judiciary: A Brief History* (Washington, D.C.: Senate Historical Office, 2007).
129   **unregenerate racist:** Charles Ludlam oral history, 2004, 4, Senate Historical Center.
129   **"It's ironic":** "Kennedy to Keep Tight Rein on Key Senate Panel," *LAT,* Dec. 10, 1978.
130   **"carefully sounding them out":** "Cautious Senate Begins."
130   **"were not left to atrophy":** Nick Thimmesch, "A Plum for Kennedy," *WP,* Jan. 7, 1979.
130   **named two allies:** Rochelle Jones, *The Private World of Congress* (New York: The Free Press, 1979), 84.
130   **change the longtime tradition:** "Why Kennedy Legend Lives On," *US News and World Report,* July 23, 1979.
130   **two-man committee:** "Kennedy Seeks to Bar Large Firms' Mergers," *WP,* Jan. 16, 1979.
131   **financial war chest:** Thimmesch, "Plum for Kennedy."
131   **forced him to move:** "Kennedy Touch at Judiciary: Bright, Fractious Staff," *WP,* July 20, 1979.
131   **Biden, a committee member:** Ibid.
131   **enraged Howard Cannon:** "Why Kennedy Legend Lives On."
131   **"Eyebrows raise, pulses quicken":** Thimmesch, "Plum for Kennedy."
131   **"He didn't want to be just":** Carey Parker int., Sept. 22, 2008, Miller Center, UVA.
132   **"to be looking for employment":** "Kennedy to Keep Tight Rein."
132   **called the Plantation:** Stephen Breyer int., June 17, 2008, Miller Center, UVA.
132   **"when people ask":** Ibid.
133   **"awfully full legislative platter":** "Kennedy to Keep Tight Rein."
133   **hearing for each nominee:** Thad Cochran int., Sept. 19, 2006, Miller Center, UVA.
134   **Winberry became the first:** Breyer int.
134   **"day they threw the rubber":** "The Day They Threw the Rubber Stamp Away," *CSM,* Mar. 7, 1980.
135   **"unquestioned leader of":** "Cautious Senate Begins"; "Kennedy Touch at Judiciary."
136   **could not get them passed:** "Cautious Senate Begins."
136   **"not sure they want":** Elizabeth Drew, *Portrait of an Election: The 1980 Presidential Campaign* (New York: Simon & Schuster, 1981), 19.
137   **"cadences that summoned up":** "What's Teddy Up To?" *Newsweek,* Jan. 29, 1979.
137   **"throw out an idea":** "Big Oil, a Fig Leaf and Baloney," *Time,* May 14, 1979.
138   **"That is a lot of baloney":** "Jimmy Versus Teddy," *Newsweek,* May 14, 1979.
138   **"confused":** "Kennedy Resumes Tiff with Carter," AP, May 2, 1979.
138   **"gracious":** Joseph Kraft, "The Arbiter of American Politics," *WP,* June 17, 1979.
138   **pet project of Sargent Shriver:** Joseph Califano, Jr., *Governing America: An Insider's Report from the White House and the Cabinet* (New York: Simon & Schuster, 1981), 125.
138   **not give that dispensation:** EMK int., Oct. 14, 2005, Miller Center, UVA; "Kennedy, Carter Clash on Naming Cox to Bench," *LAT,* May 17, 1979; "The Archibald Cox Dilemma," *Newsweek,* May 7, 1979.
138   **"The President isn't going to":** EMK int., Oct. 31, 1997, EMK Interviews 1997–99 Folder, Box 5, Series 2, Clymer Papers, JFK Lib.
139   **"I'm just not going to do it":** EMK int., Mar. 23, 2005, Miller Center, UVA.
139   **"disaster":** Larry Horowitz int., June 23, 1995, H folder, Interviews, Box 3, Series 2, Clymer Papers, JFK Lib.

139 launched the Progressive Alliance: Timothy Stanley, *Kennedy vs. Carter: The 1980 Battle for the Democratic Party's Soul* (Lawrence: Univ. of Kansas Press, 2010), 66–77.

139 "Kennedy fever": Richard Bergholz, "Kennedy Legions 'Ready to March' —If He Will Lead," *LAT*, May 27, 1979.

139 "wedge into party ranks": "Draft-Kennedy Advocates Denounced," *WP*, May 24, 1979.

140 administrative assistant Rick Burke: Bergholz, "Kennedy Legions."

140 "irresistible national mandate": "ADA Joins Draft-Kennedy Movement," *WP*, June 25, 1979.

140 "just not putting out the effort": "Carter Campaign Pitch Meets Resistance at NAACP Convention," *WP*, June 28, 1979.

140 "made a big point": EMK int., Oct. 31, 1997; Califano, *Governing*, 425; Thomas Oliphant int. by author.

140 turnout in big states would: Drew, *Portrait*, 189.

140 "popular favorite of the Democratic": Tom Wicker, "Carter and Kennedy," *NYT*, June 17, 1979.

141 "To the public he appeared": James Abourezk, *Advise and Dissent: Memoirs of an Ex-Senator* (Lincoln: Univ. of Nebraska Press, 2013), 145.

142 "Asserting his independence": Milton Gwirtzman int., Jan. 30, 1993, G Folder, Box 3, Series 2, Clymer Papers, JFK Lib.

142 "challenge now is to find": "Kennedy Gets Ovation at University of Mississippi," *LAT*, May 15, 1978.

142 46 percent maximum: "Spreading Consensus to Cut, Cut, Cut," *Time*, Sept. 25, 1978.

142 "There are two sides": "Big Oil, a Fig Leaf and Baloney."

143 "clean break with the New Deal": "The Kennedy Challenge," *Time*, Nov. 5, 1979.

143 "pragmatist, not an ideologue": "Big Oil, a Fig Leaf and Baloney."

144 bills failed to pass: "Senators Updating 200 Years of Dusty Criminal Law," *WP*, Oct. 31, 1977.

144 "a prosecutor's laundry list": "Still Reforming the Criminal Code," *NYT*, Jan. 8, 1978.

144 "You may find, Ken": Kenneth Feinberg int., July 8, 2008, Miller Center, UVA.

144 needed immediate attention: Burton Hersh, *The Shadow President: Ted Kennedy in Opposition* (South Royalton, Vt.: Steerforth Press, 1997), 145.

144 "very powerful impression": EMK int., Oct. 9, 1995, EMK Interviews 1996–99 Folder, Box 5, Series 2, Clymer Papers, JFK Lib.

144 "A roll of the dice": Parker int.

144 "important kind of opportunity": EMK int., Oct. 9, 1995.

145 Ted Kennedy joined forces: Feinberg int.

145 "Let us not confuse": "Sen. Kennedy Urges Liberals to Change Crime Code," *WP*, Apr. 3, 1977.

146 "bridge differences and get something": Feinberg int.

146 His pleas, however, went unheeded: "Judiciary Panel Factions May Be Nearing Compromise," *LAT*, Apr. 7, 1976.

146 He reintroduced it: "U.S. Crime Code Reforms Revised," *LAT*, May 2, 1977.

147 "Ehrlichman Defense": "Bill to Revise U.S. Criminal Laws Is to Be Introduced Today," *WP*, May 2, 1977.

147 compromise reinstated: "U.S. Crime Code Reforms Revised."

147 worked closely with Norman Dorsen: EMK int., Oct. 9, 1995.

147 reform included individuals violating: Charles Dale, "Analysis of the Civil Rights Sections of S.1437 of the 'Criminal Code Reform Act of 1977,'" UNT Digital Library, Apr. 23, 1978, https://digital.library.unt.edu/ark:/67531/metadc992963/m1/2/?q=%22law%22

147 mischaracterized or would be revised: EMK, "Criminal Code Reform Would Aid Liberty," *LAT*, Sept. 27, 1977.

148 markups on which the attorney general: "Senators Updating 200 Years of Dusty Criminal Law."

148 "It was the only way": EMK int., Oct. 9, 1995.

148 "The perfect is the enemy": Quoted in Peter Canellos, *Last Lion: The Fall and Rise of Ted Kennedy* (New York: Simon & Schuster, 2009), 204.

148 "One of the best examples": "Senate Begins Debate on Bill to Make Sweeping Changes in U.S. Criminal Code," *LAT*, Jan. 20, 1978; "Revision of Federal Criminal Code Is Adopted by the Senate," *NYT*, Jan. 31, 1978.

148 "every day, for ten hours": Feinberg int.

149 "It would have never passed": James Eastland int., n.d., James O. Eastland Papers, J. D. Williams Lib., Univ. of Mississippi.

149 "He cut some deals there": "Kennedy Touch at Judiciary."

149   "There were a number of": Bill Stall, "In the Senate, An Ability to Compromise," *LAT*, Dec. 18, 1979.

149   "one of the greatest legislative": "Senate's Crime Code Revision," *WP*, Feb. 5, 1978.

149   "extremely disappointed": "House Kills Criminal Code Reform," *LAT*, Oct. 5, 1978.

150   "great confidence in Kennedy's": Feinberg int.

150   "his eye on 1980": Ibid.

150   "nonglamorous": Breyer int.; Martha Derthick and Paul Quirk, *The Politics of Deregulation* (Washington, D.C.: Brookings Institution, 1985), 40–41.

151   "one of the best things": "Spotlight," *NYT*, Apr. 8, 1973.

151   fares that were generally: Derthick and Quirk, *Deregulation*, 58–59.

151–52 "would help average people": Breyer int.

152   AdPrac deregulation hearings: Stephen Breyer, *Regulation and Its Reform* (Cambridge, Mass.: Harvard Univ. Press, 1982), 323.

152   big financial clout with senators: Anthony Brown, *The Politics of Airline Deregulation* (Knoxville: Univ. of Tennessee Press, 1987), 108–9.

152   he and Thurmond wanted deregulation: Theo Lippman, *Senator Ted Kennedy: The Career Behind the Image* (New York: Norton, 1976), 166.

153   Breyer said he received a call: Breyer int.

153   "I think he got a big kick": Lippman, *Senator Kennedy*, 165.

153   "They play a tough game": Jones, *Private World*, 65–67.

154   Timm and O'Melia then both: "C.A.B. Officials Differ on Inquiry," *NYT*, Mar. 22, 1975.

154   answer was competition: Breyer, *Regulation*, 336.

154   "really aimed at substance": Derthick and Quirk, *Deregulation*, 44.

154   "crucial factor in the emergence": Stephen Breyer and Leonard Stein, "Airline Deregulation: The Anatomy of Reform," in Robert Poole, Jr., ed., *Instead of Regulation: Alternatives to Federal Regulatory Agencies* (Lexington, Mass.: Lexington Books, 1982), 16; Breyer, *Regulation*, 339.

154   "delay . . . suggests to some": Ibid., 51–52; Brown, 110–13; EMK to Ford, June 26, 1975, Box 32, Smults Papers, Ford Lib., cited in Derthick and Quirk, *Deregulation*, 52.

154   "Deregulation played a big role": Breyer int.

155   "I am convinced": T. A. Repak and Murray Levin, *Edward Kennedy: The Myth of Leadership* (Boston: Houghton Mifflin, 1980), 87.

155   "You could really call him": "Kennedy, Carter Seen Nearing Confrontation," *LAT*, Nov. 20, 1978.

155   more intensive deregulation: "Airline Industry Deregulation Bill is Introduced," *WP*, Apr. 7, 1976.

156   "A year-long process of stroking": Jones, *Private World*, 70–74.

156   pressuring them to endorse: Breyer int.

156   "massive bribe": Charles Ludlam oral history, Dec. 2, 10, 2003, Oct. 18, 20, 2004, Senate Historical Office.

157   "skeptical": "Carter, Kennedy Send Trucking Bill to Congress," *WP*, June 22, 1979; "Carter Proposes Sweeping Bill Deregulating Trucking Industry," *NYT*, June 22, 1978.

157   "What will be next?": "Senators Clashing on Trucking Bill," *NYT*, Jan. 25, 1978.

157   went on the road: "Kennedy Takes Truck Issue to People," *WP*, Mar. 24, 1978.

158   trucking industry had contributed: "Campaign Gifts Tied to a Senate Dispute," *NYT*, Feb. 18, 1979.

158   "open mind": "Senate Rift on Truck Bill," *NYT*, Feb. 8, 1979.

158   "There's one person": "Carter Signs Bill for Deregulation of Truck Lines," *NYT*, July 2, 1980.

158   no health insurance whatsoever: Repak and Levin, 58.

159   president pursued his own plan: Califano, *Governing*, 127–32.

159   "It's almost impossible": Jimmy Carter int., May 15, 1998, C Folder, Box 3, Series 2, Clymer Papers, JFK Lib. Carter was reading from his diary, which Clymer was not allowed to quote verbatim. The diary was later published. See Jimmy Carter, *White House Diary* (New York: Farrar, Straus & Giroux, 2010), 305–6.

159   "To hold out for comprehensive": Eizenstat to Carter, Mar. 20, 1979, Jan. 1, 1979 to June 30, 1979, Name file: Kennedy, Edward, Jimmy Carter Papers, Jimmy Carter Lib.

160   "under different leadership": EMK int., Oct. 31, 1997.

160   "I wasn't going to kiss": Quoted in Canellos, *Last Lion*, 212.

160   discuss healthcare at McLean all night: Doug Fraser int., May 2, 1997, F Folder, Box 3, Series 2, Clymer Papers, JFK Lib.

160 **Falk's new plan:** "Kennedy, Labor Ready Health Care Plan," *WP,* Apr. 2, 1979; "Health-Care Battle," *Newsweek,* May 28, 1979; Toby Cohen, "The Battle of Health Care," *Nation,* Nov. 10, 1979.

160 **pegged its cost:** "New Kennedy Health Plan Linked to Private Insurers," *LAT,* May 15, 1979.

160 **"with an eye for drama":** "What Limit?" *Time,* May 28, 1979.

160 **The proposal grabbed:** "Kennedy Offers Broad Health Plan," *NYT,* May 15, 1979.

161 **"The exercise is moving":** "Coming on Strong," *Newsweek,* May 28, 1979.

161 **"Kennedy leveraged Carter":** "Kennedy's Intensified Rhetoric Fuels '80 Speculation," *WP,* June 11, 1979.

161 **no longer on the table:** Califano, *Governing,* 108–11.

161 **"In a time of budgetary restraint":** "Carter Proposes Limited National Health Care Plan," *LAT,* June 12, 1979.

161 **"The idea of all or nothing":** "Carter's Rx on Health," *Newsweek,* June 25, 1979.

161 **"If Carter had said":** Quoted in Canellos, *Last Lion,* 212.

161 **"continuing his irresponsible":** Carter, *White House Diary,* 325.

162 **"an elephant had of fitting":** Califano, *Governing,* 134–35.

162 **"there's no point in laying":** Stan Jones int., Mar. 9, 2007, Miller Center, UVA.

162 **"we would have had":** Carter on *60 Minutes,* Sept. 19, 2010, quoted in Stuart Altman and David Schachtman, *Power, Politics and Universal Health Care: The Inside Story of a Century-Long Battle* (Amherst, N.Y.: Prometheus Books, 2011), 215.

162 **"Kennedy saw national health":** Paul Starr, "Public Health Now and Then," *American Journal of Public Health* (Jan. 1982): 85.

164 **"My new goal":** Jimmy Carter, *Keeping Faith: Memoirs of a President* (New York: Bantam, 1982), 525–26.

164 **"From the right":** Ibid., 528–29.

165 **"Carter's economic policies":** "Campaign Politics Rule Economic Policy," *BusinessWeek,* Oct. 22, 1979.

165 **"We are in an essentially":** Anthony Lewis, "Carter and the Liberals," *NYT,* Aug. 18, 1977.

165 **"Apocalypse Now":** Theodore White, *America in Search of Itself: The Making of the President 1956–1980* (New York: Harper & Row, 1982), 259.

166 **"voluminous memorandum":** Carter, *Keeping Faith,* 115–17.

166 **"all the legislation":** Jimmy Carter, "Energy and the National Goals—A Crisis of Confidence" (speech), July 15, 1979, https://www.americanrhetoric.com/speeches/jimmycartercrisisof confidence.htm.

167 **"The response was very good":** Carter, *White House Diary,* 344.

167 **"with mounting incredulousness":** EMK, *True Compass,* 366–67.

167 **"contrary to—it was in direct":** EMK int., Oct. 31, 1997.

168 **"Any thoughts I still held":** EMK, *True Compass,* 366.

168 **"purge as complete":** "Jimmy Carter's Cabinet Purge," *Newsweek,* July 30, 1979.

169 **Carter disliked Califano:** Kai Bird, *The Outlier: The Unfinished Presidency of Jimmy Carter* (New York: Crown, 2021), 430.

169 **small lingering hope of collaboration:** EMK int., Oct. 31, 1997.

169 **"instability":** "Jackson Decries Cabinet Upheaval," *NYT,* July 25, 1979.

169 **"most logical":** "McGovern for Kennedy as Democratic Nominee," *NYT,* July 27, 1979.

169 **"President Carter has difficulties":** "Kennedy Nomination Predicted," *NYT,* July 29, 1979.

169 **dismal 32 percent:** "Jimmy Carter's Cabinet Purge."

169 **fallen to 19 percent:** Drew, *Portrait,* 18.

FIVE: "IN THE LAP OF THE GODS"

170 **with 57 percent:** "2 Polls Find Kennedy Preferred," *WP,* Jan. 8, 1979.

170 **by twenty-three points:** Sean Wilentz, *The Age of Reagan: A History 1974–2008* (New York: Harper-Collins, 2008), 113.

171 **75 percent overall:** "Kennedy Esteem Best in 10 Years," *LAT,* July 18, 1979.

171 **"basic competency to do the job":** "Kennedy Feels Chappaquiddick Would Not Rule Out Presidency," *NYT,* July 18, 1979; Timothy Stanley, *Kennedy vs. Carter: The Battle for the Democratic Party's Soul* (Lawrence: Univ. Press of Kansas, 2010), 96.

171 **larger than any Gallup had ever:** "Sen. Kennedy Leads Carter by 2 Ratio," *WP,* Aug. 3, 1979.

171 "The consensus among political": Richard Burke with William Hoffer and Marilyn Hoffer, *The Senator: My Ten Years with Ted Kennedy* (New York: St. Martin's Press, 1992), 208.

171 "presiding over the destruction": Ibid., 134.

171 "Throughout much of September": "Teddy and the Press," *Newsweek*, Oct. 8, 1979.

171 whether Carter might actually: Tom Wicker, "Will Carter Back Out?" *NYT*, July 27, 1979.

171 "Democratic politics has come": Martin Schram, "Kennedy's Intensified Rhetoric Fuels '80 Speculation," *WP*, June 11, 1979.

171 "he's kind of walked around": Elizabeth Drew, *Portrait of an Election: The 1980 Presidential Campaign* (New York: Simon & Schuster, 1981), 15.

172 "to recognize the tenth": "Surprise Party for Teddy," *Newsweek*, July 31, 1978.

172 "I enjoy the work": "Kennedy Says He Has No Desire to be President," *WP*, Aug. 7, 1978.

172 "I will let": *Issues and Answers*, ABC, August 8, 1978.

172 "That's about right": Nick Thimmesch, "Why Kennedy Doesn't Want to Run," *WP*, Aug. 20, 1978.

172 "Why should I be talking": Robert Ajemian, "When Carter Goes Down, I Go Up," *Time*, Aug. 21, 1978.

172 "in which he gave implicit": Drew, *Portrait*, 15.

173 "startled": Ajemian, "When Carter Goes Down."

173 conversation soon pivoted: "Kennedy Sounds Out Unruh, Cory on Presidential Bid," *LAT*, Sept. 16, 1978.

173 "had to cancel his speech": Jimmy Carter, *Keeping Faith: Memoirs of a President* (New York: Bantam, 1982), 401.

173 "They are clearly planning": Herby, assistant director for legislative affairs, Exec. Office of President, June 2, 1978, Box 78, Kennedy, Edward, Chief of Staff Jordan, Jimmy Carter Lib.

173 "fire in the belly": John Tunney int., Mar. 6, 1995, T folder, Interviews, Box 5, Series 2, Clymer Papers, JFK Lib.

173 "an event that had": Quoted in Peter Canellos, *Last Lion: The Fall and Rise of Ted Kennedy* (New York: Simon & Schuster, 2009), 211.

173 "programmed by history": Harris Wofford, *Of Kennedys and Kings: Making Sense of the Sixties* (New York: Farrar, Straus & Giroux, 1980), 454.

174 "large laugh": George Will, "Heavy Hitter in the Dugout," *Newsweek*, Sept. 4, 1978.

174 "He always gave the impression": Lewis Lapham, "Edward Kennedy and the Romance of Death," *Harper's*, Dec. 1979.

174 "I think competition": "Kennedy Sees No Threat to Democrats If He Runs," *LAT*, Sept. 12, 1979.

175 "The Kennedys never shit": Al Novak quoted in Burton Hersh, *The Education of Edward Kennedy: A Family Biography* (New York: Morrow, 1972), 27.

175 "I asked him if he really": Victoria R. Kennedy int., Apr. 8, 2010, Miller Center, UVA.

175 raised that very issue: "Kennedy Sounds Out Unruh, Cory."

175 "I have always noticed": Chris Matthews, *Jack Kennedy: Elusive Hero* (New York: Simon & Schuster, 2011), 384.

175 "legendary quality of the Irish": William vanden Heuvel int., July 19, 2005, Miller Center, UVA.

175 "he hid pretty well": John Tunney int., Oct. 12, 2009, Miller Center, UVA.

176 "his fellow citizens to enjoy": Lewis Lapham, "Edward Kennedy and the Romance of Death," *Harper's*, Dec. 1979.

176 "Do you know what it's": Hersh, *Education*, 382.

176 "Over and over, Joan keeps": Lester David, *Joan: The Reluctant Kennedy* (New York: Funk & Wagnalls, 1974), 252–53.

176 show them that he hadn't suffered: Patrick Kennedy int. by author; Barbara Souliotis int., Nov. 9, 2009, Miller Center, UVA.

176 he doubled over: Lester David, *Ted Kennedy: Triumph and Tragedy* (New York: Grosset & Dunlap, 1972), 270–71.

176 quorum buzzer call: Myra MacPherson, "Senator Kennedy: Alone with the Legacy," *WP*, June 4, 1978; Melody Miller int., July 15, 2008, Miller Center, UVA.

176 "If you took it": William Honan, *Ted Kennedy: Profile of a Survivor* (New York: Quadrangle Books, 1972), 41.

176 "All I want—if someone's": "Why Kennedy Legend Lives On," *US News & World Report*, July 23, 1979.

176 hundreds of threats: Honan, *Ted Kennedy*, 39.

176 **might take vengeance:** Special agent, Butte, Mont., to director, March 11, 1964, Edward Kennedy FBI File, part 1, 20.

177 **allegedly made by Sonny:** FBI file, "Edward Kennedy. The Capone Threat," June 25, 1968, part 1, 147–48.

177 **police provided a heavy guard:** "Heavy Guard Set Up for Sen. Kennedy," *LAT*, June 8, 1964.

177 **flew to Florida and back:** "Constant Threat of Death Affects Kennedy's Life, Career," *WP*, Feb. 7, 1971.

177 **"blasted":** Miller int.

177 **mentally disturbed woman:** "Woman Draws Knife in Sen. Kennedy's Office," *WP*, Nov. 29, 1979; "Woman Wielding Hunting Knife Is Subdued in Kennedy Senate Office," *NYT*, Nov. 29, 1979.

177 **sign with an arrow:** Bob Bates quoted in Canellos, *Last Lion*, 179.

177 **"My parents and siblings":** Edward Kennedy, *True Compass* (New York: Twelve, 2009), 183–84.

178 **she was an alcoholic:** Joan Braden, "Joan Kennedy Tells Her Own Story," *McCall's*, Aug. 1978.

178 **"The truth is, I just":** Joan Kennedy int., May 12, 1998, K Folder, Box 4, Series 2, Clymer Papers, JFK Lib.

178 **"I like going to a party":** "Joan Kennedy Publicly Says She's an Alcoholic," *People*, July 9, 1978.

178 **"She realized that the only way":** "Camelot After Dark," *People*, May 27, 1991.

178 **"to find out who I am":** Braden, "Her Own Story."

178 **"They don't want any":** Laurence Leamer, *The Kennedy Women: The Saga of an American Family* (New York: Villard Books, 1994), 678.

178 **"Our family has always":** "When Carter Goes Down, I Go Up."

179 **"starts to creep up":** Braden, "Her Own Story."

179 **rumors of her husband's womanizing:** "A Second Chance," *People*, Aug. 7, 1978.

179 **smelled a woman in her bed:** Leamer, *Kennedy Women*, 677.

179 **"Kennedy is essential":** "Skier Suzy Chaffee Denies Romance with Kennedy," *LAT*, Apr. 27, 1978.

179 **"People think I'm living":** "The Talk About Teddy," *Newsweek*, May 8, 1978.

179 **"I hadn't left him":** Joan Kennedy int.

179 **new life in Boston:** "Joan Kennedy," *People*, Dec. 24, 1979.

180 **"It's brought us so much":** "Kennedy's Candid Mate," *WP*, Dec. 6, 1979.

180 **"In Washington, when we":** Braden, "Her Own Story."

180 **"At 41, Joan Kennedy":** "Second Chance."

180 **"badly":** "The Vulnerable Soul of Joansie," *Time*, Nov. 5, 1979.

180 **room was reserved:** Marcia Chellis, *Living with the Kennedys: The Joan Kennedy Story* (New York: Simon & Schuster, 1985), 59–60, 66.

180 **all communications between:** Ibid., 113.

180 **"I think she's making great":** "The Vulnerable Soul of Joansie," *Time*, Nov. 5, 1979.

180 **new daily routine:** "The Kennedy Challenge," *Time*, Nov. 5, 1979.

181 **"You'd drive in the driveway":** Lee Fentress int., Oct. 16, 2009, Miller Center, UVA.

181 **made an effort to be home:** Patrick Kennedy int.; "The Kennedy Challenge."

181 **"Honestly, I don't remember":** Patrick Kennedy int.

181 **"I knew the older children":** "One Personal Triumph on Kennedy Campaign," *WP*, Mar. 11, 1980.

181 **"Both Mom and Dad to Patrick":** "What Only Joan Can Do," *WP*, Feb. 23, 1980.

182 **"sensitive":** EMK int., July 19, 1997, EMK Interviews 1997–99 Folder, Box 5, Series 2, Clymer Papers, JFK Lib.

182 **"awkward, anxious, separate":** Patrick Kennedy and Stephen Fried, *A Common Struggle: A Personal Journey Through the Past and Future of Mental Illness and Addiction* (New York: Blue Rider Press, 2015), 34.

182 **"He felt that I was his":** Patrick Kennedy int.

182 **"looked like a nuclear meltdown":** EMK int., Mar. 28, 2008, Miller Center, UVA.

182 **virulent form of asthma:** "Ready for Teddy?" *Newsweek*, June 2, 1975; Kennedy and Fried, *Common Struggle*, 49; EMK int., July 19, 1997.

182 **"ruin everything":** Kennedy and Fried, *Common Struggle*, 49.

182 **group of asthma experts:** EMK int., Mar. 28, 2008.

182 **"You're just giving in to him":** Leamer, 698.

182 **"emotional turmoil":** Patrick Kennedy int.

182 **"lucky":** Ibid.; Kennedy and Fried, *Common Struggle*, 35.

183 **terrible headaches:** "Kennedy Funeral Service," CNN, Aug. 29, 2009.

183 **Other times he slept:** "Ready for Teddy?"
183 **four-day camping trip:** Patrick Kennedy int.
183 **"would stop whatever":** Burke with Hoffer and Hoffer, *Senator,* 21.
183 **"just hugged me all the time":** Ibid.
183 **"kind of intimacy":** Patrick Kennedy int.
183 **parade of them:** Larry Horowitz int., June 23, 1995, H folder, Interviews, Box 3, Series 2, Clymer Papers, JFK Lib.
183 **"A number of sessions":** "Ted Kennedy Enjoying Cat-and-Mouse Game," *WP,* Feb. 4, 1979.
184 **"much higher tempo":** Horowitz int.
184 **"It wasn't about personal safety":** Ibid.
184 **"delighted":** Joan Kennedy int.
184 **"I am not ambitious":** "Joan Kennedy's Worries," *People Weekly,* June 24, 1974.
184 **had their doubts:** Kennedy and Fried, *Common Struggle,* 53–54.
184 **"loose lips":** Arthur Schlesinger, Jr., *Journals: 1952–2000,* ed. Andrew Schlesinger and Stephen Schlesinger (New York: Penguin Press, 2007), 466.
184 **"I had to get the green-light":** EMK int., Oct. 14, 2005, Miller Center, UVA.
185 **"We spent a lot of time":** Ibid.; Horowitz int.
185 **expressed some hesitation:** Burke with Hoffer and Hoffer, *Senator,* 190–92.
185 **"If you want to mark time":** Paul Kirk, Jr., int., Nov. 23, 2005, Miller Center, UVA.
186 **prompt to join the draft:** "Senator's Own Signal Sets Off Draft-Kennedy Drive," *WP,* Sept. 16, 1979.
186 **"Pressure is building":** Schlesinger, *Journals,* 464–65.
186 **"you feel you've eaten it":** "Kennedy Challenge."
186 **"biggest tease":** "Carter: His Rival Plays Tease," *Time,* June 4, 1979.
186 **"moving along the same":** "Kennedy's Intensified Rhetoric Fuels '80s Speculation," *WP,* June 11, 1979.
186 **"It is hard being president":** "Carter: His Rival Plays Tease."
187 **"This Kennedy game":** "Big Oil, a Fig Leaf and Baloney," *Time,* May 14, 1979.
187 **"I'll whip his ass":** "Carter Misquoted—Kennedy," *LAT,* June 13, 1979; Carter, *Keeping Faith,* 464.
187 **"I always felt the White House":** "Kennedy Ready with a Riposte," *WP,* June 16, 1979.
187 **"I can't think of":** Carey Parker int., Oct. 13, 2008, Miller Center, UVA.
187 **"If you had to do it":** Kirk int.
187 **"Now, I ask you":** "Kennedy Courts Blacks in Urban League Speech," *NYT,* July 24, 1979.
187 **discussing the presidency:** EMK int., Oct. 31, 1997, EMK Interviews 1997–99 Folder, Box 5, Series 2, Clymer Papers, JFK Lib.
187 **"still be sort of back":** Ibid.
187 **"cheerful and unconcerned":** Schlesinger, *Journals,* 469.
187 **cookout on Squaw Island:** Burke with Hoffer and Hoffer, *Senator,* 205.
188 **only fifty-fifty:** Horowitz int.
188 **"It just seemed to me":** "Kennedy Cites Failed Economic Policies," *LAT,* May 29, 1980.
188 **"The Carter campaign will be":** Rick Stearns quoted in Canellos, *Last Lion,* 211–12.
188 **heading toward recession:** "Kennedy Confirms He Is Considering Race," *WP,* Sept. 12, 1979.
188 **"I've always been mindful":** "Is Teddy Ready?" *People,* July 2, 1979.
188 **"If the thing doesn't work":** Jack Germond and Jules Witcover, *Blue Smoke and Mirrors: How Reagan Won and Why Carter Lost the Election of 1980* (New York: Viking Press, 1981), 54.
188 **"overconfident":** Carey Parker int., Oct. 13, 2008, Miller Center, UVA.
188 **expect his poll numbers:** Ted Sorensen, "Kennedy New Leadership for the 80s," n.d. [1979], Box 118, Edward Kennedy, Series 19, Democratic Party, Theodore C. Sorensen Personal Papers, JFK Lib.
189 **"wouldn't have run if":** Milton Gwirtzman int., Apr. 3, 1993, G Folder, Box 3, Series 2, Clymer Papers, JFK Lib.
189 **"It's beginning to be":** "Carter: His Rival Plays Tease."
189 **"poisoning the political atmosphere":** "On the Rival Circuit," *Newsweek,* Aug. 13, 1979.
189 **"lap of the gods":** Theodore Sorensen int., June 1, 1996, S Folder, Box 5, Series 2, Clymer Papers, JFK Lib.
189 **approval rating that:** "Carter's Job Rating at 19%," *WP,* Sept. 14, 1979.
190 **"if Carter was willing":** Horowitz int.
190 **"Sherman-like":** Schlesinger, *Journals,* 470–71.
190 **two went to the Map Room:** Burke with Hoffer and Hoffer, *Senator,* 207.

190 **Ted and California governor:** Jimmy Carter int., May 15, 1998, C Folder, Box 3, Series 2, Clymer Papers, JFK Lib.

191 **"there had been no work":** Horowitz int.

191 **as if his candidacy were:** "Teddy Gets Ready," *Newsweek*, Sept. 17, 1979.

191 **"You'll be hearing my":** "Kennedy Details His Proposals on the Economy," *WP*, Sept. 20, 1979; "Kennedy Delivers Strong Indication That He Will Run," *LAT*, Sept. 29, 1979; "Well-Oiled Kennedy Campaign Machine Starts Rolling with Some Early Creaks," *WP*, Oct. 1, 1979.

191 **"As a student he":** Jimmy Carter, *White House Diary* (New York: Farrar, Straus & Giroux, 2010), Sept. 17, 1979 entry, 356.

192 **"I think Jack":** Gladys Gifford int. by author; John Culver int., Sept. 22, 2009, Miller Center, UVA; see also Charles Haar int., Oct. 10, 2005, Miller Center, UVA. Haar worked closely with Ted on the Harvard location and prepared an extensive report for him.

192 **"you don't trash people":** Horowitz int.; Martin Schram, "Making the Opponent the Issue," *WP*, June 9, 1980.

192 **"Well, the answer":** Robert Shrum, *No Excuses: Concessions of a Serial Campaigner* (New York: Simon & Schuster, 2007), 78.

192 **"Sort of a paralyzed":** EMK int., Oct. 31, 1997.

192 **to notify them:** "Kennedy Calls Prominent Democrats," *LAT*, Oct. 24, 1979.

192 **"We want action":** "Kennedy Disputes Carter on 'Malaise,'" *WP*, Oct. 23, 1979.

193 **"We want Teddy!":** "Kennedy Challenge."

193 **"disjointed and acrimonious":** William Honan, "The Kennedy Network," *NYT*, Nov. 11, 1979.

193 **didn't even have a campaign:** Schram, "Making the Opponent."

193 **"battle of the buses":** "Premature Poll," *Time*, Oct. 22, 1979; "Carter Holds Lead in Fla. Caucus Vote," *WP*, Oct. 13, 1979; Stanley, *Kennedy vs. Carter*, 120.

193 **"Carter did what he":** Anthony Lewis, "Next Move to Kennedy," *NYT*, Oct. 18, 1979.

193 **"very large, major":** Quoted in "Florida Caucuses: Media or Message?" *WP*, Oct. 12, 1979; "Jimmy in Camelot," *Time*, Oct. 29, 1979.

194 **"I'm somewhere between":** Miller int.

194 **"Kennedy's decision would":** Hamilton Jordan, *Crisis: The Last Year of the Carter Presidency* (New York: G. P. Putnam, 1982), 20–21.

194 **"There's just nothing":** Thomas Oliphant int. by author.

195 **"literally foaming":** Patrick Caddell int., Jan. 1, 1998, C Folder, Box 3, Series 2, Clymer Papers, JFK Lib.

195 **"Kennedy seemed to be":** Joseph Califano, Jr., *Governing America: An Insider's Report from the White House and the Cabinet* (New York: Simon & Schuster, 2007), 125–26.

195 **"doctrinally identical":** Robert Novak and Rowland Evans, "A Tack Toward the Center," *WP*, Sept. 19, 1979.

195 **two really substantive:** Carter int.

195 **taken the same position:** William Schaffer, "A Discriminant Function Analysis of Position-Taking: Carter vs. Kennedy," *Presidential Studies Quarterly* 10, no. 3 (Summer 1980): 451–68.

196 **voted with Carter 156 times:** Bill Stall, "In the Senate, An Ability to Compromise," *LAT*, Dec. 18, 1979.

196 **didn't differ substantially:** "Kennedy Says that Leadership, Not Economic Policy, Is at Issue," *NYT*, Sept. 14, 1979.

196 **"The American people will":** "A Talk with Teddy," *Newsweek*, Sept. 24, 1979.

196 **"feeling of progress":** Drew, *Portrait*, 34.

196 **"passionless presidency":** "Carter's Low Polls: A Passionless Presidency," *WP*, July 9, 1979.

196 **"very simply, the growing":** Theodore White, *America in Search of Itself: The Making of the President 1956–1980* (New York: Harper & Row, 1982), 274–75.

197 **"I did not become Speaker":** John A. Farrell, *Tip O'Neill and the Democratic Century* (Boston: Little, Brown, 2001), 528.

197 **"come to grips":** Drew, *Portrait*, 33.

198 **"weakness will deliver":** Anthony Lewis, "Senator Kennedy's Choice," *NYT*, July 2, 1979.

198 **"things that are troubling":** "New Solutions Must Be Found," *Time*, Sept. 24, 1979.

198 **"heavy weather":** Kilvert Dun Gifford int., Feb. 2, 1996, G Folder, Box 3, Series 2, Clymer Papers, JFK Lib.

198 **"Carter people had a massage":** "Price for Kennedy's Quick Entry into Campaign," *NYT*, Nov. 15, 1979.

198 **"I want to get it done":** "Teddy Makes It Official," *Newsweek*, Nov. 5, 1979.

199 **"beehive of activity":** Drew, *Portrait*, 26–27.

199 **collected $150,000 of pledges:** "Teddy Makes It Official."

199 **"He had always felt that":** Carter, *White House Diary*, 365.

199 **"The best way to discourage":** Martin Schram, "The Campaign," *WP*, June 8, 1980.

199 **finally chicken out:** Ibid.

199 **"gleam in his eye":** Jordan to Carter, memo, n.d., Box 78, Kennedy, Edward, Chief of Staff Jordan, Jimmy Carter Lib.

199 **"Like a morgue":** Schram, "Making the Opponent."

199 **"steady hand":** "Carter Accepts Kennedy Gauntlet for 1st Skirmish," *WP*, Sept. 26, 1979.

199 **"I asked my mama":** "Kennedy Challenge."

200 **"If they are not loyal":** "White House Plans Purge of Kennedy Supporters," *LAT*, Oct. 13, 1979.

200 **"I'm very sorry to hear":** Walter Mondale int., Mar. 20, 2006, Miller Center, UVA.

200 **family would be accompanying:** Miller int.

200 **interview with Ted alone:** EMK int., Oct. 14, 2005.

200 **"friendly interview":** Miller int.

201 **"it was not going to be":** "Ill-Starred, Stumbling, Ever Gutsy," *WP*, June 4, 1980; Horowitz int.

201 **"It's just Roger":** Burke with Hoffer and Hoffer, *Senator*, 213.

201 **"There are no pieces":** "Mudd Kennedy Recollection a Fantasy," *Politico*, Sept. 18, 2009.

201 **"this was to be a serious":** Roger Mudd, *The Place to Be: Washington, CBS and the Glory Days of Television News* (New York: PublicAffairs, 2008), 348–54.

202 **"disaster":** Ibid., 349.

202 **"I'm just going to clam up":** Miller int.

202 **"slowest pitch":** Mudd, *Place to Be*, 354.

202 **"trouble":** EMK int., Oct. 31, 1997.

202 **phoned Southwick:** Miller int.

202 **"I should have stayed":** "Kennedy's TV Style, or Lack of It, Is a Surprise," *LAT*, Jan. 21, 1980.

202 **"But he just kept shaking":** Kennedy and Fried, *Common Struggle*, 60.

203 **phoned Joan:** Chellis, *Living*, 83–84.

203 **"just as bad if not worse":** Horowitz int.

203 **"He doesn't know why":** Mudd, *Place to Be*, 355–56.

203 **"It was like I want":** *BG*, Oct. 4, 1981, quoted in Burton Hersh, *The Shadow President: Ted Kennedy in Opposition* (South Royalton, Vt.: Steerforth Press, 1997), 41.

203 **"I suddenly found him":** Jimmy Breslin, "Now Teddy Comes to a Bridge That He'll Have to Cross," *NY Daily News*, Nov 6, 1979.

204 **"cold and lifeless":** Richard Cohen, "Kennedy's Campaign: The Fun Has Gone," *WP*, Dec. 2, 1979.

204 **"stumbling, inarticulate":** Anthony Lewis, "Abroad at Home," *NYT*, Nov. 8, 1979.

204 **"It showed him not able":** Carter, *White House Diary*, 367.

204 **"I wanted everybody to see":** Jordan, *Crisis*, 21.

204 **"An instant embarrassment":** Parker int.

204 **"He had never really":** Gwirtzman int.

204 **"because he would have":** Dave Burke int., Apr. 9, 2008, Miller Center, UVA.

204 **"always getting himself":** Tunney int., Mar. 6, 1995; Tunney int., May 3, 2007, Miller Center, UVA.

205 **"slow to accelerate":** EMK, *True Compass*, 368.

205 **"EMK's vision of the nation":** Sorensen, "Kennedy New Leadership for the '80s."

205 **"based on the premise":** Shrum, *No Excuses*, 80.

206 **"The very charm of John":** Garry Wills, *The Kennedy Imprisonment: A Meditation on Power* (Boston: Houghton Mifflin, 2002), 151.

206 **"What did you think":** Jack Newfield, *Robert Kennedy: A Memoir* (New York: E. P. Dutton, 1969), 35.

206 **"moving and electrifying":** Tom Shales, "Teddy's Torment," *WP*, Nov. 22, 1979.

206 **long-awaited announcement:** EMK, *True Compass*, 371–72.

206 **"I don't want nostalgia":** "Kennedy Challenge."

206 **"Enveloped in the moment":** EMK, *True Compass*, 371.

206 **total crowd of five thousand:** Ibid.; "Kennedy Begins Campaign with Wife at His Side," *LAT*, Nov. 8, 1979; Hedrick Smith, "Kennedy Declares His Candidacy," *NYT*, Nov. 8, 1979.

207 **Somber was the tone:** Peter Hart quoted in Stanley, *Kennedy vs. Carter*, 114–15.

207 "For many months, we have": Smith, "Kennedy Declares."

207 as if she weren't present: Chellis, *Living*, 76–80.

208 "you could have cut": Burke with Hoffer and Hoffer, *Senator*, 217; Patrick Kennedy int.

208 "I look forward to campaigning": "Kennedy Begins Campaign with Wife at His Side."

208 "the beginning of the last": Haynes Johnson, "Taking the Course Compelled by Events," *WP*, Nov. 8, 1979.

208 "whole phalanx": Carter, *Keeping Faith*, 455; Carter int.

209 "It'll be over in a few": Jordan, *Crisis*, 189.

209 while 80 percent of Americans: Stanley, *Kennedy vs. Carter*, 125; E. J. Dionne, Jr., *Why Americans Hate Politics* (New York: Simon & Schuster, 1991), 137–38.

209 "The days of infamy": Thomas Matthews, "America Closes Ranks," *Newsweek*, Dec. 17, 1979.

210 "The Kennedy campaign": Drew, *Portrait*, 40.

210 "You go up to the Hill": Ibid., 39.

210 he himself underestimated: EMK, *True Compass*, 373.

210 "We didn't see it": Mark Schneider int., March 4, 2009, Miller Center, UVA.

SIX: "JUST ANOTHER CLARK KENT"

211 "Everybody wanted him": Quoted in Peter Canellos, *Last Lion: The Fall and Rise of Ted Kennedy* (New York: Simon & Schuster, 2009), 216.

211 "Kennedy had been drafted": Quoted in Burton Hersh, *The Shadow President: Ted Kennedy in Opposition* (South Royalton, Vt.: Steerforth Press, 1997), 46.

211 things kept going wrong: "Well-Oiled Campaign Machine Starts Rolling with Some Early Creaks," *WP*, Oct. 1, 1979.

211 pilot couldn't find an airport: Hersh, *Shadow President*, 49.

212 "Ted himself lacks the grasp": Arthur Schlesinger, Jr., *Journals: 1952–2000*, ed. Andrew Schlesinger and Stephen Schlesinger (New York: Penguin Press, 2007), 478–79.

212 "I say it isn't the American": "Candidate Kennedy," *WP*, Nov. 8, 1979; "Kennedy Discovers a Personification of His Case," *WP*, Nov. 9. 1979.

212 campaign headquarters: Melody Miller int., July 15, 2008, Miller Center, UVA; Paul Kirk, Jr., int., Nov. 23, 2005, Miller Center, UVA; "Kennedy's Decision to Stay in Race," *WP*, Feb. 5, 1980.

212–13 "When their things worked": Arthur Schlesinger, Jr., *Robert Kennedy and His Times* (Boston: Houghton Mifflin, 1978), 193.

213 anything but efficient: For a comparison of Jack's and Bobby's campaigns, see Lawrence O'Brien int., July 21, 1987, Interview 23, LBJ Lib.

213 "He was like the Robert": Christopher Lawford, *Symptoms of Withdrawal: A Memoir of Snapshots and Redemption* (New York: Morrow, 2005), 165.

213 "who had been very successful": Milton Gwirtzman int., Aug. 5, 2009, Miller Center, UVA.

214 "living in a fantasy world": Bernard Weinraub, "Troubled Kennedy TV Effort Changes Direction," *NYT*, May 18, 1980.

214 "You could win West Virginia": Timothy Hanan int., May 7, 2009, Miller Center, UVA.

214 "Decentralized": Peter Hart int., Jan. 8, 1998, H Folder, Box 3, Series 2, Clymer Papers, JFK Lib.

214 could never quite wrangle: Hersh, *Shadow President*, 48.

214 "Everything was sort of": Kirk, Jr., int.

214 "In the old days": Hedrick Smith, "Kennedy Problems: At Top and Afield," *NYT*, Mar. 11, 1980.

214 "embarrassment, probably": Weinraub.

215 led Carter by twenty-two points: "Post Pol Shows Potentially Sharp Democratic Split," *WP*, Nov. 18, 1979.

215 "running against a myth": Quoted in Hamilton Jordan, *Crisis: The Last Year of the Carter Presidency* (New York: G. P. Putnam, 1982), 57–58.

215 cautious not to undermine: Peter Goldman, "Kennedy's Blooper," *Newsweek*, Dec. 17, 1979.

215 "The more time one spends": David Broder, "Not the Way He Imagined It," *WP*, Dec. 26, 1979.

216 "ran one of the most violent": "Kennedy Makes a Goof," *Time*, Dec. 17, 1979; "Kennedy Seeks to Clarify Remarks About Shah," *LAT*, Dec. 5, 1979.

216 "You do not say something": Jan Kalicki int., Mar. 18, 2009, Miller Center, UVA.

216 shift in the American position: "Kennedy Makes a Goof."

217 "Worse than Chappaquiddick": Goldman, "Kennedy's Blooper."

217 tried to clarify: "Kennedy Sharply Criticized for Denunciation of Shah," *LAT*, Dec. 4, 1979.

217 "delicate": "Kennedy, After Criticizing Shah, Supports Carter's Efforts," *NYT*, Dec. 4, 1979.

217 "It wasn't right": "Kennedy Makes a Goof."

217 "I pledge my blood": "Bogus Kennedy Letter Circulated by Iran," *NYT*, Dec. 13, 1979.

217 "Kennedy's performance": Goldman, "Kennedy's Blooper."

217 "there is a problem moving": "Kennedy Makes a Goof."

218 led him by two points: "Carter Surges in New Poll," *WP*, Dec. 4, 1979.

218 "He came to me in the dark": Ted Sorensen int., Dec. 7, 2006, Miller Center, UVA; Ted Sorensen, *Counselor: A Life at the Edge of History* (New York: HarperCollins, 2008), 448.

218 "Kennedy is a good man": "Abourezk Went to Iran in '79 to Free Hostages," *WP*, Apr. 22, 1986.

218 contacting European liaisons: Richard Burke with William Hoffer and Marilyn Hoffer, *The Senator: My Ten Years with Ted Kennedy* (New York: St. Martin's Press, 1992), 224.

219 "All it means": Elizabeth Drew, *Portrait of an Election: The 1980 Presidential Campaign* (New York: Simon & Schuster, 1981), 52–53.

219 "We must understand": "Exit the Shah: Will It Help?" *Newsweek*, Dec. 24, 1979.

219 "Carter seems to be getting": "He Wasn't in Touch," *Time*, Feb. 25, 1980.

219 forswear actively campaigning: Jimmy Carter, *Keeping Faith: Memoirs of a President* (New York: Bantam paperback rep., 1982), 473.

219 "We worked very hard": Kalicki int.

220 "The striking development": T. R. Reid, "Invincible Image Fades," *WP*, Dec. 10, 1979.

220 "The initial strategy": "Kennedy Manager: An Insider 'Hangs In,' " *LAT*, Feb. 15, 1980.

220 "small window": Drew, *Portrait*, 161.

220 "just awful at the beginning": Larry Horowitz int., June 23, 1995, H folder, Interviews, Box 3, Series 2, Clymer Papers, JFK Lib.

220 "seems undecided whether": B. Drummond Ayres, "Reporter's Notebook: Style Eludes Kennedy," *NYT*, Dec. 7, 1979.

220 expectations for his speaking: B. Drummond Ayres int., Aug. 28, 1997, A Folder, Box 3, Series 2, Clymer Papers, JFK Lib.

221 issue had already died: "Not the Way He Imagined It."

221 "I feel embarrassed": Ellen Goodman, "It's Very Plain to See: Ted Doesn't Want It," *BG*, Jan. 24, 1980.

221 summit with fourteen: "A Helping Hand for Teddy," *Newsweek*, Dec. 17, 1979; "Kennedy on Vacation Meets Campaign Aides," *NYT*, Dec. 27, 1979.

221 "The first reviews": Mark Shields, "His First Real Campaign," *WP*, Dec. 10, 1979.

221 fighting a campaign of attrition: "Early Knockout Unlikely," *WP*, Dec. 10, 1979.

221 "He saw everything": Hart int.; Timothy Stanley, *Kennedy vs. Carter: The Battle for the Democratic Party's Soul* (Lawrence: Univ. Press of Kansas, 2010), 116–17.

222 "More doesn't necessarily": Bill Stall, "In the Senate, An Ability to Compromise," *LAT*, Dec. 18, 1979; *Meet the Press*, Nov. 23, 1979.

222 "It's time to have a real": Adam Clymer, *Edward M. Kennedy: A Biography* (New York: Harper Perennial, 2000), 294.

222 "The Kennedys feel": "Kennedy Makes a Goof."

222 "capacity to promulgate": Norman Birnbaum, "How Much of the Way with E.M.K.?" *Nation*, Dec. 22, 1979.

222 "He just hasn't given": "Kennedy Lowers His Voice Amid Crisis," *LAT*, Jan. 13, 1980.

223 "I think he psychologically": John Siegenthaler int., Sept. 25, 1995, R-Edward Kennedy Folder, Box 5, Series 2, Clymer Papers, JFK Lib.

223 "Each day Kennedy was faced": Drew, *Portrait*, 40–41.

223 "Kennedy was being forced": Garry Wills, *The Kennedy Imprisonment: A Meditation on Power* (Boston: Houghton Mifflin, 2002), 11.

223 "witty aside that reinforced": Ibid., 287.

223 "rattled": Murray Levin and T. A. Repak, *Edward Kennedy: The Myth of Leadership* (Boston: Houghton Mifflin, 1980), 180.

223 "He can't be as good": "Kennedy's TV Style, or Lack of It is a Surprise," *LAT*, Jan. 21, 1980.

224 ached bending to get in: "Ted's Aching Back," *Time*, Mar. 19, 1980.

224 soak the back in a hot bath: Drew, *Portrait*, 68–69.

224 "He would be limping": Barbara Souliotis int., Nov. 9, 2009, Miller Center, UVA.

224 stiff bulletproof vest: Ayres int.

224 **woman hurled an egg:** "Kennedy Campaigns in Carter Territory," *NYT*, Nov. 9, 1979.

224 **two-pound cheese:** Hersh, *Shadow President*, 49.

225 **"Kennedy's face is pale":** Drew, *Portrait*, 162.

225 **"masculinity thing":** Burke with Hoffer and Hoffer, *Senator*, 227.

225 **"a few other political has-beens":** James Ralph Sasser int., May 25, 2006, Miller Center, UVA.

225 **campaign that was awry:** "Kennedy Discovers Pain of Running as an Underdog," *NYT*, Jan. 27, 1980.

225 **"An enormous inhibition":** "Teddy's Ragged Start," *Newsweek*, Dec. 10, 1979.

225 **"It was clear to me":** "Political Insiders Cite Increasing Doubts that Kennedy Has Heart for Campaign," *LAT*, Dec. 18, 1979.

226 **"he didn't want to be":** William vanden Heuvel int., Dec. 7, 2006, Miller Center, UVA.

226 **"He did not so much declare":** "Kennedy's Theme," *WP*, Jan. 31, 1980.

226 **"It's as if he's doing some":** Sally Quinn, "Teddy on the High Wire," *WP*, Mar. 21, 1980.

227 **"No one is ever to see them":** Pat Caddell int., Jan. 1, 1998, C Folder, Box 3, Series 2, Clymer Papers, JFK Lib.; Canellos, *Last Lion*, 214.

227 **"Senator's compassion":** Joy Falk, Cheryl Beil, and Stephen Wayne, "Public Perceptions About Ted Kennedy and the Presidency," *Presidential Studies Quarterly* 12, no. 1 (1982): 88.

228 **"moral threats which cut":** Ira Shapiro, *The Last Great Senate: Courage and Statesmanship in a Time of Crisis* (New York: PublicAffairs, 2012), 302.

229 **"Movements become powerful":** Rick Perlstein, *Reaganland: America's Right Turn, 1976–1980* (New York: Simon & Schuster, 2020), 313.

229 **People vote on character:** Drew, *Portrait*, 162.

229 **"Character is the only":** "Last Chance for Kennedy," *Newsweek*, Mar. 10, 1980.

229 **"American people will see":** Drew, *Portrait*, 161.

229 **character issue was paramount:** B. Drummond Ayres, "Kennedy Race Ends But the Cause Continues," *NYT*, Aug. 13, 1980.

229 **"more people thought":** Falk, Beil, and Wayne, 87.

229 **"Kennedy's main problem":** William Schneider, "Kennedy Fights for His Own Sake," *LAT*, May 12, 1980.

230 **79 percent of Americans:** Canellos, *Last Lion*, 205.

230 **express his regrets:** "Kennedy Feels Chappaquiddick Would Not Rule Out Presidency," *NYT*, July 18, 1979.

230 **"good judgment under pressure":** Ibid.

230 **"more or less":** "Kopechnes Say They Don't Have 'The Whole Story,' " *NYT*, July 18, 1979.

230 **"everyone makes mistakes":** "Chappaquiddick: How Big an Issue?" *Newsweek*, Oct. 8, 1979.

230 **"essence of the event":** "A Night That Haunts Him," *Time*, Nov. 5, 1979.

231 **"Ted Kennedy should adopt":** *Chicago Tribune*, Jan. 17, 1980; Bob Weidrich, "Kennedy Short on Character," *Chicago Tribune*, Nov. 18, 1979.

231 **"We don't have to attack":** Theodore White, *America in Search of Itself: The Making of the President 1956–1980* (New York: Harper & Row, 1982), 296.

231 **eight of the thirteen:** T. R. Reid, "Kennedy on Tour, Is Seldom Questioned About Chappaquiddick," *WP*, Dec. 2, 1979.

231 **"Hey, how's *your* first wife":** "Kennedy Warm to Media," *WP*, Mar. 25, 1980.

231 **"It is time to forget":** "Kennedy's Lead is Shrinking," *Time*, Nov. 12, 1979; "The Tide in Ted's Life," *Time*, Jan. 28, 1980.

232 **"The Drag on Teddy":** "The Drag on Teddy (1)," *Newsweek*, Jan. 14, 1980.

232 **"I think there is a deep resentment":** Schlesinger, *Journals*, 491.

232 **"If it's Carter versus Kennedy":** Quoted in E. J. Dionne, Jr., *Why Americans Hate Politics* (New York: Simon & Schuster, 1991), 138.

233 **"They expected Camelot":** Weinraub.

233 **"He loved the back and forth":** Thomas Oliphant int. by author.

233 **"getting swept up in the magical":** "Teddy and the Press," *Newsweek*, Oct. 8, 1979.

233 **called him "Senator" or "Sir":** Ibid.

233 **"got into it":** Ayres int.

233 **"capable of fairly covering":** Haynes Johnson, "On Arm's-Length Coverage of the Kennedy Caravan," *WP*, Nov. 11, 1979.

234 **"another case of the press":** Tom Shales, "Petty for Teddy," *WP*, Jan. 30, 1980; Charles Seib, "Enough of Chappaquiddick," *WP*, Nov. 16, 1979. See also Michael Robinson and Margaret

Sheehan, *Over the Wire and on TV: CBS and UPI in Campaign '80* (New York: Russell Sage, 1983), 120–21.

234   **suddenly sympathetic:** Robinson and Sheehan, *Over the Wire,* 107.

234   **"Kennedy versus the boys":** Tom Shales, "Teddy's Torment," *WP,* Nov. 22, 1979.

234   **"The people who chewed":** Arlie Schardt, "Rating Campaign Coverage," *Newsweek,* Mar. 24, 1980.

234   **"illiberal times":** Myra MacPherson, "Teddy the Underdog Flies into Maine Event," *WP,* Feb. 10, 1980.

234   **so-called progressive press:** See Ronnie Dugger, "The Trashing of Teddy," *Nation,* June 21, 1980.

235   **"Such a story represents":** Haynes Johnson, "Kennedy Myth Gives Way to Hard Political Realities," *WP,* Jan. 22, 1980.

235   **"a candidate is leading":** Thomas Patterson, *Out of Order* (New York: Knopf, 1993), 116–23.

235   **"every news story should":** Ibid., 60, 80.

235   **"slide away from surprise":** Robinson and Sheehan, *Over the Wire,* 86.

236   **"If I give a funny remark":** "Kennedy Warm to Media," *WP,* Mar. 25, 1980.

236   **"Journalists see themselves":** Robinson and Sheehan, *Over the Wire,* 43.

236   **"Journalists reason from":** Patterson, *Out of Order,* 130.

236   **"A man who had become":** Drew, *Portrait,* 40.

237   **deception or weakness:** Shales, "Petty for Teddy."

237   **portraying him as inarticulate:** Drew, *Portrait,* 67.

237   **"laughed as loud":** "For Kennedy, It's Been a Mad Dash," *WP,* Dec. 17, 1979.

237   **"phenomenal":** Shales, "Petty for Teddy."

237   **"Pack pressure":** MacPherson, "Teddy the Underdog."

237   **"The trend in wolf-pack":** William Safire, "Kennedy's Certain Trumpet," *NYT,* Jan. 31, 1980.

237   **Chappaquiddick was cited:** "Kennedy Rating Drops 34 Points in Poll," *LAT,* Dec. 20, 1979.

238   **"one of the most dramatic":** "Gallup Poll Cites Big Turnabout," *WP,* Dec. 12, 1979.

238   **"Carter's low point":** Drew, *Portrait,* 18.

238   **noncommittal and refused:** "A Vicious Circle in the Kennedy Campaign," *NYT,* Dec. 12, 1979.

238   **"We're going to do the same":** EMK int., Oct. 14, 2005, Miller Center, UVA.

238   **privileged Brahmins:** Martin Tolchin int. by author; EMK int., Jan. 6, 2007, Miller Center, UVA.

239   **"With an incumbent":** Schlesinger, *Robert Kennedy,* 837.

239   **"if we win the early":** Martin Schram, "The Campaign," *WP,* June 8, 1980.

239   **"Step one was":** Quoted in Canellos, *Last Lion,* 214.

239   **wisdom of facing Ted:** Jody Powell to James Gannon, Nov. 6, 1979, "Debate (Iowa-Carter/Kennedy Cancelled)," Box 8, Staff Officers Press—Powell, Jimmy Carter Lib.; Greg Schneider to Rafshoon and Powell, Dec. 28, 1979, Box 8, Staff Officers Press—Powell, Jimmy Carter Lib.

239   **"I go out there as":** Jordan, *Crisis,* 99–100.

239   **"we will just have to take":** Martin Schram, "Making the Opponent the Issue," *WP,* June 9, 1980.

240   **"non-political, non-campaign matters":** EMK to Carter, Jan. 31, 1980, Office of Staff Sec., Box 168, Staff Offices, Jimmy Carter Lib.

240   **"This campaign could get very bloody":** Schram, "Making the Opponent."

240   **"Big Spender":** Kennedy, Carter vs. Kennedy, n.d., Susan Clough File [Carter Delegate Selections], Box 35, Jimmy Carter Lib.

240   **"I don't think there's any way":** Drew, *Portrait,* 54.

240   **ads exploited the foreign crises:** Steven Roberts, "Ted Kennedy: Haunted by the Past," *NYT Magazine,* Feb. 3, 1980.

240   **packed houses:** "Kennedy Lowers His Voice Amid Crisis," *LAT,* Jan. 13, 1980.

241   **"if he had never seen it":** "Teddy's Ragged Start," *Newsweek,* Dec. 10, 1979.

241   **"tender time":** "Kennedy Lowers His Voice Amid Crisis."

241   **"taken aback":** Ibid.

241   **"Programmed and reprogrammed":** Drew, *Portrait,* 62.

241   **"Cold and lifeless":** Richard Cohen, "Kennedy's Campaign: The Fun Has Gone," *WP,* Dec. 2, 1979.

241   **"more I went to these towns":** EMK int., Oct. 14, 2005; EMK, *True Compass,* 374.

242   **"Kennedy excitement would":** "He Wasn't in Touch," *Time,* Feb. 25, 1980.

242   **"to defend his honor":** Leonard Woodcock int., Feb. 12, 1996, V-Z Folder, Box 5, Series 2, Clymer Papers, JFK Lib.

242   **"Ted's makeup":** "Kennedy Camp Working on Farmer Anger," *NYT,* Jan. 14, 1980.

242 "windy": Robert Shrum, *No Excuses: Concessions of a Serial Campaigner* (New York: Simon & Schuster, 2007), 89.

242 internal poll in December: Drew, *Portrait*, 49.

243 "delighted you are going": "Squaring Off in Iowa," *Newsweek*, Nov. 26, 1979.

243 "spirit of unity": "Kennedy Says Unity on Iran Refutes Carter on Malaise," *WP*, Dec. 19, 1980.

243 "It is time to put": Shrum, *No Excuses*, 86.

243 "inner leisure is gone": James Reston, "A Talk with Kennedy," *NYT*, Jan. 9, 1980.

243 "reasonable expectation": T. R. Reid, "Kennedy Adjusts to Role as an Underdog in Iowa," *WP*, Jan. 17, 1980.

244 "not so bad a performer": Hugh Sidey, "On the Frosted Campaign Trail," *Time*, Jan. 21, 1980.

244 "The Kennedy on the stump": Johnson, "Kennedy Myth Gives Way."

244 "brilliant—clear": Tom Oliphant, int. by author.

244 "He delivers it as if": Drew, *Portrait*, 85.

245 "I can't tell you": Horowitz int.

245 evidence to rebut the charges: John Barron, "Chappaquiddick: The Still Unanswered Questions," *Reader's Digest*, Feb. 1980; "The Tide in Ted's Life," *Time*, Jan. 28, 1980; "Kennedy Moves to Rebut Articles on Chappaquiddick," *WP*, Jan. 16, 1980; "New Question Arises on Chappaquiddick," *NYT*, Jan. 16, 1980; "Kennedy, Citing Data, Says He Didn't Lie About Swim," *LAT*, Jan. 16, 1980.

245 "If there were new facts": "Talking Politics," *NYT*, Jan. 10, 1980.

246 "It may already be fatal": Drew, *Portrait*, 50.

246 approval rating stood at 52 percent: "Poll Shows Carter Gaining Support," *NYT*, Jan. 16, 1980.

246 "There was some sensitivity": John Culver int., Sept. 22, 2009, Miller Center, UVA.

246 "Whoooosh!": Johnson, "Kennedy Myth Gives Way."

246 said he sensed it: EMK, *True Compass*, 374.

247 "put out his hand": Shrum, *No Excuses*, 90.

247 "We're in debt": EMK int., Oct. 14, 2005.

247 "Oh, that's all right, Teddy": Ibid.

247 anti-abortion protesters: Drew, *Portrait*, 87.

247 "incompetent and confused": Carter, *Keeping Faith*, 482; Jordan, *Crisis*, 121.

248 "There's a death rattle": "Carter Pushing for Kennedy to Bow Out," *LAT*, Feb. 6, 1980.

248 draft of a statement: "Kennedy: We're in It to Stay," *Time*, Mar. 10, 1980.

248 "You represent the hopes": Martin Schram, "Kennedy's Decision to Stay in Race," *WP*, Feb. 5, 1980; "Kennedy Trims and Recasts Drive in Move to Rescue Presidential Bid," *NYT*, Mar. 1, 1980.

249 "Let's get ready": Shrum, *No Excuses*, 90–91.

249 destroy the Democratic Party: "Untroubled, Ted Kennedy Looks Ahead," *WP*, Aug. 17, 1980; Vanden Heuvel int.

249 "strong message": EMK, *True Compass*, 375.

SEVEN: "KEEP THE RUDDER TRUE"

250 "one of the most dramatic": Steven Roberts, "Ted Kennedy: Haunted by the Past," *NYT Magazine*, Feb. 3, 1980.

250 "new type of campaign": Carey Parker int., Oct. 13, 2008, Miller Center, UVA.

250 snapped in irritation: Adam Clymer, "Kennedy Discovers the Pain of Running as an Underdog," *NYT*, Jan. 27, 1980.

251 "Once it became apparent": Burton Hersh, *The Shadow President: Ted Kennedy in Opposition* (South Royalton, Vt.: Steerforth Press, 1997), 51.

251 "It's been like punching": "Kennedy's Campaign Shift," *NYT*, Jan. 30, 1980.

251 classic liberal speech: Richard Burke with William Hoffer and Marilyn Hoffer, *The Senator: My Ten Years with Ted Kennedy* (New York: St. Martin's Press 1992), 230.

251 "restrain pay increases": Jimmy Carter, State of the Union Address 1980, https://www .jimmycarterlibrary.gov/assets/documents/speeches/su80jec.phtml

251 "Kennedy was determined": Robert Shrum, *No Excuses: Concessions of a Serial Campaigner* (New York: Simon & Schuster, 2007), 92–93.

252 "go down honorably": "What Makes Teddy Run?" *Time*, Apr. 21, 1980.

252 "let it all hang out": "As Campaign Falters, Kennedy Turns to Liberal Formulas," *WP*, Jan. 29, 1980.

252 **"last-ditch effort":** Clymer, "Kennedy Discovers the Pain."

252 **"foreign policy is swallowing":** Arthur Schlesinger, Jr., *Journals: 1952–2000*, ed. Andrew Schlesinger and Stephen Schlesinger (New York: Penguin Press, 2007), 488–89.

252 **showed up at Ted's house:** Peter Goldman, "Ted Tries, Tries Again," *Newsweek*, Feb. 11, 1980; "As Campaign Falters, Kennedy Turns to Liberal Formulas"; Shrum, *No Excuses*, 92–93.

252 **instead taking briefings:** "Kennedy Plans for Talk with Top-Level Briefings," *WP*, Jan. 27, 1980; "Kennedy Talks with Waldheim to Prepare for Speech," *NYT*, Jan. 26, 1980.

252 **"strain of indifference":** Goldman, "Ted Tries, Tries Again."

252 **Georgetown's Gaston Hall:** Transcript, *NYT*, Jan. 29, 1980.

254 **wage and price controls would not:** "Politics First for Kennedy," *Newsweek*, Feb. 11, 1980.

254 **"roiling sea":** Shrum, *No Excuses*, 94; "Claque at Georgetown," *Newsweek*, Mar. 10, 1980.

254 **"elegantly drawn":** Goldman, "Ted Tries, Tries Again."

254 **"old Kennedy people":** William Raspberry, "A Gamble Kennedy Had to Take," *WP*, Feb. 1, 1980.

254 **"but he has said it":** Joseph Kraft, "Kennedy's Theme," *WP*, Jan. 31, 1980.

255 **"man who could not shake":** Mary McGrory, "Kennedy Comes Home a Challenger," *BG*, Feb. 4, 1980.

255 **"revived the art of political":** William Safire, "Kennedy's Certain Trumpet," *NYT*, Jan. 31, 1980.

255 **"genuine lift":** Schlesinger, *Journals*, 489.

255 **"There's a sharp edge":** B. Drummond Ayres, "Kennedy Smiles Despite Distress," *NYT*, Feb. 6, 1980.

255 **"Voices should not be muffled":** "Kennedy Demanding Debate with Carter," *NYT*, Jan. 31, 1980.

255 **"really rallied people":** Quoted in Peter Canellos, *Last Lion: The Fall and Rise of Ted Kennedy* (New York: Simon & Schuster, 2009), 221.

255 **Reverend Ralph Abernathy:** "Kennedy's Campaign Shift."

255 **"We kept knocking him":** Hamilton Jordan, *Crisis: The Last Year of the Carter Presidency* (New York: G. P. Putnam, 1982), 130, 141.

256 **"it represented the latest":** Elizabeth Drew, *Portrait of an Election: The 1980 Presidential Campaign* (New York: Simon & Schuster, 1981), 127.

256 **staff checks had been canceled:** "Kennedy Facing Painful Choices About Finances," *WP*, Feb. 28, 1980.

256 **"deluxe campaign":** "Funds Depleted, Kennedy Juggles Campaign Plans," *WP*, Jan. 25, 1980; "Kennedy Plane Too Expensive," *NYT*, Dec. 20, 1979; "Sinking Feeling in Camelot," *Newsweek*, Feb. 18, 1980.

256 **gave a grant to Lynn:** Theodore White, *America in Search of Itself: The Making of the President 1956–1980* (New York: Harper & Row, 1982), 295.

256 **"We can keep going":** Goldman, "Ted Tries, Tries Again."

256 **"sprinkled some dust":** EMK int., Oct. 14, 2005, Miller Center, UVA.

257 **"The swing is all":** "Carter's New Momentum," *NYT*, Jan. 25, 1980.

257 **still dogged him:** "Kennedy Effort to Stress Issues Found Lagging," *NYT*, Feb. 20, 1980.

257 **"I know there are people":** "Kennedy Takes Chappaquiddick Initiative," *NYT*, Jan. 30, 1980.

257 **"Who was that man":** Myra MacPherson, "Teddy the Underdog Flies into the Maine Event," *WP*, Feb. 10, 1980.

257 **"Now for a comment":** "Kennedy 'Debates' a Carter 1978 Tape," *NYT*, Feb. 9, 1980.

258 **"He has now laid out":** Raspberry, "Gamble."

258 **"He got his groove":** Patrick Kennedy int. by author.

258 **"more relaxed and humorous":** T. R. Reid, "Underdog Kennedy: Relaxed, Humorous," *WP*, Feb. 6, 1980.

258 **"When your sister-in-law":** "As Maine Goes, So May Go Teddy," *Newsweek*, Feb. 11, 1980.

258 **"weren't cushioned in caution":** Shrum, *No Excuses*, 95.

259 **"disarray":** Albers to Jordan, memo, Feb. 8, 1980, Subj: EMK, Box 78, Kennedy, Edward, Chief of Staff Jordan, Jimmy Carter Lib.

259 **"The momentum this morning":** "Democrats See Maine as Kennedy Resurgence," *NYT*, Feb. 12, 1980.

259 **"most strident attack":** "A Bitter Personal Vendetta," *Newsweek*, Feb. 25, 1980.

259 **despite a poll that showed:** "A *Newsweek* Poll on the Issues," *Newsweek*, Mar. 3, 1980.

260 **old school bus:** "Kennedy: A More Relaxed Campaigner Since Iowa," *LAT*, Feb. 20, 1980.

260 **"See that? The first one":** Goldman, "Ted Tries, Tries Again."

260 **wished for a New Hampshire:** "Kennedy Snuffing All Candles," *WP*, Feb. 22, 1980.

260   "Why is he, how can he": Garry Wills, *The Kennedy Imprisonment: A Meditation in Power* (Boston: Houghton Mifflin, 2002), 5.

260   "one of the best concealed": T. R. Reid, "Don't Count Out Kennedy," *WP*, Mar. 2, 1980.

261   "ugly reminder": "Kennedy Facing Painful Choices About Finances"; "Kennedy: We're in It to Stay," *Time*, Mar. 10, 1980.

261   was only helping Carter: Shrum, *No Excuses*, 97.

261   only group he carried was the young: "Kennedy: We're in It to Stay."

261   "There will be no more polls": Burke with Hoffer and Hoffer, *Senator*, 245.

262   "moodily": White, *America*, 297.

262   debated strategy for twelve hours: "Last Chance for Kennedy," *Newsweek*, Mar. 10, 1980.

262   "Well, you haven't missed": "A Tired Kennedy Returns to First Stumping Ground," *WP*, Mar. 4, 1980.

262   "We got almost no goose": "Can Teddy Build on His First Hurrah?" *Newsweek*, Mar. 17, 1980.

262   "I told the President": "Mayor Byrne Supports Kennedy," *WP*, Oct. 28, 1979.

263   "feared any challenge": Drew, *Portrait*, 20.

263   "Teddy's no Jack or Bobby": Roberts.

263   "He's in trouble": "Kennedy: Skidding in Illinois," *WP*, Jan. 13, 1980.

263   "contained enough negative": Elsa Walsh, "Inhospitable Day a Gloomy Omen for Sen. Kennedy," *WP*, Mar. 18, 1980.

263   "I remember being so embarrassed": Shrum, *No Excuses*, 100–1; Joan Kennedy int., May 12, 1998, K Folder, Box 4, Series 2, Clymer Papers, JFK Lib.

263   "ugly scar": Walter Isaacson, "That Which We Are, We Are," *Time*, Aug. 25, 1980.

263   lost overwhelmingly: Untitled, *Newsweek*, Mar. 31, 1980; "Kennedy's One-Note Message," *Time*, Mar. 24, 1980; "Carter Says He'll Accept Higher Unemployment," *LAT*, Mar. 9, 1980.

263   "character": "Kennedy's One-Note Message."

263   "campaign out of Kafka": Sally Quinn, "Teddy on the High Wire," *WP*, Mar. 21, 1980.

264   "His rhetoric about": Tom Wicker, "Kennedy Carries On," *NYT*, Mar. 18, 1980.

264   "Advertising its and his own": Wills, *Kennedy Imprisonment*, 5.

264   "All campaigns involve": George Will, "Kennedy's Comeback," *WP*, Mar. 30, 1980.

264   "Probably nowhere is": David Broder, "Kennedy: Skidding in Illinois," *WP*, Jan. 13, 1980.

265   Congressman Morris Udall: Martin Schram, "Rise and Fall of the Protest Vote," *WP*, June 10, 1980; Jordan, *Crisis*, 200; Curtis Gans, "A Force. Not a Candidate," *WP*, Apr. 8, 1980.

265   running out of money: "Underpaid Staffers Resigning," *WP*, Mar. 14, 1980.

265   significant lead among Black people: "Blacks in Survey Prefer Kennedy," *NYT*, Jan. 23, 1980.

265   endorsed the president: "Kennedy Woos the Jewish Vote," *Newsweek*, Mar. 24, 1980.

265   "People say the civil rights": Ben Brown quoted in "Blacks Not Rushing to Support Kennedy," *NYT*, Dec. 26, 1979.

265   Mine Workers wound up: Timothy Stanley, *Kennedy vs. Carter: The 1980 Battle for the Democratic Party's Soul* (Lawrence: Univ. Press of Kansas, 2010), 128–29.

265–66 "strong partisan motivations": Alan Abramowitz, John McGlennon, and Ronald Rapoport, "The Party Isn't Over: Incentives for Activism in the 1980 Presidential Nominating Campaign," *Journal of Politics* 45, no. 4 (Nov. 1983): 1012–13.

266   free to vent: Schram, "Rise and Fall of Protest Vote."

266   "it doesn't feel good": Jordan, *Crisis*, 200.

266   "tired but resolute": Quinn, "Teddy on High Wire."

266   "sputtered, coughed, cleared": T. R. Reid, "Laughing on a Day When All Else Seems to Fail," *WP*, Mar. 22, 1980.

267   "You'll never find yourself": "Kennedy Ads Stress Tragedies in Family," *NYT*, Mar. 18, 1980.

267   voted for General Assembly: "U.S. Shift at U.N.: A Matter of Consistency," *NYT*, Mar. 14, 1980.

267   "gang of five": "Kennedy Upstate Deplores Economy," *NYT*, Mar. 20, 1980.

267   voters thought Carter's handling: "Political Experts Decide—Tentatively—What Went Wrong," *WP*, Mar. 27, 1980.

268   "For weeks and months": Jordan, *Crisis*, 234–35.

268   "found his stride": "Carter Is in Trouble Again," *Newsweek*, Apr. 7, 1980.

268   leading Ted two to one: Shrum, *No Excuses*, 103; Reid, "Laughing on a Day"; Martin Schram, "Kennedy Upsets Carter in N.Y., Conn.," *WP*, Mar. 26, 1980.

268   "My own sense is that you": T. R. Reid, "Kennedy: Whether to Press on or Quit," *WP*, Mar. 23, 1980.

269 "We had those crying": "Astonishment and a New Campaign Course," *WP*, Mar. 26, 1980.

269 "Look, this is crazy": Paul Kirk, Jr., int., Nov. 23, 2005, Miller Center, UVA.

269 "Can you believe this?": Shrum, *No Excuses*, 103–4.

269 voted four to one for Ted: Schram, "Rise and Fall of Protest Vote."

269 only 10 percent of the electorate said: Stanley, *Kennedy vs. Carter*, 140.

270 "whenever it seemed obvious": Jimmy Carter, *Keeping Faith: Memoirs of a President* (New York: Bantam, 1982), 530–31.

270 "trustworthy": "Carter Is in Trouble Again."

270 personal morality didn't count: Schram, "Kennedy Upsets Carter."

270 could not handle the presidency: Schram, "Rise and Fall of Protest Vote."

270 carried the Catholic vote: Stanley, *Kennedy vs. Carter*, 143.

271 "It put a little puff": Quoted in Canellos, *Last Lion*, 224.

271 "We felt as if we had": "Kennedy's Startling Victory," *Time*, Apr. 7, 1980.

271 fifteen thousand people crammed: "Carter Is in Trouble Again."

271 "teenage squeals and hoarse": B. Drummond Ayres, "Reporter's Notebook: Kennedy Draws Support," *NYT*, Mar. 31, 1980.

271 "blitz": "Carter: A Worried Winner," *Newsweek*, Apr. 14, 1980.

271 36 percent of voters made: Stanley, *Kennedy vs. Carter*, 144.

272 won 54 percent: "Kennedy Falters," *WP*, Apr. 2, 1980.

272 Refugee Act of 1980: See EMK, "Refugee Act of 1980," *International Migration Review* 15, no. 1–2 (Spring–Summer 1981): 141–56.

272 "traveling show that": T. R. Reid, " 'New' Kennedy: More Jokes, Fewer Issues," *WP*, Apr. 21, 1980.

273 "dramatic improvement": "Kennedy's Startling Victory."

273 The campaign even released: Schram, "Rise and Fall of Protest Vote"; Mark Shields, "The Remainderman," *WP*, Apr. 18, 1980.

273 leaning toward Ted: Jane Farrell, "Memories of Mary Jo," *Ladies' Home Journal*, July 1989; "Mother of Miss Kopechne Leaning Toward Kennedy," *NYT*, Apr. 10, 1980.

273 "These spots are designed": "Kennedy and Carter TV Attacks Become Acerbic," *NYT*, Apr. 16, 1980.

273 "Urging citizens to vote": Shields, "Remainderman."

273 "He'll never forgive us": Quoted in Canellos, *Last Lion*, 225.

273 issue a protest against Carter: "The Outlook in Pennsylvania," *Newsweek*, Apr. 14, 1980.

273 won the Pennsylvania primary: E. J. Dionne, Jr., "The Kennedy Coalition," *NYT*, Apr. 25, 1980.

274 likely to rank jobs and inflation: "The Day of the Underdogs," *Time*, May 5, 1980.

274 "Carter is now falling": Stanley, *Kennedy vs. Carter*, 146.

274 "Not a victory for a candidate": "A New Ted Kennedy," *Newsweek*, Aug. 25, 1980.

274 "slightest concession": Robert Novak and Rowland Evans, "Kennedy's New Deal Pitch," *WP*, Apr. 18, 1980.

275 "Kennedy's task during": Wills, *Kennedy Imprisonment*, 51.

275 "soul-searched": "Joan Kennedy," *People*, Dec. 24, 1979.

275 sufficient condition not to capsize: Marcia Chellis, *Living with the Kennedys: The Joan Kennedy Story* (New York: Simon & Schuster, 1985), 112.

275 "I know how hard": Myra MacPherson, "Joan's Journey," *WP*, Dec. 14, 1979.

275 "I'm really starting": "Joan Kennedy: Back on Board," *WP*, Dec. 14, 1979.

275 "The result of this": MacPherson, "Joan's Journey."

275 "bout of hell": "Kennedy's Candid Mate," *WP*, Dec. 6, 1979.

275 "The members of the audience": Drew, *Portrait*, 57.

275 "Mrs. Kennedy's speeches": T. R. Reid, "One Personal Triumph on Kennedy Campaign," *WP*, Mar. 11, 1980.

276 "passionate defense": T. R. Reid, "Joan Kennedy Silences Reporters," *WP*, Jan. 19, 1980.

276 "two acted more like": Allan Mayer, "A Born-Again Politician," *Newsweek*, Apr. 7, 1980.

276 "His charm disappeared": Chellis, *Living*, 146.

276 "he doesn't notice me": Ibid., 129.

276 "That's just his style": Mayer, "Born-Again Politician."

276 stayed in separate suites: Chellis, *Living*, 138.

277 more decorous wardrobe: Burke with Hoffer and Hoffer, *Senator*, 227.

277 "puppet": Chellis, *Living*, 146, 148–49.

277 traveled with Ted only: Shrum, *No Excuses*, 82.

277 **"born-again politician":** "Born-Again Politician."

277 **"I just love my whole":** Bella Stumbo, "Joan Kennedy: Living 'a Day at a Time,'" *LAT*, June 9, 1980.

277 **"The 1980 campaign was":** Laurence Leamer, *The Kennedy Women: The Saga of an American Family* (New York: Villard Books, 1994), 705–6.

277 **good for the marriage:** MacPherson, "Joan's Journey"; "Reporter's Notebook: Kennedy Draws Support."

278 **"debacle":** See Mark Bowden, "The Desert One Debacle," *Atlantic*, May 2006.

279 **"model of somber restraint":** David M. Alpern, "Kennedy Soldiers On," *Newsweek*, May 5, 1980.

279 **"Manageable enough":** "Carter Drops 'Rose Garden Strategy,'" *NYT*, May 1, 1980.

279 **dropped by a factor:** Michael Robinson and Margaret Sheehan, *Over the Wire and on TV: CBS and UPI in Campaign '80* (New York: Russell Sage, 1983), 186.

279 **"I think the people are":** "Candidate Kennedy Edges Toward Direct Criticism of Carter Foreign Policy," *WP*, May 3, 1980.

279–80 **"which I think were":** EMK int., Sept. 11, 1998, EMK Interviews 1997–99 Folder, Box 5, Series 2, Clymer Papers, JFK Lib.

280 **"death watch":** Wills, *Kennedy Imprisonment*, 7.

280 **"subliminal mother instinct":** "Rating the Coverage," *Newsweek*, Mar. 24, 1980.

280 **"sort of a Rube Goldberg":** "Aides of Kennedy Tell Plan to Win," *LAT*, Apr. 18, 1980.

280 **"self-destruction":** David Broder, "Kennedy Withdrawal Urged," *WP*, May 24, 1980.

281 **"positive":** Parker int.

281 **"There's this thing":** Burke with Hoffer and Hoffer, *Senator*, 251.

281 **"He's trying to salvage":** "Kennedy Fights for His Own Sake," *LAT*, May 12, 1980.

281 **"series of bruising":** "What Makes Teddy Run?" *Time*, April 21, 1980.

281 **"You're peering down":** EMK int., Oct. 14, 2005.

281 **"There has been a certain":** "A Force. Not a Candidate," *WP*, Apr. 8, 1980.

281 **"metaphysical":** "The Sinking of the Kennedy Star," *WP*, Aug. 14, 1980.

281 **"from klutz to class":** Robinson and Sheehan, *Over the Wire*, 118.

281 **"brave and determined":** Ibid., 108, 120.

282 **"inner peace and self-confidence":** B. Drummond Ayres, "Kennedy's Mood Upbeat," *NYT*, Mar. 21, 1980.

282 **"happy, confident":** T. R. Reid. "A Tuned-Up Kennedy Machine Hits Its Cruising Speed," *WP*, Apr. 1, 1980.

282 **"man unpracticed in contempt":** Colman McCarthy, "Writing Kennedy's Candidacy into an Early Grave," *WP*, Apr. 6, 1980.

282 **"In adversity, Edward":** Anthony Lewis, "Kennedy Under Stress," *NYT*, Mar. 17, 1980.

282 **"different person":** Peter Hart int., Jan. 8, 1998, H Folder, Box 3, Series 2, Clymer Papers, JFK Lib.

282 **"He used to make":** Eunice Shriver int., Dec. 13, 1993, R-Edward Kennedy, S Folder, Box 5, Series 2, Clymer Papers, JFK Lib.

283 **"less he thought he could":** Hersh, *Shadow President*, 51.

283 **"made Edward Kennedy":** Antony Lewis, "Kennedy Redux," *NYT*, Mar. 27, 1980.

283 **"not to quit":** John Tunney int., May 3, 2007, Miller Center, UVA.

283 **"I spent a long time":** "What Makes Teddy Run?"

283 **"Prince has been humbled":** Ronnie Dugger, "The Trashing of Teddy," *Nation*, June 21, 1980.

284 **"a campaign of the heart":** Quoted in Tom Matthews, "Teddy's Long-Shot Scenario," *Newsweek*, May 12, 1980.

284 **"hurried effort":** "Kennedy Now Describes President as 'Pale Carbon Copy of Reagan,'" *NYT*, Apr. 11, 1980.

284 **"The moral issues":** "Kennedy Says President Failing on 'Moral Issues,'" *NYT*, May 4, 1980.

284 **"failing the historical":** "Kennedy Cites Failed Economic Policies," *LAT*, May 29, 1980.

284 **"A man brings two":** Martin Schram, "Making the Opponent the Issue," *WP*, June 9, 1980.

284 **"prevailing wind":** "What Makes Teddy Run?"

284 **"I'm talking about issues":** Reid, "Laughing on a Day."

284 **"My deepest fears":** Lou Cannon, "Kennedy's Behavior Is Now Oddly Reminiscent of Reagan's Four Years Ago," *WP*, May 26, 1980.

285 **"I am a liberal":** "Duty, Keeping of Faith Fuel his Quest," *LAT*, July 3, 1980.

285 **"Whether he wins or loses":** Colman McCarthy, "Kennedy's Liberal Light Still Shines," *WP*, June 1, 1980.

285 **"To help give the Democratic"**: "A New Ted Kennedy?" *Newsweek*, Aug. 25, 1980.

285 **"He's fighting for the soul"**: "Kennedy Fights for His Own Sake," *LAT*, May 12, 1980.

285 **"He thinks he's going to be"**: "Last Chance for Kennedy," *Newsweek*, Mar. 10, 1980.

285 **how valuable liberalizing**: T. R. Reid, "The Big Question: Will Kennedy Tackle the Convention?" *WP*, May 29, 1980.

285 **"I learned many years ago"**: Drew, *Portrait*, 164.

286 **"Was John Kennedy"**: "Kennedy Runs as If There's a Tomorrow," *WP*, June 3, 1980.

286 **typically start with**: EMK int., Oct. 14, 2005; "Kennedy Stepping Up Pace as Prospects Grow Dimmer," *NYT*, May 25, 1980.

286 **"The candidate's ruddy face"**: T. R. Reid, "Kennedy on Stump: Frenetic to the End," *WP*, June 3, 1980.

286 **"It did not look like a loser's"**: Ibid.

287 **"Kennedy seems to actually"**: Drew, *Portrait*, 165.

287 **intended to vote for Carter**: Peter Goldman, "Fighting After the Final Bell," *Newsweek*, June 16, 1980.

287 **"kamikaze mission"**: Jordan, *Crisis*, 293–97.

287 **"Today, Democrats from coast"**: Drew, *Portrait*, 187.

288 **men were not amused**: Goldman, "Fighting After the Final Bell."

288 **declared on primary night**: Paul Kirk, Jr., int., June 3, 1998, K Folder, Box 4, Series 2, Clymer Papers, JFK Lib.

288 **it was time to fold**: Ibid.

288 **"I'm not getting out"**: "White House Face Off," *Time*, June 16, 1980; Shrum 114–15.

289 **"amiable"**: Goldman, "Fighting After the Final Bell."

289 **"formal tone"**: EMK, *True Compass* (New York: Twelve, 2009), 378; Shrum, *No Excuses*, 114–15.

289 **"looked irritated"**: Jordan, *Crisis*, 299.

290 **"I'm planning to be"**: "Kennedy Snubs Carter," *LAT*, June 6, 1980.

290 **"like a spoiled brat"**: Jimmy Carter int., May 15, 1998, C Folder, Box 3, Series 2, Clymer Papers, JFK Lib.

290 **"elusive"**: B. Drummond Ayres, "Kennedy the Campaigner," *NYT*, Apr. 7, 1980; Patrick Kennedy int.

EIGHT: "EVERYTHING BUT THE NOMINATION"

291 **"absolutely berserk"**: Pat Caddell int., Jan. 1, 1998, C Folder, Box 3, Series 2, Clymer Papers, JFK Lib.

291 **"those forces out there"**: Elizabeth Drew, *Portrait of an Election: The 1980 Presidential Campaign* (New York: Simon & Schuster, 1981), 34.

291 **"very basic and fundamental"**: "Vowing Defiance to the End," *Time*, July 21, 1980.

292 **"If I stay in the race"**: "Kennedy Cheered at ADA Meeting," *LAT*, June 15, 1980.

292 **"preaching"**: "Tired Kennedy Gets Lift at N.A.A.C.P. Meeting," *NYT*, July 3, 1980.

292 **"Nobody was pounding"**: "Kennedy—Little Pressure to Drop Out," *WP*, June 17, 1980.

292 **"feels good"**: T. R. Reid, "The Campaign Feels Good," *WP*, June 29, 1980.

292 **"enervated"**: Bill Stall, "Kennedy Campaign Mood on a Seesaw," *LAT*, June 28, 1980.

292 **"confrontational"**: Frank Moore, Bill Cable to Hamilton Jordan, memo, June 5, 1980, Box 78, Kennedy, Edward, Chief of Staff Jordan, Jimmy Carter Lib.

293 **agreed with the prescription**: Richard Moe to Jordan, n.d., "Re: Post June 3, Conversations with Kennedy," Box 87, Kennedy, Edward, Chief of Staff Jordan, Jimmy Carter Lib.

293 **"Democratic in name only"**: "Teddy May Just Go Fishing," *Newsweek*, July 7, 1980.

293 **"Graciousness and conciliation"**: Moe to Carter, memo, June 5, 1980, Box 9, Kennedy, Sen. Edward M., Press Powell, Staff Offices, Jimmy Carter Lib.

293 **"significant"**: "The Mutinous Democrats," *Newsweek*, Aug. 4, 1980.

293 **"adamantly against it"**: Jimmy Carter, *Keeping Faith: Memoirs of a President* (New York: Bantam paperback rep., 1982), 541.

293 **"concede almost anything"**: Robert Shrum, *No Excuses: Concessions of a Serial Campaigner* (New York: Simon & Schuster, 2007), 112.

294 **"validates our contention"**: "Teddy May Just Go Fishing."

294 **"The jobless do not have"**: "Floor Fight Is Pledged by Kennedy," *WP*, June 25, 1980.

294 **"You've heard about"**: "Hard Times Tales Unfold for Kennedy," *WP*, July 25, 1980.

295 **at 26 percent of the vote:** Jim Mason, *No Holding Back: The 1980 Presidential Campaign of John B. Anderson* (Lanham, Md.: Univ. Press of America, 2011); "Anderson Could Win, Pollsters Agree," *WP*, June 18, 1980.

295 **"reach a responsible solution":** Peter Goldman, "The Drive to Dump Carter," *Newsweek*, Aug. 11, 1980; Hamilton Jordan, *Crisis: The Last Year of the Carter Presidency* (New York: G. P. Putnam, 1982), 314.

295 **work for an open convention:** Adam Clymer, *Edward M. Kennedy: A Biography* (New York: Harper Perennial, 2000), 315.

295 **Carter actually ran third:** "Carter Rating in Two Polls Lowest Ever," *WP*, Aug. 5, 1980.

295 **"Never before in":** Hedrick Smith, "Carter Aides Yield on TV Debate Time and Win Unity Vow," *NYT*, Aug. 6, 1980.

296 **"Mr. Norm":** Lou Cannon, *Governor Reagan: His Rise to Power* (New York: PublicAffairs, 2003), 83.

296 **"No, Jimmy Stewart for governor":** "Ronald for Real," *Time*, Oct. 7, 1966. Elsewhere the anecdote was relayed as "No, Bob Cummings for governor. Ronald Reagan for best friend."

296 **"He didn't know it yet":** H. W. Brands, *Reagan: The Life* (New York: Doubleday, 2015), 97.

296 **"A New Dealer to the core":** Ibid., 60–61.

296 **"A near-hopeless hemophiliac":** Cannon, *Governor Reagan*, 93.

297 **"I knew from the experience":** Ronald Reagan, *An American Life: The Autobiography* (New York: Simon & Schuster, 1990), 115.

297 **"I'd always thought":** Ibid., 117.

297 **"exposure to the business-as-usual":** Ibid., 119.

297 **"He sounded as though":** Bob Spitz, *Reagan: An American Journey* (New York: Penguin Press, 2018), 290.

298 **"We have so many":** Ronald Reagan, "Address on Behalf of Senator Barry Goldwater: 'A Time for Choosing,'" October 27, 1964, at https://www.presidency.ucsb.edu/documents/address-behalf-senator-barry-goldwater-time-for-choosing

299 **"one of the most important":** Reagan, *American Life*, 143.

299 **"Goldwater's doctrine with":** Brands, *Reagan: The Life*, 146.

299 **"same socialist goals":** Ibid., 139.

300 **"I will not stand by":** Ronald Reagan, "Address Accepting the Presidential Nomination at the Republican National Convention, July 1, 1980," https://www.presidency.ucsb.edu/documents/address-accepting-the-presidential-nomination-the-republican-national-convention-detroit

301 **"cowardly little bums":** Brands, *Reagan: The Life*, 175, 210.

301 **"everyone seemed to like":** Lou Cannon, *President Reagan: The Role of a Lifetime* (New York: Simon & Schuster, 1991), 11.

301 **"because an actor knows":** Ibid., 38.

301 **"There are not two Ronald":** Quoted in Michael Paul Rogin, *Ronald Reagan, the Movie, and Other Episodes in Political Demonology* (Berkeley: Univ. of Calf. Press, 1987), 7.

302 **55 to 24 percent lead:** Theodore White, *America in Search of Itself: The Making of the President 1956–1980* (New York: Harper & Row, 1982), 328.

302 **"Some people enter politics":** Brands, *Reagan: The Life*, 131.

302 **"sounding as strident":** Drew, *Portrait*, 227.

302 **greeted a large crowd:** "Upbeat but Facing Loss, Kennedy Arrives in N.Y.," *WP*, Aug. 9, 1980.

302 **really could win:** Timothy Stanley, *Kennedy vs. Carter: The 1980 Battle for the Democratic Party's Soul* (Lawrence: Univ. Press of Kansas, 2010), 158.

302 **pulling on that pipe:** Ibid., 160.

302 **65 percent for to 31 percent against:** Ibid.

302 **no attempt to coordinate:** Hedrick Smith, "Disgruntled Democrats in Congress Weigh Bid for New Party Nominee," *NYT*, July 26, 1980; Goldman, "Drive to Dump Carter."

303 **capture the nomination:** Drew, *Portrait*, 223; Shrum, *No Excuses*, 115.

303 **"Have you ever heard":** Peter Canellos, *Last Lion: The Fall and Rise of Ted Kennedy* (New York: Simon & Schuster, 2009), 228.

303 **"Nothing is certain":** Smith, "Carter Aides Yield."

303 **"I think we may be":** Drew, *Portrait*, 229–30.

303 **his staff scotched the idea:** "Upbeat but Facing Loss, Kennedy Arrives in N.Y."

303 **come down to a few votes:** Jon Ward, *Camelot's End: Kennedy vs. Carter and the Fight That Broke the Democratic Party* (New York: Twelve, 2019), 252.

304 **vote for a rules change:** Smith, "Carter Aides Yield."

304 **"outside chance":** EMK int., Oct. 14, 2005, Miller Center, UVA.

304 **"All of them wanted":** Jordan, *Crisis*, 322.

304 **lured those delegates:** EMK int., Sept. 11, 1998, EMK Interviews 1997–99 Folder, Box 5, Series 2, Clymer Papers, JFK Lib.

304 **"We just can't do it":** EMK int., Oct. 14, 2005.

304 **"it's a President-candidate":** Drew, *Portrait*, 225.

304 **"No, no, no!":** Ibid., 243.

304 **"grim smile":** Richard Burke with William Hoffer and Marilyn Hoffer, *The Senator: My Ten Years with Ted Kennedy* (New York: St. Martin's Press, 1992), 272–73.

305 **"by almost everyone's measure":** B. Drummond Ayres, "Kennedy Race Ends But Cause Continues," *NYT*, Aug. 13, 1980.

305 **"That's it":** Shrum, *No Excuses*, 116; "Call to President," *NYT*, Aug. 12, 1980; "Facing Up to Defeat," *WP*, Aug. 12, 1980; " 'Realist' Kennedy Tells Supporters It's All Over," *LAT*, Aug. 12, 1980.

305 **"This is getting to be":** "Day of Confusion," *WP*, Aug. 11, 1980.

306 **"I wouldn't be here":** "Strauss Predicting Some Carter Losses on Party Platform," *NYT*, Aug. 9, 1980.

306 **"peace agreement":** Paul Kirk, Jr., int., Nov. 23, 2005, Miller Center, UVA.

306 **"there will be another":** Barbara Mikulski int., Sept. 26, 2006, Miller Center, UVA.

306 **"good talk":** EMK int., Oct. 14, 2005.

307 **"I'm not sure this does it":** Shrum, *No Excuses*, 118–19.

307 **there would be a struggle:** "Day of Confusion."

307 **"At one point":** Robert Scheer, "In the Defense of Liberalism," *LAT*, Aug. 14, 1980.

307 **"Look, Teddy, you have":** EMK int., Oct. 14, 2005.

307 **"a rambling attack on Reagan":** Arthur Schlesinger, Jr. *Journals: 1952–2000*, ed. Andrew Schlesinger and Stephen Schlesinger (New York: Penguin Press, 2007), 496–97.

308 **"If Ted gives that speech":** Ibid.

308 **"jovial":** Scheer, "In the Defense."

308 **"Well, it worked out a little":** Edward Kennedy, 1980 Convention Speech, August 11, 1980, https://www.c-span.org/video/?3439-1/senator-edward-kennedy-1980-convention-speech

310 **"Kennedy delegates, the successful":** Francis X. Clines, "Backers Roar for Kennedy as He Hails Party's Cause," *NYT*, Aug. 13, 1980.

310 **"enormous triumph":** Schlesinger, *Journals*, 497.

310 **"more magnificent than":** Tom Shales, "The Gripper," *WP*, Aug. 13, 1980.

311 **"Sense of the Occasion":** White, *America*, 337–38.

311 **"The words have enormous":** EMK int., Oct. 14, 2005.

311 **"He had salvaged a failed":** Mark Shields, "How Kennedy Got Even," *WP*, Aug. 17, 1980.

311 **"We're all voting for":** "Carter Wins Votes, Kennedy Wins Hearts," *National Journal*, June 19, 2000.

311 **"We threw in the towel":** Quoted in Canellos, *Last Lion*, 230.

312 **"we had seven deaf mutes":** "How Deal Was Struck to Get Kennedy Planks," *LAT*, Aug. 14, 1980.

312 **ignore the platform:** "Kennedy Appeals for Unity," *LAT*, Aug. 13, 1980.

312 **"After the June primaries":** "Kennedy Kept Bid Alive for Concessions," *LAT*, Aug. 15, 1980.

312 **"We had all this tension":** EMK int., Oct. 14, 2005.

313 **"many of my supporters":** Ibid.

313 **hesitant to raise Carter's hand:** Shrum, *No Excuses*, 127–29.

313 **"Hubert Horatio Hornblower":** Jack Germond and Jules Witcover, *Blue Smoke and Mirrors: How Reagan Won and Why Carter Lost the Election of 1980* (New York: Viking Press, 1981), 192.

314 **"It's almost as if they are":** Ward, *Camelot's End*, 268.

314 **"Come on up":** Germond and Witcover, *Blue Smoke*, 192.

314 **"He's not going to do it":** Ibid., 193.

314 **"Everybody knew it":** Ward, *Camelot's End*, 1.

314 **"while he didn't have":** "Carter Wins Votes, Kennedy Wins Hearts"; Shrum, *No Excuses*, 128–29; Kirk int.; EMK int., Oct. 14, 2005.

314 **"as if he had appeared":** White, *America*, 342.

315 **"Seldom in modern history":** B. Drummond Ayres, "Kennedy Race Ends But Cause Continues," *NYT*, Aug. 13, 1980.

315 **"The fact is that":** Joseph Kraft, "The Sinking of the Kennedy Star," *WP*, Aug. 14, 1980.

315 "A big reason": "As Humphrey, As Stevenson, As Kennedy," *NYT*, Aug. 14, 1980.

316 80 percent of the public: "Edward Kennedy: The Politician as Paradox," *LAT*, Sept. 16, 1979.

316 "become a leader": "A New Ted Kennedy?" *Newsweek*, Aug. 25, 1980.

316 "not only revived": Stanley, *Kennedy vs. Carter*, 6, 142.

316 "promise, above all else": Hunter S. Thompson, *The Great Shark Hunt: Strange Tales From a Strange Time* (1979; reprint New York: Simon & Schuster, 2003), 476.

317 "There's been this whole": White, *America*, 290.

318 72 percent of respondents: "1980 Presidential Election," Roper Center, Ropercenter.cornell .edu/1980PresidentialElection

318 its sharpest dive: "Public Trust in Government, 1958–2021," Pew Research Center, May 17, 2021.

318 "If there was a single": Germond and Witcover, *Blue Smoke*, 316.

319 "did not look or sound": T. R. Reid, "Untroubled, Ted Kennedy Looks Ahead," *WP*, Aug. 17, 1980; "A New Ted Kennedy?"

320 punish him for: "Kennedy's Staff, After the Dream," *WP*, Aug. 15, 1980.

320 "more contented man": Ayres, "Kennedy Race Ends But Cause Continues."

320 "best thing that ever happened": David Burke int., Apr. 9, 2008, Miller Center, UVA.

320 "does not understand Ted": Schlesinger, *Journals*, 501–2.

320 "There is something deeply": Kraft, "Sinking of Kennedy Star."

320 "great personal victory": Theodore Sorensen, *Counselor: A Life at the Edge of History* (New York: HarperCollins, 2008), 258.

321 "redeem the President's apparent": Shrum, *No Excuses*, 77.

321 substantial postconvention bump: "Carter Gains in Gallup Poll," *NYT*, Aug. 19, 1980.

321 "The President has serious political": "Upbeat but Facing Loss, Kennedy Arrives in N.Y."

321 "Carter demonstrated that": E. J. Dionne, Jr., *Why Americans Hate Politics* (New York: Simon & Schuster, 1991), 131.

321 divided state parties: Jordan, *Crisis*, 307.

321 34 percent of Ted's: Stanley, *Kennedy vs. Carter*, 151.

321–22 "What I really do": B. Drummond Ayres, Jr., int., Aug. 28, 1997, A Folder, Box 3, Series 2, Clymer Papers, JFK Lib.

322 "need to be friends": Carter, *Keeping Faith*, 556.

322 "these stances might enable": Ibid., 555.

322 "blackmail": Jordan, *Crisis*, 334; Jack English to Jordan, Tim Finchem, Tom Donilon, Sept. 9, 1980, Box 78, Kennedy, Edward M., Chief of Staff Jordan, Jimmy Carter Lib.

322 two more disliked candidates: Stanley, *Kennedy vs. Carter*, 172–74.

322 beset by myriad problems: Carter, *Keeping Faith*, 543–44.

323 "vacation money for the lazy": Spitz, *Reagan*, 461.

323 "Americans are conservatives": Cannon, *Role of a Lifetime*, 21.

323 "There is no fun": Anthony Lewis, "Carter Against Himself," *NYT*, Oct. 16, 1980.

323 scenes from movies: "In the Garden, An Evocation of 1948 Spirit," *NYT*, Aug. 15, 1980.

323 "world of tinsel": Spitz, *Reagan*, 461.

324 "It has never before": Walter Dean Burnham, "The 1980 Earthquake: Realignment, Reaction, or What?" in *The Hidden Election: Politics and Economics in the 1980 Presidential Campaign*, ed. Thomas Ferguson and Joel Rogers (New York: Pantheon, 1981), 110.

324 "He just got killed": Ward, *Camelot's End*, 286.

325 attack John Anderson: Eugene Robinson, "Kennedy, Mindful of Future, Is Going All-Out for Carter," *WP*, Oct. 12, 1980.

325 an eight-point lead: Lydia Saad, 'Late Upsets Are Rare But Have Happened," Gallup, Oct. 27, 2008, https://news.gallup.com/poll/111451/late-upsets-rare-happened.aspx

325 Reagan was suddenly: Spitz, *Reagan*, 468.

325 "our party had always": Carter, *Keeping Faith*, 567.

325 "to concentrate almost": Ibid., 561.

325 "Carter thinks he [Ted] elected": Larry Horowitz int., June 23, 1995, H folder, Interviews, Box 3, Series 2, Clymer Papers, JFK Lib.

325 "Quite bitter": White, *America*, 417.

326 "If the election was": Carter, *Keeping Faith*, 568.

326 third lowest: Burnham, "1980 Earthquake," 103.

326 "Carter, the preeminent": Leo Ribuffo, "Jimmy Carter and the Ironies of American Liberalism," *Gettysburg Review* (Autumn 1988): 738–49.

326 "He was more than a candidate": EMK, *True Compass* (New York: Twelve, 2009), 382.

326 38 percent of Reagan's voters: Burnham, "1980 Earthquake," 109.

326 behind Gerald Ford's numbers: Dionne, *Why Americans*, 139.

326 Democratic defections: Burnham, "1980 Earthquake," 104.

326 fewer votes among liberals: Dionne, *Why Americans*, 139.

327 "The liberal bogeyman": Stanley, *Kennedy vs. Carter*, 7.

327 beat Carter among white voters: White, *America*, 415.

327 nearly one-third of those: Dionne, *Why Americans*, 138.

328 "less from what he is": George Will, "Heavy Hitter in the Dugout," *Newsweek*, Sept. 4, 1978.

328 "What happened in 1980": Jordan, *Crisis*, 378.

328 "One thing that is not": Germond and Witcover, *Blue Smoke*, 313.

329 less than 4 percent: Garry Wills, *The Kennedy Imprisonment: A Meditation on Power* (Boston: Houghton Mifflin, 2002), 292.

329 "It is almost not too": Burnham, "1980 Earthquake," 99.

329 "The New Deal died": John A. Farrell, *Tip O'Neill and the Democratic Century* (Boston: Little, Brown, 2001), 22.

329 "almost child-like self-centeredness": Ward, *Camelot's End*, 257.

NINE: LIFE AFTER DISASTER

330 "Democrats might have": Lance Morrow, "Is There Life After Disaster?" *Time*, Nov. 17, 1980.

330 "New Dealism": Quoted in Godfrey Hodgson, *America in Our Time: From World War II to Nixon* (1976; New York: Vintage, 1978), 82.

331 "What happened to the": Carl Solberg, *Hubert Humphrey: A Biography* (New York: Norton, 1984), 469.

331 "Everybody talks": Jeffrey Toobin, "The Dirty Trickster," *New Yorker*, May 23, 2008.

331 "The predicate to the conservative": Stanley Greenberg, *The Two Americas: Our Current Political Deadlock and How to Break It* (New York: St. Martin's Griffin, 2005), 50–51.

332 "The point that the Democrats": Toobin, "Dirty Trickster."

332 A Gallup poll in 1964: Andrew Kohut, "Mixed Views About Civil Rights But Support for Selma Demonstrations," *Pew Report*, Mar. 5, 2015, https://www.pewresearch.org/fact-tank/2020/01/16/50-years-ago-mixed-views-about-civil-rights-but-support-for-selma-demonstrators/

332 moving too fast on integration: Ibid.

333 "blacks should not push": Lawrence Bobo et al., "The *Real* Record on Racial Attitudes," in *Social Trends in American Life*, ed. Peter Marsden (Princeton: Princeton Univ. Press, 2012), 46.

333 only 19 percent of white: "Public Opinion on Civil Rights: Reflections on the Civil Rights Act of 1964," Roper Center, n.d., https://ropercenter.cornell.edu/public-opinion-civil-rights-reflections-civil-rights-act-1964.

333 Nearly 60 percent of white: Bobo et al., "*Real* Record," 54, 57.

333 roughly 15 percent of white: Charlotte Steeh and Maria Krysan, "Affirmative Action and the Public, 1970–1995," *The Public Opinion Quarterly* 60, no. 1 (Spring 1996): 131. Steeh and Krysan are careful to state that how polling questions were phrased had a significant effect on the responses and that Gallup polling was several percentage points below other polls.

334 "The American people were": Theodore White, *America in Search of Itself: The Making of the President 1956–1980* (New York: Harper & Row, 1982), 419.

334 "He's been speaking a lot": Lou Cannon, *Governor Reagan: His Rise to Power* (New York: PublicAffairs, 2003), 264.

334 "traditional forum": Lou Cannon, "Reagan Campaigning from County Fair to Urban League," *WP*, Aug. 4, 1980; "Reagan Campaigns at Mississippi Fair," *NYT*, Aug. 4, 1980.

335 "Government is the problem": "Bigger Than Bush," *NYT*, Jan. 2, 2009.

335 "You start out in 1954 by saying": Rick Perlstein, "Lee Atwater's Infamous 1981 Interview on the Southern Strategy," *Nation*, Nov. 13, 2012.

335 heard the abstractions: "Mrs. Harris Quotes Klan in Its Backing of Reagan," *NYT*, Aug. 7, 1980.

336 "all those who believe": Quoted in William Rusher, *The Rise of the Right* (New York: Morrow, 1984), 84.

336 opposed to labor unions: Barry Goldwater, *The Conscience of a Conservative* (1960; reprint Princeton: Princeton Univ. Press, 2007), 1.

336 "Yet anytime you and I question": Ronald Reagan, "A Time for Choosing," Oct. 17, 1964, https://www.reaganlibrary.gov/reagans/ronald-reagan/time-choosing-speech-october-27-1964

337 "the American people think": Rick Perlstein, *Reaganland: America's Right Turn, 1976–1980* (New York: Simon & Schuster, 2021), 494.

337 "If Christians do not master": Ibid., 491.

337 "all political problems are really": Theodore Lowi, *The End of the Republican Era* (Norman: Univ. of Oklahoma Press, 1995), 117.

337 "transcendent moral order": Russell Kirk, "Conservatism: A Succinct Description," *National Review*, Sept. 3, 1982.

338 halt racial progress: Sean Wilentz, *The Age of Reagan: A History 1974–2008* (New York: Harper-Collins, 2008), 92–93.

338 "shrugged, like the fellow": Perlstein, *Reaganland*, 608.

338 "might be the generation": Ibid., 846.

339 "Ronald Reagan is not": Rick Perlstein, *The Invisible Bridge: The Fall of Nixon and the Rise of Reagan* (New York: Simon & Schuster, 201), xvi.

339 "vacation money for the lazy": Bob Spitz, *Reagan: An American Journey* (New York: Penguin Press, 2018), 461.

339 "welfare queen": Josh Levin, "The Myth Was $150,000 in Fraud; The Real Story Is More Interesting," *NYT*, May 17, 2019.

339 favored handgun registration: Yankelovich poll cited in Timothy Stanley, *Kennedy vs. Carter: The 1980 Battle for the Democratic Party's Soul* (Lawrence: Univ. Press of Kansas, 2010), 155.

340 "Pat had the grays": Rick Perlstein, *Nixonland: The Rise of a President and the Fracturing of America* (New York: Simon & Schuster, 2008), 85.

340 "Reagan had the excellent fortune": Wilentz, *Age of Reagan*, 137.

341 "We're so sorry to see": Carey Parker int., Oct. 27, 2008, Miller Center, UVA.

341 "more than mild trepidation": "Remembering Ted Kennedy," *National Journal*, Sept. 5, 2009; Parker int.; Stephen Breyer int., Sept. 28, 2008, Miller Center, UVA.

342 "With regret, yet with respect": "Teddy and Joan Split Up," *Newsweek*, Feb. 2, 1981.

342 "How are you going": Marcia Chellis, *Living with the Kennedys: The Joan Kennedy Story* (New York: Simon & Schuster, 1985), 187, 210–11.

343 "I want to be married": Joan Kennedy int., May 12, 1998, K Folder, Box 4, Series 2, Clymer Papers, JFK Lib.

343 psychiatrist had advised: Ibid.

343 irretrievably broken: "Joan Kennedy: Life Without Ted," *Ladies' Home Journal*, Apr. 1981.

343 "I guess I felt like I": Adam Clymer, *Edward M. Kennedy: A Biography* (New York: Harper Perennial, 2000), 325.

343 in love with another man: "Kennedy: Life Without Ted."

343 "Except for one visit": Robert Shrum, *No Excuses: Concessions of a Serial Campaigner* (New York: Simon & Schuster, 2007), 131.

343 "Rock bottom is a good": Peter Canellos, *Last Lion: The Fall and Rise of Ted Kennedy* (New York: Simon & Schuster, 2009), 232.

343 "great strains in the marriage": Myra MacPherson, "Closing Scenes from a Kennedy Marriage," *WP*, Jan. 22, 1981.

343 seven-room Boston apartment: "Resident Kennedy," *WP*, June 26, 1976.

343 "Republican friends": Clymer, *Kennedy*, 354.

344 substantial financial settlement: Gioia Diliberto, "After 24 Years, Joan Kennedy Ends Her Marriage," *People*, Dec. 30, 1982.

344 "Vulnerable": "Joan Kennedy's Worries," *People Weekly*, June 24, 1974.

344 "They would all write": Sally Jacobs, "Prime Time with Joan Kennedy," *BG Magazine*, July 9, 2000.

344 "I mean, my God": "Joan Kennedy: Life Without Ted."

344 "I regret my failings": EMK, *True Compass* (New York: Twelve, 2009), 184.

345 "It seemed to me that": Ronald Reagan, *An American Life* (New York: Simon & Schuster, 1990), 205–6.

345 "Tell me the last time": Perlstein, *Invisible Bridge*, 563.

346 "Yes, I'm a Republican": John Taylor, *Circus of Ambition: The Culture of Wealth and Power in the Eighties* (New York: Warner Books, 1989), 11.

346 impressed with how effectively: EMK int., June 17, 2005, Miller Center, UVA.

347   "Not one day sooner": EMK, *True Compass*, 382.

347   "we can realize some": John Culver int., Sept. 22, 2009, Miller Center, UVA.

347   "He roused the comfortable": EMK, *True Compass*, 383–84; Clymer, *Kennedy*, 327.

347   "gracious": EMK int., Aug. 7, 2007, Miller Center, UVA; Ronald Reagan, *The Reagan Diaries, ed.* Douglas Brinkley (New York: HarperCollins, 2007), 49.

347   "He lit up a room": EMK, *True Compass*, 388–90; Shrum, *No Excuses*, 132.

348   draw up separate plans of action: "The Kennedy Prescription," *WP Health*, Apr. 21, 1987.

349   "small group of conservative": "Senate Stifles Housing Rights Bill," *WP*, Dec. 10, 1980.

349   "Look, I'll guarantee": EMK int., Mar. 23, 2005, Miller Center, UVA.

349   "stunned that he would": Kenneth Feinberg int., July 8, 2008, Miller Center, UVA.

349   "closer to the surface": EMK int., Mar. 27, 1998, EMK Interviews, 1997–99 Folder, Box 5, Series 2, Clymer Papers, JFK Lib.

349   "I never doubted for": "The Kennedy Prescription."

350   programs just withered: Edward Kennedy int., Sept. 11, 1998, EMK Interviews 1997–99 Folder, Box 5, Series 2, Clymer Papers, JFK Lib.

350   able to hold the line: EMK int., Mar. 28, 2008, Miller Center, UVA.

350   social programs were in jeopardy: Lowell Weicker, Jr., with Barry Sussman, *Maverick: A Life in Politics* (Boston: Little, Brown, 1995), 141.

350   enough moderate Republicans: "Rating the Senate Bosses," *Newsweek*, July 13, 1981.

351   "combination sycophant": Thomas Sussman, May 23, 2007, Miller Center, UVA.

351   "tried to act like": Ibid.

351   "perfect enabler": Thomas Oliphant int. by author.

351   "Devious and underhanded": Quoted in David Streitfield, "The Man Behind the Senator," *WP*, Sept. 24, 1992.

351   "He cracked under the strain": Ibid.

352   Burke had fabricated them: Ibid.

352   fly back each week: Larry Horowitz int., May 29, 1992, H Folder, Box 3, Series 2, Clymer Papers, JFK Lib.

352   severe asthma attack: "A Strategist Aids Kennedy Once More," *BG*, June 2, 2008.

352   "really, really smart": Thomas Rollins int., Apr. 22, 2009, Miller Center, UVA.

352   "Throw all the fish": Ibid.

352   "Machiavellian": Nancy Soderberg int., Oct. 9, 2008, Miller Center, UVA; Rollins int., Oct. 9, 2008.

352   reorganized the office: Anne Strauss int., Apr. 10, 2008, Miller Center, UVA.

352   "Larry Horowitz": Tom Oliphant int. by author.

353   "this was an historic": Stan Jones int., Sept. 14, 2007, Miller Center, UVA.

353   "If you weren't so goddamned": Horowitz int.

353   "sense of pessimism": Carey Parker int., Oct. 20, 2008, Miller Center, UVA.

354   "pretty oblique guy": Thomas Rollins int., May 14, 2009, Miller Center, UVA.

354   "hugely stung": Thomas Rollins int., Mar. 10, 2009, Miller Center, UVA.

354   "Oh, Tom. That's a great": Ibid.

354   "He seemed to have": Quoted in Canellos, *Last Lion*, 264.

355   even considering leaving: Oliphant int.

355   clearest sign of his disaffection: Richard Burke with William Hoffer and Marilyn Hoffer, *The Senator: My Ten Years with Ted Kennedy* (New York: St. Martin's Press, 1992), 296.

355   "The American people to this": Lowell Weicker int., June 19, 2009, Miller Center, UVA.

355   use his seniority to chair: Ibid.

355   pleasure in thwarting him: Orrin Hatch int., Dec. 1, 2006, Miller Center, UVA.

355   "Reagan's men now realize": "Rating the Senate Bosses."

355   "darkness": Canellos, *Last Lion*, 235.

355   "political Siberia": Patrick Kennedy int. by author.

356   "It's one thing to be America's": William Carrick int., May 27, 1992, C Folder, Box 3, Series 2, Clymer Papers, JFK Lib.

356   "We had a new definition": Robert Byrd, *The Senate 1789–1989: Addresses on the History of the United States Senate* (Washington, D.C.: U.S. Govt. Printing Office, 1988), 4:611.

356   "Democrats lost not just": Bill Bradley, *Time Present, Time Past: A Memoir* (New York: Knopf, 1996), 49–50.

357   conservative words burned: EMK, *True Compass*, 408–9.

357 **"because he was a handsome"**: John A. Farrell int., July 13, 2006, Miller Center, UVA.

357 **"My friends are going"**: Ralph Neas int. by author.

358 **"neo-nihilists"**: EMK, "Reconsidering Social Welfare Policy: Introduction," *Yale Law and Policy Review* 4, no. 1 (1985): 4.

358 **"Reagan believed in getting"**: Gil Troy, *Morning in America: How Reagan Invented the 1980s* (Princeton: Princeton Univ. Press, 2005), 8.

358 **"Lower taxes along with"**: Stanley Greenberg, *The Two Americas: Our Current Political Deadlock and How to Break It* (New York: St. Martin's Griffin, 2005), 56.

358 **"A tax cut not only increases"**: Jude Wanniski quoted in Spitz, *Reagan*, 487.

358 **"God's way of blessing people"**: Perlstein, *Reaganland*, 469.

359 **introduced his own tax plan**: "Alternative Tax Plan to Help the Needy Offered by Kennedy," *WP*, Mar. 8, 1981.

359 **no surplus but instead a deficit**: Wilentz, *Age of Reagan*, 144; Troy, *Morning*, 70.

359 **planted a kiss on his forehead**: Spitz, *Reagan*, 514.

359 **Reagan's polling skyrocketed**: Ibid., 515.

359 **"When everybody else"**: Quoted in Burton Hersh, *The Shadow President: Ted Kennedy in Opposition* (South Royalton, Vt.: Steerforth Press, 1997), 55.

359 **"Scorched-earth economics"**: EMK, *True Compass*, 385; Clymer, *Kennedy*, 329.

359 **"Now is not the time"**: "Kennedy Criticizes GOP for 'Backward' Priorities," *LAT*, June 9, 1981.

360 **"envisions the elimination"**: "Senate, 78–20, Votes $700 Billion Budget," *NYT*, May 13, 1981.

360 **commandeered the floor**: "Ted Kennedy Persists," *WP*, Apr. 8, 1981.

360 **"Anti-health, anti-education"**: Ibid.

360 **"politically unwise"**: Shrum, *No Excuses*, 132–33.

361 **"Don't give me an essay"**: "Reagan in Speech, Asks Tax Cut Help," *NYT*, July 28, 1981.

361 **"great day for the aristocracy"**: *LAT*, July 30, 1981.

362 **"We are asking schoolchildren"**: "Senate Spurns Kennedy Pleas," *LAT*, Aug. 4, 1981; "Senate Approves Tax Cut Bill, 67–8," *NYT*, Aug. 4, 1981.

362 **"many colleagues whom"**: EMK, *True Compass*, 384.

362 **"completion of the basic"**: Thomas B. Edsall, "Conferees Agree on $750 Billion Tax Cut Package," *WP*, Aug. 2, 1981.

362 **"tree ripe with the richest"**: "Why Isn't It Kennedyism?" *WP*, Aug. 14, 1981.

362 **"You're standing up"**: Rollins int., May 14, 2009.

363 **"Work it out"**: Quoted in Hersh, *Shadow President*, 239.

363 **things happened incrementally**: Melody Miller int., Oct. 7, 2008, Miller Center, UVA.

363 **"technical work"**: Quoted in Hersh, *Shadow President*, 59.

363 **"wading against the tide"**: Ibid., 58–59.

363 **White House bill signing**: Carey Parker int., Oct. 20, 2008.

363 **"You know, it would be"**: Horowitz int.

363 **use of baby formula**: "Furor Over Baby Formulas," *NYT*, May 24, 1981; "Senate Asks Administration to Back Baby Formula Code," *NYT*, June 19, 1981; "Ted Kennedy's Public Forums," *Newsweek*, June 1, 1981.

364 **"Nothing gave him more"**: Horowitz int.

365 **"paralyzed"**: EMK int., Aug. 7, 2007.

366 **expected more than fifty**: EMK int., Nov. 11, 1998, Box 5, Series 2, EMK interviews, 1997–99, Clymer Papers, JFK Lib.

366 **most effective means of securing**: "President Seeks Assessment of Voting Rights Act," *NYT*, June 16, 1981.

366 **opt out of the preclearance strictures**: "Reagan Backs Modified Plan," *NYT*, Nov. 13, 1981.

367 **"didn't have a discriminatory"**: "Senate Panel is Told Reagan Supports Voting Rights Act," *NYT*, Jan. 28, 1982.

369 **"taxing power of the Government"**: "U.S. Drops Rule on Tax Penalty," *NYT*, Jan. 9, 1982.

369 **"I don't think any Republican"**: "President Backs Bipartisan Plan on Voting Law," *NYT*, May 4, 1982.

369 **"little sticker"**: EMK int., Aug. 7, 2007.

370 **"totality of circumstances"**: James Forman, "Victory by Surrender: The Voting Rights Amendment of 1982 and the Civil Rights Act of 1991," *Yale Law and Policy Review* (1992): 133–50; "Compromise Likely on Voting Rights," *NYT*, May 1, 1982.

370 **"The House had really"**: EMK int., Aug. 7, 2007.

370–71 **"If that battle had not":** Neas int.

372 **"EMK's vision of the nation":** Theodore Sorensen, "Kennedy New Leadership for the '80s," n.d. [1979], Box 118, Edward Kennedy, Series 19, Democratic Party, Theodore C. Sorensen Personal Papers, JFK Lib.

373 **"Enough is enough":** "Randall Forsberg: Fought Against Nuclear Arms," *BG*, Oct. 21, 2007; "Randall Forsberg," *People*, Dec. 27, 1982.

373 **159 voted to support a freeze:** "A Vote for Nuclear Freeze," *Newsweek*, Mar. 15, 1982; "Heated Support for a Nuclear Freeze," *WP*, Mar. 21, 1982.

373 **"It's sort of doubling":** William Schneider, "Politicians Who Read the Polls Know the Nuclear Freeze Is a Hot Issue," *LAT*, Apr. 18, 1982.

373 **"magnificent and would think":** Quoted in Theo Lippman, *Senator Ted Kennedy: The Career Behind the Image* (New York: Norton, 1976), 183–84.

374 **moratorium on nuclear weapons:** Ibid., 180–81.

374 **rogue foreign policy:** EMK int., Mar. 27, 1998.

374 **"Why can't we have":** E. J. Kahn III, "The Making of the Remaking of Edward M. Kennedy," *Boston*, Aug. 28, 2009.

374 **"hottest new issue":** David Broder, "A Deadly Dilemma," *Time*, Apr. 12, 1982.

375 **"because Hatfield and Kennedy":** EMK int., June 5, 2005, Miller Center, UVA.

375 **sold 200,000 copies by June:** Shrum, *No Excuses*, 135–36.

375 **"The freeze has really energized":** "Kennedy in Vanguard on Nuclear Freeze," *LAT*, May 5, 1982.

375 **freeze didn't go far enough:** "Reagan Proposes a Nuclear Freeze," *LAT*, Apr. 1, 1982.

375 **"No one in authority":** " 'Voodoo Arms Control' Assailed by Kennedy," *WP*, Apr. 2, 1982.

376 **KGB-inspired plot:** "Magazine Articles Cited in KGB-Freeze Link," *WP*, Nov. 13, 1982.

376 **"More families are more desperate now":** *LAT*, Apr. 3, 1982.

376 **had to adjust his tax cuts:** Wilentz, *Age of Reagan*, 146–47.

377 **"The dawn is near":** "Democrats End Meeting Unified," *LAT*, June 28, 1982; "Basking in Reagan's Troubles," *Time*, July 12, 1982.

377 **"opportunity to make some":** "Ted Kennedy Reflects on His Life, His Family and His Political Future," *People*, Mar. 1, 1982.

377 **"After nearly 20 years of landslides":** Mark Shields, "A Hopeless and Perhaps Permanent Infatuation," *WP*, Aug. 28, 1981.

378 **"has been criticized for many":** "Kennedy Airing His Trials to Test the Waters for Compassion," *WP*, Sept. 26, 1982; EMK, *True Compass*, 395.

378 **"red-faced and shaking":** "Irate, Shaking Kennedy Confronts Editor," *LAT*, Oct. 28, 1982.

378 **"There is no corner":** David Broder, "Final Round," *WP*, Oct. 31, 1982.

378 **"one-year phenomenon":** Quoted in Wilentz, *Age of Reagan*, 7.

379 **"When you can put out as much":** Melody Miller int., July 15, 2008, Miller Center, UVA.

379 **"brutalizing experience":** Horowitz int.

379 **"looking down the line":** Carrick quoted in Canellos, *Last Lion*, 244.

380 **contingent on his family's approval:** Horowitz int.

380 **"gracious":** Martin Schram, "Running for Office in Massachusetts, Kennedy Stumps the Whole Country," *WP*, Oct. 26, 1982.

380 **"He was very definitely":** Quoted in Canellos, *Last Lion*, 244.

380 **"calmer speaking style":** David Broder, "Ted Kennedy Back in Business," *WP*, Apr. 26, 1982.

380 **"massive study":** Martin Schram, "At Summit, Younger Kennedys Prevailed over Political Pros," *WP*, Dec. 2, 1982.

380 **interview with Roger Mudd:** Canellos, *Last Lion*, 245.

381 **"could be the biggest breakthrough":** Martin Schram, "Kennedy Poll Finds New Hampshire Ads Effective," *WP*, Nov. 8, 1982.

381 **"I mean genuinely no doubt":** Horowitz int.

381 **leading Mondale two to one:** "Kennedy Tops Mondale," *WP*, July 18, 1982; Shrum, *No Excuses*, 136.

381 **"process of restoration":** Horowitz int.

381 **told Carrick the same:** Carrick int.

381 **"in a box":** Tip O'Neill with William Novak, *Man of the House: The Life and Political Memoirs of Speaker Tip O'Neill* (New York: Random House, 1987), 327.

381 **"Really raring to go":** Milton Gwirtzman int., Aug. 5, 2009, Miller Center, UVA.

382 **"puzzled Ted":** Horowitz int.

382 Reagan was no Herbert Hoover: Carrick int.

382 Ted took it out: Shrum, *No Excuses*, 136–37.

382 "You know how I knew": Pat Caddell int., Box 3, Series 2, C Folder, JFK Lib., Jan. 1, 1998.

382 "month-by-month battle": "Teddy Makes a Father's Decision," *Newsweek*, Dec. 13, 1982; "A Strategist Aids Kennedy Once More," *BG*, June 2, 2008; Thomas Oliphant, "Behind Kennedy's Decision Not to Run," *BG*, Dec. 5, 1982.

383 "adamant": Gwirtzman int., Aug. 5, 2009.

383 "all sort of teary-eyed": EMK int., Oct. 14, 2005, Miller Center, UVA.

383 children over Thanksgiving: EMK, *True Compass*, 400–3.

383 "more than a few severely": Horowitz int.

383 Caddell made a presentation: Schram, "Younger Kennedys Prevailed."

383 "devil's advocate": Patrick Kennedy int.; Horowitz int.

384 Ted pressed Horowitz about: Steve Smith, Jr., int., Sept. 16, 1992, S Folder, Box 5, Series 2, Clymer Papers, JFK Lib.

384 "Well, Teddy, we all know": Oliphant, "Behind Kennedy's Decision."

384 "I'm not most concerned": Schram, "Younger Kennedys Prevailed."

384 "strong consensus": Oliphant, "Behind Kennedy's Decision."

384 "he basically said to me": Horowitz int.

384 "We just sat down": Oliphant, "Behind Kennedy's Decision."

384 "On one side": Richard Cohen, "Family," *WP*, Dec. 2, 1982.

384 told his children he would not: Oliphant, "Behind Kennedy's Decision."

384 "You should have seen Patrick": "There Won't Be Any Regrets," *Newsweek*, Dec. 13, 1982.

384 "It wasn't on the level": Patrick Kennedy int.; Patrick Kennedy and Stephen Fried, *A Common Struggle: A Personal Journey Through the Past and Future of Mental Illness and Addiction* (New York: Blue Rider Press, 2015), 67.

385 "My children and I have": O'Neill and Novak, *Man of the House*, 327.

385 "I want to hear again": "Teddy Makes a Father's Decision," *Newsweek*, Dec. 13, 1982.

385 "small and comparatively humble": "Not a Launching but a Scuttling," *NYT*, Dec. 13, 1982.

385 phoning some of his closest: Oliphant, "Behind Kennedy's Decision."

385 "very specific conversation": John Tunney int., Mar. 6, 1995, T folder, Box 5, Series 2, Clymer Papers, JFK Lib.

386 "He's easy with himself": Joseph Kraft, "Kennedy's Withdrawal: A Service to His Party," *WP*, Dec. 2, 1982.

386 "I really felt this": EMK, *True Compass*, 400–3.

386 "very, very longshot": Horowitz int.

386 "Maybe the secret": Ellen Goodman, "He May Not Want to Be President," *WP*, Dec. 4, 1982.

386 "I could clearly detect": EMK, *True Compass*, 403.

TEN: "THE POWERFUL APPEAL OF OUR MOST DECENT VALUES"

387 "So quickly?": Gioia Diliberto, "After 24 Years, Joan Kennedy Ends Her Marriage," *People*, Dec. 30, 1982; "Kennedy Divorce Hearing Produces 'Fair' Settlement," *Sumter Daily Item*, Dec. 7, 1982.

387 "I think his career": Carey Parker int., Sept. 22, 2008, Miller Center, UVA.

388 "He found a form": Jack Newfield, "The Senate's Fighting Liberal," *Nation*, Mar. 25, 2002.

388 "When the Republicans": Thomas Oliphant, "Kennedy Urges Middle Line," *BG*, Mar. 30, 1985.

388 "enormous vacuum": Eileen McNamara, "Kennedy the Floor Fighter," *BG*, Apr. 6, 1984.

388 Trade unions had been: Paul Krugman, *The Conscience of a Liberal* (New York: Norton, 2007), 51.

389 Fifty-seven percent: Bob Spitz, *Reagan: An American Journey* (New York: Penguin Press, 2018), 521–22, 525–26.

389 "more government programs": Bill Bradley, *Time Present, Time Past: A Memoir* (New York: Knopf, 1996), 48–49.

390 "Ted has done much": Kenneth Auchincloss, "Family Ties That Bind," *Newsweek*, Dec. 13, 1982.

391 hovered in the low forties: "Ronald Reagan from the People's Perspective: A Gallup Poll Review," June 7, 2004. https://news.gallup.com/poll/11887/ronald-reagan-from-peoples-perspective -gallup-poll-review.aspx

391 tie the hands of his arms: "Meeting Forced on Nuclear Freeze," *WP*, July 28, 1983; "Senate Rejects Demand for Immediate Nuclear Freeze," *LAT*, Nov. 1, 1983.

391 "Ronald Reagan, who was": Jan Kalicki int., Mar. 18, 2009, Miller Center, UVA.

392 "The only way we have seen": "Ted Kennedy Cites Lasting Legacy of the New Frontier," *LAT*, Nov. 21, 1983.

392 "he rejected the cold": "Text of Memorial Tribute," *NYT*, Nov. 23, 1983.

392 departed to Hyannis: "Family, Friends Pay Tribute to Kennedy at Mass," *WP*, Nov. 23, 1983.

392 "Did many of us much notice": Murray Kempton, "The Kennedy Brothers," *New York Review of Books*, Jan. 19, 1984.

393 "Orwellian doublespeak": "Kennedy Proposes Aid for Hungry," *WP*, Dec. 23, 1983; "Reagan Task Force Finds No Evidence of Great Hunger," *WP*, Jan. 10, 1984.

393 "There's been a wave": Rick Perlstein, *The Invisible Bridge: The Fall of Nixon and the Rise of Reagan* (New York: Simon & Schuster, 2014), 705–6.

393 "Wherever possible": Theodore Lowi, *The End of the Republican Era* (Norman: Univ. of Oklahoma Press, 1995), 160.

393 new relationship with god: Richard Harley, "The Evangelical Vote and the Presidency," *CSM*, June 25, 1980.

394 "born again" Christians: Steve Gillon, "Reagan Tied Republicans to White Christians and Now the Party Is Trapped," *WP*, Mar. 22, 2021.

394 57 percent of evangelicals: "Carter Found the Clear Favorite Among Evangelicals," *WP*, Sept. 7, 1980.

394 denounce gay marriage: Kai Bird, *The Outlier: The Unfinished Presidency of Jimmy Carter* (New York: Crown, 2021), 568.

395 "It's right down the line": Steven Miller, "The Evangelical Presidency: Reagan's Dangerous Love Affair with the Christian Right," *Salon*, May 18, 2014.

395 Reagan won two-thirds: Clyde Haberman, "Religion and Right-Wing Politics: How Evangelicals Reshaped Elections," *NYT*, Oct. 28, 2018.

395 "Since 1860, Catholics have": Mark Shields, "Keeping the Catholics," *WP*, Feb. 19, 1982.

396 "Well, as you know": Bird, 184.

396 78 percent of Americans: Rick Perlstein, *Reaganland: America's Right Turn 1976–1980* (New York: Simon & Schuster, 2021), 796; https://news.gallup.com/poll/1576/abortion.aspx

396 he hoped to lure from: Perlstein, *Invisible Bridge*, 445–46.

396 "The heart of the": E. J. Dionne, Jr., "There is No Catholic Vote, And Yet it Matters," Brookings Institution, June 18, 2000, https://www.brookings.edu/opinions/there-is-no-catholic-vote-and-yet-it-matters/

397 bought eighty-eight copies: "Fairfax Library Stocks Up on Kennedy 'Biography'" *WP*, March 8, 1980; "Anti-Kennedy Book Stirs Protest in Maryland," *Library Journal*, Apr. 15, 1980.

397 "it's kind of an unwritten law": Richard Clasby int., Oct. 11, 2005, Miller Center, UVA.

397 pressured John Tunney: Thomas Morgan, "Teddy," *Esquire*, Apr. 1962.

397 practiced his religion: Doris Reggie int., Aug. 8, 2005, Miller Center, UVA.

397 "That seems to be": Abigail McCarthy, *Private Faces, Public Places* (Garden City, N.Y.: Doubleday, 1972), 242.

397 invited a priest: Melissa Leudtke int. by author.

397 "The teachings become": EMK int., Aug. 15, 2006, Miller Center, UVA.

398 "life of service": EMK int., June 3, 2005, Miller Center, UVA.

398 "most influential opponent": Philip Lawler, "The Lion as Catholic," *American Spectator*, Feb. 2010.

398 refused to baptize the fetuses: Edmund Reggie int., Dec. 16, 2008, Miller Center, UVA.

398 made a point of gathering: Melody Miller int., Aug. 16, 2006, Miller Center, UVA.

398 "turn it into a source": Laurence Tribe int., Apr. 27, 2009, Miller Center, UVA.

399 The amendment failed: Theo Lippman, *Senator Ted Kennedy: The Career Behind the Image* (New York: Norton, 1976), 231.

399 "The next thing I knew": Stan Jones int., Sept. 14, 2007, Miller Center, UVA.

399 "ultraliberals such as": EMK, *True Compass* (New York: Twelve, 2009), 396–98.

400 "white as a sheet": "Remembering Ted Kennedy," *National Journal*, Sept. 5, 2009; Phil Gailey, "Kennedy Tells Falwell Group of Tolerance," *NYT*, Oct. 4, 1983.

400 "in the minds of many": Gailey, "Kennedy Tells Falwell Group"; "Kennedy Lectures Falwell," *LAT*, Oct. 4, 1983.

401 "It was very difficult": EMK int., Aug. 7, 2007, Miller Center, UVA.

401 **"Although there is no"**: Jeane Kirkpatrick, "Dictatorships and Double Standards," *Commentary*, Nov. 1979, 34–45.

401 **"America has never gotten"**: Andrew Busch, *Reagan's Victory: The Presidential Election of 1980 and the Rise of the Right* (Lawrence: Univ. Press of Kansas, 2005), 116.

402 **"Our days of weakness"**: Joan Didion, *Political Fictions* (New York: Knopf, 2001), 101.

402 **two truck bombs detonated**: Spitz, *Reagan*, 562–63.

402 **Ted introduced legislation**: "Kennedy Bill Would Halt Military Aid to El Salvador," *WP*, Mar. 7, 1981.

403 **"our Founding Fathers"**: Spitz, *Reagan*, 548. See also Cynthia Arnson, *Crossroads: Congress, the Reagan Administration, and Central America* (New York: Pantheon, 1989) for a detailed account of Reagan's policies and of Congress's concessions.

403 **"implicitly"**: "The Kissinger Report Could Sharpen Latin Policy Dispute," *NYT*, Jan. 15, 1984; Arnson, *Crossroads*, 139–40.

404 **he was fully engaged**: Gregory Craig int., July 13, 2010, Miller Center, UVA.

404 **"forces of reaction"**: Adam Clymer, *Edward M. Kennedy: A Biography* (New York: Harper Perennial, 2000), 355–56.

404 **"morally right thing"**: "Reagan Endorses Proposal for Aid to Latin America," *NYT*, Jan. 15, 1984.

404 **"The United States does not seek"**: Clymer, *Kennedy*, 357.

404 **Reagan would later admit**: Arnson, *Crossroads*, 158.

404 **wasn't a single other senator**: Craig int.

405 **"littered with notes"**: Eileen McNamara, "Kennedy the Floor Fighter," *BG*, Apr. 6, 1984.

405 **"In my twenty-two years"**: "Senate OKs Arms Aid to El Salvador," *LAT*, Apr. 6, 1984.

406 **"You know, we went"**: Greg Craig int., July 13, 2010, Miller Center, UVA.

406 **"A first step"**: "Rebuke to Reagan," *NYT*, Apr. 11, 1984.

406 **"hideous embarrassment"**: Mary McGrory, "Kennedy Gave President a Dose of Bipartisan Foreign Policy," *WP*, Apr. 12, 1984.

407 **"This is all brand new"**: Craig int.

407 **unemployment rate 7.5 percent**: Sean Wilentz, *The Age of Reagan: A History 1974–2008* (New York: HarperCollins, 2008), 170–71.

408 **fired up the economy**: Gil Troy, *Morning in America: How Ronald Reagan Invented the 1980s* (Princeton: Princeton Univ. Press, 2005), 210–11.

408 **"If we allow any Democrat"**: Ibid., 148.

408 **"I don't think he said"**: Walter Mondale int., Mar. 20, 2006, Miller Center, UVA.

408 **"essential"**: Larry Horowitz int., May 29, 1992, H folder, Box 3, Series 2, Clymer Papers, JFK Lib.; Thomas Oliphant, "Hart Drops Delegate Fight," *BG*, June 26, 1984.

409 **"Boy, this Ted Kennedy"**: Oliphant, "Hart Drops Fight."

409 **"Tell that to Tom"**: David Nexon to EMK, memo, July 11, 1986, Kennedy-Stark, Box 1, 98th Cong., Legislative Files of Dr. Stephen Keith, Senate Labor and Human Resources, Senate Records, National Archives.

409 **"shake up the race"**: Horowitz int.

409 **"jarring the rafters"**: "Once Again, a Kennedy Rouses the Democrats," *WP*, July 20, 1984.

409 **"disposal"**: "Teddy Hits the Road for Mondale," *Newsweek*, Sept. 17, 1984.

409 **"Ronald Reagan, he's no good"**: " 'City Is Yours,' Kennedy Assures Ferraro in Boston," *LAT*, Sept. 27, 1984.

409 **"forever harping"**: Ronald Reagan, *An American Life* (New York: Simon & Schuster, 1990), 329.

410 **"conglomeration of blocs"**: Ibid., 325.

410 **"race, religion, and negation"**: Lowi, *End of Republican Era*, 196.

410 **"You ain't seen nothing"**: "Reagan Wins by Landslide," *NYT*, Nov. 7, 1984.

410 **He had a tremor**: EMK int., Feb. 1992, EMK Interviews 1992–94 Folder, Box 5, Series 2, Clymer Papers, JFK Lib.

410 **hospitalized early in 1984 for an ulcer**: "Kennedy Hospitalized," *LAT*, Jan. 3, 1984.

410 **"no clear agenda about"**: Thomas Rollins int., Mar. 10, 2009, Miller Center, UVA.

411 **Ted supported Byrd**: Craig int.

411 **"blame the voters"**: "Kennedy Urges Party to Reappraise Policies," *LAT*, Mar. 30, 1985; Thomas Oliphant, "Kennedy Urges Middle Line," *BG*, Mar. 30, 1985; Dan Balz, "Kennedy Challenges Party to Change," *WP*, Mar. 30, 1985.

412 **"There is nothing subtle"**: David Broder, "Ted Kennedy: Shifting Ground," *WP*, June 26, 1985.

413 **"it was something of a symbol"**: Horowitz int.; "Reagan Treasures a Symbol of Camelot," *Newsweek*, July 29, 1985.

413 **"The whole family was most"**: Ronald Reagan, *The Reagan Diaries*, ed. Douglas Brinkley (New York: HarperCollins, 2007), 338.

414 **"Congress has too much power"**: *Congressional Record*, Senate, 99th Cong., 1st sess., July 23, 1985, S19946–48.

414 **responsibility for hurting vulnerable**: Robert Kuttner, "Failing to Give Kennedy the Credit," *BG*, July 26, 1985.

414 **"act of legislative desperation"**: "Bill to End Budget Deficits Voted by House and Senate," *NYT*, Dec. 12, 1985.

414 **"balanced-budget sham"**: David Broder, "The Rudman-Gramm Balanced Budget Sham," *WP*, Dec. 11, 1985.

415 **"balanced baloney"**: "The Balanced Baloney Act of 1985," *NYT*, Oct. 4, 1985.

415 **"We have an elemental"**: *Congressional Record*, Senate, 99th Cong., 1st sess., Dec. 11, 1985, S35870.

415 **"Let him explain it"**: "Three Senators: Gramm, Rudman Hollings and the Budget Revolution They Wrought," *WP*, Jan. 22, 1986.

415 **"We are all crying"**: "Senate Adopts Plan to End Deficits," *WP*, Oct. 10, 1985.

416 **"evolving understanding"**: "Fiscal Credibility Vital for Party," *BG*, Oct. 11, 1985.

416 **"blunt weapon"**: "Face-Off" Gramm-Rudman-Hollings Law and Deficit (sound), Aug. 14, 1989, JFK Lib., https://www.jfklibrary.org/asset-viewer/archives/EMKSEN/AU0008/EMKSEN -AU0008-006/EMKSEN-AU0008-006-006/EMKSEN-AU0008-006-006.

417 **"only way to protect important"**: *Congressional Record*, Senate, 99th Cong., 1st sess., Dec. 11, 1985, S35906.

417 **"He operates"**: Martin Tolchin, "Watching Kennedy Not Run for President," *NYT*, March 27, 1986.

417 **"Senator, we're asking you"**: "Kennedy Visits Farm Community to Learn About Hunger," AP, Dec. 21, 1985.

418 **"throwback to a shameful"**: "Race Issues Key to Judicial Nominee," *NYT*, Mar. 14, 1986; *Hearings Before the Committee on Judiciary, U.S. Senate, Nomination of Jefferson B. Sessions III to Be Federal District Judge*, 99th Cong., 2nd sess., Mar. 13, 1986, 2–3.

418 **"appalling surrender"**: "Panel Hands Reagan First Defeat on Nominee for Judgeship," *NYT*, June 6, 1986.

418 **"Most of these countries"**: Nancy Soderberg int., July 13, 2010, Miller Center, UVA.

419 **"scream"**: Lawrence Haas, *The Kennedys in the World: How Jack, Bobby, and Ted Remade America's Empire* (Sterling, Va.: Potomac Books, 2021), 219.

419 **"human rights"**: "Protest Hinders Kennedy in Chile," *NYT*, Jan. 16, 1986.

419 **photographs of their children**: Clymer, *Kennedy*, 388.

419 **"You have spoken out"**: Ibid., 389.

420 **"hesitantly"**: Ibid.; Mark Schneider int., Feb. 2, 2009, Miller Center, UVA.

420 **"rave reviews"**: "Sen. Kennedy Steals Quayle's Thunder," *BG*, Mar. 14, 1990.

420 **Another bill sponsored**: Tolchin, "Watching Kennedy"; "11 Democrats, 42 Republicans Join to Give Victory to Reagan," *WP*, Mar. 28, 1986.

421 **"Kidnapped"**: Craig int.

421 **"Each time a man stands up"**: Robert F. Kennedy, Day of Affirmation Address, University of Cape Town, South Africa, June 6, 1966, https://www.jfklibrary.org/learn/about-jfk/the-kennedy -family/robert-f-kennedy/robert-f-kennedy-speeches/day-of-affirmation-address-university-of -capetown-capetown-south-africa-june-6-1966

422 **"significant moral gesture"**: EMK, "Washington Letter," *Africa Today*, Apr./May 1969.

422 **"very strong speech"**: EMK int., Aug. 7, 2007; Craig int.

423 **"disturb the particles"**: EMK int., Sept. 10, 1992, EMK Interviews 1992–94 Folder, Box 5, Series 2, Clymer Papers, JFK Lib.

423 **he would be in Oslo**: Craig int.; EMK int., Mar. 26, 1999, EMK Interviews 1997–99 Folder, Box 5, Series 2, Clymer Papers, JFK Lib.

423 **"foremost spokesman"**: "Feuding Blacks Greet Kennedy in South Africa," *LAT*, Jan. 6, 1985.

424 **"I give you the assurance"**: EMK int., Jan. 7, 2008, Miller Center, UVA; Craig int.; "S. Africans Jeer, Cheer Sen. Kennedy," *WP*, Jan. 6, 1985.

424 **"We want you to visit"**: "S. Africans Jeer, Cheer Sen. Kennedy."

424 **"One of the most distressing":** "Kennedy Visits Soweto, Is Told of Bleak Lives," *LAT*, Jan. 7, 1985.

424 **"Please, madam":** "Kennedy is Moved, Shocked by Soweto," *BG*, Jan. 7, 1985.

424 **"I have shaken the hand":** "Kennedy Describes 'Despairing' Visit in Soweto," *WP*, Jan. 7, 1985.

424 **"whirlwind tour":** Robert Shrum, *No Excuses: Concessions of a Serial Campaigner* (New York: Simon & Schuster, 2007), 151.

424 **"very tense meeting":** "Kennedy Urges S. African Reform," *LAT*, Jan. 8, 1985.

425 **Ted refused the offer:** Craig int.

425 **"How can you bring up children":** EMK int., Aug. 7, 2007.

425 **"If they jail me":** "Kennedy Visits Test S. Africa," *WP*, Jan. 10, 1985.

426 **government actually flew:** EMK int., Aug. 7, 2007.

426 **"this enormously interesting":** Ibid.

427 **equate capitalism with repression:** "Kennedy Cancels S. African Rally After Protest," *WP*, Jan. 14, 1985; Craig int.; EMK int., Jan. 7, 2008.

427 **"arrogant talent to outrage":** "Kennedy Trip Leaves Foes of Apartheid in Disarray," *LAT*, Jan. 16, 1985.

427 **"chortling":** Richard Cohen, "Chortling Over Kennedy's Trip," *WP*, Jan. 16, 1985.

427 **"supercharged":** EMK int., Jan. 7, 2008.

427 **"South Africa is eventually":** "Kennedy Vows to Push Vote on S. Africa," *WP*, Feb. 7, 1985; EMK int., Mar. 26, 1999.

428 **faced with finding a way:** EMK int., Mar. 26, 1999.

429 **"Sullivan Principles":** "Apartheid Opponents Launch Fresh Campaign," *WP*, May 15, 1985.

429 **Tutu called him a racist:** "Tutu Denounces Reagan as Racist," *NYT*, Aug. 18, 1985.

429 **"We are going to pass this bill":** "Reagan and Aides Review Policy on South Africa," *NYT*, Sept. 6, 1985.

430 **"America's view of apartheid":** "Reagan in Reversal Orders Sanctions on South Africa," *NYT*, Sept. 10, 1985; Spitz, *Reagan*, 611.

430 **"Too little, too late":** Tom Wicker, "Saving Reagan from Reagan," *NYT*, Sept. 13, 1985.

430 **"I don't care when":** "Senate Fails to Halt Sanctions Filibuster," *WP*, Sept. 12, 1985.

430 **lost by seven votes:** Clymer, *Kennedy*, 377–79.

430 **physically taking the bill:** Richard Lugar int., Mar. 6, 2009, Miller Center, UVA.

430 **"least well-kept secret":** "Kennedy Tells of '88 Ambitions," *LAT*, Apr. 1, 1985.

430 **scheduling speeches for the period:** "Burden of Kennedy Family Heritage Weighed Too Heavily on Senator," *WP*, Dec. 21, 1985; "Kennedy Sets Foot on '88 Trail," *BG*, Nov. 10, 1985.

431 **"softened up a little":** "Ted's Back in Shape," *BG*, Aug. 18, 1985.

431 **"save both his party":** "Kennedy Builds a Record, and He Is Going to Run," *LAT*, Sept. 19, 1985.

431 **"I thought there was":** "The Kennedy Prescription," *WP Health*, Apr. 21, 1987.

431 **"It bothered him that":** Parker int.

431 **"crescendo of my own thinking":** EMK int., Sept. 10, 1992.

431 **"He asked me where":** Thomas Oliphant, "Few Knew of Kennedy's Decision," *BG*, Dec. 20, 1985.

432 **by the end of that Thanksgiving:** EMK int., Mar. 26, 1999; Thomas Oliphant, "Kennedy Says Politics Played No Role in Decision Not to Run," *BG*, Dec. 22, 1985.

432 **"if we could demonstrate":** Phil Gailey, "Kennedy Reportedly Bowed Out Because He Foresaw '88 Defeat," *NYT*, Dec. 21, 1985.

432 **"Well, I realize this means":** Paul Taylor, "Burden of Kennedy Family Heritage Weighed Too Heavily on Senator," *WP*, Dec. 21, 1985.

432 **he and Horowitz wrote it:** Oliphant, "Few Knew"; Shrum, *No Excuses*, 151–52.

432 **"He was almost apoplectic":** Horowitz int.

433 **"I have decided that":** "Kennedy Announces He Will Not Enter '88 Race," *BG*, Dec. 20, 1985.

433 **"Well, here I don't go":** "A Dream Deferred," *Newsweek*, Dec. 30, 1985; "I Know I May Never Be President," *Time*, Dec. 30, 1985.

433 **intended to get married:** Taylor, "Burden of Family Heritage."

433 **"drifts between cycles":** Oliphant, "Kennedy Says Politics Played No Role."

433 **"He's perceived as a candidate":** "The Campaigns of Edward Kennedy," *BG*, Nov. 24, 1985.

434 **"embodiment of all that the rightwing":** Ibid.

434 **thought he could win the nomination:** Gailey, "Kennedy Reportedly Bowed Out."

434 **"that we are really three":** "Kennedy Sets Foot on '88 Trail."

434 **"My sense of him is":** Quoted in Peter Canellos, *Last Lion: The Fall and Rise of Ted Kennedy* (New York: Simon & Schuster, 2009), 247.

434 **"I haven't regretted it":** Tolchin, "Watching Kennedy."

435 **"He knew very clearly":** Horowitz int.

435 **"When you're a presidential":** Burton Hersh, *The Shadow President: Ted Kennedy in Opposition* (South Royalton, Vt.: Steerforth Press, 1997), 64.

435 **"reluctant grandee":** Lippman, *Senator,* 275–76.

435 **"He operates as a national senator":** Tolchin, "Watching Kennedy."

435 **"Ted Kennedy was in Albright":** "Ted Kennedy on Holiday," *LAT,* Dec. 24, 1985.

435 **"Frankly, I don't mind":** Tolchin, "Watching Kennedy."

436 **"much happier person":** "One Year After Decision on '88, Kennedy Can Count Accomplishments," *BG,* Dec. 25, 1986.

436 **"I love the Senate":** Elsa Walsh, "Kennedy's Hidden Campaign," *New Yorker,* Mar. 31, 1997.

436 **"I've been around politics":** Sidney Blumenthal, "Ted Kennedy: No Regrets as the Torch Is Passed," *WP,* July 18, 1988.

436 **"I don't think he didn't":** Horowitz int.

436 **"he need not be president":** Theodore Sorensen, *Counselor: Life at the Edge of History* (New York: HarperCollins, 2008), 258.

436 **"You look back and see":** Lippman, *Senator,* 274.

436 **"For Ted, How I wish that it":** Walsh, "Hidden Campaign."

437 **"After more than 18 months":** Anthony Lewis, "Perceiving South Africa," *NYT,* June 16, 1986.

437 **It passed unopposed:** "The Squeeze on Pretoria Gets Tighter," *Newsweek,* June 30, 1986.

437 **issue should be left:** "Key Senator Cool to Strict Sanctions on South Africa," *NYT,* June 16, 1986.

437 **"It's hard to think":** "Transcript," *NYT,* July 24, 1986.

438 **"The West, for my part":** "Falling Short," *Time,* Aug. 4, 1986.

438 **"not adopted as her ruling":** Patrick Buchanan, "Destroy South Africa to Save It?" *NYT,* Sept. 18, 1986.

438 **"Are the women of America":** "South Africa Playing for Time," *Time,* July 28, 1986.

438 **"disgrace and an embarrassment":** Ibid.

438 **warned of a bloodbath:** "Reagan Faces Sanctions Battle with Congress," *LAT,* July 23, 1986.

438 **"If Not Now, When?":** *Time,* Aug. 4, 1986.

438 **"Mr. Botha":** "How America Stands on South Africa," *NYT,* Aug. 15, 1986.

439 **"Before we get his halo":** "Senate Votes Strict Sanctions on South Africa," *NYT,* Aug. 2, 1986.

439 **this time he won passage:** "Senate Approves Sanctions, 844," *LAT,* Aug. 16, 1986.

439 **"Had it been any other senator":** Craig int.

440 **"it wasn't going to happen":** EMK int., Jan. 7, 2008.

440 **"impaled on this thing":** "Reagan Faces Sanctions Battle with Congress."

440 **Reagan was unmoved:** Lugar int.

440 **wrote a letter to Bob Dole:** "Senate Overrides Reagan's Veto," *NYT,* Oct. 3, 1986.

440 **"a day late and a dollar short":** "House Affirms Sanctions, 313–83, on South Africa," *NYT,* Sept. 30, 1986.

441 **"one of those moments":** "Senate Rebuffs Reagan," *BG,* Oct. 3, 1986.

441 **halted the congratulations:** "Topic A," *WP,* Aug. 27, 2009.

441 **"You were decisive":** Lugar int.

441 **"grinding away at this thing":** Lowell Weicker int., June 19, 2009, Miller Center, UVA.

ELEVEN: A NEW MAN

442 **"You can't be a national candidate":** Thomas Oliphant, "Kennedy Says Politics Played No Role in Decision Not to Run," *BG,* Dec. 22, 1985.

443 *Murder in the Air:* Sanford Lakoff and Herbert York, *A Shield in Space?: Technology, Politics and the Strategic Defense Initiative* (Berkeley: Univ. of Calf. Press, 1989), 7.

443 **"It kind of amuses me":** Ibid., 6–7.

443 **"Star Wars":** Bob Spitz, *Reagan: An American Journey* (New York: Penguin Press, 2018), 544–46.

444 **might be some accommodation:** EMK int., Mar. 27, 1998, EMK interviews, 1997–99, Box 5, Series 2, Clymer Papers, JFK Lib.

444 **dinner honoring Shultz:** Carey Parker int., Oct. 20, 2008, Miller Center, UVA.

444 **"considered these matters":** Jack Matlack, Jr., *Reagan and Gorbachev: How the Cold War Ended* (New York: Random House, 2004), 94–95.

445 **"There seemed to be"**: Ronald Reagan, *The Reagan Diaries*, ed. Douglas Brinkley (New York: HarperCollins, 2007), 306.

445 **call from the CIA:** Gregory Craig int., July 13, 2010, Miller Center, UVA.

446 **rid the world of nuclear:** See Karen Tumulty, *The Triumph of Nancy Reagan* (New York: Simon & Schuster, 2021), 433–65.

446 **"special relationship":** Max Kampelman, *Entering New Worlds: The Memoirs of a Private Man in Public Life* (New York: HarperCollins, 1991), 350–51.

446 **"no non-president":** Larry Horowitz int., May 29, 1992, H Folder, Box 3, Series 2, Clymer Papers, JFK Lib.

446 **"I believe the negotiations":** Kampelman, *Entering New Worlds*, 350–51.

447 **arms reduction was decoupled:** See Spitz, *Reagan*, 621–29.

447 **"wanted to check in":** Horowitz int.; Reagan, 386.

448 **"It was like setting off":** "Kennedy Says Soviets to Let 19 Refuseniks to Leave," AP, Feb. 8, 1986.

448 **"The indispensable value of science":** "Arms Offer Shift Seen," *WP,* Feb. 7, 1986.

448 **admired the Kennedy family:** Adam Clymer, *Edward M. Kennedy: A Biography* (New York: Harper Perennial, 2000), 392–93.

448 **"bridged":** Michael Gordon, "Kennedy Reports Gain in Soviet Emigration Cases," *NYT,* Feb. 9, 1986.

448 **"Let's keep your guy":** Horowitz int.

448 **"real sense of hope":** "Kremlin Eases 'Star Wars' Stand," *LAT,* Feb. 9, 1986.

449 **"worst mistake of his presidency":** "Kennedy Faults Arms Move," *NYT,* June 3, 1986.

449 **"playing":** Horowitz int.

449 **"Although the Soviets wouldn't":** Parker int., Oct. 20, 2008.

449 **Gorbachev was using Ted:** "Kennedy Says Summit Tied to Arms Pact," *WP,* Feb. 9, 1986; EMK, "The Russians Are Ready to Bargain on Arms Control," *WP,* Feb. 16, 1986.

450 **"The greatest task of our time":** " 'Eternal Optimist' Kennedy Talks to Soviets on TV," *Chicago Tribune,* Feb. 10, 1986.

450 **"was kind of the end":** Rashi Fein int., Mar. 21, 2007, Miller Center, UVA.

450 **"During the testimony":** Martha Bebinger, "Kennedy Remembered as Senate's Hardest-Working Man," WBUR, August 26, 2009.

451 **"For however important questions":** Paul Starr, "Public Health: Then and Now," *American Journal of Public Health* 72, no. 1 (Jan. 1982): 86.

451 **proposed a bill early in 1984:** "Kennedy to Seek Limits on Medical Costs," *LAT,* Feb. 14, 1984.

451 **required an employer mandate:** Bebinger, "Kennedy Remembered."

451 **require employers to continue:** "Bill Would Aid Millions Without Health Coverage," *WP,* July 2, 1986; "Statement of Sen. Edward Kennedy at Hearings on Barriers to Healthcare and Children's Health" (press release), July 16, 1986, EMK Statements, Box 1, 98th Cong., Legislative Files of Dr. Stephen Keith, Senate Labor and Human Resources Committee, Senate Records, National Archives.

452 **"very modest step":** EMK int., Nov. 11, 1998, EMK Interviews 1997–99 Folder, Box 5, Series 2, Clymer Papers, JFK Lib.

452 **"totally eliminated for years":** Bernard Weinraub, "The Reagan Legacy," *NYT Magazine,* June 22, 1986.

454 **"country has a tiny bit":** E. J. Dionne, Jr., "Democrats Rejoice at 55–45," *NYT,* Nov. 6, 1986.

454 **"To conservatives, liberalism":** Russell Baker, "Tell Me No Coattails," *NYT,* Nov. 12, 1986.

454 **"exorcised the war, the riots":** Dionne, "Democrats Rejoice."

454 **"If there was a Reagan Revolution":** Ibid.

454 **"Virtually every successful":** Mark Penn and Douglas Schoen, "Reagan's Revolution Ended?" *NYT,* Nov. 9, 1986.

455 **waiting anxiously to retake:** Martin Tolchin, "Watching Kennedy Not Run for President," *NYT,* Mar. 27, 1989.

455 **"When we took the Senate":** Burton Hersh, *The Shadow President: Ted Kennedy in Opposition* (South Royalton, Vt.: Steerforth Press, 1997), 71.

455 **"Some people have said":** "One Year After Decision on '88, Kennedy Can Count Accomplishments," *BG,* Dec. 25, 1986.

455 **"lit up":** Thomas Rollins int., Apr. 22, 2009, Miller Center, UVA.

456 **"felt that the Labor Committee":** Parker int., Oct. 20, 2008.

456 **"The point I'd like to make":** Rollins int.

456 **"an unusual opportunity"**: Senator Edward Kennedy, statement, Nov. 8, 1986, EMK Statements, 98th Congress, Labor and Human Resources Committee, Senate Records, National Archives; "Kennedy Opts to Head Labor and Human Resources Committee," *WP,* Nov. 9, 1986.

456 **if he got the job:** Ethan Bronner, *Battle for Justice: How the Bork Nomination Shook America* (New York: Union Square Press, 1989), 135.

456 **"cranked out this book":** Thomas Rollins int., Mar. 10, 2009, Miller Center, UVA; Hersh, *Shadow President,* 71.

458 **binder titled "Must Do":** Rollins int., Mar. 10, 2009; Rollins int., Apr. 22, 2009.

458 **"major player":** "New Era for Kennedy and Social Initiatives," *WP,* Jan. 6, 1987; "Kennedy Welfare Plan Stresses Job Training," *WP,* Feb. 4, 1987.

459 **"Biscuits and Muffins":** Myra MacPherson, "Senator Kennedy: Alone with the Legacy," *WP,* June 4, 1978.

459 **"Teddy now has to go":** Rick Atkinson, "Why Ted Kennedy Can't Stand Still," *WP Magazine,* Apr. 29, 1990.

459 **"whole fistful":** Thad Cochran int., Sept. 19, 2006, Miller Center, UVA.

459 **"little extra hot fudge":** Charles Tretter int., Aug. 8, 2005, Miller Center, UVA.

459 **poking his head through:** Max Fine int. by author.

459 **lose weight only to regain it:** EMK to Nancy Korman, May 6, 1985, Corr. 1985, Nancy Korman Papers, JFK Lib.

459 **He lost twenty-five pounds:** "Senator Kennedy Helps Trim Fat on Capitol Hill," *People,* Apr. 13, 1987.

460 **"You can't do that":** Rollins int., Mar. 10, 2009; Melody Miller int., Oct. 7, 2008, Miller Center, UVA.

460 **as deputy administrative assistants:** "Personalities," *WP,* Mar. 19, 1986.

460 **"he was just not up to the task":** Nancy Soderberg int., Oct. 9, 2008, Miller Center, UVA.

460 **"If you're good":** Ibid.

460 **"A snake pit":** Rollins int., Apr. 22, 2009.

461 **"More junior senators":** Nick Littlefield int., May 3, 2008, Miller Center, UVA.

461 **"Then you might have a fight":** Rollins int., Mar. 10, 2009.

461 **"Everybody got a say":** Thomas Susman int., May 23, 2007, Miller Center, UVA.

462 **"He'll drive me nuts":** Michael Myers int., Aug. 28, 2006, Miller Center, UVA.

462 **"*He* was his time manager":** Susman int.

462 **"he really decided":** Paul Kirk, Jr., int., June 20, 2007, Miller Center, UVA.

462 **"My sense is that":** Carey Parker int., Nov. 17, 2008, Miller Center, UVA.

463 **"How many co-sponsors":** Rollins int., Mar. 10, 2009.

463 **"If we do this thing":** Ibid.

464 **"mellow and a bit":** George Will, "A Liberal's Waiting Game," *Newsweek,* Mar. 16, 1987.

464 **"Moderation, pragmatism":** "The Kennedy Prescription," *WP Health,* Apr. 21, 1987.

464 **"The great age of bipartisanship":** Paul Krugman, *The Conscience of a Liberal* (New York: Norton, 2007), 154–55.

465 **"Senate's modern decline":** George Packer, "The Empty Chamber," *New Yorker,* Aug. 9, 2010.

465 **"simply rammed bills":** Trent Lott, *Herding Cats: A Life in Politics* (New York: HarperCollins/ReganBooks, 2005), 113.

465 **"could not fight guerrilla":** J. Lee Annis, Jr., *Howard Baker: Conciliator in an Age of Crisis* (Nashville, Tenn.: Madison Books, 1995), 277.

465 **"That's the way you":** Lowell Weicker int., June 19, 2009, Miller Center, UVA.

465 **"loved the idea that":** James Manley int., Sept. 28, 2009, Miller Center, UVA.

466 **"He had that good laugh":** John Podesta int. by author.

466 **"this exuberance":** Ralph Neas int. by author.

466 **"We can work together":** Parker int., Nov. 17, 2008.

466 **"loved":** Robert Dove int. by author.

466 **"In politics you don't":** Quoted in Rose Fitzgerald Kennedy, *Times to Remember* (Garden City, N.Y.: Doubleday, 1974), 21.

466 **"Senator Kennedy was a people":** Michael Myers int. in "Obama's Deal," *Frontline,* PBS-TV, Dec. 15, 2009.

466 **"He had a good sense":** George Mitchell int., Sept. 6, 2006, Miller Center, UVA.

467 **"Tending to his relationships":** Littlefield int.

467 **"Completely disorganized":** Richard Fenno, *The Making of a Senator: Dan Quayle* (Washington, D.C.: CQ Press, 1989), 43–44.

467 **leave him a message:** Paul Donovan int., Nov. 14, 1988, D Folder, Box 3, Series 2, Clymer Papers, JFK Lib.

468 **money for his neighborhood health centers:** EMK int., Mar. 28, 2008, Miller Center, UVA.

468 **agreed to sign off on the approval:** Nick Littlefield int., May 3, 2008.

468 **"those moments were magical":** Michael Myers, "Obama's Deal."

468 **"He never started across":** Patrick Kennedy int. by author.

469 **"master of detail":** Podesta int.

469 **"If there's a reasonable chance":** Carey Parker int., Oct. 6, 2008, Miller Center, UVA.

469 **"There are forty guys":** Rollins int., Mar. 10, 2009.

469 **"this little provision":** Thomas Rollins int., May 14, 2009, Miller Center, UVA.

470 **And that was guile:** Ibid.

470 **"best period he or almost":** Michael Kelly, "Ted Kennedy on the Rocks," *GQ*, Feb. 1990.

470 **"all we did was hearings":** Rollins int., Mar. 10, 2009; Rollins int., Apr. 22, 2009.

472 **stripping them of funds:** *Grove City College v. Bell et al.*, 465 U.S. 555 (1984), https://scholar .google.com/scholar_case?case=4332416657209656272

472 **"absolutely extraordinary":** Edward Kennedy int., August 7, 2007, Miller Center, UVA.

473 **"This bill has been portrayed":** "Bill to Expand Rights Coverage Sets Off Dispute," *NYT*, May 7, 1984.

473 **"intrusion":** "Rights Bill Draws Criticism," *NYT*, May 23, 1984.

473 **"I have served in the Senate":** "Baker Tries to Mediate Dispute," *NYT*, Sept. 21, 1984.

473 **vigorously opposed:** Ibid.

473 **"major defeat for the enemies":** *NYT*, Oct. 3, 1984.

473 **"I think the Senate":** "Senate Crushes a Move to Block Civil Rights Bill," *NYT*, Sept. 30, 1984.

474 **"with a heavy heart":** Tolchin, "Civil Rights Plan Shelved."

474 **"lights went out":** "Bipartisan Coalition to Push Two Rights Bills in Congress," *NYT*, Feb. 20, 1987.

474 **Ted was tireless:** Neas int.

475 **every Democrat voting for it:** "Senate, to Override Court, Votes a Bill Extending Anti-Bias Laws," *NYT*, Jan. 29, 1988.

475 **"kick in the teeth":** "Reagan Vetoes Civil Rights Restoration Act," *WP*, Mar. 17, 1988.

476 **"this is not a civil rights":** "House and Senate Vote to Override Reagan on Rights," *NYT*, Mar. 22, 1988.

476 **progressive forces had:** "Leading the Charge," *WP*, Sept. 15, 1987.

476 **"pragmatic version":** Sean Wilentz, *The Age of Reagan: A History 1974–2008* (New York: Harper-Collins, 2008), 117.

477 **"infrastructure":** EMK int., Feb. 12, 2007, Miller Center, UVA.

477 **"They were all in lockstep":** EMK int., Jan. 6, 2007, Miller Center, UVA.

477 **"racists to the federal":** "Meese and Democrats Spar at Hearing," *WP*, Feb. 5, 1987.

477 **"Too extreme to be":** EMK, *True Compass* (New York: Twelve, 2009), 404–5.

478 **values that William Rehnquist:** "Kennedy Calls Rehnquist 'Too Extreme,'" *WP*, July 30, 1986; "He's Too Extreme on Race, Women's Rights, Speech . . . ," *LAT*, July 30, 1986.

478 **"persistent and appalling":** "Senate Opens Debate on Rehnquist Nomination," *WP*, Sept. 12, 1986.

478 **"lynch mob":** Reagan, 428.

478 **"Don't worry about":** EMK int., Aug. 7, 2007, Miller Center, UVA.

478 **"single most influential":** Herman Schwartz quoted in Michael Pertschuk and Wendy Schaetzel, *The People Rising: The Campaign Against the Bork Nomination* (New York: Thunder's Mouth Press, 1989), 238–39.

478 **"right-wing zealot":** Ibid., 118.

479 **"Conservatives have waited":** W. G. Myers III, "The Role of Special Interest Groups in the Supreme Court Nomination of Robert Bork," *Hastings Constitutional Law Quarterly* 17 (1989–90): 411.

479 **delivering it before:** Ethan Bonner, *Battle for Justice: How the Bork Nomination Shook America* (New York: Union Square Press, 1989), 21, 94–95.

479 **"The passion was because":** Parker int., Oct. 20, 2008.

480 **"The rhythms of these battles":** EMK int., Feb. 12, 2007.

480 **"Well, I think I may":** Jeffrey Blattner int., Mar. 30, 2007, Miller Center, UVA.

480 **didn't see why not:** Bronner, *Battle*, 94.

480 "like biting into a jalapeno": Former Aide B int., Sept. 25, 1998, Unnamed Sources Folder, Box 5, Series 2, Clymer Papers, JFK Lib. This is almost certainly Blattner, judging from the surrounding information.

480 "red-hot": EMK, *True Compass*, 405.

481 "The deed devolved": *Congressional Record*, Senate, 100th Cong., 1st sess., July 1, 1987, S18518–19.

481 "We better win": Peter Canellos, *Last Lion: The Fall and Rise of Ted Kennedy* (New York: Simon & Schuster, 2009), 252.

481 "wretched excess": Alan Simpson int., May 10, 2006, Miller Center, UVA; Canellos, *Last Lion*, 252–53.

482 "With Senator Kennedy": Mark Gitenstein, *Matters of Principle: An Insider's Account of America's Rejection of Robert Bork's Nomination to the Supreme Court* (New York: Simon & Schuster, 1992), 57.

482 felt that Ted had prejudged Bork: Ibid., 139.

482 "He's extremely smart": Laurence Tribe int., Apr. 27, 2009, Miller Center, UVA.

482 "Kennedy would get his headline": Quoted in Gitenstein, *Matters of Principle*, 70.

482 "Paul Revere's ride": Pertschuck and Schaetzel, 124.

482 "I'm not Ted Kennedy": Bronner, *Battle*, 121–22.

482 "pivotal moment": Qutoed in Canellos, *Last Lion*, 253.

482 "landmark for judicial nominations": Bronner, *Battle*, 84–86.

483 "We know what cheaters": Ibid., 90.

483 "Who is the swimmer": Ibid., 167.

483 "The guy goes in there": Jay Urwtiz quoted in "25 Years of Charisma," *BG*, Nov. 7, 1987.

483 "Tony, this guy Bork": "Remembering Ted Kennedy," *National Journal*, Sept. 5, 2009.

484 asked People for the American: Pertschuk and Schaetzel, *People Rising*, 66.

484 "command center": EMK, *True Compass*, 406.

484 kept working the phones: Bronner, *Battle*, 91–92.

484 "This is the most important": Ibid.

484 "This campaign can't be": Pertschuk and Schaetzel, *People Rising*, 283.

484 "added a cosmic dimension": Bronner, *Battle*, 36–39; Neas int.

484 "Vicious": Simpson int.

485 made common cause: Pertschuk and Schaetzel, *People Rising*, 41–43.

485 yet another group formed: Ibid., 37–38.

485 phoned mayors all across the South: Bronner, *Battle*, 91–92.

485 held a conference call: "Kennedy Galvanized Opposition to Bork," UPI, Oct. 11, 1987; EMK int., Feb. 12, 2007; Bronner, *Battle*, 91–92.

485 "We spent hours sitting": "Remembering Ted Kennedy."

485 "join me in actively opposing": Rick Atkinson, "Why Ted Kennedy Can't Stand Still," *WP Magazine*, Apr. 29, 1990.

485 asking them to apply pressure: Bronner, *Battle*, 93.

485 ultimately got nineteen hundred: EMK int., Feb. 12, 2007.

485 conducted their own letter-writing: Pertschuk and Schaetzel, *People Rising*, 90.

486 weighed in on Supreme Court nominations: W. G. Myers III, "The Role of Special Interest Groups in the Supreme Court Nomination of Robert Bork," *Hastings Constitutional Law Quarterly* 17, no. 1 (1989–90): 404–5.

486 "The record shows": Robert Bork TV ad, narrated by Gregory Peck (1987), https://www.youtube.com/watch?v=NpFe1olkF3Y.

486 attacked the ad: Pertschuk and Shaetzel, *People Rising*, 175.

487 lasted for forty-one days: See Theodore Draper, *A Very Thin Line: The Iran-Contra Affair* (New York: Hill & Wang, 1991), for the most exhaustive account.

487 gained thirty pounds: Former Aide B int.

487 "The principle of such": Robert Bork, "Civil Rights—A Challenge," *New Republic*, Aug. 31, 1963.

488 "Look, the masses": Bronner, *Battle*, 90.

488 "not all that important": "Kennedy, 'Who is the Real Robert Bork?'" *WP*, Sept. 19, 1987.

488 "The Book of Bork": Caroline Osolinik int., Mar. 27, 2007, Miller Center, UVA.

488 "It was the 'Book of Bork'": Pertschuk and Schaetzel, *People Rising*, 251.

489 undergo one more conversion: Bronner, *Battle*, 41–83.

489 Bork might talk and charm: "Kennedy Tells How He Roused Opposition," *BG*, Oct. 11, 1987.

489 "Part of the mind-set": Quoted in Gitenstein, *Matters of Principle*, 100.

489 "What if Bork says": Former Aide B int.

489 "murder board": Bronner, *Battle*, 119–20.

489 dinners at Hyannis: Blattner int.

489 "long, long dinners": Tribe int.

489 fellow Judiciary Committee senators: Osolinik int.

490 Blattner and Osolinik were: Bronner, *Battle*, 179.

490 "notebook open": Quoted in Canellos, *Last Lion*, 257; Bronner, *Battle*, 179.

490 "contempt for law": Kenneth B. Noble, "Fervor over Bork Nomination Intensifies as Start of Senate Hearings Nears," *NYT*, Sept. 12, 1987.

490 "irrational and totally": "Anti-Bork Rhetoric Called 'Irrational' by President," *WP*, Sept. 12, 1987.

490 Bork's legal acumen: Joseph Califano, *Inside: A Public and Private Life* (New York: PublicAffairs, 2004), 430–31.

490 "echoing temple of marble": Richard Ben Cramer, *What It Takes* (1992; New York: Vintage, 1993), 643.

490 coax Cox to testify: Blattner int.

490 "ferocity": "Leading the Charge," *WP*, Sept. 15, 1987.

490 "Without question": Ibid.

491 leading role in the questioning: Gitenstein, *Matters of Principle*, 260–61.

491 "as close as you could": Simpson int.

491 "neutral principles": "The Bork Hearings: A War of Words," *NYT*, Sept. 19, 1987.

492 "is protected from having": William Safire, "Tongue-Tied Inquisitor," *NYT*, Sept. 20, 1987.

493 he would fail: "The Bork Hearings; for Biden, Epoch of Belief, Epoch of Incredulity," *NYT*, Oct. 8, 1987.

493 "he wasn't much": EMK int., Feb. 12, 2007.

493 "30–0 if he keeps on": "Kennedy Tells How He Roused Opposition"; Blattner said that Biden had passed the notes to him, not to Ted, Former Aide B int.

493 "matter of plain arithmetic": *Hearings on the Nomination of Robert Bork*, 100th Cong., 1st sess., U.S. Senate, Part 1, Sept. 16, 1987, 313.

493 "They offered a choice": Pertschuk and Schaetzel, *People Rising*, 224–25.

493 "quest of certitudes": *Hearings on the Nomination of Robert Bork*, 100th Cong., 1st sess., U.S. Senate, Part 2, Sept. 25, 1987, 2333.

494 "intellectual feast": Nat Hentoff, "What Robert Bork Never Understood," *WP*, Oct. 11, 1987.

494 "Scholarship devoid": Gitenstein, *Matters of Principle*, 290.

494 "perhaps the deepest": Stuart Taylor, Jr., "Of Bork and Tactics," *NYT*, Oct. 21, 1987.

494 more than half were less: Daniel Golden, "Bork Affair Reflects Attitudinal Changes," *BG*, Oct. 11, 1987.

495 Southerners were evenly : Noble, "Fervor over Bork Nomination."

495 "How can they tear": Simpson int.

495 harangued him for two: Bronner, *Battle*, 288.

495 "Our efforts will be": Ronald Reagan, Statement, Oct. 9, 1987, Box 3, Justice Bork nomination, Baker, Howard, Jr., Reagan Lib.

495 "When I run into": Former Aide B int.

496 cocktails at the Madison: Bronner, *Battle*, 297.

496 "As America watched Bork": Quoted in Gitenstein, *Matters of Principle*, 248.

496 liked his conservatism less: Golden, "Bork Affair."

496 "The right wing lost": Pertschuk and Schaetzel, *People Rising*, 241.

496 "Constitution won": Quoted in Canellos, *Last Lion*, 258.

TWELVE: "WE NEED THE RESULTS"

498 ratings remained low: "Ronald Reagan From the People's Perspective," https://news.gallup .com/poll/11887/ronald-reagan-from-peoples-perspective-gallup-poll-review.aspx

498 "slam dunk for Ted [Jr.]": Mark Leibovich, "Ted Kennedy, Jr., Is (Finally) Ready for the Family Business," *NYT Magazine*, Mar. 13, 2013.

498 "what-am-I-doing-here?": Pat Caddell int., Jan. 1, 1998, C Folder, Box 3, Series 2, Clymer Papers, JFK Lib.

499 keep politics at bay: Ibid.

499 cousin wanted the seat more: "A Dynasty in Decline," *Newsweek*, June 23, 1997.

499   "**ward politician**": Patrick Kennedy int. by author.

499   **won the primary:** John Podesta int. by author.

500   "**He never hesitated**": Michael Dukakis int., Nov. 9, 2009, Miller Center, UVA.

500   "**It may be difficult**": Sidney Blumenthal, "Ted Kennedy: No Regrets as the Torch Is Passed," *WP*, July 19, 1988.

500   "**post-liberal**": Walter Shapiro, "The Party's New Soul," *Time*, July 25, 1988.

500   "**The last man standing**": Sean Wilentz, *The Age of Reagan: A History 1974–2008* (New York: HarperCollins, 2008), 268.

500   "**wimp**": "Fighting the Wimp Factor," *Newsweek*, Oct. 19, 1987.

501   "**In this house**": EMK int., Aug. 7, 2007, Miller Center, UVA.

501   "**The race issue**": Ibid.

502   "**voter must know**": Quoted in Jon Meacham, *Destiny and Power: The American Odyssey of George H. W. Bush* (New York: Random House, 2015), 335.

502   "**Bush's major theme**": Arthur Schlesinger, Jr., *Journals: 1952–2000*, ed. Andrew Schlesinger and Stephen Schlesinger (New York: Penguin Press, 2007), 659.

502   "**awareness of a new**": Joan Didion, *Political Fictions* (2001; New York: Vintage, 2002), 42.

502   "**Is there a soul**": Shapiro, "Party's New Soul."

503   "**lousy campaign**": Dukakis int.

503   "**hook going deeper**": EMK int., June 5, 2005, Miller Center, UVA.

503   "**I wanted to be seen**": EMK, *True Compass* (New York: Twelve, 2009), 413–14; Patrick Kennedy and Stephen Fried, *A Common Struggle: A Personal Journey Through the Past and Future of Mental Illness and Addiction* (New York: Blue Rider Press, 2015), 89.

503   "**There's a consciousness**": Blumenthal, "No Regrets."

504   "**embraced the 'liberal' label**": Quoted in Adam Clymer, *Edward M. Kennedy: A Biography* (New York: Harper Perennial, 2000), 444.

504   "**Competence was not**": "Kennedy: Administration 'Has No Agenda,'" *WP*, Mar. 7, 1989.

504   **His average rating:** "Presidential Approval Ratings—Gallup Historical Statistics and Trends," Gallup, n.d., https://news.gallup.com/poll/116677/presidential-approval-ratings-gallup-historical-statistics-trends.aspx

505   "**good luck**": Alan Blinder and Mark Watson, "Presidents and the U.S. Economy: An Econometric Exploration," July 2014, https://www.princeton.edu/~mwatson/papers/Presidents_Blinder_Watson_July2014.pdf

505   **no economic wizard:** See Wilentz, *Age of Reagan*, 275–76; Stanley Greenberg, *The Two Americas: Our Current Political Deadlock and How to Break It* (New York: St. Martin's Griffin, 2005), 61–62.

506   "**tax and tax**": George Will, "How Reagan Changed America," *Newsweek*, Jan. 9, 1989.

506   "**liberals will regain control**": William Schneider, "The Political Legacy of the Reagan Years," in *The Reagan Legacy*, ed. Thomas Byrne Edsall and Sidney Blumenthal (New York: Pantheon, 1988), 57–58.

507   "**used it cleverly**": EMK int., May 30, 2007, Miller Center, UVA.

507   "**mischievous force**": Theodore Lowi, *The End of the Republican Era* (Norman: Univ. of Oklahoma Press, 1995), 93.

507   "**The Reaganites were**": David Stockman, *The Triumph of Politics: Why the Reagan Revolution Failed* (New York: Harper & Row, 1986), 385–86.

507   **higher in 1989 than:** Wilentz, *Age of Reagan*, 204.

507   **caught in a moral contradiction:** See E. J. Dionne, Jr., *Why Americans Hate Politics* (New York: Simon & Schuster, 1991), 13.

507   "**Self-aggrandizement wrapped**": Blumenthal, "No Regrets."

508   "**I'm going to dismantle**": Laurence Tribe int., Apr. 27, 2009, Miller Center, UVA.

508   "**American sensibilities changed**": Philip Jenkins, *Decade of Nightmares: The End of the Sixties and the Making of Eighties America* (New York: Oxford Univ. Press, 2006), 10–11.

508   **thinking of it as a movie:** See Michael Paul Rogin, *Ronald Reagan the Movie and Other Episodes in Political Demonology* (Berkeley: Univ. of Calif. Press, 1988).

509   "**it is more illuminating**": Gil Troy, *Morning in America: How Ronald Reagan Invented the 1980s* (Princeton: Princeton University Press, 2005), 20.

509   **reduced to supernumeraries:** See Will Bunch, *Tear Down This Myth: How the Reagan Legacy Has Distorted Our Politics and Haunts Our Future* (New York: Free Press, 2009).

509   "**failed to meet**": EMK, *True Compass*, 407–8.

509   "**At his worst, Reagan**": "Goodbye to the Gipper," *Newsweek*, Jan. 9, 1989.

510 "vision thing": "Where Is the Real George Bush?" *Time*, Jan. 26, 1987.

510 "Bush holds office": "Kennedy Says Lack of Vision Threatening Bush," *BG*, Mar. 7, 1989.

510 "make sure the underdog": Nick Littlefield int., May 3, 2008, Miller Center, UVA.

511 tight committee: Ibid.

511 "onto the barricades": Rick Atkinson, "Why Ted Kennedy Can't Stand Still," *WP Magazine*, Apr. 29, 1990.

511 "What are you doing": Paul Kirk, Jr., int., June 20, 2007, Miller Center, UVA.

512 "shot at showing macho": "The Minimum Wage Fight Isn't Really About Pay," *NYT*, May 7, 1989.

512 "ceremony": "Battle for Last Laugh on Minimum Wage Bill," *NYT*, Apr. 27, 1989.

512–13 "crocodile tears": Clymer, *Kennedy*, 447.

513 forty-five-cent-per-year increase: Nick Littlefield and David Nexon, *Lion of the Senate: When Ted Kennedy Rallied the Democrats in a GOP Congress* (New York: Simon & Schuster, 2015), 142–43.

513 "We perceive it to be": "Senate Votes to Raise Wage Base," *NYT*, May 18, 1989.

513 bill easily passed: "Minimum Wage Rise Wins Final Senate Vote," *NYT*, Nov. 9, 1989.

513 "neurological disturbance": Rose Fitzgerald Kennedy, *Times to Remember* (Garden City, N.Y.: Doubleday, 1974), 286.

514 "no clarity": John Tunney int., May 3, 2007, Miller Center, UVA.

514 "other children's games": EMK int., Mar. 28, 2008, Miller Center, UVA.

514 "We have to do this": Carey Parker int., Oct. 27, 2008, Miller Center, UVA.

516 champion Weicker's bill: Carolyn Osolinik int., Mar. 27, 2007, Miller Center, UVA.

516 little sensitivity to the politics: Lennard Davis, *Enabling Acts: The Story of How the Americans with Disabilities Act Gave America's Largest Minorities Their Rights* (New York: Beacon Press, 2015), 83.

516 "He wanted to retrofit": EMK int., Aug. 7, 2007.

516 "one of the most generous": Quoted in Peter Canellos, *Last Lion: The Fall and Rise of Ted Kennedy* (New York: Simon & Schuster, 2009), 318–19.

516 chairmanship of a new Subcommittee: Davis, *Enabling Acts*, 105–6.

517 "you can't start": Ibid.

517 "I live in agony": Dr. Mary Lynn Fletcher, testimony on the ADA, Committee on Labor and Human Resources, Robert Dole Archives, Kansas University, May 9–10, 1989.

518 "groups couldn't agree": Lowell Weicker int., June 19, 2009, Miller Center, UVA.

518 "Sometimes he would call": Parker int.

518 administration point man: Dick Thornburgh, "Disability and the Prophet's Call," *The Christian Citizen*, July 26, 2017.

518 "did it": Osolinik int.

519 did nothing to advance it: Weicker int.

519 "move": EMK int., Aug. 7, 2007.

519 going to cooperate: Osolinik int.

519 "piss off Kennedy": Davis, *Enabling Acts*, 147–48.

520 bidding of White House counsel: Ibid., 124.

520 "very abrupt": EMK int., Aug. 7, 2007.

520 "Well, that's of some interest": Ibid.

520 "they were going to get": Osolinik int.

521 "Every time I say something": Davis, *Enabling Acts*, 1–6.

521 "long, tough, hard bargaining": "Bush and Senate Leaders Support Sweeping Protection for Disabled," *NYT*, Aug. 3, 1989.

521–22 "No politician can vote": "Bill Barring Bias Against Disabled Holds Wide Impact," *NYT*, Aug. 14, 1989.

522 "What's it going to mean": Osolinik int.; EMK int., Aug. 7, 2007.

523 "Drafting a bill like this": Quoted in Davis, *Enabling Acts*, 155.

523 "This is the play": EMK int., Mar. 26, 1999, EMK Interviews, 1997–99, Box 5, Series 2, Clymer Papers, JFK Lib.

523 "I plan to read and read": EMK int., Aug. 7, 2007.

524 "My brother owns": EMK int., Aug. 7, 2007, Miller Center, UVA.

524 "we have to resolve": Osolinik int.

524 "I could just see": EMK int., Mar. 26, 1999; Parker int.

524 "disorders": See Ruth Colker, "The ADA's Journey Through Congress," *Wake Forest Law Review*, Spring 2004.

525 "This legislation will go down": "How the Disabled Sold Congress on a New Bill of Rights," *NYT*, Sept. 17, 1989.

525 "sight to behold": Bob Dole int., May 15, 2006, Miller Center, UVA.

527 "homosexual rights bill": Colker, "ADA's Journey," 6, 12, 18.

527 "AIDS is God's judgement": Quoted in H. W. Brands, *Reagan: The Life* (New York: Doubleday, 2015), 655.

527 "If you come out for gay rights": Quoted in Richard Burke with William Hoffer and Marilyn Hoffer, *The Senator: My Ten Years with Ted Kennedy* (New York: St. Martin's Press, 1992), 197.

527 "You have to be comfortable": EMK int., Aug. 8, 2007, Miller Center, UVA.

528 "place-marker in the movement": Ibid.

528 "Well, that would be you": Davis, *Enabling Acts*, 78.

528 "superstars": EMK int., Aug. 8, 2007; EMK int., Mar. 26, 1999.

528 "I wanted to get": EMK int., Sept. 11, 1998, EMK Interviews Folder, Box 5, Series 2, Clymer Papers, JFK Lib.

529 "managed to take possession": "Washington at Work: Orrin Hatch's Journey," *NYT*, Mar. 2, 1990.

529 "I think they made": Ibid.

529 "big heart-to-heart": Thomas Rollins int., Apr. 22, 2009, Miller Center, UVA.

529 introduced his first AIDS bill: See Orrin Hatch, Statement on S.1220 [1986] Committee on Labor and Human Resources: Republican Memos, 99th Cong., 2nd sess., Box 93–38.

530 Ted introduced his bill: "Congress Takes Up 8 AIDS Bills Today," *WP*, Aug. 6, 1987.

531 "ludicrous and deadly effect": "Program to Fight AIDS Cleared by Senate," *NYT*, Apr. 29, 1988.

531 "homosexual crowd": "Senate Passes Bill for Assault on AIDS," *Chicago Tribune*, Apr. 29, 1988.

531 "You distort and misrepresent!": Thomas Rollins int., May 14, 2009, Miller Center, UVA.

532 Ted's and Hatch's amendment carried: Ibid.

532 "Someway, somehow": Atkinson, "Why Ted Kennedy Can't."

533 farm family in Sparta: Littlefield int.

533 "disaster relief": Littlefield and Nexon, *Lion*, 129–30

533 "most vocal enemy": William Link, *Righteous Warrior: Jesse Helms and the Rise of Modern Conservatism* (New York: St. Martin's Press, 2008), 347.

533 nursery at Jackson Memorial Hospital: "How the Politics Shifted on AIDS Funds," *NYT*, May 20, 1990.

533 moved by the story of Ryan White: EMK int., Mar. 26, 1999.

534 "dignity, compassion, care": "Bush, in First Address on AIDS, Backs a Bill to Support Its Victims," *NYT*, Mar. 30, 1990.

534 rename the bill the Ryan White Act: Sheridan says it was Hatch. Thomas Sheridan, *Helping the Good Do Better: How a White Hat Lobbyist Advocates for Social Change* (New York: Twelve, 2019), 35.

534 getting Senator Dan Coats: Joshua Green, "The Heroic Story of How Congress First Confronted AIDS," *Atlantic*, June 8, 2011.

534 "This one's for you, Ryan": Michael Iskowitz quoted in Sheridan, 53.

535 "this frail little boy": Barbara Mikulski int., Sept. 26, 2006, Miller Center, UVA.

535 "nasty time": EMK int., Aug. 8, 2007.

535 lobby Bush to sign it: Orrin Hatch int., Feb. 27, 1992, H Folder, Box 3, Series 2, Clymer Papers, JFK Lib.

536 "Bush wasn't going to": Nick Littlefield int., June 30, 2008, Miller Center, UVA.

536 became law in the first two years: Littlefield ints., June 30, 2008, Feb. 15, 2009, Miller Center, UVA.

536 Ruscha won a large settlement: Katherine Marik, "Visual Artists Rights Act of 1990: The United States Recognizes Artists and Their Rights," *Entertainment and Sports Lawyer* (Winter 1991): 7–14.

536 created a Select Commission: EMK, "Foreword," *San Diego Law Review* 19, no. 1 (December 1981): 1–8, https://digital.sandiego.edu/cgi/viewcontent.cgi?article=1734&context=sdlr.

537 calling for an amnesty since 1980: "Kennedy Cites Failed Economic Policies," *LAT*, May 29, 1980.

537 "if there's a possibility": Michael Myers int., Aug. 28, 2006, Miller Center, UVA.

537 "Ted and I would come": Alan Simpson int., May 10, 2006, Miller Center, UVA.

537 Simpson was grateful: Myers int.

538 **"Let's maximize where"**: Ibid.

538 **"heartache"**: Ibid.

538 **"It's spreading like wildfire"**: Meacham, *Destiny*, 383

539 ***"Ich bin ein Berliner"***: "In Berlin, Echoes of JFK," *WP*, Nov. 29, 1989.

539 **"trademark bellow"**: Atkinson, "Why Ted Kennedy Can't."

539 **"timid"**: "Kennedy Chides 'Timid' Democrats," *WP*, Apr. 10, 1990.

540 **"We ought to be"**: Atkinson, "Why Ted Kennedy Can't."

540 **"This will not stand"**: Jeremy Sharp, "Congressional Action on Iraq, 1990–2003," CRS, January 30, 2003, https://www.everycrsreport.com/files/20030130_RS21324_c932aa7805859263e86 e6dcf3f846de1766b96d1.pdf; "Senate Gives Bush Limited Backing On Gulf Policy," *NYT*, Oct. 3, 1990.

541 **"Nobody is particularly happy"**: Meacham, *Destiny*, 448.

THIRTEEN: THE UNDERTOW

542 **"change the focus"**: Nick Littlefield int., June 30, 2008, Miller Center, UVA.

542 **"He would ask whether"**: Rick Atkinson, "Why Ted Kennedy Can't Stand Still," *WP Magazine*, Apr. 29, 1990.

542 **"between colleagues to lobby"**: Ibid.

542 **"sycophantic"**: John R. Hibbing and Sue Thomas, "The Modern United States Senate: What Is Accorded Respect?" *Journal of Politics* 52, no. 1 (Feb. 1990): 142–43.

543 **"one of the great"**: Atkinson, "Why Kennedy Can't."

543 **fretted that he might be impeached**: Jon Meacham, *Destiny and Power: The American Odyssey of George Herbert Walker Bush* (New York: Random House, 2015), 451–52.

543 **"We have not seen such"**: "On the Fence," *Time*, Jan. 14, 1991.

543 **"At this historic moment"**: "War and Peace, A Sampling from the Debate on Capitol Hill," *NYT*, Jan. 11, 1991.

544 **American aircraft attacked**: For the best account of Bush's deliberations, see Meacham, *Destiny*, 454–58.

544 **"It is time for this"**: "Democrats Open Battle on Blame for Recession," *NYT*, Jan. 8, 1991.

544 **"continues to neglect"**: Nick Littlefield int., Feb. 15, 2009, Miller Center, UVA.

544 **Bush's popularity was soaring**: R. J. Reinhart, "George H. W. Bush Retrospective," Gallup, Dec. 1, 2018, https://news.gallup.com/opinion/gallup/234971/george-bush-retrospective.aspx

545 **"effervescent"**: Quoted in Burton Hersh, *The Education of Edward Kennedy: A Family Biography* (New York: Morrow, 1972), 103.

545 **"If you want to find"**: Atkinson, "Why Kennedy Can't."

545 **"two giant characters"**: John Podesta int. by author.

545 **"From then on"**: Nick Littlefield int., May 3, 2008, Miller Center, UVA.

545 **"He'll sing at the drop"**: Carey Parker int., Oct. 13, 2008, Miller Center, UVA.

545 **impression of presidential adviser**: Lee Fentress int., Oct. 16, 2009, Miller Center, UVA.

545 **"ultimate Christmas party"**: Richard Clasby int., Oct. 11, 2005, Miller Center, UVA; "At McLean Castle, Kennedy's Birthday Bash," *WP*, Feb. 23, 1988; Melody Miller int., July 1, 2008, Miller Center, UVA.

546 **"That's *Batman*"**: Atkinson, "Why Kennedy Can't."

546 **lip-synching their songs**: Carey Parker int., Oct. 13, 2008.

546 **"quite a bit"**: Ibid.

546 **"walks in and lights up"**: Robert P. Fitzgerald int., June 18, 2009, Miller Center, UVA.

546 **"The most public"**: Atkinson, "Why Kennedy Can't."

546 **"The most profound thing"**: Howard Baker int., Jan. 13, 1994, B Folder, Box 3, Series 2, Clymer Papers, JFK Lib.

546 **"He had been trained"**: Ethan Bronner, *Battle for Justice: How the Bork Nomination Shook America* (New York: Union Square Press, 1989), 89–90.

547 **"You still stutter"**: Nancy Korman to EMK, c. 1982, Box 1, Nancy Korman Personal Papers, JFK Lib.

547 **"He wasn't any good"**: Patrick Kennedy int. by author.

547 **"When Teddy is after"**: Burton Hersh, *The Shadow President: Ted Kennedy in Opposition* (South Royalton, Vt.: Steerforth Press, 1997), 189.

547 **"technically a marriage"**: Thomas Oliphant int. by author.

547 **"We just didn't have"**: George Colt, "Is Ted Kennedy's Midlife Crisis Finally Over?" *Life*, Aug. 1994.

547 **"I think he was terribly"**: John Culver int., Sept. 22, 2009, Miller Center, UVA.

547 **"sitting in an armchair"**: Lance Morrow, "The Trouble with Teddy," *Time*, Apr. 29, 1991.

547 **taken up painting again**: Roland Flamini, "Inside Edward M. Kennedy's House in Washington D.C.," *Architectural Digest*, Nov. 1999.

547 **"And he turned around"**: Edmund and Doris Reggie int., Dec. 16, 2008, Miller Center, UVA.

548 **"extremely lonely man"**: Quoted in Peter Canellos, *Last Lion: The Fall and Rise of Ted Kennedy* (New York: Simon & Schuster, 2009), 232.

548 **"he constantly was"**: Patrick Kennedy int.

548 **"I mean, the things"**: Colt, "Midlife Crisis Over?"

548 **"I remember watching"**: Melody Miller int., Oct. 7, 2008, Miller Center, UVA.

548 **"Occasionally, you'd be sitting"**: Charles Pierce, "Kennedy Unbound After 40 Years in the Senate," *BG Magazine*, Jan. 5, 2003.

548 **"I loved your brothers"**: Quoted in Colt, "Midlife Crisis Over?"

548 **"Do you mind?"**: Edmund and Doris Reggie int.

548 **"how lonely Teddy must"**: Fentress int.

549 **"center of our lives"**: Quoted in Canellos, *Last Lion*, 194.

549 **"Believe me, he could scare"**: "The Torchbearer," *People*, Aug. 16, 1999.

549 **"greatest historians"**: Robert Shriver III int., Jan. 29, 2010, Miller Center, UVA.

549 **"scoutmaster"**: "In School or Congress, It's Sad When Recess Ends," *People*, Sept. 1, 1975.

549 **made replicas of it**: Kerry Kennedy, "Reflections on Senator Ted Kennedy," Robert F. Kennedy Center; EMK int., Dec. 1, 2006, Miller Center, UVA.

549 **"he knew his role"**: Quoted in Canellos, *Last Lion*, 196.

550 **propel a cherry tomato**: Christopher Lawford, *Symptoms of Withdrawal: A Memoir of Snapshots and Redemption* (New York: Morrow, 2005), 33.

550 **"Fee, fi, fo, fum"**: Miller int., Oct. 7, 2008.

550 **"Ted Sox"**: Melody Miller int., July 15, 2008, Miller Center, UVA.

550 **"The Grand Fromage"**: Lawford, *Symptoms*, 379.

550 **"chaos and laughter"**: Ibid., 117.

550 **"My dad was unbelievable"**: Ted Kennedy, Jr., on *Oprah Winfrey Show*, Nov. 25, 2009.

550 **"about what should be"**: Kathleen Kennedy Townsend int., Nov. 3, 2007, T Folder, Box 5, Series 2, Clymer Papers, JFK Lib.

550 **"Tremendous demands"**: James Manley int., Sept. 28, 2009, Miller Center, UVA.

550 **"emotional and pragmatic"**: Lawford, *Symptoms*, 289.

551 **paralyzed from the chest down**: "Another Kennedy Accident Victim Remains a Friend," *Cape Cod Times*, July 25, 1999.

551 **"long, long"**: "Joseph Kennedy Is Found Guilty of Negligence in Road Mishap," *NYT*, Aug. 21, 1973; Milton Gwirtzman int., Apr. 3, 1993, G Folder, Box 3, Series 2, Clymer Papers, JFK Lib.

551 **"I've been full of pain"**: "Friends Say David Kennedy was Drinking and Depressed," *NYT*, Oct. 13, 1984.

551 **"seemed vulnerable to it"**: Patrick Kennedy and Stephen Fried, *A Common Struggle: A Personal Journey Through the Past and Future of Mental Illness and Addiction* (New York: Blue Rider Press, 2015), 72–73.

551 **"grieved properly"**: Maria Shriver int., Jan. 29, 2010, Miller Center, UVA.

551 **"seriously impaired"**: Kennedy and Fried, *Common Struggle*, 79.

552 **"loser"**: Patrick Kennedy int.

553 **"ensure a continuum"**: EMK, *True Compass* (New York: Twelve, 2009), 283.

553 **"link between the future"**: Lawford, *Symptoms*,167.

554 **"stopped looking forward"**: EMK, *True Compass*, 421.

554 **period of conservative ascendance**: Carey Parker int., Dec. 1, 2008, Miller Center, UVA.

554 **"He genuinely gets sick"**: Quoted in Michael Kelly, "Ted Kennedy on the Rocks," *GQ*, Feb. 1990.

554 **"I kept moving"**: EMK, *True Compass*, 506.

554 **"The man cannot stand still"**: Richard Rhodes, "Things as They Are, Things That Never Were," *Audience*, Nov.–Dec. 1971.

554 **"as active as a third-base coach"**: Colt, "Midlife Crisis Over?"

554 **"man consigned to perpetual"**: Atkinson, "Why Kennedy Can't."

554 "He had as much energy": "Remembering Ted Kennedy," *National Journal*, Sept. 5, 2009.

554 "I have to do work": David Burke int., June 19, 2007, Miller Center, UVA.

555 "to keep ahead": See Jim Young comment in Culver int.

555 "Keep moving": Quoted in Mark Leibovich, "The Kennedy Factor," *WP*, July 13, 2004.

555 forbade any liquor: EMK int., Aug. 15, 2006.

555 in one two-hour period: Atkinson, "Why Kennedy Can't."

555 "One way Ted Kennedy": Arthur Schlesinger, Jr., *Journals: 1952–2000*, ed. Andrew Schlesinger and Stephen Schlesinger (New York: Penguin Press, 2007), 308.

555 "Kennedy's face sometimes": Morrow, "Trouble with Teddy."

555 "He looked bad and felt bad": Quoted in Canellos, *Last Lion*, 266.

555 "His head was always there": John A. Farrell int., July 13, 2006, Miller Center, UVA.

555 "feeling no pain": Richard Burke with William Hoffer and Marilyn Hoffer, *The Senator: My Ten Years with Ted Kennedy* (New York: St. Martin's Press, 1992), 5.

556 "Hmm, martinis at lunch": Terri Haddad Robinson int., Aug. 25, 2009, Miller Center, UVA.

556 abstain from alcohol: "Sobering Times," *Newsweek*, Dec. 9, 1991.

556 "He returned in time": Laurence Leamer, *The Kennedy Women: The Saga of an American Family* (New York: Villard Books, 1994), 748.

556 Ted's decline began: Oliphant int.

556 testing the limits: Joseph Kraft, "The Sinking of the Kennedy Star," *WP*, Aug. 14, 1980.

556 "The wild driving": Steven Roberts, "Ted Kennedy: Haunted by the Past," *NYT Magazine*, Feb. 3, 1980.

556 "Can you imagine": William Honan, *Ted Kennedy: Profile of a Survivor* (New York: Quadrangle Books, 1972), 4–5.

556 "My dad definitely": Patrick Kennedy int.

557 "put a new curl": *Boston Herald*, Oct. 20, 1984; June 17, 1985; Aug. 9, 1986; Apr. 10, 1986; Sept. 2, 1987; Sept. 13, 1987; May 2, 1988; Aug. 9, 1989; Aug. 6, 1992.

557 Barbara Borin: "The Sportscaster and the Senator," *WP*, June 28, 1991.

557 "Well, Teddy": "Overheard," *Newsweek*, Apr. 30, 1990.

557 Sometimes in his isolation: Patrick Kennedy int.

558 "You know, it's wonderful": Elsa Walsh, "Kennedy's Hidden Campaign," *New Yorker*, Mar. 31, 1997.

558 "men over 50 who": Korman to EMK, Dec. 4, 1983, Box 1, Nancy Korman Papers, JFK Lib.

558 "uncomfortable": Robinson int.

559 "He couldn't have been": Elizabeth Shannon int., Apr. 28, 2009, Miller Center, UVA.

559 "I faced the fact": EMK, *True Compass*, 421.

560 "for a full hour and a half": Cited in "Sex and the Senior Senator," *Time*, Nov. 12, 1979.

560 Ted's errant behavior: Atkinson, "Why Kennedy Can't."

560 Murdoch sent the *Herald*: "Kennedy and Paper Battle in Boston," *NYT*, Jan. 7, 1988.

560 "The oldest juvenile": *Boston Herald*, Aug. 14, 1987, Jan. 6, 1988.

560 "bit of a joke": Burke with Hoffer and Hoffer, *Senator*, 123–24.

560 "It is our duty": Atkinson, "Why Kennedy Can't."

561 "gallantly": Schlesinger, *Journals*, 822.

561 "He was worried": Jane Farrell, "Memories of Mary Jo," *Ladies' Home Journal*, July 1989.

562 assumption that Kennedy: Suzannah Lessard, "Kennedy's Women Problem, Women's Kennedy Problem," *Washington Monthly*, Dec. 1979, 10–14.

562 "like other accounts": Jon Margolis, "Kennedy's Problem with Women," *Chicago Tribune*, 1979.

562 "Up close the face": Michael Kelly, "Ted Kennedy on the Rocks," *GQ*, Feb. 1990.

563 article on Kelly's: "A Disintegrating Teddy?" *Newsweek*, Feb. 5, 1990.

563 "it was like he might": For a fuller discussion, see Neal Gabler, "The Press and Edward Kennedy: A Case Study in Journalistic Behavior," Shorenstein Center, Harvard University, Fall 2011.

564 "Quite upset": Patrick Kennedy int.; Atkinson, "Why Kennedy Can't."

564 "What's in it for me?": Oliphant int.

564 "He loved being in nature": Patrick Kennedy int.

565 "lot of laughing": Melissa Leudkte int. by author.

565 "way a teenager nurses": "The Kennedy Challenge," *Time*, Nov. 5, 1979.

565 sail up the coast of Maine: Fentress int.

565 "It was all part of my desire": EMK, *True Compass*, 422.

565 "If that's what we're going": Hersh, *Shadow President*, 86.

565   **"I never felt I had":** EMK int., Feb. 1992, EMK Interviews 1992–94 Folder, Box 5, Series 2, Clymer Papers, JFK Lib.

565   **refused to speak to him:** "Sobering Times."

566   **The once-grand house:** See Rita Dallas, *The Kennedy Case* (New York: G. P. Putnam, 1973), 24.

566   **"If it was my house":** Michelle Cassone quoted in "Views of the Kennedy House: Poignant Past, Busy Present," *NYT*, Apr. 10, 1991.

566   **"emotional conversation":** "Excerpts from Senator's Testimony," *BG*, Dec. 7, 1991; EMK int., Nov. 29, 2006, Miller Center, UVA.

566   **"chichi nightspot":** Michelle Green, "Boys' Night Out in Palm Beach," *People*, Apr. 22, 1991.

566   **"dressed with a double-breasted":** Farrell int.

567   **"very drunk":** "Senator Kennedy's Nephew Identified as Suspect," *WP*, Apr. 6, 1991.

567   **between four-thirty and five a.m.:** Green, "Boys' Night Out"; Larry Martz, "What Happened in Palm Beach?" *Newsweek*, Apr. 15, 1991.

568   **seemed agitated or nervous:** Green, "Boys' Night Out."

568   **"You know, she's going":** "Unanswered Questions in Palm Beach," *Newsweek*, Apr. 29, 1991; "Witness Backs Sen. Kennedy's Version of Palm Beach Meal," *BG*, Sept. 24, 1991.

568   **"clearly":** Margaret Carlson, "When in Doubt, Obfuscate," *Time*, May 27, 1991.

568   **"I was never, never":** "Kennedy Says He Was Not Told of Rape Probe at First," *WP*, May 11, 1991.

568   **ask him about an urn:** "Spotlight on the Senator: What Did Teddy Know?" *Newsweek*, May 27, 1991.

568   **"sexual harassment":** "Kennedy Defends Avoiding Police Questions," *NYT*, May 11, 1991.

568   **"sexual battery":** "Kennedy Houseguest Saw '10 Seconds' of Incident," *WP*, May 15, 1991.

568   **"we ought to get":** Felicity Barringer, "Kennedy Insists That He Did Not Avoid Palm Beach Police," *NYT*, May 16, 1991.

569   **"I think you better talk":** "Kennedy Actions in Florida Just After Incident Are in Spotlight," *NYT*, May 15, 1991.

569   **"You know there's been":** "Kennedy's Statements on Rape Case Contradictory," *WP*, May 16, 1991.

569   **heard about the rape allegations:** Carlson, "When in Doubt."

569   **"There goes my ride":** "Smith Tells Rapt Courtroom His Side of Story," *NYT*, Dec. 11, 1991.

571   **"He looked at me":** "Accuser in Smith Trial Tells of Fear and Rape," *NYT*, Dec. 5, 1991; Dominick Dunne, "The Verdict," *Vanity Fair*, Mar. 1992.

571   **three hundred by one estimate:** "Of Sex, a Senator and a Press Circus," *NYT*, Apr. 6, 1991.

571   **"greatest assemblage":** Margaret Carlson, "The Kennedy Boys' Night Out," *Time*, Apr. 15, 1991.

571   **"So many reporters":** Michael Isikoff, "Palm Beach Revels in Latest Scandal," *WP*, Apr. 8, 1991.

571   **"Do you get the sense":** Meg Greenfield, "Palm Beach Runaround," *Newsweek*, Apr. 29, 1991.

571   **"The *Enquirer* is turning":** Quoted in Howard Kurtz, "The Ethics of Identifying Rape Victims," *WP*, Apr. 18, 1991.

571   **"*The Washington Post* and other":** Ibid.

571–72 **"It's gotten totally":** "Key Details of Weekend at Kennedy Estate Remain Mysterious," *WP*, Apr. 22, 1991.

572   **"junkyard journalism":** Larry Sabato, *Feeding Frenzy: How Attack Journalism Has Transformed American Politics.* NY: The Free Press, 1991), 26. See also Stephen Hess, "Decline and Fall of Congressional News," *Society* 31, no. 2 (1993).

572   **"Of course the case would not":** Dunne, "Verdict."

572   **"It was the Senator's presence":** "Key Details of Weekend at Kennedy Estate Remain Mysterious," *WP*, Apr. 22, 1991.

572   **"You hear something delicious":** Quoted in Kurtz, "Ethics of Identifying."

573   **"tar ball massive enough":** "Legal Sleaze in Palm Beach," *Newsweek*, Apr. 22, 1991.

573   **"family fighting for its life":** Dunne, "Verdict."

573   **"It would be sad enough":** "What Happened in Palm Beach?" *Newsweek*, Apr. 14, 1991.

573   **"In the long downward slope":** Green, "Boys' Night Out."

573   **"lightning rod":** Morrow, "Trouble with Teddy."

575   **"Nobody suggests Senator":** William Safire, "Be Thou as Chaste as Ice . . ." *NYT*, Apr. 11, 1991.

575   **"Teddy may well":** Richard Cohen, "Ducking the Cops in Palm Beach," *WP*, May 16, 1991.

575   **"Surrounded by sycophants":** Mike Barnicle, "What No One Tells Kennedy," *BG*, April 9, 1991.

575   **"First, confine risky behavior":** Carlson, "When in Doubt, Obfuscate."

576   **"girls all over the place":** Mike McAlary, *NY Post*, Apr. 8, 1991.

576 **"How many other 59-year-old":** Quoted in Vincent Bzdek, *The Kennedy Legacy: Jack, Bobby and a Family Dream Fulfilled* (New York: Palgrave Macmillan, 2009), 201.

576 **"The temperature drops":** Canellos, *Last Lion,* 260.

576 **"Not the kind of person":** David Letterman et al., *An Altogether New Book of Top Ten Lists* (New York: Pocket Books, 1991), 64.

576 **"one more scene":** "For Kennedy, No Escaping a Dark Cloud," *NYT,* Apr. 17, 1991.

577 **"picture of conduct":** Ellen Goodman, "Talk of Ted," *WP,* May 18, 1991.

577 **"The dualism in which":** James Carroll, "The End of the Dream," *New Republic,* June 24, 1991.

577 **"The sadness is that Ted's":** Schlesinger, *Journals,* 710.

577 **"He is the Left to much":** Garry Wills, *The Kennedy Imprisonment: A Meditation on Power* (Boston: Houghton Mifflin, 2002), 289.

FOURTEEN: MEA CULPA

578 **became a predator:** "Then There Were Three," *Time,* Aug. 5, 1991; "Legal Sleaze in Palm Beach," *Newsweek,* Apr. 22, 1991; "Willy Smith, The Independent Kennedy, Anonymous No More," *WP,* May 10, 1991.

578 **ordered to an inpatient program:** "Joan Kennedy in Court on DWI Charge," *WP,* May 16, 1991; "Joan Kennedy Ordered to Treatment Center," *BG,* May 31, 1991.

578 **wanted to end her life:** "Kennedy Spoke to Nephew About Rape Allegations," *NYT,* Sept. 7, 1991.

578 **sinking in drugs and alcohol:** Patrick Kennedy and Steven Fried, *A Common Struggle: A Personal Journey Through the Past and Future of Mental Illness and Addiction* (New York: Blue Rider Press, 2015), 96.

579 **attended noon Mass:** Jack Thomas, "Victoria Reggie: The Next Kennedy," *BG,* Apr. 2, 1992.

579 **transferred his allegiance:** Edmund and Doris Reggie int., Aug. 8, 2005, Miller Center, UVA.

579 **"I could never vote":** Peter Canellos, *Last Lion: The Fall and Rise of Ted Kennedy* (New York: Simon & Schuster, 2009), 282.

579 **"made on that deal":** Edmund and Doris Reggie ints., Aug. 8, 2005, and Dec. 16, 2008, Miller Center, UVA; Vicki Kennedy, on *Oprah Winfrey Show,* Nov. 25, 2009.

580 **"in rapt attention":** Edmund and Doris Reggie int., Aug. 8, 2005; Vicki Kennedy, on *Oprah Winfrey Show,* Nov. 25, 2009.

580 **bottle of fine wine:** Tom Gliatto, "Time to Marry? Right, Said Ted," *People,* Mar. 30, 1992.

580 **"What's the matter?":** EMK, *True Compass* (New York: Twelve, 2009), 422–23.

580 **"We just had that banter":** Vicki Kennedy, on *Oprah Winfrey Show,* Nov. 25, 2009.

580 **"A delightful evening":** Edmund and Doris Reggie int., Aug. 8, 2005.

581 **"I had known Vicki":** Vicki Kennedy, on *Oprah Winfrey Show,* Nov. 25, 2009.

581 **"I hadn't felt that relaxed":** EMK, *True Compass,* 423.

581 **"There was such a":** Lila Lambert quoted in Thomas, "Victoria Reggie."

581 **"everything to keep them":** Edmund and Doris Reggie int., Aug. 8, 2005.

581 **"How lucky we are":** Thomas, "Victoria Reggie."

581 **straight A student:** Ibid.

581 **She had memorized:** Ibid.

582 **Keck, Mahin & Cate:** "Kennedy Engagement," *BG,* Mar. 16, 1992.

582 **"She eats a lot of salads":** Gliatto.

582 **wondered why she had agreed:** EMK, *True Compass,* 423.

582 **"I mean, I wasn't expecting":** Elsa Walsh, "Kennedy's Hidden Campaign," *New Yorker,* Mar. 31, 1997.

582 **"I never wanted to marry":** Victoria Reggie Kennedy int., in EMK int., Nov. 29, 2006, Miller Center, UVA.

582 **"I never thought I was going":** Vicki Kennedy, on *Oprah Winfrey Show,* Nov. 25, 2009.

582 **possibly through a relationship:** Patrick Kennedy int. by author.

582 **"I think there was a note":** John Tunney int., Oct. 12, 2009, Miller Center, UVA.

582 **"low key":** Vicki Kennedy, on *Oprah Winfrey Show,* Nov. 25, 2009.

582 **"Oh, Mom. We're just friends":** Canellos, *Last Lion,* 287.

582 **"It didn't happen to her":** Thomas, "Victoria Reggie."

582 **"I can't talk about":** Ibid.

582 **"We could tell that it":** Ibid.

583 **"radio silence":** EMK, *True Compass,* 425–26.

583 **"Very old-fashioned"**: Victoria Reggie Kennedy int., Apr. 8, 2010, Miller Center, UVA.

583 **"so close and connected"**: Ibid.

583 **"Just friends"**: Edmund and Doris Reggie int., Aug. 8, 2005.

584 **"Oh my. I really miss"**: Walsh, "Hidden Campaign."

584 **"awakened these feelings"**: Vicki Kennedy, on *Oprah Winfrey Show*, Nov. 25, 2009.

584 **"It just wow, boom"**: Victoria Reggie Kennedy int., Apr. 8, 2010.

584 **"It was just about Vicki"**: Ibid.

585 **almost no paper trail**: Jon Meacham, *Destiny and Power: The American Odyssey of George Herman Walker Bush* (New York: Random House, 2015), 419–20.

585 **You resolved your doubts**: Jeff Blattner int., Mar. 30, 2007, Miller Center, UVA.

585 **"not necessarily tear down"**: Meacham, *Destiny*, 420.

585 **"best qualified"**: Former Aide B int., Sept. 25, 1998, Unnamed Sources Folder, Box 5, Series 2, Clymer Papers, JFK Lib.

585 **"unqualified"**: EMK, *True Compass*, 431.

586 **"Well, this isn't a briefing"**: EMK int., Aug. 7, 2007, Miller Center, UVA.

586 **"at length"**: EMK int., Feb. 12, 2007, Miller Center, UVA.

586 **make up his mind**: Timothy Phelps, *Capitol Games: Clarence Thomas, Anita Hill, and the Story of a Supreme Court Nomination* (New York: Hyperion, 1992), 80.

586 **"It's a battle"**: Quoted in Jane Mayer and Jill Abramson, *Strange Justice: The Selling of Clarence Thomas* (Boston: Houghton Mifflin, 1994), 198–99.

587 **loath to challenge him**: Carolyn Osolinik int., Mar. 27, 2007, Miller Center, UVA.

587 **"You needed that job"**: William S. Link, *Righteous Warrior: Jesse Helms and the Rise of Modern Conservatism* (New York: St. Martin's Press, 2008), 378.

587 **"they all, to a person"**: EMK int., Feb. 12, 2007.

587 **Thomas was their Texas Western**: Ralph Neas int. by author.

588 **"shed the baggage"**: "In Trying to Clarify What He Is Not, Thomas Opens Question of What He Is," *NYT*, Sept. 13, 1991.

588 **"closet liberal, a conservative"**: "Questions for Thomas Fall Short of Mark," *NYT*, Sept. 15, 1991.

588 **"He's lying"**: Paul Simon, *P.S.: The Autobiography of Paul Simon* (n.p.: Bonus Books, 1999), 189.

588 **"hearts really weren't"**: Mayer and Abramson, *Strange Justice*, 218.

589 **"A judge must not bring"**: "Excerpts from Senate's Hearing on the Thomas Nomination," *NYT*, Sept. 11, 1991.

589 **"You've trashed the leaders"**: "Thomas Concludes Testimony," *WP*, Sept. 17, 1991; "Thomas Ends Testimony But Senators Grumble," *NYT*, Sept. 17, 1991.

589 **"triple play"**: "Excerpts from Remarks by Members of the Senate," *NYT*, Sept. 28, 1991.

589 **"I continue to have"**: *The Nomination of Judge Clarence Thomas, Hearings Before U.S. Senate Judiciary Comm.*, 102d Cong., 1st sess., Sept. 16, 1991, 444–53.

591 **"indicated she needed time"**: Michael Wines, "How the Senators Handled the Professor's Accusations," *NYT*, Oct. 8, 1991.

591 **raced to the hearing room**: Phelps, *Capitol Games*, 175.

591 **whether Hill would publicly testify**: David A. Kaplan, "Anatomy of a Debacle," *Newsweek*, Oct. 21, 1991; Mayer and Abramson, *Strange Justice*, 225, 230–31.

591 **"My first reaction was that"**: Osolinik int.

592 **"He feared his involvement"**: Mayer and Abramson, *Strange Justice*, 233–34.

592 **"utility"**: "Excerpts of Senator Biden's Chronology of the Complaint by Anita Hill," *NYT*, Oct. 8, 1991.

593 **his wristwatch flew off**: Jeffrey Blattner int., *Frontline*, PBS, Jan. 11, 2019, https://www.pbs.org/wgbh/frontline/interview/jeff-blattner/.

593 **just before the vote**: Ibid.; "Delaying the Vote: How the Senators Reached Accord," *NYT*, Oct. 10, 1991.

593 **"Any vote on the merits"**: "Comments by Senators on Thomas Nomination," *NYT*, Oct. 10, 1991.

594 **Biden permitted Thomas**: Walter V. Robinson, "A Day of Charges and Denials," *BG*, Oct. 12, 1991.

594 **"There were a number of people"**: Phelps, *Capitol Games*, 394.

594 **"I have never in all"**: *Nomination of Judge Clarence Thomas, Hearings Before U.S. Senate Judiciary Comm.*, 102d Cong., 1st sess., Oct. 11, 1991, 5–10.

595 **"greatest travesty I've ever"**: Ibid., 27–29.

595 **"began to use work situations"**: Anita Hill, "Testimony to Senate Judiciary Comm.," Oct. 11, 1991, http://www.speeches-usa.com/Transcripts/anita_hill-testimony.html.

596 **"Her life will never be"**: Blatter int. *Frontline.*

596 **"victim of the process"**: "Judge Clarence Thomas: 'My Name Has Been Harmed,' " *NYT,* Oct. 12, 1991.

596 **"invisible men"**: "Kennedy Speaks Up," *WP,* Oct. 14, 1991.

596 **"liberal activism"**: Mayer and Abramson, *Strange Justice,* 205.

596 **"If Senator Kennedy"**: Robinson, "Day of Charges and Denials."

597 **"dignity"**: *Hearings,* Oct. 11, 1991, 118.

597 **"I hope we are not going"**: Ibid., 307–8.

597 subjected to the same pressures: Mayer and Abramson, *Strange Justice,* 321–45.

598 **"There's no proof that Anita"**: "Court's 2d Black," *NYT,* Oct. 16, 1991.

598 **"There is a very strong"**: "Each Side Seeks to Get Benefit of Doubt," *NYT,* Oct. 15, 1991.

598 Only 22 percent approved: "After Judging Thomas, Senators Face the Public," *NYT,* Oct. 21, 1991.

598 **"For just a moment"**: Anna Quindlen, "Trouble With Teddy," *NYT,* Oct. 19, 1991.

599 **"severe image problem"**: Quoted in "Succor for a Wounded 'Liberal Lion,' " *BG,* Oct. 18, 1991.

599 **"I have the greatest respect"**: Barbara Ehrenreich, "Women Would Have Known," *Time,* Oct. 21, 1991.

599 **"seems to be the most"**: Michael Kranish, "Fathoming a Subdued Kennedy," *BG,* Sept. 13, 1991.

599 **"most memorable visual"**: Mark Shields, "Finally Fed Up in Massachusetts," *WP,* Sept. 20, 1991.

599 **"tragedy in slow motion"**: David Nyhan, "For Kennedy, a Tragedy in Slow Motion," *BG,* Oct. 20, 1991.

600 **"The idea that you have"**: Former Aide C int., May 11, 1998, Unnamed Sources Folder, Box 5, Series 2, Clymer Papers, JFK Lib.

600 **"Yeah, there is certainly"**: EMK int., Nov. 11, 1998, EMK Interviews 1997–99 Folder, Box 5, Series 2, Clymer Papers, JFK Lib.

600 **"This is about the time"**: EMK int., Feb. 12, 2007.

600 **"with all the background"**: EMK, *True Compass,* 433.

602 **"sank like a stone"**: Blattner int., Mar. 30, 2007.

602 **"disparate impact"**: Charles Fried, "The Civil Rights Sham of 1990," *NYT,* Oct. 4, 1990.

602–3 **"It didn't make any"**: EMK int., Aug. 7, 2007.

603 explicit intention to discriminate: See Mark Stern, "Party Alignments and Civil Rights," *Presidential Studies Quarterly* (Summer 1995): 417–20.

603 **"dramatically closer"**: Ibid.

603 Sununu kept balking: Richard Cohen, "Crumbling Committees," *National Journal,* Aug. 4, 1990.

603 **"red-faced"**: "America's 10 Best Senators," *Time,* Apr. 24, 2006.

603 **"significant relationship"**: "Civil Rights Veto Stems from Dispute Over Discrimination Ruling," *WP,* Oct. 24, 1990.

603 **"When it came down to it"**: "Exchange with Reporters in Alexandria, VA," October 31, 1990, Public Papers, George H. W. Bush, Bush Lib.

604 would have to wait: Stern, "Party Alignments," 419–20.

604 **"If Democrats want"**: Ibid., 423.

604 **"You could find the center"**: John Danforth int., Oct. 25, 2005, Miller Center, UVA.

604 **"good will"**: "G.O.P. Senators Press Accord on Rights Bill," *NYT,* June 13, 1991.

605 letting Danforth make an effort: Ibid.

605 **"long meetings with lots"**: Stern, "Party Alignments," 423.

606 **"The President says"**: "President Rejects Senate Agreement on Rights," *NYT,* Aug. 2, 1991.

606 **"stark naked"**: Danforth int.

606 **"All this innuendo"**: Ibid.

607 **"one crusty son of a bitch"**: Blattner int., Mar. 30, 2007.

607 met with Sununu and Gray: "White House and Senate in Accord on Civil Rights Bill," *BG,* Oct. 25, 1991.

607 **"We had deals many times"**: "Sununu Says He's Back," *BG,* Sept. 29, 1991.

607 **"We did not know"**: "Senator Danforth and the Snipers," *NYT,* July 10, 1991.

607 **"lurking"**: Danforth int.; Former Aide B int.

607 agreed to an amendment: Stern, "Party Alignments," 423.

607 **brought six Republicans:** Adam Clymer, "Senate Democrats Back a Compromise on Civil Rights Bill," *NYT*, Oct. 26, 1991.

608 **friendships in the Senate:** Adam Clymer, "Senators and Bush Reach Agreement on Civil Rights Bill," *NYT*, Oct. 25, 1991.

608 **signing the bill was payback:** Mayer and Abramson, *Strange Justice*, 351.

608 **"it's a no-quota bill":** Clymer, "Senators and Bush Reach."

608 **"lot of words":** Michael Frisby, "Political Signals and the Civil Rights Compromise," *BG*, Oct. 27, 1991.

608 **"job-related for the position":** "The Compromise on Civil Rights," *NYT*, Oct. 26, 1991.

609 **"That's what's really great":** Danforth int.

609 **Danforth's fellow Republicans:** Clymer, "Senators and Bush Reach."

609 **"white hot":** "Bush Endorses Senate Rights Bill," *BG*, Oct. 26, 1991.

609 **"Only one person":** Neas int.

609 **"enthusiastically":** Stern, "Party Alignments," 422.

609 **"I think that President Bush":** Clymer, "Senate Democrats Back Compromise."

610 **tried to convince Bush:** Neas int.

610 **"needed to reestablish":** EMK, *True Compass*, 434.

610 **"What's different now":** "Kennedy Slips in Poll," *WP*, Aug. 2, 1991.

611 **"He nearly took the whole":** Patrick Kennedy int.

611 **"It would not get better":** John A. Farrell, "Comeback Kid Rising from the Ashes," *BG Magazine*, Nov. 21, 1993.

611 **"I think he was very disturbed":** Charles Tretter int., Aug. 8, 2005, Miller Center, UVA.

611 **"The thing that struck me":** Ibid.

611 **"I just couldn't believe it":** Laurence Leamer, *The Kennedy Women: The Saga of an American Family* (New York: Villard Books, 1994), 769.

611 **"I don't really":** "Kennedy: I Recognize My Shortcomings," *Newsweek*, Nov. 4, 1991.

611 **"after Palm Beach":** Paul Donovan int., Nov. 14, 1998, D Folder, Box 3, Series 2, Clymer Papers, JFK Lib.

612 **"outside your ability":** E. J. Dionne, Jr., "Change for Kennedy," *WP*, Aug. 28, 1991.

612 **"settle down":** Quoted in Adam Clymer, *Edward M. Kennedy: A Biography* (New York: Harper Perennial, 2000), 489.

612 **"I'm just about ready":** Quoted in Walsh, "Hidden Campaign."

612 **"Boy, are you lucky":** Victoria Reggie Kennedy int., Apr. 8, 2010.

612 **"I want to address that":** Quoted in Canellos, *Last Lion*, 260.

613 **debated over the words:** "Kennedy Admits Personal 'Faults,'" *BG*, Oct. 26, 1991.

613 **"logical, inevitable":** Walsh, "Hidden Campaign"; "Kennedy Admits Personal 'Faults' "; "Facing Questions of Private Life, Kennedy Apologizes," *NYT*, Oct. 26, 1991; "Kennedy, in Harvard Speech, Acknowledges 'Faults,' " *WP*, Oct. 26, 1991; William J. Eaton, "Kennedy Admits Personal Frailties, Vows to Fight On," *LAT*, Oct. 26, 1991. Note Walsh wrote "a third of a century" but *NYT* a "quarter of a century."

614 **"The speech speaks for itself":** "Kennedy Admits Personal 'Faults.' "

614 **"quiet dinner":** EMK, *True Compass*, 435.

614 **"stories of excessive":** Jeff Greenfield, *Nightline*, ABC, Oct. 25, 1991.

615 **"It is never easy":** Korman to EMK, n.d. [1991], Box 1, Nancy Korman Personal Papers, JFK Lib.

615 **"To me":** Kennedy and Fried, *Common Struggle*, 98; Patrick Kennedy int.

615 **hired private investigators:** "Smith's Team Seeks to Discredit Accuser Quickly," *NYT*, Apr. 11, 1991.

615 **"very top of the Southern":** "Smith's Lawyer Exhibits a Taste for Tough Cases," *NYT*, Dec. 9, 1991.

616 **"long-standing psychological":** "Smith Lawyer: Accuser Has 'Psychological Disorder,' " *WP*, Aug. 10, 1991.

616 **flogging the discovery:** "Rape Suspect Tied to Prior Incidents," *NYT*, July 23, 1991; "Accusations Against Kennedy Nephew Detailed," *NYT*, July 24, 1991.

616 **"worst case of pretrial":** Stephen Gillers quoted in "Then There Were Three," *Time*, Aug. 5, 1991.

616 **"Ted's greatest hits":** "Willie Smith's Dogged Defender," *WP*, Dec. 2, 1991; "Sobering Times," *Newsweek*, Dec. 8, 1991; "As Selection of Smith Jurors Begins, Focus in on History of the Kennedys," *NYT*, Nov. 1, 1991.

616 **"most-watched legal":** "Case No. 91-5982 Comes to Trial," *Newsweek*, Dec. 9, 1991.

616 "Your client raped me!": "Smith Lawyers Assail Accuser's Memory," *NYT*, Dec. 6, 1991.

617 "throwing every question": Melody Miller int., July 15, 2008, Miller Center, UVA.

617 "major memorandum": Melody Miller int., Oct. 7, 2008, Miller Center, UVA.

617 "That just was not": Victoria Reggie Kennedy, Apr. 8, 2010; Craig quoted in "Kennedy to Marry Lawyer, 38," *BG*, Mar. 15, 1992.

617 "You could stake out": "Sobering Times."

617 "rock bottom": Quoted in Burton Hersh, *The Shadow President: Ted Kennedy in Opposition* (South Royalton, Vt.: Steerforth Press, 1997), 104.

618 "near riot": Dominick Dunne, "The Verdict," *Vanity Fair*, Mar. 1992.

618 "final, unavoidable collision": Robin Toner, "In the Glare of Latest Scandal, Kennedy Defends the Dynasty," *NYT*, Dec. 7, 1991.

618 "I wish I'd gone": "Kennedy Questioning Elicits Reminiscence of Tragedies," *WP*, Dec. 7, 1991.

618 "Suddenly, it wasn't": Quoted in Canellos, *Last Lion*, 281.

618 "sad smile and stiff wave": Toner, "In the Glare."

618 "boy-next-door performance": "Palm Beach Trial," *Time*, Dec. 23, 1991.

619 "When he was testifying": "Smith's Lawyer Credits Kennedy Charisma," *WP*, Dec. 13, 1991.

619 "My life was in their hands": "Jury Finds Smith Not Guilty of Rape," *WP*, Dec. 12, 1991.

619 "always believed that": "Courthouse Crowd Cheers Ex-Defendant," *WP*, Dec. 12, 1991.

619 "They'll stick by Willie": Dunne, "Verdict."

619 prayer for the accuser: Ibid.

619 forced to admit his drug use: "Senator's Son Had Drug Fling," *BG*, Dec. 10, 1991.

620 "It took me a really long time": "Ted Kennedy Jr. Quits the Fast Lane," *BG*, Oct. 7, 1993.

620 "great blow": Kennedy and Fried, *Common Struggle*, 97.

620 "The whole world": Patrick Kennedy int.; Kennedy and Fried, *Common Struggle*, 101–4.

FIFTEEN: "STABILITY AND TRANQUILITY"

622 "We'd see the two of them": "Kennedy Engagement," *BG*, Mar. 16, 1992.

622 "get used to him": Caroline Raclin int., Nov. 11, 2009, Miller Center, UVA.

622 "He loved it": Vicki Kennedy, on *Oprah Winfrey Show*, Nov. 25, 2009.

622 "were so sweet to me": Victoria Reggie Kennedy int., Apr. 8, 2010, Miller Center, UVA.

622 "I love your daughter": Edmund Reggie int., Dec. 16, 2008, Miller Center, UVA.

622 "I knew this one": Melody Miller int., July 15, 2008, Miller Center, UVA.

623 asked for their blessing: Edmund and Doris Reggie int., Aug. 8, 2005, Miller Center, UVA.

623 called John Culver: Burton Hersh, *The Shadow President: Ted Kennedy in Opposition* (South Royalton, Vt.: Steerforth Press, 1997), 108.

623 keep the engagement secret: EMK, *True Compass* (New York: Twelve, 2009), 426–27.

623 "another girlfriend of Teddy's": Victoria Reggie Kennedy int.

623 dressed as Rhett Butler: "Time to Marry? Right, Said Ted," *People*, Mar. 30, 1992.

624 "I've known her": "Kennedy Announces Plans to Wed Washington Lawyer," *WP*, Mar. 15, 1992.

624 "discovered": EMK, *True Compass*, 427.

624 "We had never discussed": Victoria Reggie Kennedy int.

624 "I think Vicki desperately": John Tunney int., Oct. 12, 2009, Miller Center, UVA.

624 "So he's got this woman": Patrick Kennedy int. by author.

625 "say a few words": Victoria Reggie Kennedy int.

625 "awkward": Terri Haddad Robinson int., Aug. 25, 2009, Miller Center, UVA.

625 "Actually, I'm really": Miller int.

626 "And then my heart": Elsa Walsh, "Kennedy's Hidden Campaign," *New Yorker*, Mar. 31, 1997; "Kennedy Quietly Ties the Knot," *BG*, July 5, 1992; Edmund and Doris Reggie int., Aug. 8, 2005; "Names and Faces," *BG*, July 8, 1992.

626 "He put it to rest": John A. Farrell, "Comeback Kid Rising from the Ashes," *BG Magazine*, Nov. 21, 1993.

626 "from a lot of other": Walsh, "Hidden Campaign."

626 "such a sense of stabilty": EMK, *True Compass*, 2.

626 "She has that wonderful": EMK int., Oct. 29, 1994, EMK Interviews 1992–94 Folder, Box 5, Series 2, Clymer Papers, JFK Lib.

627 "He just seems more": James Sasser int., May 25, 2006, Miller Center, UVA.

627 "More accessible than": Heather Campion quoted in Peter Canellos, *Last Lion: The Fall and Rise of Ted Kennedy* (New York: Simon & Schuster, 2009), 288.

627 "A healthy relationship": Miller int.

627 "chemistry": Curran Raclin int., Oct. 16, 2009, Miller Center, UVA.

627 "It's slightly scary": Caroline Raclin int.

627 "Poor Beast": Farrell, "Comeback Kid Rising."

627 "when she was cooking": Walsh, "Hidden Campaign."

627 "You don't mind": Lloyd Grove, "The Liberal Element," *WP*, July 9, 1996.

627 He even drank less: Patrick Kennedy and Steven Fried, *A Common Struggle: A Personal Journey Through the Past and Future of Mental Illness and Addiction* (New York: Blue Rider Press, 2015), 265.

627 "Just a different phase": Melissa Ludtke int. by author.

628 "his fidelity is beyond": Edmund and Doris Reggie int., Aug. 8, 2005.

628 she could tell it better: Lee Fentress int., Oct. 16, 2009, Miller Center, UVA.

628 "a bit volatile": EMK int., Nov. 29, 2006, Miller Center, UVA.

628 "I thought I was marrying": Edmund and Doris Reggie int., Aug. 8, 2005.

628 "torture her": Caroline Raclin int.

628 "He loved home": Victoria Reggie Kennedy int.

628 go back to The Bag: George Colt, "Is Ted Kennedy's Midlife Crisis Finally Over?" *Life*, Aug. 1994.

629 preferred to spend that time: Nick Littlefield int., Feb. 14, 2009, Miller Center, UVA.

629 pore over clippings: Caroline Raclin int.

629 "If there was a textbook": Curran Raclin int., Nov. 10, 2009, Miller Center, UVA.

629 signed both their names: Caroline Raclin, on *Oprah Winfrey Show*, Nov. 25, 2009.

629 "pal": Curran Raclin int., Nov. 10, 2009.

629 "childlike": Caroline Raclin int.

629 "Every night": Curran Raclin int., Nov. 10, 2009.

629 "Always calming": Ibid.

630 "It didn't really": Ibid.

630 "sports nut": "The Senator's Wife Does It All," *BG*, Nov. 11, 1993.

630 "She wanted Teddy": Tunney int.

631 "I know": Caroline Raclin int.

631 "Five minutes! Four minutes!": Ibid.

631 beam in pride: Edmund Reggie int., Dec. 16, 2008.

631 "recipe for divorce": Curran Raclin int., Nov. 10, 2009.

631 "her face pointing": Caroline Raclin int.

631 obsessed with those ospreys: Ibid.

632 "The man I used to know": Joan Kennedy int., Sept. 19, 1998, K Folder, Box 4, Series 2, Clymer Papers, JFK Lib.

633 had bonded then: Walsh, "Hidden Campaign."

633 "very first person": Ibid.

633 "moral argument I could": John A. Farrell, "Legend, Chemistry Forge Clinton-Kennedy Link," *BG*, Oct. 28, 1993.

633 "Too many of the people": Bill Clinton, DLC Keynote Address, May 6, 1991, https://www.c-span.org/video/?17869-1/democratic-leadership-council-keynote-address.

633 "talked not about what": Joan Didion, *Political Fictions* (2001; New York: Vintage, 2002), 165.

633 withhold support from Clinton: "A Winning Agenda from Kennedy," *BG*, Mar. 19, 1992.

634 "four days and four nights": Didion, *Political Fictions*, 119–20.

634 perfunctory speech: "A Favorite Son Is Recalled in RFK Film," *BG*, July 16, 1992.

634 report out a national health: "Senate Unit Backs a Health Proposal," *BG*, Jan. 23, 1992.

634 proposed a government program: "Parties Spar on Education," *BG*, Jan. 22, 1992.

634 "They don't do anything": "Bush Seen Adding to Gridlock on the Hill," *BG*, Aug. 6, 1992.

634 "To Orrin, handle": Orrin Hatch int., Feb. 27, 1992, H Folder, Box 3, Series 2, Clymer Papers, JFK Lib.

635 "Why don't we do something": Nick Littlefield int., Feb. 15, 2009, Miller Center, UVA.

635 struck a compromise: "US Senate Oks $1.9 B in Urban Aid," *BG*, May 22, 1992; "Senate Oks Education Bill," *BG*, July 1, 1992; "Bush Seen Adding to Gridlock on the Hill," *BG*, Aug. 6, 1992.

635 "You've got to do it": Nancy Soderberg int., Oct. 9, 2008, Miller Center, UVA.

636 preferred Clinton to Bush: Stanley Greenberg, *The Two Americas: Our Current Political Deadlock and How to Break It* (New York: St. Martin's Press, 2005), 64–65.

636 "It was almost as if": Sean Wilentz, *The Age of Reagan: A History 1974–2008* (New York: Harper-Collins, 2008), 314.

636 "how President Kennedy": Farrell, "Legend, Chemistry."

636 visited John and Bobby's gravesite: "Pilgrimage to the Grave of an Inspiration," *BG*, Jan. 20, 1993.

636 Kennedy's presidential style: Farrell, "Legend, Chemistry."

636 "singularly, calm, optimistic": Adam Clymer, "After Three Decades Working in the Senate, Kennedy Gets a Turn for His Agenda," *NYT*, Mar. 3, 1993.

637 "Well, Bob, I'm very": EMK int., Aug. 8, 2007, Miller Center, UVA.

637 "Normally, you just say": "Challenge Portends Hard Sell," *BG*, Feb. 4, 1993.

638 "These guys don't want": Quoted in Lewis Gould, *The Most Exclusive Club: A History of the Modern Senate* (New York: Basic Books, 2005), 281.

638 "A sacred place": Joe Biden, *Promises to Keep: On Life and Politics* (New York: Random House, 2007), xvii.

638 "Flying through": Jeffrey Blattner int., Mar. 30, 2007, Miller Center, UVA.

639 "heated exchange": Rick Atkinson, "Why Ted Kennedy Can't Stand Still," *WP Magazine*, Apr. 29, 1990.

639 "inner sanctum": Biden, *Promises*, 90–91.

639 "It's awfully difficult to say": George Packer, "The Empty Chamber," *New Yorker*, Aug. 9, 2010.

639 meet in the cocktail lounge: Robert Dove int. by author.

639 "There was just an": J. Stanley Kimmitt oral history, 2003, 99, Senate Historical Office.

640 "best way to prevent bad": George Mitchell int., Sept. 6, 2011, Miller Center, UVA.

640 "On great issues": Robert Byrd, *Leading the United States Senate* (Washington, D.C.: U.S. Govt. Printing Office, 2003), 51–52.

641 "Some of the newer": Fentress int.

641 "It's ITT": Robert Dole int., May 15, 2006, Miller Center, UVA.

641 "You never get": Ibid.

641 real motive all along: Packer, "Empty Chamber."

641 Baker changed the schedule: EMK, *True Compass*, 486–87.

641 "people listened to each other": EMK int., June 3, 2005, Miller Center, UVA.

642 "They vote and leave": William Hildenbrand oral history, 1981–85, Senate Historical Office.

642 "Everybody knew you": EMK int., Mar. 23, 2005, Miller Center, UVA.

642 "corruption of the Senate": EMK int., June 3, 2005.

642–43 "Floor debate has deteriorated": Nancy Kassebaum, "The Senate Is Not in Order," *WP*, Jan. 19, 1988.

643 "He knows the game": Farrell, "Comeback Kid Rising."

643 "independent contractor": Byrd, *Leading*, 35.

643 "The guys you try": Quoted in Kenneth Feinberg int., July 8, 2008, Miller Center, UVA.

643 "Personalistic": John Hibbing and Sue Thomas, "The Modern United States Senate: What Is Accorded Respect," *Journal of Politics* 52, no. 1 (Feb. 1990): 127.

643 "Owned lock, stock": Arthur Schlesinger, Jr., *Journals: 1952–2000*, ed. Andrew Schlesinger and Stephen Schlesinger (New York: Penguin Press, 2007), 449.

644 "getting things through": Dove int.

644 his or her own interests: Richard Cohen, "Crumbling Committees," *National Journal*, Aug. 4, 1990, 1876–77.

644 "That changed the whole": Kimmitt oral history, 19–20.

645 closed-circuit television: Robert Byrd, *The Senate: 1789–1989: Addresses on the History of the Senate* (Washington, D.C.: U.S. Govt. Printing Office, 1988), 2:615.

645 make government mediagenic: Stephen Hess, "Decline and Fall of Congressional News," *Society* 31, no. 2 (1993): 75. Hess cites a study of the *NYT* front pages that he conducted, showing a decline in government/political coverage of 30 percent from 1965 to 1992, and another by Robert Lichter of television evening news that showed a decline of 21 percent [76].

645 "What I learned over time": Nick Littlefield int., May 3, 2008, Miller Center, UVA.

645 "continuous plebiscite": Stephen Breyer int., June 17, 2008, Miller Center, UVA.

645 "No one has looked": Quoted in "Dramatic Changes in the Senate," *People*, Aug. 18, 1986.

645 Senate hearing videotapes edited: Thomas Rollins int., Mar. 10, 2009, Miller Center, UVA.

646 "Combative": Carey Parker int., Nov. 11, 2008, Miller Center, UVA.

646 "They're like football teams": Dove int.

646 "I hope you know": David Broder int., Dec. 1, 2006, Miller Center, UVA.

647 "Political polarization": Byrd, *Leading*, 51–52.

647 "Everything is so closely": "At 70, Kennedy Still a Power," *BG*, Feb. 22, 2002.

647 "It's amazing how": EMK int., Feb. 12, 2007, Miller Center, UVA.

647 "His voice cracking": Feinberg int.

648 "A handshake with Ted": Farrell, "Comeback Kid Rising."

648 "If the Department of Health": EMK int., Mar. 23, 2005.

648 "I suppose you're one": Nick Littlefield int., May 4, 2008, Miller Center, UVA.

649 parents in the waiting room: Jack Newfield, "The Senate's Fighting Liberal," *Nation*, Mar. 25, 2002.

649 Bush had vetoed it: "House Backs Bush Veto of Family Leave Bill," *NYT*, July 26, 1990.

649 another bill that Bush: Nick Littlefield int., Feb. 15, 2009, Miller Center, UVA.

650 those bills began moving: Nick Littlefield int., June 30, 2008, Miller Center, UVA.

650 compromised with Republican: "Senate OK's Bill to Outlaw Abortion Clinic Blockades," *BG*, Nov. 17, 1993.

650 "He went to the House": Littlefield int., Feb. 15, 2009.

651 "some of the most": Ana Puga, "For Sen. Kennedy, a Hectic Period of Victories," *BG*, Aug. 7, 1993.

651 "never changed his work": Littlefield int., May 3, 2008.

651 "tireless": Puga, "Hectic Period."

651 "Kennedy is walking proof": "Stacked Up Against the Rhetoric About Kennedy," *BG*, Dec. 2, 1993.

651 "He's as good at what": Walsh, "Hidden Campaign."

651 "The talk on the Hill": Farrell, "Comeback Kid Rising."

652 "to move beyond ideology": Ibid.

652 "This was a new model": Littlefield int., Feb. 15, 2009.

653 keep the federal government: Colin Gordon, *Dead on Arrival: The Politics of Health Care in Twentieth-Century America* (Princeton: Princeton Univ. Press, 2003), 37–38.

653 "It is not backdoor": "Bill Requires Employer-Provided Health Insurance," *WP*, May 20, 1987.

653 mounted a campaign: Paul Donovan int., Nov. 14, 1998, D Folder, Box 3, Series 2, Clymer Papers, JFK Lib.

653 it was later repealed: David Broder and Haynes Johnson, *The System: The American Way of Politics at the Breaking Point* (Boston: Little, Brown, 1996), 68–69.

653 there was no consensus: John Rockefeller IV, "The Pepper Commission Report on National Healthcare," *New England Journal of Medicine* 323 (Oct. 4, 1990): 1005–7.

653 derailed by business opposition: "Expanded Health Insurance Proposed," *WP*, Apr. 13, 1989; EMK int., Nov. 11, 1998, EMK Interviews 1997–99 Folder, Box 5, Series 2, Clymer Papers, JFK Lib.

653 "We are closer": "Say Ouch: Demands to Fix US Health Care Reach a Crescendo," *NYT*, May 19, 1991.

653 created tax credits: "Heeding Elections, Lawmakers Offer Health-Care Ideas," *NYT*, Nov. 8, 1991.

653 again an employer mandate bill: "The Scary Politics of Health," *Newsweek*, June 24, 1991; "Senate Democrats to Offer Plan to Restrain Health-Care Costs," *NYT*, May 25, 1991.

654 "The answer rests": Gordon, *Dead on Arrival*, 1.

654 "What we really oppose": Quoted in George Colt, "Is Ted Kennedy's Midlife Crisis Finally Over?" *Life*, Aug. 1994.

654 "wrong it was": Bill Clinton, Remarks at Northeastern University, Jan. 11, 2001, https://www.presidency.ucsb.edu/documents/remarks-northeastern-university-boston-massachusetts.

654 "The bill is ready": Littlefield int., May 3, 2008.

655 "very specific": Victoria Reggie Kennedy in EMK int., Mar. 28, 2008, Miller Center, UVA.

655 "I think we're off": "Kennedy Hails Meeting with Clinton," *BG*, Dec. 9, 1992.

655 play-or-pay plan: Littlefield int., May 3, 2008.

655 John Chafee's bill: EMK, *True Compass*, 453–54.

655 Task Force to Reform Health Care: Stuart Altman and David Schachtman, *Power, Politics and*

Universal Health Care: The Inside Story of a Century-Long Battle (Amherst, N.Y.: Prometheus Books, 2011), 62–63.

655 **moral underpinnings:** Judy Feder int., July 5, 2007, Miller Center, UVA.

656 **odds of getting health insurance:** EMK int., Feb. 5, 1993, EMK Interviews 1992–94 Folder, Box 5, Series 2, Clymer Papers, JFK Lib.

656 **"It was the economy, stupid":** "Kennedy's Forty Year Push for Universal Coverage," WBUR, Jan. 21, 2009.

656 **"Kick the health-care can":** Bill Clinton, *My Life* (New York: Knopf, 2004), 492–93.

657 **Clintons sidetracked them:** Gordon, 274.

657 **"They didn't talk to":** Rashi Fein int., Mar. 21, 2007, Miller Center, UVA.

657 **"roll" Moynihan:** John A. Farrell int., July 13, 2006, Miller Center, UVA.

657 **"dirt underneath":** EMK, *True Compass*, 454–55.

657 **"There's a difference":** Feder int.

657 **"could do this without":** Mitchell int.

658 **"The Republicans complain":** Littlefield int., May 3, 2008.

658 **"We had the perception":** Chris Jennings int. by author; Feder int.

658 **"Whoever is interested":** EMK int., Mar. 28, 2008.

658 **"this was the last opportunity":** Jennings int.

658 **conference at the Tufts School:** "Sen. Edward Kennedy to Hold Health Reform Conference" (press release), Mar. 30, 1993; "Message Mixed on Health Policies," *BG*, Apr. 6, 1993.

658 **"went a little bit":** Jennings int.

658 **"The best of all things":** Ibid.

659 **"came to appreciate":** Hillary Clinton int., May 21, 1998, C Folder, Box 3, Series 2, Clymer Papers, JFK Lib.

659 **"At one point, his":** Nick Littlefield and David Nexon, *Lion of the Senate: When Ted Kennedy Rallied the Democrats in a GOP Congress* (New York: Simon & Schuster, 2015), 26.

659 **"unprecedented access":** Jennings int.

659 **"everywhere":** Feder int.

659 **spent 90 percent of his time:** Quoted in Hersh, *Shadow President*, 112.

659 **"Relentless":** Ibid., 117.

660 **"more than probably":** Jennings int.

660 **"them all eating out":** Hillary Clinton int.

660–61 **three types of coverage:** See Nicholas Laham, *A Lost Cause: Bill Clinton's Plan for National Health Insurance* (New York: Praeger, 1996), 29–30.

661 **"new chapter":** Adam Clymer, "Clinton Asks Backing for Sweeping Change in Health Care System," *NYT*, Sept. 23, 1993; transcript, *NYT*, Sept. 23, 1993.

662 **"coolest person":** Broder and Johnson, *System*, 3–5; Clinton, *My Life*, 549.

662 **"I've waited all":** Walsh, "Hidden Campaign."

662 **"giant social experiment":** Clymer, "Clinton Asks Backing."

662 **"They are very well":** "Kennedy Vows Fast Pace on Bill to Head Off Special Interests," *BG*, Sept. 24, 1993.

662 **"You have added your":** "GOP's Jeffords Backs Clinton on Care," *BG*, Sept. 30, 1993.

662 **"She was a rock star":** Jennings int.

663 **favorability rating had risen:** "Job Performance Ratings for President Clinton," Roper Center, https://web.archive.org/web/20121023010425/http://webapps.ropercenter.uconn.edu/CFIDE/roper/presidential/webroot/presidential_rating_detail.cfm?allRate=True&presidentName=Clinton.

663 **"government-run":** EMK, *True Compass*, 455.

663 **hard for him to refuse Ted:** Robert Byrd int., Feb. 12, 1993, B Folder, Box 3, Series 2, Clymer Papers, JFK Lib.

664 **"It was all to find out":** EMK int., Mar. 28, 2008.

664 **"He hated the Clintons":** Jennings int.

664 **"He couldn't have been":** Ibid.

664 **"Completely uncooperative":** EMK int., Mar. 28, 2008.

665 **"in his prime":** Tom Daschle int., Apr. 29, 2009, Miller Center, UVA.

665 **"pitched a fit":** Littlefield int., May 3, 2008; "Kennedy Gains in Turf War on Health Bill," *BG*, Nov. 23, 1993.

665 **hold the bill at his desk:** Daschle int.

665 "huge fight": Dove int.

665 urged him to wait: Broder and Johnson, *System*, 346–48.

665 scrutinize the bill: Ibid.

666 "*political* threat": William Kristol to Republican leaders, "Defeating President Clinton's Health Care Proposal" (memo), Dec. 2, 1993, https://www.scribd.com/document/12926608/William -Kristol-s-1993-Memo-Defeating-President-Clinton-s-Health-Care-Proposal.

666 "big enchilada": Farrell, "Comeback Kid Rising."

666 "If you send me": John Harris, *The Survivor: Bill Clinton in the White House* (New York: Random House, 2005), 110–11.

666 "In '93, the opposition": EMK int., Nov. 11, 1998.

666 "exhilarating and promising": Broder and Johnson, *System*, 347–48.

667 "Time is not our friend": Jennings int.

667 "to achieve some success": Nancy Kassebaum int., Apr. 6, 2009, Miller Center, UVA.

667 only abet Bill Clinton: Littlefield int., May 3, 2008.

667 "This is really going": Kassebaum int.

667 no healthcare crisis: Laham, *Lost Cause*, 89. He had made the statement on *Meet the Press*, Jan. 9, 1994.

667 "potentially hurt many": Broder and Johnson, *System*, 393.

668 "many conversations": Sheila Burke int., July 27, 2007, Miller Center, UVA.

668 He felt he could do it: Broder and Johnson, *System*, 352–53.

668 "One small step": "Kennedy Move Advances Health Bill," *BG*, May 20, 1994.

668 made other concessions: Adam Clymer, *Edward M. Kennedy: A Biography* (New York: Harper Perennial, 2000), 538–39.

668 listing the compromises: Ibid., 302–3.

668 "You have essentially given": Quoted in Broder and Johnson, *System*, 352–53.

669 "You've got to make": Blattner int.

669 "We're going to lose": Former Aide B int., Sept. 25, 1998, Unnamed Sources Folder, Box 5, Series 2, Clymer Papers, JFK Lib.

669 "We are going to have": Blattner int.

669 favoring a federal: Laham, *Lost Cause*, 7.

669 "But now people will say": EMK int., Oct. 29, 1994.

669–70 "at the top of his lungs": Broder and Johnson, *System*, 284–85.

670 they would be voting: "Is This the Last Best Hope?" *Time*, July 4, 1994.

670 less-than-universal coverage: Jennings int.

670 "more and more frantic": Broder int.

670 "more emotion than anybody": Broder and Johnson, *System*, 446–47.

670 "smelled blood": Jennings int.

670 "The whole focus shifted": Mitchell int.

671 Mitchell's bill called for: "Mitchell Airs Health Care Plan," *BG*, Aug. 3, 1994.

671 "Very good and very clever": EMK int., Mar. 28, 2008.

671 "Could you have taken": Clymer Notes on Health Care, n.d., Clymer Papers, JFK Lib.

671 "He's devastated": Broder and Johnson, *System*, 446–47.

671 "rally the troops": Chris Jennings to et al., "Meeting with Senators," July 27, 1994, OA ID #18537, Clinton Lib.

671 "Health care belongs": "Hillary Clinton in Boston," *BG*, Aug. 1, 1994.

671 "The guy was incredible": Jennings int.

672 "Chafee was prepared": Shelia Burke int.

672 "packing the room": John Danforth int., Oct. 25, 2005, Miller Center, UVA; Broder and Johnson, *System*, 518–20.

672 "bedraggled": Jennings int.

672 "blistering attack": Broder and Johnson, *System*, 490–91; Clymer Notes on Health Care; EMK, *True Compass*, 457–58.

673 "They defeated it without": EMK int., Mar. 28, 2008.

673 "devastating": Parker int.

673 never debated: Mitchell int.

673 "Look, do you understand": Broder and Johnson, *System*, 525.

673 "Chris, it's over": Jennings int.

674 "striking distance": "Mitchell Formally Gives Up Health Care Effort," *BG*, Sept. 27, 1994.

674 **"We've killed health reform"**: Clymer, *Kennedy*, 547.

674 **"policy process in which"**: See Theda Skocpol, "The Rise and Resounding Demise of the Clinton Plan," *Health Affairs* 14, no. 1 (Spring 1995): 66–85.

675 **"What killed health care?"**: "The Health Care Debate in Their Own Words," *NYT*, Sept. 27, 1994.

SIXTEEN: "THE BATTLE OF HIS POLITICAL LIFE"

676 **with a huge lead**: "Poll Finds Kennedy's Base Firm," *BG*, July 24, 1994.

676 **comfortably ahead**: "Kennedy Launches His Media Campaign, *BG*, July 6, 1994; Carey Parker int., Nov. 10, 2008, Miller Center, UVA.

676 **"jittery"**: "Kennedy Girds for Test," *BG*, Mar. 12, 1993.

677 **"Kennedy haters"**: Debra Rosenberg, "See Teddy Run Scared," *Newsweek*, Aug. 1, 1994.

677 **voters were evenly split**: "Poll Finds Kennedy's Base Firm."

677 **"nastiness out on"**: Quoted in Adam Clymer, *Edward M. Kennedy: A Biography* (New York: Harper Perennial, 2000), 549.

677 **"ugly moments"**: Victoria Reggie Kennedy int., Apr. 8, 2010, Miller Center, UVA.

677 **younger voters didn't know**: EMK, *True Compass* (New York: Twelve, 2009), 429–30.

677 **"Kennedy. He's in"**: "Unsettling Political Climate Has Kennedy Running Hard," *BG*, June 2, 1994.

677 **"lost his touch"**: EMK int., June 3, 2005, Miller Center, UVA.

677 **"And all that time"**: Ibid.

677 **"whole different"**: Quoted in EMK int., Nov. 29, 2006, Miller Center, UVA.

677 **one of the five priority contests**: "GOP Places Priority on Kennedy Race," *BG*, May 21, 1993.

678 **"right out of central casting"**: Peter Canellos, *Last Lion: The Fall and Rise of Ted Kennedy* (New York: Simon & Schuster, 2009), 295.

678 **"particularly vicious irony"**: Jill Smolowe, "Tough Time for Teddy," *Time*, Oct. 10, 1994.

678 **"Mr. Clean image"**: EMK, *True Compass*, 437.

678 **"He was rich"**: Robert Shrum, *No Excuses: Concessions of a Serial Campaigner* (New York: Simon & Schuster, 2007), 244.

678 **"certainly knows a good"**: "GOP Candidates Raise Character Issue," *BG*, Feb. 7, 1994.

679 **"Very early these things"**: Gerard Doherty int., Oct. 10, 2005, Miller Center, UVA.

679 **fifteen times as many**: "Unsettling Political Climate Has Kennedy Running Hard."

679 **"like this big rocket"**: Victoria Reggie Kennedy int.

679 **"not fatal but bad"**: "Kennedy, Romney Deadlocked in Poll," *BG*, Sept. 17, 1994.

679 **"Claiborne, you don't"**: Jeffrey Blattner int., Mar. 30, 2007, Miller Center, UVA.

679 **"If you get elected"**: Patrick Kennedy and Stephen Fried, *A Common Struggle: A Personal Journey Through the Past and Future of Mental Illness and Addiction* (New York: Blue Rider Press, 2015), 120.

680 **defer the issue until**: "Joan Kennedy's Lawyer Denies Pressure Play," *BG*, Sept. 9, 1994; "Joan Kennedy Defers Her Campaign for His," *BG*, Oct. 5, 1994.

680 **"Contrary to statements"**: "Senate Panel Calls Allegations Against Kennedy Baseless," *BG*, Oct. 25, 1994.

681 **Safe Schools Act**: Nick Littlefield int., June 30, 2008, Miller Center, UVA.

681 **"I worked hard"**: John A. Farrell, "Comeback Kid Rising from the Ashes," *BG Magazine*, Nov. 21, 1993.

681 **"The strengths of the agreement"**: "Senate OK Finalizes NAFTA Pact," *BG*, Nov. 21, 1993.

681 **"Clinton was a charmer"**: Parker int., Nov. 10, 2008.

681 **"He's a real pro"**: Farrell, "Comeback Kid Rising."

681 **"Borked"**: Laurence Tribe int., Apr. 27, 2009, Miller Center, UVA.

682 **"Everything I'd ever done"**: Stephen Breyer int., June 17, 2008, Miller Center, UVA.

682 **Western governors pleaded**: Mark Kranish, "Boston Judge Went from Back-Up to Front-Runner Then to Also-Ran," *BG*, June 15, 1993.

682 **"and a little too eager"**: Richard Lacayo, "On Second Thought," *Time*, May 23, 1994.

682 **"Kind of fell in love"**: John Podesta int. by author.

682 **"Just unbelievably effusive"**: John A. Farrell int., July 13, 2006, Miller Center, UVA; Farrell, "Comeback Kid Rising."

683 **wanted to name Senate majority**: Bill Clinton, *My Life* (New York: Knopf, 2004), 592.

683 **"resuscitated Breyer"**: Blattner int.

683 turned the conversation: Kenneth Feinberg int., Mar. 13, 1995, F Folder, Box 3, Series 2, Clymer Papers, JFK Lib.

684 "If we ever have another": Nick Littlefield int., May 4, 2008, Miller Center, UVA.

684 "made enemies in his life": Bill Clinton, "Remarks by the President at Senator Kennedy's Fundraiser," Sept. 29, 1994, Clinton Lib.

684 version of *The Last Hurrah:* Clymer, *Kennedy*, 553.

685 "He looked bad": Andy Hiller quoted in "The Choice 2012," *Frontline*, PBS, Oct. 20, 2012.

685 "homeless man in a $1000 suit": "The Last Liberal Lion," *Economist*, Oct. 15, 1994.

685 "Pudgy, silver-haired": Rosenberg, "See Teddy Run."

685 "Oh, he's heavy": EMK int., Oct. 15, 1994, EMK Interviews 1992–94 Folder, Box 5, Series 2, Clymer Papers, JFK Lib.; Victoria Reggie Kennedy int.

685 "On the screen": Scot Lehigh, "Kennedy Outliving Family Charisma," *BG*, June 14, 1994.

685 "We have no template": George Colt, "Is Ted Kennedy's Midlife Crisis Finally Over?" *Life*, Aug. 1994.

685 "well-oiled Kennedy": Martin Nolan, "Senator's Machine Sputtering at Start," *BG*, Sept. 21, 1994.

686 "very pivotal": Tad Devine int. by author.

686 "Vintage 1970": Nolan, "Senator's Machine Sputtering."

686 too big a claim for Ted: Devine int.

686 "all drawn to a quiet": "Last Liberal Lion."

687 vicinity of $20 million: "With a Fortune Over $20 Million, Kennedy Is Wealthiest in '80 Race," *NYT*, Dec. 30, 1979; "Kennedy and Wife Report $702,697 in Income for 1978," *WP*, Nov. 8, 1979.

687 "Romney will not be": "Teddy's Test," *Newsweek*, July 25, 1994; Nolan, "Senator's Machine Sputtering."

687 raised $8 million: "Kennedy Borrows $2 Million for Campaign," *BG*, Oct. 22, 1994.

687 "He's taking the race": "Teddy's Test."

687 "people who the last time": David Burke int., June 19, 2007, Miller Center, UVA.

688 "You know, Teddy's in some": Ibid.

688 "What a difference": Victoria Reggie Kennedy int.

688 joined the campaign: Nolan, "Senator's Machine Sputtering."

688 "I'm going to sleep": Victoria Reggie Kennedy int.

688 "We need some back-up": Devine int.

688 "like reliving my whole life": David Broder int., Dec. 1, 2006, Miller Center, UVA.

689 adding tens of thousands: EMK int., June 3, 2005.

689 "Well, I could": Victoria Reggie Kennedy int.

689 "desperate": Farrell int.

689 "perversity": "Romney Hits Kennedy on Faith Issue," *BG*, Sept. 28, 1994.

689 "religion should not be": "Separation of Politics, Religion Is Often Elusive," *BG*, Oct. 2, 1994.

689 "We were in the bunker": "Rep. Kennedy Apologizes to Romney," *BG*, Sept. 24, 1994.

690 "Are you guys": "Remembering Ted Kennedy," *National Journal*, Sept. 5, 2009; Devine int.; Shrum, *No Excuses*, 247–48.

690 "cynical marriage": Farrell int.

690 Even she would joke: Burton Hersh, *The Shadow President: Ted Kennedy in Opposition* (South Royalton, Vt.: Steerforth Press, 1997), 108.

690 two of them nuzzling: Paul Donovan int., Nov. 14, 1998, D Folder, Box 3, Series 2, Clymer Papers, JFK Lib.

690 "life now is one of": "Kennedy Says His Lifestyle Has Changed," *BG*, May 10, 1994.

690 "She was very much involved": Elsa Walsh, "Kennedy's Hidden Campaign," *New Yorker*, Mar. 31, 1997.

690–91 "She can express it": "Wife Playing Key Role," *BG*, July 9, 1994.

691 "trade stories": Victoria Reggie Kennedy int.; *True Compass*, 441.

691 "You couldn't watch Ted": Farrell int.

691 "The steady beating": "Bay State Again Takes Kennedy," *BG*, Nov. 9, 1994.

691 "put all his eggs": "Black Clergy Hold Talks with Aide to Senator," *BG*, Oct. 16, 1994.

692 "Oh, well, he had": Victoria Reggie Kennedy int.

692 "She was key": Sara Rimer, "Kennedy's Closest Confidante," *NYT*, Aug. 28, 2009.

692 International Paper Workers: "Romney Firm Tied to Labor Fight," *BG*, Sept. 23, 1994.

692 collecting information: "Ind. Strikers Taking Fight to Romney," *BG*, Oct. 3, 1994.

692 **"If you had to say"**: Devine int.

693 **"He leaped right in"**: Ibid.

693 **"This is not fantasy land"**: "Romney Firm Tied to Labor Fight."

693 **"continuous distortions"**: "Romney Lashes Out at Kennedy," *BG*, Oct. 14, 1994.

693 **"What I said was from"**: "Ind. Strikers Taking Fight to Romney."

694 **"And that's when the bottom"**: Devine int.

694 **negatives rose to 31 percent**: Shrum, *No Excuses*, 246–47.

694 **"And Ted just reveled"**: Devine int.

694 **had forgone any profit**: Hersh, *Shadow President*, 142–43.

694 **"by virtue of those slick"**: "Romney Lashes Out at Kennedy."

694 **"Nothing works for me"**: Colt, "Midlife Crisis Over?"

695 **"I'd like *you* to sit in"**: David Burke int.

695 **"liberated and every strength"**: Ibid.

695 **"He's never seen a jugular"**: Ibid.

696 **take a look at those podiums**: Paul Kirk, Jr., int. Nov. 23, 2005, Miller Center, UVA.

696 **"That place is awful hot"**: Doherty int.

696 **"The expectation was"**: "The Choice," *Frontline*.

696 **"apropos of nothing"**: Rimer, "Kennedy's Closest Confidante."

696 **"just absorbing whatever"**: Kirk int.

696 **"ready to beat off anybody"**: "The Choice," *Frontline*.

697 **all he had to do**: David Burke int.; Doherty int.; EMK, *True Compass*, 445–46.

697 **"Mr. Romney, the Kennedys"**: "The Choice," *Frontline*.

698 **"Is that the way"**: Ted Kennedy and Mitt Romney, Massachusetts Senatorial Debate, Oct. 25, 1994, https://www.youtube.com/watch?v=aNiIEKhAF1k.

698 **"It was like pitching"**: Hersh, *Shadow President*, 148.

698 **"There are some people"**: Doherty int.

698 **"He may have been right"**: Quoted in Canellos, *Last Lion*, 295.

698 **"He killed him"**: David Burke int.

698 **"you could feel in the room"**: EMK, *True Compass*, 447.

698–99 **"Romney won points"**: Martin Nolan, "This *Time*, 32 Years of Baggage Carried the Day," *BG*, Oct. 26, 1994.

699 **thought Ted had won**: "Kennedy Opens Up 20-Point Lead in Poll," *BG*, Oct. 27, 1994.

699 **"people were crossing"**: EMK, *True Compass*, 447.

699 **"People say the ads"**: Joe Kennedy II int., Jan. 10, 1995, K Folder, Box 4, Series 2, Clymer Papers, JFK Lib.

699 **"event that comes down"**: Robert Healy, "Kennedy and Liberalism Won in First Debate," *BG*, Oct. 29, 1994.

699 **"Ted Kennedy is one debate"**: "Kennedy Opens Up 20-point Lead in Poll."

700 **"anti-climactic"**: "Round 2—Sound Without the Fury," *BG*, Oct. 28, 1994.

700 **"off stride"**: Hersh, *Shadow President*, 149–50.

700 **"tide of change is rising"**: "Romney Run Comes to Bittersweet End," *BG*, Nov. 9, 1994.

700 **"those who believe"**: "Bay State Again Takes Kennedy," *BG*, Nov. 9, 1994.

700 **"Inevitably, the voters"**: Hersh, *Shadow President*, 153.

700 **"battle of his political"**: Adam Clymer, "An Icon of '60s Liberalism Goes on the Attack," *NYT*, Oct. 19, 1994.

701 **"It was the first election"**: Quoted in Canellos, *Last Lion*, 301.

701 **"Bullshit!"**: EMK, *True Compass*, 449.

701 **"Senate's last great liberal"**: "Last Liberal Lion."

702 **"Big Dig"**: Farrell, "Comeback Kid Rising"; "Mass Delegation Copes With Diminishing Clout," *BG*, Aug. 30 1994.

702 **"To me, the sublime trick"**: Farrell int.

702 **"He said, 'The first thing'"**: Thomas Rollins int., May 12, 2009, Miller Center, UVA.

702 **"Listen, you fellows"**: Paul Donovan quoted in Hersh, *Shadow President*, 117; "Unsettling Political Climate Has Kennedy Running Hard," *BG*, June 2, 1994.

703 **"Kennedy country"**: "Kennedy Offensive Fueled Comeback," *BG*, Oct. 30, 1994.

703 **"He was the best politician"**: Devine int.

703 **took her hand and stayed**: Mrs. Robert Healy in Robert Healy int., Aug. 10, 2005, Miller Center, UVA.

703–4 **plane from Washington:** Doherty int.

704 **reinstituted the experimental therapy:** Ibid.

704 **"It wasn't like he was":** Ken Jones quoted in Martha Bebinger, "Kennedy Remembered as Senate's Hardest-Working Man," WBUR, Aug. 26, 2009.

704 **"proudest father in America":** Patrick Kennedy int. by author; "Another Kennedy Calls House Home," *BG*, Jan. 5, 1995.

704 **"He was as surprised":** Parker int., Nov. 10, 2008.

705 **"We got the living":** Clinton, *My Life*, 629.

705 **"proved to be a better":** Ibid., 631.

705 **"Contract with America":** See Steve Gillon, *The Pact: Bill Clinton, Newt Gingrich, and the Rivalry That Defined a Generation* (New York: Oxford Univ. Press, 2008), 124. A CBS/NYT poll taken the week of the election showed that 71 percent of Americans had never heard of Gingrich's Contract.

706 **"The nationalization of midterm":** Ibid., 628–31.

706 **plummeted to a historically low:** Theda Skocpol, "The Rise and Resounding Demise of the Clinton Plan," *Health Affairs* 14, no. 1 (Spring 1995): 66–85.

706 **"They look back":** Arthur Schlesinger, Jr., *Journals: 1952–2000*, ed. Andrew Schlesinger and Stephen Schlesinger (New York: Penguin Press, 2007), 775.

706 **"express a profound":** Quoted in Peter Brown, *Minority Party: Why Democrats Face Defeat in 1992 and Beyond* (New York: Regnery Gateway, 1991), 25–26.

707 **incomes remained static:** Stanley Greenberg, *The Two Americas: Our Current Political Deadlock and How to Break It* (New York: St. Martin's Griffin, 2005), 82.

707 **"dismantle the welfare-state":** Joe Klein, "Wither Liberalism," *Newsweek*, Nov. 21, 1994; Gingrich quoted in Sean Wilentz, *The Age of Reagan: A History 1974–2008* (New York: HarperCollins, 2008), 348.

707 **"Open warfare against":** Thomas Daschle with Michael D'Orso, *Like No Other Time: The 107th Congress and the Two Years That Changed America Forever* (New York: Crown, 2003), 16.

707 **"most consequential non-presidential":** James Traub, "Party Like It's 1994," *NYT Magazine*, Mar. 12, 2006.

708 **Republicans in the House distributed:** Littlefield int., June 30, 2008.

708 **chosen by the caucus by secret ballot:** Lewis Gould, *The Most Exclusive Club: A History of the Modern Senate* (New York: Basic Books, 2005), 304.

708 **"Put simply":** E. J. Dionne, Jr., *Why Americans Hate Politics* (New York: Simon & Schuster, 1991), 73.

708 **"starve the beast":** Carey Parker int., Dec. 1, 2008, Miller Center, UVA.

709 **"His mandate, he declared":** Gillon, *Pact*, 133.

709 **"The core of his argument":** Clinton, *My Life*, 635.

SEVENTEEN: STIFFENING THEIR SPINES

710 **"I was profoundly distressed":** Bill Clinton, *My Life* (New York: Knopf, 2004), 630.

710 **"I don't know which":** Steve Gillon, *The Pact: Bill Clinton, Newt Gingrich, and the Rivalry That Defined a Generation* (New York: Oxford Univ. Press, 2008), 131–32.

710 **"The only thing the Clintons":** Robert Shrum, *No Excuses: Concessions of a Serial Campaigner* (New York: Simon & Schuster, 2007), 443.

710 **"Immediately upon getting back":** Nick Littlefield int., May 4, 2008, Miller Center, UVA.

711 **"There were senators":** Carey Parker int., Nov. 10, 2008, Miller Center, UVA.

711 **"allowed him to reconnect":** Jack Newfield, "The Senate's Fighting Liberal," *Nation*, Mar. 25, 2002.

711 **"I just got reelected":** Littlefield int., May 4, 2008.

712 **"rub the faces":** Nick Littlefield and David Nexon, *Lion of the Senate: When Ted Kennedy Rallied the Democrats in a GOP Congress* (New York: Simon & Schuster, 2015), 72–75.

712 **"Republicans cultivate":** Nick Littlefield int., June 30, 2008, Miller Center, UVA.

713 **"Government is always":** Littlefield int., May 4, 2008; Nick Littlefield int., June 30, 2008, Miller Center, UVA.

713 **"taking their temperature":** Littlefield int., May 4, 2008.

713 **"We work with you":** Tom Daschle int., Apr. 29, 2009, Miller Center, UVA.

713 **"They needed to see":** Carey Parker int., Nov. 17, 2008, Miller Center, UVA.

714   "The breakdown in the community": EMK int., Oct. 29, 1994, EMK Interviews 1992–94 Folder, Box 5, Series 2, Clymer Papers, JFK Lib.

714   "I don't think he was concerned": Parker int., Nov. 17, 2008.

714   everything he possibly could: Littlefield int., May 4, 2008.

715   to urge them to urge: Burton Hersh, *The Shadow President: Ted Kennedy in Opposition* (South Royalton, Vt.: Steerforth Press, 1997), 161–62; Littlefield int., June 30, 2008.

715   "one of the most unforgettable": Littlefield int., May 4, 2008; Elsa Walsh, "Kennedy's Hidden Campaign," *New Yorker*, Mar. 31, 1997.

715   "stick with the working": Walsh, "Hidden Campaign"; Littlefield and Nexon, *Lion*, 114–18; Littlefield int., May 4, 2008.

716   "Economic statistics": Bill Clinton, Presidential Address to the Nation, Dec. 15, 1994, https://www.c-span.org/video/?62227-1/presidential-address-nation.

717   "flirtatious": Barbara Gibson and Ted Schwarz, *Rose Kennedy and Her Family: The Best and Worst of Their Lives and Times* (New York: Birch Lane Press, 1995), 97–98.

717   "Teddy was always open": Rita Dallas, *The Kennedy Case* (New York: G. P. Putnam, 1973), 317.

718   "first thing he would do": Hersh, *Shadow President*, 170.

718   visit them on Nantucket: Edmund and Doris Reggie int., Aug. 8, 2005, Miller Center, UVA.

718   "her voice would lilt": EMK, "Tribute to Rose Kennedy," Jan. 24, 1995, Box 1, Nancy Korman Personal Papers, JFK Lib.

718   "Well, you'll have your": Elizabeth Shannon int., Apr. 28, 2009, Miller Center, UVA.

718   "I'm like old wine": Laurence Leamer, *The Kennedy Women: The Saga of an American Family* (New York: Villard Books, 1994), 747.

719   "merciless with him": Laurence Tribe int., Apr. 27, 2009, Miller Center, UVA.

719   "You will be pleased to know": Ted to Rose, n.d., Family Corr.: EMK 1958–72, Box 59, Rose Kennedy Papers, JFK Lib.

719   "What happened, mother?": Gibson and Schwarz, 8.

719   bring along videotapes: Hersh, *Shadow President*, 162.

719   "Indomitable for all": Tribute to Rose Kennedy.

719   "self-hypnosis": Robert Coughlan quoted in Leamer, *Kennedy Women*, 673.

719   "she was ambitious": Tribute to Rose Kennedy.

719   And they gathered: "The Last Matriarch," *People*, Feb. 6, 1995.

719   "even more heartbreaking": EMK, *True Compass* (New York: Twelve, 2009), 476.

719–20   annulled his marriage: Joan Kennedy int., Oct. 12, 1998, K Folder, Box 4, Series 2, Clymer Papers, JFK Lib. See also EMK int., June 3, 2005, Miller Center, UVA. Ted says that during his Senate campaign, Cardinal Bernard Law, in what Ted called "inappropriate comments," had said Ted would be denied an annulment.

720   "spark": Tribute to Rose Kennedy.

720   "I ran as a Democrat": "Kennedy Charts Strategy for Democrats," *WP*, Jan. 12, 1995; Littlefield int., June 30, 2008.

721   "It was a losing game": Nick Littlefield int., July 1, 2008, Miller Center, UVA.

721   doing the right thing: "Remembering Ted Kennedy," *National Journal*, Sept. 5, 2009.

721   "That's when you see": Chris Jennings int. by author.

722   "sigh in relief": Carey Parker int., Dec. 1, 2008, Miller Center, UVA.

722   "I'm not sure we can do this": Littlefield and Nexon, *Lion*, 146–47.

723   "air is sucked out": Nick Littlefield int., Feb. 14, 2009, Miller Center, UVA; Walsh, "Hidden Campaign"; Adam Clymer, *Edward M. Kennedy: A Biography* (New York: Harper Perennial, 2000), 565.

723   "He kibitzed with senators": Littlefield and Nexon, *Lion*, 149.

724   introduced a formal proposal: Ibid., 149–52; Littlefield int., May 4, 2008.

725   met every Monday morning: Littlefield int., May 4, 2008.

725   explained why a raise: Ibid.

725   "We were jubilant": Ibid.

726   "I will not blink": Gillon, *Pact*, 148.

727   "Gingrich is Reaganism": Marianne Gingrich quoted in John Richardson, "Newt Gingrich: The Indispensable Republican," *Esquire*, Aug. 2010.

727   needed Young Turks: Ibid.

727   "moralistic rhetoric": For the best account of Gingrich's political awakening, see Gillon, *Pact*, 3–49.

727 **leading a crusade:** For the fullest account of Gingrich's political rise, see Julian Zelizer, *Burning Down the House: Newt Gingrich, the Fall of a Speaker, and the Rise of the New Republican Party* (New York: Penguin Press, 2020).

728 **"If they could cut funding":** Clinton, *My Life*, 681.

729 **"assault on working families":** Littlefield int., July 1, 2008; Littlefield and Nexon, *Lion*, 191, 193–95.

729 **forty-eight votes for cloture:** Littlefield and Nexon, *Lion*, 237–38.

731 **only after those cuts:** Ibid., 200–5.

733 **"cuts":** Elizabeth Drew, *Showdown: The Struggle Between the Gingrich Congress and the Clinton White House* (New York: Simon & Schuster, 1996), 206.

734 **"This is a budget that Marie":** Walsh, "Hidden Campaign."

734 **"Kennedy junkie":** Quote in Charles Pierce, "Kennedy Unbound After 40 Years in U.S. Senate," *BG Magazine*, Jan. 5, 2003.

735 **banter with the president:** Gillon, *Pact*, 153.

735 **"more of a peer":** Walsh, "Hidden Campaign."

735 **"Mr. President":** John Podesta int. by author.

735 **"His big thing was":** Jennings int.

735 **"He never cared about":** Ibid.

735 **"Do it!":** Ibid.; Podesta int.

735 **"loves to go before":** Parker int., Nov. 17, 2008.

736 **"He has what he has":** Walsh, "Hidden Campaign."

736 **"we're very close":** Ibid.

736 **"Kennedy could find":** Jennings int.; Podesta int.

736 **"key player":** Walsh, "Hidden Campaign."

736 **"debacle":** Drew, *Showdown*, 224.

736 **"insisted on having":** Walsh, "Hidden Campaign."

737 **week's postponement:** Littlefield int., May 4, 2008.

737 **$124 billion cut in Medicare:** See Doug Badger, "Medicaid Per Capita Caps: When Democrats Supported and Republicans Opposed Them, 1995–1997," Mercatus Center, George Mason Univ., 2017, https://www.mercatus.org/system/files/mercatus-badger-medicaid-per-capita-caps-v2.pdf.

737 **"turning point":** Drew, *Showdown*, 234.

737 **"I think the President *wanted*":** Ibid., 236.

737 **"We don't need a balanced":** Littlefield int., July 1, 2008.

738 **"President's direction":** Ibid.

738 **"I deeply resent":** Quoted in Ibid.

739 **had to repeat again:** Littlefield and Nexon, *Lion*, 256–60.

739 **"Republicans are being":** Ibid., 264.

740 **"most historic moment":** "Battle Over the Budget: The Overview," *NYT*, Oct. 28, 1995; Littlefield and Nexon, *Lion*, 264.

741 **"virulent hatred":** "Radical Right's Fury Boiling Over," *NYT*, Apr. 23, 1995.

741 **"promoters of paranoia":** "Shifting Debate to the Political Climate, Clinton Condemns Promoters of Paranoia," *NYT*, Apr. 25, 1995.

741 **"The full political significance":** Sean Wilentz, *The Age of Reagan: A History 1974–2008* (New York: HarperCollins, 2008), 353–54.

741 **"chaperone":** Gillon, *Pact*, 155.

741 **toughened his budget bill:** Clinton, *My Life*, 683.

741 **holding a baby bottle:** Littlefield and Nexon, *Lion*, 264–65.

742 **"You'll have to get":** Clinton, *My Life*, 682.

742 **Clinton vetoed:** "As Long Promised, the President Vetoes GOP Budget," *NYT*, Dec. 7, 1995.

742 **"With this, the Republican":** Ibid.

742 **government was shut down:** Littlefield and Nexon, *Lion*, 285–88.

742 **public sided with Clinton:** "Clinton's Ratings Over 50% in Poll as GOP Declines," *NYT*, Dec. 14, 1995.

743 **plummeted to under 30 percent:** "Government Shutdown: Polls Showed Voters Blamed GOP for 1995 Crisis," *Huffington Post*, Mar. 30, 2011.

743 **under tremendous pressure:** For the best discussion, see Littlefield and Nexon, *Lion*, 300–6.

743 **only 36 percent felt:** "Clinton's Ratings Over 50% in Poll as GOP Declines."

744   "There were things": Melody Barnes int., Aug. 16, 2006, Miller Center, UVA.

744   "They had the votes": Hersh, *Shadow President*, 156.

744   "When you get": Quoted in Littlefield int., July 1, 2008.

744   "He'd talk for two hours": Quoted in Hersh, *Shadow President*, 161.

745   blasting Republican cuts: Jill Zuckman, "Sen. Kennedy's Salvage Mission," *BG*, Oct. 3, 1995.

745   "many times there was": Daschle int.

745   "Democrats came out way": Littlefield int., July 1, 2008.

745   "sharp, clear distinctions": Thad Cochran int., Sept. 19, 2006, Miller Center, UVA.

EIGHTEEN: RUNNING THE SENATE

746   only sixty-six of them: Jill Zuckman, "GOP's Contract Has a Year of Activity, but Few Results," *BG*, Dec. 25, 1995.

746   "cultural revolution": Elizabeth Drew, *Showdown: The Struggle Between the Gingrich Congress and the Clinton White House* (New York: Simon & Schuster, 1996), 275.

746   "If you read the Gingrich": EMK int., Aug. 7, 2007, Miller Center, UVA.

746   "We can't go back": Bill Clinton, State of the Union Address, January 23, 1996, https://clintonwhitehouse4.archives.gov/WH/New/other/sotu.html.

747   "The President has to realize": "As Long Promised, the President Vetoes the GOP Budget," *NYT*, Dec. 7, 1995.

747   "rushing from crisis": Zuckman, "GOP's Contract."

748   "if Senator Kennedy": Ibid.

748   "new big idea": Nick Littlefield and David Nexon, *Lion of the Senate: When Ted Kennedy Rallied the Democrats in a GOP Congress* (New York: Simon & Schuster, 2015), 307–11.

749   "Make him seem": Ibid., 313.

749   "We had times we couldn't": Robert Dole int., May 15, 2006, Miller Center, UVA.

750   "ruined our party": Quoted in Sean Wilentz, *The Age of Reagan: A History 1974–2008* (New York: HarperCollins, 2008), 368.

750   "That was our moment": Elsa Walsh, "Kennedy's Hidden Campaign," *New Yorker*, Mar. 31, 1997.

751   "two years of college": *Congressional Record*, Senate, 104th Cong., 2nd sess., Mar. 26, 1996, S2849–50.

752   highly technical parliamentary: Nick Littlefield int., May 4, 2008, Miller Center, UVA.

752   "America Needs a Raise": James Manley int., Sept. 28, 2009, Miller Center, UVA; Littlefield and Nexon, *Lion*, 322.

752   "Little legislative traps": John A. Farrell int., July 13, 2006, Miller Center, UVA.

752   "He's having just": Lloyd Grove, "The Liberal Element: Ted Kennedy Is in the Minority But Republicans Are Finding Him Mighty Hard to Ignore," *WP*, July 9, 1996.

752   "for a very long time": Scott Ferson quoted in Martha Bebinger, "Kennedy Remembered as Senate's Hardest-Working Man," WBUR, Aug. 26, 2009.

752   "We used to think": Dole int.

753   "Where is *that* Bob Dole?": *Congressional Record*, Senate, 104th Cong., 2nd sess., Mar. 28, 1996, S3099.

753   "Speaker Gingrich": Ibid., S3097–98.

753   minimum wage amendment: Littlefield and Nexon, *Lion*, 338–42.

754   exhibit his ability: Ibid., 363–64.

754   "sooner or later the issue": "Dole Blocks Vote Raising Minimum Wage," *NYT*, Mar. 27, 1996.

754   "Dole threw up his hands": Nick Littlefield int., May 3, 2008, Miller Center, UVA.

754   "probably something": Farrell int.

755   slim presidential chances: "Dole Says He Will Leave Senate to Focus on Senate Race," *NYT*, May 16, 1996.

755   "It was the perfect vehicle": Walsh, "Hidden Campaign."

755   "I feel sort of sad": Ibid.

755   Kennedy treatment: Nancy Kassebaum int., Apr. 6, 2009, Miller Center, UVA.

756   "job lock": Littlefield int., May 4, 2008; Stuart Altman and David Schachtman, *Power, Politics and Universal Health Care: The Inside Story of a Century-Long Battle* (Amherst, N.Y.: Prometheus Books, 2011), 164.

756   wanted to leave her job: Kassebaum int.

756   seven Republican co-sponsors: "Supporters Tout Health Care Legislation's Moderate Approach,"

WP, Apr. 21, 1996; "The Health Insurance Reform Act of 1995," Senate, 104th Cong., 1st sess., Oct. 12, 1995, https://www.congress.gov/104/crpt/srpt156/CRPT-104srpt156.pdf.

756 **coverage for preexisting conditions:** Jane Hiebert-White, "Who Won What in Kennedy/Kassebaum Struggle?" *Health Progress*, Sept.–Oct. 1996.

756 **"lowest common denominator":** Robert Moffitt quoted in "Supporters Tout Health Care Legislation's Moderate Approach."

757 **fretted that it would sink:** Walsh, "Hidden Campaign."

757 **unless Dole scheduled a vote:** Ibid.

757 **"Why aren't we taking":** EMK int., Mar. 28, 2008, Miller Center, UVA.

758 **help undercut Medicare:** "G.O.P. Pushes Medical Savings Accounts to Replace Health Insurance," *NYT*, Sept. 28, 1995.

758 **benefit from high-deductible:** "G.O.P. Plan Would Profit Insurer with Ties to Party," *NYT*, Apr. 14, 1996.

758 **"payoff to the Golden Rule":** Ibid.

758 **"Healthy and wealthy":** Littlefield and Nexon, *Lion*, 346.

759 **"Senator Dole needs":** "Dole Plan on Health Bill May Encounter Resistance," *NYT*, Apr. 18, 1996.

759 **"This is very bad":** Littlefield and Nexon, *Lion*, 353.

759 **"certainly sink the bill":** "Dole Plan on Health Bill May Encounter Resistance."

759 **"could very well restore":** "Senate Defeats Dole Revision to Health Bill," *NYT*, Apr. 19, 1996.

760 **negotiate a pre-compromise:** Littlefield and Nexon, *Lion*, 359.

760 **"Now, Ted, don't get too":** Grove, "Liberal Element."

760 **"We might as well recognize":** Ibid.

761 **gotten wind of Ted's:** Walsh, "Hidden Campaign."

761 **"I guess they don't want":** Most of this account comes from Littlefield and Nexon, *Lion*. Littlefield was intimately involved in these deliberations. See 381–98.

762 **make it with Ted Kennedy:** Ibid., 399.

762 **"in a spirit of generosity":** *Congressional Record*, Senate, 104th Cong., 2nd sess., July 9, 1996, S7425–26.

763 **"They need our help":** Ibid., S7469.

764 **which Ted autographed:** EMK int., Mar. 28, 2008.

764 **hammer out their differences:** Littlefield and Nexon, *Lion*, 404–5.

764 **Ted would accept MSAs:** "Deal in Congress Gives Health Care New Momentum," *NYT*, July 26, 1996.

764 **"calling the shots":** "Kennedy Again May Star in GOP Ads," *WP*, July 25, 1996.

764 **steered Kennedy-Kassebaum:** Trent Lott, *Herding Cats* (New York: ReganBooks, 2005), 132–34.

764 **"Republicans have decided":** "House Votes to Protect Health Insurance Access," *WP*, Aug. 2, 1996.

765 **"I'm introducing a new bill":** Peter Canellos, *Last Lion: The Fall and Rise of Ted Kennedy* (New York: Simon & Schuster, 2009), 314.

765 **"double-header victory":** "Wages and Health Lead the Agenda as Congress Acts," *NYT*, Aug. 3, 1996.

765 **"very tangible":** Adam Clymer, "Big Man in Congress: Kennedy, Of All People," *NYT*, Aug. 11, 1996.

765 **clubbed Democrats:** *Congressional Record*, Senate, 104th Cong., 1st sess., Sept. 19, 1995, S13751.

765 **"Stopping the insanity of entitlement":** Ibid., S13750.

765 **"legislative child abuse":** Ibid., S13775.

766 **"decent welfare bill":** George Church, "Ripping Up Welfare," *Time*, Aug. 12, 1996.

766 **"He knows where I'm":** Walsh, "Hidden Campaign."

766 **"mean-spirited form":** Adam Clymer, *Edward M. Kennedy: A Biography* (New York: Harper Perennial, 2000), 583.

766 **"We were not going":** Melody Barnes int., Aug. 16, 2006, Miller Center, UVA.

767 **twenty-three-point lead:** "Poll Trends: The 1996 Presidential Election," Gallup News Service, Aug. 14–15, 1996, http://library.law.columbia.edu/urlmirror/CLR/100CLR524/ptpreselec.html.

768 **"It was he who identified":** Littlefield and Nexon, *Lion*, 377.

768 **"Virtually as effective":** Walsh, "Hidden Campaign."

768 **"precisely what being":** *Congressional Record*, Senate, 104th Cong., 2nd sess., Aug. 2, 1996, S9530.

768   "professional's professional": Ibid.

769   "curiously lacking in self-confidence": Walsh, "Hidden Campaign."

769   "scar tissue is so frayed": Melody Miller int., Oct. 7, 2008, Miller Center, UVA.

769   "Probably not since": Clymer, "Big Man in Congress."

769   "What did Webster do?": Edmund Reggie int., Dec. 16, 2008, Miller Center, UVA.

769   "with the whitening mane": Grove, "Liberal Element."

770   "Ted Kennedy, a new man": See Littlefield int., May 3, 2008.

770   "This is not the Republican": Burton Hersh, *The Shadow President: Ted Kennedy in Opposition* (South Royalton, Vt.: Steerforth Press, 1997), 174.

770   "In the end, it didn't": Lott, *Herding Cats*, 135.

770   "I'll talk to him": John Tunney int., May 3, 2007, Miller Center, UVA.

770   "He had no doubt": David Burke int., June 19, 2007, Miller Center, UVA.

771   He was in command: Milton Gwirtzman int., Apr. 3, 1993, G Folder, Box 3, Series 2, Clymer Papers, JFK Lib.

771   "enormously different phase": Walsh, "Hidden Campaign."

771   "Ted Kennedy is still the man": Quoted in Rick Atkinson, "Why Ted Kennedy Can't Stand Still," *WP Magazine*, Apr. 29, 1990.

771   "utterly shameless": Howard Phillips, chairman of the Conservative Caucus, quoted ibid.

771   "No one in America": Peter Brown, *Minority Party: Why Democrats Face Defeat in 1992 and Beyond* (Washington, D.C.: Regnery Gateway, 1991), 151.

771   "political religion": Howard Baker, *Leading the United States Senate* (Washington, D.C.: U.S. Govt. Printing Office, 2003), 32.

773   "He could give the most partisan": John McCain int., Oct. 16, 2009, Miller Center, UVA.

773   "I know about those letters": Patrick Leahy int., Aug. 5, 2009, Miller Center, UVA.

773   "Once he started to see": George Miller int., Oct. 13, 2009, Miller Center, UVA.

774   "We're going to kill it": Grove, "Liberal Element."

774   "He studies the subject": Lawrence Goodrich, "Senate Icon Shows Off Skills," *CSM*, Oct. 27, 1997.

774   "best briefed senator": Manley int.

774   answers he needed point by point: Barnes int.

774   "We were ready for floor": Thomas Rollins int., Mar. 10, 2009, Miller Center, UVA.

774   "give-and-take on the floor": Manley int.

775   "We passed it in '89": Grove, "Liberal Element."

775   "When Kennedy got up to speak": Dole int.

775   "Who do I need to": Barnes int.

775   "most comfortable": Manley int.

775   "such a home to him": David Burke int., Apr. 9, 2008, Miller Center, UVA.

776   handing them the card: Jeffrey Blattner int., Mar. 30, 2007, Miller Center, UVA; Carey Parker int., Nov. 17, 2008, Miller Center, UVA; Barnes int.

776   "degree to which he is familiar": Parker int., Nov. 17, 2008.

776   "He'll find five Democrats": Ibid.

776   "great speeches": Robert Dove int. by author.

776   "It was usually very": Martin Tolchin int. by author.

777   "When I'd see Kennedy": Dole int.

777   "One had the impression": Richard Lugar int., Mar. 6, 2009, Miller Center, UVA.

777   Eunice had also complained: Kassebaum int.

777   "His blood pressure goes": Mike Enzi int. by author.

777   "The argument would unspool": Barack Obama, *A Promised Land* (New York: Crown, 2021), 68.

777   "How was that, Orrin?": "Topic A," *WP*, Aug. 29, 2009.

777   "stem-winder": Manley int.

778   "he really cared": Dove int.

778   "How Long? How long": McCain int.

779   sent seventy roses: Carey Parker int., Oct. 27, 2008, Miller Center, UVA.

779   Biden's Delaware home: "Kennedy Memorial Service," CNN, Aug. 28, 2009.

779   "something changed once": Quoted in Ethan Bronner, *Battle for Justice: How the Bork Nomination Shook America* (New York: Norton, 1989), 306.

779   senator who would visit: Melody Miller int., July 15, 2008, Miller Center, UVA.

779   cane that Joe Kennedy: Ibid.

780   "even Mitchell is only": George Mitchell int., Sept. 6, 2011, Miller Center, UVA.

780   "His mother trained him": Terri Haddad Robinson int., Aug. 25, 2009, Miller Center, UVA.

780   "When people ask about him": Nancy Pelosi int., Apr. 30, 2010, Miller Center, UVA.

780   "just told me about all": Nancy Soderberg int., Oct. 9, 2009, Miller Center, UVA.

780   what a good job: Esther Olavarria, Aug. 28, 2006, Miller Center, UVA.

780   "And there was no camera": Jan Kalicki int., Mar. 18, 2009, Miller Center, UVA.

780   "Hey, how are you doing": McCain int.

781   dollar for each one: Michael Johnson, deputy assistant sergeant at arms, oral history, Nov. 8, 19, Dec. 1, 2006, Senate Historical Office.

781   conversation with him: D. A. Pollack, "Reflections on Working for Senator EMK," *Community Mental Health Journal* 46, no. 2 (April 2010): 103–11.

NINETEEN: ENDINGS AND EPILOGUES

782   "radical wish list": "Kennedy Night on the Podium," *BG*, Aug. 19, 1996.

782   "message of the Clinton": Elsa Walsh, "Kennedy's Hidden Campaign," *New Yorker*, Mar. 31, 1997.

782   "way too liberal": "Some Hopefuls Find Use for a Kennedy," *BG*, Oct. 16, 1996.

783   "from grand to homelier": "The Small Deal," *Newsweek*, Nov. 18, 1996.

783   "Medicare, education": Stanley Greenberg, *The Two Americas: Our Current Political Deadlock and How to Break It* (New York: St. Martin's Griffin, 2005), 88.

783   "vital center": John Harris, *The Survivor: Bill Clinton in the White House* (New York: Random House, 2005), 253.

783   "victory without": Robert Shrum, *No Excuses: Concessions of a Serial Campaigner* (New York: Simon & Schuster, 2007), 254.

783   "What has been developing": Burton Hersh, *The Shadow President: Ted Kennedy in Opposition* (South Royalton, Vt.: Steerforth Press, 1997), 183–84.

784   "repairer of the breach": Don Baer in Russell Riley, *Inside the Clinton White House: An Oral History* (New York: Oxford Univ. Press, 2016), 304.

784   "strategy of personal": Shrum, *No Excuses*, 256–57.

784   "shell shocked": Steve Gillon, *The Pact: Bill Clinton, Newt Gingrich and the Rivalry That Defined a Generation* (New York: Oxford Univ. Press, 2008), 198.

784   "man who had run": Harris, *Survivor*, 329.

784   "achievement of a generation": "Bills to Balance the Budget and Cut Taxes Pass the Senate," *NYT*, Aug. 1, 1997.

784   "Are the wealthy": "Sen. Kennedy Takes Budget Deal to Task," *BG*, May 7, 1997.

785   "very suspicious of those": "Vermont's Jeffords Was Warned on Joining Kennedy Health Bill," *BG*, Nov. 6, 1997.

786   "Kennedy went to the mat": Nexon quoted in "Remembering Ted Kennedy," *National Journal*, Sept. 5, 2009; Lawrence Goodrich, "Senate Icon Shows Off Skills," *CSM*, Oct. 27, 1997.

787   "I want to be": Quoted in Alan Derickson, *Health Security for All: Dreams of Universal Health Care in America* (Baltimore: Johns Hopkins Univ. Press, 2005), 134.

788   "I thought he stood": Quoted in Peter Canellos, *Last Lion: The Fall and Rise of Ted Kennedy* (New York: Simon & Schuster, 2009), 330.

788   "And he bent over": Walsh, "Hidden Campaign."

788   only senator who called: Canellos, *Last Lion*, 333.

788   have his medical experts: Ibid., 333–34.

789   find some accommodation: Nick Littlefield and David Nexon, *Lion of the Senate: When Ted Kennedy Rallied the Democrats in a GOP Senate* (New York: Simon & Schuster, 2015), 411–17. Much of the following account is taken from Littlefield and Nexon, since they were intimately involved in the children's health insurance effort and had information that was not available elsewhere.

789   "friendly teasing": EMK int., Mar. 28, 2008, Miller Center, UVA.

789   "But, Orrin, there are so": Littlefield and Nexon, *Lion*, 418–19.

790   "Hatch is ecstatic": Nick Littlefield int., May 3, 2008, Miller Center, UVA. This was Littlefield's version in his interview. In his book, he told a slightly different version that seemed more plausible, and I have chosen to separate the two because I suspect that is the way it happened.

790   "We high-fived each other": Ibid., 421–24.

791   "latter-day liberal": "Despite His Credentials, Hatch Is Derided by Conservatives," *BG*, Mar. 15, 1997.

792 "A Kennedy big-government": Littlefield and Nexon, *Lion*, 429.

792 "You gotta do kids": Chris Jennings int. by author.

792 They lobbied legislators: Littlefield and Nexon, *Lion*, 427–29.

793 found 72 percent in favor: *Congressional Record*, Senate, 105th Cong., 1st sess., May 1, 1997, S4784.

793 rule didn't apply: EMK int., Mar. 28, 2008; Littlefield and Nexon, *Lion*, 432.

793 "cool": EMK int., Mar. 28, 2008; Judy Feder int., July 5, 2007, Miller Center, UVA.

794 worried about the same thing: Jennings int.

794 "Who are the Hatch-Kennedy": *Congressional Record*, Senate, 105th Cong., 1st sess., May 21, 1997, S4783.

794 "Our plan has broad": Ibid., S4785.

794 "There can be no more": Ibid., S4789.

795 Neither returned his call: "Administration Tries to Atone to Sen. Kennedy," *BG*, May 23, 1997.

795 five of them decided: Nick Littlefield int., Feb. 14, 2009, Miller Center, UVA; "Child Health Care Plan Defeated in Senate," *WP*, May 22, 1997.

795 "Let us not lose sight": *Congressional Record*, Senate, 105th Cong., 1st sess., May 21, 1997, S4799.

795 "Yes, yes. I can only bite": "White House Helps Ditch Kennedy Bill," *BG*, May 22, 1997.

795 "applauded": Mike McCurry, Press Briefing, May 21, 1997, https://www.presidency.ucsb.edu/documents/press-briefing-mike-mccurry-166.

796 immediately phoned his nephew: Albert Hunt, "Ted Kennedy Forged Legacy with Joyful Magic," *Bloomberg*, Aug. 27, 2009.

796 "hate him": Jennings int.

797 "clean their clocks": Littlefield and Nexon, *Lion*, 437.

797 "laid into him": Ibid.; EMK int., Mar. 28, 2008.

797 apologize for his tirade: Canellos, *Last Lion*, 336–37.

798 one more individual: Stuart Altman and David Schachtman, *Power, Politics and Universal Health Care: The Inside Story of a Century-Long Battle* (Amherst, N.Y.: Prometheus Books, 2011), 171–75.

798 But Ted was unconvinced: "Administration Tries to Atone to Sen. Kennedy."

798 another tense meeting: "Through Senate Alchemy, Tobacco Is Turned into Gold for Children's Health," *NYT*, Aug. 11, 1997.

798 "making Kennedy very happy": Jennings int.

798 "It can be understood": Sara Rosenbaum, "Slouching Toward Health Reform: Insights from the Battle Over SCHIP," *Journal on Poverty, Law and Policy* 15 (2008): 705–13.

799 added a provision: Jill Quadagno, *One Nation Uninsured: Why the U.S. Had No National Health Insurance* (New York: Oxford Univ. Press, 2005), 196.

799 "If the defeat": Littlefield and Nexon, *Lion*, 442–43.

799 "[There] were guys": Quoted in Riley, *Inside*, 308.

800 presumably to harm Clinton: See Michael Isikoff, *Uncovering Clinton: A Reporter's Story* (New York: Crown, 1999).

801 "I have sinned": See Peter Baker and Susan Schmidt, "Starr Alleges Abundant Lies," in *The Starr Report: The Findings of Indpendent Counsel Kenneth W. Starr on President Clinton and the Lewinsky Affair* (New York: PublicAffairs, 1998), ix.

801 "It is a Clinton pattern": Quoted in Riley, *Inside*, 307.

801 "poisonous": EMK, *True Compass* (New York: Twelve, 2009), 465–66.

801 "Often the great advances": EMK, "America Should Work for All Americans," *BG*, Dec. 12, 1997; "Kennedy Offers Quality of Life Wish List for Congress," *WP*, Dec. 12, 1997.

802 "interrogators did their": Bill Clinton, *My Life* (New York: Knopf, 2004), 801.

802 "better than most": John Podesta int. by author.

802 "I felt that this kind": EMK, *True Compass*, 465.

802 "functioning on all cylinders": Ibid., 466.

803 Sam Beer: Ibid., 465.

803 consulted legal scholars: Carey Parker int., Nov. 17, 2008, Miller Center, UVA.

804 "not because he lacked": J. H. Ahtes, "The Kennedys, Ireland and Irish America," *Irish Review* 11 (Winter 1991–92): 23–24, 30.

804 could co-sponsor Ribicoff's: Carey Parker int., Oct. 20, 2008, Miller Center, UVA.

804 "ignorant outburst": Andrew Wilson, *Irish America and the Ulster Conflict, 1968–1995* (Washington, D.C.: Catholic Univ. of America Press, 1995), 58–61.

804 reports he had been: Ibid., 77.

804 "began the great education": EMK int., Feb. 27, 2006, Miller Center, UVA.

805 now came out forcefully: Ibid.

805 "most passionate, articulate": EMK int., Mar. 20, 2006, Miller Center, UVA.

805 "quite dramatic effect": Ibid.

806 Northern Ireland's troubles: Ibid.

806 "constitutional nationalist": R. J. Briand, "Bush, Clinton, Irish America and the Irish Peace Process," *Political Quarterly* 73, no. 2 (2002): 172–80.

806 "There are many men": John Hume, "The Irish Question: A British Problem," *Foreign Affairs* (Winter 1979–80): 312.

806 "implement reforms": Wilson, 193.

806 Protestant Unionists vehemently: EMK int., Feb. 27, 2006; Mar. 20, 2006; Parker int., Oct. 20, 2008.

807 "You had to get Kennedy": Trina Vargo int., Nov. 7, 2008, Miller Center, UVA.

807 O'Dowd talked to Vargo : Conor O'Clery, *The Greening of the White House: The Inside Story of How America Tried to Bring Peace to Ireland* (Dublin: Gill & Macmillan, 1996), 59–60; Nancy Soderberg int., Oct. 9, 2008, Miller Center, UVA.

808 "We were constantly": Vargo int.

808 "I left Ireland": O'Clery, *Greening*, 79–80; EMK int., Mar. 20, 2006.

808 visa would damage America's: Parker int., Oct. 20, 2008.

809 "Out of hand": EMK int., Mar. 20, 2006.

809 Clinton granted the visa: Clinton, *My Life*, 578–81.

809 "See what the Brits": O'Clery, *Greening*, 119.

810 "Trina, he's Irish": Vargo int.

810 "If the Sinn Fein": O'Clery, *Greening*, 163.

810 ban against Sinn Fein: Ibid., 167, 169.

810 "every kind of opportunity": EMK int., Mar. 20, 2006.

810 "There was a several-year": Ibid.

810 "I gave him about three": Vargo int.

810 helped guide a process: For a full and detailed account of Mitchell's role, see George Mitchell, *Making Peace* (New York: Knopf, 1999).

811 "basically to keep": Clinton, *My Life*, 784.

811 "seemed privately to plummet": EMK, *True Compass*, 468–69.

811 "His advice is always": Adam Clymer, *Edward M. Kennedy: A Biography* (New York: Harper Perennial, 2000), 603.

811 couldn't find those thirty-five: EMK, *True Compass*, 468–69.

812 Clinton's favorability: "Presidential Job Approval: Bill Clinton's High Ratings in the Midst of Crisis," Gallup, Jun. 4, 1999, https://news.gallup.com/poll/4609/presidential-job-approval-bill -clintons-high-ratings-midst.aspx.

812 rating stood at 66 percent: "Presidential Approval Ratings—Bill Clinton," Gallup, n.d., https:// news.gallup.com/poll/116584/presidential-approval-ratings-bill-clinton.aspx.

812 "Newt Gingrich, my dear": "Gingrich Steps Down in Face of Rebellion," *WP*, Nov. 7, 1998.

813 "The president's success": Harris, *Survivor*, 352.

813 "No matter how many": Joan Didion, *Political Fictions* (2001; New York: Vintage, 2002), 277–79.

814 should ask for a test vote: EMK, *True Compass*, 469–70.

814 "restore some order": Peter Baker, *The Breach: Inside the Impeachment and Trial of William Jefferson Clinton* (New York: Scribner, 2000), 291–92.

814 "senators were practically": Parker int., Nov. 17, 2008.

815 converting that verbal agreement: Trent Lott, *Herding Cats* (New York: ReganBooks, 2005), 195–96; EMK, *True Compass*, 417–72.

815 "going back and forth": Melody Barnes int., Aug. 16, 2006, Miller Center, UVA.

815 "bring some folks over": James Manley int., Sept. 28, 2009, Miller Center, UVA; Barnes int.

816 week of his acquittal: "Presidential Approval Ratings—Bill Clinton," Gallup, n.d., https://news .gallup.com/poll/116584/presidential-approval-ratings-bill-clinton.aspx.

816 "challenge his party's orthodoxies": Harris, *Survivor*, 354.

816 "Rank didn't matter": Hunt, "Kennedy Forged Legacy."

816 first-class air travel: Dale Bumpers int., May 20, 1998, B Folder, Box 3, Series 2, Clymer Papers, JFK Lib.

816 **Black people ought to block:** Bob Bates int., Sept. 21, 1994, B Folder, Box 3, Series 2, Clymer Papers, JFK Lib.

816 **"old shit cans":** Robert Healy int., Aug. 10, 2005, Miller Center, UVA.

817 **"Our housekeeper was so":** Doris Reggie int., Dec. 16, 2008, Miller Center, UVA.

817 **Comic Relief:** Thomas Rollins int., May 12, 2009, Miller Center, UVA.

817 **"It was never very easy":** "Kennedy Son Treated at Alcohol Clinic," *WP*, July 12, 1991; John Robinson, "Ted Kennedy Jr. Quits the Fast Lane," *BG*, Oct. 7, 1993.

817 **"reduced from mythology":** "The Camelot Curse," *Newsweek*, Jan. 12, 1998.

818 **"command performance":** Melody Miller int., July 15, 2008, Miller Center, UVA.

818 **"Today, the Republicans paid":** "Senate Kills a Patients Rights Bill," *WP*, Oct. 10, 1998.

819 **"ribbing him for his":** "Kennedy Gets Back to Senate," *BG*, July 28, 1999.

819 **Clinton threatened:** "Senate Backs GOP's Modest Steps on Protecting Rights of Patient," *WP*, July 15, 1999.

819 **left the floor and headed:** D. A. Pollack, "Reflections on Working for Senator Edward Kennedy," *Community Mental Health Journal* 46, no. 2 (April 2010): 103–11.

819 **never arrived:** Vicki Kennedy, on *Oprah Winfrey Show*, Nov. 25, 2009.

819 **appeared with a three-wheel buggy:** "A Desperate Search at Sea," *Newsweek*, July 26, 1999.

819 **"The world stands motionless":** "Rescue Search in Kennedy Crash Ends," *NYT*, July 19, 1999.

819 **thirteen years to the day:** Canellos, *Last Lion*, 344–45.

819 **where they waited hours:** Patrick Kennedy and Stephen Fried, *A Common Struggle: A Personal Journey Through the Past and Future of Mental Illness and Addiction* (New York: Blue Rider Press, 2015), 166–67.

820 **scattered at sea off Martha's Vineyard:** "Every Gift But Length of Years," *WP*, July 24, 1999.

820 **"We are tied to the ocean":** "Bodies From Kennedy Crash Are Found," *NYT*, July 22, 1999.

820 **"He was so deep":** Kennedy and Fried, *Common Struggle*, 166–67.

820 **"I have never seen him":** "The Torchbearer," *People*, Aug. 16, 1999.

820 **large public ceremony:** "JFK Jr.'s Final Journey," *Newsweek*, Aug. 2, 1999.

820 **"to the American family":** "He Had Amazing Grace," *Newsweek*, Aug. 2, 1999.

TWENTY: THE CHARM OFFENSIVE/THE WAR OFFENSIVE

821 **"back in the Senate family":** "Kennedy Gets Back to Senate," *BG*, July 28, 1999.

821 **"who carries the clan":** "The Torchbearer," *People*, Aug. 16, 1999.

821 **"supposed to be the kid":** Ken Ringle, "Ted Kennedy's Strength in Sorrow," *WP*, July 21, 1999.

821 **Mass at St. Joseph's Church:** "To Have and to Hold," *People*, July 24, 2000.

822 **"loud and boisterous faith":** EMK, *True Compass* (New York: Twelve, 2009), 477–79.

822 **wanted to be closer to her work:** Adam Clymer, *Edward M. Kennedy: A Biography* (New York: Harper Perennial, 2000), 592.

822 **Hong Kong industrialist:** "6BR, riv. Vu., Kennedy Must Sell, 4.9 m," *BG*, Jan. 17, 1997; "Kennedy House Fetches $1m over Asking Price," *BG*, Feb. 6, 1997.

822 **"quite possibly the most":** Mark David, "Senator Kennedy's Kalorama Mansion Up for Grabs," *Variety*, Jan. 19, 2010.

823 **"A warm welcoming house":** Ibid.; Roland Flamini, "Inside Senator Edward M. Kennedy's House in Washington, D.C.," *Architectural Digest*, Nov. 1999.

823 **"years in which":** EMK, *True Compass*, 475.

824 **"He loved those dogs":** John Tunney int., May 3, 2007, Miller Center, UVA.

824 **precluded Ted getting a dog:** EMK, "The Cause of My Life," *Newsweek*, July 27, 2009.

824 **"visions of sugarplums":** Caroline Raclin int., Nov. 11, 2009, Miller Center, UVA; Art Sterna int. by author.

825 **"antsy":** Sharon Waxman int., Dec. 19, 2008, Miller Center, UVA.

825 **"You're completely wrong":** George Miller int., Oct. 13, 2009, Miller Center, UVA.

825 **"freaking out":** David Sutphen in "Remembering Ted Kennedy," *National Journal*, Sept. 5, 2009.

825 **"part of the landscape":** Sandy Kress quoted in "Kennedy's Dogs Will Be Missed on Hill," *Politico*, Aug. 30, 2009.

825 **tore at the shrubbery:** Ibid.

825 **"Now whaddya want":** Mark Leibovich, "The Kennedy Factor," *WP*, July 13, 2004.

826 **"sailing on the *Mya*":** "Proust Questionnaire," *Vanity Fair*, May 2006.

826 **"One elephant too much":** "Lawmakers Drop Hate Crimes Bill," AP, Oct. 18, 1999.

826   jobs program for people: Gene Sperling, Chris Jennings, et al., "New Initiative to Provide Eco-
        nomic Opportunities for Americans with Disabilities" Jan. 12, 1999, NLWJC-Kagan DPC Box 4,
        Folder 13, Clinton Lib.
826   preferring funds be given: "Kennedy Proposes Youth Crime Program," AP, Oct. 29, 1999.
826   "Gore seemed to catch": Robert Shrum, No Excuses: Concessions of a Serial Campaigner (New
        York: Simon & Schuster, 2007), 323.
826   "Senator, it wasn't me": Tad Devine int. by author.
827   "The people versus the powerful": Nick Littlefield int., May 3, 2008, Miller Center, UVA.
827   "America, in this apocalyptic": Joan Didion, Political Fictions (2001; New York: Vintage, 2002),
        336–37.
827   "Al, there's not a single": John Harris, The Survivor: Bill Clinton in the White House (New York:
        Random House, 2005), 389.
827   waging a populist campaign: See Stanley Greenberg, The Two Americas: Our Current Political
        Deadlock and How to Break It (New York: St. Martin's Griffin, 2005), 86.
828   "I have waited for": Harris, Survivor, 393.
830   "We fell short of our": EMK, True Compass, 473.
830   "boozy kid": George W. Bush, Decision Points (New York: Crown, 2010), 21.
830   Nixon victory sign: Peter Baker, Days of Fire: Bush and Cheney in the White House (New York:
        Doubleday, 2013), 27.
831   "I like Bush personally": Jack Newfield, "The Senate's Fighting Liberal," Nation, Mar. 25, 2002.
831   known his grandfather: Anne Kornblut, "Bush Tries to Build Ties with Kennedy," BG, Jan. 11,
        2001.
831   "I've heard of you": Ibid.
831   "Jack the Tongue": "Kennedy's Kamikaze Challenger," WP, Mar. 24, 2000.
832   called him ten minutes later: Kornblut.
832   "Senator Kennedy was really": Melody Barnes int., Aug. 16, 2006, Miller Center, UVA.
833   "I don't retreat": "Kennedy Continues Ashcroft Attack," BG, Jan. 18, 2001.
833   "throughout his career": Congressional Record, Senate, 107th Cong., 1st sess., Jan. 31, 2001,
        S891.
833   "expressing outrage": Ibid., S899–S900.
834   "I'd have to say that": "Excerpts from Remarks on the Senate Debate on the Ashcroft Nomina-
        tion," NYT, Feb. 2, 2001.
834   "He should think twice": "The Ashcroft Message," NYT, Feb. 2, 2001.
835   would not heed that warning: R. W. Apple, Jr., "The Inauguration: Tradition and Legitimacy,"
        NYT, Jan. 20, 2001.
835   "You know your way": Jean Edward Smith, Bush (New York: Simon & Schuster, 2016), 164.
835   "every intention": EMK to G.H.W. Bush, Feb. 5, 2001, Bush Presidential Papers, Bush Lib.
835   Bush's main target: Anne Kornblut, "Bush Outreach Runs on Persistence, Charm," BG, Feb. 3,
        2001.
835   "also has friends": "Kennedy Joins Bush in Unveiling Aid for Disabled," WP, Feb. 2, 2001.
836   "Bush and his advisers": Gary Gerstle, "Minorities, Multiculturalism, and the Presidency of
        George W. Bush," in The Presidency of George W. Bush, ed. Julian Zelizer, (Princeton: Princeton
        Univ. Press, 2010), 272.
836   standards-based reforms: See Robert Schwartz and Marian Robinson, "Goals 2 and the Stan-
        dards Movement," Brookings Papers on Educational Policy, 2000.
836   "Higher standards, testing": Littlefield int.
837   "Ted Kennedy was public": Margaret Spellings int., Aug. 27, 2008, Miller Center, UVA.
837   "He is an ornery S.O.B.": David Broder, "Long Road to Reform," WP, Dec. 17, 2001.
837   "I want to help": Robert Draper, Dead Certain: The Presidency of George W. Bush (New York: Free
        Press, 2007), 115–17.
838   "some areas of difference": "Bush Ties School Aid, Test Scores," BG, Jan. 24, 2001.
838   "A mating dance": Spellings int.
838   "I don't think we need": Draper, Dead Certain, 116–17.
838   "We can't ask for it now": Tom Daschle int., Apr. 29, 2009, Miller Center, UVA.
839   "sweet talker": Dana Milbank, "Bush's Democratic Weapon," WP, May 10, 2001.
839   "Bush's Democratic Weapon": Ibid.
839   "We need to work with": Michael Myers int., Aug. 28, 2006, Miller Center, UVA.
839   "we could work well": Carey Parker int., Dec. 1, 2008, Miller Center, UVA.

839 **"good deal of time":** Quoted in Darren Samuelsohn and Danny Vinik, "No Child Left Behind: The Oral History," *Politico,* Sept. 23, 2015.

839 **"trying to reassure":** Parker int.

839 **"I think his":** George Miller int.

840 **"We can't have vouchers":** EMK int., Oct. 8, 2007, Miller Center, UVA.

840 **"loves to go to the":** Parker int.

840 **"Kennedy just read us":** Broder, "Long Road."

840 **"gets the reform":** Milbank, "Bush's Democratic Weapon."

841 **richest one percent:** David Rosenbaum, "Doing the Math on Bush's Tax Cut," *NYT,* Mar. 4, 2001.

841 **"Every dollar in tax cuts":** James Jeffords with Yvonne Daley and Howard Coffin, *An Independent Man: Adventures of a Public Servant* (New York: Simon & Schuster, 2003), 264.

842 **hardly afford to reject it:** See Smith, *Bush,* 160–61.

842 **plan of their own:** "Democrats Struggle to Find Stance on Tax Cut," *NYT,* Feb. 11, 2001.

842 **"football game":** *Congressional Record,* Senate, 107th Cong., 1st sess., May 23, 2001, S5512–13.

842 **tax cuts passed the Senate:** "Senators Vote to Slash Bush Tax Cut," *BG,* Apr. 5, 2001; "Democrats Dig in Heels on Tax Bill," *BG,* May 23, 2001; "Senate Approves Tax Cut," *BG,* May 24, 2001.

843 **"Jeffords problem":** Draper, *Dead Certain,* 117.

843 **"Bill Clinton's favorite":** Garrison Nelson, "Jim Jeffords's Long Goodbye," *NYT,* May 25, 2001.

843 **"loose cannon":** Trent Lott, *Herding Cats* (New York: ReganBooks, 2005), 213–16.

843 **"If you're a Republican":** "While a Restless Senator Stirred, the Bush Team May Have Slept," *NYT,* May 24, 2001.

843 **"I felt that if":** Jeffords, *Independent Man,* 172.

844 **caucus with the Democrats:** "Senate Faces Sea Change," *WP,* May 27, 2001.

844 **another minimum wage increase:** Ibid.

844 **fought for the bill:** "Senate Again Rejects Patient Protection Bill," *Modern Healthcare,* June 12, 2000.

844 **"Bipartisan talk is fine":** "Bush Threatens to Veto Health Bill," *BG,* Mar. 22, 2001.

845 **"I think we underestimated":** John McCain int., Oct. 16, 2009, Miller Center, UVA.

845 **"A lot of press conferences":** James Manley int., Sept. 28, 2009, Miller Center, UVA.

845 **did make a concession:** "Senate Sides Square Off Over Patients' Rights," *WP,* June 17, 2001.

846 **pull it back when it had:** Amy Goldstein, "Patients' Rights Talks Hit Impasse," *WP,* Aug. 2, 2002.

846 **"If it is brought up":** "New Bill on Patients' Rights Is Both Hailed and Criticized," *NYT,* May 16, 2001.

847 **"The bottom line":** "Deal Is Reached on a Bill to Set Patients' Rights," *NYT,* Aug. 2, 2001.

847 **"unenforceable":** "Remembering Ted Kennedy," *National Journal,* Sept. 5, 2009.

847 **"If they had been willing":** Goldstein, "Patients' Rights Talks Hit Impasse."

848 **"A radicalized form of Reaganism":** Sean Wilentz, *The Age of Reagan: A History 1974–2008* (New York: HarperCollins, 2008), 434–35.

849 **"A pretty traumatic day":** EMK, *True Compass,* 492; Peter Canellos, *Last Lion: The Fall and Rise of Ted Kennedy* (New York: Simon & Schuster, 2009), 355; EMK int., Dec. 9, 2007, Miller Center, UVA; Victoria Reggie Kennedy int., Dec. 9, 2007, Miller Center, UVA; Waxman int.; Parker int.

850 **show of strength:** EMK int., Dec. 9, 2007.

850 **"I hope I can survive":** "Back Home a Member of the Family Has Been Lost," *BG,* Aug. 27, 2009.

850 **"Whenever one of your":** Newfield, "Senate's Fighting Liberal."

851 **"They've just run out of steam":** EMK int., June 3, 2005, Miller Center, UVA; Canellos, *Last Lion,* 360; Barbara Souliotis int., July 12, 2005, Miller Center, UVA.

851 **soared to 86 percent:** "Presidential Approval Ratings—George W. Bush," Gallup, n.d., https://news.gallup.com/poll/116500/presidential-approval-ratings-george-bush.aspx.

852 **working in his Capitol hideaway:** "In Cramped Digs, Senators Go On With Business," *BG,* Oct. 19, 2001.

852 **"dozens of press conferences":** Manley int.

852 **read every single word:** Michael Myers int., Aug. 28, 2006, Miller Center, UVA.

852 **"legendary":** Manley int.

852 **"put up the money":** George Miller int.

853 **"You've just got to get":** Ibid.

853 **"Bush hasn't won":** Michael Duffy, "When Dynasties Call a Truce," *Time,* Nov. 26, 2001.

854 **thirty-six-hour conference:** Broder, "Long Road."

854 **"There were two moments":** Quoted in Samuelsohn and Vinik, "No Child."

854 **Daschle once again concurred:** Thomas Daschle with Michael D'Orso, *Like No Other Time: The 107th Congress and the Two Years That Changed America Forever* (New York: Crown, 2003), 97–98.

854 **"protested vigorously":** "Congress Reaches Compromise on Education Bill," *NYT*, Dec. 12, 2001; "Kennedy the Pragmatist," *National Journal*, Dec. 8, 2001.

854 **"Yesterday's libertine":** "King of the Hill: In Praise of Ted Kennedy," *Economist*, Jan. 12, 2002.

854 **"The folks at Crawford":** "With Fanfare Bush Signs Education Bill," *WP*, Jan. 9, 2002.

855 **"likely the most":** Gerstle, "Minorities, Multiculturalism," 253.

855 **"may well be the most":** Broder, "Long Road."

855 **"The bill lays a solid foundation":** "Landmark Legislation Gets Final Approval," *WP*, Dec. 19, 2001.

855 **average of 13.4 percent:** Newfield, "Senate's Fighting Liberal."

855 **"I remember the Senator":** Melody Miller int., July 15, 2008, Miller Center, UVA.

856 **"A spectacular broken promise":** "Democrats Criticizing Bush Budget on Education," *NYT*, Feb. 13, 2002.

856 **gloated over Ted's surrender:** Melody Miller int.

856 **"We had to uncover":** Bush, *Decision Points*, 154.

857 **"Kennedy supported the resolution":** Waxman int.

857 **international response to the attacks:** EMK int., Dec. 9, 2007.

858 **resolved the differences:** Esther Olavarria int., Aug. 28, 2006, Miller Center, UVA.

858 **civil libertarians had:** See "Letter to the Senate on the Enhanced Border Security and Visa Entry Reform Act of 2001," ACLU, Dec. 17, 2001, https://www.aclu.org/letter/letter-senate-enhanced -border-security-and-visa-entry-reform-act-2001.

858 **"Dealing with Iraq":** Bush, *Decision Points*, 189.

859 **"Unless I received":** Ibid., 191.

859 **"Before 9/11, Saddam":** Ibid., 229.

859 **"We would confront":** Ibid.

859 **"we were looking for":** Baker, *Days of Fire*, 191.

860 **"Bush needed something":** Smith, *Bush*, 277.

860 **"The 'axis of evil' speech":** Baker, *Days of Fire*, 189.

860 **77 percent of Americans:** Ibid., 191.

861 **"seemed aimed at preparing":** Elisabeth Bumiller, "U.S. Must Act First to Battle Terror," *NYT*, June 2, 2002.

861 **"would put some common sense":** EMK int., Dec. 9, 2007.

861 **"Don't Attack Saddam":** Baker, *Days of Fire*, 211.

861 **"something big was coming":** Waxman int.

862 **"Doing nothing is not":** "Bush to Seek OK of Congress Before Taking Action on Iraq," *BG*, Sept. 5, 2002.

862 **attacked Saddam relentlessly:** "Bush Urges UN to Join Action Against Iraq," *WP*, Sept. 13, 2002.

862 **"virtually unanimous":** EMK int., Dec. 9, 2007.

862 **"last fifteen minutes":** EMK, *True Compass*, 495.

862 **"longstanding and continuing":** "US Says New Data Tie Iraq to Qaeda," *BG*, Sept. 27, 2002.

863 **was being disingenuous:** Waxman int.

863 **"void":** Ibid.

863 **"most sweeping criticism":** "Kennedy Criticizes Bush on Iraq Policy," *BG*, Sept. 28, 2002; "Liberals Object to Bush Policy on Iraq Attack," *NYT*, Sept. 28, 2002.

863 **"Every day we were tracking":** Waxman int.

864 **"He wasn't giving these speeches":** Ibid.

864 **"glass of wine too much":** David Burke int., Apr. 9, 2008, Miller Center, UVA.

864 **briefings with former secretary:** EMK int., Dec. 9, 2007.

864 **"deliberately provoked":** William vanden Heuvel int., Dec. 7, 2006, Miller Center, UVA.

865 **"already made up his mind":** Gregory Craig int., July 13, 2010, Miller Center, UVA.

865 **"just war":** EMK, *True Compass*, 495–96.

865 **group had doubled in size:** EMK int., Dec. 9, 2007.

865 **"one of the most important":** *Congressional Record*, Senate, 107th Cong., 2nd sess., Oct. 4, 2002, S9934.

866 **"Let them make a decision":** Ibid., S9956–61.

866 **"We don't want the smoking":** Smith, *Bush*, 316.

866 **"passionately contending":** Shrum, *No Excuses*, 388.

866 "I have been in the Senate": "Congress Gives Bush OK to Act Alone Against Iraq," *BG*, Oct. 11, 2002.

TWENTY-ONE: "A FRAUD COOKED UP IN TEXAS"

868 "liked nothing more": Jean Edward Smith, *Bush* (New York: Simon & Schuster, 2016), 329; Robert Draper, *Dead Certain: The Presidency of George W. Bush* (New York: Free Press, 2007), 185.

868 "security of our country": Thomas Daschle with Michael D'Orso, *Like No Other Time: The 107th Congress and the Two Years That Changed America* (New York: Crown, 2003), 226.

868 "different wave": "Kennedy: The Attacks Transformed Our Politics," *BG*, Jan. 19, 2002.

869 answer the call and run: Daschle, *Like No Other Time*, 256–57.

869 "consumed": Ibid., 4.

869 "very unsatisfactory": EMK int., Mar. 28, 2008, Miller Center, UVA; "Kara Kennedy Treated for Lung Cancer," *BG*, Jan. 3, 2003; Sally Jacobs, "Kennedy, His Children and Cancer," *People*, May 25, 2008; Melody Miller int., Oct. 7, 2008, Miller Center, UVA.

869 "felt a little left behind": Melody Miller int.

870 "When Kara got lung cancer": Ibid.; Jacobs, "Kennedy, His Children."

870 "We cannot say": "Kennedy Assails Bush Policies," *WP*, Jan. 22, 2002.

870 "chip-on-the-shoulder": "Kennedy Attacks Bush on Iraq, Drugs," *BG*, Jan. 25, 2003.

871 "stick to what we know": Draper, *Dead Certain*, 186.

871 63 percent of Americans: "Seventy-two Percent of Americans Support War Against Iraq," Gallup, March 24, 2003, https://news.gallup.com/poll/8038/seventytwo-percent-americans -support-war-against-iraq.aspx.

871 "wavered": Sharon Waxman int., May 11, 2009, Miller Center, UVA.

871 "strong presentation": EMK, "Level With Us, Mr. President," *BG*, Feb. 8, 2003.

871 welcome American soldiers: Draper, *Dead Certain*, 186–89.

872 prophecies were far less rosy: Sharon Waxman int., Dec. 19, 2008, Miller Center, UVA.

872 "If you really want": Ibid.

873 "Why weren't there more": EMK int., Dec. 9, 2007, Miller Center, UVA.

873 "two old bulls": James Manley int., Sept. 28, 2009, Miller Center, UVA.

873 "unnecessary": "At Methodist Meeting, Kennedy Blasts War Planning," *National Catholic Reporter*, Mar. 21, 2003.

873 administration didn't listen: See Smith, *Bush*, 347–48.

874 "It was gross incompetence": EMK int., Dec. 9, 2007.

874 "police officers in a shooting gallery": "Rebuilding Iraq," *BG*, July 16, 2003.

874 wanted to push back: "Partisan Battle Builds in Congress Over Bush's Spending Request," *NYT*, Sept. 24, 2003.

874 "fraud cooked up": EMK int., Dec. 9, 2007; "Backtrack Time for Kennedy?" *Time*, Sept. 29, 2003; "Kennedy Says Case for War Built on 'Fraud,' " *WP*, Sept. 19, 2003.

875 "My god! What did": Waxman int., May 11, 2009.

875 "I would have had": EMK int., Dec. 9, 2007.

875 "uncivil": "Kennedy Says Case for War Built on 'Fraud.' "

876 "administration's rationale": "In Senate, Kennedy Fuels Sharp Debate," *WP*, Sept. 24, 2003.

876 "You don't have to get": Mark Leibovich, "The Kennedy Factor," *WP*, July 13, 2004.

876 "mindless, senseless": Anne E. Kornblut, "Kennedy to Assail Bush over Iraq War," *BG*, Oct. 16, 2003.

876 decided instead to phone him: EMK int., Dec. 9, 2007.

877 "This is how it's going": April Witt, "Fatal Inaction," *WP*, June 18, 2006.

877 continued to fight: Mike Barnicle, "Of Memory and the Sea," *Time*, Aug. 27, 2009.

878 consider it done: See "Edward Kennedy was Set Fast in the Family Mould," *Sunday Times*, Aug. 30, 2009.

878 "They blew it": Kornblut, "Kennedy to Assail Bush."

878 went through private insurers: Amy Goldstein and Helen Dewar, "Drug Plan for Seniors Defeated," *WP*, Aug. 1, 2002; "Senior Drug Plan Falls to Two Parties' Rivalry," *BG*, Aug. 1, 2002.

878 "How many of us": Goldstein and Dewar, "Drug Plan for Seniors Defeated."

879 "solemn promise between": "Kennedy Attacks Bush on Iraq, Drugs."

879 privatize Medicare: Stuart Altman and David Schachtman, *Power, Politics, and Universal Health Care: The Inside Story of a Century-Long Battle* (Amherst, N.Y.: Prometheus Books, 2011), 181.

879 "create an opportunity": George W. Bush, *Decision Points* (New York: Crown, 2010), 282.

879 making the private plan: Ibid.; "Senators Reach Agreement on Drug Plan for Elderly," *NYT*, June 6, 2003. The *Times's* account mentions neither Ted nor Breaux.

879 pass it by the July Fourth: David Blumenthal and James Morone, *The Heart of Power: Health and Politics in the Oval Office* (Berkeley: Univ. of California Press, 2009), 402–4.

880 "pathetic bill": "Ted and Hillary's Health Care Split," *WP*, June 24, 2003.

880 "huddled in the well": "Medicare Expansion Reaches Last Hurdle," *WP*, June 28, 2003.

880 "greatest action in": "Medicare Drug Plan Passes Senate," *BG*, June 27, 2003; Robin Toner and Robert Pear, "House and Senate Pass Measures for Broad Overhaul of Medicare," *NYT*, June 27, 2003.

880 not happy about his own: Elisabeth Bumiller, "A Final Push in Congress," *NYT*, Nov. 23, 2003.

881 "donut hole": Toner and Pear, "House and Senate Pass Measures."

881 "reasonable compromises": "10 Questions for Ted Kennedy," *Time*, Aug. 4, 2003.

881 "life support": "Prescription Drug Bill in Peril," *NYT*, Nov. 5, 2003.

881 "It is the beginning": "Medicare Bill Near Senate Passage," *WP*, Nov. 25, 2003; See also Paul Krugman, "The Trojan Horse," *NYT*, Nov. 14, 2003.

882 "Let's face it": Manley int.

882 "When you're dealing with": Carey Parker int., Dec. 1, 2008, Miller Center, UVA.

882 tough ideologue: See Gary Jacobson, *A Divider, Not a Uniter: George W. Bush and the American People, the 2006 Election and Beyond* (New York: Longman Press, 2007).

882 "basically a slush fund": "Kennedy Vows Fight Over GOP Drug Bill," *BG*, Nov. 17, 2003.

882 "made a mistake": "Six Democratic Candidates Attack Medicare Measure," *NYT*, Nov. 19, 2003.

882 "We're here to say": "Counting Votes and Attacks in Final Push for Medicare Bill," *NYT*, Nov. 20, 2003.

882 "Virtually overnight": "Ted Kennedy Gets a Little Republican Respect," *WP*, May 30, 2007.

883 "Give this bill a fair": "A Medicare Bill Squeezed Through House at Dawn," *WP*, Nov. 23, 2003.

883 "This vote has been held": Peter Baker, *Days of Fire: Bush and Cheney in the White House* (New York: Doubleday, 2013), 294–95.

884 compared the tactic: Bumiller, "Final Push in Congress."

884 shaking his head: Trent Lott, *Herding Cats* (New York: ReganBooks, 2005), 290–93.

884 parliamentary avenue: Altman and Schachtman, *Power, Politics*, 194–95; Baker, *Days of Fire*, 295.

885 left the floor fuming: Susan Milligan, "Saying GOP Broke Word, Kennedy Vows New Tactics," *BG*, Nov. 27, 2003.

885 "You sold us out!": "Medicare Bill Near Senate Passage," *WP*, Nov. 25, 2003.

885 "A 40-ton chunk": E. J. Dionne, Jr., "The Democrats Take a Dive," *WP*, Nov. 25, 2003.

885 "He and I opposed": Tom Daschle int., Apr. 29, 2009, Miller Center, UVA.

885 "When the President": Milligan, "Saying GOP Broke Word."

885 "Republicans controlled": Dionne, "Democrats Take a Dive."

886 "Too ready to compromise": Michael Myers int., Aug. 28, 2006, Miller Center, UVA.

886 "The key to his legacy": "America's Ten Best Senators," *Time*, Apr. 24, 2006.

886 was the anachronism: Milligan, "Saying GOP Broke Word."

886 "proves that Republicans": Dionne, "Democrats Take a Dive."

886 "pre-conferenced": Milligan, "Saying GOP Broke Word."

886 "Who do you trust": Altman and Schachtman, *Power, Politics*, 194–95; "President Signs Medicare Drug Bill," *WP*, Dec. 19, 2003.

886 "most antisenior": "Bush Signs Bill to Add Medicare Drug Benefit," *BG*, Dec. 9, 2003.

887 "It has changed": "On Hill, Relations Take a Turn for the Worse," *BG*, Dec. 1, 2003.

887 "We never imagined they": "Democrats Forced to Work on Margins," *WP*, Dec. 22, 2003.

888 "Personally burned": Leibovich, "Kennedy Factor."

888 seldom spoke on the phone: "Not So Strange Bedfellows Despite Differences," *BG*, Jan. 8, 2002.

888 "greatly imperiled": "Bush and Former Allies Differ on School Law," *BG*, Jan. 9. 2003.

888 "breathtakingly arrogant": David Broder and Dana Milbank, "Hopes for Civility in Washington Are Dashed," *WP*, Jan. 18, 2004; "Kennedy Accuses Bush of 'Credibility Gap,'" *WP*, Apr. 6, 2004.

888 "We had endless trouble": Parker int.

888 "We're doing absolutely": EMK int., June 3, 2005, Miller Center, UVA.

889 "non-functioning institution": "Senate Deadlocks on Wages, Welfare," *WP*, Apr. 2, 2004.

889 "Can you believe what": Myers int.
890 "There is no precedent": Quoted in Ron Suskind, "Why Are These Men Laughing?" *Esquire*, Jan. 2003.
890 "maybe the single most": John Dilulio, "John Dilulio's Letter," *Esquire*, May 23, 2007.
890 "relished the 'us versus them' thing": Broder and Milbank, "Hopes for Civility."
890 "Why would you want": Sean Wilentz, *The Age of Reagan: A History 1974–2008* (New York: HarperCollins, 2008), 448.
890 "It's basically a result": Charles Pierce, "Kennedy Unbound After 40 Years in the US Senate," *BG Magazine*, Jan. 5, 2003.
891 "nuclear option": See Jeffrey Toobin, "Blowing Up the Senate," *New Yorker*, Feb. 27, 2006.
891 "aggressive way of imposing": EMK int., June 3, 2005.
891 "They think it's politically": EMK int., May 8, 2006, Miller Center, UVA.
891 some 55 percent: "Public Attitudes Toward the War in Iraq: 2003–2008," Pew Research Center, March 18, 2008, https://www.pewresearch.org/2008/03/19/public-attitudes-toward-the-war-in-iraq-20032008/.
892 "The agenda was clear": "In Speech, Kennedy Toughens War Stance," *BG*, Jan. 15, 2004; "Kennedy Hits Bush on War," *WP*, Jan. 15, 2004.
892 "gutsy speech": Waxman int., May 11, 2009.
892 "state of facts": "Kennedy Says Bush Skewed Iraq Data," *WP*, Mar. 6, 2004.
892 "what was said before": "Kyl Rebuts Kennedy on Prewar Data," *WP*, Mar. 14, 2004.
892 never have taken our eye off: *Meet the Press*, Mar. 21, 2004.
892 "Bush's Vietnam": "Kennedy an Attribute in Democratic Effort," *BG*, Apr. 7, 2004.
893 "What? Is he crazy?": Waxman int., May 11, 2009.
893 It was personal: Manley int.
893 "how personal it was": Waxman int., Dec. 19, 2008.
893 spoke of Private John Hart: Leibovich, "Kennedy Factor."
893 read the names slowly: Waxman int., May 11, 2009.
894 continued to insist otherwise: Myers int.
894 "Senator Kennedy is the": Waxman int., May 11, 2009.
894 "I long ago stopped": "Ted Kennedy's Lesson for Kerry," *WP*, Sept. 14, 2004.
894 "The Democrats were convinced": William vanden Heuvel int., Dec. 7, 2006, Miller Center, UVA.
895 deserved a reward: John Kerry int., June 21, 2010, Miller Center, UVA.
895 "the first person to dare": Kerry int.; Leibovich, "Kennedy Factor."
895 "properly submissive": John Farrell int., July 13, 2006, Miller Center, UVA.
895 miffed that Kerry spoke: "For Kennedy and Kerry, Chill is Gone," *BG*, May 10, 2003; "Ending His Silence, Kennedy Says He'll Back Kerry," *BG*, Jan. 22, 2003.
896 blowup with Ted: Patrick Healy, "Kennedy Gives Kerry Campaign a Lift in Iowa," *BG*, Sept. 28, 2003.
896 have a bill to point to: Farrell int.
896 "master of the personal": John Kerry, *Every Day Is Extra* (New York: Simon & Schuster, 2018), 156, 240.
896 fundament of politics: "Fits and Starts," *Newsweek*, Nov. 15, 2004.
896 "impassioned": Robert Shrum, *No Excuses: Concessions of a Serial Campaigner* (New York: Simon & Schuster, 2007), 389.
896 ride to the rescue: Ibid., 424.
896 reassert liberal values: Healy, "Kennedy Gives Kerry Campaign."
896 "magnet for Iowa Democrats": Shrum, *No Excuses*, 424.
896 "Are you going to": Healy, "Kennedy Gives Kerry Campaign"; "Senior Senator Leads Rally," *BG*, Jan. 11, 2004; Tad Devine int. by author; Leibovich, "Kennedy Factor."
897 "It was like going back": Peter Canellos, *Last Lion: The Fall and Rise of Ted Kennedy* (New York: Simon & Schuster, 2009), 374.
897 "campaign for you": Devine int.
897 "He worked his heart": "Ted Kennedy Memorial Service," ABC News, Aug. 28, 2009.
897 "I think everybody's wrong": Shrum, *No Excuses*, 424.
897 "See how he's not gone": Charles Pierce, "Kennedy Unbound After 40 Years in the US Senate," *BG Magazine*, Jan. 5, 2003.
898 "AM radio stuck on scan": Ibid.
898 "He looks all of his": Leibovich, "Kennedy Factor."

898   "eeriness": Joan Vennochi, "Kennedy's Two-Edged Mystique," *BG*, May 27, 2004.

898   good for Boston generally: Barbara Souliotis int., July 12, 2005, Miller Center, UVA.

899   "Yeah, I've been out": Leibovich, "Kennedy Factor."

899   "Iraq. Jobs. Medicare.": "Kennedy Likens Bush to Nixon," *BG*, Apr. 6, 2004.

899   "Kerry's lead hatchet man": "Kennedy an Attribute in Democratic Effort," *BG*, Apr. 7, 2004.

899   "most important election": Leibovich, "Kennedy Factor."

899   "stem-winder while": Ibid.; "For Kerry and Kennedy, Chill is Gone."

900   select John Edwards: "Inside the Decision: The Gleam Team," *Time*, July 19, 2004.

900   "greatest fall from grace": "Kennedy Rallies Democrats with Bush Barbs," *USA Today*, July 28, 2004.

900   "fiery attack": "Kennedy Launches an Attack on Bush on Convention's Second Day," *NYT*, July 27, 2004.

900   "near farewell": Ibid.

901   "All of us are connected": "Master of the Senate," *BG*, July 28, 2004.

901   "celebration of all": "The Life of the Party," *BG*, Apr. 13, 2004.

901   "going bananas": Richard Dyer, "Celebrities Serenade Kennedy with Style," *BG*, July 28, 2004.

901   "I think you vote": EMK int., Dec. 9, 2007.

902   "Money, lies and television": Kerry, *Every Day*, 302.

902   "If you're explaining": Ibid., 306.

902   "conservative senator": "Both Campaigns Invoke an Image: The Liberal's Liberal," *BG*, Oct. 28, 2004.

903   "wafer watch": Kerry, *Every Day*, 294.

903   being denied communion: Victoria Reggie Kennedy in EMK int., Aug. 15, 2006, Miller Center, UVA.

903   "I think we've lost it": Kerry, *Every Day*, 326.

903   "There are so many things": EMK, *True Compass* (New York: Twelve, 2009), 498–99.

TWENTY-TWO: "THE MORAL CHALLENGE OF DOING THE RIGHT THING"

904   "I was furious about": John Kerry, *Every Day Is Extra* (New York: Simon & Schuster, 2018), 326.

904   essentially divided equally: Stanley Greenberg, *The Two Americas: Our Current Political Deadlock and How to Break It* (New York: St. Martin's Griffin, 2005), 21.

904   If it's about national: Robert Draper, *Dead Certain: The Presidency of George W. Bush* (New York: Free Press, 2007), 297.

905   traditional moral values: "Stunned Democrats Look to the Internal Debate Ahead," *NYT*, Nov. 4, 2004.

905   "very thoughtful conversation": Jim Wallis, "Honoring the Greatest Commitment of Sen. EMK," *Huffington Post*, Aug. 26, 2009; EMK int., June 3, 2005, Miller Center, UVA.

906   "He pushed back": "Topic A," *WP*, Aug. 27, 2009.

906   visited with wounded soldiers: "Senator Kennedy Visits Wounded Soldiers," *BG*, Dec. 24, 2004.

906   "privatizing social security": Draper, *Dead Certain*, 293–94.

906   "I've got political capital": Ibid., 294.

906   "nothing but a shameful": "Bush Stumps to Cap Malpractice Awards," *BG*, Jan. 6, 2005.

906   wielded an ax: "Bush Spending Plan Hits Social Programs," *BG*, Feb. 8, 2005.

907   "faith guides and sustains me": Wallis, "Honoring."

907   National Press Club address: "Kennedy Exhorts Democrats on Social Programs," *WP*, Jan. 13, 2005.

907   "No doubt, we must": EMK int., June 3, 2005; "Kennedy Vows to Fight on Values," *BG*, Jan. 13, 2005.

907   "equal opportunity": Eileen McNamara, "Liberal Lion Needs a Tiger," *BG*, Jan. 16, 2005.

908   troops should stay in Iraq: "Public Attitudes Toward the War in Iraq: 2003–2008," Pew Research Center, Mar. 18, 2008, https://www.pewresearch.org/2008/03/19/public-attitudes-toward-the-war-in-iraq-20032008/.

908   dramatic step of discussing: Michael Myers int., Aug. 28, 2006, Miller Center, UVA.

908   "We need a political military": "Kennedy Calls on US to Begin Troop Pullout," *BG*, Jan. 28, 2005; Sharon Waxman int., Dec. 19, 2008, Miller Center, UVA.

908   "Why can't we expect": "Kennedy Sticks to War Criticism," *BG*, Feb. 7, 2005.

908   "The Senate went crazy": Waxman int., Dec. 19, 2008.

909 "What do you mean": Ibid.

909 "power point essentially": Ibid.

909 felt the Bush administration: Sharon Waxman int., May 11, 2009, Miller Center, UVA.

909 that of congressional Democrats: "Democrats Split over Position on Iraq War," WP, Aug. 22, 2005, https://news.gallup.com/poll/116500/presidential-approval-ratings-george-bush.aspx.

910 "his Social Security initiative": Draper, Dead Certain, 300–3.

911 "Neanderthals": "Senate Filibuster Ends with Talk of Next Stage in Fight," WP, Nov. 15, 2003.

911 Pickering finally decided: Melody Barnes int., Aug. 16, 2006, Miller Center, UVA.

911 "Nominations do not get": "For Rights, a Wrong Choice," WP, Apr. 2, 2004.

912 "It isn't the career jurists": EMK int., Aug. 8, 2007, Miller Center, UVA.

912 "The idea that we want": EMK int., Feb. 12, 2007, Miller Center, UVA.

912 "undermined the work": Ibid.

912 "fragile": "Many Republicans Are Already Eager to Challenge Agreement on Filibusters," NYT, May 25, 2005.

913 "distraction": Ibid.

913 "big blowup": John Danforth int., Oct. 25, 2005, Miller Center, UVA.

913 biographer Robert Caro: Rick Klein, "Kennedy Opposition Carries Risks for Supreme Court Fight," BG, July 17, 2005.

914 "The American people deserve": Ibid.

914 not one of them: "Ted Kennedy Eyes the Court," Progressive, Sept. 2005.

914 "real and serious reasons": Confirmation Hearing on the Nomination of John G. Roberts Jr. to be Chief Justice of the Supreme Court, 109th Cong., Senate, 1st sess., Sept. 12–15, 2005, 167, 933.

914 "narrow and cramped": Ibid., 170.

914 "architect": EMK int., Aug. 7, 2007, Miller Center, UVA.

915 never felt that way: "Roberts Reacts Cautiously as Senators Press Him on Abortion," NYT, Sept. 13, 2005.

915 "exorcising the ghost": Peter Baker, Days of Fire: Bush and Cheney in the White House (New York: Doubleday, 2013), 401.

915 "Well, I am just getting": Ibid.

915 withdraw her nomination: Ibid., 417–24.

915 "hard look": Barnes int.

916 "deep disagreement": EMK, "Alito's Credibility Problem," WP, Jan. 7, 2006; EMK int., Feb. 12, 2007.

916 "all-powerful presidency": "Kennedy Makes a Weapon of McCain's Torture Law," WP, Jan. 11, 2006.

916 Reid was opposed: Ralph Neas int. by author.

916 "I had difficulty": EMK int., Aug. 7, 2007.

917 "people who have been": Ibid.

918 "our mission and our goal": Baker, Days of Fire, 394.

918 "Doing something good": Ibid., 395.

919 "perhaps the single": Otis Graham, "Tracing Liberal Woes to '65 Immigration Act," CSM, Dec. 28, 1995.

919 "noble" and "revolutionary": Theodore White, America in Search of Itself: The Making of the President, 1956–1980 (New York: Harper & Row, 1982), 363.

919 divided refugees from immigrants: EMK int., Oct. 8, 2007, Miller Center, UVA.

920 "Many businesses found": Carey Parker int., Dec. 1, 2008, Miller Center, UVA.

920 Irish immigration bill: Adam Clymer, Edward M. Kennedy: A Biography (New York: Harper Perennial, 2000), 442–43.

920 "without departing": Ibid., 479.

920 "very good bill": EMK int., Oct. 8, 2007, Miller Center, UVA.

921 "We're here for you": Alan Simpson int., May 10, 2006, Miller Center, UVA.

921 not a winning issue: Esther Olavarria int., Aug. 28, 2006, Miller Center, UVA.

921 desisted rather than pursue: Frank Sharry int. by author.

922 "We must make our": "Bush on Immigration," NYT, Jan. 8, 2004.

922 "As governor and as": George W. Bush, Decision Points (New York: Crown, 2010), 301.

922 Safe, Orderly, and Legal: S.2381, May 4, 2004, https://www.congress.gov/108/bills/s2381/BILLS-108s2381is.pdf; "Democrats Urge Immigration Changes," BG, May 2, 2004.

923 "We wanted to counterbalance": Sharry int.

923 **shared a deep commitment:** John McCain int., Oct. 16, 2009, Miller Center, UVA.

923 **relationship strengthened:** John McCain and Mark Salter, *The Restless Wave* (New York: Simon & Schuster, 2018), 199–200.

923 **"cynical":** Ibid., 203–4.

923 **"match made in Heaven":** Sharry int.

923 **"very strong nucleus":** McCain int.

924 **"One of the greatest":** Bush, *Decision Points*, 300.

924 **"McCain didn't sweat":** "GOP Senators' Proposal Would Force Out Illegal Immigrants," *BG*, July 20, 2005.

925 **"Report to deport":** Sharry int.

925 **"toughest border security":** Ibid.

925 **hadn't compromised enough:** Ibid.

925 **clutter of bills:** EMK int., Oct. 8, 2007.

926 **"at least a pathway":** "Lawmakers at Odds on Immigration," *BG*, Mar. 21, 2006; "Showdown on Immigration," *BG*, Mar. 27, 2006.

926 **Tens of thousands of others gathered:** "Los Angeles Sees Record Day of Pro-Immigration Rallies," *BG*, Mar. 26, 2006; Rick Klein, "Panel Acts to Extend Immigrant Rights," *BG*, Mar. 28, 2006.

926 **"nation-shaking event":** Klein, "Panel Acts to Extend."

926 **"day and night":** Sharry int.

927 **"welcoming the stranger":** "A GOP Faceoff Over Illegal Immigration," *Christian Science Monitor* Mar. 29, 2006.

927 **"She had 500,000 good":** Sharry int.

927 **applause and cheers:** Ibid.

927 **"So much for your":** Ibid.

927 **"Ted Kennedy hasn't won":** Massimo Calabresi, "The Playmaker: How Kennedy Got His Way," *Time*, Apr. 2, 2006.

928 **"We want to try":** Ibid.

928 **struck a compromise:** "Senate Pact Offers Permits to Most Illegal Immigrants," *WP*, Apr. 7, 2006.

929 **wresting a concession:** David Brooks, "Scuttling Toward Sanity," *NYT*, Apr. 6, 2006.

929 **"hard rocks and inhospitable":** Harry Reid with Mark Warren, *The Good Fight: Hard Lessons from Searchlight to Washington* (New York: G. P. Putnam, 2008), 23–56.

929 **also suspicions:** Carl Hulse, "Kennedy Tactics on Immigration Vex Democrats," *NYT*, Apr. 12, 2006.

929 **amendments that Reid:** "Senate GOP Poised to Offer Compromise on Immigration," *BG*, Apr. 6, 2006.

930 **"This is a bullshit amendment":** EMK int., Oct. 8, 2007.

930 **"foul odor that's coming":** Brooks, "Scuttling."

931 **"Politics got in front":** "Immigration Deal Fails in Senate," *WP*, Apr. 8, 2006; "Deal on Immigration Bill Collapses," *BG*, Apr. 8, 2006.

931 **"We're starting to feel":** James Sasser int., May 25, 2006, Miller Center, UVA.

931 **"if there's a sense":** Myers int.

931 **"Just about everyone":** Hulse, "Kennedy Tactics."

932 **"This debate goes":** "Immigrants' Voice: We're in a Fight," *BG*, Apr. 11, 2006.

932 **"There is too much velocity":** Hulse, "Kennedy Tactics."

932 **Bush glanced over:** EMK int., Mar. 20, 2006, Miller Center, UVA.

932 **"The president":** "Bush Blames Democrat for Immigration Impasse," *NYT*, Apr. 13, 2006.

932 **"top priority":** "Senators to Reignite the Debate on Immigration," *NYT*, Apr. 24, 2006; "Bush Begins Push for Immigration Deal with Congress," *WP*, Apr. 25, 2006.

933 **"We cannot build":** "Bush Calls for Compromise on Immigration," *NYT*, May 16, 2006.

933 **"I have been working":** Ralph Blumenthal and Monica Davey, "President's Middle Path Disappoints Both Sides," *NYT*, May 16, 2006.

934 **opposed the latter:** "Senate Backs Fence, Guest-Worker Curbs," *WP*, May 18, 2006.

934 **"You don't know how":** Sharry int.

934 **"out of control":** Ibid.

935 **eight-thirty every morning:** *Congressional Record*, Senate, 109th Cong., 2nd sess., May 25, 2006, S5183.

935 **"Very spirited discussions":** McCain int.

935 **"Why don't you pitch in":** McCain and Salter, *Restless Wave*, 223.

936 **all those old trepidations:** Sharry int.

936 **"absolutely punitive, mean-spirited,":** EMK int., Oct. 8, 2007.

936 **"yeoman's work to sort":** *Congressional Record*, Senate, 109th Cong., 2nd sess., May 25, 2006, S5181.

936 **"matter of life and death":** Ibid., S5183.

936 **"I can't wait until":** *The Senators' Bargain*, dir. Shari Robertson and Michael Camerini, HBO Films, aired Mar. 24, 2010.

937 **"pulled down":** "Senate Bill on Immigration to Set up Clash," *NYT*, May 25, 2006.

937 **"this is the way":** *Congressional Record*, Senate, 109th Cong., 2nd sess., May 25, 2006, S1582.

937 **"dark clouds forming":** John M. Broder, "Immigration, from a Simmer to a Scream," *NYT*, May 21, 2006.

937 **send bricks to their congressmen:** "A Build-a-Protest Approach to Immigration," *NYT*, May 31, 2006.

937 **roused the immigration activists:** Broder, "Immigration, Simmer to Scream."

938 **"Suicide for some":** "Bush Turns to House in Immigration Debate," *NYT*, June 7, 2006; "Bush's Immigration Plan Stalled as House G.O.P. Grew More Anxious," *NYT*, June 25, 2006.

938 **"worst period":** Bush, *Decision Points*, 367.

939 **declined to 31 percent:** "Presidential Approval Ratings—George W. Bush," Gallup, n.d., https://news.gallup.com/poll/116500/presidential-approval-ratings-george-bush.aspx.

939 **"We had people who":** Baker, *Days of Fire*, 474.

939 **stood the president up :** Jean Edward Smith, *Bush* (New York: Simon & Schuster, 2016), 521.

939 **House majority in jeopardy:** Baker, *Days of Fire*, 498.

939 **"Remember the revenge":** Andrew Kohut, "The Real Message of the Midterms," *NYT*, Nov. 13, 2006.

940 **"Ruling parties":** Matt Bai, "The Last 20th Century Election," *NYT Magazine*, Nov. 19, 2006.

940 **raised millions of dollars:** Frank Phillips, "Kennedy Seeking Clear Run in '06," *BG*, Feb. 20, 2005.

940 **"That makes a big":** EMK int., June 3, 2005.

940 **"Their presence helped":** EMK int., Dec. 1, 2006, Miller Center, UVA.

940 **"Finding someone to run":** Phillips, "Kennedy Seeking Clear Run"; "No More Mr. Nice Guy," *BG*, June 28, 2005.

940 **Chase stressed enforcement:** "Kennedy-Chase Mini-Debate," *BG*, Oct. 11, 2006.

940 **"I'm to stay until":** "Kennedy and Pups Vote," *BG*, Nov. 7, 2006.

941 **returning to his office:** Robert Fitzgerald, Sr., int., June 18, 2009, Miller Center, UVA.

941 **"acted as though":** Susan Milligan, "Gleeful Democrats Celebrate Perks," *BG*, Jan. 5, 2007.

941 **"most ambivalent press":** EMK int., Nov. 29, 2006, Miller Center, UVA.

941 **hundred-hour legislative offensive:** "After 42 Hours (or So) House Democrats Complete 100-Hour Push," *NYT*, Jan. 19, 2007.

941 **"trying to get the minimum":** EMK int., Nov. 29, 2006; "Universal Health Coverage Attracts New Support," *WP*, Jan. 22, 2007; "Gay Rights Proposals Gain in Congress," *BG*, Apr. 25, 2007.

942 **"This is the day":** "House By a Wide Margin Backs Minimum Wage Rise," *NYT*, Jan. 11, 2007.

942 **"Why can't we do just":** "Minimum Wage Hike Hits Snag," *BG*, Jan. 25, 2007.

943 **"What is it that":** "GOP Senator Rebuffs Kennedy," *BG*, Jan. 30. 2007.

943 **grudging approval:** "Familiar Problem Stalls Minimum Wage Bill," *NYT*, Feb. 17, 2007.

943 **"bruising debate":** "Minimum Wage Hike OK'd in Senate," *BG*, Feb. 2, 2007.

943 **"fortunately":** "Bush Budget Puts Pinch on Domestic Spending," *BG*, Feb. 6, 2007.

943 **"Rome wasn't built":** EMK, "What a Difference an Election Makes," *WP*, Mar. 11, 2007.

944 **"The dynamics are right":** "Bush Seeks Unity on Immigration," *BG*, Nov. 27, 2006.

944 **three Congresses:** Peter Canellos, *Last Lion: The Fall and Rise of Ted Kennedy* (New York: Simon & Schuster, 2009), 379.

944 **"moral issue":** *Senators' Bargain*.

944 **finished drafting a bill:** "Kennedy, McCain Try Again on Immigration," *BG*, Feb. 28, 2007.

944 **"comprehensive":** "Bush's Last Chance on Immigration," *Time*, Mar. 2, 2007.

945 **"Can't you do something?":** EMK int., Oct. 8, 2007.

945 **objected to a provision:** "Kennedy McCain Partnership Falters," *BG*, Mar. 22, 2007.

945 **convened a group of senators:** Canellos, *Last Lion*, 377; Milligan, "Gleeful Democrats Celebrate Perks."

945 **"You could just see how":** "Closing the Door on Russell 317," *Politico*, Oct. 23, 2009.

946   "upholding Republican positions": EMK int., Oct. 8, 2007; Susan Milligan, "Adversaries Praise a Relentless Kennedy," *BG*, May 18, 2007.

946   stayed out of the deliberations: "Bush Pushes to End Immigration Logjam," *BG*, Apr. 10, 2007.

946   "The president has got": "Reid Forces New Senate Debate on Immigration," *WP*, May 10, 2007.

947   "There were times he blew": Milligan, "Adversaries Praise."

947   "We'll take care of you": Ibid.

947   Even labor was divided: Olavarria int.

948   "last best chance": *Senators' Bargain.*

948   "Every one of them": EMK int., Oct. 8, 2007; Milligan, "Adversaries Praise."

949   "When I told them": Milligan, "Adversaries Praise."

950   "This is not the": "Immigration Reform Overhaul Is Closer to Senate Floor," *WP*, May 17, 2007; "Senators Reach Deal on Immigration," *USA Today*, May 18, 2007; "Deal on Immigration Reached," *WP*, May 18, 2007.

950   "Here's a note for you": EMK int., Oct. 8, 2007.

950   detect threats to the bill: "Senators to Debate Immigration Bill," *BG*, May 22, 2007.

950   imprimatur might have made: EMK int., Oct. 8, 2007.

951   nudging the bill: "Ted Kennedy Gets a Little Republican Respect," *WP*, May 30, 2007.

951   "before Rush Limbaugh": "Immigrant Bill Dies in Senate," *NYT*, June 29, 2007.

951   "I know that we've got": "Backers of Immigration Bill More Optimistic," *WP*, June 4, 2007.

952   "filled the tree": EMK int., Oct. 8, 2007.

952   "atmosphere had been": Carl Hulse, "Kennedy Plea Was Last Gasp for Immigration Bill," *NYT*, June 9, 2007.

952   "When they do that": EMK int., Oct. 8, 2007.

952   "I've been trying to kill": "Immigration Overhaul Bill Stalls in Senate," *WP*, June 8, 2007.

952–53   "Hope is a powerful thing": Ibid.

953   if he let them: Hulse, "Kennedy Tactics."

953   debate would be too protracted: EMK int., Oct. 8, 2007.

953   "This place is a very": *Senators' Bargain.*

953   "The headlines are going": "Bush, Senators to Meet on Immigration," *WP*, June 12, 2007.

953   whittle the number: Ibid.; "Bush Tries to Save Immigration Bill," *Time*, June 11, 2007.

953   "inundated": "Broad Effort to Resurrect Immigration Bill," *NYT*, June 16, 2007.

954   "made it harder on the left": Sharry int.

954   "nodding and nodding": EMK int., Oct. 8, 2007.

954   "right at the border": Ibid.

954   "I want you to know": Ibid.

955   "Unless you move toward": EMK, int., Oct. 8, 2007.

955   "perhaps the most important": Sharry int.

955   "It was in this Chamber": *Congressional Record*, 110th Cong., Senate, 1st sess., June 28, 2007, S8642, S8947.

956   "Intense": "Immigration Bill Dies in Senate," *WP*, June 29, 2007.

956   "The bill now dies": Ibid.

956   "Thank you, my friend": "Determined Foes, Heavy Pressure Decisive," *BG*, June 29, 2007.

956   "There were lots of tears": Cecilia Muñoz, in "Remembering Ted Kennedy," *National Journal*, Sept. 5, 2009.

TWENTY-THREE: HOPE

957   "Congress must no longer": "Democrats Step Up Battle Over Troops," *BG*, Jan. 10, 2007.

958   "This was all done quietly": Sharon Waxman int., May 11, 2009, Miller Center, UVA; "US Pressed to Admit More Iraqi Refugees," *BG*, Jan. 17, 2007.

958   "When is enough enough": "Iraq Funds Approved in Senate Budget Bill," *WP*, Dec. 19, 2007.

958   as high as 40 percent: "Presidential Approval Ratings —George W. Bush," Gallup, n.d., https://news.gallup.com/poll/116500/presidential-approval-ratings-george-bush.aspx.

958   set of protocols: "US Adopts Rules for Softening Treatment of Some Illegals," *BG*, Nov. 25, 2007.

958   "If you were to give": Carey Parker int., Dec. 1, 2008, Miller Center, UVA; EMK, "How to Fix 'No Child,'" *WP*, Jan. 7, 2008.

959   "With each coming day": "Veto Fight Looms on Healthcare," *BG*, Sept. 28, 2007.

959 "This is all a matter of priorities": "Democrats Build Plan to Override Heath Bill Veto," *NYT*, Sept. 29, 2007.

959 "George Bush just vetoed Abby": "Democrats See Wedge Issue in Health Bill," *NYT*, Oct. 8, 2007.

960 "indefinitely": "Kennedy Wants Signs of Kerry's Plans for '08," *BG*, Dec. 12, 2006.

960 "I'm really trying to absorb": "Kennedy Smooths Senate Path for Clinton," *BG*, Feb. 22, 2001.

961 "That's not going to happen": EMK int., Mar. 28, 2008, Miller Center, UVA.

961 "The thing is": Barack Obama, "Remarks Celebrating Edward M. Kennedy Institute," Oct. 14, 2009, Daily Compilation of Presidential Documents.

961 "lot of personal relationship": John McCain int., Oct. 16, 2009, Miller Center, UVA.

961 "with the shades drawn": Glen Johnson, "Chance of Obama Visit Highlights Bond with Kennedy," AP, Aug. 21, 2009.

961 "The brass ring doesn't": Victoria Reggie Kennedy int., Apr. 8, 2010, Miller Center, UVA.

962 "Go for it": "Kennedy Poised to Endorse Obama," *BG*, Jan. 28, 2008.

962 "The power to inspire is rare": Barack Obama, *A Promised Land* (New York: Crown, 2021), 69.

963 talking up Obama: Karen Tumulty, "Why the Kennedys Went for Obama," *Time*, Jan. 28, 2008.

963 "We've got to call up Ted": Peter Canellos, *Last Lion: The Fall and Rise of Ted Kennedy* (New York: Simon & Schuster, 2009), 381.

963 miffed over Obama's behavior: Evan Thomas, "How He Did It," *Newsweek*, Nov. 17, 2008.

963 "Dr. King's dream began": Paul Kane and Mary Ann Akers, "Kennedy Endorsement of Obama Had Family Roots," *WP*, Jan. 31, 2008.

963 "I was waiting to see": EMK, *True Compass* (New York: Twelve, 2009), 502–3.

964 "monitor and generally": Tom Daschle int., Apr. 29, 2009, Miller Center, UVA.

964 "I'm looking for someone": Michael Myers quoted in "Obama's Deal," *Frontline*, PBS, Dec. 15, 2009.

964 "I'm thinking of doing": Gregory Craig int., July 13, 2010, Miller Center, UVA.

965 "difficult": Thomas, "How He Did It."

965 "Caroline": Ibid.

965 "Listen, pal": EMK, *True Compass*, 502–3; Karen Tumulty, "How the Kennedy Nod Helps Obama," *Time*, Jan. 28, 2008.

965 "We need a change": "A President Like My Father," *NYT*, Jan. 27, 2008.

965 "Oh, my God. We're done": Thomas, "How He Did It."

966 "You know, Barack": Laurence Tribe int., Apr. 27, 2009. Miller Center, UVA.

966 got Patrick to reconsider: Craig int.

966–67 "connect with people from": "Ted Kennedy Endorses Barack Obama," Jan. 28, 2008, https://www.youtube.com/watch?v=oEawu8pQxRI; "Ted Kennedy Endorses Obama," *LAT*, Jan. 29, 2008; "Kennedy Backs Obama with 'Old Politics' Attack," *NYT*, Jan. 29, 2008.

967 "educated, upper income": George Packer, "The Fall of Conservatism," *New Yorker*, May 26, 2008.

967 "has had the Starbucks": Dan Payne quoted in "Obama-Kennedy Alliance Sets Focus," *BG*, Jan. 29, 2008.

968 "Nobody's better than him": Tumulty, "Why Kennedys Went for Obama."

968 "in the stories I heard": "Teddy Ready for Prez Obama," *NYP*, Jan. 29, 2008.

968 "It was a moment packed": *CBS Evening News*, Jan. 28, 2008.

968 "Kennedy name still has": *NBC Nightly News*, Jan. 28, 2008.

968 "audacity of hope had": *Nightline*, ABC, Jan. 28, 2008.

968 "added poetry to": Obama, *Promised Land*, 129.

968 "served that institution": David Brooks, "The Kennedy Mystique," *NYT*, Jan. 29, 2008.

969 "hot, hot, hot on the trail": Mark Leibovich, "Kennedy Revels in Limelight as He Campaigns for Obama," *NYT*, Feb. 2, 2008; Susan Milligan, "Kennedy Stumps for Obama," *BG*, Feb. 2, 2008; Adam Cohen, "Ted Kennedy's Pitch for Obama: '60s Nostalgia," *NYT*, Feb. 2, 2008; EMK, *True Compass*, 504.

970 "Because the Clintons": John McCain and Mark Salter, *The Restless Wave* (New York: Simon & Schuster, 2018), 229.

970 "Maybe, Hillary, I should": "Kennedy Helps Clinton and Obama Break Ice," *WP*, Feb. 7, 2008; EMK, *True Compass*, 503.

971 "lying through my teeth": Victoria Reggie Kennedy int.

971 "very high-grade blockage": "Kennedy Surgery Routine, Successful," *BG*, Oct. 13, 2007.

971 choked up with emotion: Jonathan Alter, "How We Really Help Ted," *Newsweek*, June 2, 2008.

972 **"I would think that's bad"**: EMK, *True Compass*, 3–4; Canellos, *Last Lion*, 2–3; "More Hospital Tests for Kennedy," *NYT*, May 20, 2008.

972 **"sounded like the Ted"**: "Kennedy Upbeat Day After Seizure," *BG*, May 19, 2008; "More Hospital Tests for Kennedy"; *Andrea Mitchell*, MSNBC, May 20, 2008.

973 **"small earthquake"**: "In the Senate, Ted Kennedy Still Rules," *Time*, May 17, 2008.

973 **"I said a lot of people"**: "More Hospital Tests for Kennedy."

973 **"preliminary results"**: "Ted Kennedy Released from Hospital Awaits Further Tests," *Huffington Post*, May 20, 2008.

973 **"one of the worst kinds"**: *NBC Nightly News*, May 20, 2008.

973 **"very pessimistic prognosis"**: Vicki Kennedy, on *Oprah Winfrey Show*, Nov. 25, 2009.

973 **"last several days"**: "A Curveball," *BG*, May 21, 2008.

974 **"plotting his course"**: "Kennedy Has Malignant Tumor," *BG*, May 21, 2008.

974 **"It's nothing compared"**: "A Strategist Aids Kennedy Once More," *BG*, June 2, 2008.

974 **"having a very difficult"**: "Kennedy, His Children and Cancer," *BG*, May 25, 2008.

974 **put his affairs in order**: Vicki Kennedy, on *Oprah Winfrey Show*, Nov. 25, 2009.

974 **there was stunned silence**: MSNBC, May 5, 2008.

974 **"Ted Kennedy spent"**: "Senator Kennedy Has Malignant Brain Tumor," *NYT*, May 21, 2008.

974 **"My dear friend, I love you"**: "Kennedy Diagnosed with Malignant Brain Tumor," *PBS NewsHour*, May 20, 2008, https://www.pbs.org/newshour/politics/politics-jan-june08-kennedy_05-20; "Kennedy Has Malignant Brain Tumor," *Politico*, May 20, 2008.

975 **"He's not just the patriarch"**: "Despite Absence, His Efforts Bear Fruit," *BG*, May 22, 2008.

975 **"why the mere thought"**: Carl Hulse, "Kennedy: A Little Like Everyone, A Lot Like No One," *NYT*, May 22, 2008.

975 **"who just wanted to talk"**: Bob Herbert, "Tears for Teddy," *NYT*, May 24, 2008.

975 **"made a lot of Americans think"**: *NBC Nightly News*, May 20, 2008.

975 **overwhelming Ted's office phones**: "Kennedy Returns to Cape Cod," *WP*, May 22, 2008.

975–76 **"Senator Kennedy's toughest fight"**: Herbert, "Tears for Teddy."

976 **"Get Well" banner**: "Kennedy Returns to Cape Cod," *WP*, May 22, 2008.

976 **"Remarkably quickly"**: "Kennedy Released from Hospital, Heads to Cape," AP, May 21, 2008.

976 **"shuffling"**: "Showing Resolve to Fight, a Family Takes to the Sea," *BG*, May 22, 2008; "Senator Kennedy Interview Following Surgery," video, May 22, 2008, www.youtube.com/watch?v=MxPCH21vLjA.

976 **"*affirmation* of life"**: EMK, *True Compass*, 6.

976 **"Considering what he's done"**: "Obama to Fill in for Kennedy at Ceremony," *NYT*, May 23, 2008.

977 **"I have a feeling that Ted"**: "Obama Urges Wesleyan Grads to Enter Public Service," *WP*, May 25, 2008.

977 **"it couldn't be a more"**: "Kennedy Opts to Sit Out Annual Figawi Race," *BG*, May 25, 2008; "Kennedy Sailing Mya in Figawi Today," *Cape Cod Today*, May 26, 2008; "Sen. Kennedy Competes in Annual Figawi Sailboat Race," *Boston Herald*, May 26, 2008; "Kennedy Competes in Figawi Race," *BG*, May 26, 2008.

977 **"We were taught never"**: EMK, *True Compass*, 6.

977 **"Live each day"**: Vicki Kennedy, on *Oprah Winfrey Show*, Nov. 25, 2009.

978 **"Life is a bowl"**: "Remembering Ted Kennedy," *National Journal*, Sept. 5, 2009.

978 **stay at Hyannis with Vicki**: EMK int., Apr. 12, 1996, EMK Interviews 1997–99 Folder, Box 5, Series 2, Clymer Papers, JFK Lib.

978 **"dozens of discussions"**: Matt Viser, "A Strategist Aids Kennedy Once More," *BG*, June 2, 2008.

979 **crowd stood and applauded**: Lawrence Altman, "The Story Behind Kennedy's Surgery," *NYT*, July 29, 2008.

979 **called Barbara Mikulski**: Mark Leibovich, "After Diagnosis, Determined to Make a Good Ending," *NYT*, Aug. 26, 2009.

979 **"good sign"**: "Kennedy's Surgery for Tumor Called Success," *NYT*, June 3, 2008.

979 **"Better than anyone expected"**: "Kennedy Leaves Hospital, Goes Sailing," AP, June 9, 2008.

979 **"they don't get up"**: Caroline Raclin int., Nov. 11, 2009, Miller Center, UVA.

980 **up and walking the hospital**: "Kennedy Is Recuperating," *NYT*, June 4, 2008.

980 **"That is what he is talking"**: "Kennedy Released from N.C. Hospital."

980 **"we just didn't know what"**: Barbara Souliotis int., Nov. 9, 2009, Miller Center, UVA.

980 **"pleased with his progress"**: "Kennedy Released from N.C. Hospital."

980 **"moments of quiet"**: "Sen. Kennedy Preparing to 'Do Battle,' Son Says," AP, June 15, 2008.

980 **sail virtually every day:** EMK, *True Compass*, 9.

980 **congregated at the compound:** Ibid.

980 **"She basically put my uncle":** Sara Rimer, "Kennedy's Closest Confidante," *NYT*, Aug. 28, 2008.

981 **drafting a national service act:** "Ailing Kennedy Aims to Return to Senate in January," AP, Sept. 7, 2008.

981 **Kennedys loaned the family:** Daschle int.

981 **Ted and Vicki phoned him:** Albert Hunt, "Ted Kennedy Forged Legacy with Joyful Magic," *Bloomberg*, Aug. 27, 2009.

981 **"The news is really all":** Matt Viser, "Kennedy's Wife Says Senator Is Doing Well," *BG*, July 8, 2008.

981 **"betting on the lion":** "Kennedy's Wife Says Treatment Going Well," AP, July 7, 2008.

981 **"It was like [he] was":** Canellos, *Last Lion*, 393.

982 **couldn't afford to practice:** "Doctors Press Senate to Undo Medicare Cuts," *NYT*, July 7, 2008.

982 **"I'll be there":** Mark Leibovich, "After Diagnosis, Determined to Make a Good Ending," *NYT*, Aug. 26, 2009.

982 **"I may be the only patient":** EMK, *True Compass*, 9.

983 **"spectators rained down":** Susan Milligan, "Stunning Return and a Vital Vote," *BG*, July 10, 2008; David Herszenhorn, "Kennedy Returns to Senate," *NYT*, July 9, 2008; "With Nudge by Kennedy, Medicare Bill Passes," *WP*, July 10, 2008; Patrick Kennedy and Stephen Fried, *A Common Struggle: A Personal Journey Through the Past and Future of Mental Illness and Addiction* (New York: Blue Rider Press, 2015), 287; Altman, "Kennedy's Surgery."

983 **"stayed at the forefront":** "A Kennedy Surprise?" *Politico*, Aug. 24, 2009.

984 **"He's truly humbled":** Leibovich, "After Diagnosis."

985 **"He knew it all along":** Susan Milligan, "Kidney Stones Nearly Derailed Speech," *BG*, Aug. 27, 2008.

985 **"pay tribute to two men":** Adam Nagourney, "Democrats Meet and Kennedy Adds an Opening Spark," *NYT*, Aug. 26, 2008.

985 **"My fellow Democrats":** EMK, Democratic National Convention Tribute and Speech, 2008, https://www.youtube.com/watch?v=f4fh8oZkVNk.

986 **"Triumphant":** Nagourney, "Democrats Meet."

986 **father stopped to wave:** Kennedy and Fried, *Common Struggle*, 288–89.

986 **Aguila Azteca:** "Kennedy's Harvard Honor is Latest Among Accolades," *BG*, Nov. 30, 2008.

987 **"one of the true friends":** Glen Johnson, "Kennedy Talks Politics After Getting Award," AP, Sept. 23, 2008.

987 **"giant camera":** Curran Raclin int., Nov. 10, 2009, Miller Center, UVA.

987 **Serve America Act:** Johnson, "Kennedy Talks Politics After Getting Award."

987 **"He's getting people":** Melody Miller int., Oct. 7, 2008, Miller Center, UVA.

987 **"regrouping now because":** Nancy Soderberg int., Oct. 9, 2008, Miller Center, UVA.

988 **"I know you're hearing":** Thomas Rollins int., May 14, 2009, Miller Center, UVA; Rollins to Kennedy, n.d., shared with author; Kennedy to Rollins, Sept. 9, 2008, shared with author.

988 **"forcefully":** Johnson, "Kennedy Talks Politics."

988 **"mild seizure":** "Kennedy Treated for Mild Seizure," *WP*, Sept. 27, 2008; "Mild Seizure Sends Kennedy to Hospital," *Boston Herald*, Sept. 26, 2008.

989 **"Together, the global pool":** George W. Bush, *Decision Points* (New York: Crown, 2010), 439–49.

989 **"Wall Street got drunk":** Ibid., 448.

990 **"The political atmosphere":** "Republican Election Losses Stir Fall Fears," *NYT*, May 15, 2008.

990 **"It's not about the war":** Matt Taibbi, "Full Metal McCain," *Rolling Stone*, June 26, 2008.

990 **crushed by Democrats:** Benjamin Wallace-Wells, "A Case of the Blues," *NYT Magazine*, Mar. 30, 2008.

990 **"embrace of a radical":** "GOP Struggles to Reinvent Itself Without Losing Itself," *LAT*, May 18, 2008.

991 **"John McCain, raised in":** Howard Wolfson, "The End of Nixonland," *New Republic*, Oct. 18, 2008.

991 **"By the end of the campaign":** George Packer, "The New Liberalism," *New Yorker*, Nov. 17, 2008.

992 **"inflection point":** John Harwood, "Is the Era of Dominance Over for Conservatives?" *NYT*, Oct. 6, 2008; Nicholas Kristof, "The Obama Dividend," *NYT*, Nov. 6, 2008; Joe Klein, "Obama's Victory Ushers in New America," *Time*, Nov. 5, 2008.

992 **"least conservative":** George Packer, "The Fall of Conservatism," *New Yorker*, May 26, 2008.

992 **"increasingly as an aging":** Stanley Greenberg, "The Emerging Center-Left Majority," *American Prospect,* Nov. 13, 2008.

993 **"Republican strength":** Ronald Brownstein, "For GOP, a Southern Exposure," *National Journal,* May 22, 2009.

993 **"Republican coalition of the 1980s":** Michael Gerson, "How My Party Lost Its Way," *Newsweek,* Jan. 28, 2008.

993 **"With the heavy lifting":** Tom Davis, "The Way Back," *Ripon Forum,* Jan. 15, 2009.

993 **"What had been contained":** Thomas Frank, "Conservatism Isn't Finished," *Wall Street Journal,* Nov. 5, 2008.

993 **"lower taxes, stronger defense":** Evan Thomas, "In the Shadow of Bush," *Newsweek,* Jan. 28, 2008.

993 **"final grade":** Ron Brownstein, "Bush's Final Failing Grade," *National Journal,* Nov. 7, 2008.

994 **"distance between those two":** Peter Beinart, "The New Liberal Order," *Time,* Nov. 13, 2008.

994 **"You're really talking":** "New Beginning for a Party in Power," *BG,* Nov. 5, 2008.

994 **"momentous moment":** "President Obama," *WP,* Nov. 5, 2008.

994 **"new majority":** Greenberg, "Emerging Center-Left Majority."

994 **typically chose the Republicans:** Mark Penn, "Most Affluent Voters Key to Obama Sweep," *Politico,* Nov. 11, 2008.

995 **declined 15 percent:** John Judis, "America the Liberal," *New Republic,* Nov. 5, 2008; Ruy Teixeira, "New Progressive America," Center for American Progress, Mar. 9, 2009.

995 **"irrepressible moral conflict":** E. J. Dionne, Jr., "Yes, We Did," *New Republic,* Nov. 5, 2008.

995 **"new kind of politics":** "America Turns the Page," *BG,* Nov. 5, 2008.

995 **"His election in and of":** Laurence Tribe, "Morning-After Pride," *Forbes,* Nov. 5, 2008.

995 **"There was a rush of noise":** Nancy Gibbs, "How Obama Rewrote the Book," *Time,* Nov. 5, 2008.

995 **"never thought they would":** Anna Quindlen, "Living History," *Newsweek,* Nov. 17, 2008.

995 **"moment so powerful":** John Harris, "The Obama Revolution," *Politico,* Nov. 5, 2008.

995 **"Let cynics sleep":** Marc Ginsberg, "Return of the Jedi," *Huffington Post,* Nov. 5, 2008.

996 **"The torch is being passed":** Evan Thomas, "How He Did It," *Newsweek,* Nov. 17, 2008.

996 **"We lost our way":** EMK, *True Compass,* 501.

TWENTY-FOUR: RETURN TO THE SEA

997 **"beaming":** Susan Milligan, "Kennedy Returns to Senate," *BG,* Nov. 18, 2008.

997 **"I feel fine":** Ibid.; Dana Milbank, "First Rule for Freshmen," *WP,* Nov. 18, 2008.

998 **"He was thinking":** John Podesta int. by author.

998 **"shot heard round":** Steven Brill, *America's Bitter Pill: Money, Politics, Backroom Deals, and the Fight to Fix Our Broken Healthcare System* (New York: Random House, 2015), 34–35; "A Campaign Commercial in the Making," *BG,* Apr. 13, 2006.

999 **"He was like a professor":** Susan Milligan and Lisa Wangsness, "The Man at the Center," *BG,* May 10, 2009.

999 **"build a fair amount":** Lisa Wangsness, "Kennedy Leads Renewed Effort on Universal Health Care," *BG,* July 2, 2008.

999 **three working groups:** Kathy Kiely, "Kennedy Set for Major Health Care Push," *USA Today,* Nov. 21, 2008.

999 **issue of insurance coverage:** "Kennedy Creates Healthcare Working Groups," *BG,* Nov. 18, 2008.

999 **"empowering us to carry":** Ibid.

999 **iron out details:** Stuart Altman and David Schachtman, *Power, Politics and Universal Health Care: The Inside Story of a Century-Long Battle* (Amherst, N.Y.: Prometheus Books, 2011), 254–55.

1000 **"We're hopeful this will":** "Teddy: I'd Like to See Obama Sign Health Care Bill in First Year," *Talking Points Memo,* Nov. 17, 2008.

1000 **before Obama appointed her:** Milligan, "Kennedy Returns to Senate."

1000 **"He wanted to do something":** Elizabeth Fowler quoted in Brill, *America's Bitter Pill,* 44.

1000 **"In three decades as":** Barack Obama, *A Promised Land* (New York: Crown, 2021), 384.

1001 **prevented Clinton's plan:** Brill, *America's Bitter Pill,* 80.

1001 **"very complimentary":** "Democrats Focus on Healthcare Reform," *BG,* Nov. 13, 2008.

1001 **meeting and forging ahead:** Milligan and Wangsness, "Man at the Center."

1001 **"Very significant":** Kiely, "Kennedy Set."

1001 **"We're carrying it out":** "Kennedy Focuses from Home on Healthcare Overhaul," AP, Oct. 24, 2008.

1001 **"His presence is felt":** Milligan and Wangsness, "Man at the Center."

1002 **Baucus held negotiations:** Jonathan Cohn, "How They Did It," *New Republic*, June 10, 2010.

1002 **"North Star by which":** Patrick Kennedy and Stephen Fried, *A Common Struggle: A Personal Journey Through the Past and Future of Mental Illness and Addiction* (New York: Blue Rider Press, 2015), 3.

1002 **insisted on being admitted:** Ibid., 221.

1003 **"It looked to me like":** "Kennedy Enters Rehab," *BG*, May 6, 2006.

1003 **combination of a sleeping pill:** "Rep. Kennedy in 3 a.m. Crash Near Capitol," *BG*, May 5, 2006.

1003 **"overwhelming sense":** Kennedy and Fried, *Common Struggle*, 233.

1003 **"You did a good job":** Ibid.

1003 **"Sometimes I think":** Ibid., 240.

1004 **"I tearfully admitted":** Ibid., 265.

1004 **"He was not comfortable":** Patrick Kennedy int. by author.

1004 **intimate form of intimacy:** Kennedy and Fried, *Common Struggle*, 188–89.

1004 **"livid":** Ibid., 4; Mark Leibovich, "Ted Kennedy, Jr., Is (Finally) Ready for the Family Business," *NYT Magazine*, Mar. 13, 2013.

1004 **"so toothless":** Laurie Joan Aron, "Empty Gain for Mental Health," *NYT*, Dec. 14, 1997.

1005 **"Over a period":** Carey Parker int., Oct. 27, 2008, Miller Center, UVA.

1005 **slowly began to gain momentum:** "Bailout Provides More Mental Health Coverage," *NYT*, Oct. 5, 2008.

1005 **"the need to accept":** Carey Parker int., Dec. 1, 2008, Miller Center, UVA.

1005 **"The bill was written":** Patrick Kennedy int.

1006 **"You keep this up":** Ibid.

1006 **"He needs time alone":** Kennedy and Fried, *Common Struggle*, 291–92.

1006 **"there was concern":** Parker int., Oct. 27, 2008.

1007 **that sort of offer from:** Patrick Kennedy int.

1007 **Chris Dodd who came up:** Kennedy and Fried, *Common Struggle*, 291.

1007 **"You know, it's pretty tough":** Ibid., 295–97; Carey Parker int., Dec. 1, 2008.

1008 **"ultimate safety net":** Mike Barnicle, "Of Memory and the Sea," *Time*, Aug. 27, 2009.

1008 **Kennedy would join them:** James Carroll, "Ted Kennedy, The Champion," *BG*, Dec. 1, 2008.

1009 **"lifelong commitment to public":** "Kennedy's Honor Is Latest Among Accolades," *BG*, Nov. 30, 2008; Peter Schworm, "For Kennedy, a Rare Privilege," *BG*, Dec. 2, 2008.

1009 **contacts and connections:** "Ted Wants Caroline," *NYP*, Dec. 7, 2008.

1009 **special election two years hence:** "Kennedy Is Said to be Politicking for his Niece," *NYT*, Dec. 8, 2008.

1009 **denied he had made:** "Senator Kennedy Denies Politicking for Niece," *NYT*, Dec. 9, 2008.

1009 **"I think they know enough":** "Aide to Senator Kennedy Is Said to Make Contacts on Ms. Kennedy's Behalf," *NYT*, Dec. 19, 2008.

1009 **planning a statewide tour:** "Caroline Kennedy Seeking Senate Seat Held by Clinton," *NYT*, Dec. 16, 2008.

1010 **less than articulate:** "Resistance to Kennedy's Senate Bid Emerging," *NYT*, Dec. 24, 2008.

1010 **"it makes him look":** Karen Tumulty, "Ted Kennedy's Circle Upset by Caroline's Awkward Exit," *Time*, Jan. 22, 2009.

1010 **"serious training":** Vicki Kennedy, on *Oprah Winfrey Show*, Nov. 25, 2009.

1010 **"He really looked":** Susan Milligan, "Eager to Work, Kennedy Makes Emotional Return," *BG*, Jan. 7, 2009.

1011 **fulfillment of Bobby's effort:** CNN Inauguration Coverage, Jan. 20, 2009.

1011 **"It's a great day":** Mark Leibovich, "Hold the Eulogies, Kennedy Says," *NYT*, Feb. 21, 2009.

1011 **filled the National Mall:** Tim Wallace, Karen Yourish, and Troy Griggs, "Trump's Inauguration vs. Obama's: Comparing the Crowds," *NYT*, Jan. 20, 2017.

1011 **"very happy, jocular":** Susan Milligan, "Kennedy Takes Ill at Luncheon," *BG*, Jan. 21, 2009; Kennedy and Fried, *Common Struggle*, 297.

1012 ***"Oh God, don't let this happen":*** John Kerry, *Every Day Is Extra* (New York: Simon & Schuster, 2018), 352.

1012 "remarkably different": Inauguration Coverage, MSNBC, Jan. 20, 2009.

1012 "warrior for justice": David Welna, "Kennedy, Byrd Taken from Inaugural Luncheon," *All Things Considered*, NPR, Jan. 20, 2009.

1012 "When he bellows": Milligan, "Kennedy Takes Ill."

1012 "I caahn't believe it": Kennedy and Fried, *Common Struggle*, 297.

1012 "I'm so sorry I upset": Leibovich, "Hold the Eulogies."

1012 "Kennedy, reporting": Lisa Wangsness, "Kennedy Returns for Vote on Stimulus Bill," *BG*, Feb. 10, 2009.

1012 "People were walking": Milligan and Wangsness, "Man at the Center."

1012 "Here comes my hero": Wangsness, "Kennedy Returns for Vote."

1013 signaling his "aye": Laurie Kellman, "Stimulus Bill Draws Kennedy Back to Senate," AP, Feb. 9, 2009.

1013 cited scripture by heart: Lee Fentress int., Oct. 16, 2009, Miller Center, UVA.

1013 "I have to pace myself": Leibovich, "Hold the Eulogies."

1013 "Some days are better": Wangsness, "Kennedy Returns for Vote."

1013 "cancer is in its cage": Eleanor Clift, "His Time Is Now," *Newsweek*, Mar. 6, 2009.

1014 "probably the last time": "Obama Leads Salute to Ted Kennedy," *Today*, Mar. 8, 2009, https://www.today.com/popculture/obama-leads-salute-ted-kennedy-1C9416321; Susan Milligan, "Obama Leads Star-Studded Birthday Salute to Kennedy," *BG*, Mar. 9, 2009; Barbara Souliotis int., Nov. 9, 2009, Miller Center, UVA.

1014 corps of 175,000 Americans: "Kennedy Set to Offer Bill Today," *BG*, Sept. 12, 2008.

1014 passed a cloture vote: "Kennedy Returns to Hill," *BG*, Mar. 24, 2009.

1015 "spirit of the man for whom": "President Signs $5.7 Billion Measure to Boost Volunteerism," *BG*, Apr. 22, 2009.

1015 "Miracles still happen": "House Gives FDA More Powers Over Tobacco," *BG*, Apr. 3, 2009; "Pushing Health Agenda," *BG*, June 10, 2009; "Senate Approves Tobacco Measure," *BG*, June 12, 2009.

1016 "This is the time": Obama, *Promised Land*, 375.

1016 "That's what keeps him going": Leibovich, "Hold the Eulogies."

1016 "Move very early": Michael Myers int. on "Obama's Deal," *Frontline*, PBS, Dec. 15, 2009.

1017 "This is the opportunity": "Kennedy to Step Down from Judiciary Panel," *BG*, Dec. 6, 2008.

1017 "He's working tirelessly": Jeffrey Birnbaum, "Kennedy Secretly Crafts Health Care Plan," *Washington Times*, Oct. 24, 2008.

1017 "Everyone was on red alert": Ralph Neas int. by author.

1017 "While there was some": "Health Care Industry in Talks to Shape Policy," *NYT*, Feb. 20, 2009.

1018 "Kennedy is squeezing": Clift, "His Time Is Now."

1018 "There is a moral component": Brill, *America's Bitter Pill*, 89.

1018 "There were good days": Michael Myers int., "Obama's Deal."

1018 "That's the kind of greeting": "Kennedy Back in Washington for Health Summit," AP, Mar. 5, 2009.

1018 "Teddy's walk was unsteady": Obama, *Promised Land*, 374.

1018 "The status quo is": "Obama Stands Aside, Slightly, at Health Summit," *Time*, Mar. 6, 2009.

1018 "I'm looking forward": "Kennedy Back in Washington for Health Summit."

1019 "There was a sense": Cohn, "How They Did It."

1019 "I was impressed": Milligan and Wangsness, "Man at the Center."

1019 "He's impatient": Ibid.

1019 "man at the center": Milligan and Wangsness, "Man at the Center"; Michael Myers int., "Obama's Deal."

1019 "There are very few": Cohn, "How They Did It."

1020 "Take it or leave it": Mike Enzi int. by author.

1020 "quickly merged into a single": "US Senators Hope to Have Health Bills by June," *Talking Points Memo*, Apr. 20, 2009.

1020 immovably opposed: "Obama Urges Senate Democrats to Settle Healthcare Issues," *BG*, June 3, 2009.

1020 "Bad Max": Altman and Schachtman, *Power, Politics*, 256.

1020 "a few final words": EMK to Barack Obama, May 12, 2009, https://obamawhitehouse.archives.gov/blog/2015/06/08/letter-senator-kennedy-sent-me.

1021 "If this were easy": Michael Myers int., "Obama's Deal."

1021 He previewed it: EMK, "Health Bill Would Fix What's Broken," *BG*, May 28, 2009.

1022 "Senator Kennedy is on the cusp": "Kennedy's Health Care Measure to Require Employers to Chip In," *WP*, May 29, 2009; "Kennedy Readies Health-Care Bill, *WP*, June 6, 2009; "Kennedy Details Vision for Health Care," *WP*, June 7, 2009.

1022 "run-up to major": "Senate Feels Absence on Health Bill," *NYT*, June 9, 2009; "Health Bill Highlighted," *BG*, June 9, 2009.

1022 make some progress: "Democrats Pushing Healthcare Agenda," *BG*, June 10, 2009; Cohn, "How They Did It."

1022 "What are people": Michael Myers int., "Obama's Deal."

1023 "hours of sharpness": Milligan and Wangsness, "Man at the Center."

1023 "We had crossed": Michael Myers int., "Obama's Deal."

1023 "We're going to get": Nancy Pelosi int., Apr. 30, 2010, Miller Center, UVA.

1023 restored the public option: "Kennedy, Dodd Unveil Trimmer Senate Healthcare Bill," *BG*, July 3, 2009.

1023 "It has never been": EMK, "The Cause of My Life," *Newsweek*, July 27, 2009.

1024 "place he associated": Victoria Reggie Kennedy, Apr. 8, 2010, Miller Center, UVA.

1024 "I have good days": EMK, *True Compass*, 504.

1024 throughout his illness: Curran Raclin int., Nov. 10, 2009, Miller Center, UVA.

1024 "You know, all of us": Caroline Raclin int., Nov. 11, 2009, Miller Center, UVA.

1024 old friends visited: Patrick Kennedy int.

1024 "Teddy wanted it": Kennedy and Fried, *Common Struggle*, 302.

1024 barely speak at all: Michael Levenson, "In Last Days a Quest for Joy," *BG*, Aug. 27, 2009.

1024–25 "in ways that were impossible": John Tunney int., Oct. 12, 2009, Miller Center, UVA.

1025 "thump on the back": Kerry, *Every Day*, 355–56.

1025 "I had the sense": Souliotis int.

1025 "Toward the end": Levenson, "In Last Days."

1025 "for weeks and weeks": Caroline Raclin int.

1025 "paired off": Maria Shriver int., Jan. 29, 2010, Miller Center, UVA.

1025 "just crack each other": Caroline Raclin int.

1025 "very involved in her care": Shriver int.

1026 another stroke in August: Kennedy and Fried, *Common Struggle*, 302.

1026 "She understood deeply": "Eunice Kennedy Shriver, Trailblazer Who Changed Lives, Dies," *BG*, Aug. 12, 2009.

1026 returned to Hyannis: "Patrick Kennedy Discusses Rehab," *BG*, July 9, 2009.

1026 "big gift": "Rep. Kennedy: Dad's Illness Has United Family," AP, Aug. 13, 2009.

1026 "I took as some form": Kennedy and Fried, *Common Struggle*, 303.

1026 his cane for a wheelchair: Levenson, "In Last Days."

1026 "The sea does": Edmund Reggie int., Dec. 16, 2008, Miller Center, UVA.

1027 "in an emotional way": Nick Littlefield int., May 3, 2008, Miller Center, UVA.

1027 "many contented hours": EMK, *True Compass*, 506.

1027 calling his memoir: Ted Kennedy, Jr., on *Oprah Winfrey Show*, Nov. 25, 2009.

1028 "Remind me, Vicki": Leibovich, "Hold the Eulogies."

1028 "poignant acknowledgment": Frank Phillips, "Kennedy Looking Ahead Urges that Senate Seat Be Filled Quickly," *BG*, Aug. 20, 2009.

1028 "two voices speaking": "Kennedy Asks to Alter Law on His Successor," *NYT*, Aug. 20, 2009.

1028 Deval Patrick to appoint: "Ted Kennedy: I'd Like Wife to Take Seat," *NY Daily News*, May 22, 2008.

1028 "fully engaged": Phillips, "Kennedy Looking Ahead."

1029 "death panels": "Rep. Kennedy: Dad's Illness Has United Family."

1029 "Every day is a gift": Mark Leibovich, "After Diagnosis, Determined to Make a Good Ending," *NYT*, Aug. 26, 2009.

1029 "I had a wonderful life": Ibid.

1029 called to wish him: "Ted Kennedy Memorial Service," C-SPAN, Aug. 28, 2009, https://www.c-span.org/video/?288589-2/senator-edward-kennedy-memorial-service.

1029 "The last couple of times": Fentress int.

1029 drove him around Hyannis Port: Levenson, "In Last Days."

1029 "The end was so quick": Curran Raclin int.

1030 "I've got to get it right": Leibovich, "After Diagnosis."

1030 **"ruff-tuff-'em"**: Caroline Raclin int.

1030 **"greatest senator in the last"**: Littlefield int., May 3, 2008.

1030 **"every detail"**: Fentress int.

1030 **canvass the country**: Theodore Sorensen int., May 19, 2005, Miller Center, UVA.

1031 **"salute to him"**: "Kennedy Steps Up Plan for Institute at UMass," *BG*, Aug. 12, 2008.

1031 **"Blessed are the poor"**: Luke 14:13.

1031 **sent the president a sealed letter**: "Ailing Kennedy Sends Letter to Pope," *BG*, July 11, 2009; "After Kennedy's Death, Silence from the Pope," *Time*, Aug. 28, 2009.

1031 **"penitent on a deathbed"**: Thomas Oliphant, "The Lion at Rest," *Democracy*, no. 15 (Winter 2010), https://democracyjournal.org/magazine/15/the-lion-at-rest/.

1031 **"sustained and nurtured"**: EMK to Pope Benedict XVI, August 30, 2009, https://fratres.word press.com/2009/08/30/full-text-edward-m-kennedy-letter-to-pope-benedict-xvi/.

1032 **"a man in full"**: Richard Reeves, "A Publicly Moral Man," *USA Today*, Aug. 27, 2009.

1032 **"had she not helped me"**: EMK, *True Compass*, 509.

1033 **"Ted seemed incredibly peaceful"**: Kerry, *Every Day*, 355–56.

1033 **"There were a lot"**: Leibovich, "After Diagnosis."

1033 **He spent his last days in repose**: Ibid.

1033 **He didn't look good**: Souliotis int.

1033 **"Viva Kennedy"**: Kennedy and Fried, *Common Struggle*, 306; Levenson, "In Last Days."

1033 **"He was ready to go"**: "Kennedy Memorial Service," Aug. 28, 2009, https://www.youtube.com/watch?v=03jzJkSxLjU.

1033 **"seemed to be in mourning"**: Kerry, *Every Day*, 356.

1034 **"peaceful departure"**: Levenson, "In Last Days."

As in the bibliography for *Catching the Wind*, the following bibliography is necessarily selected. Those of us who attempt to capture a life must always proceed with modesty. A life is a nearly infinite construction, and no matter how much data we collect, it will always, finally, evade us, not only because the data is always insufficient, but because a life is more than data, much more. Every biographer has to make peace with his or her own failure. Still, we try. The literature on the Kennedys generally and on Edward Kennedy specifically is vast. It comprises hundreds of books and interviews, thousands of magazine articles, and tens of thousands of newspaper articles, along with public addresses, legal documents, manuscripts, papers, journal articles, audio recordings, and videotapes. No single individual could possibly consume all of it. Indeed, examining the life would take a lifetime. But I tried. I did my very best to work my way through five decades of *The Boston Globe, The New York Times, The Washington Post,* and *The Los Angeles Times,* and less sedulously, which is to say more selectively, through a number of other papers. I did my best to work my way through the magazine articles and other available materials as well. There is simply not enough space to cite every source I used, hence the selectivity, but one will find all the prominent sources in the notes if not in the bibliography itself. There was also a great deal of material I read that dealt with the larger context of this story, and much that dealt with its underpinnings—on conservatism and liberalism. I spent the better part of my public policy scholarship at the Woodrow Wilson Center in Washington exploring those issues before I even dug into Edward Kennedy. Very little of that material is cited here—also for reasons of space—though some of it can be found in the endnotes.

I did not, for reasons I explained in *Catching the Wind*, work with the Kennedy family on these volumes. The books are not official or authorized. Frankly, I would not write such a book because I think it might cede control of the project to the family or, at the very least, give the appearance of my having ceded control. Under those circumstances, I am not sure the reader would or could trust the book. I did ask the family for their cooperation—the sort of cooperation I was fortunate enough to have received from my subjects' families for my previous books—though I asked only with the provision that there be no quid pro quo other than the instruction I received from a Disney vice president when the Disney company decided to give me access to Walt Disney's papers for my biography of the artist: "Write a good book." That is always my intention. In any case, quid pro quo or not, I did not receive the cooperation I sought. Before his illness, I had corresponded with the senator, and as I wrote in the "Note on Sources" in *Catching the Wind*, the senator sent me a lovely note encouraging my "own venture (or adventure!)" even as he was working on his memoir. Understandably, his diagnosis ended that correspondence and any cooperation he might have provided, but Vicki Kennedy later sent me a handwritten note in response to one of my own saying that the senator was "doing well and looking forward to giving you a lot more material for your book." Even so, my subsequent attempts to reach Mrs. Kennedy were thwarted, and I never heard back from those who offered to intercede with her on my behalf. It will be no surprise to anyone who has read these volumes that the Kennedys are, by their own admission, secretive and protective. They have been the targets of misinformation, disinformation, and plain malice. They are press-shy, even biographer-shy. Still, even without the family imprimatur, I was fortunate enough to speak with many individuals who worked for the senator or had known him. I spoke with Ted Jr. several times hoping to encourage him to sit for an interview and, I hoped, a number of interviews. He demurred. As I wrote in *Catching the Wind*, the only family member with whom I spoke was Patrick Kennedy, in a lengthy, candid, and illuminating interview that was one of the highlights of my work on this project.

This *omertà* would have been a crippling obstacle were it not for the Edward Kennedy Oral History Project at the Miller Center at the University of Virginia, which had been planned by Senator Kennedy and which holds nearly two dozen multihour interviews with the senator himself and several hundred with family members, friends, associates, and staff members. As those who read the endnotes will see, I relied heavily on this material. I relied heavily, too, on the interviews left for scholars by the late

Adam Clymer, a *New York Times* reporter and Kennedy biographer, who donated his interviews and notes to the John F. Kennedy Presidential Library. They were invaluable—in part because some of the interview subjects had died, in part because Clymer *did* work with the authorization of the senator, so he had access to people who likely would not have been accessible without that authorization.

Finally, like most biographers, I love to pore over the papers of my subjects, and Senator Kennedy's papers are, as one might imagine after his forty-seven years in the Senate, extensive. By one account, the boxes laid end to end would stretch for a mile. Unfortunately for me, those papers began being released—piecemeal—only after I entered the writing stage, and even then slowly, with the first tranches being letters pertaining to the senator's constituent services. It was agony not having his documents, which presumably include his diaries, and admittedly, the book might be very different if I had had them. But as with the copious materials in print that were beyond my capacity to read in their entirety, I had to make peace with the insufficiency. Some future biographer *will* have access to those papers, and as I said in the source notes to *Catching the Wind*, that ongoing investigation, in which new items are always added and analyses are always revised, is integral to the larger biographical enterprise. A life is the raw material. We examine it as best we can with what we have available at the time, and we give our interpretations and draw our conclusions— interpretations and conclusions that are likely to be different for each biographer and that are always provisional. Taken together, one hopes these biographies will allow one to see the complexity of the subject and understand more about him or her and what he or she might say about us. This bibliography is likely to grow with time, as it should with a life as large and complex as Edward Kennedy's. And, one hopes, his life will continue to illuminate our politics and our nation for decades to come.

BIBLIOGRAPHY

BOOKS

Abourezk, James. *Advise and Dissent: Memoirs of an Ex-Senator*. Lincoln: University of Nebraska Press, 2013.

Alter, Jonathan. *The Very Best: Jimmy Carter, A Life*. New York: Simon & Schuster, 2020.

Altman, Stuart, and David Shachtman. *Power, Politics, and Universal Health Care: The Inside Story of a Century-Long Battle*. Amherst, N.Y.: Prometheus Books, 2011.

Annis, J. Lee, Jr. *Howard Baker: Conciliator in an Age of Crisis*. Nashville, Tenn.: Madison Books, 1995.

Arnson, Cynthia. *Crossroads: Congress, the Reagan Administration, and Central America*. New York: Pantheon Books, 1989.

Baker, Howard. *Leading the United States Senate*. Washington, D.C.: Government Printing Office, 2003.

Baker, Peter, and Susan Schmidt. "Starr Alleges Abundant Lies." In *The Starr Report: The Findings of Independent Counsel Kenneth W. Starr on President Clinton and the Lewinsky Affair*. New York: PublicAffairs, 1998.

Baker, Peter. *The Breach: Inside the Impeachment and Trial of William Jefferson Clinton*. New York: Scribner, 2000.

———. *Days of Fire: Bush and Cheney in the White House*. New York: Doubleday, 2013.

Biden, Joe. *Promises to Keep: On Life and Politics*. New York: Random House, 2007.

Bird, Kai. *The Outlier: The Unfinished Presidency of Jimmy Carter*. New York: Crown, 2021.

Blumenthal, David, and James Morone. *The Heart of Power: Health and Politics in the Oval Office*. Berkeley: University of California Press, 2009.

Bobo, Lawrence, Camille Charles, Maria Krysan, and Alicia Simmons. "The *Real* Record on Racial Attitudes." In *Social Trends in American Life*, edited by Peter Marsden. Princeton, N.J.: Princeton University Press, 2012.

Bradley, Bill. *Time Present, Time Past: A Memoir*. New York: Knopf, 1996.

Brands, H. W. *Reagan: The Life*. New York: Doubleday, 2015.

Breyer, Stephen, and Leonard Stein. "Airline Deregulation: The Anatomy of Reform." In *Instead of Regulation: Alternatives to Federal Regulatory Agencies*, edited by Robert Poole, Jr. Lanham, Md.: Lexington Books, 1982.

Breyer, Stephen. *Regulation and Its Reform*. Cambridge, Mass.: Harvard University Press, 1982.

Brill, Steven. *America's Bitter Pill: Money, Politics, Backroom Deals, and the Fight to Fix Our Broken Healthcare System*. New York: Random House, 2015.

Broder, David, and Haynes Johnson. *The System: The American Way of Politics at the Breaking Point*. Boston: Little, Brown, 1996.

Bronner, Ethan. *Battle for Justice: How the Bork Nomination Shook America*. New York: Union Square Press, 1989.

Brooke, Edward. *Bridging the Divide: My Life*. New Brunswick, N.J.: Rutgers University Press, 2007.

Brown, Anthony. *The Politics of Airline Deregulation*. Knoxville: University of Tennessee Press, 1987.

Brown, Peter. *Minority Party: Why Democrats Face Defeat in 1992 and Beyond*. Washington, D.C.: Regnery Gateway, 1991.

Bunch, Will. *Tear Down This Myth: How the Reagan Legacy Has Distorted Our Politics and Haunts Our Future*. New York: Free Press, 2009.

Burke, Richard, with William and Marilyn Hoffer. *The Senator: My Ten Years with Ted Kennedy*. New York: St. Martin's Press, 1992.

Burnham, Walter Dean. "The 1980 Earthquake: Realignment, Reaction, or What?" In *The Hidden Election: Politics and Economics in the 1980 Presidential Campaign*, edited by Thomas Ferguson and Joel Rogers. New York: Pantheon, 1981.

Burns, James MacGregor. *Edward Kennedy and the Camelot Legacy*. New York: Norton, 1976.

Busch, Andrew. *Reagan's Victory: The Presidential Election of 1980 and the Rise of the Right*. Lawrence: University Press of Kansas, 2005.

Bush, George W. *Decision Points*. New York: Crown, 2010.

Byrd, Robert. *Leading the United States Senate*. Washington, D.C.: U.S. Government Printing Office, 2003.

———. *The Senate: 1789–1989: Addresses on the History of the United States Senate, Volume 2*. Washington, D.C.: U.S. Government Printing Office, 1988.

———. *The Senate: 1789–1989: Historical Statistics, 1789–1992, Volume 4*. Washington, D.C.: U.S. Government Printing Office, 1993.

Bzdek, Vincent. *The Kennedy Legacy: Jack, Bobby and Ted and a Family Dream Fulfilled*. New York: Palgrave Macmillan, 2009.

Califano, Joseph, Jr. *Governing America: An Insider's Report from the White House and the Cabinet*. New York: Simon & Schuster, 1981.

———. *Inside: A Public and Private Life*. New York: PublicAffairs, 2004.

Canellos, Peter. *Last Lion: The Fall and Rise of Ted Kennedy*. New York: Simon & Schuster, 2009.

Cannon, Lou. *Governor Reagan: His Rise to Power*. New York: PublicAffairs, 2003.

———. *President Reagan: The Role of a Lifetime*. New York: Simon & Schuster, 1991.

Caro, Robert. *Master of the Senate*. New York: Knopf, 2002.

Carter, Jimmy. *Keeping Faith: Memoirs of a President*. New York: Bantam, 1982.

———. *White House Diary*. New York: Farrar, Straus & Giroux, 2010.

Chellis, Marcia. *Living with the Kennedys: The Joan Kennedy Story*. New York: Simon & Schuster, 1985.

Clinton, Bill. *My Life*. New York: Knopf, 2004.

Clymer, Adam. *Edward M. Kennedy: A Biography*. New York: Harper Perennial, 2000.

Cramer, Richard Ben. *What It Takes*. New York: Vintage Books, 1993.

Dallas, Rita. *The Kennedy Case*. New York: G. P. Putnam's Sons, 1973.

Daschle, Thomas, with Michael D'Orso. *Like No Other Time: The 107th Congress and the Two Years That Changed America Forever*. New York: Crown, 2003.

David, Lester. *Joan: The Reluctant Kennedy*. New York: Funk & Wagnalls, 1974.

———. *Ted Kennedy: Triumph and Tragedy*. New York: Grosset & Dunlap, 1972.

Davis, Lennard. *Enabling Acts: The Story of How the Americans with Disabilities Act Gave America's Largest Minorities Their Rights*. New York: Beacon Press, 2015.

Derickson, Alan. *Health Security for All: Dreams of Universal Health Care in America*. Baltimore: Johns Hopkins University Press, 2005.

Derthick, Martha, and Paul Quirk. *The Politics of Deregulation*. Washington, D.C.: Brookings Institution, 1985.

Didion, Joan. *Political Fictions*. New York: Vintage, 2002.

Dionne, E. J., Jr. *Why Americans Hate Politics*. New York: Simon & Schuster, 1991.

Draper, Robert. *Dead Certain: The Presidency of George W. Bush*. New York: Free Press, 2007.

Draper, Theodore. *A Very Thin Line: The Iran-Contra Affair*. New York: Hill & Wang, 1991.

Drew, Elizabeth. *Portrait of an Election: The 1980 Presidential Campaign*. New York: Simon & Schuster, 1981.

———. *Showdown: The Struggle Between the Gingrich Congress and the Clinton White House*. New York: Simon & Schuster, 1996.

Eizenstat, Stuart. *President Carter: The White House Years*. New York: Thomas Dunne Books, 2018.

Fairlie, Henry. *The Kennedy Promise: The Politics of Expectation*. Garden City, N.Y.: Doubleday, 1973.

Farrell, John Aloysius. *Tip O'Neill and the Democratic Century*. Boston: Little, Brown, 2001.

Fenno, Richard. *The Making of a Senator: Dan Quayle*. Washington, D.C.: CQ Press, 1989.

Formisano, Ronald. *Boston Against Busing: Race, Class, and Ethnicity in the 1960s and 1970s*. Chapel Hill: University of North Carolina Press, 1991.

Germond, Jack, and Jules Witcover. *Blue Smoke and Mirrors: How Reagan Won and Why Carter Lost the Election of 1980*. New York: Viking Press, 1981.

Gerstle, Gary. "Minorities, Multiculturalism, and the Presidency of George W. Bush." In *The Presidency of George W. Bush*, edited by Julian Zelizer. Princeton, N.J.: Princeton University Press, 2010.

Gibson, Barbara, and Ted Schwarz. *Rose Kennedy and Her Family: The Best and Worst of Their Lives and Times*. New York: Birch Lane Press, 1995.

Gillon, Steve. *The Pact: Bill Clinton, Newt Gingrich, and the Rivalry That Defined a Generation*. New York: Oxford University Press, 2008.

Gitenstein, Mark. *Matters of Principle: An Insider's Account of America's Rejection of Robert Bork's Nomination to the Supreme Court*. New York: Simon & Schuster, 1992.

Goldwater, Barry. *The Conscience of a Conservative*. 1960; reprint Princeton, N.J.: Princeton University Press, 2007.

Gordon, Colin. *Dead on Arrival: The Politics of Health Care in Twentieth-Century America*. Princeton, N.J.: Princeton University Press, 2003.

Gould, Lewis. *The Most Exclusive Club: A History of the Modern Senate*. New York: Basic Books, 2005.

Greenberg, Stanley. *The Two Americas: Our Current Political Deadlock and How to Break It*. 2004; reprint New York: St. Martin's Griffin, 2005.

Haas, Lawrence. *The Kennedys in the World: How Jack, Bobby, and Ted Remade America's Empire*. Sterling, Va.: Potomac Books, 2021.

Harris, John. *The Survivor: Bill Clinton in the White House*. New York: Random House, 2005.

Hersh, Burton. *The Education of Edward Kennedy: A Family Biography*. New York: William Morrow, 1972.

———. *Edward Kennedy: An Intimate Biography*. Berkeley, Calif.: Counterpoint, 2010.

———. *The Shadow President: Ted Kennedy in Opposition*. South Royalton, Vt.: Steerforth Press, 1997.

Hodgson, Godfrey. *America in Our Time: From World War II to Nixon*. 1976; reprint New York: Vintage Books, 1978.

Hollings, Ernest, and Kirk Victor. *Making Government Work*. Columbia: University of South Carolina Press, 2008.

Honan, William. *Ted Kennedy: Profile of a Survivor*. New York: Quadrangle Books, 1972.

Isikoff, Michael. *Uncovering Clinton: A Reporter's Story*. New York: Crown, 1999.

Jacobson, Gary. *A Divider, Not a Uniter: George W. Bush and the American People, the 2006 Election, and Beyond*. New York: Longman Press, 2007.

Jeffords, James, with Yvonne Daley and Howard Coffin. *An Independent Man: Adventures of a Public Servant*. New York: Simon & Schuster, 2003.

Jenkins, Philip. *Decade of Nightmares: The End of the Sixties and the Making of Eighties America*. New York: Oxford University Press, 2006.

Jones, Rochelle. *The Private World of Congress*. New York: Free Press, 1979.

Jordan, Hamilton. *Crisis: The Last Year of the Carter Presidency*. New York: G. P. Putnam's Sons, 1982.

Kampelman, Max. *Entering New Worlds: The Memoirs of a Private Man in Public Life*. New York: HarperCollins, 1991.

Kennedy, Edward. *True Compass*. New York: Twelve, 2009.

Kennedy, Patrick, and Stephen Fried. *A Common Struggle: A Personal Journey Through the Past and Future of Mental Illness and Addiction*. New York: Blue Rider Press, 2015.

Kennedy, Rose Fitzgerald. *Times to Remember*. Garden City, N.Y.: Doubleday, 1974.

Kerry, John. *Every Day Is Extra*. New York: Simon & Schuster, 2018.

Koed, Betty. *Committee on the Judiciary: A Brief History*. Washington, D.C.: Senate Historical Office, 2007.

Krugman, Paul. *The Conscience of a Liberal*. New York: Norton, 2007.

Laham, Nicholas. *A Lost Cause: Bill Clinton's Plan for National Health Insurance*. New York: Praeger, 1996.

Lakoff, Sanford, and Herbert York. *A Shield in Space?: Technology, Politics, and the Strategic Defense Initiative: How the Reagan Administration Set Out to Make Nuclear Weapons "Impotent and Obsolete" and Succumbed to the Fallacy of the Last Move*. Berkeley: University of California Press, 1989.

Lawford, Christopher. *Symptoms of Withdrawal: A Memoir of Snapshots and Redemption*. New York: William Morrow, 2005.

Leamer, Laurence. *The Kennedy Women: The Saga of an American Family*. New York: Villard Books, 1994.

Letterman, David, et al. *An Altogether New Book of Top Ten Lists*. New York: Pocket Books, 1991.

Link, William S. *Righteous Warrior: Jesse Helms and the Rise of Modern Conservatism*. New York: St. Martin's Press, 2008.

Lippman, Theo. *Senator Ted Kennedy: The Career Behind the Image.* New York: Norton, 1976.

Littlefield, Nick, and David Nexon. *Lion of the Senate: When Ted Kennedy Rallied the Democrats in a GOP Congress.* New York: Simon & Schuster, 2015.

Lott, Trent. *Herding Cats: A Life in Politics.* New York: HarperCollins/ReganBooks, 2005.

Lowi, Theodore. *The End of the Republican Era.* Norman: University of Oklahoma Press, 1995.

Lukas, J. Anthony. *Common Ground: A Turbulent Decade in the Lives of Three American Families.* New York: Knopf, 1985.

Mason, Jim. *No Holding Back: The 1980 Presidential Campaign of John B. Anderson.* Lanham, Md.: University Press of America, 2011.

Matlack, Jack, Jr. *Reagan and Gorbachev: How the Cold War Ended.* New York: Random House, 2004.

Matthews, Chris. *Jack Kennedy: Elusive Hero.* New York: Simon & Schuster, 2011.

Mayer, Jane, and Jill Abramson. *Strange Justice: The Selling of Clarence Thomas.* Boston: Houghton Mifflin, 1994.

McCain, John, and Mark Salter. *The Restless Wave.* New York: Simon & Schuster, 2018.

McCarthy, Abigail. *Private Faces, Public Places.* Garden City, N.Y.: Doubleday, 1972.

Meacham, Jon. *Destiny and Power: The American Odyssey of George Herbert Walker Bush.* New York: Random House, 2015.

Mitchell, George. *Making Peace.* New York: Knopf, 1999.

Mudd, Roger. *The Place to Be: Washington, CBS and the Glory Days of Television News.* New York: PublicAffairs, 2008.

Newfield, Jack. *Robert Kennedy: A Memoir.* New York: E. P. Dutton, 1969.

Obama, Barack. *A Promised Land.* New York: Crown, 2021.

O'Brien, Michael. *Philip Hart: The Conscience of the Senate.* East Lansing: Michigan State University Press, 1995.

O'Clery, Conor. *The Greening of the White House: The Inside Story of How America Tried to Bring Peace to Ireland.* Dublin: Gill & Macmillan, 1996.

O'Neill, Tip, with William Novak. *Man of the House: The Life and Political Memoirs of Speaker Tip O'Neill.* New York: Random House, 1987.

Patterson, Thomas. *Out of Order.* New York: Knopf, 1993.

Perlstein, Rick. *The Invisible Bridge: The Fall of Nixon and the Rise of Reagan.* New York: Simon & Schuster, 2014.

———. *Nixonland: The Rise of a President and the Fracturing of America.* New York: Simon & Schuster, 2008.

———. *Reaganland: America's Right Turn, 1976–1980.* New York: Simon & Schuster, 2021.

Pertschuk, Michael, and Wendy Schaetzel. *The People Rising: The Campaign Against the Bork Nomination.* New York: Thunder's Mouth Press, 1989.

Phelps, Timothy. *Capitol Games: Clarence Thomas, Anita Hill, and the Story of a Supreme Court Nomination.* New York: Hyperion, 1992.

Polsby, Nelson. "Goodbye to the Inner Club." In *Congressional Behavior,* edited by Nelson Polsby. New York: Random House, 1971.

Quadagno, Jill. *One Nation, Uninsured: Why the U.S. Has No National Health Insurance.* New York: Oxford University Press, 2005.

Reagan, Ronald. *An American Life.* New York: Simon & Schuster, 1990.

———. *The Reagan Diaries.* Edited by Douglas Brinkley. New York: HarperCollins, 2007.

Reid, Harry, with Mark Warren. *The Good Fight: Hard Lessons from Searchlight to Washington.* New York: G. P. Putnam's Sons, 2008.

Repak, T. A., and Murray Levin. *Edward Kennedy: The Myth of Leadership.* Boston: Houghton Mifflin, 1980.

Riley, Russell. *Inside the Clinton White House: An Oral History.* New York: Oxford University Press, 2016.

Robinson, Michael, and Margaret Sheehan. *Over the Wire and on TV: CBS and UPI in Campaign '80.* New York: Russell Sage Foundation, 1983.

Rogin, Michael Paul. *Ronald Reagan, the Movie, and Other Episodes in Political Demonology.* Berkeley: University of California Press, 1987.

Rusher, William. *The Rise of the Right.* New York: William Morrow, 1984.

Sabato, Larry. *Feeding Frenzy: How Attack Journalism Transformed American Politics.* New York: The Free Press, 1991.

Schlesinger, Arthur, Jr. *Journals: 1952–2000.* Edited by Andrew Schlesinger and Stephen Schlesinger. New York: Penguin Press, 2007.

Schlesinger, Arthur, Jr. *Robert Kennedy and His Times*. Boston: Houghton Mifflin, 1978.

Schneider, William. "The Political Legacy of the Reagan Years." In *The Reagan Legacy*, edited by Thomas Byrne Edsall and Sidney Blumenthal. New York: Pantheon Books, 1988.

Shannon, William. *The American Irish: A Political and Social Portrait*. 1989; reprint Amherst: University of Massachusetts Press, 2003.

Shapiro, Ira. *The Last Great Senate: Courage and Statesmanship in a Time of Crisis*. New York: PublicAffairs, 2012.

Sheridan, Thomas. *Helping the Good Do Better: How a White Hat Lobbyist Advocates for Social Change*. New York: Twelve, 2019.

Shrum, Robert. *No Excuses: Concessions of a Serial Campaigner*. New York: Simon & Schuster, 2007.

Simon, Paul. *P.S.: The Autobiography of Paul Simon*. N.p.: Bonus Books, 1999.

Smith, Jean Edward. *Bush*. New York: Simon & Schuster, 2016.

Solberg, Carl. *Hubert Humphrey: A Biography*. New York: Norton, 1984.

Sorensen, Ted. *Counselor: A Life at the Edge of History*. New York: HarperCollins, 2008.

Spitz, Bob. *Reagan: An American Journey*. New York: Penguin Press, 2018.

Stanley, Timothy. *Kennedy vs. Carter: The 1980 Battle for the Democratic Party's Soul*. Lawrence: University Press of Kansas, 2010.

Stockman, David. *The Triumph of Politics: Why the Reagan Revolution Failed*. New York: Harper & Row, 1986.

Taylor, John. *Circus of Ambition: The Culture of Wealth and Power in the Eighties*. New York: Warner Books, 1989.

Thompson, Hunter S. *The Great Shark Hunt: Gonzo Papers*. 1979; reprint New York: Simon & Schuster, 2003.

Troy, Gil. *Morning in America: How Ronald Reagan Invented the 1980s*. Princeton, N.J.: Princeton University Press, 2005.

Tumulty, Karen. *The Triumph of Nancy Reagan*. New York: Simon & Schuster, 2021.

Ward, Jon. *Camelot's End: Kennedy vs. Carter and the Fight That Broke the Democratic Party*. New York: Twelve, 2019.

Weicker, Lowell, Jr., with Barry Sussman. *Maverick: A Life in Politics*. Boston: Little, Brown, 1995.

White, Theodore. *America in Search of Itself: The Making of the President 1956–1980*. New York: Harper & Row, 1982.

White, William S. *Citadel: The Story of the U.S. Senate*. New York: Harper & Brothers, 1957.

Wilentz, Sean. *The Age of Reagan: A History 1974–2008*. New York: HarperCollins, 2008.

Wills, Garry. *The Kennedy Imprisonment: A Meditation on Power*. Boston: Houghton Mifflin, 2002.

Wilson, Andrew. *Irish America and the Ulster Conflict, 1968–1995*. Washington, D.C.: Catholic University of America Press, 1995.

Wofford, Harris. *Of Kennedys and Kings: Making Sense of the Sixties*. New York: Farrar, Straus & Giroux, 1980.

Zelizer, Julian. *Burning Down the House: Newt Gingrich, the Fall of a Speaker, and the Rise of the New Republican Party*. New York: Penguin Press, 2020.

INTERVIEWS AND ORAL HISTORIES

Adam Clymer Personal Papers, JFK Library

Abrams, George, int. June 17, 1992. Folder A, Box 3, Series 2.

Ayres, B. Drummond, int. August 28, 1997. Folder A, Box 3, Series 2.

Baker, Howard, int. January 13, 1994. Folder B, Box 3, Series 2.

Bates, Bob, int. September 21, 1994. Folder B, Box 3, Series 2.

Breyer, Stephen, int. July 26, 1997. Folder B, Box 3, Series 2.

Bumpers, Dale, int. May 20, 1998. Folder B, Box 3, Series 2.

Byrd, Robert, int. February 12, 1993. Folder B, Box 3, Series 2.

Caddell, Patrick, int. January 1, 1998. Folder C, Box 3, Series 2.

Carrick, William, int. May 27, 1992. Folder C, Box 3, Series 2.

Carter, Jimmy, int. May 15, 1998. Folder C, Series 2, Box 3.

Clinton, Hillary, int. May 21, 1998. Folder C, Box 3, Series 2.

Donovan, Paul, int. November 14, 1998. Folder D, Box 3, Series 2.

Feinberg, Kenneth, int. March 13, 1995. Folder F, Box 3, Series 2.

Ferris, Charles, int. April 10, 1992. Folder F, Box 3, Series 2.

Former Aide B, int. September 25, 1998. Unnamed Sources Folder. Box 5, Series 2.

Former Aide C, int. May 11, 1998. Unnamed Sources Folder. Box 5, Series 2.

Fraser, Doug, int. May 2, 1997. Folder F, Box 3, Series 2.

Gifford, Kilvert Dun, int. February 2, 1996. Folder G, Box 3, Series 2.

Gwirtzman, Milton, int. January 30, 1993. Folder G, Box 3, Series 2.

Gwirtzman, Milton, int. April 3, 1993. Folder G, Box 3, Series 2.

Hart, Peter, int. January 8, 1998. Folder H, Box 3, Series 2.

Hatch, Orrin, int. February 27, 1992. Folder H, Box 3, Series 2.

Horowitz, Larry, int. May 29, 1992. Folder H, Box 3, Series 2.

Horowitz, Larry, int. June 23, 1995. Folder H, Box 3, Series 2.

Jones, Stan, int. November 11, 1993. Folder I–J, Box 4, Series 2.

Kennedy, Edward, int. February 1992. Edward M. Kennedy Interviews, 1992–1994 Folder, Box 5, Series 2,

Kennedy, Edward, int. September 10, 1992. Edward M. Kennedy Interviews, 1992–1994 Folder. Box 5, Series 2.

Kennedy, Edward, int. February 5, 1993. Edward M. Kennedy Interviews, 1992–1994 Folder, Box 5, Series 2.

Kennedy, Edward, int. October 15, 1994. Edward M. Kennedy Interviews, 1992–1994 Folder, Box 5, Series 2.

Kennedy, Edward, int. October 29, 1994. Edward M. Kennedy Interviews, 1992–1994 Folder, Box 5, Series 2.

Kennedy, Edward, int. October 9, 1995. Edward M. Kennedy Interviews, 1995–1996 Folder, Box 5, Series 2.

Kennedy, Edward, int. April 12, 1996. Edward M. Kennedy Interviews, 1995–1996 Folder, Box 5, Series 2.

Kennedy, Edward, int. July 19, 1997. Edward M. Kennedy Interviews, 1997–1999 Folder, Box 5, Series 2.

Kennedy, Edward, int. October 31, 1997. Edward M. Kennedy Interviews, 1997–1999 Folder. Box 5, Series 2, Edward M. Kennedy Interviews,

Kennedy, Edward, int. March 27, 1998. Edward M. Kennedy Interviews, 1997–1999 Folder, Box 5, Series 2.

Kennedy, Edward, int. September 11, 1998. Edward M. Kennedy Interviews, 1997–1999 Folder. Box 5, Series 2.

Kennedy, Edward, int. November 11, 1998. Edward M. Kennedy Interviews, 1997–1999 Folder, Box 5, Series 2.

Kennedy, Edward, int. March 26, 1999. Edward M. Kennedy Interviews, 1997–1999 Folder, Box 5, Series 2.

Kennedy, Joan, int. May 12, 1998. Folder K, Box 4, Series 2.

Kennedy, Joan, int. September 19, 1998. Folder K, Box 4, Series 2.

Kennedy, Joan, int. October 12, 1998. Folder K, Box 4, Series 2.

Kennedy, Joe II, int. January 10, 1995. Folder K, Box 4, Series 2.

Kirk, Paul, Jr., int. June 3, 1998. Folder K, Box 4, Series 2.

Shriver, Eunice, int. December 13, 1993. Folder S, Box 5, Series 2.

Siegenthaler, John, int. September 25, 1995. Folder R-Edward Kennedy, Box 5, Series 2.

Smith, Steve, Jr., int. September 16, 1992. Folder S, Box 5, Series 2.

Sorensen, Ted, int. June 17, 1996. Folder S, Box 5, Series 2.

Townsend, Kathleen Kennedy, int. November 3, 2007. Folder T, Box 5, Series 2.

Tunney, John, int. March 6, 1995. Folder T, Box 5, Series 2.

Woodcock, Leonard, int. February 12, 1996. Folder V–Z, Box 5, Series 2.

James O. Eastland Collection, University of Mississippi

Eastland, James, int. n.d.

Miller Center, University of Virginia

Barnes, Melody, int. August 16, 2006.

Bates, Robert, int. May 8, 2007.

Bates, Robert, int. July 26, 2007.

Blattner, Jeffrey, int. March 30, 2007.
Boies, David, int. September 23, 2008.
Breyer, Stephen, int. June 17, 2008.
Breyer, Stephen, int. September 28, 2008.
Broder, David, int. December 1, 2006.
Burke, David, int. June 19, 2007.
Burke, David, int. April 9, 2008.
Burke, Sheila, int. July 27, 2007.
Caper, Philip, int. March 20, 2007.
Clasby, Richard, int. October 11, 2005.
Cochran, Thad, int. September 19, 2006.
Craig, Gregory, int. July 13, 2010.
Culver, John, int. September 22, 2009.
Danforth, John, int. October 25, 2005.
Daschle, Tom, int. April 29, 2009.
Doherty, Gerard, int. October 10, 2005.
Dole, Robert, int. May 15, 2006.
Dukakis, Michael, int. November 9, 2009.
Farrell, John A., int. July 13, 2006.
Feder, Judy, int. July 5, 2007.
Fein, Rashi, int. March 21, 2007.
Feinberg, Kenneth, int. July 8, 2008.
Fentress, Lee, int. October 16, 2009.
Fitzgerald, Robert P., int. June 18, 2009.
Gifford, Kilvert Dun, int. July 13, 2005.
Goldman, Leroy, int. May 5, 2007.
Gwirtzman, Milton, int. August 5, 2009.
Haar, Charles, int. October 10, 2005.
Hannan, Timothy, int. May 7, 2009.
Healy, Robert, int. August 10, 2005.
Jones, Stan, int. March 9, 2007.
Jones, Stan, int. September 14, 2007.
Kalicki, Jan, int. March 18, 2009.
Kassebaum, Nancy, int. April 6, 2009.
Kennedy, Edward, int. March 23, 2005.
Kennedy, Edward, int. June 3, 2005.
Kennedy, Edward, int. June 5, 2005.
Kennedy, Edward, int. June 17, 2005.
Kennedy, Edward, int. October 14, 2005.
Kennedy, Edward, int. February 27, 2006.
Kennedy, Edward, int. March 20, 2006.
Kennedy, Edward, int. May 8, 2006.
Kennedy, Edward, int. August 15, 2006.
Kennedy, Edward, int. November 29, 2006.
Kennedy, Edward, int. December 1, 2006.
Kennedy, Edward, int. January 6, 2007.
Kennedy, Edward, int. February 12, 2007.
Kennedy, Edward, int. May 30, 2007.
Kennedy, Edward, int. August 7, 2007.
Kennedy, Edward, int. August 8, 2007.
Kennedy, Edward, int. October 8, 2007.
Kennedy, Edward, int. December 9, 2007.
Kennedy, Edward, int. January 7, 2008.
Kennedy, Edward, int. March 28, 2008.
Kennedy, Victoria Reggie, int. April 8, 2010.
Kennedy, Victoria Reggie, int. December 9, 2007.
Kerry, John, int. June 21, 2010.
Kirk, Paul, Jr., int. November 23, 2005.

Kirk, Paul, Jr., int. June 20, 2007.
Leahy, Patrick, int. August 5, 2009 .
Littlefield, Nick, int. May 3, 2008.
Littlefield, Nick, int. May 4, 2008.
Littlefield, Nick, int. June 30, 2008.
Littlefield, Nick, int. July 1, 2008.
Littlefield, Nick, int. February 14, 2009.
Littlefield, Nick, int. February 15, 2009.
Lugar, Richard, int. March 6, 2009.
Lyons, Nance, int. May 9, 2008.
Manley, James, int. September 28, 2009.
Martin, Ed, int. April 20, 2005.
Mathias, Charles, int. March 10, 2006.
McCain, John, int. October 16, 2009.
Mikulski, Barbara, int. September 26, 2006.
Miller, George, int. October 13, 2009.
Miller, Melody, int. August 16, 2006.
Miller, Melody, int. July 1, 2008.
Miller, Melody, int. July 15, 2008.
Miller, Melody, int. October 7, 2008.
Mitchell, George, int. September 6, 2006.
Mitchell, George, int. September 6, 2011.
Mondale, Walter, int. March 20, 2006.
Myers, Michael, int. August 28, 2006.
Olavarria, Esther, int. August 28, 2006.
Osolinik, Carolyn, int. March 27, 2007.
Parker, Carey, int. September 22, 2008.
Parker, Carey, int. October 6, 2008.
Parker, Carey, int. October 13, 2008.
Parker, Carey, int. October 20, 2008.
Parker, Carey, int. October 27, 2008.
Parker, Carey, int. November 10, 2008.
Parker, Carey, int. November 11, 2008.
Parker, Carey, int. November 17, 2008.
Parker, Carey, int. December 1, 2008.
Pelosi, Nancy, int. April 30, 2010.
Raclin, Caroline, int. November 11, 2009.
Raclin, Curran, int. November 10, 2009.
Reggie, Edmund, and Doris Reggie, int. August 8, 2005.
Reggie, Edmund, and Doris Reggie, int. December 16, 2008.
Robinson, Terri Haddad, int. August 25, 2009.
Rollins, Thomas, int. October 9, 2008.
Rollins, Thomas, int. March 10, 2009.
Rollins, Thomas, int. April 22, 2009.
Rollins, Thomas, int. May 12, 2009.
Rollins, Thomas, int. May 14, 2009.
Sasser, James, int. May 2, 2006.
Sasser, James, int. May 25, 2006.
Schneider, Mark, int. February 2, 2009.
Shannon, Elizabeth, int. April 28, 2009.
Shriver, Maria, int. January 29, 2010.
Shriver, Robert III, int. January 29, 2010.
Simpson, Alan, int. May 10, 2006.
Soderberg, Nancy, int. October 9, 2008.
Soderberg, Nancy, int. July 13, 2010.
Sorensen, Ted, int. May 19, 2005.
Sorensen, Ted, int. December 7, 2006.
Souliotis, Barbara, int. July 12, 2005.

Souliotis, Barbara, int. November 9, 2009.
Spellings, Margaret, int. August 27, 2008.
Strauss, Anne, int. April 10, 2008.
Susman, Thomas, int. May 23, 2007.
Taymor, Betty, int. July 8, 2005.
Tretter, Charles, int. August 8, 2005.
Tribe, Laurence, int. April 27, 2009.
Tunney, John, int. May 3, 2007.
Tunney, John, int. October 12, 2009.
Vanden Heuvel, William, int. July 19, 2005.
Vanden Heuvel, William, int. December 7, 2006.
Vargo, Trina, int. November 7, 2008.
Waxman, Sharon, int. December 19, 2008.
Waxman, Sharon, int. May 11, 2009.
Weicker, Lowell, int. June 19, 2009.

U.S. Senate Historical Office

Hildenbrand, William, int. Oral History Interview. 1981–1985.
Johnson, Michael. Oral History.
Kimmitt, J. Stanley. Oral History. 2003.
Ludlam, Charles E. Oral History.
Shuman, Howard. Oral History.
Valeo, Francis, int. Oral History Interviews. n.d.

ARCHIVES, PRESIDENTIAL LIBRARIES, FILES, AND PAPERS

Adam Clymer Personal Papers, JFK Library.
Center for Legislative Archives, National Archives.
Edward Kennedy, FBI Files.
George H.W. Bush Presidential Library.
George W. Bush Presidential Center.
Gerald R. Ford Presidential Library.
James O. Eastland Papers, J.D. Williams Library, University of Mississippi.
Jimmy Carter Presidential Papers, Jimmy Carter Presidential Library.
Joseph L. Rauh Papers, Library of Congress.
LBJ Presidential Library.
Nancy F. Korman Personal Papers, JFK Library.
Robert Dole Archives, University of Kansas.
Ronald Reagan Presidential Library.
Rose Fitzgerald Kennedy Personal Papers, JFK Library.
Senate Records, National Archives.
Theodore C. Sorensen Personal Papers, JFK Library.
United Auto Workers Collection, Walter P. Reuther Library, Wayne State University.
William J. Clinton Presidential Library.

ACADEMIC JOURNALS/ARTICLES AND THINK TANK REPORTS

Abramowitz, Alan, John McGlennon, and Ronald Rapoport. "The Party Isn't Over: Incentives for Activism in the 1980 Presidential Nominating Campaign." *Journal of Politics* 45, no. 4 (November 1983).
Ahtes, J. H. "The Kennedys, Ireland and Irish America." *Irish Review* 11 (Winter 1991–92): 23–34.
Badger, Doug. "Medicaid Per Capita Caps: When Democrats Supported and Republicans Opposed Them, 1995–1997." Mercatus Center, George Mason University, 2017. https://www.mercatus.org/system/files/mercatus-badger-medicaid-per-capita-caps-v2.pdf.
Blinder, Alan, and Mark Watson. "Presidents and the U.S. Economy: An Econometric Exploration." Woodrow Wilson School and Department of Economics, Princeton University, July 2014. https://www.princeton.edu/~mwatson/papers/Presidents_Blinder_Watson_July2014.pdf.

Briand, R. J. "Bush, Clinton, Irish America and the Irish Peace Process." *Political Quarterly* 73, no. 2 (2002): 172–80.

Cohen, Jerome. "Ted Kennedy's Role in Restoring Diplomatic Relations with China." *New York University Journal of Legislation and Public Policy* 14, no. 2 (2011).

Colker, Ruth. "The ADA's Journey Through Congress." *Wake Forest Law Review* (Spring 2004).

Dale, Charles. "Analysis of the Civil Rights Sections of S.1437, the 'Criminal Code Reform Act of 1977.'" UNT Digital Library, April 23, 1978. https://digital.library.unt.edu/ark:/67531/metadc992963/m1/2/?q=%22law%22.

Davis, Tom. "The Way Back." *Ripon Forum*, January 15, 2009, https://riponsociety.org/article/the-way-back.

Dionne, E. J., Jr. "There Is No Catholic Vote, And Yet, It Matters." Brookings Institution, June 18, 2000. https://www.brookings.edu/opinions/there-is-no-catholic-vote-and-yet-it-matters.

Forman, James, Jr. "Victory by Surrender: The Voting Rights Amendment of 1982 and the Civil Rights Act of 1991." *Yale Law and Policy Review* 10 (1992): 133–50.

Fox, Harrison W., Jr., and Susan Webb Hammond. "The Growth of Congressional Staffs." *Proceedings of the Academy of Political Science* 32, no. 1 (1975): 112–24.

Gabler, Neal. "The Press and Edward Kennedy: A Case Study in Journalistic Behavior." Shorenstein Center on Media, Politics and Public Policy, Harvard University, Fall 2011.

Hess, Stephen. "Decline and Fall of Congressional News." *Society* 31, no. 2 (1994): 72–79.

Hibbing, John R., and Sue Thomas. "The Modern United States Senate: What Is Accorded Respect." *Journal of Politics* 52, no. 1 (February 1990): 126–45.

Hiebert-White, Jane. "Who Won What in Kennedy/Kassebaum Struggle?" *Health Progress* (September–October 1996).

Hume, John. "The Irish Question: A British Problem." *Foreign Affairs* (Winter 1979–80).

Kennedy, Edward. "Foreword," *San Diego Law Review* 19, no. 1 (December 1981): 1–8. https://digital.sandiego.edu/cgi/viewcontent.cgi?article=1734&context=sdlr.

———. "Reconsidering Social Welfare Policy: Introduction." *Yale Law and Policy Review* 4, no. 1 (1985).

———. "Refugee Act of 1980." *International Migration Review* 15, no. 1–2 (Spring–Summer 1981): 141–56.

———. "Washington Letter." *Africa Today* 16, no. 2 (April–May 1969).

Kirkpatrick, Jeane. "Dictatorships and Double Standards." *Commentary*, Nov. 1979, 34–45.

Kohut, Andrew. "Mixed Views About Civil Rights But Support for Selma Demonstrations." Pew Research Center, March 5, 2015. https://www.pewresearch.org/fact-tank/2020/01/16/50-years-ago-mixed-views-about-civil-rights-but-support-for-selma-demonstrators.

Marik, Katherine. "Visual Artists Rights Act of 1990: The United States Recognizes Artists and Their Rights." *Entertainment and Sports Lawyer* (Winter 1991): 7–14.

Myers, G. William, III. "The Role of Special Interest Groups in the Supreme Court Nomination of Robert Bork." *Hastings Constitutional Law Quarterly* 17 (1990): 399.

Newport, Frank, Jeffrey M. Jones, and Lydia Saad. "Ronald Reagan from the People's Perspective: A Gallop Poll Review." *Gallup*, June 7, 2004. https://news.gallup.com/poll/11887/ronald-reagan-from-peoples-perspective-gallup-poll-review.aspx.

Oliphant, Thomas. "The Lion at Rest." *Democracy*, no. 15 (Winter 2010). https://democracyjournal.org/magazine/15/the-lion-at-rest.

Patterson, Samuel. "Party Leadership in the U.S. Senate." *Legislative Studies Quarterly* 14 (August 1989): 393–413.

Pollack, David A. "Reflections on Working for Senator Edward Kennedy." *Community Mental Health Journal* 46, no. 2 (April 2010): 103–11.

"Public Opinion on Civil Rights: Reflections on the Civil Rights Act of 1964." Roper Center for Public Opinion Research, n.d. https://ropercenter.cornell.edu/public-opinion-civil-rights-reflections-civil-rights-act-1964.

"Public Trust in Government, 1958–2021." Pew Research Center, May 17, 2021.

Ribuffo, Leo P. "From Carter to Clinton: The Latest Crisis of American Liberalism." *American Studies International* 35, no. 2 (June 1997): 4–29.

———. "Jimmy Carter and the Ironies of American Liberalism." *Gettysburg Review* (Autumn 1988).

Rockefeller, John IV. "The Pepper Commission Report on National Healthcare." *New England Journal of Medicine* 323 (October 4, 1990).

Rosenbaum, Sara. "Slouching Toward Health Reform: Insights from the Battle Over SCHIP." *Georgetown Journal on Poverty, Law and Policy* 15 (Fall 2008): 703–13.

Schaffer, William. "A Discriminant Function Analysis of Position-Taking: Carter vs. Kennedy." *Presidential Studies Quarterly* 10, no. 3 (Summer 1980): 451–68.

Schwartz, Robert, and Marian Robinson. "Goals 2000 and the Standards Movement." *Brookings Papers on Educational Policy* (2000): 173–214.

Sinclair, Barbara. "Senate Styles and Senate Decision Making, 1955–1980." *Journal of Politics* 48, no. 4 (November 1986): 877–908.

Skocpol, Theda. "The Rise and Resounding Demise of the Clinton Plan." *Health Affairs* 14, no. 1 (Spring 1995): 66–85.

Starr, Paul. "Transformation in Defeat: The Changing Objectives of National Health Insurance, 1915–1980." *American Journal of Public Health* 72, no. 1 (January 1982): 78–88.

Steeh, Charlotte, and Maria Krysan. "Affirmative Action and the Public, 1970–1995." *Public Opinion Quarterly* 60, no. 1 (Spring 1996): 128–58.

Stern, Mark. "Party Alignments and Civil Rights." *Presidential Studies Quarterly* 25, no. 3 (Summer 1995): 413–27.

Supel, Thomas. "The U.S. Economy in 1977 and 1978." *Federal Reserve Bank of Minneapolis Quarterly Review* 211 (Winter 1978).

Teixeira, Ruy. "New Progressive America." Center for American Progress, March 9, 2009.

Wayne, Stephen, Cheryl Beil, and Joy Falk. "Public Perceptions About Ted Kennedy and the Presidency." *Presidential Studies Quarterly* 12, no. 1 (1982): 84–90.

MAJOR MAGAZINE ARTICLES

Atkinson, Rick. "Why Ted Kennedy Can't Stand Still." *Washington Post Magazine*, April 29, 1990.

Bai, Matt. "The Last 20th Century Election." *New York Times Magazine*, November 19, 2006.

Barnicle, Mike. "Of Memory and the Sea." *Time*, August 27, 2009.

Barron, John. "Chappaquiddick: The Still Unanswered Questions." *Reader's Digest*, February 1980.

Beinart, Peter. "The New Liberal Order." *Time*, November 13, 2008.

Birnbaum, Norman. "How Much of the Way with E.M.K.?" *Nation*, December 22, 1979.

Bork, Robert. "Civil Rights—A Challenge." *New Republic*, August 31, 1963.

Bowden, Mark. "The Desert One Debacle." *Atlantic*, May 2006.

Braden, Joan. "Joan Kennedy Tells Her Own Story." *McCall's*, August 1978.

Brownstein, Ron. "Bush's Final Failing Grade." *National Journal*, November 7, 2008.

Calabresi, Massimo. "The Playmaker: How Kennedy Got His Way." *Time*, April 2, 2006.

"Carter Wins Votes, Kennedy Wins Hearts." *National Journal*, June 19, 2000.

Cohn, Jonathan. "How They Did It." *New Republic*, June 10, 2010.

Colt, George Howe. "Is Ted Kennedy's Midlife Crisis Finally Over?" *Life*, August 1994.

Diliberto, Gioia. "After 24 Years, Joan Kennedy Ends Her Marriage." *People*, December 30, 1982.

Dilulio, John. "John Dilulio's Letter." *Esquire*, May 23, 2007. https://www.esquire.com/news-politics/a2880/dilulio/.

Dionne, E. J., Jr. "Yes, We Did." *New Republic*, November 5, 2008.

Duffy, Michael. "When Dynasties Call a Truce." *Time*, November 26, 2001.

Dunne, Dominick. "The Verdict." *Vanity Fair*, March 1992.

Farrell, Jane. "Memories of Mary Jo." *Ladies' Home Journal*, July 1989.

Farrell, John Aloysius. "Comeback Kid Rising from the Ashes." *Boston Globe Magazine*, November 21, 1993.

Flamini, Roland. "Inside Edward M. Kennedy's House in Washington, D.C." *Architectural Digest*, November 1999.

Fritchey, Clayton. "Who Belongs to the Senate's Inner Club?" *Harper's Magazine*, May 1967.

Gerson, Michael. "How My Party Lost Its Way." *Newsweek*, January 28, 2008.

Gibbs, Nancy. "How Obama Rewrote the Book." *Time*, November 5, 2008.

Green, Joshua. "The Heroic Story of How Congress First Confronted AIDS." *Atlantic*, June 8, 2011.

Greenberg, Stanley. "The Emerging Center-Left Majority." *American Prospect*, November 13, 2008.

"I Know I Cannot Run Now." *Time*, May 31, 1976.

Isaacson, Walter. "That Which We Are, We Are." *Time*, August 25, 1980.

Jacobs, Sally. "Prime Time with Joan Kennedy." *Boston Globe Magazine*, July 9, 2000.

"Joan Kennedy: Life Without Ted." *Ladies' Home Journal*, April 1981.

Judis, John. "America the Liberal." *New Republic*, November 5, 2008.

Kahn, E. J. III. "The Making of the Remaking of Edward M. Kennedy." *Boston*, August 28, 2009.

Kelly, Michael. "Ted Kennedy on the Rocks." *GQ*, February 1990.

Kempton, Murray. "The Kennedy Brothers." *New York Review of Books*, January 19, 1984.

Kennedy, Edward. "The Cause of My Life." *Newsweek*, July 27, 2009.

"King of the Hill: In Praise of Ted Kennedy." *Economist*, January 12, 2002.

Kirk, Russell. "Conservatism: A Succinct Description." *National Review*, September 3, 1982.

Klein, Joe. "Obama's Victory Ushers in New America." *Time*, November 5, 2008.

Lapham, Lewis. "Edward Kennedy and the Romance of Death." *Harper's Magazine*, December 1979.

Lawler, Philip. "The Lion as Catholic." *American Spectator*, February 2010.

Leibovich, Mark. "Ted Kennedy, Jr., Is (Finally) Ready for the Family Business." *New York Times Magazine*, March 13, 2013.

Mayer, Allan. "A Born-Again Politician." *Newsweek*, April 7, 1980.

Morgan, Thomas. "Teddy." *Esquire*, April 1962.

Morrow, Lance. "Is There Life After Disaster?" *Time*, November 17, 1980.

———. "The Trouble with Teddy." *Time*, April 29, 1991.

Newfield, Jack. "The Senate's Fighting Liberal." *Nation*, March 25, 2002.

Packer, George. "The Empty Chamber." *New Yorker*, August 9, 2010.

———. "The Fall of Conservatism." *New Yorker*, May 26, 2008.

———. "The New Liberalism." *New Yorker*, November 17, 2008.

Perlstein, Rick. "Lee Atwater's Infamous 1981 Interview on the Southern Strategy." *Nation*, November 13, 2012.

Pierce, Charles. "Kennedy Unbound After 40 Years in the U.S. Senate." *Boston Globe Magazine*, January 5, 2003.

Quindlen, Anna. "Living History." *Newsweek*, November 17, 2008.

"Ready for Teddy?" *Newsweek*, June 2, 1975.

Reeves, Richard. "Teddy or Not." *New York*, April 22, 1974.

"Remembering Ted Kennedy." *National Journal*, September 5, 2009.

Rhodes, Richard. "Things as They Are, Things That Never Were: The Last Kennedy." *Audience*, November–December 1971.

Richardson, John. "Newt Gingrich: The Indispensable Republican." *Esquire*, August 2010.

Roberts, Steven. "Ted Kennedy: Haunted by the Past." *New York Times Magazine*, February 3, 1980.

Shapiro, Walter. "The Party's New Soul." *Time*, July 25, 1988.

"Sobering Times." *Newsweek*, December 9, 1991.

Suskind, Ron. "Why Are These Men Laughing?" *Esquire*, January 2003.

Taibbi, Matt. "Full Metal McCain." *Rolling Stone*, June 26, 2008.

"Then There Were Three." *Time*, August 5, 1991.

Thomas, Evan. "How He Did It." *Newsweek*, November 17, 2008.

———. "In the Shadow of Bush." *Newsweek*, January 28, 2008.

Thornburgh, Dick. "Disability and the Prophet's Call." *Christian Citizen*, July 26, 2017.

Toobin, Jeffrey. "Blowing Up the Senate." *New Yorker*, February 27, 2006.

———. "The Dirty Trickster." *New Yorker*, June 2, 2008.

Traub, James. "Party Like It's 1994." *New York Times Magazine*, March 12, 2006.

Tribe, Laurence. "Morning-After Pride." *Forbes*, November 5, 2008.

Tumulty, Karen. "Why the Kennedys Went for Obama." *Time*, January 28, 2008.

Wallace-Wells, Benjamin. "A Case of the Blues." *New York Times Magazine*, March 30, 2008.

Walsh, Elsa. "Kennedy's Hidden Campaign." *New Yorker*, March 31, 1997.

Weaver, Warren, Jr. "By His Deeds . . ." *Esquire*, February 1972.

Weinraub, Bernard. "The Reagan Legacy." *New York Times Magazine*, June 22, 1986.

"What Makes Teddy Run?" *Time*, April 21, 1980.

"Why Kennedy Legend Lives On." *U.S. News and World Report*, July 23, 1979.

Wolfson, Howard. "The End of Nixonland." *New Republic*, October 18, 2008.

MAJOR NEWSPAPER ARTICLES

Alsop, Joseph. "Kennedy's Experiment." *Washington Post*, September 27, 1974.

Altman, Lawrence. "The Story Behind Kennedy's Surgery." *New York Times*, July 29, 2008.

"At 70, Kennedy Still a Power." Boston Globe, February 22, 2002.

Blumenthal, Sidney. "Ted Kennedy: No Regrets as the Torch Is Passed." *Washington Post*, July 19, 1988.

Broder, David, and Dana Milbank. "Hopes for Civility in Washington Are Dashed." *Washington Post*, January 18, 2004.

Clymer, Adam. "After Three Decades Working in the Senate, Kennedy Gets a Turn for His Agenda." *New York Times*, March 3, 1993.

———. "An Icon of '60s Liberalism Goes on the Attack." *New York Times*, October 19, 1994.

———. "Big Man in Congress: Kennedy, Of All People." *New York Times*, August 11, 1996.

———. "Carter's Clash with Kennedy." *New York Times*, December 13, 1978.

Dionne, E. J., Jr. "The Democrats Take a Dive." *Washington Post*, November 25, 2003.

Edsall, Thomas. "Why Trump Still Has Millions of Americans in His Grip." *New York Times*, May 5, 2021.

Farrell, John Aloysius. "Legend, Chemistry Forge Clinton-Kennedy Link." *Boston Globe*, October 28, 1993.

Frank, Thomas. "Conservatism Isn't Finished." *Wall Street Journal*, November 5, 2008.

Gillon, Steve. "Reagan Tied Republicans to White Christians and Now the Party Is Trapped." *Washington Post*, March 22, 2021.

Goodrich, Lawrence. "Senate Icon Shows Off Skills." *Christian Science Monitor*, October 27, 1997.

Graham, Otis. "Tracing Liberal Woes to '65 Immigration Act." *Christian Science Monitor*, December 28, 1995.

Grove, Lloyd. "The Liberal Element: Ted Kennedy Is in the Minority But Republicans are Finding Him Mighty Hard to Ignore." *Washington Post*, July 9, 1996.

Haberman, Clyde. "Religion and Right-Wing Politics: How Evangelicals Reshaped Elections." *New York Times*, October 28, 2018.

Harley, Richard. "The Evangelical Vote and the Presidency." *Christian Science Monitor*, June 25, 1980.

Harwood, John. "Is the Era of Dominance Over for Conservatives?" *New York Times*, October 6, 2008.

Herbert, Bob. "Tears for Teddy." *New York Times*, May 24, 2008.

Hulse, Carl. "Kennedy: A Little Like Everyone, A Lot Like No One." *New York Times*, May 22, 2008.

Isikoff, Michael. "Palm Beach Revels in Latest Scandal." *Washington Post*, April 8, 1991.

Johnson, Haynes. "Kennedy Myth Gives Way to Hard Political Realities." *Washington Post*, January 22, 1980.

Kassebaum, Nancy Landon. "The Senate Is Not in Order." *Washington Post*, January 19, 1988.

Kennedy, Edward. "Alito's Credibility Problem." *Washington Post*, January 7, 2006.

———. "America Should Work for All Americans." *Boston Globe*, December 12, 1997.

———. "Criminal Code Reform Would Aid Liberty." *Los Angeles Times*, September 27, 1977.

———. "Health Bill Would Fix What's Broken." *Boston Globe*, May 28, 2009.

———. "How to Fix 'No Child.'" *Washington Post*, January 7, 2008.

———. "Level With Us, Mr. President." *Boston Globe*, February 8, 2003.

———. "What a Difference an Election Makes." *Washington Post*, March 11, 2007.

Kornblut, Anne. "Bush Tries to Build Ties with Kennedy." *Boston Globe*, January 11, 2001.

Kurtz, Howard. "The Ethics of Identifying Rape Victims." *Washington Post*, April 18, 1991.

Leibovich, Mark. "After Diagnosis, Determined to Make a Good Ending." *New York Times*, August 26, 2009.

———. "Hold the Eulogies, Kennedy Says." *New York Times*, February 21, 2009.

———. "The Kennedy Factor." *Washington Post*, July 13, 2004.

Levenson, Michael. "In Last Days a Quest for Joy." *Boston Globe*, August 27, 2009.

MacPherson, Myra. "Closing Scenes from a Kennedy Marriage." *Washington Post*, January 22, 1981.

———. "Joan's Journey." *Washington Post*, December 14, 1979.

———. "Senator Kennedy: Alone with the Legacy." *Washington Post*, June 4, 1978.

McNamara, Eileen. "Kennedy the Floor Fighter." *Boston Globe*, April 6, 1984.

———. "Liberal Lion Needs a Tiger." *Boston Globe*, January 16, 2005.

Milligan, Susan. "Adversaries Praise a Relentless Kennedy." *Boston Globe*, May 18, 2007.

Milligan, Susan, and Lisa Wangsness. "The Man at the Center." *Boston Globe*, May 10, 2009.

Oliphant, Thomas. "Behind Kennedy's Decision Not to Run." *Boston Globe*, December 5, 1982.

Puga, Ana. "For Sen. Kennedy, a Hectic Period of Victories." *Boston Globe*, August 7, 1993.

Quindlen, Anna. "Trouble With Teddy." *New York Times*, Oct. 19, 1991.

Reeves, Richard. "A Publicly Moral Man." *USA Today*, August 27, 2009.

Rimer, Sarah. "Kennedy's Closest Confidante." *New York Times*, August 28, 2009.

Scheer, Robert. "In the Defense of Liberalism." *Los Angeles Times*, August 14, 1980.

Schram, Martin. "At Summit, Younger Kennedys Prevailed over Political Pros." *Washington Post*, December 2, 1982.

———. "Making the Opponent the Issue." *Washington Post*, June 9, 1980.

———. "Rise and Fall of the Protest Vote." *Washington Post*, June 10, 1980.

———. "The Campaign." *Washington Post*, June 8, 1980.

Stall, Bill. "In the Senate, An Ability to Compromise." *Los Angeles Times*, December 18, 1979.

Streitfield, David. "The Man Behind the Senator." *Washington Post*, September 24, 1992.

Taylor, Paul. "Burden of Kennedy Family Heritage Weighed Too Heavily on Senator." *Washington Post*, December 21, 1985.

"The Sinking of the Kennedy Star." *Washington Post*, August 14, 1980.

Thimmesch, Nick. "A Plum for Kennedy." *Washington Post*, January 7, 1979.

Thomas, Jack. "Victoria Reggie: The Next Kennedy." *Boston Globe*, April 2, 1992.

Tolchin, Martin. "Watching Kennedy Not Run for President." *New York Times*, March 27, 1986.

Witt, April. "Fatal Inaction." *Washington Post*, June 18, 2006.

SPEECHES AND EVENTS

Barack Obama Inauguration Coverage. CNN, January 20, 2009.

———. MSNBC, January 20, 2009.

Biden, Joe. Remarks at Edward Kennedy Memorial Service. MSNBC, August 26, 2009.

———. Remarks at Edward Kennedy Memorial Service, August 28, 2009. https://www.youtube.com/watch?v=o3jzJkSxLjU.

Carter, Jimmy. State of the Union Address, January 19, 1978. https://www.presidency.ucsb.edu/documents/the-state-the-union-address-delivered-before-joint-session-the-congress-1.

———. State of the Union Address, January 23, 1980. https://www.jimmycarterlibrary.gov/assets/documents/speeches/su8ojec.phtml.

———. "Energy and the National Goals—A Crisis of Confidence." Speech, July 15, 1979. https://www.americanrhetoric.com/speeches/jimmycartercrisisofconfidence.htm.

Clinton, Bill. Democratic Leadership Council Keynote Address, May 6, 1991. https://www.c-span.org/video/?17869-1/democratic-leadership-council-keynote-address.

———. State of the Union Address, January 23, 1996. https://clintonwhitehouse4.archives.gov/WH/New/other/sotu.html.

———. Remarks at Northeastern University, January 11, 2001. https://www.govinfo.gov/content/pkg/PPP-2000-book3/html/PPP-2000-book3-doc-pg2892-2.htm.

Edward Kennedy Funeral Service. CNN, August 9, 2009.

Edward Kennedy Memorial Service. C-SPAN, August 28, 2009. https://www.c-span.org/video/?288589-2/senator-edward-kennedy-memorial-service.

Hill, Anita. Testimony to Senate Judiciary Committee, October 11, 1991. http://www.speeches-usa.com/Transcripts/anita_hill-testimony.html.

Kennedy, Edward. Democratic National Convention Speech, August 11, 1980. https://www.c-span.org/video/?3439-1/senator-edward-kennedy-1980-convention-speech.

———. Memorial Tribute to John F. Kennedy (text). *New York Times*, November 23, 1983.

———. "Ted Kennedy Endorses Barack Obama," January 28, 2008. https://www.youtube.com/watch?v=oEawu8pQxRI.

———. Democratic National Committee Tribute and Speech, August 25, 2008. https://www.youtube.com/watch?v=f4fh8oZkVNk.

Kennedy, Edward, and Mitt Romney. Massachusetts Senatorial Debate, October 25, 1994. https://www.youtube.com/watch?v=aNiIEKhAF1k.

Kennedy, Robert F. Day of Affirmation Address, June 6, 1966. https://www.jfklibrary.org/learn/about-jfk/the-kennedy-family/robert-f-kennedy/robert-f-kennedy-speeches/day-of-affirmation-address-university-of-capetown-capetown-south-africa-june-6-1966.

Reagan, Ronald. "A Time for Choosing," October 27, 1964. https://www.reaganlibrary.gov/reagans/ronald-reagan/time-choosing-speech-october-27-1964.

———. Address Accepting the Presidential Nomination at the Republican National Convention in Detroit, July 17, 1980. https://www.presidency.ucsb.edu/documents/address-accepting-the-presidential-nomination-the-republican-national-convention-detroit.

Roosevelt, Franklin D. Address Accepting the Presidential Nomination at the Democratic National

Convention in Chicago, July 2, 1932. https://www.presidency.ucsb.edu/documents/address-accepting-the-presidential-nomination-the-democratic-national-convention-chicago-1.

U.S. SENATE HEARINGS

Hearing Before the Judiciary Committee on the nomination of Jefferson B. Sessions III to be Federal District Judge. 99th Congress, 2nd session, March 13, 1986.

Hearing Before the Judiciary Committee on the nomination of Robert Bork to be Justice of the Supreme Court. 100th Congress, 1st session, Part 1, September 16, 1987; Part 2, September 25, 1987.

Hearing Before the Judiciary Committee on the nomination of Judge Clarence Thomas to be Justice of the Supreme Court. 102nd Congress, 1st session, September 16, 1991; October 11, 1991.

Hearing Before the Judiciary Committee on the nomination of John G. Roberts, Jr., to be Chief Justice of the Supreme Court. 109th Congress, 1st session, September 12–15, 2005.

OTHER MEDIA AND SOURCES

ACLU. Letter to the Senate on the Enhanced Border Security and Visa Entry Reform Act of 2001, December 17, 2001. https://www.aclu.org/letter/letter-senate-enhanced-border-security-and-visa-entry-reform-act-2001.

Bebinger, Martha. "Kennedy Remembered as the Senate's Hardest-Working Man." WBUR, August 26, 2009. wbur.org/2009/08/26/kennedy-tributes.

"The Choice 2012." *Frontline*, PBS, October 20, 2012.

Harris, John. "The Obama Revolution." *Politico*, November 5, 2008.

Kennedy, Edward, and Alan Simpson. "Face-Off" on Gramm-Rudman-Hollings Law and Deficit, August 14, 1989, John F. Kennedy Presidential Library. https://www.jfklibrary.org/asset-viewer/archives/EMKSEN/AU0008/EMKSEN-AU0008-006/EMKSEN-AU0008-006-006/EMKSEN-AU0008-006-006.

Kennedy, Kerry. "Reflections on Senator Ted Kennedy." Robert F. Kennedy Center, n.d.

Kennedy, Vicki, Ted Kennedy, Jr., and Caroline Rachlin. Appearance on The Oprah Winfrey Show, November 25, 2009.

"Kennedy's Forty Year Push for Universal Coverage." WBUR, January 21, 2009. https://www.wbur.org/news/2009/01/21/kennedys-40-year-push-for-universal-coverage.

Kristol, William, to Republican Leaders. "Defeating President Clinton's Health Care Proposal." December 2, 1993. https://www.scribd.com/document/12926608/William-Kristol-s-1993-Memo-Defeating-President-Clinton-s-Health-Care-Proposal.

Lovley, Erika. "Kennedy's Dogs Will be Missed on Hill." *Politico*, August 30, 2009.

Miller, Steven. "The Evangelical Presidency: Reagan's Dangerous Love Affair with the Christian Right." *Salon*, May 18, 2014.

"Obama's Deal." *Frontline*. PBS, December 15, 2009.

Greenfield, Jeff. Appearance on *Nightline*, ABC, October 25, 1991.

Penn, Mark. "Most Affluent Voters Key to Obama Sweep." *Politico*, November 11, 2008.

People for the American Way. Robert Bork TV ad, narrated by Gregory Peck," 1987. https://www.youtube.com/watch?v=NpFe10lkF3Y.

Reinhart, R. J. "George H. W. Bush Retrospective," *Gallup*, December 1, 2018. https://news.gallup.com/opinion/gallup/234971/george-bush-retrospective.aspx.

Samuelsohn, Darren, and Danny Vinik. "No Child Left Behind: The Oral History." *Politico*, September 23, 2015.

Robertson, Shari, and Michael Camerini, dir. *The Senators' Bargain*. HBO Films, aired March 24, 2010.

Sharp, Jeremy. "Congressional Action on Iraq: 1990–2003, A Compilation of Legislation." CRS Report for Congress, February 14, 2003. https://www.everycrsreport.com/files/20030130_RS21324_c932aa7805859263e86e6dcf3f846de1766b96d1.pdf.

Wallis, Jim. "Honoring the Greatest Commitment of Sen. Edward Kennedy." *Huffington Post*, August 26, 2009.

Wolfson, Roger. "A Former Counsel to Ted Kennedy on Kennedy." *Huffington Post*, August 26, 2009.

INDEX

NEAL GABLER is the author of six books, including four biographies: *An Empire of Their Own*, which won the *Los Angeles Times* Book Prize; *Winchell*, which was named *Time* magazine's nonfiction book of the year and was nominated for the National Book Critics Circle Award; and *Walt Disney*, which won him his second *Los Angeles Times* Book Prize and was named biography of the year by *USA Today*. The first volume of his Edward Kennedy biography, *Catching the Wind*, was a *New York Times* Notable Book. He has been the recipient of a Guggenheim Fellowship, a Shorenstein Fellowship from Harvard, and a Woodrow Wilson Public Policy scholarship, and was the chief nonfiction judge of the National Book Awards.